	Chapter Title	Focus Company	Managerial Focus	Contrast Companies	[illegible]
1	Financial Statements and Business Decisions	**Maxidrive Corporation** Manufacturer of computer disks	Valuing an acquisition	Appl[illegible]	
2	Investing and Financing Decisions and the Balance Sheet	PIZZA PAPA JOHNS Better Ingredients. Better Pizza. Pizza restaurant chain (food service)	Investing and financing decisions	Domino's Pizza Yum! Brands Pizza Inn Inc. Wendy's International Lance, Inc.	**Current Ratio**
3	Operating Decisions and the Income Statement	PIZZA PAPA JOHNS Better Ingredients. Better Pizza. Pizza restaurant chain	Operating decisions	GlaxoSmithKline Unilever BMW Group Domino's Pizza Mattel Yum! Brands	**Total Asset Turnover**
4	Adjustments, Financial Statements, and the Quality of Earnings	PIZZA PAPA JOHNS Better Ingredients. Better Pizza. Pizza restaurant chain	Year-end accounting activities	Whole Foods, Inc. Domino's Pizza Yum! Brands Toys R Us	**Net Profit Margin**
5	Communicating and Interpreting Accounting Information	Callaway GOLF Manufacturer of golf clubs	Corporate communication	Adams Golf Apple, Inc. Microsoft Corporation Hewlett-Packard Verizon	**Return on Assets**
6	Reporting and Interpreting Sales Revenue, Receivables, and Cash	DECKERS outdoor corporation Shoe manufacturer and clothing merchandiser	Marketing strategy	Skechers U.S.A. Timberland Co.	**Gross Profit Percentage** **Receivables Turnover**
7	Reporting and Interpreting Cost of Goods Sold and Inventory	HARLEY-DAVIDSON, INC. Motorcycle manufacturer and clothing merchandiser	Inventory management	Apple Inc. Dell Computer Deere & Company Caterpillar Polaris Honda Motor	**Inventory Turnover**
8	Reporting and Interpreting Property, Plant, and Equipment; Natural Resources; and Intangibles	SOUTHWEST.COM Major air carrier	Planning productive capacity	US Airways United Airlines Singapore Airlines International Paper ExxonMobil Corporation Sony Cisco IBM Corporation	**Fixed Asset Turnover**

Chapter Title	Focus Company	Managerial Focus	Contrast Companies	Key Ratios
9 Reporting and Interpreting Liabilities	STARBUCKS Retailer and roaster of specialty coffee	Capital structure	Peet's Coffee Caribou Coffee Krispy Kreme General Mills Toyota Motor Ford Motor Co. Harley-Davidson, Inc.	**Quick Ratio** **Accounts Payable Turnover**
10 Reporting and Interpreting Bonds	BNSF Railroad	Long-term debt financing	CSX Rail Union Pacific Home Depot Outback Steakhouse General Mills	**Debt-to-Equity** **Times Interest Earned**
11 Reporting and Interpreting Owners' Equity	Kroger Supermarket chain	Corporate ownership	Whole Foods Lone Star Ind. Lowe's Starbucks Home Depot	**Dividend Yield** **Earnings per Share**
12 Reporting and Interpreting Investments in Other Corporations	THE WASHINGTON POST COMPANY Publishing, broadcasting, and education company	Strategic investment in other companies	The Buckle	**Economic Return from Investing**
13 Statement of Cash Flows	National Beverage Corp. Beverage company	Management of cash	CocaCola Pepsi Dr. Pepper Snapple Continental Airlines Redhook Ale	**Quality of Income** **Capital Acquisitions**
14 Analyzing Financial Statements	THE HOME DEPOT Home improvement retailer	Financial statement analysis	Hechinger.com Lowe's	**Ratio Summary**

Ratios Used for Financial Analyses

Ratio		Basic Computation	Chapter
Current Ratio	=	$\frac{\text{Current Assets}}{\text{Current Liabilities}}$	2
Total Asset Turnover	=	$\frac{\text{Sales (or Operating) Revenues}}{\text{Average Total Assets}}$	3
Net Profit Margin	=	$\frac{\text{Net Income}}{\text{Net Sales}}$	4
Return on Assets (ROA)*	=	$\frac{\text{Net Income}}{\text{Average Total Assets}}$	5
Gross Profit Percentage	=	$\frac{\text{Gross Profit}}{\text{Net Sales}}$	6
Receivables Turnover	=	$\frac{\text{Net Sales}}{\text{Average Net Trade Accounts Receivable}}$	6
Inventory Turnover	=	$\frac{\text{Cost of Goods Sold}}{\text{Average Inventory}}$	7
Fixed Asset Turnover	=	$\frac{\text{Net Sales}}{\text{Average Net Fixed Assets}}$	8
Quick Ratio	=	$\frac{\text{Quick Assets}}{\text{Current Liabilities}}$	9
Accounts Payable Turnover	=	$\frac{\text{Cost of Goods Sold}}{\text{Average Accounts Payable}}$	9
Debt-to-Equity	=	$\frac{\text{Total Liabilities}}{\text{Stockholders' Equity}}$	10
Times Interest Earned	=	$\frac{\text{Net Income} + \text{Interest Expense} + \text{Income Tax Expense}}{\text{Interest Expense}}$	10
Earnings per Share	=	$\frac{\text{Net Income**}}{\text{Average Number of Shares of Common Stock Outstanding During the Period}}$	11
Dividend Yield	=	$\frac{\text{Dividend per Share}}{\text{Market Price per Share}}$	11
Economic Return from Investing	=	$\frac{\text{Dividends and Interest Received} + \text{Change in Fair Value***}}{\text{Fair Value of Investments (beginning of period)}}$	12
Quality of Income	=	$\frac{\text{Cash Flow from Operating Activities}}{\text{Net Income}}$	13
Capital Acquisitions	=	$\frac{\text{Cash Flow from Operating Activities}}{\text{Cash Paid for Property, Plant, and Equipment}}$	13

*As shown in Chapter 14, in most complex analytical situations, interest expense net of tax is added back to net income in the numerator of the ratio.

**If there are preferred dividends, the amount is subtracted from the Net Income in the numerator.

***Beginning Balance of Investments—Ending Balance of Investments

SELECT MATERIAL FROM

FINANCIAL ACCOUNTING

Northeastern University

Financial Accounting & Reporting

ACCT 1201

SEVENTH EDITION

Robert Libby
Cornell University

Patricia A. Libby
Ithaca College

Daniel G. Short
Texas Christian University

McGraw-Hill Learning Solutions

Boston Burr Ridge, IL Dubuque, IA New York San Francisco St. Louis
Bangkok Bogotá Caracas Lisbon London Madrid
Mexico City Milan New Delhi Seoul Singapore Sydney Taipei Toronto

The McGraw·Hill Companies

Financial Accounting & Reporting
ACCT 1201
Northeastern University

This book is a McGraw-Hill Learning Solutions textbook and contains select material from *Financial Accounting*, Seventh Edition by Robert Libby, Patricia A. Libby and Daniel G. Short. Copyright © 2011, 2009, 2007, 2004, 2001, 1998, 1996 by The McGraw-Hill Companies, Inc. Reprinted with permission of the publisher. Many custom published texts are modified versions or adaptations of our best-selling textbooks. Some adaptations are printed in black and white to keep prices at a minimum, while others are in color.

4 5 6 7 8 9 0 DIG DIG 13

ISBN-13: 978-0-07-763598-5
ISBN-10: 0-07-763598-1
Part of
ISBN-13: 978-0-07-763599-2
ISBN-10: 0-07-763599-X

Learning Solutions Consultant: Jessica Watts
Production Editor: Jennifer Pickel
Printer/Binder: Digital Impressions

ABOUT THE AUTHORS

ROBERT LIBBY

Robert Libby is the David A. Thomas Professor of Accounting at Cornell University, where he teaches the introductory financial accounting course. He previously taught at the University of Illinois, Pennsylvania State University, the University of Texas at Austin, the University of Chicago, and the University of Michigan. He received his BS from Pennsylvania State University and his MAS and PhD from the University of Illinois; he is also a CPA.

Bob is a widely published author and researcher specializing in behavioral accounting. He was selected as the AAA Outstanding Educator in 2000, received the AAA Outstanding Service Award in 2006, and received the AAA Notable Contributions to the Literature Award in 1985 and 1996. He is the only person to have received all three of the Association's highest awards for teaching, service, and research. He has published numerous articles in *The Accounting Review; Journal of Accounting Research; Accounting, Organizations, and Society*; and other accounting journals. He has held a variety of offices including vice president in the American Accounting Association and is a member of the American Institute of CPAs and the editorial boards of *The Accounting Review; Accounting, Organizations, and Society; Journal of Accounting Literature*; and *Journal of Behavioral Decision Making*.

PATRICIA A. LIBBY

Patricia Libby is associate professor of accounting at Ithaca College, where she teaches the undergraduate financial accounting course. She previously taught graduate and undergraduate financial accounting at Eastern Michigan University and the University of Texas. Before entering academe, she was an auditor with Price Waterhouse (now PricewaterhouseCoopers) and a financial administrator at the University of Chicago. She is also faculty advisor to Beta Alpha Psi and Ithaca College Accounting Association. She received her BS from Pennsylvania State University, her MBA from DePaul University, and her PhD from the University of Michigan; she is also a CPA.

Pat conducts research on using cases in the introductory course and other parts of the accounting curriculum. She has published articles in *The Accounting Review*, *Issues in Accounting Education*, and *The Michigan CPA*.

DANIEL G. SHORT

Daniel Short is professor of accounting and former dean of the M.J. Neeley School of Business at Texas Christian University in Fort Worth, Texas. Before he joined TCU, he was dean at the Richard T. Farmer School of Business at Miami University and the College of Business at Kansas State University. Prior to that, he was associate dean at the University of Texas at Austin, where he taught the undergraduate and graduate financial accounting courses. He also taught at the University of Michigan and the University of Chicago. He received his undergraduate degree from Boston University and his MBA and PhD from the University of Michigan.

Dan has won numerous awards for his outstanding teaching abilities and has published articles in *The Wall Street Journal*, *The Accounting Review*, the *Journal of Accounting Research*, and other business journals. He has worked with a number of Fortune 500 companies, commercial banks, and investment banks to develop and teach executive education courses on the effective use of accounting information. Dan has also served on boards of directors in several industries, including manufacturing, commercial banking, and medical services.

A TRUSTED LEADER FOR

The award-winning author team of Bob Libby, Pat Libby, and Dan Short has made *Financial Accounting* a best-selling textbook by helping the instructor and student become partners in learning. Libby/Libby/Short uses a remarkable learning approach that keeps students engaged and involved in the material from the first day of class.

Libby/Libby/Short's *Financial Accounting* maintains its leadership by focusing on three key attributes:

THE PIONEERING FOCUS COMPANY APPROACH:

The Libby/Libby/Short authors' trademark focus company approach is the best method for helping students understand financial statements and the real-world implications of financial accounting for future managers. **This approach shows that accounting is relevant and motivates students by explaining accounting in a real-world context.** Throughout each chapter, the material is integrated around a familiar focus company, its decisions, and its financial statements. This provides the perfect setting for discussing the importance of accounting and how businesses use accounting information.

A BUILDING-BLOCK APPROACH TO TEACHING TRANSACTION ANALYSIS:

Most faculty agree that mastery of the accounting cycle is critical to success in financial accounting. And yet all other financial books introduce and develop transaction analysis in one chapter, bombarding a student early in the course with an overload of new concepts and terms. The authors believe that most faculty take more time with the accounting cycle, but other financial accounting textbooks don't. **By slowing down the introduction of transactions and giving students time to practice and gain mastery, this building-block approach leads to greater student success in their study of later topics in financial accounting such as adjusting entries.**

POWERFUL TECHNOLOGY FOR TEACHING AND STUDY:

Students have different learning styles and conflicting time commitments, so they want technology tools that will help them study more efficiently and effectively. The 7th edition includes even more technology features, including McGraw-Hill Connect Accounting, Self-Quiz and Study, and Tegrity Campus. See pages xiv–xviii for more details.

STUDENTS AND INSTRUCTORS

"Libby, Libby, Short does a **great job in explaining financial accounting concepts at a level that introductory students can grasp and understand.**"

—*Marci Butterfield, University of Utah*

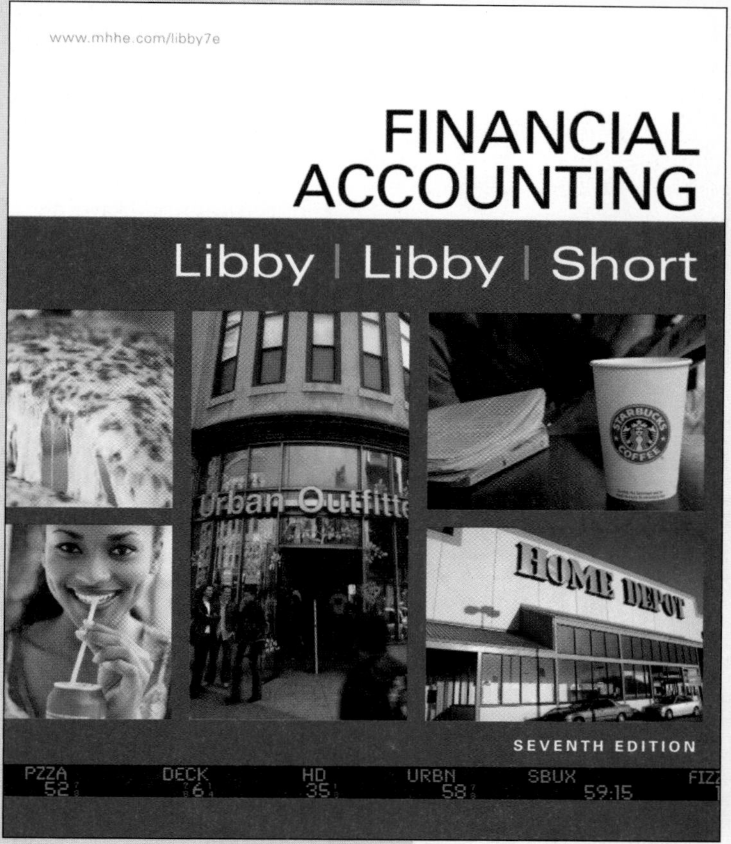

"The text has **some of the best discussions that I have seen in introductory texts of statement of cash flows and financial statement analysis topics.**"

—*Marilyn Misch, Pepperdine University*

"A **solid textbook with a decision-making focus.**"

—*Chao-Shin Liu, Notre Dame*

"The book does an excellent job of using real-world examples to highlight the importance of understanding financial accounting to students who may or may not be interested in pursuing accounting careers. One challenge with traditional courses and textbooks is that students who might not be interested in accounting careers lose interest quickly. I think this book will hold their attention, without sacrificing the technical information that provides the foundation for further accounting coursework. **Exceptionally well written and nicely organized.**"

—*Paul Hribar, University of Iowa*

MARKET-LEADING PEDAGOGY

Financial Accounting, 7e, offers a host of pedagogical tools that complement the different ways you like to teach and the ways your students like to learn. Some offer information and tips that help you present a complex subject; others highlight issues relevant to what your students read online or see on television. Either way, *Financial Accounting*'s pedagogical support will make a real difference in your course and in your students' learning.

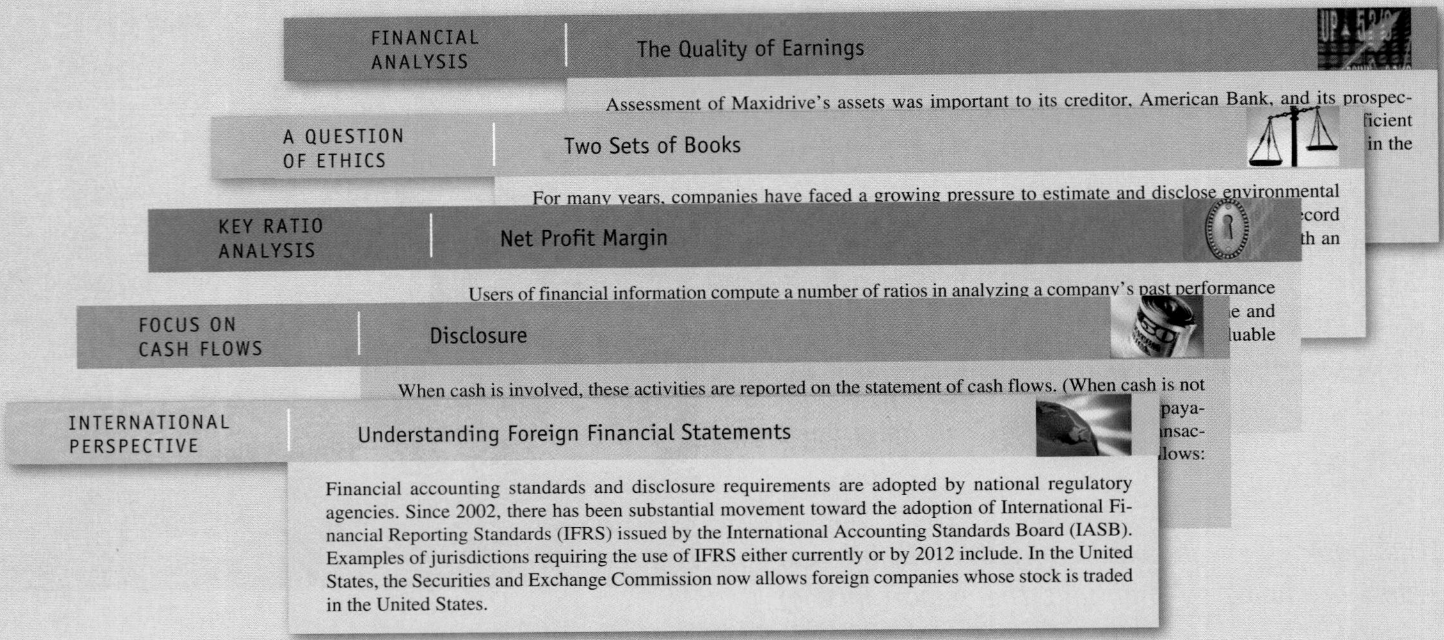

FINANCIAL ANALYSIS BOXES—These features tie important chapter concepts to real-world decision-making examples. They also highlight alternative viewpoints and add to the critical-thinking and decision-making focus of the text.

A QUESTION OF ETHICS BOXES—These boxes appear throughout the text, conveying the importance and the consequences of acting responsibly in business practice.

KEY RATIO ANALYSIS BOXES—Each box presents ratio analysis for the focus company in the chapter as well as for comparative companies. Cautions are also provided to help students understand the limitations of certain ratios.

FOCUS ON CASH FLOWS BOXES—Each of the first twelve chapters includes a discussion and analysis of changes in the cash flow of the focus company and explores the decisions that caused those changes.

INTERNATIONAL PERSPECTIVE BOXES—These boxes highlight the emergence of global accounting standards (IFRS) at a level appropriate for the introductory student.

AND CONTENT

NEW! Anticipating a greater emphasis on International Financial Reporting Standards (IFRS) in the United States and recognizing its presence in more than 100 countries worldwide, selected IFRS topics are integrated in appropriate chapters at a level suitable for introductory financial accounting so students will be well-prepared to use statements prepared under IFRS in their careers. The coverage in Libby/Libby/Short exceeds the standards suggested by the PricewaterhouseCoopers (PwC) IFRS Ready program (2010) for sophomores and juniors presented below:

- Sophomores interviewing for summer programs and internships and who have had at least one term of accounting should have a pre-awareness of IFRS by being able to define what IFRS stands for and why it could be important to their future careers.
- Juniors and above interviewing for internships or full time positions should be able to demonstrate an awareness of IFRS by being able to articulate which global organization establishes IFRS, what an example of a difference between US GAAP and IFRS may be, and generally where it is used in the world.

The following table outlines the coverage chapter by chapter.

CHAPTER	TOPIC
1 Financial Statements and Business Decisions, p.19	The IASB and Global Convergence of Accounting Standards
2 Investing and Financing Decisions and the Balance Sheet, p.46, 67	The IASB/FASB Project on the Conceptual Framework Financial Statement Titles and Balance Sheet Format Differences
3 Operating Decisions and the Income Statement, p.107	Income Statement Format Differences
5 Communicating and Interpreting Accounting Information, p.237	Differences in Accounting Methods Acceptable under IFRS and U.S. GAAP Treatment of Extraordinary Items
7 Cost of Goods Sold and Inventory, p.342	Use of Last-In First-Out Method for Inventory
8 Property, Plant, and Equipment; Natural Resources; and Intangibles, p.405, 414	Measurement Basis of Property, Plant, & Equipment Accounting for Development Costs
9 Reporting and Interpreting Liabilities, p.464, 466	Classification of Refinanced Debt Contingent Liabilities
11 Reporting and Interpreting Owners' Equity, p.565	Stockholders' Equity Terminology
13 Statement of Cash Flows, p.649	Treatment of Interest Received and Paid

*"The textbook focuses on the key accounting concepts and is **written clearly so that it is easy for students to understand.**"*

—Rada Brooks, University of California Berkeley, Haas School of Business

*"The **real-life examples are an excellent way to draw in the student** and I thought that **the ethics components and IFRS components were an excellent addition.**"*

—Tammy Metzke, Milwaukee Area Technical College

PRACTICE IS KEY TO SUCCESS

NEW! PAUSE FOR FEEDBACK AND SELF-STUDY QUIZ

Research shows that students learn best when they are actively engaged in the learning process. This active learning feature engages the student, provides interactivity, and promotes efficient learning. These quizzes ask students to pause at strategic points throughout each chapter to ensure they understand key points before moving ahead.

14 CHAPTER 1 Financial Statements and Business Decisions

STOP PAUSE FOR **FEEDBACK**

The **statement of retained earnings** explains changes to the retained earnings balance caused by net income and dividends during the reporting period. Check your understanding of these relationships by completing the following question.

SELF-STUDY **QUIZ**

1. Maxidrive's statement of retained earnings reports the way that net income and the distribution of dividends affected the financial position of the company during the accounting period. In a prior period, Maxidrive's financial statements reported the following amounts: beginning retained earnings, $5,510; total assets, $20,450; dividends, $900; cost of goods sold expense, $19,475; net income, $1,780. Without referring to Exhibit 1.4, compute ending retained earnings.

After you have completed your answer, check it with the solution at the bottom of the page.

Statement of Cash Flows

Structure

The STATEMENT OF CASH FLOWS (Cash Flow Statement) reports inflows and outflows of cash during the accounting period in the categories of operating, investing, and financing.

Maxidrive's statement of cash flows is presented in Exhibit 1.5. The statement of cash flows (cash flow statement) divides Maxidrive's cash inflows and outflows (receipts and payments) into the three primary categories of cash flows in a typical business: cash flows from operating, investing, and financing activities. The heading identifies the name of the entity, the title of the report, and the unit of measure used in the statement. Like the income statement, the cash flow statement covers a specified period of time (the accounting period), which in this case is one year.

As discussed earlier in this chapter, reported revenues do not always equal cash collected from customers because some sales may be on credit. Also, expenses reported on the income statement may not be equal to the cash paid out during the period because expenses may be incurred in one period and paid for in another. Because the income statement does not provide information concerning cash flows, accountants prepare the statement of cash flows to report inflows and outflows of cash. The cash flow statement equation describes the causes of the change in cash reported on the balance sheet from the end of last period to the end of the current period:

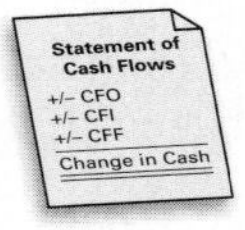

+ / – Cash Flows from Operating Activities (CFO)
+ / – Cash Flows from Investing Activities (CFI)
+ / – Cash Flows from Financing Activities (CFF)
Change in Cash

Note that each of the three cash flow sources can be positive or negative.

Elements

Cash flows from operating activities are cash flows that are directly related to earning income. For example, when Dell, Apple, and other customers pay Maxidrive for the disk drives it has delivered to them, it lists the amounts collected as cash collected from

Solution to SELF-STUDY QUIZ

1. Beginning Retained Earnings ($5,510) + Net Income ($1,780) – Dividends ($900) = Ending Retained Earnings ($6,390).

CHAPTER TAKE-AWAYS

Bulleted end-of-chapter summaries complement the learning objectives outlined at the beginning of the chapter.

CHAPTER **TAKE-AWAYS**

1. Recognize the information conveyed in each of the four basic financial statements and the way that it is used by different decision makers (investors, creditors, and managers). p. 4

   The **balance sheet** is a statement of financial position that reports dollar amounts for the assets, liabilities, and stockholders' equity at a specific point in time.

   The **income statement** is a statement of operations that reports revenues, expenses, and net income for a stated period of time.

   The **statement of retained earnings** explains changes to the retained earnings balance that occurred during the reporting period.

   The **statement of cash flows** reports inflows and outflows of cash for a stated period of time.

   The statements are used by investors and creditors to evaluate different aspects of the firm's financial position and performance.

2. Identify the role of generally accepted accounting principles (GAAP) in determining the content of financial statements. p. 18

   GAAP are the measurement rules used to develop the information in financial statements. Knowledge of GAAP is necessary for accurate interpretation of the numbers in financial statements.

3. Distinguish the roles of managers and auditors in the accounting communication process. p. 20

   Management has primary responsibility for the accuracy of a company's financial information. Auditors are responsible for expressing an opinion on the fairness of the financial statement presentations based on their examination of the reports and records of the company.

4. Appreciate the importance of ethics, reputation, and legal liability in accounting. p. 21

   Users will have confidence in the accuracy of financial statement numbers only if the people associated with their preparation and audit have reputations for ethical behavior and competence. Management and auditors can also be held legally liable for fraudulent financial statements and malpractice.

In this chapter, we studied the basic financial statements that communicate financial information to external users. Chapters 2, 3, and 4 provide a more detailed look at financial statements and examine how

NEW! COMPREHENSIVE PROBLEMS

Selected chapters include problems that cover topics from earlier chapters to refresh, reinforce, and build an integrative understanding of the course material.

connect ACCOUNTING PROBLEMS

Identifying Accounts on a Classified Balance Sheet and Their Normal Debit or Credit Balances (AP2-1) — **P2-1** LO1, 2

Exxon Mobil Corporation explores, produces, refines, markets, and supplies crude oil, natural gas, and petroleum products in the United States and around the world. The following are accounts from a recent balance sheet of Exxon Mobil Corporation:

ExxonMobil

COMPREHENSIVE **PROBLEM (CHAPTERS 9–11)**

Complete the following requirements for each independent case.

Case A: The charter for Rogers, Incorporated, authorized the following capital stock:

Common stock, par $10, 103,000 shares

Preferred stock, 9 percent, par value $8 per share, 4,000 shares

ALTERNATE **PROBLEMS**

Preparing an Income Statement, Statement of Retained Earnings, and Balance Sheet (P1-1) — **AP1-1** LO1

Assume that you are the president of Influence Corporation. At the end of the first year (June 30, 2011) of operations, the following financial data for the company are available:

IN FINANCIAL ACCOUNTING

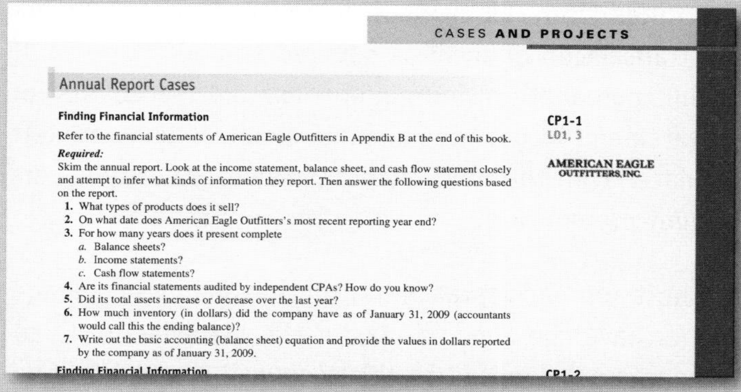

CASES AND PROJECTS

Annual Report Cases

Finding Financial Information

CP1-1
LO1, 3

AMERICAN EAGLE OUTFITTERS, INC.

Refer to the financial statements of American Eagle Outfitters in Appendix B at the end of this book.

Required:

Skim the annual report. Look at the income statement, balance sheet, and cash flow statement closely and attempt to infer what kinds of information they report. Then answer the following questions based on the report.

1. What types of products does it sell?
2. On what date does American Eagle Outfitters's most recent reporting year end?
3. For how many years does it present complete
   a. Balance sheets?
   b. Income statements?
   c. Cash flow statements?
4. Are its financial statements audited by independent CPAs? How do you know?
5. Did its total assets increase or decrease over the last year?
6. How much inventory (in dollars) did the company have as of January 31, 2009 (accountants would call this the ending balance)?
7. Write out the basic accounting (balance sheet) equation and provide the values in dollars reported by the company as of January 31, 2009.

Finding Financial Information

CP1-2

CASES AND PROJECTS

This section includes annual report cases, financial reporting and analysis cases, critical thinking cases, and financial reporting and analysis projects.

IPOD DOWNLOADABLE CONTENT

Photo Courtesy of Apple.®

You are holding a *media-integrated textbook* that provides students with portable educational content—just right for those students who want to study when and where it's most convenient for them. *Financial Accounting* 7e gives students the option to download content for review and study to their Apple® iPods and most other MP3/MP4 devices. iPod icons appear throughout the text pointing students to audio and video lecture presentation slides, and course-related videos.

QUICK REFERENCE TO IPOD ICON:

Lecture Presentations available for download to your **iPod, Zune,** or **MP3** device (audio and visual depending on your device).

Topical videos available for download to your **iPod, Zune,** or **MP3** (depending on your device).

A PROVEN TEACHING AND LEARNING METHODOLOGY

Faculty agree the accounting cycle is the most critical concept to learn and master for students studying financial accounting. Libby/Libby/Short believes students struggle with the accounting cycle when transaction analysis is covered in one chapter. If students are exposed to the accounting equation, journal entries, and T-accounts for both balance sheet and income statement accounts in a single chapter, many are left behind and are unable to grasp material in the next chapter, which typically covers adjustments and financial statement preparation.

The market-leading Libby/Libby/Short approach spreads transaction analysis coverage over two chapters so that students have the time to master the material. In Chapter 2 of *Financial Accounting*, students are exposed to the accounting equation and transaction analysis for investing and financing transactions that only affect balance sheet accounts. This provides students with the opportunity to learn the basic structure and tools used in accounting in a simpler setting. In Chapter 3, students are exposed to more complex operating transactions that also affect income statement accounts. As a result of this slower building-block approach to transaction analysis, students are better prepared and ready to learn adjustments, financial statement preparation, and more advanced topics. After the students have developed an understanding of the complete accounting cycle and the resulting statements, Chapter 5 takes students through the corporate reporting and analysis process.

Accounting Cycle

Start Early	Compress Coverage	Extend Coverage (Libby/Libby/Short approach)
Overview of F/S and Users, B/S and I/S Transactions with Accounting Equation	Overview of F/S and Users	Overview of F/S and Users
	F/S, Ratios, and Conceptual Framework	**B/S** Transactions with Accounting Equation, Journal Entries, and T-accounts
B/S and I/S Transactions with Journal Entries and T-accounts	B/S and I/S Transactions with Accounting Equation, Journal Entries, and T-accounts	**B/S** and **I/S** Transactions with Accounting Equation, Journal Entries, and T-accounts
Adjustments, Closing Entries, F/S Preparation	Adjustments, Closing Entries, F/S Preparation	Adjustments, Closing Entries, F/S Preparation

The graphic to the left shows a detailed comparison of the Libby/Libby/Short approach to the accounting cycle chapters compared to the approach taken by other financial accounting texts.

The Libby/Libby/Short approach is better because it gives students more time to master transaction analysis, which is the foundation for the rest of the course.

WHAT'S NEW IN THE 7th EDITION?

One reason Libby/Libby/Short's *Financial Accounting* is a best-selling textbook is because instructors can trust the flexibility in key topical coverage, the simplified explanations of complex topics, and end-of-chapter material that relates directly to the chapter's text and engages the students with concepts and decision-making using details from the chapter.

Chapter 1

- Contrast company information updated.
- New Pause for Feedback feature added to self-study quizzes.
- New and updated real companies, as well as modified accounts, names, and amounts for fictional companies in end-of-chapter material.
- Updated feature on the IASB and international convergence.

Chapter 2

- Expanded Exhibit 2.1 and discussion.
- Updated Papa John's financial information.
- Simplified additional account titles in balance sheet.
- Updated International Perspective features on status of integrating IFRS.
- New Pause for Feedback feature added to Self-Study Quiz feature.
- Added explanation bubbles in Exhibit 2.3.
- Modified journal entry illustrations by moving equality checks to margin.
- Changed Key Ratio feature to current ratio (moved financial leverage ratio to later chapter).
- Substantial revision of end-of-chapter material: new numerical data for 95 percent of exercises, problems and alternate problems; 60 percent new annual report cases.

Chapter 3

- Updated International Perspective with focus on IFRS.
- Revised Exhibits 3.2 and 3.3 plus discussion of the exhibits for improved clarity, including adding journal entry illustrations.
- Continued to simplify the account titles in financial statements.
- New Pause for Feedback feature added to Self-Study Quiz feature.
- Updated Financial Analysis feature on stock market reactions.
- Embedded new summaries in explaining the effect of recognizing revenues and expenses on the accounting equation.
- Revised Exhibit 3.5 and the related discussion on steps in analyzing transactions.
- Modified journal entry illustrations by moving equality checks to margin (as in Chapter 2).
- Revised section *How Are Financial Statements Prepared and Analyzed?* with modified illustrations and marginal comments on statements for clarity.
- Replaced Statement of Retained Earnings illustration and discussion with the more realistic Statement of Stockholders' Equity.
- Added new Pause for Feedback–Self-Study Quiz following Focus on Cash Flows to provide an example of certain end-of-chapter questions.
- Substantial revision of end-of-chapter material: new numerical data for 95 percent of mini-exercises, exercises, problems and alternate problems; 60 percent new annual report cases.

Chapter 4

- Reorganized topics to begin with trial balance.
- Created new Exhibit 4.3 for types of adjustments and modified names to deferred and accrued revenues and expenses, adding clarity to graphic.
- Revised steps in the adjustment process to be systematic and created new graphic summarizing the pattern for adjusting entries.
- Illustrated new three-step analysis for adjusting entries with embedded journal entries highlighting the steps.

- Revised discussion of accounting for the use of property and equipment to location of illustration.
- New Pause for Feedback feature added to Self-Study Quiz feature.
- Deleted reference to Appendix E on the Web.
- Substantial revision of end-of-chapter material: new numerical data for 100 percent of mini-exercises, exercises, problems and alternate problems; 70 percent new annual report cases.
- Added two ***NEW*** Comprehensive Cases.

Chapter 5

- Focus and contrast company information updated.
- Expanded IFRS coverage on differences in accounting methods acceptable under IFRS and U.S. GAAP and the treatment of extraordinary measures.
- New Pause for Feedback feature added to Self-Study quizzes.
- Notes added emphasizing key formatting details for balance sheet and income statement in Exhibits 5.5 and 5.6.
- Operating section of cash flow statement simplified in Exhibit 5.7.
- Return on assets analysis substituted for return on equity analysis to postpone the discussion of leverage until the liabilities chapters. Maintains same discussion of strategy and levers of profitability in simpler presentation.
- New inferring financial information exercise focusing on the income statement equation and income statement format.

Chapter 6

- Focus and contrast company information updated.
- New Pause for Feedback feature added to Self-Study quizzes.
- New and updated real companies, as well as modified accounts, names, and amounts for fictional companies in end of chapter material.
- New exercise on recording, reporting, and evaluating a bad debt estimate.
- New case on the effects of choosing between alternative revenue recognition points.

Chapter 7

- Focus changed from expansion to managing in an economic downturn.
- Focus and contrast company information updated.
- New Pause for Feedback feature added to Self-Study quizzes.
- New and updated real companies, as well as modified accounts, names, and amounts for fictional companies in end-of-chapter material.
- Eliminated Exhibit 7.2.
- Cost of goods sold equation added to Exhibit 7.3.
- New, clearer inventory flow exhibit (Exhibit 7.4).
- New coverage of U.S. GAAP/IFRS differences in accounting for inventories.
- End-of-chapter supplement A on effects of LIFO liquidations shortened and simplified.
- New case based on Seneca Foods illustrating the effects on income taxes and net income of a change to LIFO.

Chapter 8

- Updated Southwest Airlines' information (financial and other) and information for contrast companies.
- New Pause for Feedback feature added to Self-Study quizzes.
- Added explanation bubbles in depreciation formulae and clarity in discussion.
- Added summary on steps for asset impairment.
- Substantial revision of end-of-chapter material: new numerical data for 90 percent of multiple-choice questions, mini-exercises, exercises, problems and alternate problems; and all new annual report cases.
- Added ***NEW*** Comprehensive Problem covering Chapters 6, 7, and 8.

Chapter 9

- Added new annual report cases.
- Updated focus company information.
- Added two new sections on IFRS.
- Incorporated numerous revisions suggested by reviewers.
- New Pause for Feedback feature added to Self-Study quizzes.

- Introduced the quick ratio in the discussion of liquidity.
- Eliminated chapter supplement showing computation of federal corporate income taxes.
- Eliminated supplement on retirement benefits.
- Added focused discussion of deferred taxes to chapter.

Chapter 10

- Added new focus company, BNSF.
- Added new comparison companies.
- Incorporated many revisions suggested by reviewers.
- Added new annual report cases.
- New Pause for Feedback feature added to Self-Study quizzes.
- Revised Excel discussion to show computation of the present value of a bond in a single step.

Chapter 11

- Added new focus company, Kroger.
- Added new comparison companies.
- Incorporated many small revisions recommended by reviewers.
- Added new section on IFRS.
- New Pause for Feedback feature added to Self-Study quizzes.
- Added ***NEW*** Comprehensive Problem covering Chapters 9, 10, 11.

Chapter 12

- Updated Washington Post's information (financial and other) and information for contrast companies.
- New Pause for Feedback feature added to Self-Study Quiz feature.
- Simplified Self-Study quizzes.
- Simplified accounting for passive investments by directly adjusting the investment account to fair value.
- Added Financial Analysis feature on fair value accounting.
- Changed ratio to economic return from investing as a more relevant analytical tool.
- Simplified section on mergers and acquisitions and reporting for combined companies.
- Moved Supplement A on Preparing Consolidated Statements to the Web.
- Substantial revision of end-of-chapter material: new numerical data for 100 percent of multiple-choice questions, mini-exercises, exercises, problems and alternate problems; added two new problems, and all new annual report cases.

Chapter 13

- Added new focus company, National Beverage, and changed contrast companies to Coca-Cola, PepsiCo and Dr Pepper Snapple.
- Changed from quarterly to annual cash flow statement to simplify presentation and focus on differences between income and cash flows.
- New illustration added to emphasize that cash flow from operations is the same under both the direct and indirect methods.
- Expanded IFRS coverage on classification of interest paid and received.
- New Pause for Feedback feature added to Self-Study quizzes.
- New Supplement B added showing the detailed computations and statement presentation issues related to gains and losses on sale of plant and equipment. The simple discussion remains in the main chapter material.
- Included additional exercise showing simple inclusion of gain and loss on sale of plant and equipment in the operating section.
- Added new problem requiring complete preparation of the cash flow statement, including computation of gain or loss on sale of equipment.
- Updated information in end-of-chapter material and changed some numbers in material based on fictitious companies.

Chapter 14

- Incorporated numerous small revisions recommended by reviewers.
- Financial analysis for The Home Depot and Lowe's revised.
- Added new annual report cases.
- Updated comparison companies and financial examples.
- New Pause for Feedback feature added to Self-Study quizzes.

MARKET-LEADING

MCGRAW-HILL *CONNECT ACCOUNTING*

Connect Learn Succeed™

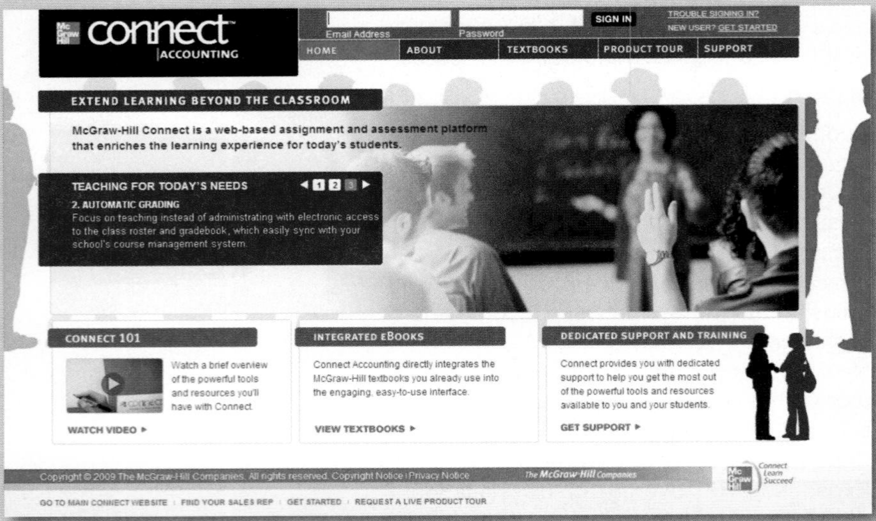

Less Managing. More Teaching. Greater Learning.

McGraw-Hill *Connect Accounting* is an online assignment and assessment solution that connects students with the tools and resources they'll need to achieve success.

McGraw-Hill *Connect Accounting* helps prepare students for their future by enabling faster learning, more efficient studying, and higher retention of knowledge.

McGraw-Hill *Connect Accounting* Features

Connect Accounting offers a number of powerful tools and features to make managing assignments easier, so faculty can spend more time teaching. With *Connect Accounting* students can engage with their coursework anytime and anywhere, making the learning process more accessible and efficient. *Connect Accounting* offers you the features described below.

Simple Assignment Management

With *Connect Accounting* creating assignments is easier than ever, so you can spend more time teaching and less time managing. The assignment management function enables you to:

- Create and deliver assignments easily with selectable end-of-chapter questions and test bank items.
- Streamline lesson planning, student progress reporting, and assignment grading to make classroom management more efficient than ever.
- Go paperless with the eBook and online submission and grading of student assignments.

TECHNOLOGY

Smart Grading

When it comes to studying, time is precious. *Connect Accounting* helps students learn more efficiently by providing feedback and practice material when they need it, where they need it. When it comes to teaching, your time also is precious. The grading function enables you to:

- Have assignments scored automatically, giving students immediate feedback on their work and side-by-side comparisons with correct answers.
- Access and review each response; manually change grades or leave comments for students to review.
- Reinforce classroom concepts with practice tests and instant quizzes.

Instructor Library

The *Connect Accounting* Instructor Library is your repository for additional resources to improve student engagement in and out of class. You can select and use any asset that enhances your lecture. The *Connect Accounting* Instructor Library includes:

- eBook
- PowerPoint files

Student Study Center

The *Connect Accounting* Student Study Center is the place for students to access additional resources. The Student Study Center:

- Offers students quick access to lectures, practice materials, eBooks, and more.
- Provides instant practice material and study questions, easily accessible on the go.

Self-Quiz and Study

The Self-Quiz and Study (SQS) connects each student to the learning resources needed for success in the course. For each chapter, students:

- Take a practice test to initiate the Self-Quiz and Study.
- Immediately upon completing the practice test, see how their performance compares to chapter learning objectives within chapters.
- Receive a Self-Quiz and Study that recommends specific readings from the text, supplemental study material, and practice work that will improve their understanding and mastery of each learning objective.

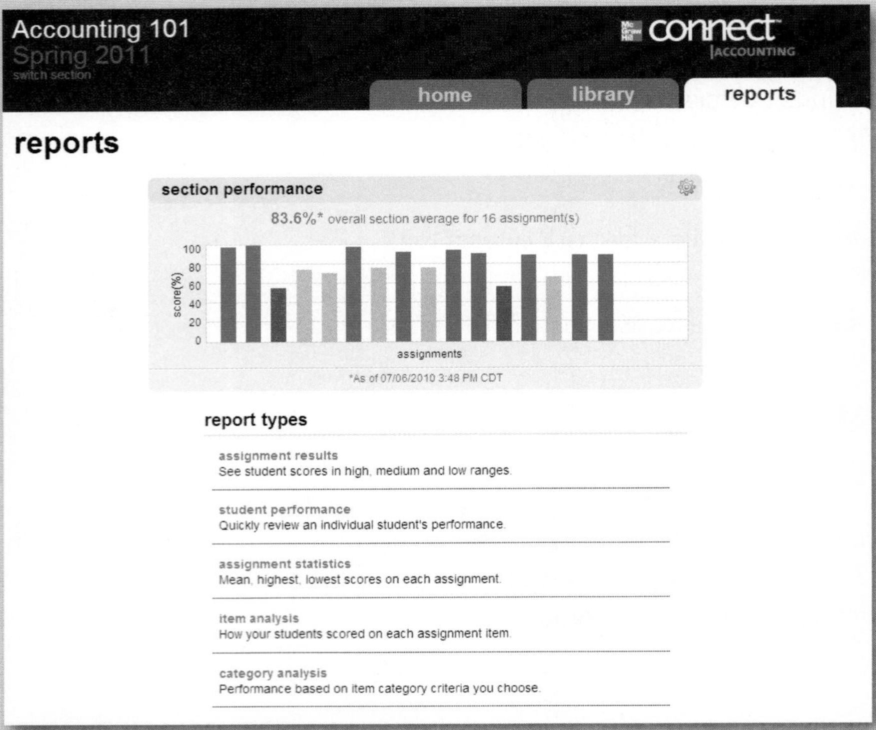

Student Progress Tracking

Connect Accounting keeps instructors informed about how each student, section, and class is performing, allowing for more productive use of lecture and office hours. The progress-tracking function enables you to:

- View scored work immediately and track individual or group performance with assignment and grade reports.
- Access an instant view of student or class performance relative to learning objectives.
- Collect data and generate reports required by many accreditation organizations, such as the AACSB and AICPA.

TEGRITY CAMPUS: LECTURES 24/7

Tegrity Campus is a service that makes class time available 24/7 by automatically capturing every lecture in a searchable format for students to review when they study and complete assignments. With a simple one-click start-and-stop process, you capture all computer screens and corresponding audio. Students can replay any part of any class with easy-to-use browser-based viewing on a PC or Mac.

Educators know that the more students can see, hear, and experience class resources, the better they learn. In fact, studies prove it. With Tegrity Campus, students quickly recall key moments by using Tegrity Campus's unique search feature. This search helps students efficiently find what they need, when they need it, across an entire semester of class recordings. Help turn all your students' study time into learning moments immediately supported by your lecture.

To learn more about Tegrity, watch a 2-minute Flash demo at http://tegritycampus.mhhe.com.

MCGRAW-HILL CONNECT PLUS ACCOUNTING

McGraw-Hill reinvents the textbook learning experience for the modern student with *Connect Plus Accounting*. A seamless integration of an eBook and *Connect Accounting, Connect Plus Accounting* provides all of the *Connect Accounting* features plus the following:

- An integrated eBook, allowing for anytime, anywhere access to the textbook.
- Dynamic links between the problems or questions you assign to your students and the location in the eBook where that problem or question is covered.
- A powerful search function to pinpoint and connect key concepts in a snap.

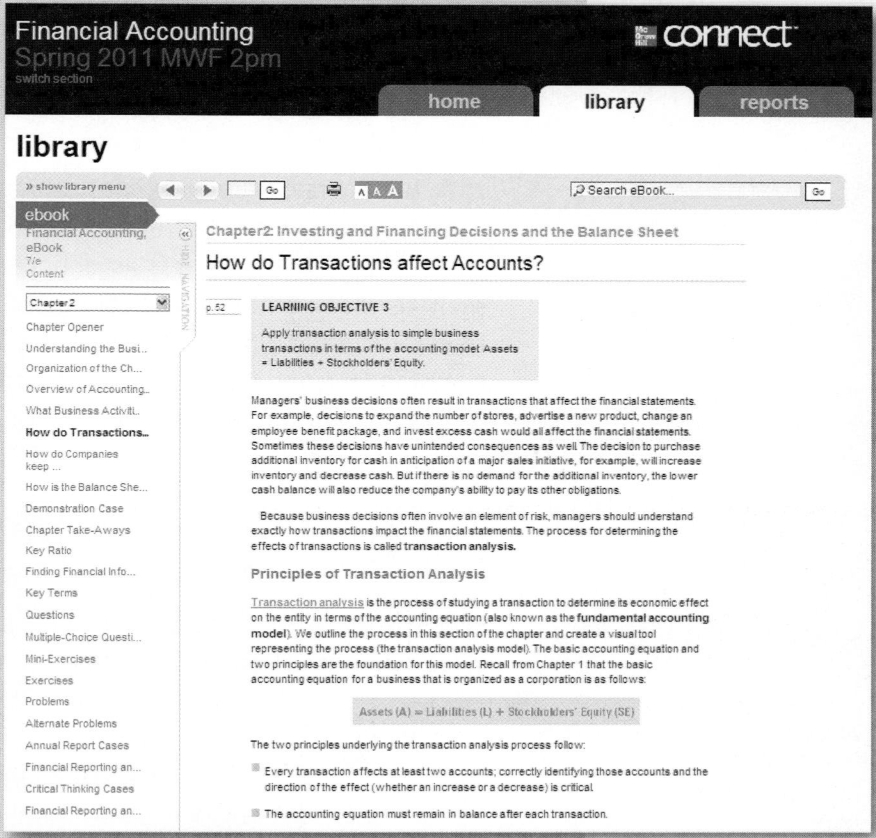

In short, *Connect Plus Accounting* offers you and your students powerful tools and features that optimize your time and energies, enabling you to focus on course content, teaching, and student learning. *Connect Plus Accounting* also offers a wealth of content resources for both instructors and students. This state-of-the-art, thoroughly tested system supports you in preparing students for the world that awaits.

For more information about Connect, go to www.mcgraw-hillconnect.com, or contact your local McGraw-Hill sales representative.

COURSESMART ISBN 0077329112

Learn Smart. Choose Smart.

CourseSmart is a new way for faculty to find and review eTextbooks. It's also a great option for students who are interested in accessing their course materials digitally and saving money.

CourseSmart offers thousands of the most commonly adopted textbooks across hundreds of courses from a wide variety of higher education publishers. It is the only place for faculty to review and compare the full text of a textbook online, providing immediate access without the environmental impact of requesting a print exam copy.

With the CourseSmart eTextbook, students can save up to 45 percent off the cost of a print book, reduce their impact on the environment, and access powerful Web tools for learning. CourseSmart is an online eTextbook, which means users access and view their textbook online when connected to the Internet. Students can also print sections of the book for maximum portability. CourseSmart eTextbooks are available in one standard online reader with full text search, notes and highlighting, and email tools for sharing notes between classmates.

http://www.coursesmart.com

ALEKS® FOR THE ACCOUNTING CYCLE AND ALEKS® FOR FINANCIAL ACCOUNTING

ALEKS is an assessment and learning program that provides individualized instruction in accounting. Available online in partnership with McGraw-Hill/Irwin, ALEKS interacts with students much like a skilled human tutor, with the ability to precisely assess a student's knowledge and provide instruction on the exact topics the student is most ready to learn. By providing topics to meet individual students' needs, allowing students to move between explanation and practice, correcting and analyzing errors, and defining terms, ALEKS helps students to master course content quickly and easily.

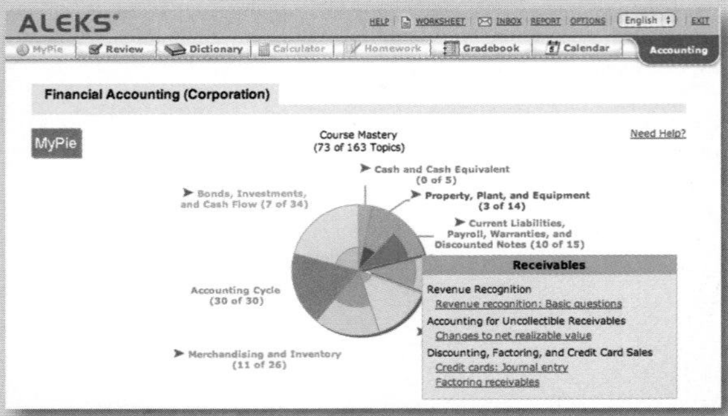

ALEKS also includes a new instructor module with powerful, assignment-driven features and extensive content flexibility. The complimentary Instructor Module provides a course calendar, a customizable gradebook with automatically graded homework, improved textbook integration, and dynamic reports to monitor student and class progress. ALEKS simplifies course management and allows instructors to spend less time with administrative tasks and more time directing student learning.

To learn more about ALEKS, visit www.aleks.com.

COMPLETE TEACHING PACKAGE FOR INSTRUCTORS

☑ Instructor CD-ROM

ISBN 007732904X

Access to the instructor's key text ancillary materials is at your fingertips. You can find all of the instructor ancillaries available on one convenient CD-ROM: Presentation Slides, Solutions Manual, Test Bank and Computerized Test Bank, Instructor's Resource Manual, Solutions to Excel Templates, and text exhibits.

☑ Presentation Slides

Prepared by Susan Galbreath at David Lipscomb University, Jon Booker and Charles Caldwell at Tennessee Technological University, and Cynthia Rooney. Completely customized PowerPoint presentations for use in your classroom. Available on the Instructor CD-ROM and the text website.

☑ Solutions Manual

Prepared by Robert Libby, Patricia Libby, and Daniel Short. Provides solutions to end-of-chapter questions, mini-exercises, exercises, problems, alternate problems and cases. Available on the Instructor CD-ROM and the text website.

☑ Test Bank

Prepared by Randy Johnston at the University of Colorado. Available on the Instructor CD-ROM and password-protected Instructor site, this comprehensive test bank includes more than 1,500 true/false, multiple-choice, and matching questions and problems, each tagged by learning objective, topic area, difficulty level, and AACSB, Bloom's, and AICPA categories.

☑ Instructor's Resource Manual

Prepared by Jeannie Folk at College of DuPage. Includes overviews of chapter topics and resources to help you prepare for class. It describes the ready-to-use resources that support the text and presents other enrichment resources, including innovative active learning exercises that you can use in class. This manual is a must-read for any instructor interested in improving teaching evaluations. Available on the Instructor CD-ROM and the text website.

☑ Instructor Excel Templates

Solutions to the student Excel Templates used to solve selected end-of-chapter exercises and problems. These assignments are designated by the Excel icon. Available on the text website.

EZ Test

McGraw-Hill's EZ Test is a flexible and easy-to-use electronic testing program that allows instructors to create tests from book-specific items. EZ Test accommodates a wide range of question types and allows instructors to add their own questions. Multiple versions of the test can be created and any test can be exported for use with course management systems such as BlackBoard/WebCT. EZ Test Online is a new service that gives instructors a place to easily administer EZ Test-created exams and quizzes online. The program is available for Windows and Macintosh environments.

ASSURANCE OF LEARNING READY

Many educational institutions today are focused on the notion of *assurance of learning*, an important element of some accreditation standards. *Financial Accounting* is designed specifically to support your assurance of learning initiatives with a simple, yet powerful solution.

Each test bank question for *Financial Accounting* maps to a specific chapter learning outcome/objective listed in the text. You can use our test bank software, EZ Test and EZ Test Online, or *Connect Accounting* to easily query for learning outcomes/ objectives that directly relate to the learning objectives for your course. You can then use the reporting features of EZ Test or *Connect Accounting* to aggregate student results in similar fashion, making the collection and presentation of assurance of learning data simple and easy.

AACSB STATEMENT

AACSB INTERNATIONAL

The McGraw-Hill Companies is a proud corporate member of AACSB International. Understanding the importance and value of AACSB accreditation, *Financial Accounting* recognizes the curricula guidelines detailed in the AACSB standards for business accreditation by connecting selected questions in the test bank to the six general knowledge and skill guidelines in the AACSB standards.

The statements contained in *Financial Accounting* are provided only as a guide for the users of this textbook. The AACSB leaves content coverage and assessment within the purview of individual schools, the mission of the school, and the faculty. While *Financial Accounting* and the teaching package make no claim of any specific AACSB qualification or evaluation, we have labeled selected questions within the Test Bank to accompany *Financial Accounting* according to the six general knowledge and skill areas.

COMPLETE STUDY PACKAGE FOR STUDENTS

☑ Online Learning Center

www.mhhe.com/libby7e

Financial Accounting's Online Learning Center offers students additional study resources, including Self-Study quizzes, B set exercises, PowerPoint slides, and Excel templates tied to the end-of-chapter material, all organized by chapter.

☑ Student PowerPoint Presentations

Selected presentation slides reproduced in student version. Presentation slides are located on the text's website.

☑ Check Figures

Prepared by Betty David. This resource provides answers to select problems and cases. Check Figures are located on the text's Online Learning Center.

☑ Study Guide ISBN 0077329090

Prepared by Jeannie Folk at College of DuPage. An outstanding learning tool, this guide gives students a deeper understanding of the course material and reinforces, step by step, what they are learning in the main text.

☑ Working Papers ISBN 0077329104

Working Papers are provided to assist students in solving complex text assignments. The Working Papers are available both in print and as Excel spreadsheets.

☑ Excel Templates

Available on the text website www.mhhe.com/libby7e. These templates are tied to selected end-of-chapter material and are available on the text website. These assignments are designated by the Excel icon.

☑ *Understanding Corporate Annual Reports,* by William R. Pasewark

ISBN 0073526932

This financial analysis project emphasizes the interpretation and analysis of financial statements. It contains extensive instructions for obtaining an annual report from a publicly traded corporation. Students gain hands-on experience working with annual reports and are then better prepared to understand financial accounting concepts and their use in the business world.

☑ McGraw-Hill Customer Care Contact Information

At McGraw-Hill, we understand that getting the most from new technology can be challenging. That's why our services don't stop after you purchase our products. You can email our Product Specialists 24 hours a day to get product training online. Or you can search our knowledge bank of Frequently Asked Questions on our support website. For Customer Support, call 800-331-5094, email hmsupport@mcgraw-hill.com, or visit www.mhhe.com/support. One of our Technical Support Analysts will be able to assist you in a timely fashion.

ACKNOWLEDGMENTS

Many dedicated instructors have devoted their time and effort to help us make each edition better. We would like to acknowledge and thank all of our colleagues who have helped guide our development decisions for this and previous editions. This text would not be the success it is without the help of all of you.

Board of Reviewers

Dawn Addington, *Central New Mexico Community College*
Ajay Adhikari, *American University*
Gary Adna Ames, *Brigham Young University*
Peter Aghimien, *Indiana University—South Bend*
Nas Ahadiat, *California Polytechnic University*
John Ahern, *DePaul University*
Pervaiz Alam, *Kent State University*
Vern Allen, *Central Florida Community College*
Bridget Anakwe, *Plattsburgh State University of New York*
Brenda Anderson, *Boston University*
Joseph Antenucci, *Youngstown State University*
Frank Aquilino, *Montclair State University*
Florence Atiase, *University of Texas—Austin*
Jane Baird, *Minnesota State University Mankato*
Laurel Barfitt, *Delta State University*
Ira W. Bates, *Florida A&M University*
Deborah Beard, *Southeast Missouri State University*
Daisy Beck, *Louisiana State University*
John Bedient, *Albion College*
S. Douglas Beets, *Wake Forest University*
Michael Bitter, *Stetson University*
Eric Blazer, *Millersville University*
Michael G. Booth, *Cabrillo College*
Scott Boylan, *Washington & Lee University*
Mark Bradshaw, *Harvard Business School*
Christopher Brandon, *Indiana University—Purdue University Columbus*
Rodger Brannan, *University of Minnesota Duluth*
Rada Brooks, *University of California at Berkeley*
Nina Brown, *Tarrant County College*
Amy Browning, *Ivy Technical Community College*
Helen Brubeck, *San Jose State University*
Terri Brunsdon, *The University of Akron*
Marci Butterfield, *University of Utah*
Kay Carnes, *Gonzaga University*
Nancy Cassidy, *Texas A&M University*
Michael Cathey, *The George Washington University*
Kam Chan, *Pace University*
Chiaho Chang, *Montclair State University*
Gretchen Charrier, *University of Texas—Austin*
Agnes Cheng, *University of Houston*
Antoinette Clegg, *Palm Beach Community College*
Anne Clem, *Iowa State University*
Judy Colwell, *Northern Oklahoma College*
Teresa Conover, *University of North Texas*
Marcia Croteau, *University of Maryland—Baltimore*
Sue Cullers, *Tarleton State University*
Dori Danko, *Grand Valley State University*
Betty David, *Francis Marion University*
Harold Davis, *Southeastern Louisiana University*
Paquita Davis-Friday, *Bernard M. Baruch College*
Marinus DeBruine, *Grand Valley State University*
Mark DeFond, *University of Southern California*
Elizabeth Demers, *University of Rochester*
Bettye Desselle, *Prairie View A&M University*
Allan Drebin, *Northwestern University*
Carolyn Dreher, *Southern Methodist University*
Sheri Erickson, *Minnesota State University Moorehead*
Harlan Etheridge, *University of Louisiana—Lafayette*
Thomas Finnegan, *University of Illinois at Urbana—Champaign*
Richard Fleischman, *John Carroll University*
Virginia Fullwood, *Texas A&M University—Commerce*
Cheryl Furbee, *Cabrillo College*
Joseph Galante, *Millersville University of Pennsylvania*
Carolyn Galantine, *Pepperdine University*
Andy Garcia, *Bowling Green State University*
David Gelb, *Seton Hall University*
Lisa Gillespie, *Loyola University, Chicago*
Anthony Greig, *Purdue University*
A. Kay Guess, *St. Edward's University*
Jeffrey Haber, *Iona College*
Leon Hanouille, *Syracuse University*
Russell Hardin, *Pittsburgh State University*
Sheila Hardy, *Lafayette College*
Betty Harper, *Middle Tennessee State*
Bob Hartman, *University of Iowa*
Carla Hayn, *University of California—Los Angeles*
Haihong He, *California State University—Los Angeles*
Kenneth R. Henry, *Florida International University*
Ann Ownby Hicks, *North Park University*
Lori Holder-Webb, *University of Wisconsin*
Pamela Hopcroft, *Florida Community College*
Paul Hribar, *University of Iowa*
Courtland Huber, *University of Texas—Austin*
Dawn Hukai, *University of Wisconsin—River Falls*
Bob Hurt, *California State Polytechnic University Pomona*
Carol Hutchinson, *AB Tech*
Constance M. Hylton, *George Mason University*
Marc Hyman, *University of California—Berkeley*
Laura Ilcisin, *University of Nebraska—Omaha*
Norma Jacobs, *Austin Community College*
Scott Jerris, *San Francisco State University*
Carol Johnson, *Oklahoma State University*
Eric Johnson, *Indiana University—Purdue University Columbus*
Shondra Johnson, *Bradley University*
Christopher Jones, *The George Washington University*
John Karayan, *California State Polytechnic University Pomona*
Robert Kasmir, *The George Washington University*
Beth Kern, *Indiana University—South Bend*
Janet Kimbrell, *Oklahoma State University*
Janice Klimek, *University of Central Missouri*
Dennis Lee Kovach, *Community College of Allegheny*
Tammy Kowalczyk, *Western Washington University*
Charles Ladd, *University of St. Thomas*
Steven J. LaFave, *Augsburg College*
Terry Lease, *Sonoma State*

Marc Lebow, *Christopher Newport University*
Deborah Lee, *Northeastern State University*
Patsy Lee, *University of North Texas*
Christy Lefevers-Land, *Catawba Valley Community College*
Seth Levine, *University of Miami*
Elliott Levy, *Bentley University*
Phil Lewis, *Eastern Michigan University*
June Li, *University of Wisconsin—River Falls*
Daniel Litt, *University of California—Los Angeles*
Chao-Shin Liu, *University of Notre Dame*
Joshua Livnat, *New York University*
Lawrence Logan, *University of Massachusetts—Dartmouth*
Patricia Lopez, *Valencia Community College*
Barbara Lougee, *University of San Diego*
Joseph Lupino, *St. Mary's College of California*
Lori Mason-Olson, *University of Northern Iowa*
Larry McCabe, *Muhlenberg College*
Nick McGaughey, *San Jose State University*
Florence McGovern, *Bergen Community College*
Noel McKeon, *Florida Community College—Jacksonville*
Michael G. McMillan, *Johns Hopkins University*
L. Kevin McNelis, *New Mexico State University*
Tammy Metzke, *Milwaukee Area Technical College*
Paulette Miller, *Collin County Community College*
Tim Mills, *Eastern Illinois University*
Marilyn Misch, *Pepperdine University*
Birendra Mishra, *University of California at Riverside*
Earl Mitchell, *Santa Ana College*
Dennis P. Moore, *Worcester State College*
Haim Mozes, *Fordham University*
Brian Nagle, *Duquesne University*
Ramesh Narasimhan, *Montclair State University*
Presha Neidermeyer, *Union College*
Samir Nissan, *California Sate University Chico*
Tom Nunamaker, *Washington State University*
John O'Shaughnessy, *San Francisco State University*
Janet L. O'Tousa, *University of Notre Dame*
Olga Quintanta, *University of Miami*
Donald Pagach, *North Carolina State—Raleigh*
Sharon Parrish, *Kentucky State University*
Catherine Plante, *University of New Hampshire*
Grace Pownall, *Emory University*
Rama Ramamurthy, *College of William & Mary*
Charles Ransom, *Oklahoma State University*
Keith Richardson, *Bellarmine University*
Laura Rickett, *Kent State University*
Brandi Roberts, *Southeastern Louisiana University*
Joanne Rockness, *University of North Carolina—Wilmington*
Lawrence Roman, *Cuyahoga Community College*
John Rossi III, *Moravian College*
John Rude, *Bloomsburg University*
Angela Sandberg, *Jacksonville State University*
Amy Santos, *Manatee Community College*
Andrew Schmidt, *Columbia University*
Richard Schroeder, *University of North Carolina—Charlotte*
Joann Segovia, *Minnesota State University Moorhead*
Cindy Seipel, *New Mexico State University*
Ann Selk, *University of Wisconsin—Green Bay*
Kathy Sevigny, *Bridgewater State College*
Howard Shapiro, *Eastern Washington University*
Warren Smock, *Ivy Technical Community College—Lafayette*
Sri Sridhanen, *Northwestern University*
David Stein, *Metropolitan State University*
Phillip Stocken, *Dartmouth College*
Dennis Stovall, *Grand Valley State University*
Joel Strong, *St. Cloud State University*
Gina Sturgill, *Concord College*
Susan Sullivan, *University of Massachusetts—Dartmouth*
Martin Taylor, *University of Texas—Arlington*
Mack Tennyson, *College of Charleston*
Peter Theuri, *Northern Kentucky University*
Lynda Thompson, *Massasoit Community College*
Theresa Tiggeman, *University of the Incarnate Word*
Theodore Tully, *DeVry University*
Michael Ulinski, *Pace University*
Ingrid Ulstad, *University of Wisconsin—Eau Claire*
Marcia Veit, *University of Central Florida*
Charles Wain, *Babson College*
Charles Wasley, *University of Rochester*
David Weiner, *University of San Francisco*
Cheryl Westen, *Western Illinois University*
David Wiest, *Western Illinois University*
Patrick Wilkie, *University of Virginia*
Jefferson Williams, *University of Michigan*
Peter Woodlock, *Youngstown State University*
Kathryn Yarbrough, *University of North Carolina—Charlotte*
Zhang (May) Yue, *Northeastern University*
Xiao-Jun Zhang, *University of California at Berkeley*

We are grateful to the following individuals who helped develop, critique, and shape the extensive ancillary package: Randy Johnston, University of Colorado; Jeannie Folk, College of DuPage; Kimberly Temme, Maryville University, Beth Woods; LuAnn Bean, Florida Technical Institute; Sara Melendy, Gonzaga University; Rada Brooks, University of California at Berkeley; Susan Galbreath, David Lipscomb University; Jon Booker, Tennessee Technological University; Charles Caldwell, Tennessee Technological University; and Jack Terry, ComSource Associates, Inc.

We also have received invaluable input and support through the years from present and former colleagues and students. We also appreciate the additional comments, suggestions, and support of our students and our colleagues at Cornell University, Ithaca College, and Texas Christian University.

Last, we applaud the extraordinary efforts of a talented group of individuals at McGraw-Hill/Irwin who made all of this come together. We would especially like to thank Stewart Mattson, our editorial director; Tim Vertovec, our publisher; Dana Woo, our senior sponsoring editor; Kimberly Hooker, our senior developmental editor; Rebecca Mann, our developmental editor; Kathleen Klehr, our senior marketing manager; Bruce Gin, our senoir project manager; Cara Hawthorne, our designer; Michael McCormick, our production supervisor; Allison Souter, our media production manager; Jeremy Cheshareck, our senior photo research coordinator; and David Tietz, our photo researcher.

Robert Libby
Patricia A. Libby
Daniel G. Short

TO OUR STUDENT READERS

THIS BOOK IS AIMED AT TWO GROUPS OF READERS:

Future managers, who will need to interpret and use financial statement information in business decisions.

Future accountants, who will prepare financial statements for those managers.

Future managers need a firm basis for using financial statement information in their careers in marketing, finance, banking, manufacturing, human resources, sales, information systems, or other areas of management. Future accountants need a solid foundation for further professional study.

Both managers and accountants must understand how to *use financial statements in real business decisions* to perform their duties successfully. The best way to learn to do this is to study accounting in real business contexts. This is the key idea behind our *focus company approach*, which we introduce in the first chapter and which integrates each chapter's material around a focus company, its decisions, and its financial statements. The focus companies are drawn from 12 different industries, providing you with a broad range of experience with realistic business and financial accounting practices. In each chapter, *you will actually work with these real companies' statements* and those of additional contrast companies.

When you complete this book, you will be able to read and understand financial statements of real companies. We help you achieve this goal by:

- Selecting learning objectives and content based on the way that seasoned managers use financial statements in modern businesses. *We emphasize the topics that count.*
- Recognizing that students using this book have no previous exposure to accounting and financial statements and often little exposure to the business world. We take you through the financial statements three times at increasing levels of detail (in Chapter 1, Chapters 2 through 5, and Chapters 6 through 14). This is the secret to our "*building block approach*."

- Helping you "*learn how to learn*" by teaching efficient and effective approaches for learning the material. Keep these learning hints in mind as you work your way through each chapter.

- Providing regular feedback in Self-Study Quizzes, which occur throughout each chapter. *Complete the quizzes before you move on*. Then check your answers against the solution provided in the footnote. If you are still unclear about any of the answers, you should refer back to the chapter material preceding the quiz before moving on.

- Highlighting the *Key Terms* in **bold print** and repeating their definitions in the margins. You should pay special attention to the definitions of these terms and review them at the end of the chapter. A handy glossary is provided at the end of the book; consult it if you forget the meaning of an important term.

- Introducing the *Key Financial Ratios* used to assess different elements of financial performance at the same time you are learning how to measure and report those elements. These will show you what kinds of accounting information managers use and how they interpret it.

At the end of each chapter you can test what you have learned by working the Demonstration Cases. *Working problems is one of the keys to learning accounting*. Good luck in your first accounting course.

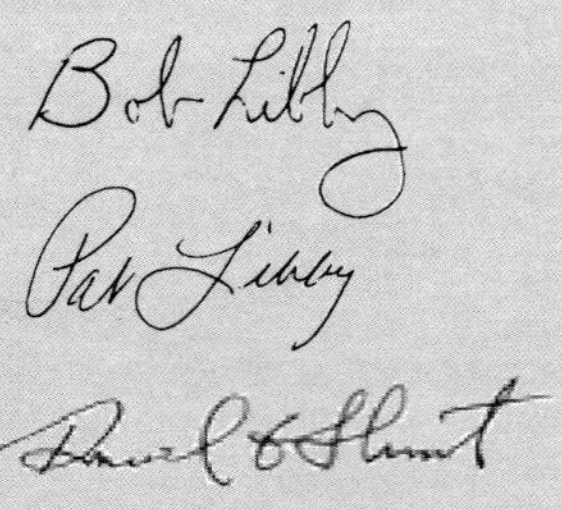

CONTENTS **IN BRIEF**

CONTENTS

Chapter Eleven

Reporting and Interpreting Owners' Equity 550

Chapter Thirteen

Statement of Cash Flows 636

SEVENTH EDITION

FINANCIAL ACCOUNTING

LEARNING OBJECTIVES

Lecture Presentation LP-1
www.mhhe.com/libby7e

After studying this chapter, you should be able to:

1. Recognize the information conveyed in each of the four basic financial statements and the way that it is used by different decision makers (investors, creditors, and managers). p. 4
2. Identify the role of generally accepted accounting principles (GAAP) in determining the content of financial statements. p. 18
3. Distinguish the roles of managers and auditors in the accounting communication process. p. 20
4. Appreciate the importance of ethics, reputation, and legal liability in accounting. p. 21

FINANCIAL STATEMENTS AND BUSINESS DECISIONS

FOCUS COMPANY:

Maxidrive Corporation

VALUING AN ACQUISITION USING FINANCIAL STATEMENT INFORMATION*

In January, Exeter Investors purchased Maxidrive Corp., a fast-growing manufacturer of personal computer disk drives, for $33 million. The price Exeter paid was determined by considering the value of Maxidrive's assets, its debts to others, its ability to sell goods for more than the cost to produce them, and its ability to generate the cash necessary to pay its current bills. Much of this assessment was based on financial information that Maxidrive provided to Exeter in the form of financial statements. By July, Exeter had discovered a variety of problems in the company's operations and its financial statements. Maxidrive appeared to be worth only about half of what Exeter had paid for the company. Furthermore, Maxidrive did not have enough cash to pay its debt to American Bank. Exeter Investors filed a lawsuit against the previous owners and others responsible for Maxidrive's financial statements to recover its losses.

UNDERSTANDING THE BUSINESS

The Players

Maxidrive was founded by two engineers who had formerly worked for General Data, then a manufacturer of large computers. Predicting the rise in demand for personal computers with a hard disk drive, they started a company to manufacture this component. The founders invested a major portion of their savings, becoming the sole owners of Maxidrive. As is common in new businesses, the founders also functioned as managers of the business (they were **owner-managers**).

*The Maxidrive case is a realistic representation of an actual case of fraud. No names in the case are real. The actual fraud is discussed in the epilogue to the chapter.

The founders soon discovered that they needed additional money to develop the business. Based on the recommendation of a close friend, they asked American Bank for a loan. American Bank continued to lend to Maxidrive as the need arose, becoming its largest lender, or **creditor.** Early last year, one of the founders of the business became gravely ill. This event, plus the stresses of operating in their highly competitive industry, led the founders to search for a buyer for their company. In January of this year, they struck a deal for the sale of the company to Exeter Investors, a small group of wealthy private **investors.** Both founders retired and a new manager was hired to run Maxidrive for the new owners. The new **manager** worked on behalf of Exeter Investors but was not an owner of the company.

Whether investors are groups such as Exeter who recently bought all of Maxidrive Corp. or individuals who buy small percentages of large corporations, they make their purchases hoping to gain in two ways. They hope to receive a portion of what the company earns in the form of cash payments called **dividends** and eventually sell their share of the company at a higher price than they paid. As the Maxidrive case suggests, not all companies increase in value or have sufficient cash to pay dividends. Creditors lend money to a company for a specific length of time. They hope to gain by charging interest on the money they lend. As American Bank, Maxidrive's major creditor, has learned, some borrowers cannot repay their debts. When Maxidrive borrows additional money or pays back money to its lenders and receives additional funds or pays dividends to owners, these are called **financing activities.** When Maxidrive buys or sells items such as plant and equipment used in producing disk drives, these are called **investing activities.**

The Business Operations

To understand any company's financial statements, you must first understand its **operating activities.** As noted, Maxidrive designs and manufactures hard disk drives for personal computers. The major parts that go into the drive include the disks on which information is stored, the motors that spin the disks, the heads that read and write to the disks, and the computer chips that control the operations of the drive. Maxidrive purchases the disks and motors from other companies, called **suppliers.** It designs and manufactures the heads and chips and then assembles the drives. Maxidrive does not sell disk drives directly to the public. Instead, its **customers** are computer manufacturers such as Dell Inc. and Apple Inc. which install the drives in machines they sell to retailers such as Best Buy and to consumers. Thus, Maxidrive is a supplier to Dell and Apple.

The Accounting System

ACCOUNTING is a system that collects and processes (analyzes, measures, and records) financial information about an organization and reports that information to decision makers.

Like all businesses, Maxidrive has an **accounting** system that collects and processes financial information about an organization and reports that information to decision makers. Maxidrive's managers (often called **internal decision makers**) and parties outside the firm such as Exeter Investors and American Bank (often called **external decision makers**) use the reports produced by this system. Exhibit 1.1 outlines the two parts of the accounting system. Internal managers typically require continuous, detailed information because they must plan and manage the day-to-day operations of the organization. Developing accounting information for internal decision makers, called **managerial** or **management accounting,** is the subject of a separate accounting course. The focus of this text is accounting for external decision makers, called **financial accounting,** and the four basic financial statements and related disclosures that are the output of that system.

LEARNING OBJECTIVE 1

Recognize the information conveyed in each of the four basic financial statements and the way that it is used by different decision makers (investors, creditors, and managers).

We begin with a brief but comprehensive overview of the information reported in the four basic financial statements and the people and organizations involved in their preparation and use. This overview provides a context in which you can learn the more detailed material presented in the chapters that follow. In particular, we focus on how two primary users of the statements, investors (owners) and creditors (lenders), relied on each

EXHIBIT 1.1

The Accounting System and Decision Makers

of Maxidrive's four basic financial statements in their ill-fated decisions to buy and lend money to Maxidrive. Then we discuss the ethical and legal responsibilities of various parties for those errors.

To understand the way in which Exeter Investors used Maxidrive's financial statements in its decision and the way it was misled, we must first understand what specific information is presented in the four basic financial statements for a company such as Maxidrive. **Rather than trying to memorize the definitions of every term used in this chapter, try to focus your attention on learning the general structure and content of the statements. Specifically:**

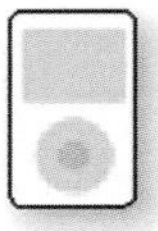

Video 1-1
www.mhhe.com/libby7e

1. What categories of items (often called **elements**) are reported on each of the four statements? (What type of information does a statement convey, and where can you find it?)
2. How are the elements within a statement related? (These relationships are usually described by an equation that tells you how the elements fit together.)
3. Why is each element important to owners' or creditors' decisions? (How important is the information to decision makers?)

The pause for feedback-self-study quizzes will help you assess whether you have reached these goals. Remember that since this chapter is an overview, each concept discussed here will be discussed again in Chapters 2 through 5.

ORGANIZATION of the Chapter

- **The Four Basic Financial Statements: An Overview**
  - Balance Sheet
  - Income Statement
  - Statement of Retained Earnings
  - Statement of Cash Flows
  - Relationships Among the Statements
  - Notes
- **Responsibilities for the Accounting Communication Process**
  - Generally Accepted Accounting Principles
  - Management Responsibility and the Demand for Auditing
  - Ethics, Reputation, and Legal Liability

THE FOUR BASIC FINANCIAL STATEMENTS: AN OVERVIEW

Both Exeter Investors (Maxidrive's new owner) and American Bank (Maxidrive's largest creditor) used Maxidrive's financial statements to learn more about the company before making their purchase and lending decisions. In doing so, Exeter and American Bank assumed that the statements accurately represented Maxidrive's financial condition. As they soon learned, and now have claimed in their lawsuits, the statements were in error.

1. On its **balance sheet,** Maxidrive overstated the economic resources it owned and understated its debts to others.
2. On its **income statement,** Maxidrive overstated its ability to sell goods for more than the cost to produce and sell them.
3. On its **statement of retained earnings,** Maxidrive overstated the amount of income it reinvested in the company for future growth.
4. On its **statement of cash flows,** Maxidrive overstated its ability to generate from sales of disk drives the cash necessary to meet its current debts.

These four financial statements are the basic statements normally prepared by profit-making organizations for use by investors, creditors, and other external decision makers.

The four basic statements summarize the financial activities of the business. They can be prepared at any point in time (such as the end of the year, quarter, or month) and can apply to any time span (such as one year, one quarter, or one month). Like most companies, Maxidrive prepares financial statements for investors and creditors at the end of each quarter (known as **quarterly reports**) and at the end of the year (known as **annual reports**).

EXHIBIT 1.2

Balance Sheet

MAXIDRIVE CORP.		*name of the entity*
Balance Sheet		*title of the statement*
At December 31, 2010		*specific date of the statement*
(in thousands of dollars)		*unit of measure*
Assets		
Cash	$ 4,895	*the amount of cash in the company's bank accounts*
Accounts receivable	5,714	*amounts owed by customers from prior sales*
Inventories	8,517	*parts and completed but unsold disk drives*
Plant and equipment	7,154	*factories and production machinery*
Land	981	*land on which the factories are built*
Total assets	$27,261	
Liabilities		
Accounts payable	$ 7,156	*amounts owed to suppliers for prior purchases*
Notes payable	9,000	*amounts owed on written debt contracts*
Total liabilities	16,156	
Stockholders' Equity		
Contributed capital	2,000	*amounts invested in the business by stockholders*
Retained earnings	9,105	*past earnings not distributed to stockholders*
Total stockholders' equity	11,105	
Total liabilities and stockholders' equity	$27,261	

The notes are an integral part of these financial statements.

The Balance Sheet

The purpose of the **balance sheet** is to report the financial position (amount of assets, liabilities, and stockholders' equity) of an accounting entity at a particular point in time. We can learn a great deal about what the balance sheet reports just by reading the statement from the top. The balance sheet of Maxidrive Corp., presented by its former owners to Exeter Investors, is shown in Exhibit 1.2.

A BALANCE SHEET (Statement of Financial Position) reports the amount of assets, liabilities, and stockholders' equity of an accounting entity at a point in time.

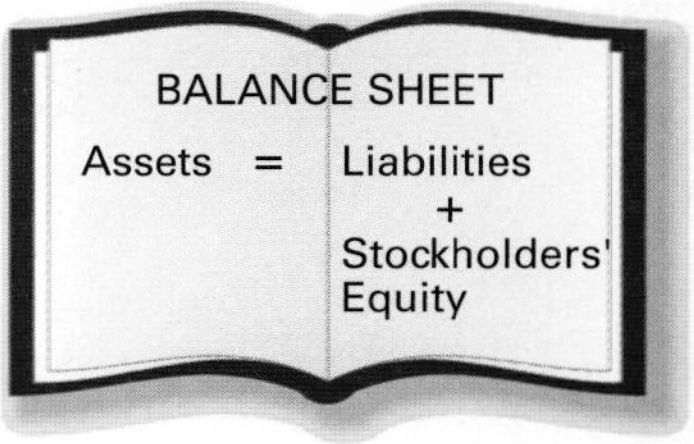

Structure

Notice that the **heading** specifically identifies four significant items related to the statement:

1. **Name of the entity,** Maxidrive Corp.
2. **Title of the statement,** Balance Sheet.
3. **Specific date of the statement,** At December 31, 2010.
4. **Unit of measure** (in thousands of dollars).

The organization for which financial data are to be collected, called an **accounting entity,** must be precisely defined. On the balance sheet, the business entity itself, not the business owners, is viewed as owning the resources it uses and as owing its debts. The heading of each statement indicates the time dimension of the report. The balance sheet is like a financial snapshot indicating the entity's financial position at a specific point in time—in this case, December 31, 2010—which is stated clearly on the balance sheet. Financial reports are normally denominated in the currency of the country in which they are located. U.S. companies report in U.S. dollars, Canadian companies in Canadian dollars, and Mexican companies in Mexican pesos. Medium-sized companies such as Maxidrive often report in thousands of dollars; that is, they round the last three digits to the nearest thousand. The listing of Cash $4,895 on Maxidrive's balance sheet actually means $4,895,000.

An ACCOUNTING ENTITY is the organization for which financial data are to be collected.

Maxidrive's balance sheet first lists the company's assets. Assets are economic resources owned by the entity. It next lists its liabilities and stockholders' equity. They are the sources of financing or claims against the company's economic resources. Financing provided by creditors creates a liability. Financing provided by owners creates owners' equity. Since Maxidrive is a corporation, its owners' equity is designated as stockholders' equity.[1] Since each asset must have a source of financing, a company's assets must, by definition, equal the combined total of its liabilities and stockholders' equity. This **basic accounting equation,** often called the balance sheet equation, is written:

BASIC ACCOUNTING EQUATION (Balance Sheet Equation): Assets = Liabilities + Stockholders' Equity.

Assets	=	**Liabilities + Stockholders' Equity**
Economic resources (e.g., cash, inventory)		Sources of financing for the economic resources Liabilities: From creditors Stockholders' Equity: From stockholders

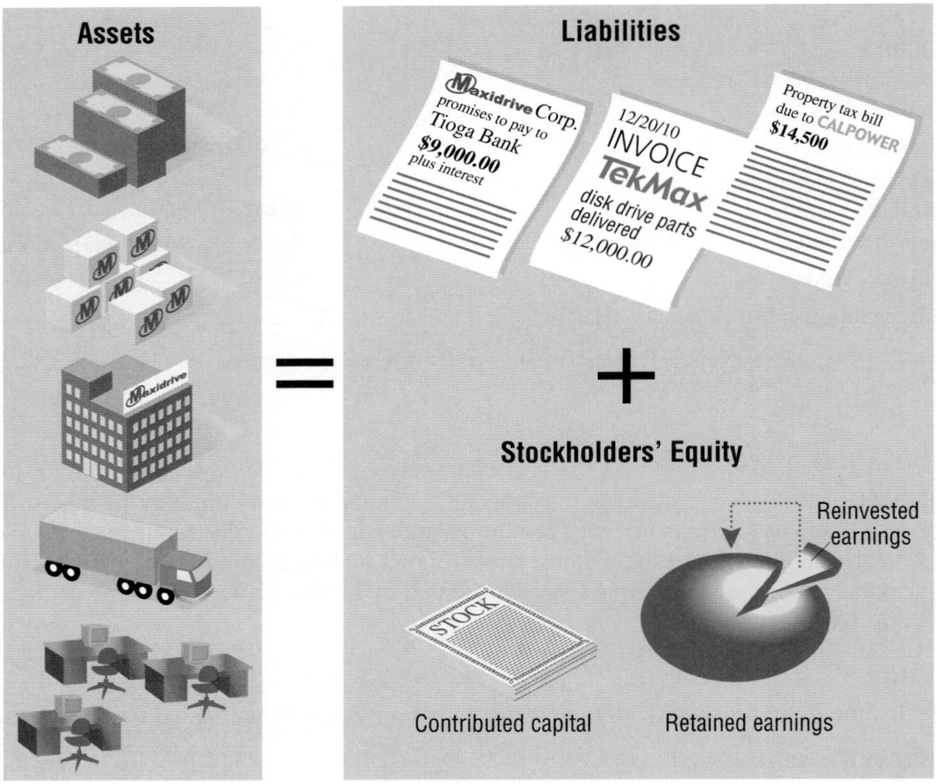

The basic accounting equation shows what we mean when we refer to a company's **financial position:** the economic resources that the company owns and the sources of financing for those resources.

Elements

Assets are the economic resources owned by the company. Maxidrive lists five items under the category Assets. The exact items listed as assets on a company's balance sheet depend on the nature of its operations. But these are common names used by many companies. The five items listed by Maxidrive are the economic resources needed to manufacture and sell disk drives to companies such as Dell. Each of these economic resources is expected to provide future

[1]A corporation is a business that is incorporated under the laws of a particular state. The owners are called **stockholders** or **shareholders.** Ownership is represented by shares of capital stock that usually can be bought and sold freely. The corporation operates as a separate legal entity, separate and apart from its owners. The stockholders enjoy limited liability; they are liable for the debts of the corporation only to the extent of their investments. Chapter Supplement A discusses forms of ownership in more detail.

benefits to the firm. To prepare to manufacture the drives, Maxidrive first needed cash to purchase land on which to build factories and install production machinery (plant and equipment). Maxidrive then began purchasing parts and producing disk drives, which led to the balance assigned to inventories. When Maxidrive sells its disk drives to Dell and others, it sells them on credit and receives promises to pay called accounts receivable, which are collected in cash later.

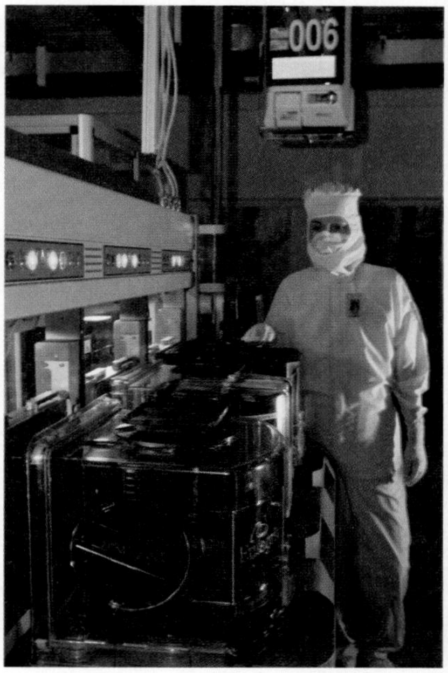

Every asset on the balance sheet is initially measured at the total cost incurred to acquire it. For example, the balance sheet for Maxidrive reports Land, $981; this is the amount paid (in thousands) for the land when it was acquired. Balance sheets do not generally show the amounts for which the assets could currently be sold.

Liabilities are the company's debts or obligations. Under the category Liabilities, Maxidrive lists two items. The accounts payable arise from the purchase of goods or services from suppliers on credit without a formal written contract (or a note). The notes payable result from cash borrowings based on a formal written debt contract with lending institutions such as banks.

Stockholders' equity indicates the amount of financing provided by owners of the business and earnings. The investment of cash and other assets in the business by the owners is called contributed capital. The amount of earnings (profits) reinvested in the business (and thus not distributed to stockholders in the form of dividends) is called retained earnings.

In Exhibit 1.2, the Stockholders' Equity section reports two items. The two founding stockholders' investment of $2,000,000 is reported as contributed capital. Maxidrive's total earnings (or losses incurred) less all dividends paid to the stockholders since formation of the corporation equals $9,105,000 and is reported as retained earnings. Total stockholders' equity is the sum of the contributed capital plus the retained earnings.

Interpreting Assets, Liabilities, and Stockholders' Equity on the Balance Sheet

FINANCIAL ANALYSIS

Assessment of Maxidrive's assets was important to its creditor, American Bank, and its prospective investor, Exeter, because assets provide a basis for judging whether the company has sufficient resources available to operate. Assets were also important because they could be sold for cash in the event that Maxidrive went out of business.

Exeter Investors was interested in Maxidrive's debts because of its concern about whether the company has sufficient sources of cash to pay its debts. Maxidrive's debts were also relevant to American Bank's decision to lend money to the company because existing creditors share American Bank's claim against Maxidrive's assets. If a business does not pay its creditors, the creditors may force the sale of assets sufficient to meet their claims. The sale of assets often fails to cover all of a company's debts, and some creditors may take a loss.

Maxidrive's stockholders' equity or net worth is important to American Bank because creditors' claims legally come before those of owners. If Maxidrive goes out of business and its assets are sold, the proceeds of that sale must be used to pay back creditors such as American Bank before the owners receive any money. Thus, creditors consider stockholders' equity a protective "cushion."

PAUSE FOR **FEEDBACK**

We just learned the **balance sheet** is a statement of financial position that reports dollar amounts for a company's assets, liabilities, and stockholders' equity at a specific point in time. These elements are related in the basic accounting equation: **Assets = Liabilities + Stockholders' Equity.** Before you move on, complete the following questions to test your understanding of these concepts.

SELF-STUDY QUIZ

1. Maxidrive's **assets** are listed in one section and **liabilities** and **stockholders' equity** in another. Notice that the two sections balance in conformity with the basic accounting equation. In the following chapters, you will learn that the basic accounting equation is the basic building block for the entire accounting process. Your task here is to verify that total assets ($27,261,000) is correct using the numbers for liabilities and stockholders' equity presented in Exhibit 1.2.
2. Learning which items belong in each of the balance sheet categories is an important first step in understanding their meaning. Without referring to Exhibit 1.2, mark each balance sheet item in the following list as an asset (A), liability (L), or stockholders' equity (SE).

_____ Accounts payable	_____ Inventories
_____ Accounts receivable	_____ Land
_____ Cash	_____ Notes payable
_____ Contributed capital	_____ Retained earnings
_____ Plant and equipment	

After you have completed your answers, check them with the solutions at the bottom of the page.

The Income Statement

Structure

The INCOME STATEMENT (Statement of Income, Statement of Earnings, Statement of Operations) reports the revenues less the expenses of the accounting period.

The **income statement** (statement of income, statement of earnings, or statement of operations) reports the accountant's primary measure of performance of a business, revenues less expenses during the accounting period. While the term profit is used widely for this measure of performance, accountants prefer to use the technical terms **net income** or net earnings. Maxidrive's net income measures its success in selling disk drives for more than the cost to generate those sales.

A quick reading of Maxidrive's income statement (Exhibit 1.3) indicates a great deal about its purpose and content. The heading identifies the name of the entity, the title of the report, and the unit of measure used in the statement. Unlike the balance sheet, however, which reports as of a certain date, the income statement reports for a specified period of time (for the year ended December 31, 2010). The time period covered by the financial statements (one year in this case) is called an **accounting period.** Notice that Maxidrive's income statement has three major captions: revenues, expenses, and net income. The income statement equation that describes their relationship is:

Revenues − Expenses = Net Income

The ACCOUNTING PERIOD is the time period covered by the financial statements.

Solutions to SELF-STUDY QUIZ

1. Assets ($27,261,000) = Liabilities ($16,156,000) + Stockholders' Equity ($11,105,000).
2. L, A, A, SE, A, A, A, L, SE (reading down the columns).

EXHIBIT 1.3

Income Statement

MAXIDRIVE CORP. **Income Statement** **For the Year Ended December 31, 2010** **(in thousands of dollars)**		*name of the entity* *title of the statement* *accounting period* *unit of measure*
Revenues		
Sales revenue	$37,436	*cash and promises received from sale of disk drives*
Total revenues	37,436	
Expenses		
Cost of goods sold expense	26,980	*cost to produce disk drives sold*
Selling, general, and administrative expense	3,624	*operating expenses not directly related to production*
Research and development expense	1,982	*expenses incurred to develop new products*
Interest expense	450	*cost of using borrowed funds*
Total expenses	33,036	
Pretax income	4,400	
Income tax expense	1,100	*income taxes on period's pretax income ($4,400 × 25%)*
Net income	$ 3,300	

The notes are an integral part of these financial statements.

Elements

Companies earn **revenues** from the sale of goods or services to customers (in Maxidrive's case, from the sale of disk drives). Revenues normally are reported for goods or services that have been sold to a customer **whether or not they have yet been paid for.** Retail stores such as Walmart and McDonald's often receive cash at the time of sale. However, when Maxidrive sells its disk drives to Dell and Apple, it receives a promise of future payment called an account receivable, which later is collected in cash. In either case, the business recognizes total sales (cash and credit) as revenue for the period. Various terms are used in income statements to describe different sources of revenue (e.g., provision of services, sale of goods, rental of property). Maxidrive lists only one, sales revenue, in its income statement.

Expenses represent the dollar amount of resources the entity used to earn revenues during the period. Expenses reported in one accounting period may actually be paid for in another accounting period. Some expenses require the payment of cash immediately while others require payment at a later date. Some may also require the use of another resource, such as an inventory item, which may have been paid for in a prior period. Maxidrive lists five types of expenses on its income statement, which are described in Exhibit 1.3. These expenses include income tax expense, which, as a corporation, Maxidrive must pay on pretax income.[2]

Net income or net earnings (often called "the bottom line") is the excess of total revenues over total expenses. If total expenses exceed total revenues, a net loss is reported.[3] We noted earlier that revenues are not necessarily the same as collections from customers and expenses are not necessarily the same as payments to suppliers. As a result, net income normally **does not equal** the net cash generated by operations. This latter amount is reported on the cash flow statement discussed later in this chapter.

[2]This example uses a 25 percent rate. Federal tax rates for corporations actually ranged from 15 percent to 35 percent at the time this book was written. State and local governments may levy additional taxes on corporate income, resulting in a higher total income tax rate.

[3]Net losses are normally noted by parentheses around the income figure.

FINANCIAL ANALYSIS | Analyzing the Income Statement: Beyond the Bottom Line

Investors such as Exeter and creditors such as American Bank closely monitor a firm's net income because it indicates the firm's ability to sell goods and services for more than they cost to produce and deliver. Investors buy stock when they believe that future earnings will improve and lead to a higher stock price. Lenders also rely on future earnings to provide the resources to repay loans. The details of the statement also are important. For example, Maxidrive had to sell more than $37 million worth of disk drives to make just over $3 million. If a competitor were to lower prices just 10 percent, forcing Maxidrive to do the same, its net income could easily turn into a net loss. These factors and others help investors and creditors estimate the company's future earnings.

PAUSE FOR **FEEDBACK**

As noted above, the **income statement** is a statement of operations that reports revenues, expenses, and net income for a stated period of time. To practice your understanding of these concepts, complete the following questions.

SELF-STUDY **QUIZ**

1. Learning which items belong in each of the income statement categories is an important first step in understanding their meaning. Without referring to Exhibit 1.3, mark each income statement item in the following list as a revenue (R) or an expense (E).

   _____ Cost of goods sold   _____ Sales
   _____ Income tax   _____ Selling, general, and administrative

2. During the period 2010, Maxidrive delivered disk drives for which customers paid or promised to pay amounts totaling $37,436,000. During the same period, it collected $33,563,000 in cash from its customers. Without referring to Exhibit 1.3, indicate which of these two amounts will be shown on Maxidrive's income statement as **sales revenue** for 2010. Why did you select your answer?
3. During the period 2010, Maxidrive **produced** disk drives with a total cost of production of $27,130,000. During the same period, it **delivered** to customers disk drives that had cost a total of $26,980,000 to produce. Without referring to Exhibit 1.3, indicate which of the two numbers will be shown on Maxidrive's income statement as **cost of goods sold expense** for 2010. Why did you select your answer?

After you have completed your answers, check them with the solutions at the bottom of the page.

The STATEMENT OF RETAINED EARNINGS reports the way that net income and the distribution of dividends affected the financial position of the company during the accounting period.

Statement of Retained Earnings

Structure

Maxidrive prepares a separate statement of retained earnings, shown in Exhibit 1.4. The heading identifies the name of the entity, the title of the report, and the unit of measure used in the statement. Like the income statement, the statement of retained earnings covers a specified period of time (the accounting period), which in this case is one year. The statement reports the

Solutions to SELF-STUDY QUIZ

1. E, E, R, E (reading down the columns).
2. Sales revenue in the amount of $37,436,000 is recognized. Sales revenue is normally reported on the income statement when goods or services have been delivered to customers who have either paid or promised to pay for them in the future.
3. Cost of goods sold expense is $26,980,000. Expenses are the dollar amount of resources used up to earn revenues during the period. Only those disk drives that have been delivered to customers have been used up. Those disk drives that are still on hand are part of the asset inventory.

EXHIBIT 1.4

Statement of Retained Earnings

MAXIDRIVE CORP. **Statement of Retained Earnings** **For the Year Ended December 31, 2010** **(in thousands of dollars)**		
		name of the entity *title of the statement* *accounting period* *unit of measure*
Retained earnings, January 1, 2010	$ 6,805	*last period's ending retained earnings*
Net income for 2010	3,300	*net income reported on the income statement*
Dividends for 2010	(1,000)	*dividends declared during the period*
Retained earnings, December 31, 2010	$ 9,105	*ending retained earnings on the balance sheet*

The notes are an integral part of these financial statements.

way that net income and the distribution of dividends affected the company's financial position during the accounting period.[4] Net income earned during the year increases the balance of retained earnings, showing the relationship of the income statement to the balance sheet.[5] The declaration of dividends to the stockholders decreases retained earnings.

The retained earnings equation that describes these relationships is:

Beginning Retained Earnings + Net Income − Dividends = Ending Retained Earnings

Statement of Retained Earnings
Beginning RE
+ Net Income
− Dividends
Ending RE

Elements

The statement of retained earnings in Exhibit 1.4 begins with Maxidrive's **beginning-of-the-year retained earnings.** The current year's **net income** reported on the income statement is added and the current year's **dividends** are subtracted from this amount. During 2010, Maxidrive earned $3,300,000, as shown on the income statement (Exhibit 1.3). This amount was added to the beginning-of-the-year retained earnings. Also, during 2010, Maxidrive declared and paid a total of $1,000,000 in dividends to its two original stockholders. This amount was subtracted in computing **end-of-the-year retained earnings** on the balance sheet. Note that retained earnings increased by the portion of income reinvested in the business ($3,300,000 − $1,000,000 = $2,300,000). The ending retained earnings amount of $9,105,000 is the same as that reported in Exhibit 1.2 on Maxidrive's balance sheet. Thus, the retained earnings statement indicates the relationship of the income statement to the balance sheet.

Interpreting Retained Earnings

FINANCIAL ANALYSIS

Reinvestment of earnings, or retained earnings, is an important source of financing for Maxidrive, representing more than one-third of its financing. Creditors such as American Bank closely monitor a firm's retained earnings statement because the firm's policy on dividend payments to the stockholders affects its ability to repay its debts. Every dollar Maxidrive pays to stockholders as a dividend is not available for use in paying back its debt to American Bank. Investors examine retained earnings to determine whether the company is reinvesting a sufficient portion of earnings to support future growth.

[4]Other corporations report these changes at the end of the income statement or in a more general statement of stockholders' equity, which we discuss in Chapter 4.
[5]Net losses are subtracted.

PAUSE FOR **FEEDBACK**

The **statement of retained earnings** explains changes to the retained earnings balance caused by net income and dividends during the reporting period. Check your understanding of these relationships by completing the following question.

SELF-STUDY **QUIZ**

1. Maxidrive's statement of retained earnings reports the way that net income and the distribution of dividends affected the financial position of the company during the accounting period. In a prior period, Maxidrive's financial statements reported the following amounts: beginning retained earnings, $5,510; total assets, $20,450; dividends, $900; cost of goods sold expense, $19,475; net income, $1,780. Without referring to Exhibit 1.4, compute ending retained earnings.

After you have completed your answer, check it with the solution at the bottom of the page.

Statement of Cash Flows

Structure

The STATEMENT OF CASH FLOWS (Cash Flow Statement) reports inflows and outflows of cash during the accounting period in the categories of operating, investing, and financing.

Maxidrive's statement of cash flows is presented in Exhibit 1.5. The **statement of cash flows** (cash flow statement) divides Maxidrive's cash inflows and outflows (receipts and payments) into the three primary categories of cash flows in a typical business: cash flows from operating, investing, and financing activities. The heading identifies the name of the entity, the title of the report, and the unit of measure used in the statement. Like the income statement, the cash flow statement covers a specified period of time (the accounting period), which in this case is one year.

As discussed earlier in this chapter, reported revenues do not always equal cash collected from customers because some sales may be on credit. Also, expenses reported on the income statement may not be equal to the cash paid out during the period because expenses may be incurred in one period and paid for in another. Because the income statement does not provide information concerning cash flows, accountants prepare the statement of cash flows to report inflows and outflows of cash. The cash flow statement equation describes the causes of the change in cash reported on the balance sheet from the end of last period to the end of the current period:

+ / − Cash Flows from Operating Activities (CFO)
+ / − Cash Flows from Investing Activities (CFI)
+ / − Cash Flows from Financing Activities (CFF)
Change in Cash

Note that each of the three cash flow sources can be positive or negative.

Elements

Cash flows from operating activities are cash flows that are directly related to earning income. For example, when Dell, Apple, and other customers pay Maxidrive for the disk drives it has delivered to them, it lists the amounts collected as cash collected from

Solution to SELF-STUDY QUIZ

1. Beginning Retained Earnings ($5,510) + Net Income ($1,780) − Dividends ($900) = Ending Retained Earnings ($6,390).

EXHIBIT 1.5

Statement of Cash Flows

MAXIDRIVE CORP. **Statement of Cash Flows** **For the Year Ended December 31, 2010** **(in thousands of dollars)**		*name of the entity* *title of the statement* *accounting period* *unit of measure*
Cash flows from operating activities		*cash flows directly related to earning income*
Cash collected from customers	$ 33,563	
Cash paid to suppliers and employees	(30,854)	
Cash paid for interest	(450)	
Cash paid for taxes	(1,190)	
Net cash flow from operating activities	1,069	
Cash flows from investing activities		*cash flows from purchase/sale of productive assets*
Cash paid to purchase manufacturing equipment	(1,625)	
Net cash flow from investing activities	(1,625)	
Cash flows from financing activities		*cash flows from investors and creditors*
Cash received from bank loan	1,400	
Cash paid for dividends	(1,000)	
Net cash flow from financing activities	400	
Net decrease in cash during the year	(156)	*change in cash during the period ($1,069 − 1,625 + 400)*
Cash at beginning of year	5,051	*last period's ending cash balance*
Cash at end of year	$ 4,895	*ending cash on the balance sheet*

The notes are an integral part of these financial statements.

customers. When Maxidrive pays salaries to its employees in research and development or pays bills received from its parts suppliers, it includes the amounts in cash paid to suppliers and employees.[6]

Cash flows from investing activities include cash flows related to the acquisition or sale of the company's productive assets. This year, Maxidrive had only one cash outflow from investing activities, the purchase of additional manufacturing equipment to meet growing demand for its products. **Cash flows from financing activities** are directly related to the financing of the enterprise itself. They involve the receipt or payment of money to investors and creditors (except for suppliers). This year, Maxidrive borrowed an additional $1,400,000 from the bank to purchase most of the new manufacturing equipment. It also paid out $1,000,000 in dividends to the founding stockholders.

Interpreting the Cash Flow Statement

FINANCIAL ANALYSIS

Many analysts believe that the statement of cash flows is particularly useful in predicting future cash flows that may be available for payment of debt to creditors and dividends to investors. Bankers often consider the Operating Activities section to be most important because it indicates the company's ability to generate cash from sales to meet its current cash needs. Any amount left over can be used to pay back the bank debt or expand the company. Stockholders will invest in a company only if they believe that it will eventually generate more cash from operations than it uses so that cash will become available to pay dividends and expand.

[6]Alternative ways to present cash flows from operations are discussed in Chapter 5.

STOP

PAUSE FOR **FEEDBACK**

The **statement of cash flows** reports inflows and outflows of cash for a stated period of time classified into three categories: operating, investing, and financing activities. Answer the following questions to test your understanding of the concepts involved.

SELF-STUDY **QUIZ**

1. During the period 2010, Maxidrive delivered disk drives to customers who paid or promised to pay a total of $37,436,000. During the same period, it collected $33,563,000 in cash from customers. Without referring to Exhibit 1.5, indicate which of the two amounts will be shown on Maxidrive's cash flow statement for 2010.
2. Your task here is to verify that Maxidrive's cash balance decreased by $156 during the year using the totals for cash flows from operating, investing, and financing activities presented in Exhibit 1.5. Recall the cash flow statement equation:

+/− Cash Flows from Operating Activities (CFO)
+/− Cash Flows from Investing Activities (CFI)
+/− Cash Flows from Financing Activities (CFF)
Change in Cash

After you have completed your answers, check them with the solutions at the bottom of the page.

Relationships Among the Statements

Our discussion of the four basic financial statements has focused on what elements are reported in each statement, how the elements are related by the equation for each statement, and how the elements are important to the decisions of investors, creditors, and others. We have also discovered how the statements, all of which are outputs from the same system, are related to one another. In particular, we learned:

1. Net income from the income statement results in an increase in ending retained earnings on the statement of retained earnings.
2. Ending retained earnings from the statement of retained earnings is one of the two components of stockholders' equity on the balance sheet.
3. The change in cash on the cash flow statement added to the beginning-of-the-year balance in cash equals the end-of-year balance in cash on the balance sheet.

Thus, we can think of the income statement as explaining, through the statement of retained earnings, how the operations of the company improved or harmed the financial position of the company during the year. The cash flow statement explains how the operating, investing, and financing activities of the company affected the cash balance on the balance sheet during the year. These relationships are illustrated in Exhibit 1.6 for Maxidrive's financial statements.

Notes

NOTES (Footnotes) provide supplemental information about the financial condition of a company, without which the financial statements cannot be fully understood.

At the bottom of each of Maxidrive's four basic financial statements is this statement: **"The notes are an integral part of these financial statements."** This is the accounting equivalent of the Surgeon General's warning on a package of cigarettes. It warns users that failure to read the **notes** (or footnotes) to the financial statements will result in an incomplete picture of the

Solutions to SELF-STUDY QUIZ

1. The firm recognizes $33,563,000 on the cash flow statement because this number represents the actual cash collected from customers related to current and prior years' sales.

2.

+/− Cash Flows from Operating Activities (CFO)	$1,069
+/− Cash Flows from Investing Activities (CFI)	− 1,625
+/− Cash Flows from Financing Activities (CFF)	+ 400
Change in Cash	$ (156)

EXHIBIT 1.6

Relationships Among Maxidrive's Statements

Income Statement

Revenues	$ 37,436
− Expenses	34,136
Net Income	$ 3,300

1 (Net Income → Statement of Retained Earnings)

Statement of Retained Earnings

Beginning Retained Earnings	$ 6,805
+ Net Income	3,300
− Dividends	(1,000)
Ending Retained Earnings	$ 9,105

2 (Ending Retained Earnings → Balance Sheet Retained Earnings)

Statement of Cash Flows

+/− Cash Flows from Operating Activities	$ 1,069
+/− Cash Flows from Investing Activities	(1,625)
+/− Cash Flows from Financing Activities	400
Change in Cash	(156)
+ Cash at Beginning of Period	5,051
Cash at End of Period	$ 4,895

3 (Cash at End of Period → Balance Sheet Cash)

Balance Sheet

Cash	$ 4,895
Other Assets	22,366
Total Assets	$ 27,261
Liabilities	$ 16,156
Contributed Capital	2,000
Retained Earnings	9,105
Total Liabilities & Stockholders' Equity	$ 27,261

company's financial health. Notes provide supplemental information about the financial condition of a company without which the financial statements cannot be fully understood.

There are three basic types of notes. The first type provides descriptions of the accounting rules applied in the company's statements. The second presents additional detail about a line on the financial statements. For example, Maxidrive's inventory note indicates the amount of parts, drives under construction, and finished disk drives included in the total inventory amount listed on the balance sheet. The third type of note provides additional financial disclosures about items not listed on the statements themselves. For example, Maxidrive leases one of its production facilities; terms of the lease are disclosed in a note. Throughout this book, we will discuss many note disclosures because understanding their content is critical to understanding the company.

A few additional formatting conventions are worth noting here. Assets are listed on the balance sheet by ease of conversion to cash. Liabilities are listed by their maturity (due date). Most financial statements include the monetary unit sign (in the United States, the $) beside the first dollar amount in a group of items (e.g., the cash amount in the assets). Also, it is common to place a single underline below the last item in a group before a total or subtotal (e.g., land). A dollar sign is also placed beside group totals (e.g., total assets) and a double underline below. The same conventions are followed in all four basic financial statements.

Management Uses of Financial Statements

FINANCIAL ANALYSIS

In our discussion of financial analysis thus far, we have focused on the perspectives of investors and creditors. Managers within the firm also make direct use of financial statements. For example, Maxidrive's **marketing managers** and **credit managers** use customers' financial statements to decide whether to extend credit for purchases of disk drives. Maxidrive's **purchasing managers** analyze parts suppliers' financial statements to see whether the suppliers have the resources to meet Maxidrive's demand and invest in the development of new parts. Both the **employees' union** and Maxidrive's **human resource managers** use Maxidrive's financial statements as a basis for contract negotiations over pay rates. The net income figure even serves as a basis for calculating **employee bonuses.** Regardless of the functional area of management in which you are employed, you will use financial statement data. You also will be evaluated based on the impact of your decisions on your company's financial statement data.

EXHIBIT 1.7

Summary of the Four Basic Financial Statements

Financial Statement	Purpose	Structure	Examples of Content
Balance Sheet (Statement of Financial Position)	Reports the financial position (economic resources and sources of financing) of an accounting entity *at a point in time.*	BALANCE SHEET Assets = Liabilities + Stockholders' Equity	Cash, accounts receivable, plant and equipment, notes payable, contributed capital
Income Statement (Statement of Income, Statement of Earnings, Statement of Operations)	Reports the accountant's primary measure of economic performance *during the accounting period.*	**Income Statement** Revenues – Expenses Net Income	Sales revenue, cost of goods sold, selling expense, interest expense
Statement of Retained Earnings	Reports the way that net income and the distribution of dividends have affected the financial position of the company *during the accounting period.*	**Statement of Retained Earnings** Beginning RE + Net Income – Dividends Ending RE	Net income is taken from the income statement; Dividends are distributions to stockholders
Statement of Cash Flows (Cash Flow Statement)	Reports inflows (receipts) and outflows (payments) of cash *during the accounting period* in the categories operating, investing, and financing.	**Statement of Cash Flows** +/– CFO +/– CFI +/– CFF Change in Cash	Cash collected from customers, cash paid to suppliers, cash paid to purchase equipment, cash borrowed from banks

Summary of the Four Basic Financial Statements

We have learned a great deal about the content of the four basic financial statements. Exhibit 1.7 summarizes this information. Take a few minutes to review the information in the exhibit before you move on to the next section of the chapter.

RESPONSIBILITIES FOR THE ACCOUNTING COMMUNICATION PROCESS

LEARNING OBJECTIVE 2

Identify the role of generally accepted accounting principles (GAAP) in determining the content of financial statements.

For the decision makers at Exeter to use the information in Maxidrive's financial statements effectively, they had to understand what information each of the statements conveyed. Decision makers also need to understand the **measurement rules** applied in computing the numbers on the statements. A swim coach would never try to evaluate a swimmer's time in the 100 freestyle without first asking if the time was for a race in meters or in yards. Likewise, a decision maker should never attempt to use accounting information without first understanding the measurement rules that were used to develop the information. These measurement rules are called **generally accepted accounting principles,** or GAAP.

GENERALLY ACCEPTED ACCOUNTING PRINCIPLES (GAAP) are the measurement rules used to develop the information in financial statements.

Generally Accepted Accounting Principles

How Are Generally Accepted Accounting Principles Determined?

The accounting system in use today has a long history. Its foundations are normally traced back to the works of an Italian monk and mathematician, Fr. Luca Pacioli, published in 1494.

However, prior to 1933, each company's management largely determined its financial reporting practices. Thus, little uniformity in practice existed among companies.

Following the dramatic stock market decline of 1929, the Securities Act of 1933 and the Securities Exchange Act of 1934 were passed into law by the U.S. Congress. These acts created the **Securities and Exchange Commission (SEC)** and gave it broad powers to determine the measurement rules for financial statements that companies issuing stock to the public (publicly traded companies) must provide to stockholders.[7] The SEC has worked with organizations of professional accountants to establish groups that are given the primary responsibilities to work out the detailed rules that become generally accepted accounting principles. Today, the **Financial Accounting Standards Board (FASB)** has this responsibility. The Board has five full-time voting members and a permanent staff who consider the appropriate financial reporting responses to ever-changing business practices. The official pronouncements of the FASB **(Financial Accounting Standards)** and its predecessors total thousands of pages of very fine print. Such detail is made necessary by the enormous diversity and complexity of current business practices.

The SECURITIES AND EXCHANGE COMMISSION (SEC) is the U.S. government agency that determines the financial statements that public companies must provide to stockholders and the measurement rules that they must use in producing those statements.

The FINANCIAL ACCOUNTING STANDARDS BOARD (FASB) is the private sector body given the primary responsibility to work out the detailed rules that become generally accepted accounting principles.

Most managers do not need to learn all the details included in these standards. Our approach is to focus on those details that have the greatest impact on the numbers presented in financial statements and are appropriate for an introductory course.

Why Is GAAP Important to Managers and External Users?

Generally accepted accounting principles (GAAP) are of great interest to the companies that must prepare financial statements, their auditors, and the readers of the statements. Companies and their managers and owners are most directly affected by the information presented in financial statements. Companies incur the cost of preparing the statements and bear the major economic consequences of their publication, which include, among others,

1. Effects on the selling price of a company's stock.
2. Effects on the amount of bonuses received by management and employees.
3. Loss of competitive information to other companies.

As a consequence of these and other concerns, changes in GAAP are actively debated, political lobbying often takes place, and final rules are a compromise among the wishes of interested parties.

The International Accounting Standards Board and Global Convergence of Accounting Standards

INTERNATIONAL PERSPECTIVE

Financial accounting standards and disclosure requirements are adopted by national regulatory agencies. Since 2002, there has been substantial movement toward the adoption of **International Financial Reporting Standards (IFRS)** issued by the **International Accounting Standards Board (IASB).** Examples of jurisdictions requiring the use of IFRS either currently or by 2012 include:

- **European Union (United Kingdom, Germany, France, Netherlands, Belgium, Bulgaria, Poland, etc.)**
- **Australia and New Zealand**
- **Hong Kong (S.A.R. of China), India, Malaysia, and South Korea**
- **Israel and Turkey**
- **Brazil and Chile**
- **Canada and Mexico**

In the United States, the Securities and Exchange Commission now allows foreign companies whose stock is traded in the United States to use IFRS and is considering requiring the use of IFRS for U.S. domestic companies by 2015. To prepare you for this eventuality, we will point out key differences between IFRS and U.S. GAAP starting in Chapter 6. The basic principles and practices we discuss in Chapters 1 through 5 apply equally to both sets of standards.

SOURCE: Deloitte IAS PLUS website.

REAL WORLD EXCERPT
Deloitte IAS Plus Website

[7] Contrary to popular belief, these rules are different from those that companies follow when filing their income tax returns. We discuss these differences further in later chapters.

LEARNING OBJECTIVE 3

Distinguish the roles of managers and auditors in the accounting communication process.

Management Responsibility and the Demand for Auditing

Exeter's owners and managers were well aware of the details of U.S. GAAP, but they were still misled. Although the measurement rules that Maxidrive had used to produce its financial statements were consistent with GAAP, the underlying figures were fictitious. Who was responsible for the accuracy of the numbers in Maxidrive's financial statements?

Primary responsibility for the information in the financial statements lies with management, represented by the highest officer of the company and the highest financial officer. Companies take three important steps to assure investors that the company's records are accurate: (1) they maintain a system of controls over both the records and the assets of the company, (2) they hire outside independent auditors to verify the fairness of the financial statements, and (3) they form a committee of the board of directors to oversee the integrity of these other two safeguards. These responsibilities are often reiterated in a formal **report of management** or **management certification** in the annual report. These three safeguards and a management certification are required for companies with publicly traded stock. These safeguards failed in Maxidrive's case. Managers of companies that prepare fraudulent financial statements are subject to criminal and civil penalties.

The role of the independent auditor is described in more detail in the **audit report** in Exhibit 1.8 (report of independent accountants or independent registered public accounting firm). The audit report describes the auditor's opinion of the fairness of the financial statements and the evidence gathered to support that opinion. An accountant may be licensed as a **certified public accountant,** or **CPA,** only on completion of requirements specified by each state. Only a licensed CPA can issue an audit report. In this role, accountants are known as **independent CPAs** (or **independent accountants**) because they have certain responsibilities that extend to the general public as well as to the specific business that pays for this service.

An AUDIT is an examination of the financial reports to ensure that they represent what they claim and conform with GAAP.

The PUBLIC COMPANY ACCOUNTING OVERSIGHT BOARD (PCAOB) is the private sector body given the primary responsibility to issue detailed auditing standards.

An **audit** involves the examination of the financial reports (prepared by the management of the entity) to ensure that they represent what they claim to and conform with generally accepted accounting principles (GAAP). In performing an audit, the independent CPA examines the underlying transactions and the accounting methods used to account for these transactions. Because of the enormous number of transactions involving a major enterprise such as Apple, the CPA does not examine each of these transactions. Rather, professional approaches are used to ascertain beyond reasonable doubt that transactions were measured and reported properly. The **Public Company Accounting Oversight Board (PCAOB),** in consultation with the SEC, sets standards for these tests for the audits of public companies.

EXHIBIT 1.8

Report of Independent Accountants

Report of Independent Accountants to the Stockholders and Board of Directors of Maxidrive Corp.

We have audited the accompanying balance sheet of Maxidrive Corp. as of December 31, 2010, and the related statements of income, retained earnings, and cash flows for the period ended December 31, 2010. These financial statements are the responsibility of the Company's management. Our responsibility is to express an opinion on these financial statements based on our audits.

We conducted our audits in accordance with generally accepted auditing standards in the United States of America. Those standards require that we plan and perform the audit to obtain reasonable assurance about whether the financial statements are free of material misstatement. An audit includes examining, on a test basis, evidence supporting the amounts and disclosures in the financial statements. An audit also includes assessing the accounting principles used and significant estimates made by management, as well as evaluating the overall financial statement presentation. We believe that our audits provide a reasonable basis for our opinion.

In our opinion, the financial statements referred to above present fairly, in all material respects, the financial position of Maxidrive Corp. at December 31, 2010, and the results of its operations and its cash flows for the year ended December 31, 2010, in conformity with generally accepted accounting principles in the United States of America.

Smith and Walker, CPAs
February 26, 2011

Using Financial Statements to Determine Maxidrive's Value

FINANCIAL ANALYSIS

Maxidrive's current and prior years' income statements played a particularly important part in the price Exeter was willing to pay for Maxidrive Corp. Prior years' income statements (which were not presented here) indicated that the company had earned income every year since its founding except for the first year. Furthermore, both sales revenue and net income had risen every year. One method for estimating the value of a company that relies on net income and growth in net income is the **price/earnings ratio** (P/E ratio, or P/E multiple). The P/E ratio measures how many times current year's earnings investors are willing to pay for a company's stock. A higher P/E ratio means that investors have more confidence in the company's ability to produce higher profits in future years. A first approximation of Exeter's overpayment, and the amount it would hope to recover from the perpetrators of the fraud would be:

$$\text{Income Overstatement} \times \text{P/E Ratio} = \text{Overpayment}$$

If income was overstated by $1,650,000 and Maxidrive's P/E ratio was 10, Exeter would have overpaid $16.5 million for the purchase of Maxidrive. The role of net income in determining the value of a company will be discussed in more detail in your corporate finance course and more advanced courses in financial statement analysis.

Ethics, Reputation, and Legal Liability

LEARNING OBJECTIVE 4

Appreciate the importance of ethics, reputation, and legal liability in accounting.

If financial statements are to be of any value to decision makers, users must have confidence in the fairness of the information they present. Users will have greater confidence in the information if they know that the people who audited the statements were required to meet professional standards of ethics and competence.

The American Institute of Certified Public Accountants (AICPA) requires all of its members to adhere to a professional code of ethics and professional auditing standards, and auditors of public companies must register with and comply with standards set by the Public Company Accounting Oversight Board (PCAOB). Failure to comply with the rules of conduct can result in serious professional penalties. CPAs' reputations for honesty and competence are their most important assets. The potential economic effects of damage to reputation, malpractice liability, and potential fines provide even stronger incentives to abide by professional standards.

In case of malpractice, the independent CPA may be held liable for losses suffered by those who relied on the statements the CPA examined. As a result of the fraud, Maxidrive filed for bankruptcy and will likely be sold in an attempt to pay off creditors. In a civil lawsuit, Exeter Investors and American Bank claimed losses of $16.5 million and $9 million, respectively, charging that the officers of Maxidrive had "perpetrated a massive fraud" and the auditors had "overlooked the errors" in the audit. Exeter and American Bank also have asked for punitive damages for gross negligence. In addition, the president and the chief financial officer of Maxidrive were convicted by a federal jury on three counts of criminal securities fraud for which they were fined and imprisoned.

EPILOGUE

Although financial statement fraud is a fairly rare event, the misrepresentations in Maxidrive's statements aptly illustrate the importance of fairly presented financial statements to investors and creditors. They also indicate the crucial importance of the public accounting profession in ensuring the integrity of the financial reporting system. The recent Enron and WorldCom debacles have brought the importance of these issues to the attention of the general public.

As noted at the beginning of this chapter, Maxidrive is not a real company but is based on a real company that perpetrated a similar fraud. (The focus companies and contrasting examples in the remaining chapters are *real* companies.) Maxidrive is loosely based on the infamous fraud at MiniScribe, a real disk drive manufacturer. The size of the real fraud, however, was more than 10 times as great as that in the fictional case, as were the losses incurred and the damages claimed in the lawsuits that followed. (Many of the numbers in Maxidrive's financial statements are simply one-tenth the amounts presented in MiniScribe's fraudulent statements.) The nature of the fraud also was quite similar. At MiniScribe, sales revenue was overstated by transferring nonexistent inventory between two facilities and creating phony documents to make it look as though the inventory was transferred to customers. MiniScribe even packaged bricks as finished products, shipped them to distributors, and counted them as sold. Cost of goods sold was understated by activities such as counting scrap parts and damaged drives as usable inventory. MiniScribe managers even broke into the auditors' locked trunks to change numbers on their audit papers.

As a consequence, MiniScribe reported net income of $31 million, which was subsequently shown to be $9 million. MiniScribe's investors and creditors filed lawsuits claiming more than $1 billion in damages. Actual damages in the hundreds of millions were paid. Both the chairman and the chief financial officer of MiniScribe were convicted of federal securities and wire fraud charges and sentenced to jail. Although most managers and owners act in an honest and responsible fashion, this incident, and the much larger frauds at Enron and WorldCom, are stark reminders of the economic consequences of lack of fair presentation in financial reports. Both companies were forced into bankruptcy when their fraudulent financial reporting practices were brought to light. Penalties against their audit firm, Arthur Andersen, also led to its bankruptcy and dissolution. A sampling of firms that have recently been involved in financial statement misrepresentations follows:

Enron	Parmalat
WorldCom	Nortel
Adelphia	General Electric
Satyam	Cardinal Health

Computer Associates	Homestore.com
Tyco	Dynegy
HealthSouth	Fannie Mae
McKesson	Freddie Mac
Beazer Homes	Royal Ahold NV
Rite-Aid	Gerber Scientific
Aurora Foods	Stanley Works
Halliburton	AIG

DEMONSTRATION CASE

Apple Inc.

At the end of most chapters, one or more demonstration cases are presented. These cases provide an overview of the primary issues discussed in the chapter. Each demonstration case is followed by a recommended solution. You should read the case carefully and then prepare your own solution before you study the recommended solution. This self-evaluation is highly recommended. The introductory case presented here reviews the elements reported on the income statement and balance sheet and how the elements within the statements are related.

Apple's iPods, iPhones, and iTunes stores have become the center of the digital lifestyle for professionals and consumers alike. Extensive iPod content is even available for this textbook. The ease-of-use, seamless integration, and innovative design of Apple's products have produced record profits and stock prices for Apple's shareholders. Following is a list of the financial statement items and amounts adapted from a recent Apple income statement and balance sheet. The numbers are presented in millions of dollars for the year ended September 26, 2009.

Accounts payable	$ 6,471	Property and equipment	2,954
Accounts receivable	3,361	Research and development expenses	1,333
Cash	5,263	Retained earnings	19,622
Contributed capital	8,210	Sales revenues	36,537
Cost of sales	23,397	Selling, general, and administrative expenses	4,149
Income tax expense	2,280		
Inventories	455	Total assets	53,851
Investments	28,729	Total expenses	28,879
Net income	5,704	Total liabilities	26,019
Notes payable	6,737	Total liabilities and stockholders' equity	53,851
Other assets	13,089		
Other revenues	326	Total revenues	36,863
Pretax income	7,984	Total stockholders' equity	27,832

Required:

1. Prepare a balance sheet and an income statement for the year following the formats in Exhibits 1.2 and 1.3.
2. Specify what information these two statements provide.
3. Indicate the other two statements that would be included in Apple's annual report.
4. Securities regulations require that Apple's statements be subject to an independent audit. Suggest why Apple might voluntarily subject its statements to an independent audit if there were no such requirement.

SUGGESTED SOLUTION

1.

APPLE INC.
Balance Sheet
At September 26, 2009
(in millions of dollars)

Assets	
Cash	$ 5,263
Accounts receivable	3,361
Inventories	455
Investments	28,729
Property and equipment	2,954
Other assets	13,089
Total assets	$53,851
Liabilities	
Accounts payable	$19,282
Notes payable	6,737
Total liabilities	26,019
Stockholders' Equity	
Contributed capital	8,210
Retained earnings	19,622
Total stockholders' equity	27,832
Total liabilities and stockholders' equity	$53,851

APPLE INC.
Income Statement
For the Year Ended September 26, 2009
(in millions of dollars)

Revenues	
Sales revenues	$36,537
Other revenues	326
Total revenues	36,863
Expenses	
Cost of sales	23,397
Selling, general, and administrative expenses	4,149
Research and development expenses	1,333
Total expenses	28,879
Pretax income	7,984
Income tax expense	2,280
Net income	$ 5,704

2. The balance sheet reports the amount of assets, liabilities, and stockholders' equity of an accounting entity at a point in time. The income statement reports the accountant's primary measure of performance of a business, revenues less expenses, during the accounting period.
3. Apple would also present a statement of retained earnings and a statement of cash flows.
4. Users will have greater confidence in the accuracy of financial statement information if they know that the people who audited the statements were required to meet professional standards of ethics and competence.

Chapter Supplement A

Types of Business Entities

This textbook emphasizes **accounting for profit-making business entities**. The three main types of business entities are sole proprietorship, partnership, and corporation. A **sole proprietorship** is an unincorporated business owned by one person; it usually is small in size and is common in the service, retailing, and farming industries. Often the owner is the manager. Legally, the business and the owner are not separate entities. Accounting views the business as a separate entity, however, that must be accounted for separately from its owner.

A **partnership** is an unincorporated business owned by two or more persons known as **partners.** The agreements between the owners are specified in a partnership contract. This contract deals with matters such as division of income each reporting period and distribution of resources of the business on termination of its operations. A partnership is not legally separate from its owners. Legally, each partner in a general partnership is responsible for the debts of the business (each general partner has **unlimited liability**). The partnership, however, is a separate business entity to be accounted for separately from its several owners.

A **corporation** is a business incorporated under the laws of a particular state. The owners are called **stockholders** or **shareholders.** Ownership is represented by shares of capital stock that usually can be bought and sold freely. When the organizers file an approved application for incorporation, the state issues a charter. This charter gives the corporation the right to operate as a separate legal entity, separate and apart from its owners. The stockholders enjoy **limited liability.** Stockholders are liable for the corporation's debts only to the extent of their investments. The corporate charter specifies the types and amounts of capital stock that can be issued. Most states require a minimum of two or three stockholders and a minimum amount of resources to be contributed at the time of organization. The stockholders elect a governing board of directors, which in turn employs managers and exercises general supervision of the corporation. Accounting also views the corporation as a separate business entity that must be accounted for separately from its owners.

In terms of economic importance, the corporation is the dominant form of business organization in the United States. This dominance is caused by the many advantages of the corporate form: (1) limited liability for the stockholders, (2) continuity of life, (3) ease in transferring ownership (stock), and (4) opportunities to raise large amounts of money by selling shares to a large number of people. The primary disadvantage of a corporation is that its income may be subject to double taxation (income is taxed when it is earned and again when it is distributed to stockholders as dividends). In this textbook, we emphasize the corporate form of business. Nevertheless, the accounting concepts and procedures that we discuss also apply to other types of businesses.

Chapter Supplement B

Employment in the Accounting Profession Today

Since 1900, accounting has attained the stature of professions such as law, medicine, engineering, and architecture. As with all recognized professions, accounting is subject to professional competence requirements, is dedicated to service to the public, requires a high level of academic study, and rests on a common body of knowledge. An accountant may be licensed as a certified public accountant, or CPA. This designation is granted only on completion of requirements specified by the state that issues the license. Although CPA requirements vary among states, they include a college degree with a specified number of accounting courses, good character, one to five years of professional experience, and successful completion of a professional examination. The CPA examination is prepared by the American Institute of Certified Public Accountants.

Accountants (including CPAs) commonly are engaged in professional practice or are employed by businesses, government entities, nonprofit organizations, and so on. Accountants employed in these activities may take and pass a professional examination to become a certified management accountant, or CMA (the CMA examination is administered by the Institute of Management Accountants), or a certified internal auditor, or CIA (the CIA examination is administered by the Institute of Internal Auditors).

Practice of Public Accounting

Although an individual may practice public accounting, usually two or more individuals organize an accounting firm in the form of a partnership (in many cases, a limited liability partnership, or LLP). Accounting firms vary in size from a one-person office, to regional firms, to the Big Four firms (Deloitte & Touche, Ernst & Young, KPMG, and PricewaterhouseCoopers), which have hundreds of offices located worldwide. Accounting firms usually render three types of services: audit or assurance services, management consulting services, and tax services.

Audit or Assurance Services

Audit or assurance services are independent professional services that improve the quality of information, or its context, for decision makers. The most important assurance service performed by the CPA in public practice is financial statement auditing. The purpose of an audit is to lend credibility to the financial reports, that is, to ensure that they fairly represent what they claim. An audit involves an examination of the financial reports (prepared by the management of the entity) to ensure that they conform with GAAP. Other areas of assurance services include electronic commerce integrity and security and information systems reliability.

Management Consulting Services

Many independent CPA firms offer management consulting services. These services usually are accounting based and encompass such activities as the design and installation of accounting, data processing, and profit-planning and control (budget) systems; financial advice; forecasting; inventory controls; cost-effectiveness studies; and operational analysis. To maintain their independence, CPAs are prohibited from performing certain consulting services for the public companies that they audit.

Tax Services

CPAs in public practice usually provide income tax services to their clients. These services include both tax planning as a part of the decision-making process and the determination of the income tax liability (reported on the annual income tax return). Because of the increasing complexity of state and federal tax laws, a high level of competence is required, which CPAs specializing in taxation can provide. The CPA's involvement in tax planning often is quite significant. Most major business decisions have significant tax impacts; in fact, tax-planning considerations often govern certain business decisions.

Employment by Organizations

Many accountants, including CPAs, CMAs, and CIAs, are employed by profit-making and nonprofit organizations. An organization, depending on its size and complexity, may employ from a few to hundreds of accountants. In a business enterprise, the chief financial officer (usually a vice president or controller) is a member of the management team. This responsibility usually entails a wide range of management, financial, and accounting duties.

In a business entity, accountants typically are engaged in a wide variety of activities, such as general management, general accounting, cost accounting, profit planning and control (budgeting), internal auditing, and computerized data processing. A primary function of the accountants in organizations is to provide data that are useful for internal managerial decision making and for controlling operations. The functions of external reporting, tax planning, control of assets, and a host of related responsibilities normally are also performed by accountants in industry.

Employment in the Public and Not-for-Profit Sector

The vast and complex operations of governmental units, from the local to the international level, create a need for accountants. The same holds true for other not-for-profit organizations such as hospitals and universities. Accountants employed in the public and not-for-profit sector perform functions similar to those performed by their counterparts in private organizations. The Government Accountability Office (GAO) and the regulatory agencies, such as the SEC and Federal Communications Commission (FCC), also use the services of accountants in carrying out their regulatory duties.

CHAPTER TAKE-AWAYS

1. **Recognize the information conveyed in each of the four basic financial statements and the way that it is used by different decision makers (investors, creditors, and managers).** p. 4

   The **balance sheet** is a statement of financial position that reports dollar amounts for the assets, liabilities, and stockholders' equity at a specific point in time.

   The **income statement** is a statement of operations that reports revenues, expenses, and net income for a stated period of time.

   The **statement of retained earnings** explains changes to the retained earnings balance that occurred during the reporting period.

   The **statement of cash flows** reports inflows and outflows of cash for a stated period of time.

   The statements are used by investors and creditors to evaluate different aspects of the firm's financial position and performance.

2. **Identify the role of generally accepted accounting principles (GAAP) in determining the content of financial statements.** p. 18

   GAAP are the measurement rules used to develop the information in financial statements. Knowledge of GAAP is necessary for accurate interpretation of the numbers in financial statements.

3. **Distinguish the roles of managers and auditors in the accounting communication process.** p. 20

   Management has primary responsibility for the accuracy of a company's financial information. Auditors are responsible for expressing an opinion on the fairness of the financial statement presentations based on their examination of the reports and records of the company.

4. **Appreciate the importance of ethics, reputation, and legal liability in accounting.** p. 21

   Users will have confidence in the accuracy of financial statement numbers only if the people associated with their preparation and audit have reputations for ethical behavior and competence. Management and auditors can also be held legally liable for fraudulent financial statements and malpractice.

In this chapter, we studied the basic financial statements that communicate financial information to external users. Chapters 2, 3, and 4 provide a more detailed look at financial statements and examine how to translate data about business transactions into these statements. Learning how to translate back and forth between business transactions and financial statements is the key to using financial statements in planning and decision making. Chapter 2 begins our discussion of the way that the accounting function collects data about business transactions and processes the data to provide periodic financial statements, with emphasis on the balance sheet. To accomplish this purpose, Chapter 2 discusses key accounting concepts, the accounting model, transaction analysis, and analytical tools. We examine the typical business activities of an actual service-oriented company to demonstrate the concepts in Chapters 2, 3, and 4.

FINDING FINANCIAL INFORMATION

Balance Sheet

Assets = Liabilities + Stockholders' Equity

Income Statement

Revenues
− Expenses
Net Income

Statement of Retained Earnings

Retained Earnings, beginning of the period
+ Net Income
− Dividends
Retained Earnings, end of the period

Statement of Cash Flows

+/− Cash Flows from Operating Activities
+/− Cash Flows from Investing Activities
+/− Cash Flows from Financing Activities
Net Change in Cash

KEY TERMS

Accounting p. 4
Accounting Entity p. 7
Accounting Period p. 10
Audit p. 20
Balance Sheet (Statement of Financial Position) p. 7
Basic Accounting Equation (Balance Sheet Equation) p. 8
Financial Accounting Standards Board (FASB) p. 19
Generally Accepted Accounting Principles (GAAP) p. 18
Income Statement (Statement of Income, Statement of Earnings, or Statement of Operations) p. 10
Notes (Footnotes) p. 16
Public Company Accounting Oversight Board (PCAOB) p. 20
Securities and Exchange Commission (SEC) p. 19
Statement of Cash Flows p. 14
Statement of Retained Earnings p. 12

QUESTIONS

1. Define **accounting.**
2. Briefly distinguish financial accounting from managerial accounting.
3. The accounting process generates financial reports for both internal and external users. Identify some of the groups of users.
4. Briefly distinguish investors from creditors.
5. What is an accounting entity? Why is a business treated as a separate entity for accounting purposes?
6. Complete the following:

Name of Statement	Alternative Title
a. Income statement	*a.* ________
b. Balance sheet	*b.* ________
c. Audit report	*c.* ________

7. What information should be included in the heading of each of the four primary financial statements?
8. What are the purposes of (*a*) the income statement, (*b*) the balance sheet, (*c*) the statement of cash flows, and (*d*) the statement of retained earnings?

9. Explain why the income statement and the statement of cash flows are dated "For the Year Ended December 31, 2010," whereas the balance sheet is dated "At December 31, 2010."
10. Briefly explain the importance of assets and liabilities to the decisions of investors and creditors.
11. Briefly define **net income** and **net loss.**
12. Explain the equation for the income statement. What are the three major items reported on the income statement?
13. Explain the equation for the balance sheet. Define the three major components reported on the balance sheet.
14. Explain the equation for the statement of cash flows. Explain the three major components reported on the statement of cash flows.
15. Explain the equation for the statement of retained earnings. Explain the four major items reported on the statement of retained earnings.
16. Financial statements discussed in this chapter are aimed at **external** users. Briefly explain how a company's **internal** managers in different functional areas (e.g., marketing, purchasing, human resources) might use financial statement information from their own and other companies.
17. Briefly describe the way that accounting measurement rules (generally accepted accounting principles) are determined in the United States.
18. Briefly explain the responsibility of company management and the independent auditors in the accounting communication process.
19. (Supplement A) Briefly differentiate between a sole proprietorship, a partnership, and a corporation.
20. (Supplement B) List and briefly explain the three primary services that CPAs in public practice provide.

MULTIPLE-CHOICE **QUESTIONS**

1. Which of the following is **not** one of the four basic financial statements?
   a. Balance sheet
   b. Audit report
   c. Income statement
   d. Statement of cash flows
2. As stated in the audit report, or **Report of Independent Accountants,** the primary responsibility for a company's financial statements lies with
   a. The owners of the company.
   b. Independent financial analysts.
   c. The auditors.
   d. The company's management.
3. Which of the following is true?
   a. FASB creates SEC.
   b. GAAP creates FASB.
   c. SEC creates AICPA.
   d. FASB creates GAAP.
4. Which of the following regarding retained earnings is false?
   a. Retained earnings is increased by net income and decreased by a net loss.
   b. Retained earnings is a component of stockholders' equity on the balance sheet.
   c. Retained earnings is an asset on the balance sheet.
   d. Retained earnings represents earnings not distributed to stockholders in the form of dividends.
5. Which of the following is **not** one of the four items required to be shown in the heading of a financial statement?
   a. The financial statement preparer's name.
   b. The title of the financial statement.
   c. The unit of measure in the financial statement.
   d. The name of the business entity.
6. Which of the following statements regarding the statement of cash flows is true?
   a. The statement of cash flows separates cash inflows and outflows into three major categories: operations, investing, and financing.
   b. The ending cash balance shown on the statement of cash flows must agree with the amount shown on the balance sheet for the same fiscal period.
   c. The total increase or decrease in cash shown on the statement of cash flows must agree with the "bottom line" (net income or net loss) reported on the income statement.
   d. "a" and "b."
   e. All of the above.

7. Which of the following is **not** a typical note included in an annual report?
   a. A note describing the auditor's opinion of the management's past and future financial planning for the business.
   b. A note providing more detail about a specific item shown in the financial statements.
   c. A note describing the accounting rules applied in the financial statements.
   d. A note describing financial disclosures about items not appearing in the financial statements.
8. Which of the following is true regarding the income statement?
   a. The income statement is sometimes called the **statement of operations.**
   b. The income statement reports revenues, expenses, and liabilities.
   c. The income statement reports only revenue for which cash was received at the point of sale.
   d. The income statement reports the financial position of a business at a particular point in time.
9. Which of the following is false regarding the balance sheet?
   a. The accounts shown on a balance sheet represent the basic accounting equation for a particular business entity.
   b. The retained earnings balance shown on the balance sheet must agree with the ending retained earnings balance shown on the statement of retained earnings.
   c. The balance sheet reports the changes in specific account balances over a period of time.
   d. The balance sheet reports the amount of assets, liabilities, and stockholders' equity of an accounting entity at a point in time.
10. Which of the following regarding GAAP is true?
   a. U.S. GAAP is the body of accounting knowledge followed by all countries in the world.
   b. Changes in GAAP can affect the interests of managers and stockholders.
   c. GAAP is the abbreviation for generally accepted auditing procedures.
   d. Changes to GAAP must be approved by the Senate Finance Committee.

For more practice with multiple-choice questions, go to the text website at **www.mhhe.com/libby7e**.

MINI-EXERCISES

Matching Elements with Financial Statements

M1-1
LO1

Match each element with its financial statement by entering the appropriate letter in the space provided.

Element	Financial Statement
___ (1) Expenses	A. Balance sheet
___ (2) Cash flow from investing activities	B. Income statement
___ (3) Assets	C. Statement of retained earnings
___ (4) Dividends	D. Statement of cash flows
___ (5) Revenues	
___ (6) Cash flow from operating activities	
___ (7) Liabilities	
___ (8) Cash flow from financing activities	

Matching Financial Statement Items to Financial Statement Categories

M1-2
LO1

Mark each item in the following list as an asset (A), liability (L), or stockholders' equity (SE) item that would appear on the balance sheet or a revenue (R) or expense (E) that would appear on the income statement.

___ (1) Retained earnings	___ (6) Inventories
___ (2) Accounts receivable	___ (7) Interest expense
___ (3) Sales revenue	___ (8) Accounts payable
___ (4) Property, plant, and equipment	___ (9) Land
___ (5) Cost of goods sold expense	

M1-3
LO2, 3

Identifying Important Accounting Abbreviations

The following is a list of important abbreviations used in the chapter. These abbreviations also are used widely in business. For each abbreviation, give the full designation. The first one is an example.

Abbreviation	Full Designation
(1) CPA	Certified Public Accountant
(2) GAAP	____________
(3) AICPA	____________
(4) SEC	____________
(5) FASB	____________

EXERCISES

E1-1
LO1, 2, 3

Matching Definitions with Terms or Abbreviations

Match each definition with its related term or abbreviation by entering the appropriate letter in the space provided.

Term or Abbreviation

___ (1) SEC
___ (2) Audit
___ (3) Sole proprietorship
___ (4) Corporation
___ (5) Accounting
___ (6) Accounting entity
___ (7) Audit report
___ (8) Cost principle
___ (9) Partnership
___ (10) FASB
___ (11) CPA
___ (12) Unit of measure
___ (13) GAAP
___ (14) Publicly traded

Definition

A. A system that collects and processes financial information about an organization and reports that information to decision makers.
B. Measurement of information about an entity in terms of the dollar or other national monetary unit.
C. An unincorporated business owned by two or more persons.
D. The organization for which financial data are to be collected (separate and distinct from its owners).
E. An incorporated entity that issues shares of stock as evidence of ownership.
F. Initial recording of financial statement elements at acquisition cost.
G. An examination of the financial reports to ensure that they represent what they claim and conform with generally accepted accounting principles.
H. Certified public accountant.
I. An unincorporated business owned by one person.
J. A report that describes the auditor's opinion of the fairness of the financial statement presentations and the evidence gathered to support that opinion.
K. Securities and Exchange Commission.
L. Financial Accounting Standards Board.
M. A company with stock that can be bought and sold by investors on established stock exchanges.
N. Generally accepted accounting principles.

E1-2
LO1

Matching Financial Statement Items to Financial Statement Categories

According to its annual report, "P&G's more than 250 brands include Pampers, Tide, Ariel, Always, Whisper, Pantene, Bounty, Pringles, Folgers, Charmin, Downy, Lenor, Iams, Olay, Crest, Vicks and Actonel." The following are items taken from its recent balance sheet and income statement. Note that different companies use slightly different titles for the same item. Mark each item in the following list as an asset (A), liability (L), or stockholders' equity (SE) item that would appear on the balance sheet, or a revenue (R) or expense (E) that would appear on the income statement.

P&G

___ (1) Accounts receivable
___ (2) Cash and cash equivalents
___ (3) Net sales
___ (4) Notes payable
___ (5) Taxes payable
___ (6) Retained earnings
___ (7) Cost of products sold
___ (8) Marketing, administrative, and other operating expenses
___ (9) Income taxes
___ (10) Accounts payable
___ (11) Land
___ (12) Property, plant, and equipment
___ (13) Long-term debt
___ (14) Inventories
___ (15) Interest expense

E1-3
LO1

Matching Financial Statement Items to Financial Statement Categories

Tootsie Roll Industries is engaged in the manufacture and sale of candy. Major products include Tootsie Roll, Tootsie Roll Pops, Tootsie Pop Drops, Tootsie Flavor Rolls, Charms, and Blow-Pop lollipops. The following items were listed on Tootsie Roll's recent income statement and balance sheet. Mark each item from the balance sheet as an asset (A), liability (L), or shareholders' equity (SE) and each item from the income statement as a revenue (R) or expense (E).

Tootsie
Tootsie Roll Industries

___ (1) Notes payable to banks
___ (2) General and administrative
___ (3) Accounts payable
___ (4) Dividends payable
___ (5) Retained earnings
___ (6) Cash and cash equivalents
___ (7) Accounts receivable
___ (8) Provision for income taxes*
___ (9) Cost of goods sold
___ (10) Machinery and equipment
___ (11) Net sales
___ (12) Inventories
___ (13) Marketing, selling, and advertising
___ (14) Buildings
___ (15) Land
___ (16) Income taxes payable
___ (17) Distribution and warehousing costs
___ (18) Investments (in other companies)

E1-4
LO1

Preparing a Balance Sheet

Honda Motor Corporation of Japan is a leading international manufacturer of automobiles, motorcycles, all-terrain vehicles, and personal watercraft. As a Japanese company, it follows Japanese GAAP and reports its financial statements in billions of yen (the sign for yen is ¥). Its recent balance sheet contained the following items (in billions). Prepare a balance sheet as of March 31, 2009, solving for the missing amount. (**Hint:** Exhibit 1.2 in the chapter provides a good model for completing this exercise.)

Honda Motor Co.

Cash and cash equivalents	¥ 690
Contributed capital	259
Accounts payable and other current liabilities	4,237
Inventories	1,244
Investments	639
Long-term debt	1,933
Net property, plant, and equipment	2,148
Other assets	6,244
Other liabilities	1,519
Retained earnings	3,871
Total assets	11,819
Total liabilities and stockholders' equity	?
Trade accounts, notes, and other receivables	854

E1-5
LO1

Completing a Balance Sheet and Inferring Net Income

Carlos Ramirez and Camila Garza organized New World Book Store as a corporation; each contributed $70,000 cash to start the business and received 4,000 shares of common stock. The store completed its first year of operations on December 31, 2011. On that date, the following financial items for the year were determined: December 31, 2011, cash on hand and in the bank, $68,350; December 31, 2011, amounts

*In the United States, "provision for income taxes" is most often used as a synonym for "income tax expense."

due from customers from sales of books, $39,000; unused portion of store and office equipment, $72,000; December 31, 2011, amounts owed to publishers for books purchased, $12,000; one-year note payable to a local bank for $3,000. No dividends were declared or paid to the stockholders during the year.

Required:

1. Complete the following balance sheet as of the end of 2011.
2. What was the amount of net income for the year? (**Hint:** Use the retained earnings equation [Beginning Retained Earnings + Net Income − Dividends = Ending Retained Earnings] to solve for net income.)

Assets		Liabilities		
Cash	$	Accounts payable	$	
Accounts receivable		Note payable		
Store and office equipment		Interest payable	120	
		Total liabilities		$
		Stockholders' Equity		
		Contributed capital		
		Retained earnings	24,230	
		Total stockholders' equity		
Total assets	$	Total liabilities and stockholders' equity		$

E1-6 LO1 Analyzing Revenues and Expenses and Preparing an Income Statement

Assume that you are the owner of College Connection, which specializes in items that interest students. At the end of January 2011, you find (for January only) this information:

a. Sales, per the cash register tapes, of $110,000, plus one sale on credit (a special situation) of $3,000.
b. With the help of a friend (who majored in accounting), you determine that all of the goods sold during January cost $50,000 to purchase.
c. During the month, according to the checkbook, you paid $37,000 for salaries, rent, supplies, advertising, and other expenses; however, you have not yet paid the $900 monthly utilities for January on the store and fixtures.

Required:

On the basis of the data given (disregard income taxes), what was the amount of net income for January? Show computations. (**Hint:** A convenient form to use has the following major side captions: Revenue from Sales, Expenses, and the difference—Net Income.)

E1-7 LO1 Preparing an Income Statement and Inferring Missing Values

Walgreens

Walgreen Co. is one of the nation's leading drugstore chains. Its recent quarterly income statement contained the following items (in millions). Solve for the missing amounts and prepare an income statement for the quarter ended May 31, 2009. (**Hint:** First order the items as they would appear on the income statement and then solve for the missing values. Exhibit 1.3 in the chapter provides a good model for completing this exercise.)

Cost of sales	$11,751
Provision for income taxes*	299
Interest expense	25
Net earnings	?
Net sales	16,210
Pretax income	?
Selling, occupancy, and administration expense	3,613
Total expenses	?
Total revenues	?

E1-8 LO1 Analyzing Revenues and Expenses and Completing an Income Statement

Neighborhood Realty, Incorporated, has been operating for three years and is owned by three investors. S. Bhojraj owns 60 percent of the total outstanding stock of 9,000 shares and is the managing executive in

*In the United States, "provision for income taxes" is a common synonym for "income tax expense."

charge. On December 31, 2012, the following financial items for the entire year were determined: commissions earned and collected in cash, $150,900, plus $16,800 uncollected; rental service fees earned and collected, $20,000; salaries expense paid, $62,740; commissions expense paid, $35,330; payroll taxes paid, $2,500; rent paid, $2,475 (not including December rent yet to be paid); utilities expense paid, $1,600; promotion and advertising paid, $7,750; income taxes paid, $24,400; and miscellaneous expenses paid, $500. There were no other unpaid expenses at December 31. Also during the year, the company paid the owners "out-of-profit" cash dividends amounting to $12,000. Complete the following income statement:

____

____

____

Revenues		
Commissions earned	$ _____	
Rental service fees	_____	
Total revenues		$ _____
Expenses		
Salaries expense	_____	
Commission expense	_____	
Payroll tax expense	_____	
Rent expense	_____	
Utilities expense	_____	
Promotion and advertising expense	_____	
Miscellaneous expenses	_____	
Total expenses (excluding income taxes)		_____
Pretax income		_____
Income tax expense		_____
Net income		$50,180

Inferring Values Using the Income Statement and Balance Sheet Equations

E1-9
LO1

Review the chapter explanations of the income statement and the balance sheet equations. Apply these equations in each independent case to compute the two missing amounts for each case. Assume that it is the end of 2012, the first full year of operations for the company. (**Hint:** Organize the listed items as they are presented in the balance sheet and income statement equations and then compute the missing amounts.)

Independent Cases	Total Revenues	Total Expenses	Net Income (Loss)	Total Assets	Total Liabilities	Stockholders' Equity
A	$91,700	$76,940	$	$140,200	$69,000	$
B		74,240	14,740	107,880		79,010
C	69,260	76,430		97,850	69,850	
D	58,680		21,770		17,890	78,680
E	84,840	78,720			25,520	79,580

Inferring Values Using the Income Statement and Balance Sheet Equations

E1-10
LO1

Review the chapter explanations of the income statement and the balance sheet equations. Apply these equations in each independent case to compute the two missing amounts for each case. Assume that it is the end of 2012, the first full year of operations for the company. (**Hint:** Organize the listed items as they are presented in the balance sheet and income statement equations and then compute the missing amounts.)

Independent Cases	Total Revenues	Total Expenses	Net Income (Loss)	Total Assets	Total Liabilities	Stockholders' Equity
A	$231,820	$196,700	$	$294,300	$75,000	$
B		175,780	29,920	590,000		348,400
C	72,990	91,890		258,200	190,760	
D	36,590		9,840		189,675	97,525
E	224,130	210,630			173,850	361,240

E1-11 Preparing an Income Statement and Balance Sheet

LO1

Painter Corporation was organized by five individuals on January 1, 2011. At the end of January 2011, the following monthly financial data are available:

Total revenues	$299,000
Total expenses (excluding income taxes)	189,000
Income tax expense (all unpaid as of January 31)	34,500
Cash balance, January 31, 2011	65,150
Receivables from customers (all considered collectible)	34,500
Merchandise inventory (by inventory count at cost)	96,600
Payables to suppliers for merchandise purchased from them (will be paid during February 2011)	26,450
Contributed capital (2,600 shares)	59,800

No dividends were declared or paid during 2011.

Required:

Complete the following two statements:

PAINTER CORPORATION
Income Statement
For the Month of January 2011

Total revenues	$ ____
Less: Total expenses (excluding income tax)	____
Pretax income	____
Less: Income tax expense	____
Net income	$ ____

PAINTER CORPORATION
Balance Sheet
At January 31, 2011

Assets	
Cash	$ ____
Receivables from customers	____
Merchandise inventory	____
Total assets	$ ____
Liabilities	
Payables to suppliers	$ ____
Income taxes payable	____
Total liabilities	____
Stockholders' Equity	
Contributed capital	____
Retained earnings	____
Total stockholders' equity	____
Total liabilities and stockholders' equity	$ ____

E1-12 Preparing a Statement of Retained Earnings

LO1

Clint's Stonework Corporation was organized on January 1, 2011. For its first two years of operations, it reported the following:

Net income for 2011	$ 31,000
Net income for 2012	42,000
Dividends for 2011	14,200
Dividends for 2012	18,700
Total assets at the end of 2011	130,000
Total assets at the end of 2012	250,000

Required:
On the basis of the data given, prepare a statement of retained earnings for 2012. Show computations.

E1-13
LO1

Focus on Cash Flows: Matching Cash Flow Statement Items to Categories

The following items were taken from a recent cash flow statement. Note that different companies use slightly different titles for the same item. Without referring to Exhibit 1.5, mark each item in the list as a cash flow from operating activities (O), investing activities (I), or financing activities (F). Also place parentheses around the letter only if it is a cash outflow.

___ (1) Purchases of property, plant, and equipment
___ (2) Cash received from customers
___ (3) Cash paid for dividends to stockholders
___ (4) Cash paid to suppliers
___ (5) Income taxes paid
___ (6) Cash paid to employees
___ (7) Cash proceeds received from sale of investment in another company
___ (8) Repayment of borrowings

E1-14
LO1

Preparing a Statement of Cash Flows

LAH Manufacturing Corporation is preparing the annual financial statements for the stockholders. A statement of cash flows must be prepared. The following data on cash flows were developed for the entire year ended December 31, 2011: cash collections from sales, $270,000; cash expended for operating expenses, $175,000; sale of unissued LAH stock for cash, $30,000; cash dividends declared and paid to stockholders during the year, $18,000; and payments on long-term notes payable, $80,000. During the year, a tract of land held as an investment was sold for $25,000 cash (which was the same price that LAH had paid for the land in 2010), and $48,000 cash was expended for two new machines. The machines were used in the factory. The beginning-of-the-year cash balance was $63,000.

Required:
Prepare the statement of cash flows for 2011. Follow the format illustrated in the chapter.

To practice with more exercises, go to the text website at **www.mhhe.com/libby7e**.

PROBLEMS

P1-1
LO1

Preparing an Income Statement, Statement of Retained Earnings, and Balance Sheet (AP1-1)

excel
www.mhhe.com/libby7e

Assume that you are the president of Gaslight Company. At the end of the first year (December 31, 2011) of operations, the following financial data for the company are available:

Cash	$ 24,500
Receivables from customers (all considered collectible)	10,800
Inventory of merchandise (based on physical count and priced at cost)	81,000
Equipment owned, at cost less used portion	40,700
Accounts payable owed to suppliers	46,140
Salary payable for 2011 (on December 31, 2011, this was owed to an employee who was away because of an emergency; will return around January 10, 2012, at which time the payment will be made)	1,800
Total sales revenue	126,000
Expenses, including the cost of the merchandise sold (excluding income taxes)	80,200
Income taxes expense at 30% × pretax income; all paid during 2011	?
Contributed capital, 7,000 shares outstanding	87,000
Dividends declared and paid during 2011	10,000

Required:

Using the financial statement exhibits in the chapter as models and showing computations:

1. Prepare a summarized income statement for the year 2011.
2. Prepare a statement of retained earnings for the year 2011.
3. Prepare a balance sheet at December 31, 2011.

P1-2 LO1

Analyzing a Student's Business and Preparing an Income Statement (AP1-2)

eXcel www.mhhe.com/libby7e

During the summer between her junior and senior years, Bridget Lewis needed to earn sufficient money for the coming academic year. Unable to obtain a job with a reasonable salary, she decided to try the lawn care business for three months. After a survey of the market potential, Bridget bought a used pickup truck on June 1 for $1,500. On each door she painted "Bridget's Lawn Service, Phone 471-4487." She also spent $900 for mowers, trimmers, and tools. To acquire these items, she borrowed $2,500 cash by signing a note payable promising to pay the $2,500 plus interest of $65 at the end of the three months (ending August 31).

At the end of the summer, Bridget realized that she had done a lot of work, and her bank account looked good. This fact prompted her to become concerned about how much profit the business had earned.

A review of the check stubs showed the following: Bank deposits of collections from customers totaled $12,300. The following checks had been written: gas, oil, and lubrication, $940; pickup repairs, $250; mower repair, $110; miscellaneous supplies used, $80; helpers, $5,400; payroll taxes, $190; payment for assistance in preparing payroll tax forms, $25; insurance, $125; telephone, $110; and $2,565 to pay off the note including interest (on August 31). A notebook kept in the pickup, plus some unpaid bills, reflected that customers still owed her $700 for lawn services rendered and that she owed $180 for gas and oil (credit card charges). She estimated that the cost for use of the truck and the other equipment (called **depreciation**) for three months amounted to $600.

Required:

1. Prepare a quarterly income statement for Bridget's Lawn Service for the months June, July, and August 2011. Use the following main captions: Revenues from Services, Expenses, and Net Income. Because this is a sole proprietorship, the company will not be subject to income tax.
2. Do you see a need for one or more additional financial reports for this company for 2011 and thereafter? Explain.

P1-3 LO1

Comparing Income with Cash Flow (A Challenging Problem) (AP1-3)

Huang Trucking Company was organized on January 1, 2011. At the end of the first quarter (three months) of operations, the owner prepared a summary of its activities as shown in the first row of the following tabulation:

	Computation of	
Summary of Transactions	**Income**	**Cash**
a. Services performed for customers, $66,000, of which $11,000 remained uncollected at the end of the quarter.	+$66,000	+$55,000
b. Cash borrowed from the local bank, $45,000 (one-year note).		
c. Small service truck purchased at the end of the quarter to be used in the business for two years starting the next quarter: cost, $9,500 cash.		
d. Wages earned by employees, $21,000, of which one-half remained unpaid at the end of the quarter.		
e. Service supplies purchased for use in the business, $3,800 cash, of which $900 were unused (still on hand) at the end of the quarter.		
f. Other operating expenses, $39,000, of which $6,500 remained unpaid at the end of the quarter.	______	______
Based only on these transactions, compute the following for the quarter:		
Income (or loss)	======	
Cash inflow (or outflow)		======

Required:

1. For each of the six transactions given in this tabulation, enter what you consider the correct amounts. Enter a zero when appropriate. The first transaction is illustrated.
2. For each transaction, explain the basis for your dollar responses.

Evaluating Data to Support a Loan Application (A Challenging Problem)

P1-4
LO1

On January 1, 2011, three individuals organized Northwest Company as a corporation. Each individual invested $10,000 cash in the business. On December 31, 2011, they prepared a list of resources owned (assets) and a list of the debts (liabilities) to support a company loan request for $70,000 submitted to a local bank. None of the three investors had studied accounting. The two lists prepared were as follows:

Company resources	
Cash	$ 12,000
Service supplies inventory (on hand)	7,000
Service trucks (four, practically new)	57,000
Personal residences of organizers (three houses)	190,000
Service equipment used in the business (practically new)	30,000
Bills due from customers (for services already completed)	15,000
Total	$311,000
Company obligations	
Unpaid wages to employees	$ 19,000
Unpaid taxes	8,000
Owed to suppliers	10,000
Owed on service trucks and equipment (to a finance company)	45,000
Loan from organizer	10,000
Total	$ 92,000

Required:

Prepare a short memo indicating:

1. Which of these items do not belong on the balance sheet? (Bear in mind that the company is considered to be separate from the owners.)
2. What additional questions would you raise about the measurement of items on the list? Explain the basis for each question.
3. If you were advising the local bank on its loan decision, which amounts on the list would create special concerns? Explain the basis for each concern and include any recommendations that you have.
4. In view of your responses to (1) and (2), what do you think the amount of stockholders' equity (i.e., assets minus liabilities) of the company would be? Show your computations.

ALTERNATE **PROBLEMS**

Preparing an Income Statement, Statement of Retained Earnings, and Balance Sheet (P1-1)

AP1-1
LO1

Assume that you are the president of Influence Corporation. At the end of the first year (June 30, 2011) of operations, the following financial data for the company are available:

Cash	$13,150
Receivables from customers (all considered collectible)	10,900
Inventory of merchandise (based on physical count and priced at cost)	27,000
Equipment owned, at cost less used portion	66,000
Accounts payable owed to suppliers	31,500
Salary payable for 2011 (on June 30, 2011, this was owed to an employee who was away because of an emergency; will return around July 7, 2011, at which time the payment will be made)	1,500
Total sales revenue	100,000
Expenses, including the cost of the merchandise sold (excluding income taxes)	68,500
Income taxes expense at 30% × pretax income; all paid during 2011	?
Contributed capital, 5,000 shares outstanding	62,000

No dividends were declared or paid during 2011.

Required:

Using the financial statement exhibits in the chapter as models and showing computations:

1. Prepare a summarized income statement for the year ended June 30, 2011.
2. Prepare a statement of retained earnings for the year ended June 30, 2011.
3. Prepare a balance sheet at June 30, 2011.

AP1-2 LO1 Analyzing a Student's Business and Preparing an Income Statement (P1-2)

Upon graduation from high school, Sam List immediately accepted a job as an electrician's assistant for a large local electrical repair company. After three years of hard work, Sam received an electrician's license and decided to start his own business. He had saved $12,000, which he invested in the business. First, he transferred this amount from his savings account to a business bank account for List Electric Repair Company, Incorporated. His lawyer had advised him to start as a corporation. He then purchased a used panel truck for $9,000 cash and secondhand tools for $1,500; rented space in a small building; inserted an ad in the local paper; and opened the doors on October 1, 2011. Immediately, Sam was very busy; after one month, he employed an assistant.

Although Sam knew practically nothing about the financial side of the business, he realized that a number of reports were required and that costs and collections had to be controlled carefully. At the end of the year, prompted in part by concern about his income tax situation (previously he had to report only salary), Sam recognized the need for financial statements. His wife Janet developed some financial statements for the business. On December 31, 2011, with the help of a friend, she gathered the following data for the three months just ended. Bank account deposits of collections for electric repair services totaled $32,000. The following checks had been written: electrician's assistant, $7,500; payroll taxes, $175; supplies purchased and used on jobs, $9,500; oil, gas, and maintenance on truck, $1,200; insurance, $700; rent, $500; utilities and telephone, $825; and miscellaneous expenses (including advertising), $600. Also, uncollected bills to customers for electric repair services amounted to $3,500. The $250 rent for December had not been paid. Sam estimated the cost of using the truck and tools (depreciation) during the three months to be $1,200. Income taxes for the three-month period were $3,930.

Required:

1. Prepare a quarterly income statement for List Electric Repair for the three months October through December 2011. Use the following main captions: Revenues from Services, Expenses, Pretax Income, and Net Income.
2. Do you think that Sam may need one or more additional financial reports for 2011 and thereafter? Explain.

AP1-3 LO1 Comparing Income with Cash Flow (A Challenging Problem) (P1-3)

Choice Chicken Company was organized on January 1, 2011. At the end of the first quarter (three months) of operations, the owner prepared a summary of its activities as shown in the first row of the following tabulation:

	Computation of	
Summary of Transactions	Income	Cash
a. Services performed for customers, $85,000, of which $15,000 remained uncollected at the end of the quarter.	+$85,000	+$70,000
b. Cash borrowed from the local bank, $25,000 (one-year note).		
c. Small service truck purchased at the end of the quarter to be used in the business for two years starting the next quarter: cost, $8,000 cash.		
d. Wages earned by employees, $36,000, of which one-sixth remained unpaid at the end of the quarter.		
e. Service supplies purchased for use in the business, $4,000 cash, of which $1,000 were unused (still on hand) at the end of the quarter.		
f. Other operating expenses, $31,000, of which one-half remained unpaid at the end of the quarter.	______	______
Based only on these transactions, compute the following for the quarter: Income (or loss) Cash inflow (or outflow)		

Required:

1. For each of the six transactions given in this tabulation, enter what you consider the correct amounts. Enter a zero when appropriate. The first transaction is illustrated.
2. For each transaction, explain the basis for your dollar responses.

CASES AND PROJECTS

Annual Report Cases

Finding Financial Information

CP1-1
LO1, 3

AMERICAN EAGLE OUTFITTERS, INC.

Refer to the financial statements of American Eagle Outfitters in Appendix B at the end of this book.

Required:
Skim the annual report. Look at the income statement, balance sheet, and cash flow statement closely and attempt to infer what kinds of information they report. Then answer the following questions based on the report.

1. What types of products does it sell?
2. On what date does American Eagle Outfitters's most recent reporting year end?
3. For how many years does it present complete
   a. Balance sheets?
   b. Income statements?
   c. Cash flow statements?
4. Are its financial statements audited by independent CPAs? How do you know?
5. Did its total assets increase or decrease over the last year?
6. How much inventory (in dollars) did the company have as of January 31, 2009 (accountants would call this the ending balance)?
7. Write out the basic accounting (balance sheet) equation and provide the values in dollars reported by the company as of January 31, 2009.

Finding Financial Information

CP1-2
LO1, 3

URBAN OUTFITTERS INC.

Refer to the financial statements of Urban Outfitters in Appendix C at the end of this book.

Required:

1. What is the amount of net income for the most recent year?
2. What amount of revenue was earned in the most recent year?
3. How much inventory (in dollars) does the company have as of January 31, 2009?
4. By what amount did cash and cash equivalents* change during the most recent year?
5. Who is the auditor for the company?

Comparing Companies within an Industry

CP1-3
LO1

AMERICAN EAGLE OUTFITTERS, INC.

URBAN OUTFITTERS INC.

eXcel
www.mhhe.com/libby7e

Refer to the financial statements of American Eagle Outfitters in Appendix B and Urban Outfitters in Appendix C.

Required:

1. Total assets is a common measure of the size of a company. Which company had the higher total assets at the end of the most recent year? **(Note: some companies will label a year that has a January year-end as having a fiscal year-end dated one year earlier. For example, a January 2009 year-end may be labeled as Fiscal 2008 since the year actually has more months that fall in the 2008 calendar year than in the 2009 calendar year.)**
2. Net sales is also a common measure of the size of a company. Which company had the higher net sales for the most recent year?
3. Growth during a period is calculated as:

$$\frac{\text{Ending amount} - \text{Beginning amount}}{\text{Beginning amount}} \times 100 = \text{Growth rate}$$

***Cash equivalents** are short-term investments readily convertible to cash whose value is unlikely to change.

Which company had the highest growth in total assets during the most recent year? Which company had the highest growth in net sales during the most recent year?

Financial Reporting and Analysis Cases

CP1-4 LO1 Using Financial Reports: Identifying and Correcting Deficiencies in an Income Statement and Balance Sheet

Performance Corporation was organized on January 1, 2009. At the end of 2009, the company had not yet employed an accountant; however, an employee who was "good with numbers" prepared the following statements at that date:

PERFORMANCE CORPORATION **December 31, 2009**	
Income from sales of merchandise	$175,000
Total amount paid for goods sold during 2009	(90,000)
Selling costs	(25,000)
Depreciation (on service vehicles used)	(10,000)
Income from services rendered	52,000
Salaries and wages paid	(62,000)

PERFORMANCE CORPORATION **December 31, 2009**		
Resources		
Cash		$ 32,000
Merchandise inventory (held for resale)		42,000
Service vehicles		50,000
Retained earnings (profit earned in 2009)		30,000
Grand total		$154,000
Debts		
Payables to suppliers		$ 22,000
Note owed to bank		25,000
Due from customers		13,000
Total		$ 60,000
Supplies on hand (to be used in rendering services)	$15,000	
Accumulated depreciation* (on service vehicles)	10,000	
Contributed capital, 6,500 shares	65,000	
Total		90,000
Grand total		$150,000

Required:

1. List all deficiencies that you can identify in these statements. Give a brief explanation of each one.
2. Prepare a proper income statement (correct net income is $30,000 and income tax expense is $10,000) and balance sheet (correct total assets are $142,000).

Critical Thinking Cases

CP1-5 LO3 Making Decisions as an Owner: Deciding about a Proposed Audit

You are one of three partners who own and operate Mary's Maid Service. The company has been operating for seven years. One of the other partners has always prepared the company's annual

*Accumulated depreciation represents the used portion of the asset and should be subtracted from the asset's balance.

financial statements. Recently you proposed that the statements be audited each year because it would benefit the partners and preclude possible disagreements about the division of profits. The partner who prepares the statements proposed that his Uncle Ray, who has a lot of financial experience, can do the job and at little cost. Your other partner remained silent.

Required:

1. What position would you take on the proposal? Justify your response.
2. What would you strongly recommend? Give the basis for your recommendation.

Evaluating an Ethical Dilemma: Ethics and Auditor Responsibilities

CP1-6
LO3, 4

A key factor that an auditor provides is independence. The **AICPA Code of Professional Conduct** states that "a member in public practice should be independent in fact and appearance when providing auditing and other attestation services."

Required:

Do you consider the following circumstances to suggest a lack of independence? Justify your position. (Use your imagination. Specific answers are not provided in the chapter.)

1. Jack Jones is a partner with a large audit firm and is assigned to the Ford audit. Jack owns 10 shares of Ford.
2. Melissa Chee has invested in a mutual fund company that owns 500,000 shares of Sears stock. She is the auditor of Sears.
3. Bob Franklin is a clerk/typist who works on the audit of AT&T. He has just inherited 50,000 shares of AT&T stock. (Bob enjoys his work and plans to continue despite his new wealth.)
4. Nancy Sodoma worked on weekends as the controller for a small business that a friend started. Nancy quit the job in midyear and now has no association with the company. She works full-time for a large CPA firm and has been assigned to do the audit of her friend's business.
5. Mark Jacobs borrowed $100,000 for a home mortgage from First City National Bank. The mortgage was granted on normal credit terms. Mark is the partner in charge of the First City audit.

Financial Reporting and Analysis Team Project

Team Project: Examining an Annual Report

CP1-7

As a team, select an industry to analyze. *Reuters* provides lists of industries under Sectors and Industries at www.reuters.com. (Click on an industry and then select Company Rankings for a list of members of that industry.) Each team member should acquire the annual report or 10-K for one publicly traded company in the industry, with each member selecting a different company. (Library files, the SEC EDGAR service at www.sec.gov, or the company itself are good sources.)

Required:

On an individual basis, each team member should write a short report answering the following questions about the selected company. Discuss any patterns across the companies that you as a team observe. Then, as a team, write a short report comparing and contrasting your companies.

1. What types of products or services does it sell?
2. On what day of the year does its fiscal year end?
3. For how many years does it present complete
   a. Balance sheets?
   b. Income statements?
   c. Cash flow statements?
4. Are its financial statements audited by independent CPAs? If so, by whom?
5. Did its total assets increase or decrease over last year? By what percentage? [Percentage change is calculated as (Current year − Last year) ÷ Last year. Show supporting computations.]
6. Did its net income increase or decrease over last year? By what percentage?

LEARNING OBJECTIVES

After studying this chapter, you should be able to:

Lectured Presentation LP–2
www.mhhe.com/libby7e

1. Define the objective of financial reporting, the elements of the balance sheet, and the related key accounting assumptions and principles. p. 45
2. Identify what constitutes a business transaction and recognize common balance sheet account titles used in business. p. 50
3. Apply transaction analysis to simple business transactions in terms of the accounting model: Assets = Liabilities + Stockholders' Equity. p. 52
4. Determine the impact of business transactions on the balance sheet using two basic tools, journal entries and T-accounts. p. 57
5. Prepare a simple classified balance sheet and analyze the company using the current ratio. p. 66
6. Identify investing and financing transactions and demonstrate how they are reported on the statement of cash flows. p. 70

INVESTING AND FINANCING DECISIONS AND THE BALANCE SHEET

In the pizza segment of the highly competitive restaurant business, Papa John's continues to fight the battle to become the No. 1 pizza brand in the world, taking on industry leader Pizza Hut as its primary target. In 2000, through aggressive expansion, Papa John's moved ahead of Little Caesar's to rank third in sales behind giants Pizza Hut and Domino's.

FOCUS COMPANY:

Papa John's International

EXPANSION STRATEGY IN THE "PIZZA WARS"

www.papajohns.com

With more than 3,300 restaurants in the United States and abroad, the company has grown tremendously since its beginnings in 1983 when John Schnatter, founder and chief executive officer, knocked down closet walls at a bar he was tending to install a pizza oven. Ten years later, Papa John's became a public company with stock trading on the NASDAQ exchange (under the symbol PZZA). The company's balance sheet at the end of 2008 compared to the end of 1994 (in millions of dollars*) highlights its growth:

	Assets	=	Liabilities	+	Stockholders' Equity
End of 2008	$387		$257		$130
End of 1994	76		13		63
Change	+ $311		+ $244		+ $ 67

In recent years, competition has stiffened not only from traditional pizza chains but also from niche dwellers—take-and-bake pizza chains, frozen pizza companies, carry-out initiatives from restaurants such as Applebee's and Chili's, and restaurants seeking to meet the shift in consumer interests by offering healthier menu options. While addressing the competition and meeting changing consumer interests, Papa John's continues to expand, with plans to add up to 265 new restaurants in 2009 in the United States and abroad. The Pizza Wars continue.

*These totals are rounded amounts from the actual financial statements for the respective years. Amounts used in illustrations throughout Chapters 2, 3, and 4 are realistic estimates of actual monthly amounts.

UNDERSTANDING THE BUSINESS

Pizza is a global commodity, generating more than $34 billion in sales annually.[1] While the business depends heavily on human capital, companies can compete through product quality and marketing. Papa John's strategy is to offer "Better Ingredients. Better Pizza." To do so requires an almost fanatical focus on testing ingredients and checking product quality, right down to the size of the black olives and the fat content of the mozzarella and meat. The company keeps operations simple, sticking to a focused menu of pizza with side items including breadsticks, cheesesticks, chicken strips, wings, dessert items, and soft drinks for pickup or delivery. To control quality and increase efficiency, the company builds regional commissaries (called its Quality Control Center system) that make the dough and sell it to the stores. Development of the commissaries and new company-owned stores plus the sale of franchises[2] explain most of the change in Papa John's assets and liabilities from year to year.

To understand how the results of Papa John's growth strategy are communicated in the balance sheet, we must answer the following questions:

- What business activities cause changes in the balance sheet amounts from one period to the next?
- How do specific business activities affect each of the balance sheet amounts?
- How do companies keep track of the balance sheet amounts?

Once we have answered these questions, we will be able to perform two key analytical tasks:

1. Analyze and predict the effects of business decisions on a company's financial statements.
2. Use the financial statements of other companies to identify and evaluate the activities managers engaged in during a past period. This is a key task in **financial statement analysis**.

In this chapter, we focus on some typical asset acquisition activities (often called **investing activities**), along with related **financing activities,** such as borrowing funds from creditors or selling stock to investors to acquire the assets. We examine only those activities that affect balance sheet amounts. Operating activities that affect both the income statement and the balance sheet are covered in Chapters 3 and 4. To begin, let's return to the basic concepts introduced in Chapter 1.

[1]Source: www.franchisedirect.com/foodfranchises/pizzafranchises/snapshotofthepizzafranchiseindustry2009/80/126.

[2]Franchises are contracts in which a franchisor (such as Papa John's International) provides rights to franchisees (in this case, local restaurant operators) to sell or distribute a specific line of products or provide a particular service. In return, franchisees usually pay an initial fee to obtain the franchise, along with annual payments for ongoing services such as accounting, advertising, and training. Approximately 82 percent of Papa John's restaurants worldwide are franchises.

ORGANIZATION of the Chapter

Overview of Accounting Concepts
- Concepts Emphasized in Chapter 2

What Business Activities Cause Changes in Financial Statement Amounts?
- Nature of Business Transactions
- Accounts

How Do Transactions Affect Accounts?
- Principles of Transaction Analysis
- Analyzing Papa John's Transactions

How Do Companies Keep Track of Account Balances?
- The Direction of Transaction Effects
- Analytical Tools
- Transaction Analysis Illustrated

How Is the Balance Sheet Prepared and Analyzed?
- Classified Balance Sheet
- Current Ratio

Objective of External Financial Reporting:
To provide useful economic information to external users for decision making
Qualitative Characteristics of Financial Information:
Useful information is:
- **Relevant, Reliable,** Comparable, and Consistent

Elements to Be Measured and Reported:
- **Assets, Liabilities, Stockholders' Equity,** Revenues, Expenses, Gains, and Losses

Concepts for Measuring and Reporting Information:
- **Assumptions:** **Separate-entity, Unit-of-measure, Continuity,** Time Period
- **Principles:** **Historical Cost,** Revenue Recognition, Matching, Full Disclosure
- **Exceptions:** Cost-benefit, **Materiality, Conservatism,** Industry Practices

EXHIBIT 2.1

Financial Accounting and Reporting—Conceptual Framework

Concepts in red are discussed in Chapters 1 and 2. Those in black will be discussed in future chapters.

OVERVIEW OF ACCOUNTING CONCEPTS

LEARNING OBJECTIVE 1
Define the objective of financial reporting, the elements of the balance sheet, and the related key accounting assumptions and principles.

The key accounting terms and concepts defined in Chapter 1 are part of a theoretical framework developed over many years and synthesized by the Financial Accounting Standards Board (FASB). This conceptual framework is presented in Exhibit 2.1 as an overview of the key concepts that will be discussed in each of the next four chapters. An understanding of these accounting concepts will be helpful as you study. That's because learning and remembering **how** the accounting process works is much easier if you know **why** it works a certain way. A clear understanding of these concepts will also help you in future chapters as we examine more complex business activities.

Concepts Emphasized in Chapter 2

Objective of Financial Reporting

The **primary objective of external financial reporting** that guides the remaining sections of the conceptual framework is to provide useful economic information about a business to help external parties, primarily investors and creditors, make sound financial decisions. The users of accounting information are identified as **decision makers.** These decision makers include average investors, creditors, and experts who provide financial advice. They are all expected to have a reasonable understanding of accounting concepts and procedures (this may be one of the reasons you are studying accounting). Of course, as we discussed in Chapter 1, many other groups, such as suppliers and customers, also use external financial statements.

The PRIMARY OBJECTIVE OF EXTERNAL FINANCIAL REPORTING is to provide useful economic information about a business to help external parties make sound financial decisions.

Most users are interested in information to help them **project a business's future cash inflows and outflows.** For example, creditors and potential creditors need to assess an entity's ability to (1) pay interest on a loan over time and also (2) pay back the principal on the loan when it is due. Investors and potential investors want to assess the entity's ability to (1) pay dividends in the future and (2) be successful so that the stock price rises, enabling investors to sell their stock for more than they paid.

RELEVANT information can influence a decision; it is timely and has predictive and/or feedback value.

Qualitative Characteristics of Financial Information

To fulfill the primary objective of providing useful information, the conceptual framework provides guidance on what characteristics are essential. Overall, information should be **relevant** to the decision (that is, it provides feedback and predictive value on a timely basis) and **reliable** (that is, it is accurate, unbiased, and verifiable).

RELIABLE information is accurate, unbiased, and verifiable.

SEPARATE-ENTITY ASSUMPTION states that business transactions are accounted for separately from the transactions of owners.

Accounting Assumptions

Three of the four basic assumptions that underlie accounting measurement and reporting relate to the balance sheet. The **separate-entity assumption** states that each business's activities must be accounted for separately from the activities of its owners, all other persons, and other entities. This means that, when an owner purchases property for personal use, the property is not an asset of the business. Under the **unit-of-measure assumption,** each business entity accounts for and reports its financial results primarily in terms of the national monetary unit (e.g., dollars in the United States, yen in Japan, and euros in Germany).

UNIT-OF-MEASURE ASSUMPTION states that accounting information should be measured and reported in the national monetary unit.

Under the **continuity assumption** (sometimes called the **going-concern assumption**), a business normally is assumed to continue operating long enough to meet its contractual commitments and plans. If a company was not expected to continue, for example, due to the likelihood of bankruptcy, then its assets and liabilities should be valued and reported on the balance sheet as if the company were to be liquidated (that is, discontinued, with all of its assets sold and all debts paid). In future chapters, unless otherwise indicated, we assume that businesses meet the continuity assumption. The fourth assumption, the time period assumption, provides guidance on measuring revenues and expenses that we will introduce in Chapter 3.

CONTINUITY (or going-concern) ASSUMPTION states that businesses are assumed to continue to operate into the foreseeable future.

INTERNATIONAL PERSPECTIVE

Reconsidering the Conceptual Framework

The Financial Accounting Standards Board (FASB) and the International Accounting Standards Board (IASB) are working on a joint project to develop a common conceptual framework toward convergence of accounting standards. In December 2009, the final draft of the first phase of the joint project was being written on "The Objective of Financial Reporting and Qualitative Characteristics and Constraints of Decision-Useful Financial Reporting Information." The following is a summary:

- ***Objective of Financial Reporting:*** To provide financial information about the reporting entity that is useful to present and potential equity investors, lenders, and other creditors in making decisions in their capacity as capital providers.
- ***Qualitative Characteristics*** (limited by materiality and costs):

Fundamental (to be useful):	*Enhancing* (degrees of usefulness):
• Relevance	• Comparability
• Faithful representation	• Verifiability
	• Timeliness
	• Understandability

For the latest updates on the joint project, go to www.iasb.org *or* www.fasb.org.

Elements of the Balance Sheet

The four financial statements—balance sheet, income statement, statement of retained earnings, and statement of cash flows—and the notes to the statements provide the structure for the information communicated to users. The elements of the financial statements are defined as part of the conceptual framework. As we learned in Chapter 1, assets, liabilities, and stockholders' equity are the elements of a corporation's balance sheet. Let's examine their definitions in more detail.

Assets are economic resources with probable future benefits owned or controlled by an entity as a result of past transactions. In other words, they are the acquired resources the entity can use to operate in the future. To be reported, assets must have a measurable, verifiable value, usually based on the purchase price. However, subsequent to acquisition, so as not to mislead users by reporting a value for the assets that is too high, managers use judgment (and past experience) to determine an acquired asset's most likely future benefit. For example, a company may have a list of customers who owe $10,000. History suggests, however, that only $9,800 is likely to be collected. The lower, more probable, and more conservative figure is reported to users for purposes of projecting future cash flows. In future chapters, we discuss the estimation process to determine the amount to report.

ASSETS are economic resources with probable future benefits owned by the entity as a result of past transactions.

Assets are measured initially under the **historical cost principle** (or cost principle). That is, on the acquisition date, cash paid plus the dollar value of all noncash considerations (any assets, privileges, or rights) given in the exchange become the historical cost of a new asset

The HISTORICAL COST PRINCIPLE (or cost principle) requires assets to be recorded at historical cost–cash paid plus the current dollar value of all noncash considerations given on the date of the exchange.

(i.e., its fair market value on the exchange date). For example, what would be the measured historical cost of a new delivery van when trading in an old delivery van with a market value of $2,000 and paying $15,000 cash? The new van's cost would be $17,000 (the sum of what was exchanged). Thus, in most cases, cost is relatively easy to determine and can be verified due to the arm's length exchange.

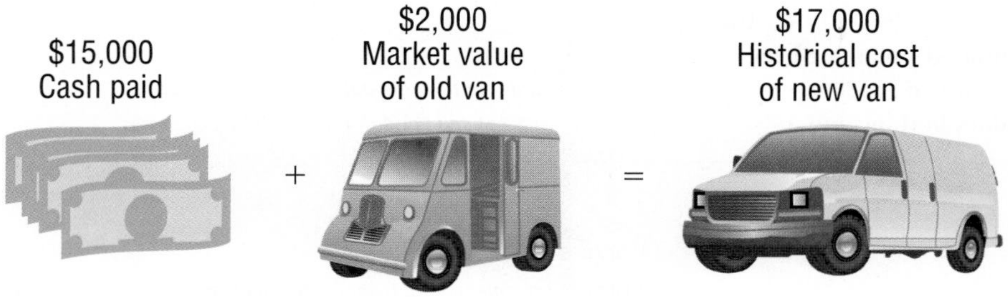

As shown in Papa John's balance sheet presented in Exhibit 2.2, most companies list assets **in order of liquidity,** or how soon an asset is expected by management to be turned into cash or used. Notice that several of Papa John's assets are categorized as **current assets.** Current assets are those resources that Papa John's will use or turn into cash within one year (the next 12 months). Note that inventory is always considered a current asset, regardless of how long it takes to produce and sell the inventory. As indicated in Exhibit 2.2, Papa John's current assets include Cash, Accounts Receivable, Supplies, Prepaid Expenses, and Other Current Assets (a summary of several current assets with individually smaller balances). These are typical titles utilized by most entities.

CURRENT ASSETS are assets that will be used or turned into cash within one year. Inventory is always considered a current asset regardless of the time needed to produce and sell it.

All other assets are considered long term (or noncurrent). That is, they are to be used or turned into cash beyond the coming year. For Papa John's, that includes Long-Term Investments, Property and Equipment (net of amounts used in the past), Notes Receivable (to be paid to Papa John's by its franchisees over several years), Intangibles (such as trademarks and patents), and Other Assets. As with other franchisers,[3] Papa John's balance sheet includes assets of its company-owned restaurants only, about 18 percent of all Papa John's restaurants. The assets of the remaining 82 percent belong to franchisees and are appropriately reported in each franchisee's own financial statements.

Unrecorded but Valuable Assets

FINANCIAL ANALYSIS

Many very valuable intangible assets, such as trademarks, patents, and copyrights, that are developed inside a company (not purchased) are not reported on the balance sheet. For example, General Electric's balance sheet reveals no listing for the GE trademark because it was developed internally over time through research, development, and advertising (it was not purchased). Likewise, the Coca-Cola Company does not report any asset for its patented Coke formulae, although it does report more than $2 billion in various trademarks that it has purchased.

Liabilities are probable debts or obligations (claims to a company's resources) that result from a company's past transactions and will be paid with assets or services. Entities that a company owes money to are called **creditors.** Papa John's balance sheet includes five liabilities: Accounts Payable, Accrued Expenses Payable, Unearned Franchise Fees, Long-Term Notes Payable, and Other Long-Term Liabilities. These and other liabilities will be discussed in subsequent chapters.

LIABILITIES are probable debts or obligations of the entity that result from past transactions, which will be paid with assets or services.

[3]Companies that sell franchises include Subway, Choice Hotels, Supercuts, GolfUSA, Marble Slab Creamery, and Arco ampm. To identify other franchise companies, go to a company's website or www.franchisedirect.com.

EXHIBIT 2.2

Papa John's Balance Sheet

	PAPA JOHN'S INTERNATIONAL, INC. **Consolidated Balance Sheet** **December 31, 2008** **(dollars in thousands)**		point in time the balance sheet is prepared (at year-end in this case)
	ASSETS		
	Current Assets		
Current assets	Cash	$ 11,000	
Current assets	Accounts receivable	24,000	*payments due from franchisees and others on account*
Current assets	Supplies	17,000	*food, beverages, and paper supplies on hand*
Current assets	Prepaid expenses	10,000	*rent, advertising, and/or insurance paid in advance*
Current assets	Other current assets	13,000	*a summary of several current assets with smaller balances*
	Total current assets	75,000	
Noncurrent assets	Investments	1,000	*another company's stocks and bonds purchased with excess cash*
Noncurrent assets	Property and equipment (net)	190,000	*the remaining cost of long-lived assets to be used in future operations (original cost $388,000 minus $198,000, the estimated portion of cost already used in the past)*
Noncurrent assets	Notes receivable	8,000	*long-term amounts due from franchisees*
Noncurrent assets	Intangibles	77,000	*patents, trademarks, and goodwill*
Noncurrent assets	Other assets	36,000	*a summary of several long-term assets with smaller balances*
	Total assets	$387,000	
	LIABILITIES AND STOCKHOLDERS' EQUITY		
	Current Liabilities		
Current liabilities	Accounts payable	$ 29,000	*payments due to suppliers*
Current liabilities	Accrued expenses payable	71,000	*a summary of payroll, rent, and other obligations*
	Total current liabilities	100,000	
Noncurrent liabilities	Unearned franchise fees	6,000	*amounts paid by franchisees for services they will receive*
Noncurrent liabilities	Notes payable	124,000	*loans from creditors*
Noncurrent liabilities	Other long-term liabilities	27,000	
	Total liabilities	257,000	
	Stockholders' Equity*		
	Contributed capital	7,000	*amounts received from contributors (investors)*
	Retained earnings	123,000	*cumulative profits not distributed to investors*
	Total stockholders' equity	130,000	
	Total liabilities and stockholders' equity	$387,000	

*Stockholders' equity amounts have been simplified.

CURRENT LIABILITIES are obligations that will be settled by providing cash, goods, or services within the coming year.

Just as assets are reported in order of liquidity, liabilities are usually listed on the balance sheet **in order of maturity** (how soon an obligation is to be paid). Liabilities that Papa John's will need to pay or settle within the coming year (with cash, services, or other current assets) are classified as **current liabilities.** Distinguishing current assets and current liabilities assists external users of the financial statements in assessing the amounts and timing of future cash flows.

Environmental Liabilities: The "Greening of GAAP"

A QUESTION OF ETHICS

For many years, companies have faced a growing pressure to estimate and disclose environmental liabilities, such as the cleanup of hazardous waste sites. Current GAAP require companies to record and report a reasonable estimate of any **probable** future environmental liabilities associated with an asset, if a reasonable amount can be projected.

Changing attitudes toward environmental stewardship along with recent federal and state legislative initiatives are adding to the challenge of recording and disclosing environmental liabilities. As this text is being written, new accounting rules have been proposed to estimate **possible** losses. This could likely cause companies to disclose more potential environmental liabilities at higher amounts. However, more uncertainty will exist as to identifying, calculating, and disclosing relevant information.

Stockholders' equity (also called **owners' equity** or **shareholders' equity**) is the financing provided by the owners and by business operations. Owner-provided cash (and sometimes other assets) is referred to as contributed capital. Owners invest in the business and receive shares of stock as evidence of ownership. The largest investor in Papa John's International, Inc., is John Schnatter, founder and CEO, who owns approximately 21 percent of the stock. Mutual funds, other corporate employees, directors, and the general public own the rest.

Owners who invest (or buy stock) in a company hope to benefit from their investment in two ways: receipts of **dividends,** which are a distribution of a company's earnings (a return on the shareholders' investment), and gains from selling the stock for more than they paid (known as **capital gains**). Earnings that are not distributed to the owners but instead are reinvested in the business by management are called retained earnings.[4] Companies with a growth strategy often pay little or no dividends to retain funds for expansion. A look at Papa John's balance sheet (Exhibit 2.2) indicates that its growth has been financed by substantial reinvestment of earnings ($123 million).

STOCKHOLDERS' EQUITY (also called owners' equity or shareholders' equity) is the financing provided by the owners and business operations.

CONTRIBUTED CAPITAL results from owners providing cash (and sometimes other assets) to the business.

RETAINED EARNINGS refers to the cumulative earnings of a company that are not distributed to the owners and are reinvested in the business.

[4]Retained earnings can increase only from profitable operations. Retained earnings decrease when a firm has a loss. Also, as we discuss in Chapter 3, a company's annual income from operations is usually not equal to the net cash flows for the year.

PAUSE FOR FEEDBACK

We just learned the elements of the balance sheet (assets, liabilities, and stockholders' equity) and how assets and liabilities are usually classified (current or noncurrent). Current assets (including inventory) are expected to be used or turned into cash within the next 12 months and current liabilities are expected to be paid or satisfied within the next 12 months with cash, services, or other current assets.

SELF-STUDY QUIZ

The following is a list of items from a recent Wendy's International, Inc., balance sheet. Indicate on the line provided whether each of the following is categorized on the balance sheet as a current asset (CA), noncurrent asset (NCA), current liability (CL), noncurrent liability (NCL), or stockholders' equity (SE).

______ Accrued Expenses Payable	______ Long-Term Debt	______ Properties (land, building, and equipment)
______ Inventories	______ Retained Earnings	______ Notes Receivable (due in five years)
______ Accounts Receivable	______ Accounts Payable	______ Cash

After you have completed your answers, check them with the solutions at the bottom of the page.

Column 1: CL; CA; CA. Column 2: NCL; SE; CL. Column 3: NCA; NCA; CA.

Solutions to SELF-STUDY QUIZ

Exceptions to the Measurement and Reporting Principles

The conceptual framework also contains exceptions to measurement and reporting rules that allow for variations in practice while continuing to provide relevant and reliable information to users. Two of the exceptions are materiality and conservatism.

MATERIALITY exception suggests that small amounts that are not likely to influence a user's decision can be accounted for in the most cost-beneficial manner.

The **materiality** exception suggests that when relatively small (immaterial) dollar amounts are not likely to influence a user's decision, the item can be accounted for in the most cost-beneficial manner. For example, pencil sharpeners that a company purchases represent equipment with a life that usually is greater than one year—a noncurrent asset. However, the cost of keeping track of, measuring, and reporting these inexpensive items as a noncurrent asset likely exceeds any value to users' decisions. Instead, the pencil sharpeners can be recorded as an expense when purchased. For expediency, many companies have a threshold limit that is applied to low-cost equipment acquisitions (e.g., anything under $500 is expensed, not recorded as an asset). Throughout the text, unless told otherwise, assume all amounts are material to users' decisions.

CONSERVATISM exception suggests that care should be taken not to overstate assets and revenues or understate liabilities and expenses.

For information to be useful, it must not mislead users. The **conservatism** exception suggests that, when options in measurement exist and no option is better than any other, accountants should apply the methods that do not overstate assets and revenues or understate liabilities and expenses—that is, they should choose conservative methods. Measurement options will be presented beginning in Chapter 6. Now that we have reviewed the basic elements of the balance sheet as part of the conceptual framework, let's see what economic activities cause changes in the amounts reported on the balance sheet.

LEARNING OBJECTIVE 2

Identify what constitutes a business transaction and recognize common balance sheet account titles used in business.

WHAT BUSINESS ACTIVITIES CAUSE CHANGES IN FINANCIAL STATEMENT AMOUNTS?

Nature of Business Transactions

A TRANSACTION is (1) an exchange of assets or services for assets, services, or promises to pay between a business and one or more external parties to a business or (2) a measurable internal event such as the use of assets in operations.

Video 2-1
www.mhhe.com/libby7e

Accounting focuses on certain events that have an economic impact on the entity. Those events that are recorded as part of the accounting process are called **transactions.** The first step in translating the results of business events to financial statement numbers is determining which events to include. As the definitions of assets and liabilities indicate, only economic resources and debts **resulting from past transactions** are recorded on the balance sheet. Transactions include two types of events:

1. **External events:** These are **exchanges** of assets, goods, or services by one party for assets, services, or promises to pay (liabilities) by one or more other parties. Examples include the purchase of a machine from a supplier, sale of merchandise to customers, borrowing cash from a bank, and investment of cash in the business by the owners.
2. **Internal events:** These include certain events that are not exchanges between the business and other parties but nevertheless have a direct and measurable effect on the entity. Examples include using up insurance paid in advance and using buildings and equipment over several years.

Throughout this textbook, the word *transaction* is used in the broad sense to include both types of events.

Some important events that have a future economic impact on a company, however, are **not** reflected in the financial statements. In most cases, signing a contract is not considered to be a transaction because it involves **only the exchange of promises,** not of assets such as cash, goods, services, or property. For example, assume that Papa John's signs an employment contract with a new regional manager. From an accounting perspective, no transaction has occurred because no exchange of assets, goods, or services has been made. Each party to the contract has exchanged promises—the manager agrees to work; Papa John's agrees to pay the manager for the work. For each day the new manager works, however, the exchange of services for pay results in a transaction that Papa John's must record. Because of their importance, long-term employment contracts, leases, and other commitments may need to be disclosed in notes to the financial statements.

EXHIBIT 2.3

Typical Account Titles

Assets	Liabilities	Stockholders' Equity	Revenues	Expenses
Cash	Accounts Payable	Contributed Capital	Sales Revenue	Cost of Goods Sold
Short-Term Investments	Accrued Expenses Payable	Retained Earnings	Fee Revenue	Wages Expense
Accounts Receivable	Notes Payable		Interest Revenue	Rent Expense
Notes Receivable	Taxes Payable		Rent Revenue	Interest Expense
Inventory (to be sold)	Unearned Revenue		Service Revenue	Depreciation Expense
Supplies	Bonds Payable			Advertising Expense
Prepaid Expenses				Insurance Expense
Long-Term Investments				Repair Expense
Equipment				Income Tax Expense
Buildings				
Land				
Intangibles				

Accounts with "receivable" in the title are always assets; they represent amounts owed by (receivable from) customers and others to the business.

Prepaid Expenses is always an asset; it represents amounts paid by the company to others for future benefits, such as future insurance coverage, rental of property, or advertising.

Accounts with "payable" in the title are always liabilities and represent amounts owed by the company to be paid to others in the future.

Accounts with "unearned" in the title are always liabilities representing amounts paid in the past to the company by others who expect future goods or services from the company.

Title revenue accounts by their source followed by the word "revenue."

Title expense accounts by what was incurred or used followed by the word "expense," except for inventory sold, which is titled Cost of Goods Sold.

Accounts

To accumulate the dollar effect of transactions on each financial statement item, organizations use a standardized format called an **account.** The resulting balances are kept separate for financial statement purposes. To facilitate the recording of transactions, each company establishes a **chart of accounts,** a list of all account titles and their unique numbers. The accounts are usually organized by financial statement element, with asset accounts listed first, followed by liability, stockholders' equity, revenue, and expense accounts in that order. Exhibit 2.3 lists various account titles that are quite common and are used by most companies. The exhibit also provides special notes to help you in learning account titles. When you are completing assignments and are unsure of an account title, refer to this listing for help.

An ACCOUNT is a standardized format that organizations use to accumulate the dollar effect of transactions on each financial statement item.

Every company creates its own chart of accounts to fit the nature of its business activities. For example, a small lawn care service may have an asset account titled Lawn Mowing Equipment, but a large corporation such as Dell is unlikely to report such an account. These differences in accounts will become more apparent as we examine the balance sheets of various companies. Because each company has its own chart of accounts, you should **not** try to memorize a typical chart of accounts, but understand the nature of each typical account. Then when you see a company that uses a slightly different title, you will understand what it means. For example, some companies use the terms Trade Accounts Receivable (same as Accounts Receivable) or Merchandise Inventory (same as Inventory). In homework problems, you will either be given the account names or be expected to select appropriate names, similar to the ones in Exhibit 2.3. Once you select a name for an account, you must use that exact name in all transactions affecting that account.

The accounts you see in the financial statements of most large corporations are actually summations (or aggregations) of a number of specific accounts in their recordkeeping system. For example, Papa John's keeps separate accounts for paper supplies, food supplies, and beverage supplies, but combines them under **Supplies** on the balance sheet. Equipment, buildings, and land are also combined into an account called **Property and Equipment.** Since our aim is to understand financial statements of actual entities, we will focus on aggregated accounts.

HOW DO TRANSACTIONS AFFECT ACCOUNTS?

LEARNING OBJECTIVE 3

Apply transaction analysis to simple business transactions in terms of the accounting model: Assets = Liabilities + Stockholders' Equity.

Managers' business decisions often result in transactions that affect the financial statements. For example, decisions to expand the number of stores, advertise a new product, change an employee benefit package, and invest excess cash would all affect the financial statements. Sometimes these decisions have unintended consequences as well. The decision to purchase additional inventory for cash in anticipation of a major sales initiative, for example, will increase inventory and decrease cash. But if there is no demand for the additional inventory, the lower cash balance will also reduce the company's ability to pay its other obligations.

Because business decisions often involve an element of risk, managers should understand exactly how transactions impact the financial statements. The process for determining the effects of transactions is called **transaction analysis.**

Principles of Transaction Analysis

TRANSACTION ANALYSIS is the process of studying a transaction to determine its economic effect on the business in terms of the accounting equation.

Transaction analysis is the process of studying a transaction to determine its economic effect on the entity in terms of the accounting equation (also known as the **fundamental accounting model**). We outline the process in this section of the chapter and create a visual tool representing the process (the transaction analysis model). The basic accounting equation and two principles are the foundation for this model. Recall from Chapter 1 that the basic accounting equation for a business that is organized as a corporation is as follows:

Assets (A) = Liabilities (L) + Stockholders' Equity (SE)

The two principles underlying the transaction analysis process follow:

- Every transaction affects at least two accounts; correctly identifying those accounts and the direction of the effect (whether an increase or a decrease) is critical.
- The accounting equation must remain in balance after each transaction.

Success in performing transaction analysis depends on a clear understanding of these principles. Study the following material well.

Dual Effects

The idea that every transaction has **at least two effects** on the basic accounting equation is known as the **dual effects** concept.[5] Most transactions with external parties involve an **exchange** by which the business **entity both receives something and gives up something in return.** For example, suppose Papa John's purchased some paper napkins for cash. In this exchange, Papa John's would receive supplies (an increase in an asset) and in return would give up cash (a decrease in an asset).

Transaction	Papa John's Received	Papa John's Gave
Purchased paper napkins for cash	Supplies (increased)	Cash (decreased)

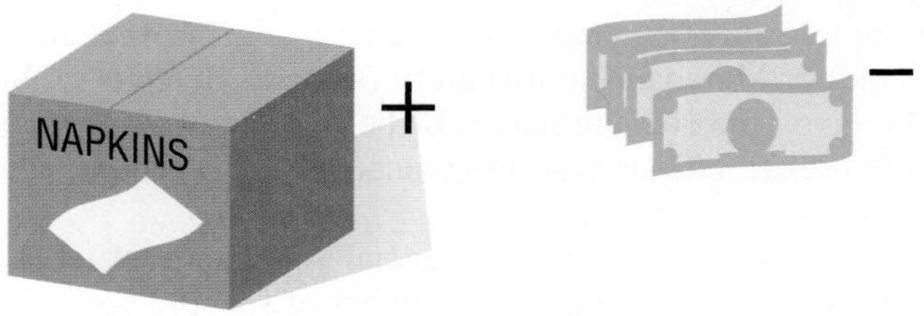

[5]From this concept, accountants have developed what is known as the *double-entry system* of recordkeeping.

In analyzing this transaction, we determined that the accounts affected were Supplies and Cash. As we discussed in Chapter 1, however, most supplies are purchased on credit (that is, money is owed to suppliers). In that case, Papa John's would engage in *two* transactions:

1. The purchase of an asset on credit	In the first transaction, Papa John's would receive Supplies (an increase in an asset) and would give in return a promise to pay later called **Accounts Payable** (an increase in a liability).
2. The eventual payment	In the second transaction, Papa John's would eliminate or receive back its promise to pay (a decrease in the Accounts Payable liability) and would give up Cash (a decrease in an asset).

Transactions	Papa John's Received	Papa John's Gave
(1) Purchased paper napkins on credit	Supplies (increased)	Accounts Payable (increased) [a promise to pay]

Transactions	Papa John's Received	Papa John's Gave
(2) Paid on its accounts payable	Accounts Payable (decreased) [a promise was eliminated]	Cash (decreased)

As noted earlier, not all important business activities result in a transaction that affects the financial statements. Most importantly, signing a contract involving **the exchange of two promises to perform does not result in an accounting transaction** that is recorded. For example, if Papa John's sent an order for more napkins to its paper supplier and the supplier accepted the order but did not fill it immediately, no transaction took place. As soon as the goods are shipped to Papa John's, however, the supplier has given up its inventory in exchange for a promise from Papa John's to pay for the items in the near future, and Papa John's has exchanged its promise to pay for the supplies it receives. Because a **promise** has been exchanged for **goods,** a transaction has taken place. Both Papa John's and the supplier's statements will be affected.

Balancing the Accounting Equation

The accounting equation must remain in balance after each transaction. That is, total assets (resources) must equal total liabilities and stockholders' equity (claims to resources). If all correct accounts have been identified and the appropriate direction of the effect on each account has been determined, the equation should remain in balance. A systematic transaction analysis includes the following steps, in this order:

Step 1: Identify and classify accounts and effects

- **Identify the accounts (by title) affected,** making sure that at least two accounts change. Ask yourself: What was received and what was given?
- **Classify them by type of account.** Was each account an asset (A), a liability (L), or a stockholders' equity (SE)?
- **Determine the direction of the effect.** Did the account increase (+) or decrease (−)?

Step 2: Verify accounting equation is in balance

- **Verify that the accounting equation (A = L + SE) remains in balance.**

Analyzing Papa John's Transactions

To illustrate the use of the transaction analysis process, let's consider some typical transactions of Papa John's that are also common to most businesses. Remember that this chapter presents transactions that affect only the balance sheet accounts. Assume that Papa John's engages in the following events during January 2009, the month following the balance sheet in Exhibit 2.2. Account titles are from that balance sheet, and remember that, for simplicity, all amounts are in **thousands of dollars:**

***(a)* Papa John's issues $2,000 of additional common stock shares, receiving cash from investors.**

Step 1: **Identify and classify accounts and effects.**

Received: Cash (+A) $2,000

Given: Additional stock shares, Contributed Capital (+SE) $2,000

Step 2: **Is the accounting equation in balance?**

Yes. The left side and the right side increased by $2,000.

	Assets	=	Liabilities	+	Stockholders' Equity
	Cash				**Contributed Capital**
(a)	**+2,000**	=			**+2,000**

***(b)* Papa John's borrows $6,000 from its local bank, signing a note to be paid in three years.**

Step 1: **Identify and classify accounts and effects.**

Received: Cash (+A) $6,000

Given: Written promise to the bank, Notes Payable (+L) $6,000

Step 2: **Is the accounting equation in balance?**

Yes. The left side and the right side increased by $6,000.

	Assets	=	Liabilities	+	Stockholders' Equity
	Cash		**Notes Payable**		**Contributed Capital**
(a)	+2,000	=			+2,000
(b)	**+6,000**	=	**+6,000**		

Events *(a)* and *(b)* are **financing** transactions. Companies that need cash for **investing** purposes (to buy or build additional facilities) often seek funds by selling stock to investors as in event *(a)* or by borrowing from creditors as in event *(b)*.

(c) Papa John's purchases new ovens, counters, refrigerators, and other equipment costing $10,000, paying $2,000 in cash and signing a two-year note payable to the equipment manufacturer for the rest.

Step 1: Identify and classify accounts and effects.
Received: Property and Equipment (+A) $10,000 **Given:** (1) Cash (−A) $2,000
(2) Notes Payable (+L) $8,000

Step 2: Is the accounting equation in balance?
Yes. The left side and the right side increased by $8,000.

	Assets		=	Liabilities	+	Stockholders' Equity
	Cash	Property and Equipment		Notes Payable		Contributed Capital
(a)	+2,000		=			+2,000
(b)	+6,000		=	+6,000		
(c)	**−2,000**	**+10,000**	=	**+8,000**		

Notice that more than two accounts were affected by transaction (*c*).

***(d)* Papa John's lends $3,000 cash to new franchisees who sign notes agreeing to repay the loans in five years.**

Step 1: Identify and classify accounts and effects.
Received: Notes Receivable (+A) $3,000 **Given:** Cash (−A) $3,000

Step 2: Is the accounting equation in balance?
Yes. The equation stays in balance because assets increase and decrease by the same amount, $3,000.

The effects are included in the chart that follows transaction (*f*).

***(e)* Papa John's purchases the stock of other companies as a long-term investment, paying $1,000 in cash.**

Step 1: Identify and classify accounts and effects.
Received: Investments (+A) $1,000 **Given:** Cash (−A) $1,000

Step 2: Is the accounting equation in balance?
Yes. The equation stays in balance because assets increase and decrease by the same amount, $1,000.

The effects are included in the chart that follows transaction (*f*).

***(f)* Papa John's board of directors declares that the Company will pay $3,000 in cash dividends to shareholders next month.[6]** Retained Earnings represent the profits available to shareholders. When a company's board of directors declares a cash dividend, Retained Earnings is reduced. Thus, the company receives a reduction in the profits it has available to distribute to shareholders. On the other hand, until the dividends are paid, the company gives shareholders a promise to pay the dividends (called Dividends Payable).

Step 1: Identify and classify accounts and effects.
Received: Retained Earnings (−SE) $3,000 **Given:** Dividends Payable (+L) $3,000

Step 2: Is the accounting equation in balance?
Yes. The equation stays in balance because liabilities increase and stockholders' equity decreases by the same amount, $3,000.

The effects are included in the chart that follows.

[6]At the time this chapter is being written, Papa John's has not declared dividends; this transaction, as well as later similar ones, is included for purposes of illustration only.

	Assets				=	Liabilities		+ Stockholders' Equity	
	Cash	Notes Receivable	Property and Equipment	Investments		Dividends Payable	Notes Payable	Contributed Capital	Retained Earnings
(a)	+2,000				=			+2,000	
(b)	+6,000				=		+6,000		
(c)	−2,000		+10,000		=		+8,000		
(d)	−3,000	+3,000			=	No Change			
(e)	−1,000			+1,000	=	No Change			
(f)				No Change	=	+3,000			−3,000
Totals	**+2,000**	**+3,000**	**+10,000**	**+1,000**	**=**	**+3,000**	**+14,000**	**+2,000**	**−3,000**
			+16,000		**=**			**+16,000**	

STOP

PAUSE FOR **FEEDBACK**

Transaction analysis involves identifying accounts (by title) affected in a transaction, recognizing that at least two accounts are affected, classifying the accounts (asset, liability, or stockholders' equity), and determining the direction of the effect on the account (increase or decrease). If all accounts and effects are correct, then the fundamental accounting equation (A = L + SE) will remain in balance. **Practice is the most effective way to develop your transaction analysis skills.**

SELF-STUDY **QUIZ**

Review the analysis in events (*a*) through (*f*) above, complete the analysis of the following transactions, and indicate the effects in the chart below. Answer from the standpoint of the business.

(*a*) **Paul Knepper contributes $50,000 cash to establish Florida Flippers, Inc., a new scuba business organized as a corporation; he receives stock in exchange.**

Step 1: Identify and classify accounts and effects.
Received: ____________________ **Given:** ____________________

Step 2: Is the accounting equation in balance? Yes or No? ____________

(*b*) **Florida Flippers buys a small building near the ocean for $250,000, paying $25,000 cash and signing a 10-year note payable for the rest.**

Step 1: Identify and classify accounts and effects.
Received: ____________________ **Given:** ____________________

Step 2: Is the accounting equation in balance? Yes or No? ____________

	Assets		=	Liabilities	+	Stockholders' Equity
	Cash	**Building**		**Notes Payable**		**Contributed Capital**
(a)			=			
(b)			=			

After you have completed your answers, check them with the solutions at the bottom of page 57. If your answers did not agree with ours, we recommend that you go back to each event to make sure that you have completed each of the steps of transaction analysis.

HOW DO COMPANIES KEEP TRACK OF ACCOUNT BALANCES?

LEARNING OBJECTIVE 4

Determine the impact of business transactions on the balance sheet using two basic tools, journal entries and T-accounts.

For most organizations, recording transaction effects and keeping track of account balances in the manner just presented is impractical. To handle the multitude of daily transactions that a business generates, companies establish accounting systems, usually computerized, that follow a cycle. The accounting cycle, illustrated in Exhibit 2.4, highlights the primary activities performed during the accounting period to analyze, record, and post transactions. In Chapters 2 and 3, we will illustrate these activities during the period. In Chapter 4, we will complete the accounting cycle by discussing and illustrating activities at the end of the period to adjust the records, prepare financial statements, and close the accounting records.

During the accounting period, transactions that result in exchanges between the company and other external parties are analyzed and recorded in the **general journal** in chronological order, and the related accounts are updated in the **general ledger.** These formal records are based on two very important tools used by accountants: journal entries and T-accounts. From the standpoint of accounting systems design, these analytical tools are a more efficient way to reflect the effects of transactions, determine account balances, and prepare financial statements. As future business managers, you should develop your understanding and use of these tools in financial analysis. For those studying accounting, this knowledge is the foundation for an understanding of the accounting system and future accounting coursework. After we explain how to perform transaction analysis using these tools, we illustrate their use in financial analysis.

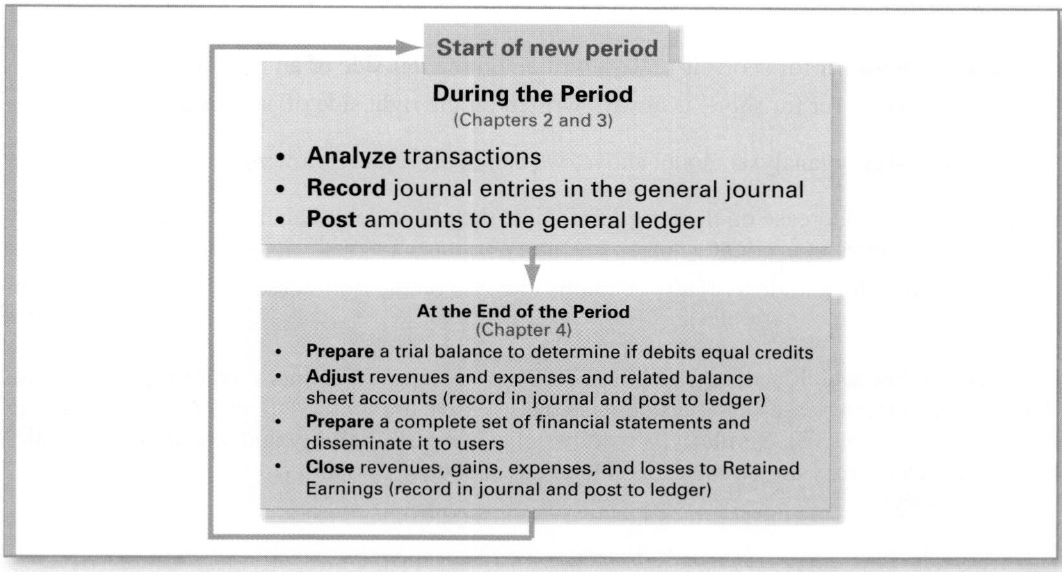

EXHIBIT 2.4

The Accounting Cycle

Solutions to SELF-STUDY QUIZ

(*a*) Step 1: Received: Cash (+A) $50,000; Given: Contributed Capital (+SE) $50,000.
Step 2: Yes. The equation remains in balance; assets (on the left) and stockholders' equity (on the right) increase by the same amount, $50,000.

(*b*) Step 1: Received: Building (+A) $250,000; Given: Cash (−A) $25,000 and Notes Payable (+L) $225,000.
Step 2: Yes. Assets (on the left) increase by $225,000 and liabilities (on the right) increase by $225,000.

	Assets		=	Liabilities	+	Stockholders' Equity
	Cash	**Building**		**Notes Payable**		**Contributed Capital**
(a)	+50,000		=			+50,000
(b)	−25,000	+250,000	=	+225,000		

EXHIBIT 2.5

Transaction Analysis Model

Assets (many accounts)		=	Liabilities (many accounts)		+	Stockholders' Equity (two accounts)			
						Contributed Capital		Retained Earnings	
+	−		−	+		−	+	−	+
debit	credit		debit	credit		debit	credit	debit	credit
							Investments by owners	Dividends declared	Net income of business

The Direction of Transaction Effects

As we saw earlier, transaction effects increase and decrease assets, liabilities, and stockholders' equity. To reflect these effects efficiently, we need to structure the transaction analysis model in a manner that shows the **direction** of the effects. As shown in Exhibit 2.5, the critical structural factor is the following:

- **The increase symbol + is located on the left side of the T for accounts on the left side of the accounting equation (assets).**
- **The increase symbol + is located on the right side of the T for accounts on the right side of the equation (liabilities and stockholders' equity).**

Also notice that:

DEBIT (dr) is on the left side of an account.

CREDIT (cr) is on the right side of an account.

- The term debit (dr for short) is always written on the left side of an account.
- The term credit (cr for short) is always written on the right side of an account.

From the transaction analysis model above, we can observe the following:

- Asset accounts increase on the left (debit) side; they have debit balances. It would be highly unusual for an asset account, such as Inventory, to have a negative (credit) balance.
- Liability and stockholders' equity accounts increase on the right (credit) side, creating credit balances.

To remember which accounts debits increase and which accounts credits increase, recall that a debit (left) increases asset accounts because assets are on the left side of the accounting equation (A = L + SE). Similarly, a credit (right) increases liability and stockholders' equity accounts because they are on the right side of the accounting equation.

In summary:

Assets	=	Liabilities	=	Stockholders' Equity
↑ with Debits		↑ with Credits		↑ with Credits
Accounts have debit balances		Accounts have credit balances		Accounts have credit balances

In Chapter 3, we will add revenue and expense account effects. Until then, as you are learning to perform transaction analysis, **you should refer to the transaction analysis model in Exhibit 2.5 often until you can construct it on your own without assistance.**

Many students have trouble with accounting because they forget that the term **debit** is simply the left side of an account and the term **credit** is simply the right side of an account. Perhaps someone once told you that you were a credit to your school or your family. As a result, you may think that credits are good and debits are bad. Such is not the case. Just remember that **debit is on the left** and **credit is on the right.**

If you have identified the correct accounts and effects through transaction analysis, the accounting equation will remain in balance. **The total dollar value of all debits will equal the total dollar value of all credits** in a transaction. For an extra measure of assurance, add this equality check (Debits = Credits) to the transaction analysis process.

PAUSE FOR **FEEDBACK**

From Exhibit 2.5, we learned that each account can increase and decrease. In the transaction analysis model, the effect of a transaction on each element can be represented with a T with one side increasing and the other side decreasing. Asset accounts on the left side of the fundamental accounting equation increase their balances on the left side of the T. Liability and stockholders' equity accounts are on the right side of the fundamental accounting equation and increase their balance on the right side of the T. In accounting, the left side of the T is called the debit side and the right is called the credit side. Most accounts have a balance on the positive side.

SELF-STUDY **QUIZ**

The following is a list of accounts from a recent Wendy's International, Inc., balance sheet. Indicate on the line provided whether each of the following usually has a debit (DR) or credit (CR) balance.

______ Accrued Expenses Payable	______ Long-Term Debt	______ Properties (land, building, and equipment)
______ Inventories	______ Retained Earnings	______ Notes Receivable (due in five years)
______ Accounts Receivable	______ Accounts Payable	______ Cash

After you have completed your answers, check them with the solutions at the bottom of the page.

Analytical Tools

The Journal Entry

In a bookkeeping system, transactions are recorded in chronological order in a **general journal** (or simply, journal). After analyzing the business documents (such as purchase invoices, receipts, and cash register tapes) that describe a transaction, the bookkeeper enters the effects on the accounts in the journal using debits and credits. The **journal entry,** then, is an accounting method for expressing the effects of a transaction on accounts. It is written in a debits-equal-credits format. The journal entry for event (*c*) in the Papa John's illustration is as follows:

A JOURNAL ENTRY is an accounting method for expressing the effects of a transaction on accounts in a debits-equal-credits format.

Account Titles:
Debited accounts on top.
Credited accounts on bottom, usually indented.

Reference:
Letter, number, or date

		Debit	Credit
(*c*)	Property and Equipment (+A)	10,000	
	Cash (−A)		2,000
	Notes Payable (+L)		8,000

Amounts:
Debited amounts on left. Credited amounts on right.

Column 1: CR; DR; DR. Column 2: CR; CR; CR. Column 3: DR; DR; DR.

Solutions to SELF-STUDY QUIZ

Notice the following:

- It is useful to include a date or some form of reference for each transaction. The debited accounts are written first (on top) with the amounts recorded in the left column. The credited accounts are written below the debits and are usually indented in manual records; the credited amounts are written in the right column. The order of the debited accounts or credited accounts does not matter, as long as the debits are on top and the credits are on the bottom and indented to the right.
- Total debits ($10,000) equal total credits ($2,000 + $8,000).
- Three accounts are affected by this transaction. Any journal entry that affects more than two accounts is called a **compound entry.** Although this is the only transaction in the Papa John's illustration that affects more than two accounts, many transactions in subsequent chapters require a compound journal entry.

While you are learning to perform transaction analysis, use the symbols A, L, and SE next to each account title, as in the preceding journal entry. Specifically identifying accounts as assets (A), liabilities (L), or stockholders' equity (SE) clarifies the transaction analysis and makes journal entries easier to write. For example, if Cash is to be increased, we write Cash (+A). Throughout subsequent chapters, we include the direction of the effect along with the symbol to help you understand the effects of each transaction on the financial statements. In transaction (*c*) above, we can see that assets are affected by +$8,000 (increase of $10,000 in Property and Equipment and decrease of $2,000 in Cash) and liabilities are affected by +$8,000. The accounting equation A = L + SE remains in balance.

Many students try to memorize journal entries without understanding or using the transaction analysis model. As more detailed transactions are presented in subsequent chapters, the task becomes increasingly more difficult. In the long run, **memorizing, understanding, and using the transaction analysis model** presented here will save you time and prevent confusion.

The T-Account

By themselves, journal entries do not provide the balances in accounts. After the journal entries have been recorded, the bookkeeper posts (transfers) the dollar amounts to each account affected by the transaction to determine the new account balances. (In most computerized accounting systems, this happens automatically.)

As a group, the accounts are called a **general ledger.** In the manual accounting system used by some small organizations, the ledger is often a three-ring binder with a separate page for each account. In a computerized system, accounts are stored on a disk. See Exhibit 2.6 for an illustration of a journal page and the related ledger pages. Note that the cash effects from the journal entries have been posted to the Cash ledger page.

The T-ACCOUNT is a tool for summarizing transaction effects for each account, determining balances, and drawing inferences about a company's activities.

One very useful tool for summarizing the transaction effects and determining the balances for individual accounts is a **T-account,** a simplified representation of a ledger account. Exhibit 2.7 shows the T-accounts for Papa John's Cash and Notes Payable accounts based on Events (*a*) through (*c*). Notice that, for Cash, which is classified as an asset, increases are shown on the left and decreases appear on the right side of the T-account. For Notes Payable, however, increases are shown on the right and decreases on the left since Notes Payable is a liability. Many small businesses still use handwritten or manually maintained accounts in this T-account format. Computerized systems retain the concept but not the format of the T-account.

In Exhibit 2.7, notice that the ending balance is indicated on the positive side with a double underline. To find the account balances, we can express the T-accounts as equations:

	Cash	Notes Payable
Beginning balance	$ 11,000	$ 124,000
plus "+" side	+ 8,000	+ 14,000
minus "−" side	− 2,000	− 0
Ending balance	$ 17,000	$ 138,000

EXHIBIT 2.6

Posting Transaction Effects from the Journal to the Ledger

General Journal Page G1

Date	Account Titles and Explanation (in thousands)	Ref.	Debit	Credit
Jan. 2	Cash	101	2,000	
	Contributed Capital			2,000
	(Investment by stockholders.)			
Jan. 6	Cash	101	6,000	
	Notes Payable	201		6,000
	(Borrowed from bank.)			
Jan. 8	Property and Equipment	140	**10,000**	
	Cash	101		**2,000**
	Notes Payable	201		**8,000**
	(Purchased equipment paying part cash and the rest due on a note payable.)			

General Ledger — **CASH** 101

Date	Explanation	Ref.	Debit	Credit	Balance
	Balance				11,000
Jan. 2		G1	2,000		13,000
Jan. 6		G1	6,000		19,000
Jan. 8		G1		**2,000**	17,000

General Ledger — **PROPERTY AND EQUIPMENT** 140

Date	Explanation	Ref.	Debit	Credit	Balance
	Balance				190,000
Jan. 8		G1	**10,000**		200,000

General Ledger — **NOTES PAYABLE** 201

Date	Explanation	Ref.	Debit	Credit	Balance
	Balance				124,000
Jan. 6		G1		6,000	130,000
Jan. 8		G1		**8,000**	138,000

EXHIBIT 2.7

T-Accounts Illustrated

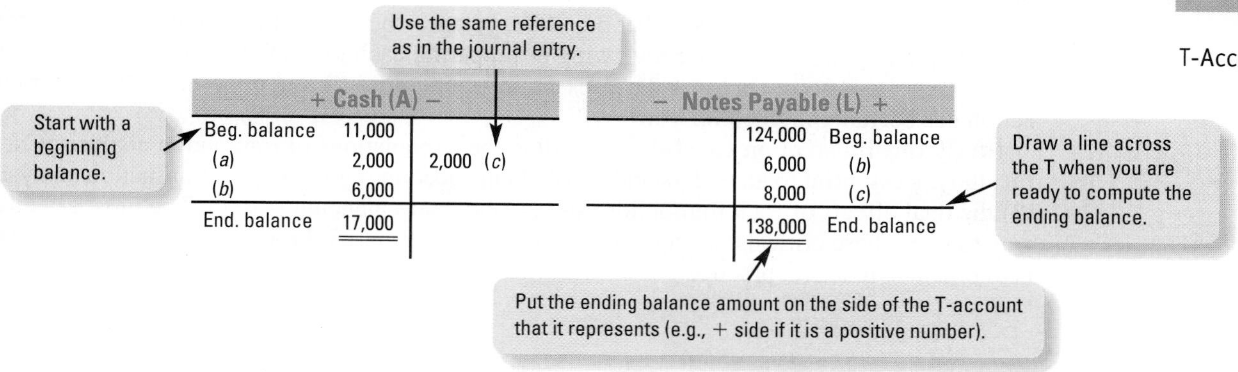

A word on terminology: The words **debit** and **credit** may be used as verbs, nouns, and adjectives. For example, we can say that Papa John's Cash account was debited (verb) when stock was issued to investors, meaning that the amount was entered on the left side of the T-account. Or we can say that a credit (noun) was entered on the right side of an account. Notes Payable may be described as a credit account (adjective). These terms will be used instead of **left** and **right** throughout the rest of this textbook. The next section illustrates the steps to follow in analyzing the effects of transactions, recording the effects in journal entries, and determining account balances using T-accounts.

FINANCIAL ANALYSIS

Inferring Business Activities from T-Accounts

T-accounts are useful primarily for instructional and analytical purposes. In many cases, we will use T-accounts to determine what transactions a company engaged in during a period. For example, the primary transactions affecting Accounts Payable for a period are purchases of assets on account and cash payments to suppliers. If we know the beginning and ending balances of Accounts Payable and all the amounts that were purchased on credit during a period, we can determine the amount of cash paid. A T-account analysis would include the following:

− Accounts Payable (L)		+
	600	Beg. bal.
Cash payments to suppliers ?	1,500	Purchases on account
	300	End. bal.

Solution:

Beginning Balance	+	Purchases on Account	−	Cash Payments to Suppliers	=	Ending Balance
$600	+	$1,500	−	?	=	$ 300
		$2,100	−	?	=	$ 300
				?	=	$1,800

Transaction Analysis Illustrated

In this section, we will use the monthly transactions for Papa John's that were presented earlier to demonstrate transaction analysis and the use of journal entries and T-accounts. We analyze each transaction, checking to make sure that the accounting equation remains in balance and that debits equal credits. In the T-accounts, located together at the end of the illustration, the amounts from Papa John's December 31, 2008, balance sheet (Exhibit 2.2) have been inserted as the beginning balances. After reviewing or preparing each journal entry, trace the effects to the appropriate T-accounts using the transaction letters (*a*) to (*f*) as a reference. The first transaction has been highlighted for you.

Study this illustration carefully, including the explanations of transaction analysis. Careful study is **essential** to an understanding of (1) the accounting model, (2) transaction analysis, (3) the dual effects of each transaction, and (4) the dual-balancing system. The most effective way to learn these critical concepts, which are basic to material throughout the rest of the text, is to practice, practice, practice.

(*a*) Papa John's issues $2,000 of additional common stock shares, receiving cash from investors.

	Debit	Credit
(a) Cash (+A)	2,000	
Contributed Capital (+SE)		2,000

Assets		=	Liabilities	+	Stockholders' Equity	
Cash	+2,000				Contributed Capital	+2,000

Equality checks:
(1) Debits $2,000 = Credits $2,000;
(2) The accounting equation is in balance.

These effects have been posted to the appropriate T-accounts at the end of the illustration. To post the amounts, transfer or copy the debit or credit amount on each line to the appropriate T-account. For example, the $2,000 debit is listed in the debit (increase) column of the Cash T-account.

(*b*) Papa John's borrows $6,000 from its local bank, signing a note to be paid in three years.

	Debit	Credit
(b) Cash (+A)	6,000	
Notes Payable (+L)		6,000

Assets		=	Liabilities		+	Stockholders' Equity
Cash	+6,000		Notes Payable	+6,000		

Equality checks:
(1) Debits $6,000 = Credits $6,000;
(2) The accounting equation is in balance.

(*c*) Papa John's purchases new ovens, counters, refrigerators, and other equipment costing $10,000, paying $2,000 in cash and signing a two-year note payable to the equipment manufacturer for the rest.

	Debit	Credit
(c) Property and Equipment (+A)	10,000	
Cash (−A)		2,000
Notes Payable (+L)		8,000

Assets		=	Liabilities		+	Stockholders' Equity
Property and Equipment	+10,000		Notes Payable	+8,000		
Cash	−2,000					

Equality checks:
(1) Debits $10,000 = Credits $10,000;
(2) The accounting equation is in balance.

(*d*) Papa John's lends $3,000 cash to new franchisees who sign notes agreeing to repay the loans in five years.

	Debit	Credit
(d) Notes Receivable (+A)	3,000	
Cash (−A)		3,000

Assets		=	Liabilities	+	Stockholders' Equity
Cash	−3,000				
Notes Receivable	+3,000				

Equality checks:
(1) Debits $3,000 = Credits $3,000;
(2) The accounting equation is in balance.

***(e)* Papa John's purchases the stock of other companies as a long-term investment, paying $1,000 in cash.**

Equality checks:
(1) Debits $1,000 = Credits $1,000;
(2) The accounting equation is in balance.

	Debit	Credit
(e) Investments (+A)	1,000	
Cash (−A)		1,000

Assets		=	Liabilities	+	Stockholders' Equity
Investments	+1,000				
Cash	−1,000				

***(f)* Papa John's board of directors declares that the Company will pay $3,000 in cash dividends to shareholders next month.** When a company's board of directors declares a cash dividend, a legal obligation is created.

Equality checks:
(1) Debits $3,000 = Credits $3,000;
(2) The accounting equation is in balance.

	Debit	Credit
(f) Retained Earnings (−SE)	3,000	
Dividends Payable (+L)		3,000

Assets	=	Liabilities		+	Stockholders' Equity	
		Dividends Payable	+3,000		Retained Earnings	−3,000

Following are the T-accounts (in thousands of dollars) that **changed** during the period because of these transactions. The beginning balances are the amounts from the December 31, 2008, Papa John's balance sheet. The balances of all other accounts remained the same.

+ Cash (A) −

12/31/08 bal.	11,000		
(a)	2,000	2,000	(c)
(b)	6,000	3,000	(d)
		1,000	(e)
1/31/09 bal.	13,000		

+ Investments (A) −

12/31/08 bal.	1,000	
(e)	1,000	
1/31/09 bal.	2,000	

+ Property and Equipment, Net (A) −

12/31/08 bal.	190,000	
(c)	10,000	
1/31/09 bal.	200,000	

+ Notes Receivable (A) −

12/31/08 bal.	8,000	
(d)	3,000	
1/31/09 bal.	11,000	

− Notes Payable (L) +

	124,000	12/31/08 bal.
	6,000	(b)
	8,000	(c)
	138,000	1/31/09 bal.

− Dividends Payable (L) +

	0	12/31/08 bal.
	3,000	(f)
	3,000	1/31/09 bal.

− Contributed Capital (SE) +

	7,000	12/31/08 bal.
	2,000	(a)
	9,000	1/31/09 bal.

− Retained Earnings (SE) +

		123,000	12/31/08 bal.
(f)	3,000		
		120,000	1/31/09 bal.

PAUSE FOR **FEEDBACK**

Accountants record transactions first in the general journal in chronological order in journal entry form. Debited accounts are written on top with amounts in the left column and credited accounts are written on the bottom with amounts in the right column. Then the effects are posted in the general ledger. Each page of the ledger represents a different account that has a debit (left) side and a credit (right) side. To post transaction effects, the amount for each account in a journal entry is written in the appropriate debit or credit column on the ledger page to obtain account balances.

SELF-STUDY **QUIZ**

Review the analysis in events (*a*) and (*b*). Then record the following transactions and post the effects to the T-accounts.

(*a*) **Paul Knepper contributes $50,000 cash to establish Florida Flippers, Inc., a new scuba business organized as a corporation; he receives stock in exchange.**

	Debit	Credit
____________ ( )	______	
____________ ( )		______

(*b*) **Florida Flippers buys a small building near the ocean for $250,000, paying $25,000 cash and signing a 10-year note payable for the rest.**

	Debit	Credit
____________ ( )	______	
____________ ( )		______
____________ ( )		______

+ Cash (A) −

Beg. 0	
End.	

+ Building (A) −

Beg. 0	
End.	

− Notes Payable (L) +

	0 Beg.
	End.

− Contributed Capital (SE) +

	0 Beg.
	End.

After you have completed your answers, check them with the solutions at the bottom of the page.

Solutions to SELF-STUDY QUIZ

		Debit	Credit
(*a*)	Cash (+A)	50,000	
	Contributed Capital (+SE)		50,000
(*b*)	Building (+A)	250,000	
	Cash (−A)		25,000
	Notes Payable (+L)		225,000

+ Cash (A) −

Beg. 0	
(*a*) 50,000	25,000 (*b*)
End. 25,000	

+ Building (A) −

Beg. 0	
(*b*) 250,000	
End. 250,000	

− Notes Payable (L) +

	0 Beg.
	225,000 (*b*)
	225,000 End.

− Contributed Capital (SE) +

	0 Beg.
	50,000 (*a*)
	50,000 End.

LEARNING OBJECTIVE 5

Prepare a simple classified balance sheet and analyze the company using the current ratio.

HOW IS THE BALANCE SHEET PREPARED AND ANALYZED?

As discussed in Chapter 1, a balance sheet is one of the financial statements that will be communicated to users, especially those external to the business. It is possible to prepare a balance sheet at any point in time using the balances in the accounts.

Classified Balance Sheet

The balance sheet in Exhibit 2.8 was prepared using the new balances shown in the T-accounts in the preceding Papa John's illustration. As such, it needs a good heading (name of the company, title of the statement, date, and if the dollars are in thousands or millions). The accounts

EXHIBIT 2.8

Papa John's Balance Sheet

PAPA JOHN'S INTERNATIONAL, INC.
Consolidated Balance Sheets
(dollars in thousands)

	January 31, 2009	December 31, 2008
ASSETS		
Current Assets		
Cash	$ 13,000	$ 11,000
Accounts receivable	24,000	24,000
Supplies	17,000	17,000
Prepaid expenses	10,000	10,000
Other current assets	13,000	13,000
Total current assets	77,000	75,000
Investments	2,000	1,000
Property and equipment (net)	200,000	190,000
Notes receivable	11,000	8,000
Intangibles	77,000	77,000
Other assets	36,000	36,000
Total assets	$403,000	$387,000
LIABILITIES AND STOCKHOLDERS' EQUITY		
Current Liabilities		
Accounts payable	$ 29,000	$ 29,000
Dividends payable	3,000	0
Accrued expenses payable	71,000	71,000
Total current liabilities	103,000	100,000
Unearned franchise fees	6,000	6,000
Notes payable	138,000	124,000
Other long-term liabilities	27,000	27,000
Total liabilities	274,000	257,000
Stockholders' Equity		
Contributed capital	9,000	7,000
Retained earnings	120,000	123,000
Total stockholders' equity	129,000	130,000
Total liabilities and stockholders' equity	$403,000	$387,000

Many companies do not provide a total liabilities line on the balance sheet. To determine total liabilities, add total current liabilities and each of the noncurrent liabilities.

and the balances that have changed since December 31, 2008, are highlighted. Notice in Exhibit 2.8 several additional features:

- The assets and liabilities are classified into two categories: **current** and **noncurrent.** Current assets are those to be used or turned into cash within the upcoming year, whereas noncurrent assets are those that will last longer than one year. Current liabilities are those obligations to be paid or settled within the next 12 months with current assets.
- Dollar signs are indicated at the top and bottom of the asset section and top and bottom of the liabilities and shareholders' equity section.
- The statement includes comparative data. That is, it compares the account balances at January 31, 2009, with those at December 31, 2008. When multiple periods are presented, the most recent balance sheet amounts are usually listed on the left.

At the beginning of the chapter, we presented the changes in Papa John's balance sheets from the end of 1994 to the end of 2008. We questioned what made the accounts change and what the process was for reflecting the changes. Now we can see that the accounts have changed again in one month due to the transactions illustrated in this chapter:

(in millions)	Assets	=	Liabilities	+	Stockholders' Equity
End of January 2009	$403		$274		$129
End of 2008	387		257		130
Change	+$ 16		+$ 17		−$ 1

Understanding Foreign Financial Statements

INTERNATIONAL PERSPECTIVE

Although IFRS differ from GAAP, they use the same system of analyzing, recording, and summarizing the results of business activities that you have learned in this chapter. One place where IFRS differ from GAAP is in the formatting of financial statements.

Although financial statements prepared using GAAP and IFRS include the same elements (assets, liabilities, revenues, expenses, etc.), a single, consistent format has not been mandated. Consequently, various formats have evolved over time, with those in the U.S. differing from those typically used internationally. The formatting differences include:

	GAAP	IFRS
Financial Statement Titles • The financial statements report similar items but under different titles	**Balance Sheet** **Income Statement** **Statement of Stockholders' Equity** **Statement of Cash Flows**	**Statement of Financial Position** **Statement of Operations** **Statement of Shareholders' Equity** **Statement of Cash Flows**
Balance Sheet Order • Similar accounts are shown, but the order of liquidity (for assets) and the order of maturity (for liabilities) differ	**Assets** **Current** **Noncurrent** **Liabilities** **Current** **Noncurrent** **Stockholders' Equity**	**Assets** **Noncurrent** **Current** **Stockholders' Equity** **Liabilities** **Noncurrent** **Current**

Of the differences listed, balance sheet order is the most striking. GAAP begins with current items whereas IFRS begins with noncurrent items. Consistent with this, **assets are listed in decreasing order of liquidity under GAAP, but internationally are usually listed in increasing order of liquidity.** IFRS similarly emphasize longer-term financing sources by listing equity before liabilities and, within liabilities, by listing noncurrent liabilities before current liabilities (**decreasing time to maturity**). The key to avoiding confusion is to be sure to **pay attention to the subheadings** in the statement. Any account under the heading "liabilities" must be a liability.

KEY RATIO ANALYSIS

Current Ratio

Users of financial information compute a number of ratios in analyzing a company's past performance and financial condition as input in predicting its future potential. How ratios change over time and how they compare to the ratios of the company's competitors or industry averages provide valuable information about a company's strategies for its operating, investing, and financing activities.

We introduce here the first of many ratios that will be presented throughout the rest of this textbook, with a final summary of ratio analysis in Chapter 14. In Chapters 2, 3, and 4, we present three ratios that provide information about management's effectiveness at managing short-term debt (**current ratio**), utilizing assets (**total asset turnover ratio**), and controlling revenues and costs (**net profit margin**), all for the purpose of enhancing returns to shareholders. The remaining chapters discuss the additional ratios for a more precise assessment of a company's strategies, strengths, and areas for concern.

As we discussed earlier in the chapter, companies raise large amounts of money to acquire additional assets by issuing stock to investors and borrowing funds from creditors. These additional assets are used to generate more income. However, since debt must be repaid, taking on increasing amounts of liabilities carries increased risk. The current ratio provides one measure for analysts to examine this financing strategy.

ANALYTICAL QUESTION

Does the company currently have the resources to pay its short-term debt?

RATIO AND COMPARISONS

$$\textbf{Current Ratio} = \frac{\textbf{Current Assets}}{\textbf{Current Liabilities}}$$

The 2008 ratio for Papa John's is (dollars are in thousands):

$$\frac{\$75{,}000}{\$100{,}000} = .75$$

Comparisons over Time

Papa John's International, Inc.		
2006	2007	2008
.83	.68	.75

Comparisons with Competitors

Domino's Pizza, Inc.	Pizza Inn, Inc.
2008	2008
1.02	1.81

Domino's Pizza, Inc., is the second largest pizza company and number one delivery pizza business in the world, with over 8,366 stores (approximately 7 percent company-owned). Its core business focuses on delivering quality pizza and other related menu items from stores with low capital requirements.

Pizza Inn, Inc., has over 323 buffet, delivery, and express restaurants (only one is company-owned), primarily in the southern half of the United States and internationally primarily in the United Arab Emirates and Saudi Arabia.

INTERPRETATIONS

In General The current ratio is a very common ratio. Creditors and security analysts use the current ratio to measure the ability of the company to pay its short-term obligations with short-term assets. Generally, the higher the ratio, the more cushion a company has to pay its current obligations if future economic conditions take a downturn. While a high ratio normally suggests good liquidity, too high of a ratio suggests inefficient use of resources. An old rule of thumb was that companies should have a current ratio between 1.0 and 2.0. Today, many strong companies use sophisticated management techniques to minimize funds invested in current assets and, as a result, have current ratios below 1.0.

Focus Company Analysis The current ratio for Papa John's shows a low level of liquidity, below 1.0, and the ratio has decreased since 2006, although there was an improvement in the ratio between 2007 and 2008. The primary causes for the overall decrease were a decrease in inventories (a current asset) and an increase in debt due in the current period (a current liability) for stock repurchases and restaurant acquisitions as part of its growth strategy. In some cases, analysts would be concerned about both the level and trend, but the situation is understandable when considering the nature of the business. In addition, the company has over $10 million in cash and was able to generate over $73 million in cash from operating activities in 2008. On balance, most analysts would not be concerned about Papa John's liquidity.

The ratio for Papa John's is lower than both of its competitors, Domino's Pizza and Pizza Inn. Domino's and Pizza Inn have higher current ratios, both above 1.0. This suggests that both companies have sufficient liquidity. Reuters reports that the restaurant industry has an average current ratio of 1.23 (approximately 23 percent more current assets than current liabilities). Compared to the industry average, Domino's and Papa John's have lower liquidity and Pizza Inn, the smallest of the three, has higher liquidity. It is also likely that all of these companies have sophisticated cash management systems that enable them to maintain lower current asset balances.

A Few Cautions The current ratio may be a misleading measure of liquidity if significant funds are tied up in assets that cannot be easily converted into cash. A company with a high current ratio might still have liquidity problems if the majority of its current assets consists of slow-moving inventory. Analysts also recognize that managers can manipulate the current ratio by engaging in certain transactions just before the close of the fiscal year. In most cases, for example, the current ratio can be improved by paying creditors immediately prior to preparation of financial statements.

Selected Focus Companies' Financial Leverage Ratios

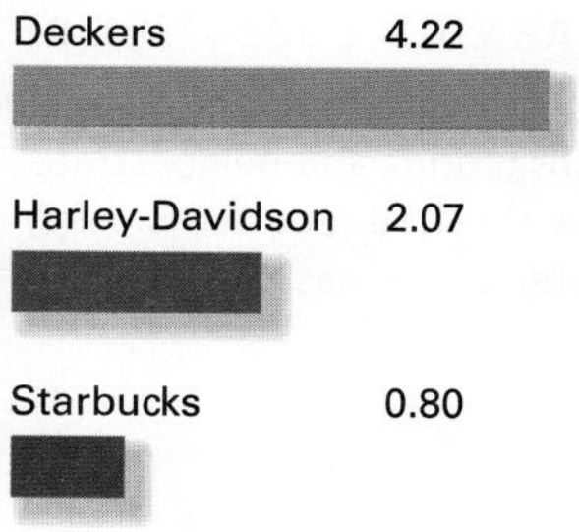

PAUSE FOR FEEDBACK

We just learned that the current ratio measures a company's ability to pay short-term obligations with short-term assets—a liquidity measure. It is computed by dividing current assets by current liabilities. A ratio between 1.0 and 2.0 is normally considered good, although some may need a higher ratio and others with good cash management systems can have a ratio below 1.0 (i.e., more current liabilities than current assets).

SELF-STUDY QUIZ

Yum! Brands, Inc., the world's largest quick-service restaurant company that develops, franchises, and operates 36,000 units in more than 110 countries and territories through five restaurant concepts (KFC, Pizza Hut, Taco Bell, Long John Silver's, and A&W), reported the following balances on its recent balance sheets (in millions). Compute Yum Brands's current ratio for the three years.

	Current Assets	Current Liabilities	Current Ratio
December 31, 2008	$ 951	$1,722	
December 31, 2007	1,481	2,062	
December 31, 2006	901	1,724	

What does this ratio suggest about Yum! Brands's liquidity in the current year and over time?

After you have completed your answers, check them with the solutions at the bottom of the page.

Solutions to SELF-STUDY QUIZ

Current Ratio:

December 31, 2008	$ 951 ÷ $1,722 =	.55
December 31, 2007	$ 1,481 ÷ $2,062 =	.72
December 31, 2006	$ 901 ÷ $1,724 =	.52

Yum! Brands has a low level of liquidity and has remained below 1.0 over the three years. Its ratio is below Papa John's. As a cash-oriented business and with a strong cash management system, Yum! Brands's low ratio is not a concern.

FOCUS ON CASH FLOWS | Investing and Financing Activities

LEARNING OBJECTIVE 6

Identify investing and financing transactions and demonstrate how they are reported on the statement of cash flows.

Recall from Chapter 1 that companies report cash inflows and outflows over a period in their statement of cash flows. This statement divides all transactions that affect cash into three categories: operating, investing, and financing activities:

- Operating activities are covered in Chapter 3.
- Investing activities include buying and selling noncurrent assets and investments.
- Financing activities include borrowing and repaying debt, including short-term bank loans, issuing and repurchasing stock, and paying dividends.

When cash is involved, these activities are reported on the **statement of cash flows.** (When cash is not included in the transaction, such as when a building is acquired with a long-term mortgage note payable, there is no cash effect to include on the statement of cash flows. **You must see cash in the transaction for it to affect the statement of cash flows.**) In general, the effects of such activities are as follows:

	Effect on Cash Flows
Operating activities	
(None of the transactions in this chapter have been operating activities.)	
Investing activities	
Purchasing long-term assets and investments for cash	−
Selling long-term assets and investments for cash	+
Lending cash to others	−
Receiving principal payments on loans made to others	+
Financing activities	
Borrowing cash from banks	+
Repaying the principal on borrowings from banks	−
Issuing stock for cash	+
Repurchasing stock with cash	−
Paying cash dividends	−

Focus Company Analysis Exhibit 2.9 shows a statement of cash flows for Papa John's based on the activities listed in this chapter. It reports the sources and uses of cash that created the $2,000 increase in cash (from $11,000 to $13,000) in January 2009. **Remember that only transactions that affect cash are reported on the cash flow statement.**

The pattern of cash flows shown in Exhibit 2.9 (net cash outflows for investing activities and net cash inflows from financing activities) is typical of Papa John's past several annual statements of cash flows. Companies seeking to expand usually report cash outflows for investing activities.

EXHIBIT 2.9

Papa John's Statement of Cash Flows

PAPA JOHN'S INTERNATIONAL, INC.
Consolidated Statement of Cash Flows
For the month ended January 31, 2009
(in thousands)

Items are referenced to events (a) through (f) illustrated in this chapter.

Operating activities	
(None in this chapter.)	
Investing activities	
Purchased property and equipment (*c*)	$(2,000)
Purchased investments (*e*)	(1,000)
Lent funds to franchisees (*d*)	(3,000)
Net cash used in investing activities	**(6,000)**
Financing activities	
Issued common stock (*a*)	2,000
Borrowed from banks (*b*)	6,000
Net cash provided by financing activities	**8,000**
Net increase in cash	2,000
Cash at beginning of month	11,000
Cash at end of month	**$ 13,000**

Also called capital expenditures. (Purchased property and equipment)

Agrees with the amount on the balance sheet. (Cash at end of month)

PAUSE FOR **FEEDBACK**

As we discussed, every transaction affecting cash can be classified either as an operating (discussed in Chapter 3), investing, or financing effect. Investing effects relate to purchasing/selling investments or property and equipment or lending funds to/receiving repayment from others. Financing effects relate to borrowing or repaying banks, issuing stock to investors, repurchasing stock from investors, or paying dividends to investors.

SELF-STUDY **QUIZ**

Lance, Inc., manufactures and sells snack products. Indicate whether these transactions from a recent annual statement of cash flows were investing (I) or financing (F) activities and the direction of their effects on cash (+ for increases; – for decreases):

TRANSACTIONS	TYPE OF ACTIVITY (I OR F)	EFFECT ON CASH FLOWS (+ OR –)
1. Paid dividends.	______	______
2. Sold property.	______	______
3. Repaid debt.	______	______
4. Purchased property and equipment.	______	______
5. Issued common stock.	______	______

After you have completed your answers, check them with the solutions at the bottom of this page.

Solutions to SELF-STUDY QUIZ

1. F – 2. I + 3. F – 4. I – 5. F +

DEMONSTRATION CASE

On April 1, 2010, three ambitious college students started Terrific Lawn Maintenance Corporation. A summary of transactions completed through April 7, 2010, for Terrific Lawn Maintenance Corporation follows:

a. Issued 500 shares of stock (1,500 shares in total) to each of the three investors in exchange for $9,000 cash.

b. Acquired rakes and other hand tools (equipment) with a list price of $690 for $600; paid the hardware store $200 cash and signed a three-month note for the balance.

c. Ordered three lawn mowers and two edgers from XYZ Lawn Supply, Inc., for $4,000.

d. Purchased four acres of land for the future site of a storage garage; paid cash, $5,000.

e. Received the mowers and edgers that had been ordered, signing a note to pay XYZ Lawn Supply in full in 30 days.

f. Sold for $1,250 one acre of land to the city for a park. Accepted a note from the city for payment by the end of the month.

g. One of the owners borrowed $3,000 from a local bank for personal use.

Required:

1. Set up T-accounts for Cash, Notes Receivable (from the city), Equipment (hand tools and mowing equipment), Land, Notes Payable (to equipment supply companies), and Contributed Capital. Beginning balances are $0; indicate these beginning balances in the T-accounts. Analyze each transaction using the process outlined in the chapter. Prepare journal entries in chronological order. Enter the effects of the transactions in the appropriate T-accounts; identify each amount with its letter in the preceding list.

2. Use the amounts in the T-accounts developed in requirement (1) to prepare a classified balance sheet for Terrific Lawn Maintenance Corporation at April 7, 2010. Show the account balances for all assets, liabilities, and stockholders' equity. Use the following transaction analysis model.

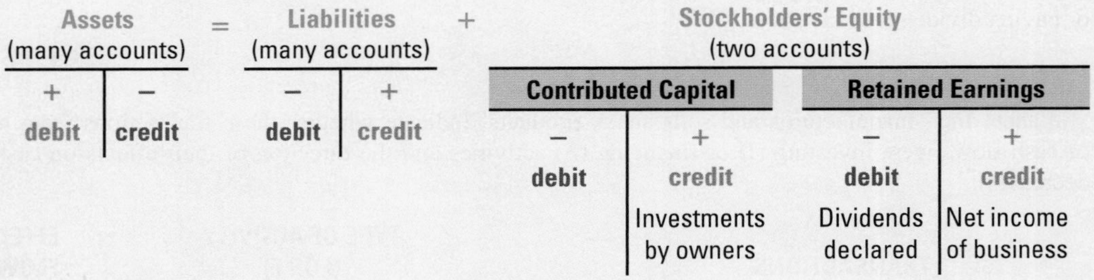

3. Prepare the investing and financing sections of the statement of cash flows. Check your answers with the solution in the following section.

SUGGESTED SOLUTION

1. Transaction analysis, journal entries, and T-accounts:

Equality checks:
(1) Debits $9,000 = Credits $9,000;
(2) The accounting equation is in balance.

(*a*)	Cash (+A)	9,000	
	Contributed Capital (+SE)		9,000

Assets		=	Liabilities	+	Stockholders' Equity	
Cash	+9,000				Contributed Capital	+9,000

(*b*) Equipment (+A)	600	
Cash (−A)		200
Notes Payable (+L)		400

Assets		=	Liabilities		+	Stockholders' Equity
Equipment*	+600		Notes Payable	+400		
Cash	−200					

*The historical cost principle states that assets should be recorded at the amount paid on the date of the transaction, or $600, rather than at the $690 list price.

Equality checks:
(1) Debits $600 = Credits $600;
(2) The accounting equation is in balance.

(*c*) This is not an accounting transaction; no exchange has taken place. No accounts are affected.

(*d*) Land (+A)	5,000	
Cash (−A)		5,000

Assets		=	Liabilities	+	Stockholders' Equity
Land	+5,000				
Cash	−5,000				

Equality checks:
(1) Debits $5,000 = Credits $5,000;
(2) The accounting equation is in balance.

(*e*) Equipment (+A)	4,000	
Notes Payable (+L)		4,000

Assets		=	Liabilities		+	Stockholders' Equity
Equipment	+4,000		Notes Payable	+4,000		

Equality checks:
(1) Debits $4,000 = Credits $4,000;
(2) The accounting equation is in balance.

(*f*) Notes Receivable (+A)	1,250	
Land (−A)		1,250

Assets		=	Liabilities	+	Stockholders' Equity
Notes Receivable	+1,250				
Land*	−1,250				

*One acre of land cost the company $1,250 when it was purchased ($5,000 total cost ÷ 4 acres). When an asset is sold, the account is reduced by the asset's historical cost.

Equality checks:
(1) Debits $1,250 = Credits $1,250;
(2) The accounting equation is in balance.

(*g*) There is no transaction for the company. The separate-entity assumption states that transactions of the owners are separate from transactions of the business.

+ (dr)	Cash (A)		(cr) −
4/1/10 bal.	0		
(*a*)	9,000	200	(*b*)
		5,000	(*d*)
4/7/10 bal.	3,800		

+ (dr)	Notes Receivable (A)		(cr) −
4/1/10 bal.	0		
(*f*)	1,250		
4/7/10 bal.	1,250		

+ (dr)	Equipment (A)		(cr) −
4/1/10 bal.	0		
(*b*)	600		
(*e*)	4,000		
4/7/10 bal.	4,600		

+ (dr)	Land (A)		(cr) −
4/1/10 bal.	0		
(*d*)	5,000	1,250	(*f*)
4/7/10 bal.	3,750		

− (dr)	Notes Payable (L)		(cr) +
		0	4/1/10 bal.
		400	(*b*)
		4,000	(*e*)
		4,400	4/7/10 bal.

− (dr)	Contributed Capital (SE)		(cr) +
		0	4/1/10 bal.
		9,000	(*a*)
		9,000	4/7/10 bal.

2. Balance sheet:

TERRIFIC LAWN MAINTENANCE CORPORATION
Balance Sheet
At April 7, 2010

Assets		**Liabilities**	
Current Assets		*Current Liabilities*	
Cash	$ 3,800	Notes payable	$ 4,400
Notes receivable	1,250	Total current liabilities	4,400
Total current assets	5,050		
Equipment	4,600	**Stockholders' Equity**	
Land	3,750	Contributed capital	9,000
Total assets	$13,400	Total liabilities and stockholders' equity	$13,400

Notice that the balance sheets presented earlier in the text listed assets on the top and liabilities and stockholders' equity on the bottom. It is also acceptable practice to prepare a balance sheet with assets on the left side and liabilities and stockholders' equity on the right side, as in the preceding example.

3. Investing and financing effects of the statement of cash flows:

TERRIFIC LAWN MAINTENANCE CORPORATION
Statement of Cash Flows
For the Period Ended April 7, 2010

Operating activities		
(none in this case)		
Investing activities		
Purchased land	$(5,000)	*Transaction (d)*
Purchased equipment	(200)	*Transaction (b)*
Net cash used in investing activities	**(5,200)**	
Financing activities		
Issued common stock	9,000	*Transaction (a)*
Net cash provided by financing activities	**9,000**	
Change in cash	3,800	
Beginning cash balance	0	
Ending cash balance	$ 3,800	

CHAPTER TAKE-AWAYS

1. **Define the objective of financial reporting, the elements of the balance sheet, and the related key accounting assumptions and principles.** p. 45
   - The primary objective of external financial reporting is to provide useful economic information about a business to help external parties, primarily investors and creditors, make sound financial decisions.
   - Qualitative characteristics of useful financial information are relevancy (possessing predictive and feedback value and being timely) and reliability (neutral, representative of reality, and verifiable). Information should also be comparable to other companies and be consistent over time.
   - Elements of the balance sheet:
     a. Assets—probable future economic benefits owned by the entity as a result of past transactions.
     b. Liabilities—probable debts or obligations acquired by the entity as a result of past transactions, to be paid with assets or services.
     c. Stockholders' equity—the financing provided by the owners and by business operations.
   - Key accounting assumptions, principles, and constraints:
     a. Separate-entity assumption—transactions of the business are accounted for separately from transactions of the owner.
     b. Unit-of-measure assumption—financial information is reported in the national monetary unit.
     c. Continuity (going-concern) assumption—a business is expected to continue to operate into the foreseeable future.
     d. Historical cost principle—financial statement elements should be recorded at the cash-equivalent cost on the date of the transaction.
     e. Constraints—the benefits of providing information should outweigh the costs, immaterial amounts (those that do not affect a decision) can be accounted for in the least costly, most expedient manner, information should be conservative (assets and revenues are not overstated and liabilities and expenses are not understated), and industry practices are acceptable.

2. **Identify what constitutes a business transaction and recognize common balance sheet account titles used in business.** p. 50

   A transaction includes:
   - An exchange of cash, goods, or services for cash, goods, services or promises between a business and one or more external parties to a business,

   or
   - A measurable internal event, such as adjustments for the use of assets in operations.

   An account is a standardized format that organizations use to accumulate the dollar effects of transactions related to each financial statement item. Typical balance sheet account titles include the following:
   - *Assets:* Cash, Accounts Receivable, Inventory, Prepaid Expenses, and Buildings and Equipment.
   - *Liabilities:* Accounts Payable, Notes Payable, Accrued Expenses Payable, Unearned Revenues, and Taxes Payable.
   - *Stockholders' Equity:* Contributed Capital and Retained Earnings.

3. **Apply transaction analysis to simple business transactions in terms of the accounting model: Assets = Liabilities + Stockholders' Equity.** p. 52

   To determine the economic effect of a transaction on an entity in terms of the accounting equation, each transaction must be analyzed to determine the accounts (at least two) that are affected. In an exchange, the company receives something and gives up something. If the accounts, direction of the effects, and amounts are correctly analyzed, the accounting equation will stay in balance. The transaction analysis model is:

ASSETS (many accounts) = **LIABILITIES** (many accounts) + **STOCKHOLDERS' EQUITY** (two accounts)

ASSETS +	ASSETS −	LIABILITIES −	LIABILITIES +	Contributed Capital −	Contributed Capital +	Retained Earnings −	Retained Earnings +
debit	credit	debit	credit	debit	credit	debit	credit
					Investments by owners	Dividends declared	Net income of business

4. Determine the impact of business transactions on the balance sheet using two basic tools, journal entries and T-accounts. p. 57

- Journal entries express the effects of a transaction on accounts in a debits-equal-credits format. The accounts and amounts to be debited are listed first. Then the accounts and amounts to be credited are listed below the debits and indented, resulting in debit amounts on the left and credit amounts on the right.

		Debit	Credit
(date or reference)	Property and Equipment (+A)	10,000	
	Cash (−A)		2,000
	Notes Payable (+L)		8,000

- T-accounts summarize the transaction effects for each account. These tools can be used to determine balances and draw inferences about a company's activities.

+ (dr) Assets	(cr) −
Beginning balance Increases	Decreases
Ending balance	

− (dr) Liabilities and Stockholders' Equity	(cr) +
Decreases	Beginning balance Increases
	Ending balance

5. Prepare a simple classified balance sheet and analyze the company using the current ratio. p. 66

Classified balance sheets are structured as follows:

- Assets are categorized as current assets (those to be used or turned into cash within the year, with inventory always considered a current asset) and noncurrent assets, such as long-term investments, property and equipment, and intangible assets.
- Liabilities are categorized as current liabilities (those that will be paid with current assets) and long-term liabilities.
- Stockholders' equity accounts are listed as Contributed Capital first, followed by Retained Earnings.

The current ratio (Current Assets ÷ Current Liabilities) measures a company's liquidity, that is, the ability of the company to pay its short-term obligations with current assets.

6. Identify investing and financing transactions and demonstrate how they are reported on the statement of cash flows. p. 70

A statement of cash flows reports the sources and uses of cash for the period by the type of activity that generated the cash flow: operating, investing, and financing. Investing activities include purchasing and selling long-term assets and making loans and receiving principal repayments from others. Financing activities are borrowing and repaying to banks the principal on loans, issuing and repurchasing stock, and paying dividends.

In this chapter, we discussed the fundamental accounting model and transaction analysis. Journal entries and T-accounts were used to record the results of transaction analysis for investing and financing decisions that affect balance sheet accounts. In Chapter 3, we continue our detailed look at the financial statements, in particular the income statement. The purpose of Chapter 3 is to build on your knowledge by discussing the measurement of revenues and expenses and illustrating the transaction analysis of operating decisions.

KEY RATIO

Current ratio measures the ability of the company to pay its short-term obligations with current assets. Although a ratio between 1.0 and 2.0 indicates sufficient current assets to meet obligations when they come due, many companies with sophisticated cash management systems have ratios below 1.0. (p. 68):

$$\text{Current Ratio} = \frac{\text{Current Assets}}{\text{Current Liabilities}}$$

FINDING FINANCIAL INFORMATION

Balance Sheet

Current Assets	Current Liabilities
Cash	Accounts payable
Accounts receivable	Notes payable
Notes receivable	Accrued expenses payable
Inventory	Unearned revenue
Prepaid expenses	*Noncurrent Liabilities*
Noncurrent Assets	Long-term debt
Long-term investments	*Stockholders' Equity*
Property and equipment	Contributed capital
Intangibles	Retained earnings

Income Statement

To be presented in Chapter 3

Statement of Cash Flows

Operating Activities
To be presented in Chapter 3

Investing Activities
+ Sales of noncurrent assets for cash
− Purchases of noncurrent assets for cash
− Loans to others
+ Receipt of loan principal payments from others

Financing Activities
+ Borrowing from banks
− Repayment of loan principal to banks
+ Issuance of stock
− Repurchasing stock
− Dividends paid

Notes

To be discussed in future chapters

KEY TERMS

Account p. 51
Assets p. 46
Conservatism p. 50
Continuity (Going-Concern) Assumption p. 46
Contributed Capital p. 49
Credit p. 58
Current Assets p. 47
Current Liabilities p. 48
Debit p. 58
Historical Cost Principle p. 46
Journal Entry p. 59
Liabilities p. 47
Materiality p. 50
Primary Objective of External Financial Reporting p. 45
Relevant Information p. 45
Reliable Information p. 45
Retained Earnings p. 49
Separate-Entity Assumption p. 45
Stockholders' Equity (Owners' or Shareholders' Equity) p. 49
T-account p. 60
Transaction p. 50
Transaction Analysis p. 52
Unit-of-Measure Assumption p. 46

QUESTIONS

1. What is the primary objective of financial reporting for external users?
2. Define the following:
   a. Asset
   b. Current asset
   c. Liability
   d. Current liability
   e. Contributed capital
   f. Retained earnings
3. Explain what the following accounting terms mean:
   a. Separate-entity assumption
   b. Unit-of-measure assumption
   c. Continuity assumption
   d. Historical cost principle
4. Why are accounting assumptions necessary?
5. For accounting purposes, what is an account? Explain why accounts are used in an accounting system.
6. What is the fundamental accounting model?
7. Define a business transaction in the broad sense, and give an example of two different kinds of transactions.
8. Explain what *debit* and *credit* mean.
9. Briefly explain what is meant by *transaction analysis*. What are the two steps in transaction analysis?
10. What two accounting equalities must be maintained in transaction analysis?
11. What is a journal entry?
12. What is a T-account? What is its purpose?
13. How is the current ratio computed and interpreted?
14. What transactions are classified as investing activities in a statement of cash flows? What transactions are classified as financing activities?

MULTIPLE-CHOICE QUESTIONS

1. If a publicly traded company is trying to maximize its perceived value to decision makers external to the corporation, the company is most likely to understate which of the following on its balance sheet?
   a. Assets
   b. Liabilities
   c. Retained Earnings
   d. Contributed Capital
2. Which of the following is not an asset?
   a. Investments
   b. Land
   c. Prepaid Expense
   d. Contributed Capital
3. Total liabilities on a balance sheet at the end of the year are $150,000, retained earnings at the end of the year is $80,000, net income for the year is $60,000, and contributed capital is $35,000. What amount of total assets would be reported on the balance sheet at the end of the year?
   a. $290,000
   b. $265,000
   c. $205,000
   d. $15,000
4. The dual effects concept can best be described as follows:
   a. When one records a transaction in the accounting system, at least two effects on the basic accounting equation will result.
   b. When an exchange takes place between two parties, both parties must record the transaction.
   c. When a transaction is recorded, both the balance sheet and the income statement must be impacted.
   d. When a transaction is recorded, one account will always increase and one account will always decrease.
5. The T-account is a tool commonly used for analyzing which of the following?
   a. Increases and decreases to a single account in the accounting system.
   b. Debits and credits to a single account in the accounting system.
   c. Changes in specific account balances over a time period.
   d. All of the above describe how T-accounts are used by accountants.
6. Which of the following describes how assets are listed on the balance sheet?
   a. In alphabetical order
   b. In order of magnitude, lowest value to highest value
   c. From most liquid to least liquid
   d. From least liquid to most liquid

7. The Cash T-account has a beginning balance of $21,000. During the year, $98,000 was debited and $110,000 was credited to the account. What is the ending balance of Cash?
   a. $33,000 debit balance
   b. $9,000 credit balance
   c. $33,000 credit balance
   d. $9,000 debit balance
8. Which of the following statements are true regarding the balance sheet?
   1. One cannot determine the true fair market value of a company by reviewing its balance sheet.
   2. Certain internally generated assets, such as a trademark, are not reported on a company's balance sheet.
   3. A balance sheet shows only the ending balances, in a summarized format, of all balance sheet accounts in the accounting system as of a particular date.

   a. None are true.
   b. Statements 1 and 2 only are true.
   c. Statements 2 and 3 only are true.
   d. All statements are true.
9. At the end of a recent year, The Gap, Inc., reported total assets of $7,564 million, current assets of $4,005 million, total liabilities of $3,177 million, current liabilities of $2,158 million, and stockholders' equity of $4,387 million. What is its current ratio and what does this suggest about the company?
   a. The ratio of 2.38 suggests that The Gap has liquidity problems.
   b. The ratio of 1.86 suggests that The Gap has sufficient liquidity.
   c. The ratio of 2.38 suggests that The Gap has greater current assets than current liabilities.
   d. The ratio of 1.86 suggests that The Gap is not able to pay its short-term obligations with current assets.
10. Which of the following is *not* a financing activity on the statement of cash flows?
   a. When the company lends money.
   b. When the company borrows money.
   c. When the company pays dividends.
   d. When the company issues stock to shareholders.

For more practice with multiple-choice questions, go to the text website at **www.mhhe.com/libby7e**.

Mc Graw Hill connect ACCOUNTING

MINI-EXERCISES

Matching Definitions with Terms

M2-1
LO1, 4

Match each definition with its related term by entering the appropriate letter in the space provided. There should be only one definition per term (that is, there are more definitions than terms).

Term	Definition
___ (1) Separate-entity assumption	A. = Liabilities + Stockholders' Equity.
___ (2) Historical cost principle	B. Reports assets, liabilities, and stockholders' equity.
___ (3) Credits	C. Accounts for a business separate from its owners.
___ (4) Assets	D. Increase assets; decrease liabilities and stockholders' equity.
___ (5) Account	E. An exchange between an entity and other parties.
	F. The concept that businesses will operate into the foreseeable future.
	G. Decrease assets; increase liabilities and stockholders' equity.
	H. The concept that assets should be recorded at the amount paid on the date of the transaction.
	I. A standardized format used to accumulate data about each item reported on financial statements.

M2-2
LO1, 2, 3, 4

Matching Definitions with Terms

Match each definition with its related term by entering the appropriate letter in the space provided. There should be only one definition per term (that is, there are more definitions than terms).

Term	Definition
___ (1) Journal entry	A. Accounting model.
___ (2) A = L + SE, and Debits = Credits	B. Four periodic financial statements.
___ (3) Assets = Liabilities + Stockholders' Equity	C. The two equalities in accounting that aid in providing accuracy.
___ (4) Liabilities	D. The results of transaction analysis in accounting format.
___ (5) Income statement, balance sheet, statement of retained earnings, and statement of cash flows	E. The account that is debited when money is borrowed from a bank.
	F. Probable future economic benefits owned by an entity.
	G. Cumulative earnings of a company that are not distributed to the owners.
	H. Every transaction has at least two effects.
	I. Probable debts or obligations to be paid with assets or services.

M2-3
LO2

Identifying Events as Accounting Transactions

For each of the following events, which ones result in an exchange transaction for Dittman Company (Y for yes and N for no)?

___ (1) Dittman Company purchased a machine that it paid for by signing a note payable.
___ (2) The founding owner, Megan Dittman, purchased additional stock in another company.
___ (3) The company borrowed $1,000,000 from a local bank.
___ (4) Six investors in Dittman Company sold their stock to another investor.
___ (5) The company lent $150,000 to a member of the board of directors.
___ (6) Dittman Company ordered supplies from Staples to be delivered next week.

M2-4
LO2

Classifying Accounts on a Balance Sheet

The following are accounts of Rosa-Perez Company:

___ (1) Accounts Payable	___ (9) Long-Term Investments
___ (2) Accounts Receivable	___ (10) Notes Payable (due in three years)
___ (3) Buildings	___ (11) Notes Receivable (due in six months)
___ (4) Cash	___ (12) Prepaid Rent
___ (5) Contributed Capital	___ (13) Retained Earnings
___ (6) Land	___ (14) Supplies
___ (7) Merchandise Inventory	___ (15) Utilities Payable
___ (8) Income Taxes Payable	___ (16) Wages Payable

In the space provided, classify each as it would be reported on a balance sheet. Use:

CA for current asset	CL for current liability	SE for stockholders' equity
NCA for noncurrent asset	NCL for noncurrent liability	

M2-5
LO3

Determining Financial Statement Effects of Several Transactions

For each of the following transactions of Pitt Inc. for the month of January 2012, indicate the accounts, amounts, and direction of the effects on the accounting equation. A sample is provided.

a. *(Sample)* Borrowed $20,000 from a local bank.
b. Lent $7,000 to an affiliate; accepted a note due in one year.
c. Sold additional stock to investors for $1,000 cash.
d. Purchased $15,000 of equipment, paying $6,000 cash and the rest on a note due in one year.
e. Declared and paid $2,000 in dividends to stockholders.

Assets		=	Liabilities		+	Stockholders' Equity
a. Sample: Cash	+20,000		Notes Payable	+20,000		

M2-6
LO4

Identifying Increase and Decrease Effects on Balance Sheet Elements

Complete the following table by entering either the word *increases* or *decreases* in each column.

	Debit	Credit
Assets	______	______
Liabilities	______	______
Stockholders' equity	______	______

M2-7
LO4

Identifying Debit and Credit Effects on Balance Sheet Elements

Complete the following table by entering either the word *debit* or *credit* in each column.

	Increase	Decrease
Assets	______	______
Liabilities	______	______
Stockholder's equity	______	______

M2-8
LO4

Recording Simple Transactions

For each transaction in M2-5 (including the sample), write the journal entry in the proper form.

M2-9
LO4

Completing T-Accounts

For each transaction in M2-5 (including the sample), post the effects to the appropriate T-accounts and determine ending account balances. Beginning balances are provided.

Cash	
Beg. bal. 800	
═══	

Notes Receivable	
Beg. bal. 900	
═══	

Equipment	
Beg. bal. 15,000	
═══	

Notes Payable	
	Beg. bal. 2,700
	═══

Contributed Capital	
	Beg. bal. 5,000
	═══

Retained Earnings	
	Beg. bal. 9,000
	═══

M2-10
LO5

Preparing a Simple Classified Balance Sheet

Starting with the beginning balances in M2-9 and given the transactions in M2-5 (including the sample), prepare a balance sheet for Pitt Inc. as of January 31, 2012, classified into current and noncurrent assets and liabilities.

M2-11
LO5

Computing and Interpreting the Current Ratio

Calculate the current ratio for Sal's Pizza Company at the end of 2007 and 2008, based on the following data:

	Current Assets	Current Liabilities
End of 2007	\$240,000	\$160,000
End of 2008	\$260,000	\$220,000

What does the result suggest about the company over time? What can you say about Sal's Pizza Company's ratio when compared to Papa John's 2008 ratio?

M2-12
LO6

Identifying Transactions as Investing or Financing Activities on the Statement of Cash Flows

For the transactions in M2-5, identify each as an investing (I) activity or financing (F) activity on the statement of cash flows.

EXERCISES

connect ACCOUNTING

E2-1
LO1, 2, 3, 4

Matching Definitions with Terms

Match each definition with its related term by entering the appropriate letter in the space provided. There should be only one definition per term (that is, there are more definitions than terms).

Term

___ (1) Transaction
___ (2) Continuity assumption
___ (3) Balance sheet
___ (4) Liabilities
___ (5) Assets = Liabilities + Stockholders' Equity
___ (6) Note payable
___ (7) Conservatism
___ (8) Historical cost principle
___ (9) Account
___ (10) Dual effects
___ (11) Retained earnings
___ (12) Current assets
___ (13) Separate-entity assumption
___ (14) Reliability
___ (15) Debits
___ (16) Accounts receivable
___ (17) Unit-of-measure assumption
___ (18) Materiality
___ (19) Relevance
___ (20) Stockholders' equity

Definition

A. Economic resources to be used or turned into cash within one year.
B. Reports assets, liabilities, and stockholders' equity.
C. Business transactions are separate from the transactions of the owners.
D. Increase assets; decrease liabilities and stockholders' equity.
E. An exchange between an entity and other parties.
F. The concept that businesses will operate into the foreseeable future.
G. Decrease assets; increase liabilities and stockholders' equity.
H. The concept that assets should be recorded at the amount paid on the exchange date.
I. A standardized format used to accumulate data about each item reported on financial statements.
J. Amounts owed from customers.
K. The fundamental accounting model.
L. The two equalities in accounting that aid in providing accuracy.
M. The account that is credited when money is borrowed from a bank.
N. The concept that states that accounting information should be measured and reported in the national monetary unit.
O. Cumulative earnings of a company that are not distributed to the owners.
P. Probable debts or obligations to be paid with assets or services.
Q. Every transaction has at least two effects.
R. Financing provided by owners and by business operations.
S. The concept to exercise care not to overstate assets and revenues or understate liabilities and expenses.
T. Useful information has predictive and feedback value.
U. Relatively small amounts not likely to influence users' decisions are to be recorded in the most cost-beneficial way.
V. Probable economic resources expected to be used or turned into cash beyond the next 12 months.
W. Useful information should be verifiable, unbiased, and representative of reality.

Identifying Account Titles

E2-2
LO2

The following are independent situations.

a. A new company is formed and sells 100 shares of stock for $12 per share to investors.
b. A company purchases for $18,000 cash a new delivery truck that has a list, or sticker, price of $21,000.
c. A women's clothing retailer orders 30 new display stands for $300 each for future delivery.
d. A company orders and receives 10 personal computers for office use for which it signs a note promising to pay $25,000 within three months.
e. A construction company signs a contract to build a new $500,000 warehouse for a corporate customer. At the signing, the corporation writes a check for $50,000 to the construction company as the initial payment for the construction (receiving construction in progress). Answer from the standpoint of the corporation.
f. A publishing firm purchases for $40,000 cash the copyright (an intangible asset) to a manuscript for an introductory accounting text.
g. A manufacturing firm pays stockholders a $100,000 cash dividend.
h. A company purchases a piece of land for $50,000 cash. An appraiser for the buyer values the land at $52,500.
i. A manufacturing company acquires the patent (an intangible asset) on a new digital satellite system for television reception, paying $500,000 cash and signing a $400,000 note payable due in one year.
j. A local company is a sole proprietorship (one owner); its owner buys a car for $10,000 for personal use. Answer from the company's point of view.
k. A company purchases 100 shares of Apple Inc. common stock as an investment for $5,000 cash.
l. A company borrows $1,000 from a local bank and signs a six-month note for the loan.
m. A company pays $1,500 principal on its note payable (ignore interest).

Required:

1. Indicate the appropriate account titles, if any, affected in each of the preceding events. Consider what is received and what is given.
2. At what amount would you record the truck in (*b*)? The land in (*h*)? What measurement principle are you applying?
3. For (*c*), what accounting concept did you apply? For (*j*), what accounting concept did you apply?

Classifying Accounts and Their Usual Balances

E2-3
LO2, 4

Verizon Communications, Inc.

As described in a recent annual report, Verizon Wireless provides wireless voice and data services across one of the most extensive wireless networks in the United States. Verizon now serves more than 80 million customers, making it the largest wireless service provider in the United States in terms of the total number of customers. The following are accounts from a recent balance sheet for Verizon.

(1) Accounts Receivable	(6) Long-Term Investments
(2) Retained Earnings	(7) Plant, Property, and Equipment
(3) Taxes Payable	(8) Accounts Payable
(4) Prepaid Expenses	(9) Short-Term Investments
(5) Contributed Capital	(10) Long-Term Debt

Required:

For each account, indicate whether the account is classified as a current asset (CA), noncurrent asset (NCA), current liability (CL), noncurrent liability (NCL), or stockholders' equity (SE), and whether the account usually has a debit or credit balance.

Determining Financial Statement Effects of Several Transactions

E2-4
LO3

The following events occurred for Christensen Company:

a. Received investment of $34,000 cash by organizers and distributed stock to them.
b. Purchased $8,000 of equipment, paying $1,000 in cash and signing a note for the rest.
c. Borrowed $9,000 cash from a bank.
d. Loaned $500 to an employee who signed a note.
e. Purchased $15,000 of land; paid $4,000 in cash and signed a mortgage note for the balance.

Required:
For each of the events *(a)* through *(e),* perform transaction analysis and indicate the account, amount, and direction of the effect (+ for increase and − for decrease) on the accounting equation. Check that the accounting equation remains in balance after each transaction. Use the following headings:

Event	Assets	=	Liabilities	+	Stockholders' Equity

E2-5 LO3 Determining Financial Statement Effects of Several Transactions

Nike, Inc., with headquarters in Beaverton, Oregon, is one of the world's leading manufacturers of athletic shoes and sports apparel. The following activities occurred during a recent year. The amounts are rounded to millions of dollars.

a. Purchased additional buildings for $212 and equipment for $30.4; paid $43.2 in cash and signed a long-term note for the rest.
b. Issued $186.6 in additional stock for cash.
c. Declared $121.4 in dividends to be paid in the following year.
d. Purchased additional short-term investments for $2,908.7 cash.
e. Several Nike investors sold their own stock to other investors on the stock exchange for $53.
f. Sold $2,390 in short-term investments for cash.

Required:
1. For each of the events (*a*) through (*f*), perform transaction analysis and indicate the account, amount, and direction of the effect on the accounting equation. Check that the accounting equation remains in balance after each transaction. Use the following headings:

Event	Assets	=	Liabilities	+	Stockholders' Equity

2. Explain your response to event (*e*).

E2-6 LO4 Recording Investing and Financing Activities

Refer to E2-4.

Required:
For each of the events (*a*) through (*e*) in E2-4, prepare journal entries, checking that debits equal credits.

E2-7 LO4 Recording Investing and Financing Activities

Refer to E2-5.

Required:
1. For each of the events (*a*) through (*f*) in E2-5, prepare journal entries, checking that debits equal credits.
2. Explain your response to event (*e*).

E2-8 LO4 Analyzing the Effects of Transactions in T-Accounts

Granger Service Company, Inc., was organized by Ted Granger and five other investors. The following activities occurred during the year:

a. Received $63,000 cash from the investors; each was issued 1,400 shares of capital stock.
b. Purchased equipment for use in the business at a cost of $20,000; one-fourth was paid in cash and the company signed a note for the balance (due in six months).
c. Signed an agreement with a cleaning service to pay $120 per week for cleaning the corporate offices.
d. Received an additional contribution from investors who provided $4,000 in cash and land valued at $13,000 in exchange for stock in the company.
e. Lent $2,500 to one of the investors who signed a note due in six months.
f. Ted Granger borrowed $10,000 for personal use from a local bank, signing a one-year note.

Required:
1. Create T-accounts for the following accounts: Cash, Note Receivable, Equipment, Land, Note Payable, and Contributed Capital. Beginning balances are $0. For each of the preceding transactions,

record the effects of the transaction in the appropriate T-accounts. Include good referencing and totals for each T-account.

2. Using the balances in the T-accounts, fill in the following amounts for the accounting equation:

   Assets $________ = Liabilities $________ + Stockholders' Equity $________

3. Explain your response to events (*c*) and (*f*).

Inferring Investing and Financing Transactions and Preparing a Balance Sheet

E2-9
LO4, 5

During its first week of operations ending January 7, 2011, FastTrack Sports Inc. completed six transactions with the dollar effects indicated in the following schedule:

	Dollar Effect of Each of the Six Transactions						
Accounts	1	2	3	4	5	6	Ending Balance
Cash	$15,000	$75,000	$(5,000)	$(4,000)	$(9,500)		
Note receivable (short-term)				4,000			
Store fixtures					9,500		
Land			16,000			$4,000	
Note payable (due in three months)		75,000	11,000			4,000	
Contributed capital	15,000						

Required:

1. Write a brief explanation of each transaction. Explain any assumptions that you made.
2. Compute the ending balance in each account and prepare a classified balance sheet for FastTrack Sports Inc. on January 7, 2011.

Inferring Investing and Financing Transactions and Preparing a Balance Sheet

E2-10
LO4, 5

During its first month of operations in March 2011, Volz Cleaning, Inc., completed six transactions with the dollar effects indicated in the following schedule:

	Dollar Effect of Each of the Six Transactions						
Accounts	1	2	3	4	5	6	Ending Balance
Cash	$50,000	$(6,000)	$(4,000)	$(7,000)	$2,000		
Investments (short-term)				7,000	(2,000)		
Notes receivable (due in six months)			4,000				
Computer equipment						$4,000	
Delivery truck		30,000					
Notes payable (due in 10 years)		24,000					
Contributed capital	50,000					4,000	

Required:

1. Write a brief explanation of transactions (1) through (6). Explain any assumptions that you made.
2. Compute the ending balance in each account and prepare a classified balance sheet for Volz Cleaning, Inc., at the end of March 2011.

Recording Journal Entries

E2-11
LO4

Jefferson Corporation was organized on May 1, 2011. The following events occurred during the first month.

a. Received $65,000 cash from the five investors who organized Jefferson Corporation.
b. Ordered store fixtures costing $20,000.

c. Borrowed $10,000 cash and signed a note due in two years.
d. Purchased $13,000 of equipment, paying $1,500 in cash and signing a six-month note for the balance.
e. Lent $1,000 to an employee who signed a note to repay the loan in three months.
f. Received and paid for the store fixtures ordered in (*b*).

Required:
Prepare journal entries for each transaction. (Remember that debits go on top and credits go on the bottom, indented.) Be sure to use good referencing and categorize each account as an asset (A), liability (L), or stockholders' equity (SE). If a transaction does not require a journal entry, explain the reason.

E2-12 LO4

Recording Journal Entries

BMW Group, headquartered in Munich, Germany, manufactures several automotive brands including BMW Group, MINI, and Rolls-Royce. Financial information is reported in the euro (€) monetary unit using International Financial Reporting Standards (IFRS) as applicable to the European Union. The following transactions were adapted from the annual report of the BMW Group; amounts are in millions of euros.
a. Declared €197 in dividends to be paid next month.
b. Ordered €1,255 of equipment.
c. Paid €694 in dividends declared in prior months.
d. Borrowed €2,655 in cash from banks.
e. Sold equipment at its cost of €285 for cash.
f. Received the equipment ordered in event (*b*), paying €970 in cash and signing a note for the balance.
g. Purchased investments for €2,220 cash.

Required:
Prepare journal entries for each transaction. Be sure to use good referencing and categorize each account as an asset (A), liability (L), or stockholders' equity (SE). If a transaction does not require a journal entry, explain the reason.

E2-13 LO4, 5

Analyzing the Effects of Transactions Using T-Accounts and Interpreting the Current Ratio as a Manager of the Company

Zeber Company has been operating for one year (2011). You are a member of the management team investigating expansion ideas that will require borrowing funds from banks. At the start of 2012, Zeber's T-account balances were as follows:

Assets:

Cash	
4,000	

Short-Term Investments	
2,000	

Property and Equipment	
2,500	

Liabilities:

Short-Term Notes Payable	
	2,200

Long-Term Notes Payable	
	300

Stockholders' Equity:

Contributed Capital	
	4,000

Retained Earnings	
	2,000

Required:
1. Using the data from these T-accounts, determine the amounts for the following on January 1, 2012:

Assets $________ = Liabilities $________ + Stockholders' Equity $________

2. Enter the following 2012 transactions in the T-accounts:
   (a) Borrowed $3,000 from a local bank, signing a note due in three years.
   (b) Sold $1,000 of the investments for $1,000 cash.
   (c) Sold one-half of the property and equipment for $1,250 in cash.
   (d) Paid $300 in cash dividends to stockholders.

3. Compute ending balances in the T-accounts to determine amounts for the following on December 31, 2012:

   Assets $________ = Liabilities $________ + Stockholders' Equity $________

4. Calculate the current ratio at December 31, 2012. If the industry average for the current ratio is 1.50, what does your computation suggest to you about Zeber Company? Would you suggest that Zeber Company increase its short-term liabilities? Why or why not?

Preparing a Balance Sheet

E2-14
L05

Refer to E2-13.

Required:
From the ending balances in the T-accounts in E2-13, prepare a classified balance sheet at December 31, 2012, in good form.

Analyzing the Effects of Transactions Using T-Accounts, Preparing a Balance Sheet, and Evaluating the Current Ratio over Time as a Bank Loan Officer

E2-15
L04, 5

Strauderman Delivery Company, Inc., was organized in 2011 in Wisconsin. The following transactions occurred during year 2011:

a. Received $40,000 cash from organizers in exchange for stock in the new company.
b. Purchased land in Wisconsin for $16,000, signing a one-year note (ignore interest).
c. Bought two used delivery trucks for operating purposes at the start of the year at a cost of $10,000 each; paid $4,000 cash and signed a note due in three years for the rest (ignore interest).
d. Paid $1,000 cash to a truck repair shop for a new motor for one of the trucks. (*Hint:* Increase the account you used to record the purchase of the trucks since the productive life of the truck has been improved.)
e. Sold one-fourth of the land for $4,000 to Pablo Moving, which signed a six-month note.
f. Stockholder Melissa Strauderman paid $27,600 cash for a vacant lot (land) in Canada for her personal use.

Required:
1. Set up appropriate T-accounts with beginning balances of zero for Cash, Short-Term Notes Receivable, Land, Equipment, Short-Term Notes Payable, Long-Term Notes Payable, and Contributed Capital. Using the T-accounts, record the effects of these transactions by Strauderman Delivery Company.
2. Prepare a classified balance sheet for Strauderman Delivery Company at December 31, 2011.
3. At the end of the next two years, Strauderman Delivery Company reported the following amounts on its balance sheets:

	December 31, 2012	December 31, 2013
Current Assets	$52,000	$ 47,000
Long-Term Assets	38,000	73,000
Total Assets	**90,000**	**120,000**
Short-Term Notes Payable	23,000	40,000
Long-Term Notes Payable	17,000	20,000
Total Liabilities	**40,000**	**60,000**
Stockholders' Equity	**50,000**	**60,000**

   Compute the company's current ratio for 2011, 2012, and 2013. What is the trend and what does this suggest about the company?
4. At the beginning of year 2014, Strauderman Delivery Company applied to your bank for a $50,000 short-term loan to expand the business. The vice president of the bank asked you to review the information and make a recommendation on lending the funds based solely on the results of the current ratio. What recommendation would you make to the bank's vice president about lending the money to Strauderman Delivery Company?

Explaining the Effects of Transactions on Balance Sheet Accounts Using T-Accounts

E2-16
L04

Waltman Furniture Repair Service, a company with two stockholders, began operations on June 1, 2011. The following T-accounts indicate the activities for the month of June.

Cash (A)

6/1/11	0		
a.	16,000	c.	10,000
d.	800	b.	1,500

Notes Receivable (A)

6/1/11	0		
b.	1,500		

Tools and Equipment (A)

6/1/11	0		
a.	4,000	d.	800

Building (A)

6/1/11	0		
c.	50,000		

Notes Payable (L)

		6/1/11	0
		c.	40,000

Contributed Capital (SE)

		6/1/11	0
		a.	20,000

Required:
Explain events *(a)* through *(d)* that resulted in the entries in the T-accounts. That is, for each account, what transactions made it increase and/or decrease?

E2-17 LO4 Inferring Typical Investing and Financing Activities in Accounts

The following T-accounts indicate the effects of normal business transactions:

Equipment

1/1	500		
	250	?	
12/31	100		

Notes Receivable

1/1	150		
	?	225	
12/31	170		

Notes Payable

		100	1/1
	?	170	
		160	12/31

Required:
1. Describe the typical investing and financing transactions that affect each T-account. That is, what economic events occur to make each of these accounts increase and decrease?
2. For each T-account, compute the missing amounts.

E2-18 LO6 Identifying Investing and Financing Activities Affecting Cash Flows

Foot Locker, Inc.

Foot Locker, Inc., is a large global retailer of athletic footwear and apparel selling directly to customers and through the Internet. It includes the Foot Locker family of stores, Champs Sports, and Eastbay. The following are several of Foot Locker's investing and financing activities as reflected in a recent annual statement of cash flows.

a. Reduction of long-term debt.
b. Sale of short-term investments.
c. Issuance of common stock.
d. Capital expenditures (for property, plant, and equipment).
e. Dividends paid on common stock.

Required:
For each of these, indicate whether the activity is investing (I) or financing (F) and the direction of the effect on cash flows (+ for increases cash; − for decreases cash).

E2-19 LO6 Preparing the Investing and Financing Sections of the Statement of Cash Flows

starwood Hotels and Resorts

Starwood Hotels & Resorts Worldwide, Inc., is one of the world's largest hotel and leisure companies. It conducts business both directly and through its subsidiaries, including the following hotel brands: Sheraton, Four Points, W, Aloft, The Luxury Collection, Le Meridien, Element, Westin, and St. Regis.* Information adapted from the company's recent annual statement of cash flows indicates the following investing and financing activities during that year (simplified, in millions of dollars):

*Sheraton, Four Points, W, Aloft, The Luxury Collection, Le Meridien, Element, Westin, St. Regis and their respective logos are the trademarks of Starwood Hotels & Resorts Worldwide, Inc., or its affiliates.

Additional borrowing from banks	$986
Purchase of investments	37
Sale of assets and investments (assume sold at cost)	359
Issuance of stock	120
Purchase and renovation of properties	476
Payment of debt principal	574
Receipt of principal payment on a note receivable	172

Required:
Prepare the investing and financing sections of the statement of cash flows for Starwood Hotels. Assume that year-end is December 31, 2012.

Finding Financial Information as a Potential Investor

E2-20
LO2, 5, 6

You are considering investing the cash you inherited from your grandfather in various stocks. You have received the annual reports of several major companies.

Required:
For each of the following, indicate where you would locate the information in an annual report. The information may be in more than one location.

1. Total current assets.
2. Amount of debt principal repaid during the year.
3. Summary of significant accounting policies.
4. Cash received from sales of noncurrent assets.
5. Amount of dividends paid during the year.
6. Short-term obligations.
7. Date of the statement of financial position.

To practice with more exercises, go to the text website at **www.mhhe.com/libby7e**.

connect ACCOUNTING

PROBLEMS

Identifying Accounts on a Classified Balance Sheet and Their Normal Debit or Credit Balances (AP2-1)

P2-1
LO1, 2, 4

ExxonMobil

Exxon Mobil Corporation explores, produces, refines, markets, and supplies crude oil, natural gas, and petroleum products in the United States and around the world. The following are accounts from a recent balance sheet of Exxon Mobil Corporation:

	Balance Sheet Classification	Debit or Credit Balance
(1) Notes and Loans Payable (short-term)	CL	C
(2) Materials and Supplies	CA	D
(3) Contributed Capital	SE	C
(4) Patents (an intangible asset)	NCA	D
(5) Income Taxes Payable	CL	C
(6) Long-Term Debt	NCL	C
(7) Marketable Securities (short-term)	CA	D
(8) Property, Plant, and Equipment	NCA	D
(9) Retained Earnings	SE	C
(10) Notes and Accounts Receivable (short-term)	CA	D
(11) Investments (long-term)	NCA	D
(12) Cash and Cash Equivalents	CA	D
(13) Accounts Payable	CL	C
(14) Crude Oil Products and Merchandise	CA	D

Required:
For each account, indicate how it normally should be categorized on a classified balance sheet. Use CA for current asset, NCA for noncurrent asset, CL for current liability, NCL for noncurrent liability, and SE for stockholders' equity. Also indicate whether the account normally has a debit or credit balance.

P2-2 Determining Financial Statement Effects of Various Transactions (AP2-2)

LO2, 3, 5

www.mhhe.com/libby7e

East Hill Home Healthcare Services was organized on January 1, 2011, by four friends. Each organizer invested $10,000 in the company and, in turn, was issued 8,000 shares of stock. To date, they are the only stockholders. At the end of 2012, the accounting records reflected total assets of $700,000 ($50,000 cash; $500,000 land; $50,000 equipment; and $100,000 buildings), total liabilities of $200,000 (short-term notes payable of $100,000 and long-term notes payable of $100,000), and stockholders' equity of $500,000 ($100,000 contributed capital and $400,000 retained earnings). During the current year, 2013, the following summarized events occurred:

a. Sold 9,000 additional shares of stock to the original organizers for a total of $90,000 cash.
b. Purchased a building for $60,000, equipment for $15,000, and four acres of land for $14,000; paid $9,000 in cash and signed a note for the balance (due in 15 years). (*Hint:* Five different accounts are affected.)
c. Sold one acre of land acquired in (*b*) for $3,500 cash to another company.
d. Purchased short-term investments for $18,000 cash.
e. One stockholder reported to the company that 300 shares of his East Hill stock had been sold and transferred to another stockholder for $3,000 cash.
f. Lent one of the shareholders $5,000 for moving costs, receiving a signed six-month note from the shareholder.

Required:

1. Was East Hill Home Healthcare Services organized as a sole proprietorship, a partnership, or a corporation? Explain the basis for your answer.
2. During 2013, the records of the company were inadequate. You were asked to prepare the summary of the preceding transactions. To develop a quick assessment of their economic effects on East Hill Home Healthcare Services, you have decided to complete the tabulation that follows and to use plus (+) for increases and minus (−) for decreases for each account. The first event is used as an example.

	ASSETS						=	LIABILITIES		+	STOCKHOLDERS' EQUITY	
	Cash	Short-Term Investments	Notes Receivable	Land	Buildings	Equipment		Short-Term Notes Payable	Long-Term Notes Payable		Contributed Capital	Retained Earnings
Beg.	50,000			500,000	100,000	50,000	=	100,000	100,000		100,000	400,000
(a)	+90,000						=				+ 90,000	

3. Did you include the transaction between the two stockholders—event (*e*)—in the tabulation? Why?
4. Based only on the completed tabulation, provide the following amounts (show computations):
   a. Total assets at the end of the month.
   b. Total liabilities at the end of the month.
   c. Total stockholders' equity at the end of the month.
   d. Cash balance at the end of the month.
   e. Total current assets at the end of the month.
5. Compute the current ratio for 2013. What does this suggest about the company?

P2-3 Recording Transactions in T-Accounts, Preparing the Balance Sheet, and Evaluating the Current Ratio (AP2-3)

LO2, 4, 5

www.mhhe.com/libby7e

Cougar Plastics Company has been operating for three years. At December 31, 2011, the accounting records reflected the following:

Cash	$19,000	Intangibles	$ 3,000
Investments (short-term)	2,000	Accounts payable	15,000
Accounts receivable	3,000	Accrued liabilities payable	2,000
Inventory	24,000	Notes payable (short-term)	7,000
Notes receivable (long-term)	1,000	Long-term notes payable	46,000
Equipment	48,000	Contributed capital	90,000
Factory building	90,000	Retained earnings	30,000

During the year 2012, the company had the following summarized activities:

a. Purchased short-term investments for $9,000 cash.
b. Lent $7,000 to a supplier who signed a two-year note.
c. Purchased equipment that cost $18,000; paid $6,000 cash and signed a one-year note for the balance.
d. Hired a new president at the end of the year. The contract was for $85,000 per year plus options to purchase company stock at a set price based on company performance.

e. Issued an additional 2,000 shares of capital stock for $12,000 cash.
f. Borrowed $12,000 cash from a local bank, payable in three months.
g. Purchased a patent (an intangible asset) for $3,000 cash.
h. Built an addition to the factory for $25,000; paid $9,000 in cash and signed a three-year note for the balance.
i. Returned defective equipment to the manufacturer, receiving a cash refund of $1,000.

Required:

1. Create T-accounts for each of the accounts on the balance sheet and enter the balances at the end of 2011 as beginning balances for 2012.
2. Record each of the events for 2012 in T-accounts (including referencing) and determine the ending balances.
3. Explain your response to event (*d*).
4. Prepare a classified balance sheet at December 31, 2012.
5. Compute the current ratio for 2012. What does this suggest about Cougar Plastics?

P2-4
LO6

Identifying Effects of Transactions on the Statement of Cash Flows (AP2-4)

Refer to P2-3.

Required:

Using the events (*a*) through (*i*) in P2-3, indicate whether each is an investing (I) or financing (F) activity for the year and the direction of the effect on cash flows (+ for increase and − for decrease). If there is no effect on cash flows, write NE.

P2-5
LO2, 4, 5

Recording Transactions, Preparing Journal Entries, Posting to T-Accounts, Preparing the Balance Sheet, and Evaluating the Current Ratio

excel
www.mhhe.com/libby7e

Dell Inc., headquartered in Austin, Texas, is the global leader in selling computer products and services. The following is Dell's (simplified) balance sheet from a recent year.

DELL INC.
Balance Sheet
at January 30, 2009
(dollars in millions)

ASSETS	
Current assets	
Cash	$ 8,352
Short-term investments	740
Receivables and other assets	6,443
Inventories	867
Other	3,749
	20,151
Noncurrent assets	
Property, plant, and equipment	2,277
Long-term investments	454
Other noncurrent assets	3,618
Total assets	**$26,500**
LIABILITIES AND STOCKHOLDERS' EQUITY	
Current Liabilities	
Accounts payable	$ 8,309
Other short-term obligations	6,550
	14,859
Long-term liabilities	**7,370**
Stockholders' equity	
Contributed capital	11,189
Retained earnings	20,986
Other stockholders' equity items	(27,904)
Total stockholders' equity and liabilities	**$26,500**

Assume that the following transactions (in millions of dollars) occurred during the remainder of 2009 (ending on January 29, 2010):

a. Borrowed $30 from banks due in two years.
b. Lent $250 to affiliates, who signed a six-month note.
c. Purchased additional investments for $13,000 cash; one-fifth were long term and the rest were short term.
d. Purchased property, plant, and equipment; paid $875 in cash and $1,410 with additional long-term bank loans.
e. Issued additional shares of stock for $200 in cash.
f. Sold short-term investments costing $10,000 for $10,000 cash.
g. Dell does not actually pay dividends; it reinvests its earnings into the company for growth purposes. Assume instead for this problem that Dell declared and paid $52 in dividends during 2009.

Required:

1. Prepare a journal entry for each transaction.
2. Create T-accounts for each balance sheet account and include the January 30, 2009, balances. Post each journal entry to the appropriate T-accounts.
3. Prepare a balance sheet from the T-account ending balances for Dell at January 29, 2010, based on these transactions.
4. Compute Dell's current ratio for 2009 (year ending on January 29, 2010). What does this suggest about the company?

P2-6
LO6

DELL

Preparing the Investing and Financing Sections of a Statement of Cash Flows

Refer to P2-5.

Required:

Based on the activities for the year ended January 29, 2010, prepare the investing and financing sections of a statement of cash flows.

ALTERNATE PROBLEMS

AP2-1
LO1, 2, 4

MATTEL

Identifying Accounts on a Classified Balance Sheet and Their Normal Debit or Credit Balances (P2-1)

According to a recent Form 10-K report of Mattel, Inc., the company "designs, manufactures, and markets a broad variety of toy products worldwide." Mattel's brands include Barbie, Hot Wheels, Fisher-Price toys, and American Girl brand dolls and accessories. The following are several of the accounts from a recent balance sheet:

	Balance Sheet Classification	Debit or Credit Balance
(1) Prepaid Expenses	______	______
(2) Inventories	______	______
(3) Accounts Receivable	______	______
(4) Long-Term Debt	______	______
(5) Cash and Cash Equivalents	______	______
(6) Goodwill (an intangible asset)	______	______
(7) Accounts Payable	______	______
(8) Income Taxes Payable	______	______
(9) Property, Plant, and Equipment	______	______
(10) Retained Earnings	______	______
(11) Contributed Capital	______	______
(12) Short-Term Borrowings	______	______
(13) Accrued Liabilities	______	______

Required:

Indicate how each account normally should be categorized on a classified balance sheet. Use CA for current asset, NCA for noncurrent asset, CL for current liability, NCL for noncurrent liability, and SE for stockholders' equity. Also indicate whether the account normally has a debit or credit balance.

Determining Financial Statement Effects of Various Transactions (P2-2)

AP2-2
LO2, 3, 5

Adamson Incorporated is a small manufacturing company that makes model trains to sell to toy stores. It has a small service department that repairs customers' trains for a fee. The company has been in business for five years. At December 31, 2011 (the company's fiscal year-end), the accounting records reflected total assets of $500,000 (cash, $120,000; equipment, $70,000; buildings, $310,000), total liabilities of $200,000 (short-term notes payable, $140,000; long-term notes payable, $60,000), and total stockholders' equity of $300,000 (contributed capital, $220,000; retained earnings, $80,000). During the current year, 2012, the following summarized events occurred:

a. Borrowed $110,000 cash from the bank and signed a 10-year note.
b. Purchased equipment for $30,000, paying $3,000 in cash and signing a note due in six months for the balance.
c. Issued an additional 10,000 shares of capital stock for $100,000 cash.
d. Purchased a delivery truck (equipment) for $10,000; paid $5,000 cash and signed a short-term note payable for the remainder.
e. Lent $2,000 cash to the company president, Clark Adamson, who signed a note with terms showing the principal plus interest due in one year.
f. Built an addition on the factory for $200,000 and paid cash to the contractor.
g. Purchased $85,000 in long-term investments.
h. Returned a $3,000 piece of equipment purchased in (*b*) because it proved to be defective; received a reduction of its short-term note payable.
i. A stockholder sold $5,000 of his capital stock in Adamson Incorporated to his neighbor.

Required:

1. Was Adamson Incorporated organized as a sole proprietorship, a partnership, or a corporation? Explain the basis for your answer.
2. During 2012, the records of the company were inadequate. You were asked to prepare the summary of the preceding transactions. To develop a quick assessment of their economic effects on Adamson Incorporated, you have decided to complete the tabulation that follows and to use plus (+) for increases and minus (−) for decreases for each account. The first transaction is used as an example.

	ASSETS					=	LIABILITIES		+	STOCKHOLDERS' EQUITY	
	Cash	Notes Receivable	Long-Term Investments	Equipment	Buildings		Short-Term Notes Payable	Long-Term Notes Payable		Contributed Capital	Retained Earnings
Beg.	120,000			70,000	310,000	=	140,000	60,000		220,000	80,000
(a)	+110,000					=		+110,000			

3. Did you include event (*i*) in the tabulation? Why?
4. Based on beginning balances plus the completed tabulation, provide the following amounts (show computations):
   a. Total assets at the end of the year.
   b. Total liabilities at the end of the year.
   c. Total stockholders' equity at the end of the year.
   d. Cash balance at the end of the year.
   e. Total current assets at the end of the year.
5. Compute the current ratio for 2012. What does this suggest about the company?

AP2-3
LO2, 4, 5

ETHAN ALLEN

Recording Transactions in T-Accounts, Preparing the Balance Sheet, and Evaluating the Current Ratio (P2-3)

Ethan Allen Interiors, Inc., is a leading manufacturer and retailer of home furnishings in the United States and abroad. The following is adapted from Ethan Allen's June 30, 2008, annual financial report. Dollars are in thousands.

Cash and cash equivalents	$ 74,376	Other assets	$ 4,540
Short-term investments	0	Accounts payable	26,444
Accounts receivable	12,672	Accrued expenses payable	109,017
Inventories	186,265	Long-term debt (includes the current portion of $41)	203,029
Prepaid expenses and other current assets	36,865	Other long-term liabilities	47,710
Property, plant, and equipment	350,432	Contributed capital	21,048
Intangibles	96,823	Retained earnings	354,725

Assume that the following events occurred in the first quarter ended September 30, 2008:

a. Issued additional shares of stock for $1,020 in cash.
b. Purchased $3,400 in additional intangibles for cash.
c. Ordered $43,500 in wood and other raw materials for the manufacturing plants.
d. Sold equipment at its cost for $4,020 cash.
e. Purchased $2,980 in short-term investments for cash.
f. Purchased property, plant, and equipment; paid $1,830 in cash and signed additional long-term notes for $9,400.
g. Sold at cost other assets for $310 cash.
h. Declared and paid $300 in dividends.

Required:

1. Create T-accounts for each of the accounts on the balance sheet; enter the balances at June 30, 2008.
2. Record each of the transactions for the first quarter ended September 30, 2008, in the T-accounts (including referencing) and determine the ending balances.
3. Explain your response to event (*c*).
4. Prepare a classified balance sheet at September 30, 2008.
5. Compute the current ratio for the quarter ended September 30, 2008. What does this suggest about Ethan Allen Interiors, Inc.?

AP2-4
LO6

ETHAN ALLEN

Identifying Effects of Transactions on the Statement of Cash Flows (P2-4)

Refer to AP2-3.

Required:

Using the events (*a*) through (*h*) in AP2-3, indicate whether each transaction is an investing (I) or financing (F) activity for the quarter and the direction of the effect on cash flows (+ for increase and − for decrease). If there is no effect on cash flows, write NE.

CASES AND PROJECTS

Annual Report Cases

CP2-1
LO1, 2, 5, 6

AMERICAN EAGLE OUTFITTERS, INC.

Finding Financial Information

Refer to the financial statements of American Eagle Outfitters in Appendix B at the end of this book.

Required:

1. Is the company a corporation, a partnership, or a sole proprietorship? How do you know?
2. The company shows on the balance sheet that inventories are worth $294,928,000. Does this amount represent the expected selling price? Why or why not?

3. List the types of current obligations this company has. You need not provide the amounts.
4. Compute the company's current ratio and explain its meaning.
5. How much cash did the company spend on purchasing property and equipment each year (capital expenditures)? Where did you find the information?

CP2-2
LO1, 2, 5, 6

Finding Financial Information

Refer to the financial statements of Urban Outfitters in Appendix C at the end of this book.

URBAN OUTFITTERS INC.

Required:

1. Use the company's balance sheet to determine the amounts in the accounting equation (A = L + SE) as of January 31, 2009.
2. If the company were liquidated at the end of the current year (January 31, 2009), are the shareholders guaranteed to receive $1,053,775,000?
3. What are the company's noncurrent liabilities?
4. What is the company's current ratio?
5. Did the company have a cash inflow or outflow from investing activities? Of how much?

CP2-3
LO2, 5, 6

Comparing Companies within an Industry

Refer to the financial statements of American Eagle Outfitters in Appendix B, Urban Outfitters in Appendix C, and the Industry Ratio Report in Appendix D at the end of this book.

AMERICAN EAGLE OUTFITTERS, INC.

URBAN OUTFITTERS INC.

Required:

1. Compute the current ratio for both companies. Compared to the industry average (from the Industry Ratio Report), are these two companies more or less able to satisfy short-term obligations with current assets? How is the current ratio influenced by these companies' choice to rent space instead of buying it?
2. In the most recent year, how much cash, if any, was spent buying back (repurchasing) each company's own common stock?
3. How much, if any, did each company pay in dividends for the most recent year?
4. What account title or titles does each company use to report any land, buildings, and equipment it may have?

excel
www.mhhe.com/libby7e

Financial Reporting and Analysis Cases

CP2-4
LO2, 5, 6

Broadening Financial Research Skills: Locating Financial Information on the SEC's Database

The Securities and Exchange Commission (SEC) regulates companies that issue stock on the stock market. It receives financial reports from public companies electronically under a system called EDGAR (Electronic Data Gathering and Retrieval Service). Using the Internet, anyone may search the database for the reports that have been filed.

Using your Web browser, access the EDGAR database at www.sec.gov. To search the database, click on "Search" at the top of the page on the right side, type in "Papa Johns" for the company name," and then click on "Find Companies."

PIZZA PAPA JOHNS
Better Ingredients. Better Pizza.

Required:

To look at SEC filings, type in "10-Q" in the space indicating "Filing Type" and click on "Retrieve Selected Filings." Skim down the left side until you locate the Form 10-Q (quarterly report) filed May 5, 2009. Click on the "documents" for that report, click on the 10-Q document (first item), and skim to the Table of Contents.

1. Click on "Condensed Consolidated Balance Sheets."
   a. What was the amount of Papa John's total assets for the most recent quarter reported?
   b. Did long-term debt increase or decrease for the quarter?
   c. Compute the current ratio. How does it compare to the ratio indicated for Papa John's in the chapter? What does this suggest about the company?

2. Return to the Table of Contents and click on "Consolidated Statements of Cash Flow."
   a. What amount did Papa John's spend on property and equipment for the period?
   b. What was the total amount of cash flows from financing activities?

CP2-5 Using Financial Reports: Evaluating the Reliability of a Balance Sheet

LO1, 5

Frances Sabatier asked a local bank for a $50,000 loan to expand her small company. The bank asked Frances to submit a financial statement of the business to supplement the loan application. Frances prepared the following balance sheet.

FS COMPUTING
Balance Sheet
June 30, 2012

Assets	
Cash and investments	$ 9,000
Inventory	30,000
Equipment	46,000
Personal residence (monthly payments, $2,800)	300,000
Remaining assets	20,000
Total assets	$405,000
Liabilities	
Short-term debt to suppliers	$ 62,000
Long-term debt on equipment	38,000
Total debt	100,000
Stockholders' Equity	305,000
Total liabilities and stockholders' equity	$405,000

Required:
The balance sheet has several flaws. However, there is at least one major deficiency. Identify it and explain its significance.

CP2-6 Using Financial Reports: Analyzing the Balance Sheet

LO2, 4, 5

Recent balance sheets of Dell, Inc., a leading producer and marketer of a broad range of personal computers, mobility products, software, and related tools and services, are provided.

Required:
1. Is Dell a corporation, sole proprietorship, or partnership? Explain the basis of your answer.
2. Use the company's balance sheet (consolidated statement of financial position) to determine the amounts in the accounting equation (A = L + SE) at the end of the most recent year.
3. Calculate the company's current ratio on January 30, 2009. Interpret the ratio that you calculated. What other information would make your interpretation more useful?
4. Give the journal entry the company will make in 2009 when it pays its fiscal year 2008 accounts payable (fiscal year 2008 ends on January 30, 2009).
5. Does the company appear to have been profitable over its years in business? On what account are you basing your answer? Assuming no dividends were paid, how much was net income (or net loss) in the most recent year? If it is impossible to determine without an income statement, state so.

DELL INC.
Consolidated Statements of Financial Position
(dollars in millions)

	January 30, 2009	February 1, 2008
ASSETS		
Current assets		
Cash and cash equivalents	$ 8,352	$ 7,764
Short-term investments	740	208
Accounts receivable	6,443	7,693
Inventories	867	1,180
Other	3,749	3,035
Total current assets	20,151	19,880
Property, plant and equipment, net	2,277	2,668
Investments	454	1,560
Intangibles	2,461	2,428
Other noncurrent assets	1,157	1,025
	$ 26,500	$ 27,561
LIABILITIES AND STOCKHOLDERS' EQUITY		
Current liabilities		
Short-term debt	$ 113	$ 225
Accounts payable	8,309	11,492
Accrued and other liabilities	3,788	4,323
Deferred service revenue	2,649	2,486
Total current liabilities	14,859	18,526
Long-term debt	1,898	362
Long-term deferred service revenue	3,000	2,774
Other noncurrent liabilities	2,472	2,070
Total liabilities	22,229	23,732
Stockholders' equity		
Contributed capital	11,189	10,589
Retained earnings	20,677	18,199
Other	(27,595)	(24,959)
Total stockholders' equity	4,271	3,829
	$ 26,500	$ 27,561

Critical Thinking Cases

Making a Decision as a Financial Analyst: Preparing and Analyzing a Balance Sheet

CP2-7
LO1, 5

Your best friend from home writes you a letter about an investment opportunity that has come her way. A company is raising money by issuing shares of stock and wants her to invest $20,000 (her recent inheritance from her great-aunt's estate). Your friend has never invested in a company before and, knowing that you are a financial analyst, asks that you look over the balance sheet and send her some advice. An **unaudited** balance sheet, in only moderately good form, is enclosed with the letter.

DEWEY, CHEETUM, AND HOWE, INC.
Balance Sheet
For the Year Ending December 31, 2012

Accounts receivable	$ 8,000
Cash	1,000
Inventory	8,000
Furniture and fixtures	52,000
Delivery truck	12,000
Buildings (estimated market value)	98,000
Total assets	**$179,000**
Accounts payable	$ 16,000
Payroll taxes payable	13,000
Notes payable (due in three years)	15,000
Mortgage payable	50,000
Total liabilities	**$ 94,000**
Contributed capital	$ 80,000
Retained earnings	5,000
Total stockholders' equity	**$ 85,000**

There is only one footnote, and it states that the building was purchased for $65,000, has been depreciated by $5,000 on the books, and still carries a mortgage (shown in the liability section). The footnote also states that, in the opinion of the company president, the building is "easily worth $98,000."

Required:

1. Draft a new balance sheet for your friend, correcting any errors you note. (If any of the account balances need to be corrected, you may need to adjust the retained earnings balance correspondingly.) If there are no errors or omissions, so state.
2. Write a letter to your friend explaining the changes you made to the balance sheet, if any, and offer your comments on the company's apparent financial condition based only on this information. Suggest other information your friend might want to review before coming to a final decision on whether to invest.

CP2-8 Evaluating an Ethical Dilemma: Analyzing Management Incentives

U.S. Foodservice, Inc.

In July 2004, the U.S. government filed civil and criminal charges against four former executives of Netherlands-based Ahold's subsidiary U.S. Foodservice, Inc., an operator of supermarkets such as Bi-Lo and Giant Food Stores. Two of the four executives have pleaded guilty, and the other two were indicted. The alleged widespread fraud included recording completely fictitious revenues for false promotions and persuading vendors to confirm to auditors the false promotional payments. U.S. Attorney David Kelley suggested the fraud was motivated by the greed of the executives to reap fat bonuses if the company met certain financial goals. The auditors did not uncover the fraud.

Required:

1. Describe the parties who were harmed or helped by this fraud.
2. Explain how greed may have contributed to the fraud.
3. Why do you think the independent auditors failed to catch the fraud?

Financial Reporting and Analysis Team Project

Team Project: Analysis of Balance Sheets and Ratios

CP2-9
LO2, 5, 6

As a team, select an industry to analyze. Reuters provides lists of industries under Sectors and Industries at www.reuters.com. (Click on an industry and then select Company Rankings for a list of members of that industry.) Each team member should acquire the annual report or 10-K for one publicly traded company in the industry, with each member selecting a different company. (Library files, the SEC EDGAR service at www.sec.gov, or the company itself are good sources.)

Required:

On an individual basis, each team member should write a short report answering the following questions about the selected company. Discuss any patterns across the companies that you as a team observe. Then, as a team, write a short report comparing and contrasting your companies.

1. For the most recent year, what are the top three asset accounts by size? What percentage is each of total assets? (Calculated as Asset A ÷ Total Assets)
2. What are the major investing and financing activities (by dollar size) for the most recent year? (Look at the Statement of Cash Flows.)
3. Ratio Analysis:
   a. What does the current ratio measure in general?
   b. Compute the current ratio for each of the last three years. (You may find prior years' information in the section of the annual report or 10-K called "Selected Financial Information," or you may search for prior years' annual reports.)
   c. What do your results suggest about the company?
   d. If available, find the industry ratio for the most recent year, compare it to your results, and discuss why you believe your company differs or is similar to the industry ratio.

Lecture Presentation LP-3
www.mhhe.com/libby7e

LEARNING OBJECTIVES

After studying this chapter, you should be able to:

1. Describe a typical business operating cycle and explain the necessity for the time period assumption. p. 103
2. Explain how business activities affect the elements of the income statement. p. 104
3. Explain the accrual basis of accounting and apply the revenue and matching principles to measure income. p. 108
4. Apply transaction analysis to examine and record the effects of operating activities on the financial statements. p. 113
5. Prepare financial statements. p. 122
6. Compute and interpret the total asset turnover ratio. p. 127

OPERATING DECISIONS AND THE INCOME STATEMENT

Papa John's and Pizza Hut follow different operating strategies:

- Number-one Pizza Hut regularly creates new pizza varieties (such as the Big New Yorker, the Twisted Crust, the Stuffed Crust pizza you can eat backwards, the "P'Zone" calzone, and the "4forALL" with four individually topped pizzas in one) to attract customers to its eat-in, take-out, and delivery services. It now also offers a variety of pasta dishes. The company releases a new variety, advertises like crazy, waits for the customers to rush in, and hopes they will return.
- Papa John's focuses on producing a limited variety of pizzas for pickup or delivery. The company believes it can build strong customer loyalty and repeat business by advertising the simple slogan, "Better Ingredients. Better Pizza."

FOCUS COMPANY:

Papa John's International

IT'S MORE THAN DOUGH, CHEESE, AND TOMATOES

www.papajohns.com

Despite these different strategies, Papa John's, ranked number three through aggressive expansion, aims to become the number-one pizza brand in the world by building the strongest brand loyalty. Papa John's believes this requires extensive local marketing efforts supplemented with radio and television advertising. In 2008, for instance, Papa John's aired nine national television campaigns to compete against its rivals. In 2009, as part of its 25th anniversary, Papa John's launched a new reality TV-style "Papa's in the House" ad campaign in which founder John Schnatter personally delivered pizzas to real customers' homes.

To reach new markets, the company continues to expand its company-owned and franchising operations. By adding new restaurants, Papa John's quality control centers increase their efficiency, taking advantage of volume purchasing of food and supplies and thus lowering operating costs. At the same time, Papa John's spends additional resources in developing and motivating its team members.

However, one of the most significant effects on a pizza restaurant's financial performance for a period is the cost of cheese. When cheese prices are low, the pizza chains compete by offering low-price deals. When cheese prices are high, they use other gimmicks. For example, Papa John's became the first pizza chain to offer 24/7 online ordering and text ordering from mobile phones for all its restaurants. Embracing technology, Papa John's also used a new website, Facebook, Twitter, and YouTube integration to promote its 25th anniversary.

UNDERSTANDING THE BUSINESS

To become the number-one pizza brand globally, Papa John's executives develop strategies, plans, and measurable indicators of progress toward their goals. For example, their growth plan in 2009 was to add approximately 280 new restaurants (while closing 145 low-performing franchises) and continue to tell customers about their fresh dough, tomato sauce, and high-quality cheese in various promotional advertising programs. In developing their growth strategies, companies such as Papa John's plan their companywide operations in terms of the elements of the income statement (specific revenues and expenses).

Financial analysts develop their own set of expectations about Papa John's future performance. Its published income statement provides the primary basis for comparing analysts' projections to the actual results of operations. We will discuss these comparisons and the stock market's reactions to Papa John's results throughout this chapter as we learn about income recognition and measurement. To understand how business plans and the results of operations are reflected on the income statement, we need to answer the following questions:

1. How do business activities affect the income statement?
2. How are business activities measured?
3. How are business activities reported on the income statement?

In this chapter we focus on Papa John's operating activities that involve the sale of food to the public and the sale of ingredients and services to franchisees. The results of these activities are reported on the income statement.

ORGANIZATION OF THE CHAPTER

How Do Business Activities Affect the Income Statement?

- The Operating Cycle
- Elements on the Income Statement

How Are Operating Activities Recognized and Measured?

- Accrual Accounting
  - Revenue Principle
  - Matching Principle

The Expanded Transaction Analysis Model

- Transaction Analysis Rules
- Analyzing Papa John's Transactions

How Are Financial Statements Prepared and Analyzed?

- Classified Income Statement
- Statement of Stockholders' Equity
- Classified Balance Sheet
- Focus on Cash Flows
- Total Asset Turnover Ratio

HOW DO BUSINESS ACTIVITIES AFFECT THE INCOME STATEMENT?

The Operating Cycle

LEARNING OBJECTIVE 1

Describe a typical business operating cycle and explain the necessity for the time period assumption.

The long-term objective for any business is to **turn cash into more cash.** If a company is to stay in business, this excess cash must be generated from operations (that is, from the activities for which the business was established), not from borrowing money or selling long-lived assets.

Companies (1) acquire inventory and the services of employees and (2) sell inventory or services to customers. The **operating (or cash-to-cash) cycle** begins when a company receives goods to sell (or, in the case of a service company, has employees work), pays for them, and sells to customers; it ends when customers pay cash to the company. The length of time for completion of the operating cycle depends on the nature of the business.

The OPERATING (CASH-TO-CASH) CYCLE is the time it takes for a company to pay cash to suppliers, sell goods and services to customers, and collect cash from customers.

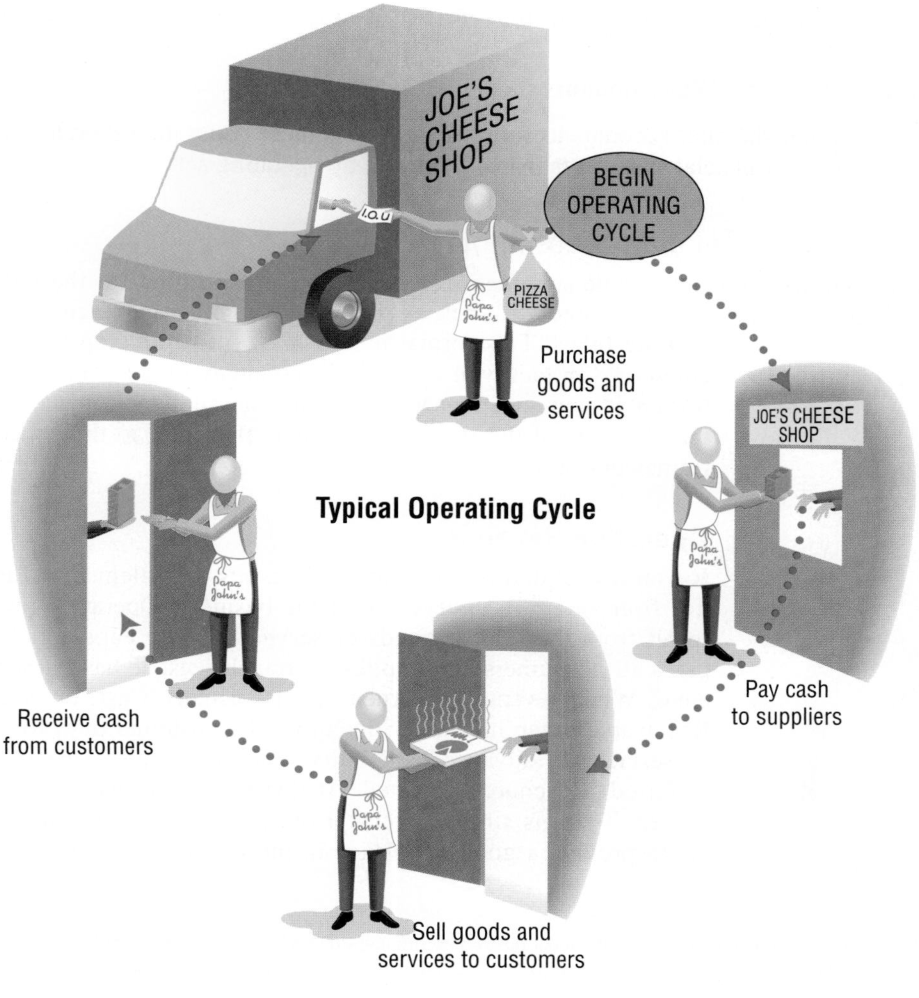

The operating cycle for Papa John's is relatively short. It spends cash to purchase fresh ingredients, makes pizzas, and sells them to customers for cash. In some companies, inventory is paid for well before it is sold. Toys R Us, for example, builds its inventory for months preceding the year-end holiday season. It borrows funds from banks to pay for the inventory and repays the loans with interest when it receives cash from customers. In other companies, cash is received from customers well after a sale takes place. For example, furniture retailers often allow customers to make monthly payments over several years. Shortening the operating cycle by creating incentives that encourage customers to buy sooner and/or pay faster improves a company's cash flows.

Managers know that reducing the time needed to turn cash into more cash (that is, shortening the operating cycle) means higher profit and faster growth. With the excess cash, managers may purchase additional inventory or other assets for growth, repay debt, or distribute it to owners as dividends.

The TIME PERIOD ASSUMPTION indicates that the long life of a company can be reported in shorter time periods.

Until a company ceases its activities, the operating cycle is repeated continuously. However, decision makers require information periodically about the company's financial condition and performance. As indicated in the conceptual framework in Exhibit 2.1, to measure income for a specific period of time, accountants follow the **time period assumption,** which assumes that the long life of a company can be reported in shorter time periods, such as months, quarters, and years.[1] Two types of issues arise in reporting periodic income to users:

1. Recognition issues: **When** should the effects of operating activities be recognized (recorded)?
2. Measurement issues: **What amounts** should be recognized?

Before we examine the rules accountants follow in resolving these issues, however, let's examine the elements of financial statements that are affected by operating activities.

LEARNING OBJECTIVE 2

Explain how business activities affect the elements of the income statement.

Elements on the Income Statement

Exhibit 3.1 shows a recent income statement for Papa John's, simplified for the purposes of this chapter.[2] It has multiple subtotals, such as **operating income** and **income before income taxes.** This format is known as **multiple step** and is very common.[3] In fact, you can tell if a company uses the multiple step format if you see the Operating Income subtotal. As we discuss the elements of the income statement, also refer to the conceptual framework outlined in Exhibit 2.1.

REVENUES are increases in assets or settlements of liabilities from ongoing operations.

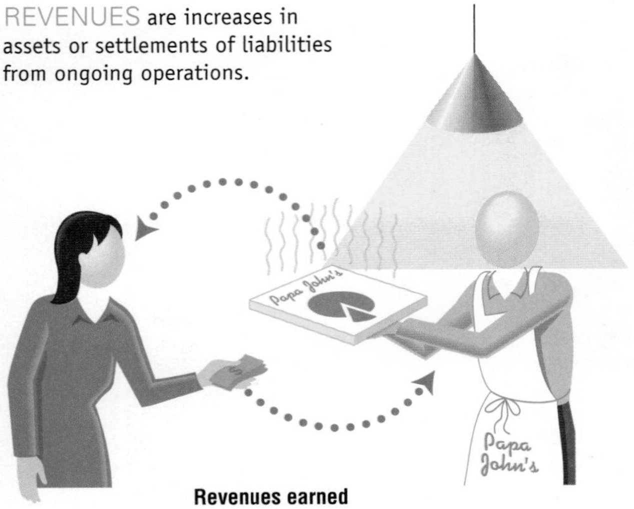

Revenues earned

Operating Revenues

Revenues are defined as increases in assets or settlements of liabilities from **ongoing operations** of the business. Operating revenues result from the sale of goods or services. When Papa John's sells pizza to consumers or supplies to franchisees, it has earned revenue. When revenue is earned, assets, usually Cash or Accounts Receivable, often increase. Sometimes if a customer pays for goods or services in advance, a liability account, usually Unearned (or Deferred) Revenue, is created. At this point, no revenue has been earned. There is simply a receipt of cash in exchange for a promise to provide a good or service in the future. When the company

[1]In addition to the audited annual statements, most businesses prepare quarterly financial statements (also known as **interim reports** covering a three-month period) for external users. The Securities and Exchange Commission requires public companies to do so.

[2]For simplification, dollar amounts have been rounded and several accounts in the original statement have been combined with other accounts and/or shown in a different section of the statement in the exhibit. In addition, only one year's income statement is presented. Publicly traded companies such as Papa John's are actually required to present income information for three years to help users assess trends over time.

[3]Another common format, **single step,** reorganizes all accounts on the multiple-step format. All revenues and gains are listed together and all expenses and losses except taxes are listed together. The expense subtotal is then subtracted from the revenue subtotal to arrive at income before income taxes, the same subtotal as on the multiple-step statement.

EXHIBIT 3.1

Income Statement

PAPA JOHN'S INTERNATIONAL, INC.
Consolidated Statement of Income
For the Year Ended December 31, 2008
(dollars in thousands)

Operating Revenues		
Restaurant sales revenue	$ 996,000	
Franchise fee revenue	136,000	
Total revenues	1,132,000	
Operating Expenses		
Cost of sales	483,000	
Salaries expense	193,000	***Operating activities*** *(central focus of the business)*
Rent expense	35,000	
Advertising expense	49,000	
General and administrative expenses	100,000	← *Includes insurance, repairs, utilities, and fuel expenses*
Depreciation expense	33,000	
Other operating expenses	172,000	
Total expenses	1,065,000	
Operating Income	67,000	← *Subtotal of operating revenues minus operating expenses*
Other Items		
Investment income	1,000	
Interest expense	(8,000)	***Peripheral activities*** *(not the main focus of the business)*
Loss on restaurants sold	(3,000)	
Income before Income Taxes	57,000	← *Subtotal of all revenues minus all expenses except taxes*
Income tax expense	20,000	
Net Income	**$ 37,000**	
Earnings per Share	**$ 1.32**	← *= $37,000,000 Net Income ÷ 28,100,000 Average Number of Shares Outstanding (from Papa John's annual report)*

provides the promised goods or services to the customer, the revenue is recognized and the liability settled.

Like most companies, Papa John's generates revenues from a variety of sources. Exhibit 3.1 shows operating revenues from two primary sources:

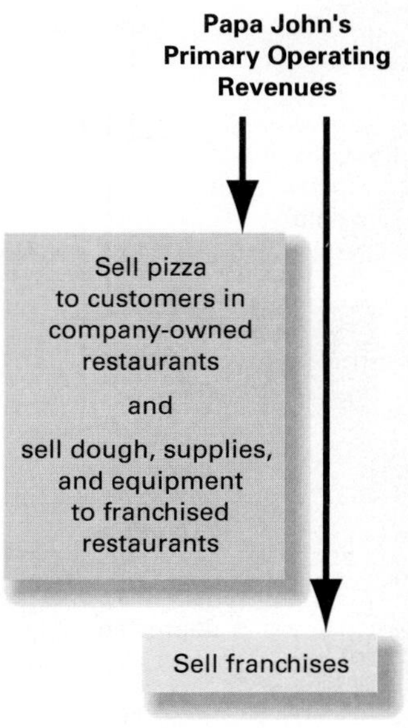

- **Restaurant Sales Revenue.** Approximately 18 percent of Papa John's stores are owned by the company, while 82 percent are owned by others through franchise agreements. Included in Restaurant Sales Revenue, the largest revenue account, are the sales of pizza ingredients and supplies to all of the chain's restaurants, including the franchised stores, and sales of pizzas in company-owned stores. Pizza sales revenue for the franchised restaurants is reported in each of the franchisees' financial statements, not Papa John's.
- **Franchise Fee Revenue.** Approximately 12 percent of all Papa John's revenues in 2008 came from selling franchises. Franchisees pay initial fees that Papa John's records as a liability (Unearned Franchise Fees) until it provides pre-opening services to the franchisees. As part of the franchise agreement, franchisees also pay Papa John's a fixed percentage (between 4 and 5 percent) of their store sales as franchise royalties. Both the earned portion of initial fees and annual royalty payments are reported on Papa John's income statement as Franchise Fee Revenue.

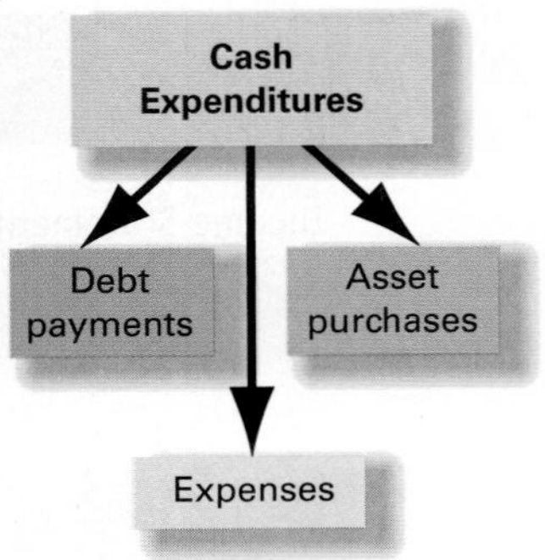

EXPENSES are decreases in assets or increases in liabilities from ongoing operations incurred to generate revenues during the period.

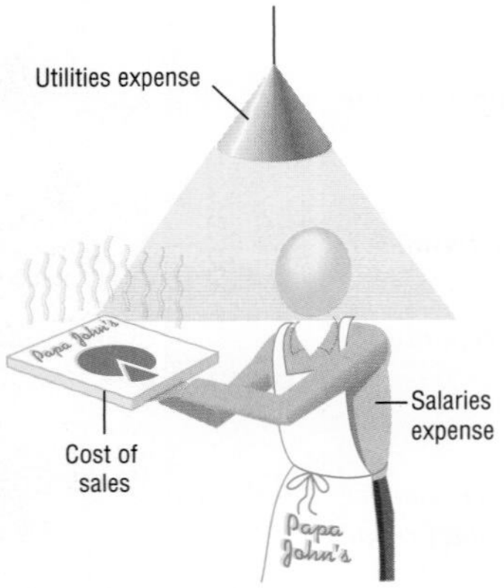

Expenses incurred to generate revenues

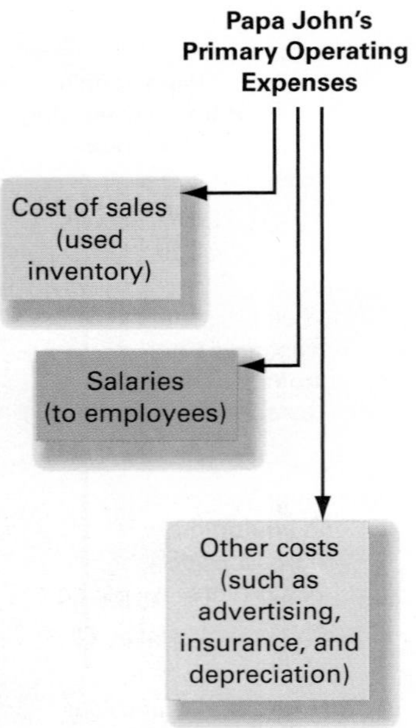

Operating Expenses

Some students confuse the terms **expenditures** and **expenses.** An expenditure is any outflow of cash for any purpose, whether to buy equipment, pay off a bank loan, or pay employees their wages. Expenses are decreases in assets or increases in liabilities from **ongoing operations** incurred to generate revenues during the period. Therefore, while **not all cash expenditures are expenses, expenses are necessary to generate revenues.**

Papa John's pays employees to make and serve food, uses electricity to operate equipment and light its facilities, advertises its pizza, and uses food and paper supplies. Without incurring these expenses, Papa John's could not generate revenues. Although some of the expenses may result from expenditures of cash at the time they are incurred, some expenses may be incurred after cash has been paid and others may be incurred before cash is paid. When an expense is incurred, assets such as Supplies decrease (are used up) **or** liabilities such as Salaries Payable or Utilities Payable increase.

The following are Papa John's primary operating expenses:

- **Cost of Sales.** In Papa John's restaurant operations, any ingredients or supplies that are used to produce meals are expensed as they are used. In addition, any ingredients and supplies that are sold to company-owned and franchised restaurants from the Quality Control Centers are expensed as they are provided to the restaurants. In companies with a manufacturing or merchandising focus, Cost of Goods Sold (or Cost of Sales) representing the cost of inventory used in generating sales is usually the most significant expense.
- **Salaries Expense.** When employees work and generate pizza sales for Papa John's, the company incurs an expense, although salaries will be paid later. Salaries Expense of $193,000,000 is Papa John's second largest expense. In purely service-oriented companies in which no products are produced or sold, the cost of using employees to generate revenues is usually the largest expense.
- **All other operating expenses.** The remaining large expenses include Rent Expense, Advertising Expense, General and Administrative Expenses (for insurance, executive salaries, and rental of headquarters facilities), and Depreciation Expense, reflecting the use of a part of long-lived assets such as buildings and equipment.

Subtracting operating expenses from operating revenues gives **Operating Income** (also called Income from Operations)—a measure of the profit from central ongoing operations.

Other Items

Not all activities affecting an income statement are, however, central to ongoing operations. Any revenues, expenses, gains, or losses that result from these other activities are not included as part of operating income, but are instead categorized as Other Items. Typically, these include:

- **Investment Income** (or **Investment, Interest,** or **Dividend Revenue**). Using excess cash to purchase stocks or bonds in other companies is an investing activity for Papa John's, not a central operation (making and selling pizza). Therefore, any interest or dividends earned on the investment are not included as operating revenue.
- **Interest Expense.** Likewise, since borrowing money is a financing activity, any cost of using that money (called interest) is not an operating expense. Except for financial institutions, incurring interest expense or earning investment income are **not** the central operations of most businesses, including Papa John's. We say these are peripheral (normal but not central) transactions.
- **Gains (or Losses) on Sales of Assets.** Companies sell property, plant, and equipment from time to time to maintain modern facilities. Selling land for more than the original purchase price does not result in earning revenue because the transaction is not the central operating focus for the business. Gains (with an account called Gain on Sale of Assets) result in an increase in assets or decrease in liabilities from a **peripheral** transaction. Losses are decreases in assets or increases in liabilities from **peripheral** transactions. In 2008, Papa John's sold restaurants costing $12 million for $9 million, recognizing a Loss on Restaurants Sold of $3 million.

Income Tax Expense

Adding and subtracting other items to operating income gives a subtotal of **Income before Income Taxes** (or pretax income). Income Tax Expense (also called Provision for Income Taxes) is the last expense listed on the income statement before determining net income. All profit-making corporations are required to compute income taxes owed to federal, state, and foreign governments. Income tax expense is calculated as a percentage of pretax income determined by applying the tax rates of the federal, state, local, and foreign taxing authorities. Papa John's effective tax rate in 2008 was 35 percent ($20 million in income tax expense divided by $57 million in income before income taxes). This indicates that, for every dollar of income before taxes that Papa John's made in 2008, the company paid $0.35 to taxing authorities.

GAINS are increases in assets or decreases in liabilities from peripheral transactions.

LOSSES are decreases in assets or increases in liabilities from peripheral transactions.

Earnings per Share

Corporations are required to disclose earnings per share on the income statement or in the notes to the financial statements. This ratio is widely used in evaluating the operating performance and profitability of a company. At this introductory level, we can compute earnings per share simply as net income divided by the average number of shares of stock outstanding (Net Income ÷ Average Number of Shares of Stock Outstanding). Please note, however, that the calculation of the ratio is actually much more complex and beyond the scope of this course. Instead, we used the actual number computed by Papa John's. For 2008, Papa John's reported $1.32 in earnings for each share of stock owned by investors.

Income Statement Differences

INTERNATIONAL PERSPECTIVE

As indicated in Chapter 2, under IFRS, the income statement is usually titled the Statement of Operations. There is also a difference in how expenses may be reported:

	GAAP	IFRS
Presentation of Expenses		
• Similar expenses are reported, but they may be grouped in different ways.	Public companies categorize expenses by business **function** (e.g., production, research, marketing, general operations).	Companies can categorize expenses by either **function or nature** (e.g., salaries, rent, supplies, electricity).

In addition, foreign companies often use account titles that differ from those used by U.S. companies. For example, GlaxoSmithKline (a U.K. pharmaceutical company), Parmalat (an Italian food producer of milk, dairy products, and fruit-based beverages), and Unilever (a U.K. and Netherlands-based company supplying food, home, and personal care products such as Hellman's mayonnaise, Dove soap, and Popsicle treats) use the term *turnover* to refer to sales revenue, *finance income* for income from investments, and *finance cost* for interest expense. BMW Group, on the other hand, reports *revenues* and uses *financial result* for the difference between income from investments and interest expense. All four companies follow IFRS.

GlaxoSmithKline
Parmalat
Unilever Group

HOW ARE OPERATING ACTIVITIES RECOGNIZED AND MEASURED?

You probably determine your personal financial position by the cash balance in your bank account. Your financial performance is measured as the difference between your cash balance at the beginning of the period and the cash balance at the end of the period (that is, whether you end up with more or less cash). If you have a higher cash balance, cash receipts exceeded cash disbursements for the period. Many local retailers, medical offices, and other small businesses

CASH BASIS
Income Measurement
Revenues (= cash receipts)
- Expenses (= cash payments)
Net Income (cash basis)

CASH BASIS ACCOUNTING records revenues when cash is received and expenses when cash is paid.

use **cash basis accounting** in which revenues are recorded when cash is received, and expenses are recorded when cash is paid, regardless of when the revenues were earned or the expenses incurred. This basis is often quite adequate for organizations that do not need to report to external users.

LEARNING OBJECTIVE 3

Explain the accrual basis of accounting and apply the revenue and matching principles to measure income.

Accrual Accounting

Financial statements created under cash basis accounting normally postpone or accelerate recognition of revenues and expenses long before or after goods and services are produced and delivered (when cash is received or paid). They also do not necessarily reflect all assets or liabilities of a company on a particular date. For these reasons, cash basis financial statements are not very useful to external decision makers. Therefore, generally accepted accounting principles require **accrual basis accounting** for financial reporting purposes.

In accrual basis accounting, revenues and expenses are recognized when the transaction that causes them occurs, not necessarily when cash is received or paid. That is, **revenues are recognized when they are earned and expenses when they are incurred.** The two basic accounting principles that determine when revenues and expenses are recorded under accrual basis accounting are the **revenue principle** and the **matching principle.**

ACCRUAL BASIS
Income Measurement

Revenues (= when earned)
-Expenses (= when incurred)
Net Income (accrual basis)

ACCRUAL BASIS ACCOUNTING records revenues when earned and expenses when incurred, regardless of the timing of cash receipts or payments.

The REVENUE PRINCIPLE states that revenues are recognized when (1) goods or services are delivered, (2) there is persuasive evidence of an arrangement for customer payment, (3) the price is fixed or determinable, and (4) collection is reasonably assured.

Revenue Principle

Under the **revenue principle,** four criteria or conditions must normally be met for revenue to be recognized. If **any** of the following criteria are **not** met, revenue normally is **not** recognized and cannot be recorded.

1. **Delivery has occurred or services have been rendered.** The company has performed or substantially performed the acts promised to the customer by providing goods or services.
2. **There is persuasive evidence of an arrangement for customer payment.** In exchange for the company's performance, the customer has provided cash or a promise to pay cash (a receivable).
3. **The price is fixed or determinable.** There are no uncertainties as to the amount to be collected.
4. **Collection is reasonably assured.** For cash sales, collection is not an issue since it is received on the date of the exchange. For sales on credit, the company reviews the customer's ability to pay. If the customer is considered creditworthy, collecting cash from the customer is reasonably likely.

These conditions normally occur when the title, risks, and rewards of ownership have transferred to the customers. For most businesses, these conditions are met at the point of delivery of goods or services, **regardless of when cash is received.**

Although businesses expect to receive cash in exchange for their goods and services at the time of delivery, the timing of cash receipts from customers does not dictate when businesses report revenues. Instead, the key to determining when to report revenue is whether the business has done what it promised to do. Exhibit 3.2 illustrates that revenue is earned when the business delivers goods or services, although cash can be received from customers (1) in a period **before** delivery, (2) in the **same** period as delivery, or (3) in a period **after** delivery. Let's see how to handle each of these cases.

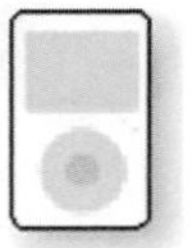

Video 3-1
www.mhhe.com/libby7e

On receipt of a $100 cash deposit:

Cash (+A)	100	
Unearned Restaurant Revenue (+L) ...		100

On delivery of ordered pizza:

Unearned Restaurant Revenue (−L)	100	
Restaurant Sales Revenue (+R)		100

1 **Cash is received *before* the goods or services are delivered.** Papa John's may receive cash from customers who provide a deposit toward a large future pizza order. Since Papa John's has not at that point delivered the pizza, it records **no revenue.** Instead it creates a liability account (Unearned Restaurant Revenue) representing

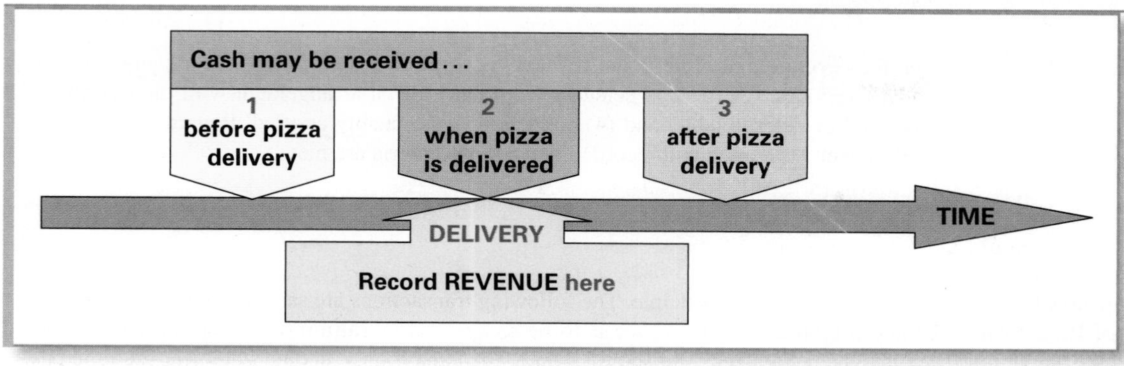

EXHIBIT 3.2

Recording Revenues versus Cash Receipts

the amount of pizza service owed to the customers. Later, when Papa John's delivers the pizza, it earns and records the revenue while reducing the liability account since it has satisfied its promise to deliver.

2 **Cash is received *in the same period as* the goods or services are delivered.** As is a typical timing of cash receipts and revenue recognition in the fast-food and restaurant industry, Papa John's receives cash from most customers within a few minutes of them receiving their pizza. Papa John's delivers the pizza to the customer as ordered, **earning revenue** in the process in exchange for cash.

On delivery of ordered pizza for $12 cash:		
Cash (+A)	12	
Restaurant Sales Revenue (+R)		12

3 **Cash is received *after* the goods or services are delivered.** When a business sells goods or services on account, the revenue is earned when the goods or services are delivered, not when cash is received at a later date. To boost business, Papa John's delivers pizza when ordered by certain customers, such as departments at area colleges or businesses, that pay for the pizza when Papa John's bills them at the end of the month, not when the customers receive the pizza. When delivered, Papa John's records both Restaurant Sales Revenue and the asset Accounts Receivable, representing the customer's promise to pay in the future for past pizza deliveries. When the customer pays its monthly bill, Papa John's will increase its Cash account and decrease Accounts Receivable.

On delivery of ordered pizza for $50 on account:		
Accounts Receivable (+A)	50	
Restaurant Sales Revenue (+R)		50
On receipt of cash after delivery:		
Cash (+A)	50	
Accounts Receivable (−A)		50

Companies usually disclose their revenue recognition practices in a note to the financial statements. The following excerpt from a note to the financial statements describes how Papa John's recognizes its two forms of revenue (from pizza sales in company-owned stores and from franchises sold to franchisees):

2. SIGNIFICANT ACCOUNTING POLICIES

Revenue Recognition

Franchise fees are recognized when a franchised restaurant begins operations, at which time we have performed our obligations related to such fees. Fees received pursuant to development agreements which grant the right to develop franchised restaurants in future periods in specific geographic areas are deferred and recognized on a pro rata basis as the franchised restaurants subject to the development agreements begin operations. . . . Retail sales from Company-owned restaurants and franchise royalties, which are based on a percentage of franchised restaurant sales, are recognized as revenue when the products are delivered to or carried out by customers.

Better Ingredients. Better Pizza.

REAL WORLD EXCERPT

Annual Report

STOP

PAUSE FOR **FEEDBACK**

We just learned the **revenue principle's** four revenue recognition criteria: (1) The company delivers goods or performs services, (2) there is persuasive evidence of an arrangement with the customer, (3) the price is fixed or determinable, and (4) collection is reasonably assured. Regardless of when cash is received, revenue is earned and recorded when these criteria are met.

SELF-STUDY **QUIZ**

Complete this quiz now to make sure you can apply the principle. The following transactions are samples of typical monthly operating activities of Papa John's (dollars in thousands). If revenue is to be recognized in **January,** indicate the title of the revenue account and the amount of revenue to be recognized. You should refer to the Papa John's income statement presented in Exhibit 3.1 for account titles.

Activity	Revenue Account Title	Amount of Revenue Recognized in January
(*a*) In January, Papa John's company-owned restaurants sold food to customers for $32,000 cash.		
(*b*) In January, Papa John's sold new franchises for $625 cash, providing $400 in services to these new franchisees during January; the remainder of services will be provided over the next three months.		
(*c*) In January, franchisees paid Papa John's $2,750 in cash for royalties based on the franchisees' weekly sales; $750 related to December sales and the rest to January sales.		
(*d*) In January, Papa John's commissaries sold sauce and dough to restaurants for $30,000, of which $20,000 was in cash and the rest was on account.		
(*e*) In January, customers paid $1,200 on account to Papa John's from December deliveries of pizza.		

After you have completed your answers, check them with the solutions at the bottom of the page.

Solutions to
SELF-STUDY QUIZ

Revenue Account Title	Amount of Revenue Recognized in January
(*a*) Restaurant Sales Revenue	$32,000
(*b*) Franchise Fee Revenue	$ 400
(*c*) Franchise Fee Revenue	$ 2,000
(*d*) Restaurant Sales Revenue	$30,000
(*e*) No revenue earned in January	—

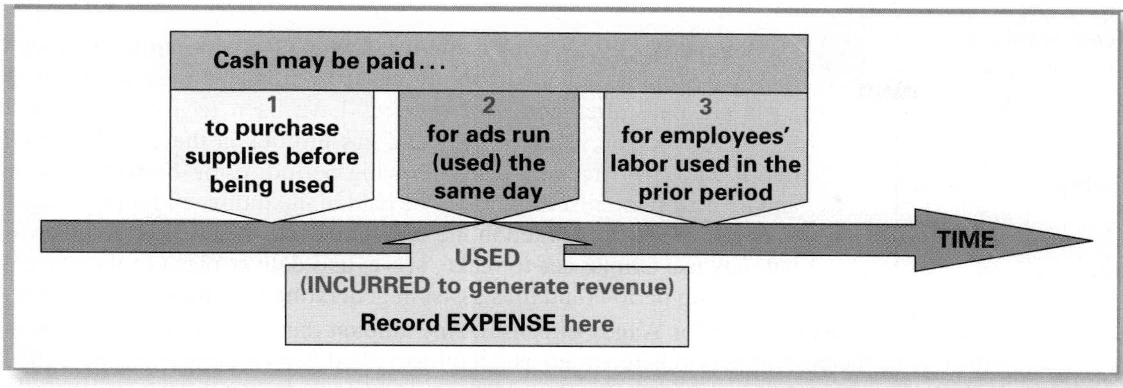

EXHIBIT 3.3

Recording Expenses versus Cash Payments

Matching Principle

The **matching principle** requires that costs incurred to generate revenues be recognized in the same period—a matching of costs with benefits. For example, when Papa John's restaurants provide food service to customers, revenue is earned. The costs of generating the revenue include expenses incurred such as these:

The MATCHING PRINCIPLE requires that expenses be recorded when incurred in earning revenue.

- Wages to employees who worked **during the period** (Wages Expense)
- Utilities for the electricity used **during the period** (Utilities Expense)
- Food and paper products used **during the period** (Cost of Sales)
- Facilities rental **during the period** (Rent Expense)
- The use of ovens and other equipment **during the period** (Depreciation Expense)

As with revenues and cash receipts, expenses are recorded as incurred, **regardless of when cash is paid.** Cash may be paid (1) **before,** (2) **during,** or (3) **after** an expense is incurred (see Exhibit 3.3). An entry will be made on the date the expense is incurred and another on the date the cash is paid, if they occur at different times. Let's see how to handle each of these cases related to the matching principle.

1 **Cash is paid *before* the expense is incurred to generate revenue.** Companies purchase many assets that are used to generate revenues in future periods. Examples include buying insurance for future coverage, paying rent for future use of space, and acquiring supplies and equipment for future use. When revenues are generated in the future, the company records an expense for the portion of the cost of the assets used—costs are matched with the benefits. As an example, Papa John's buys paper supplies (napkins, boxes, cups, etc.) in one month, but uses them the following month. When acquired, the supplies are recorded as an asset (called Supplies or Prepaid Expenses) because they will benefit future periods. When they are used the following month, Supplies Expense (or Cost of Sales) is recorded for the month and the asset Supplies is reduced to the amount yet to be used.

On payment of $200 cash for supplies:		
Supplies (+A)	200	
Cash (−A)		200
On subsequent use of half of the supplies:		
Supplies Expense (+E)	100	
Supplies (−A).............		100

2 **Cash is paid *in the same period* as the expense is incurred to generate revenue.** Expenses are sometimes incurred and paid for in the period in which they arise. Examples are paying for repair or delivery service the day of the service. If Papa John's spends $75 cash for newspaper advertising for the opening of a new restaurant on that day, the company records Advertising Expense because the advertising is used to generate revenue in the current accounting period.

On payment of $75 cash for newspaper ads run (used) the same day:		
Advertising Expense (+E)......	75	
Cash (−A)		75

On use of $400 in employees' services during the period:		
Salaries Expense (+E)	400	
Salaries Payable (+L).		400
On payment of cash after using employees:		
Salaries Payable (−L)	400	
Cash (−A)		400

3 **Cash is paid *after* the cost is incurred to generate revenue.** Although rent and supplies are typically purchased before they are used, many costs are paid after goods or services have been received and used. Examples include using electric and gas utilities in the current period that are not paid for until the following period, using borrowed funds and incurring Interest Expense to be paid in the future, and owing wages to employees who worked in the current period. When Papa John's restaurants use employees to make, serve, and deliver pizza in the current accounting period (and thus assist in generating revenues), the company records Salaries Expense (or Wages Expense). Any amount that is owed to employees at the end of the current period is recorded as a liability called Salaries Payable (also called Wages Payable or Accrued Expenses Payable).

STOP PAUSE FOR FEEDBACK

The **matching principle** requires that costs incurred to generate revenues be recognized in the same period—that costs be matched with revenues. Regardless of when cash is paid, expense is recorded when incurred.

SELF-STUDY QUIZ

Complete this quiz now to make sure you can apply the principle. The following transactions are samples of typical monthly operating activities of Papa John's (dollars in thousands). If an expense is to be recognized in **January,** indicate the title of the expense account and the amount of expense to be recognized. You should refer to the Papa John's income statement presented in Exhibit 3.1 for account titles. Note that Papa John's combines Insurance Expense, Repairs Expense, Utilities Expense, and Fuel Expense into General and Administrative Expenses on the income statement. Use the more descriptive account titles in your responses, not General and Administrative Expenses.

Activity	Expense Account Title	Amount of Expense Recognized in January
(*a*) At the beginning of January, Papa John's restaurants paid $3,000 in rent for the months of January, February, and March.		
(*b*) In January, Papa John's paid suppliers $10,000 on account for supplies received in December.		
(*c*) In January, the food and paper products inventory used in selling pizza products to customers was $9,500.		
(*d*) In late January, Papa John's received a $400 utility bill for electricity used in January. The bill will be paid in February.		

After you have completed your answers, check them with the solutions at the bottom of the page.

Solutions to SELF-STUDY QUIZ

Expense Account Title	Amount of Expense Recognized in January
(*a*) Rent Expense	$1,000 ($3,000 ÷ 3 months)
(*b*) No expense in January	Supplies will be expensed when used.
(*c*) Supplies Expense (or Cost of Supplies)	$9,500
(*d*) Utilities Expense (General and Administrative Expenses)	$400

Management's Incentives to Violate Accounting Rules

A QUESTION OF ETHICS

Investors in the stock market base their decisions on their expectations of a company's future earnings. When companies announce quarterly and annual earnings information, investors evaluate how well the companies have met expectations and adjust their investing decisions accordingly. Companies that fail to meet expectations often experience a decline in stock price. Thus, managers are motivated to produce earnings results that meet or exceed investors' expectations to bolster stock prices. Greed may lead some managers to make unethical accounting and reporting decisions, often involving falsifying revenues and expenses. While this sometimes fools people for a short time, it rarely works in the long run and often leads to very bad consequences.

Fraud is a criminal offense for which managers may be sentenced to jail. Samples of fraud cases, a few involving faulty revenue and expense accounting, are shown below. Just imagine what it must have been like to be 65-year-old Bernie Ebbers or 21-year-old Barry Minkow, both sentenced to 25 years in prison for accounting fraud.

The CEO	The Fraud	Conviction/Plea	The Outcome
Bernard Madoff, 71 Madoff Investment Securities	Scammed $50 billion from investors in a Ponzi scheme in which investors receive "returns" from money paid by subsequent investors.	Confessed, December 2008	Sentenced to 150 years
Bernie Ebbers, 65 Worldcom	Recorded $11 billion in operating expenses as if they were assets.	Convicted, July 2005	Sentenced to 25 years
Sanjay Kumar, 44 Computer Associates	Recorded sales in the wrong accounting period.	Pleaded guilty, April 2006	Sentenced to 12 years
Martin Grass, 49 Rite Aid Corporation	Recorded rebates from drug companies before they were earned.	Pleaded guilty, June 2003	Sentenced to 8 years
Barry Minkow, 21 ZZZZ Best	Made up customers and sales to show profits when, in reality, the company was a sham.	Convicted, December 1988	Sentenced to 25 years

Many others are affected by fraud. Shareholders lose stock value, employees may lose their jobs (and pension funds, as in the case of Enron), and customers and suppliers may become wary of dealing with a company operating under the cloud of fraud. As a manager, you may face an ethical dilemma in the workplace. The ethical decision is the one you will be proud of 20 years later.

THE EXPANDED TRANSACTION ANALYSIS MODEL

LEARNING OBJECTIVE 4

Apply transaction analysis to examine and record the effects of operating activities on the financial statements.

We have discussed the variety of business activities affecting the income statement and how they are measured. Now we need to determine how these business activities are recorded in the accounting system and reflected in the financial statements. Chapter 2 covered investing and financing activities that affect assets, liabilities, and contributed capital. We now expand the transaction analysis model to include operating activities.

Transaction Analysis Rules

The complete transaction analysis model presented in Exhibit 3.4 includes **all five elements:** assets, liabilities, stockholders' equity, revenues, and expenses. Recall that the

EXHIBIT 3.4

Expanded Transaction Analysis Model

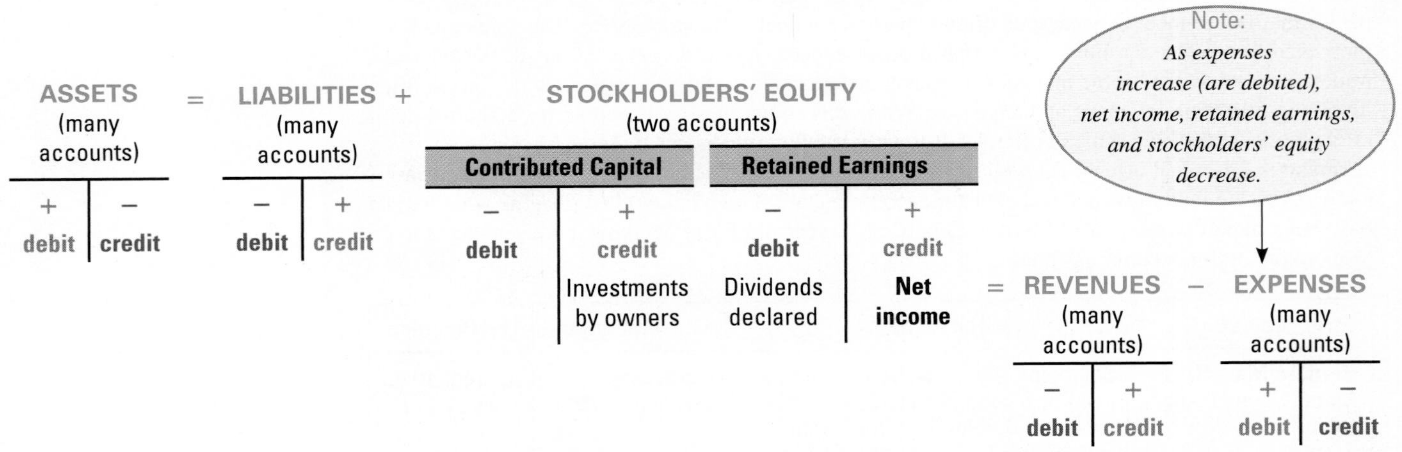

Video 3-2
www.mhhe.com/libby7e

REVENUES

- Increase net income and stockholders' equity
- ↑ with Credits
- Accounts have credit balances

EXPENSES

- Decrease net income and stockholders' equity
- ↑ with Debits
- Accounts have debit balances

Retained Earnings account is the accumulation of all past revenues and expenses minus any income distributed to stockholders as dividends (that is, earnings not retained in the business).[4] When net income is positive, Retained Earnings increase; a net loss decreases Retained Earnings.

Some students attempt to memorize journal entries in the introductory accounting course. However, they are often overwhelmed by the number and complexity of transactions as the course progresses. To avoid this pitfall, you should instead be able to construct the transaction analysis model in Exhibit 3.4 on your own without assistance and use it to analyze transactions. It will be very beneficial in completing assignments and analyzing more complex transactions in future chapters. Now let's study Exhibit 3.4 carefully to remember how the model is constructed and to understand the impact of operating activities on both the balance sheet and income statement:

- All accounts can increase or decrease, although revenues and expenses tend to increase throughout a period. For accounts on the left side of the accounting equation, the increase symbol + is written on the left side of the T-account. For accounts on the right side of the accounting equation, the increase symbol + is written on the right side of the T-account, **except for expenses, which increase on the left side of the T-account.**
- Debits (dr) are written on the left of each T-account and credits (cr) are written on the right.
- Every transaction affects at least two accounts.

---

[4]Instead of reducing Retained Earnings directly when dividends are declared, companies may use the account Dividends Declared, which has a debit balance.

- Revenues increase stockholders' equity through the account Retained Earnings and therefore have **credit** balances. Recording revenue results in either increasing an asset (such as Cash or Accounts Receivable) or decreasing a liability (such as Unearned Subscriptions Revenue).

A	=	L	+	SE
+ or −				+ (+ revenue ↑ RE)

- Expenses decrease net income, thus decreasing Retained Earnings and stockholders' equity. Therefore, they have **debit** balances (opposite of the balance in Retained Earnings). That is, to increase an expense, you debit it, thereby decreasing net income and Retained Earnings. Recording an expense results in either decreasing an asset (such as Supplies when used) or increasing a liability (such as Wages Payable when money is owed to employees).

A	=	L	+	SE
− or +				− (+ expense ↓ RE)

- When revenues exceed expenses, the company reports net income, increasing Retained Earnings and stockholders' equity. However, when expenses exceed revenues, a net loss results that decreases Retained Earnings and thus stockholders' equity.

The steps to follow in analyzing transactions presented in Chapter 2 are now modified to determine the effects of earning revenues and incurring expenses. Now, as shown in Exhibit 3.5, when a transaction occurs, the questions to ask are:

- ***Is a revenue earned (i.e., did the company perform or deliver to customers)?*** If the answer is yes, then a **revenue** account is increased (credited). Then identify what the company **received** in the exchange and the other accounts affected.
- ***Is an expense incurred (i.e., did the company incur an expense to generate the revenue)?*** If the answer is yes, then an **expense** is increased (debited). Then identify what the company **gave** in the exchange and the other accounts affected.
- ***If revenue was not earned or expense was not incurred, what was received and what was given?***

EXHIBIT 3.5

Steps in Analyzing the Effects of Transactions

Step 1: Identify and Classify Accounts and Effects

- **Identify the accounts (by title) affected,** making sure that at least two accounts change.
  Ask yourself: Was revenue earned (if so, then what was received)?
  Was an expense incurred (if so, then what was given)?
  If no revenue or expense was affected, what was received and given?
- **Classify them by type of account.** Was each account an asset (A), a liability (L), a stockholders' equity (SE), a revenue (R), or an expense (E)?
- **Determine the direction of the effect.** Did the account increase [+] or decrease [−]?

Step 2: Verify Entries and Accounting Equation Balance

- **Verify that debits = credits.**
- **Verify that the accounting equation (A = L + SE) remains in balance.**

Analyzing Papa John's Transactions

Now we continue activities for Papa John's, building on the company's balance sheet presented at the end of Chapter 2. It included only investing and financing transactions occurring during the January accounting cycle. Using the transaction analysis steps in Exhibit 3.5, we analyze, record, and post to the T-accounts the effects of this chapter's operating activities that also occurred during the month of January. In Chapter 4, we complete the accounting cycle with the activities at the end of the period (on January 31). All amounts are in thousands of dollars and the effects are posted to the appropriate T-accounts at the end of the illustration.

(*a*) Papa John's restaurants sold pizza to customers for $36,000 cash and sold $30,000 in supplies to franchised restaurants, receiving $21,000 cash with the rest due on account.

Equality checks:
(1) Debits $66,000 = Credits $66,000;
(2) The accounting equation is in balance.

		Debit	Credit
(a)	Cash (+A) [$36,000 + $21,000]	57,000	
	Accounts Receivable (+A)	9,000	
	Restaurant Sales Revenue (+R, +SE)		66,000

Assets		=	Liabilities	+	Stockholders' Equity	
Cash	+57,000				Restaurant Sales Revenue (+R)	+66,000
Accounts Receivable	+ 9,000					

(*b*) The cost of the dough, sauce, cheese, and other supplies for the restaurant sales in *(a)* was $30,000.

Equality checks:
(1) Debits $30,000 = Credits $30,000;
(2) The accounting equation is in balance.

		Debit	Credit
(b)	Cost of Sales (+E, −SE)	30,000	
	Supplies (−A)		30,000

Assets		=	Liabilities	+	Stockholders' Equity	
Supplies	−30,000				Cost of Sales (+E)	−30,000

(*c*) Papa John's sold new franchises for $400 cash, earning $100 immediately by performing services for franchisees; the rest will be earned over the next several months.

Equality checks:
(1) Debits $400 = Credits $400;
(2) The accounting equation is in balance.

		Debit	Credit
(c)	Cash (+A)	400	
	Franchise Fee Revenue (+R, +SE)		100
	Unearned Franchise Fees (+L)		300

Assets		=	Liabilities		+	Stockholders' Equity	
Cash	+400		Unearned Franchise Fees	+300		Franchise Fee Revenue (+R)	+100

(*d*) In January, Papa John's paid $7,000 for utilities, repairs, and fuel for delivery vehicles, all considered general and administrative expenses incurred during the month.

	Debit	Credit
(d) General and Administrative Expenses (+E, −SE)	7,000	
Cash (−A)		7,000

Assets		=	Liabilities	+	Stockholders' Equity	
Cash	−7,000				General and Administrative Expenses (+E)	−7,000

Equality checks:
(1) Debits $7,000 = Credits $7,000;
(2) The accounting equation is in balance.

(*e*) Papa John's commissaries ordered and received $29,000 in supplies, paying $9,000 in cash and owing the rest on account to suppliers.

	Debit	Credit
(e) Supplies (+A)	29,000	
Cash (−A)		9,000
Accounts Payable (+L)		20,000

Assets		=	Liabilities		+	Stockholders' Equity
Cash	− 9,000		Accounts Payable	+20,000		
Supplies	+29,000					

Equality checks:
(1) Debits $29,000 = Credits $29,000;
(2) The accounting equation is in balance.

(*f*) Papa John's paid $14,000 cash to employees for their work in January.

	Debit	Credit
(f) Salaries Expense (+E, −SE)	14,000	
Cash (−A)		14,000

Assets		=	Liabilities	+	Stockholders' Equity	
Cash	−14,000				Salaries Expense (+E)	−14,000

Equality checks:
(1) Debits $14,000 = Credits $14,000;
(2) The accounting equation is in balance.

(*g*) At the beginning of January, Papa John's paid the following, all of which are considered prepaid expenses when paid (any adjustments will be made in Chapter 4):

- $2,000 for insurance (covering the next four months beginning January 1),
- $6,000 for renting space in shopping centers (over the next three months beginning January 1), and
- $1,000 for advertising (to be run in February).

	Debit	Credit
(g) Prepaid Expenses (+A)	9,000	
Cash (-A)		9,000

Assets		=	Liabilities	+	Stockholders' Equity
Cash	−9,000				
Prepaid Expenses	+9,000				

Equality checks:
(1) Debits $9,000 = Credits $9,000;
(2) The accounting equation is in balance.

(*h*) Papa John's sold land with an historical cost of $1,000 for $4,000 cash.[5]

Equality checks:
(1) Debits $4,000 = Credits $4,000;
(2) The accounting equation is in balance.

		Debit	Credit
(h)	Cash (+A)	4,000	
	Property and Equipment (−A)		1,000
	Gain on Sale of Land (+R, +SE)		3,000

Assets		=	Liabilities	+	Stockholders' Equity	
Cash	+4,000				Gain on Sale of Land (+R)	+3,000
Property and Equipment	− 1,000					

(*i*) Papa John's received $15,500 in franchisee fees based on their weekly sales; $12,800 of the amount was due from franchisees' sales recorded as accounts receivable in December and the rest is from January sales.

Equality checks:
(1) Debits $15,500 = Credits $15,500;
(2) The accounting equation is in balance.

		Debit	Credit
(i)	Cash (+A)	15,500	
	Accounts Receivable (−A)		12,800
	Franchise Fee Revenue (+R, +SE)		2,700

Assets		=	Liabilities	+	Stockholders' Equity	
Cash	+15,500				Franchise Fee Revenue (+R)	+2,700
Accounts Receivable	− 12,800					

(*j*) Papa John's paid $10,000 on accounts owed to suppliers.

Equality checks:
(1) Debits $10,000 = Credits $10,000;
(2) The accounting equation is in balance.

		Debit	Credit
(j)	Accounts Payable (−L)	10,000	
	Cash (−A)		10,000

Assets		=	Liabilities		+	Stockholders' Equity
Cash	−10,000		Accounts Payable	−10,000		

(*k*) Papa John's received $1,000 in cash for interest earned on investments.

Equality checks:
(1) Debits $1,000 = Credits $1,000;
(2) The accounting equation is in balance.

		Debit	Credit
(k)	Cash (+A)	1,000	
	Investment Income (+R, +SE)		1,000

Assets		=	Liabilities	+	Stockholders' Equity	
Cash	+1,000				Investment Income (+R)	+1,000

[5]This is an example of a peripheral activity; it will be covered in more depth in Chapter 8.

EXHIBIT 3.6

T-Accounts

Balance Sheet Accounts (beginning balances are the ending balances in Exhibit 2.8)

+ Cash (A) −			
Bal.	13,000		
(*a*)	57,000	7,000	(*d*)
(*c*)	400	9,000	(*e*)
(*h*)	4,000	14,000	(*f*)
(*i*)	15,500	9,000	(*g*)
(*k*)	1,000	10,000	(*j*)
Bal.	41,900		

+ Accounts Receivable (A) −			
Bal.	24,000		
(*a*)	9,000	12,800	(*i*)
Bal.	20,200		

+ Supplies (A) −			
Bal.	17,000		
(*e*)	29,000	30,000	(*b*)
Bal.	16,000		

+ Prepaid Expenses (A) −			
Bal.	10,000		
(*g*)	9,000		
Bal.	19,000		

+ Property and Equipment (A) −			
Bal.	200,000		
		1,000	(*h*)
Bal.	199,000		

− Accounts Payable (L) +			
		29,000	Bal.
(*j*)	10,000	20,000	(*e*)
		39,000	Bal.

− Unearned Franchise Fees (L) +			
		6,000	Bal.
		300	(*c*)
		6,300	Bal.

Income Statement Accounts (beginning balances start at zero)

− Restaurant Sales Revenue (R) +			
		0	Bal.
		66,000	(*a*)
		66,000	Bal.

− Franchise Fee Revenue (R) +			
		0	Bal.
		100	(*c*)
		2,700	(*i*)
		2,800	Bal.

− Gain on Sale of Land (R) +			
		0	Bal.
		3,000	(*h*)
		3,000	Bal.

− Investment Income (R) +			
		0	Bal.
		1,000	(*k*)
		1,000	Bal.

+ Cost of Sales (E) −			
Bal.	0		
(*b*)	30,000		
Bal.	30,000		

+ Salaries Expense (E) −			
Bal.	0		
(*f*)	14,000		
Bal.	14,000		

+ General and Administrative Expenses (E) −			
Bal.	0		
(*d*)	7,000		
Bal.	7,000		

Exhibit 3.6 shows the T-accounts that changed during the period because of transactions (*a*) through (*k*). The balances of all other accounts remained the same. Note that the amounts from Papa John's balance sheet at the end of Chapter 2 (Exhibit 2.8) have been included as the beginning balances in Exhibit 3.6 for assets, liabilities, and stockholders' equity accounts. On the other hand, income statement accounts have a zero beginning balance so that revenue and expense activities can accumulate over the period.

PAUSE FOR **FEEDBACK**

We just illustrated the steps in analyzing and recording transactions, including those involving earning revenue and incurring expenses.

SELF-STUDY **QUIZ**

Step 1: Identify and Classify Accounts and Effects

- **Identify the accounts (by title) affected,** making sure that at least two accounts change. Ask yourself:
  Was revenue earned (if so, then what was received)
  Was an expense incurred (if so, then what was given)?
  If no revenue or expense was affected, what was received and given?
- **Classify them by type of account.** Was each account an asset (A), a liability (L), a stockholders' equity (SE), a revenue (R), or an expense (E)?
- **Determine the direction of the effect.** Did the account increase [+] or decrease [–]?

Step 2: Verify Entries and Accounting Equation Balance

- **Verify that debits = credits.**
- **Verify that the accounting equation (A = L + SE) remains in balance.**

Now it's your turn. Analyze and record the journal entries for each of the selected **June** transactions for Florida Flippers, Inc., a scuba diving and instruction business. Then post the effects to the T-accounts. Account titles and beginning balances are provided in the T-accounts. Be sure to check that debits equal credits in each journal entry and that the accounting equation remains in balance.

a. In June, new customers paid Florida Flippers $8,200 in cash for diving trips; $5,200 was for trips made in June, and the rest is for trips that will be provided in July.

b. In June, customers paid $3,900 in cash for instruction they received in May.

c. At the beginning of June, Florida Flippers paid a total of $6,000 cash for insurance to cover the months of June, July, and August.

d. In June, Florida Flippers paid $4,000 in wages to employees who worked in June.

Journal Entries:

	Account Titles	Debit	Credit
a.			

b.			

c.			

d.			

+ Cash (A) –	
Beg. 25,000	
End.	

+ Accounts Receivable (A) –	
Beg. 4,500	
End.	

– Prepaid Insurance (L) +	
Beg. 0	
End.	

– Unearned Revenue (L) +	
	0 Beg.
	End.

– Diving Trip Revenue (R) +	
	0 Beg.
	End.

+ Wages Expense (E) –	
Beg. 0	
End.	

After you have completed your answers, check them with the solutions at the bottom of the page.

Solutions to SELF-STUDY QUIZ

	Account Titles	Debit	Credit
a.	Cash (+A)	8,200	
	Diving Trip Revenue (+R, +SE)		5,200
	Unearned Revenue (+L)		3,000
b.	Cash (+A)	3,900	
	Accounts Receivable (+A)		3,900

	Account Titles	Debit	Credit
c.	Prepaid Insurance (+A)	6,000	
	Cash (−A)		6,000
d.	Wages Expense (+E, −SE)	4,000	
	Cash (−A)		4,000

+ Cash (A) –			
Beg.	25,000		
(*a*)	8,200	6,000	(*c*)
(*b*)	3,900	4,000	(*d*)
End.	27,100		

+ Accounts Receivable (A) –			
Beg.	4,500		
		3,900	(*b*)
End.	600		

– Prepaid Insurance (L) +			
Beg.	0		
(*c*)	6,000		
End.	6,000		

– Unearned Revenue (L) +			
		0	Beg.
		3,000	(*a*)
		3,000	End.

– Diving Trip Revenue (R) +			
		0	Beg.
		5,200	(*a*)
		5,200	End.

+ Wages Expense (E) –			
Beg.	0		
(*d*)	4,000		
End.	4,000		

LEARNING OBJECTIVE 5
Prepare financial statements.

HOW ARE FINANCIAL STATEMENTS PREPARED AND ANALYZED?

Based on the January transactions that have just been posted to the T-accounts, we can now prepare financial statements reflecting the operating activities for January. Recall from prior chapters what the four statements are and how they relate to each other.

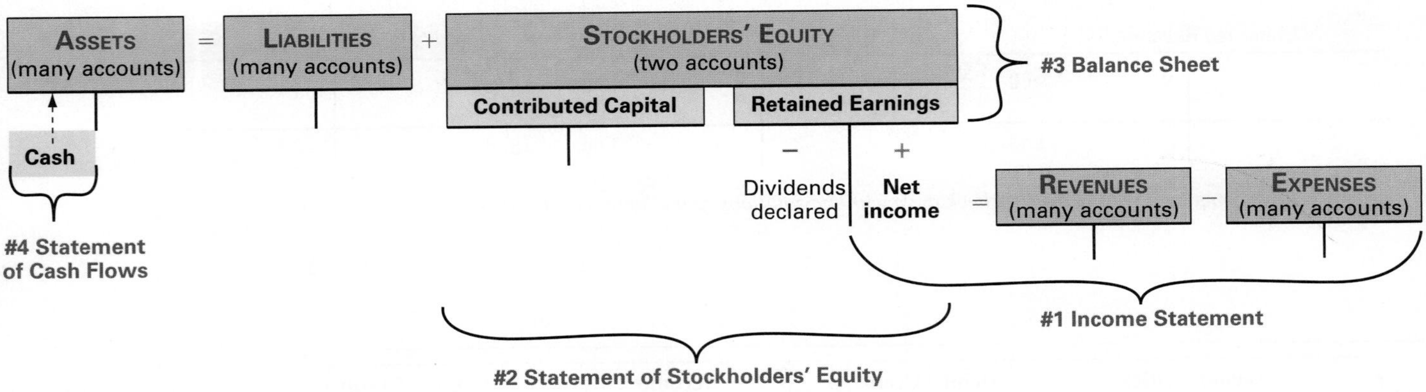

Because net income is a component of Retained Earnings on the balance sheet, it is necessary to compute net income first by preparing the income statement (#1). The statement of stockholders' equity (#2) is then prepared because it reports the changes and ending balances in Contributed Capital and Retained Earnings, providing the connection to the balance sheet (#3). Finally, the sources and uses of cash are reported on the statement of cash flows (#4), and the ending balance for Cash on the statement equals the Cash balance on the balance sheet.

Statement	Formula
#1 Income Statement	Revenues − Expenses = **Net Income**
#2 Statement of Stockholders' Equity	Beginning Retained Earnings + **Net Income** − Dividends Declared = Ending Retained Earnings Beginning Contributed Capital + Stock Issuances − Stock Repurchases = Ending Contributed Capital Ending **Stockholders' Equity**
#3 Balance Sheet	Assets = Liabilities + **Stockholders' Equity** (includes **Cash**)
#4 Statement of Cash Flows	Cash provided by (or used in) Operating Activities +/− Cash provided by (or used in) Investing Activities +/− Cash provided by (or used in) Financing Activities Change in Cash + Beginning Cash Ending **Cash**

It is important to note that the statements we are about to present for Papa John's at the end of January **do not at this point reflect all revenues earned or expenses incurred in January.** For example:

- The account Prepaid Expenses includes rent and insurance covering January and future months, but the expenses are not yet recorded for the amounts used in January. This is true of the equipment used during the month as well. Until adjusted, assets are overstated and expenses are understated.

- We have not calculated income taxes for the amount incurred in January and owed within the next quarter. Thus, both liabilities and expenses are understated.
- Unearned Franchise Fees (a liability account) has not been updated for any amount of Franchise Fee Revenue earned in January. In this case, the liability is overstated and revenues are understated.

Chapter 4 will describe the adjustment process to update the accounting records. After the adjustments are recorded, the amount of tax expense will be determined and the statements will reflect generally accepted accounting principles following accrual basis accounting. Until then, here are the **unadjusted financial statements for Papa John's at the end of January.**

Classified Income Statement

PAPA JOHN'S INTERNATIONAL, INC.
Consolidated Statement of Income (before adjustments)
For the Month Ended January 31, 2009
(dollars in thousands)

Operating Revenues	
Restaurant sales revenue	$66,000
Franchise fee revenue	2,800
Total revenues	68,800
Operating Expenses	
Cost of sales	30,000
Salaries expense	14,000
General and administrative expenses	7,000
Supplies expense	0
Rent expense	0
Insurance expense	0
Utilities expense	0
Depreciation expense	0
Other operating expenses	0
Total expenses	51,000
Operating Income	17,800
Other Items	
Investment income	1,000
Interest expense	(0)
Gain on sale of land	3,000
Income before Income Taxes	21,800
Income tax expense	0
Net Income	**$21,800**
Earnings per Share (for the month)	$ 0.78

Note:
Normally, accounts with zero balances are not included on formal statements. However, we include them here to indicate that there are numerous expenses and revenues to be determined and recorded in the adjustment process described in Chapter 4.

$21,800,000 unadjusted net income divided by approximately 28,100,000 shares (from Papa John's annual report)

In our illustration for Papa John's, the company earned positive income before income taxes of $21,800,000 in January, nearly 32% of operating revenues ($21,800,000 income before income taxes ÷ $68,800,000 total revenues) before adjustments.

Statement of Stockholders' Equity

The statement of stockholders' equity ties the information on Papa John's income statement to the balance sheet. Any additional stock issuances affect Contributed Capital; net income (from the income statement) and any declared dividends affect Retained Earnings.

PAPA JOHN'S INTERNATIONAL, INC.
Consolidated Statement of Stockholders' Equity (before adjustments)
Month Ended January 31, 2009
(dollars in thousands)

		Contributed Capital	Retained Earnings	Total Stockholders' Equity
	Beginning balance, December 31, 2008	$7,000	$123,000	$130,000
From Event (a) in Chapter 2 →	Additional stock issuances	2,000		2,000
From the income statement →	Net income (prior to adjustments)		21,800	21,800
From Event (f) in Chapter 2 →	Dividends declared		(3,000)	(3,000)
Included on the balance sheet that follows →	Ending balance, January 31, 2009	$9,000	$141,800	$150,800

Classified Balance Sheet

Finally, we can revise the balance sheet from Chapter 2 to reflect the effects of the operating activities discussed in this chapter. Accounts that were not affected by operating activities in this chapter retain the same balances as in Exhibit 2.8, except for Retained Earnings. The $141,800,000 ending balance of Retained Earnings in the statement of stockholders' equity flows into the Stockholders' Equity section of the balance sheet. Accounts that were affected by this chapter's operating activities reflect the revised balances from the T-accounts in Exhibit 3.6. We explore the relationships among the financial statements further in the next chapter.

PAPA JOHN'S INTERNATIONAL, INC.
Consolidated Balance Sheet (before adjustments)
January 31, 2009
(dollars in thousands)

ASSETS		
Current Assets		
Cash	$ 41,900	
Accounts receivable	20,200	
Supplies	16,000	
Prepaid expenses	19,000	
Other current assets	13,000	
Total current assets	110,100	
Investments	2,000	
Property and equipment (net)	199,000	
Notes receivable	11,000	
Intangibles	77,000	
Other assets	36,000	
Total Assets	**$435,100**	
LIABILITIES AND STOCKHOLDERS' EQUITY		
Current Liabilities		
Accounts payable	$ 39,000	
Dividends payable	3,000	
Accrued expenses payable	71,000	
Total current liabilities	113,000	
Unearned franchise fees	6,300	
Notes payable	138,000	
Other long-term liabilities	27,000	
Total liabilities	284,300	
Stockholders' Equity		
Contributed capital	9,000	} *From the Statement of Stockholders' Equity*
Retained earnings	141,800	}
Total stockholders' equity	150,800	
Total liabilities and stockholders' equity	**$435,100**	

Reporting More Detailed Financial Information in the Notes

FINANCIAL ANALYSIS

Many companies, especially very large ones, operate in more than one geographic area. These companies are often called **multinationals**. A consolidated income statement that is based on aggregated data may not prove useful to investors seeking to assess possible risks and returns from companies operating in foreign markets. The same may be true if a company operates more than a single business. Therefore, many companies provide additional information about geographic and business segments in notes to the financial statements. An excerpt from Papa John's 2008 annual report provides information on its geographic segments:

Notes to Consolidated Financial Statements

21. Segment Information

We have defined five reportable segments: domestic restaurants, domestic commissaries, domestic franchising, international operations, and variable interest entities. . . .

(in thousands)	**2008**	**2007**	**2006**
Revenues from external customers:			
Domestic company-owned restaurants	$ 533,255	$ 504,330	$ 447,938
Domestic commissaries	429,068	399,099	413,075
Domestic franchising	61,304	60,041	58,971
International	38,717	31,174	23,209
Variable interest entities	8,328	7,131	7,859
All others	61,415	61,820	50,505
Total revenues from external customers	$1,132,087	$1,063,595	$1,001,557

Better Ingredients. Better Pizza.

REAL WORLD EXCERPT

Annual Report

Operating Activities

FOCUS ON CASH FLOWS

Chapter 2 presented a partial statement of cash flows for Papa John's—only its investing and financing activities. Recall that investing activities relate primarily to transactions affecting long-term assets; financing activities are those from bank borrowings, stock issuances, and dividend payments to stockholders.

In this chapter, we focus on cash flows from operating activities reporting **cash from** operating sources, primarily customers, and **cash to** suppliers and others involved in operations. The accounts most often associated with operating activities are current assets, such as Accounts Receivable, Inventories, and Prepaid Expenses, and current liabilities, such as Accounts Payable, Wages Payable, and Unearned Revenue.

We present the Cash Flows from Operating Activities section of the statement of cash flows using the **direct method**—cash receipts and cash disbursements. However, most companies report cash from operations using the **indirect method,** which will be discussed in later chapters.

		Effect on Cash Flows
Operating activities		
Cash received:	Customers	+
	Interest and dividends on investments	+
Cash paid:	Suppliers	−
	Employees	−
	Interest on debt obligations	−
	Income taxes	−
Investing activities	(see Chapter 2)	
Financing activities	(see Chapter 2)	

(continued)

When a transaction affects cash, it is included on the statement of cash flows. When a transaction does not affect cash, such as acquiring a building with a long-term mortgage note payable or selling goods on account to customers, there is no cash effect to include on the statement. **If you see Cash in a transaction, it will be reflected on the statement of cash flows.** Therefore, when preparing the Cash Flows from Operating Activities section of the statement of cash flows using the direct method, it is easiest to look at the activities in the Cash T-account. We use O for operating activities, I for investing activities, and F for financing activities for the transactions in this chapter affecting cash.

			+ Cash (A)	−			
		Bal.	13,000				
From customers	O	(*a*)	57,000	7,000	(*d*)	O	To suppliers
From franchisees	O	(*c*)	400	9,000	(*e*)	O	To suppliers
Investing activity	I	(*h*)	4,000	14,000	(*f*)	O	To employees
From franchisees	O	(*i*)	15,500	9,000	(*g*)	O	To suppliers
From investment income	O	(*k*)	1,000	10,000	(*j*)	O	To suppliers
		Bal.	41,900				

PAUSE FOR **FEEDBACK**

As we discussed, every transaction affecting cash can be classified either as an operating, investing, or financing effect.

Operating effects relate to receipts of cash from customers, payments to suppliers (employees, utilities, and other suppliers of goods and services for operating the business), and any interest paid or investment income received.

Investing effects relate to purchasing/selling investments or property and equipment or lending funds to/receiving repayment from others.

Financing effects relate to borrowing or repaying banks, issuing stock to investors, repurchasing stock from investors, or paying dividends to investors.

SELF-STUDY **QUIZ**

Mattel, Inc., designs, manufactures, and markets a broad variety of toys (e.g., Barbie, Hot Wheels, Fisher-Price brands, and American Girl dolls) worldwide. Indicate whether these transactions from a recent statement of cash flows were operating (O), investing (I), or financing (F) activities and the direction of their effects on cash (+ for increases in cash; − for decreases in cash):

Transactions	Type of Activity (O, I, or F)	Effect on Cash Flows (+ or −)
1. Purchases of property, plant, and equipment		
2. Receipts from customers		
3. Payments of dividends		
4. Payments to employees		
5. Receipts of investment income		

After you have completed your answers, check them with the solutions at the bottom of the page.

Solutions to SELF-STUDY QUIZ

1. I − 2. O + 3. F − 4. O − 5. O +

Total Asset Turnover Ratio

KEY RATIO ANALYSIS

LEARNING OBJECTIVE 6

Compute and interpret the total asset turnover ratio.

In Chapter 2, we discussed the current ratio, a tool to evaluate the company's ability to pay its short-term obligations with current assets—a liquidity measure. We now introduce a ratio to assess managers' use of all of the company's assets to improve earnings. As we will see in other chapters, similar analysis of the use of each specific type of asset (for example, inventory turnover and receivables turnover) provides additional information for decision makers.

ANALYTICAL QUESTION

How effective is management in generating sales from assets (resources)?

RATIO AND COMPARISONS

$$\textbf{Total Asset Turnover Ratio} = \frac{\textbf{Sales (or Operating) Revenues}}{\textbf{Average Total Assets*}}$$

*To compute "average": (Beginning balance + Ending balance)/2

The 2008 ratio for Papa John's is (dollars in thousands):

$$\frac{\$1{,}132{,}000}{(\$402{,}000 + \$387{,}000)/2} = \frac{\$1{,}132{,}000}{\$394{,}000} = 2.87$$

COMPARISONS OVER TIME		
Papa John's		
2006	**2007**	**2008**
2.74	2.72	2.87

COMPARISONS WITH COMPETITORS	
Domino's Inc.	**Yum! Brands***
2008	**2008**
3.04	1.64

*Yum! Brands is the parent company of Pizza Hut, KFC, Taco Bell, and others.

Selected Focus Companies' Total Asset Turnover Ratios for 2008

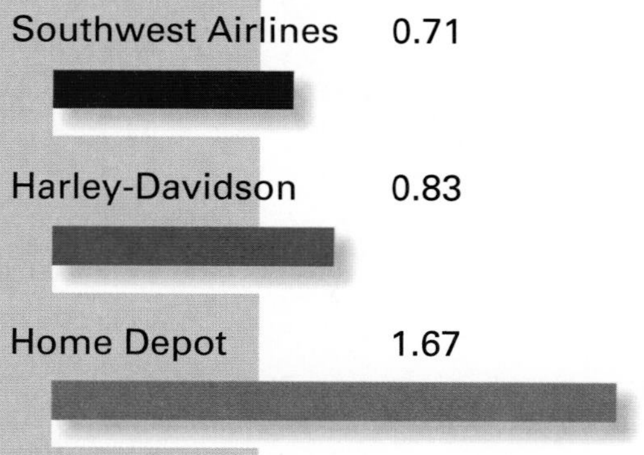

INTERPRETATIONS

In General The total asset turnover ratio measures the sales generated per dollar of assets. A high asset turnover ratio signifies efficient management of assets; a low asset turnover ratio signifies less efficient management. A company's products and business strategy contribute significantly to its asset turnover ratio. However, when competitors are similar, management's ability to control the firm's assets is vital in determining its success. Stronger financial performance improves the asset turnover ratio.

Creditors and security analysts use this ratio to assess a company's effectiveness at controlling both current and noncurrent assets. In a well-run business, creditors expect the ratio to fluctuate due to seasonal upswings and downturns. For example, as inventory is built up prior to a heavy sales season, companies need to borrow funds. The asset turnover ratio declines with this increase in assets. Eventually, the season's high sales provide the cash needed to repay the loans. The asset turnover ratio then rises with the increased sales.

Focus Company Analysis Papa John's asset turnover ratio has increased slightly since 2006, suggesting an increase in management effectiveness in using assets to generate sales. In fact, Papa John's reported that as the number of stores in a geographic area increased, regional commissaries showed higher sales, allowing management to use the commissary assets more efficiently.

Compared to its main competitors, Papa John's 2008 total asset turnover ratio falls in the middle. The difference in ratios is due in part to differences in operating strategy: Yum! Brands (which includes Pizza Hut, KFC, and Taco Bell) operates primarily eat-in restaurants, so it must invest more in its facilities (that is, it is more asset-intensive). Domino's, the leading pizza delivery company, operates primarily from rented facilities (that is, it is less asset-intensive) and is much larger than Papa John's, thus allowing for greater efficiencies.

A Few Cautions While the total asset turnover ratio may decrease due to seasonal fluctuations, a declining ratio may also be caused by changes in corporate policies leading to a rising level of assets. Examples include relaxing credit policies for new customers or reducing collection efforts in accounts receivable. A detailed analysis of the changes in the key components of assets is needed to determine the causes of a change in the asset turnover ratio and thus management's decisions.

DEMONSTRATION CASE

This case is a continuation of the Terrific Lawn Maintenance Corporation case introduced in Chapter 2. In that chapter, the company was established and supplies, property, and equipment were purchased. Terrific Lawn is now ready for business. The balance sheet at April 7, 2010, based on the first week of investing and financing activities (from Chapter 2) is as follows:

TERRIFIC LAWN MAINTENANCE CORPORATION
Balance Sheet
At April 7, 2010

Assets		**Liabilities**	
Current Assets		*Current Liabilities*	
Cash	$ 3,800	Notes payable	$ 4,400
Notes receivable	1,250	Total current liabilities	4,400
Total current assets	5,050		
Equipment	4,600	**Stockholders' Equity**	
Land	3,750	Contributed capital	9,000
Total assets	$13,400	Total liabilities and stockholders' equity	$13,400

The additional following activities occurred during the rest of April 2010:

a. Purchased and used gasoline for mowers and edgers, paying $90 in cash at a local gas station.

b. In early April, received from the city $1,600 cash in advance for lawn maintenance service for April through July ($400 each month). The entire amount was recorded as Unearned Revenue.

c. In early April, purchased $300 of insurance covering six months, April through September. The entire payment was recorded as Prepaid Expenses.

d. Mowed lawns for residential customers who are billed every two weeks. A total of $5,200 of service was billed in April.

e. Residential customers paid $3,500 on their accounts.

f. Paid wages every two weeks. Total cash paid in April was $3,900.

g. Received a bill for $320 from the local gas station for additional gasoline purchased on account and used in April.

h. Paid $700 principal and $40 interest on notes owed to XYZ Lawn Supply and the hardware store.

i. Paid $100 on accounts payable.

j. Collected $1,250 principal and $12 interest on the note owed by the city to Terrific Lawn Maintenance Corporation.

Required:

1. *a.* On a separate sheet of paper, set up T-accounts for Cash, Accounts Receivable, Notes Receivable, Prepaid Expenses, Equipment, Land, Accounts Payable, Notes Payable, Unearned Revenue (same as deferred revenue), Contributed Capital, Retained Earnings, Mowing Revenue, Interest Revenue, Wages Expense, Fuel Expense, and Interest Expense. Beginning balances for the balance sheet accounts should be taken from the preceding balance sheet. Beginning balances for operating accounts are $0. Indicate these balances on the T-accounts.

b. Analyze each transaction, referring to the expanded transaction analysis model presented in this chapter.

c. On a separate sheet of paper, prepare journal entries in chronological order and indicate their effects on the accounting model (Assets = Liabilities + Stockholders' Equity). Include the equality checks: (1) Debits = Credits, and (2) the accounting equation is in balance.

d. Enter the effects of each transaction in the appropriate T-accounts. Identify each amount with its letter in the preceding list of activities.

e. Compute balances in each of the T-accounts.

2. On the Cash T-account, identify each transaction as O for operating activity, I for investing activity, or F for financing activity.
3. Use the amounts in the T-accounts to prepare a full set of financial statements—income statement, statement of stockholders' equity, balance sheet, and statement of cash flows—for Terrific Lawn Maintenance Corporation at April 30, 2010. Refer to the cash flow statement presented in Chapter 2 for the investing and financing activities. (Adjustments to accounts will be presented in Chapter 4.)

Now check your answers with the following suggested solution.

SUGGESTED SOLUTION

1. Transaction analysis, journal entries, and T-accounts:

(*a*) Fuel Expense (+E, − SE)	90	
Cash (−A)		90

Assets		=	Liabilities	+	Stockholders' Equity	
Cash	−90				Fuel Expense (+E)	−90

Equality checks:
(1) Debits $90 = Credits $90;
(2) The accounting equation is in balance.

(*b*) Cash (+A)	1,600	
Unearned Revenue (+L)		1,600

Assets		=	Liabilities		+	Stockholders' Equity
Cash	+1,600		Unearned Revenue	+1,600		

Equality checks:
(1) Debits $1,600 = Credits $1,600;
(2) The accounting equation is in balance.

(*c*) Prepaid Expenses (+A)	300	
Cash (−A)		300

Assets		=	Liabilities	+	Stockholders' Equity
Cash	−300				
Prepaid Expenses	+300				

Equality checks:
(1) Debits $300 = Credits $300;
(2) The accounting equation is in balance.

(*d*) Accounts Receivable (+A)	5,200	
Mowing Revenue (+R, +SE)		5,200

Assets		=	Liabilities	+	Stockholders' Equity	
Accounts Receivable	+5,200				Mowing Revenue (+R)	+ 5,200

Equality checks:
(1) Debits $5,200 = Credits $5,200;
(2) The accounting equation is in balance.

(*e*) Cash (+A)	3,500	
Accounts Receivable (−A)		3,500

Assets		=	Liabilities	+	Stockholders' Equity
Cash	+3,500				
Accounts Receivable	−3,500				

Equality checks:
(1) Debits $3,500 = Credits $3,500;
(2) The accounting equation is in balance.

Equality checks:
(1) Debits $3,900 = Credits $3,900;
(2) The accounting equation is in balance.

(*f*)	Wages Expense (+E, −SE)	3,900	
	Cash (−A)		3,900

Assets		=	Liabilities		+	Stockholders' Equity	
Cash	−3,900					Wages Expense (+E)	−3,900

Equality checks:
(1) Debits $320 = Credits $320;
(2) The accounting equation is in balance.

(*g*)	Fuel Expense (+E, −SE)	320	
	Accounts Payable (+L)		320

Assets		=	Liabilities		+	Stockholders' Equity	
			Accounts Payable	+320		Fuel Expense (+E)	−320

Equality checks:
(1) Debits $740 = Credits $740;
(2) The accounting equation is in balance.

(*h*)	Interest Expense (+E, −SE)	40	
	Notes Payable (−L)	700	
	Cash (−A)		740

Assets		=	Liabilities		+	Stockholders' Equity	
Cash	−740		Notes Payable	−700		Interest Expense (+E)	−40

Equality checks:
(1) Debits $100 = Credits $100;
(2) The accounting equation is in balance.

(*i*)	Accounts Payable (−L)	100	
	Cash (−A)		100

Assets		=	Liabilities		+	Stockholders' Equity	
Cash	−100		Accounts Payable	−100			

Equality checks:
(1) Debits $1,262 = Credits $1,262;
(2) The accounting equation is in balance.

(*j*)	Cash (+A)	1,262	
	Notes Receivable (−A)		1,250
	Interest Revenue (+R, +SE)		12

Assets		=	Liabilities		+	Stockholders' Equity	
Cash	+1,262					Interest Revenue (+R)	+12
Notes Receivable	−1,250						

T-Accounts:

Assets

+ Cash –			
Beg.	3,800		
(*b*)	1,600	90	(*a*)
(*e*)	3,500	300	(*c*)
(*j*)	1,262	3,900	(*f*)
		740	(*h*)
		100	(*i*)
Bal.	5,032		

+ Accounts Receivable –			
Beg.	0		
(*d*)	5,200	3,500	(*e*)
Bal.	1,700		

+ Notes Receivable –			
Beg.	1,250	1,250	(*j*)
Bal.	0		

+ Prepaid Expenses –			
Beg.	0		
(*c*)	300		
Bal.	300		

+ Equipment –			
Beg.	4,600		
Bal.	4,600		

+ Land –			
Beg.	3,750		
Bal.	3,750		

Liabilities

– Accounts Payable +			
		0	Beg.
(*i*)	100	320	(*g*)
		220	Bal.

– Notes Payable +			
		4,400	Beg.
(*h*)	700		
		3,700	Bal.

– Unearned Revenue +			
		0	Beg.
		1,600	(*b*)
		1,600	Bal.

Stockholders' Equity

– Contributed Capital +			
		9,000	Beg.
		9,000	Bal.

– Retained Earnings +			
		0	Beg.
		0	Bal.

Revenues

– Mowing Revenue +			
		0	Beg.
		5,200	(*d*)
		5,200	Bal.

– Interest Revenue +			
		0	Beg.
		12	(*j*)
		12	Bal.

Expenses

+ Wages Expense –			
Beg.	0		
(*f*)	3,900		
Bal.	3,900		

+ Fuel Expense –			
Beg.	0		
(*a*)	90		
(*g*)	320		
Bal.	410		

+ Interest Expense –			
Beg.	0		
(*h*)	40		
Bal.	40		

2. Cash flow activities identified (O = operating, I = investing, and F = financing):

	+ Cash –				
	Beg.	3,800			
O	(*b*)	1,600	90	(*a*)	O
O	(*e*)	3,500	300	(*c*)	O
$12 O and $1,250 I	(*j*)	1,262	3,900	(*f*)	O
			740	(*h*)	$40 O and $700 F
			100	(*i*)	O
	Bal.	5,032			

3. Financial statements:

TERRIFIC LAWN MAINTENANCE CORPORATION
Income Statement
For the Month Ended April 30, 2010

Operating Revenues	
Mowing revenue	$5,200
Operating Expenses	
Fuel expense	410
Wages expense	3,900
	4,310
Operating income	**890**
Other items	
Interest revenue	12
Interest expense	(40)
Pretax income	862
Income tax expense	0
Net Income	**$ 862**
Earnings per share for the month	**$ .57**

($862 net income divided by 1,500 shares outstanding)

TERRIFIC LAWN MAINTENANCE CORPORATION
Statement of Stockholders' Equity
For the Month Ended April 30, 2010

	Contributed Capital	Retained Earnings	Total Stockholders' Equity
Balance, April 1, 2010	$ 0	$ 0	$ 0
Additional contributions	9,000		9,000
Net income		862	862
Dividends declared		(0)	(0)
Balance, April 30, 2010	$9,000	$ 862	$9,862

TERRIFIC LAWN MAINTENANCE CORPORATION
Balance Sheet
April 30, 2010

Assets		**Liabilities**	
Current Assets		*Current Liabilities*	
Cash	$ 5,032	Accounts payable	$ 220
Accounts receivable	1,700	Notes payable	3,700
Prepaid expenses	300	Unearned revenue	1,600
Total current assets	7,032	Total current liabilities	5,520
Equipment	4,600	**Stockholders' Equity**	
Land	3,750	Contributed capital	9,000
		Retained earnings	862
		Total stockholders' equity	9,862
Total assets	**$15,382**	**Total liabilities and stockholders' equity**	**$15,382**

TERRIFIC LAWN MAINTENANCE CORPORATION
Statement of Cash Flows
For the Month Ended April 30, 2010

			From Events:
Cash Flows from Operating Activities			
Cash received from:	Customers	$5,100	(*b*) and (*e*)
	Interest on notes receivable	12	(*j*)
Cash paid to:	Suppliers	(490)	(*a*), (*c*), and (*i*)
	Employees	(3,900)	(*f*)
	Interest on notes payable	(40)	(*h*)
Cash flows provided by operations		**682**	
Cash Flows from Investing Activities			
Purchased land		(5,000)	
Purchased equipment		(200)	
Received principal payment on note receivable		1,250	(*j*)
Cash flows used in investing activities		**(3,950)**	
Cash Flows from Financing Activities			
Issued common stock		9,000	
Paid principal on notes payable		(700)	(*h*)
Cash flows provided by financing activities		**8,300**	
Change in cash		5,032	
Beginning cash balance		0	
Ending cash balance		**$5,032**	

CHAPTER TAKE-AWAYS

1. **Describe a typical business operating cycle and explain the necessity for the time period assumption.** p. 103
   - The operating cycle, or cash-to-cash cycle, is the time needed to purchase goods or services from suppliers, sell the goods or services to customers, and collect cash from customers.
   - Time period assumption—to measure and report financial information periodically, we assume the long life of a company can be cut into shorter periods.
2. **Explain how business activities affect the elements of the income statement.** p. 104
   - Elements of the income statement:
     a. Revenues—increases in assets or settlements of liabilities from ongoing operations.
     b. Expenses—decreases in assets or increases in liabilities from ongoing operations.
     c. Gains—increases in assets or settlements of liabilities from peripheral activities.
     d. Losses—decreases in assets or increases in liabilities from peripheral activities.
3. **Explain the accrual basis of accounting and apply the revenue and matching principles to measure income.** p. 108

   In accrual basis accounting, revenues are recognized when earned and expenses are recognized when incurred.
   - Revenue principle—recognize revenues when (1) delivery has occurred, (2) there is persuasive evidence of an arrangement for customer payment, (3) the price is fixed or determinable, and (4) collection is reasonably assured.
   - Matching principle—recognize expenses when they are incurred in generating revenue.
4. **Apply transaction analysis to examine and record the effects of operating activities on the financial statements.** p. 113

   The expanded transaction analysis model includes revenues and expenses:

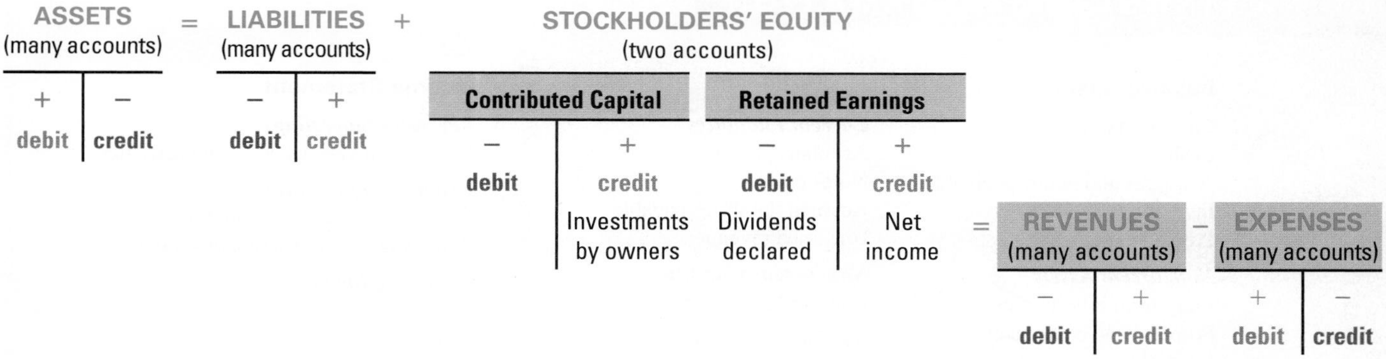

5. **Prepare financial statements.** p. 122

   Until the accounts have been updated to include all revenues earned and expenses incurred in the period (due to a difference in the time when cash is received or paid), the financial statements are unadjusted:
   - Classified income statement—net income is needed to determine ending Retained Earnings; classifications include Operating Revenues, Operating Expenses (to determine Operating Income), Other Items (to determine Pretax Income), Income Tax Expense, Net Income, and Earnings per Share.
   - Statement of stockholders' equity—connects the income statement to the balance sheet.
   - Classified balance sheet—classified into current and noncurrent assets, current and noncurrent liabilities, and stockholders' equity.
   - Statement of cash flows—classifies sources and uses of cash into operating, investing, and financing activities.

6. **Compute and interpret the total asset turnover ratio.** p. 127

   The total asset turnover ratio (Sales ÷ Average Total Assets) measures the sales generated per dollar of assets. The higher the ratio, the more efficient the company is at managing assets.

In this chapter, we discussed the operating cycle and accounting concepts relevant to income determination: the time period assumption, definitions of the income statement elements (revenues, expenses, gains, and losses), the revenue principle, and the matching principle. The accounting principles are defined in accordance with the accrual basis of accounting, which requires revenues to be recorded when earned and expenses to be recorded when incurred in the process of generating revenues. We expanded the transaction analysis model introduced in Chapter 2 by adding revenues and expenses and prepared unadjusted financial statements. In Chapter 4, we discuss the activities that occur at the end of the accounting period: the adjustment process, the preparation of adjusted financial statements, and the closing process.

KEY RATIO

Total asset turnover ratio measures the sales generated per dollar of assets. A high ratio suggests that a company is managing its assets (the resources used to generate revenues) efficiently. The ratio is computed as follows (p. 127):

$$\text{Total Asset Turnover Ratio} = \frac{\text{Sales (or Operating) Revenues}}{\text{Average Total Assets}}$$

"Average" is (Beginning Balance + Ending Balance) ÷ 2

FINDING FINANCIAL INFORMATION

Balance Sheet

Current Assets
Cash
Accounts and notes receivable
Inventory
Prepaid expenses

Noncurrent Assets
Long-term investments
Property and equipment
Intangibles

Current Liabilities
Accounts payable
Notes payable
Accrued liabilities payable
Unearned revenue

Noncurrent Liabilities
Long-term debt

Stockholders' Equity
Contributed capital
Retained earnings

Income Statement

Revenues (operating)
Sales (from various operating activities)

Expenses (operating)
Cost of sales (used inventory)
Rent, wages, depreciation, insurance, etc.

Operating Income
Other Items
Interest expense
Investment income
Gains on sale of assets
Losses on sale of assets

Pretax Income
Income tax expense

Net Income
Earnings per Share

Statement of Cash Flows

Under Operating Activities
+ Cash from customers
+ Cash from interest and dividends
− Cash to suppliers
− Cash to employees
− Interest paid
− Income taxes paid

Notes

Under Summary of Significant Accounting Policies
Description of the company's revenue recognition policy.

KEY TERMS

Accrual Basis Accounting p. 108
Cash Basis Accounting p. 108
Expenses p. 106
Gains p. 106
Losses p. 106
Matching Principle p. 111
Operating (Cash-to-Cash) Cycle p. 103
Revenues p. 104
Revenue Principle p. 108
Time Period Assumption p. 104

QUESTIONS

1. Describe a typical business operating cycle.
2. Explain what the time period assumption means.
3. Write the income statement equation and define each element.
4. Explain the difference between
a. Revenues and gains.
b. Expenses and losses.
5. Define **accrual accounting** and contrast it with cash basis accounting.
6. What four criteria must normally be met for revenue to be recognized under accrual basis accounting?
7. Explain the matching principle.
8. Explain why stockholders' equity is increased by revenues and decreased by expenses.
9. Explain why revenues are recorded as credits and expenses as debits.
10. Complete the following matrix by entering either **debit** or **credit** in each cell:

Item	Increase	Decrease
Revenues		
Losses		
Gains		
Expenses		

11. Complete the following matrix by entering either **increase** or **decrease** in each cell:

Item	Debit	Credit
Revenues		
Losses		
Gains		
Expenses		

12. Identify whether the following transactions affect cash flow from operating, investing, or financing activities, and indicate the effect of each on cash (+ for increase and − for decrease). If there is no cash flow effect, write "None."

Transaction	Operating, Investing, or Financing Effect on Cash	Direction of the Effect on Cash
Cash paid to suppliers		
Sale of goods on account		
Cash received from customers		
Purchase of investments		
Cash paid for interest		
Issuance of stock for cash		

13. State the equation for the total asset turnover ratio and explain how it is interpreted.

7/10

MULTIPLE-CHOICE QUESTIONS

1. Which of the following is **not** a specific account in a company's chart of accounts?
   a. Gains
   b. Revenue
   c. Net Income
   d. Unearned Revenue
2. Which of the following is **not** one of the four criteria that normally must be met for revenue to be recognized according to the revenue principle for accrual basis accounting?
   a. Cash has been collected.
   b. Services have been performed.
   c. The price is determinable.
   d. Evidence of an arrangement exists.
3. The matching principle controls
   a. Where on the income statement expenses should be presented.
   b. When costs are recognized as expenses on the income statement.
   c. The ordering of current assets and current liabilities on the balance sheet.
   d. How costs are allocated between Cost of Sales (sometimes called Cost of Goods Sold) and general and administrative expenses.
4. When expenses exceed revenues in a given period,
   a. Retained earnings are not impacted.
   b. Retained earnings are decreased.
   c. Retained earnings are increased.
   d. One cannot determine the impact on retained earnings without additional information.
5. On January 1, 2011, Anson Company started the year with a $250,000 credit balance in Retained Earnings and a $300,000 balance in Contributed Capital. During 2011, the company earned net income of $50,000, declared a dividend of $15,000, and issued more stock for $12,500. What is total stockholders' equity on December 31, 2011?
   a. $692,500.
   b. $597,500.
   c. $585,000.
   d. None of the above.
6. During 2011, CliffCo Inc. incurred operating expenses of $200,000, of which $150,000 was paid in cash; the balance will be paid in January 2012. Transaction analysis of operating expenses for 2011 should reflect only the following:
   a. Decrease stockholders' equity, $150,000; decrease assets, $150,000.
   b. Decrease assets, $200,000; decrease stockholders' equity, $200,000.
   c. Decrease stockholders' equity, $200,000; decrease assets, $150,000; increase liabilities, $50,000.
   d. Decrease assets, $200,000; increase liabilities, $50,000; decrease stockholders' equity, $150,000.
   e. None of the above is correct.
7. Which of the following is the entry to be recorded by a law firm when it receives a $2,000 retainer from a new client at the initial client meeting?
   a. Debit to Cash, $2,000; credit to Legal Fees Revenue, $2,000.
   b. Debit to Accounts Receivable, $2,000; credit to Legal Fees Revenue, $2,000.
   c. Debit to Unearned Revenue, $2,000; credit to Legal Fees Revenue, $2,000.
   d. Debit to Cash, $2,000; credit to Unearned Revenue, $2,000.
   e. Debit to Unearned Revenue, $2,000; credit to Cash, $2,000.
8. You have observed that the total asset turnover ratio for a retail chain has increased steadily over the last three years. The **most** likely explanation is which of the following?
   a. Salaries for upper management as a percentage of total expenses have decreased over the last three years.
   b. A successful advertising campaign increased sales companywide, but no new store locations were added over the last three years.
   c. New stores were added throughout the last three years, and sales increased as a result of the additional new locations.
   d. The company began construction of a new, larger main office location three years ago that was put into use at the end of the second year.
9. Cash payments for salaries are reported in what section of the Statement of Cash Flows?
   a. Operating.
   b. Investing.
   c. Financing.
   d. None of the above.

10. This period a company collects $100 cash on an account receivable from a customer for a sale last period. How would the receipt of cash impact the following two financial statements this period?

	Income Statement	Statement of Cash Flows
a.	Revenue + $100	Inflow from investing
b.	No impact	Inflow from operations
c.	Revenue − $100	Inflow from operations
d.	No impact	Inflow from financing

For more practice with multiple-choice questions, go to the text website at **www.mhhe.com/libby7e**.

connect ACCOUNTING

MINI-EXERCISES

Matching Definitions with Terms

M3-1
LO1, 2, 3

Match each definition with its related term by entering the appropriate letter in the space provided. There should be only one definition per term (that is, there are more definitions than terms).

Term	Definition
___ (1) Losses	A. Record revenues when earned and measurable (delivery of goods or services has been performed, there is persuasive evidence of an arrangement, the price is fixed or determinable, and collection is reasonably assured).
___ (2) Matching principle	B. The time it takes to purchase goods or services from suppliers, sell goods or services to customers, and collect cash from customers.
___ (3) Revenues	C. Record expenses when incurred in earning revenue.
___ (4) Time period assumption	D. Decreases in assets or increases in liabilities from ongoing operations.
___ (5) Operating cycle	E. Report the long life of a company in shorter time periods.
	F. Increases in assets or decreases in liabilities from ongoing operations.
	G. Decreases in assets or increases in liabilities from peripheral transactions.

Reporting Cash Basis versus Accrual Basis Income

M3-2
LO3

Skidmore Music Company had the following transactions in March:

a. Sold instruments to customers for $15,000; received $10,000 in cash and the rest on account. The cost of the instruments was $9,000.
b. Purchased $3,000 of new instruments inventory; paid $1,000 in cash and owed the rest on account.
c. Paid $750 in wages for the month.
d. Received $3,000 from customers as deposits on orders of new instruments to be sold to the customers in April.
e. Received a $200 bill for March utilities that will be paid in April.

Complete the following statements:

Cash Basis Income Statement		Accrual Basis Income Statement	
Revenues		Revenues	
Cash sales		Sales to customers	
Customer deposits			
Expenses		Expenses	
Inventory purchases		Cost of sales	
Wages paid		Wages expense	
	______	Utilities expense	______
Net income	______	Net income	______

M3-3 **Identifying Revenues**
LO2, 3

The following transactions are July 2011 activities of Craig's Bowling, Inc., which operates several bowling centers (for games and equipment sales). If revenue is to be recognized in **July,** indicate the revenue account title and amount. If revenue is not to be recognized in July, explain why.

Activity	Revenue Account Title and Amount
a. Craig's collected $13,000 from customers for games played in July.	
b. Craig's sold bowling equipment inventory for $7,000; received $3,000 in cash and the rest on account. [The cost of goods sold (expense) related to these sales is in M3-4*e.*]	
c. Craig's received $2,500 from customers on account who purchased merchandise in June.	
d. The men's and ladies' bowling leagues gave Craig's a deposit of $2,600 for the upcoming fall season.	

M3-4 **Identifying Expenses**
LO2, 3

The following transactions are July 2011 activities of Craig's Bowling, Inc., which operates several bowling centers (for games and equipment sales). If expense is to be recognized in **July,** indicate the expense account title and amount. If expense is not to be recognized in July, explain why.

Activity	Expense Account Title and Amount
e. Craig's sold bowling merchandise costing $3,890. [The sale related to the use of this merchandise is in M3-3*b.*]	
f. Craig's paid $1,900 on the electricity bill for June (recorded as expense in June).	
g. Craig's paid $4,700 to employees for work in July.	
h. Craig's purchased $1,800 in insurance for coverage from July 1 to October 1.	
i. Craig's paid $1,400 to plumbers for repairing a broken pipe in the restrooms.	
j. Craig's received the July electricity bill for $2,600 to be paid in August.	

M3-5 **Recording Revenues**
LO4

For each of the transactions in M3-3, write the journal entry in good form.

M3-6 **Recording Expenses**
LO4

For each of the transactions in M3-4, write the journal entry in good form.

M3-7 **Determining the Financial Statement Effects of Operating Activities Involving Revenues**
LO4

The following transactions are July 2011 activities of Craig's Bowling, Inc., which operates several bowling centers (for games and equipment sales). For each of the following transactions, complete the tabulation, indicating the amount and effect (+ for increase and − for decrease) of each transaction. (Remember that A = L + SE, R − E = NI, and NI affects SE through Retained Earnings.) Write NE if there is no effect. The first transaction is provided as an example.

	BALANCE SHEET			INCOME STATEMENT		
Transaction	Assets	Liabilities	Stockholders' Equity	Revenues	Expenses	Net Income
a. Craig's collected $13,000 from customers for games played in July.	+13,000	NE	+13,000	+13,000	NE	+13,000
b. Craig's sold bowling equipment inventory for $7,000; received $3,000 in cash and the rest on account. [The cost of goods sold (expense) related to these sales is in M3-8*e.*]						
c. Craig's received $2,500 from customers on account who purchased merchandise in June.						
d. The men's and ladies' bowling leagues gave Craig's a deposit of $2,600 for the upcoming fall season.						

Determining the Financial Statement Effects of Operating Activities Involving Expenses

M3-8
L04

The following transactions are July 2011 activities of Craig's Bowling, Inc., which operates several bowling centers (for games and equipment sales). For each of the following transactions, complete the tabulation, indicating the amount and effect (+ for increase and − for decrease) of each transaction. (Remember that A = L + SE, R − E = NI, and NI affects SE through Retained Earnings.) Write NE if there is no effect. The first transaction is provided as an example.

	BALANCE SHEET			INCOME STATEMENT		
Transaction	Assets	Liabilities	Stockholders' Equity	Revenues	Expenses	Net Income
e. Craig's sold bowling merchandise costing $3,890. [The sale related to the use of this merchandise is in M3-3*b.*]	−3,890	NE	−3,890	NE	+3,890	−3,890
f. Craig's paid $1,900 on the electricity bill for June (recorded as expense in June).						
g. Craig's paid $4,700 to employees for work in July.						
h. Craig's purchased $1,800 in insurance for coverage from July 1 to October 1.						
i. Craig's paid $1,400 to plumbers for repairing a broken pipe in the restrooms.						
j. Craig's received the July electricity bill for $2,600 to be paid in August.						

Preparing a Simple Income Statement

M3-9
L05

Given the transactions in M3-7 and M3-8 (including the examples), prepare an income statement for Craig's Bowling, Inc., for the month of July 2011.

Preparing the Operating Activities Section of a Statement of Cash Flows

M3-10
L05

Given the transactions in M3-7 and M3-8 (including the examples), prepare the Operating Activities section of the statement of cash flows for Craig's Bowling, Inc., for the month of July 2011.

M3-11
LO6

Computing and Explaining the Total Asset Turnover Ratio

The following data are from annual reports of Jen's Jewelry Company:

	2012	2011	2010
Total assets	$ 60,000	$ 53,000	$ 41,000
Total liabilities	14,000	11,000	6,000
Total stockholders' equity	46,000	42,000	35,000
Sales revenue	163,000	151,000	132,000
Net income	51,000	40,000	25,000

Compute Jen's total asset turnover ratio for 2012 and 2011. What do these results suggest to you about Jen's Jewelry Company?

EXERCISES

connect ACCOUNTING

E3-1
LO1, 2, 3

Matching Definitions with Terms

Match each definition with its related term by entering the appropriate letter in the space provided. There should be only one definition per term (that is, there are more definitions than terms).

Term	Definition
____ (1) Expenses	A. Report the long life of a company in shorter periods.
____ (2) Gains	B. Record expenses when incurred in earning revenue.
____ (3) Revenue principle	C. The time it takes to purchase goods or services from suppliers, sell goods or services to customers, and collect cash from customers.
____ (4) Cash basis accounting	D. Record revenues when earned and expenses when incurred.
____ (5) Unearned revenue	E. Increases in assets or decreases in liabilities from peripheral transactions.
____ (6) Operating cycle	F. An asset account used to record cash paid before expenses have been incurred.
____ (7) Accrual basis accounting	G. Record revenues when earned and measurable (delivery of goods or services has occurred, there is persuasive evidence of an arrangement for customer payment, the price is fixed or determinable, and collection is reasonably assured).
____ (8) Prepaid expenses	H. Decreases in assets or increases in liabilities from peripheral transactions.
____ (9) Revenues − Expenses = Net Income	I. Record revenues when received and expenses when paid.
____ (10) Ending Retained Earnings = Beginning Retained Earnings + Net Income − Dividends Declared	J. The income statement equation.
	K. Decreases in assets or increases in liabilities from ongoing operations.
	L. The retained earnings equation.
	M. A liability account used to record cash received before revenues have been earned.

E3-2
LO3

Reporting Cash Basis versus Accrual Basis Income

Payson Sports, Inc., sells sports equipment to customers. Its fiscal year ends on December 31. The following transactions occurred in 2012:

a. Purchased $314,000 of new sports equipment inventory; paid $90,000 in cash and owed the rest on account.

b. Paid employees $164,200 in wages for work during the year; an additional $4,800 for 2012 wages will be paid in January 2013.

c. Sold sports equipment to customers for $630,000; received $520,000 in cash and the rest on account. The cost of the equipment was $387,000.

d. Paid $17,200 cash for utilities for the year.

e. Received $35,000 from customers as deposits on orders of new winter sports equipment to be sold to the customers in January 2013.

f. Received a $1,740 bill for December 2012 utilities that will be paid in January 2013.

Required:

1. Complete the following statements:

Cash Basis Income Statement		Accrual Basis Income Statement	
Revenues		Revenues	
Cash sales		Sales to customers	
Customer deposits			
Expenses		Expenses	
Inventory purchases		Cost of sales	
Wages paid		Wages expense	
Utilities paid		Utilities expense	
Net income		Net income	

2. Which basis of accounting (cash or accrual) provides more useful information to investors, creditors, and other users? Why?

Identifying Revenues

E3-3
LO2, 3

Revenues are normally recognized when the delivery of goods or services has occurred, there is persuasive evidence of an arrangement for customer payment, the price is fixed or determinable, and collection is reasonably assured. The amount recorded is the cash-equivalent sales price. The following transactions occurred in **September** 2013:

a. A popular ski magazine company receives a total of $11,980 today from subscribers. The subscriptions begin in the next fiscal year. Answer from the magazine company's standpoint.

b. On September 1, 2013, a bank lends $1,200 to a company; the note principal and $144 ($1,200 × 12 percent) annual interest are due in one year. Answer from the bank's standpoint.

c. Fucillo Hyundai, Inc., sells a truck with a list, or "sticker," price of $20,050 for $18,050 cash.

d. Macy's department store orders 1,000 men's shirts for $15 each for future delivery from Phillips-Van Heusen Corporation, manufacturer of Izod, Arrow, Van Heusen, and Calvin Klein shirts. The terms require payment in full within 30 days of delivery. Answer from Phillips-Van Heusen's standpoint.

e. Phillips-Van Heusen Corporation completes production of the shirts described in (*d*) and delivers the order. Answer from Phillips-Van Heusen's standpoint.

f. Phillips-Van Heusen receives payment from Macy's for the events described in (*d*) and (*e*). Answer from Phillips-Van Heusen's standpoint.

g. A customer purchases a ticket from American Airlines for $610 cash to travel the following January. Answer from American Airlines's standpoint.

h. Ford Motors issues $20 million in new common stock.

i. Penn State University receives $18,300,000 cash for 80,000 five-game season football tickets.

j. Penn State plays the first football game referred to in (*i*).

k. Precision Builders signs a contract with a customer for the construction of a new $1,500,000 warehouse. At the signing, Precision receives a check for $150,000 as a deposit on the future construction. Answer from Precision's standpoint.

l. A customer orders and receives 10 personal computers from Dell; the customer promises to pay $18,400 within three months. Answer from Dell's standpoint.

m. Sears, a retail store, sells a $100 lamp to a customer who charges the sale on his store credit card. Answer from Sears's standpoint.

Required:

For each of the transactions, if revenue is to be recognized in September, indicate the revenue account title and amount. If revenue is not to be recognized in September, explain why.

E3-4 LO2, 3

Identifying Expenses

Revenues are normally recognized when goods or services have been provided and payment or promise of payment has been received. Expense recognition is guided by an attempt to match the costs associated with the generation of those revenues to the same time period. The following transactions occurred in **January** 2013:

a. The McGraw-Hill Companies use $2,754 worth of electricity and natural gas in its headquarters building for which it has not yet been billed.
b. At the beginning of January, Turner Construction Company pays $846 for magazine advertising to run in monthly publications each of the first three months of the year.
c. Dell pays its computer service technicians $379,500 in salaries for the two weeks ended January 7. Answer from Dell's standpoint.
d. The University of Florida orders 60,000 season football tickets from its printer and pays $7,610 in advance for the custom printing. The first game will be played in September. Answer from the university's standpoint.
e. The campus bookstore receives 500 accounting texts at a cost of $89 each. The terms indicate that payment is due within 30 days of delivery.
f. During the last week of January, the campus bookstore sold 450 accounting texts received in (*e*) at a sales price of $150 each.
g. Fucillo Hyundai, Inc., pays its salespersons $13,200 in commissions related to December automobile sales. Answer from Fucillo's standpoint.
h. On January 31, Fucillo Hyundai, Inc., determines that it will pay its salespersons $14,470 in commissions related to January sales. The payment will be made in early February. Answer from Fucillo's standpoint.
i. A new grill is purchased and installed at a Wendy's restaurant at the end of the day on January 31; a $12,750 cash payment is made on that day.
j. Carousel Center Mall had janitorial supplies costing $4,000 in storage. An additional $2,600 worth of supplies was purchased during January. At the end of January, $1,410 worth of janitorial supplies remained in storage.
k. An Iowa State University employee works eight hours, at $13 per hour, on January 31; however, payday is not until February 3. Answer from the university's point of view.
l. Wang Company paid $3,600 for a fire insurance policy on January 1. The policy covers 12 months beginning on January 1. Answer from Wang's point of view.
m. Darrius Incorporated has its delivery van repaired in January for $300 and charges the amount on account.
n. Haas Company, a farm equipment company, receives its phone bill at the end of January for $202 for January calls. The bill has not been paid to date.
o. Martin Company receives and pays in January a $1,285 invoice (bill) from a consulting firm for services received in January.
p. Parillo's Taxi Company pays a $595 invoice from a consulting firm for services received and recorded in December.
q. Phillips-Van Heusen Corporation, manufacturer of Izod, Arrow, Van Heusen, and Calvin Klein shirts, completes production of 500 men's shirts ordered by Macy's department stores at a cost of $10 each and delivers the order. Answer from Phillips-Van Heusen's standpoint.

Required:
For each of the transactions, if an expense is to be recognized in January, indicate the expense account title and the amount. If an expense is not to be recognized in January, indicate why.

E3-5 LO4

Determining Financial Statement Effects of Various Transactions

The following transactions occurred during a recent year:

a. Issued stock to organizers for cash (example).
b. Purchased equipment on credit.
c. Declared and paid cash dividends.
d. Earned revenue, collected cash.
e. Incurred expenses, on credit.
f. Earned revenue, on credit.
g. Paid cash on account.
h. Incurred expenses; paid cash.
i. Earned revenue; collected three-fourths in cash, balance on credit.
j. Borrowed cash from local bank.
k. Collected cash from customers on account.
l. Experienced theft (a loss) of $100 cash.
m. Incurred expenses; paid four-fifths in cash, balance on credit.
n. Paid income tax expense for the period.

Required:
For each of the transactions, complete the tabulation, indicating the effect (+ for increase and − for decrease) of each transaction. (Remember that A = L + SE, R − E = NI, and NI affects SE through Retained Earnings.) Write NE if there is no effect. The first transaction is provided as an example.

	BALANCE SHEET			INCOME STATEMENT		
Transaction	Assets	Liabilities	Stockholders' Equity	Revenues	Expenses	Net Income
(*a*) (example)	+	NE	+	NE	NE	NE

Determining Financial Statement Effects of Various Transactions

E3-6
LO4
Wolverine World Wide, Inc.

Wolverine World Wide, Inc., manufactures military, work, sport, and casual footwear and leather accessories under a variety of brand names, such as Hush Puppies, Wolverine, and Bates, to a global market. The following transactions occurred during a recent year. Dollars are in thousands.

a. Issued common stock to investors for $7,047 cash (example).
b. Purchased $765,472 of additional inventory on account.
c. Borrowed $59,500.
d. Sold $1,220,568 of products to customers on account; cost of the products sold was $734,547.
e. Paid cash dividends of $20,758.
f. Purchased for cash $24,126 in additional property, plant, and equipment.
g. Incurred $345,183 in selling expenses, paying three-fourths in cash and owing the rest on account.
h. Earned $1,757 interest on investments, receiving 90 percent in cash.
i. Incurred $2,850 in interest expense to be paid at the beginning of next year.

Required:
For each of the transactions, complete the tabulation, indicating the effect (+ for increase and − for decrease) of each transaction. (Remember that A = L + SE, R − E = NI, and NI affects SE through Retained Earnings.) Write NE if there is no effect. The first transaction is provided as an example.

	BALANCE SHEET			INCOME STATEMENT		
Transaction	Assets	Liabilities	Stockholders' Equity	Revenues	Expenses	Net Income
(*a*) (example)	+7,047	NE	+7,047	NE	NE	NE

Recording Journal Entries

E3-7
LO4
Sysco

Sysco, formed in 1969, is North America's largest marketer and distributor of food service products, serving approximately 400,000 restaurants, hotels, schools, hospitals, and other institutions. The following summarized transactions are typical of those that occurred in a recent year (dollars are in thousands).

a. Purchased plant and equipment for $515 in cash.
b. Borrowed $758 from a bank, signing a short-term note.
c. Provided $37,522 in service to customers during the year, with $27,250 on account and the rest received in cash.
d. Paid $4,300 cash on accounts payable.
e. Purchased $30,449 inventory on account.
f. Paid payroll, $3,500 during the year.
g. Received $37,410 on account paid by customers.
h. Purchased and used fuel of $750 in delivery vehicles during the year (paid for in cash).
i. Declared and paid $497 in dividends for the year.
j. Incurred $68 in utility usage during the year; paid $55 in cash and owed the rest on account.

Required:
For each of the transactions, prepare journal entries. Determine whether the accounting equation remains in balance and debits equal credits after each entry.

E3-8
LO4
Vail Resorts, Inc.

Recording Journal Entries

Vail Resorts, Inc., owns and operates five premier year-round ski resort properties (Vail Mountain, Beaver Creek Resort, Breckenridge Mountain, and Keystone Resort, all located in the Colorado Rocky Mountains, and Heavenly Valley Mountain Resort, located in the Lake Tahoe area of California/Nevada). The company also owns a collection of luxury hotels, resorts, and lodging properties. The company sells lift tickets, ski lessons, and ski equipment. The following hypothetical December transactions are typical of those that occur at the resorts.

a. Borrowed $2,500,000 from the bank on December 1, signing a note payable due in six months.
b. Purchased a new snowplow for $95,000 cash on December 31.
c. Purchased ski equipment inventory for $40,000 on account to sell in the ski shops.
d. Incurred $62,000 in routine maintenance expenses for the chairlifts; paid cash.
e. Sold $372,000 of January through March season passes and received cash.
f. Sold a pair of skis from a ski shop to a customer for $750 on account. (The cost of the skis was $450.)
g. Sold daily lift passes in December for a total of $270,000 in cash.
h. Received a $3,200 deposit on a townhouse to be rented for five days in January.
i. Paid half the charges incurred on account in (*c*).
j. Received $400 on account from the customer in (*f*).
k. Paid $258,000 in wages to employees for the month of December.

Required:
1. Prepare journal entries for each transaction. (Remember to check that debits equal credits and that the accounting equation is in balance after each transaction.)
2. Assume that Vail Resorts had a $1,200 balance in Accounts Receivable at the beginning of December. Determine the ending balance in the Accounts Receivable account at the end of December based on transactions (*a*) through (*k*). Show your work in T-account format.

E3-9
LO4

Recording Journal Entries

Blaine Air Transport Service, Inc., has been in operation for three years. The following transactions occurred in February:

February 1	Paid $275 for rent of hangar space in February.
February 2	Purchased fuel costing $490 on account for the next flight to Dallas.
February 4	Received customer payment of $820 to ship several items to Philadelphia next month.
February 7	Flew cargo from Denver to Dallas; the customer paid $910 for the air transport.
February 10	Paid $175 for an advertisement in the local paper to run on February 19.
February 14	Paid pilot $2,300 in wages for flying in January (recorded as expense in January).
February 18	Flew cargo for two customers from Dallas to Albuquerque for $3,800; one customer paid $1,600 cash and the other asked to be billed.
February 25	Purchased on account $2,550 in spare parts for the planes.
February 27	Declared a $200 cash dividend to be paid in March.

Required:
Prepare journal entries for each transaction. Be sure to categorize each account as an asset (A), liability (L), stockholders' equity (SE), revenue (R), or expense (E).

E3-10
LO3, 4

Analyzing the Effects of Transactions in T-Accounts and Computing Cash Basis versus Accrual Basis Net Income

Stacey's Piano Rebuilding Company has been operating for one year (2010). At the start of 2011, its income statement accounts had zero balances and its balance sheet account balances were as follows:

Cash	$ 6,200	Accounts payable	$ 9,600
Accounts receivable	30,000	Unearned fee revenue (deposits)	3,840
Supplies	1,440	Note payable (long-term)	48,000
Equipment	9,600	Contributed capital	8,600
Land	7,200	Retained earnings	10,800
Building	26,400		

Required:

1. Create T-accounts for the balance sheet accounts and for these additional accounts: Rebuilding Fees Revenue, Rent Revenue, Wages Expense, and Utilities Expense. Enter the beginning balances.
2. Enter the following January 2011 transactions in the T-accounts, using the letter of each transaction as the reference:
   a. Rebuilt and delivered five pianos in January to customers who paid $18,400 in cash.
   b. Received a $600 deposit from a customer who wanted her piano rebuilt.
   c. Rented a part of the building to a bicycle repair shop; received $820 for rent in January.
   d. Received $7,200 from customers as payment on their accounts.
   e. Received an electric and gas utility bill for $520 to be paid in February.
   f. Ordered $960 in supplies.
   g. Paid $2,140 on account in January.
   h. Received from the home of Stacey Eddy, the major shareholder, a $920 tool (equipment) to use in the business.
   i. Paid $15,000 in wages to employees who worked in January.
   j. Declared and paid a $2,600 dividend.
   k. Received and paid cash for the supplies in (*f*).
3. Using the data from the T-accounts, amounts for the following on January 31, 2011, were

   Revenues $ _______ − Expenses $ _______ = Net Income $ _______
   Assets $ _______ = Liabilities $ _______ + Stockholders' Equity $ _______

4. What is net income if Stacey's used the cash basis of accounting? Why does this differ from accrual basis net income (in requirement 3)?

Preparing an Income Statement, Statement of Stockholders' Equity, and Classified Balance Sheet

E3-11
LO5

Refer to E3-10.

Required:

Use the ending balances in the T-accounts in E3-10 to prepare the following:

1. An income statement for January 2011 in good form (ignore income taxes).
2. A statement of stockholders' equity for January 2011.
3. A classified balance sheet as of January 31, 2011, in good form.

Preparing a Statement of Cash Flows

E3-12
LO5

Refer to E3-10.

Required:

Use the transactions in E3-10 to prepare a statement of cash flows in good form.

Analyzing the Effects of Transactions in T-Accounts

E3-13
LO4

Lisa Frees and Amelia Ellinger had been operating a catering business for several years. In March 2011, the partners were planning to expand by opening a retail sales shop and decided to form the business as a corporation called Traveling Gourmet, Inc. The following transactions occurred in March 2011:

a. Received $80,000 cash from each of the two shareholders to form the corporation, in addition to $2,000 in accounts receivable, $5,300 in equipment, a van (equipment) appraised at a fair market value of $13,000, and $1,200 in supplies.
b. Purchased a vacant store for sale in a good location for $360,000, making a $72,000 cash down payment and signing a 10-year mortgage from a local bank for the rest.
c. Borrowed $50,000 from the local bank on a 10 percent, one-year note.
d. Purchased and used food and paper supplies costing $10,830 in March; paid cash.
e. Catered four parties in March for $4,200; $1,600 was billed, and the rest was received in cash.
f. Made and sold food at the retail store for $11,900 cash.
g. Received a $420 telephone bill for March to be paid in April.
h. Paid $363 in gas for the van in March.

i. Paid $6,280 in wages to employees who worked in March.
j. Paid a $300 dividend from the corporation to each owner.
k. Purchased $50,000 of equipment (refrigerated display cases, cabinets, tables, and chairs) and renovated and decorated the new store for $20,000 (added to the cost of the building); paid cash.

Required:

1. Set up appropriate T-accounts for Cash, Accounts Receivable, Supplies, Equipment, Building, Accounts Payable, Note Payable, Mortgage Payable, Contributed Capital, Retained Earnings, Food Sales Revenue, Catering Sales Revenue, Supplies Expense, Utilities Expense, Wages Expense, and Fuel Expense.
2. Record in the T-accounts the effects of each transaction for Traveling Gourmet, Inc., in March. Identify the amounts with the letters starting with (*a*). Compute ending balances.

E3-14 LO5 Preparing an Income Statement, Statement of Stockholders' Equity, and Classified Balance Sheet

Refer to E3-13.

Required:

Use the balances in the completed T-accounts in E3-13 to respond to the following:

1. Prepare an income statement in good form for the month of March 2011.
2. Prepare a statement of retained earnings for the month of March 2011.
3. Prepare a classified balance sheet in good form as of March 2011.
4. What do you think about the success of this company based on the results of the first month of operations?

E3-15 LO5 Preparing a Statement of Cash Flows

Refer to E3-13.

Required:

Use the transactions in E3-13 to prepare a statement of cash flows in good form.

E3-16 LO2, 3, 4, 5 Inferring Operating Transactions and Preparing an Income Statement and Balance Sheet

Kate's Kite Company (a corporation) sells and repairs kites from manufacturers around the world. Its stores are located in rented space in malls and shopping centers. During its first month of operations ended April 30, 2011, Kate's Kite Company completed eight transactions with the dollar effects indicated in the following schedule:

	DOLLAR EFFECT OF EACH OF THE EIGHT TRANSACTIONS								
Accounts	**(a)**	**(b)**	**(c)**	**(d)**	**(e)**	**(f)**	**(g)**	**(h)**	**Ending Balance**
Cash	$63,300	$(13,700)	$(6,200)	$8,680		$(1,240)	$(2,480)	$3,720	
Accounts Receivable				3,720					
Inventory			24,800	(6,510)					
Prepaid Expenses							1,860		
Store Fixtures		13,700							
Accounts Payable			18,600		$1,480				
Unearned Revenue								2,480	
Contributed Capital	63,300								
Sales Revenue				12,400				1,240	
Cost of Sales				6,510					
Wages Expense						1,240			
Rent Expense							620		
Utilities Expense					1,480				

Required:

1. Write a brief explanation of transactions (*a*) through (*h*). Include any assumptions that you made.
2. Compute the ending balance in each account and prepare an income statement and a classified balance sheet for Kate's Kite Company on April 30, 2011.

Analyzing the Effects of Transactions Using T-Accounts and Interpreting the Total Asset Turnover Ratio as a Financial Analyst

E3-17
LO4, 6

Massa Company, which has been operating for three years, provides marketing consulting services worldwide for dot-com companies. You are a financial analyst assigned to report on the Massa management team's effectiveness at managing its assets efficiently. At the start of 2012 (its fourth year), Massa's T-account balances were as follows. Dollars are in thousands.

Assets

Cash	
3,200	

Accounts Receivable	
8,000	

Long-Term Investments	
6,400	

Liabilities

Accounts Payable	
	2,400

Unearned Revenue	
	5,600

Long-Term Notes Payable	
	1,600

Stockholders' Equity

Contributed Capital	
	4,800

Retained Earnings	
	3,200

Revenues

Consulting Fee Revenue	

Investment Income	

Expenses

Wages Expense	

Travel Expense	

Utilities Expense	

Rent Expense	

Required:

1. Using the data from these T-accounts, amounts for the following on January 1, 2012, were

   Assets $ ________ = Liabilities $ ________ + Stockholders' Equity $ ________

2. Enter the following 2012 transactions in the T-accounts:
   a. Provided $58,000 in services to clients who paid $48,000 in cash and owed the rest on account.
   b. Received $5,600 cash from clients on account.
   c. Received $400 in cash as income on investments.
   d. Paid $36,000 in wages, $12,000 in travel, $7,600 in rent, and $1,600 on accounts payable.
   e. Received $1,600 in cash from clients in advance of services Massa will provide next year.

f. Received a utility bill for $800 for 2012 services.
g. Paid $480 in dividends to stockholders.

3. Compute ending balances in the T-accounts to determine amounts for the following on December 31, 2012:

   Revenues $ ________ − Expenses $ ________ = Net Income $ ________
   Assets $ ________ = Liabilities $ ________ + Stockholders' Equity $ ________

4. Calculate the total asset turnover ratio for 2012. If the company had an asset turnover ratio of 2.00 in 2011 and 1.80 in 2010, what does your computation suggest to you about Massa Company? What would you say in your report?

E3-18
LO4
The New York Times Company

Inferring Transactions and Computing Effects Using T-Accounts

A recent annual report of The New York Times Company, a diversified media company that currently includes newspapers (including *The New York Times*), Internet businesses, and television and radio stations, included the following accounts. Dollars are in millions:

Accounts Receivable		
1/1	438	
	2,949	?
12/31	404	

Prepaid Expenses		
1/1	90	
	313	?
12/31	126	

Unearned Subscriptions		
	81	1/1
?	151	
	84	12/31

Required:
1. For each T-account, describe the typical transactions that affect each account (that is, the economic events that occur to make these accounts increase and decrease).
2. For each T-account, compute the missing amounts.

E3-19
LO5, 6

Finding Financial Information as an Investor

You are evaluating your current portfolio of investments to determine those that are not performing to your expectations. You have all of the companies' most recent annual reports.

Required:
For each of the following, indicate where you would locate the information in an annual report. (**Hint:** The information may be in more than one location.)
1. Description of a company's primary business(es).
2. Income taxes paid.
3. Accounts receivable.
4. Cash flow from operating activities.
5. Description of a company's revenue recognition policy.
6. The inventory sold during the year.
7. The data needed to compute the total asset turnover ratio.

To practice with more exercises, go to the text website at **www.mhhe.com/libby7e**.

PROBLEMS

connect ACCOUNTING

P3-1
LO4

Recording Nonquantitative Journal Entries (AP3-1)

The following list includes a series of accounts for Sanjeev Corporation, which has been operating for three years. These accounts are listed and numbered for identification. Following the accounts is a series of transactions. For each transaction, indicate the account(s) that should be debited and credited by entering the appropriate account number(s) to the right of each transaction. If no journal entry is needed, write **none** after the transaction. The first transaction is used as an example.

Account No.	Account Title	Account No.	Account Title
1	Cash	9	Wages Payable
2	Accounts Receivable	10	Income Taxes Payable
3	Supplies	11	Contributed Capital
4	Prepaid Expenses	12	Retained Earnings
5	Equipment	13	Service Revenue
6	Patents	14	Operating Expenses (wages, supplies)
7	Accounts Payable	15	Income Tax Expense
8	Note Payable	16	Interest Expense

Transactions	Debit	Credit
a. Example: Purchased equipment for use in the business; paid one-third cash and signed a note payable for the balance.	5	1, 8
b. Paid cash for salaries and wages earned by employees this period.	~~9~~ 14	~~7~~ 1
c. Paid cash on accounts payable for expenses incurred last period.	7	1
d. Purchased supplies to be used later; paid cash.	3	1
e. Performed services this period on credit.	2	13
f. Collected cash on accounts receivable for services performed last period.	1	2
g. Issued stock to new investors.	1	11
h. Paid operating expenses incurred this period.	14	1
i. Incurred operating expenses this period to be paid next period.	14	7
j. Purchased a patent (an intangible asset); paid cash.	6	1
k. Collected cash for services performed this period.	1	13
l. Used some of the supplies on hand for operations.	14	3
m. Paid three-fourths of the income tax expense incurred for the year; the balance will be paid next year.	~~7~~ 15	~~1~~ 1, 10
n. Made a payment on the equipment note in (*a*); the payment was part principal and part interest expense.	~~8~~ 8, 16	~~1~~ 1
o. On the last day of the current period, paid cash for an insurance policy covering the next two years.	4	1

Recording Journal Entries (AP3-2)

P3-2
LO4

Ryan Terlecki organized a new Internet company, CapUniverse, Inc. The company specializes in baseball-type caps with logos printed on them. Ryan, who is never without a cap, believes that his target market is college and high school students. You have been hired to record the transactions occurring in the first two weeks of operations.

a. Issued 2,000 shares of stock to investors for cash at $20 per share.
b. Borrowed $60,000 from the bank to provide additional funding to begin operations; the note is due in two years.
c. Paid $1,500 for the current month's rent of a warehouse and another $1,500 for next month's rent.
d. Paid $2,400 for a one-year fire insurance policy on the warehouse (recorded as a prepaid expense).
e. Purchased furniture and fixtures for the warehouse for $15,000, paying $3,000 cash and the rest on account. The amount is due within 30 days.
f. Purchased for $2,800 cash The University of Florida, UCLA, Texas A&M, and Michigan State University baseball caps as inventory to sell online.
g. Placed advertisements on Google for a total of $350 cash.
h. Sold caps totaling $1,700, half of which was charged on account. The cost of the caps sold was $900.
i. Made full payment for the furniture and fixtures purchased on account in (*e*).
j. Received $210 from a customer on account.

Required:
For each of the transactions, prepare journal entries. Be sure to categorize each account as an asset (A), liability (L), stockholders' equity (SE), revenue (R), or expense (E). Note that transaction (*h*) will require two entries, one for revenue and one for the related expense.

P3-3 LO4 Determining Financial Statement Effects of Various Transactions and Identifying Cash Flow Effects (AP3-3)

According to its annual report, Wendy's International serves "the best hamburgers in the business" and other fresh food including salads, chicken sandwiches, and baked potatoes in more than 6,600 restaurants worldwide. The company operates its own restaurants and sells franchises to others. The following activities were inferred from a recent annual report.

a. Purchased food and paper products; paid part in cash and the rest on account.
b. Purchased additional investments.
c. Incurred restaurant operating costs in company-owned facilities; paid part in cash and the rest on account.
d. Served food to customers for cash.
e. Used food and paper products.
f. Paid cash dividends.
g. Sold franchises, receiving part in cash and the rest in notes due from franchisees.
h. Paid interest on debt incurred and due during the period.

Required:

1. For each of the transactions, complete the tabulation, indicating the effect (+ for increase and − for decrease) of each transaction. (Remember that A = L + SE, R − E = NI, and NI affects SE through Retained Earnings.) Write NE if there is no effect. The first transaction is provided as an example.

	BALANCE SHEET			INCOME STATEMENT		
Transaction	Assets	Liabilities	Stockholders' Equity	Revenues	Expenses	Net Income
(*a*) (example)	+/−	+	NE	NE	NE	NE

2. Where, if at all, would each transaction be reported on the statement of cash flows? Use O for operating activities, I for investing activities, F for financing activities, and NE if the transaction would not be included on the statement.

P3-4 LO4, 5, 6 Analyzing the Effects of Transactions Using T-Accounts, Preparing Financial Statements, and Evaluating the Total Asset Turnover Ratio as a Manager (AP3-4)

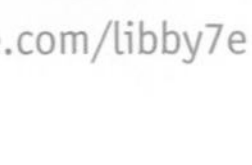

eXcel
www.mhhe.com/libby7e

Brianna Webb, a connoisseur of fine chocolate, opened Bri's Sweets in Collegetown on February 1, 2011. The shop specializes in a selection of gourmet chocolate candies and a line of gourmet ice cream. You have been hired as manager. Your duties include maintaining the store's financial records. The following transactions occurred in February 2011, the first month of operations.

a. Received four shareholders' contributions totaling $27,600 cash to form the corporation; issued stock.
b. Paid three months' rent for the store at $1,880 per month (recorded as prepaid expenses).
c. Purchased and received candy for $5,500 on account, due in 60 days.
d. Purchased supplies for $1,430 cash.
e. Negotiated and signed a two-year $11,000 loan at the bank.
f. Used the money from (*e*) to purchase a computer for $2,750 (for recordkeeping and inventory tracking); used the balance for furniture and fixtures for the store.
g. Placed a grand opening advertisement in the local paper for $500 cash.
h. Made sales on Valentine's Day totaling $3,000; $2,675 was in cash and the rest on accounts receivable. The cost of the candy sold was $1,200.
i. Made a $550 payment on accounts payable.
j. Incurred and paid employee wages of $1,500.
k. Collected accounts receivable of $155 from customers.
l. Made a repair to one of the display cases for $130 cash.
m. Made cash sales of $2,400 during the rest of the month. The cost of the candy sold was $1,210.

Required:

1. Set up appropriate T-accounts for Cash, Accounts Receivable, Supplies, Inventory, Prepaid Expenses, Equipment, Furniture and Fixtures, Accounts Payable, Notes Payable, Contributed Capital, Sales Revenue, Cost of Goods Sold (expense), Advertising Expense, Wage Expense, and Repair Expense. All accounts begin with zero balances.
2. Record in the T-accounts the effects of each transaction for Bri's Sweets in February, referencing each transaction in the accounts with the transaction letter. Show the ending balances in the T-accounts. Note that transactions (*h*) and (*m*) require two types of entries, one for revenue recognition and one for the expense.
3. Prepare financial statements at the end of the month ended February 28, 2011 (income statement, statement of stockholders' equity, and balance sheet).
4. Write a short memo to Brianna offering your opinion on the results of operations during the first month of business.
5. After three years in business, you are being evaluated for a promotion. One measure is how efficiently you managed the assets of the business. The following data are available:

	2013*	2012	2011
Total assets	$88,000	$49,500	$38,500
Total liabilities	49,500	22,000	16,500
Total stockholders' equity	38,500	27,500	22,000
Total sales	93,500	82,500	55,000
Net income	22,000	11,000	4,400

**At the end of 2013, Brianna decided to open a second store, requiring loans and inventory purchases prior to the store's opening in early 2014.*

Compute the total asset turnover ratio for 2012 and 2013 and evaluate the results. Do you think you should be promoted? Why?

P3-5
LO5

excel
www.mhhe.com/libby7e

Preparing a Statement of Cash Flows (AP3-5)

Refer to P3-4.

Required:

For the transactions listed in P3-4, prepare a statement of cash flows for the month.

P3-6
LO4, 5, 6
FedEx

excel
www.mhhe.com/libby7e

Analyzing the Effects of Transactions Using T-Accounts, Preparing Financial Statements, and Evaluating the Total Asset Turnover Ratio (AP3-6)

Following are account balances (in millions of dollars) from a recent FedEx annual report, followed by several typical transactions. Assume that the following are account balances on May 31, 2011:

Account	Balance	Account	Balance
Property and equipment (net)	$8,362	Contributed capital	$ 492
Retained earnings	5,827	Receivables	1,162
Accounts payable	835	Other current assets	1,196
Prepaid expenses	82	Cash	360
Accrued expenses payable	1,675	Spare parts, supplies, and fuel	294
Long-term notes payable	667	Other noncurrent liabilities	3,513
Other noncurrent assets	1,850	Other current liabilities	297

These accounts are not necessarily in good order and have normal debit or credit balances. Assume the following transactions (in millions of dollars) occurred the next year ending May 31, 2012:

a. Provided delivery service to customers, receiving $4,567 in accounts receivable and $17,600 in cash.
b. Purchased new equipment costing $1,345; signed a long-term note.
c. Paid $4,598 cash to rent equipment and aircraft, with $3,067 for rental this year and the rest for rent next year.
d. Spent $1,348 cash to maintain and repair facilities and equipment during the year.
e. Collected $4,824 from customers on account.

f. Repaid $18 on a long-term note (ignore interest).
g. Issued additional stock for $16.
h. Paid employees $10,031 during the year.
i. Purchased for cash and used $5,348 in fuel for the aircraft and equipment during the year.
j. Paid $784 on accounts payable.
k. Ordered $72 in spare parts and supplies.

Required:

1. Prepare T-accounts for May 31, 2011, from the preceding list; enter the respective beginning balances. You will need additional T-accounts for income statement accounts; enter zero for beginning balances.
2. For each transaction, record the 2012 effects in the T-accounts. Label each using the letter of the transaction. Compute ending balances.
3. Prepare an income statement, statement of stockholders' equity, balance sheet, and statement of cash flows in good form for May 31, 2012.
4. Compute the company's total asset turnover ratio for the year ended May 31, 2012. What does it suggest to you about FedEx?

P3-7 Recording Journal Entries and Identifying Cash Flow Effects

LO4

Cedar Fair, L.P.

excel

www.mhhe.com/libby7e

Cedar Fair, L.P. (Limited Partnership) is one of the largest regional amusement park operators in the world, owning 12 amusement parks, five outdoor water parks, one indoor water park, and six hotels. The parks include Cedar Point in Ohio, Valleyfair near Minneapolis/St. Paul, Dorney Park and Wildwater Kingdom near Allentown, Pennsylvania, Worlds of Fun/Oceans of Fun in Kansas City, Great America in Santa Clara, California, and Canada's Wonderland near Toronto, Canada, among others. The following are summarized transactions similar to those that occurred in a recent year (assume 2011). Dollars are in thousands:

a. Guests at the parks paid $566,266 cash in admissions.
b. The primary operating expenses (such as employee wages, utilities, and repairs and maintenance on buildings and equipment) for the year were $450,967, with $412,200 paid in cash and the rest on account.
c. Cedar Fair paid $58,962 principal on notes payable.
d. The parks sell food and merchandise and operate games. The cash received during the year for these combined activities was $335,917. The cost of merchandise sold during the year was $90,626.
e. Cedar Fair purchased and built additional buildings, rides, and equipment during the year, paying $83,841 in cash.
f. Guests may stay in the parks at accommodations owned by the company. During the year, accommodations revenue was $74,049; $72,910 was paid by the guests in cash and the rest was owed on account.
g. Interest paid on long-term debt was $125,838.
h. The company purchased $146,100 in food and merchandise inventory for the year, paying $118,000 in cash and owing the rest on account.
i. The selling, general, and administrative expenses, such as the president's salary and advertising for the parks, were $131,882 for the year and were classified as operating expenses; $125,500 was paid in cash, and the rest was owed on account.
j. Cedar Fair paid $9,600 on accounts payable during the year.

Required:

1. For each of these transactions, record journal entries. Use the letter of each transaction as its reference. Note that transaction (*d*) will require two entries, one for revenue recognition and one for the related expense.
2. Use the following chart to identify whether each transaction results in a cash flow effect from operating (O), investing (I), or financing (F) activities, and indicate the direction and amount of the effect on cash (+ for increase and − for decrease). If there is no cash flow effect, write **none.** The first transaction is provided as an example.

Transaction	Operating, Investing, or Financing Effect	Direction and Amount of the Effect (in thousands)
(*a*)	O	+566,266

ALTERNATE PROBLEMS

Recording Nonquantitative Journal Entries (P3-1)

AP3-1
LO4

The following is a series of accounts for Kruger & Laurenzo, Incorporated, which has been operating for two years. The accounts are listed and numbered for identification. Following the accounts is a series of transactions. For each transaction, indicate the account(s) that should be debited and credited by entering the appropriate account number(s) to the right of each transaction. If no journal entry is needed, write **none** after the transaction. The first transaction is given as an example.

Account No.	Account Title	Account No.	Account Title
1	Cash	9	Wages Payable
2	Accounts Receivable	10	Income Taxes Payable
3	Supplies	11	Contributed Capital
4	Prepaid Expenses	12	Retained Earnings
5	Buildings	13	Service Revenue
6	Land	14	Other Expenses (wages, supplies, interest)
7	Accounts Payable	15	Income Tax Expense
8	Mortgage Payable		

Transactions	Debit	Credit
a. *Example:* Issued stock to new investors.	1	11
b. Incurred and recorded operating expenses on credit to be paid next period.	14	7
c. Purchased on credit but did not use supplies this period.	3	7
d. Performed services for customers this period on credit.	2	13
e. Prepaid a fire insurance policy this period to cover the next 12 months.	4	1
f. Purchased a building this period by making a 20 percent cash down payment and signing a mortgage loan for the balance.	5	1, 8
g. Collected cash this year for services rendered and recorded in the prior year.	1	2
h. Collected cash for services rendered this period.	1	13
i. Paid cash this period for wages earned and recorded last period.	9	1
j. Paid cash for operating expenses charged on accounts payable in the prior period.	7	1
k. Paid cash for operating expenses incurred in the current period.	14	1
l. Made a payment on the mortgage loan, which was part principal repayment and part interest.	8, 14	1
m. This period a shareholder sold some shares of her stock to another person for an amount above the original issuance price.	None	
n. Used supplies on hand to clean the offices.	14	3
o. Recorded income taxes for this period to be paid at the beginning of the next period.	15	10
p. Declared and paid a cash dividend this period.	12	1

Recording Journal Entries (P3-2)

AP3-2
LO4

Jimmy Langenberger is the president of TemPro, Inc., a company that provides temporary employees for not-for-profit companies. TemPro has been operating for five years; its revenues are increasing with each passing year. You have been hired to help Jimmy analyze the following transactions for the first two weeks of April:

a. Billed the local United Way office \$23,500 for temporary services provided.
b. Paid \$3,005 for supplies purchased and recorded on account last period.
c. Purchased office supplies for \$2,600 on account.
d. Purchased a new computer for the office costing \$3,800 cash.
e. Placed an advertisement in the local paper for \$1,400 cash.

f. Paid employee wages of $11,900. Of this amount, $3,800 had been earned by employees and recorded in the Wages Payable account in the prior period.
g. Issued 3,000 additional shares of capital stock for cash at $45 per share in anticipation of building a new office.
h. Received $12,500 on account from the local United Way office from the services provided in (*a*).
i. Billed Family & Children's Service $14,500 for services rendered.
j. Purchased land as the site of a future office for $10,000. Paid $3,000 cash as a down payment and signed a note payable for the balance.
k. Received the April telephone bill for $1,950 to be paid next month.

Required:
For each of the transactions, prepare journal entries. Be sure to categorize each account as an asset (A), liability (L), stockholders' equity (SE), revenue (R), or expense (E).

AP3-3 LO4 Determining Financial Statement Effects of Various Transactions and Identifying Cash Flow Effects (P3-3)

Big Dog Holdings, Inc.

Big Dog Holdings, Inc., is the parent company of Big Dog USA, a company that develops, markets, and retails a collection of consumer products centered around the signature BIG DOGS name, logo, and "Big Dog" characters. The following activities were inferred from a recent annual report.

a. *Example:* Incurred expenses; paid part in cash and part on credit.
b. Paid interest on long-term debt.
c. Sold merchandise to customers on account. (**Hint:** Indicate the effects of the sale; then reduce inventory for the amount sold—two transactions.)
d. Sold investments for cash for more than their cost.
e. Collected cash on account.
f. Used supplies.
g. Repaid long-term debt principal.
h. Received dividends and interest on investments.
i. Purchased equipment; paid part in cash and part on credit.
j. Paid cash on account.
k. Issued additional stock.
l. Paid rent to outlet mall owners.

Required:
1. For each of the transactions, complete the tabulation, indicating the effect (+ for increase and − for decrease) of each transaction. (Remember that A = L + SE, R − E = NI, and NI affects SE through Retained Earnings.) Write NE if there is no effect. The first transaction is provided as an example.

	BALANCE SHEET			INCOME STATEMENT		
Transaction	Assets	Liabilities	Stockholders' Equity	Revenues	Expenses	Net Income
(*a*) (example)	−	+	−	NE	+	−

2. For each transaction, indicate where, if at all, it would be reported on the statement of cash flows. Use O for operating activities, I for investing activities, F for financing activities, and NE if the transaction would not be included on the statement.

AP3-4 LO 4, 5, 6 Analyzing the Effects of Transactions Using T-Accounts, Preparing Financial Statements, and Evaluating the Total Asset Turnover Ratio as a Manager (P3-4)

Alpine Stables, Inc., was established in Denver, Colorado, on April 1, 2011. The company provides stables, care for animals, and grounds for riding and showing horses. You have been hired as the new assistant controller. The following transactions for April 2011 are provided for your review.

a. Received contributions from five investors of $60,000 in cash ($12,000 each), a barn valued at $100,000, land valued at $90,000, and supplies valued at $12,000. Each investor received 3,000 shares of stock.
b. Built a small barn for $62,000. The company paid half the amount in cash on April 1, 2011, and signed a three-year note payable for the balance.

c. Provided $35,260 in animal care services for customers, all on credit.
d. Rented stables to customers who cared for their own animals; received cash of $13,200.
e. Received from a customer $2,400 to board her horse in May, June, and July (record as unearned revenue).
f. Purchased hay and feed supplies on account for $3,810 to be used in the summer.
g. Paid $1,240 in cash for water utilities incurred in the month.
h. Paid $2,700 on accounts payable for previous purchases.
i. Received $10,000 from customers on accounts receivable.
j. Paid $6,000 in wages to employees who worked during the month.
k. At the end of the month, purchased a two-year insurance policy for $3,600.
l. Received an electric utility bill for $1,800 for usage in April; the bill will be paid next month.
m. Paid $100 cash dividend to each of the investors at the end of the month.

Required:

1. Set up appropriate T-accounts. All accounts begin with zero balances.
2. Record in the T-accounts the effects of each transaction for Alpine Stables in April, referencing each transaction in the accounts with the transaction letter. Show the ending balances in the T-accounts.
3. Prepare financial statements at the end of April (income statement, statement of stockholders' equity, and balance sheet).
4. Write a short memo to the five owners offering your opinion on the results of operations during the first month of business.
5. After three years in business, you are being evaluated for a promotion to chief financial officer. One measure is how efficiently you have managed the assets of the business. The following annual data are available:

	2013*	2012	2011
Total assets	$480,000	$320,000	$300,000
Total liabilities	125,000	28,000	30,000
Total stockholders' equity	355,000	292,000	270,000
Total revenues	450,000	400,000	360,000
Net income	50,000	30,000	(10,000)

**At the end of 2013, Alpine Stables decided to build an indoor riding arena for giving lessons year-round. The company borrowed construction funds from a local bank in 2013, and the arena was opened in early 2014.*

Compute the total asset turnover ratio for 2012 and 2013 and evaluate the results. Do you think you should be promoted? Why?

Preparing a Statement of Cash Flows (P3-5)

AP3-5
LO5

Refer to AP3-4.

Required:
For the transactions listed in AP3-4, prepare a statement of cash flows for the month.

Analyzing the Effects of Transactions Using T-Accounts, Preparing Financial Statements, and Evaluating the Total Asset Turnover Ratio (P3-6)

AP3-6
LO4, 5, 6

ExxonMobil

The following are the summary account balances from a recent balance sheet of Exxon Mobil Corporation. The accounts have normal debit or credit balances, but they are not necessarily listed in good order. The amounts are shown in millions of dollars. Assume the year-end is December 31, 2010.

Cash	$ 31,437	Marketable securities (short-term investments)	$ 570
Notes payable (long-term)	7,025	Accounts payable	36,640
Accounts receivable	24,702	Income tax payable	10,060
Inventories	9,331	Prepaid expenses	2,315
Other long-term debt	58,962	Investments	28,556
Property and equipment, net	121,346	Other assets and intangibles, net	5,884
Contributed capital	5,314	Notes payable (short-term)	2,400
Other current assets	3,911		
Retained earnings	107,651		

The following is a list of hypothetical transactions for January 2011 (in millions of dollars):

a. Purchased on account $1,610 of new equipment.
b. Received $3,100 on accounts receivable.
c. Received and paid $3 for utility bills.
d. Earned $39,780 in sales on account with customers; cost of sales was $5,984.
e. Paid employees $1,238 for wages earned during the month.
f. Paid three-fourths of the income taxes payable.
g. Purchased $23 in supplies on account (include in Inventories).
h. Prepaid $82 to rent a warehouse next month.
i. Paid $10 of other long-term debt principal and $1 in interest expense on the debt.
j. Purchased a patent (an intangible asset) for $6 cash.

Required:

1. Prepare T-accounts for December 31, 2010, from the preceding list; enter the beginning balances. You will need additional T-accounts for income statement accounts; enter zero for beginning balances.
2. For each transaction, record the effects in the T-accounts. Label each using the letter of the transaction. Compute ending balances. (**Note:** Record two transactions in (*d*), one for revenue recognition and one for the expense.)
3. Prepare an income statement, statement of stockholders' equity, balance sheet, and statement of cash flows in good form for January 2011.
4. Compute the company's total asset turnover ratio for the month ended January 31, 2011. What does it suggest to you about Exxon Mobil?

CASES AND PROJECTS

Annual Report Cases

CP3-1
LO2, 4, 6

AMERICAN EAGLE OUTFITTERS, INC.

Finding Financial Information

Refer to the financial statements of American Eagle Outfitters in Appendix B at the end of the book.

Required:

1. State the amount of the largest expense on the income statement for the year ended January 31, 2009, and describe the transaction represented by the expense.
2. Assuming that all net sales are on credit, how much cash did American Eagle Outfitters collect from customers?* (**Hint:** Use a T-account of accounts receivable to infer collection.)
3. A shareholder has complained that "more dividends should be paid because the company had net earnings of $179,061,000. Since this amount is all cash, more of it should go to the owners." Explain why the shareholder's assumption that earnings equal net cash inflow is valid. If you believe that the assumption is **not** valid, state so and support your position concisely.
4. Describe and contrast the purpose of an income statement versus a balance sheet.
5. Compute the company's total asset turnover for the year ended January 31, 2009. Explain its meaning.

CP3-2
LO2, 4, 6

URBN
URBAN OUTFITTERS INC.

Finding Financial Information

Refer to the financial statements of Urban Outfitters in Appendix C at the end of the book.

*Note that most retailers settle sales in cash at the register and would not have accounts receivable related to sales unless they had layaway or private credit. For American Eagle, the accounts receivable on the balance sheet primarily relates to amounts owed from landlords for their construction allowances for building new American Eagle stores in malls.

Required:

1. What is the company's revenue recognition policy? (**Hint:** Look in the notes to the financial statements.)
2. Assuming that $50 million of cost of sales was due to noninventory purchase expenses (distribution and occupancy costs), how much inventory did the company buy during the year? (**Hint:** Use a T-account of inventory to infer how much was purchased.)
3. Calculate general, administrative, and selling expenses as a percent of sales for the years ended January 31, 2009, and January 31, 2008. By what percent did these expenses increase or decrease from fiscal year 2007 to 2008? The company's 2008 fiscal year ends on January 31, 2009. (**Hint:** Percentage Change = [Current Year Amount − Prior Year Amount]/Prior Year Amount.)
4. Compute the company's total asset turnover for the year ended January 31, 2009, and explain its meaning.

Comparing Companies within an Industry

CP3-3
LO2, 4, 6

Refer to the financial statements of American Eagle Outfitters in Appendix B, Urban Outfitters in Appendix C, and the Industry Ratio Report in Appendix D at the end of this book.

Required:

1. By what title does each company call its income statement? Explain what "Consolidated" means.
2. Which company had higher net income for the fiscal year?
3. Compute the total asset turnover ratio for both companies for the year. Which company is utilizing assets more effectively to generate sales? State why this is so and support your position.
4. Compare the total asset turnover ratio for both companies to the industry average. On average, are these two companies utilizing assets to generate sales better or worse than their competitors?
5. How much cash was provided by operating activities for each year by each company? What was the percentage change in operating cash flows (1) from fiscal year ended 2007 to 2008 and (2) from fiscal year ended 2008 to 2009? (**Hint:** Percentage Change = [Current Year Amount − Prior Year Amount]/Prior Year Amount.)

eXcel
www.mhhe.com/libby7e

Financial Reporting and Analysis Cases

Analyzing a Company over Time

CP3-4
LO6

Refer to the annual report for American Eagle Outfitters in Appendix B.

Required:

1. The annual report or 10-K report for American Eagle Outfitters provides selected financial data for the last five years. Compute the total asset turnover ratio for each of the most recent four years. (**Hint:** See Item 6 from the 10-K, which is disclosed within the annual report for the data. **Note:** Some companies will label a year that has a January year-end as having a fiscal year-end dated one year earlier. For example, a January 2009 year-end may be labeled as Fiscal 2008 since the year actually has more months that fall in the 2008 calendar year than in the 2009 calendar year.)
2. In Chapter 2, we discussed the current ratio. Compute this ratio for the most recent four years from information in Item 6.
3. What do your results from the trends in the two ratios suggest to you about American Eagle Outfitters?

Interpreting the Financial Press

CP3-5
LO3

The October 4, 2004, edition of *BusinessWeek* presented an article titled "Fuzzy Numbers" on issues related to accrual accounting and its weaknesses that have led some corporate executives to manipulate estimates in their favor, sometimes fraudulently. You can access the article on the text's website at **www.mhhe.com/libby7e**.

Required:

Read the article and then answer the following questions:

1. What is accrual accounting?
2. What does the article's title "Fuzzy Numbers" mean?
3. What does the article suggest about the reforms adopted by Congress and the SEC?

CP3-6
LO4, 5

Using Financial Reports: Analyzing Changes in Accounts and Preparing Financial Statements

Pete's Painting Service was organized as a corporation on January 20, 2011, by three individuals, each receiving 5,000 shares of stock from the new company. The following is a schedule of the **cumulative** account balances immediately after each of the first 10 transactions ending on January 31, 2011.

	CUMULATIVE BALANCES									
Accounts	*(a)*	*(b)*	*(c)*	*(d)*	*(e)*	*(f)*	*(g)*	*(h)*	*(i)*	*(j)*
Cash	$75,000	$70,000	$85,000	$71,000	$61,000	$64,000	$60,000	$49,000	$44,000	$60,000
Accounts Receivable			12,000	12,000	12,000	26,000	26,000	26,000	26,000	10,000
Office Fixtures		22,000	22,000	22,000	22,000	22,000	22,000	22,000	22,000	22,000
Land				18,000	18,000	18,000	18,000	18,000	18,000	18,000
Accounts Payable					3,000	3,000	3,000	10,000	5,000	5,000
Note Payable (long-term)		17,000	17,000	21,000	21,000	21,000	21,000	21,000	21,000	21,000
Contributed Capital	75,000	75,000	75,000	75,000	75,000	75,000	75,000	75,000	75,000	75,000
Retained Earnings							(4,000)	(4,000)	(4,000)	(4,000)
Paint Revenue			27,000	27,000	27,000	44,000	44,000	44,000	44,000	44,000
Supplies Expense					5,000	5,000	5,000	8,000	8,000	8,000
Wages Expense					8,000	8,000	8,000	23,000	23,000	23,000

Required:

1. Analyze the changes in this schedule for each transaction; then explain the transaction. Transaction *(a)* is an example:
   a. Cash increased $75,000, and Contributed Capital (stockholders' equity) increased $75,000. Therefore, transaction *(a)* was an issuance of the capital stock of the corporation for $75,000 cash.
2. Based only on the preceding schedule after transaction *(j)*, prepare an income statement, a statement of stockholders' equity, and a balance sheet.
3. For each of the transactions, indicate the type of effect on cash flows (O for operating, I for investing, or F for financing) and the direction (+ for increase and – for decrease) and amount of the effect. If there is no effect, write none. The first transaction is provided as an example.

Transaction	Operating, Investing, or Financing Effect	Direction and Amount of the Effect
(a)	F	+75,000

Critical Thinking Cases

CP3-7
LO3, 4, 5

Making a Decision as a Bank Loan Officer: Analyzing and Restating Financial Statements That Have Major Deficiencies (A Challenging Case)

Julio Estela started and operated a small boat repair service company during 2012. He is interested in obtaining a $100,000 loan from your bank to build a dry dock to store boats for customers in the winter months. At the end of the year, he prepared the following statements based on information stored in a large filing cabinet:

ESTELA COMPANY **Profit for 2012**		
Service fees collected during 2012		$ 55,000
Cash dividends received		10,000
Total		65,000
Expense for operations paid during 2012	$22,000	
Cash stolen	500	
New tools purchased during 2012 (cash paid)	1,000	
Supplies purchased for use on service jobs (cash paid)	3,200	
Total		26,700
Profit		$ 38,300
Assets Owned at the End of 2012		
Cash in checking account		$ 29,300
Building (at current market value)		32,000
Tools and equipment		18,000
Land (at current market value)		30,000
Stock in ABC Industrial		130,000
Total		$239,300

The following is a summary of completed transactions:

a. Received the following contributions (at fair market value) to the business from the owner when it was started in exchange for 1,000 shares of stock in the new company:

Building	$21,000	Land	$20,000
Tools and equipment	17,000	Cash	1,000

b. Earned service fees during 2012 of $87,000; of the cash collected, $20,000 was for deposits from customers on work to be done by Julio in the next year.

c. Received the cash dividends on shares of ABC Industrial stock purchased by Julio Estela six years earlier (the stock was not owned by the company).

d. Incurred expenses during 2012 of $61,000.

e. Determined amount of supplies on hand (unused) at the end of 2012 as $700.

Required:

1. Did Julio prepare the income statement on a cash basis or an accrual basis? Explain how you can tell. Which basis should be used? Explain why.
2. Reconstruct the correct entries under accrual accounting principles and post the effects to T-accounts.
3. Prepare an accrual-based income statement, balance sheet, and statement of cash flows. Explain (using footnotes) the reason for each change that you make to the income statement.
4. What additional information would assist you in formulating your decision regarding the loan to Julio?
5. Based on the revised statements and additional information needed, write a letter to Julio explaining your decision at this time regarding the loan.

Evaluating an Ethical Dilemma

CP3-8
LO3

Mike Lynch is the manager of an upstate New York regional office for an insurance company. As the regional manager, his compensation package comprises a base salary, commissions, and a bonus when the region sells new policies in excess of its quota. Mike has been under enormous pressure lately, stemming largely from two factors. First, he is experiencing a mounting personal debt due to a family member's illness. Second, compounding his worries, the region's sales of new policies have dipped below the normal quota for the first time in years.

You have been working for Mike for two years, and like everyone else in the office, you consider yourself lucky to work for such a supportive boss. You also feel great sympathy for his personal problems over the last few months. In your position as accountant for the regional office, you are only too aware of the drop in new policy sales and the impact this will have on the manager's bonus. While you are working late at year-end, Mike stops by your office.

Mike asks you to change the manner in which you have accounted for a new property insurance policy for a large local business. A substantial check for the premium came in the mail on December 31, the last day of the reporting year. The premium covers a period beginning on January 5. You deposited the check and correctly debited Cash and credited an **unearned revenue** account. Mike says, "Hey, we have the money this year, so why not count the revenue this year? I never did understand why you accountants are so picky about these things anyway. I'd like you to change the way you have recorded the transaction. I want you to credit a *revenue* account. And anyway, I've done favors for you in the past, and I am asking for such a small thing in return." With that, he leaves for the day.

Required:

1. How should you handle this situation?
2. What are the ethical implications of Mike's request?
3. Who are the parties who would be helped or harmed if you complied with the request?
4. If you fail to comply with his request, how will you explain your position to him in the morning?

Financial Reporting and Analysis Team Project

CP3-9
LO2, 3, 6

Team Project: Analysis of Income Statements and Ratios

As a team, select an industry to analyze. Reuters provides lists of industries under Sectors and Industries at www.reuters.com. (Click on an industry and then select Company Rankings for a list of members of that industry.) Each team member should acquire the annual report or 10-K for one publicly traded company in the industry, with each member selecting a different company. (Library files, the SEC EDGAR service at www.sec.gov, or the company itself are good sources.)

Required:

On an individual basis, each team member should write a short report answering the following questions about the selected company. Discuss any patterns across the companies that you as a team observe. Then, as a team, write a short report comparing and contrasting your companies.

1. For the most recent year, what is (are) the major revenue account(s)? What percentage is each to total operating revenues? (Calculated as Revenue A ÷ Total revenues.)
2. For the most recent year, what is (are) the major expense account(s)? What percentage is each to total operating expenses? (Calculated as Expense A ÷ Total expenses.)
3. Ratio Analysis:
   a. What does the total asset turnover ratio measure in general?
   b. Compute the ratio for the last three years.
   c. What do your results suggest about the company?
   d. If available, find the industry ratio for the most recent year, compare it to your results, and discuss why you believe your company differs or is similar to the industry ratio.
4. Describe the company's revenue recognition policy, if reported. (Usually in the Significant Accounting Policies footnote.)
5. The ratio of Cash from Operating Activities divided by Net Income measures how liberal (that is, speeding up revenue recognition or delaying expense recognition) or conservative (that is, taking care not to record revenues too early or expenses too late) management is in choosing among various revenue and expense recognition policies. A ratio above 1.0 suggests more conservative policies and below 1.0, more liberal policies. Compute the ratio for each of the last three years. What do your results suggest about the company's choice in accounting policies?

LEARNING OBJECTIVES

After studying this chapter, you should be able to:

1. Explain the purpose of a trial balance. p. 165
2. Explain the purpose of adjustments and analyze the adjustments necessary at the end of the period to update balance sheet and income statement accounts. p. 167
3. Present an income statement with earnings per share, statement of stockholders' equity, balance sheet, and statement of cash flows. p. 177
4. Compute and interpret the net profit margin. p. 182
5. Explain the closing process. p. 183

Lecture Presentation LP-4
www.mhhe.com/libby7e

CHAPTER FOUR

ADJUSTMENTS, FINANCIAL STATEMENTS, AND THE QUALITY OF EARNINGS

The end of the accounting period is a very busy time for Papa John's. Although the last day of the fiscal year for Papa John's falls on the last Sunday of December each year, the financial statements are not distributed to users until management and the external auditors (independent CPAs) make many critical evaluations.

FOCUS COMPANY:

Papa John's International

ESTIMATING REVENUES AND EXPENSES AT YEAR-END

www.papajohns.com

- Management must ensure that the correct amounts are reported on the balance sheet and income statement. This often requires estimations, assumptions, and judgments about the timing of revenue and expense recognition and values for assets and liabilities.
- The auditors have to (1) assess the strength of the controls established by management to safeguard the company's assets and ensure the accuracy of the financial records, and (2) evaluate the appropriateness of estimates and accounting principles used by management in determining revenues and expenses.

Managers of most companies understand the need to present financial information fairly so as not to mislead users. However, since end-of-period adjustments are the most complex portion of the annual recordkeeping process, they are prone to error. External auditors examine the company's records on a test, or sample, basis. To maximize the chance of detecting any errors significant enough to affect users' decisions, CPAs allocate more of their testing to transactions most likely to be in error.

Several accounting research studies have documented the most error-prone transactions for medium-size manufacturing companies. End-of-period adjustment errors such as failure to provide adequate product warranty liability, failure to include items that should be expensed, and end-of-period transactions recorded in the wrong period (called cut-off errors) are in the top category and thus receive a great deal of attention from the auditors.

For 2008, Papa John's year-end estimation and auditing process took until February 23, 2009, the date on which the auditor Ernst & Young LLP completed the audit work and signed its audit opinion. At that point, the financial statements were made available to the public.

UNDERSTANDING THE BUSINESS

Managers are responsible for preparing financial statements that are useful to investors, creditors, and others. Financial information is most useful for analyzing the past and predicting the future when it is considered by users to be of **high quality.** High-quality information should be relevant (that is, important in the analysis and available in a timely manner) and reliable (that is, verifiable and unbiased in portraying economic reality).

Users expect revenues and expenses to be reported in the proper period based on the revenue and matching principles discussed in Chapter 3. Revenues are to be recorded when earned, and expenses are to be recorded when incurred regardless of when cash receipts or payments occur. Many operating activities take place over a period of time or over several periods, such as using insurance that has been prepaid or owing wages to employees for past work. Because recording these and similar activities daily is often very costly, most companies wait until the end of the period (usually monthly, quarterly, or annually) to make **adjustments** to record related revenues and expenses in the correct period. These entries update the records and are the focus of this chapter.

In this chapter, we emphasize the use of the same analytical tools illustrated in Chapters 2 and 3 (T-accounts and journal entries) to understand how common adjustments are analyzed and recorded at the end of the accounting period. These tools provide the foundation for understanding adjustments requiring additional estimation and judgments by management that will be discussed in future chapters. Then, in this chapter, we prepare financial statements using adjusted accounts, and finally, illustrate how to prepare the accounting records for the next period by performing a process called **closing the books.**

ORGANIZATION of the Chapter

Adjusting Revenues and Expenses

- Accounting Cycle
- Unadjusted Trial Balance
- Purpose of Adjustments
- Types of Adjustments
- Adjustment Process

Preparing Financial Statements

- Income Statement
- Statement of Stockholders' Equity
- Balance Sheet
- Net Profit Margin Ratio

Closing the Books

- End of the Accounting Cycle
- Post-Closing Trial Balance

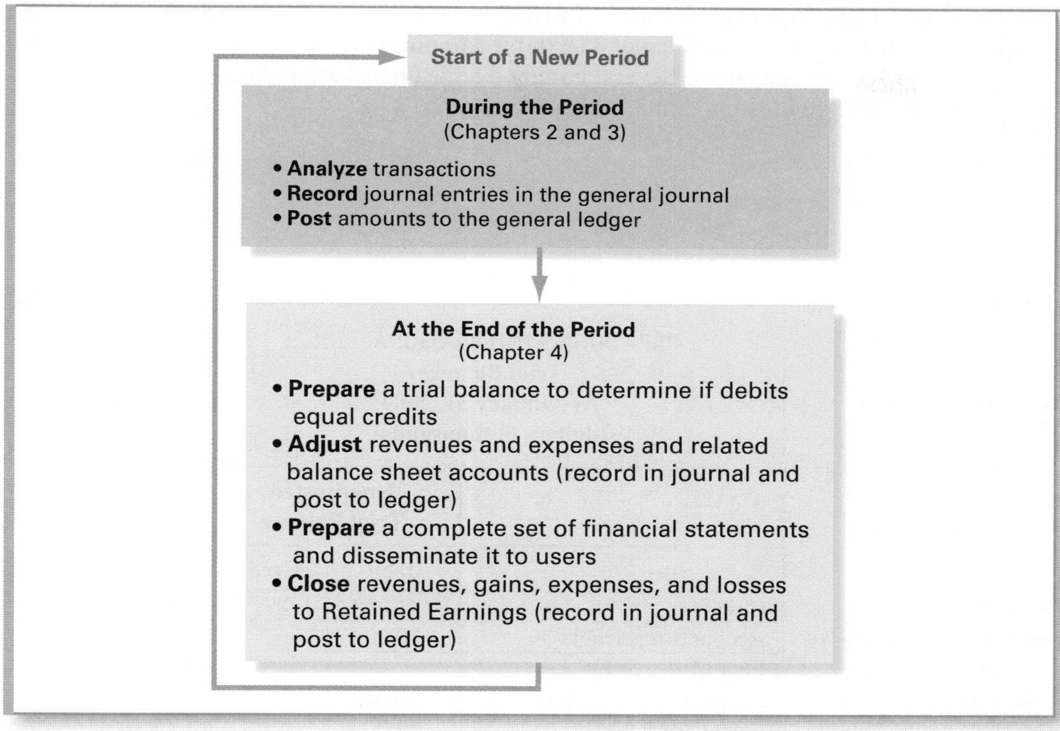

EXHIBIT 4.1

The Accounting Cycle

ADJUSTING REVENUES AND EXPENSES

Accounting Cycle

Exhibit 4.1 presents the basic steps in the **accounting cycle.** As initially discussed in Chapter 2, the accounting cycle is the process followed by entities to analyze and record transactions, adjust the records at the end of the period, prepare financial statements, and prepare the records for the next cycle. **During** the accounting period, transactions that result in exchanges between the company and other external parties are analyzed and recorded in the general journal in chronological order (journal entries), and the related accounts are updated in the general ledger (T-accounts), similar to our Papa John's illustrations in Chapters 2 and 3. In this chapter, we examine the **end-of-period** steps that focus primarily on adjustments to record revenues and expenses in the proper period and to update the balance sheet accounts for reporting purposes.

The ACCOUNTING CYCLE is the process followed by entities to analyze and record transactions, adjust the records at the end of the period, prepare financial statements, and prepare the records for the next cycle.

Unadjusted Trial Balance

LEARNING OBJECTIVE 1

Explain the purpose of a trial balance.

Before adjusting the accounting records, managers normally review an unadjusted trial balance. A **trial balance** is a spreadsheet that lists the names of the T-accounts in one column, usually in financial statement order, with their ending debit or credit balances in the next two columns. Debit balances are indicated in the left column and credit balances are indicated in the right column. Then the two columns are totaled to provide a check on the equality of the debits and credits. Errors in a computer-generated trial balance may exist if wrong accounts and/or amounts are used in the journal entries.[1] Once equality is established, the accounts on the trial balance can be reviewed to determine if there are any adjustments that need to be recorded.

A TRIAL BALANCE is a list of all accounts with their balances to provide a check on the equality of the debits and credits.

[1]In homework assignments, if you have an error in your trial balance (the two column totals are not equal), errors can be traced and should be corrected before adjusting the records. To find errors, reverse your steps. Check that you:

- Copied the ending balances in all of the T-accounts (both amount and whether a debit or credit) correctly to the trial balance.
- Computed the ending balances in the T-accounts correctly.
- Posted the transaction effects correctly from the journal entries to the T-accounts (amount, account, and whether a debit or credit).
- Prepared the journal entries correctly (amount, account, and whether a debit or credit).

Video 4-1
www.mhhe.com/libby7e

Papa John's unadjusted trial balance is presented in Exhibit 4.2. It is based on the T-account balances from the illustration in Chapter 3 (Exhibit 3.6) plus other accounts that may be needed but currently have zero balances. Several common adjustments are indicated in the margin of Exhibit 4.2 and will be illustrated in this chapter.

EXHIBIT 4.2

Unadjusted Trial Balance for Papa John's International

PAPA JOHN'S INTERNATIONAL, INC.
Trial Balance
At January 31, 2009
(dollars in thousands)

Margin note	Account	Unadjusted Trial Balance Debit	Unadjusted Trial Balance Credit	
	Cash	41,900		Assets
May need an accrual for any amount earned from franchisees but not yet recorded	Accounts receivable	20,200		Assets
May need an accrual for any investment income earned but not yet recorded	Interest receivable	0		Assets
May need an adjustment for the amount of supplies used during the period	Supplies	16,000		Assets
May need an adjustment for the amount of rent and insurance used during period	Prepaid expenses	19,000		Assets
	Other current assets	13,000		Assets
	Investments (long-term)	2,000		Assets
Represents the historical cost of property and equipment →	Property and equipment	388,000		Assets
Represents the total amount of the cost of property and equipment used in the past →	Accumulated depreciation		189,000	Assets
	Notes receivable (long-term)	11,000		Assets
	Intangibles	77,000		Assets
	Other assets	36,000		Assets
	Accounts payable		39,000	Liabilities
	Dividends payable		3,000	Liabilities
May need an accrual for any wages, utilities, and interest incurred	Accrued expenses payable		71,000	Liabilities
Needs an accrual for the amount of income tax expense incurred during period	Income tax payable		0	Liabilities
May need an adjustment for the amount earned during period	Unearned franchise fees		6,300	Liabilities
	Notes payable (long-term)		138,000	Liabilities
	Other long-term liabilities		27,000	Liabilities
	Contributed capital		9,000	Stockholders' Equity
Represents the beginning balance of retained earnings minus dividends declared during the month ($123,000 − $3,000) →	Retained earnings		120,000	Stockholders' Equity
Revenue from selling pizza and ingredients plus equipment to franchisees	Restaurant sales revenue		66,000	Revenues and Gains
Revenue from selling franchises during the period	Franchise fee revenue		2,800	Revenues and Gains
Revenue on investments earned during the period	Investment income		1,000	Revenues and Gains
	Gain on sale of land		3,000	Revenues and Gains
	Cost of sales	30,000		Expenses and Losses
Expense for wages incurred during the period	Salaries expense	14,000		Expenses and Losses
Summary for many operating expenses	General and administrative expenses	7,000		Expenses and Losses
Expense for supplies used during period	Supplies expense	0		Expenses and Losses
Expense for rent used during period	Rent expense	0		Expenses and Losses
Expense for insurance used during period	Insurance expense	0		Expenses and Losses
Expense for utilities used during period	Utilities expense	0		Expenses and Losses
Expense for property and equipment used during period	Depreciation expense	0		Expenses and Losses
Expense for interest incurred on debt during period	Interest expense	0		Expenses and Losses
Expense for income taxes incurred during period	Income tax expense	0		Expenses and Losses
Debits = Credits →	Total	$675,100	$675,100	

For reporting purposes:		
Property and Equipment	(cost)	$388,000
− Accumulated Depreciation	(used cost)	189,000
Net book value	(unused cost)	$199,000

Purpose of Adjustments

LEARNING OBJECTIVE 2
Explain the purpose of adjustments and analyze the adjustments necessary at the end of the period to update balance sheet and income statement accounts.

Accounting systems are designed to record most recurring daily transactions, particularly those involving cash. As cash is received or paid, it is recorded in the accounting system. In general, this focus on cash works well, especially when cash receipts and payments occur in the same period as the activities that produce revenues and expenses. However, cash is not always received in the period in which the company earns revenue; likewise, cash is not always paid in the period in which the company incurs an expense.

How does the accounting system record revenues and expenses when one transaction is needed to record a cash receipt or payment and another transaction is needed to record revenue when it is earned or an expense when it is incurred? The solution to the problem created by such differences in timing is to record **adjusting entries** at the end of every accounting period, so that

- Revenues are recorded when they are earned (the **revenue principle**),
- Expenses are recorded when they are incurred to generate revenue (the **matching principle**),
- **Assets** are reported at amounts that represent the probable future benefits remaining at the end of the period, and
- **Liabilities** are reported at amounts that represent the probable future sacrifices of assets or services owed at the end of the period.

ADJUSTING ENTRIES are entries necessary at the end of the accounting period to measure all revenues and expenses of that period.

Companies wait until the **end of the accounting period** to adjust their accounts in this way because adjusting the records daily would be very costly and time-consuming. Adjusting entries are required every time a company wants to prepare financial statements for external users.

Types of Adjustments

Exhibit 4.3 describes the four types of adjustments (two in which cash was already received or paid and two in which cash will be received or paid). Each of these types of adjustments involves two entries:

1. One for the cash receipt or payment.
2. One for recording the revenue or expense in the proper period through the adjusting entry.

EXHIBIT 4.3

Four Types of Adjustments

Adjusting Entries that Increase Revenues:

- **Deferred Revenues** – Previously recorded liabilities that were created when cash was received in advance, and that must be reduced for the amount of revenue actually earned during the period.
- **Accrued Revenues** – Revenues that have been earned but not yet recorded because cash will be received after the services are performed or goods are delivered.

Adjusting Entries that Increase Expenses:

- **Deferred Expenses** – Previously recorded assets, such as Prepaid Rent, Supplies, and Equipment, that were created when cash was paid in advance and that must be reduced for the amount of expense actually incurred during the period through use of the asset.
- **Accrued Expenses** – Expenses that have been incurred but not yet recorded because cash will be paid after the goods or services are used.

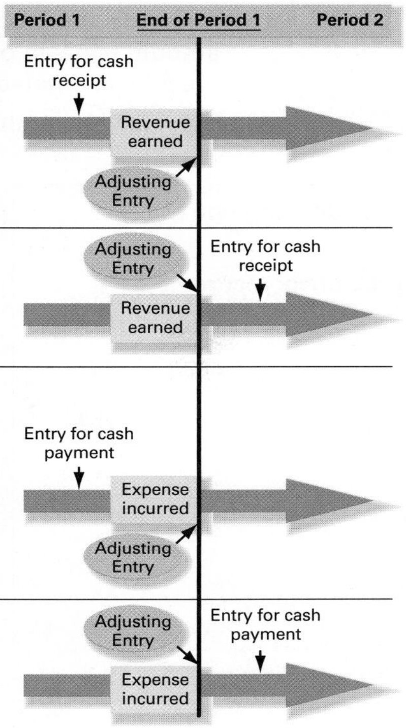

In practice, almost every account could require an adjustment. Rather than trying to memorize an endless list of specific examples, you should focus instead on learning the general types of adjustments that are needed and the process that is used to determine how to adjust the accounts. We will illustrate the process involved in analyzing and adjusting the accounts by reviewing all the adjustments needed for Papa John's before preparing January's financial statements based on adjusted balances.

Adjustment Process

In analyzing adjustments at the end of the period, there are three steps:

Step 1 **Ask: Was revenue earned or an expense incurred that is not yet recorded?**

If the answer is YES, credit the revenue account or debit the expense account in the adjusting entry.

Step 2 **Ask: Was the related cash received or paid in the past or will it be received or paid in the future?**

If cash **was received** in the past (creating a deferred revenue [liability] account in the past) → Reduce the liability account (usually Unearned Revenue) that was recorded when cash was received because some or all of the liability has been earned since then.

If cash **will be received** in the future → Increase the receivable account (such as Interest Receivable or Rent Receivable) to record what is owed by others to the company (creates an accrued revenue).

If cash **was paid** in the past (creating a deferred expense account [asset] in the past) → Reduce the asset account (such as Supplies or Prepaid Expenses) that was recorded in the past because some or the entire asset has been used since then.

If cash **will be paid** in the future → Increase the payable account (such as Interest Payable or Wages Payable) to record what is owed by the company to others (creates an accrued expense).

Step 3 **Compute the amount of revenue earned or expense incurred.** Sometimes the amount is given or known, sometimes it must be computed, and sometimes it must be estimated.

In summary, the pattern that results when the adjusting entry is recorded is as follows:

When revenue is earned, the adjusting entry is:

DEFERRED REVENUE
if cash was received and previously recorded
↓

Unearned Revenue (–L)	xx	
Revenue (+R, +SE)		xx

OR

ACCRUED REVENUE
if cash will be received
↓

Receivable (+A)	xx	
Revenue (+R, +SE)		xx

When expense is incurred, the adjusting entry is:

Expense (+E, –SE)	xx	
Prepaid Expense (–A)		xx

↑
DEFERRED EXPENSE
if cash was paid and previously recorded

OR

Expense (+E, –SE)	xx	
Payable (+L)		xx

↑
ACCRUED EXPENSE
if cash will be paid

Now let's illustrate the adjustment process for Papa John's at the end of January. From a review of the unadjusted trial balance in Exhibit 4.2, we identify several accounts to adjust:

- One unearned revenue account: Unearned Franchise Fees
- Two accrued revenue accounts:
  - Interest Receivable
  - Accounts Receivable
- Three prepaid expense accounts:
  - Prepaid Expenses (related to rent and insurance)
  - Supplies
  - Property and Equipment (used during the period)
- Two accrued expense accounts:
  - Accrued Expenses Payable (for wages, utilities, and interest)
  - Income Tax Payable

For each of the following adjustments, we shorten the term **adjusting journal entry** to AJE for ease of labeling. Also, as you learned in Chapters 2 and 3, it is important to continue to check that debits equal credits in each entry and that the accounting equation remains in balance. In the following adjustments, all entries and the accounting equation are in balance.

Deferred Revenues

When a customer pays for goods or services before the company delivers them, the company records the amount of cash received in a **deferred (or unearned) revenue** account. This unearned revenue is a liability representing the company's promise to perform or deliver the goods or services in the future. Recognition of (recording) the revenue is postponed (deferred) until the company meets its obligation.

DEFERRED (OR UNEARNED) REVENUES are previously recorded liabilities that need to be adjusted at the end of the accounting period to reflect the amount of revenue earned.

AJE 1 **Unearned Franchise Fees** Papa John's received cash last period and recorded an increase in Cash and an increase in Unearned Franchise Fees, a liability, to recognize the business's obligation to provide future services to franchisees. During January, Papa John's performed $1,100 in services for franchisees who had previously paid fees.

AJE 1:	Debit	Credit
Unearned Franchise Fees (−L) (Step 2)	1,100	
Franchise Fee Revenue (+R, +SE) (Step 1)		1,100 (Step 3)

Assets	=	Liabilities	+	Stockholders' Equity	
		−1,100		+1,100	Franchise Fee Revenue (+R)

Step 1: Was revenue earned that is not yet recorded? Yes. Because Papa John's provided services to franchisees, the company has earned Franchise Fee Revenue that is not yet recorded. Record an increase in the revenue account.

Step 2: Was the related cash received in the past or will it be received in the future? In the past. Papa John's received cash in the past from franchisees for future services. At the end of the period, there was $6,300 in the liability account Unearned Franchise Fees. Because some of the services have been performed in the current period, reduce the deferred revenue account.

Step 3: Compute the amount of revenue earned. The amount of the revenue that was earned is given as $1,100. Record this amount in the adjusting journal entry.

For other companies, additional examples of deferred revenues include magazine subscriptions; season tickets to sporting events, plays, and concerts; airplane tickets sold in advance; and rent paid in advance by renters. Each of these requires an adjusting entry at the end of the accounting period to report the amount of revenue earned during the period.

Accrued Revenues

ACCRUED REVENUES are previously unrecorded revenues that need to be adjusted at the end of the accounting period to reflect the amount earned and the related receivable account.

Sometimes companies perform services or provide goods (that is, earn revenue) before customers pay. Because the cash that is owed for these goods and services has not yet been received and the customers have not yet been billed, the revenue that was earned has not been recorded. Revenues that have been earned but have not yet been recorded at the end of the accounting period are called **accrued revenues.**

AJE 2 **Accounts Receivable** Papa John's franchisees owe Papa John's $830 in royalties for sales the franchisees made in the last week of January.

Step 2 (→ Accounts Receivable); Step 1 (→ Franchise Fee Revenue); Step 3 (→ 830 credit)

AJE 2:	Debit	Credit
Accounts Receivable (+A)	830	
Franchise Fee Revenue (+R, +SE)		830

Assets	=	Liabilities	+	Stockholders' Equity	
+830				+830	Franchise Fee Revenue (+R)

Step 1: **Was revenue earned that is not yet recorded? Yes.** The franchise agreement requires franchisees to pay Papa John's royalties on a percentage of weekly sales. Papa John's has earned the royalties for the last week of January. Record an increase in the revenue account.

Step 2: **Was the related cash received in the past or will it be received in the future? In the future.** Papa John's will receive payment from franchisees for royalties on past sales. Because cash will be received, a receivable needs to be increased. Increase Accounts Receivable.

Step 3: **Compute the amount of revenue earned.** The amount of the revenue that was earned is given as $830. Add this amount to the adjusting journal entry.

AJE 3 **Interest Receivable** Papa John's loaned $3,000 to franchisees on December 31 (one month ago) at 6 percent interest per year with interest to be paid at the end of each year. There was also $8,000 in notes receivable outstanding all month from prior loans. There are two components when lending or borrowing money: **principal** (the amount loaned or borrowed) and **interest** (the cost of borrowing). Notes Receivable (the principal) was recorded properly when the money was loaned. Its balance does not need to be adjusted. However, interest revenue is earned by Papa John's over time as the money is used by the franchisees.

Step 2 (→ Interest Receivable); Step 1 (→ Investment Income); Step 3 (→ 70 credit)

AJE 3:	Debit	Credit
Interest Receivable (+A)	70	
Investment Income (+R, +SE)		70

Assets	=	Liabilities	+	Stockholders' Equity	
+70				+70	Investment Income (+R)

Step 1: **Was revenue earned that is not yet recorded? Yes.** Papa John's earns interest revenue over time as the franchisees use the money they borrowed. Record an increase in the revenue account.

Step 2: **Was the related cash received in the past or will it be received in the future? In the future.** Papa John's will receive interest payments from franchisees in the future.

Because cash will be received, a receivable account needs to be increased. Increase Interest Receivable.

Step 3: **Compute the amount of revenue earned. Note:** Unless told otherwise, **the interest rate on loans and borrowings is always given as an annual percentage.** To compute interest revenue for less than a full year, the number of months needed in the calculation is divided by 12. Because the loan was made on December 31, only one month has passed. The formula to compute interest is:

Principal	×	Rate per Year	×	Number of Months (since last computation)/12	=	Interest for the Period
$3,000	×	.06	×	1 month /12 months	=	$15
Assume interest on the other $8,000 in notes receivable					=	55
				Total interest earned		$70

Add this $70 amount to the adjusting journal entry.

Deferred Expenses

Assets represent resources with probable future benefits to the company. Many assets are used over time to generate revenues, including supplies, buildings, equipment, prepaid insurance, and prepaid rent. These assets are **deferred expenses.** At the end of every period, an adjustment must be made to record the amount of the asset that was used during the period.

DEFERRED EXPENSES are previously acquired assets that need to be adjusted at the end of the accounting period to reflect the amount of expense incurred in using the asset to generate revenue.

AJE 4 **Prepaid Rent and Insurance** The Prepaid Expenses account includes $2,000 paid on January 1 for insurance coverage for four months (January through April) and $6,000 paid on January 1 for the rental of space at shopping centers over three months (January through March).

Step 1: **Was expense incurred that is not yet recorded? Yes.** The company used insurance coverage for one month and rental space for one month, but no entry has been made to record either. Record an increase in the appropriate expense accounts, Insurance Expense and Rent Expense.

Step 2: **Was the related cash paid in the past or will it be paid in the future? In the past.** At the beginning of January, Papa John's acquired insurance coverage for the next four months and prepaid rent for the next three months. The payments were recorded in the asset account, Prepaid Expenses, that must now be reduced at month-end because insurance and rent for one month have been used. Reduce Prepaid Expenses.

Step 1 → Insurance Expense; Step 2 → Prepaid Expenses; Step 3 → amounts

AJE 4:	Debit	Credit
Insurance Expense (+E, −SE)	500	
Rent Expense (+E, −SE)	2,000	
Prepaid Expenses (−A)		2,500

Assets	=	Liabilities	+	Stockholders' Equity	
−2,500				−500	Insurance Expense (+E)
				−2,000	Rent Expense (+E)

Step 3: **Compute the amount of expense incurred.** One month has expired for each of the prepaid amounts:

(1) Insurance: $2,000 × 1 month/4 months = $500 used in January.

(2) Rent: $6,000 × 1 month/3 months = $2,000 used in January.

AJE 5 **Supplies** Supplies include food and paper products. At the end of the month, Papa John's counted $12,000 in supplies on hand, but the Supplies account indicated a balance of $16,000 (from Exhibit 4.2).

Step 1

AJE 5:	Debit	Credit
Supplies Expense (+E, −SE)	4,000	
Supplies (−A)		4,000

Step 2 Step 3

Assets	=	Liabilities	+	Stockholders' Equity	
−4,000				−4,000	Supplies Expense (+E)

Step 1: **Was expense incurred that is not yet recorded? Yes.** Supplies were used during the period, but no entry has been made to record the amount used. Record an increase in the expense account.

Step 2: **Was the related cash paid in the past or will it be paid in the future? In the past.** Papa John's purchased supplies during the month and recorded the acquisition in the Supplies account. Some of these supplies have been used during the month, but no entry has yet been made to reduce the account. Reduce Supplies.

Step 3: **Compute the amount of expense incurred.** The easiest way to determine the dollar amount of supplies used is to add the dollar amount of supplies available at the beginning of the period plus any purchases made during the period, and then subtract the dollar amount of supplies remaining on hand at the end of the period.

Computation of Supplies Expense:	
Beginning balance of supplies + Supply purchases during period	$ 16,000 unadjusted balance
− Ending amount of supplies on hand	−12,000
= Supplies used during the period	$ 4,000

The balance on Papa John's trial balance is $16,000, which includes purchases during the month. With a count of supplies on hand of $12,000, the amount of supplies used during the period is $4,000. Add this amount to the adjusting journal entry.

AJE 6 **Property and Equipment** Before illustrating the adjustment process for buildings and equipment, notice that the Property and Equipment account is stated at the original cost of $388,000 in the trial balance in Exhibit 4.2 but was shown at $199,000 on the balance sheet in previous chapters. Unlike supplies, which are purchased and then used over a relatively short period, buildings and equipment represent deferred expenses that will be used over many years. Building and equipment accounts increase when the assets are **acquired** and decrease when they are **sold.** However, these assets are also **used** over time to generate revenue. Thus, a part of their cost should be expensed in the same period (the matching principle). Accountants say that buildings and equipment **depreciate** over time as they are used. In accounting, **depreciation is an allocation of an asset's cost over its estimated useful life to the company.**

To keep track of the asset's historical cost, the amount that has been used is not subtracted directly from the asset account. Instead, it is accumulated in a new kind of account called a **contra-account.** Contra-accounts are accounts that are **directly linked to another account, but with an opposite balance.** For Property and Equipment, the contra-account for the total cost used to date is called **Accumulated Depreciation.** This is the first of several contra-accounts you will learn throughout the text. We will designate contra-accounts with an X in front of the type of account to which it is related. For example, this first contra-account will be shown as Accumulated Depreciation (XA).

A CONTRA-ACCOUNT is an account that is an offset to, or reduction of, the primary account.

Since assets have debit balances, Accumulated Depreciation has a credit balance. On the balance sheet, the amount that is reported for Property and Equipment is its **net book value** (also called the **book value** or **carrying value**), which equals the ending balance in the Property and Equipment account minus the ending balance in the Accumulated Depreciation account.

The NET BOOK VALUE (BOOK VALUE, CARRYING VALUE) of an asset is the difference between its acquisition cost and accumulated depreciation, its related contra-account.

+ Property and Equipment (A) −	
Beginning bal. Buy	Sell
Ending bal.	

−

− Accumulated Depreciation (XA) +	
	Beginning bal. Used
	Ending bal.

= Net book value

Amount reported on the balance sheet

For Papa John's, Accumulated Depreciation has a credit balance of $189,000.

On the balance sheet:	
Property and equipment (net of accumulated depreciation of $189,000)	$199,000

Depreciation is discussed in much greater detail in Chapter 8. Until then, we will give you the amount of depreciation estimated by the company for the period. Papa John's estimates depreciation to be $30,000 per year.

Step 1: **Was expense incurred that is not yet recorded? Yes.** The company used buildings and equipment during January. Record an increase in the expense account, Depreciation Expense.

Step 2: **Was the related cash paid in the past or will it be paid in the future? In the past.** Papa John's purchased property and equipment in the past to be used over several years. The acquisitions were recorded in the asset account Property and Equipment. The amount to be used in the future (net book value) must now be reduced for the depreciation for January. Reduce the net book value by increasing the contra-account Accumulated Depreciation.

Step 3: **Compute the amount of expense incurred.** The property and equipment has been used to generate revenues for one month. Thus, we need to calculate only one month of Depreciation Expense:

Monthly depreciation = $30,000 annual depreciation × 1/12 months
= $ 2,500

AJE 6:	Debit	Credit
Depreciation Expense (+E, −SE) (Step 1)	2,500	
Accumulated Depreciation (+XA, −A) (Step 2)		2,500 (Step 3)

Assets	=	Liabilities	+	Stockholders' Equity	
−2,500				−2,500	Depreciation Expense (+E)

Accrued Expenses

Numerous expenses are incurred in the current period without being paid for until the next period. Common examples include Salaries Expense for the wages owed to employees, Utilities Expense for the water, gas, and electricity used during the period, and the Interest Expense incurred on debt. These **accrued expenses** accumulate (accrue) over time but are not recognized until the end of the period in an adjusting entry.

ACCRUED EXPENSES are previously unrecorded expenses that need to be adjusted at the end of the accounting period to reflect the amount incurred and the related payable account.

AJE 7 **Accrued Expenses Payable (Salaries, Utilities, and Interest)** Papa John's owed (1) its employees salaries for working four days at the end of January at $500 per day, (2) $610 for utilities used in January, and (3) interest on its long-term notes payable borrowed at a 6 percent annual rate.

AJE 7:	Debit	Credit
Salaries Expense (+E, −SE)	2,000	
Utilities Expense (+E, −SE)	610	
Interest Expense (+E, −SE)	690	
Accrued Expenses Payable (+L)		3,300

Step 1 → Salaries Expense (+E, −SE); Step 2 → Accrued Expenses Payable (+L); Step 3 → amounts

Assets	=	Liabilities	+	Stockholders' Equity	
		+3,300		−2,000	Salaries Expense (+E)
				−610	Utilities Expense (+E)
				−690	Interest Expense (+E)

Step 1: **Was expense incurred that is not yet recorded? Yes.** During January, the company used employee labor, utilities, and money borrowed from a bank, but by the end of January, not all of these expenses have been recorded. Expenses on the income statement are understated. Record an increase in each of the following expense accounts: Salaries Expense, Utilities Expense, and Interest Expense.

Step 2: **Was the related cash paid in the past or will it be paid in the future? In the future.** Each of the expenses will need to be paid in the next period, but no liability has yet been recorded. Thus liabilities on the balance sheet need to be increased. Although individual liability accounts such as Salaries Payable, Utilities Payable, and Interest Payable could be increased, Papa John's records all of these types of expenses in one account, Accrued Expenses Payable. Increase the liability.

Step 3: **Compute the amount of expense incurred.** Each of these amounts is computed or estimated as follows:

(1) Salaries: \$500 per day × 4 days = \$2,000

(2) Utilities: Amount is given as \$610, which is estimated by Papa John's based on reviewing prior utility bills

(3) Interest on debt: Like interest earned (in AJE 3), interest incurred on borrowed funds is computed using the same formula:

Principal	×	Rate per Year	×	Number of Months (since last computation)/12	=	Interest for the Period
\$138,000	×	.06	×	1 month/12 months	=	\$690

AJE 8 **Income Taxes Payable** The final adjusting journal entry is to record the accrual of income taxes that will be paid in the next quarter. This requires computing adjusted pretax income (that is, balances from the unadjusted trial balance plus the effects of all of the other adjustments):

	Revenues and Gains		Expenses and Losses		
Unadjusted totals	\$72,800		\$51,000		From Exhibit 4.2
AJE 1	1,100				
AJE 2	830				
AJE 3	70				
AJE 4			2,500		
AJE 5			4,000		
AJE 6			2,500		
AJE 7			3,300		
	\$74,800	−	\$63,300	=	**\$11,500 Pretax income**

Papa John's average income tax rate is 34 percent.

Step 1: **Was expense incurred that is not yet recorded? Yes.** Companies incur taxes on income. Until an adjusting entry is recorded at the end of the period based on all adjusted revenues, gains, expenses, and losses, expenses on the income statement are understated. Record an increase in the expense Income Tax Expense.

AJE 8:

	Debit	Credit
Income Tax Expense (+E, −SE) (Step 1)	3,910	
Income Tax Payable (+L) (Step 2)		3,910 (Step 3)

Assets	=	Liabilities	+	Stockholders' Equity	
		+3,910		−3,910	Income Tax Expense (+E)

Step 2: **Was the related cash paid in the past or will it be paid in the future? In the future.** Income taxes are due at the end of each quarter. So the tax liabilities on the balance sheet must be increased. Increase the liability Income Tax Payable.

Step 3: **Compute the amount of expense incurred.** Income taxes are computed on the pretax income after all other adjustments:

$11,500 pretax income × .34 = $3,910 income tax expense for January

In all of the above adjustments, you may have noticed that **the Cash account was never adjusted.** The cash has already been received or paid by the end of the period, or will be received or paid in the next period. Adjustments are required to record revenues and expenses in the proper period because the cash part of the transaction is at a different point in time. In addition, **each adjusting entry always included one income statement account and one balance sheet account.** Now it's your turn to practice the adjustment process.

Adjustments and Incentives

A QUESTION OF ETHICS

Owners and managers of companies are most directly affected by the information presented in financial statements. If the financial performance and condition of the company appear strong, the company's stock price rises. Shareholders usually receive dividends and increase their investment value. Managers often receive bonuses based on the strength of a company's financial performance, and many in top management are compensated with options to buy their company's stock at prices below market value. The higher the market value, the more compensation they earn. When actual performance lags behind expectations, managers and owners may be tempted to manipulate accruals and deferrals to make up part of the difference. For example, managers may record cash received in advance of being earned as revenue in the current period or may fail to accrue certain expenses at year-end.

Evidence from studies of large samples of companies indicates that some managers do engage in such behavior. This research is borne out by enforcement actions of the Securities and Exchange Commission against companies and sometimes against their auditors. In January 2003, an SEC study reported that, in a five-year period, there were 227 enforcement investigations. Of these, "126 involved improper revenue recognition and 101 involved improper expense recognition. . . . Of the 227 enforcement matters during the Study period, 157 resulted in charges against at least one senior manager. . . . Furthermore, the Study found that 57 enforcement matters resulted in charges for auditing violations. . . ." (p. 47).*

In many of these cases, the firms involved, their managers, and their auditors are penalized for such actions. Furthermore, owners suffer because news of an SEC investigation negatively affects the company's stock price.

*These statistics are reported in the Securities and Exchange Commission's study, "Report Pursuant to Section 704 of the Sarbanes-Oxley Act of 2002," January 27, 2003.

PAUSE FOR **FEEDBACK**

Adjustments are necessary at the end of the accounting cycle to record all revenues and expenses in the proper period and to reflect the proper valuation for assets and liabilities.

- **Deferred revenues** (liabilities) have balances at the end of the period because cash was received before it was earned. If all or part of the liability has been satisfied by the end of the period, revenue needs to be recorded and the liability reduced.
- **Accrued revenue** adjustments are necessary when the company has earned revenue, but the cash will be received in the next period. Since nothing has yet been recorded, revenue needs to be recognized and an asset (a receivable) increased.
- **Deferred expenses** (assets) have balances at the end of the period because cash was paid in the past by the company for the assets. If all or part of the asset has been used to generate revenues in the period, an expense needs to be recorded and the asset reduced.
- **Accrued expense** adjustments are necessary when the company has incurred an expense but the cash will be paid in the next period. Since nothing has yet been recorded, an expense needs to be recognized and a liability (a payable) increased.

SELF-STUDY **QUIZ**

For practice, complete the following adjustments using the three-step process outlined in the chapter: (1) Determine if a revenue was earned or an expense incurred; (2) determine if cash was received or paid in the past or will be received or paid in the future; and (3) compute the amount.

Florida Flippers, a scuba diving and instruction business, completed its first year of operations on December 31, 2010.

AJE 1: Florida Flippers received $6,000 from customers on November 15, 2010, for diving trips to the Bahamas in December and January. The $6,000 was recorded in Unearned Revenue on that date. By the end of December, one-third of the diving trips had been completed.

AJE 2: On December 31, 2010, Florida Flippers provided advanced diving instruction to 10 customers who will pay the business $800 in January. No entry was made when the instruction was provided.

AJE 3: On September 1, 2010, Florida Flippers paid $24,000 for insurance for the 12 months beginning on September 1. The amount was recorded as Prepaid Insurance on September 1.

AJE 4: On March 1, 2010, Florida Flippers borrowed $300,000 at 12 percent. Interest is payable each March 1 for three years.

	(1) Revenue earned or expense incurred?	(2) Cash received/paid in the past or cash to be received/paid in the future?	(3) Amount	Adjusting Journal Entry Accounts	Debit	Credit
AJE 1						
AJE 2						
AJE 3						
AJE 4						

After you have completed your answers, check them with the solutions at the bottom of the next page.

PREPARING FINANCIAL STATEMENTS

LEARNING OBJECTIVE 3

Present an income statement with earnings per share, statement of stockholders' equity, balance sheet, and statement of cash flows.

Before we prepare a complete set of financial statements, let's update the trial balance to reflect the adjustments and provide us with adjusted balances for the statements. In Exhibit 4.5, four new columns are added. Two are used to reflect the adjustments to each of the accounts. The other two are the updated balances, determined by adding (or subtracting) across each row. Again, we note that the total debits equal the total credits in each of the columns. It is from these adjusted balances that we will prepare an income statement, a statement of stockholders' equity (which includes a column for Retained Earnings), and a balance sheet.

As you learned in Chapter 1, the financial statements are interrelated—that is, the numbers from one statement flow into the next statement. Exhibit 4.4 illustrates the interconnections among the statements using the fundamental accounting equation. Starting on the bottom right, notice that

- Revenues minus expenses yields net income on the **Income Statement.**
- Net income (or net loss) and dividends to stockholders affect Retained Earnings and any additional issuances of stock during the period affect the balance in Contributed Capital, both on the **Statement of Stockholders' Equity.**
- Stockholders' Equity is a component of the **Balance Sheet.**

Thus, if a number on the income statement changes or is in error, it will impact the other statements.

Exhibit 4.4 also includes special labels for the accounts. Balance sheet accounts are considered **permanent,** indicating that they retain their balances from the end of one period to the beginning of the next. Revenue, expense, gain, and loss accounts are **temporary** accounts because their balances accumulate for a period, but start with a zero balance at the beginning of the next period. These labels will be discussed in the section on closing the books, which follows our presentation of Papa John's financial statements.

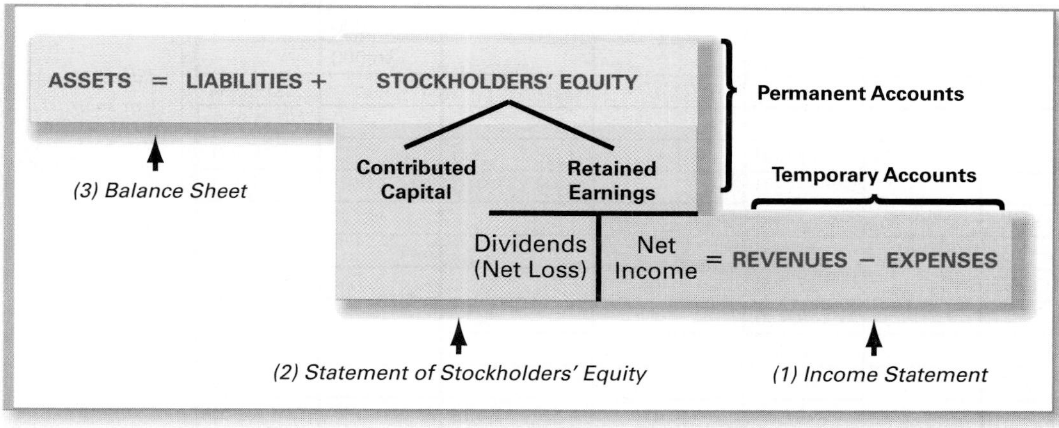

EXHIBIT 4.4

Relationships of the Financial Statements Using the Transaction Analysis Model

Solutions to SELF-STUDY QUIZ

	(1) Revenue earned or expense incurred?	(2) Cash received/paid in the past or cash to be received/paid in the future?	(3) Amount	Adjusting Journal Entry Accounts	Debit	Credit
AJE 1	Trip Revenue earned	Received in past: *Unearned Revenue*	$6,000 × 1/3 = $2,000 earned	Unearned Revenue (−L) Trip Revenue (+R, +SE)	2,000	2,000
AJE 2	Instruction Revenue earned	To be received: *Accrued Revenue*	$800 earned (given)	Accounts Receivable (+A) Instruction Revenue (+R, +SE)	800	800
AJE 3	Insurance Expense incurred	Paid in past: *Prepaid Expense*	$24,000 × 4 months/12=$8,000 used	Insurance Expense (+E, −SE) Prepaid Insurance (−A)	8,000	8,000
AJE 4	Interest Expense incurred	To be paid: *Accrued Expense*	$300,000 × .12 × 10/12 = $30,000 incurred and owed	Interest Expense (+E, −SE) Interest Payable (+L)	30,000	30,000

EXHIBIT 4.5

Adjusted Trial Balance for Papa John's International

Effects of the adjusting entries

PAPA JOHN'S INTERNATIONAL, INC.
Trial Balance at January 31, 2009
(dollars in thousands)

		Unadjusted Trial Balance		Adjustments		Adjusted Trial Balance		
		Debit	**Credit**	**Debit**	**Credit**	**Debit**	**Credit**	
Assets	Cash	41,900				41,900		
	Accounts receivable	20,200		*AJE 2* 830		21,030		
	Interest receivable	0		*AJE 3* 70		70		
	Supplies	16,000			*AJE 5* 4,000	12,000		
	Prepaid expenses	19,000			*AJE 4* 2,500	16,500		*= 19,000 − 2,500*
	Other current assets	13,000				13,000		
	Investments (long-term)	2,000				2,000		
	Property and equipment	388,000				388,000		
	Accumulated depreciation		189,000		*AJE 6* 2,500		191,500	
	Notes receivable (long-term)	11,000				11,000		
	Intangibles	77,000				77,000		
	Other assets	36,000				36,000		
Liabilities	Accounts payable		39,000				39,000	
	Dividends payable		3,000				3,000	
	Accrued expenses payable		71,000		*AJE 7* 3,300		74,300	
	Income tax payable		0		*AJE 8* 3,910		3,910	
	Unearned franchise fees		6,300	*AJE 1* 1,100			5,200	
	Notes payable (long-term)		138,000				138,000	
	Other long-term liabilities		27,000				27,000	
Stockholders' Equity	Contributed capital		9,000				9,000	
	Retained earnings		120,000				120,000	
Revenues and Gains	Restaurant sales revenue		66,000				66,000	
	Franchise fee revenue		2,800		*AJE 1* 1,100 *AJE 2* 830		4,730	*= 2,800 + 1,100 + 830*
	Investment income		1,000		*AJE 3* 70		1,070	
	Gain on sale of land		3,000				3,000	
Expenses and Losses	Cost of sales	30,000				30,000		
	Salaries expense	14,000		*AJE 7* 2,000		16,000		
	General and administrative expenses	7,000				7,000		
	Supplies expense	0		*AJE 5* 4,000		4,000		
	Rent expense	0		*AJE 4* 2,000		2,000		
	Insurance expense	0		*AJE 4* 500		500		
	Utilities expense	0		*AJE 7* 610		610		
	Depreciation expense	0		*AJE 6* 2,500		2,500		
	Interest expense	0		*AJE 7* 690		690		
	Income tax expense	0		*AJE 8* 3,910		3,910		
	Total	$675,100	$675,100	$18,210	$18,210	$685,710	$685,710	

To compute adjusted balances, add or subtract across each row: unadjusted balance +/− adjustment(s). See examples.

Another way of presenting the relationships among the statements is illustrated below. If a number on the income statement changes, it will impact the other statements.

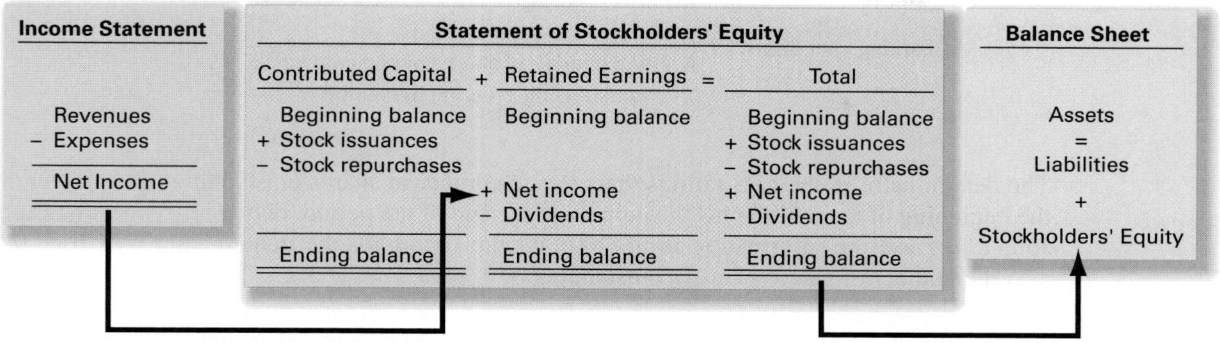

Income Statement

The income statement is prepared first because net income is a component of Retained Earnings. The January income statement for Papa John's based on transactions in Chapters 2 and 3 and adjustments in Chapter 4 follows.

PAPA JOHN'S INTERNATIONAL, INC., AND SUBSIDIARIES
Consolidated Statement of Income
For the Month Ended January 31, 2009
(dollars in thousands)

Operating Revenues	
Restaurant sales revenue	$66,000
Franchise fee revenue	4,730
Total revenues	70,730
Operating Expenses	
Cost of sales	30,000
Salaries expense	16,000
General and administrative expenses	7,000
Supplies expense	4,000
Rent expense	2,000
Insurance expense	500
Utilities expense	610
Depreciation expense	2,500
Total expenses	62,610
Operating Income	8,120
Other Items	
Investment income	1,070
Interest expense	(690)
Gain on sale of land	3,000
Income before Income Taxes	11,500
Income tax expense	3,910
Net Income	$ 7,590
Earnings per Share (EPS)	$ .27 ← *For the month*

You will note that the earnings (EPS) ratio is reported on the income statement. It is widely used in evaluating the operating performance and profitability of a company, and it is the only ratio required to be disclosed on the statement or in the notes to the statements. The actual computation of the ratio is quite complex and appropriate for more advanced accounting courses. In this text, we simplify the earnings per share computation as:

$$\text{Earnings per Share*} = \frac{\text{Net income}}{\text{Average number of shares of common stock outstanding** during the period}}$$

The denominator in the EPS ratio is the average number of shares outstanding (the number at the beginning of the period plus the number at the end of the period, divided by two). For Papa John's, we use the information in its 2008 annual report for the denominator—28,100,000 average number of shares of stock outstanding.

$7,590,000 Net income ÷ 28,100,000 shares = $.27 earnings per share for the month

Statement of Stockholders' Equity

The final total from the income statement, net income, is carried forward to the Retained Earnings column of the statement of stockholders' equity. To this, the additional elements of the statement are added. Dividends declared and an additional stock issuance (from prior chapters) are also included in the statement:

PAPA JOHN'S INTERNATIONAL, INC., AND SUBSIDIARIES
Consolidated Statement of Stockholders' Equity
Month Ended January 31, 2009
(dollars in thousands)

		Contributed Capital	Retained Earnings	Total Stockholders' Equity
	Beginning balance, December 31, 2008	$7,000	$123,000	$130,000
From Event (a) in Chapter 2 →	Additional stock issuances	2,000		2,000
From the income statement →	Net income		7,590	7,590
From Event (f) in Chapter 2 →	Dividends declared		(3,000)	(3,000)
Included on the balance sheet →	Ending balance, January 31, 2009	$9,000	$127,590	$136,590

Balance Sheet

The ending balances for Contributed Capital and Retained Earnings from the statement of stockholders' equity are included on the balance sheet that follows. You will notice that the contra-asset account, Accumulated Depreciation, has been subtracted from the Property and Equipment account to reflect **net book value** (or carrying value) at month-end for balance sheet purposes. Also recall that assets are listed in order of liquidity, and liabilities are listed in order of due dates. Current assets are those used or turned into cash within one year (as well as inventory). Current liabilities are obligations to be paid with current assets within one year.

---

*If there are preferred dividends (discussed in Chapter 11), the amount is subtracted from net income in the numerator. In addition, the denominator is the weighted average of shares outstanding, a complex computation.

**Outstanding shares are those that are currently held by the shareholders.

PAPA JOHN'S INTERNATIONAL, INC., AND SUBSIDIARIES
Consolidated Balance Sheet
January 31, 2009
(dollars in thousands)

ASSETS	
Current Assets	
Cash	$ 41,900
Accounts receivable	21,030
Interest receivable	70
Supplies	12,000
Prepaid expenses	16,500
Other current assets	13,000
Total current assets	104,500
Investments	2,000
Property and equipment (net of accumulated depreciation of $191,500)	196,500
Notes receivable	11,000
Intangibles	77,000
Other assets	36,000
Total assets	$427,000
LIABILITIES AND STOCKHOLDERS' EQUITY	
Current Liabilities	
Accounts payable	$ 39,000
Dividends payable	3,000
Accrued expenses payable	74,300
Income tax payable	3,910
Total current liabilities	120,210
Unearned franchise fees	5,200
Notes payable	138,000
Other long-term liabilities	27,000
Total liabilities	290,410
Stockholders' Equity	
Contributed capital	9,000
Retained earnings	127,590
Total stockholders' equity	136,590
Total liabilities and stockholders' equity	$427,000

From the Statement of Stockholders' Equity

Cash Flows from Operations, Net Income, and the Quality of Earnings

FOCUS ON CASH FLOWS

As presented in the previous chapters, the statement of cash flows explains the difference between the ending and beginning balances in the Cash account on the balance sheet during the accounting period. Put simply, the cash flow statement is a categorized list of all transactions of the period that affected the Cash account. The three categories are operating, investing, and financing activities. **Since no adjustments made in this chapter affected cash, Papa John's statement of cash flows discussed in Chapter 3 has not changed.**

Many standard financial analysis texts warn analysts to look for unusual deferrals and accruals when they attempt to predict future periods' earnings. They often suggest that wide disparities

(continued)

between net income and cash flow from operations are a useful warning sign. For example, Subramanyan suggests the following:

> Accounting accruals determining net income rely on estimates, deferrals, allocations, and valuations. These considerations sometimes allow more subjectivity than do the factors determining cash flows. For this reason we often relate cash flows from operations to net income in assessing its quality. **Some users consider earnings of higher quality when the ratio of cash flows from operations divided by net income is greater.** This derives from a concern with revenue recognition or expense accrual criteria yielding high net income but low cash flows (emphasis added).*

The cash flows from operations to net income ratio is illustrated and discussed in more depth in Chapter 13.

*K. Subramanyan, *Financial Statement Analysis* (New York, McGraw-Hill/Irwin, 2009), p. 412.

KEY RATIO ANALYSIS | Net Profit Margin

LEARNING OBJECTIVE 4

Compute and interpret the net profit margin.

ANALYTICAL QUESTION

How effective is management in generating profit on every dollar of sales?

RATIO AND COMPARISONS

$$\textbf{Net Profit Margin} = \frac{\textbf{Net Income}}{\textbf{Net Sales (or Operating Revenues)*}}$$

The 2008 ratio for Papa John's using actual reported amounts is (dollars in thousands):

$$\frac{\$36{,}796{,}000}{\$1{,}132{,}087{,}000} = .0325\ (3.25\%)$$

COMPARISONS OVER TIME		
Papa John's		
2006	2007	2008
6.33%	3.08%	3.25%

COMPARISONS WITH COMPETITORS	
Domino's Inc.	Yum! Brands, Inc.†
2008	2008
3.79%	8.55%

Selected Focus Companies' Net Profit Margin Ratios for 2008

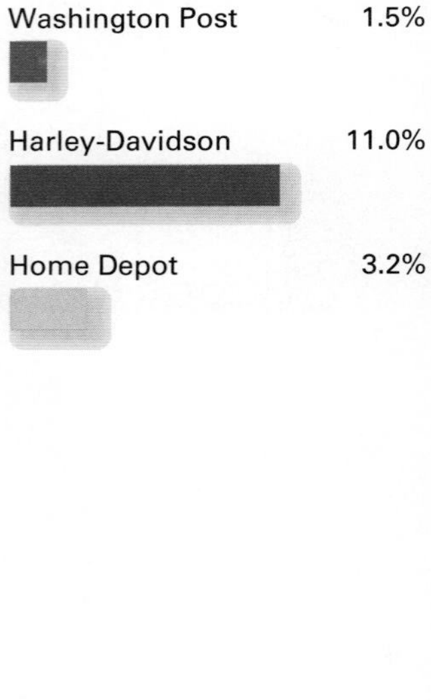

INTERPRETATIONS

In General Net profit margin measures how much of every sales dollar generated during the period is profit. A rising net profit margin signals more efficient management of sales and expenses. Differences among industries result from the nature of the products or services provided and the intensity of competition. Differences among competitors in the same industry reflect how each company responds to changes in competition (and demand for the product or service) and changes in managing sales volume, sales price, and costs. Financial analysts expect well-run businesses to maintain or improve their net profit margin over time.

Focus Company Analysis Papa John's net profit margin decreased significantly between 2006 and 2007 to 3.08 percent. As indicated in the annual report, the primary changes were in higher labor costs due to a federal minimum wage increase and higher cheese costs. Although cheese, wheat, rent, and utility costs were higher in 2008, the ratio improved in 2008 to 3.25 percent due to an increase in franchise sales on the revenue side and staffing efficiencies and a lower level of advertising on the cost side. Papa John's management did a better job of controlling sales and costs in 2008.

Domino's is Papa John's main competitor in the delivery segment of the pizza business. Domino's has an almost 17 percent higher net profit margin at 3.79 percent. This may suggest increased efficiency in commissary activities by Domino's. Similarly, Yum! Brands has an 8.55 percent net profit margin, more than two times greater than that of Papa John's and Domino's. Yum! Brands operates dine-in, take-out, and delivery restaurants that rely more heavily on facilities. Differences in business strategies explain some of the wide variation in the ratio analysis.

A Few Cautions The decisions that management makes to maintain the company's net profit margin in the current period may have negative long-run implications. Analysts should perform additional analysis of the ratio to identify trends in each component of revenues and expenses. This involves dividing each line on the income statement by net sales. Statements presented with these percentages are called **common-sized income statements.** Changes in the percentages of the individual components of net income provide information on shifts in management's strategies.

*Net sales is sales revenue less any returns from customers and other reductions. For companies in the service industry, total operating revenues is equivalent to net sales.
†Yum! Brands is the parent company of Pizza Hut, KFC, A&W, Long John Silver's, and Taco Bell.

CLOSING THE BOOKS

End of the Accounting Cycle

LEARNING OBJECTIVE 5
Explain the closing process.

The ending balance in each of the asset, liability, and stockholders' equity accounts becomes the beginning account balance for the next period. These accounts, called **permanent (real) accounts** (shown in Exhibit 4.5), are not reduced to a zero balance at the end of the accounting period. For example, the ending Cash balance of the prior accounting period is the beginning Cash balance of the next accounting period. The only time a permanent account has a zero balance is when the item it represents is no longer owned or owed.

PERMANENT (REAL) ACCOUNTS are the balance sheet accounts that carry their ending balances into the next accounting period.

On the other hand, revenue, expense, gain, and loss accounts are used to accumulate data for the **current accounting period only;** they are called **temporary (nominal) accounts** (see Exhibit 4.5). The final step in the accounting cycle, closing the books, is done to prepare income statement accounts for the next accounting cycle. Therefore, at the end of each period, the balances in the temporary accounts are transferred, or **closed,** to the Retained Earnings account by recording a closing entry.

TEMPORARY (NOMINAL) ACCOUNTS are income statement accounts that are closed to Retained Earnings at the end of the accounting period.

The **closing entry** has two purposes:

A CLOSING ENTRY transfers balances in temporary accounts to Retained Earnings and establishes zero balances in temporary accounts.

1. To transfer the balances in the temporary accounts (income statement accounts) to Retained Earnings.[2]
2. To establish a zero balance in each of the temporary accounts to start the accumulation in the next accounting period.

In this way, the income statement accounts are again ready for their temporary accumulation function for the next period. The closing entry is dated the last day of the accounting period, entered in the usual debits-equal-credits format (in the journal), and immediately posted to the ledger (or T-accounts). **Temporary accounts with debit balances are credited and temporary accounts with credit balances are debited.** The net amount, equal to net income, affects Retained Earnings.

Video 4-2
www.mhhe.com/libby7e

[2]Companies may close income statement accounts to a special temporary summary account, called **Income Summary,** which is then closed to Retained Earnings.

To illustrate the process, we create an example using just a few accounts. The journal entry amounts are taken from the pre-closing balances in the T-accounts:

Revenues have credit balances. Close them with debits.

Sales Revenue (−R)	100	
Gain on Sale of Assets (−R)	30	
Wages Expense (−E)		40
Loss on Sale of Assets (−E)		10
Retained Earnings (+SE)		80

Expenses have debit balances. Close them with credits.

=Net income

CE is short for closing entry.

Wages Expense			
Bal.	40	40	CE
Closed	0		

Loss on Sale of Assets			
Bal.	10	10	CE
Closed	0		

Retained Earnings			
		6,000	Bal.
		80	CE
		6,080	Bal.

130 revenues − 50 expenses = 80 Net income

Sales Revenue			
CE	100	100	Bal.
		0	Closed

Gain on Sale of Assets			
CE	30	30	Bal.
		0	Closed

We will now prepare the closing entry for Papa John's at January 31, 2009, although companies close their records only at the end of the fiscal year.[3] These amounts are taken from the adjusted trial balance in Exhibit 4.5.

Restaurant Sales Revenue (−R)	66,000	
Franchise Fee Revenue (−R)	4,730	
Investment Income (−R)	1,070	
Gain on Sale of Land (−R)	3,000	
Cost of Sales (−E)		30,000
Salaries Expense (−E)		16,000
General and Administrative Expenses (−E)		7,000
Supplies Expense (−E)		4,000
Rent Expense (−E)		2,000
Insurance Expense (−E)		500
Utilities Expense (−E)		610
Depreciation Expense (−E)		2,500
Interest Expense (−E)		690
Income Tax Expense (−E)		3,910
Retained Earnings (+SE)		7,590

[3]Most companies use computerized accounting software to record journal entries, produce trial balances and financial statements, and close the books.

PAUSE FOR **FEEDBACK**

The process of closing the books (after adjustments) includes making all temporary account balances (from the income statement) zero and transferring the difference to Retained Earnings. The following is an adjusted trial balance from a recent year for Toys R Us. Dollars are in millions. Record the journal entry at the end of the accounting cycle to close the books.

SELF-STUDY **QUIZ**

	Debit	Credit
Cash	783	
Accounts receivable	251	
Merchandise inventories	1,781	
Buildings	7,226	
Accumulated depreciation		3,039
Other assets	1,409	
Accounts payable		1,412
Accrued expenses payable		847
Long-term debt		5,447
Other liabilities		979
Contributed capital		19
Retained earnings (accumulated deficit)	399	
Sales revenue		13,724
Interest income		16
Gain on sale of business		5
Other income		130
Cost of sales	8,976	
Selling, general, and administrative expenses	3,968	
Depreciation expense	399	
Interest expense	419	
Income tax expense	7	
Totals	25,618	25,618

Closing entry:

After you have completed your answers, check them with the solutions at the bottom of the page.

Solutions to SELF-STUDY QUIZ

	Debit	Credit
Sales revenue (−R)	13,724	
Interest income (−R)	16	
Gain on sale of business (−R)	5	
Other income (−R)	130	
Cost of sales (−E)		8,976
Selling, general, and administrative expenses (−E)		3,968
Depreciation expense (−E)		399
Interest expense (−E)		419
Income tax expense (−E)		7
Retained earnings (+SE)		106

Post-Closing Trial Balance

A POST-CLOSING TRIAL BALANCE should be prepared as the last step of the accounting cycle to check that debits equal credits and all temporary accounts have been closed.

After the closing process is complete, all income statement accounts have a zero balance. These accounts are then ready for recording revenues and expenses in the new accounting period. The ending balance in Retained Earnings now is up-to-date (matches the amount on the balance sheet) and is carried forward as the beginning balance for the next period. As the last step of the accounting information processing cycle, a **post-closing trial balance** should be prepared as a check that debits still equal credits and that all temporary accounts have been closed.

DEMONSTRATION CASE

We take our final look at the accounting activities of Terrific Lawn Maintenance Corporation by illustrating the activities at the end of the accounting cycle: the adjustment process, financial statement preparation, and the closing process. No adjustments had been made to the accounts to reflect all revenues earned and expenses incurred in April. The trial balance for Terrific Lawn on April 30, 2010, based on the unadjusted balances in Chapter 3, is as follows:

TERRIFIC LAWN MAINTENANCE CORPORATION
Unadjusted Trial Balance at April 30, 2010

		Debit	Credit
	Cash	5,032	
	Accounts receivable	1,700	
	Notes receivable	0	
	Prepaid expenses	300	
	Equipment	4,600	
	Accumulated depreciation		0
	Land	3,750	
	Accounts payable		220
	Wages payable		0
	Utilities payable		0
	Notes payable		3,700
	Interest payable		0
	Income tax payable		0
	Unearned revenue		1,600
	Contributed capital		9,000
	Retained earnings		0
$5,212 in total revenues	Mowing revenue		5,200
	Interest revenue		12
$4,350 in total expenses	Wages expense	3,900	
	Fuel expense	410	
	Insurance expense	0	
	Utilities expense	0	
	Depreciation expense	0	
	Interest expense	40	
	Income tax expense	0	
	Total	$19,732	$19,732

Additional information follows:

a. One-fourth of the $1,600 cash received from the city at the beginning of April for future mowing service has been earned in April. The $1,600 in Unearned Revenues represents four months of service (April through July).

b. Insurance costing $300 providing coverage for six months (April through September) paid by Terrific Lawn at the beginning of April has been partially used in April.

c. Mowers, edgers, rakes, and hand tools (equipment) have been used in April to generate revenues. The company estimates $300 in depreciation each year.

d. Wages have been paid through April 28. Employees worked the last two days of April and will be paid in May. Wages accrue at $200 per day.

e. An extra telephone line was installed in April at an estimated cost of $52, including hookup and usage charges. The bill will be received and paid in May.

f. Interest accrues on the outstanding notes payable at an annual rate of 12 percent. The $3,700 in principal has been outstanding all month.

g. The estimated income tax rate for Terrific Lawn is 35 percent.

Required:

1. Using the three-step process outlined in this chapter, (1) determine if a revenue was earned or an expense incurred that needs to be recorded for the period, (2) determine whether cash was or will be received or paid, and (3) compute the amount. Prepare the adjusting journal entries for April.

2. Prepare an adjusted trial balance.

3. Prepare an income statement, statement of stockholders' equity, and balance sheet from the amounts in the adjusted trial balance. Include earnings per share on the income statement. The company issued 1,500 shares.

4. Prepare the closing entry for April 30, 2010.

5. Compute the company's net profit margin for the month.

Now you can check your answers with the following solutions.

SUGGESTED SOLUTION

1. *a.* **Step 1: Was revenue earned?**
Yes. A portion of the unearned revenue liability has been earned. Mowing Revenue is understated.

AJE a	Debit	Credit
Unearned Revenue (−L)	400	
Mowing Revenue (+R, +SE)		400

Step 2: Was cash received in the past or will it be received in the future?
In the past. The Unearned Revenue account is currently overstated. —*Deferred Revenue*

Assets	=	Liabilities	+	Stockholders' Equity	
		−400		+400	Mowing Revenue (+R)

Step 3: Compute the amount.
$1,600 × 1/4 = $400 earned.

b. **Step 1: Was expense incurred?**
Yes. A portion of the prepaid insurance asset has been used. Insurance Expense is understated.

AJE b	Debit	Credit
Insurance Expense (+E, −SE)	50	
Prepaid Expenses (−A)		50

Step 2: Was cash paid in the past or will it be paid in the future?
In the past. The Prepaid Expenses account is currently overstated. —*Deferred Expense*

Assets	=	Liabilities	+	Stockholders' Equity	
−50				−50	Insurance Expense (+E)

Step 3: Compute the amount.
$300 × 1/6 = $50 insurance used in April.

AJE c	Debit	Credit
Depreciation Expense (+E, −SE)	25	
Accumulated Depreciation (+XA, −A)		25

Assets	=	Liabilities	+	Stockholders' Equity	
−25				−25	Depreciation Expense (+E)

c. **Step 1: Was expense incurred?**
Yes. A portion of the equipment has been used. Depreciation Expense is understated.

Step 2: Was cash paid in the past or will it be paid in the future?
In the past. The equipment account is not directly reduced when the asset is used. Instead, the contra-account Accumulated Depreciation is increased, thus reducing the equipment's net book value. —*Deferred Expense*

Step 3: Compute the amount.
$300 × 1/12 = $25 depreciation on equipment in April.

AJE d	Debit	Credit
Wages Expense (+E, −SE)	400	
Wages Payable (+L)		400

Assets	=	Liabilities	+	Stockholders' Equity	
		+400		−400	Wages Expense (+E)

d. **Step 1: Was expense incurred?**
Yes. The company used employees' labor, incurring Wages Expense that is not yet recorded. It is understated.

Step 2: Was cash paid in the past or will it be paid in the future?
In the future. The employees will be paid next period for work this period. Because no entry has yet been recorded, Wages Payable is understated. —*Accrued Expense*

Step 3: Compute the amount.
$200 per day × 2 days = $400 incurred in April.

AJE e	Debit	Credit
Utilities Expense (+E, −SE)	52	
Utilities Payable (+L)		52

Assets	=	Liabilities	+	Stockholders' Equity	
		+52		−52	Utilities Expense (+E)

e. **Step 1: Was expense incurred?**
Yes. The company used utilities in April, incurring Utilities Expense that is not yet recorded. It is understated.

Step 2: Was cash paid in the past or will it be paid in the future?
In the future. The utility company will be paid next period when the bill is received. Because no entry has yet been recorded, Utilities Payable is understated. –*Accrued Expense*

Step 3: Compute the amount.
$52 is estimated as incurred in April.

f. **Step 1: Was expense incurred?**
Yes. The company used borrowed funds in April, incurring Interest Expense (the cost of borrowing) that is not yet recorded. It is understated.

AJE f

	Debit	Credit
Interest Expense (+E, −SE)	37	
Interest Payable (+L)		37

Assets	=	Liabilities	+	Stockholders' Equity	
		+37		−37	Interest Expense (+E)

Step 2: Was cash paid in the past or will it be paid in the future?
In the future. The interest on debt will be paid in the future when due. Because no entry has yet been recorded, Interest Payable is understated. *–Accrued Expense*

Step 3: Compute the amount.
$3,700 principal × .12 rate × 1/12 = $37 interest incurred in April.

g. **Step 1: Was expense incurred?**
Yes. The company incurs Income Tax Expense for earning net income in April. The expense is understated.

AJE g

	Debit	Credit
Income Tax Expense (+E, −SE)	244	
Income Tax Payable (+L		244

Assets	=	Liabilities	+	Stockholders' Equity	
		+244		−244	Income Tax Expense (+E)

Step 2: Was cash paid in the past or will it be paid in the future?
In the future. Income taxes will be paid in the next period. Because no entry has yet been recorded, Income Tax Payable is understated. *–Accrued Expense*

Step 3: Compute the amount.

COMPUTATION OF PRETAX INCOME

	Revenues		Expenses	
Unadjusted amounts	$5,212		$4,350	From trial balance
a	400			
b			50	
c			25	
d			400	
e			52	
f			37	
Adjusted amounts	$5,612	–	$4,914	= $698 pretax income

$698 pretax income × .35 tax rate = $244 tax expense (rounded)

2. Adjusted trial balance:

TERRIFIC LAWN MAINTENANCE CORPORATION
Adjusted Trial Balance
At April 30, 2010

	Unadjusted Trial Balance		Adjustments		Adjusted Trial Balance	
	Debit	**Credit**	**Debit**	**Credit**	**Debit**	**Credit**
Cash	5,032				5,032	
Accounts receivable	1,700				1,700	
Notes receivable	0				0	
Prepaid expenses	300			*(b)* 50	250	
Equipment	4,600				4,600	
Accumulated depreciation		0		*(c)* 25		25
Land	3,750				3,750	
Accounts payable		220				220
Wages payable		0		*(d)* 400		400
Utilities payable		0		*(e)* 52		52
Notes payable		3,700				3,700
Interest payable		0		*(f)* 37		37
Income tax payable		0		*(g)* 244		244
Unearned revenues		1,600	*(a)* 400			1,200
Contributed capital		9,000				9,000
Retained earnings		0				0
Mowing revenue		5,200		*(a)* 400		5,600
Interest revenue		12				12
Wages expense	3,900		*(d)* 400		4,300	
Fuel expense	410				410	
Insurance expense	0		*(b)* 50		50	
Utilities expense	0		*(e)* 52		52	
Depreciation expense	0		*(c)* 25		25	
Interest expense	40		*(f)* 37		77	
Income tax expense	0		*(g)* 244		244	
Total	$19,732	$19,732	$1,208	$1,208	$20,490	$20,490

3. Financial statements:

TERRIFIC LAWN MAINTENANCE CORPORATION
Income Statement
For the Month Ended April 30, 2010

Operating revenues	
Mowing revenue	$5,600
Operating expenses	
Wages expense	4,300
Fuel expense	410
Insurance expense	50
Utilities expense	52
Depreciation expense	25
	4,837
Operating income	763
Other items	
Interest revenue	12
Interest expense	(77)
Pretax income	698
Income tax expense	244
Net Income	$ 454
Earnings per share (for the month) ($454 ÷ 1,500 shares)	$ .30

TERRIFIC LAWN MAINTENANCE CORPORATION
Statement of Stockholders' Equity
For the Month Ended April 30, 2010

	Contributed Capital	Retained Earnings	Total
Beginning April 1, 2010	$ 0	$ 0	$ 0
Stock issuance	9,000		9,000
Net income		454	454
Dividends declared		0	0
Balance, April 30, 2010	$9,000	$454	$9,454

TERRIFIC LAWN MAINTENANCE CORPORATION
Balance Sheet
April 30, 2009

Assets		**Liabilities**	
Current Assets:		Current Liabilities:	
Cash	$ 5,032	Accounts payable	$ 220
Accounts receivable	1,700	Wages payable	400
Prepaid expenses	250	Utilities payable	52
Total current assets	6,982	Notes payable	3,700
		Interest payable	37
		Income tax payable	244
		Unearned revenue	1,200
Equipment (net of $25 accumulated depreciation)	4,575	Total current liabilities	5,853
Land	3,750	**Stockholders' Equity**	
		Contributed Capital	9,000
		Retained earnings	454
		Total stockholders' equity	9,454
Total assets	**$15,307**	**Total liabilities and stockholders' equity**	**$15,307**

4. Closing entry:

Mowing Revenue (−R)	5,600	
Interest Revenue (−R)	12	
Wages Expense (−E)		4,300
Fuel Expense (−E)		410
Insurance Expense (−E)		50
Utilities Expense (−E)		52
Depreciation Expense (−E)		25
Interest Expense (−E)		77
Income Tax Expense (−E)		244
Retained Earnings (+SE)		454

5. Net Profit Margin for April:

$$\frac{\text{Net Income}}{\text{Net Sales Revenue}} = \$454 \div \$5{,}600 = 0.081\text{, or } 8.1\% \text{ for the month of April}$$

CHAPTER TAKE-AWAYS

1. Explain the purpose of a trial balance. p. 165

A trial balance is a list of all accounts with their debit or credit balances indicated in the appropriate column to provide a check on the equality of the debits and credits. The trial balance may be

- Unadjusted—before adjustments are made.
- Adjusted—after adjustments are made.
- Post-closing—after revenues and expenses are closed to Retained Earnings.

2. Explain the purpose of adjustments and analyze the adjustments necessary at the end of the period to update balance sheet and income statement accounts. p. 167

- Adjusting entries are necessary at the end of the accounting period to measure income properly, correct errors, and provide for adequate valuation of balance sheet accounts. There are four types:
  - Deferred revenues—previously recorded liabilities created when cash was received in advance that must be adjusted for the amount of revenue earned during the period.
  - Accrued revenues—revenues that were earned during the period but have not yet been recorded (cash will be received in the future).
  - Deferred expenses—previously recorded assets (Prepaid Rent, Supplies, and Equipment) that must be adjusted for the amount of expense incurred during the period.
  - Accrued expenses—expenses that were incurred during the period but have not yet been recorded (cash will be paid in the future).

The analysis involves:

Step 1: Determining if revenue was earned or an expense was incurred. Record an increase in the revenue or expense account.

Step 2: Determining whether cash was received or paid in the past or will be received or paid in the future. If in the past, the existing asset or liability is overstated and needs to be reduced. If in the future, the related receivable or payable account needs to be increased.

Step 3: Compute the amount of revenue earned or expense incurred in the period.

- Recording adjusting entries has no effect on the Cash account.

3. Present an income statement with earnings per share, statement of stockholders' equity, balance sheet, and statement of cash flows. p. 177

Adjusted account balances are used in preparing the following financial statements:

- Income Statement: Revenues − Expenses = Net Income (including earnings per share, computed as net income divided by the average number of shares of common stock outstanding during the period).
- Statement of Stockholders' Equity: (Beginning Contributed Capital + Stock Issuances − Stock Repurchases) + (Beginning Retained Earnings + Net Income − Dividends Declared) = Ending Total Stockholders' Equity.
- Balance Sheet: Assets = Liabilities + Stockholders' Equity.
- Statement of Cash Flows: Since adjustments never affect cash, the statement of cash flows is not changed.

4. Compute and interpret the net profit margin. p. 182

Net profit margin (Net Income ÷ Net Sales) measures how much of every dollar of sales generated during the period is profit. A rising net profit margin signals more efficient management of sales and expenses.

5. Explain the closing process. p. 183

Temporary accounts (revenues, expenses, gains, and losses) are closed to a zero balance at the end of the accounting period to allow for the accumulation of income items in the following period and to update Retained Earnings for the period's net income. To close these accounts, debit each revenue and gain account, credit each expense and loss account, and record the difference (equal to net income) to Retained Earnings.

Closing Entry:

Each revenue	xx	
Each gain	xx	
Each expense		xx
Each loss		xx
Retained earnings . . .		xx
(assumes net income is positive) . . .		

This chapter discussed the important steps in the accounting process that take place at year-end. These include the adjustment process, the preparation of the basic financial statements, and the closing process that prepares the records for the next accounting period. This end to the internal portions of the accounting process, however, is just the beginning of the process of communicating accounting information to external users.

In the next chapter we take a closer look at more sophisticated financial statements and related disclosures. We also examine the process by which financial information is disseminated to professional analysts, investors, the Securities and Exchange Commission, and the public, and the role each plays in analyzing and interpreting the information. These discussions will help you consolidate much of what you have learned about the financial reporting process from previous chapters. It will also preview many of the important issues we address in later chapters. These later chapters include many other adjustments that involve difficult and complex estimates about the future, such as estimates of customers' ability to make payments to the company for purchases on account, the useful lives of new machines, and future amounts that a company may owe on warranties of products sold in the past. Each of these estimates and many others can have significant effects on the stream of net earnings that companies report over time.

KEY RATIO

Net profit margin measures how much of every sales dollar generated during the period is profit. A high or rising ratio suggests that the company is managing its sales and expenses efficiently. It is computed as follows (p. 182):

$$\text{Net Profit Margin} = \frac{\text{Net Income}}{\text{Net Sales (or Operating Revenues)}}$$

FINDING FINANCIAL INFORMATION

Balance Sheet

Current Assets
Accrued revenues include:
- Interest receivable
- Rent receivable

Deferred expenses include:
- Supplies
- Prepaid insurance

Noncurrent Assets
Deferred expenses include:
- Property and equipment
- Intangibles

Current Liabilities
Accrued expenses include:
- Interest payable
- Wages payable
- Utilities payable
- Income tax payable

Deferred revenues include:
- Unearned revenue

Income Statement

Revenues
Increased by adjusting entries

Expenses
Increased by adjusting entries

Pretax Income
Income tax expense

Net Income

Statement of Cash Flows

Adjusting Entries Do Not Affect Cash

Notes

In Various Notes (if not on the balance sheet)
Details of accrued expenses payable
Interest paid, income taxes paid

KEY TERMS

Accounting Cycle p. 165
Accrued Expenses p. 173
Accrued Revenues p. 170
Adjusting Entries p. 167
Closing Entry p. 183
Contra-Account p. 172
Deferred Expenses p. 171
Deferred (Unearned) Revenues p. 169
Net Book Value (Book Value, Carrying Value) p. 173
Permanent (Real) Accounts p. 183
Post-Closing Trial Balance p. 186
Temporary (Nominal) Accounts p. 183
Trial Balance p. 165

QUESTIONS

1. What is a trial balance? What is its purpose?
2. What is the purpose of recording adjusting entries?
3. List the four types of adjusting entries, and give an example of each type.
4. What is a contra-asset? Give an example of one.
5. Explain how the financial statements relate to each other.
6. What is the equation for each of the following statements: (*a*) income statement, (*b*) balance sheet, (*c*) statement of cash flows, and (*d*) statement of stockholders' equity?
7. Explain the effect of adjusting entries on cash.
8. How is earnings per share computed and interpreted?
9. How is net profit margin computed and interpreted?
10. Contrast an unadjusted trial balance with an adjusted trial balance. What is the purpose of each?
11. What are the purposes for closing the books?
12. Differentiate among (*a*) permanent, (*b*) temporary, (*c*) real, and (*d*) nominal accounts.
13. Why are the income statement accounts closed but the balance sheet accounts are not?
14. What is a post-closing trial balance? Is it a useful part of the accounting information processing cycle? Explain.

MULTIPLE-CHOICE QUESTIONS

1. Which of the following accounts would not appear in a closing entry?
   a. Salary Expense
   b. Interest Income
   c. Accumulated Depreciation
   d. Retained Earnings
2. Which account is least likely to appear in an adjusting journal entry?
   a. Interest Receivable
   b. Cash
   c. Property Tax Expense
   d. Salaries Payable
3. On October 1, 2011, the $12,000 premium on a one-year insurance policy for the building was paid and recorded as Prepaid Insurance. On December 31, 2011 (end of the accounting period), what adjusting entry is needed?

a.	Insurance Expense (+E)	2,000	
	Prepaid Insurance (−A)		2,000
b.	Insurance Expense (+E)	3,000	
	Prepaid Insurance (−A)		3,000
c.	Prepaid Insurance (+A)	3,000	
	Insurance Expense (−E)		3,000
d.	Prepaid Insurance (+A)	9,000	
	Insurance Expense (−E)		9,000

4. On June 1, 2010, Oakcrest Company signed a three-year $100,000 note payable with 9 percent interest. Interest is due on June 1 of each year beginning in 2011. What amount of interest expense should be reported on the income statement for the year ended December 31, 2010?
   a. $5,250
   b. $6,000
   c. $6,750
   d. $9,000
5. Failure to make an adjusting entry to recognize accrued salaries payable would cause which of the following?
   a. An understatement of expenses, liabilities, and stockholders' equity.
   b. An understatement of expenses and liabilities and an overstatement of stockholders' equity.
   c. An overstatement of assets and stockholders' equity.
   d. An overstatement of assets and liabilities.
6. An adjusted trial balance
   a. Shows the ending account balances in a "debit" and "credit" format before posting the adjusting journal entries.
   b. Is prepared after closing entries have been posted.
   c. Shows the ending account balances resulting from the adjusting journal entries in a "debit" and "credit" format.
   d. Is a tool used by financial analysts to review the performance of publicly traded companies.
7. JJ Company owns a building. Which of the following statements regarding depreciation as used by accountants is false?
   a. As depreciation is recorded, stockholders' equity is reduced.
   b. As depreciation is recorded, the net book value of the asset is reduced.
   c. As the value of the building decreases over time, it "depreciates."
   d. Depreciation is an estimated expense to be recorded over the building's estimated useful life.
8. At the beginning of 2011, Donna Company had $1,000 of supplies on hand. During 2011, the company purchased supplies amounting to $6,400 (paid for in cash and debited to Supplies). At December 31, 2011, a count of supplies reflected $2,600. The adjusting entry Donna Company would record on December 31, 2011, to adjust the Supplies account would include a
   a. Debit to Supplies for $2,600.
   b. Credit to Supplies Expense for $4,800.
   c. Credit to Supplies for $2,600.
   d. Debit to Supplies Expense for $4,800.
9. What ratio is required by GAAP to be reported on the financial statements or in the notes to the statements?
   a. Return on equity ratio.
   b. Net profit margin ratio.
   c. Earnings per share ratio.
   d. Current ratio.

10. If a company is successful in reducing selling and administrative costs while maintaining sales volume and the sales price of its product, what is the effect on the net profit margin ratio?

a. The ratio will increase.
b. The ratio will not change.
c. The ratio will decrease.
d. Either (a) or (c).

For more practice with multiple-choice questions, go to the text website at **www.mhhe.com/libby7e**.

MINI-EXERCISES

connect ACCOUNTING

M4-1 Preparing a Trial Balance
LO1

Hagadorn Company has the following adjusted accounts and balances at year-end (June 30, 2011):

Accounts Payable	$ 250	Interest Expense	$ 70
Accounts Receivable	420	Interest Income	60
Accrued Expenses Payable	160	Inventories	710
Accumulated Depreciation	250	Land	300
Buildings and Equipment	1,400	Long-Term Debt	1,460
Cash	175	Prepaid Expenses	30
Contributed Capital	400	Salaries Expense	640
Cost of Sales	780	Sales Revenue	2,400
Depreciation Expense	150	Rent Expense	460
Income Taxes Expense	135	Retained Earnings	150
Income Taxes Payable	50	Unearned Fees	90

Prepare an adjusted trial balance in good form for the Hagadorn Company at June 30, 2011.

M4-2 Matching Definitions with Terms
LO2

Match each definition with its related term by entering the appropriate letter in the space provided.

Definition	Term
___ (1) A revenue not yet earned; collected in advance.	A. Accrued expense
___ (2) Rent not yet collected; already earned.	B. Deferred expense
___ (3) Property taxes incurred; not yet paid.	C. Accrued revenue
___ (4) Rent revenue collected; not yet earned.	D. Deferred revenue
___ (5) An expense incurred; not yet paid or recorded.	
___ (6) Office supplies on hand to be used next accounting period.	
___ (7) An expense not yet incurred; paid in advance.	
___ (8) A revenue earned; not yet collected.	

M4-3 Matching Definitions with Terms
LO2

Match each definition with its related term by entering the appropriate letter in the space provided.

Definition	Term
___ (1) At year-end, service revenue of $1,000 was collected in cash but was not yet earned.	A. Accrued expense
___ (2) Interest of $550 on a note receivable was earned at year-end, although collection of the interest is not due until the following year.	B. Deferred expense
___ (3) At year-end, wages payable of $5,600 had not been recorded or paid.	C. Accrued revenue
___ (4) Office supplies were purchased during the year for $700, and $100 of them remained on hand (unused) at year-end.	D. Deferred revenue

Recording Adjusting Entries (Deferred Accounts)

M4-4
LO2

In each of the following transactions (*a*) through (*c*) for Romney's Marketing Company, use the three-step process illustrated in the chapter to record the adjusting entry at year-end December 31, 2012. The process includes (1) determining if revenue was earned or an expense incurred, (2) determining whether cash was received or paid in the past or will be received or paid in the future, and (3) computing the amount of the adjustment.

a. Collected $1,000 rent for the period December 1, 2012, to April 1, 2013, which was credited to Unearned Rent Revenue on December 1, 2012.
b. Purchased a machine for $32,000 cash on January 1, 2008. The company estimates annual depreciation at $3,000.
c. Paid $4,200 for a two-year insurance premium on July 1, 2012; debited Prepaid Insurance for that amount.

Determining Financial Statement Effects of Adjusting Entries (Deferred Accounts)

M4-5
LO2

For each of the transactions in M4-4, indicate the amounts and direction of effects of the adjusting entry on the elements of the balance sheet and income statement. Using the following format, indicate + for increase, − for decrease, and NE for no effect.

	BALANCE SHEET			INCOME STATEMENT		
Transaction	Assets	Liabilities	Stockholders' Equity	Revenues	Expenses	Net Income
a.						
b.						
c.						

Recording Adjusting Entries (Accrued Accounts)

M4-6
LO2

In each of the following transactions (*a*) through (*c*) for Romney's Marketing Company, use the three-step process illustrated in the chapter to record the adjusting entry at year-end December 31, 2012. The process includes (1) determining if revenue was earned or an expense incurred, (2) determining whether cash was received or paid in the past or will be received or paid in the future, and (3) computing the amount of the adjustment.

a. Estimated electricity usage at $380 for December; to be paid in January 2013.
b. On September 1, 2012, loaned $5,000 to an officer who will repay the loan principal and interest in one year at an annual interest rate of 14 percent.
c. Owed wages to 10 employees who worked four days at $150 each per day at the end of December. The company will pay employees at the end of the first week of January 2013.

Determining Financial Statement Effects of Adjusting Entries (Accrued Accounts)

M4-7
LO2

For each of the transactions in M4-6, indicate the amounts and direction of effects of the adjusting entry on the elements of the balance sheet and income statement. Using the following format, indicate + for increase, − for decrease, and NE for no effect.

	BALANCE SHEET			INCOME STATEMENT		
Transaction	Assets	Liabilities	Stockholders' Equity	Revenues	Expenses	Net Income
a.						
b.						
c.						

M4-8 Reporting an Income Statement with Earnings per Share
LO3

Romney's Marketing Company has the following adjusted trial balance at December 31, 2012. No dividends were declared. However, 500 shares issued at the end of the year for $3,000 are included below:

	Debit	Credit
Cash	$ 1,500	
Accounts receivable	2,200	
Interest receivable	100	
Prepaid insurance	1,600	
Notes receivable (long-term)	2,800	
Equipment	15,000	
Accumulated depreciation		$ 3,000
Accounts payable		2,400
Accrued expenses payable		3,920
Income taxes payable		2,700
Unearned rent revenue		500
Contributed capital (800 shares)		3,700
Retained earnings		2,000
Sales revenue		37,650
Interest revenue		100
Rent revenue		750
Wages expense	19,000	
Depreciation expense	1,800	
Utilities expense	320	
Insurance expense	700	
Rent expense	9,000	
Income tax expense	2,700	
Total	$56,720	$56,720

Prepare a multi-step income statement in good form for 2012. Include earnings per share.

M4-9 Reporting a Statement of Stockholders' Equity
LO3

Refer to M4-8. Prepare a statement of stockholders' equity in good form for 2012.

M4-10 Reporting a Balance Sheet and Explaining the Effects of Adjustments on the Statement of Cash Flows
LO3

1. Prepare a classified balance sheet in good form at December 31, 2012 from the information in M4-8.
2. Explain how the adjustments in M4-4 and M4-6 affected the operating, investing, and financing activities on the statement of cash flows.

M4-11 Analyzing Net Profit Margin
LO4

Compute net income based on the adjusted trial balance in M4-8. Then compute Romney's Marketing Company's net profit margin for 2012.

M4-12 Recording Closing Entries
LO5

Refer to the adjusted trial balance in M4-8. Prepare the closing entry on December 31, 2012.

EXERCISES

Preparing a Trial Balance

E4-1
LO1

Paige Consultants, Inc., provides marketing research for clients in the retail industry. The company had the following unadjusted balances at September 30, 2012:

Account	Debit	Credit
Accumulated Depreciation		18,100
Accrued Expenses Payable		25,650
Cash	153,000	
General and Administrative Expenses	321,050	
Supplies	12,200	
Wages and Benefits Expense	1,610,000	
Prepaid Expenses	10,200	
Interest Expense	17,200	
Accounts Receivable	225,400	
Consulting Fees Revenue		2,564,200
Retained Earnings		?
Income Taxes Payable		3,030
Travel Expense	23,990	
Buildings and Equipment	323,040	
Utilities Expense	25,230	
Gain on Sale of Land		6,000
Unearned Consulting Fees		32,500
Investment Income		10,800
Accounts Payable		96,830
Land	60,000	
Other Operating Expenses	188,000	
Contributed Capital		223,370
Professional Development Expense	18,600	
Notes Payable		160,000
Rent Expense (on leased computers)	152,080	
Investments	145,000	

Required:

Prepare in good form an unadjusted trial balance for Paige Consultants, Inc., at September 30, 2012.

Identifying Adjusting Entries from Unadjusted Trial Balance

E4-2
LO1, 2, 5
Hewlett-Packard Company

In its annual report, Hewlett-Packard Company states, "We are a leading global provider of products, technologies, solutions and services to individual consumers, small- and medium-sized businesses, and large enterprises, including customers in the public and education sectors." Its offerings span personal computing and other access drivers, imaging and printing-related products and services, enterprise information technology infrastructure, and multi-vendor customer services. Following is a trial balance listing accounts that Hewlett-Packard uses. Assume that the balances are unadjusted at the end of a recent fiscal year ended October 31.

HEWLETT-PACKARD COMPANY
Unadjusted Trial Balance
(dollars in millions)

	Debit	Credit
Cash	$ 10,200	
Short-term investments	100	
Accounts receivable	19,300	
Inventory	7,900	
Other current assets	14,400	
Property, plant, and equipment	18,900	
Accumulated depreciation		$ 8,100
Other assets	50,700	
Short-term note payable		10,100
Accounts payable		14,100
Accrued liabilities		17,300
Deferred revenue		6,200
Income tax payable		900
Long-term debt		7,700
Other liabilities		17,000
Contributed capital		14,000
Retained earnings		17,800
Product revenue		91,700
Service revenue		26,300
Interest revenue		400
Cost of products	69,300	
Cost of services	20,300	
Interest expense	300	
Research and development expense	3,600	
Selling, general, and administrative expense	13,100	
Other expenses	1,400	
Income tax expense	2,100	
Total	$231,600	$231,600

Required:

1. Based on the information in the unadjusted trial balance, list types of adjustments on the balance sheet that may need to be adjusted at October 31 and the related income statement account for each (no computations are necessary). You may need to make assumptions.
2. Which accounts should be closed at the end of the year? Why?

E4-3 Recording Adjusting Entries
LO2

Ramos Company completed its first year of operations on December 31, 2011. All of the 2011 entries have been recorded except for the following:

a. At year-end, employees earned wages of $7,000, which will be paid on the next payroll date, January 6, 2012.

b. At year-end, the company had earned interest revenue of $2,000. The cash will be collected March 1, 2012.

Required:

1. What is the annual reporting period for this company?
2. Identify whether each transaction results in adjusting a deferred or an accrued account. Using the process illustrated in the chapter, give the required adjusting entry for transactions (*a*) and (*b*). Include appropriate dates and write a brief explanation of each entry.
3. Why are these adjustments made?

Recording Adjusting Entries and Reporting Balances in Financial Statements

E4-4
LO2, 3

Aubrae Company is making adjusting entries for the year ended December 31, 2011. In developing information for the adjusting entries, the accountant learned the following:

a. A two-year insurance premium of $3,600 was paid on October 1, 2011, for coverage beginning on that date.
b. At December 31, 2011, the following data relating to Shipping Supplies were obtained from the records and supporting documents.

Shipping supplies on hand, January 1, 2011	$11,000
Purchases of shipping supplies during 2011	60,000
Shipping supplies on hand, counted on December 31, 2011	20,000

Required:

1. Using the process illustrated in the chapter, record the adjusting entry for insurance at December 31, 2011, assuming that the premium was paid on October 1, 2011, and the bookkeeper debited the full amount to Prepaid Insurance.
2. Using the process illustrated in the chapter, record the adjusting entry for supplies at December 31, 2011, assuming that the purchases of shipping supplies were debited in full to Shipping Supplies.
3. What amount should be reported on the 2011 income statement for Insurance Expense? For Shipping Supplies Expense?
4. What amount should be reported on the December 31, 2011, balance sheet for Prepaid Insurance? For Shipping Supplies?

Determining Financial Statement Effects of Adjusting Entries

E4-5
LO2

Refer to E4-3 and E4-4.

Required:

For each of the transactions in E4-3 and E4-4, indicate the amount and direction of effects of the adjusting entry on the elements of the balance sheet and income statement. Using the following format, indicate + for increase, − for decrease, and NE for no effect.

	BALANCE SHEET			INCOME STATEMENT		
Transaction	Assets	Liabilities	Stockholders' Equity	Revenues	Expenses	Net Income
E4-3 (*a*)						
E4-3 (*b*)						
E4-4 (*a*)						
E4-4 (*b*)						

Recording Seven Typical Adjusting Entries

E4-6
LO2

Dittman's Variety Store is completing the accounting process for the year just ended, December 31, 2011. The transactions during 2011 have been journalized and posted. The following data with respect to adjusting entries are available:

a. Wages earned by employees during December 2011, unpaid and unrecorded at December 31, 2011, amounted to $2,700. The last payroll was December 28; the next payroll will be January 6, 2012.
b. Office supplies on hand at January 1, 2011, totaled $450. Office supplies purchased and debited to Office Supplies during the year amounted to $500. The year-end count showed $275 of supplies on hand.

c. One-fourth of the basement space is rented to Heald's Specialty Shop for $560 per month, payable monthly. On December 31, 2011, the rent for November and December 2011 had not been collected or recorded. Collection is expected January 10, 2012.

d. The store used delivery equipment that cost $60,500; $12,100 was the estimated depreciation for 2011.

e. On July 1, 2011, a two-year insurance premium amounting to $2,400 was paid in cash and debited in full to Prepaid Insurance. Coverage began on July 1, 2011.

f. The remaining basement of the store is rented for $1,600 per month to another merchant, M. Carlos, Inc. Carlos sells compatible, but not competitive, merchandise. On November 1, 2011, the store collected six months' rent in the amount of $9,600 in advance from Carlos; it was credited in full to Unearned Rent Revenue when collected.

g. Dittman's Variety Store operates a repair shop to meet its own needs. The shop also does repairs for M. Carlos. At the end of December 31, 2011, Carlos had not paid $800 for completed repairs. This amount has not yet been recorded as Repair Shop Revenue. Collection is expected during January 2012.

Required:

1. Identify each of these transactions as a deferred revenue, deferred expense, accrued revenue, or accrued expense.
2. Prepare the adjusting entries that should be recorded for Dittman's Variety Store at December 31, 2011.

E4-7 Recording Seven Typical Adjusting Entries

LO2

Cardon's Boat Yard, Inc., repairs, stores, and cleans boats for customers. It is completing the accounting process for the year just ended, November 30, 2012. The transactions during 2012 have been journalized and posted. The following data with respect to adjusting entries are available:

a. Cardon's winterized (cleaned and covered) three boats for customers at the end of November, but did not record the service for $2,700.

b. On October 1, 2012, Cardon's paid $1,200 to the local newspaper for an advertisement to run every Thursday for 12 weeks. All ads have been run except for three Thursdays in December to complete the 12-week contract.

c. Cardon's borrowed $250,000 at a 12 percent annual interest rate on April 1, 2012, to expand its boat storage facility. The loan requires Cardon's to pay the interest quarterly until the note is repaid in three years. Cardon's paid quarterly interest on July 1 and October 1.

d. The Johnson family paid Cardon's $4,500 on November 1, 2012, to store its sailboat for the winter until May 1, 2013. Cardon's credited the full amount to Unearned Storage Revenue on November 1.

e. Cardon's used boat-lifting equipment that cost $220,000; $22,000 was the estimated depreciation for 2012.

f. Boat repair supplies on hand at December 1, 2011, totaled $16,500. Repair supplies purchased and debited to Supplies during the year amounted to $46,000. The year-end count showed $12,400 of the supplies on hand.

g. Wages earned by employees during November 2012, unpaid and unrecorded at November 30, 2012, amounted to $3,800. The next payroll date will be December 5, 2012.

Required:

1. Identify each of these transactions as a deferred revenue, deferred expense, accrued revenue, or accrued expense.

2. Prepare the adjusting entries that should be recorded for Cardon's at November 30, 2012.

E4-8 Determining Financial Statement Effects of Seven Typical Adjusting Entries

LO2

Refer to E4-6.

Required:
For each of the transactions in E4-6, indicate the amount and direction of effects of the adjusting entry on the elements of the balance sheet and income statement. Using the following format, indicate + for increase, − for decrease, and NE for no effect.

	BALANCE SHEET			INCOME STATEMENT		
Transaction	Assets	Liabilities	Stockholders' Equity	Revenues	Expenses	Net Income
a.						
b.						
c.						
(etc.)						

Determining Financial Statement Effects of Seven Typical Adjusting Entries

E4-9
LO2

Refer to E4-7.

Required:
For each of the transactions in E4-7, indicate the amount and direction of effects of the adjusting entry on the elements of the balance sheet and income statement. Using the following format, indicate + for increase, − for decrease, and NE for no effect.

	BALANCE SHEET			INCOME STATEMENT		
Transaction	Assets	Liabilities	Stockholders' Equity	Revenues	Expenses	Net Income
a.						
b.						
c.						
(etc.)						

Recording Transactions Including Adjusting and Closing Entries (Nonquantitative)

E4-10
LO2, 5

The following accounts are used by Britt's Knits, Inc.

Codes	Accounts	Codes	Accounts
A	Cash	J	Contributed Capital
B	Office Supplies	K	Retained Earnings
C	Accounts Receivable	L	Service Revenue
D	Office Equipment	M	Interest Revenue
E	Accumulated Depreciation	N	Wage Expense
F	Note Payable	O	Depreciation Expense
G	Wages Payable	P	Interest Expense
H	Interest Payable	Q	Supplies Expense
I	Unearned Service Revenue	R	None of the above

Required:
For each of the following nine independent situations, give the journal entry by entering the appropriate code(s) and amount(s). The first transaction is used as an example.

Independent Situations	DEBIT		CREDIT	
	Code	Amount	Code	Amount
a. Accrued wages, unrecorded and unpaid at year-end, $400 (example).	N	400	G	400
b. Service revenue earned but not yet collected at year-end, $600.				
c. Dividends declared and paid during the year, $900.				
d. Office supplies on hand during the year, $400; supplies on hand at year-end, $160.				
e. Service revenue collected in advance, $800.				
f. Depreciation expense for the year, $1,000.				
g. At year-end, interest on note payable not yet recorded or paid, $220.				
h. Balance at year-end in Service Revenue account, $56,000. Give the closing entry at year-end.				
i. Balance at year-end in Interest Expense account, $460. Give the closing entry at year-end.				

E4-11
LO2, 3

Determining Financial Statement Effects of Three Adjusting Entries

Terbish Company started operations on January 1, 2012. It is now December 31, 2012, the end of the annual accounting period. The part-time bookkeeper needs your help to analyze the following three transactions:

a. During 2012, the company purchased office supplies that cost $1,600. At the end of 2012, office supplies of $400 remained on hand.
b. On January 1, 2012, the company purchased a special machine for cash at a cost of $12,000. The machine's cost is estimated to depreciate at $1,200 per year.
c. On July 1, 2012, the company paid cash of $600 for a two-year premium on an insurance policy on the machine; coverage begins on July 1, 2012.

Required:
Complete the following schedule with the amounts that should be reported for 2012:

Selected Balance Sheet Accounts at December 31, 2012	Amount to Be Reported
Assets	
Equipment	$ ______
Accumulated depreciation	______
Net book value of equipment	______
Office supplies	______
Prepaid insurance	______
Selected Income Statement Accounts for the Year Ended December 31, 2012	
Expenses	
Depreciation expense	$ ______
Office supplies expense	______
Insurance expense	______

E4-12
LO2

Determining Financial Statement Effects of Adjustments for Interest on Two Notes

Note 1: On April 1, 2011, Warren Corporation received a $30,000, 10 percent note from a customer in settlement of a $30,000 open account receivable. According to the terms, the principal of the note and interest are payable at the end of 12 months. The annual accounting period for Warren ends on December 31, 2011.

Note 2: On August 1, 2011, to meet a cash shortage, Warren Corporation obtained a $30,000, 12 percent loan from a local bank. The principal of the note and interest expense are payable at the end of six months.

Required:

For the relevant transaction dates of each note, indicate the amounts and direction of effects on the elements of the balance sheet and income statement. Using the following format, indicate + for increase, − for decrease, and NE for no effect. (**Reminder:** Assets = Liabilities + Stockholders' Equity; Revenues − Expenses = Net Income; and Net Income accounts are closed to Retained Earnings, a part of Stockholders' Equity.)

	BALANCE SHEET			INCOME STATEMENT		
Date	Assets	Liabilities	Stockholders' Equity	Revenues	Expenses	Net Income
Note 1 April 1, 2011						
December 31, 2011						
March 31, 2012						
Note 2 August 1, 2011						
December 31, 2011						
January 31, 2012						

Inferring Transactions

E4-13
LO2
Deere & Company

Deere & Company is the world's leading producer of agricultural equipment; a leading supplier of a broad range of industrial equipment for construction, forestry, and public works; a producer and marketer of a broad line of lawn and grounds care equipment; and a provider of credit, managed health care plans, and insurance products for businesses and the general public. The following information is from a recent annual report (in millions of dollars):

Income Taxes Payable	
	Beg. bal. 135
(*a*) ?	(*b*) 656
	End. bal. 79

Dividends Payable	
	Beg. bal. 110
(*c*) ?	(*d*) 456
	End. bal. 118

Interest Payable	
	Beg. bal. 140
(*e*) 1,127	(*f*) ?
	End. bal. 150

Required:

1. Identify the nature of each of the transactions (*a*) through (*f*). Specifically, what activities cause the accounts to increase and decrease?
2. For transactions (*a*), (*c*), and (*f*), compute the amount.

Analyzing the Effects of Errors on Financial Statement Items

E4-14
LO2

Cohen & Boyd, Inc., publishers of movie and song trivia books, made the following errors in adjusting the accounts at year-end (December 31):

a. Did not accrue $1,400 owed to the company by another company renting part of the building as a storage facility.
b. Did not record $15,000 depreciation on the equipment costing $115,000.
c. Failed to adjust the Unearned Fee Revenue account to reflect that $1,500 was earned by the end of the year.
d. Recorded a full year of accrued interest expense on a $17,000, 9 percent note payable that has been outstanding only since November 1.
e. Failed to adjust Prepaid Insurance to reflect that $650 of insurance coverage has been used.

Required:

1. For each error, prepare the adjusting journal entry (*a*) that was made, if any, and (*b*) that should have been made at year-end.
2. Using the following headings, indicate the effect of each error and the amount of the effect (that is, the difference between the entry that was or was not made and the entry that should have been made). Use O if the effect overstates the item, U if the effect understates the item, and NE if there is no effect. (**Reminder:** Assets = Liabilities + Stockholders' Equity; Revenues − Expenses = Net Income; and Net Income accounts are closed to Retained Earnings, a part of Stockholders' Equity.)

	BALANCE SHEET			INCOME STATEMENT		
Transaction	Assets	Liabilities	Stockholders' Equity	Revenues	Expenses	Net Income
a.						
b.						
c.						
(etc.)						

E4-15
LO2, 3

Analyzing the Effects of Adjusting Entries on the Income Statement and Balance Sheet

On December 31, 2011, Yates Company prepared an income statement and balance sheet and failed to take into account four adjusting entries. The income statement, prepared on this incorrect basis, reflected pretax income of $60,000. The balance sheet (before the effect of income taxes) reflected total assets, $170,000; total liabilities, $80,000; and stockholders' equity, $90,000. The data for the four adjusting entries follow:

a. Wages amounting to $39,000 for the last three days of December 2011 were not paid and not recorded (the next payroll will be on January 10, 2012).
b. Depreciation of $17,000 for the year on equipment that cost $170,000 was not recorded.
c. Rent revenue of $9,600 was collected on December 1, 2011, for office space for the period December 1, 2011, to February 28, 2012. The $9,600 was credited in full to Unearned Rent Revenue when collected.
d. Income taxes were not recorded. The income tax rate for the company is 30 percent.

Required:

Complete the following tabulation to correct the financial statements for the effects of the four errors (indicate deductions with parentheses):

Items	Net Income	Total Assets	Total Liabilities	Stockholders' Equity
Balances reported	$60,000	$170,000	$80,000	$90,000
Additional adjustments:				
a. Wages	______	______	______	______
b. Depreciation	______	______	______	______
c. Rent revenue	______	______	______	______
Adjusted balances	______	______	______	______
d. Income taxes	______	______	______	______
Correct balances	______	______	______	______

E4-16
LO2, 3

Recording the Effects of Adjusting Entries and Reporting a Corrected Income Statement and Balance Sheet

On December 31, 2011, the bookkeeper for Grillo Company prepared the following income statement and balance sheet summarized here but neglected to consider three adjusting entries.

	As Prepared	Effects of Adjusting Entries	Corrected Amounts
Income Statement			
Revenues	$ 97,000		
Expenses	(73,000)		
Income tax expense			
Net income	$ 24,000		
Balance Sheet			
Assets			
Cash	$ 20,000		
Accounts receivable	22,000		
Rent receivable			
Equipment	50,000		
Accumulated depreciation	(10,000)		
	$ 82,000		
Liabilities			
Accounts payable	$ 10,000		
Income taxes payable			
Stockholders' Equity			
Contributed capital	40,000		
Retained earnings	32,000		
	$ 82,000		

Data on the three adjusting entries follow:

a. Rent revenue of $2,500 earned for December 2011was neither collected nor recorded.
b. Depreciation of $4,500 on the equipment for 2011 was not recorded.
c. Income tax expense of $5,100 for 2011 was neither paid nor recorded.

Required:

1. Prepare the three adjusting entries that were omitted. Use the account titles shown in the income statement and balance sheet data.
2. Complete the two columns to the right in the preceding tabulation to show the correct amounts on the income statement and balance sheet.

Reporting a Correct Income Statement with Earnings per Share to Include the Effects of Adjusting Entries and Evaluating the Net Profit Margin as an Auditor

E4-17
LO2, 3, 4

Tyson, Inc., a party rental business, completed its first year of operations on December 31, 2011. Because this is the end of the annual accounting period, the company bookkeeper prepared the following tentative income statement:

Income Statement, 2011	
Rental revenue	$109,000
Expenses:	
Salaries and wages expense	26,500
Maintenance expense	12,000
Rent expense	8,800
Utilities expense	4,300
Gas and oil expense	3,000
Miscellaneous expenses (items not listed elsewhere)	1,000
Total expenses	55,600
Income	$ 53,400

You are an independent CPA hired by the company to audit the company's accounting systems and review the financial statements. In your audit, you developed additional data as follows:

a. Wages for the last three days of December amounting to $730 were not recorded or paid.
b. Tyson estimated telephone usage at $440 for December 2011, but nothing has been recorded or paid.
c. Depreciation on rental autos, amounting to $24,000 for 2011, was not recorded.
d. Interest on a $15,000, one-year, 8 percent note payable dated October 1, 2011, was not recorded. The 8 percent interest is payable on the maturity date of the note.
e. Maintenance expense excludes $1,100 representing the cost of maintenance supplies used during 2011.
f. The Unearned Rental Revenue account includes $4,100 of revenue to be earned in January 2012.
g. The income tax expense is $5,800. Payment of income tax will be made in 2012.

Required:

1. What adjusting entry for each item (*a*) through (*g*) should Tyson record at December 31, 2011? If none is required, explain why.
2. Prepare a corrected income statement for 2011 in good form, including earnings per share assuming that 7,000 shares of stock are outstanding all year. Show computations.
3. Compute the net profit margin based on the corrected information. What does this ratio suggest? If the average net profit margin for the industry is 18 percent, what might you infer about Tyson?

E4-18 LO1, 2 Recording Four Adjusting Entries and Completing the Trial Balance Worksheet

Red River Company prepared the following trial balance at the end of its first year of operations ending December 31, 2011. To simplify the case, the amounts given are in thousands of dollars.

	UNADJUSTED		ADJUSTMENTS		ADJUSTED	
Account Titles	Debit	Credit	Debit	Credit	Debit	Credit
Cash	35					
Accounts receivable	9					
Prepaid insurance	6					
Machinery	80					
Accumulated depreciation						
Accounts payable		9				
Wages payable						
Income taxes payable						
Contributed capital (4,000 shares)		73				
Retained earnings	4					
Revenues (not detailed)		84				
Expenses (not detailed)	32					
Totals	166	166				

Other data not yet recorded at December 31, 2011 include:

a. Insurance expired during 2011, $4.
b. Wages payable, $5.
c. Depreciation expense for 2011, $8.
d. Income tax expense, $9.

Required:

1. Prepare the adjusting entries for 2011.
2. Complete the trial balance Adjustments and Adjusted columns.

E4-19 LO3 Reporting an Income Statement, Statement of Stockholders' Equity, and Balance Sheet

Refer to E4-18.

Required:
Using the adjusted balances in E4-18, prepare an income statement, statement of stockholders' equity, and balance sheet for 2011.

Recording Closing Entries

E4-20
LO5

Refer to E4-18.

Required:
1. What are the purposes of "closing the books" at the end of the accounting period?
2. Using the adjusted balances in E4-18, give the closing entry for 2011.

For more practice with exercises, go to the text website at **www.mhhe.com/libby7e**.

connect ACCOUNTING

PROBLEMS

Preparing a Trial Balance (AP4-1)

P4-1
LO1

Dell Inc. is the world's largest computer systems company selling directly to customers. Products include desktop computer systems, notebook computers, workstations, network server and storage products, and peripheral hardware and software. The following is a list of accounts and amounts reported in a recent year. The accounts have normal debit or credit balances and the dollars are rounded to the nearest million. Assume the company's year ended on January 31, 2012.

Accounts Payable	$ 8,309	Marketable Securities (investments)	$ 740
Accounts Receivable	6,443	Other Assets	7,821
Accrued Expenses Payable	3,788	Other Income	134
Accumulated Depreciation	2,233	Other Liabilities	8,234
Cash	8,352	Property, Plant, and Equipment	4,510
Contributed Capital	11,189	Research and Development Expense	665
Cost of Sales	50,144	Retained Earnings	?
Income Tax Expense	846	Sales Revenue	61,101
Inventories	867	Selling, General,	
Long-Term Debt	1,898	and Administrative Expenses	7,102

Required:
1. Prepare an adjusted trial balance at January 31, 2012.
2. How did you determine the amount for retained earnings?

Recording Adjusting Entries (AP4-2)

P4-2
LO2

Zimmerman Company's annual accounting year ends on December 31. It is December 31, 2011, and all of the 2011 entries except the following adjusting entries have been made:

a. On September 1, 2011, Zimmerman collected six months' rent of $8,400 on storage space. At that date, Zimmerman debited Cash and credited Unearned Rent Revenue for $8,400. deferred revenue

b. On October 1, 2011, the company borrowed $18,000 from a local bank and signed a 12 percent note for that amount. The principal and interest are payable on the maturity date, September 30, 2012. accrued expense

c. Depreciation of $2,500 must be recognized on a service truck purchased on July 1, 2011, at a cost of $15,000. deferred expense

d. Cash of $3,000 was collected on November 1, 2011, for services to be rendered evenly over the next year beginning on November 1. Unearned Service Revenue was credited when the cash was received. deferred revenue

e. On November 1, 2011, Zimmerman paid a one-year premium for property insurance, $9,000, for coverage starting on that date. Cash was credited and Prepaid Insurance was debited for this amount. deferred expense

f. The company earned service revenue of $4,000 on a special job that was completed December 29, 2011. Collection will be made during January 2012. No entry has been recorded. accrued revenue

g. At December 31, 2011, wages earned by employees totaled $14,000. The employees will be paid on the next payroll date, January 15, 2012. accrued expense

h. On December 31, 2011, the company estimated it owed $500 for 2011 property taxes on land. The tax will be paid when the bill is received in January 2012. accrued expense

Required:

1. Indicate whether each transaction relates to a deferred revenue, deferred expense, accrued revenue, or accrued expense.
2. Give the adjusting entry required for each transaction at December 31, 2011.

P4-3 LO2 Recording Adjusting Entries (AP4-3)

Brayden Towing Company is at the end of its accounting year, December 31, 2011. The following data that must be considered were developed from the company's records and related documents:

a. On January 1, 2011, the company purchased a new hauling van at a cash cost of $24,600. Depreciation estimated at $4,000 for the year has not been recorded for 2011.

b. During 2011, office supplies amounting to $1,000 were purchased for cash and debited in full to Supplies. At the end of 2010, the count of supplies remaining on hand was $400. The inventory of supplies counted on hand at December 31, 2011, was $250.

c. On December 31, 2011, Lanie's Garage completed repairs on one of the company's trucks at a cost of $1,200; the amount is not yet recorded and by agreement will be paid during January 2012.

d. On December 31, 2011, property taxes on land owned during 2011 were estimated at $1,500. The taxes have not been recorded, and will be paid in 2012 when billed.

e. On December 31, 2011, the company completed a contract for an out-of-state company for $6,000 payable by the customer within 30 days. No cash has been collected, and no journal entry has been made for this transaction.

f. On July 1, 2011, a three-year insurance premium on equipment in the amount of $1,200 was paid and debited in full to Prepaid Insurance on that date. Coverage began on July 1.

g. On October 1, 2011, the company borrowed $11,000 from the local bank on a one-year, 14 percent note payable. The principal plus interest is payable at the end of 12 months.

h. The income before any of the adjustments or income taxes was $30,000. The company's federal income tax rate is 30 percent. (**Hint:** Compute adjusted income based on *(a)* through *(g)* to determine income tax expense.)

Required:

1. Indicate whether each transaction relates to a deferred revenue, deferred expense, accrued revenue, or accrued expense.
2. Give the adjusting entry required for each transaction at December 31, 2011.

P4-4 LO2 Determining Financial Statement Effects of Adjusting Entries (AP4-4)

www.mhhe.com/libby7e

Refer to P4-2.

Required:

1. Indicate whether each transaction relates to a deferred revenue, deferred expense, accrued revenue, or accrued expense.
2. Using the following headings, indicate the effect of each adjusting entry and the amount of the effect. Use + for increase, − for decrease, and NE for no effect. (**Reminder:** Assets = Liabilities + Stockholders' Equity; Revenues − Expenses = Net Income; and Net Income accounts are closed to Retained Earnings, a part of Stockholders' Equity.)

	BALANCE SHEET			INCOME STATEMENT		
Transaction	Assets	Liabilities	Stockholders' Equity	Revenues	Expenses	Net Income
a.		−	+	+		+
b.		+	−		+	−
(etc.)						

Determining Financial Statement Effects of Adjusting Entries (AP4-5)

P4-5
LO2

eXcel
www.mhhe.com/libby7e

Refer to P4-3.

Required:

1. Indicate whether each transaction relates to a deferred revenue, deferred expense, accrued revenue, or accrued expense.
2. Using the following headings, indicate the effect of each adjusting entry and the amount of each. Use + for increase, − for decrease, and NE for no effect. (**Reminder:** Assets = Liabilities + Stockholders' Equity; Revenues − Expenses = Net Income; and Net Income accounts are closed to Retained Earnings, a part of Stockholders' Equity.)

	BALANCE SHEET			INCOME STATEMENT		
Transaction	Assets	Liabilities	Stockholders' Equity	Revenues	Expenses	Net Income
a.						
b.						
(etc.)						

Inferring Year-End Adjustments, Computing Earnings per Share and Net Profit Margin, and Recording Closing Entries (AP4-6)

P4-6
LO1, 2, 4, 5

Ramirez Company is completing the information processing cycle at its fiscal year-end, December 31, 2012. Following are the correct balances at December 31, 2012, for the accounts both before and after the adjusting entries for 2012.

Trial Balance, December 31, 2012						
	Before Adjusting Entries		Adjustments		After Adjusting Entries	
Items	Debit	Credit	Debit	Credit	Debit	Credit
a. Cash	$ 12,600				$ 12,600	
b. Accounts receivable					560	
c. Prepaid insurance	840				560	
d. Equipment	168,280				168,280	
e. Accumulated depreciation, equipment		$ 42,100				$ 54,000
f. Income taxes payable						6,580
g. Contributed capital		112,000				112,000
h. Retained earnings, January 1, 2012		19,600				19,600
i. Service revenue		64,400				64,960
j. Salary expense	56,380				56,380	
k. Depreciation expense					11,900	
l. Insurance expense					280	
m. Income tax expense					6,580	
	$238,100	$238,100			$257,140	$257,140

Required:

1. Compare the amounts in the columns before and after the adjusting entries to reconstruct the adjusting entries made in 2012. Provide an explanation of each.

2. Compute the amount of income assuming that it is based on the amounts (*a*) before adjusting entries and (*b*) after adjusting entries. Which income amount is correct? Explain why.
3. Compute earnings per share, assuming that 3,000 shares of stock are outstanding all year.
4. Compute the net profit margin. What does this suggest to you about the company?
5. Record the closing entry at December 31, 2012.

P4-7
LO1, 2, 3, 5

Recording Adjusting and Closing Entries and Preparing a Balance Sheet and Income Statement Including Earnings per Share (AP4-7)

Ellis, Inc., a small service company, keeps its records without the help of an accountant. After much effort, an outside accountant prepared the following unadjusted trial balance as of the end of the annual accounting period, December 31, 2011:

Account Titles	Debit	Credit
Cash	$ 46,000	
Accounts receivable	10,400	
Supplies	640	
Prepaid insurance	800	
Service trucks	16,000	
Accumulated depreciation		$ 9,600
Other assets	8,960	
Accounts payable		2,400
Wages payable		
Income taxes payable		
Note payable (3 years; 10% interest due each December 31)		16,000
Contributed capital (5,000 shares outstanding)		20,560
Retained earnings		6,000
Service revenue		61,600
Remaining expenses (not detailed; excludes income tax)	33,360	
Income tax expense		
Totals	$116,160	$116,160

Data not yet recorded at December 31, 2011, included:

a. The supplies count on December 31, 2011, reflected $240 remaining supplies on hand to be used in 2012.
b. Insurance expired during 2011, $400.
c. Depreciation expense for 2011, $4,200.
d. Wages earned by employees not yet paid on December 31, 2011, $720.
e. Income tax expense, $5,880.

Required:

1. Record the 2011 adjusting entries.
2. Prepare an income statement and a classified balance sheet that include the effects of the preceding five transactions.
3. Record the 2011 closing entry.

ALTERNATE PROBLEMS

AP4-1
LO1

Starbucks Corporation

Preparing a Trial Balance (P4-1)

Starbucks Corporation purchases and roasts high-quality whole bean coffees and sells them along with fresh-brewed coffees, Italian-style espresso beverages, a variety of pastries and confections, coffee-related accessories and equipment, and a line of premium teas. In addition to sales through its company-operated retail stores, Starbucks also sells coffee and tea products through other channels of distribution. The following is a simplified list of accounts and amounts reported in recent financial statements. The accounts have normal debit or credit balances, and the dollars are rounded to the nearest million. Assume that the year ended on September 30, 2012.

Accounts Payable	$ 325	Inventories	$ 693
Accounts Receivable	330	Long-Term Investments	374
Accrued Liabilities	1,152	Long-Term Liabilities	992
Accumulated Depreciation	2,761	Net Revenues	10,497
Cash	270	Other Current Assets	234
Contributed Capital	40	Other Long-Lived Assets	594
Cost of Sales	4,645	Other Operating Expenses	330
Depreciation Expense	549	Prepaid Expenses	169
General and Administrative Expense	723	Property, Plant, and Equipment	5,717
		Retained Earnings	?
Income Tax Expense	144	Short-Term Bank Debt	713
Interest Expense	53	Short-Term Investments	43
Interest Income	9	Store Operating Expenses	3,745

Required:

1. Prepare an adjusted trial balance at September 30, 2012.
2. How did you determine the amount for retained earnings?

Recording Adjusting Entries (P4-2)

AP4-2
LO2

Hannah Company's annual accounting year ends on June 30. It is June 30, 2012, and all of the entries for the current year have been made except the following adjusting entries:

a. On March 30, 2012, Hannah paid a six-month premium for property insurance, $3,200, for coverage starting on that date. Cash was credited and Prepaid Insurance was debited for this amount.

b. On June 1, 2012, Hannah collected two months' maintenance revenue of $450. At that date, Hannah debited Cash and credited Unearned Maintenance Revenue for $450.

c. At June 30, 2012, wages of $900 were earned by employees but not yet paid. The employees will be paid on the next payroll date, July 15, 2012.

d. Depreciation of $3,000 must be recognized on a service truck that cost $15,000 when purchased on July 1, 2011.

e. Cash of $4,200 was collected on May 1, 2012, for services to be rendered evenly over the next year beginning on May 1. Unearned Service Revenue was credited when the cash was received.

f. On February 1, 2012, the company borrowed $18,000 from a local bank and signed a 9 percent note for that amount. The principal and interest are payable on the maturity date, January 31, 2013.

g. On June 30, 2012, the company estimated that it owed $500 in property taxes on land it owned in the first half of 2012. The taxes will be paid when billed in August 2012.

h. The company earned service revenue of $2,000 on a special job that was completed June 29, 2012. Collection will be made during July 2012; no entry has been recorded.

Required:

1. Indicate whether each transaction relates to a deferred revenue, deferred expense, accrued revenue, or accrued expense.
2. Give the adjusting entry required for each transaction at June 30, 2012.

AP4-3 **Recording Adjusting Entries** (P4-3)
LO2

Bill's Catering Company is at its accounting year-end, December 31, 2011. The following data that must be considered were developed from the company's records and related documents:

a. During 2011, office supplies amounting to $1,200 were purchased for cash and debited in full to Supplies. At the beginning of 2011, the count of supplies on hand was $450; at December 31, 2011, the count of supplies on hand was $400.
b. On December 31, 2011, the company catered an evening gala for a local celebrity. The $7,500 bill was payable by the end of January 2012. No cash has been collected, and no journal entry has been made for this transaction.
c. On October 1, 2011, a one-year insurance premium on equipment in the amount of $1,200 was paid and debited in full to Prepaid Insurance on that date. Coverage began on November 1.
d. On December 31, 2011, repairs on one of the company's delivery vans were completed at a cost estimate of $600; the amount has not yet been paid or recorded. The repair shop will bill Bill's Catering at the beginning of January 2012.
e. In November 2011, Bill's Catering signed a lease for a new retail location, providing a down payment of $2,100 for the first three months' rent that was debited in full to Prepaid Rent. The lease began on December 1, 2011.
f. On July 1, 2011, the company purchased new refrigerated display counters at a cash cost of $18,000. Depreciation of $2,600 has not been recorded for 2011.
g. On November 1, 2011, the company loaned $4,000 to one of its employees on a one-year, 12 percent note. The principal plus interest is payable by the employee at the end of 12 months.
h. The income before any of the adjustments or income taxes was $22,400. The company's federal income tax rate is 30 percent. (**Hint:** Compute adjusted income based on (*a*) through (*g*) to determine income tax expense.)

Required:

1. Indicate whether each transaction relates to a deferred revenue, deferred expense, accrued revenue, or accrued expense.
2. Give the adjusting entry required for each transaction at December 31, 2011.

AP4-4 **Determining Financial Statement Effects of Adjusting Entries** (P4-4)
LO2

Refer to AP4-2.

Required:

1. Indicate whether each transaction relates to a deferred revenue, deferred expense, accrued revenue, or accrued expense.
2. Using the following headings, indicate the effect of each adjusting entry and the amount of the effect. Use + for increase, − for decrease, and NE for no effect. (**Reminder:** Assets = Liabilities + Stockholders' Equity; Revenues − Expenses = Net Income; and Net Income accounts are closed to Retained Earnings, a part of Stockholders' Equity.)

	BALANCE SHEET			INCOME STATEMENT		
Transaction	Assets	Liabilities	Stockholders' Equity	Revenues	Expenses	Net Income
a.						
b.						
(etc.)						

Determining Financial Statement Effects of Adjusting Entries (P4-5)

AP4-5
LO2

Refer to AP4-3.

Required:

1. Indicate whether each transaction relates to a deferred revenue, deferred expense, accrued revenue, or accrued expense.
2. Using the following headings, indicate the effect of each adjusting entry and the amount of each. Use + for increase, − for decrease, and NE for no effect. (**Reminder:** Assets = Liabilities + Stockholders' Equity; Revenues − Expenses = Net Income; and Net Income accounts are closed to Retained Earnings, a part of Stockholders' Equity.)

	BALANCE SHEET			INCOME STATEMENT		
Transaction	Assets	Liabilities	Stockholders' Equity	Revenues	Expenses	Net Income
a.						
b.						
(etc.)						

Inferring Year-End Adjustments, Computing Earnings per Share and Net Profit Margin, and Recording Closing Entries (P4-6)

AP4-6
LO1, 2, 4, 5

Taos Company is completing the information processing cycle at the end of its fiscal year, December 31, 2011. Following are the correct balances at December 31, 2011, for the accounts both before and after the adjusting entries for 2011.

Trial Balance, December 31, 2011						
	Before Adjusting Entries		Adjustments		After Adjusting Entries	
Items	Debit	Credit	Debit	Credit	Debit	Credit
a. Cash	$ 18,000				$ 18,000	
b. Accounts receivable					1,500	
c. Prepaid rent	1,200				800	
d. Property, plant, and equipment	208,000				208,000	
e. Accumulated depreciation		$ 52,500				$ 70,000
f. Income taxes payable						6,500
g. Unearned revenue		16,000				8,000
h. Contributed capital		110,000				110,000
i. Retained earnings, January 1, 2011		21,700				21,700
j. Service revenue		83,000				92,500
k. Salary expense	56,000				56,000	
l. Depreciation expense					17,500	
m. Rent expense					400	
n. Income tax expense					6,500	
	$283,200	$283,200			$308,700	$308,700

Required:

1. Compare the amounts in the columns before and after the adjusting entries to reconstruct the adjusting entries made in 2011. Provide an explanation of each.
2. Compute the amount of income, assuming that it is based on the amount (*a*) before adjusting entries and (*b*) after adjusting entries. Which income amount is correct? Explain why.
3. Compute earnings per share, assuming that 5,000 shares of stock are outstanding.
4. Compute the net profit margin ratio. What does this suggest to you about the company?
5. Record the closing entry at December 31, 2011.

AP4-7 Recording Adjusting and Closing Entries and Preparing a Balance Sheet and Income Statement Including Earnings per Share (P4-7)

LO1, 2, 3, 5

South Bend Repair Service Co. keeps its records without the help of an accountant. After much effort, an outside accountant prepared the following unadjusted trial balance as of the end of the annual accounting period, December 31, 2011:

Account Titles	Debit	Credit
Cash	$19,600	
Accounts receivable	7,000	
Supplies	1,300	
Prepaid insurance	900	
Equipment	27,000	
Accumulated depreciation		$12,000
Other assets	5,100	
Accounts payable		2,500
Wages payable		
Income taxes payable		
Note payable (two years; 12% interest due each December 31)		5,000
Contributed capital (3,000 shares outstanding all year)		16,000
Retained earnings		10,300
Service revenue		48,000
Remaining expenses (not detailed; excludes income tax)	32,900	
Income tax expense		
Totals	$93,800	$93,800

Data not yet recorded at December 31, 2011 include:

a. Depreciation expense for 2011, $3,000.
b. Insurance expired during 2011, $450.
c. Wages earned by employees but not yet paid on December 31, 2011, $2,100.
d. The supplies count on December 31, 2011, reflected $800 remaining supplies on hand to be used in 2012.
e. Income tax expense was $3,150.

Required:

1. Record the 2011 adjusting entries.
2. Prepare an income statement and a classified balance sheet for 2011 to include the effects of the preceding five transactions.
3. Record the 2011 closing entry.

COMPREHENSIVE PROBLEMS (CHAPTERS 1–4)

Recording Transactions (Including Adjusting and Closing Entries), Preparing a Complete Set of Financial Statements, and Performing Ratio Analysis

COMP4-1
LO1, 2, 3, 4, 5

Brothers Mike and Tim Hargen began operations of their tool and die shop (H & H Tool, Inc.) on January 1, 2011. The annual reporting period ends December 31. The trial balance on January 1, 2012, follows:

Account Titles	Debit	Credit
Cash	$ 4,000	
Accounts receivable	7,000	
Supplies	16,000	
Land		
Equipment	78,000	
Accumulated depreciation (on equipment)		$ 8,000
Other assets (not detailed to simplify)	5,000	
Accounts payable		
Wages payable		
Interest payable		
Income taxes payable		
Long-term notes payable		
Contributed capital (85,000 shares)		85,000
Retained earnings		17,000
Service revenue		
Depreciation expense		
Supplies expense		
Wages expense		
Interest expense		
Income tax expense		
Remaining expenses (not detailed to simplify)		
Totals	$110,000	$110,000

Transactions during 2012 follow:

a. Borrowed $12,000 cash on a five-year, 10 percent note payable, dated March 1, 2012.
b. Purchased land for a future building site; paid cash, $12,000.
c. Earned $208,000 in revenues for 2012, including $52,000 on credit and the rest in cash.
d. Sold 4,000 additional shares of capital stock for cash at $1 market value per share on January 1, 2012.
e. Incurred $111,000 in Remaining Expenses for 2012, including $20,000 on credit and the rest paid in cash.
f. Collected accounts receivable, $34,000.
g. Purchased other assets, $13,000 cash.
h. Paid accounts payable, $19,000.
i. Purchased supplies on account for future use, $23,000.
j. Signed a three-year $33,000 service contract to start February 1, 2013.
k. Declared and paid cash dividends, $22,000.

Data for adjusting entries:

l. Supplies counted on December 31, 2012, $18,000.
m. Depreciation for the year on the equipment, $8,000.

n. Interest accrued on notes payable (to be computed).
o. Wages earned by employees since the December 24 payroll but not yet paid, $16,000.
p. Income tax expense, $10,000, payable in 2013.

Required:

1. Set up T-accounts for the accounts on the trial balance and enter beginning balances.
2. Prepare journal entries for transactions (*a*) through (*k*) and post them to the T-accounts.
3. Journalize and post the adjusting entries (*l*) through (*p*).
4. Prepare an income statement (including earnings per share), statement of stockholders' equity, balance sheet, and statement of cash flows.
5. Journalize and post the closing entry.
6. Compute the following ratios for 2012 and explain what the results suggest about the company:
   a. Current ratio
   b. Total asset turnover
   c. Net profit margin

COMP4-2
LO1, 2, 3, 4, 5

Recording Transactions (Including Adjusting and Closing Entries), Preparing a Complete Set of Financial Statements, and Performing Ratio Analysis

Josh and Kelly McKay began operations of their furniture repair shop (Furniture Refinishers, Inc.) on January 1, 2012. The annual reporting period ends December 31. The trial balance on January 1, 2013, was as follows:

Account Titles	Debit	Credit
Cash	$ 5,000	
Accounts receivable	4,000	
Supplies	2,000	
Small tools	6,000	
Equipment		
Accumulated depreciation (on equipment)		
Other assets (not detailed to simplify)	9,000	
Accounts payable		$ 7,000
Notes payable		
Wages payable		
Interest payable		
Income taxes payable		
Unearned revenue		
Contributed capital (15,000 shares)		15,000
Retained earnings		4,000
Service revenue		
Depreciation expense		
Wages expense		
Interest expense		
Income tax expense		
Remaining expenses (not detailed to simplify)		
Totals	$26,000	$26,000

Transactions during 2013 follow:

a. Borrowed $20,000 cash on July 1, 2013, signing a one-year, 10 percent note payable.
b. Purchased equipment for $18,000 cash on July 1, 2013.

c. Sold 5,000 additional shares of capital stock for cash at $1 market value per share at the beginning of the year.
d. Earned $70,000 in revenues for 2013, including $14,000 on credit and the rest in cash.
e. Incurred remaining expenses of $35,000 for 2013, including $7,000 on credit and the rest paid with cash.
f. Purchased additional small tools, $3,000 cash.
g. Collected accounts receivable, $8,000.
h. Paid accounts payable, $11,000.
i. Purchased $10,000 of supplies on account.
j. Received a $3,000 deposit on work to start January 15, 2014.
k. Declared and paid a cash dividend, $10,000.

Data for adjusting entries:

l. Supplies of $4,000 and small tools of $8,000 were counted on December 31, 2013 (debit Remaining Expenses).
m. Depreciation for 2013, $2,000.
n. Interest accrued on notes payable (to be computed).
o. Wages earned since the December 24 payroll but not yet paid, $3,000.
p. Income tax expense was $4,000, payable in 2014.

Required:

1. Set up T-accounts for the accounts on the trial balance and enter beginning balances.
2. Prepare journal entries for transactions (*a*) through (*k*) and post them to the T-accounts.
3. Journalize and post the adjusting entries (*l*) through (*p*).
4. Prepare an income statement (including earnings per share), statement of stockholders' equity, balance sheet, and statement of cash flows.
5. Journalize and post the closing entry.
6. Compute the following ratios for 2013 and explain what the results suggest about the company:
   a. Current ratio
   b. Total asset turnover
   c. Net profit margin

CASES AND PROJECTS

Annual Report Cases

Finding Financial Information

CP4-1
LO3, 4, 5

AMERICAN EAGLE OUTFITTERS, INC.

Refer to the financial statements of American Eagle Outfitters in Appendix B at the end of this book.

Required:
(**Hint:** The notes to the financial statements may be helpful for many of these questions.)

1. How much cash did the company pay for income taxes in its 2008 fiscal year (for the year ended January 31, 2009)?
2. What was the company's best quarter in terms of sales in its 2008 fiscal year? Where did you find this information?
3. Give the closing entry for the Other Income (net) account.
4. What does Accounts and Note Receivable consist of? Provide the names of the accounts and their balances as of January 31, 2009. Where did you find this information?
5. Compute the company's net profit margin for the three years reported. What does the trend suggest to you about American Eagle Outfitters?

CP4-2
LO3, 4, 5

URBAN OUTFITTERS INC.

Finding Financial Information

Refer to the financial statements of Urban Outfitters in Appendix C at the end of this book.

Required:

1. How much is in the Prepaid Expenses and Other Current Assets account at the end of the most recent year (for the year ended January 31, 2009)? Where did you find this information?
2. What did the company report for Deferred Rent and Other liabilities at January 31, 2009? Where did you find this information?
3. What is the difference between prepaid rent and deferred rent?
4. Describe in general terms what accrued liabilities are.
5. What would generate the interest income that is reported on the income statement?
6. What company accounts would not have balances on a post-closing trial balance?
7. Give the closing entry, if any, for Prepaid Expenses.
8. What is the company's earnings per share (basic only) for the three years reported?
9. Compute the company's net profit margin for the three years reported. What does the trend suggest to you about Urban Outfitters?

CP4-3
LO3, 4

AMERICAN EAGLE OUTFITTERS, INC.

URBAN OUTFITTERS INC.

excel

www.mhhe.com/libby7e

Comparing Companies within an Industry and Over Time

Refer to the financial statements of American Eagle Outfitters in Appendix B, Urban Outfitters in Appendix C, and the Industry Ratio Report in Appendix D at the end of this book.

Required:

1. What was Advertising Expense for each company for the most recent year? Where did you find the information?
2. Compute the percentage of Advertising Expense to Net Sales for the most recent year for both companies. Which company incurred the higher percentage? Show computations. Are you able to perform the same comparison for the previous two years? If so, show the computations. If not, explain why not.
3. Compare the Advertising Expense to Net Sales ratio for the most recent year computed in requirement (2) to the industry average found in the Industry Ratio Report (Appendix D). Were these two companies spending more or less than their average competitor on advertising (on a relative basis)? What does this ratio tell you about the general effectiveness of each company's advertising strategy?
4. Both companies include a note to the financial statements explaining the accounting policy for advertising. How do the policies differ, if at all?
5. Compute each company's net profit margin for the three years reported. What do your results suggest to you about each company over time and in comparison to each other?
6. Compare each company's net profit margin for the most recent year to the industry average net profit margin in the Industry Ratio Report. Were these two companies performing better or worse than the average company in the industry?

Financial Reporting and Analysis Cases

CP4-4
LO2, 3

Computing Amounts on Financial Statements and Finding Financial Information

The following information was provided by the records of Elm Tree Apartments (a corporation) at the end of the annual fiscal period, December 31, 2011:

Rent

a. Rent revenue collected in cash during 2011 for occupancy in 2011, $492,000.
b. Rent revenue earned for occupancy in December 2011; not collected until 2012, $16,000.
c. In December 2011, rent revenue collected in advance for January 2012, $12,000.

Salaries

d. Cash payment in January 2011 to employees for work in December 2010 (accrued in 2010), $4,000.
e. Salaries incurred and paid during 2011, $68,000.
f. Salaries earned by employees during December 2011 that will be paid in January 2012, $3,000.
g. Cash advances to employees in December 2011 for salaries that will be earned in January 2012, $1,500.

Supplies

h. Maintenance supplies on January 1, 2011 (balance on hand), $3,000.
i. Maintenance supplies purchased for cash during 2011, $8,000.
j. Maintenance supplies counted on December 31, 2011, $1,850.

Required:

For each of the following accounts, compute the balance to be reported in 2011, the statement the account will be reported on, and the effect (direction and amount) on cash flows (+ for increases cash and − for decreases cash). (**Hint:** Create T-accounts to determine balances.)

Account	2011 Balance	Financial Statement	Effect on Cash Flows
1. Rent revenue			
2. Salary expense			
3. Maintenance supplies expense			
4. Rent receivable			
5. Receivables from employees			
6. Maintenance supplies			
7. Unearned rent revenue			
8. Salaries payable			

Using Financial Reports: Inferring Adjusting Entries and Information Used in Computations and Recording Closing Entries

CP4-5
LO1, 2, 5

The pre-closing balances in the T-accounts of Waldman Company at the end of the third year of operations, December 31, 2011, follow. The 2011 adjusting entries are identified by letters.

Cash

Debit	Credit
Bal. 20,000	

Note Payable (8%)

Debit	Credit
	Bal. 10,000

Contributed Capital (10,000 shares)

Debit	Credit
	Bal. 50,000

Maintenance Supplies

Debit	Credit
Bal. 500	(*a*) 300

Interest Payable

Debit	Credit
	(*b*) 800

Retained Earnings

Debit	Credit
	Bal. 9,000

Service Equipment

Debit	Credit
Bal. 90,000	

Income Taxes Payable

Debit	Credit
	(*f*) 13,020

Service Revenue

Debit	Credit
	Bal. 214,000
	(*c*) 6,000

Accumulated Depreciation, Service Equipment

Debit	Credit
	Bal. 18,000
	(*d*) 9,000

Wages Payable

Debit	Credit
	(*e*) 500

Expenses

Debit	Credit
Bal. 160,000	
(*a*) 300	
(*b*) 800	
(*d*) 9,000	
(*e*) 500	
(*f*) 13,020	

Remaining Assets

Debit	Credit
Bal. 42,500	

Unearned Revenue

Debit	Credit
(*c*) 6,000	Bal. 12,000

Required:

1. Develop three 2011 trial balances for Waldman Company using the following format:

Account	UNADJUSTED TRIAL BALANCE		ADJUSTED TRIAL BALANCE		POST-CLOSING TRIAL BALANCE	
	Debit	Credit	Debit	Credit	Debit	Credit

2. Write an explanation for each adjusting entry for 2011.
3. Record the closing journal entry at the end of 2011.
4. What was the average income tax rate for 2011?
5. What was the average issue (sale) price per share of the capital stock?

CP4-6 Using Financial Reports: Analyzing the Effects of Adjustments

LO2, 3

Carey Land Company, a closely held corporation, invests in commercial rental properties. Carey's annual accounting period ends on December 31. At the end of each year, numerous adjusting entries must be made because many transactions completed during current and prior years have economic effects on the financial statements of the current and future years. Assume that the current year is 2013.

Required:
This case concerns four transactions that have been selected for your analysis. Answer the questions for each.

Transaction (*a*): On January 1, 2011, the company purchased office equipment costing $14,000 for use in the business. The company estimates that the equipment's cost should be allocated at $1,000 annually.

1. Over how many accounting periods will this transaction directly affect Carey's financial statements? Explain.
2. How much depreciation expense was reported on the 2011 and 2012 income statements?
3. How should the office equipment be reported on the 2013 balance sheet?
4. Would Carey make an adjusting entry at the end of each year during the life of the equipment? Explain your answer.

Transaction (*b*): On September 1, 2013, Carey collected $30,000 rent on office space. This amount represented the monthly rent in advance for the six-month period, September 1, 2013, through February 28, 2014. Unearned Rent Revenue was increased (credited) and Cash was increased (debited) for $30,000.

1. Over how many accounting periods will this transaction affect Carey's financial statements? Explain.
2. How much rent revenue on this office space should Carey report on the 2013 income statement? Explain.
3. Did this transaction create a liability for Carey as of the end of 2013? Explain. If yes, how much?
4. Should Carey make an adjusting entry on December 31, 2014? Explain why. If your answer is yes, give the adjusting entry.

Transaction (*c*): On December 31, 2013, Carey owed employees unpaid and unrecorded wages of $7,500 because the employees worked the last three days in December 2013. The next payroll date is January 5, 2014.

1. Over how many accounting periods will this transaction affect Carey's financial statements? Explain.
2. How will this $7,500 affect Carey's 2013 income statement and balance sheet?
3. Should Carey make an adjusting entry on December 31, 2013? Explain why. If your answer is yes, give the adjusting entry.

Transaction (*d*): On January 1, 2013, Carey agreed to supervise the planning and subdivision of a large tract of land for a customer, J. Signanini. This service job that Carey will perform involves four separate phases. By December 31, 2013, three phases had been completed to Signanini's satisfaction. The remaining phase will be performed during 2014. The total price for the four phases (agreed on in advance by both parties) was $60,000. Each phase involves about the same amount of services. On December 31, 2013, Carey had collected no cash for the services already performed.

1. Should Carey record any service revenue on this job for 2013? Explain why. If yes, how much?
2. If your answer to part (1) is yes, should Carey make an adjusting entry on December 31, 2013? If yes, give the entry. Explain.
3. What entry will Carey make when it completes the last phase, assuming that the full contract price is collected on the completion date, February 15, 2014?

Using Financial Reports: Inferring Adjusting and Closing Entries and Answering Analytical Questions

CP4-7
LO1, 2, 4, 5

Waddell Company was organized on January 1, 2011. At the end of the first year of operations, December 31, 2011, the bookkeeper prepared the following trial balances (amounts in thousands of dollars):

Account Titles	UNADJUSTED TRIAL BALANCE Debit	UNADJUSTED TRIAL BALANCE Credit	ADJUSTMENTS Debit	ADJUSTMENTS Credit	ADJUSTED TRIAL BALANCE Debit	ADJUSTED TRIAL BALANCE Credit
Cash	40				40	
Accounts Receivable	17				17	
Prepaid Insurance	2				1	
Rent Receivable					2	
Property, Plant, and Equipment	46				46	
Accumulated Depreciation						11
Other Assets	6				6	
Accounts Payable		27				27
Wages Payable						3
Income Taxes Payable						5
Unearned Rent Revenue		7				4
Note Payable (10% interest, dated January 1, 2011)		20				20
Contributed Capital (1,000 shares)		30				30
Retained Earnings	3				3	
Revenues (total)		98				103
Expenses (total including interest)	68				83	
Income Tax Expense					5	
Totals	182	182			203	203

Required:

1. Based on inspection of the two trial balances, give the 2011 adjusting entries developed by the bookkeeper (provide brief explanations).
2. Based on these data, give the 2011 closing entry with a brief explanation.
3. Answer the following questions (show computations):
   a. How many shares of stock were outstanding at year-end?
   b. What was the amount of interest expense included in total expenses?
   c. What was the balance of Retained Earnings on December 31, 2011 after closing the books?
   d. What was the average income tax rate?
   e. How would the two accounts Rent Receivable and Unearned Rent Revenue be reported on the balance sheet?
   f. Explain why cash increased by $40,000 during the year even though net income was comparatively very low.
   g. What was the amount of earnings per share for 2011?
   h. What was the average selling price of the shares?
   i. When was the insurance premium paid and over what period of time did the coverage extend?
   j. What was the net profit margin for the year?

CP4-8 LO2, 3

eXcel

www.mhhe.com/libby7e

Using Financial Reports: Analyzing Financial Information in a Sale of a Business (A Challenging Case)

Crystal Mullinex owns and operates Crystal's Day Spa and Salon, Inc. She has decided to sell the business and retire. She has had discussions with a representative from a regional chain of day spas. The discussions are at the complex stage of agreeing on a price. Among the important factors have been the financial statements of the business. Crystal's secretary, Kenya, under Crystal's direction, maintained the records. Each year they developed a statement of profits on a cash basis; no balance sheet was prepared. Upon request, Crystal provided the other company with the following statement for 2012 prepared by Kenya:

CRYSTAL'S DAY SPA AND SALON, INC.
Statement of Profits
2012

Spa fees collected		$1,215,000
Expenses paid:		
Rent for office space	$130,000	
Utilities expense	43,600	
Telephone expense	12,200	
Salaries expense	562,000	
Supplies expense	31,900	
Miscellaneous expenses	12,400	
Total expenses		792,100
Profit for the year		$ 422,900

Upon agreement of the parties, you have been asked to examine the financial figures for 2012. The other company's representative said, "I question the figures because, among other things, they appear to be on a 100 percent cash basis." Your investigations revealed the following additional data at December 31, 2012:

a. Of the $1,215,000 in spa fees collected in 2012, $142,000 was for services performed prior to 2012.
b. At the end of 2012, spa fees of $29,000 for services performed during the year were uncollected.
c. Office equipment owned and used by Crystal cost $205,000. Depreciation was estimated at $20,500 annually.
d. A count of supplies at December 31, 2012, reflected $5,200 worth of items purchased during the year that were still on hand. Also, the records for 2011 indicated that the supplies on hand at the end of that year were $3,125.
e. At the end of 2012, the secretary whose salary is $18,000 per year had not been paid for December because of a long trip that extended to January 15, 2013.
f. The December 2012 telephone bill for $1,400 has not been received or paid. In addition, the $12,200 amount on the statement of profits includes payment of the December 2011 bill of $1,800 in January 2012.
g. The $130,000 office rent paid was for 13 months (it included the rent for January 2013).

Required:

1. On the basis of this information, prepare a corrected income statement for 2012 (ignore income taxes). Show your computations for any amounts changed from those in the statement prepared by Crystal's secretary. (**Suggestion:** Format solution with four column headings: Items; Cash Basis per Crystal's Statement, $; Explanation of Changes; and Corrected Basis, $.)
2. Write a memo to support your schedule prepared in requirement (1). The purpose should be to explain the reasons for your changes and to suggest other important items that should be considered in the pricing decision.

Critical Thinking Cases

Using Financial Reports: Evaluating Financial Information as a Bank Loan Officer

CP4-9
LO2, 3, 4

Stoscheck Moving Corporation has been in operation since January 1, 2012. It is now December 31, 2012, the end of the annual accounting period. The company has not done well financially during the first year, although revenue has been fairly good. The three stockholders manage the company, but they have not given much attention to recordkeeping. In view of a serious cash shortage, they have applied to your bank for a $30,000 loan. You requested a complete set of financial statements. The following 2012 annual financial statements were prepared by a clerk and then were given to the bank.

STOSCHECK MOVING CORP.
Balance Sheet
At December 31, 2012

Assets	
Cash	$ 2,000
Receivables	3,000
Supplies	4,000
Equipment	40,000
Prepaid insurance	6,000
Remaining assets	27,000
Total assets	$82,000
Liabilities	
Accounts payable	$ 9,000
Stockholders' Equity	
Contributed capital (10,000 shares outstanding)	35,000
Retained earnings	38,000
Total liabilities and stockholders' equity	$82,000

STOSCHECK MOVING CORP.
Income Statement
For the Period Ended December 31, 2012

Transportation revenue	$85,000
Expenses:	
Salaries expense	17,000
Supplies expense	12,000
Other expenses	18,000
Total expenses	47,000
Net income	$38,000

After briefly reviewing the statements and "looking into the situation," you requested that the statements be redone (with some expert help) to "incorporate depreciation, accruals, inventory counts, income taxes, and so on." As a result of a review of the records and supporting documents, the following additional information was developed:

a. The Supplies of $4,000 shown on the balance sheet has not been adjusted for supplies used during 2012. A count of the supplies on hand on December 31, 2012, showed $1,800.
b. The insurance premium paid in 2012 was for years 2012 and 2013. The total insurance premium was debited in full to Prepaid Insurance when paid in 2012 and no adjustment has been made.
c. The equipment cost $40,000 when purchased January 1, 2012. It had an estimated annual depreciation of $8,000. No depreciation has been recorded for 2012.
d. Unpaid (and unrecorded) salaries at December 31, 2012, amounted to $3,200.
e. At December 31, 2012, transportation revenue collected in advance amounted to $7,000. This amount was credited in full to Transportation Revenue when the cash was collected earlier during 2012.
f. The income tax rate is 35 percent.

Required:

1. Record the six adjusting entries required on December 31, 2012, based on the preceding additional information.
2. Recast the preceding statements after taking into account the adjusting entries. You do not need to use classifications on the statements. Suggested form for the solution:

Items	Amounts Reported	CHANGES Debit	CHANGES Credit	Corrected Amounts
(List here each item from the two statements)				

3. Omission of the adjusting entries caused:
   a. Net income to be overstated or understated (select one) by $ _______ .
   b. Total assets on the balance sheet to be overstated or understated (select one) by $ _______.
   c. Total liabilities on the balance sheet to be overstated or understated (select one) by $ _______.
4. For both of the unadjusted and adjusted balances, calculate these ratios for the company: (*a*) earnings per share and (*b*) net profit margin. There were 10,000 shares outstanding all year. Explain the causes of the differences and the impact of the changes on financial analysis.
5. Write a letter to the company explaining the results of the adjustments, your analysis, and your decision regarding the loan.

CP4-10 LO2 Evaluating the Effect of Adjusting Unearned Subscriptions on Cash Flows and Performance as a Manager

You are the regional sales manager for Miga News Company. Miga is making adjusting entries for the year ended March 31, 2013. On September 1, 2012, customers in your region paid $24,000 cash for three-year magazine subscriptions beginning on that date. The magazines are published and mailed to customers monthly. These were the only subscription sales in your region during the year.

Required:

1. What amount should be reported as cash from operations on the statement of cash flows for the year ended March 31, 2013?
2. What amount should be reported on the income statement for subscriptions revenue for the year ended March 31, 2013?
3. What amount should be reported on the March 31, 2013, balance sheet for unearned subscriptions revenue?
4. Give the adjusting entry at March 31, 2013, assuming that the subscriptions received on September 1, 2012, were recorded for the full amount in Unearned Subscriptions Revenue.
5. The company expects your region's annual revenue target to be $6,000.
   a. Evaluate your region's performance, assuming that the revenue target is based on cash sales.
   b. Evaluate your region's performance, assuming that the revenue target is based on accrual accounting.

Financial Reporting And Analysis Team Project

CP4-11 LO2, 3, 4 Team Project: Analysis of Accruals, Earnings per Share, and Net Profit Margin

As a team, select an industry to analyze. Reuters provides lists of industries under Sectors and Industries at www.reuters.com. (Click on an industry and then select Company Rankings for a list of members of that industry.) Each team member should acquire the annual report or 10-K for one publicly traded company in the industry, with each member selecting a different company. (Library files, the SEC EDGAR service at www.sec.gov, or the company itself are good sources.)

Required:

On an individual basis, each team member should write a short report answering the following questions about the selected company. Discuss any patterns across the companies that you as a team observe. Then, as a team, write a short report comparing and contrasting your companies.

1. From the income statement, what is the company's basic earnings per share for each of the last three years?
2. Ratio analysis:
   a. What does the net profit margin ratio measure in general?
   b. Compute the net profit margin ratio for the last three years.
   c. What do your results suggest about the company? (You may refer to the Management Discussion and Analysis section of the 10-K or annual report to read what the company says about the reasons for any change over time.)
   d. If available, find the industry ratio for the most recent year, compare it to your results, and discuss why you believe your company differs or is similar to the industry ratio.
3. List the accounts and amounts of accrued expenses payable on the most recent balance sheet. (You may find the detail in the notes to the statements.) What is the ratio of the total accrued expenses payable to total liabilities?

Lecture Presentation LP-5
www.mhhe.com/libby7e

LEARNING OBJECTIVES

After studying this chapter, you should be able to:

1. Recognize the people involved in the accounting communication process (regulators, managers, directors, auditors, information intermediaries, and users), their roles in the process, and the guidance they receive from legal and professional standards. p. 231
2. Identify the steps in the accounting communication process, including the issuance of press releases, annual reports, quarterly reports, and SEC filings, as well as the role of electronic information services in this process. p. 238
3. Recognize and apply the different financial statement and disclosure formats used by companies in practice. p. 240
4. Analyze a company's performance based on return on assets and its components. p. 249

COMMUNICATING AND INTERPRETING ACCOUNTING INFORMATION

Founded by heralded entrepreneur Ely Callaway, the company that bears his name is the number one manufacturer of premium golf clubs. In just 20 years, Mr. Callaway took a small manufacturer of specialty golf clubs with $500,000 in annual sales and built it into the industry leader with sales of more than $800 million. Callaway Golf's growth was based on its laserlike focus on product innovations that make the game easier to learn and play. Both touring pros like three-time Masters champion Phil Mickelson and average golfers, including former presidents Bill Clinton and George Bush, use Callaway clubs.

FOCUS COMPANY:

Callaway Golf

COMMUNICATING FINANCIAL INFORMATION AND CORPORATE STRATEGY

www.callawaygolf.com

Financing this type of growth requires an equal commitment to satisfying the highest standards of integrity in corporate governance and communication with the financial markets. In 1989, Callaway and then chief financial officer (CFO) Carol Kerley applied that commitment to integrity in communication when they persuaded managers of the General Electric Pension Fund to invest $10 million in the company, and during the company's initial public offering (first stock issuance to the public, or IPO) in 1992. The CFO and her accounting staff worked tirelessly with the company's outside auditor, PricewaterhouseCoopers, and its investment bankers at Merrill Lynch to prepare the financial information necessary for the IPO.

As a publicly traded company, Callaway Golf is required to provide detailed information in regular filings with the Securities and Exchange Commission. As the certifying officers of the company, current President and CEO George Fellows and Bradley J. Holiday, Senior Executive Vice President and Chief Financial Officer, are responsible for the accuracy of the filings. The board of directors and auditors monitor the integrity of the system that produces the disclosures. Integrity in communication with investors and other users of financial statements is a key to maintaining relationships with suppliers of capital.

UNDERSTANDING THE BUSINESS

Callaway Golf Company designs, manufactures, and markets high-quality innovative golf clubs and golf balls that sell at premium prices. Its Fusion Technology woods and irons account for most of its sales. The company manufactures most of its clubs in its Carlsbad, California, factories using clubheads, shafts, and grips supplied by independent vendors. The clubs are sold at pro shops and sporting goods stores. Callaway Golf invests considerable sums in research and development and is known for introducing new and innovative products long before the end of existing products' life cycles.

CORPORATE GOVERNANCE refers to the procedures designed to ensure that the company is managed in the interests of the shareholders.

Callaway Golf also invests in **corporate governance:** the procedures designed to ensure that the company is managed in the interests of the shareholders. Much of its corporate governance system is aimed at ensuring integrity in the financial reporting process. Good corporate governance eases the company's access to capital, lowering both the costs of borrowing (interest rates) and the perceived riskiness of Callaway Golf's stock.

Callaway Golf knows that when investors lose faith in the truthfulness of a firm's accounting numbers, they also normally punish the company's stock. Disclosure of an accounting fraud causes, on average, a 20 percent drop in the price of a company's stock. The extreme accounting scandals at Enron and WorldCom caused their stock to become worthless. In an attempt to restore investor confidence, Congress passed the Public Accounting Reform and Investor Protection Act (the Sarbanes-Oxley Act), which strengthens financial reporting and corporate governance for public companies. Even with these added safeguards, the wisdom of famed analyst Jack Ciesielski's warning to financial statement users is still evident:

REAL WORLD EXCERPT

Analyst's Accounting Observer

> One usual answer to the question "why does accounting matter?" is that it helps to avoid "blow-ups": the unpleasant outcome when a stock crashes because the firm's management engaged in accounting chicanery that subsequently becomes visible. . . . the analyst who understands accounting matters will know . . . where the "soft spots" are in financial reporting, the ones that can be manipulated in order to meet an expected earnings target or avoid breaking a loan covenant.
>
> Source: *Analyst's Accounting Observer,* www.accountingobserver.com.

While even the savviest analysts can still be surprised by fraudulent reports in some cases, accounting knowledge and healthy skepticism are the best protection from such surprises.

Chapters 2 through 4 focused on the mechanics of preparing the income statement, balance sheet, statement of stockholders' equity, and cash flow statement. Based on our better understanding of financial statements, we will next take a more detailed look at the people involved and the regulations that govern the process that conveys accounting information to statement users in the Internet age. We will also take a more detailed look at statement formats and additional disclosures provided in financial reports to help you learn how to find relevant information. Finally, we will examine a general framework for assessing a company's performance based on these reports.

ORGANIZATION of the Chapter

Players in the Accounting Communication Process

- Regulators (SEC, FASB, PCAOB, Stock Exchanges)
- Managers (CEO, CFO, and Accounting Staff)
- Boards of Directors (Audit Committee)
- Auditors
- Information Intermediaries: Financial Analysts and Information Services
- Users: Institutional and Private Investors, Creditors, and Others
- Guiding Principles for Communicating Useful Information

The Disclosure Process

- Press Releases
- Annual Reports
- Quarterly Reports
- SEC Reports—10-K, 10-Q, 8-K

A Closer Look at Financial Statement Formats and Notes

- Classified Balance Sheet
- Classified Income Statement
- Statement of Stockholders' Equity
- Statement of Cash Flows
- Notes to Financial Statements
- Voluntary Disclosures

ROA Analysis: A Framework for Evaluating Company Performance

- Return on Assets (ROA)
- ROA Profit Driver Analysis
- Profit Drivers and Business Strategy

PLAYERS IN THE ACCOUNTING COMMUNICATION PROCESS

LEARNING OBJECTIVE 1

Recognize the people involved in the accounting communication process (regulators, managers, directors, auditors, information intermediaries, and users), their roles in the process, and the guidance they receive from legal and professional standards.

Exhibit 5.1 summarizes the major actors involved in ensuring the integrity of the financial reporting process.

Regulators (SEC, FASB, PCAOB, Stock Exchanges)

The mission of the **U.S. Securities and Exchange Commission** (SEC) is to protect investors and maintain the integrity of the securities markets. As part of this mission, the SEC oversees the work of the Financial Accounting Standards Board (FASB), which sets generally accepted accounting principles (GAAP), the Public Company Accounting Oversight Board (PCAOB), which sets auditing standards for independent auditors (CPAs) of public companies, and the stock exchanges (e.g., New York Stock Exchange), which, along with state governments, set overall corporate governance standards.

The SEC staff also reviews the reports filed with it for compliance with its standards, investigates irregularities, and punishes violators. During 2004 through 2008, the SEC brought 875 enforcement actions related to financial reporting.[1] As a consequence, a number of

[1]Source: registeredrep.com.

EXHIBIT 5.1

Ensuring the Integrity of Financial Information

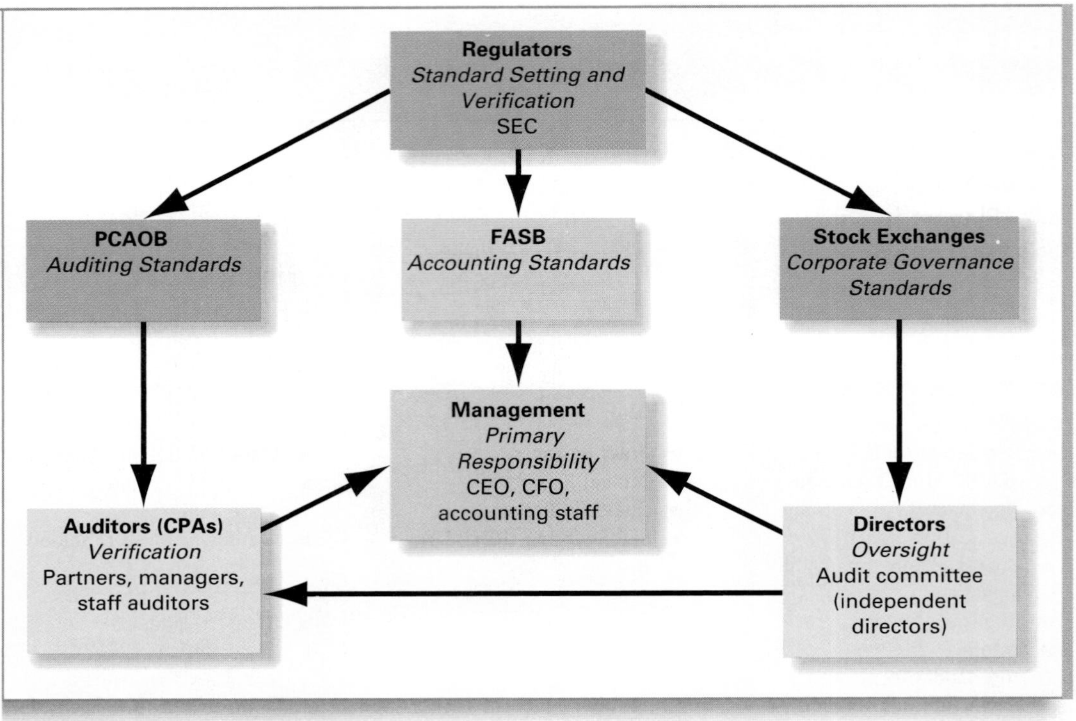

high-profile company officers have recently been fined and sentenced to jail. Consequences to the company can include enormous financial penalties as well as bankruptcy, as in the cases of Enron and WorldCom. You can read about recent SEC enforcement actions at

www.sec.gov/divisions/enforce/friactions.shtml.

Managers (CEO, CFO, and Accounting Staff)

The primary responsibility for the information in Callaway Golf's financial statements and related disclosures lies with management, specifically the highest officer in the company, often called the **chairman and chief executive officer** (CEO), and the highest officer associated with the financial and accounting side of the business, often called the **chief financial officer** (CFO). At Callaway and all public companies, these two officers must personally certify that:

- Each report filed with the Securities and Exchange Commission does not contain any untrue material statement or omit a material fact and fairly presents in all material respects the financial condition, results of operations, and cash flows of the company.
- There are no significant deficiencies and material weaknesses in the internal controls over financial reporting.
- They have disclosed to the auditors and audit committee of the board any weaknesses in internal controls or any fraud involving management or other employees who have a significant role in financial reporting.

Executives who knowingly certify false financial reports are subject to a fine of $5 million and a 20-year prison term. The members of the **accounting staff,** who actually prepare the details of the reports, also bear professional responsibility for the accuracy of this information, although their legal responsibility is smaller. Their future professional success depends heavily on their reputation for honesty and competence. Accounting managers responsible for financial statements with material errors are routinely fired and often have difficulty finding other employment.

Board of Directors (Audit Committee)

As Callaway Golf's statement on corporate governance indicates, the **board of directors** (elected by the stockholders) is responsible for ensuring that processes are in place for maintaining the integrity of the company's accounting, financial statement preparation, and financial reporting. The audit committee of the board, which must be composed of nonmanagement (independent) directors with financial knowledge, is responsible for hiring the company's independent auditors. They also meet separately with the auditors to discuss management's compliance with their financial reporting responsibilities.

The BOARD OF DIRECTORS, elected by the stockholders to represent their interests, is responsible for maintaining the integrity of the company's financial reports.

Auditors

The SEC requires publicly traded companies to have their statements and their control systems over the financial reporting process audited by an independent registered public accounting firm (independent auditor) following auditing standards established by the PCAOB. Many privately owned companies also have their statements audited. By signing an **unqualified** (or **clean**) **audit opinion,** a CPA firm assumes part of the financial responsibility for the fairness of the financial statements and related presentations. This opinion, which adds credibility to the statements, is also often required by agreements with lenders and private investors. Subjecting the company's statements to independent verification reduces the risk that the company's financial condition is misrepresented in the statements. As a result, rational investors and lenders should lower the rate of return (interest) they charge for providing capital.

An UNQUALIFIED (clean) AUDIT OPINION is an auditor's statement that the financial statements are fair presentations in all material respects in conformity with GAAP.

Deloitte & Touche is currently Callaway Golf's auditor. This firm, along with KPMG, PricewaterhouseCoopers, and Ernst & Young, make up what are referred to as the "Big 4" CPA firms. Each of these firms employs thousands of CPAs in offices scattered throughout the world. They audit the great majority of publicly traded companies as well as many that are privately held. Some public companies and most private companies are audited by smaller CPA firms. A list of the auditors for selected focus companies follows.

Focus Company	Industry	Auditor
Starbucks	Coffee	Deloitte & Touche
Deckers Outdoor	Footwear	KPMG
Papa John's	Fast food	Ernst & Young

Information Intermediaries: Financial Analysts and Information Services

Students often view the communication process between companies and financial statement users as a simple process of mailing the report to individual shareholders who read the report and then make investment decisions based on what they have learned. This simple picture is far from today's reality. Now most investors rely on sophisticated financial analysts and information services to gather and analyze information. Exhibit 5.2 summarizes this process.

Financial analysts receive accounting reports and other information about the company from electronic information services. They also gather information through conversations with company executives and visits to company facilities and competitors. The results of their analyses are combined into analysts' reports. Analysts' reports normally include forecasts of future quarterly and annual earnings per share and share price; a buy, hold, or sell recommendation for the company's shares; and explanations for these judgments. In making their **earnings forecasts,** the analysts rely heavily on their knowledge of the way the accounting system translates business events into the numbers on a company's financial statements, which is the subject matter of this text. Individual analysts often specialize in particular industries (such as sporting goods or energy companies). Analysts are regularly evaluated based on the accuracy of their forecasts, as well as the profitability of their stock picks. At the time this

EARNINGS FORECASTS are predictions of earnings for future accounting periods.

EXHIBIT 5.2

Using Financial Reports

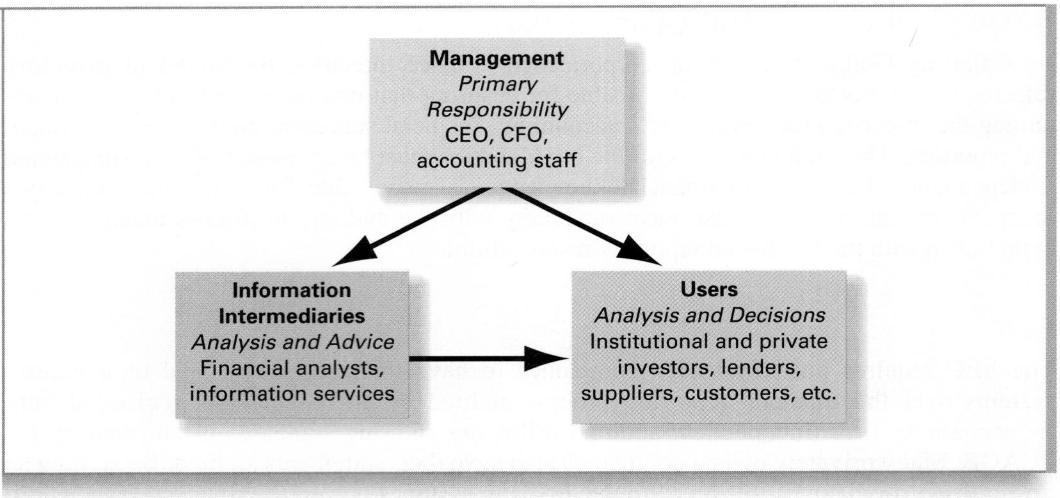

chapter was written, five major firms provided the following forecasts and recommendations for Callaway Golf:

REAL WORLD EXCERPT
Analysts' Reports

Firm	Stock Recommendation	Earnings Forecast for 2009	Earnings Forecast for 2010
Wedbush Morgan	Hold	0.10	0.45
Barrington Research	Market Perform	0.09	0.60
Wachovia Capital Markets	Market Perform	0.04	0.65
Gilford Securities	Buy	0.04	0.69
Morgan Joseph & Co.	Hold	0.00	0.82

Analysts often work in the research departments of brokerage and investment banking houses such as Merrill Lynch, mutual fund companies such as Fidelity Investments, and investment advisory services such as Value Line that sell their advice to others. Through their reports and recommendations, analysts are transferring their knowledge of accounting, the company, and the industry to their customers who lack this expertise. Many believe that decisions made based on analysts' advice cause stock market prices to react quickly to information in financial statements. A quick, unbiased reaction to information is called **market efficiency** in finance. It is highly unlikely that unsophisticated investors can glean more information from financial statements than the sophisticated analysts have already learned. The **information services** discussed next allow investors to gather their own information about the company and monitor the recommendations of a variety of analysts.

Companies actually file their SEC forms electronically through the EDGAR (Electronic Data Gathering and Retrieval) Service, which is sponsored by the SEC. Users can retrieve information from EDGAR within 24 hours of its submission, long before it is available through the mail. EDGAR is a free service available on the Web under "Filings & Forms" at

www.sec.gov.

Most companies also provide direct access to their financial statements and other information over the Web. You can contact Callaway Golf by clicking on "Investor Relations" at

www.callawaygolf.com.

Financial analysts and other sophisticated users obtain much of the information they use from the wide variety of commercial online information services. Services such as Compustat and Thomson Research provide broad access to financial statements and news information.

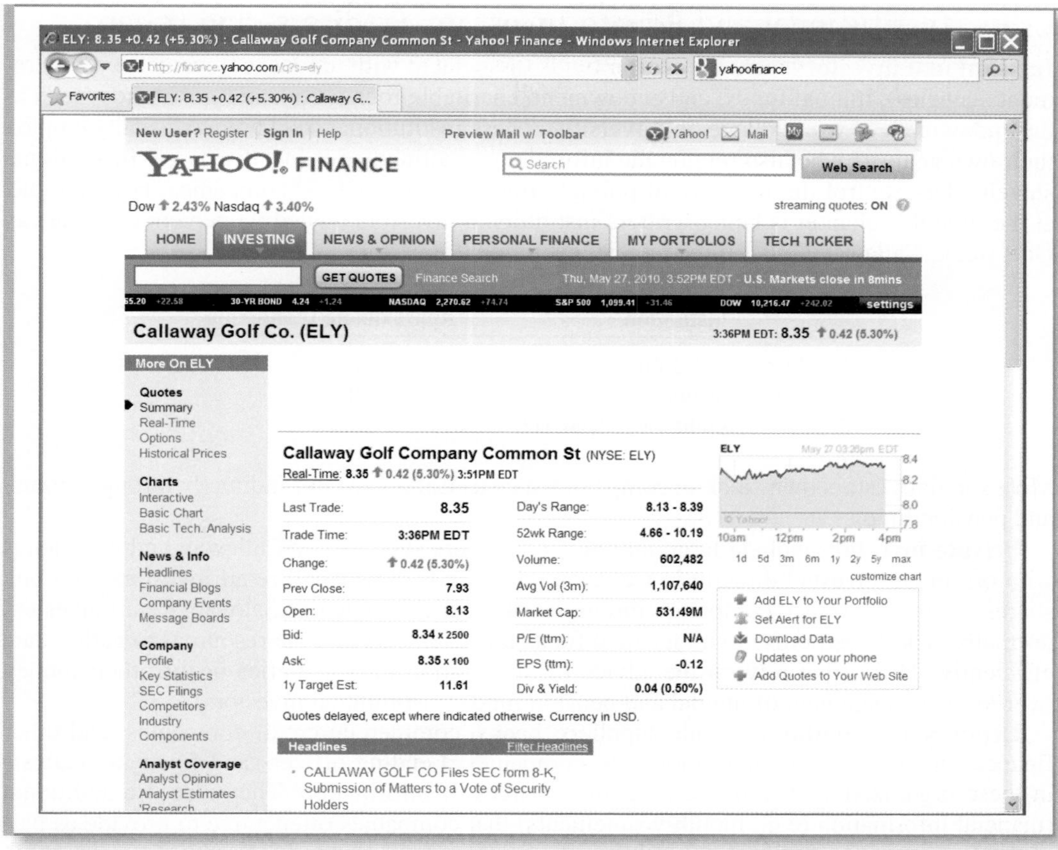

EXHIBIT 5.3

Yahoo! Finance Information on Callaway Golf

REAL WORLD EXCERPT

Yahoo! Finance

They also allow users to search the database by key words, including various financial statement terms. Their websites describe their services in more detail.

www.compustat.com
www.thomson.com

Readers should be aware that the definitions used to compute key ratios often differ across these sources.

A growing number of other resources offering a mixture of free and fee-based information exist on the Web. These include:

www.bloomberg.com
www.reuters.com/finance
finance.yahoo.com

Exhibit 5.3 suggests the wide range of information on Callaway Golf available on the Yahoo! Finance website.

Information Services and Your Job Search

FINANCIAL ANALYSIS

Information services have become the primary tool for professional analysts who use them to analyze competing firms. Information services are also an important source of information for job seekers. Potential employers expect job applicants to demonstrate knowledge of their companies during an interview, and electronic information services are an excellent source of company information. The best place to begin learning about potential employers is to visit their websites. Be sure to read the material in the employment section and the investor relations section of the site. To learn more about electronic information services, contact the business or reference librarian at your college or university or explore the websites discussed in this section.

Users: Institutional and Private Investors, Creditors, and Others

INSTITUTIONAL INVESTORS are managers of pension, mutual, endowment, and other funds that invest on the behalf of others.

Institutional investors include pension funds (associated with unions, companies, or government agencies); mutual funds; and endowment, charitable foundation, and trust funds (such as the endowment of your college or university). These institutional stockholders usually employ their own analysts who also rely on the information intermediaries just discussed. Institutional shareholders control the majority of publicly traded shares of U.S. companies. For example, at the time this chapter is being written, institutional investors owned 93 percent of Callaway Golf stock. Callaway Golf's three largest institutional investors follow:

Institution	Approximate Ownership
NFJ Investment Group LLC	7.0%
AXA Financial, Inc.	5.9%
Cramer, Rosenthal, McGlynn, LLC	5.7%

Most small investors own stock in companies such as Callaway Golf indirectly through mutual and pension funds.

PRIVATE INVESTORS include individuals who purchase shares in companies.

Private investors include large individual investors such as Ely Callaway and his friends who originally invested directly in Callaway Golf, as well as small retail investors who buy shares of publicly traded companies through brokers such as Charles Schwab. Retail investors normally lack the expertise to understand financial statements and the resources to gather data efficiently. They often rely on the advice of information intermediaries or turn their money over to the management of mutual and pension funds (institutional investors).

LENDERS (CREDITORS) include suppliers and financial institutions that lend money to companies.

Lenders, or **creditors,** include suppliers, banks, commercial credit companies, and other financial institutions that lend money to companies. Lending officers and financial analysts in these organizations use the same public sources of information. They also use additional financial information (e.g., monthly statements) that companies often agree to provide as part of the lending contract. Lenders are the primary external user group for financial statements of private companies. Institutional and private investors also become creditors when they buy a company's publicly traded bonds.

The COST-BENEFIT CONSTRAINT suggests that the benefits of accounting for and reporting information should outweigh the costs.

Financial statements also play an important role in the relationships between suppliers and customers. Customers evaluate the financial health of suppliers to determine whether they will be reliable, up-to-date sources of supply. Suppliers evaluate their customers to estimate their future needs and ability to pay debts. Competitors also attempt to learn useful information about a company from its statements. The potential loss of competitive advantage is one of the costs of public financial disclosures. Accounting regulators consider these costs as well as the direct costs of preparation when they consider requiring new disclosures. They apply what is called the **cost-benefit constraint,** which suggests that the benefits of accounting for and reporting information should outweigh the costs.

RELEVANT INFORMATION can influence a decision; it is timely and has predictive and/or feedback value.

RELIABLE INFORMATION is accurate, unbiased, and verifiable.

CONSISTENT INFORMATION can be compared over time because similar accounting methods have been applied.

COMPARABLE INFORMATION allows comparisons across businesses because similar accounting methods have been applied.

Guiding Principles for Communicating Useful Information

For accounting information to be useful, it must be relevant and reliable. **Relevant information** is capable of influencing decisions by allowing users to assess past activities and/or predict future activities. **Reliable information** is accurate, unbiased, and verifiable (independent parties can agree on the nature of the transaction and amount). Our discussions of ratio analysis have emphasized the importance of comparing ratios for the same company over time, as well as with those of competitors. Such comparisons are valid only if the information is prepared on a consistent and comparable basis.**Consistent information** means that within a company, similar accounting methods have been applied over time. **Comparable information** means that similar accounting methods have been applied across companies. These characteristics of useful information, along with the full-disclosure principle, guide the FASB in deciding what financial information should be reported.

Accurate interpretation of financial statements requires that the statement reader be aware of important constraints of accounting measurement. First, small amounts do not have to be reported separately or accounted for precisely according to GAAP if they would not influence users' decisions. Accountants usually designate such items and amounts as **immaterial.** Determining **material amounts** is often very subjective.

Second, **conservatism** requires that special care be taken to avoid (1) overstating assets and revenues and (2) understating liabilities and expenses. This guideline attempts to offset managers' natural optimism about their operations, which sometimes creeps into the financial reports they prepare. This constraint produces more conservative income statement and balance sheet amounts. Finally, in certain industries such as public utilities, special industry reporting practices are followed to better reflect the economics of those industries.

MATERIAL AMOUNTS are amounts that are large enough to influence a user's decision.

CONSERVATISM suggests that care should be taken not to overstate assets and revenues or understate liabilities and expenses.

Differences in Accounting Methods Acceptable under IFRS and U.S. GAAP

INTERNATIONAL PERSPECTIVE

Financial accounting standards and disclosure requirements are adopted by national regulatory agencies. Many countries, including the members of the European Union, have adopted international financial reporting standards (IFRS) issued by the International Accounting Standards Board (IASB). IFRS are similar to U.S. GAAP, but there are several important differences. A partial list of the differences at the time this chapter is being written is presented below, along with the chapter in which these issues will be addressed:

Difference	U.S. GAAP	IFRS	Chapter
Extraordinary items	Permitted	Prohibited	5
Last-in first-out (LIFO) method for inventory	Permitted	Prohibited	7
Reversal of inventory write-downs	Prohibited	Required	7
Basis for property, plant, and equipment	Historical cost	Fair value or historical cost	8
Development costs	Expensed	Capitalized	8
Debt to be refinanced	Current	Noncurrent	9
Recognition of contingent liabilities	Probable	More likely than not	9
Stockholders' equity accounts	Capital stock	Share capital	11
	Paid-in capital	Share premium	
Interest received on cash flow statement	Operating	Operating or investing	13
Interest paid on cash flow statement	Operating	Operating or financing	13

The FASB and IASB are working together to eliminate these and other differences.

PAUSE FOR **FEEDBACK**

In this section, we learned the roles of different parties in the accounting communication process and the guidance they receive from legal and professional standards. Management of the reporting company decides the appropriate format and level of detail to present in its financial reports. Independent audits increase the credibility of the information. Directors monitor managers' compliance with reporting standards and hire the auditor. Financial statement announcements from public companies usually are first transmitted to users through electronic information services. The SEC staff reviews public financial reports for compliance with legal and professional standards and punishes violators. Analysts play a major role in making financial statement and other information available to average investors through their stock recommendations and earnings forecasts. Before you move on, complete the following exercise to test your understanding of these concepts.

(continued)

SELF-STUDY **QUIZ**

Match the key terms in the left column with their definitions in the right column.

1. Relevant information	*a.* Management primarily responsible for accounting information.
2. CEO and CFO	*b.* An independent party who verifies financial statements.
3. Financial analyst	*c.* Information that influences users' decisions.
4. Auditor	*d.* Reporting only information that provides benefits in excess of costs.
5. Cost-benefit constraint	*e.* An individual who analyzes financial information and provides advice.

After you have completed your answers, check them with the solutions at the bottom of the page.

THE DISCLOSURE PROCESS

LEARNING OBJECTIVE 2

Identify the steps in the accounting communication process, including the issuance of press releases, annual reports, quarterly reports, and SEC filings, as well as the role of electronic information services in this process.

As noted in our discussion of information services and information intermediaries, the accounting communication process includes more steps and participants than one would envision in a world in which annual and quarterly reports are simply mailed to shareholders. SEC regulation FD, for "Fair Disclosure," requires that companies provide all investors equal access to all important company news. Managers and other insiders are also prohibited from trading their company's shares based on nonpublic (insider) information so that no party benefits from early access.

Press Releases

A PRESS RELEASE is a written public news announcement normally distributed to major news services.

To provide timely information to external users and to limit the possibility of selective leakage of information, Callaway Golf and other public companies announce quarterly and annual earnings through a **press release** as soon as the verified figures (audited for annual and reviewed for quarterly earnings) are available. Callaway Golf normally issues its earnings press releases within four weeks of the end of the accounting period. The announcements are sent electronically to the major print and electronic news services, including *DowJones, Reuters,* and *Bloomberg,* which make them immediately available to subscribers. Exhibit 5.4 shows an excerpt from a typical earnings press release for Callaway Golf that includes key financial figures. This excerpt is followed by management's discussion of the results and condensed income statements and balance sheets, which will be included in the formal report to shareholders, distributed after the press release.

Many companies, including Callaway Golf, follow these press releases with a conference call during which senior managers answer analysts' questions about the quarterly results. These calls are open to the investing public. Listening to these recordings is a good way to learn about a company's business strategy and its expectations for the future, as well as key factors that analysts consider when they evaluate a company.

FINANCIAL ANALYSIS — How Does the Stock Market React to Earnings Announcements?

For actively traded stocks such as Callaway Golf, most of the stock market reaction (stock price increases and decreases from investor trading) to the news in the press release usually occurs quickly. Recall that a number of analysts follow Callaway Golf and regularly predict the company's earnings. When the actual earnings are published, the market reacts **not** to the amount of earnings but to the difference between expected earnings and actual earnings. This amount is called **unexpected earnings.** In July, analysts expected Callaway Golf to report a profit of $.12 per share. Callaway's actual earnings per share for the quarter ended up being a profit of $.10 per share. Unexpected earnings (Actual − Expected) were thus −2 cents per share (10 cents − 12 cents), and, as a result, the share price fell around $.46 or 8 percent, to $5.19.

Solutions to SELF-STUDY QUIZ

1. *c;* 2. *a;* 3. *e;* 4. *b;* 5. *d.*

EXHIBIT 5.4

Earnings Press Release Excerpt for Callaway Golf Company

REAL WORLD EXCERPT

Press release

CALLAWAY GOLF COMPANY ANNOUNCES SECOND QUARTER AND FIRST HALF 2009 RESULTS

CARLSBAD, Calif.—Business Wire—July 29, 2009—Callaway Golf Company (NYSE:ELY) today announced its financial results for the second quarter and first half of the year ended June 30, 2009. For the second quarter, the Company reported net sales of $302 million, a decrease of 17% compared to $366 million for the second quarter of 2008. On a currency neutral basis, net sales would have been $321 million, a decrease of 12% compared to the second quarter of 2008. The Company also reported gross profit for the second quarter of 2009 of $110 million (36% of net sales), compared to gross profit of $171 million (47% of net sales) in the second quarter of 2008, and reported operating expenses of $100 million (33% of net sales) compared to $111 million (30% of net sales) for the same period in 2008. Fully diluted earnings per share were $0.10 (on 66.8 million shares outstanding), compared to $0.58 (on 63.9 million shares outstanding) in 2008. Fully diluted earnings per share for the second quarter include after-tax charges for gross margin improvement initiatives of $0.02 per share in 2009 and $0.05 per share in 2008.

Companies such as Callaway Golf also issue press releases concerning other important events such as new product announcements and new endorsement contracts with professional golfers. Press releases related to annual earnings and quarterly earnings often precede the issuance of the quarterly or annual report by 15 to 45 days. This time is necessary to prepare the additional detail and to print and distribute those reports.

Annual Reports

For privately held companies, **annual reports** are relatively simple documents photocopied on white bond paper. They normally include only the following:

1. Four basic financial statements: income statement, balance sheet, stockholders' equity or retained earnings statement, and cash flow statement.
2. Related notes (footnotes).
3. Report of Independent Accountants (Auditor's Opinion) if the statements are audited.

The annual reports of public companies are significantly more elaborate, both because of additional SEC reporting requirements and because many companies use their annual reports as public relations tools.

The annual reports of public companies are normally split into two sections. The first, "nonfinancial," section usually includes a letter to stockholders from the Chairman and CEO; descriptions of the company's management philosophy, products, successes (and occasionally failures); and exciting prospects and challenges for the future. Beautiful photographs of products, facilities, and personnel often are included. The second, "financial," section includes the core of the report. The SEC sets minimum disclosure standards for the financial section of the annual reports of public companies. The principal components of the financial section include:

1. Summarized financial data for a 5- or 10-year period.
2. Management's Discussion and Analysis of Financial Condition and Results of Operations and Disclosures about Market Risk.
3. The four basic financial statements.
4. Notes (footnotes).
5. Report of Independent Accountants (Auditor's Opinion) and the Management Certification.
6. Recent stock price information.
7. Summaries of the unaudited quarterly financial data (described later).
8. Lists of directors and officers of the company and relevant addresses.

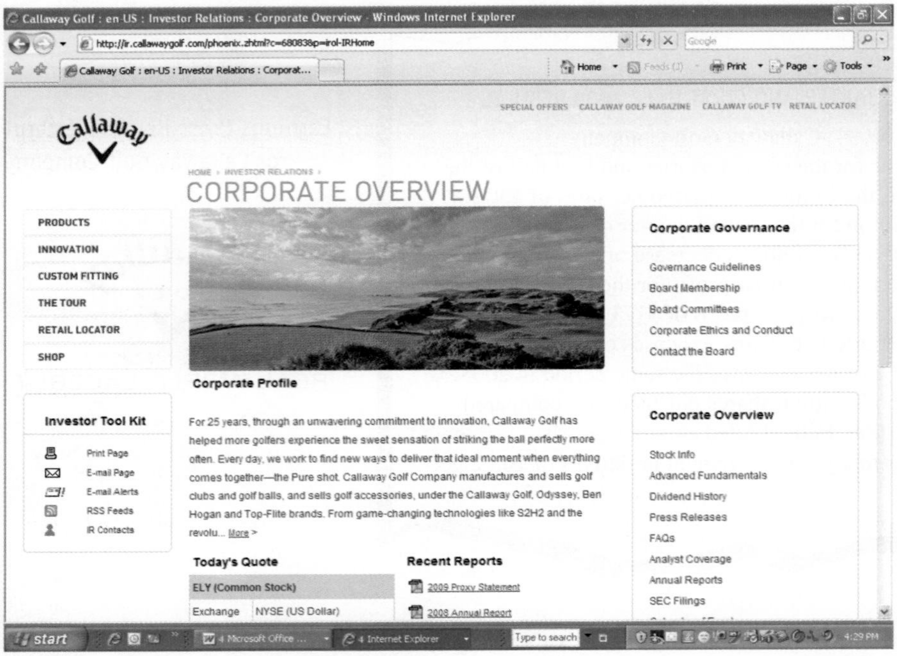

The order of these components varies.

Except for the Management's Discussion and Analysis and Disclosures about Market Risks, most of these elements have been covered in earlier chapters. This element includes an explanation of key figures on the financial statements and the risks the company faces in the future.

Quarterly Reports

Quarterly reports normally begin with a short letter to shareholders. This is followed by a condensed income statement for the quarter, which often shows less detail than the annual income statement, and a condensed balance sheet dated at the end of the quarter (e.g., March 31 for the first quarter). These condensed financial statements are not audited and so are marked **unaudited.** Often the cash flow statement, statement of stockholders' equity (or retained earnings statement), and some notes to the financial statements are omitted. Private companies also normally prepare quarterly reports for their lenders.

SEC Reports—10-K, 10-Q, 8-K

The FORM 10-K is the annual report that publicly traded companies must file with the SEC.

The FORM 10-Q is the quarterly report that publicly traded companies must file with the SEC.

The FORM 8-K is used by publicly traded companies to disclose any material event not previously reported that is important to investors (e.g., auditor changes, mergers).

Public companies must file periodic reports with the SEC. They include the annual report on **Form 10-K,** quarterly reports on **Form 10-Q,** and current event reports on **Form 8-K.** These reports are normally referred to by number (for example, the "10-K"). In general, the 10-K and 10-Q present all information in the annual and quarterly reports, respectively, along with additional management discussion and several required schedules.

For example, the Form 10-K provides a more detailed description of the business including its products, product development, sales and marketing, manufacturing, and competitors. It also lists properties owned or leased, any legal proceedings it is involved in, and significant contracts it has signed. The 10-K also provides more detailed schedules concerning various figures on the income statement and balance sheet, including bad debts, warranties, inventories, and advertising. There has been a recent trend to combine the information in the 10-K into the company annual reports. Callaway's current annual report includes seven pages featuring product details and the president's letter to shareholders followed by the complete 10-K for that year.

A CLOSER LOOK AT FINANCIAL STATEMENT FORMATS AND NOTES

LEARNING OBJECTIVE 3

Recognize and apply the different financial statement and disclosure formats used by companies in practice.

To make financial statements more useful to investors, creditors, and analysts, specific **classifications** of information are included on the statements. Various classifications are used in practice. You should not be confused when you notice slightly different formats used by different companies. In this section, we will focus on similarities and differences in the classifications and line items presented on Callaway Golf's and Papa John's balance sheet, income statement, and cash flow statement. We also discuss some of Callaway Golf's note disclosures in more detail.

Classified Balance Sheet

Exhibit 5.5 shows the December 31, 2008, balance sheet for Callaway Golf. Its balance sheet looks very similar in structure to Papa John's presented in Chapter 4. Its balance sheet is classified as follows:

EXHIBIT 5.5

Balance Sheet of Callaway Golf

REAL WORLD EXCERPT

Annual Report

CALLAWAY GOLF COMPANY **Consolidated Balance Sheets*** **At December 31, 2008 and 2007** **(dollars in thousands, except share and per share data)**	**December 31**		
	2008	**2007**	
Assets			
Current assets:			
Cash and cash equivalents	$ 38,337	$ 49,875	*Assets that will be used or turned into cash within one year*
Accounts receivable, net	120,067	112,064	
Inventories	257,191	253,001	
Other current assets	74,408	81,641	
Total current assets	490,003	496,581	
Property, plant, and equipment, net	142,145	128,036	*Assets that will be used or turned into cash beyond one year*
Intangible assets, net	176,689	173,045	
Other assets	46,501	40,416	
Total assets	$855,338	$838,078	
Liabilities and Shareholders' Equity			
Current liabilities:			
Accounts payable and accrued expenses	$126,167	$130,410	*Obligations that will be paid or settled within one year*
Accrued employee compensation and benefits	25,630	44,245	
Accrued warranty expense	11,614	12,386	
Notes payable, current portion	90,000	36,507	
Total current liabilities	253,411	223,548	
Long-term liabilities:			
Other long-term liabilities	23,772	46,300	*Obligations that will be paid or settled after one year*
Commitments and contingencies (Note 15)			
Shareholders' equity:			
Common Stock, $.01 par value, 240,000,000 shares authorized, 66,276,236 shares and 66,281,693 shares issued at December 31, 2008, and 2007, respectively	663	663	*Capital contributed by shareholders*
Additional paid-in capital	58,641	97,098	
Retained earnings	518,851	470,469	*Earnings reinvested in the company*
Total shareholders' equity	578,155	568,230	
Total liabilities and shareholders' equity	$855,338	$838,078	

**Callaway's statements have been simplified for purposes of our discussion.*

Assets (by order of liquidity)
- Current assets (short-term)
- Noncurrent assets
  - Total assets

Liabilities (by order of time to maturity)
- Current liabilities (short-term)
- Long-term liabilities
  - Total liabilities

Stockholders' equity (by source)
- Contributed capital (by owners)
- Retained earnings (accumulated earnings minus accumulated dividends declared)
  - Total stockholders' equity
  - Total liabilities and stockholders' equity

These classifications will play a major role in our discussions of ratio analysis in later chapters.

Callaway Golf's balance sheet contains two items, not included in Papa John's, that are worthy of additional discussion. **Intangible assets** have no physical existence and a long life. Examples are patents, trademarks, copyrights, franchises, and goodwill from purchasing other companies. Most intangibles, except goodwill, trademarks, and other intangibles with indefinite lives, are amortized as they are used, in a manner similar to the depreciation of tangible assets. They are reported net of accumulated amortization on the balance sheet.

PAR VALUE is a legal amount per share established by the board of directors; it establishes the minimum amount a stockholder must contribute and has no relationship to the market price of the stock.

ADDITIONAL PAID-IN CAPITAL (Paid-In Capital, Contributed Capital in Excess of Par) is the amount of contributed capital less the par value of the stock.

Until this chapter, we have identified the financing by investors as **Contributed Capital.** In practice, however, this account often is shown as two accounts: Common Stock and Additional Paid-In Capital.[2] Each share of common stock usually has a nominal (low) **par value** printed on the face of the certificate. Par value is a legal amount per share established by the board of directors; it has no relationship to the market price of the stock. Its significance is that it establishes the minimum amount that a stockholder must contribute. Callaway Golf's common stock has a par value of \$.01 per share, but the 1,000,000 shares were sold in its 1992 initial public offering at a market price of \$16 per share.[3] When a corporation issues capital stock, the amount received is recorded in part as Common Stock (Number of Shares × Par Value per Share) and the excess above par is recorded as **Additional Paid-In Capital** (also called Paid-In Capital or Contributed Capital in Excess of Par). The journal entry to record Callaway Golf's 1992 initial public offering follows:

Cash (+A) (\$16 × 1,000,000 Shares)	16,000,000	
Common stock (+SE) (\$.01 per Share × 1,000,000 shares) . . .		10,000
Additional paid-in capital (+SE) (\$16,000,000 − \$10,000) . . .		15,990,000

Assets		=	Liabilities	+	Stockholders' Equity	
Cash	+16,000,000				Common Stock	+10,000
					Additional Paid-In Capital	+15,990,000

Classified Income Statement

Callaway Golf's 2008 consolidated income statement is reprinted for you in Exhibit 5.6. Income statements have two major sections. The first presents the income statement as we have in prior chapters. The second presents net income on a per share basis or earnings per share.

Continuing Operations

Callaway Golf's income statements are prepared using the following basic structure.

	Net sales
−	Cost of goods sold
	Gross profit
−	Operating expenses
	Income from operations
+/−	Nonoperating revenues/expenses and gains/losses
	Income before income taxes
−	Income tax expense
	Net income

Callaway Golf is a manufacturing company, whereas Papa John's is a service firm. Consequently, Callaway Golf's income statement includes one subtotal not included in Papa John's.

[2]Callaway's actual statement lists an amount as treasury stock that is the shares that have been repurchased by the company from shareholders. Chapter 11 discusses these terms in more detail.

[3]These numbers are rounded.

EXHIBIT 5.6

Income Statement of Callaway Golf

REAL WORLD EXCERPT

Annual Report

CALLAWAY GOLF COMPANY
Consolidated Statement of Operations
For the Years Ended December 31, 2006–2008
(dollars in thousands, except per share data)

	Years Ended December 31		
	2008	**2007**	**2006**
Net sales	$1,117,204	$1,124,591	$1,017,907
Cost of sales	630,371	631,368	619,832
Gross profit	486,833	493,223	398,075
Selling expenses	287,802	281,960	254,526
General and administrative expenses	85,473	89,060	79,709
Research and development expenses	29,370	32,020	26,785
Total operating expenses	402,645	403,040	361,020
Income from operations	84,188	90,183	37,055
Interest and other income, net	21,785	3,455	3,364
Interest expense	(4,666)	(5,363)	(5,421)
Income before income taxes	101,307	88,275	34,998
Provision for income taxes	35,131	33,688	11,708
Net income	$ 66,176	$ 54,587	$ 23,290
Earnings per common share:	$1.05	$0.82	$0.34
Common equivalent shares:	63,055	66,371	67,732

Operating activities (central focus of the business)

Peripheral activities (not the main focus of the business)

Income tax expense

= Net Income/Average Number of Shares Outstanding

Like most manufacturing and merchandising companies,[4] Callaway Golf reports the subtotal **Gross Profit** (gross margin) which is the difference between net sales and cost of goods sold. Another subtotal—**Income from Operations** (also called operating income)—is computed by subtracting operating expenses from gross profit.

Nonoperating (other) Items are income, expenses, gains, and losses that do not relate to the company's primary operations. Examples include interest income, interest expense, and gains and losses on the sale of fixed assets and investments. These nonoperating items are added to or subtracted from income from operations to obtain **Income before Income Taxes,** also called Pretax Earnings. At this point, Income Tax Provision (Income Tax Expense) is normally subtracted to obtain Net Income. Some companies show fewer subtotals on their income statements. No difference exists in the revenue, expense, gain, and loss items reported using the different formats. Only the categories and subtotals differ.

GROSS PROFIT (GROSS MARGIN) is net sales less cost of goods sold.

INCOME FROM OPERATIONS (OPERATING INCOME) equals net sales less cost of goods sold and other operating expenses.

INCOME BEFORE INCOME TAXES (PRETAX EARNINGS) is revenues minus all expenses except income tax expense.

Nonrecurring Items

Companies may also report one or both of two nonrecurring items on their income statements:

1. Discontinued operations
2. Extraordinary items

If any one of these items exists, an additional subtotal is presented for Income from Continuing Operations (or Income before Nonrecurring Items), after which the nonrecurring items are presented. These two items are presented separately because they are not useful in predicting the future income of the company given their nonrecurring nature.

When a major component of a business is sold or abandoned, income or loss from that component, as well as any gain or loss on disposal, are included as discontinued operations. Extraordinary Items are gains or losses incurred that are both unusual and infrequent in occurrence.

[4]A merchandiser buys products from a manufacturer for resale, and a manufacturer produces goods for sale to wholesalers or retail merchandisers.

The Chapter Supplement explains and presents an example income statement from Verizon Communications illustrating these two nonrecurring items.

Earnings per Share

As we discussed in Chapter 4, simple computations for earnings per share (EPS) are as follows:

$$\text{Earnings per Share} = \frac{\text{Net Income*}}{\text{Average Number of Shares of Common Stock Outstanding during the Period}}$$

FINANCIAL ANALYSIS | Statement of Comprehensive Income

Both the FASB and IASB have proposed requiring a single performance statement entitled the Statement of Comprehensive Income. The first portion of this statement would include all of the components and the same total (Net Income) now included on the income statement. Following this total would be the components and total for Other Comprehensive Income. Other comprehensive income includes unrealized gains and losses on certain investment securities (discussed in Chapter 12), as well as other items discussed in more advanced accounting classes. The Net Income and Other Comprehensive Income totals are then combined to create a final total called Comprehensive Income (the bottom line for this statement). This form of presentation is currently an option under both US GAAP and IFRS, but is used by few public companies. Other comprehensive income and its typical current presentation in the statement of stockholders' equity are discussed in Chapter 12.

PAUSE FOR **FEEDBACK**

As Callaway's statements suggest, most statements are classified and include subtotals that are relevant to analysis. On the balance sheet, the most important distinctions are between current and noncurrent assets and liabilities. On the income statement, the distinction between operating and nonoperating items is most important. So the next step in preparing to analyze financial statements is to see if you understand the effects of transactions you have already studied on these subtotals. The following questions will test your ability to do so.

SELF-STUDY **QUIZ**

1. Prepare a journal entry for the following transaction: Issued 1,000 shares of $1 par value stock for $12 per share.
2. Complete the following tabulation, indicating the direction (+ for increase, − for decrease, and NE for no effect) and amount of the effect of each transaction. Consider each item independently.
   a. Recorded and paid rent expense of $200.
   b. Recorded the sale of goods on account for $400 and cost of goods sold of $300.

Transaction	Current Assets	Gross Profit	Income from Operations
a.			
b.			

After you have completed your answers, check them with the solutions at the bottom of the next page.

*If there are preferred dividends (discussed in Chapter 11), the amount is subtracted from Net Income in the numerator.

Statement of Stockholders' Equity

The statement of stockholders' (shareholders') equity reports the changes in each of the company's stockholders' equity accounts during the accounting period. We will discuss this statement in more detail in Chapter 11.

Statement of Cash Flows

We introduced the three cash flow statement classifications in prior chapters:

Cash Flows from Operating Activities. This section reports cash flows associated with earning income.

Cash Flows from Investing Activities. Cash flows in this section are associated with the purchase and sale of (1) productive assets (other than inventory) and (2) investments in other companies.

Cash Flows from Financing Activities. These cash flows are related to financing the business through borrowing and repaying loans, stock (equity) issuances and repurchases, and dividend payments.

Exhibit 5.7 presents Callaway Golf's 2008 consolidated statement of cash flows. The first section (Cash Flows from Operating Activities) can be reported using either the **direct** or **indirect** method. For Callaway Golf, this first section is reported using the indirect method, which presents a reconciliation of net income on an accrual basis to cash flows from operations. This more common format differs from the format in the statement prepared for Papa John's in Chapter 3, which was constructed using the direct method.

Operating Activities (Indirect Method)

FOCUS ON CASH FLOWS

The Operating Activities section prepared using the indirect method helps the analyst understand the **causes of differences** between a company's net income and its cash flows. Net income and cash flows from operating activities can be quite different. Remember that the income statement is prepared under the accrual concept. Revenues are recorded when earned without regard to when the related cash flows occur. Likewise, expenses are matched with revenues and recorded in the same period without regard to when the related cash flows occur.

In the indirect method, the operating activities section starts with net income computed under the accrual concept and then eliminates noncash items, leaving cash flow from operating activities:

Net income
+/−Adjustments for noncash items
―――――――――――――
Cash provided by operating activities

The items listed between these two amounts explain the reasons they differ. For example, since no cash is paid during the current period for Callaway Golf's depreciation expense reported on the income statement, this amount is added back in the conversion process. Similarly, increases and decreases in certain current assets and liabilities also account for some of the difference between net income and cash flow from operations. For example, sales on account increase net income as well as the current asset accounts receivable, but sales on account do not increase cash. As we cover different portions of the income statement and balance sheet in more detail in Chapters 6 through 12, we will also discuss the relevant sections of the cash flow statement. Then we discuss the complete cash flow statement in detail in Chapter 13.

Solutions to SELF-STUDY QUIZ

1. Cash (+A) ($12 × 1,000 Shares)	12,000	
Common stock (+SE) ($1 per Share × 1,000 shares)		1,000
Additional paid-in capital (+SE) ($12,000 − 1,000)		11,000

2. *a.* −200, NE, −200; *b.* +100, +100, +100

EXHIBIT 5.7

Cash Flow Statement of Callaway Golf

REAL WORLD EXCERPT

Annual Report

CALLAWAY GOLF COMPANY
Consolidated Statement of Cash Flows
For the Years Ended December 31, 2006–2008
(dollars in thousands)

	Year Ended December 31			
	2008	**2007**	**2006**	
Cash flows from operating activities:				
Net income	$66,176	$ 54,587	$23,290	*Cash flows associated with earning income*
Adjustments to reconcile net income to net cash provided by operating activities:				
Depreciation	37,963	35,326	32,274	
Other noncash items	940	15,167	13,729	
Changes in operating assets and liabilities	(63,374)	46,902	(52,312)	
Net cash provided by operating activities	41,705	151,982	16,981	
Cash flows from investing activities:				
Capital expenditures	(51,005)	(32,930)	(32,453)	*Cash flows associated with purchase and sale of productive assets and investments*
Acquisitions, net of cash acquired	(9,797)		374	
Proceeds from sale of capital assets	45	11,460	469	
Investment in golf-related ventures	(763)	(3,698)	(10,008)	
Net cash used in investing activities	(61,520)	(25,168)	(41,618)	
Cash flows from financing activities:				
Issuance of common stock	4,708	48,035	9,606	*Cash flows associated with borrowing and repaying loans and issuing and repurchasing stock*
Acquisition of common stock	(23,650)	(114,795)	(52,872)	
Dividends paid, net	(17,794)	(18,755)	(19,212)	
Proceeds from (payments on) bank loans	53,493	(43,493)	80,000	
Other financing activities	(8,480)	5,707	3,996	
Net cash provided by (used in) financing activities	8,277	(123,301)	21,518	
Net (decrease) increase in cash and cash equivalents	(11,538)	3,513	(3,119)	*Total change in cash*
Cash and cash equivalents at beginning of year	49,875	46,362	49,481	*Beginning of year cash*
Cash and cash equivalents at end of year	$38,337	$ 49,875	$46,362	*End of year cash on balance sheet*

Notes to Financial Statements

While the numbers reported on the various financial statements provide important information, users require additional details to facilitate their analysis. All financial reports include additional information in notes that follow the statements. Callaway Golf's 2008 notes include three types of information:

1. Descriptions of the key accounting rules applied to the company's statements.
2. Additional detail supporting reported numbers.
3. Relevant financial information not disclosed on the statements.

Accounting Rules Applied in the Company's Statements

One of the first notes is typically a summary of significant accounting policies. As you will see in your study of subsequent chapters, generally accepted accounting principles (GAAP) permit companies to select from alternative methods for measuring the effects of transactions. The summary of significant accounting policies tells the user which accounting methods the company has adopted. Callaway Golf's accounting policy for property, plant, and equipment is as follows:

NOTE 2: SIGNIFICANT ACCOUNTING POLICIES

Property, Plant, and Equipment

Property, plant, and equipment are stated at cost less accumulated depreciation. Depreciation is computed using the straight-line method over estimated useful lives as follows:

Buildings and improvements	10–30 years
Machinery and equipment	5–15 years
Furniture, computers, and equipment	3–5 years
Production molds	2 years

Callaway GOLF

REAL WORLD EXCERPT

Annual Report

Without an understanding of the various accounting methods used, it is impossible to analyze a company's financial results effectively.

Alternative Accounting Methods and GAAP

FINANCIAL ANALYSIS

Many people mistakenly believe that GAAP permits only one accounting method to be used to compute each value on the financial statements (e.g., inventory). Actually, GAAP often allows a selection of an accounting method from a menu of acceptable methods. This permits a company to choose the methods that most closely reflect its particular economic circumstances. This flexibility complicates the financial statement users' task, however. Users must understand how the company's choice of accounting methods affects its financial statement presentations. As renowned financial analysts Gabrielle Napolitano, Michael Moran, and Abby Joseph Cohen of the investment banking firm of Goldman, Sachs & Co. note in their recent research report,

> Discretionary choices in financial reporting that can ultimately lead to or create future earnings shocks that drive stock prices must be identified; analysts must make adjustments to minimize or eliminate the impact of these drivers on corporate performance. As a result, financial statement users must (1) develop a keen understanding of the fundamentals underlying each firm's business operations and (2) familiarize themselves with the corporate reporting practices of the companies they are analyzing.*
>
> *Gabrielle Napolitano, Michael A. Moran, and Abby Joseph Cohen, "Demand for Forensic Accounting Intensifies," *Global Strategy Research* (New York: Goldman, Sachs & Co).

REAL WORLD EXCERPT

Goldman, Sachs & Co.

Analysts' reports

For example, before analyzing two companies' statements prepared using different accounting methods, one company's statements must be converted to the other's methods to make them comparable. Otherwise, the reader is in a situation analogous to comparing distances in kilometers and miles without converting to a common scale. In later chapters, we will focus on developing the ability to make these conversions.

Additional Detail Supporting Reported Numbers

The second category of notes provides supplemental information concerning the data shown on the financial statements. Among other information, these notes may show revenues broken out by geographic region or business segment, describe unusual transactions, and/or offer expanded detail on a specific classification. For example, in Note 6, Callaway Golf indicates the makeup of accounts receivable; inventory; property, plant, and equipment; and other items presented on the balance sheet. Note 17, which follows, shows sales reported on the income statement and long-lived assets from the balance sheet divided by geographic region:

REAL WORLD EXCERPT
ANNUAL REPORT

NOTE 17: SEGMENT INFORMATION

	Sales	Long-Lived Assets
	(In thousands)	
2008		
United States	$ 554,029	$320,594
Europe	191,089	7,354
Japan	166,476	8,180
Rest of Asia	80,011	3,171
Other foreign countries	125,599	13,750
	$1,117,204	$353,049

Relevant Financial Information Not Disclosed on the Statements

The final category includes information that impacts the company financially but is not shown on the statements. Examples include information on legal matters and any material event that occurred subsequent to year-end but before the financial statements were published. In Note 15, Callaway Golf disclosed the details of its lease commitments:

REAL WORLD EXCERPT
ANNUAL REPORT

NOTE 15: LEASE COMMITMENTS

The Company leases certain warehouse, distribution and office facilities, vehicles as well as office equipment under operating leases, and certain computer and telecommunication equipment under capital leases. Lease terms range from 1 to 9 years expiring at various dates through November 2017, with options to renew at varying terms. Commitments for minimum lease payments under noncancelable operating leases as of December 31, 2008, are as follows (in thousands):

2009	$10,679
2010	6,668
2011	4,422
2012	3,049
2013	1,512
Thereafter	5,411
	$31,741

Voluntary Disclosures

GAAP and SEC regulations set only the minimum level of required financial disclosures. Many companies provide important disclosures beyond those required. For example, in its annual report, 10-K, and recent earnings press release, Callaway Golf discloses sales by major product category, which helps investors track the success of new products.

Accounting and Sustainable Development

A QUESTION OF ETHICS

A growing area of voluntary disclosure in the United States is sustainability reporting, as described by *CFO* magazine:

REAL WORLD EXCERPT
CFO Magazine

> The idea that a company should conduct its business in ways that benefit not just shareholders but the environment and society, too, is called **sustainability,** or sustainable development. It's an idea championed by a small but growing number of companies around the globe. One business group, the World Business Council for Sustainable Development, lists some 170 international members, including more than 30 Fortune 500 companies. According to the council's website, these companies share the belief that "the pursuit of sustainable development is good for business and business is good for sustainable development."
>
> To tell their stakeholders about that pursuit, companies are issuing sustainability reports. Many, like Suncor, are doing so following the strict guidelines of the Global Reporting Initiative (GRI), an independent institution founded in 1997, to develop a common framework for sustainability reporting. Enter the words "sustainability reporting" into your favorite search engine and you'll find such well-known company names as Alcoa, Alcan, Bristol-Myers Squibb, General Motors, Baxter International, and FedEx Kinko's. In all, some 500 organizations publish sustainability reports according to GRI guidelines. Some countries, such as France, South Africa, and the Netherlands, now mandate environmental or social sustainability reporting as a condition for being listed on their stock exchanges.
>
> Source: *CFO* magazine.

Such reports are voluntary disclosures in the United States. However, many believe that managing a company in the interests of a wider group of stakeholders and reporting on these efforts is an ethical imperative.

RETURN ON ASSETS ANALYSIS: A FRAMEWORK FOR EVALUATING COMPANY PERFORMANCE

LEARNING OBJECTIVE 4
Analyze a company's performance based on return on assets and its components.

Evaluating company performance is the primary goal of financial statement analysis. Company managers, as well as competitors, use financial statements to better understand and evaluate a company's business strategy. Analysts, investors, and creditors use these same statements to judge company performance when they estimate the value of the company's stock and its creditworthiness. Our discussion of the financial data contained in accounting reports has now reached the point where we can develop an overall framework for using that data to evaluate company performance. The most general framework of this type is called return on assets (ROA) analysis.

KEY RATIO ANALYSIS

Return on Assets (ROA)

ANALYTICAL QUESTION

During the period, how well has management used the company's total invested capital provided by both debt holders and stockholders?

RATIO AND COMPARISONS

$$\textbf{Return on Assets} = \frac{\textbf{Net Income*}}{\textbf{Average Total Assets}^{\dagger}}$$

The 2008 ratio for Callaway Golf:

$$\frac{\$66{,}176}{(\$838{,}078 + \$855{,}338) \div 2} = 0.078\ (7.8\%)$$

COMPARISIONS OVER TIME		
Callaway Golf		
2006	**2007**	**2008**
2.9%	6.5%	7.8%

COMPARISON WITH COMPETITOR
Adams Golf
2008
−2.2%

Selected Focus Companies' Return on Assets Ratios for 2008

Papa John's	9.3%
Harley-Davidson	9.7%
Deckers Outdoor	15.6%

INTERPRETATIONS

In General ROA measures how much the firm earned for each dollar of investment. It is the broadest measure of profitability and management effectiveness, independent of financing strategy. Firms with higher ROA are doing a better job of selecting and managing investments, all other things equal. Since it is independent of the source of financing (debt vs. equity), it can be used to evaluate performance at any level within the organization. It is often computed on a division-by-division or product line basis and used to evaluate division or product line managers' relative performance.

Focus Company Analysis The increase in return on assets between 2006 and 2007 was mainly due to an increase in overall sales and a change in product mix to newer products with higher gross margin percentages, as well as the disposal of some unproductive assets. The first half of 2008 was also very positive in terms of sales growth and margins, but sales were negatively affected in the second half by overall deterioration in the world economy. The company is doing much better in these difficult times than its smaller rival Adams Golf.

A Few Cautions Like all ratios, the key to interpreting change is to dig deeper to understand the reason for each change. Inspection of the income statement reveals that the only reason for the increase in ROA between 2007 and 2008 was an increase in "Other Income" from investing activities which cannot be repeated in future periods. Unless consumer discretionary spending increases, it will be very difficult for Callaway to continue to improve its ROA.

*In more complex return on assets analyses, interest expense (net of tax) and minority interest are added back to net income in the numerator of the ratio, since the measure assesses return on capital independent of its source.
†Average Total Assets = (Beginning Total Assets + Ending Total Assets) ÷ 2.

EXHIBIT 5.8

ROA Profit Driver Analysis

$$\text{ROA} = \text{Net Profit Margin} \times \text{Total Asset Turnover}$$

$$\frac{\text{Net Income}}{\text{Average Total Assets}} = \frac{\text{Net Income}}{\text{Net Sales}} \times \frac{\text{Net Sales}}{\text{Average Total Assets}}$$

ROA Profit Driver Analysis

Effective analysis of Callaway Golf's performance also requires understanding **why** its ROA differs both from prior levels and from those of its competitors. ROA profit driver analysis (also called **ROA decomposition** or **DuPont analysis**) breaks down ROA into the two factors shown in Exhibit 5.8. These factors are often called **profit drivers** or **profit levers** because they describe the two ways that management can improve ROA. They are measured by the key ratios you learned in Chapters 3 and 4.

1. **Net profit margin.** Net profit margin is Net Income ÷ Net Sales. It measures how much of every sales dollar is profit. It can be increased by
   a. Increasing sales volume.
   b. Increasing sales price.
   c. Decreasing cost of goods sold and operating expenses.
2. **Total asset turnover (efficiency).** Total asset turnover is Net Sales ÷ Average Total Assets. It measures how many sales dollars the company generates with each dollar of assets. It can be increased by
   a. Collecting accounts receivable more quickly.
   b. Centralizing distribution to reduce inventory kept on hand.
   c. Consolidating production facilities in fewer factories to reduce the amount of assets necessary to generate each dollar of sales.

These two ratios report on the effectiveness of the company's operating and investing activities, respectively.

Profit Drivers and Business Strategy

Successful manufacturers often follow one of two business strategies. The first is a **high-value** or **product-differentiation** strategy. Companies following this strategy rely on research and development and product promotion to convince customers of the superiority or distinctiveness of their products. This allows the company to charge higher prices and earn a higher net profit margin. The second is a **low-cost strategy,** which relies on efficient management of accounts receivable, inventory, and productive assets to produce high asset turnover.

Callaway Golf follows a classic high-value strategy. The ROA profit driver analysis presented in Exhibit 5.9 indicates the sources of its ROA, as well as reasons for its recent increase. The analysis shows continuing improvement in net profit margin from 2006 to 2008, as well as an improvement in asset turnover. This indicates that Callaway Golf is generating higher profits on each dollar of sales, as well as more sales dollars for each dollar of assets.

EXHIBIT 5.9

Callaway Golf ROA Profit Driver Analysis

Fiscal Year Ending	12/31/2006	12/31/2007	12/31/2008
Net Profit Margin	0.023	0.049	0.059
× Total Asset Turnover	1.26	1.32	1.32
= Return on Assets	0.029	0.065	0.078

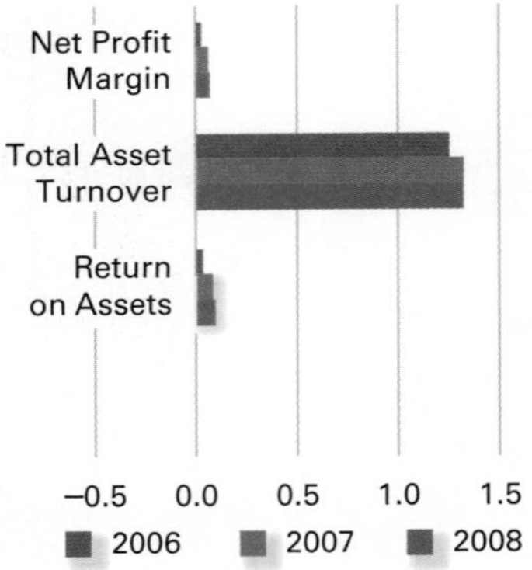

If Callaway Golf follows the same strategy it has in the past, the secret to increasing ROA must be continued product development to support premium selling prices. In 2008, Callaway Golf made major strides in new product development and expense reduction, and the success of new product introductions bodes well for further improvements in ROA in the longer term. But the lingering recession has led to a very tough 2009 for the company.

As the preceding discussion indicates, a company can take many different actions to try to affect its profit drivers. To understand the impact of these actions, financial analysts disaggregate each of the profit drivers into more detailed ratios. For example, the total asset turnover ratio is further disaggregated into turnover ratios for specific assets such as accounts receivable, inventory, and fixed assets. We will develop our understanding of these more specific ratios in the next eight chapters of the book. Then, in Chapter 14, we will combine the ratios in a comprehensive review.

STOP

PAUSE FOR **FEEDBACK**

SELF-STUDY **QUIZ**

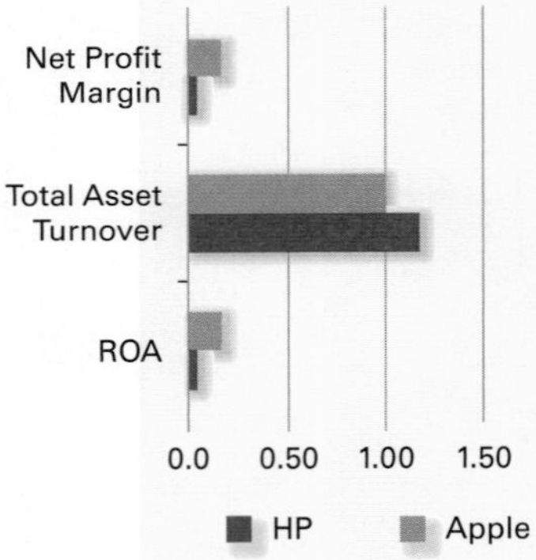

We used profit driver analysis in Exhibit 5.9 to understand how changes in net profit margin (Net Income/Net Sales) and total asset turnover (Net Sales/Average Total Assets) changed Callaway Golf's ROA over the last three years. This type of analysis is often called **time-series analysis.** Profit driver analysis can also be used to explain why a company has an ROA different from its competitors at a single point in time. This type of analysis is called **cross-sectional analysis.** Following is the recent year's ROA analysis for Apple Inc. and Hewlett-Packard Co. Apple uses a product differentiation strategy, developing a reputation for the most innovative products in its markets. HP primarily follows a low-cost strategy by offering good products and service at competitive prices. Apple has produced a higher ROA than HP and its stock price has responded accordingly. Using profit driver analysis, explain how Apple has produced its higher ROA.

Apple Inc.

Hewlett-Packard Co.

ROA Profit Drivers	Apple	HP
Net Income/Net Sales	.149	.070
× Net Sales/Average Total Assets	1.00	1.17
= Net Income/Average Total Assets	.149	.082

After you have completed your answers, check them with the solutions at the bottom of the page.

Solutions to SELF-STUDY QUIZ

Both Apple and HP have high net profit margins, but Apple's unique products result in a significantly higher net profit margin. They both are also well known for the efficiency of their operations, which is reflected in their high asset turnover ratios, but HP has the edge in asset efficiency. However, HP's edge in asset efficiency is not sufficient to make up for its lower net profit margin.

Epilogue

In 2009, citing declining sales and gross profits as well as costs related to its restructuring initiatives, Callaway reported a $0.33 per share loss. While predicting continuing difficult economic times, CEO George Fellows also noted that its responsible expense management and new product developments, together with its increase in market share, have positioned the company to generate a meaningful turnaround and return to profitability in 2010. You can evaluate Callaway Golf's progress by going to the Web at www.callawaygolf.com to check its latest annual and quarterly reports.

DEMONSTRATION CASE

MICROSOFT CORPORATION

Microsoft Corporation

Complete the following requirements before proceeding to the suggested solution. Microsoft Corporation, developer of a broad line of computer software, including the Windows operating systems, Word (word processing), and Excel (spreadsheet) programs, is now the largest computer-related company in the world. Following is a list of the financial statement items and amounts adapted from a recent Microsoft income statement and balance sheet. These items have normal debit and credit balances and are reported in millions of dollars. For that year, 8,908 million (weighted average) shares of stock were outstanding. The company closed its books on June 30, 2009.

Accounts payable	$ 3,324
Accounts receivable (net)	11,192
Accrued compensation	3,156
Cash and short-term investments	31,447
Common stock and paid-in capital	62,382
Cost of goods sold	12,155
General and administrative	4,030
Income taxes payable	725
Net revenues	58,437
Other current assets	$ 6,641
Other current liabilities	6,826
Other income (expense)	(542)
Other investments	4,933
Other noncurrent assets	16,140
Property, plant, and equipment (net)	7,535
Provision for income taxes	5,252
Research and development	9,010
Retained earnings (deficit)	(22,824)
Sales and marketing	12,879
Unearned revenue	13,003
Long-term liabilities	11,296

Required:

1. Prepare in good form a classified (multiple-step) income statement (showing gross profit, operating income, and income before income taxes) and a classified balance sheet for the year.
2. Compute the company's ROA. Briefly explain its meaning using ROA profit driver analysis. (Microsoft's total assets at the beginning of the year were $72,793 million.)

SUGGESTED SOLUTION

1.

MICROSOFT CORPORATION
Income Statement
For the Year Ended June 30, 2009
(dollars in millions)

Net revenues	$58,437
Cost of goods sold	12,155
Gross profit	46,282
Operating expenses:	
Research and development	9,010
Sales and marketing	12,879
General and administrative	4,030
Total operating expenses	25,919
Operating income	20,363
Nonoperating income and expenses:	
Other income (expense)	(542)
Income before income taxes	19,821
Provision for income taxes	5,252
Net income	$14,569
Earnings per share	$ 1.63*

MICROSOFT CORPORATION
Balance Sheet
June 30, 2009
(dollars in millions)

ASSETS	
Current assets	
Cash and short-term investments	$31,447
Accounts receivable (net)	11,192
Other current assets	6,641
Total current assets	49,280
Noncurrent assets	
Property, plant, and equipment (net)	7,535
Other investments	4,933
Other noncurrent assets	16,140
Total assets	$77,888
LIABILITIES	
Current liabilities	
Accounts payable	$ 3,324
Accrued compensation	3,156
Income taxes payable	725
Unearned revenue	13,003
Other current liabilities	6,826
Total current liabilities	27,034
Long-term liabilities	11,296
Stockholders' equity	
Common stock and paid-in capital	62,382
Retained earnings (deficit)	(22,824)
Total stockholders' equity	39,558
Total liabilities and stockholders' equity	$77,888

2.

Fiscal Year Ending June 30, 2009	
Net Income/Net Sales	0.25
× Net Sales/Average Total Assets	0.78
= Net Income/Average Total Assets	0.19

For the year ended June 30, Microsoft earned an ROA of 19 percent. Microsoft maintains high profit margins, earning $0.25 of net income for every $1 of net sales, but the company has a lower asset efficiency with only $0.78 in sales generated for each $1 of assets. The analysis also indicates Microsoft's dominance of the computer software business, which allows the company to charge premium prices for its products.

*With the numbers given, this computes as $1.64 because of rounding error.

Chapter Supplement

Nonrecurring Items

As noted in the chapter, companies may report any of two nonrecurring items: discontinued operations and extraordinary items. The income statement of Verizon Communications, Inc., the largest wireless communication provider in the United States, contains both of these items. It is presented in Exhibit 5.10.

Discontinued Operations

Discontinued operations result from abandoning or selling a major business component. Operating income generated by the discontinued component and any gain or loss on the disposal (the difference between the book value of the net assets being disposed of and the sale price or the abandonment costs) are included. These amounts may be separately disclosed in a note or on the face of the income statement. Each amount is reported net of the income tax effects. Separate reporting of discontinued operations informs users that these results are not predictive of the company's future.

DISCONTINUED OPERATIONS result from the disposal of a major component of the business and are reported net of income tax effects.

Verizon recognized income from discontinued operations primarily due to the sale of its interest in TELPRI (Telecomunicaciones de Puerto Rico, Inc.). The results of the operations of that business and the loss on sale of the business are listed as discontinued operations, net of tax, on the income statement shown in Exhibit 5.10.

Extraordinary Items

Extraordinary items are gains or losses that are considered both unusual in nature and infrequent in occurrence. Examples include losses suffered from natural disasters such as floods and hurricanes in geographic areas where such disasters are rare. These items must be reported separately on the income statement net of income tax effects. Separate reporting again informs decision makers that these items are not likely to recur, and so are not predictive of the company's future. Note disclosure is needed to explain the nature of the extraordinary item. **Companies report such items very rarely.**[5] For example, only 4 of the 600 companies followed by *Accounting Trends and Techniques* reported extraordinary items.

EXTRAORDINARY ITEMS are gains and losses that are both unusual in nature and infrequent in occurrence; they are reported net of tax on the income statement.

EXHIBIT 5.10

Income Statement for Verizon Communications, Inc.

REAL WORLD EXCERPT

Verizon Communications, Inc.

Annual Report

VERIZON COMMUNICATIONS, INC.
Consolidated Statement of Operations
Fiscal Year Ended December 31, 2007

Operating revenues	$93,469
Cost of services and sales	37,547
Selling, general, and administrative	25,967
Depreciation and amortization expense	14,377
Operating income	15,578
Equity in earnings of unconsolidated businesses	585
Other income (expense), net	211
Interest expense	(1,829)
Minority interest	(5,053)
Income from continuing operations before taxes	9,492
Provision for income taxes	(3,982)
Income from continuing operations	5,510
Income from discontinued operations, net of tax	142
Extraordinary item, net of tax	(131)
Net income	5,521

See notes to consolidated financial statements.

[5] Most extraordinary gains result from mergers and acquisitions. Gains and losses on early retirement of debt are separately disclosed (if material) as part of income from continuing operations. They are no longer considered extraordinary items.

CHAPTER TAKE-AWAYS

1. **Recognize the people involved in the accounting communication process (regulators, managers, directors, auditors, information intermediaries, and users), their roles in the process, and the guidance they receive from legal and professional standards. p. 231**

   Management of the reporting company must decide on the appropriate format (categories) and level of detail to present in its financial reports. Independent audits increase the credibility of the information. Directors monitor managers' compliance with reporting standards and hire the auditor. Financial statement announcements from public companies usually are first transmitted to users through electronic information services. The SEC staff reviews public financial reports for compliance with legal and professional standards, investigates irregularities, and punishes violators. Analysts play a major role in making financial statement and other information available to average investors through their stock recommendations and earnings forecasts.

2. **Identify the steps in the accounting communication process, including the issuance of press releases, annual reports, quarterly reports, and SEC filings, as well as the role of electronic information services in this process. p. 238**

   Earnings are first made public in press releases. Companies follow these announcements with annual and quarterly reports containing statements, notes, and additional information. Public companies must file additional reports with the SEC, including the 10-K, 10-Q, and 8-K, which contain more details about the company. Electronic information services are the key source of dissemination of this information to sophisticated users.

3. **Recognize and apply the different financial statement and disclosure formats used by companies in practice. p. 240**

   Most statements are classified and include subtotals that are relevant to analysis. On the balance sheet, the most important distinctions are between current and noncurrent assets and liabilities. On the income and cash flow statements, the distinction between operating and nonoperating items is most important. The notes to the statements provide descriptions of the accounting rules applied, add more information about items disclosed on the statements, and present information about economic events not included in the statements.

4. **Analyze a company's performance based on return on assets and its components. p. 249**

   ROA measures how well management used the company's invested capital during the period. Its two determinants, net profit margin and asset turnover, indicate why ROA differs from prior levels or the ROAs of competitors. They also suggest strategies to improve ROA in future periods.

In Chapter 6, we will begin our in-depth discussion of individual items presented in financial statements. We will start with two of the most liquid assets, cash and accounts receivable, and transactions that involve revenues and certain selling expenses. Accuracy in revenue recognition and the related recognition of cost of goods sold (discussed in Chapter 7) are the most important determinants of the accuracy—and, thus, the usefulness—of financial statements. We will also introduce concepts related to the management and control of cash and receivables, a critical business function. A detailed understanding of these topics is crucial to future managers, accountants, and financial analysts.

KEY RATIO

Return on assets (ROA) measures how much the firm earned for each dollar of investment. It is computed as follows (p. 250):

$$\textbf{Return on Assets} = \frac{\textbf{Net Income}}{\textbf{Average Total Assets}}$$

FINDING FINANCIAL INFORMATION

Balance Sheet

Key Classifications
Current and noncurrent assets and liabilities
Contributed capital and retained earnings

Income Statement

Key Subtotals
Gross profit
Income from operations
Income before income taxes
Net income
Earnings per share

Statement of Cash Flows

Under Operating Activities (indirect method)
Net income
± Adjustments for noncash items
Cash provided by operating activities

Notes

Key Classifications
Descriptions of accounting rules applied in the statements
Additional detail supporting reported numbers
Relevant financial information not disclosed on the statements

KEY TERMS

QUESTIONS

1. Describe the roles and responsibilities of management and independent auditors in the financial reporting process.
2. Define the following three users of financial accounting disclosures and the relationships among them: (*a*) financial analysts, (*b*) private investors, and (*c*) institutional investors.
3. Briefly describe the role of information services in the communication of financial information.
4. Explain why information must be relevant and reliable to be useful.
5. What basis of accounting does GAAP require on the (*a*) income statement, (*b*) balance sheet, and (*c*) statement of cash flows?
6. Briefly explain the normal sequence and form of financial reports produced by private companies in a typical year.
7. Briefly explain the normal sequence and form of financial reports produced by public companies in a typical year.
8. What are the four major subtotals or totals on the income statement?
9. Define extraordinary items. Why should they be reported separately on the income statement?
10. List the six major classifications reported on a balance sheet.
11. For property, plant, and equipment, as reported on the balance sheet, explain (*a*) cost, (*b*) accumulated depreciation, and (*c*) net book value.

12. Briefly explain the major classifications of stockholders' equity for a corporation.
13. What are the three major classifications on a statement of cash flows?
14. What are the three major categories of notes or footnotes presented in annual reports? Cite an example of each.
15. Briefly define return on assets and what it measures.

MULTIPLE-CHOICE QUESTIONS

1. If average total assets increase, but net income, net sales, and average stockholders' equity remain the same, what is the impact on the return on assets ratio?
   a. Increases.
   b. Decreases.
   c. Remains the same.
   d. Cannot be determined without additional information.
2. If a company plans to differentiate its products by offering low prices and discounts for items packaged in bulk (like a discount retailer that requires memberships for its customers), which component in the ROA profit driver analysis is the company attempting to boost?
   a. Net profit margin.
   b. Asset turnover.
   c. Financial leverage.
   d. All of the above.
3. If a company reported the following items on its income statement (cost of goods sold $5,000, income tax expense $2,000, interest expense $500, operating expenses $3,500, sales revenue $14,000), what amount would be reported for the subtotal "income from operations"?
   a. $9,000
   b. $3,000
   c. $5,000
   d. $5,500
4. Which of the following is **not** one of the possible nonrecurring items that must be shown in a separate line item below the Income from Continuing Operations subtotal in the income statement?
   a. Gains and losses from the sale of fixed assets.
   b. Discontinued operations.
   c. Extraordinary items.
   d. Both a and b.
5. Which of the following reports is filed annually with the SEC?
   a. Form 10-Q
   b. Form 10-K
   c. Form 8-K
   d. Press release
6. Which of the following would normally **not** be found in the notes to the financial statements?
   a. Accounting rules applied in the company's financial statements.
   b. Additional detail supporting numbers reported in the company's financial statements.
   c. Relevant financial information not presented in the company's financial statements.
   d. All of the above would be found in the notes to the financial statements.
7. Which of the following is **not** a normal function of a financial analyst?
   a. Issue earnings forecasts.
   b. Examine the records underlying the financial statements to certify their conformance with GAAP.
   c. Make buy, hold, and sell recommendations on companies' stock.
   d. Advise institutional investors on their securities holdings.
8. The classified balance sheet format allows one to ascertain quickly which of the following?
   a. The most valuable asset of the company.
   b. The specific due date for all liabilities of the company.
   c. What liabilities must be paid within the upcoming year.
   d. None of the above.
9. When companies issue par value stock for cash, which accounts are normally affected?
   a. Common Stock; Additional Paid-In Capital; and Property, Plant, and Equipment, Net.
   b. Cash; and Property, Plant, and Equipment, Net.
   c. Common Stock; Additional Paid-In Capital; and Retained Earnings.
   d. Common Stock; Additional Paid-In Capital; and Cash.
10. Net income was $900,000. Beginning and ending assets were $8,000,000 and $9,600,000, respectively. What was the return on assets (ROA)?
   a. 9.4%
   b. 10.23%
   c. 11.25%
   d. 10.41%

For more practice with multiple-choice questions, go to the text website at **www.mhhe.com/libby7e**.

connect ACCOUNTING

MINI-EXERCISES

Matching Players in the Accounting Communication Process with Their Definitions

M5-1
LO1

Match each player with the related definition by entering the appropriate letter in the space provided.

Players	Definitions
___ (1) Independent auditor	A. Adviser who analyzes financial and other economic information to form forecasts and stock recommendations.
___ (2) CEO and CFO	B. Institutional and private investors and creditors (among others).
___ (3) Users	C. Chief executive officer and chief financial officer who have primary responsibility for the information presented in financial statements.
___ (4) Financial analyst	D. Independent CPA who examines financial statements and attests to their fairness.

Identifying the Disclosure Sequence

M5-2
LO2

Indicate the order in which the following disclosures or reports are normally issued by public companies.

No.	Title
______	Form 10-K
______	Earnings press release
______	Annual report

Finding Financial Information: Matching Financial Statements with the Elements of Financial Statements

M5-3
LO3

Match each financial statement with the items presented on it by entering the appropriate letter in the space provided.

Elements of Financial Statements	Financial Statements
___ (1) Expenses	A. Income statement
___ (2) Cash from operating activities	B. Balance sheet
___ (3) Losses	C. Cash flow statement
___ (4) Assets	D. None of the above
___ (5) Revenues	
___ (6) Cash from financing activities	
___ (7) Gains	
___ (8) Owners' equity	
___ (9) Liabilities	
___ (10) Assets personally owned by a stockholder	

Determining the Effects of Transactions on Balance Sheet and Income Statement Categories

M5-4
LO3

Complete the following tabulation, indicating the sign of the effect (+ for increase, − for decrease, and NE for no effect) of each transaction. Consider each item independently.

a. Recorded sales on account of $120 and related cost of goods sold of $80.
b. Recorded advertising expense of $10 incurred but not paid for.

Transaction	Current Assets	Gross Profit	Current Liabilities
(*a*)			
(*b*)			

M5-5 **Determining Financial Statement Effects of Sales and Cost of Goods Sold and Issuance of Par Value Stock**
LO3

Using the following categories, indicate the effects of the following transactions. Use + for increase and − for decrease and indicate the accounts affected and the amounts.

a. Sales on account were $800 and related cost of goods sold was $350.
b. Issued 5,000 shares of $1 par value stock for $80,000 cash.

Event	Assets	=	Liabilities	+	Stockholders' Equity
(*a*)					
(*b*)					

M5-6 **Recording Sales and Cost of Goods Sold and Issuance of Par Value Stock**
LO3

Prepare journal entries for each transaction listed in M5-5.

M5-7 **Computing and Interpreting Return on Assets**
LO4

Saunders, Inc., recently reported the following December 31 amounts in its financial statements (dollars in thousands):

	Current Year	Prior Year
Gross profit	$ 170	$120
Net income	80	40
Total assets	1,000	900
Total shareholders' equity	800	600

Compute return on assets for the current year. What does this ratio measure?

EXERCISES

connect ACCOUNTING

E5-1 **Matching Players in the Accounting Communication Process with Their Definitions**
LO1

Match each player with the related definition by entering the appropriate letter in the space provided.

Players

___ (1) Financial analyst
___ (2) Creditor
___ (3) Independent auditor
___ (4) Private investor
___ (5) SEC
___ (6) Information service
___ (7) Institutional investor
___ (8) CEO and CFO

Definitions

A. Financial institution or supplier that lends money to the company.
B. Chief executive officer and chief financial officer who have primary responsibility for the information presented in financial statements.
C. Manager of pension, mutual, and endowment funds that invest on the behalf of others.
D. Securities and Exchange Commission, which regulates financial disclosure requirements.
E. A company that gathers, combines, and transmits (paper and electronic) financial and related information from various sources.
F. Adviser who analyzes financial and other economic information to form forecasts and stock recommendations.
G. Individual who purchases shares in companies.
H. Independent CPA who examines financial statements and attests to their fairness.

Matching Definitions with Information Releases Made by Public Companies

E5-2
LO2

Following are the titles of various information releases. Match each definition with the related release by entering the appropriate letter in the space provided.

Information Release	Definitions
___ (1) Form 10-Q	A. Report of special events (e.g., auditor changes, mergers) filed by public companies with the SEC.
___ (2) Quarterly report	B. Brief unaudited report for quarter normally containing summary income statement and balance sheet.
___ (3) Press release	C. Quarterly report filed by public companies with the SEC that contains additional unaudited financial information.
___ (4) Annual report	D. Written public news announcement that is normally distributed to major news services.
___ (5) Form 10-K	E. Annual report filed by public companies with the SEC that contains additional detailed financial information.
___ (6) Form 8-K	F. Report containing the four basic financial statements for the year, related notes, and often statements by management and auditors.

Finding Financial Information: Matching Information Items to Financial Reports

E5-3
LO2

Following are information items included in various financial reports. Match each information item with the report(s) where it would most likely be found by entering the appropriate letter(s) in the space provided.

Information Item	Report
___ (1) Summarized financial data for 5- or 10-year period.	A. Form 10-Q
___ (2) Notes to financial statements.	B. Annual report
___ (3) The four basic financial statements for the year.	C. Form 8-K
___ (4) Summarized income statement information for the quarter.	D. Press release
___ (5) Detailed discussion of the company's competition.	E. Quarterly report
___ (6) Initial announcement of hiring of new vice president for sales.	F. Form 10-K
___ (7) Initial announcement of quarterly earnings.	G. None of the above
___ (8) Description of those responsible for the financial statements.	
___ (9) Complete quarterly income statement, balance sheet, and cash flow statement.	
___ (10) Announcement of a change in auditors.	

Ordering the Classifications on a Typical Balance Sheet

E5-4
LO3

Following is a list of classifications on the balance sheet. Number them in the order in which they normally appear on a balance sheet.

No.	Title
___	Long-term liabilities
___	Current liabilities
___	Long-term investments
___	Intangible assets
___	Contributed capital
___	Current assets
___	Retained earnings
___	Property, plant, and equipment
___	Other noncurrent assets

E5-5
LO3

Campbell Soup Co.

Preparing a Classified Balance Sheet

Campbell Soup Company is the world's leading maker and marketer of soup and sells other well-known brands of food in 120 countries. Presented here are the items listed on its recent balance sheet (dollars in millions) presented in alphabetical order:

Accounts payable	$ 569	Other assets	$ 105
Accounts receivable	528	Other current assets	148
Accrued expenses	579	Other current debt	480
Cash and cash equivalents	51	Other noncurrent liabilities	3,700
Common stock, $0.0375 par value	352	Property, plant, and equipment, net	1,977
Intangible assets	2,423	Retained earnings	376
Inventories	824		

Required:
Prepare a classified consolidated balance sheet for Campbell Soup for the current year (ended August 2) using the categories presented in the chapter.

E5-6
LO3

Preparing and Interpreting a Classified Balance Sheet with Discussion of Terminology (Challenging)

Lance, Inc., manufactures, markets, and distributes a variety of snack foods. Product categories include sandwich crackers, cookies, restaurant crackers and bread basket items, candy, chips, meat snacks, nuts, and cake items. These items are sold under trade names including Lance, Toastchee, Toasty, Choc-O-Lunch, Captain's Wafers, and Cape Cod. Presented here are the items listed on its recent balance sheet (dollars in millions) in alphabetical order:

Accounts payable	$25,939	Other assets (noncurrent)	$ 4,949
Accounts receivable, net	74,406	Other current assets	9,778
Accrued compensation	26,312	Other intangible assets, net	23,966
Additional paid-in capital	49,138	Other long-term liabilities	48,070
Cash and cash equivalents	807	Other payables and accrued liabilities	32,318
Common stock, 28,947,222 shares outstanding	26,268	Prepaid expenses and other	12,933
Goodwill	80,110	Property, plant, and equipment, net	216,085
Inventories	43,112	Retained earnings	160,101
Long-term debt	91,000	Short-term debt	7,000

Required:
1. Prepare a classified consolidated balance sheet for Lance, Inc., for the current year (ended December 31) using the categories presented in the chapter.
2. Three of the items end in the term **net.** Explain what this term means in each case.

E5-7
LO3

Coach, Inc.

Recording Stock Issuances with Par Value

In a recent year, Coach, Inc., a designer and marketer of handbags and other accessories, issued 10,200 shares of its $0.01 par value stock for $43,000 (these numbers are rounded). These additional shares were issued under an employee stock option plan. Prepare the journal entry required to record the stock issuance.

E5-8
LO3

Inferring Stock Issuances and Cash Dividends from Changes in Stockholders' Equity

The Kroger Co. is one of the largest retailers in the United States and also manufactures and processes some of the food for sale in its supermarkets. Kroger reported the following January 31 balances in its stockholders' equity accounts (dollars in millions):

	Current Year	Prior Year
Common stock	$ 955	$ 947
Paid-in capital	3,266	3,031
Retained earnings	7,489	6,480

During the current year, Kroger reported net income of $1,249.

Required:

1. How much did Kroger declare in dividends for the year?
2. Assume that the only other transaction that affected stockholders' equity during the current year was a single stock issuance. Recreate the journal entry reflecting the stock issuance.

Matching Definitions with Income Statement Related Terms

E5-9
LO3

Following are terms related to the income statement. Match each definition with its related term by entering the appropriate letter in the space provided.

Terms	Definitions
___ (1) Net income	A. Revenues + Gains − Expenses − Losses including effects of discontinued operations and extraordinary items (if any).
___ (2) Income tax expense on operations	B. Income Tax on Revenues − Operating Expenses.
___ (3) Income before extra-ordinary items	C. Sales Revenue − Cost of Goods Sold
___ (4) Cost of goods sold	D. Sales of services for cash or on credit.
___ (5) Operating expenses	E. Amount of resources used to purchase or produce the goods that were sold during the reporting period.
___ (6) Gross margin on sales	F. Total expenses directly related to operations.
___ (7) EPS	G. Income before all income tax and before discontinued operations and extraordinary items (if any).
___ (8) Interest expense	H. Cost of money (borrowing) over time.
___ (9) Service revenue	I. Item that is both unusual and infrequent.
___ (10) Pretax income from operations	J. Net Income ÷ Average Shares Outstanding.
	K. Income before unusual and infrequent items and the related income tax.
	L. None of the above.

Inferring Income Statement Values

E5-10
LO3

Supply the missing dollar amounts for the 2012 income statement of NexTech Company for each of the following independent cases. (**Hint:** Organize each case in the format of the classified or multiple-step income statement discussed in the chapter. Rely on the amounts given to infer the missing values.)

	Case A	Case B	Case C	Case D	Case E
Sales revenue	$900	$750	$420	$?	$?
Selling expense	?	100	80	390	240
Cost of goods sold	?	300	?	500	320
Income tax expense	?	30	20	50	20
Gross margin	375	?	?	?	430
Pretax income	200	200	?	190	?
Administrative expense	125	?	70	120	90
Net income	120	?	60	?	80

Inferring Income Statement Values

E5-11
LO3

Supply the missing dollar amounts for the 2012 income statement of BGT Company for each of the following independent cases. (**Hint:** Organize each case in the format of the classified or multiple-step income statement discussed in the chapter. Rely on the amounts given to infer the missing values.)

	Case A	Case B	Case C	Case D	Case E
Sales revenue	$770	$?	$?	$600	$1,050
Pretax income	?	?	150	130	370
Income tax expense	65	210	60	45	?
Cost of goods sold	?	320	125	250	?
Gross margin	?	880	?	?	630
Selling expense	90	275	45	70	?
Net income	115	275	?	?	240
Administrative expense	200	120	80	?	175

E5-12 LO3 Preparing a Multiple-Step Income Statement

The following data were taken from the records of Township Corporation at December 31, 2012:

Sales revenue	$79,000
Gross profit	28,000
Selling (distribution) expense	7,000
Administrative expense	?
Pretax income	13,000
Income tax rate	35%
Shares of stock outstanding	3,500

Required:
Prepare a complete multiple-step income statement for the company (showing both gross profit and income from operations). Show all computations. (**Hint:** Set up the side captions or rows starting with sales revenue and ending with earnings per share; rely on the amounts and percentages given to infer missing values.)

E5-13 LO3 Preparing a Multiple-Step Income Statement

The following data were taken from the records of Cofelt Appliances, Incorporated, at December 31, 2011:

Sales revenue	$130,000
Administrative expense	17,000
Selling (distribution) expense	19,000
Income tax rate	30%
Gross profit	60,000
Shares of stock outstanding	2,500

Required:
Prepare a complete multiple-step income statement for the company (showing both gross profit and income from operations). Show all computations. (**Hint:** Set up the side captions or rows starting with sales revenue and ending with earnings per share; rely on the amounts and percentages given to infer missing values.)

E5-14 LO3 Determining the Effects of Transactions on Balance Sheet and Income Statement Categories

Hasbro

Hasbro is one of the world's leading toy manufacturers and maker of such popular board games as Monopoly, Scrabble, and Clue, among others. Listed here are selected aggregate transactions from the first quarter of a recent year (dollars in millions). Complete the following tabulation, indicating the sign (+ for increase, − for decrease, and NE for no effect) and amount of the effect of each transaction. Consider each item independently.

a. Recorded sales on account of $792.2 and related cost of goods sold of $319.5.
b. Issued debt with a principle amount of $425.0.
c. Incurred research and development expense of $43.5, which was paid in cash.

Transaction	Current Assets	Gross Profit	Current Liabilities
a.			
b.			
c.			

E5-15 LO3 Determining the Effects of Transactions on Balance Sheet, Income Statement, and Statement of Cash Flows Categories

Listed here are selected aggregate transactions for ModernStyle Furniture Company from the first quarter of a recent year (dollars in millions). Complete the following tabulation, indicating the sign (+ for increase, − for decrease, and NE for no effect) and amount of the effect of each additional transaction. Consider each item independently.

a. Recorded collections of cash from customers owed on open account of $35.2.
b. Repaid $3.1 in principal on line of credit with a bank with principal payable within one year.

Transaction	Current Assets	Gross Profit	Current Liabilities	Cash Flow from Operating Activities
a.				
b.				

E5-16
LO3

Preparing a Simple Statement of Cash Flows Using the Indirect Method

Avalos Corporation is preparing its annual financial statements at December 31, 2011. Listed here are the items on its statement of cash flows presented in alphabetical order. Parentheses indicate that a listed amount should be subtracted on the cash flow statement. The beginning balance in cash was $25,000 and the ending balance was $50,000.

Cash borrowed on three-year note	$30,000
Decrease in accounts payable	(3,000)
Decrease in inventory	1,000
Increase in accounts receivable	(9,000)
Land purchased	(36,000)
Net income	25,000
New delivery truck purchased for cash	(7,000)
Stock issued for cash	24,000

Required:
Prepare the 2011 statement of cash flows for Avalos Corporation. The section reporting cash flows from operating activities should be prepared using the indirect method discussed in the chapter.

E5-17
LO4

TIFFANY & CO.

Analyzing and Interpreting Return on Assets

Tiffany & Co. is one of the world's premier jewelers and a designer of other fine gifts and housewares. Presented here are selected income statement and balance sheet amounts (dollars in thousands).

	Current Year	Prior Year
Net sales	$2,859,997	$2,938,771
Net income	220,022	323,478
Average shareholders' equity	1,652,243	1,721,131
Average total assets	3,051,594	2,883,833

Required:
1. Compute ROA for the current and prior years and explain the meaning of the change.
2. Explain the major cause(s) of the change in ROA using ROA profit driver analysis.

E5-18
LO4

Analyzing and Evaluating Return on Assets from a Security Analyst's Perspective

Papa John's is one of the fastest-growing pizza delivery and carry-out restaurant chains in the country. Presented here are selected income statement and balance sheet amounts (dollars in thousands).

	Current Year	Prior Year
Net sales	$1,132,087	$1,063,595
Net income	36,796	32,735
Average shareholders' equity	128,445	136,536
Average total assets	394,143	390,728

Required:
1. Compute ROA for the current and prior years and explain the meaning of the change.
2. Would security analysts more likely increase or decrease their estimates of share value on the basis of this change? Explain.

To practice with more exercises, go to the text website at **www.mhhe.com/libby7e**.

PROBLEMS

connect ACCOUNTING

P5-1 Matching Transactions with Concepts

LO1, 2

Following are the concepts of accounting covered in Chapters 2 through 5. Match each transaction or definition with its related concept by entering the appropriate letter in the space provided. Use one letter for each blank.

Concepts

____ (1) Users of financial statements
____ (2) Objective of financial statements

Qualitative Characteristics

____ (3) Relevance
____ (4) Reliability

Assumptions

____ (5) Separate entity
____ (6) Continuity
____ (7) Unit of measure
____ (8) Time period

Elements of Financial Statements

____ (9) Revenues
____ (10) Expenses
____ (11) Gains
____ (12) Losses
____ (13) Assets
____ (14) Liabilities
____ (15) Stockholders' equity

Principles

____ (16) Cost
____ (17) Revenue
____ (18) Matching
____ (19) Full disclosure

Constraints of Accounting

____ (20) Materiality threshold
____ (21) Cost-benefit constraint
____ (22) Conservatism constraint
____ (23) Special industry practices

Transactions/Definitions

A. Recorded a $1,000 sale of merchandise on credit.
B. Counted (inventoried) the unsold items at the end of the period and valued them in dollars.
C. Acquired a vehicle for use in operating the business.
D. Reported the amount of depreciation expense because it likely will affect important decisions of statement users.
E. The investors, creditors, and others interested in the business.
F. Used special accounting approaches because of the uniqueness of the industry.
G. Sold and issued bonds payable of $1 million.
H. Used services from outsiders; paid cash for some and put the remainder on credit.
I. Engaged an outside independent CPA to audit the financial statements.
J. Sold an asset at a loss that was a peripheral or incidental transaction.
K. Established an accounting policy that sales revenue shall be recognized only when ownership to the goods sold passes to the customer.
L. To design and prepare the financial statements to assist the users in making decisions.
M. Established a policy not to include in the financial statements the personal financial affairs of the owners of the business.
N. Sold merchandise and services for cash and on credit during the year; then determined the cost of those goods sold and the cost of rendering those services.
O. The user value of a special financial report exceeds the cost of preparing it.
P. Valued an asset, such as inventory, at less than its purchase cost because the replacement cost is less.
Q. Dated the income statement "For the Year Ended December 31, 2011."
R. Paid a contractor for an addition to the building with $10,000 cash and $20,000 market value of the stock of the company ($30,000 was deemed to be the cash-equivalent price).
S. Acquired an asset (a pencil sharpener that will have a useful life of five years) and recorded it as an expense when purchased for $1.99.
T. Disclosed in the financial statements all relevant financial information about the business; necessitated the use of notes to the financial statements.
U. Sold an asset at a gain that was a peripheral or incidental transaction.
V. Assets of $500,000 − Liabilities of $300,000 = ?
W. Accounting and reporting assume a "going concern."

Matching Definitions with Balance Sheet–Related Terms

P5-2
LO3

Following are terms related to the balance sheet that were discussed in Chapters 2 through 5. Match each definition with its related term by entering the appropriate letter in the space provided.

Terms	Definitions
____ (1) Capital in excess of par	A. Nearness of assets to cash (in time).
____ (2) Assets	B. Liabilities expected to be paid out of current assets normally within the next year.
____ (3) Retained earnings	C. All liabilities not classified as current liabilities.
____ (4) Book value	D. Total assets minus total liabilities.
____ (5) Other assets	E. Probable future economic benefits owned by the entity from past transactions.
____ (6) Shares outstanding	F. Debts or obligations from past transactions to be paid with assets or services.
____ (7) Shareholders' equity	G. Assets expected to be collected in cash within one year or the operating cycle, if longer.
____ (8) Liquidity	H. Assets that do not have physical substance.
____ (9) Normal operating cycle	I. Balance of the Common Stock account divided by the par value per share.
____ (10) Current assets	J. A miscellaneous category of assets.
____ (11) Current liabilities	K. Sum of the annual depreciation expense on an asset from its acquisition to the current date.
____ (12) Long-term liabilities	L. Asset offset account (subtracted from asset).
____ (13) Fixed assets	M. Accumulated earnings minus accumulated dividends.
____ (14) Liabilities	N. Property, plant, and equipment.
____ (15) Contra-asset account	O. Same as carrying value; cost less accumulated depreciation to date.
____ (16) Accumulated depreciation	P. Amount of contributed capital less the par value of the stock.
____ (17) Intangible assets	Q. The average cash-to-cash time involved in the operations of the business.
	R. None of the above.

Preparing a Balance Sheet and Analyzing Some of Its Parts (AP5-1)

P5-3
LO3

excel
www.mhhe.com/libby7e

Exquisite Jewelers is developing its annual financial statements for 2012. The following amounts were correct at December 31, 2012: cash, \$58,000; accounts receivable, \$71,000; merchandise inventory, \$154,000; prepaid insurance, \$1,500; investment in stock of Z corporation (long-term), \$36,000; store equipment, \$67,000; used store equipment held for disposal, \$9,000; accumulated depreciation, store equipment, \$19,000; accounts payable, \$52,500; long-term note payable, \$42,000; income taxes payable, \$9,000; retained earnings, \$164,000; and common stock, 100,000 shares outstanding, par value \$1.00 per share (originally sold and issued at \$1.10 per share).

Required:

1. Based on these data, prepare a December 31, 2012 balance sheet. Use the following major captions (list the individual items under these captions):
   a. Assets: Current Assets, Long-Term Investments, Fixed Assets, and Other Assets.
   b. Liabilities: Current Liabilities and Long-Term Liabilities.
   c. Stockholders' Equity: Contributed Capital and Retained Earnings.
2. What is the net book value of the store equipment? Explain what this value means.

P5-4 LO3 Reporting Stockholders' Equity on a Balance Sheet and Recording the Issuance of Stock (AP5-2)

excel
www.mhhe.com/libby7e

At the end of the 2011 annual reporting period, Barnard Corporation's balance sheet showed the following:

BARNARD CORPORATION **Balance Sheet** **At December 31, 2011**	
Stockholders' Equity	
Contributed capital	
Common stock (par $15; 6,000 shares)	$ 90,000
Paid-in capital	13,000
Total contributed capital	103,000
Retained earnings	44,000
Total stockholders' equity	$147,000

During 2012, the following selected transactions (summarized) were completed:

a. Sold and issued 1,000 shares of common stock at $25 cash per share (at year-end).
b. Determined net income, $43,000.
c. Declared and paid a cash dividend of $3 per share on the beginning shares outstanding.

Required:

1. Prepare the stockholders' equity section of the balance sheet at December 31, 2012.
2. Give the journal entry to record the sale and issuance of the 1,000 shares of common stock.

P5-5 LO3 Preparing a Multiple-Step Income Statement

AÉROPOSTALE

excel
www.mhhe.com/libby7e

Aeropostale, Inc., is a mall-based specialty retailer of casual apparel and accessories. The company concept is to provide the customer with a focused selection of high-quality, active-oriented fashions at compelling values. The items reported on its income statement for a recent year (ended March 31) are presented here (dollars in thousands) in alphabetical order:

Cost of goods sold	$1,231,349
Interest income	510
Net revenue	1,885,531
Other selling, general, and administrative expenses	405,883
Provision for income taxes	99,387
Weighted average shares outstanding	66,832

Required:

Prepare a multiple-step consolidated income statement (showing gross profit, operating income, and income before income taxes). Include a presentation of basic earnings per share.

P5-6 LO3 Preparing Both an Income Statement and a Balance Sheet from a Trial Balance (AP5-3)

excel
www.mhhe.com/libby7e

Jordan Sales Company (organized as a corporation on April 1, 2011) has completed the accounting cycle for the second year, ended March 31, 2013. Jordan also has completed a correct trial balance as follows:

JORDAN SALES COMPANY **Trial Balance** **At March 31, 2013**		
Account Titles	**Debit**	**Credit**
Cash	$ 58,000	
Accounts receivable	49,000	
Office supplies inventory	1,000	
Automobiles (company cars)	34,000	
Accumulated depreciation, automobiles		$ 14,000
Office equipment	3,000	
Accumulated depreciation, office equipment		1,000
Accounts payable		22,000
Income taxes payable		0
Salaries and commissions payable		2,000
Note payable, long-term		33,000
Capital stock (par $1; 33,000 shares)		33,000
Paid-in capital		5,000
Retained earnings (on April 1, 2012)		7,500
Dividends declared and paid during the current year	10,500	
Sales revenue		99,000
Cost of goods sold	33,000	
Operating expenses (detail omitted to conserve time)	19,000	
Depreciation expense (on autos and including $500 on office equipment)	8,000	
Interest expense	1,000	
Income tax expense (not yet computed)		
Totals	$216,500	$216,500

Required:

Complete the financial statements as follows:

a. Classified (multiple-step) income statement for the reporting year ended March 31, 2013. Include income tax expense, assuming a 25 percent tax rate. Use the following subtotals: Gross Profit, Total Operating Expenses, Income from Operations, Income before Income Taxes, and Net Income, and show EPS.

b. Classified balance sheet at the end of the reporting year, March 31, 2013. Include (1) income taxes for the current year in Income Taxes Payable and (2) dividends in Retained Earnings. Use the following captions (list each item under these captions).

Assets

Current assets
Noncurrent assets

Liabilities

Current liabilities
Long-term liabilities

Stockholders' Equity

Contributed capital
Retained earnings

P5-7
LO3, 4
Creative Technology

Determining and Interpreting the Effects of Transactions on Income Statement Categories and Return on Assets (AP5-4)

Creative Technology, a computer hardware company based in Singapore, developed the modern standard for computer sound cards in the early 1990s. Recently, Creative has released a line of portable audio products to directly compete with Apple's popular iPod. Presented here is a recent income statement (dollars in millions).

Net sales	$915
Costs and expenses	
Cost of sales	737
Research and development	64
Selling, general, and administrative	175
Operating income (loss)	(61)
Interest and other income (expenses), net	112
Income (loss) before provision (benefit) for income taxes	51
Provision (benefit) for income taxes	23
Net income (loss)	$ 28

Its beginning and ending assets were $393 and $409, respectively.

Required:

Listed here are hypothetical **additional** transactions. Assuming that they **also** occurred during the fiscal year, complete the following tabulation, indicating the sign of the effect of each **additional** transaction (+ for increase, − for decrease, and NE for no effect). Consider each item independently and ignore taxes.

a. Recorded sales on account of $500 and related cost of goods sold of $475.
b. Incurred additional research and development expense of $100, which was paid in cash.
c. Issued additional shares of common stock for $200 cash.
d. Declared and paid dividends of $90.

Transaction	Gross Profit	Operating Income (Loss)	Return on Assets
a.			
b.			
c.			
d.			

P5-8 (Supplement) Preparing a Multiple-Step Income Statement with Discontinued Operations and Cumulative Effects of Accounting Changes

Newell Rubbermaid
Brands That Matter

Newell Rubbermaid Inc. manufactures and markets a broad array of office products, tools and hardware, and home products under a variety of brand names, including Sharpie, Paper Mate, Rolodex, Rubbermaid, Levolor, and others. The items reported on its income statement for the year ended December 31, 2008, are presented here (dollars in thousands) in alphabetical order:

Cost of Products Sold	$4,347.4
Income Tax Expense	53.6
Interest and Other Non-operating Expense	199.0
Loss on Sale of Discontinued Operations, Net of Income Taxes	(0.5)
Net Sales	6,470.6
Other Expense	419.7
Selling, General, and Administrative Expenses	1,502.7

Required:

Using appropriate headings and subtotals, prepare a multiple-step consolidated income statement (showing gross profit, operating income, and any other subheadings you deem appropriate).

ALTERNATE PROBLEMS

Preparing a Balance Sheet and Analyzing Some of Its Parts (P5-3)

AP5-1
L03

TangoCo is developing its annual financial statements for 2012. The following amounts were correct at December 31, 2012: cash, $48,800; investment in stock of PIL Corporation (long-term), $36,400; store equipment, $67,200; accounts receivable, $71,820; inventory, $154,000; prepaid rent, $1,120; used store equipment held for disposal, $9,800; accumulated depreciation, store equipment, $13,440; income taxes payable, $9,800; long-term note payable, $32,000; accounts payable, $58,800; retained earnings, $165,100; and common stock, 100,000 shares outstanding, par value $1 per share (originally sold and issued at $1.10 per share).

Required:

1. Based on these data, prepare a 2012 balance sheet. Use the following major captions (list the individual items under these captions):
   a. Assets: Current Assets, Long-Term Investments, Fixed Assets, and Other Assets.
   b. Liabilities: Current Liabilities and Long-Term Liabilities.
   c. Stockholders' Equity: Contributed Capital and Retained Earnings.
2. What is the net book value of the store equipment? Explain what this value means.

Reporting Stockholders' Equity on a Balance Sheet and Recording the Issuance of Stock (P5-4)

AP5-2
L03

At the end of the 2011 annual reporting period, Mesa Industries's balance sheet showed the following:

MESA INDUSTRIES Balance Sheet At December 31, 2011	
Stockholders' Equity	
Common stock (par $15; 7,000 shares)	$105,000
Additional paid-in capital	9,000
Retained earnings	48,000
Total stockholders' equity	$162,000

During 2012, the following selected transactions (summarized) were completed:

a. Sold and issued 1,500 shares of common stock at $26 cash per share (at year-end).
b. Determined net income, $46,000.
c. Declared and paid a cash dividend of $1 per share on the beginning shares outstanding.

Required:

1. Prepare the stockholders' equity section of the balance sheet at December 31, 2012.
2. Give the journal entry to record the sale and issuance of the 1,500 shares of common stock.

Preparing Both an Income Statement and a Balance Sheet from a Trial Balance (P5-6)

AP5-3
L03

Dynamite Sales (organized as a corporation on September 1, 2010) has completed the accounting cycle for the second year, ended August 31, 2012. Dynamite also has completed a correct trial balance as follows:

DYNAMITE SALES
Trial Balance
At August 31, 2012

Account Titles	Debit	Credit
Cash	$ 47,700	
Accounts receivable	38,320	
Office supplies	270	
Company vehicles (delivery vans)	27,000	
Accumulated depreciation, company vehicles		$ 9,000
Equipment	2,700	
Accumulated depreciation, equipment		900
Accounts payable		16,225
Income taxes payable		0
Salaries payable		1,350
Long-term debt		25,000
Capital stock (par $1; 29,000 shares)		29,000
Paid-in capital		4,500
Retained earnings (on September 1, 2011)		6,615
Dividends declared and paid during the current year	7,200	
Sales revenue		81,000
Cost of goods sold	27,000	
Operating expenses (detail omitted to conserve time)	16,200	
Depreciation expense (on vehicles and including $3,450 on equipment)	4,950	
Interest expense	2,250	
Income tax expense (not yet computed)		
Totals	$173,590	$173,590

Required:
Complete the financial statements, as follows:

a. Classified (multiple-step) income statement for the reporting year ended August 31, 2012. Include income tax expense, assuming a 30 percent tax rate. Use the following subtotals: Gross Profit, Total Operating Expenses, Income from Operations, Income before Income Taxes, and Net Income, and show EPS.
b. Classified balance sheet at the end of the reporting year, August 31, 2012. Include (1) income taxes for the current year in Income Taxes Payable and (2) dividends in Retained Earnings. Use the following captions (list each item under these captions).

Assets
Current assets
Noncurrent assets

Liabilities
Current liabilities
Long-term liabilities

Stockholders' Equity
Contributed capital
Retained earnings

AP5-4
LO3, 4
Avon

Determining and Interpreting the Effects of Transactions on Income Statement Categories and Return on Assets (P5-7)

Avon Products, Inc., is a leading manufacturer and marketer of beauty products and related merchandise. The company sells its products in 110 countries through a combination of direct selling and use of individual sales representatives. Presented here is a recent income statement (dollars in millions).

Net sales	$10,690
Costs and expenses	
Cost of sales	3,949
Selling, general, and administrative	5,402
Operating income (loss)	1,339
Interest and other income (expenses), net	(101)
Income (loss) before provision (benefit) for income taxes	1,238
Provision (benefit) for income taxes	363
Net income (loss)	$ 875

Its beginning and ending total assets were $5,716 and $6,074, respectively.

Required:

1. Listed here are hypothetical **additional** transactions. Assuming that they **also** occurred during the fiscal year, complete the following tabulation, indicating the sign of the effect of each **additional** transaction (+ for increase, − for decrease, and NE for no effect). Consider each item independently and ignore taxes.
   a. Recorded and received additional interest income of $7.
   b. Purchased $80 of additional inventory on open account.
   c. Recorded and paid additional advertising expense of $16.
   d. Issued additional shares of common stock for $40 cash.

Transaction	Operating Income (Loss)	Net Income	Return on Assets
a.			
b.			
c.			
d.			

2. Assume that next period, Avon does not pay any dividends, does not issue or retire stock, and earns 20 percent more than during the current period. If total assets increase by 5 percent, will Avon's ROA next period be higher, lower, or the same as in the current period? Why?

CASES AND PROJECTS

Annual Report Cases

Finding Financial Information

CP5-1
LO2, 3, 4

AMERICAN EAGLE OUTFITTERS, INC.

Refer to the financial statements of American Eagle Outfitters given in Appendix B at the end of this book. At the bottom of each statement, the company warns readers to "Refer to Notes to Consolidated Financial Statements." The following questions illustrate the types of information that you can find in the financial statements and accompanying notes. (**Hint:** Use the notes.)

Required:

1. What items were included as noncurrent assets on the balance sheet?
2. How much land did the company own at the end of the most recent reporting year?

3. What portion of current liabilities were "Unredeemed store value cards and gift certificates" during the current year?
4. At what point were website sales recognized as revenue?
5. The company reported cash flows from operating activities of $302,193,000. However, its cash and cash equivalents increased by $357,281,000 for the year. Explain how that happened.
6. What was the highest stock price for the company during fiscal 2008? (**Note:** Some companies will label a year that has a January year-end as having a fiscal year-end dated one year earlier. For example, a January 2009 year-end may be labeled as Fiscal 2008 since the year actually has more months that fall in the 2008 calendar year than in the 2009 calendar year.)
7. Calculate the company's ROA for fiscal 2008 and 2007. Did it increase or decrease? How would you expect the change in ROA to be reflected in the company's share price?

CP5-2
LO2, 3

URBN
URBAN OUTFITTERS INC.

Finding Financial Information

Refer to the financial statements of Urban Outfitters given in Appendix C at the end of this book. At the bottom of each statement, the company warns readers that "The accompanying notes are an integral part of these financial statements." The following questions illustrate the types of information that you can find in the financial statements and accompanying notes. (**Hint:** Use the notes.)

Required:

1. What subtotals does Urban Outfitters report on its income statement?
2. The company spent $112,553,000 on capital expenditures (property, plant, and equipment) and $809,039,000 purchasing investments during the most recent year. Were operating activities or financing activities the major source of cash for these expenditures?
3. What was the company's largest asset (net) at the end of the most recent year?
4. How does the company account for costs associated with developing its websites?
5. Over what useful lives are buildings depreciated?
6. What portion of gross "Property and Equipment" is composed of "Buildings"?

CP5-3
LO4

AMERICAN EAGLE OUTFITTERS, INC.

URBN
URBAN OUTFITTERS INC.

Comparing Companies within an Industry

Refer to the financial statements of American Eagle Outfitters (Appendix B) and Urban Outfitters (Appendix C) and the Industry Ratio Report (Appendix D) at the end of this book.

Required:

1. Compute return on assets for the most recent year. Which company provided the highest return on invested capital during the current year?
2. Use ROA profit driver analysis to determine the cause(s) of any differences. How might the ownership versus the rental of property, plant, and equipment affect the total asset turnover ratio?
3. Compare the ROA profit driver analysis for American Eagle Outfitters and Urban Outfitters to the ROA profit driver analysis for their industry. Where does American Eagle Outfitters outperform or underperform the industry? Where does Urban Outfitters outperform or underperform the industry?

Financial Reporting and Analysis Case

CP5-4
LO3

Using Financial Reports: Financial Statement Inferences

The following amounts were selected from the annual financial statements for Genesis Corporation at December 31, 2012 (end of the third year of operations):

From the 2012 income statement:	
Sales revenue	$275,000
Cost of goods sold	(170,000)
All other expenses (including income tax)	(95,000)
Net income	$ 10,000
From the December 31, 2012, balance sheet:	
Current assets	$ 90,000
All other assets	212,000
Total assets	$302,000
Current liabilities	$ 40,000
Long-term liabilities	66,000
Capital stock (par $10)	100,000
Paid-in capital	16,000
Retained earnings	80,000
Total liabilities and stockholders' equity	$302,000

Required:
Analyze the data on the 2012 financial statements of Genesis by answering the questions that follow. Show computations.

1. What was the gross margin on sales?
2. What was the amount of EPS?
3. If the income tax rate was 25%, what was the amount of pretax income?
4. What was the average sales price per share of the capital stock?
5. Assuming that no dividends were declared or paid during 2012, what was the beginning balance (January 1, 2012) of retained earnings?

Critical Thinking Cases

Making Decisions as a Manager: Evaluating the Effects of Business Strategy on Return on Assets

CP5-5
LO4

Sony

eXcel
www.mhhe.com/libby7e

Sony is a world leader in the manufacture of consumer and commercial electronics as well as in the entertainment and insurance industries. Its ROA has decreased over the last three years.

Required:
Indicate the most likely effect of each of the changes in business strategy on Sony's ROA for the next period and future periods (+ for increase, − for decrease, and NE for no effect), assuming all other things are unchanged. Explain your answer for each. Treat each item independently.

a. Sony decreases its investment in research and development aimed at products to be brought to market in more than one year.
b. Sony begins a new advertising campaign for a movie to be released during the next year.

Strategy Change	Current Period ROA	Future Periods' ROA
a.		
b.		

Making a Decision as an Auditor: Effects of Errors on Income, Assets, and Liabilities

CP5-6
LO1, 3

Megan Company (not a corporation) was careless about its financial records during its first year of operations, 2010. It is December 31, 2010, the end of the annual accounting period. An outside CPA has examined the records and discovered numerous errors, all of which are described here. Assume that each error is independent of the others.

Required:

Analyze each error and indicate its effect on 2010 and 2011 net income, assets, and liabilities if not corrected. Do not assume any other errors. Use these codes to indicate the effect of each dollar amount: O = overstated, U = understated, and NE = no effect. Write an explanation of your analysis of each transaction to support your response. The first transaction is used as an example.

	Effect On					
	Net Income		Assets		Liabilities	
Independent Errors	2010	2011	2010	2011	2010	2011
1. Depreciation expense for 2010, not recorded in 2010, $950.	O $950	NE	O $950	O $950	NE	NE
2. Wages earned by employees during 2010 not recorded or paid in 2010 but recorded and paid in 2011, $500.						
3. Revenue earned during 2010 but not collected or recorded until 2011, $600.						
4. Amount paid in 2010 and recorded as expense in 2010 but not an expense until 2011, $200.						
5. Revenue collected in 2010 and recorded as revenue in 2010 but not earned until 2011, $900.						
6. Sale of services and cash collected in 2010. Recorded as a debit to Cash and as a credit to Accounts Receivable, $300.						
7. On December 31, 2010, bought land on credit for $8,000, not recorded until payment was made on February 1, 2011.						

Following is a sample explanation of the first error:

Failure to record depreciation in 2010 caused depreciation expense to be too low; therefore, income was overstated by $950. Accumulated depreciation also is too low by $950, which causes assets to be overstated by $950 until the error is corrected.

CP5-7
LO1, 3

Evaluating an Ethical Dilemma: Management Incentives and Fraudulent Financial Statements

Ahold

Netherlands-based Royal Ahold ranks among the world's three largest food retailers. In the United States it operates the Stop & Shop and Giant supermarket chains. Dutch and U.S regulators and prosecutors have brought criminal and civil charges against the company and its executives for overstating earnings by more than $1 billion. The nature of the fraud is described in the following excerpt:

Two Former Execs of Ahold Subsidiary Plead Not Guilty to Fraud

28 July 2004 Associated Press Newswires © 2004. The Associated Press.

NEW YORK (AP)—Two former executives pleaded not guilty Wednesday to devising a scheme to inflate the earnings of U.S. Foodservice Inc., a subsidiary of Dutch supermarket giant Royal Ahold NV. Former chief financial officer Michael Resnick and former chief marketing officer Mark Kaiser entered their pleas in a Manhattan federal court, a day after prosecutors announced fraud and conspiracy charges against them.

The government contends they worked together to boost the company's earnings by $800 million from 2000 to 2003 by reporting fake rebates from suppliers—and sweetened their own bonuses in the process. Two other defendants have already pleaded guilty in the alleged scheme: Timothy Lee, a former executive vice president, and William Carter, a former vice president. Both are set for sentencing in January. Netherlands-based Ahold's U.S. properties include the Stop & Shop and Giant supermarket chains. U.S. Foodservice is one of the largest distributors of food products in the country, providing to restaurants and cafeterias.

Ahold said last year it had overstated its earnings by more than $1 billion, mostly because of the fraud at U.S. Foodservice. Its stock lost 60 percent of its value, and about $6 billion in market value evaporated.

Required:
Using more recent news reports (*The Wall Street Journal Index, Factiva,* and *Bloomberg Business News* are good sources), answer the following questions.

1. Whom did the courts and regulatory authorities hold responsible for the misstated financial statements?
2. Did the company cooperate with investigations into the fraud? How did this affect the penalties imposed against the company?
3. How might executive compensation plans that tied bonuses to accounting earnings have motivated unethical conduct in this case?

Financial Reporting and Analysis Team Project

Analyzing the Accounting Communication Process

CP5-8
LO1, 2, 3, 4

As a team, select an industry to analyze. *Reuters* provides lists of industries under Sectors and Industries at www.reuters.com. (Click on an industry and then select Company Rankings for a list of members of that industry.) Each team member should acquire the annual report or 10-K for one publicly traded company in the industry, with each member selecting a different company. (Library files, the SEC EDGAR service at www.sec.gov, or the company itself are good sources.)

Required:
On an individual basis, each team member should write a short report answering the following questions about the selected company. Discuss any patterns across the companies that you as a team observe. Then, as a team, write a short report comparing and contrasting your companies.

1. What formats are used to present the
   a. Balance Sheets?
   b. Income Statements?
   c. Operating Activities section of the Statement of Cash Flows?
2. Find one footnote for each of the following and describe its contents in brief:
   a. An accounting rule applied in the company's statements.
   b. Additional detail about a reported financial statement number.
   c. Relevant financial information but with no number reported in the financial statements.
3. Using electronic sources, find one article reporting the company's annual earnings announcement. When is it dated and how does that date compare to the balance sheet date?
4. Using electronic sources, find two analysts' reports for your company.
   a. Give the date, name of the analyst, and his or her recommendation from each report.
   b. Discuss why the recommendations are similar or different. Look at the analysts' reasoning for their respective recommendations.
5. Using the SEC EDGAR website (www.sec.gov), what is the most recent document filed by your company with the SEC (e.g., 8-K, S-1) and what did it say in brief?
6. Ratio analysis:
   a. What does the return on total assets ratio measure in general?
   b. Compute the ROA ratio for the last three years.
   c. What do your results suggest about the company?
   d. If available, find the industry ratio for the most recent year, compare it to your results, and discuss why you believe your company differs from or is similar to the industry ratio.
7. Use the ROA profit driver analysis to determine the cause(s) of any differences in the ROA ratio over the last three years. (Remember that you computed the three profit driver ratios in the last three chapters.)

LEARNING OBJECTIVES

After studying this chapter, you should be able to:

Lecture Presentation LP-6
www.mhhe.com/libby7e

1. Apply the revenue principle to determine the accepted time to record sales revenue for typical retailers, wholesalers, manufacturers, and service companies. p. 281
2. Analyze the impact of credit card sales, sales discounts, and sales returns on the amounts reported as net sales. p. 281
3. Analyze and interpret the gross profit percentage. p. 284
4. Estimate, report, and evaluate the effects of uncollectible accounts receivable (bad debts) on financial statements. p. 286
5. Analyze and interpret the receivables turnover ratio and the effects of accounts receivable on cash flows. p. 292
6. Report, control, and safeguard cash. p. 295

CHAPTER SIX

REPORTING AND INTERPRETING SALES REVENUE, RECEIVABLES, AND CASH

Founded by then University of California, Santa Barbara, student Doug Otto, Deckers Outdoor is best known for its Teva sports sandals and UGG sheepskin boots. Deckers has become a major player in the casual, outdoor, and athletic footwear market by building on its commitment to the needs of hikers, trail runners, kayakers, surfers, and whitewater rafters for comfort, function, and performance. Its growth strategy requires building brand recognition by developing and introducing additional innovative footwear that satisfies the company's high standards of comfort, performance, and quality. "Building the brands" allows Deckers to maintain a loyal consumer following and penetrate new markets. It also has allowed Deckers to continue to grow during the worst recession in more than 25 years.

FOCUS COMPANY:

Deckers Outdoor Corporation*

BUILDING BRANDS TO BUILD GROSS PROFIT: MANAGING PRODUCT DEVELOPMENT, PRODUCTION, AND WORKING CAPITAL

www.deckers.com

There is a second key component to Deckers's successful growth strategy. Success in the ultracompetitive footwear market requires careful matching of production schedules to customers' needs and careful management of customer receivables. Deckers's successful focus on brand development, product innovation, and working capital management has allowed the company to report the highest gross profit and net income in its history.

UNDERSTANDING THE BUSINESS

The success of each element of Deckers's strategy can be seen in the information presented in the income statement in Exhibit 6.1. Net Sales (Revenue) is reported first, and Cost of Sales (Cost of Goods Sold Expense, Cost of Products Sold) is set out separately from the remaining expenses. Next, the income statement shows **gross profit (gross margin, gross profit margin),** which is net sales revenue minus cost of sales.

Planning Deckers's growth strategy requires careful coordination of sales and production activities, as well as cash collections from customers. Much of this coordination revolves

*Deckers Outdoor Corporation has not verified the data nor the information contained in this text. Therefore investors should not rely on this information in making any assessments of the company for investment or other such purposes.

EXHIBIT 6.1

Net Sales and Gross Profit on the Statement of Income

DECKERS outdoor corporation

REAL WORLD EXCERPT

Annual Report

DECKERS OUTDOOR CORPORATION AND SUBSIDIARIES
Consolidated Statements of Operations
Three Years Ended December 31, 2008, 2007, and 2006
(amounts in thousands of dollars except share data)

	2008	2007	2006
Net sales	$689,445	$448,929	$304,423
Cost of sales	384,127	241,458	163,692
Gross profit	305,318	207,471	140,731

around the use of credit card and sales discounts and managing sales returns and bad debts. These activities affect **net sales revenue** on the income statement and **cash** and **accounts receivable** on the balance sheet, which are the focus of this chapter. We will also introduce the gross profit percentage ratio as a basis for evaluating changes in gross profit, as well as the receivables turnover ratio as a measure of the efficiency of credit-granting and collection activities. Finally, since the cash collected from customers is also a tempting target for fraud and embezzlement, we will discuss how accounting systems commonly include controls to prevent and detect such misdeeds.

ORGANIZATION of the Chapter

Accounting for Sales Revenue

- Credit Card Sales to Consumers
- Sales Discounts to Businesses
- Sales Returns and Allowances
- Reporting Net Sales
- Gross Profit Percentage

Measuring and Reporting Receivables

- Classifying Receivables
- Accounting for Bad Debts
- Reporting Accounts Receivable and Bad Debts
- Estimating Bad Debts
- Control Over Accounts Receivable
- Receivables Turnover Ratio

Reporting and Safeguarding Cash

- Cash and Cash Equivalents Defined
- Cash Management
- Internal Control of Cash
- Reconciliation of the Cash Accounts and the Bank Statements

ACCOUNTING FOR SALES REVENUE

As indicated in Chapter 3, the **revenue principle** requires that revenues be recorded when they are earned (delivery has occurred or services have been rendered, there is persuasive evidence of an arrangement for customer payment, the price is fixed or determinable, and collection is reasonably assured). For sellers of goods, these criteria are most often met and sales revenue is recorded when title and risks of ownership transfer to the buyer.[1] The point at which title (ownership) changes hands is determined by the shipping terms in the sales contract. When goods are shipped **FOB (free on board) shipping point,** title changes hands at shipment, and the buyer normally pays for shipping. When they are shipped **FOB destination,** title changes hands on delivery, and the seller normally pays for shipping. Revenues from goods shipped FOB shipping point are normally recognized at shipment. Revenues from goods shipped FOB delivery are normally recognized at delivery.

LEARNING OBJECTIVE 1

Apply the revenue principle to determine the accepted time to record sales revenue for typical retailers, wholesalers, manufacturers, and service companies.

Service companies most often record sales revenue when they have provided services to the buyer. Companies disclose the revenue recognition rule they follow in the footnote to the financial statements entitled Summary of Significant Accounting Policies. In that note, Deckers reports the following:

NOTES TO CONSOLIDATED FINANCIAL STATEMENTS

1. Summary of Significant Accounting Policies

Recognition of Revenue

The Company recognizes revenue when products are shipped and the customer takes title and assumes risk of loss, collection of relevant receivable is probable, persuasive evidence of an arrangement exists, and the sales price is fixed or determinable.

DECKERS outdoor corporation

REAL WORLD EXCERPT

Annual Report

The appropriate **amount** of revenue to record is the **cash equivalent sales price.** Some sales practices differ depending on whether sales are made to businesses or consumers. Deckers sells footwear and apparel to other **businesses** (retailers), including Athlete's Foot and Eastern Mountain Sports, which then sell the goods to consumers. It also operates its own Internet and retail stores that sell footwear directly to **consumers.**

Deckers uses a variety of methods to motivate both groups of customers to buy its products and make payment for their purchases. The principal methods include (1) allowing consumers to use credit cards to pay for purchases, (2) providing business customers direct credit and discounts for early payment, and (3) allowing returns from all customers under certain circumstances. These methods, in turn, affect the way we compute **net sales revenue.**

Credit Card Sales to Consumers

Deckers accepts cash or credit card payment for its retail store and Internet sales. Deckers's managers decided to accept credit cards (mainly Visa, Mastercard, and American Express) for a variety of reasons:

LEARNING OBJECTIVE 2

Analyze the impact of credit card sales, sales discounts, and sales returns on the amounts reported as net sales.

1. Increasing customer traffic.
2. Avoiding the costs of providing credit directly to consumers, including recordkeeping and bad debts (discussed later).
3. Lowering losses due to bad checks.
4. Avoiding losses from fraudulent credit card sales. (As long as Deckers follows the credit card company's verification procedure, the credit card company [e.g., Visa] absorbs any losses.)
5. Receiving money faster. (Since credit card receipts can be directly deposited in its bank account, Deckers receives its money faster than it would if it provided credit directly to consumers.)

Video 6-1
www.mhhe.com/libby7e

[1] See SEC Staff Accounting Bulletin 101, *Revenue Recognition in Financial Statements,* 2000.

A CREDIT CARD DISCOUNT is the fee charged by the credit card company for its services.

The credit card company charges a fee for the service it provides. When Deckers deposits its credit card receipts in the bank, it might receive credit for only 97 percent of the sales price. The credit card company is charging a 3 percent fee (the **credit card discount**) for its services. If daily credit card sales were $3,000, Deckers would report the following:

Sales revenue	$3,000
Less: Credit card discounts (0.03 × 3,000)	90
Net sales (reported on the income statement)	$2,910

Sales Discounts to Businesses

Most of Deckers's sales to businesses are credit sales on open account; that is, there is no formal written promissory note or credit card. When Deckers sells footwear to retailers on credit, credit terms are printed on the sales document and invoice (bill) sent to the customer. Often credit terms are abbreviated. For example, if the full price is due within 30 days of the invoice date, the credit terms would be noted as **n/30.** Here, the **n** means the sales amount **net** of, or less, any sales returns.

Early Payment Incentive

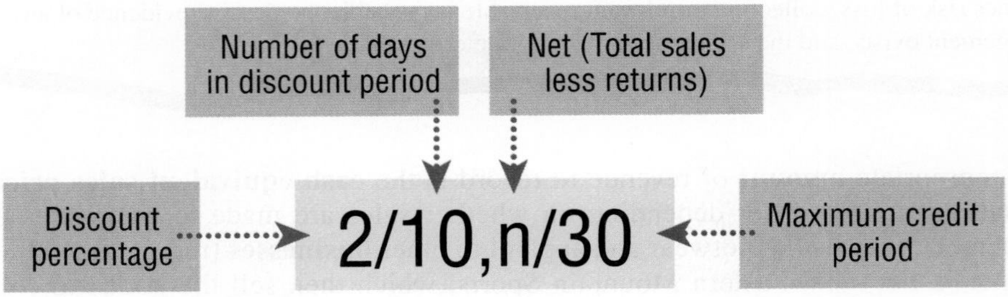

A SALES DISCOUNT (cash discount) is a cash discount offered to encourage prompt payment of an account receivable.

In some cases, a **sales discount** (often called a cash discount) is granted to the purchaser to encourage early payment.[2] For example, Deckers may offer terms of 2/10, n/30, which means that the customer may deduct 2 percent from the invoice price if cash payment is made within 10 days from the date of sale. If cash payment is not made within the 10-day discount period, the full sales price (less any returns) is due within a maximum of 30 days.

Deckers offers this sales discount to encourage customers to pay more quickly. This provides two benefits to Deckers:

1. Prompt receipt of cash from customers reduces the necessity to borrow money to meet operating needs.
2. Since customers tend to pay bills providing discounts first, a sales discount also decreases the chances that the customer will run out of funds before Deckers's bill is paid.

Companies commonly record sales discounts taken by subtracting the discount from sales if payment is made **within** the discount period (the usual case).[3] For example, if credit sales of $1,000 are recorded with terms 2/10, n/30 and payment of $980 ($1,000 × 0.98 = $980) is made within the discount period, net sales of the following amount would be reported:

Sales revenue	$1,000
Less: Sales discounts (0.02 × $1,000)	20
Net sales (reported on the income statement)	$ 980

[2]It is important not to confuse a cash discount with a trade discount. Vendors sometimes use a **trade discount** for quoting sales prices; the sales price is the list or printed catalog price **less** the trade discount.

[3]We use the gross method in all examples in this text. Some companies use the alternative net method, which records sales revenue after deducting the amount of the cash discount. Since the choice of method has little effect on the financial statements, discussion of this method is left for an advanced course.

If payment is made after the discount period, the full $1,000 would be reported as net sales. Accounting for sales discounts is discussed in more detail in the Supplement at the end of this chapter.

To Take or Not to Take the Discount, That Is the Question

FINANCIAL ANALYSIS

Customers usually pay within the discount period because the savings are substantial. With terms 2/10, n/30, customers save 2 percent by paying 20 days early (on the 10th day instead of the 30th). This translates into a 37 percent annual interest rate. To calculate the annual interest rate, first compute the interest rate for the discount period. When the 2 percent discount is taken, the customer pays only 98 percent of the gross sales price. For example, on a $100 sale with terms 2/10, n/30, $2 would be saved and $98 would be paid 20 days early.

The interest rate for the 20-day discount period and the annual interest rate are computed as follows:

$$\frac{\textbf{Amount Saved}}{\textbf{Amount Paid}} = \textbf{Interest Rate for 20 Days} \qquad \textbf{Interest Rate for 20 Days} \times \frac{\textbf{365 Days}}{\textbf{20 Days}} = \textbf{Annual Interest Rate}$$

$$\frac{\$2}{\$98} = \textbf{2.04\% for 20 Days} \qquad \textbf{2.04\%} \times \frac{\textbf{365 Days}}{\textbf{20 Days}} = \textbf{37.23\% Annual Interest Rate}$$

As long as the bank's interest rate is less than the interest rate associated with failing to take cash discounts, the customer will save by taking the cash discount. For example, even if credit customers had to borrow from that bank at a high rate such as 15 percent, they would save a great deal.

Sales Returns and Allowances

Retailers and consumers have a right to return unsatisfactory or damaged merchandise and receive a refund or an adjustment to their bill. Such returns are often accumulated in a separate account called **Sales Returns and Allowances** and must be deducted from gross sales revenue in determining net sales. This account informs Deckers's managers of the volume of returns and allowances and thus provides an important measure of the quality of customer service. Assume that Fontana Shoes of Ithaca, New York, buys 40 pairs of sandals from Deckers for $2,000 on account. Before paying for the sandals, Fontana discovers that 10 pairs of sandals are not the color ordered and returns them to Deckers.[4] Deckers computes net sales as follows:

SALES RETURNS AND ALLOWANCES is a reduction of sales revenues for return of or allowances for unsatisfactory goods.

Sales revenue	$2,000
Less: Sales returns and allowances (0.25 × $2,000)	500
Net sales (reported on the income statement)	$1,500

Cost of goods sold related to the 10 pairs of sandals would also be reduced.

Reporting Net Sales

On the company's books, credit card discounts, sales discounts, and sales returns and allowances are accounted for separately to allow managers to monitor the costs of credit card use, sales discounts, and returns. Using the numbers in the preceding examples, the amount of net sales reported on the income statement is computed in the following manner:

Sales revenue	$6,000
Less: Credit card discounts (a contra-revenue)	90
Sales discounts (a contra-revenue)	20
Sales returns and allowances (a contra-revenue)	500
Net sales (reported on the income statement)	$5,390

Deckers indicates in its revenue recognition footnote that the appropriate subtractions are made.

[4]Alternatively, Deckers might offer Fontana a $200 allowance to keep the wrong-color sandals. If Fontana accepts the offer, Deckers reports $200 as sales returns and allowances.

DECKERS outdoor corporation

REAL WORLD EXCERPT

Annual Report

NOTES TO CONSOLIDATED FINANCIAL STATEMENTS

1. The Company and Summary of Significant Accounting Policies

Revenue Recognition

. . . Allowances for estimated returns, discounts . . . are provided for when related revenue is recorded.

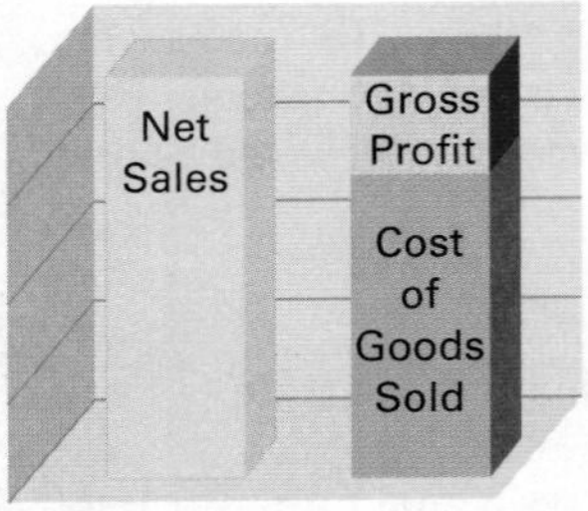

In 2008, Deckers disclosed that it provided its customers with $18,170,000 in sales discounts based on meeting certain order, shipment, and payment timelines.

As we noted earlier, net sales less cost of goods sold equals the subtotal **gross profit** or **gross margin.** Analysts often examine gross profit as a percentage of sales (the gross profit or gross margin percentage).

KEY RATIO ANALYSIS | Gross Profit Percentage

LEARNING OBJECTIVE 3

Analyze and interpret the gross profit percentage.

ANALYTICAL QUESTION

How effective is management in selling goods and services for more than the costs to purchase or produce them?

RATIO AND COMPARISONS

The gross profit percentage ratio is computed as follows:

$$\textbf{Gross Profit Percentage} = \frac{\textbf{Gross Profit}}{\textbf{Net Sales}}$$

The 2008 ratio for Deckers (see Exhibit 6.1):

$$\frac{\$305{,}318}{\$689{,}445} = 0.443\ (44.3\%)$$

COMPARISONS OVER TIME		
Deckers		
2006	2007	2008
46.2%	46.2%	44.3%

COMPARISONS WITH COMPETITORS	
Skechers U.S.A.	Timberland
2008	2008
41.4%	45.5%

Selected Focus Company Comparisons

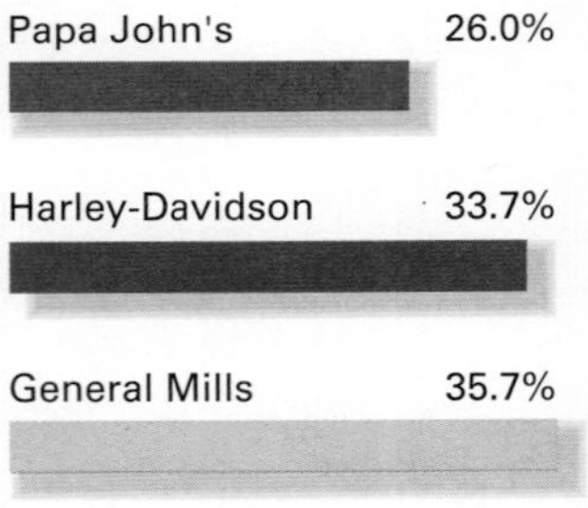

INTERPRETATIONS

In General The gross profit percentage measures a company's ability to charge premium prices and produce goods and services at low cost. All other things equal, a higher gross profit results in higher net income.

Business strategy, as well as competition, affects the gross profit percentage. Companies pursuing a product-differentiation strategy use research and development and product promotion activities to convince customers of the superiority or distinctiveness of the company's products. This allows them to charge premium prices, producing a higher gross profit percentage. Companies following a low-cost strategy rely on more efficient management of production to reduce costs and increase the gross profit percentage. Managers, analysts, and creditors use this ratio to assess the effectiveness of the company's product development, marketing, and production strategy.

Focus Company Analysis Deckers's gross profit percentage has declined slightly over the past three years and remains between its competitors Skechers and Timberland. Its Form 10-K indicates that increased factory costs associated with the UGG brand and the increased percentage of international sales, which carry lower gross margins, contributed to the decline.

At the beginning of the chapter, we discussed key elements of Deckers's business strategy that focused on introducing new technologies, product lines, and styles, as well as managing production and inventory costs. Each of these elements can have a large effect on gross margin.

A Few Cautions To assess the company's ability to sustain its gross margins, you must understand the sources of any change in the gross profit percentage. For example, an increase in margin resulting from increased sales of high-margin boots during a hard winter would be less sustainable than an increase resulting from introducing new products. Also, higher prices must often be sustained with higher R&D and advertising costs, which can eat up any increase in gross margin. Finally, be aware that a small change in the gross profit percentage can lead to a large change in net income.

PAUSE FOR **FEEDBACK**

DECKERS outdoor corporation

In the last section, we learned to analyze the impact of **credit card sales, sales discounts,** and **sales returns,** all of which reduce the amounts reported as net sales. Both credit card discounts and sales or cash discounts promote faster receipt of cash. Sales returns and allowances include refunds and adjustments to customers' bills for defective or incorrect merchandise.

We also analyzed and interpreted the **gross profit percentage,** which measures the ability to charge premium prices and produce goods and services at lower cost. Managers, analysts, and creditors use this ratio to assess the effectiveness of the company's product development, marketing, and production strategy.

Before you move on, complete the following questions to test your understanding of these concepts.

SELF-STUDY **QUIZ**

1. Assume that Deckers sold $30,000 worth of footwear to various retailers with terms 1/10, n/30 and half of that amount was paid within the discount period. Gross catalog and Internet sales were $5,000 for the same period; 80 percent of these sales were paid for with credit cards with a 3 percent discount and the rest were paid for with cash. Compute net sales for the period.

____

____

2. During the first quarter of 2008, Deckers's net sales totaled $134,226, and cost of sales was $75,313. Verify that its gross profit percentage was 43.89 percent.

____

____

After you have completed your answers, check them with the solutions at the bottom of the page.

Solutions to SELF-STUDY QUIZ

1.

Gross Sales	$35,000
Less: Sales Discounts (0.01 × 1/2 × $30,000)	150
Credit Card Discounts (0.03 × 0.80 × $5,000)	120
Net Sales	$34,730

2.

Net Sales	$134,226
Cost of Sales	75,313
Gross Profit	$ 58,913

$58,913/$134,226 = 43.89% Gross Profit Percentage

MEASURING AND REPORTING RECEIVABLES

Classifying Receivables

ACCOUNTS RECEIVABLE (Trade Receivables, Receivables) are open accounts owed to the business by trade customers.

NOTES RECEIVABLE are written promises that require another party to pay the business under specified conditions (amount, time, interest).

Receivables may be classified in three common ways. First, they may be classified as either an account receivable or a note receivable. An account receivable is created by a credit sale on an open account. For example, an account receivable is created when Deckers sells shoes on open account to Fontana Shoes in Ithaca, New York. A note receivable is a promise in writing (a formal document) to pay (1) a specified amount of money, called the **principal,** at a definite future date known as the maturity date and (2) a specified amount of **interest** at one or more future dates. The interest is the amount charged for use of the principal. We discuss the computation of interest when we discuss notes payable in a later chapter.

Second, receivables may be classified as trade or nontrade receivables. A **trade receivable** is created in the normal course of business when a sale of merchandise or services on credit occurs. A **nontrade receivable** arises from transactions other than the normal sale of merchandise or services. For example, if Deckers loaned money to a new vice president to help finance a home at the new job location, the loan would be classified as a nontrade receivable. Third, in a classified balance sheet, receivables also are classified as either **current** or **noncurrent** (short term or long term), depending on when the cash is expected to be collected. Like many companies, Deckers reports only one type of receivable account, Trade Accounts Receivable, from customers and classifies the asset as a current asset because the accounts receivable are all due to be paid within one year.

INTERNATIONAL PERSPECTIVE — Foreign Currency Receivables

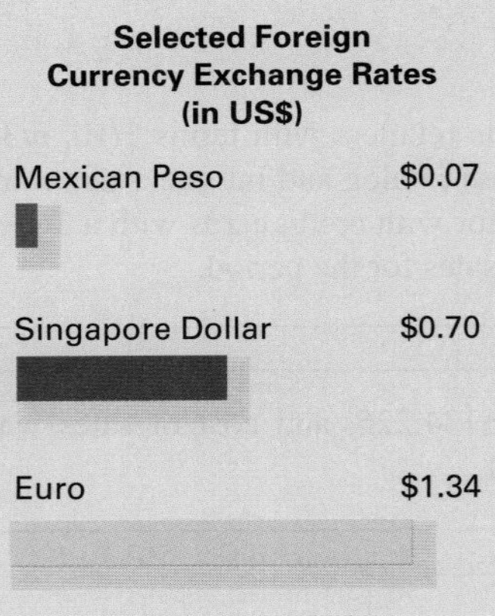

Export (international) sales are a growing part of the U.S. economy. For example, international sales amounted to 15.7 percent of Deckers's revenues in 2008. Most export sales to businesses are on credit. When a buyer agrees to pay in its local currency, Deckers cannot add the resulting accounts receivable, which are denominated in foreign currency, directly to its U.S. dollar accounts receivable. Deckers's accountants must first convert them to U.S. dollars using the end-of-period exchange rate between the two currencies. For example, if a French department store owed Deckers €20,000 (euros, the common currency of the European Monetary Union) on December 31, 2008, and each euro was worth US$1.34 on that date, it would add US$27,800 to its accounts receivable on the balance sheet.

Accounting for Bad Debts

LEARNING OBJECTIVE 4

Estimate, report, and evaluate the effects of uncollectible accounts receivable (bad debts) on financial statements.

For billing and collection purposes, Deckers keeps a separate accounts receivable account for each retailer that resells its footwear and apparel (called a **subsidiary account**). The accounts receivable amount on the balance sheet represents the total of these individual customer accounts.

When Deckers extends credit to its commercial customers, it knows that some of these customers will not pay their debts. The matching principle requires recording of bad debt expense in the **same** accounting period in which the related sales are made. This presents an important accounting problem. Deckers may not learn which particular customers will not pay until the **next** accounting period. So, at the end of the period of sale, it normally does not know which customers' accounts receivable are bad debts.

Deckers resolves this problem by using the allowance method to measure bad debt expense. The allowance method is based on **estimates** of the expected amount of bad debts. Two primary steps in employing the allowance method are:

1. Making the end-of-period adjusting entry to record estimated bad debt expense.
2. Writing off specific accounts determined to be uncollectible during the period.

The ALLOWANCE METHOD bases bad debt expense on an estimate of uncollectible accounts.

Recording Bad Debt Expense Estimates

Bad debt expense (doubtful accounts expense, uncollectible accounts expense, provision for uncollectible accounts) is the expense associated with estimated uncollectible accounts receivable. An **adjusting journal entry at the end of the accounting period** records the bad debt estimate. For the year ended December 31, 2008, Deckers estimated bad debt expense to be $27,567 (all numbers in thousands of dollars) and made the following adjusting entry:

BAD DEBT EXPENSE (Doubtful Accounts Expense, Uncollectible Accounts Expense, Provision for Uncollectible Accounts) is the expense associated with estimated uncollectible accounts receivable.

Bad debt expense (+E, −SE)	27,567	
Allowance for doubtful accounts (+XA, −A)		27,567

Assets		=	Liabilities	+	Stockholders' Equity	
Allowance for doubtful accounts	−27,567				Bad debt expense (+E)	−27,567

The Bad Debt Expense is included in the category "Selling" expenses on the income statement. It decreases net income and stockholders' equity. Accounts Receivable could not be credited in the journal entry because there is no way to know which customers' accounts receivable are involved. So the credit is made, instead, to a contra-asset account called Allowance for Doubtful Accounts (Allowance for Bad Debts or Allowance for Uncollectible Accounts). As a contra-asset, the balance in Allowance for Doubtful Accounts is always subtracted from the balance of the asset Accounts Receivable. Thus, the entry decreases the net book value of Accounts Receivable and total assets.

ALLOWANCE FOR DOUBTFUL ACCOUNTS (Allowance for Bad Debts, Allowance for Uncollectible Accounts) is a contra-asset account containing the estimated uncollectible accounts receivable.

Writing Off Specific Uncollectible Accounts

Throughout the year, when it is determined that a customer will not pay its debts (e.g., due to bankruptcy), the write-off of that individual bad debt is recorded through a journal entry. Now that the specific uncollectible customer account receivable has been identified, it can be removed with a credit. At the same time, we no longer need the related estimate in the contra-asset Allowance for Doubtful Accounts, which is removed by a debit. The journal entry summarizing Deckers's total write-offs of $25,216 during 2008 follows:

Allowance for doubtful accounts (−XA, +A)	25,216	
Accounts receivable (−A)		25,216

Assets		=	Liabilities	+	Stockholders' Equity
Allowance for doubtful accounts	+25,216				
Accounts receivable	−25,216				

Notice that this journal entry did **not affect any income statement accounts.** It did not record a bad debt expense because the estimated expense was recorded with an adjusting entry in the period of sale. Also, the entry did **not change the net book value of accounts receivable,** since the decrease in the asset account (Accounts Receivable) was offset by the decrease in the contra-asset account (Allowance for Doubtful Accounts). Thus, it also did not affect total assets.

When a customer makes a payment on an account that has already been written off, the journal entry to write off the account is reversed to put the receivable back on the books, and the collection of cash is recorded.

Summary of the Accounting Process

It is important to remember that accounting for bad debts is a two-step process:

Step	Timing	Accounts Affected		Financial Statement Effects		
1. Record estimated bad debts adjustment	End of period in which sales are made	Bad Debt Expense (E)	↑	Net Income	↓	
		Allowance for Doubtful Accounts (XA)	↑	Assets (Accounts Receivable, Net)	↓	
2. Identify and write off actual bad debts	Throughout period as bad debts become known	Accounts Receivable (A)	↓	Net Income		No effect
		Allowance for Doubtful Accounts (XA)	↓	Assets (Accounts Receivable, Net)		No effect

Deckers's complete 2008 accounting process for bad debts can now be summarized in terms of the changes in Accounts Receivable (Gross) and the Allowance for Doubtful Accounts:[5]

Accounts Receivable (Gross) (A)

Beginning balance	80,564	Collections on account	625,958
Sales on account	689,445	Write-offs	25,216
Ending balance	118,835		

Allowance for Doubtful Accounts (XA)

		Beginning balance	8,355
Write-offs	25,216	Bad debt expense adjustment	27,567
		Ending balance	10,706

Accounts Receivable Dec. 31, 2008

Accounts Receivable (Gross) (A)	$118,835
−Allowance for Doubtful Accounts (XA)	10,706
Accounts Receivable (Net) (A)	$108,129

Accounts Receivable (Gross) includes the total accounts receivable, both collectible and uncollectible. The balance in the Allowance for Doubtful Accounts is the portion of the accounts receivable balance the company estimates to be uncollectible. Accounts Receivable (Net) reported on the balance sheet is the portion of the accounts the company expects to collect (or its estimated net realizable value).

Reporting Accounts Receivable and Bad Debts

Analysts who want information on Deckers's receivables will find Accounts Receivable, net of allowance for doubtful accounts (the **net book value**), of $108,129 and $72,209 for 2008 and 2007, respectively, reported on the balance sheet (Exhibit 6.2). The balance in the Allowance for Doubtful Accounts ($10,706 in 2008 and $8,355 in 2007) is reported within the account title. Accounts Receivable (Gross), the total accounts receivable, can be computed by adding the two amounts together.

The amounts of bad debt expense and accounts receivable written off for the period if material are reported on a schedule that publicly traded companies include in their Annual Report Form 10-K filed with the SEC. Exhibit 6.3 presents this schedule from Deckers's 2008 filing.[6]

[5]This assumes that all sales are on account.

[6]Deckers's balance sheet and accompanying note also disclose the reserve for sales discounts, which is also subtracted in computing accounts receivable (net).

EXHIBIT 6.2

Accounts Receivable on the Partial Balance Sheet

DECKERS outdoor corporation

REAL WORLD EXCERPT

Annual Report

DECKERS OUTDOOR CORPORATION AND SUBSIDIARIES
Consolidated Balance Sheets
December 31, 2008 and 2007
(amounts in thousands of dollars except share data)

	2008	**2007**
Assets		
Current assets:		
Cash and cash equivalents	$176,804	$ 54,525
Restricted cash	300	250
Short-term investments	17,976	113,567
Trade accounts receivable, net of allowances of $10,706 and $8,355 in 2008 and 2007, respectively	108,129	72,209
Inventories	92,740	51,776
Prepaid expenses and other current assets	3,691	3,276
Deferred tax assets	13,324	5,964
Total current assets	$412,964	$301,567

EXHIBIT 6.3

Accounts Receivable Valuation Schedule (Form 10-K)

DECKERS outdoor corporation

REAL WORLD EXCERPT

Annual Report

DECKERS OUTDOOR CORPORATION AND SUBSIDIARIES
Valuation and Qualifying Accounts
Three Years Ended December 31, 2008, 2007, and 2006

Description	**Balance at Beginning of Year**	**Additions**	**Deductions**	**Balance at End of Year**
Allowance for doubtful account year ended:				
December 31, 2008	$8,355	$27,567	$25,216	$10,706
December 31, 2007	6,100	27,613	25,358	8,355
December 31, 2006	8,384	14,185	16,469	6,100

PAUSE FOR **FEEDBACK**

STOP

Timberland

When receivables are material, companies must employ the allowance method to account for uncollectibles. These are the steps in the process:

a. The end-of-period adjusting entry to record bad debt expense estimates and *increase* the allowance for doubtful accounts.

b. Writing off specific accounts determined to be uncollectible during the period which eliminates the specific uncollectible account receivable and *reduces* the allowance for doubtful accounts.

The adjusting entry reduces net income as well as net accounts receivable. The write-off affects neither. Before you move on, complete the following questions to test your understanding of these concepts.

(continued)

SELF-STUDY QUIZ

In a recent year, Timberland, a major Deckers competitor, had a beginning credit balance in the Allowance for Doubtful Accounts of $4,910 (all numbers in thousands of dollars). It wrote off accounts receivable totaling $1,480 during the year and made a bad debt expense adjustment for the year of $2,395.

1. What adjusting journal entry did Timberland make for bad debts at the end of the year?
2. Make the journal entry summarizing Timberland's total write-offs of bad debts during the year.
3. Compute the balance in the Allowance for Doubtful Accounts at the end of the year.

After you have completed your answers, check them with the solutions at the bottom of the page.

Estimating Bad Debts

The bad debt expense amount recorded in the end-of-period adjusting entry often is estimated based on either (1) a percentage of total credit sales for the period or (2) an aging of accounts receivable. Both methods are acceptable under GAAP and are widely used. The percentage of credit sales method is simpler to apply, but the aging method is generally more accurate. Many companies use the simpler method on a weekly or monthly basis and use the more accurate method on a monthly or quarterly basis to check the accuracy of the earlier estimates. In our example, both methods produce exactly the same estimate, which rarely occurs in practice.

Percentage of Credit Sales Method

The PERCENTAGE OF CREDIT SALES METHOD bases bad debt expense on the historical percentage of credit sales that result in bad debts.

The **percentage of credit sales method** bases bad debt expense on the historical percentage of credit sales that result in bad debts. The average percentage of credit sales that result in bad debts can be computed by dividing total bad debt losses by total **credit** sales. A company that has been operating for some years has sufficient experience to project probable future bad debt losses. For example, if we assume that, during the year 2009, Deckers expected bad debt losses of 1.0 percent of credit sales, and its credit sales were $900,000, it would estimate the current year's bad debts as:

Credit sales	$900,000
× **Bad debt loss rate** (1.0%)	× .01
Bad debt expense	$ 9,000

This amount would be directly recorded as Bad Debt Expense (and an increase in Allowance for Doubtful Accounts) in the current year. Our beginning balance in the Allowance for Doubtful Accounts for 2009 would be the ending balance for 2008. Assuming write-offs during 2009 of $7,706, the ending balance is computed as follows:

Beginning balance	$10,706
+ Bad debt expense	9,000
− Write-offs	7,706
Ending balance	$12,000

percent of credit sales estimate

Allowance for Doubtful Accounts (XA)			
		2009 Beginning balance	10,706
2009 Write-offs	7,706	2009 Bad debt expense adjustment	9,000
		2009 Ending balance	? = 12,000

Solutions to SELF-STUDY QUIZ

1. Bad debt expense (+E, −SE)	2,395	
Allowance for doubtful accounts (+XA, −A)		2,395
2. Allowance for doubtful accounts (−XA, +A)	1,480	
Accounts receivable (−A)		1,480

3. Beginning Balance + Bad Debt Expense Estimate − Write-Offs = Ending Balance, $4,910 + 2,395 − 1,480 = $5,825

Aging of Accounts Receivable

The **aging of accounts receivable method** relies on the fact that, as accounts receivable become older and more overdue, it is less likely that they will be collectible. For example, a receivable that was due in 30 days but has not been paid after 120 days is less likely to be collected, on average, than a similar receivable that remains unpaid after 45 days.

The AGING OF ACCOUNTS RECEIVABLE METHOD estimates uncollectible accounts based on the age of each account receivable.

If Deckers split its 2009 ending balance in accounts receivable (gross) of $120,000 into three age categories, it would first examine the individual customer accounts receivable and sort them into the three age categories. Based on prior experience, management would then **estimate** the probable bad debt loss rates for each category: for example, not yet due, 2 percent; 1 to 90 days past due, 10 percent; over 90 days, 30 percent.

As illustrated in the aging schedule below, this would result in an estimate of total uncollectible amounts of $12,000, the **estimated ending balance** that **should be** in the Allowance for Doubtful Accounts. From this, the adjustment to record Bad Debt Expense (and an increase in Allowance for Doubtful Accounts) for 2009 would be computed as follows:

Aging Schedule 2009

Aged Accounts Receivable			Estimated Percentage Uncollectible		Estimated Amount Uncollectible
Not yet due	$60,000	×	2%	=	$ 1,200
Up to 90 days past due	36,000	×	10%	=	3,600
Over 90 days past due	24,000	×	30%	=	7,200
Estimated ending balance in Allowance for Doubtful Accounts					$12,000
Less: Balance in Allowance for Doubtful Accounts before adjustment ($10,706 − 7,706)					3,000
Bad Debt Expense for the year					$ 9,000

Allowance for Doubtful Accounts (XA)

		2009 Beginning balance	10,706	
2009 Write-offs	7,706	2009 Bad debt expense adjustment	?	= 9,000
		2009 Ending balance	12,000	total estimated uncollectible accounts

Comparison of the Two Methods

Students often fail to recognize that the approach to recording bad debt expense using the percentage of credit sales method is different from that for the aging method:

- **Percentage of credit sales.** Directly compute the amount to be recorded as **Bad Debt Expense** on the **income statement** for the period in the adjusting journal entry.
- **Aging.** Compute the **estimated ending balance** we would like to have in the **Allowance for Doubtful Accounts** on the **balance sheet** after we make the necessary adjusting entry. The **difference** between the current balance in the account and the estimated balance is recorded as the adjusting entry for Bad Debt Expense for the period.

In either case, the balance sheet presentation for 2009 would show Accounts Receivable, less Allowance for Doubtful Accounts, of $108,000 ($120,000 − $12,000).

Actual Write-Offs Compared with Estimates

Deckers's Form 10-K provides particularly clear information on its approach to estimating uncollectible accounts and the potential effect of any errors in those estimates:

DECKERS outdoor corporation

REAL WORLD EXCERPT

Form 10-K

CRITICAL ACCOUNTING POLICIES

Allowance for Doubtful Accounts

We provide a reserve against trade accounts receivable for estimated losses that may result from customers' inability to pay. We determine the amount of the reserve by analyzing known uncollectible accounts, aged trade accounts receivables, economic conditions, historical experience and the customers' credit-worthiness. . . . Our use of different estimates and assumptions could produce different financial results. For example, a 1.0% change in the rate used to estimate the reserve for the accounts we consider to have credit risk and not specifically identified as uncollectible would change the allowance for doubtful accounts by $670.

If uncollectible accounts actually written off differ from the estimated amount previously recorded, a higher or lower amount is recorded in the next period to make up for the previous period's error in estimate. **When estimates are found to be incorrect, financial statement values for prior annual accounting periods are not corrected.**

Control Over Accounts Receivable

Many managers forget that extending credit will increase sales volume, but unless the related receivables are collected, they do not add to the bottom line. Companies that emphasize sales without monitoring the collection of credit sales soon find much of their current assets tied up in accounts receivable. The following practices can help minimize bad debts:

1. Require approval of customers' credit history by a person independent of the sales and collections functions.
2. Age accounts receivable periodically and contact customers with overdue payments.
3. Reward both sales and collections personnel for speedy collections so that they work as a team.

To assess the effectiveness of overall credit-granting and collection activities, managers and analysts often compute the receivables turnover ratio.

KEY RATIO ANALYSIS | Receivables Turnover Ratio

LEARNING OBJECTIVE 5

Analyze and interpret the receivables turnover ratio and the effects of accounts receivable on cash flows.

ANALYTICAL QUESTION

How effective are credit-granting and collection activities?

RATIO AND COMPARISONS

The receivables turnover ratio is computed as follows (see Exhibits 6.1 and 6.2):

$$\textbf{Receivables Turnover} = \frac{\textbf{Net Sales}^*}{\textbf{Average Net Trade Accounts Receivable}^\dagger}$$

The 2008 receivables turnover ratio for Deckers:

$$\frac{\$689{,}445}{(\$72{,}209 + \$108{,}129)/2} = 7.6$$

COMPARISONS OVER TIME		
Deckers		
2006	2007	2008
6.8	7.4	7.6

COMPARISONS WITH COMPETITORS	
Skechers U.S.A.	Timberland
2008	2008
6.7	7.6

INTERPRETATIONS

In General The receivables turnover ratio reflects how many times average trade receivables are recorded and collected during the period. The higher the ratio, the faster the collection of receivables. A higher ratio benefits the company because it can invest the money collected to earn interest income or reduce borrowings to reduce interest expense. Overly generous payment schedules and ineffective collection methods keep the receivables turnover ratio low. Analysts and creditors watch this ratio because a sudden decline may mean that a company is extending payment deadlines in an attempt to prop up lagging sales or is even recording sales that will later be returned by customers. Many managers and analysts compute the related number **average collection period** or **average days sales in receivables,** which is equal to 365 ÷ Receivables Turnover Ratio. It indicates the average time it takes a customer to pay its accounts. For Deckers, the amount would be computed as follows for 2008:

$$\textbf{Average Collection Period} = \frac{365}{\textbf{Receivables Turnover}} = \frac{365}{7.6} = \textbf{48.0 days}$$

Focus Company Analysis Deckers's receivables turnover increased from a 2006 low of 6.8 to 7.6 in 2008. This indicates that the company is taking less time to convert its receivables into cash. Compared to the receivables turnover ratios of its competitors, Deckers's ratio is above that of Skechers and tied with that of Timberland.

A Few Cautions Since differences across industries and between firms in the manner in which customer purchases are financed can cause dramatic differences in the ratio, a particular firm's ratio should be compared only with its prior years' figures or with other firms in the same industry following the same financing practices.

**Since the amount of net credit sales is normally not reported separately, most analysts use net sales in this equation.*

†Average Net Trade Accounts Receivable = (Beginning Net Trade Accounts Receivable + Ending Net Trade Accounts Receivable) ÷ 2.

Selected Industry Comparisons: Receivables Turnover Ratio

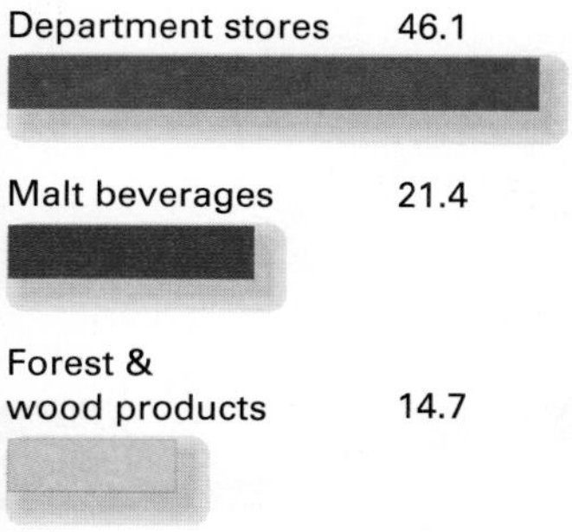

Accounts Receivable

FOCUS ON CASH FLOWS

The change in accounts receivable can be a major determinant of a company's cash flow from operations. While the income statement reflects the revenues of the period, the cash flow from operating activities reflects cash collections from customers. Since sales on account increase the balance in accounts receivable and cash collections from customers decrease the balance in accounts receivable, the change in accounts receivable from the beginning to the end of the period is the difference between sales and collections.

EFFECT ON STATEMENT OF CASH FLOWS

In General When there is a net **decrease in accounts receivable** for the period, cash collected from customers is more than revenue; thus, the decrease must be **added** in computing cash flows from operations. When a net **increase in accounts receivable** occurs, cash collected from customers is less than revenue; thus, the increase must be **subtracted** in computing cash flows from operations.*

	Effect on Cash Flows
Operating activities (indirect method)	
Net income	$ xxx
Adjusted for	
Add accounts receivable decrease	+
or	
Subtract accounts receivable increase	−

(continued)

Focus Company Analysis Exhibit 6.4 shows the Operating Activities section of Deckers's statement of cash flows. Sales growth during 2008 has resulted in an increase in Deckers's balance in receivables. This increase is subtracted in reconciling net income to cash flow from operating activities because revenues are higher than cash collected from customers for 2008. When receivables decrease, the amount of the reduction in receivables is added in reconciling net income to cash flow from operating activities because cash collected from customers is higher than revenues.

**For companies with receivables in foreign currency or business acquisitions/dispositions, the change reported on the cash flow statement will not equal the change in the accounts receivable reported on the balance sheet.*

PAUSE FOR FEEDBACK

Timberland

When using the **percentage of sales method,** you directly compute the bad debt expense for the period by multiplying the amount of credit sales by the bad debt loss rate. With the **aging method,** you compute the estimated ending balance in the allowance and solve for the bad debt expense. This process involves multiplying the amount in each age category by the estimated percentage uncollectible to produce the estimated ending balance in the allowance for doubtful accounts. The difference between the estimated ending balance and the balance in the allowance before the adjustment becomes the bad debt expense for the year. Before you move on, try an example of the more difficult aging method computations based on Timberland's numbers reported in an earlier year.

SELF-STUDY QUIZ

1. In an earlier year, Deckers's competitor Timberland reported a beginning balance in the Allowance for Doubtful Accounts of $723. It also wrote off bad debts amounting to $648 during the year. At the end of the year, it computed total estimated uncollectible accounts using the aging method to be $904 (all numbers in thousands of dollars). What amount did Timberland record as bad debt expense for the period? (**Solution approach:** Use the Allowance for Doubtful Accounts T-account or the following equation to solve for the missing value.)

Allowance for Doubtful Accounts (XA)

Estimated ending balance in Allowance for Doubtful Accounts	
Less: Current balance in Allowance for Doubtful Accounts	____
Bad Debt Expense for the year	====

The accounts receivable turnover ratio measures the effectiveness of credit-granting and collection activities. Faster turnover means faster receipt of cash from your customers. To test whether you understand this concept, answer the following question:

2. Indicate whether **granting later payment deadlines** (e.g., 60 days instead of 30 days) will most likely **increase** or **decrease** the accounts receivable turnover ratio. Explain.

After you have completed your answers, check them with the solutions at the bottom of the next page.

DECKERS OUTDOOR CORPORATION AND SUBSIDIARIES
Consolidated Statements of Cash Flows
Three Years Ended December 31, 2008, 2007, and 2006

	2008	2007	2006
Cash flows from operating activities:			
Net income	$73,948	$66,437	$30,609
Adjustments to reconcile net income to net cash provided by operating activities:			
. . . .	. . .	. . .	. . .
Changes in operating assets and liabilities:			
Trade accounts receivable, net of provision for doubtful accounts	(35,920)	(22,638)	(9,888)
Inventories	(40,964)	(19,401)	999
	. . .	. . .	. . .
	. . .	. . .	. . .
Net cash provided by operating activities	$53,276	$61,054	$48,498

EXHIBIT 6.4

Accounts Receivable on the Partial Cash Flow Statement

DECKERS outdoor corporation

REAL WORLD EXCERPT

Annual Report

LEARNING OBJECTIVE 6

Report, control, and safeguard cash.

REPORTING AND SAFEGUARDING CASH

Cash and Cash Equivalents Defined

Cash is defined as money or any instrument that banks will accept for deposit and immediate credit to a company's account, such as a check, money order, or bank draft. **Cash equivalents** are investments with original maturities of three months or less that are readily convertible to cash and whose value is unlikely to change (that is, they are not sensitive to interest rate changes). Typical instruments included as cash equivalents are bank certificates of deposit and treasury bills that the U.S. government issues to finance its activities.

Like most companies, Deckers combines all of its bank accounts and cash equivalents into one amount, Cash and Cash Equivalents, on the balance sheet. It also reports that the book values of cash equivalents on the balance sheet equal their fair market values—which we should expect given the nature of the instruments (investments whose value is unlikely to change).

CASH is money or any instrument that banks will accept for deposit and immediate credit to a company's account, such as a check, money order, or bank draft.

CASH EQUIVALENTS are short-term investments with original maturities of three months or less that are readily convertible to cash and whose value is unlikely to change.

Solutions to SELF-STUDY QUIZ

1.

Allowance for Doubtful Accounts (XA)			
		Beginning balance	723
Write-offs	648	Bad debt expense (solve)	829
		Ending balance	904

Estimated ending balance in Allowance for Doubtful Accounts	$904
Less: Current balance in Allowance for Doubtful Accounts ($723 − $648)	75
Bad Debt Expense for the year	$829

2. Granting later payment deadlines will most likely **decrease** the accounts receivable turnover ratio because later collections from customers will increase the average accounts receivable balance (the denominator of the ratio), decreasing the ratio.

Cash Management

Many businesses receive a large amount of cash, checks, and credit card receipts from their customers each day. Anyone can spend cash, so management must develop procedures to safeguard the cash it uses in the business. Effective cash management involves more than protecting cash from theft, fraud, or loss through carelessness. Other cash management responsibilities include:

1. Accurate accounting so that reports of cash flows and balances may be prepared.
2. Controls to ensure that enough cash is available to meet (*a*) current operating needs, (*b*) maturing liabilities, and (*c*) unexpected emergencies.
3. Prevention of the accumulation of excess amounts of idle cash. Idle cash earns no revenue. Therefore, it is often invested in securities to earn a return until it is needed for operations.

Internal Control of Cash

INTERNAL CONTROLS are the processes by which a company safeguards its assets and provides reasonable assurance regarding the reliability of the company's financial reporting, the effectiveness and efficiency of its operations, and its compliance with applicable laws and regulations.

The term **internal controls** refers to the process by which a company safeguards its assets and provides reasonable assurance regarding the reliability of the company's financial reporting, the effectiveness and efficiency of its operations, and its compliance with applicable laws and regulations. Internal control procedures should extend to all assets: cash, receivables, investments, plant and equipment, and so on. Controls that ensure the accuracy of the financial records are designed to prevent inadvertent errors and outright fraud such as occurred in the Maxidrive case discussed in Chapter 1. Because internal control increases the reliability of the financial statements, it is reviewed by the outside independent auditor.

Because cash is the asset most vulnerable to theft and fraud, a significant number of internal control procedures should focus on cash. You have already observed internal control procedures for cash, although you may not have known it at the time. At most movie theaters, one employee sells tickets and another employee collects them. Having one employee do both jobs would be less expensive, but that single employee could easily steal cash and admit a patron without issuing a ticket. If different employees perform the tasks, a successful theft requires participation of both.

Effective internal control of cash should include the following:

1. Separation of duties.
   a. Complete separation of the jobs of receiving cash and disbursing cash.
   b. Complete separation of the procedures of accounting for cash receipts and cash disbursements.
   c. Complete separation of the physical handling of cash and all phases of the accounting function.
2. Prescribed policies and procedures.
   a. Require that all cash receipts be deposited in a bank daily. Keep any cash on hand under strict control.
   b. Require separate approval of the purchases and the actual cash payments. Prenumbered checks should be used. Special care must be taken with payments by electronic funds transfers since they involve no controlled documents (checks).
   c. Assign the responsibilities for cash payment approval and check-signing or electronic funds transfer transmittal to different individuals.
   d. Require monthly reconciliation of bank accounts with the cash accounts on the company's books (discussed in detail in the next section).

Ethics and the Need for Internal Control

A QUESTION OF ETHICS

Some people are bothered by the recommendation that all well-run companies should have strong internal control procedures. These people believe that control procedures suggest that management does not trust the company's employees. Although the vast majority of employees are trustworthy, employee theft does cost businesses billions of dollars each year. Interviews with convicted felons indicate that in many cases they stole from their employers because they thought that it was easy and that no one cared (there were no internal control procedures).

Many companies have a formal code of ethics that requires high standards of behavior in dealing with customers, suppliers, fellow employees, and the company's assets. Although each employee is ultimately responsible for his or her own ethical behavior, internal control procedures can be thought of as important value statements from management.

Reconciliation of the Cash Accounts and the Bank Statements

Content of a Bank Statement

Proper use of the bank accounts can be an important internal cash control procedure. Each month, the bank provides the company (the depositor) with a **bank statement** that lists (1) each paper or electronic deposit recorded by the bank during the period, (2) each paper or electronic check cleared by the bank during the period, and (3) the balance in the company's account. The bank statement also shows the bank charges or deductions (such as service charges) made directly to the company's account by the bank. A typical bank statement for ROW.COM, Inc., is shown in Exhibit 6.5.

A BANK STATEMENT is a monthly report from a bank that shows deposits recorded, checks cleared, other debits and credits, and a running bank balance.

Exhibit 6.5 lists four items that need explanation. Notice the $500 and $100 items listed in the Checks and Debits column and coded **EFT.**[7] This is the code for **electronic funds transfers.** ROW.COM pays its electricity and insurance bills using electronic checking. When it orders the electronic payments, it records these items on the company's books in the same manner as a paper check. So no additional entry is needed.

Notice that listed in the Checks and Debits column there is a deduction for $18 coded **NSF.** This entry refers to a check for $18 received from a customer and deposited by ROW.COM with its bank. The bank processed the check through banking channels to the customer's bank, but the account did not have sufficient funds to cover the check. The customer's bank therefore returned it to ROW.COM's bank, which then charged it back to ROW.COM's account. This type of check often is called an **NSF check** (not sufficient funds). The NSF check is now a receivable; consequently, ROW.COM must make an entry to debit Receivables and credit Cash for the $18.

Notice the $6 listed on June 30 in the Checks and Debits column and coded **SC.** This is the code for bank service charges. The bank statement included a memo by the bank explaining this service charge (which was not documented by a check). ROW.COM must make an entry to reflect this $6 decrease in the bank balance as a debit to a relevant expense account, such as Bank Service Expense, and a credit to Cash.

Notice the $20 listed on June 18 in the Deposits and Credits column and coded **INT** for interest earned. The bank pays interest on checking account balances, and increased ROW.COM's account for interest earned during the period. ROW.COM must record the interest by making an entry to debit Cash and credit Interest Income for the $20.

Need for Reconciliation

A **bank reconciliation** is the process of comparing (reconciling) the ending cash balance in the company's records and the ending cash balance reported by the bank on the monthly bank statement. A bank reconciliation should be completed at the end of each month. Usually, the

A BANK RECONCILIATION is the process of verifying the accuracy of both the bank statement and the cash accounts of a business.

[7]These codes vary among banks.

EXHIBIT 6.5

Example of a Bank Statement

Texas Commerce Bank
Austin
NATIONAL ASSOCIATION

7TH & LAVACA
AUSTIN, TEXAS 78789
PHONE: 512/476-6611

ACCOUNT NUMBER	STATEMENT DATE	PAGE NO.
877-95861	6-30-11	1

ROW.COM Inc.
1000 Blank Road
Austin, Texas 78703

STATEMENT OF ACCOUNT
Please examine statement and checks promptly. If no error is reported within ten days, the account will be considered correct. Please report change of address.
For questions or problems call TCB-Austin's Hotline—476-6100

BALANCE LAST STATEMENT	DEPOSITS AND CREDITS No.	DEPOSITS AND CREDITS Total Amount	CHECKS AND DEBITS No.	CHECKS AND DEBITS Total Amount	BALANCE THIS STATEMENT
7,762.40	5	4,050.00	14	3,490.20	8,322.20

CHECKS AND DEBITS Date	No.	Amount	DEPOSITS AND CREDITS Date	Amount	DAILY BALANCE Date	Amount
					06-01-11	7,762.40
06-02		500.00 EFT	06-02	3,000.00	06-02-11	10,262.40
06-03	102	55.00			06-03-11	10,207.40
06-09		100.00 EFT	06-09	500.00	06-09-11	10,607.40
06-10	122	8.20			06-10-11	10,599.20
06-11	124	2,150.00			06-11-11	8,449.20
06-18	125	46.80	06-18	20.00 INT	06-18-11	8,422.40
06-19	127	208.00			06-19-11	8,214.40
06-24	128	82.70	06-24	230.00	06-24-11	8,361.70
06-25		18.00 NSF			06-25-11	8,343.70
06-25	129	144.40			06-25-11	8,199.30
06-26	132	22.52	06-26	300.00	06-26-11	8,476.78
06-27	130	96.50			06-27-11	8,380.28
06-30	126	52.08			06-30-11	8,328.20
06-30		6.00 SC			06-30-11	8,322.20

Code:
INT–Interest Earned
NSF–Not Sufficient Funds
SC–Service Charge
EFT–Electronic Funds Transfer

MEMBER F.D.I.C. IMPORTANT: SEE REVERSE SIDE OF STATEMENT

ending cash balance as shown on the bank statement does not agree with the ending cash balance shown by the related Cash ledger account on the books of the company. For example, the Cash ledger account of ROW.COM showed the following at the end of June (ROW.COM has only one checking account):

Cash (A)			
June 1 balance	7,090.00	June checks written	3,800.00
June deposits	5,750.00		
Ending balance	9,040.00		

The $8,322.20 ending cash balance shown on the bank statement (Exhibit 6.5) differs from the $9,040.00 ending balance of cash shown on the books of ROW.COM. Most of this difference exists because of timing differences in the recording of transactions:

1. Some transactions affecting cash were recorded in the books of ROW.COM but were not shown on the bank statement.
2. Some transactions were shown on the bank statement but had not been recorded in the books of ROW.COM.

Some of the difference may also be caused by errors in recording transactions.

The most common causes of differences between the ending bank balance and the ending book balance of cash are as follows:

1. **Outstanding checks.** These are checks written by the company and recorded in the company's ledger as credits to the Cash account that have not cleared the bank (they are not shown

EXHIBIT 6.6

Bank Reconciliation Illustrated

ROW.COM INC.
Bank Reconciliation
For the Month Ending June 30, 2011

Company's Books		**Bank Statement**	
Ending cash balance per books	$9,040.00	Ending cash balance per bank statement	$ 8,322.20
Additions		Additions	
Interest paid by the bank	20.00	Deposit in transit	1,800.00
Error in recording payment	9.00		
	9,069.00		10,122.20
Deductions		Deductions	
NSF check of R. Smith	18.00	Outstanding checks	1,077.20
Bank service charges	6.00		
Ending correct cash balance	$9,045.00	Ending correct cash balance	$ 9,045.00

on the bank statement as a deduction from the bank balance). The outstanding checks are identified by comparing the list of canceled checks on the bank statement with the record of checks (such as check stubs or a journal) maintained by the company.

2. **Deposits in transit.** These are deposits sent to the bank by the company and recorded in the company's ledger as debits to the Cash account. The bank has not recorded these deposits (they are not shown on the bank statement as an increase in the bank balance). Deposits in transit usually happen when deposits are made one or two days before the close of the period covered by the bank statement. Deposits in transit are determined by comparing the deposits listed on the bank statement with the company deposit records.
3. **Bank service charges.** These are expenses for bank services listed on the bank statement but not recorded on the company's books.
4. **NSF checks.** These are "bad checks" or "bounced checks" that have been deposited but must be deducted from the company's cash account and rerecorded as accounts receivable.
5. **Interest.** This is the interest paid by the bank to the company on its bank balance.
6. **Errors.** Both the bank and the company may make errors, especially when the volume of cash transactions is large.

Bank Reconciliation Illustrated

The company should make a bank reconciliation immediately after receiving each bank statement. The general format for the bank reconciliation follows:

Ending cash balance per books	$xxx	Ending cash balance per bank statement	$xxx
+ Interest paid by bank	xx	+ Deposits in transit	xx
− NSF checks/Service charges	xx	− Outstanding checks	xx
± Company errors	xx	± Bank errors	xx
Ending correct cash balance	$xxx	Ending correct cash balance	$xxx

Exhibit 6.6 shows the bank reconciliation prepared by ROW.COM for the month of June to reconcile the ending bank balance ($8,322.20) with the ending book balance ($9,040.00). On the completed reconciliation, the correct cash balance is $9,045.00. This correct balance is the amount that should be shown in the Cash account after the reconciliation. Since ROW.COM has only one checking account and no cash on hand, it is also the correct amount of cash that should be reported on the balance sheet.

ROW.COM followed these steps in preparing the bank reconciliation:

1. **Identify the outstanding checks.** A comparison of the checks and electronic payments listed on the bank statement with the company's record of all checks drawn and electronic payments made showed the following checks were still outstanding (had not cleared the bank) at the end of June:

Check No.	Amount
101	$ 145.00
123	815.00
131	117.20
Total	$1,077.20

This total was entered on the reconciliation as a deduction from the bank account. These checks will be deducted by the bank when they clear the bank.

2. **Identify the deposits in transit.** A comparison of the deposit slips on hand with those listed on the bank statement revealed that a deposit of $1,800 made on June 30 was not listed on the bank statement. This amount was entered on the reconciliation as an addition to the bank account. It will be added by the bank when it records the deposit.
3. **Record bank charges and credits:**
   a. Interest received from the bank, $20—entered on the bank reconciliation as an addition to the book balance; it already has been included in the bank balance.
   b. NSF check of R. Smith, $18—entered on the bank reconciliation as a deduction from the book balance; it has been deducted from the bank statement balance.
   c. Bank service charges, $6—entered on the bank reconciliation as a deduction from the book balance; it has been deducted from the bank balance.
4. **Determine the impact of errors.** At this point, ROW.COM found that the reconciliation did not balance by $9. Upon checking the journal entries made during the month, the electronic payment on 6-09 for $100 to pay an account payable was found. The payment was recorded in the company's accounts as $109. Therefore, $9 (i.e., $109 − $100) must be added to the book cash balance on the reconciliation; the bank cleared the electronic payment for the correct amount, $100.

Note that in Exhibit 6.6 the two sections of the bank reconciliation now agree at a correct cash balance of $9,045.00.

A bank reconciliation as shown in Exhibit 6.6 accomplishes two major objectives:

1. It checks the accuracy of the bank balance and the company cash records, which involves developing the correct cash balance. The correct cash balance (plus cash on hand, if any) is the amount of cash that is reported on the balance sheet.
2. It identifies any previously unrecorded transactions or changes that are necessary to cause the company's Cash account(s) to show the correct cash balance. Any transactions or changes on the **company's books side** of the bank reconciliation need journal entries. Therefore, the following journal entries based on the company's books side of the bank reconciliation (Exhibit 6.6) must be entered into the company's records:

Accounts of ROW.COM

(a) Cash (+A)	20	
Interest income (+R, +SE)		20
To record interest by bank.		
(b) Accounts receivable (+A)	18	
Cash (−A)		18
To record NSF check.		
(c) Bank service expense (+E, −SE)	6	
Cash (−A)		6
To record service fees charged by bank.		
(d) Cash (+A)	9	
Accounts payable (+L)		9
To correct error made in recording a check payable to a creditor.		

Assets		=	Liabilities		+	Stockholders' Equity	
Cash (+20, −18, −6, +9)	+5		Accounts payable	+9		Interest income (+R)	+20
Accounts receivable	+18					Bank service expense (+E)	−6

Notice again that all of the additions and deductions on the company's books side of the reconciliation need journal entries to update the Cash account. The additions and deductions on the bank statement side do not need journal entries because they will work out automatically when they clear the bank.

PAUSE FOR **FEEDBACK**

Cash is the most liquid of all assets, flowing continually into and out of a business. As a result, a number of critical control procedures, including the **reconciliation** of bank accounts, should be applied. Also, management of cash may be critically important to decision makers who must have cash available to meet current needs yet must avoid excess amounts of idle cash that produce no revenue. To see if you understand the basics of a bank reconciliation, answer the following questions:

SELF-STUDY **QUIZ**

Indicate which of the following items discovered while preparing a company's bank reconciliation will result in adjustment of the cash balance on the balance sheet.

1. Outstanding checks.
2. Deposits in transit.
3. Bank service charges.
4. NSF checks that were deposited.

After you have completed your answers, check them with the solution at the bottom of the page.

Solutions to SELF-STUDY QUIZ

3. Bank service charges are deducted from the company's account; thus, cash must be reduced and an expense must be recorded.
4. NSF checks that were deposited were recorded on the books as increases in the cash account; thus, cash must be decreased and the related accounts receivable increased if payment is still expected.

EPILOGUE

As we noted at the beginning of the chapter, Deckers recognized that to turn growth into profits, it had to (1) continually refresh its product lines by introducing new technologies, new styles, and new product categories; (2) become a leaner and more nimble manufacturer, taking advantage of lower-cost, more flexible production locations; and (3) focus attention on inventory management and collections of accounts receivable since an uncollected account is of no value to the company. Each of these efforts is aimed at increasing net sales and/or decreasing cost of goods sold, thereby increasing gross profit. The first quarter of 2009 has sent positive signals about the continued success of Deckers's strategy. Driven by the strength of the UGG brand, net sales have increased 38 percent and gross profit by 28 percent over the same period in 2008. You can evaluate the further success of the company's strategy by going to the Web at www.deckers.com to check Deckers's latest annual and quarterly reports.

DEMONSTRATION CASE A

(Complete the requirements before proceeding to the suggested solutions.) Wholesale Warehouse Stores sold $950,000 in merchandise during 2011. Of this amount, $400,000 was on credit with terms 2/10, n/30 (75 percent of these amounts were paid within the discount period), $500,000 was paid with credit cards (there was a 3 percent credit card discount), and the rest was paid in cash. On December 31, 2011, the Accounts Receivable balance was $80,000. The beginning balance in the Allowance for Doubtful Accounts was $9,000 and $6,000 of bad debts was written off during the year.

Required:

1. Compute net sales for 2011, assuming that sales and credit card discounts are treated as contra-revenues.
2. Assume that Wholesale uses the percentage of sales method for estimating bad debt expense and that it estimates that 2 percent of credit sales will produce bad debts. Record bad debt expense for 2011.
3. Assume instead that Wholesale uses the aging of accounts receivable method and that it estimates that $10,000 worth of current accounts is uncollectible. Record bad debt expense for 2011.

SUGGESTED SOLUTION

1. Both sales discounts and credit card discounts should be subtracted from sales revenues in the computation of net sales.

Sales revenue	$950,000
Less: Sales discounts (0.02 × 0.75 × $400,000)	6,000
Credit card discounts (0.03 × $500,000)	15,000
Net sales	$929,000

2. The percentage estimate of bad debts should be applied to credit sales. Cash sales never produce bad debts.

Bad debt expense (+E, −SE) (0.02 × $400,000)	8,000	
Allowance for doubtful accounts (+XA, −A)		8,000

Assets		=	Liabilities	+	Stockholders' Equity	
Allowance for doubtful accounts	−8,000				Bad debt expense (+E)	−8,000

3. The entry made when using the aging of accounts receivable method is the estimated balance minus the current balance.

Estimated ending balance in Allowance for Doubtful Accounts	$10,000
Less: Current balance in Allowance for Doubtful Accounts ($9,000 – $6,000)	3,000
Bad Debt Expense for the year	$ 7,000

Bad debt expense (+E, −SE)	7,000	
Allowance for doubtful accounts (+XA, −A)		7,000

Assets		=	Liabilities	+	Stockholders' Equity	
Allowance for doubtful accounts	−7,000				Bad debt expense (+E)	−7,000

DEMONSTRATION CASE B

(Complete the requirements before proceeding to the suggested solution that follows.) Heather Ann Long, a freshman at a large state university, has just received her first checking account statement. This was her first chance to attempt a bank reconciliation. She had the following information to work with:

Bank balance, September 1	$1,150
Deposits during September	650
Checks cleared during September	900
Bank service charge	25
Bank balance, October 1	875

Heather was surprised that the deposit of $50 she made on September 29 had not been posted to her account and was pleased that her rent check of $200 had not cleared her account. Her checkbook balance was $750.

Required:

1. Complete Heather's bank reconciliation.
2. Why is it important for individuals such as Heather and businesses to do a bank reconciliation each month?

SUGGESTED SOLUTION

1. Heather's bank reconciliation:

Heather's Books		Bank Statement	
October 1 cash balance	$750	October 1 cash balance	$875
Additions		Additions	
None		Deposit in transit	50
Deductions		Deductions	
Bank service charge	(25)	Outstanding check	(200)
Correct cash balance	$725	Correct cash balance	$725

2. Bank statements, whether personal or business, should be reconciled each month. This process helps ensure that a correct balance is reflected in the customer's books. Failure to reconcile a bank statement increases the chance that an error will not be discovered and may result in bad checks being written. Businesses must reconcile their bank statements for an additional reason: The correct balance that is calculated during reconciliation is recorded on the balance sheet.

Chapter Supplement

Recording Discounts and Returns

In this chapter, both **credit card discounts** and **cash discounts** have been recorded as contra-revenues. For example, if the credit card company is charging a 3 percent fee for its service and Deckers's Internet credit card sales are $3,000 for January 2, Deckers will record the following:

Cash (+A)	2,910	
Credit card discount (+XR, −R, −SE)	90	
Sales revenue (+R, +SE)		3,000

Assets		=	Liabilities	+	Stockholders' Equity	
Cash	+2,910				Sales revenue (+R)	+3,000
					Credit card discount (+XR)	−90

Similarly, if credit sales of $1,000 are recorded with terms 2/10, n/30 ($\$1{,}000 \times 0.98 = \$980$), and payment is made within the discount period, Deckers will record the following:

Accounts receivable (+A)	1,000	
Sales revenue (+R, +SE)		1,000

Assets		=	Liabilities	+	Stockholders' Equity	
Accounts receivable	+1,000				Sales revenue (+R)	+1,000

Cash (+A)	980	
Sales discount (+XR, −R, −SE)	20	
Accounts receivable (−A)		1,000

Assets		=	Liabilities	+	Stockholders' Equity	
Cash	+980				Sales discount (+XR)	−20
Accounts receivable	−1,000					

Sales returns and allowances should always be treated as a contra-revenue. Assume that Fontana Shoes of Ithaca, New York, buys 40 pairs of sandals from Deckers for $2,000 on account. On the date of sale, Deckers makes the following journal entry:

Accounts receivable (+A)	2,000	
Sales revenue (+R, +SE)		2,000

Assets		=	Liabilities	+	Stockholders' Equity	
Accounts receivable	+2,000				Sales revenue (+R)	+2,000

Before paying for the sandals, however, Fontana discovers that 10 pairs of sandals are not the color ordered and returns them to Deckers. On that date Deckers records:

Sales returns and allowances (+XR, −R, −SE)	500	
Accounts receivable (−A)		500

Assets		=	Liabilities	+	Stockholders' Equity	
Accounts receivable	−500				Sales returns and allowances (+XR)	−500

In addition, the related cost of goods sold entry for the 10 pairs of sandals would be reversed.

CHAPTER TAKE-AWAYS

1. **Apply the revenue principle to determine the accepted time to record sales revenue for typical retailers, wholesalers, manufacturers, and service companies.** p. 281

   Revenue recognition policies are widely recognized as one of the most important determinants of the fair presentation of financial statements. For most merchandisers and manufacturers, the required revenue recognition point is the time that title changes to the buyer (shipment or delivery of goods). For service companies, it is the time that services are provided.

2. **Analyze the impact of credit card sales, sales discounts, and sales returns on the amounts reported as net sales.** p. 281

   Both **credit card discounts** and **sales** or **cash discounts** can be recorded either as contra-revenues or as expenses. When recorded as contra-revenues, they reduce net sales. **Sales returns and allowances,** which should always be treated as a contra-revenue, also reduce net sales.

3. **Analyze and interpret the gross profit percentage.** p. 284

   Gross profit percentage measures the ability to charge premium prices and produce goods and services at lower cost. Managers, analysts, and creditors use this ratio to assess the effectiveness of the company's product development, marketing, and production strategy.

4. **Estimate, report, and evaluate the effects of uncollectible accounts receivable (bad debts) on financial statements.** p. 286

   When receivables are material, companies must employ the allowance method to account for uncollectibles. These are the steps in the process:

   a. The end-of-period adjusting entry to record bad debt expense estimates.

   b. Writing off specific accounts determined to be uncollectible during the period.

   The adjusting entry reduces net income as well as net accounts receivable. The write-off affects neither.

5. **Analyze and interpret the receivables turnover ratio and the effects of accounts receivable on cash flows.** p. 292

   a. **Receivables turnover ratio**—This ratio measures the effectiveness of credit-granting and collection activities. It reflects how many times average trade receivables were recorded and collected during the period. Analysts and creditors watch this ratio because a sudden decline in it may mean that a company is extending payment deadlines in an attempt to prop up lagging sales or is recording sales that later will be returned by customers.

   b. **Effects on cash flows**—When a net decrease in accounts receivable for the period occurs, cash collected from customers is always more than revenue, and cash flows from operations increases. When a net increase in accounts receivable occurs, cash collected from customers is always less than revenue. Thus, cash flows from operations declines.

6. **Report, control, and safeguard cash.** p. 295

   Cash is the most liquid of all assets, flowing continually into and out of a business. As a result, a number of critical control procedures, including the reconciliation of bank accounts, should be applied. Also, management of cash may be critically important to decision makers who must have cash available to meet current needs yet must avoid excess amounts of idle cash that produce no revenue.

Closely related to recording revenue is recording the cost of what was sold. Chapter 7 will focus on transactions related to inventory and cost of goods sold. This topic is important because cost of goods sold has a major impact on a company's gross profit and net income, which are watched closely by investors, analysts, and other users of financial statements. Increasing emphasis on quality, productivity, and costs have further focused production managers' attention on cost of goods sold and inventory. Since inventory cost figures play a major role in product introduction and pricing decisions, they also are important to marketing and general managers. Finally, since inventory accounting has a major effect on many companies' tax liabilities, this is an important place to introduce the effect of taxation on management decision making and financial reporting.

KEY RATIOS

Gross profit percentage measures the excess of sales prices over the costs to purchase or produce the goods or services sold as a percentage. It is computed as follows (p. 284):

$$\text{Gross Profit Percentage} = \frac{\text{Gross Profit}}{\text{Net Sales}}$$

Receivables turnover ratio measures the effectiveness of credit-granting and collection activities. It is computed as follows (p. 292):

$$\text{Receivables Turnover} = \frac{\text{Net Sales}}{\text{Average Net Trade Accounts Receivable}}$$

FINDING FINANCIAL INFORMATION

Balance Sheet

Under Current Assets

Accounts receivable (net of allowance for doubtful accounts)

Income Statement

Revenues

Net sales (sales revenue less discounts and sales returns and allowances)

Expenses

Selling expenses (including bad debt expense)

Statement of Cash Flows

Under Operating Activities (indirect method)

Net income
+ decreases in accounts receivable (net)
− increases in accounts receivable (net)

Notes

Under Summary of Significant Accounting Policies

Revenue recognition policy

Under a Separate Note on Form 10-K

Bad debt expense and write-offs of bad debts

KEY TERMS

Accounts Receivable (Trade Receivables or Receivables) p. 286
Aging of Accounts Receivable Method p. 291
Allowance for Doubtful Accounts (Allowance for Bad Debts or Allowance for Uncollectible Accounts) p. 287
Allowance Method p. 287
Bad Debt Expense (Doubtful Accounts Expense, Uncollectible Accounts Expense, or Provision for Uncollectible Accounts) p. 287
Bank Reconciliation p. 297
Bank Statement p. 297
Cash p. 295
Cash Equivalents p. 295
Credit Card Discount p. 282
Internal Controls p. 296
Notes Receivable p. 286
Percentage of Credit Sales Method p. 290
Sales (or Cash) Discount p. 282
Sales Returns and Allowances p. 283

QUESTIONS

1. Explain the difference between sales revenue and net sales.
2. What is gross profit or gross margin on sales? How is the gross profit ratio computed? In your explanation, assume that net sales revenue was $100,000 and cost of goods sold was $60,000.
3. What is a credit card discount? How does it affect amounts reported on the income statement?

4. What is a sales discount? Use 1/10, n/30 in your explanation.
5. What is the distinction between sales allowances and sales discounts?
6. Differentiate accounts receivable from notes receivable.
7. Which basic accounting principle is the allowance method of accounting for bad debts designed to satisfy?
8. Using the allowance method, is bad debt expense recognized in (*a*) the period in which sales related to the uncollectible account are made or (*b*) the period in which the seller learns that the customer is unable to pay?
9. What is the effect of the write-off of bad debts (using the allowance method) on (*a*) net income and (*b*) accounts receivable, net?
10. Does an increase in the receivables turnover ratio generally indicate faster or slower collection of receivables? Explain.
11. Define cash and cash equivalents in the context of accounting. Indicate the types of items that should be included and excluded.
12. Summarize the primary characteristics of an effective internal control system for cash.
13. Why should cash-handling and cash-recording activities be separated? How is this separation accomplished?
14. What are the purposes of a bank reconciliation? What balances are reconciled?
15. Briefly explain how the total amount of cash reported on the balance sheet is computed.
16. (Chapter Supplement) Under the gross method of recording sales discounts discussed in this chapter, is the amount of sales discount taken recorded (*a*) at the time the sale is recorded or (*b*) at the time the collection of the account is recorded?

6/10

MULTIPLE-CHOICE QUESTIONS

1. Sales discounts with terms 2/10, n/30 mean:
   a. 10 percent discount for payment within 30 days.
   b. 2 percent discount for payment within 10 days, or the full amount (less returns) due within 30 days.
   c. Two-tenths of a percent discount for payment within 30 days.
   d. None of the above.
2. Gross sales total $250,000, one-half of which were credit sales. Sales returns and allowances of $15,000 apply to the credit sales, sales discounts of 2% were taken on all of the net credit sales, and credit card sales of $100,000 were subject to a credit card discount of 3%. What is the dollar amount of net sales?
   a. $227,000
   b. $229,800
   c. $250,000
   d. $240,000

125,000
125,000 − 15,000 − 2,200 − 3,000
104,800 + 125,000 = 229,800

3. A company has been successful in reducing the costs of its manufacturing process by relocating the factory to another locale. What effect will this factor have on the company's gross profit percentage ratio, all other things equal?
   a. The ratio will not change.
   b. The ratio will increase.
   c. The ratio will decrease.
   d. Either (b) or (c).
4. When a company using the allowance method writes off a specific customer's $100,000 account receivable from the accounting system, which of the following statements are true?
   1. Total stockholders' equity remains the same.
   2. Total assets remain the same.
   3. Total expenses remain the same.

   a. 2
   b. 1 and 3
   c. 1 and 2
   d. 1, 2, and 3

AFDA Contra-asset
AR
A↓

5. You have determined that Company X estimates bad debt expense with an aging of accounts receivable schedule. Company X's estimate of uncollectible receivables resulting from the aging analysis equals $250. The beginning balance in the allowance for doubtful accounts was $220. Write-offs of bad debts during the period were $180. What amount would be recorded as bad debt expense for the current period?
   a. $180
   b. $250
   c. $210
   d. $220

250
+180
−220
210

6. Upon review of the most recent bank statement, you discover that you recently received an "insufficient funds check" from a customer. Which of the following describes the actions to be taken when preparing your bank reconciliation?

	Balance per Books	**Balance per Bank Statement**
a.	No change	Decrease
b.	Decrease	Increase
c.	Decrease	No change
d.	Increase	Decrease

7. Which of the following is **not** a step toward effective internal control over cash?
   a. Require signatures from a manager and one financial officer on all checks.
   b. Require that cash be deposited daily at the bank.
   c. Require that the person responsible for removing the cash from the register have no access to the accounting records.
   d. All of the above are steps toward effective internal control.
8. When using the allowance method, as bad debt expense is recorded,
   a. Total assets remain the same and stockholders' equity remains the same.
   b. Total assets decrease and stockholders' equity decreases.
   c. Total assets increase and stockholders' equity decreases.
   d. Total liabilities increase and stockholders' equity decreases.
9. Which of the following best describes the proper presentation of accounts receivable in the financial statements?
   a. Gross accounts receivable plus the allowance for doubtful accounts in the asset section of the balance sheet.
   b. Gross accounts receivable in the asset section of the balance sheet and the allowance for doubtful accounts in the expense section of the income statement.
   c. Gross accounts receivable less bad debt expense in the asset section of the balance sheet.
   d. Gross accounts receivable less the allowance for doubtful accounts in the asset section of the balance sheet.
10. Which of the following is not a component of net sales?
   a. Sales returns and allowances
   b. Sales discounts
   c. Cost of goods sold
   d. Credit card discounts

For more practice with multiple-choice questions, go to the text website at **www.mhhe.com/libby7e**.

MINI-EXERCISES

connect ACCOUNTING

M6-1 Interpreting the Revenue Principle
LO1

Indicate the most likely time you expect sales revenue to be recorded for each of the listed transactions.

Transaction	Point A	Point B
a. Sale of inventory to a business customer on open account	_____ Shipment	_____ Collection of account
b. Computer sold by mail order company on a credit card	_____ Shipment	_____ Delivery
c. Airline tickets sold by an airline on a credit card	_____ Point of sale	_____ Completion of flight

M6-2 Reporting Net Sales with Sales Discounts
LO2

Merchandise invoiced at $8,500 is sold on terms 1/10, n/30. If the buyer pays within the discount period, what amount will be reported on the income statement as net sales?

M6-3 Reporting Net Sales with Sales Discounts, Credit Card Discounts, and Sales Returns
LO2

Total gross sales for the period include the following:

Credit card sales (discount 3%)	$ 9,400
Sales on account (2/15, n/60)	$10,500

Sales returns related to sales on account were $500. All returns were made before payment. One-half of the remaining sales on account were paid within the discount period. The company treats all discounts and returns as contra-revenues. What amount will be reported on the income statement as net sales?

Computing and Interpreting the Gross Profit Percentage

M6-4
LO3

Net sales for the period was $45,000 and cost of sales was $28,000. Compute the gross profit percentage for the current year. What does this ratio measure?

Recording Bad Debts

M6-5
LO4

Prepare journal entries for each transaction listed.

a. During the period, bad debts are written off in the amount of $19,000.
b. At the end of the period, bad debt expense is estimated to be $13,000.

Determining Financial Statement Effects of Bad Debts

M6-6
LO4

Using the following categories, indicate the effects of the following transactions. Use + for increase and − for decrease and indicate the accounts affected and the amounts.

a. At the end of the period, bad debt expense is estimated to be $17,000.
b. During the period, bad debts are written off in the amount of $8,000.

Assets	=	Liabilities	+	Stockholders' Equity

Determining the Effects of Credit Policy Changes on Receivables Turnover Ratio

M6-7
LO5

Indicate the most likely effect of the following changes in credit policy on the receivables turnover ratio (+ for increase, − for decrease, and NE for no effect).

a. Granted credit with shorter payment deadlines.
b. Increased effectiveness of collection methods.
c. Granted credit to less creditworthy customers.

Matching Reconciling Items to the Bank Reconciliation

M6-8
LO6

Indicate whether the following items would be added (+) or subtracted (−) from the company's books or the bank statement during the construction of a bank reconciliation.

Reconciling Item	Company's Books	Bank Statement
a. Outstanding checks		
b. Bank service charge		
c. Deposit in transit		

(Supplement) Recording Sales Discounts

M6-9

A sale is made for $8,000; terms are 2/10, n/30. At what amount should the sale be recorded under the gross method of recording sales discounts? Give the required entry. Also give the collection entry, assuming that it is during the discount period.

EXERCISES

connect ACCOUNTING

E6-1
LO2

Reporting Net Sales with Credit Sales and Sales Discounts

During the months of January and February, Silver Corporation sold goods to three customers. The sequence of events was as follows:

Jan.	6	Sold goods for $850 to S. Green and billed that amount subject to terms 2/10, n/30.
	6	Sold goods to M. Munoz for $700 and billed that amount subject to terms 2/10, n/30.
	14	Collected cash due from S. Green.
Feb.	2	Collected cash due from M. Munoz.
	28	Sold goods for $450 to R. Reynolds and billed that amount subject to terms 2/10, n/45.

Required:
Assuming that Sales Discounts is treated as a contra-revenue, compute net sales for the two months ended February 28.

E6-2
LO2

Reporting Net Sales with Credit Sales, Sales Discounts, and Credit Card Sales

The following transactions were selected from the records of OceanView Company:

July	12	Sold merchandise to Customer R, who charged the $3,000 purchase on his Visa credit card. Visa charges OceanView a 2 percent credit card fee.
	15	Sold merchandise to Customer S at an invoice price of $9,000; terms 3/10, n/30.
	20	Sold merchandise to Customer T at an invoice price of $4,000; terms 3/10, n/30.
	23	Collected payment from Customer S from July 15 sale.
Aug.	25	Collected payment from Customer T from July 20 sale.

Required:
Assuming that Sales Discounts and Credit Card Discounts are treated as contra-revenues, compute net sales for the two months ended August 31.

E6-3
LO2

Reporting Net Sales with Credit Sales, Sales Discounts, Sales Returns, and Credit Card Sales

The following transactions were selected from among those completed by Cadence Retailers in 2011:

Nov.	20	Sold 20 items of merchandise to Customer B at an invoice price of $5,500 (total); terms 3/10, n/30.
	25	Sold two items of merchandise to Customer C, who charged the $400 sales price on her Visa credit card. Visa charges Cadence Retailers a 2 percent credit card fee.
	28	Sold 10 identical items of merchandise to Customer D at an invoice price of $9,000 (total); terms 3/10, n/30.
	29	Customer D returned one of the items purchased on the 28th; the item was defective, and credit was given to the customer.
Dec.	6	Customer D paid the account balance in full.
	20	Customer B paid in full for the invoice of November 20, 2011.

Required:
Assume that Sales Returns and Allowances, Sales Discounts, and Credit Card Discounts are treated as contra-revenues; compute net sales for the two months ended December 31, 2011.

E6-4
LO2

Determining the Effects of Credit Sales, Sales Discounts, Credit Card Sales, and Sales Returns and Allowances on Income Statement Categories

Brazen Shoe Company records Sales Returns and Allowances, Sales Discounts, and Credit Card Discounts as contra-revenues. Complete the following tabulation, indicating the effect (+ for increase, − for decrease, and NE for no effect) and amount of the effects of each transaction, including related cost of goods sold.

July	12	Sold merchandise to customer at factory store who charged the $300 purchase on her American Express card. American Express charges a 1 percent credit card fee. Cost of goods sold was $175.
July	15	Sold merchandise to Customer T at an invoice price of $5,000; terms 3/10, n/30. Cost of goods sold was $2,500.
July	20	Collected cash due from Customer T.
July	21	Before paying for the order, a customer returned shoes with an invoice price of $1,000, and cost of goods sold was $600.

Transaction	Net Sales	Cost of Goods Sold	Gross Profit
July 12			
July 15			
July 20			
July 21			

E6-5
LO2

Evaluating the Annual Interest Rate Implicit in a Sales Discount with Discussion of Management Choice of Financing Strategy

Clark's Landscaping bills customers subject to terms 3/10, n/50.

Required:

1. Compute the annual interest rate implicit in the sales discount. (Round to two decimal places.)
2. If his bank charges 15 percent interest, should the customer borrow from the bank so that he can take advantage of the discount? Explain your recommendation.

E6-6
LO3

Wolverine World Wide Inc.

Analyzing Gross Profit Percentage on the Basis of an Income Statement and Within-Industry Comparison

Wolverine World Wide Inc. prides itself as being the "world's leading marketer of U.S. branded non-athletic footwear." It competes in many markets with Deckers, often offering products at a lower price point. Its brands include Wolverine, Bates, Sebago, and Hush Puppies. The following data were taken from its recent annual report (dollars in thousands):

Sales of merchandise	$1,220,568
Income taxes	44,763
Cash dividends declared on common stock	21,500
Selling and administrative expense	345,183
Cost of products sold	734,547
Interest expense	2,850
Other income	839
Items not included in above amounts:	
Number of shares of common stock outstanding, 48,888	

Required:

1. Based on these data, prepare an income statement (showing both gross profit and income from operations). There were no extraordinary items.
2. How much was the gross profit margin? What was the gross profit percentage ratio? Explain what these two amounts mean. Compare the gross profit percentage with that of Deckers. What do you believe accounts for the difference?

E6-7
LO2, 3, 4

Analyzing Gross Profit Percentage on the Basis of an Income Statement

The following summarized data were provided by the records of Slate, Incorporated, for the year ended December 31, 2012:

Sales of merchandise for cash	$233,000
Sales of merchandise on credit	40,000
Cost of goods sold	146,000
Selling expense	47,200
Administrative expense	20,000
Sales returns and allowances	8,000
Items not included in above amounts:	
Estimated bad debt loss, 3% of credit sales	
Average income tax rate, 30%	
Number of shares of common stock outstanding, 4,500	

Required:

1. Based on these data, prepare an income statement (showing both gross profit and income from operations).
2. What was the amount of gross profit margin? What was the gross profit percentage ratio? Explain what these two amounts mean.

E6-8
LO4

Recording Bad Debt Expense Estimates and Write-Offs Using the Percentage of Credit Sales Method

During 2011, Crandell Productions, Inc., recorded credit sales of $800,000. Based on prior experience, it estimates a 1 percent bad debt rate on credit sales.

Required:

Prepare journal entries for each transaction:

a. The appropriate bad debt expense adjustment was recorded for the year 2011.

b. On December 31, 2011, an account receivable for $2,500 from March of the current year was determined to be uncollectible and was written off.

E6-9
LO4

Recording Bad Debt Expense Estimates and Write-Offs Using the Percentage of Credit Sales Method

During 2011, Soto Electronics, Incorporated, recorded credit sales of $790,000. Based on prior experience, it estimates a 2 percent bad debt rate on credit sales.

Required:

Prepare journal entries for each transaction:

a. The appropriate bad debt expense adjustment was recorded for the year 2011.

b. On December 31, 2011, an account receivable for $360 from a prior year was determined to be uncollectible and was written off.

E6-10
LO4

Determining Financial Statement Effects of Bad Debts Using the Percentage of Credit Sales Method

Using the following categories, indicate the effects of the transactions listed in E6-9. Use + for increase and − for decrease and indicate the accounts affected and the amounts.

Assets	=	Liabilities	+	Stockholders' Equity

E6-11
LO4

Recording and Determining the Effects of Bad Debt Transactions on Income Statement Categories Using the Percentage of Credit Sales Method

During 2012, Giatras Electronics recorded credit sales of $680,000. Based on prior experience, it estimates a 3.5 percent bad debt rate on credit sales.

Required:

1. Prepare journal entries for each of the following transactions.
   a. The appropriate bad debt expense adjustment was recorded for the year 2012.
   b. On December 31, 2012, an account receivable for $2,800 from a prior year was determined to be uncollectible and was written off.
2. Complete the following tabulation, indicating the amount and effect (+ for increase, − for decrease, and NE for no effect) of each transaction.

Transaction	Net Sales	Gross Profit	Income from Operations
a.			
b.			

Computing Bad Debt Expense Using Aging Analysis

E6-12
LO4

Gary's Dairy uses the aging approach to estimate bad debt expense. The balance of each account receivable is aged on the basis of three time periods as follows: (1) not yet due, $16,000, (2) up to 120 days past due, $5,500, and (3) more than 120 days past due, $2,500. Experience has shown that for each age group, the average loss rate on the amount of the receivables at year-end due to uncollectability is (1) 2 percent, (2) 14 percent, and (3) 35 percent, respectively. At December 31, 2011 (end of the current year), the Allowance for Doubtful Accounts balance is $900 (credit) before the end-of-period adjusting entry is made.

Required:

What amount should be recorded as Bad Debt Expense for the current year?

Recording and Reporting a Bad Debt Estimate Using Aging Analysis

E6-13
LO4

Casilda Company uses the aging approach to estimate bad debt expense. The balance of each account receivable is aged on the basis of three time periods as follows: (1) not yet due, $50,000, (2) up to 180 days past due, $14,000, and (3) more than 180 days past due, $4,000. Experience has shown that for each age group, the average loss rate on the amount of the receivables at year-end due to uncollectability is (1) 3 percent, (2) 12 percent, and (3) 30 percent, respectively. At December 31, 2011 (end of the current year), the Allowance for Doubtful Accounts balance is $200 (credit) before the end-of-period adjusting entry is made.

Required:

1. Prepare the appropriate bad debt expense adjusting entry for the year 2011.
2. Show how the various accounts related to accounts receivable should be shown on the December 31, 2011, balance sheet.

Recording and Reporting a Bad Debt Estimate Using Aging Analysis

E6-14
LO4

Frederick Company uses the aging approach to estimate bad debt expense. The balance of each account receivable is aged on the basis of three time periods as follows: (1) not yet due, $275,000, (2) up to 120 days past due, $50,000, and (3) more than 120 days past due, $20,000. Experience has shown that for each age group, the average loss rate on the amount of the receivables at year-end due to uncollectability is (1) 3.5 percent, (2) 10 percent, and (3) 30 percent, respectively. At December 31, 2012 (end of the current year), the Allowance for Doubtful Accounts balance is $400 (credit) before the end-of-period adjusting entry is made.

Required:

1. Prepare the appropriate bad debt expense adjusting entry for the year 2012.
2. Show how the various accounts related to accounts receivable should be shown on the December 31, 2012, balance sheet.

Interpreting Bad Debt Disclosures

E6-15
LO4
SIEMENS

Siemens is one of the world's largest electrical engineering and electronics companies. Headquartered in Germany, the company has been in business for over 160 years and operates in 190 countries. In a recent annual report, it disclosed the following information concerning its allowance for doubtful accounts (euros in millions denoted as €):

Balance at Beginning of Period	Charged to Costs and Expenses	Amounts Written Off	Balance at End of Period
€895	€271	€(153)	€1,013

Required:

1. Record summary journal entries related to the allowance for doubtful accounts for the current year.
2. If Siemens had written off an additional €10 million of accounts receivable during the period, how would receivables, net, and net income have been affected? Explain why.

E6-16 Inferring Bad Debt Write-Offs and Cash Collections from Customers

LO4

Microsoft

Microsoft develops, produces, and markets a wide range of computer software, including the Windows operating system. On its recent financial statements, Microsoft reported the following information about net sales revenue and accounts receivable (amounts in millions).

	Current Year	Prior Year
Accounts receivable, net of allowances of $153 and $117	$13,589	$11,338
Net revenues	60,420	51,122

According to its Form 10-K, Microsoft recorded bad debt expense of $88 and did not reinstate any previously written-off accounts during the current year. (**Hint:** Refer to the summary of the effects of accounting for bad debts on the Accounts Receivable (Gross) and the Allowance for Doubtful Accounts T-accounts. Use the T-accounts to solve for the missing values.)

Required:

1. What amount of bad debts was written off during the current year?
2. Based on your answer to requirement (1), solve for cash collected from customers for the current year, assuming that all of Microsoft's sales during the period were on open account.

E6-17 Inferring Bad Debt Expense and Determining the Impact of Uncollectible Accounts on Income and Working Capital

LO4

Target

A recent annual report for Target contained the following information (dollars in thousands) at the end of its fiscal year:

	Year 2	Year 1
Accounts receivable	$9,094,000	$8,624,000
Allowance for doubtful accounts	(1,010,000)	(570,000)
	$8,084,000	$8,054,000

A footnote to the financial statements disclosed that uncollectible accounts amounting to $811,000 and $428,000 were written off as bad debts during year 2 and year 1, respectively. Assume that the tax rate for Target was 30 percent.

Required:

1. Determine the bad debt expense for year 2 based on the preceding facts. (**Hint:** Use the Allowance for Doubtful Accounts T-account to solve for the missing value.)
2. **Working capital** is defined as current assets minus current liabilities. How was Target's working capital affected by the write-off of $811,000 in uncollectible accounts during year 2? What impact did the recording of bad debt expense have on working capital in year 2?
3. How was net income affected by the $811,000 write-off during year 2? What impact did recording bad debt expense have on net income for year 2?

Recording, Reporting, and Evaluating a Bad Debt Estimate

E6-18
LO4

During 2012, Robby's Camera Shop had sales revenue of $170,000, of which $75,000 was on credit. At the start of 2012, Accounts Receivable showed a $16,000 debit balance, and the Allowance for Doubtful Accounts showed a $900 credit balance. Collections of accounts receivable during 2012 amounted to $60,000.

Data during 2012 follows:

a. On December 31, 2012, an Account Receivable (J. Doe) of $1,700 from a prior year was determined to be uncollectible; therefore, it was written off immediately as a bad debt.
b. On December 31, 2012, on the basis of experience, a decision was made to continue the accounting policy of basing estimated bad debt losses on 1.5 percent of credit sales for the year.

Required:

1. Give the required journal entries for the two items on December 31, 2012 (end of the accounting period).
2. Show how the amounts related to Accounts Receivable and Bad Debt Expense would be reported on the income statement and balance sheet for 2012. Disregard income tax considerations.
3. On the basis of the data available, does the 1.5 percent rate appear to be reasonable? Explain.

Recording, Reporting, and Evaluating a Bad Debt Estimate

E6-19
LO4

During 2011, Dorothy's Ceramics Shop had sales revenue of $70,000, of which $25,000 was on credit. At the start of 2011, Accounts Receivable showed a $4,000 debit balance, and the Allowance for Doubtful Accounts showed a $300 credit balance. Collections of accounts receivable during 2011 amounted to $19,000.

Data during 2011 follows:

a. On December 31, 2011, an Account Receivable (Toby's Gift Shop) of $700 from a prior year was determined to be uncollectible; therefore, it was written off immediately as a bad debt.
b. On December 31, 2011, on the basis of experience, a decision was made to continue the accounting policy of basing estimated bad debt losses on 2.5 percent of credit sales for the year.

Required:

1. Give the required journal entries for the two items on December 31, 2011 (end of the accounting period).
2. Show how the amounts related to Accounts Receivable and Bad Debt Expense would be reported on the income statement and balance sheet for 2011. Disregard income tax considerations.
3. On the basis of the data available, does the 2.5 percent rate appear to be reasonable? Explain.

Computing and Interpreting the Receivables Turnover Ratio

E6-20
LO5

FedEx

A recent annual report for FedEx contained the following data:

	(dollars in thousands)	
	Current Year	Previous Year
Accounts receivable	$ 3,587,000	$4,517,000
Less: Allowance for doubtful accounts	196,000	158,000
Net accounts receivable	$ 3,391,000	$4,359,000
Net sales (assume all on credit)	$35,497,000	

Required:

1. Determine the receivables turnover ratio and average days sales in receivables for the current year.
2. Explain the meaning of each number.

E6-21 LO5 Computing and Interpreting the Receivables Turnover Ratio

A recent annual report for Dell, Inc., contained the following data:

DELL

	(dollars in thousands)	
	Current Year	Previous Year
Accounts receivable	$ 4,843,000	$6,064,000
Less: Allowance for doubtful accounts	112,000	103,000
Net accounts receivable	$ 4,731,000	$5,961,000
Net sales (assume all on credit)	$61,101,000	

Required:

1. Determine the receivables turnover ratio and average days sales in receivables for the current year.
2. Explain the meaning of each number.

E6-22 LO5 Interpreting the Effects of Sales Declines and Changes in Receivables on Cash Flow from Operations

Stride Rite

Stride Rite Corporation manufactures and markets shoes under the brand names Stride Rite, Keds, and Sperry Top-Sider. Three recent years produced a combination of declining sales revenue and net income culminating in a net loss of $8,430,000. Each year, however, Stride Rite was able to report positive cash flows from operations. Contributing to that positive cash flow was the change in accounts receivable. The current and prior year balance sheets reported the following:

	(dollars in thousands)	
	Current Year	Previous Year
Accounts and notes receivable, less allowances	$48,066	$63,403

Required:

1. On the current year's cash flow statement (indirect method), how would the change in accounts receivable affect cash flow from operations? Explain why it would have this effect.
2. Explain how declining sales revenue often leads to (*a*) declining accounts receivable and (*b*) cash collections from customers being higher than sales revenue.

E6-23 LO6 Preparing Bank Reconciliation, Entries, and Reporting Cash

Jackson Company's June 30, 2011, bank statement and June ledger accounts for cash are summarized below:

BANK STATEMENT			
	Checks	Deposits	Balance
Balance, June 1, 2011			$ 6,900
Deposits during June		$16,200	23,100
Checks cleared during June	$17,000		6,100
Bank service charges	40		6,060
Balance, June 30, 2011			6,060

Cash (A)					
June 1	Balance	6,900	June	Checks written	19,000
June	Deposits	18,100			

Required:

1. Reconcile the bank account. A comparison of the checks written with the checks that have cleared the bank shows outstanding checks of $2,000. A deposit of $1,900 is in transit at the end of June.
2. Give any journal entries that should be made as a result of the bank reconciliation.
3. What is the balance in the Cash account after the reconciliation entries?
4. What is the total amount of cash that should be reported on the balance sheet at June 30?

Preparing Bank Reconciliation, Entries, and Reporting Cash

E6-24
LO6

The September 30, 2011, bank statement for Bennett Company and the September ledger accounts for cash are summarized here:

BANK STATEMENT	Checks	Deposits	Balance
Balance, September 1, 2011			$ 6,500
Deposits recorded during September		$26,900	33,400
Checks cleared during September	$27,400		6,000
NSF checks—Betty Brown	170		5,830
Bank service charges	60		5,770
Balance, September 30, 2011			5,770

Cash (A)					
Sept. 1	Balance	6,500	Sept.	Checks written	28,900
Sept.	Deposits	28,100			

No outstanding checks and no deposits in transit were carried over from August; however, there are deposits in transit and checks outstanding at the end of September.

Required:

1. Reconcile the bank account.
2. Give any journal entries that should be made as the result of the bank reconciliation.
3. What should the balance in the Cash account be after the reconciliation entries?
4. What total amount of cash should the company report on the September 30 balance sheet?

(Supplement) Recording Credit Sales, Sales Discounts, Sales Returns, and Credit Card Sales

E6-25

The following transactions were selected from among those completed by Hailey Retailers in 2010:

Nov.	20	Sold two items of merchandise to Customer B, who charged the $450 sales price on her Visa credit card. Visa charges Hailey a 2 percent credit card fee.
	25	Sold 14 items of merchandise to Customer C at an invoice price of $2,800 (total); terms 2/10, n/30.
	28	Sold 12 identical items of merchandise to Customer D at an invoice price of $7,200 (total); terms 2/10, n/30.
	30	Customer D returned one of the items purchased on the 28th; the item was defective, and credit was given to the customer.
Dec.	6	Customer D paid the account balance in full.
	30	Customer C paid in full for the invoice of November 25, 2010.

Required:

Give the appropriate journal entry for each of these transactions, assuming the company records sales revenue under the gross method. Do not record cost of goods sold. Compute Net Sales.

To practice with more exercises, go to the text website at **www.mhhe.com/libby7e**.

PROBLEMS

connect ACCOUNTING

P6-1 LO1 Applying the Revenue Principle

At what point should revenue be recognized in each of the following independent cases?

Case A. For Christmas presents, a Wendy's restaurant sells coupon books for $15. Each of the $1 coupons may be used in the restaurant any time during the following 12 months. The customer must pay cash when purchasing the coupon book.

Case B. Russell Land Development Corporation sold a lot to Upland Builders to construct a new home. The price of the lot was $50,000. Upland made a down payment of $250 and agreed to pay the balance in six months. After making the sale, Russell learned that Upland Builders often entered into these agreements but refused to pay the balance if it did not find a customer who wanted a house built on the lot.

Case C. Davis Corporation has always recorded revenue at the point of sale of its refrigerators. Recently, it has extended its warranties to cover all repairs for a period of seven years. One young accountant with the company now questions whether Davis has completed its earning process when it sells the refrigerators. She suggests that the warranty obligation for seven years means that a significant amount of additional work must be performed in the future.

P6-2 LO2, 4 Reporting Net Sales and Expenses with Discounts, Returns, and Bad Debts (AP6-1)

The following data were selected from the records of Sykes Company for the year ended December 31, 2011.

Balances January 1, 2011	
Accounts receivable (various customers)	$115,000
Allowance for doubtful accounts	7,000

In the following order, except for cash sales, the company sold merchandise and made collections on credit terms 2/10, n/30 (assume a unit sales price of $500 in all transactions and use the gross method to record sales revenue).

Transactions during 2011

a. Sold merchandise for cash, $234,000.
b. Sold merchandise to R. Smith; invoice price, $11,500.
c. Sold merchandise to K. Miller; invoice price, $25,000.
d. Two days after purchase date, R. Smith returned one of the units purchased in (*b*) and received account credit.
e. Sold merchandise to B. Sears; invoice price, $26,000.
f. R. Smith paid his account in full within the discount period.
g. Collected $98,000 cash from customer sales on credit in prior year, all within the discount periods.
h. K. Miller paid the invoice in (*c*) within the discount period.
i. Sold merchandise to R. Roy; invoice price, $17,500.
j. Three days after paying the account in full, K. Miller returned seven defective units and received a cash refund.
k. After the discount period, collected $6,000 cash on an account receivable on sales in a prior year.
l. Wrote off a 2010 account of $3,000 after deciding that the amount would never be collected.
m. The estimated bad debt rate used by the company was 1.5 percent of credit sales net of returns.

Required:

1. Using the following categories, indicate the effect of each listed transaction, including the write-off of the uncollectible account and the adjusting entry for estimated bad debts (ignore cost of goods sold). Indicate the sign and amount of the effect or "NE" for "no effect." The first transaction is used as an example.

	Sales Revenue	Sales Discounts (taken)	Sales Returns and Allowances	Bad Debt Expense
(*a*)	+234,000	NE	NE	NE

2. Show how the accounts related to the preceding sale and collection activities should be reported on the 2011 income statement. (Treat sales discounts as a contra-revenue.)

Understanding the Income Statement Based on the Gross Profit Percentage

P6-3
LO3

eXcel
www.mhhe.com/libby7e

The following data presented in income statement order were taken from the year-end records of Berugu Export Company. Fill in all of the missing amounts and show computations. (**Hint:** In Case B, start from the bottom.)

Income Statement Items	Independent Cases Case A	Case B
Gross sales revenue	$259,000	$165,000
Sales returns and allowances	20,000	?
Net sales revenue	?	?
Cost of goods sold	?	(70%)?
Gross profit	(30%)?	?
Operating expenses	?	15,600
Pretax income	22,000	?
Income tax expense (20%)	?	?
Income before extraordinary items	?	?
Extraordinary gain (loss)	(2,000)	10,000
Less: Income tax (20% of extraordinary item)	?	?
Net income	?	?
EPS (10,000 shares)	?	$2.54

Recording Bad Debts and Interpreting Disclosure of Allowance for Doubtful Accounts (AP6-2)

P6-4
LO4

Peet's Coffee & Tea

Peet's Coffee & Tea, Inc., is a specialty coffee roaster and marketer of branded fresh roasted whole bean coffee. It recently disclosed the following information concerning the Allowance for Doubtful Accounts on its Form 10-K Annual Report submitted to the Securities and Exchange Commission.

A summary of the Allowance for Doubtful Accounts is as follows (dollars in thousands):

Allowance for Doubtful Accounts	Balance at Beginning of Period	Additions (Charges) to Expense	Write-Offs	Balance at End of Period
Year 1	$ 89	$?	$1	$145
Year 2	145	—	?	67
Year 3	67	7	2	72

Required:

1. Record summary journal entries related to bad debts for year 3.
2. Supply the missing dollar amounts noted by (?) for year 1 and year 2.

Determining Bad Debt Expense Based on Aging Analysis (AP6-3)

P6-5
LO4

Blue Skies Equipment Company uses the aging approach to estimate bad debt expense at the end of each accounting year. Credit sales occur frequently on terms n/60. The balance of each account receivable is aged on the basis of three time periods as follows: (1) not yet due, (2) up to one year past due, and (3) more than one year past due. Experience has shown that for each age group, the average loss rate on the amount of the receivable at year-end due to uncollectability is (*a*) 2 percent, (*b*) 7 percent, and (*c*) 30 percent, respectively.

At December 31, 2011 (end of the current accounting year), the Accounts Receivable balance was $46,700, and the Allowance for Doubtful Accounts balance was $920 (credit). In determining which accounts have been paid, the company applies collections to the oldest sales first. To simplify, only five customer accounts are used; the details of each on December 31, 2011, follow:

	B. Brown—Account Receivable			
Date	**Explanation**	**Debit**	**Credit**	**Balance**
3/11/2010	Sale	13,000		13,000
6/30/2010	Collection		4,000	9,000
1/31/2011	Collection		3,800	5,200
	D. Donalds—Account Receivable			
2/28/2011	Sale	21,000		21,000
4/15/2011	Collection		8,000	13,000
11/30/2011	Collection		5,000	8,000
	N. Napier—Account Receivable			
11/30/2011	Sale	8,000		8,000
12/15/2011	Collection		1,000	7,000
	S. Strothers—Account Receivable			
3/2/2009	Sale	4,000		4,000
4/15/2009	Collection		4,000	–0–
9/1/2010	Sale	9,000		9,000
10/15/2010	Collection		4,500	4,500
2/1/2011	Sale	21,000		25,500
3/1/2011	Collection		5,000	20,500
12/31/2011	Sale	2,000		22,500
	T. Thomas—Account Receivable			
12/30/2011	Sale	4,000		4,000

Required:

1. Compute the total accounts receivable in each age category.
2. Compute the estimated uncollectible amount for each age category and in total.
3. Give the adjusting entry for bad debt expense at December 31, 2011.
4. Show how the amounts related to accounts receivable should be presented on the 2011 income statement and balance sheet.

P6-6
LO2, 3, 4, 5

excel

www.mhhe.com/libby7e

Preparing an Income Statement and Computing the Gross Profit Percentage and Receivables Turnover Ratio with Discounts, Returns, and Bad Debts (AP6-4)

Tungsten Company, Inc., sells heavy construction equipment. There are 10,000 shares of capital stock outstanding. The annual fiscal period ends on December 31. The following condensed trial balance was taken from the general ledger on December 31, 2011:

Account Titles	Debit	Credit
Cash	$ 33,600	
Accounts receivable (net)	14,400	
Inventory, ending	52,000	
Operational assets	40,000	
Accumulated depreciation		$ 16,800
Liabilities		24,000
Capital stock		72,000
Retained earnings, January 1, 2011		9,280
Sales revenue		147,100
Sales returns and allowances	5,600	
Cost of goods sold	78,400	
Selling expense	14,100	
Administrative expense	15,400	
Bad debt expense	1,600	
Sales discounts	6,400	
Income tax expense	7,680	
Totals	$269,180	$269,180

Required:

1. Beginning with the amount for net sales, prepare an income statement (showing both gross profit and income from operations). Treat sales discounts and sales returns and allowances as a contra-revenue.
2. The beginning balance in Accounts Receivable (net) was $16,000. Compute the gross profit percentage and receivables turnover ratio and explain their meaning.

Preparing a Bank Reconciliation and Related Journal Entries

P6-7
LO6
eXcel
www.mhhe.com/libby7e

The bookkeeper at Wood Company has not reconciled the bank statement with the Cash account, saying, "I don't have time." You have been asked to prepare a reconciliation and review the procedures with the bookkeeper.

The April 30, 2011, bank statement and the April ledger accounts for cash showed the following (summarized):

BANK STATEMENT	Checks	Deposits	Balance
Balance, April 1, 2011			$31,000
Deposits during April		$36,100	67,100
Interest collected		1,180	68,280
Checks cleared during April	$44,500		23,780
NSF check—A. B. Wright	160		23,620
Bank service charges	50		23,570
Balance, April 30, 2011			23,570

Cash (A)

Apr. 1	Balance	23,500	Apr.	Checks written	41,100
Apr.	Deposits	41,500			

A comparison of checks written before and during April with the checks cleared through the bank showed outstanding checks at the end of April of $4,100. No deposits in transit were carried over from March, but a deposit was in transit at the end of April.

Required:

1. Prepare a detailed bank reconciliation for April.
2. Give any required journal entries as a result of the reconciliation. Why are they necessary?
3. What was the balance in the cash account in the ledger on May 1, 2011?
4. What total amount of cash should be reported on the balance sheet at the end of April?

Computing Outstanding Checks and Deposits in Transit and Preparing a Bank Reconciliation and Journal Entries (AP6-5)

P6-8
LO6
eXcel
www.mhhe.com/libby7e

The August 2011 bank statement for Allison Company and the August 2011 ledger account for cash follow:

BANK STATEMENT

Date	Checks	Deposits	Balance
Aug. 1			$17,510
2	$ 320		17,190
3		$11,700	28,890
4	430		28,460
5	270		28,190
9	880		27,310
10	250		27,060
15		4,000	31,060
21	350		30,710
24	20,400		10,310
25		6,500	16,810
30	850		15,960
30		2,350*	18,310
31	120†		18,190

*$2,350 interest collected.
†Bank service charge.

Cash (A)			
Aug. 1 Balance	16,490	Checks written	
Deposits		Aug. 2	250
Aug. 2	11,700	4	880
12	4,000	15	280
24	6,500	17	510
31	5,200	18	850
		20	350
		23	20,400

Outstanding checks at the end of July were for $270, $430, and $320. No deposits were in transit at the end of July.

Required:

1. Compute the deposits in transit at the end of August by comparing the deposits on the bank statement to the deposits listed on the cash ledger account.
2. Compute the outstanding checks at the end of August by comparing the checks listed on the bank statement with those on the cash ledger account and the list of outstanding checks at the end of July.
3. Prepare a bank reconciliation for August.
4. Give any journal entries that the company should make as a result of the bank reconciliation. Why are they necessary?
5. What total amount of cash should be reported on the August 31, 2011, balance sheet?

P6-9 (Supplement) Recording Sales, Returns, and Bad Debts

Use the data presented in P6-2, which were selected from the records of Sykes Company for the year ended December 31, 2011.

Required:

1. Give the journal entries for these transactions, including the write-off of the uncollectible account and the adjusting entry for estimated bad debts. Do not record cost of goods sold. Show computations for each entry.
2. Show how the accounts related to the preceding sale and collection activities should be reported on the 2011 income statement. (Treat sales discounts as a contra-revenue.)

ALTERNATE PROBLEMS

AP6-1 Reporting Net Sales and Expenses with Discounts, Returns, and Bad Debts (P6-2)

LO2, 4

The following data were selected from the records of Sharkim Company for the year ended December 31, 2012.

Balances January 1, 2012:	
Accounts receivable (various customers)	$116,000
Allowance for doubtful accounts	5,200

In the following order, except for cash sales, the company sold merchandise and made collections on credit terms 2/10, n/30 (assume a unit sales price of $500 in all transactions and use the gross method to record sales revenue).

Transactions during 2012

a. Sold merchandise for cash, $227,000.
b. Sold merchandise to Karen Corp; invoice price, $12,000.
c. Sold merchandise to White Company; invoice price, $23,500.
d. Karen paid the invoice in (*b*) within the discount period.
e. Sold merchandise to Cavendish Inc; invoice price, $26,000.

f. Two days after paying the account in full, Karen returned one defective unit and received a cash refund.
g. Collected $88,200 cash from customer sales on credit in prior year, all within the discount periods.
h. Three days after purchase date, White returned seven of the units purchased in (*c*) and received account credit.
i. White paid its account in full within the discount period.
j. Sold merchandise to Delta Corporation; invoice price, $18,500.
k. Cavendish paid its account in full after the discount period.
l. Wrote off a 2010 account of $2,400 after deciding that the amount would never be collected.
m. The estimated bad debt rate used by the company was 4 percent of credit sales net of returns.

Required:

1. Using the following categories, indicate the effect of each listed transaction, including the write-off of the uncollectible account and the adjusting entry for estimated bad debts (ignore cost of goods sold). Indicate the sign and amount of the effect or use "NE" to indicate "no effect." The first transaction is used as an example.

	Sales Revenue	Sales Discounts (taken)	Sales Returns and Allowances	Bad Debt Expense
(*a*)	+227,000	NE	NE	NE

2. Show how the accounts related to the preceding sale and collection activities should be reported on the 2012 income statement. (Treat sales discounts as a contra-revenue.)

Recording Bad Debts and Interpreting Disclosure of Allowance for Doubtful Accounts (P6-4)

AP6-2
LO4

Saucony, Inc.

Under various registered brand names, Saucony, Inc., and its subsidiaries develop, manufacture, and market bicycles and component parts, athletic apparel, and athletic shoes. It recently disclosed the following information concerning the allowance for doubtful accounts on its Form 10-K Annual Report submitted to the Securities and Exchange Commission.

Schedule II				
Valuation and Qualifying Accounts (dollars in thousands)				
Allowances for Doubtful Accounts	Balance at Beginning of Year	Additions Charged to Costs and Expenses	Deductions from Reserve	Balance at End of Year
Year 3	$1,108	$6,014	$5,941	(?)
Year 2	2,406	(?)	5,751	$1,108
Year 1	2,457	4,752	(?)	2,406

Required:

1. Record summary journal entries related to bad debts for year 3.
2. Supply the missing dollar amounts noted by (?) for year 1, year 2, and year 3.

Determining Bad Debt Expense Based on Aging Analysis (P6-5)

AP6-3
LO4

Briggs & Stratton Engines Inc. uses the aging approach to estimate bad debt expense at the end of each accounting year. Credit sales occur frequently on terms n/45. The balance of each account receivable is aged on the basis of four time periods as follows: (1) not yet due, (2) up to 6 months past due, (3) 6 to 12 months past due, and (4) more than one year past due. Experience has shown that for each age group, the average loss rate on the amount of the receivable at year-end due to uncollectability is (*a*) 1 percent, (*b*) 5 percent, (*c*) 20 percent, and (*d*) 50 percent, respectively.

At December 31, 2011 (end of the current accounting year), the Accounts Receivable balance was $39,500, and the Allowance for Doubtful Accounts balance was $1,550 (credit). In determining which accounts have been paid, the company applies collections to the oldest sales first. To simplify, only five customer accounts are used; the details of each on December 31, 2011, follow:

Date	Explanation	Debit	Credit	Balance
	R. Devens—Account Receivable			
3/13/2011	Sale	19,000		19,000
5/12/2011	Collection		10,000	9,000
9/30/2011	Collection		7,000	2,000
	C. Howard—Account Receivable			
11/01/2010	Sale	31,000		31,000
06/01/2011	Collection		20,000	11,000
12/01/2011	Collection		5,000	6,000
	D. McClain—Account Receivable			
10/31/2011	Sale	12,000		12,000
12/10/2011	Collection		8,000	4,000
	T. Skibinski—Account Receivable			
05/02/2011	Sale	15,000		15,000
06/01/2011	Sale	10,000		25,000
06/15/2011	Collection		15,000	10,000
07/15/2011	Collection		10,000	0
10/01/2011	Sale	26,000		26,000
11/15/2011	Collection		16,000	10,000
12/15/2011	Sale	4,500		14,500
	H. Wu—Account Receivable			
12/30/2011	Sale	13,000		13,000

Required:

1. Compute the total accounts receivable in each age category.
2. Compute the estimated uncollectible amount for each age category and in total.
3. Give the adjusting entry for bad debt expense at December 31, 2011.
4. Show how the amounts related to accounts receivable should be presented on the 2011 income statement and balance sheet.

AP6-4 LO2, 3, 4, 5 Preparing an Income Statement and Computing the Gross Profit Percentage and Receivables Turnover Ratio with Discounts, Returns, and Bad Debts (P6-6)

Perry Corporation is a local grocery store organized seven years ago as a corporation. At that time, a total of 10,000 shares of common stock were issued to the three organizers. The store is in an excellent location, and sales have increased each year. At the end of 2012, the bookkeeper prepared the following statement (assume that all amounts are correct; note the incorrect terminology and format):

PERRY CORPORATION
Profit and Loss
December 31, 2012

	Debit	Credit
Sales		$184,000
Cost of goods sold	$ 98,000	
Sales returns and allowances	9,000	
Selling expense	17,000	
Administrative and general expense	18,000	
Bad debt expense	2,000	
Sales discounts	8,000	
Income tax expense	10,900	
Net profit	21,100	
Totals	$184,000	$184,000

Required:

1. Beginning with the amount of net sales, prepare an income statement (showing both gross profit and income from operations). Treat sales discounts as a contra-revenue.
2. The beginning and ending balances in accounts receivable were $16,000 and $18,000, respectively. Compute the gross profit percentage and receivables turnover ratio and explain their meaning.

Computing Outstanding Checks and Deposits in Transit and Preparing a Bank Reconciliation and Journal Entries (P6-8)

AP6-5
LO6

The December 31, 2011, bank statement for Rivas Company and the December 2011 ledger accounts for cash follow.

BANK STATEMENT			
Date	**Checks**	**Deposits**	**Balance**
Dec. 1			$48,000
2	$400; 300	$17,000	64,300
4	7,000; 90		57,210
6	120; 180; 1,600		55,310
11	500; 1,200; 70	28,000	81,540
13	480; 700; 1,900		78,460
17	12,000; 8,000		58,460
23	60; 23,500	36,000	70,900
26	900; 2,650		67,350
28	2,200; 5,200		59,950
30	17,000; 1,890; 300*	19,000	59,760
31	1,650; 1,350; 150†	5,250‡	61,860

*NSF check, J. Left, a customer.
†Bank service charge.
‡Interest collected.

Cash (A)					
Dec. 1 Balance	64,100	Checks written during December:		
Deposits		60	5,000	2,650
Dec. 11	28,000	17,000	5,200	1,650
23	36,000	700	1,890	2,200
30	19,000	3,500	1,600	7,000
31	13,000	1,350	120	300
		180	90	480
		12,000	23,500	8,000
		70	500	1,900
		900	1,200	

The November 2011 bank reconciliation showed the following: correct cash balance at November 30, $64,100; deposits in transit on November 30, $17,000; and outstanding checks on November 30, $400 + $500 = $900.

Required:

1. Compute the deposits in transit December 31, 2011, by comparing the deposits on the bank statement to the deposits listed on the cash ledger account and the list of deposits in transit at the end of November.
2. Compute the outstanding checks at December 31, 2011, by comparing the checks listed on the bank statement with those on the cash ledger account and the list of outstanding checks at the end of November.
3. Prepare a bank reconciliation at December 31, 2011.
4. Give any journal entries that should be made as a result of the bank reconciliation made by the company. Why are they necessary?
5. What total amount of cash should be reported on the December 31, 2011, balance sheet?

CASES AND PROJECTS

Annual Report Cases

CP6-1
LO3, 4, 5, 6

AMERICAN EAGLE OUTFITTERS, INC.

Finding Financial Information

Refer to the financial statements of American Eagle Outfitters given in Appendix B at the end of this book.

Required:

1. What does the company include in its category of cash and cash equivalents? How close do you think the disclosed amount is to actual fair market value? (**Hint:** The notes may be helpful in answering this question.)
2. What expenses does American Eagle Outfitters subtract from net sales in the computation of gross profit? How does this differ from Deckers's practice and how might it affect the manner in which you interpret the gross profit percentage?
3. Compute American Eagle Outfitters's receivables turnover ratio for the current year. What characteristics of its business might cause it to be so high?
4. Does the company report an allowance for doubtful accounts on the balance sheet or in the notes? Explain why it does or does not. (**Hint:** Consider the makeup of its receivables.)

CP6-2
LO1, 3, 4, 6

URBAN OUTFITTERS INC.

Finding Financial Information

Refer to the financial statements of Urban Outfitters given in Appendix C at the end of this book.

Required:

1. How much cash and cash equivalents does the company report at the end of the current year?
2. What was the change in accounts receivable and how did it affect net cash provided by operating activities for the current year?
3. Compute the company's gross profit percentage for the most recent two years. Has it risen or fallen? Explain the meaning of the change.
4. Where does the company disclose its revenue recognition policy? When does the company record revenues for the "sale" of gift cards?

CP6-3
LO3, 6

AMERICAN EAGLE OUTFITTERS, INC.

URBAN OUTFITTERS INC.

excel
www.mhhe.com/libby7e

Comparing Companies within an Industry

Refer to the financial statements of American Eagle Outfitters (Appendix B) and Urban Outfitters (Appendix C) and the Industry Ratio Report (Appendix D) at the end of this book.

Required:

1. Compute the gross profit percentage for both companies for the current and previous years. What do these changes suggest?
2. Knowing that these two companies are specialty or niche retailers compared to some others in their industry (see the list of companies used in the Industry Ratio Report), do you expect their gross profit percentage to be higher or lower than the industry average? Why?
3. Compare the gross profit percentage for each company for the most recent reporting year to the industry average. Are these two companies doing better or worse than the industry average? Does this match your expectations from requirement (2)?

Financial Reporting and Analysis Cases

CP6-4
LO1

Making a Decision as a Manager: Choosing among Alternative Recognition Points

When companies involved in long-term construction projects can estimate the percentage of work completed and the total expected costs with reasonable accuracy, GAAP allows them to recognize revenues based on the incurred contract costs to date divided by the estimated total contract costs. This is called the **percentage of completion method.** When total costs cannot be accurately estimated, the companies must wait until the contract is completed to recognize all contract revenue in the period of completion. These revenue recognition points correspond to continuous recognition and the end of the earnings process.

Required:

1. Assume that a construction company works on a single construction project at a time and that each project takes three years to complete. Do you think that the choice between the two revenue recognition policies would materially affect the reported earnings? Why or why not?
2. Given your answers to requirement (1), under what conditions would that answer change?
3. Which revenue recognition rule for financial reporting purposes would you prefer as a manager? Why?

Critical Thinking Cases

CP6-5
LO1

Symbol Technologies, Inc.

Evaluating an Ethical Dilemma: Management Incentives, Revenue Recognition, and Sales with the Right of Return

Symbol Technologies, Inc., was a fast-growing maker of bar-code scanners. According to the federal charges, Tomo Razmilovic, the CEO at Symbol, was obsessed with meeting the stock market's expectation for continued growth. His executive team responded by improperly recording revenue and allowances for returns, as well as a variety of other tricks, to overstate revenues by $230 million and pretax earnings by $530 million. What makes this fraud nearly unique is that virtually the whole senior management team is charged with participating in the six-year fraud. At the time this case is being written, five have pleaded guilty, another eight are under indictment, and the former CEO has fled the country to avoid prosecution. The exact nature of the fraud is described in the following excerpt dealing with the guilty plea by the former vice president for finance:

Ex-Official at Symbol Pleads Guilty

By Kara Scannell
26 March 2003
The Wall Street Journal
(Copyright © 2003, Dow Jones & Company, Inc.)

A former finance executive at Symbol Technologies Inc. pleaded guilty to participating in a vast accounting fraud that inflated revenue at the maker of bar-code scanners by roughly 10%, or $100 million a year, from 1999 through 2001.

. . .

The criminal information and civil complaint filed yesterday accused Mr. Asti and other high-level executives of stuffing the firm's distribution channel with phony orders at the end of each quarter to meet revenue and earnings targets. Under generally accepted accounting practices, revenue can be booked only when the products are shipped to a customer. Symbol's customers include delivery services and grocery stores.

Investigators alleged that Mr. Asti and others engaged in "candy" deals, where Symbol bribed resellers with a 1% fee to "buy" products from a distributor at the end of a quarter, which Symbol would later buy back. Symbol then allegedly would convince the distributor to order more products from the company to satisfy the newly created inventory void.

The SEC said the inflated revenue figures helped boost Symbol's stock price, as well as enriching Mr. Asti. He allegedly sold thousands of shares of Symbol stock, which he received from exercising stock options, when the stock was trading at inflated levels.

Required:

1. What facts, if any, presented in the article suggest that Symbol violated the revenue principle?
2. Assuming that Symbol did recognize revenue when goods were shipped, how could it have properly accounted for the fact that customers had a right to cancel the contracts (make an analogy with accounting for bad debts)?
3. What do you think may have motivated management to falsify the statements? Why was management concerned with reporting continued growth in net income?
4. Explain who was hurt by management's unethical conduct.
5. Assume that you are the auditor for other firms. After reading about the fraud, what types of transactions would you pay special attention to in the audit of your clients in this industry? What ratio might provide warnings about possible channel stuffing?

CP6-6 LO6

Evaluating Internal Control

Cripple Creek Company has one trusted employee who, as the owner said, "handles all of the bookkeeping and paperwork for the company." This employee is responsible for counting, verifying, and recording cash receipts and payments, making the weekly bank deposit, preparing checks for major expenditures (signed by the owner), making small expenditures from the cash register for daily expenses, and collecting accounts receivable. The owners asked the local bank for a $20,000 loan. The bank asked that an audit be performed covering the year just ended. The independent auditor (a local CPA), in a private conference with the owner, presented some evidence of the following activities of the trusted employee during the past year.

a. Cash sales sometimes were not entered in the cash register, and the trusted employee pocketed approximately $50 per month.
b. Cash taken from the cash register (and pocketed by the trusted employee) was replaced with expense memos with fictitious signatures (approximately $12 per day).
c. A $300 collection on an account receivable of a valued out-of-town customer was pocketed by the trusted employee and was covered by making a $300 entry as a debit to Sales Returns and a credit to Accounts Receivable.
d. An $800 collection on an account receivable from a local customer was pocketed by the trusted employee and was covered by making an $800 entry as a debit to Allowance for Doubtful Accounts and a credit to Accounts Receivable.

Required:

1. What was the approximate amount stolen during the past year?
2. What would be your recommendations to the owner?

Financial Reporting and Analysis Team Project

CP6-7 LO4

Team Project: Analyzing Revenues and Receivables

As a team, select an industry to analyze. *Reuters* provides lists of industries under Sectors and Industries at www.reuters.com. (Click on an industry and then select Company Rankings for a list of members of that industry.) Each team member should acquire the annual report or 10-K for one publicly traded company in the industry, with each member selecting a different company. (Library files, the SEC EDGAR service at www.sec.gov, or the company itself are good sources.)

Required:

On an individual basis, each team member should write a short report answering the following questions about the selected company. Discuss any patterns across the companies that you as a team observe. Then, as a team, write a short report comparing and contrasting your companies.

1. If your company lists receivables in its balance sheet, what percentage is it of total assets for each of the last three years? If your company does not list receivables, discuss why this is so.
2. Ratio analysis
   a. What does the receivables turnover ratio measure in general?
   b. If your company lists receivables, compute the ratio for the last three years.

   c. What do your results suggest about the company?
   d. If available, find the industry ratio for the most recent year, compare it to your results, and discuss why you believe your company differs or is similar to the industry ratio.
3. If your company lists receivables, use the 10-K to determine what additional disclosure is available concerning the allowance for doubtful accounts. (Usually the information is in a separate schedule, Item 15.)
   a. What is bad debt expense as a percentage of sales for the last three years?
4. What is the effect of the change in receivables on cash flows from operating activities for the most recent year (that is, did the change increase or decrease operating cash flows)? Explain your answer.

LEARNING OBJECTIVES

After studying this chapter, you should be able to:

Lecture Presentation LP-7
www.mhhe.com/libby7e

1. Apply the cost principle to identify the amounts that should be included in inventory and the matching principle to determine cost of goods sold for typical retailers, wholesalers, and manufacturers. p. 333
2. Report inventory and cost of goods sold using the four inventory costing methods. p. 338
3. Decide when the use of different inventory costing methods is beneficial to a company. p. 343
4. Report inventory at the lower of cost or market (LCM). p. 346
5. Evaluate inventory management using the inventory turnover ratio and analyze the effects of inventory on cash flows. p. 347
6. Compare companies that use different inventory costing methods. p. 350
7. Understand methods for controlling and keeping track of inventory and analyze the effects of inventory errors on financial statements. p. 353

REPORTING AND INTERPRETING COST OF GOODS SOLD AND INVENTORY

The Harley-Davidson eagle trademark was once known best as a popular request in tattoo parlors. Now, Harley-Davidson dominates the heavyweight motorcycle market in North America with a 46.3 percent market share. Harley is also the market leader in Canada, Japan, and Australia and is a growing presence in Europe. However, the worldwide economic downturn has reduced Harley's sales and profit. Harley shipped 7.1 percent fewer units in 2008 than 2007 and expects to ship 25 to 30 percent fewer units in 2009. To close the gap between supply and demand for its products, Harley-Davidson is implementing a plan to restructure its production facilities in Wisconsin, Missouri, and Pennsylvania to reduce production capacity and reduce inventories in anticipation of lower future sales. Harley must cut costs to maintain its gross margin and net profit margin while also ensuring that it has the resources to take advantage of the economic recovery when it arrives.

FOCUS COMPANY:

Harley-Davidson, Inc.

BUILDING A LEGEND INTO A WORLD-CLASS MANUFACTURER

www.harley-davidson.com

However, cutting costs is only part of Harley's strategy. It is also introducing new and improved products to stay ahead of major competitors Honda, Yamaha, and BMW. In addition, it is focusing on controlling inventory quality and cost to maintain gross profit margin. Finally, selection of appropriate accounting methods for inventory can have a dramatic effect on the amount Harley-Davidson pays in income taxes. Continuous improvement in product development, manufacturing, inventory management, and information system design will be necessary for the Harley-Davidson eagle to survive the economic downturn and continue its rise.

UNDERSTANDING THE BUSINESS

Concerns about the cost and quality of inventory face all modern manufacturers and merchandisers and turn our attention to **cost of goods sold** (cost of sales, cost of products sold) on the income statement and **inventory** on the balance sheet. Exhibit 7.1 presents the relevant excerpts from Harley-Davidson's financial statements that include these accounts. Note that Cost of Goods Sold is subtracted from Net Sales to produce Gross Profit on its

EXHIBIT 7.1

Income Statement and Balance Sheet Excerpts

HARLEY-DAVIDSON, INC.

REAL WORLD EXCERPT

Annual Report

HARLEY-DAVIDSON, INC.
Consolidated Statements of Income
(dollars in thousands, except per share amounts)

Years Ended December 31,	2008	2007	2006
Net sales	$5,594,307	$5,726,848	$5,800,686
Cost of goods sold	3,663,488	3,612,748	3,567,839
Gross profit	1,930,819	2,114,100	2,232,847

HARLEY-DAVIDSON, INC.
Consolidated Balance Sheets
(dollars in thousands, except share amounts)

December 31,	2008	2007
Assets		
Current Assets		
Cash and cash equivalents	$ 593,558	$ 402,854
Marketable securities	—	2,475
Accounts receivable, net	296,258	181,217
Finance receivables, net	3,822,426	2,356,563
Inventories	400,908	349,697
Deferred income taxes	123,327	103,278
Prepaid expenses	141,404	71,230
Total current assets	5,377,881	3,467,314

income statement. On the balance sheet, Inventory is a current asset; it is reported below Cash, Marketable Securities, and Accounts and Finance Receivables because it is less liquid than those assets.

The primary goals of inventory management are to have sufficient quantities of high-quality inventory available to serve customers' needs while minimizing the costs of carrying inventory (production, storage, obsolescence, and financing). Low quality leads to customer dissatisfaction, returns, and a decline in future sales. Also, purchasing or producing too few units of a hot-selling item causes stock-outs that mean lost sales revenue and decreases in customer satisfaction. Conversely, purchasing too many units of a slow-selling item increases storage costs as well as interest costs on short-term borrowings that finance the purchases. It may even lead to losses if the merchandise cannot be sold at normal prices.

The accounting system plays three roles in the inventory management process. First, the system must provide accurate information for preparation of periodic financial statements and tax returns. Second, it must provide up-to-date information on inventory quantities and costs to facilitate ordering and manufacturing decisions. Third, since inventories are subject to theft and other forms of misuse, the system must also provide the information needed to help protect these important assets.

Harley's mix of product lines makes it a particularly good example for this chapter. Although best known as a **manufacturer** of motorcycles, Harley also purchases and resells completed products such as its popular line of Motorclothes apparel. In the second case, it acts as a **wholesaler.** Both the motorcycle and Motorclothes product lines are sold to their network of independent dealers. From an accounting standpoint, these independent dealers are Harley-Davidson's customers. The independent dealers are the **retailers** who sell the products to the public.

We begin this chapter with a discussion of the makeup of inventory, the important choices management must make in the financial and tax reporting process, and how these choices affect the financial statements and taxes paid. Then we discuss how managers and analysts evaluate the efficiency of inventory management. Finally, we briefly discuss how accounting systems are organized to keep track of inventory quantities and costs for decision making and control. This topic will be the principal subject matter of your managerial accounting course.

ORGANIZATION of the Chapter

- **Nature of Inventory and Cost of Goods Sold**
  - Items Included in Inventory
  - Costs Included in Inventory Purchases
  - Flow of Inventory Costs
  - Nature of Costs of Goods Sold
- **Inventory Costing Methods**
  - Specific Identification Method
  - Cost Flow Assumptions (FIFO, LIFO, Average Cost)
  - Financial Statement Effects of Inventory Methods
  - Managers' Choice of Inventory Methods
- **Valuation at Lower of Cost or Market**
- **Evaluating Inventory Management**
  - Measuring Efficiency in Inventory Management
  - Inventory Turnover Ratio
  - Inventory and Cash Flows
  - Inventory Methods and Financial Statement Analysis
- **Control of Inventory**
  - Internal Control of Inventory
  - Perpetual and Periodic Inventory Systems
  - Errors in Measuring Ending Inventory

NATURE OF INVENTORY AND COST OF GOODS SOLD

Items Included in Inventory

Inventory is tangible property that is (1) held for sale in the normal course of business or (2) used to produce goods or services for sale. Inventory is reported on the balance sheet as a current asset because it normally is used or converted into cash within one year or the next operating cycle. The types of inventory normally held depend on the characteristics of the business.

Merchandisers (wholesale or retail businesses) hold the following:

Merchandise inventory Goods (or merchandise) held for resale in the normal course of business. The goods usually are acquired in a finished condition and are ready for sale without further processing.

LEARNING OBJECTIVE 1

Apply the cost principle to identify the amounts that should be included in inventory and the matching principle to determine cost of goods sold for typical retailers, wholesalers, and manufacturers.

INVENTORY is tangible property held for sale in the normal course of business or used in producing goods or services for sale.

MERCHANDISE INVENTORY includes goods held for resale in the ordinary course of business.

RAW MATERIALS INVENTORY includes items acquired for the purpose of processing into finished goods.

WORK IN PROCESS INVENTORY includes goods in the process of being manufactured.

FINISHED GOODS INVENTORY includes manufactured goods that are complete and ready for sale.

For Harley-Davidson, merchandise inventory includes the Motorclothes line and the parts and accessories it purchases for sale to its independent dealers.

Manufacturing businesses hold three types of inventory:

Raw materials inventory Items acquired for processing into finished goods. These items are included in raw materials inventory until they are used, at which point they become part of work in process inventory.

Work in process inventory Goods in the process of being manufactured but not yet complete. When completed, work in process inventory becomes finished goods inventory.

Finished goods inventory Manufactured goods that are complete and ready for sale.

Inventories related to Harley-Davidson's motorcycle manufacturing operations are recorded in these accounts.

Harley-Davidson's recent inventory note reports the following:

HARLEY-DAVIDSON, INC.

REAL WORLD EXCERPT

Annual Report

HARLEY-DAVIDSON, INC.
Notes to Consolidated Financial Statements

2. ADDITIONAL BALANCE SHEET AND CASH FLOWS INFORMATION
(dollars in thousands)

	December 31,	
	2008	**2007**
Inventories:		
Components at the lower of FIFO cost or market:		
Raw materials and work in process	$151,896	$149,954
Motorcycle finished goods	185,464	107,768
Parts and accessories and general merchandise	103,682	124,109

Note that Harley-Davidson combines the raw materials and work in process into one number. Other companies separate the two components. The parts and accessories and general merchandise category includes purchased parts and Motorclothes and other accessories that make up merchandise inventory.[1]

Costs Included in Inventory Purchases

Goods in inventory are initially recorded at cost. Inventory cost includes the sum of the costs incurred in bringing an article to usable or salable condition and location. When Harley-Davidson purchases raw materials and merchandise inventory, the amount recorded should include the invoice price to be paid plus other expenditures related to the purchase, such as freight charges to deliver the items to its warehouses (freight-in) and inspection and preparation costs. In general, the company should cease accumulating purchase costs when the raw materials are **ready for use** or when the merchandise inventory is **ready for shipment.** Any additional costs related to selling the inventory to the dealers, such as marketing department salaries and dealer training sessions, are incurred after the inventory is ready for use. So they should be included in selling, general, and administrative expenses in the period in which they are incurred.

[1]These do not add up to the balance reported in Exhibit 7.1 because they do not include the LIFO adjustment discussed later.

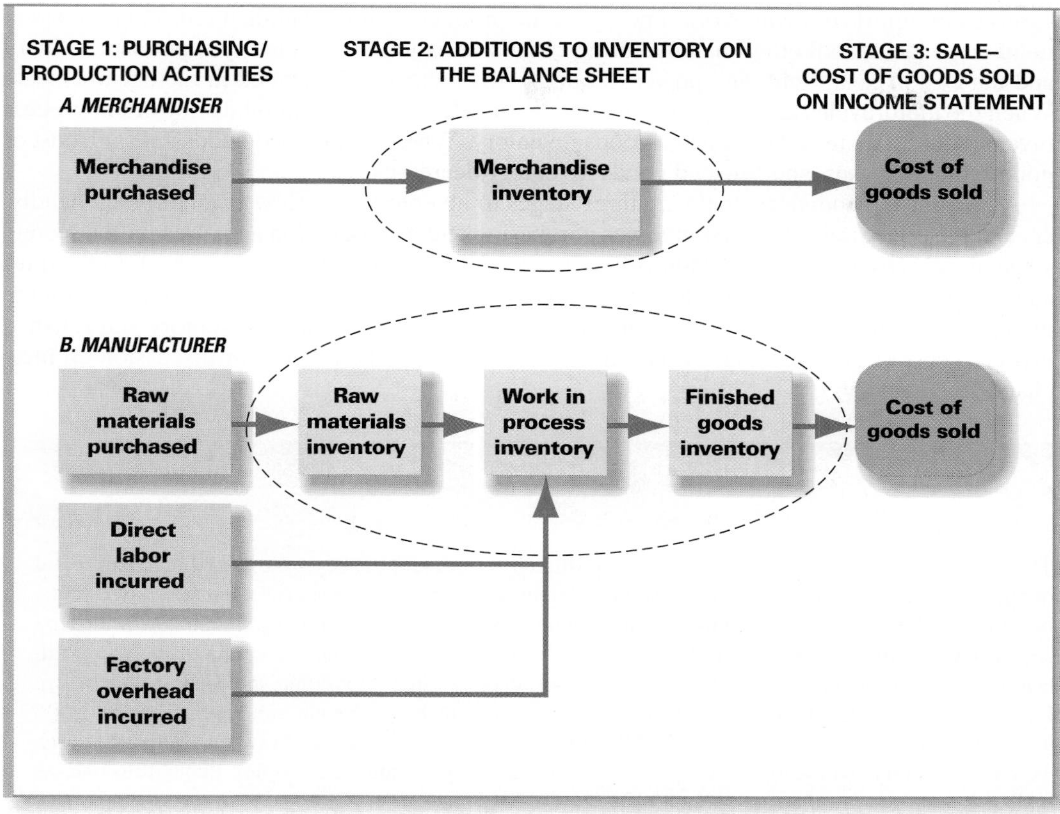

EXHIBIT 7.2

Flow of Inventory Costs

Applying the Materiality Constraint in Practice

FINANCIAL ANALYSIS

Incidental costs such as inspection and preparation costs often are not material in amount (see the discussion of the materiality constraint in Chapter 5) and do not have to be assigned to the inventory cost. Thus, for practical reasons, many companies use the invoice price, less returns and discounts, to assign a unit cost to raw materials or merchandise and record other indirect expenditures as a separate cost that is reported as an expense.

Flow of Inventory Costs

The flow of inventory costs for merchandisers (wholesalers and retailers) is relatively simple, as Exhibit 7.2A shows. When merchandise is purchased, the merchandise inventory account is increased. When the goods are sold, cost of goods sold is increased and merchandise inventory is decreased.

The flow of inventory costs in a manufacturing environment is more complex, as diagrammed in Exhibit 7.2B. First, **raw materials** (also called **direct materials**) must be purchased. For Harley-Davidson, these raw materials include steel and aluminum castings, forgings, sheet, and bars, as well as certain motorcycle component parts produced by its small network of suppliers, including carburetors, batteries, and tires. When they are used, the cost of these materials is removed from the raw materials inventory and added to the work in process inventory.

DIRECT LABOR refers to the earnings of employees who work directly on the products being manufactured.

Two other components of manufacturing cost, direct labor and factory overhead, are also added to the work in process inventory when they are used. **Direct labor** cost represents the

FACTORY OVERHEAD are manufacturing costs that are not raw material or direct labor costs.

earnings of employees who work directly on the products being manufactured. **Factory overhead** costs include all other manufacturing costs. For example, the factory supervisor's salary and the cost of heat, light, and power to operate the factory are included in factory overhead. When the motorcycles are completed and ready for sale, the related amounts in work in process inventory are transferred to finished goods inventory. When the finished goods are sold, cost of goods sold increases, and finished goods inventory decreases.

As Exhibit 7.2 indicates, there are three stages to inventory cost flows for both merchandisers and manufacturers. The first involves purchasing and/or production activities. In the second stage, these activities result in additions to inventory accounts on the balance sheet. In the third stage, the inventory items are sold and the amounts become cost of goods sold expense on the income statement. Since the flow of inventory costs from merchandise inventory and finished goods to cost of goods sold are very similar, we will focus the rest of our discussion on merchandise inventory.

FINANCIAL ANALYSIS | Managing Inventory During an Economic Downturn

The flows of inventory costs diagrammed in Exhibit 7.2 represent the keys to manufacturing cost and quality control. Since the company must pay to finance and store raw materials and purchased parts, minimizing the size of these inventories in keeping with projected manufacturing demand is the first key to the process. Even though Harley's sales have declined less than its competitors, the tough economic environment has forced the company to reduce production volume and each of the costs in Exhibit 7.2. To reduce direct labor, Harley plans to reduce its hourly production work force by 2,100 hourly positions. To reduce direct materials, it has lowered its purchases of raw materials and parts. To reduce factory overhead, it has consolidated its two engine and transmission plants into one, as well as its two paint and frame operations into a single plant.

Harley-Davidson's management accounting system is designed to monitor the success of these changes and promote continuous improvements in manufacturing. The design of such systems is the subject matter of management accounting and cost accounting courses.

Nature of Cost of Goods Sold

Cost of goods sold (CGS) expense is directly related to sales revenue. Sales revenue during an accounting period is the number of units sold multiplied by the sales price. Cost of goods sold is the same number of units multiplied by their unit costs.

GOODS AVAILABLE FOR SALE refers to the sum of beginning inventory and purchases (or transfers to finished goods) for the period.

COST OF GOODS SOLD EQUATION: BI + P − EI = CGS

Let's examine the relationship between cost of goods sold on the income statement and inventory on the balance sheet. Harley-Davidson starts each accounting period with a stock of inventory called **beginning inventory** (BI). During the accounting period, new **purchases** (P) are added to inventory. The sum of the two amounts is the **goods available for sale** during that period. What remains unsold at the end of the period becomes **ending inventory** (EI) on the balance sheet. The portion of goods available for sale that is sold becomes **cost of goods sold** on the income statement. The ending inventory for one accounting period then becomes the beginning inventory for the next period. The relationships between these various inventory amounts are brought together in the **cost of goods sold equation.**

To illustrate, assume that Harley-Davidson began the period with $40,000 worth of Motorclothes in beginning inventory, purchased additional merchandise during the period for $55,000, and had $35,000 left in inventory at the end of the period. These amounts are combined as follows to compute cost of goods sold of $60,000:

Beginning inventory	$40,000
+ Purchases of merchandise during the year	55,000
Goods available for sale	95,000
− Ending inventory	35,000
Cost of goods sold	$60,000

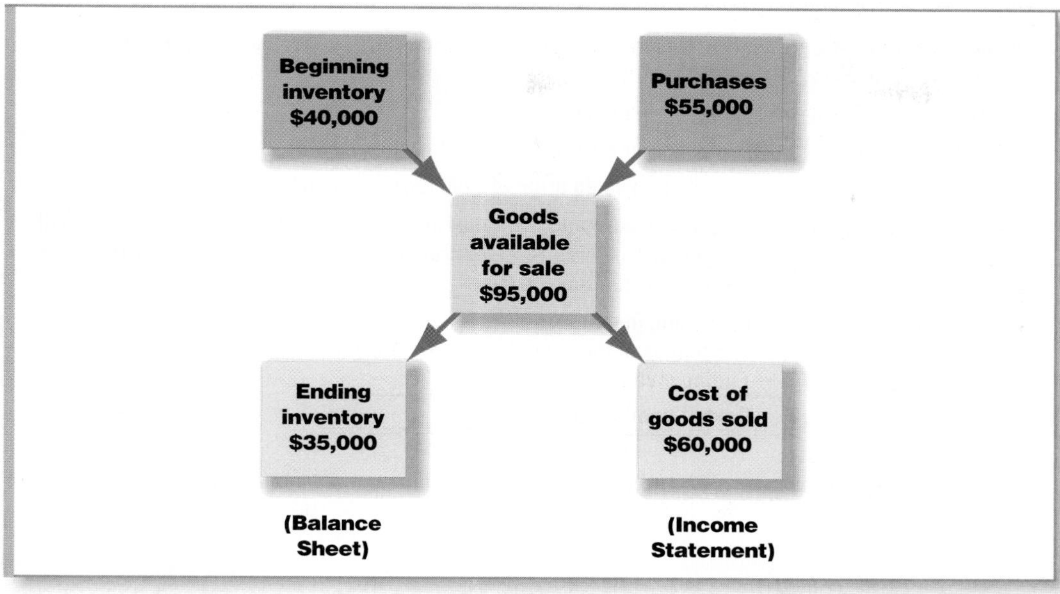

EXHIBIT 7.3

Cost of Goods Sold for Merchandise Inventory

	Beginning inventory
+	Purchases of merchandise during the year
	Goods available for sale
−	Ending inventory
	Cost of goods sold

These same relationships are illustrated in Exhibit 7.3 and can be represented in the merchandise inventory T-account as follows:

Merchandise Inventory (A)			
Beginning inventory	40,000		
Add: Purchases of inventory	55,000	Deduct: Cost of goods sold	60,000
Ending inventory	35,000		

If three of these four values are known, either the cost of goods sold equation or the inventory T-account can be used to solve for the fourth value.

PAUSE FOR **FEEDBACK**

Inventory should include all items owned that are held for resale. Costs flow into inventory when goods are purchased or manufactured. They flow out (as an expense) when they are sold or disposed of. The cost of goods sold equation describes these flows.

SELF-STUDY **QUIZ**

1. Assume the following facts for Harley-Davidson's Motorclothes leather baseball jacket product line for the year 2010.

Beginning inventory:	400 units at unit cost of $75.
Purchases:	600 units at unit cost of $75.
Sales:	700 units at a sales price of $100 (cost per unit $75).

Using the cost of goods sold equation, compute the dollar amount of **goods available for sale, ending inventory,** and **cost of goods sold** of leather baseball jackets for the period.

	Beginning inventory
+	Purchases of merchandise during the year
	Goods available for sale
−	Ending inventory
	Cost of goods sold

(continued)

2. Assume the following facts for Harley-Davidson's Motorclothes leather baseball jacket product line for the year 2011.

Beginning inventory:	300 units at unit cost of $75.
Ending inventory:	600 units at unit cost of $75.
Sales:	1,100 units at a sales price of $100 (cost per unit $75).

Using the cost of goods sold equation, compute the dollar amount of **purchases** of leather baseball jackets for the period. Remember that if three of these four values are known, the cost of goods sold equation can be used to solve for the fourth value.

Beginning inventory
\+ Purchases of merchandise during the year
− Ending inventory
Cost of goods sold

After you have completed your answers, check them with the solutions at the bottom of this page.

INVENTORY COSTING METHODS

LEARNING OBJECTIVE 2

Report inventory and cost of goods sold using the four inventory costing methods.

Video 7-1
www.mhhe.com/libby7e

In the Motorclothes example presented in the Self-Study Quiz, the cost of all units of the leather baseball jackets was the same—$75. If inventory costs normally did not change, this would be the end of our discussion. As we are all aware, however, the prices of most goods do change. In recent years, the costs of many manufactured items such as automobiles and motorcycles have risen gradually. In some industries such as computers, costs of production have dropped dramatically along with retail prices.

When inventory costs have changed, which inventory items are treated as sold or remaining in inventory can turn profits into losses and cause companies to pay or save millions in taxes. A simple example will illustrate these dramatic effects. Do not let the simplicity of our example mislead you. It applies broadly to actual company practices.

Assume that a Harley-Davidson dealer made the following purchases:

Jan. 1	Had beginning inventory of two units of a Model A leather jacket at $70 each.
March 12	Purchased four units of Model A leather jacket at $80 each.
June 9	Purchased one unit of Model A leather jacket at $100 each.
Nov. 5	Sold four units for $120 each.

Note that the **cost of the leather jacket rose** rapidly between January and June! On November 5, four units are sold for $120 each and revenues of $480 are recorded. What amount is recorded

Solutions to SELF-STUDY QUIZ

1. Beginning inventory (400 × $75)	$30,000
\+ Purchases of merchandise during the year (600 × $75)	45,000
Goods available for sale (1,000 × $75)	75,000
− Ending inventory (300 × $75)	22,500
Cost of goods sold (700 × $75)	$52,500

2. BI = 300 × $75 = $22,500 BI + P − EI = CGS
EI = 600 × $75 = $45,000 22,500 + P − 45,000 = 82,500
CGS = 1,100 × $75 = $82,500 P = 105,000

as cost of goods sold? The answer depends on which specific goods we assume are sold. Four generally accepted inventory costing methods are available for determining cost of goods sold:

1. Specific identification.
2. First-in, first-out (FIFO).
3. Last-in, first-out (LIFO).
4. Average cost.

The four inventory costing methods are alternative ways to assign the total dollar amount of goods available for sale between (1) ending inventory and (2) cost of goods sold. The first method identifies individual items that remain in inventory or are sold. The remaining three methods assume that the inventory costs follow a certain flow.

Specific Identification Method

When the **specific identification method** is used, the cost of each item sold is individually identified and recorded as cost of goods sold. This method requires keeping track of the purchase cost of each item. In the leather jacket example, any four of the items could have been sold. If we assume that one of the $70 items, two of the $80 items, and the one $100 item have been sold, the cost of those items ($70 + $80 + $80 + $100) would become cost of goods sold ($330). The cost of the remaining items would be ending inventory.

The specific identification method is impractical when large quantities of similar items are stocked. On the other hand, when dealing with expensive unique items such as houses or fine jewelry, this method is appropriate. As a consequence, most inventory items are accounted for using one of three cost flow assumptions.

The SPECIFIC IDENTIFICATION METHOD identifies the cost of the specific item that was sold.

Cost Flow Assumptions

The **choice of an inventory costing method is NOT based on the physical flow of goods** on and off the shelves. That is why they are called **cost flow assumptions.** A useful tool for representing inventory cost flow assumptions is a bin, or container. Try visualizing these inventory costing methods as flows of inventory in and out of the bin. **Following practice, we will apply the methods as if all purchases during the period take place before any sales and cost of goods sold are recorded.**

First-In, First-Out Method

The **first-in, first-out method,** frequently called **FIFO,** assumes that the earliest goods purchased (the first ones in) are the first goods sold, and the last goods purchased are left in ending inventory. Under FIFO, cost of goods sold and ending inventory are computed as if the flows in and out of the FIFO inventory bin in Exhibit 7.4A had taken place. First, each purchase is treated as if it were deposited in the bin from the top in sequence (two units of beginning inventory at $70 followed by purchases of four units at $80 and one unit at $100) producing goods available for sale of $560. Each good sold is then removed from the *bottom* in sequence (two units at $70 and two at $80); **first in is first out.** These goods totaling $300 become cost of goods sold (CGS). The remaining units (two units at $80 and one unit at $100 = $260) become ending inventory. FIFO allocates the **oldest** unit costs **to cost of goods sold** and the **newest** unit costs **to ending inventory.**

The FIRST-IN, FIRST-OUT (FIFO) METHOD assumes that the first goods purchased (the first in) are the first goods sold (the first out).

Cost of Goods Sold Calculation (FIFO)

Beginning inventory	(2 units at $70 each)	$140
+ Purchases	(4 units at $80 each)	320
	(1 unit at $100 each)	100
Goods available for sale		560
− Ending inventory	(2 units at $80 each and 1 unit at $100 each)	260
Cost of goods sold	(2 units at $70 and 2 units at $80 each)	$300

EXHIBIT 7.4

FIFO and LIFO Inventory Flows

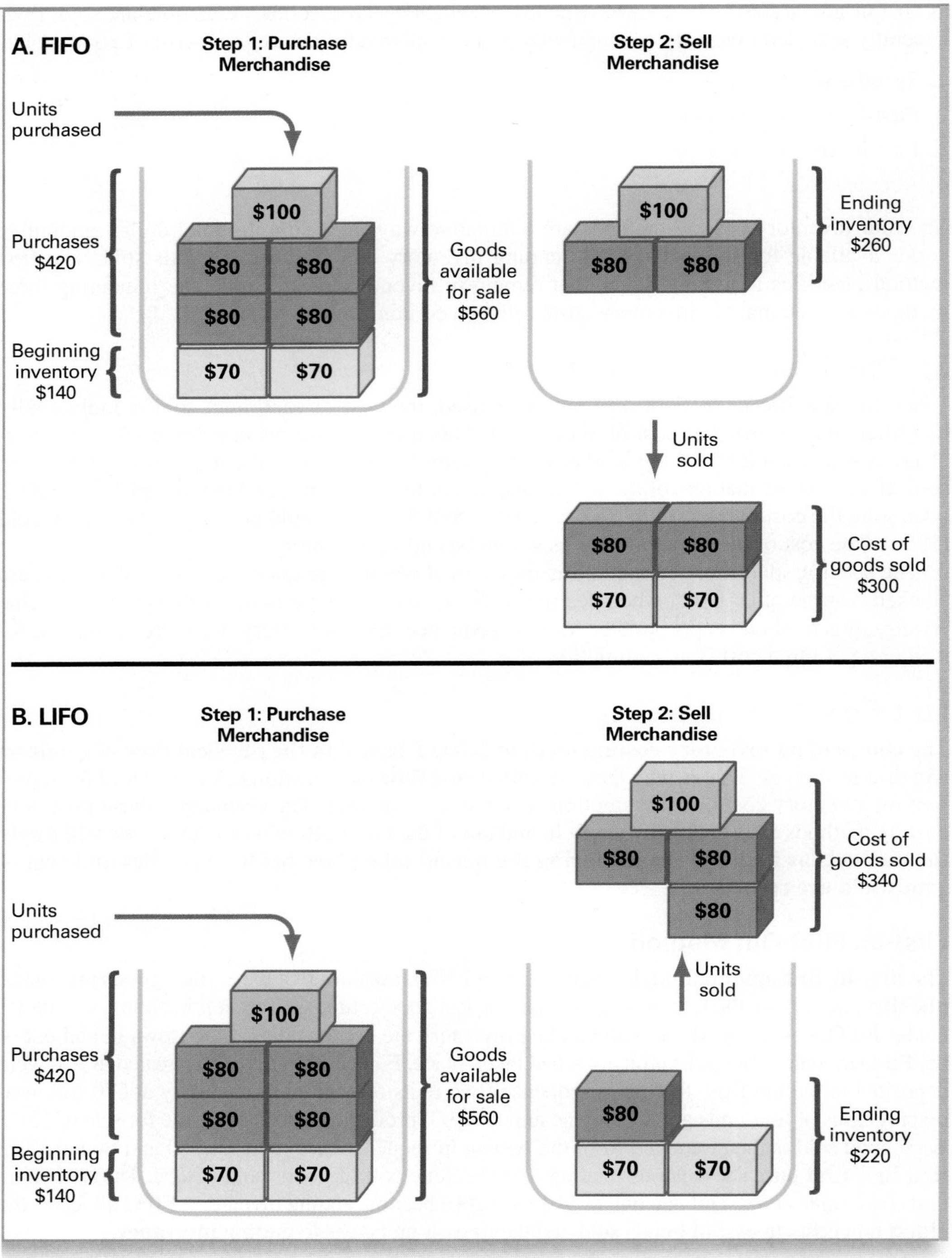

Last-In, First-Out Method

The LAST-IN, FIRST-OUT (LIFO) METHOD assumes that the most recently purchased units (the last in) are sold first (the first out).

The **last-in, first-out method,** often called **LIFO,** assumes that the most recently purchased goods (the last ones in) are sold first and the oldest units are left in ending inventory. It is illustrated by the LIFO inventory bin in Exhibit 7.4B. As in FIFO, each purchase is treated as if it were deposited in the bin from the top (two units of beginning inventory at $70 followed by purchases of four units at $80 and one unit at $100) resulting in the goods available for sale of $560.

Unlike FIFO, however, each good sold is treated as if it were removed from the *top* in sequence (one unit at $100 followed by three units at $80). These goods totaling $340 become cost of goods sold (CGS). The remaining units (one at $80 and two at $70 = $220) become ending inventory. LIFO allocates the **newest** unit costs **to cost of goods sold** and the **oldest** unit costs **to ending inventory.**

Cost of Goods Sold Calculation (LIFO)		
Beginning inventory	(2 units at $70 each)	$140
+ Purchases	(4 units at $80 each)	320
	(1 unit at $100 each)	100
Goods available for sale		560
− Ending inventory	(2 units at $70 each and 1 unit at $80 each)	220
Cost of goods sold	(3 units at $80 and 1 unit at $100 each)	$340

The LIFO cost flow assumption is the exact opposite of the FIFO cost flow assumption:

	FIFO	LIFO
Cost of goods sold on income statement	Oldest unit costs	Newest unit costs
Inventory on balance sheet	Newest unit costs	Oldest unit costs

Average Cost Method

The **average cost method** (weighted average cost method) uses the weighted average unit cost of the goods available for sale for both cost of goods sold and ending inventory. The weighted average unit cost of the goods available for sale is computed as follows.

The AVERAGE COST METHOD uses the weighted average unit cost of the goods available for sale for both cost of goods sold and ending inventory.

Number of Units	×	Unit Cost	=	Total Cost
2	×	$ 70	=	$140
4	×	$ 80	=	320
1	×	$100	=	100
7				$560

$$\text{Average cost} = \frac{\text{Cost of Goods Available for Sale}}{\text{Number of Units Available for Sale}}$$

$$\text{Average Cost} = \frac{\$560}{\text{7 Units}} = \$80 \text{ per Unit}$$

Cost of goods sold and ending inventory are assigned the same weighted average cost per unit of $80.

Cost of Goods Sold Calculation (Average Cost)		
Beginning inventory	(2 units at $70 each)	$140
+ Purchases	(4 units at $80 each)	320
	(1 unit at $100 each)	100
Goods available for sale	(7 units at $80 average cost each)	560
− Ending inventory	(3 units at $80 average cost each)	240
Cost of goods sold	(4 units at $80 average cost each)	$320

EXHIBIT 7.5

Financial Statement Effects of Inventory Costing Methods

	FIFO		LIFO		Average Cost	
Effect on the Income Statement						
Sales		$480		$480		$480
Cost of Goods Sold:						
Beginning inventory	$140		$140		$140	
Add: Purchases	420		420		420	
Goods available for sale	560		560		560	
Subtract: Ending inventory (to balance sheet)	260		220		240	
Cost of goods sold		300		340		320
Gross profit		180		140		160
Other expenses		80		80		80
Income before income taxes		100		60		80
Income tax expense (25%)		25		15		20
Net income		$ 75		$ 45		$ 60
Effect on the Balance Sheet						
Inventory		$260		$220		$240

INTERNATIONAL PERSPECTIVE

LIFO and International Comparisons

While U.S. GAAP allows companies to choose between FIFO, LIFO, and average cost inventory accounting methods, International Financial Reporting Standards (IFRS) currently prohibit the use of LIFO. U.S. GAAP also allows different inventory accounting methods to be used for different types of inventory items and even for the same item in different locations. IFRS requires that the same method be used for all inventory items that have a similar nature and use. These differences can create comparability problems when one attempts to compare companies across international borders. For example, General Motors and Ford use LIFO to value U.S. inventories and average cost or FIFO for non–U.S. inventories, while Honda (of Japan) uses FIFO for all inventories. Each individual country's tax laws determine the acceptability of different inventory methods for tax purposes.

Financial Statement Effects of Inventory Methods

Each of the four alternative inventory costing methods is in conformity with GAAP and the tax law. To understand why managers choose different methods in different circumstances, we must first understand their effects on the income statement and balance sheet. Exhibit 7.5 summarizes the financial statement effects of FIFO, LIFO, and weighted average methods in our example. Remember that the methods differ only in the dollar amount of goods available for sale allocated to cost of goods sold versus ending inventory. For that reason, the method that gives the highest ending inventory amount also gives the lowest cost of goods sold and the highest gross profit, income tax expense, and income amounts, and vice versa. The weighted average cost method generally gives income and inventory amounts that are between the FIFO and LIFO extremes.

In our example, recall that unit costs were increasing. **When unit costs are rising, LIFO produces lower income and a lower inventory valuation than FIFO.** Even in inflationary times, some companies' costs decline. **When unit costs are declining, LIFO produces**

higher income and higher inventory valuation than FIFO. These effects, which hold as long as inventory quantities are constant or rising,[2] are summarized in the following table:

Increasing Costs: Normal Financial Statement Effects

	FIFO	LIFO
Cost of goods sold on income statement	Lower	Higher
Net income	Higher	Lower
Income taxes	Higher	Lower
Inventory on balance sheet	Higher	Lower

Decreasing Costs: Normal Financial Statement Effects

	FIFO	LIFO
Cost of goods sold on income statement	Higher	Lower
Net income	Lower	Higher
Income taxes	Lower	Higher
Inventory on balance sheet	Lower	Higher

Managers' Choice of Inventory Methods

LEARNING OBJECTIVE 3

Decide when the use of different inventory costing methods is beneficial to a company.

What motivates companies to choose different inventory costing methods? Most managers choose accounting methods based on two factors:

1. Net income effects (managers prefer to report higher earnings for their companies).
2. Income tax effects (managers prefer to pay the least amount of taxes allowed by law as late as possible—the **least–latest rule**).

Any conflict between the two motives is normally resolved by choosing one accounting method for external financial statements and a different method for preparing its tax return. The choice of inventory costing methods is a special case, however, because of what is called the **LIFO conformity rule:** If LIFO is used on the income tax return, it must also be used to calculate inventory and cost of goods sold for the financial statements.

Increasing Cost Inventories

- **For inventory with increasing costs, LIFO is used on the tax return because it normally results in lower income taxes.**

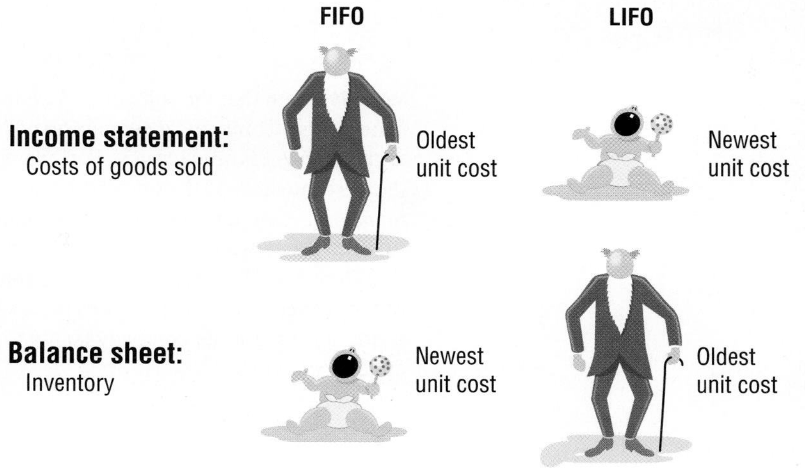

This is illustrated in Exhibit 7.5, where income before income taxes was lowered from $100 under FIFO to $60 under LIFO. On the income tax expense line, this lowers income taxes from $25 under FIFO to $15 under LIFO, generating cash tax savings of $10 under LIFO.[3] The LIFO conformity rule leads companies to adopt LIFO for **both** tax and financial reporting purposes for increasing cost inventories located in the United States. Harley-Davidson is a fairly typical company facing

[2]The impact of a decline in inventory **quantity** on LIFO amounts is discussed in Supplement A to this chapter.
[3]In theory, LIFO cannot provide permanent tax savings because (1) when inventory levels drop or (2) costs drop, the income effect reverses and the income taxes deferred must be paid. The economic advantage of deferring income taxes in such situations is due to the fact that interest can be earned on the money that otherwise would be paid as taxes for the current year.

increasing costs. It has saved approximately $14 million in taxes from the date it adopted the LIFO method through 2008.

For inventory located in countries that do not allow LIFO for tax purposes or that do not have a LIFO conformity rule, companies with increasing costs most often use FIFO or average cost to report higher income on the income statement.

Decreasing Cost Inventories

- **For inventory with decreasing costs, FIFO is most often used for both the tax return and financial statements.**

Using this method (along with lower of cost or market valuation, discussed later) produces the lowest tax payments for companies with decreasing cost inventories. Many high-technology companies are facing declining costs. In such circumstances, the FIFO method, in which the oldest, most expensive goods become cost of goods sold, produces the highest cost of goods sold, the lowest pretax earnings, and thus the lowest income tax liability. For example, Apple Inc. and Dell Inc. account for inventories using the FIFO method.

Since most companies in the same industry face similar cost structures, clusters of companies in the same industries often choose the same accounting method.

Consistency in Use of Inventory Methods

It is important to remember that regardless of the physical flow of goods, a company can use any of the inventory costing methods. Also, a company is not required to use the same inventory costing method for all inventory items, and no particular justification is needed for the selection of one or more of the acceptable methods. Harley-Davidson, and most large companies, use different inventory methods for different inventory items.[4] However, accounting rules require companies to apply their accounting methods on a consistent basis over time. A company is not permitted to use LIFO one period, FIFO the next, and then go back to LIFO. A change in method is allowed only if the change will improve the measurement of financial results and financial position.

A QUESTION OF ETHICS

LIFO and Conflicts between Managers' and Owners' Interests

We have seen that the selection of an inventory method can have significant effects on the financial statements. Company managers may have an incentive to select a method that is not consistent with the owners' objectives. For example, during a period of rising prices, using LIFO may be in the best interests of the owners, because LIFO often reduces a company's tax liability. However, if managers' compensation is tied to reported profits, they may prefer FIFO, which typically results in higher profits.

While a well-designed compensation plan should reward managers for acting in the best interests of the owners, that is not always the case. Clearly, a manager who selects an accounting method that is not optimal for the company solely to increase his or her compensation is engaging in questionable ethical behavior.

[4] *Accounting Trends & Techniques* (New York: AICPA, 2008) reported that, although 213 (35.5 percent) of the 600 companies surveyed reported using LIFO for some portion of inventories, only 14 (2.3 percent) use LIFO for all inventories.

PAUSE FOR FEEDBACK

STOP

Four different inventory costing methods may be used to allocate costs between the units remaining in inventory and the units sold, depending on economic circumstances. The methods include specific identification, FIFO, LIFO, and average cost. Each of the inventory costing methods conforms to GAAP. Remember that the cost flow assumption need not match the physical flow of inventory. The following questions test your understanding of the FIFO and LIFO methods.

SELF-STUDY QUIZ

1. Compute cost of goods sold and pretax income for **2009** under the FIFO and LIFO accounting methods. Assume that a company's beginning inventory and purchases for 2009 included:

Beginning inventory	10 units @ $ 6 each
Purchases January	5 units @ $10 each
Purchases May	5 units @ $12 each

During 2009, 15 units were sold for $20 each, and other operating expenses totaled $100.

2. Compute cost of goods sold and pretax income for **2010** under the FIFO and LIFO accounting methods. (**Hint:** The 2009 ending inventory amount from Part 1 becomes the 2010 beginning inventory amount.) Assume that the company's purchases for 2010 included:

Purchases March	6 units @ $13 each
Purchases November	5 units @ $14 each

During 2010, 10 units were sold for $24 each, and other operating expenses totaled $70.

3. Which method would you recommend that the company adopt? Why?

After you have completed your answers, check them with the solutions at the bottom of the page.

Solutions to SELF-STUDY QUIZ

1.

2009	FIFO	LIFO		FIFO	LIFO
Beginning inventory	$ 60	$ 60	Sales revenue (15 × $20)	$300	$300
Purchases (5 × $10) + (5 × $12)	110	110	Cost of goods sold	110	140
Goods available for sale	170	170	Gross profit	190	160
Ending inventory*	60	30	Other expenses	100	100
Cost of goods sold	$110	$140	Pretax income	$ 90	$ 60

*FIFO ending inventory = (5 × $12) = $60
Cost of goods sold = (10 × $6) + (5 × $10) = $110
LIFO ending inventory = (5 × $6) = $30
Cost of goods sold = (5 × $12) + (5 × $10) + (5 × $6) = $140

2.

2010	FIFO	LIFO		FIFO	LIFO
Beginning inventory	$ 60	$ 30	Sales revenue (10 × $24)	$240	$240
Purchases (6 × $13) + (5 × $14)	148	148	Cost of goods sold	125	135
Goods available for sale	208	178	Gross profit	115	105
Ending inventory*	83	43	Other expenses	70	70
Cost of goods sold	$125	$135	Pretax income	$ 45	$ 35

*FIFO ending inventory = (5 × $14) + (1 × $13) = $83
Cost of goods sold = (5 × $12) + (5 × $13) = $125
LIFO ending inventory = (5 × $6) + (1 × $13) = $43
Cost of goods sold = (5 × $14) + (5 × $13) = $135

3. LIFO would be recommended because it produces lower pretax income and lower taxes when inventory costs are rising.

VALUATION AT LOWER OF COST OR MARKET

LEARNING OBJECTIVE 4

Report inventory at the lower of cost or market (LCM).

REPLACEMENT COST is the current purchase price for identical goods.

NET REALIZABLE VALUE is the expected sales price less selling costs (e.g., repair and disposal costs).

LOWER OF COST OR MARKET (LCM) is a valuation method departing from the cost principle; it serves to recognize a loss when replacement cost or net realizable value drops below cost.

Inventories should be measured initially at their purchase cost in conformity with the cost principle. When the goods remaining in ending inventory can be replaced with identical goods at a lower cost, however, the lower **replacement cost** should be used as the inventory valuation. Damaged, obsolete, and deteriorated items in inventory should also be assigned a unit cost that represents their current estimated **net realizable value** (sales price less costs to sell) if that is below cost. This rule is known as measuring inventories at the **lower of cost or market** (LCM).

This departure from the cost principle is based on the **conservatism** constraint, which requires special care to avoid overstating assets and income. It is particularly important for two types of companies: (1) high-technology companies such as Dell Inc. that manufacture goods for which costs of production and selling price are declining and (2) companies such as American Eagle Outfitters that sell seasonal goods such as clothing, the value of which drops dramatically at the end of each selling season (fall or spring).

Under LCM, companies recognize a "holding" loss in the period in which the replacement cost of an item drops, rather than in the period the item is sold. The holding loss is the difference between the purchase cost and the lower replacement cost. It is added to the cost of goods sold for the period. To illustrate, assume that Dell Inc. had the following in the current period ending inventory:

Item	Quantity	Cost per Item	Replacement Cost (Market) per Item	Lower of Cost or Market per Item	Total Lower of Cost or Market
Intel chips	1,000	$250	$200	$200	1,000 × $200 = $200,000
Disk drives	400	100	110	100	400 × $100 = 40,000

The 1,000 Intel chips should be recorded in the ending inventory at the current market value ($200) because it is **lower** than the cost ($250). Dell makes the following journal entry to record the write-down:

	Debit	Credit
Cost of goods sold (+E, −SE) (1,000 × $50)	50,000	
Inventory (−A)		50,000

Assets		=	Liabilities	+	Stockholders' Equity
Inventory	−50,000				Cost of Goods Sold (+E) −50,000

Since the market price of the disk drives ($110) is higher than the original cost ($100), no write-down is necessary. The drives remain on the books at their cost of $100 per unit ($40,000 in total). Recognition of holding gains on inventory is not permitted by GAAP.

The write-down of the Intel chips to market produces the following effects on the income statement and balance sheet:

Effects of LCM Write-Down	Current Period	Next Period (if sold)
Cost of goods sold	Increase $50,000	Decrease $50,000
Pretax income	Decrease $50,000	Increase $50,000
Ending inventory on balance sheet	Decrease $50,000	Unaffected

Note that the effects in the period of sale are the opposite of those in the period of the write-down. Lower of cost or market changes only the timing of cost of goods sold. It transfers cost of goods sold from the period of sale to the period of write-down.

Note that in the two examples that follow, both Harley-Davidson, which is a mixed LIFO company, and Dell Inc., which is a FIFO company, report the use of lower of cost or market for financial statement purposes.[5]

[5]For tax purposes, lower of cost or market may be applied with all inventory costing methods except LIFO.

HARLEY-DAVIDSON, INC.
Notes to Consolidated Financial Statements
1. SUMMARY OF SIGNIFICANT ACCOUNTING POLICIES

Inventories—Inventories are valued at the lower of cost or market. Substantially all inventories located in the United States are valued using the last-in, first-out (LIFO) method. Other inventories totaling $174.1 million at December 31, 2008 and $112.7 million at December 31, 2007 are valued at the lower of cost or market using the first-in, first-out (FIFO) method.

HARLEY-DAVIDSON, INC.

REAL WORLD EXCERPT
Annual Report

DELL INC.
Notes to Consolidated Financial Statements
NOTE 1—Description of Business and Summary of Significant Accounting Policies

Inventories—Inventories are stated at the lower of cost or market with cost being determined on a first-in, first-out basis.

REAL WORLD EXCERPT
Annual Report

EVALUATING INVENTORY MANAGEMENT

Measuring Efficiency in Inventory Management

LEARNING OBJECTIVE 5
Evaluate inventory management using the inventory turnover ratio and analyze the effects of inventory on cash flows.

As noted at the beginning of the chapter, the primary goals of inventory management are to have sufficient quantities of high-quality inventory available to serve customers' needs while minimizing the costs of carrying inventory (production, storage, obsolescence, and financing). The inventory turnover ratio is an important measure of the company's success in balancing these conflicting goals.

Inventory Turnover

KEY RATIO ANALYSIS

ANALYTICAL QUESTION
How efficient are inventory management activities?

RATIO AND COMPARISONS

$$\textbf{Inventory Turnover} = \frac{\textbf{Cost of Goods Sold}}{\textbf{Average Inventory}}$$

The 2008 ratio for Harley-Davidson (see Exhibit 7.1 for the inputs to the equation):

$$\frac{\$3{,}663{,}488}{(349{,}697 + \$400{,}908)/2} = 9.8$$

COMPARISONS OVER TIME		
Harley-Davidson		
2006	2007	2008
14.0	11.3	9.8

COMPARISONS WITH COMPETITORS	
Polaris	Honda Motor
2008	2008
6.8	7.2

INTERPRETATIONS

In General The inventory turnover ratio reflects how many times average inventory was produced and sold during the period. A higher ratio indicates that inventory moves more quickly through the production process to the ultimate customer, reducing storage and obsolescence costs. Because less

(continued)

Selected Focus Companies' Inventory Turnover

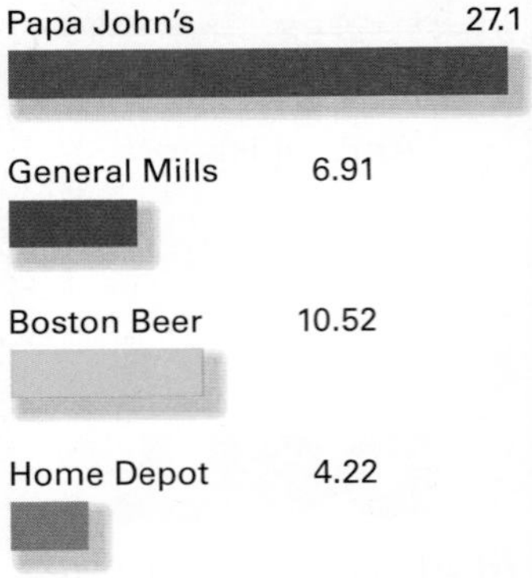

money is tied up in inventory, the excess can be invested to earn interest income or reduce borrowing, which reduces interest expense. More efficient purchasing and production techniques, such as just-in-time inventory, as well as high product demand cause this ratio to be high. Analysts and creditors also watch the inventory turnover ratio because a sudden decline may mean that a company is facing an unexpected drop in demand for its products or is becoming sloppy in its production management. Many managers and analysts compute the related number average days to sell inventory, which, for Harley-Davidson, is equal to:

$$\textbf{Average Days to Sell Inventory} = \frac{\textbf{365}}{\textbf{Inventory Turnover}} = \frac{\textbf{365}}{\textbf{9.8}} = \textbf{37.2 days}$$

It indicates the average time it takes the company to produce and deliver inventory to customers.

Focus Company Analysis Harley-Davidson's inventory turnover has decreased from 14.0 in 2006 to 9.8 in 2008. This decline reflects the unexpected decline in sales during the recent recession. Many of the changes Harley has instituted (discussed at the beginning of the chapter) are aimed at restoring its inventory turnover to previous levels. Harley's ratio is still higher than related company Polaris. Harley's turnover is even higher than the ratio for the giant Japanese auto and motorcycle manufacturer Honda.

A Few Cautions Differences across industries in purchasing, production, and sales processes cause dramatic differences in this ratio. For example, restaurants such as Papa John's, which must turn over their perishable inventory very quickly, tend to have much higher inventory turnover. A particular firm's ratio should be compared only with its figures from prior years or with figures for other firms in the same industry.

Inventory and Cash Flows

When companies expand production to meet increases in demand, this increases the amount of inventory reported on the balance sheet. However, when companies overestimate demand for a product, they usually produce too many units of the slow-selling item. This increases storage costs as well as the interest costs on short-term borrowings that finance the inventory. It may even lead to losses if the excess inventory cannot be sold at normal prices. The cash flow statement often provides the first sign of such problems.

FOCUS ON CASH FLOWS | Inventory

As with a change in accounts receivable, a change in inventories can have a major effect on a company's cash flow from operations. Cost of goods sold on the income statement may be more or less than the amount of cash paid to suppliers during the period. Since most inventory is purchased on open credit (borrowing from suppliers is normally called accounts payable), reconciling cost of goods sold with cash paid to suppliers requires consideration of the changes in both the Inventory and Accounts Payable accounts.

The simplest way to think about the effects of changes in inventory is that buying (increasing) inventory eventually decreases cash, while selling (decreasing) inventory eventually increases cash. Similarly, borrowing from suppliers, which increases accounts payable, increases cash. Paying suppliers, which decreases accounts payable, decreases cash.

EFFECT ON STATEMENT OF CASH FLOWS

In General When a net **decrease in inventory** for the period occurs, sales are greater than purchases; thus, the decrease must be **added** in computing cash flows from operations.

When a net **increase in inventory** for the period occurs, sales are less than purchases; thus, the increase must be **subtracted** in computing cash flows from operations.

When a net **decrease in accounts payable** for the period occurs, payments to suppliers are greater than new purchases; thus, the decrease must be **subtracted** in computing cash flows from operations.

When a net **increase in accounts payable** for the period occurs, payments to suppliers are less than new purchases; thus, the increase must be **added** in computing cash flows from operations.

	Effect on Cash Flows
Operating activities (indirect method)	
Net income	$xxx
Adjusted for	
Add inventory **decrease**	+
or	
Subtract inventory **increase**	−
Add accounts payable **increase**	+
or	
Subtract accounts payable **decrease**	−

Focus Company Analysis Exhibit 7.6 is the Operating Activities section of Harley-Davidson's statement of cash flows. When the inventory balance increases during the period, as was the case at Harley-Davidson in 2008 (see Exhibit 7.1), the company has purchased or produced more inventory than it has sold. Thus, the increase is subtracted in the computation of cash flow from operations. Conversely, when the inventory balance decreases during the period, the company has sold more inventory than it purchased or produced. Thus, the decrease is added in the computation of cash flow from operations. When the accounts payable balance increases during the period, the company has borrowed more from suppliers than it has paid them (or postponed payments). Thus, the increase is added in the computation of cash flow from operations.*

**For companies with foreign currency or business acquisitions/dispositions, the amount of the change reported on the cash flow statement will not equal the change in the accounts reported on the balance sheet.*

EXHIBIT 7.6

Inventories on the Cash Flow Statement

HARLEY-DAVIDSON, INC.

REAL WORLD EXCERPT

Annual Report

HARLEY-DAVIDSON, INC.
CONSOLIDATED STATEMENT OF CASH FLOWS
Years Ended December 31, 2008 and 2007
(dollars in thousands)

	2008	**2007**
Cash flows from operating activities:		
Net Income:	$ 654,718	$ 933,843
Adjustments to reconcile net income to net cash provided by operating activities:		
Depreciation and amortization	222,191	204,172
Amortization of acquisition-related intangibles	20,090	—
Provision for long-term employee benefits	76,426	75,683
....	...	...
Changes in current assets and current liabilities:		
Accounts receivable, net	(4,474)	(26,449)
Finance receivables—accrued interest and other	(7,149)	(19,680)
Inventories	(45,094)	(48,019)
Accounts payable and accrued liabilities	9,734	48,157
Other	(33,323)	(2,519)
Total adjustments	(1,339,367)	(135,697)
Net cash (used by) provided by operating activities	$ (684,649)	$ 798,146

PAUSE FOR **FEEDBACK**

The inventory turnover ratio measures the efficiency of inventory management. It reflects how many times average inventory was produced and sold during the period. Analysts and creditors watch this ratio because a sudden decline may mean that a company is facing an unexpected drop in demand for its products or is becoming sloppy in its production management. When a net **decrease in inventory** for the period occurs, sales are more than purchases; thus, the decrease must be **added** in computing cash flows from operations. When a net **increase in inventory** for the period occurs, the opposite is true. Before you move on, complete the following questions to test your understanding of these concepts.

SELF-STUDY **QUIZ**

1. Refer to the Key Ratio Analysis for Harley-Davidson's inventory turnover. Based on the computations for 2008, answer the following question. If Harley-Davidson had been able to manage its inventory more efficiently and decrease purchases and ending inventory by $10,000 for 2008, would its inventory turnover ratio have increased or decreased? Explain.
2. Based on the Focus on Cash Flows section, answer the following question. If Harley-Davidson had decreased its accounts payable, would its cash flow from operations have increased or decreased?

After you have completed your answers, check them with the solutions at the bottom of the page.

Inventory Methods and Financial Statement Analysis

LEARNING OBJECTIVE 6

Compare companies that use different inventory costing methods.

What would analysts do if they wanted to compare two companies that prepared their statements using different inventory accounting methods? Before meaningful comparisons could be made, one company's statements would have to be converted to a comparable basis. Making such a conversion is eased by the requirement that U.S. public companies using LIFO also report beginning and ending inventory on a FIFO basis in the notes if the FIFO values are materially different. We can use this information along with the cost of goods sold equation to convert the balance sheet and income statement to the FIFO basis.

Converting the Income Statement to FIFO

Recall that the choice of a cost flow assumption affects how goods available for sale are allocated to ending inventory and cost of goods sold. It does not affect the recording of purchases. Ending inventory will be different under the alternative methods, and, since last year's ending inventory is this year's beginning inventory, beginning inventory will also be different:

Beginning inventory	**Different**
+ Purchases of merchandise during the year	**Same**
− Ending inventory	**Different**
Cost of goods sold	**Different**

This equation suggests that if we know the differences between a company's inventory valued at LIFO and FIFO for both beginning and ending inventory, we can compute the difference in cost of goods sold. Exhibit 7.7 shows Harley-Davidson's 2008 disclosure of the differences

Solutions to SELF-STUDY QUIZ

1. Inventory turnover would have increased because the denominator of the ratio (average inventory) would have decreased by $5,000.

$$\frac{\$3{,}663{,}488}{(\$349{,}697 + \$390{,}908)/2} = 9.9$$

2. A decrease in accounts payable would have decreased cash flow from operations because Harley would have paid its vendors more than it had borrowed during the period.

EXHIBIT 7.7

Financial Statement Effects of Inventory Costing Methods

HARLEY-DAVIDSON, INC.

REAL WORLD EXCERPT

Annual Report

HARLEY-DAVIDSON, INC.
Notes to Consolidated Financial Statements
2. ADDITIONAL BALANCE SHEET AND CASH FLOWS INFORMATION
(in thousands)

	December 31, 2008	December 31, 2007	
Inventories:			
...			
Inventory at FIFO	441,042	381,831	
Excess of FIFO over LIFO cost	40,134	32,134	← *LIFO Reserve*
Inventory at LIFO	$400,908	$349,697	← *Inventory reported on the balance sheet*

between LIFO and FIFO values for beginning and ending inventory. These amounts, referred to as the LIFO reserve or "Excess of FIFO over LIFO," are disclosed by LIFO users in their inventory footnotes.

The LIFO RESERVE is a contra-asset for the excess of FIFO over LIFO inventory.

Using Harley-Davidson's LIFO reserve values reported in the footnote in Exhibit 7.7, we see that cost of goods sold would have been $8,000 **lower** had it used FIFO.

Beginning LIFO Reserve (Excess of FIFO over LIFO)	$32,134
− Less: Ending LIFO Reserve (Excess of FIFO over LIFO)	−40,134
Difference in Cost of Goods Sold under FIFO	($ 8,000)

Since FIFO cost of goods sold expense is **lower,** income before income taxes would have been $8,000 **higher.** Income taxes would be that amount times its tax rate of 35 percent **higher** had it used FIFO.

Difference in pretax income under FIFO	$8,000
Tax rate	× .35
Difference in taxes under FIFO	$2,800

Combining the two effects, net income would be increased by the change in cost of goods sold of $8,000 and decreased by the change in income tax expense of $2,800, resulting in an overall increase in net income of $5,200.

Decrease in Cost of Goods Sold Expense (*Income increases*)	$ 8,000
Increase in Income Tax Expense (*Income decreases*)	(2,800)
Increase in Net Income	$ 5,200

These Harley-Davidson computations are for 2008. It is important to note that even companies that usually face increasing costs occasionally face decreasing costs. For example, during 2000, Harley-Davidson's costs of new inventory declined due to manufacturing efficiencies. As a result, even though LIFO usually **saves** the company taxes, Harley paid **extra** taxes in 2000.

Converting Inventory on the Balance Sheet to FIFO

You can adjust the inventory amounts on the balance sheet to FIFO by substituting the FIFO values in the note ($441,042 and $381,831 for 2008 and 2007, respectively) for the LIFO values (see Exhibit 7.7). Alternatively, you can add the LIFO reserve to the LIFO value on the balance sheet to arrive at the same numbers.

FINANCIAL ANALYSIS | LIFO and Inventory Turnover Ratio

REAL WORLD EXCERPT
Deere & Company
Annual Report

For many LIFO companies, the inventory turnover ratio can be deceptive. Remember that, for these companies, the beginning and ending inventory numbers that make up the denominator of the ratio will be artificially small because they reflect old lower costs. Consider Deere & Co., manufacturer of John Deere farm, lawn, and construction equipment. Its inventory note lists the following values:

DEERE & COMPANY
Notes to Consolidated Financial Statements
(dollars in millions)

	2008	2007
Inventories:		
Total FIFO value	$4,366	$3,570
Adjustment to LIFO basis	1,324	1,233
Inventories	$3,042	$2,337

John Deere's cost of goods sold for 2008 was $19,574.8 million. If the ratio is computed using the reported LIFO inventory values for the ratio, it would be

$$\textbf{Inventory Turnover Ratio} = \frac{\$19{,}574.8}{(\$3{,}042 + \$2{,}337)/2} = 7.3$$

Converting cost of goods sold (the numerator) to a FIFO basis and using the more current FIFO inventory values in the denominator, it would be

$$\textbf{Inventory Turnover Ratio} = \frac{\$19{,}574.8 - 91}{(\$4{,}366 + \$3{,}570)/2} = 4.9$$

Note that the major difference between the two ratios is in the denominator. FIFO inventory values are nearly 44 percent higher than the LIFO values. The LIFO beginning and ending inventory numbers are artificially small because they reflect older lower costs.

PAUSE FOR FEEDBACK

The selection of an inventory costing method is important because it will affect reported income, income tax expense (and hence cash flow), and the inventory valuation reported on the balance sheet. In a period of rising prices, FIFO normally results in a higher income and higher taxes than LIFO; in a period of falling prices, the opposite occurs. The choice of methods is normally made to minimize taxes. Answer the following question to practice converting cost of goods sold and pretax income from the LIFO to the FIFO method for a company facing increasing prices.

SELF-STUDY QUIZ

In a recent year, Caterpillar Inc., a major manufacturer of farm and construction equipment, reported pretax earnings of $1,615 million. Its inventory note indicated "if the FIFO (first-in, first-out) method had been in use, inventories would have been $2,103 and $2,035 higher than reported at the end of the current and prior year, respectively." (The amounts noted are for the LIFO reserve.) Convert pretax earnings for the current year from a LIFO to a FIFO basis.

Beginning LIFO Reserve (Excess of FIFO over LIFO)	______
Less: Ending LIFO Reserve (Excess of FIFO over LIFO)	______
Difference in cost of goods sold under FIFO	______
Pretax income (LIFO)	______
Difference in pretax income under FIFO	______
Pretax income (FIFO)	______

After you have completed your answers, check them with the solutions at the bottom of the next page.

CONTROL OF INVENTORY

Internal Control of Inventory

LEARNING OBJECTIVE 7

Understand methods for controlling and keeping track of inventory and analyze the effects of inventory errors on financial statements.

After cash, inventory is the asset second most vulnerable to theft. Efficient management of inventory to avoid the cost of stock-outs and overstock situations is also crucial to the profitability of most companies. As a consequence, a number of control features focus on safeguarding inventories and providing up-to-date information for management decisions. Key among these are:

1. Separation of responsibilities for inventory accounting and physical handling of inventory.
2. Storage of inventory in a manner that protects it from theft and damage.
3. Limiting access to inventory to authorized employees.
4. Maintaining perpetual inventory records (described below).
5. Comparing perpetual records to periodic physical counts of inventory.

Perpetual and Periodic Inventory Systems

The amount of purchases for the period is always accumulated in the accounting system. The amount of cost of goods sold and ending inventory can be determined by using one of two different inventory systems: perpetual or periodic.

Perpetual Inventory System

In a **perpetual inventory system,** a detailed record is maintained for each type of merchandise stocked, showing (1) units and cost of the beginning inventory, (2) units and cost of each purchase, (3) units and cost of the goods for each sale, and (4) units and cost of the goods on hand at any point in time. This up-to-date record is maintained on a transaction-by-transaction basis. In a complete perpetual inventory system, the inventory record gives the amount of both ending inventory and cost of goods sold at any point in time. Under this system, a physical count should also be performed from time to time to ensure that records are accurate in case of errors or theft.

To this point in the text, all journal entries for purchase and sale transactions have been recorded using a perpetual inventory system. In a perpetual inventory system, purchase transactions are recorded directly in an inventory account. When each sale is recorded, a companion cost of goods sold entry is made, decreasing inventory and recording cost of goods sold. As a result, information on cost of goods sold and ending inventory is available on a continuous (perpetual) basis.

In a PERPETUAL INVENTORY SYSTEM, a detailed inventory record is maintained, recording each purchase and sale during the accounting period.

Periodic Inventory System

Under the **periodic inventory system,** no up-to-date record of inventory is maintained during the year. An actual physical count of the goods remaining on hand is required at the **end of each period.** The number of units of each type of merchandise on hand is multiplied by their unit cost to compute the dollar amount of the ending inventory. Cost of goods sold is calculated using the cost of goods sold equation.

Because the amount of inventory is not known until the end of the period when the inventory count is taken, the amount of cost of goods sold cannot be reliably determined until the inventory count is complete. Inventory purchases are debited to an account called **Purchases,** which is part of the asset inventory. Revenues are recorded at the time of each sale. However, cost of goods sold is not recorded until after the inventory count is completed. At other times, companies using a periodic system must estimate the amount of inventory on hand. Estimation methods are discussed in intermediate accounting courses.

In a PERIODIC INVENTORY SYSTEM, ending inventory and cost of goods sold are determined at the end of the accounting period based on a physical count.

Solutions to SELF-STUDY QUIZ

Beginning LIFO Reserve	$2,035	Pretax income (LIFO)	$1,615
Less: Ending LIFO Reserve	2,103	Difference in pretax income	68
Difference in cost of goods sold	($ 68)	Pretax income (FIFO)	$1,683

Before affordable computers and bar code readers were available, the primary reason for using a periodic inventory system was its low cost. The primary disadvantage of a periodic inventory system is the lack of inventory information. Managers are not informed about low stock or overstocked situations. Most modern companies could not survive without this information. As noted at the beginning of the chapter, cost and quality pressures brought on by increasing competition, combined with dramatic declines in the cost of computers, have made sophisticated perpetual inventory systems a requirement at all but the smallest companies. The entries made when using both systems are compared in Supplement C at the end of this chapter.

Perpetual Inventory Records and Cost Flow Assumptions in Practice

Systems that do keep track of the costs of individual items or lots normally do so on a FIFO or estimated average (or standard) cost basis. For distinguishable high-value items, specific identification may be used. Perpetual records are rarely kept on a LIFO basis for two reasons: (1) doing so is more complex and costly and (2) it can increase tax payments. LIFO companies convert the outputs of their perpetual inventory system to LIFO with an adjusting entry.

Errors in Measuring Ending Inventory

As the cost of goods sold equation indicates, a direct relationship exists between ending inventory and cost of goods sold because items not in the ending inventory are assumed to have been sold. Thus, the measurement of ending inventory quantities and costs affects both the balance sheet (assets) and the income statement (cost of goods sold, gross profit, and net income). The measurement of ending inventory affects not only the net income for that period but also the net income for the next accounting period. This two-period effect occurs because the ending inventory for one period is the beginning inventory for the next accounting period.

Greeting card maker Gibson Greetings overstated its net income by 20 percent because one division overstated ending inventory for the year. You can compute the effects of the error on both the current year's and the next year's income before taxes using the cost of goods sold equation. Assume that ending inventory was overstated by $10,000 due to a clerical error that was not discovered. This would have the following effects in the current year and next year:

Current Year	
Beginning inventory	
+ Purchases of merchandise during the year	
− Ending inventory	**Overstated $10,000**
Cost of goods sold	**Understated $10,000**

Next Year	
Beginning inventory	**Overstated $10,000**
+ Purchases of merchandise during the year	
− Ending inventory	
Cost of goods sold	**Overstated $10,000**

Because cost of goods sold was understated, **income before taxes would be overstated** by $10,000 in the **current year.** And, since the current year's ending inventory becomes next year's beginning inventory, it would have the following effects: Because cost of goods sold was overstated, **income before taxes would be understated** by $10,000 in the **next year.**

Each of these errors would flow into retained earnings so that at the end of the current year, retained earnings would be overstated by $10,000 (less the related income tax expense). This error would be offset in the next year, and retained earnings and inventory at the end of next year would be correct.

In this example, we assumed that the overstatement of ending inventory was inadvertent, the result of a clerical error. However, inventory fraud is a common form of financial statement fraud. It occurred in the Maxidrive case discussed in Chapter 1 as well as in the real MiniScribe fraud.

PAUSE FOR FEEDBACK

STOP

A company can keep track of the ending inventory and cost of goods sold for the period using (1) the perpetual inventory system, which is based on the maintenance of detailed and continuous inventory records, and (2) the periodic inventory system, which is based on a physical count of ending inventory and use of the cost of goods sold equation to determine cost of goods sold. An error in the measurement of ending inventory affects cost of goods sold on the current period's income statement and ending inventory on the balance sheet. Because this year's ending inventory becomes next year's beginning inventory, it also affects cost of goods sold in the following period by the same amount but in the opposite direction. These relationships can be seen through the cost of goods sold equation (BI + P − EI = CGS).

SELF-STUDY QUIZ

Assume that it is now the end of 2010, and for the first time, the company will undergo an audit by an independent CPA. The annual income statement prepared by the company is presented here. Assume further that the independent CPA discovered that the ending inventory for 2010 was understated by $15,000. Correct and reconstruct the income statement in the space provided.

	For the Year Ended December 31			
	2010 Uncorrected		**2010 Corrected**	
Sales revenue		$750,000		
Cost of goods sold				
Beginning inventory	$ 45,000			
Add purchases	460,000		______	
Goods available for sale	505,000			
Less ending inventory	40,000		______	
Cost of goods sold		465,000		______
Gross margin on sales		285,000		
Operating expenses		275,000		______
Pretax income		10,000		
Income tax expense (20%)		2,000		______
Net income		$ 8,000		______

After you have completed your answers, check them with the solutions at the bottom of the page.

Solutions to SELF-STUDY QUIZ

Sales revenue		$750,000
Cost of goods sold		
Beginning inventory	$ 45,000	
Add purchases	460,000	
Goods available for sale	505,000	
Less ending inventory	55,000	
Cost of goods sold		450,000
Gross margin on sales		300,000
Operating expenses		275,000
Pretax income		25,000
Income tax expense (20%)		5,000
Net income		$ 20,000

Note: An ending inventory error in one year affects pretax income by the amount of the error and in the next year affects pretax income again by the same amount, but in the opposite direction.

DEMONSTRATION CASE

(Complete the requirements before proceeding to the suggested solution that follows.) This case reviews the application of the FIFO and LIFO inventory costing methods and the inventory turnover ratio.

Balent Appliances distributes a number of household appliances. One product, microwave ovens, has been selected for case purposes. Assume that the following summarized transactions were completed during the year ended December 31, 2010, in the order given (assume that all transactions are cash):

	Units	Unit Cost
a. Beginning inventory	11	$200
b. New inventory purchases	9	220
c. Sales (selling price, $420)	8	?

Required:

1. Compute the following amounts, assuming the application of the FIFO and LIFO inventory costing methods:

	Ending Inventory		Cost of Goods Sold	
	Units	Dollars	Units	Dollars
FIFO				
LIFO				

2. Assuming that inventory cost was expected to follow current trends, which method would you suggest that Balent select to account for these inventory items? Explain your answer.

3. Assuming that other operating expenses were $500 and the income tax rate is 25 percent, prepare the income statement for the period using your selected method.

4. Compute the inventory turnover ratio for the current period using your selected method. What does it indicate?

SUGGESTED SOLUTION

1.

	Ending Inventory		Cost of Goods Sold	
	Units	Dollars	Units	Dollars
FIFO	12	$2,580	8	$1,600
LIFO	12	$2,420	8	$1,760

Computations

Beginning inventory (11 units × $200)	$2,200
+ Purchases (9 units × $220)	1,980
Goods available for sale	$4,180
FIFO inventory (costed at end of period)	
Goods available for sale (from above)	$4,180
− Ending inventory (9 units × $220) + (3 units × $200)	2,580
Cost of goods sold (8 units × $200)	$1,600
LIFO inventory (costed at end of period)	
Goods available for sale (from above)	$4,180
− Ending inventory (11 units × $200) + (1 unit × $220)	2,420
Cost of goods sold (8 units × $220)	$1,760

2. LIFO should be selected. Because costs are rising, LIFO produces higher cost of goods sold, lower pretax income, and lower income tax payments. It is used on the tax return and income statement because of the LIFO conformity rule.

3.

BALENT APPLIANCES
Statement of Income
Year Ended December 31, 2010

Sales	$3,360
Cost of goods sold	1,760
Gross profit	1,600
Other expenses	500
Income before income taxes	1,100
Income tax expense (25%)	275
Net income	$ 825

Computations

Sales = 8 × $420 = $3,360

4. Inventory turnover ratio = Cost of Goods Sold ÷ Average Inventory

= $1,760 ÷ [($2,200 + $2,420) ÷ 2 = $2,310]

= 0.76

The inventory turnover ratio reflects how many times average inventory was produced or purchased and sold during the period. Thus, Balent Appliances purchased and sold its average inventory less than one time during the year.

Chapter Supplement A

LIFO Liquidations

When a LIFO company sells more inventory than it purchases or manufactures, items from beginning inventory become part of cost of goods sold. This is called a **LIFO liquidation.** When inventory costs are rising, these lower cost items in beginning inventory produce a higher gross profit, higher taxable income, and higher taxes when they are sold. We illustrate this process by continuing our Harley-Davidson Model A leather baseball jacket example into its second year.

A LIFO LIQUIDATION is a sale of a lower-cost inventory item from beginning LIFO inventory.

Financial Statement Effects of LIFO Liquidations

Recall that, in its first year of operation, the store purchased units for $70, $80, and $100 in sequence. Then, the $100 unit and three of the $80 units were sold under LIFO, leaving one $80 unit and two $70 units in ending inventory. We will continue this illustration into a second year. The ending inventory from year 1 becomes the beginning inventory for year 2.

First, we assume that in year 2, the Harley-Davidson store purchases a total of **three** inventory units at the current $120 price, the sales price has been raised to $140, and **three** units are sold. Using LIFO, the units are allocated to ending inventory and cost of goods sold as follows.

Cost of Goods Sold Calculation (LIFO with three units purchased and three units sold)

Beginning inventory	(2 units at $70 each and 1 unit at $80)	$220
+ Purchases	(3 units at $120 each)	360
Goods available for sale		580
− Ending inventory	(2 units at $70 each and 1 unit at $80)	220
Cost of goods sold	(3 units at $120 each)	$360

Given that revenue is $140 per unit, the gross profit on the three newly purchased units is 3 units × $20 = $60.

Now assume instead that the store purchases only *two* additional units at $120 each. Using LIFO, these two new $120 units and the old $80 unit would become cost of goods sold.

Cost of Goods Sold Calculation (LIFO with two units purchased and three units sold)		
Beginning inventory	(2 units at $70 each and 1 unit at $80)	$220
+ Purchases	(2 units at $120 each)	240
Goods available for sale		460
− Ending inventory	(2 units at $70 each)	140
Cost of goods sold	(2 units at $120 each and 1 unit at $80)	$320

Given that revenue is $140 per unit, the gross profit on the newly purchased units is 2 units × $20 = $40. Since the cost of the old unit is only $80, the gross profit on this one unit is $60 ($140 − $80) instead of $20, raising total gross profit to $100. The complete income statement effects are reflected below.

	No Liquidation (purchase 3 units)	Liquidation (purchase 2 units)
Effect on the Income Statement		
Sales	$420	$420
Cost of goods sold	360	320
Gross profit	60	100
Other expenses	48	48
Income before income taxes	12	52
Income tax expense (25%)	3	13
Net income	$ 9	$ 39

This $40 change is the **pretax effect of the LIFO liquidation.** Given the assumed tax rate of 25 percent, taxes paid are $10 (0.25 × $40) higher than if no liquidation had taken place.

In practice, LIFO liquidations and extra tax payments can be avoided even if purchases of additional inventory take place **after** the sale of the item it replaces. Tax law allows LIFO to be applied **as if** all purchases during an accounting period took place before any sales and cost of goods sold were recorded. Thus, temporary LIFO liquidations can be eliminated by purchasing additional inventory before year-end. Most companies apply LIFO in this manner.

Chapter Supplement B

Additional Issues in Measuring Purchases

Purchase Returns and Allowances

PURCHASE RETURNS AND ALLOWANCES are a reduction in the cost of purchases associated with unsatisfactory goods.

Purchased goods may be returned to the vendor if they do not meet specifications, arrive in damaged condition, or are otherwise unsatisfactory. Purchase returns and allowances require a reduction in the cost of inventory purchases and the recording of a cash refund or a reduction in the liability to the vendor. For example, assume that Harley-Davidson returned to a supplier damaged harness boots that cost $1,000. The return would be recorded as follows:

	Debit	Credit
Accounts payable (−L) (or Cash +A)	1,000	
Inventory (−A)		1,000

Assets		=	Liabilities		+	Stockholders' Equity
Inventory	−1,000		Accounts Payable	−1,000		

Purchase Discounts

Cash discounts must be accounted for by both the seller and the buyer (accounting by the seller was discussed in Chapter 6). When merchandise is bought on credit, terms such as 2/10, n/30 are sometimes specified. That is, if payment is made within 10 days from the date of purchase, a 2 percent cash discount known as the **purchase discount** is granted. If payment is not made within the discount period, the full invoice cost is due 30 days after the purchase.

A PURCHASE DISCOUNT is a cash discount received for prompt payment of an account.

Assume that on January 17, Harley-Davidson bought goods that had a $1,000 invoice price with terms 2/10, n/30. The purchase would be recorded as follows (using what is called the **gross method**):

Date of Purchase

Jan. 17	Inventory (+A)	1,000	
	Accounts payable (+L)		1,000

Assets		=	Liabilities		+	Stockholders' Equity
Inventory	+1,000		Accounts Payable	+1,000		

Date of Payment, within the Discount Period

Jan. 26	Accounts payable (−L)	1,000	
	Inventory (−A)		20
	Cash (−A)		980

Assets		=	Liabilities		+	Stockholders' Equity
Inventory	−20		Accounts Payable	−1,000		
Cash	−980					

If for any reason Harley-Davidson did not pay within the 10-day discount period, the following entry would be needed:

Date of Payment, after the Discount Period

Feb. 1	Accounts payable (−L)	1,000	
	Cash (−A)		1,000

Assets		=	Liabilities		+	Stockholders' Equity
Cash	−1,000		Accounts Payable	−1,000		

Chapter Supplement C

Comparison of Perpetual and Periodic Inventory Systems

To simplify the discussion of how accounting systems keep track of these amounts, we will focus this discussion on the Motorclothes line for which Harley-Davidson is a wholesaler. Assume, for this illustration only, that Harley-Davidson stocks and sells only one item, its Eagle Harness Boots, and that only the following events occurred in 2010.

Jan. 1 Beginning inventory:	800 units, at unit cost of $50.
April 14 Purchased:	1,100 additional units, at unit cost of $50.
Nov. 30 Sold:	1,300 units, at unit sales price of $83.

In the two types of inventory systems, the following sequential steps would take place:

Perpetual Records	Periodic Records
1. Record all purchases in the Inventory account and in a detailed perpetual inventory record.	1. Record all purchases in an account called Purchases.
April 14, 2010 Inventory (+A) (1,100 units at $50)* . . . . . . 55,000 Accounts payable (+L) (or Cash−A) . . . . 55,000 *Also entered in the detailed perpetual inventory record as 1,100 harness boots at $50 each.	**April 14, 2010** Purchases (+A) (1,100 units at $50) . . . . . . 55,000 Accounts payable (+L) (or Cash−A) 55,000
2. Record all sales in the Sales Revenue account and record the cost of goods sold.	2. Record all sales in a Sales Revenue account.
November 30, 2010 Accounts receivable (+A) (or Cash+A) . . . . 107,900 Sales revenue (+R, +SE) (1,300 units at $83) . . . . 107,900 Cost of goods sold (+E, −SE) . . . . 65,000 Inventory (−A) (1,300 units at $50)* . . . . 65,000 *Also entered in the perpetual inventory record as a reduction of 1,300 units at $50 each.	**November 30, 2010** Accounts receivable (+A) (or Cash+A) . . . . 107,900 Sales revenue (+R, +SE) (1,300 units at $83) 107,900
3. Use cost of goods sold and inventory amounts. At the end of the accounting period, the balance in the Cost of Goods Sold account is reported on the income statement. It is not necessary to compute cost of goods sold because the Cost of Goods Sold account is up-to-date. Also, the Inventory account shows the ending inventory amount reported on the balance sheet. A physical inventory count is still necessary to assess the accuracy of the perpetual records and identify theft and other forms of misuse (called **shrinkage**). No entry	3. At end of period: a. Count the number of units on hand. b. Compute the dollar valuation of the ending inventory. c. Compute and record the cost of goods sold. Beginning inventory (last period's ending) $40,000 Add purchases (balance in the Purchases account) 55,000 Goods available for sale 95,000 Deduct ending inventory (physical count—600 units at $50) 30,000 Cost of goods sold $65,000 **December 31, 2010** Transfer beginning inventory and purchases to cost of goods sold: Cost of goods sold (+E, −SE) . . . . 95,000 Inventory (−A) (beginning) . . . . 40,000 Purchases (−A) . . . . 55,000 Subtract the ending inventory amount from the cost of goods sold to complete its computation and establish the ending inventory balance: Inventory (+A) (ending) . . . . 30,000 Cost of goods sold (−E, +SE) 30,000
Assets = Liabilities + Stockholders' Equity Inventory +55,000; Accts. Rec. +107,900; Inventory −65,000 = Accounts Payable +55,000 + Sales Revenue +107,900; Cost of Goods Sold −65,000	**Assets = Liabilities + Stockholders' Equity** Purchases +55,000; Accts. Rec. +107,900; Inventory −40,000; Purchases −55,000; Inventory +30,000 = Accounts Payable +55,000 + Sales Revenue +107,900; Cost of Goods Sold −95,000; Cost of Goods Sold +30,000

Note that the effects of the entries on the accounting equation are the same under both systems. Only the timing of the recording of amounts changes.

CHAPTER TAKE-AWAYS

1. **Apply the cost principle to identify the amounts that should be included in inventory and the matching principle to determine cost of goods sold for typical retailers, wholesalers, and manufacturers.** p. 333

   Inventory should include all items owned that are held for resale. Costs flow into inventory when goods are purchased or manufactured. They flow out (as an expense) when they are sold or disposed of. In conformity with the matching principle, the total cost of the goods sold during the period must be matched with the sales revenue earned during the period.

2. **Report inventory and cost of goods sold using the four inventory costing methods.** p. 338

   The chapter discussed four different inventory costing methods used to allocate costs between the units remaining in inventory and the units sold, and their applications in different economic circumstances. The methods discussed were specific identification, FIFO, LIFO, and average cost. Each of the inventory costing methods conforms to GAAP. Public companies using LIFO must provide note disclosures that allow conversion of inventory and cost of goods sold to FIFO amounts. Remember that the cost flow assumption need not match the physical flow of inventory.

3. **Decide when the use of different inventory costing methods is beneficial to a company.** p. 343

   The selection of an inventory costing method is important because it will affect reported income, income tax expense (and hence cash flow), and the inventory valuation reported on the balance sheet. In a period of rising prices, FIFO normally results in a higher income and higher taxes than LIFO; in a period of falling prices, the opposite occurs. The choice of methods is normally made to minimize taxes.

4. **Report inventory at the lower of cost or market (LCM).** p. 346

   Ending inventory should be measured based on the lower of actual cost or replacement cost (LCM basis). This practice can have a major effect on the statements of companies facing declining costs. Damaged, obsolete, and out-of-season inventory should also be written down to their current estimated net realizable value if below cost. The LCM adjustment increases cost of goods sold, decreases income, and decreases reported inventory in the year of the write-down.

5. **Evaluate inventory management using the inventory turnover ratio and analyze the effects of inventory on cash flows.** p. 347

   The inventory turnover ratio measures the efficiency of inventory management. It reflects how many times average inventory was produced and sold during the period. Analysts and creditors watch this ratio because a sudden decline may mean that a company is facing an unexpected drop in demand for its products or is becoming sloppy in its production management. When a net **decrease in inventory** for the period occurs, sales are more than purchases; thus, the decrease must be **added** in computing cash flows from operations. When a net **increase in inventory** for the period occurs, sales are less than purchases; thus, the increase must be **subtracted** in computing cash flows from operations.

6. **Compare companies that use different inventory costing methods.** p. 350

   These comparisons can be made by converting the LIFO company's statements to FIFO. Public companies using LIFO must disclose the differences between LIFO and FIFO values for beginning and ending inventory. These amounts are often called the LIFO reserve. The beginning LIFO reserve minus the ending LIFO reserve equals the difference in cost of goods sold under FIFO. Pretax income is affected by the same amount in the opposite direction. This amount times the tax rate is the tax effect.

7. **Understand methods for controlling and keeping track of inventory and analyze the effects of inventory errors on financial statements.** p. 353

   Various control procedures can limit inventory theft or mismanagement. A company can keep track of the ending inventory and cost of goods sold for the period using (1) the perpetual inventory system, which is based on the maintenance of detailed and continuous inventory records, and (2) the periodic inventory system, which is based on a physical count of ending inventory and use of the cost of goods sold equation to determine cost of goods sold. An error in the measurement of ending inventory affects cost of goods sold on the current period's income statement and ending inventory on the balance sheet. Because this year's ending inventory becomes next year's beginning inventory, it also affects cost of goods sold in the following period by the same amount but in the opposite direction. These relationships can be seen through the cost of goods sold equation (BI + P − EI = CGS).

In this and previous chapters, we discussed the current assets of a business. These assets are critical to operations, but many of them do not directly produce value. In Chapter 8, we will discuss the noncurrent assets property, plant, and equipment; natural resources; and intangibles that are the elements of productive capacity. Many of the noncurrent assets produce value, such as a factory that manufactures cars. These assets present some interesting accounting problems because they benefit a number of accounting periods.

KEY RATIO

Inventory turnover ratio measures the efficiency of inventory management. It reflects how many times average inventory was produced and sold during the period (p. 347):

$$\text{Inventory Turnover} = \frac{\text{Cost of Goods Sold}}{\text{Average Inventory}}$$

FINDING FINANCIAL INFORMATION

Balance Sheet

Under Current Assets
Inventories

Income Statement

Expenses
Cost of goods sold

Statement of Cash Flows

Under Operating Activities (indirect method):
Net income
− increases in inventory
+ decreases in inventory
+ increases in accounts payable
− decreases in accounts payable

Notes

Under Summary of Significant Accounting Policies:
Description of management's choice of inventory accounting policy (FIFO, LIFO, LCM, etc.)

In Separate Note
If not listed on balance sheet, components of inventory (merchandise, raw materials, work in progress, finished goods)
If using LIFO, LIFO reserve (excess of FIFO over LIFO)

KEY TERMS

Average Cost Method p. 341
Cost of Goods Sold Equation p. 336
Direct Labor p. 335
Factory Overhead p. 336
Finished Goods Inventory p. 334
First-In, First-Out (FIFO) Method p. 339
Goods Available for Sale p. 336
Inventory p. 333
Last-In, First-Out (LIFO) Method p. 340
LIFO Liquidation p. 357
LIFO Reserve p. 351
Lower of Cost or Market (LCM) p. 346
Merchandise Inventory p. 333
Net Realizable Value p. 346
Periodic Inventory System p. 353
Perpetual Inventory System p. 353
Purchase Discount p. 359
Purchase Returns and Allowances p. 358
Raw Materials Inventory p. 334
Replacement Cost p. 346
Specific Identification Method p. 339
Work in Process Inventory p. 334

QUESTIONS

1. Why is inventory an important item to both internal (management) and external users of financial statements?
2. What are the general guidelines for deciding which items should be included in inventory?
3. Explain the application of the cost principle to an item in the ending inventory.
4. Define goods available for sale. How does it differ from cost of goods sold?
5. Define beginning inventory and ending inventory.
6. The chapter discussed four inventory costing methods. List the four methods and briefly explain each.
7. Explain how income can be manipulated when the specific identification inventory costing method is used.
8. Contrast the effects of LIFO versus FIFO on reported assets (i.e., the ending inventory) when (*a*) prices are rising and (*b*) prices are falling.
9. Contrast the income statement effect of LIFO versus FIFO (i.e., on pretax income) when (*a*) prices are rising and (*b*) prices are falling.
10. Contrast the effects of LIFO versus FIFO on cash outflow and inflow.
11. Explain briefly the application of the LCM concept to the ending inventory and its effect on the income statement and balance sheet when market is lower than cost.
12. When a perpetual inventory system is used, unit costs of the items sold are known at the date of each sale. In contrast, when a periodic inventory system is used, unit costs are known only at the end of the accounting period. Why are these statements correct?

MULTIPLE-CHOICE **QUESTIONS**

1. Consider the following information: ending inventory, $24,000; sales, $250,000; beginning inventory, $20,000; selling and administrative expenses, $70,000; and purchases, $90,000. What is cost of goods sold?
   a. $86,000 c. $16,000
   b. $94,000 d. $84,000

2. The inventory costing method selected by a company will affect
   a. The balance sheet. c. The statement of retained earnings.
   b. The income statement. d. All of the above.

3. Which of the following is **not** a component of the cost of inventory?
   a. Administrative overhead c. Raw materials
   b. Direct labor d. Factory overhead

4. Consider the following information: beginning inventory 20 units @ $20 per unit; first purchase 35 units @ $22 per unit; second purchase 40 units @ $24 per unit; 50 units were sold. What is cost of goods sold using the **FIFO** method of inventory costing?
   a. $1,000 c. $1,180
   b. $1,060 d. $1,200

5. Consider the following information: beginning inventory 20 units @ $20 per unit; first purchase 35 units @ $22 per unit; second purchase 40 units @ $24 per unit; 50 units were sold. What is cost of goods sold using the **LIFO** method of inventory costing?
   a. $1,000 c. $1,180
   b. $1,060 d. $1,200

6. An increasing inventory turnover ratio
   a. Indicates a longer time span between the ordering and receiving of inventory.
   b. Indicates a shorter time span between the ordering and receiving of inventory.
   c. Indicates a shorter time span between the purchase and sale of inventory.
   d. Indicates a longer time span between the purchase and sale of inventory.

7. If the ending balance in accounts payable decreases from one period to the next, which of the following is true?
   a. Cash payments to suppliers exceeded current period purchases.
   b. Cash payments to suppliers were less than current period purchases.
   c. Cash receipts from customers exceeded cash payments to suppliers.
   d. Cash receipts from customers exceeded current period purchases.
8. Which of the following regarding the lower of cost or market rule for inventory are true?
   (1) The lower of cost or market rule is an example of the historical cost principle.
   (2) When the replacement cost of inventory drops below the cost shown in the financial records, net income is reduced.
   (3) When the replacement cost of inventory drops below the cost shown in the financial records, total assets are reduced.
   a. (1)
   b. (2)
   c. (2) and (3)
   d. All three
9. Which inventory method provides a better matching of current costs with sales revenue on the income statement and outdated values for inventory on the balance sheet?
   a. FIFO
   b. Average cost
   c. LIFO
   d. Specific identification
10. Which of the following is false regarding a perpetual inventory system?
   a. Physical counts are not needed since records are maintained on a transaction-by-transaction basis.
   b. The balance in the inventory account is updated with each inventory purchase and sale transaction.
   c. Cost of goods sold is increased as sales are recorded.
   d. The account Purchases is not used as inventory is acquired.

For more practice with multiple-choice questions, go to the text website at **www.mhhe.com/libby7e**.

MINI-EXERCISES

connect ACCOUNTING

M7-1 Matching Inventory Items to Type of Business
LO1

Match the type of inventory with the type of business in the following matrix:

	TYPE OF BUSINESS	
Type of Inventory	**Merchandising**	**Manufacturing**
Work in process		
Finished goods		
Merchandise		
Raw materials		

M7-2 Recording the Cost of Purchases for a Merchandiser
LO1

Elite Apparel purchased 90 new shirts and recorded a total cost of $2,735 determined as follows:

Invoice cost	$2,250
Shipping charges	185
Import taxes and duties	165
Interest (6.0%) on $2,250 borrowed to finance the purchase	135
	$2,735

Required:
Make the needed corrections in this calculation. Give the journal entry(ies) to record this purchase in the correct amount, assuming a perpetual inventory system. Show computations.

Identifying the Cost of Inventories for a Manufacturer

M7-3
LO1

Operating costs incurred by a manufacturing company become either (1) part of the cost of inventory to be expensed as cost of goods sold at the time the finished goods are sold or (2) expenses at the time they are incurred. Indicate whether each of the following costs belongs in category (1) or (2).

___ *a.* Wages of factory workers
___ *b.* Costs of raw materials purchased
___ *c.* Sales salaries
___ *d.* Heat, light, and power for the factory building
___ *e.* Heat, light, and power for the headquarters office building

Inferring Purchases Using the Cost of Goods Sold Equation

M7-4
LO1

JCPenney Company, Inc., is a major retailer with department stores in all 50 states. The dominant portion of the company's business consists of providing merchandise and services to consumers through department stores that include catalog departments. In a recent annual report, JCPenney reported cost of goods sold of $11,571 million, ending inventory for the current year of $3,259 million, and ending inventory for the previous year of $3,641 million.

Required:
Is it possible to develop a reasonable estimate of the merchandise purchases for the year? If so, prepare the estimate; if not, explain why.

Matching Financial Statement Effects to Inventory Costing Methods

M7-5
LO2

Indicate whether the FIFO or LIFO inventory costing method normally produces each of the following effects under the listed circumstances.

a. Declining costs
  Highest net income ______
  Highest inventory ______
b. Rising costs
  Highest net income ______
  Highest inventory ______

Matching Inventory Costing Method Choices to Company Circumstances

M7-6
LO3

Indicate whether the FIFO or LIFO inventory costing method would normally be selected when inventory costs are rising. Explain why.

Reporting Inventory Under Lower of Cost or Market

M7-7
LO4

Knight Company had the following inventory items on hand at the end of the year.

	Quantity	Cost per Item	Replacement Cost per Item
Item A	70	$85	$100
Item B	30	60	55

Computing the lower of cost or market on an item-by-item basis, determine what amount would be reported on the balance sheet for inventory.

Determining the Effects of Inventory Management Changes on Inventory Turnover Ratio

M7-8
LO5

Indicate the most likely effect of the following changes in inventory management on the inventory turnover ratio (use + for increase, − for decrease, and NE for no effect).

___ *a.* Have parts inventory delivered daily by suppliers instead of weekly.
___ *b.* Extend payments for inventory purchases from 15 days to 30 days.
___ *c.* Shorten production process from 10 days to 8 days.

M7-9 LO7 Determining the Financial Statement Effects of Inventory Errors

Assume the 2011 ending inventory was understated by $100,000. Explain how this error would affect the 2011 and 2012 pretax income amounts. What would be the effects if the 2011 ending inventory were overstated by $100,000 instead of understated?

EXERCISES

connect ACCOUNTING

E7-1 LO1 Analyzing Items to Be Included in Inventory

Based on its physical count of inventory in its warehouse at year-end, December 31, 2011, Madison Company planned to report inventory of $34,500. During the audit, the independent CPA developed the following additional information:

a. Goods from a supplier costing $700 are in transit with UPS on December 31, 2011. The terms are FOB shipping point (explained in the "Required" section). Because these goods had not yet arrived, they were excluded from the physical inventory count.
b. Madison delivered samples costing $1,800 to a customer on December 27, 2011, with the understanding that they would be returned to Madison on January 15, 2012. Because these goods were not on hand, they were excluded from the inventory count.
c. On December 31, 2011, goods in transit to customers, with terms FOB shipping point, amounted to $6,500 (expected delivery date January 10, 2012). Because the goods had been shipped, they were excluded from the physical inventory count.
d. On December 31, 2011, goods in transit to customers, with terms FOB destination, amounted to $1,500 (expected delivery date January 10, 2012). Because the goods had been shipped, they were excluded from the physical inventory count.

Required:
Madison's accounting policy requires including in inventory all goods for which it has title. Note that the point where title (ownership) changes hands is determined by the shipping terms in the sales contract. When goods are shipped "FOB shipping point," title changes hands at shipment and the buyer normally pays for shipping. When they are shipped "FOB destination," title changes hands on delivery, and the seller normally pays for shipping. Begin with the $34,500 inventory amount and compute the correct amount for the ending inventory. Explain the basis for your treatment of each of the preceding items. (**Hint:** Set up three columns: Item, Amount, and Explanation.)

E7-2 LO1 Inferring Missing Amounts Based on Income Statement Relationships

Supply the missing dollar amounts for the income statement for each of the following independent cases. (**Hint:** In Case B, work from the bottom up.)

	Case A		Case B		Case C	
Net sales revenue		$7,500		$?		$6,000
Beginning inventory	$11,200		$ 6,500		$ 4,000	
Purchases	5,000		?		9,500	
Goods available for sale	?		15,050		13,500	
Ending inventory	10,200		11,050		?	
Cost of goods sold		?		?		4,500
Gross profit		?		1,500		?
Expenses		400		?		700
Pretax income		$1,100		$ (400)		$ 800

E7-3 LO1 Inferring Missing Amounts Based on Income Statement Relationships

Supply the missing dollar amounts for the income statement for each of the following independent cases:

Cases	Sales Revenue	Beginning Inventory	Purchases	Total Available	Ending Inventory	Cost of Goods Sold	Gross Profit	Expenses	Pretax Income (Loss)
A	$ 650	$100	$700	$?	$500	$?	$?	$200	$?
B	1,100	200	900	?	?	?	?	150	150
C	?	150	?	?	300	200	400	100	?
D	800	?	550	?	300	?	?	200	200
E	1,000	?	900	1,100	?	?	500	?	(50)

Inferring Merchandise Purchases

E7-4
LO1

Abercrombie and Fitch

Abercrombie and Fitch is a leading retailer of casual apparel for men, women, and children. Assume that you are employed as a stock analyst and your boss has just completed a review of the new Abercrombie annual report. She provided you with her notes, but they are missing some information that you need. Her notes show that the ending inventory for Abercrombie in the current year was $372,422,000 and in the previous year was $333,153,000. Net sales for the current year were $3,540,276,000. Cost of goods sold was $1,178,584,000. Net income was $272,255,000. For your analysis, you determine that you need to know the amount of purchases for the year.

Required:
Can you develop the information from her notes? Explain and show calculations. (**Hint:** Use the cost of goods sold equation or the inventory T-account to solve for the needed value.)

Calculating Ending Inventory and Cost of Goods Sold Under FIFO, LIFO, and Average Cost

E7-5
LO2

Star Company uses a periodic inventory system. At the end of the annual accounting period, December 31, 2012, the accounting records provided the following information for product 1:

	Units	Unit Cost
Inventory, December 31, 2011	2,000	$5
For the year 2012:		
Purchase, March 21	5,000	7
Purchase, August 1	3,000	8
Inventory, December 31, 2012	4,000	

Required:
Compute ending inventory and cost of goods sold under FIFO, LIFO, and average cost inventory costing methods. (**Hint:** Set up adjacent columns for each case.)

Calculating Ending Inventory and Cost of Goods Sold Under FIFO, LIFO, and Average Cost

E7-6
LO2

Hamilton Company uses a periodic inventory system. At the end of the annual accounting period, December 31, 2012, the accounting records provided the following information for product 1:

	Units	Unit Cost
Inventory, December 31, 2011	2,000	$5
For the year 2012:		
Purchase, March 21	6,000	4
Purchase, August 1	4,000	2
Inventory, December 31, 2012	3,000	

Required:
Compute ending inventory and cost of goods sold under FIFO, LIFO, and average cost inventory costing methods. (**Hint:** Set up adjacent columns for each case.)

E7-7 Analyzing and Interpreting the Financial Statement Effects of LIFO and FIFO

LO2, 3

Element Company uses a periodic inventory system. At the end of the annual accounting period, December 31, 2012, the accounting records provided the following information for product 2:

		Units	Unit Cost
Inventory, December 31, 2011		3,000	$12
For the year 2012:			
Purchase, April 11		9,000	10
Purchase, June 1		8,000	15
Sales ($50 each)		11,000	
Operating expenses (excluding income tax expense)	$195,000		

Required:

1. Prepare a separate income statement through pretax income that details cost of goods sold for (*a*) Case A: FIFO and (*b*) Case B: LIFO. For each case, show the computation of the ending inventory. (**Hint:** Set up adjacent columns for each case.)
2. Compare the pretax income and the ending inventory amounts between the two cases. Explain the similarities and differences.
3. Which inventory costing method may be preferred for income tax purposes? Explain.

E7-8 Analyzing and Interpreting the Financial Statement Effects of LIFO and FIFO

LO2, 3

Beck Inc. uses a periodic inventory system. At the end of the annual accounting period, December 31, 2012, the accounting records provided the following information for product 2:

		Units	Unit Cost
Inventory, December 31, 2011		7,000	$ 5
For the year 2012:			
Purchase, March 5		19,000	9
Purchase, September 19		10,000	11
Sale ($28 each)		8,000	
Sale ($30 each)		16,000	
Operating expenses (excluding income tax expense)	$500,000		

Required:

1. Prepare a separate income statement through pretax income that details cost of goods sold for (*a*) Case A: FIFO and (*b*) Case B: LIFO. For each case, show the computation of the ending inventory. (**Hint:** Set up adjacent columns for each case.)
2. Compare the pretax income and the ending inventory amounts between the two cases. Explain the similarities and differences.
3. Which inventory costing method may be preferred for income tax purposes? Explain.

E7-9 Evaluating the Choice among Three Alternative Inventory Methods Based on Income and Cash Flow Effects

LO2, 3

Daniel Company uses a periodic inventory system. Data for 2012: beginning merchandise inventory (December 31, 2011), 2,000 units at $38; purchases, 8,000 units at $40; expenses (excluding income taxes), $194,500; ending inventory per physical count at December 31, 2012, 1,800 units; sales, 8,200 units; sales price per unit, $75; and average income tax rate, 30 percent.

Required:

1. Compute cost of goods sold and prepare income statements under the FIFO, LIFO, and average cost inventory costing methods. Use a format similar to the following:

		INVENTORY COSTING METHOD		
Cost of Goods Sold	Units	FIFO	LIFO	Average Cost
Beginning inventory	_____	$_____	$_____	$_____
Purchases	_____	_____	_____	_____
Goods available for sale	_____	_____	_____	_____
Ending inventory	_____	_____	_____	_____
Cost of goods sold	_____	$_____	$_____	$_____

Income Statement	FIFO	LIFO	Average Cost
Sales revenue	$______	$______	$______
Cost of goods sold	______	______	______
Gross profit	______	______	______
Expenses	______	______	______
Pretax income	______	______	______
Income tax expense	______	______	______
Net income	$______	$______	$______

2. Between FIFO and LIFO, which method is preferable in terms of (*a*) net income and (*b*) income taxes paid (cash flow)? Explain.
3. What would your answer to requirement (2) be, assuming that prices were falling? Explain.

E7-10
LO2, 3

Evaluating the Choice among Three Alternative Inventory Methods Based on Cash Flow Effects

Following is partial information for the income statement of Lumber Company under three different inventory costing methods, assuming the use of a periodic inventory system:

	FIFO	LIFO	Average Cost
Cost of goods sold			
Beginning inventory (400 units)	$11,200	$11,200	$11,200
Purchases (475 units)	17,100	17,100	17,100
Goods available for sale			
Ending inventory (545 units)	______	______	______
Cost of goods sold	$	$	$
Sales, 330 units; unit sales price, $50			
Expenses, $1,700			

Required:

1. Compute cost of goods sold under the FIFO, LIFO, and average cost inventory costing methods.
2. Prepare an income statement through pretax income for each method.
3. Rank the three methods in order of income taxes paid (favorable cash flow) and explain the basis for your ranking.

E7-11
LO4

Reporting Inventory at Lower of Cost or Market

Jones Company is preparing the annual financial statements dated December 31, 2012. Ending inventory information about the five major items stocked for regular sale follows:

	ENDING INVENTORY, 2012		
Item	Quantity on Hand	Unit Cost When Acquired (FIFO)	Replacement Cost (Market) at Year-End
A	50	$15	$12
B	80	30	40
C	10	48	52
D	70	25	30
E	350	10	5

Required:

Compute the valuation that should be used for the 2012 ending inventory using the LCM rule applied on an item-by-item basis. (**Hint:** Set up columns for Item, Quantity, Total Cost, Total Market, and LCM Valuation.)

E7-12
LO4

Reporting Inventory at Lower of Cost or Market

Parson Company was formed on January 1, 2012, and is preparing the annual financial statements dated December 31, 2012. Ending inventory information about the four major items stocked for regular sale follows:

	ENDING INVENTORY, 2012		
Item	Quantity on Hand	Unit Cost When Acquired (FIFO)	Replacement Cost (Market) at Year-End
A	20	$10	$15
B	55	40	44
C	35	57	55
D	10	27	32

Required:

1. Compute the valuation that should be used for the 2012 ending inventory using the LCM rule applied on an item-by-item basis. (**Hint:** Set up columns for Item, Quantity, Total Cost, Total Market, and LCM Valuation.)
2. What will be the effect of the write-down of inventory to lower of cost or market on cost of goods sold for the year ended December 31, 2012?

E7-13
LO5

Analyzing and Interpreting the Inventory Turnover Ratio

Dell Inc. is the leading manufacturer of personal computers. In a recent year, it reported the following in dollars in millions:

Net sales revenue	$61,101
Cost of sales	50,144
Beginning inventory	1,180
Ending inventory	867

Required:

1. Determine the inventory turnover ratio and average days to sell inventory for the current year.
2. Explain the meaning of each number.

E7-14
LO5, 6

Analyzing and Interpreting the Effects of the LIFO/FIFO Choice on Inventory Turnover Ratio

The records at the end of January 2012 for Captain Company showed the following for a particular kind of merchandise:

Inventory, December 31, 2011, at FIFO: 19 Units @ $16 = $304
Inventory, December 31, 2011, at LIFO: 19 Units @ $12 = $228

Transactions	Units	Unit Cost	Total Cost
Purchase, January 9, 2012	25	$14	$350
Purchase, January 20, 2012	50	19	950
Sale, January 21, 2012 (at $38 per unit)	40		
Sale, January 27, 2012 (at $39 per unit)	28		

Required:

Compute the inventory turnover ratio under the FIFO and LIFO inventory costing methods (show computations and round to the nearest dollar). Which costing method is the more accurate indicator of the efficiency of inventory management? Explain.

Interpreting the Effect of Changes in Inventories and Accounts Payable on Cash Flow from Operations

E7-15
LO5

First Team Sports, Inc.

First Team Sports, Inc., is engaged in the manufacture (through independent contractors) and distribution of in-line roller skates, ice skates, street hockey equipment, and related accessory products. Its recent annual report included the following on its balance sheets:

CONSOLIDATED BALANCE SHEETS		
	Current Year	Previous Year
...		
Inventory (Note 3)	$22,813,850	$20,838,171
...		
Trade accounts payable	9,462,883	9,015,376

Required:
Explain the effects of the changes in inventory and trade accounts payable on cash flow from operating activities for the current year.

Analyzing Notes to Adjust Inventory from LIFO to FIFO

E7-16
LO6

The following note was contained in a recent Ford Motor Company annual report:

NOTE 8. INVENTORIES—AUTOMOTIVE SECTOR Inventories at December 31 were as follows (dollars in millions)		
	Current Year	Previous Year
Raw material, work in process, & supplies	$3,016	$ 4,360
Finished products	6,493	6,861
Total inventories at FIFO	9,509	11,221
Less LIFO Adjustment	(891)	(1,100)
Total	$8,618	$10,121
About one-fourth of inventories were determined under the last-in, first-out method.		

Required:

1. What amount of ending inventory would have been reported in the current year if Ford had used only FIFO?
2. The cost of goods sold reported by Ford for the current year was $127,103 million. Determine the cost of goods sold that would have been reported if Ford had used only FIFO for both years.
3. Explain why Ford management chose to use LIFO for certain of its inventories.

Analyzing the Effects of an Error in Recording Purchases

E7-17
LO7

Zocco Ski Company mistakenly recorded purchases of inventory on account received during the last week of December 2011 as purchases during January of 2012 (this is called a purchases cutoff error). Zocco uses a periodic inventory system, and ending inventory was correctly counted and reported each year.

Required:
Assuming that no correction was made in 2011 or 2012, indicate whether each of the following financial statement amounts will be understated, overstated, or correct.

1. Net Income for 2011.
2. Net Income for 2012.
3. Retained Earnings for December 31, 2011.
4. Retained Earnings for December 31, 2012.

E7-18
LO7

AMERICAN GREETINGS

Analyzing the Effect of an Inventory Error Disclosed in an Actual Note to a Financial Statement

Several years ago, the financial statements of Gibson Greeting Cards, now part of American Greetings, contained the following note:

> On July 1, the Company announced that it had determined that the inventory . . . had been overstated. . . . The overstatement of inventory . . . was $8,806,000.

Gibson reported an incorrect net income amount of $25,852,000 for the year in which the error occurred and the income tax rate was 39.3 percent.

Required:

1. Compute the amount of net income that Gibson reported after correcting the inventory error. Show computations.
2. Assume that the inventory error was not discovered. Identify the financial statement accounts that would have been incorrect (*a*) for the year the error occurred and (*b*) for the subsequent year. State whether each account was understated or overstated.

E7-19
LO7

Analyzing and Interpreting the Impact of an Inventory Error

Grants Corporation prepared the following two income statements (simplified for illustrative purposes):

	First Quarter 2011		Second Quarter 2011	
Sales revenue		$11,000		$18,000
Cost of goods sold				
Beginning inventory	$4,000		$ 3,800	
Purchases	3,000		13,000	
Goods available for sale	7,000		16,800	
Ending inventory	3,800		9,000	
Cost of goods sold		3,200		7,800
Gross profit		7,800		10,200
Expenses		5,000		6,000
Pretax income		$ 2,800		$ 4,200

During the third quarter, it was discovered that the ending inventory for the first quarter should have been $4,400.

Required:

1. What effect did this error have on the combined pretax income of the two quarters? Explain.
2. Did this error affect the EPS amounts for each quarter? (See Chapter 5 for discussion of EPS.) Explain.
3. Prepare corrected income statements for each quarter.
4. Set up a schedule with the following headings to reflect the comparative effects of the correct and incorrect amounts on the income statement:

	1st Quarter			2nd Quarter		
Income Statement Item	Incorrect	Correct	Error	Incorrect	Correct	Error

E7-20

ConocoPhillips

(Supplement A) Analyzing the Effects of a Reduction in the Amount of LIFO Inventory

An annual report of ConocoPhillips contained the following note:

> During 2008, certain international inventory quantity reductions caused a liquidation of LIFO inventory values resulting in a $39 million benefit to our R&M segment net income. In 2007, a liquidation of LIFO inventory values increased net income $280 million, of which $260 million was attributable to our R&M segment.

Required:

1. Explain why the reduction in inventory quantity increased net income for ConocoPhillips.
2. If ConocoPhillips had used FIFO, would the reductions in inventory quantity during the two years have increased net income? Explain.

(Supplement B) Recording Sales and Purchases with Cash Discounts

E7-21

Brett's Cycles sells merchandise on credit terms of 2/15, n/30. A sale invoiced at $900 (cost of sales $600) was made to Shannon Allen on February 1, 2011. The company uses the gross method of recording sales discounts.

Required:

1. Give the journal entry to record the credit sale. Assume use of the perpetual inventory system.
2. Give the journal entry, assuming that the account was collected in full on February 9, 2011.
3. Give the journal entry, assuming, instead, that the account was collected in full on March 2, 2011.

On March 4, 2011, the company purchased bicycles and accessories from a supplier on credit, invoiced at $8,400; the terms were 3/10, n/30. The company uses the gross method to record purchases.

Required:

4. Give the journal entry to record the purchase on credit. Assume the use of the perpetual inventory system.
5. Give the journal entry, assuming that the account was paid in full on March 12, 2011.
6. Give the journal entry, assuming, instead, that the account was paid in full on March 28, 2011.

(Supplement C) Recording Purchases and Sales Using a Perpetual and Periodic Inventory System

E7-22

Misty Company reported beginning inventory of 100 units at a unit cost of $20. It engaged in the following purchase and sale transactions during 2011:

Jan. 14	Sold 20 units at unit sales price of $47.50 on open account.
April 9	Purchased 15 additional units at unit cost of $20 on open account.
Sept. 2	Sold 45 units at sales price of $50 on open account.

At the end of 2011, a physical count showed that Misty Company had 50 units of inventory still on hand.

Required:

Record each transaction, assuming that Misty Company uses (*a*) a perpetual inventory system and (*b*) a periodic inventory system (including any necessary entries at the end of the accounting period on December 31).

To practice with more exercises, go to the text website at **www.mhhe.com/libby7e**.

connect ACCOUNTING

PROBLEMS

Analyzing Items to Be Included in Inventory

P7-1
L01

Walker Company has just completed a physical inventory count at year-end, December 31, 2011. Only the items on the shelves, in storage, and in the receiving area were counted and costed on a FIFO basis. The inventory amounted to $65,000. During the audit, the independent CPA developed the following additional information:

a. Goods costing $750 were being used by a customer on a trial basis and were excluded from the inventory count at December 31, 2011.

b. Goods in transit on December 31, 2011, from a supplier, with terms FOB destination (explained in the "Required" section), cost $900. Because these goods had not yet arrived, they were excluded from the physical inventory count.

c. On December 31, 2011, goods in transit to customers, with terms FOB shipping point, amounted to $1,700 (expected delivery date January 10, 2012). Because the goods had been shipped, they were excluded from the physical inventory count.

d. On December 28, 2011, a customer purchased goods for cash amounting to $2,650 and left them "for pickup on January 3, 2012." Walker Company had paid $1,590 for the goods and, because they were on hand, included the latter amount in the physical inventory count.

e. On the date of the inventory count, the company received notice from a supplier that goods ordered earlier at a cost of $3,550 had been delivered to the transportation company on December 27, 2011; the terms were FOB shipping point. Because the shipment had not arrived by December 31, 2011, it was excluded from the physical inventory count.

f. On December 31, 2011, the company shipped $850 worth of goods to a customer, FOB destination. The goods are expected to arrive at their destination no earlier than January 8, 2012. Because the goods were not on hand, they were not included in the physical inventory count.

g. One of the items sold by the company has such a low volume that management planned to drop it last year. To induce Walker Company to continue carrying the item, the manufacturer-supplier provided the item on a "consignment basis." This means that the manufacturer-supplier retains ownership of the item, and Walker Company (the consignee) has no responsibility to pay for the items until they are sold to a customer. Each month, Walker Company sends a report to the manufacturer on the number sold and remits cash for the cost. At the end of December 2011, Walker Company had six of these items on hand; therefore, they were included in the physical inventory count at $950 each.

Required:

Assume that Walker's accounting policy requires including in inventory all goods for which it has title. Note that the point where title (ownership) changes hands is determined by the shipping terms in the sales contract. When goods are shipped "FOB shipping point," title changes hands at shipment and the buyer normally pays for shipping. When they are shipped "FOB destination," title changes hands on delivery, and the seller normally pays for shipping. Begin with the $65,000 inventory amount and compute the correct amount for the ending inventory. Explain the basis for your treatment of each of the preceding items. (**Hint:** Set up three columns: Item, Amount, and Explanation.)

P7-2
LO2

Analyzing the Effects of Four Alternative Inventory Methods (AP7-1)

Kirtland Corporation uses a periodic inventory system. At the end of the annual accounting period, December 31, 2012, the accounting records for the most popular item in inventory showed the following:

Transactions	Units	Unit Cost
Beginning inventory, January 1, 2012	400	$3.00
Transactions during 2012:		
a. Purchase, January 30	600	3.20
b. Purchase, May 1	460	3.50
c. Sale ($5 each)	(160)	
d. Sale ($5 each)	(700)	

Required:

Compute the amount of (*a*) goods available for sale, (*b*) ending inventory, and (*c*) cost of goods sold at December 31, 2012, under each of the following inventory costing methods (show computations and round to the nearest dollar):

1. Average cost (round the average cost per unit to the nearest cent).
2. First-in, first-out.
3. Last-in, first-out.
4. Specific identification, assuming that the first sale was selected two-fifths from the beginning inventory and three-fifths from the purchase of January 30, 2012. Assume that the second sale was selected from the remainder of the beginning inventory, with the balance from the purchase of May 1, 2012.

P7-3
LO2, 3

eXcel
www.mhhe.com/libby7e

Evaluating Four Alternative Inventory Methods Based on Income and Cash Flow (AP7-2)

At the end of January 2011, the records of Donner Company showed the following for a particular item that sold at $16 per unit:

Transactions	Units	Amount
Inventory, January 1, 2011	500	$2,500
Purchase, January 12	600	3,600
Purchase, January 26	160	1,280
Sale	(370)	
Sale	(250)	

Required:

1. Assuming the use of a periodic inventory system, prepare a summarized income statement through gross profit for the month of January under each method of inventory: (*a*) average cost, (*b*) FIFO, (*c*) LIFO, and (*d*) specific identification. For specific identification, assume that the first sale was selected from the beginning inventory and the second sale was selected from the January 12 purchase. Round the average cost per unit to the nearest cent. Show the inventory computations in detail.
2. Of FIFO and LIFO, which method would result in the higher pretax income? Which would result in the higher EPS?
3. Of FIFO and LIFO, which method would result in the lower income tax expense? Explain, assuming a 30 percent average tax rate.
4. Of FIFO and LIFO, which method would produce the more favorable cash flow? Explain.

Analyzing and Interpreting Income Manipulation Under the LIFO Inventory Method

P7-4
LO2, 3

Atlantic Company sells electronic test equipment that it acquires from a foreign source. During the year 2011, the inventory records reflected the following:

	Units	Unit Cost	Total Cost
Beginning inventory	20	$11,500	$230,000
Purchases	42	10,000	420,000
Sales (47 units at $24,500 each)			

Inventory is valued at cost using the LIFO inventory method.

Required:

1. Complete the following income statement summary using the LIFO method and the periodic inventory system (show computations):

Sales revenue	$
Cost of goods sold	
Gross profit	
Expenses	300,000
Pretax income	$
Ending inventory	$

2. The management, for various reasons, is considering buying 20 additional units before December 31, 2011, at $9,500 each. Restate the income statement (and ending inventory), assuming that this purchase is made on December 31, 2011.
3. How much did pretax income change because of the decision on December 31, 2011? Assuming that the unit cost of test equipment is expected to continue to decline in 2012, is there any evidence of income manipulation? Explain.

Evaluating the LIFO and FIFO Choice When Costs Are Rising and Falling (AP7-3)

P7-5
LO2, 3
eXcel
www.mhhe.com/libby7e

Income is to be evaluated under four different situations as follows:

a. Prices are rising:
   (1) Situation A: FIFO is used.
   (2) Situation B: LIFO is used.

b. Prices are falling:
   (1) Situation C: FIFO is used.
   (2) Situation D: LIFO is used.

The basic data common to all four situations are: sales, 500 units for $15,000; beginning inventory, 300 units; purchases, 400 units; ending inventory, 200 units; and operating expenses, $4,000. The following tabulated income statements for each situation have been set up for analytical purposes:

	PRICES RISING		PRICES FALLING	
	Situation A FIFO	Situation B LIFO	Situation C FIFO	Situation D LIFO
Sales revenue	$15,000	$15,000	$15,000	$15,000
Cost of goods sold:				
Beginning inventory	3,300	?	?	?
Purchases	4,800	?	?	?
Goods available for sale	8,100	?	?	?
Ending inventory	2,400	?	?	?
Cost of goods sold	5,700	?	?	?
Gross profit	9,300	?	?	?
Expenses	4,000	4,000	4,000	4,000
Pretax income	5,300	?	?	?
Income tax expense (30%)	1,590	?	?	?
Net income	$ 3,710			

Required:

1. Complete the preceding tabulation for each situation. In Situations A and B (prices rising), assume the following: beginning inventory, 300 units at $11 = $3,300; purchases, 400 units at $12 = $4,800. In Situations C and D (prices falling), assume the opposite; that is, beginning inventory, 300 units at $12 = $3,600; purchases, 400 units at $11 = $4,400. Use periodic inventory procedures.
2. Analyze the relative effects on pretax income and on net income as demonstrated by requirement (1) when prices are rising and when prices are falling.
3. Analyze the relative effects on the cash position for each situation.
4. Would you recommend FIFO or LIFO? Explain.

P7-6
LO4

Evaluating the Income Statement and Cash Flow Effects of Lower of Cost or Market

Harvey Company prepared its annual financial statements dated December 31, 2011. The company applies the FIFO inventory costing method; however, the company neglected to apply LCM to the ending inventory. The preliminary 2011 income statement follows:

Sales revenue		$280,000
Cost of goods sold		
Beginning inventory	$ 33,000	
Purchases	184,000	
Goods available for sale	217,000	
Ending inventory (FIFO cost)	46,500	
Cost of goods sold		170,500
Gross profit		109,500
Operating expenses		62,000
Pretax income		47,500
Income tax expense (30%)		14,250
Net income		$ 33,250

Assume that you have been asked to restate the 2011 financial statements to incorporate LCM. You have developed the following data relating to the 2011 ending inventory:

Item	Quantity	Acquisition Cost Unit	Acquisition Cost Total	Current Replacement Unit Cost (Market)
A	3,050	$3	$ 9,150	$4
B	1,500	5	7,500	3.5
C	7,100	1.5	10,650	3.5
D	3,200	6	19,200	4
			$46,500	

Required:

1. Restate this income statement to reflect LCM valuation of the 2011 ending inventory. Apply LCM on an item-by-item basis and show computations.
2. Compare and explain the LCM effect on each amount that was changed on the income statement in requirement (1).
3. What is the conceptual basis for applying LCM to merchandise inventories?
4. Thought question: What effect did LCM have on the 2011 cash flow? What will be the long-term effect on cash flow?

Evaluating the Effects of Manufacturing Changes on Inventory Turnover Ratio and Cash Flows from Operating Activities

P7-7
LO5

eXcel
www.mhhe.com/libby7e

Carter and Company has been operating for five years as an electronics component manufacturer specializing in cellular phone components. During this period, it has experienced rapid growth in sales revenue and in inventory. Mr. Carter and his associates have hired you as its first corporate controller. You have put into place new purchasing and manufacturing procedures that are expected to reduce inventories by approximately one-third by year-end. You have gathered the following data related to the changes:

	(dollars in thousands) Beginning of Year	End of Year (projected)
Inventory	$595,700	$394,310
		Current Year (projected)
Cost of goods sold		$7,008,984

Required:

1. Compute the inventory turnover ratio based on two different assumptions:
   a. Those presented in the preceding table (a decrease in the balance in inventory).
   b. No change from the beginning-of-the-year inventory balance.
2. Compute the effect of the projected change in the balance in inventory on cash flow from operating activities for the year (the sign and amount of effect).
3. On the basis of the preceding analysis, write a brief memo explaining how an increase in inventory turnover can result in an increase in cash flow from operating activities. Also explain how this increase can benefit the company.

Evaluating the Choice between LIFO and FIFO Based on an Inventory Note

P7-8
LO6

An annual report for General Motors Corporation included the following note:

> Inventories are stated generally at cost, which is not in excess of market. The cost of substantially all domestic inventories was determined by the last-in, first-out (LIFO) method. If the first-in,

first-out (FIFO) method of inventory valuation had been used by the corporation for U.S. inventories, it is estimated that they would be $2,077.1 million higher at the end of this year, compared with $1,784.5 million higher at the end of last year.

For the year, GM reported net income (after taxes) of $320.5 million. At year-end, the balance of the GM retained earnings account was $15,340 million.

Required:

1. Determine the amount of net income that GM would have reported for the year if it had used the FIFO method (assume a 30 percent tax rate).
2. Determine the amount of retained earnings that GM would have reported at year-end if it always had used the FIFO method (assume a 30 percent tax rate).
3. Use of the LIFO method reduced the amount of taxes that GM had to pay for the year compared with the amount that would have been paid if GM had used FIFO. Calculate the amount of this reduction (assume a 30 percent tax rate).

P7-9 LO7 Analyzing and Interpreting the Effects of Inventory Errors (AP7-4)

eXcel
www.mhhe.com/libby7e

The income statement for Pruitt Company summarized for a four-year period shows the following:

	2011	2012	2013	2014
Sales revenue	$2,025,000	$2,450,000	$2,700,000	$2,975,000
Cost of goods sold	1,505,000	1,627,000	1,782,000	2,113,000
Gross profit	520,000	823,000	918,000	862,000
Expenses	490,000	513,000	538,000	542,000
Pretax income	30,000	310,000	380,000	320,000
Income tax expense (30%)	9,000	93,000	114,000	96,000
Net income	$ 21,000	$ 217,000	$ 266,000	$ 224,000

An audit revealed that in determining these amounts, the ending inventory for 2012 was overstated by $18,000. The company uses a periodic inventory system.

Required:

1. Recast the income statements to reflect the correct amounts, taking into consideration the inventory error.
2. Compute the gross profit percentage for each year (*a*) before the correction and (*b*) after the correction.
3. What effect would the error have had on the income tax expense assuming a 30 percent average rate?

P7-10 (Supplement A) Analyzing LIFO and FIFO When Inventory Quantities Decline Based on an Actual Note

In a recent annual report, General Electric reported the following in its inventory note:

December 31 (dollars in millions)	Current Year	Prior Year
Raw materials and work in progress	$5,603	$5,515
Finished goods	2,863	2,546
Unbilled shipments	246	280
	8,712	8,341
Less revaluation to LIFO	(2,226)	(2,076)
LIFO value of inventories	$6,486	$6,265

It also reported a $23 million change in cost of goods sold due to "lower inventory levels."

Required:

1. Compute the increase or decrease in the pretax operating profit (loss) that would have been reported for the current year had GE employed FIFO accounting for all inventory for both years.
2. Compute the increase or decrease in pretax operating profit that would have been reported had GE employed LIFO but not reduced inventory quantities during the current year.

ALTERNATE PROBLEMS

Analyzing the Effects of Four Alternative Inventory Methods (P7-2)

AP7-1
LO2

Dixon Company uses a periodic inventory system. At the end of the annual accounting period, December 31, 2011, the accounting records for the most popular item in inventory showed the following:

Transactions	Units	Unit Cost
Beginning inventory, January 1, 2011	390	$32
Transactions during 2011:		
a. Purchase, February 20	700	34
b. Purchase, June 30	460	37
c. Sale ($50 each)	(70)	
d. Sale ($50 each)	(750)	

Required:

Compute the cost of (*a*) goods available for sale, (*b*) ending inventory, and (*c*) goods sold at December 31, 2011, under each of the following inventory costing methods (show computations and round to the nearest dollar):

1. Average cost (round average cost per unit to the nearest cent).
2. First-in, first-out.
3. Last-in, first-out.
4. Specific identification, assuming that the first sale was selected two-fifths from the beginning inventory and three-fifths from the purchase of February 20, 2011. Assume that the second sale was selected from the remainder of the beginning inventory, with the balance from the purchase of June 30, 2011.

Evaluating Four Alternative Inventory Methods Based on Income and Cash Flow (P7-3)

AP7-2
LO2, 3

At the end of January 2012, the records of NewRidge Company showed the following for a particular item that sold at $16 per unit:

Transactions	Units	Amount
Inventory, January 1, 2012	120	$ 960
Purchase, January 12	380	3,420
Purchase, January 26	200	2,200
Sale	(100)	
Sale	(140)	

Required:

1. Assuming the use of a periodic inventory system, prepare a summarized income statement through gross profit for January 2012 under each method of inventory: (*a*) weighted average cost, (*b*) FIFO, (*c*) LIFO, and (*d*) specific identification. For specific identification, assume that the first sale was selected from the beginning inventory and the second sale was selected from the January 12 purchase. Show the inventory computations (including for ending inventory) in detail.
2. Of FIFO and LIFO, which method would result in the higher pretax income? Which would result in the higher EPS?
3. Of FIFO and LIFO, which method would result in the lower income tax expense? Explain, assuming a 30 percent average tax rate.
4. Of FIFO and LIFO, which method would produce the more favorable cash flow? Explain.

Evaluating the LIFO and FIFO Choice When Costs Are Rising and Falling (P7-5)

AP7-3
LO2, 3

Income is to be evaluated under four different situations as follows:

a. Prices are rising:
  (1) Situation A: FIFO is used.
  (2) Situation B: LIFO is used.

b. Prices are falling:
  (1) Situation C: FIFO is used.
  (2) Situation D: LIFO is used.

The basic data common to all four situations are: sales, 510 units for $13,260; beginning inventory, 340 units; purchases, 410 units; ending inventory, 240 units; and operating expenses, $5,000. The following tabulated income statements for each situation have been set up for analytical purposes:

	PRICES RISING		PRICES FALLING	
	Situation A FIFO	Situation B LIFO	Situation C FIFO	Situation D LIFO
Sales revenue	$13,260	$13,260	$13,260	$13,260
Cost of goods sold:				
Beginning inventory	3,060	?	?	?
Purchases	4,100	?	?	?
Goods available for sale	7,160	?	?	?
Ending inventory	2,400	?	?	?
Cost of goods sold	4,760	?	?	?
Gross profit	8,500	?	?	?
Expenses	5,000	5,000	5,000	5,000
Pretax income	3,500	?	?	?
Income tax expense (30%)	1,050	?	?	?
Net income	$ 2,450			

Required:

1. Complete the preceding tabulation for each situation. In Situations A and B (prices rising), assume the following: beginning inventory, 340 units at $9 = $3,060; purchases, 410 units at $10 = $4,100. In Situations C and D (prices falling), assume the opposite; that is, beginning inventory, 340 units at $10 = $3,400; purchases, 410 units at $9 = $3,690. Use periodic inventory procedures.
2. Analyze the relative effects on pretax income and on net income as demonstrated by requirement (1) when prices are rising and when prices are falling.
3. Analyze the relative effects on the cash position for each situation.
4. Would you recommend FIFO or LIFO? Explain.

AP7-4 LO7 Analyzing and Interpreting the Effects of Inventory Errors (P7-9)

The income statements for four consecutive years for Colca Company reflected the following summarized amounts:

	2011	2012	2013	2014
Sales revenue	$60,000	$63,000	$65,000	$68,000
Cost of goods sold	39,000	43,000	44,000	46,000
Gross profit	21,000	20,000	21,000	22,000
Expenses	16,000	17,000	17,000	19,000
Pretax income	$ 5,000	$ 3,000	$ 4,000	$ 3,000

Subsequent to development of these amounts, it has been determined that the physical inventory taken on December 31, 2012, was understated by $2,000.

Required:

1. Recast the income statements to reflect the correct amounts, taking into consideration the inventory error.
2. Compute the gross profit percentage for each year (*a*) before the correction and (*b*) after the correction.
3. What effect would the error have had on the income tax expense, assuming a 30 percent average rate?

CASES AND PROJECTS

Annual Report Cases

Finding Financial Information

CP7-1
LO1, 2, 5

AMERICAN EAGLE OUTFITTERS, INC.

Refer to the financial statements of American Eagle Outfitters given in Appendix B at the end of this book.

Required:

1. How much inventory does the company hold at the end of the most recent year?
2. Estimate the amount of merchandise that the company purchased during the current year. (**Hint:** Use the cost of goods sold equation and ignore "certain buying, occupancy, and warehousing expenses.")
3. What method does the company use to determine the cost of its inventory?
4. Compute the inventory turnover ratio for the current year. What does an inventory turnover ratio tell you?

Finding Financial Information

CP7-2
LO2, 4, 5, 7

URBN
URBAN OUTFITTERS INC.

Refer to the financial statements of Urban Outfitters given in Appendix C at the end of this book.

Required:

1. The company uses lower of cost or market to account for its inventory. At the end of the year, do you expect the company to write its inventory down to replacement cost or net realizable value? Explain your answer.
2. What method does the company use to determine the cost of its inventory?
3. If the company overstated ending inventory by $10 million for the year ended January 31, 2009, what would be the corrected value for Income before Income Taxes?
4. Compute the inventory turnover ratio for the current year. What does an inventory turnover ratio tell you?

Comparing Companies within an Industry

CP7-3
LO5

AMERICAN EAGLE OUTFITTERS, INC.

URBN
URBAN OUTFITTERS INC.

excel
www.mhhe.com/libby7e

Refer to the financial statements of American Eagle Outfitters (Appendix B) and Urban Outfitters (Appendix C) and the Industry Ratio Report (Appendix D) at the end of this book.

Required:

1. Compute the inventory turnover ratio for both companies for the current year. What do you infer from the difference?
2. Compare the inventory turnover ratio for both companies to the industry average. Are these two companies doing better or worse than the industry average in turning over their inventory?

Financial Reporting and Analysis Cases

Using Financial Reports: Interpreting the Effect of a Change in Accounting for Production-Related Costs

CP7-4
LO1

DANA

Dana Holding Corporation designs and manufactures component parts for the vehicular, industrial, and mobile off-highway original equipment markets. In a recent annual report, Dana's inventory note indicated the following:

> Dana changed its method of accounting for inventories effective January 1 . . . to include in inventory certain production-related costs previously charged to expense. This change in accounting principle resulted in a better matching of costs against related revenues. The effect of this change in accounting increased inventories by $23.0 and net income by $12.9.

Required:

1. Under Dana's previous accounting method, certain production costs were recognized as expenses on the income statement in the period they were incurred. When will they be recognized under the new accounting method?
2. Explain how including these costs in inventory increased both inventories and net income for the year.

CP7-5
LO5, 6

CATERPILLAR®

Using Financial Reports: Interpreting Effects of the LIFO/FIFO Choice on Inventory Turnover

In its annual report, Caterpillar, Inc., a major manufacturer of farm and construction equipment, reported the following information concerning its inventories:

> Inventories are stated at the lower of cost or market. Cost is principally determined using the last-in, first-out (LIFO) method. The value of inventories on the LIFO basis represented about 70% of total inventories at December 31, 2008, and about 75% of total inventories at December 31, 2007 and 2006.
>
> If the FIFO (first-in, first-out) method had been in use, inventories would have been $3,183 million, $2,617 million, and $2,403 million higher than reported at December 31, 2008, 2007, and 2006, respectively.

On its balance sheet, Caterpillar reported:

	2008	2007	2006
Inventories	$8,781	$7,204	$6,351

	2008	2007	2006
Cost of goods sold	$38,415	$32,626	$29,549

Required:

As a recently hired financial analyst, you have been asked to analyze the efficiency with which Caterpillar has been managing its inventory and to write a short report. Specifically, you have been asked to compute inventory turnover for 2008 based on FIFO and LIFO and to compare the two ratios with two standards: (1) Caterpillar for the prior year 2007 and (2) its chief competitor, John Deere. For 2008, John Deere's inventory turnover was 4.9 based on FIFO and 7.3 based on LIFO. In your report, include:

1. The appropriate ratios computed based on FIFO and LIFO.
2. An explanation of the differences in the ratios across the FIFO and LIFO methods.
3. An explanation of whether the FIFO or LIFO ratios provide a more accurate representation of the companies' efficiency in use of inventory.

Critical Thinking Cases

CP7-6
LO6

Seneca Foods

Making a Decision as a Financial Analyst: Analysis of the Effect of a Change to LIFO

A recent press release for Seneca Foods (licensee of the Libby's brand of canned fruits and vegetables) included the following information:

> The current year's net earnings were $8,019,000 or $0.65 per diluted share, compared with $32,067,000 or $2.63 per diluted share, last year. These results reflect the Company's decision to implement the LIFO (last-in, first-out) inventory valuation method effective December 30, 2007 (fourth quarter). The effect of this change was to reduce annual pretax earnings by $28,165,000 and net earnings by $18,307,000 or $1.50 per share ($1.49 diluted) below that which would have been reported using the Company's previous inventory method. The Company believes that in this period of significant inflation, the use of the LIFO method better matches current costs with current revenues. This change also results in cash savings of $9,858,000 by reducing the Company's income taxes, based on statutory rates. If the Company had remained on the FIFO (first-in,

first-out) inventory valuation method, the pretax results, less non-operating gains and losses, would have been an all-time record of $42,644,000, up from $40,009,000 in the prior year.

Required:

As a new financial analyst at a leading Wall Street investment banking firm, you are assigned to write a memo outlining the effects of the accounting change on Seneca's financial statements. Assume a 35 percent tax rate. In your report, be sure to include the following:

1. Why did management adopt LIFO?
2. By how much did the change affect pretax earnings and ending inventory? Verify that the amount of the tax savings listed in the press release is correct.
3. As an analyst, how would you react to the decrease in income caused by the adoption of LIFO? Consider all of the information in the press release.

Evaluating an Ethical Dilemma: Earnings, Inventory Purchases, and Management Bonuses

CP7-7

Micro Warehouse

Micro Warehouse was a computer software and hardware online and catalog sales company.* A *Wall Street Journal* article disclosed the following:

> **MICRO WAREHOUSE IS REORGANIZING TOP MANAGEMENT**
>
> Micro Warehouse Inc. announced a "significant reorganization" of its management, including the resignation of three senior executives. The move comes just a few weeks after the Norwalk, Conn., computer catalogue sales company said it overstated earnings by $28 million since 1992 as a result of accounting irregularities. That previous disclosure prompted a flurry of shareholder lawsuits against the company. In addition, Micro Warehouse said it is cooperating with an "informal inquiry" by the Securities and Exchange Commission.
>
> Source: Stephan E. Frank, *The Wall Street Journal,* November 21, 1996, p. B2.

Its Form 10-Q quarterly report filed with the Securities and Exchange Commission two days before indicated that inaccuracies involving understatement of purchases and accounts payable in current and prior periods amounted to $47.3 million. It also indicated that, as a result, $2.2 million of executive bonuses for 1995 would be rescinded. Micro Warehouse's total tax rate is approximately 40.4 percent. Both cost of goods sold and executive bonuses are fully deductible for tax purposes.

Required:

As a new staff member at Micro Warehouse's auditing firm, you are assigned to write a memo outlining the effects of the understatement of purchases and the rescinding of the bonuses. In your report, be sure to include the following:

1. The total effect on pretax and after-tax earnings of the understatement of purchases.
2. The total effect on pretax and after-tax earnings of the rescinding of the bonuses.
3. An estimate of the percentage of after-tax earnings management is receiving in bonuses.
4. A discussion of why Micro Warehouse's board of directors may have decided to tie managers' compensation to reported earnings and the possible relation between this type of bonus scheme and the accounting errors.

*Micro Warehouse declared bankruptcy in 2003.

Financial Reporting and Analysis Team Project

Team Project: Analyzing Inventories

CP7-8

LO2, 3, 5

As a team, select an industry to analyze. *Reuters* provides lists of industries under Sectors and Industries at www.reuters.com. (Click on an industry and then select Company Rankings for a list of members of that industry.) Each team member should acquire the annual report or 10-K for one publicly traded company in the industry, with each member selecting a different company. (Library files, the SEC EDGAR service at www.sec.gov, and the company itself are good sources.)

Required:

On an individual basis, each team member should write a short report answering the following questions about the selected company. Discuss any patterns across the companies that you as a team observe. Then, as a team, write a short report comparing and contrasting your companies.

1. If your company lists inventories in its balance sheet, what percentage is it of total assets for each of the last three years? If your company does not list inventories, discuss why this is so.
2. If your company lists inventories, what inventory costing method is applied to U.S. inventories?
   a. What do you think motivated this choice?
   b. If the company uses LIFO, how much higher or lower would net income before taxes be if it had used FIFO or a similar method instead?
3. Ratio Analysis:
   a. What does the inventory turnover ratio measure in general?
   b. If your company reports inventories, compute the ratio for the last three years.
   c. What do your results suggest about the company?
   d. If available, find the industry ratio for the most recent year, compare it to your results, and discuss why you believe your company differs or is similar to the industry ratio.
4. What is the effect of the change in inventories on cash flows from operating activities for the most recent year (that is, did the change increase or decrease operating cash flows)? Explain your answer.

Lecture Presentation LP-8
www.mhhe.com/libby7e

LEARNING OBJECTIVES

After studying this chapter, you should be able to:

1. Define, classify, and explain the nature of long-lived productive assets and interpret the fixed asset turnover ratio. p. 389

2. Apply the cost principle to measure the acquisition and maintenance of property, plant, and equipment. p. 391

3. Apply various cost allocation methods as assets are held and used over time. p. 396

4. Explain the effect of asset impairment on the financial statements. p. 406

5. Analyze the disposal of property, plant, and equipment. p. 408

6. Apply measurement and reporting concepts for natural resources and intangible assets. p. 409

7. Explain how the acquisition, use, and disposal of long-lived assets impact cash flows. p. 414

CHAPTER EIGHT

REPORTING AND INTERPRETING PROPERTY, PLANT, AND EQUIPMENT; NATURAL RESOURCES; AND INTANGIBLES

As of December 31, 2009, Southwest Airlines operated 537 Boeing 737 aircraft, providing service to 68 domestic cities in 32 states, and was the largest U.S. air carrier in number of originating passengers boarded and number of scheduled domestic departures. Southwest is a capital-intensive company with nearly $11 billion in property, plant, and equipment reported on its balance sheet. In fiscal year 2009, Southwest spent $585 million on aircraft and other flight equipment as well as ground equipment. Since the demand for air travel is seasonal, with peak demand occurring during the summer months, planning for optimal productive capacity in the airline industry is very difficult. Southwest's managers must determine how many aircraft are needed in which cities at what points in time to fill all seats demanded. Otherwise, the company loses revenue (not enough seats) or incurs higher costs (too many seats).

FOCUS COMPANY:

Southwest Airlines

MANAGING PRODUCTIVE CAPACITY FOR THE LOW-FARE LEADER

www.southwest.com

Demand is also highly sensitive to general economic conditions and other events beyond the control of the company. Even the best corporate planners could not have predicted the September 11, 2001, terrorist attacks against the United States that rocked the airline industry. The war in Iraq led to further declines in the demand for air travel. In response to the precipitous drop in demand, many airlines accelerated retirement of various aircraft, temporarily grounded aircraft, and considered delaying the purchase of new aircraft. Then, a worsening global economic environment provided more challenges for the airline industry. With fuel prices more than doubling between 2004 and 2009, many carriers were forced to reduce capacity.

UNDERSTANDING THE BUSINESS

One of the major challenges managers of most businesses face is forecasting the company's long-term productive capacity—that is, predicting the amount of plant and equipment it will need. If managers underestimate the need, the company will not be able to produce enough goods or services to meet demand and will miss an opportunity to earn revenue. On the other hand, if they overestimate the need, the company will incur excessive costs that will reduce its profitability.

The airline industry provides an outstanding example of the difficulty of planning for and analyzing productive capacity. If an airplane takes off from Kansas City, Missouri, en route to New York City with empty seats, the economic value associated with those seats is lost for that flight. There is obviously no way to sell the seat to a customer after the airplane has left the gate. Unlike a manufacturer, an airline cannot "inventory" seats for the future.

Likewise, if an unexpectedly large number of people want to board a flight, the airline must turn away some customers. You might be willing to buy a television set from Sears even if you had to wait one week for delivery, but you probably wouldn't book a flight home on Thanksgiving weekend on an airline that told you no seats were available. You would simply pick another airline or use a different mode of transportation.

Southwest has a number of large competitors with familiar names such as US Airways, American, United, JetBlue, and Delta. Southwest's 10-K report mentions that the company "currently competes with other airlines on almost all of its routes . . . Some of these airlines have larger fleets than Southwest and some may have wider name recognition in certain markets."

Much of the battle for passengers in the airline industry is fought in terms of property, plant, and equipment. Passengers want convenient schedules (which requires a large number of aircraft), and they want to fly on new, modern airplanes. Because airlines have such a large investment in equipment but no opportunity to inventory unused seats, they work very hard to fill their aircraft to capacity for each flight. Southwest's Annual Report for 2009 describes the keys to its ability to offer low fares and generous frequent flyer benefits.

SOUTHWEST.COM
REAL WORLD EXCERPT
Annual Report

> The Company operates with a low cost structure that is designed to allow it to charge low fares. Adjusted for stage length, the Company has lower unit costs, on average, than most major carriers. The Company's low cost structure is facilitated by the Company's reliance upon a single aircraft type, its operationally efficient point-to-point route structure, and its highly productive Employees.

As you can see from this discussion, issues surrounding property, plant, and equipment have a pervasive impact on a company in terms of strategy, pricing decisions, and profitability. Managers devote considerable time to planning optimal levels of productive capacity, and financial analysts closely review a company's statements to determine the impact of management's decisions.

This chapter is organized according to the life cycle of long-lived assets—acquisition, use, and disposal. First we will discuss the measuring and reporting issues related to land, buildings, and equipment. Then we will discuss the measurement and reporting issues for natural resources and intangible assets. Among the issues we will discuss are the maintenance, use, and disposal of property and equipment over time and the measurement and reporting of assets considered impaired in their ability to generate future cash flows.

ORGANIZATION of the Chapter

Acquisition and Maintenance of Plant and Equipment

- Classifying Long-Lived Assets
- Fixed Asset Turnover Ratio
- Measuring and Recording Acquisition Cost
- Repairs, Maintenance, and Additions

Use, Impairment, and Disposal of Plant and Equipment

- Depreciation Concepts
- Alternative Depreciation Methods
- How Managers Choose
- Measuring Asset Impairment
- Disposal of Property, Plant, and Equipment

Natural Resources and Intangible Assets

- Acquisition and Depletion of Natural Resources
- Acquisition and Amortization of Intangible Assets

ACQUISITION AND MAINTENANCE OF PLANT AND EQUIPMENT

LEARNING OBJECTIVE 1

Define, classify, and explain the nature of long-lived productive assets and interpret the fixed asset turnover ratio.

Exhibit 8.1 shows the asset section of the balance sheet from Southwest's annual report for the fiscal year ended December 31, 2009. Over 74 percent of Southwest's total assets are flight and ground equipment. Southwest also reports other assets with probable long-term benefits. Let's begin by classifying these assets.

Classifying Long-Lived Assets

The resources that determine a company's productive capacity are often called **long-lived assets.** These assets, which are listed as noncurrent assets on the balance sheet, may be either tangible or intangible and have the following characteristics:

LONG-LIVED ASSETS are tangible and intangible resources owned by a business and used in its operations over several years.

TANGIBLE ASSETS (or fixed assets) have physical substance.

INTANGIBLE ASSETS have special rights but not physical substance.

1. **Tangible assets** have physical substance; that is, they can be touched. This classification is called **property, plant, and equipment** or **fixed assets.** The three kinds of long-lived tangible assets are:
   a. **Land** used in operations. As is the case with Southwest, land often is not shown as a separate item on the balance sheet.
   b. **Buildings, fixtures, and equipment** used in operations. For Southwest, this category includes aircraft, ground equipment to service the aircraft, and office space.
   c. **Natural resources** used in operations. Southwest does not report any natural resources on its balance sheet. However, companies in other industries report natural resources such as timber tracts and silver mines.
2. **Intangible assets** are long-lived assets without physical substance that confer specific rights on their owner. Examples are patents, copyrights, franchises, licenses, and trademarks. Southwest does not report any intangibles on its balance sheet.

Plant and Equipment as a Percent of Total Assets for Selected Focus Companies

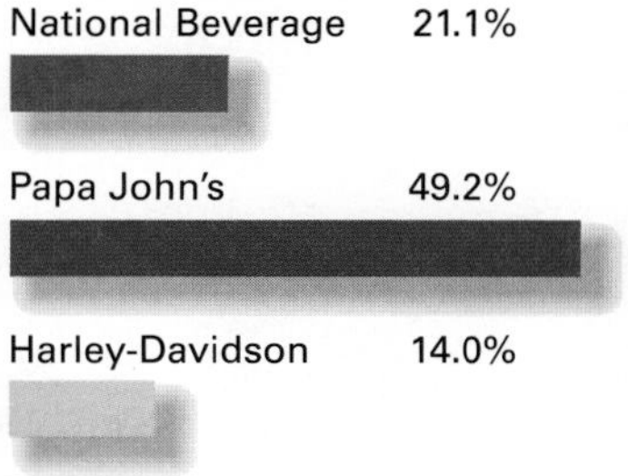

Measuring and Recording Acquisition Cost

Under the **cost principle,** all reasonable and necessary expenditures made in acquiring and preparing an asset for use (or sale, as in the case of inventory) should be recorded as the cost of the asset. We say that the expenditures are **capitalized** when they are recorded as part of the cost of an asset instead of as expenses in the current period. Any sales taxes, legal fees, transportation costs, and installation costs are then added to the purchase price of the asset.

EXHIBIT 8.1

Southwest Airlines's Asset Section of the Balance Sheet

SOUTHWEST.COM

REAL WORLD EXCERPT

Annual Report

SOUTHWEST AIRLINES CO.
Consolidated Balance Sheets (partial)
December 31, 2009 and 2008

Assets ***(dollars in millions)***	**2009**	**2008**
Current assets: *(summarized)*	$ 3,358	$ 2,653
Property and equipment:		
Flight equipment	13,719	13,722
Ground property and equipment	1,922	1,769
Deposits on flight equipment purchase contracts	247	380
	15,888	15,871
Less allowance for depreciation and amortization	5,254	4,831
Total property and equipment	10,634	11,040
Other assets	277	375
Total assets	$14,269	$14,068

KEY RATIO ANALYSIS

Fixed Asset Turnover

Selected Focus Companies' Fixed Asset Turnover Ratios for 2008

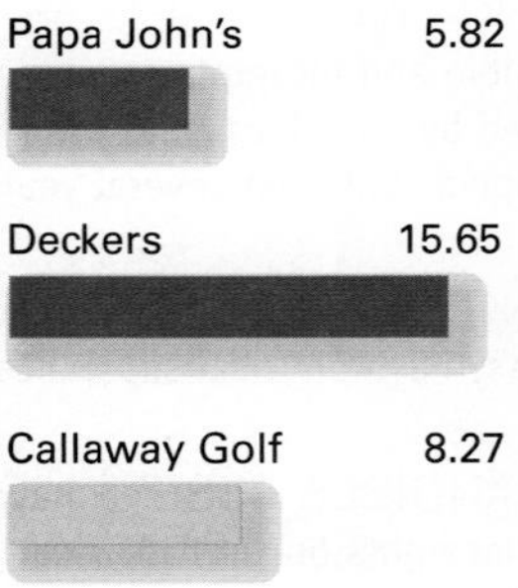

ANALYTICAL QUESTION

How effectively is management utilizing fixed assets to generate revenues?

RATIO AND COMPARISONS

$$\textbf{Fixed Asset Turnover} = \frac{\textbf{Net Sales (or Operating Revenues)}}{\textbf{Average Net Fixed Assets*}}$$

The 2009 ratio for Southwest is (dollars in millions):

Operating Revenues $10,350 ÷ [($11,040 + $10,634) ÷ 2] = 0.96 times

COMPARISIONS OVER TIME		
Southwest Airlines		
2006	**2007**	**2008**
0.94	0.94	1.01

COMPARISONS WITH COMPETITORS	
Delta	**United**
2008	**2008**
1.40	1.86

INTERPRETATIONS

In General The fixed asset turnover ratio measures the sales dollars generated by each dollar of fixed assets used. A high rate normally suggests effective management. An increasing rate over time signals more efficient fixed asset use. Creditors and security analysts use this ratio to assess a company's effectiveness in generating sales from its fixed assets.

Focus Company Analysis Southwest's fixed asset turnover ratio increased between 2007 and 2008, indicating a more efficient use of equipment, and then fell in 2009 to 0.96, a level closer to earlier years. Although at first glance it appears that Southwest is less efficient than perennial money losers Delta and United, this is not the case. Their higher fixed asset turnover is due to the greater age of their fleet (a higher percentage has been depreciated) and the fact that more planes are leased in such a way that they do not appear as fixed assets on the balance sheet.

A Few Cautions A lower or declining fixed asset turnover rate may indicate that a company is expanding (by acquiring additional productive assets) in anticipation of higher future sales. An increasing ratio could also signal that a firm has cut back on capital expenditures due to a downturn in business. This is not the case at Southwest, which continues to expand its fleet. As a consequence, appropriate interpretation of the fixed asset turnover ratio requires an investigation of related activities.

*[Beginning + Ending Fixed Asset Balance (net of accumulated depreciation)] ÷ 2

However, special discounts are subtracted and any interest charges associated with the purchase are expensed as incurred.

LEARNING OBJECTIVE 2

Apply the cost principle to measure the acquisition and maintenance of property, plant, and equipment.

In addition to purchasing buildings and equipment, a company may acquire undeveloped land, typically with the intent to build a new factory or office building. When a company purchases land, all of the incidental costs of the purchase, such as title fees, sales commissions, legal fees, title insurance, delinquent taxes, and surveying fees, should be included in its cost.

Sometimes a company purchases an old building or used machinery for the business operations. Renovation and repair costs incurred by the company prior to the asset's use should be included as a part of its cost. Also, when purchasing land, building, and equipment as a group, the total cost is allocated to each asset in proportion to the asset's market value relative to the total market value of the assets as a whole.

Video 8-1
www.mhhe.com/libby7e

For the sake of illustration, let's assume that Southwest purchased a new 737 aircraft from Boeing on January 1, 2011 (the beginning of Southwest's fiscal year), for a list price of $78 million. Let's also assume that Boeing offered Southwest a discount of $4 million for signing the purchase agreement. That means the price of the new plane to Southwest would actually be $74 million. In addition, Southwest paid $200,000 to have the plane delivered and $800,000 to prepare the new plane for use. The amount recorded for the purchase, called the **acquisition cost,** is the net cash amount paid for the asset or, when noncash assets are used as payment, the fair value of the asset given or asset received, whichever can be more clearly determined (called the **cash equivalent price**). Southwest would calculate the acquisition cost of the new aircraft as follows:

The ACQUISITION COST is the net cash equivalent amount paid or to be paid for the asset.

Invoice price	$78,000,000
Less: Discount from Boeing	4,000,000
Net cash invoice price	74,000,000
Add: Transportation charges paid by Southwest	200,000
Preparation costs paid by Southwest	800,000
Cost of the aircraft (added to the asset account)	$75,000,000

For Cash

Assuming that Southwest paid cash for the aircraft and related transportation and preparation costs, the transaction is recorded as follows:

	Debit	Credit
Flight Equipment (+A)	75,000,000	
Cash (−A)		75,000,000

Assets		=	Liabilities	+	Stockholders' Equity
Flight Equipment	+75,000,000				
Cash	−75,000,000				

It might seem unusual for Southwest to pay cash to purchase new assets that cost $75 million, but this is often the case. When it acquires productive assets, a company may pay with cash that was generated from operations or cash recently borrowed. It also is possible for the seller to finance the purchase on credit.

For Debt

Now let's assume that Southwest signed a note payable for the new aircraft and paid cash for the transportation and preparation costs. In that case, Southwest would record the following journal entry:

	Debit	Credit
Flight Equipment (+A)	75,000,000	
Cash (−A)		1,000,000
Note Payable (+L)		74,000,000

Assets		=	Liabilities		+	Stockholders' Equity
Flight Equipment	+75,000,000		Note Payable	+74,000,000		
Cash	−1,000,000					

For Equity (or Other Noncash Considerations)

Noncash consideration, such as the company's common stock or a right given by the company to the seller to purchase the company's goods or services at a special price, might also be part of the transaction. When noncash consideration is included in the purchase of an asset, the cash-equivalent cost (fair value of the asset given or received) is determined.

Assume that Southwest gave Boeing 1,000,000 shares of its $1.00 par value common stock with a market value of $50 per share and paid the balance in cash. The journal entry and transaction effects follow:

1,000,000 shares × $1 par → Common Stock

1,000,000 shares × $49 excess ($50 market value − $1 par) → Additional Paid-In Capital

	Debit	Credit
Flight Equipment (+A)	75,000,000	
Common Stock (+SE)		1,000,000
Additional Paid-In Capital (+SE)		49,000,000
Cash (−A)		25,000,000

Assets		=	Liabilities	+	Stockholders' Equity	
Flight Equipment	+75,000,000				Common Stock	+1,000,000
Cash	−25,000,000				Additional Paid-In Capital	+49,000,000

By Construction

In some cases, a company may construct an asset for its own use instead of buying it from a manufacturer. When a company does so, the cost of the asset includes all the necessary costs associated with construction, such as labor, materials, and in most situations, a portion of the interest incurred during the construction period, called **capitalized interest.** The amount of interest expense that is capitalized is recorded by debiting the asset and crediting cash when the interest is paid. The amount of interest to be capitalized is a complex computation discussed in detail in other accounting courses.

CAPITALIZED INTEREST refers to interest expenditures included in the cost of a self-constructed asset.

Capitalizing labor, materials, and a portion of interest expense has the effect of increasing assets, decreasing expenses, and increasing net income. Let's assume Southwest constructed a new hangar, paying $600,000 in labor costs and $1,300,000 in supplies and materials. Southwest also paid $100,000 in interest expense during the year related to the construction project:

Capitalized Expenditures:	
Wages paid	*600,000*
Supplies paid	*1,300,000*
Interest paid	*100,000*

	Debit	Credit
Building (+A)	2,000,000	
Cash (−A)		2,000,000

Assets		=	Liabilities	+	Stockholders' Equity
Building	+2,000,000				
Cash	−2,000,000				

US Airways includes a note on capitalized interest in a recent annual report:

NOTES TO CONSOLIDATED FINANCIAL STATEMENTS

1. Basis of Presentation and Summary of Significant Accounting Policies:

(g) Property and Equipment

Property and equipment are recorded at cost. Interest expense related to the acquisition of certain property and equipment is capitalized as an additional cost of the asset or as a leasehold improvement if the asset is leased. Interest capitalized for the years ended December 31, 2008, 2007, and 2006 was $6 million, $4 million, and $2 million, respectively.

REAL WORLD EXCERPT
US Airways Group
2008 Annual Report

PAUSE FOR **FEEDBACK**

We just learned how to measure the cost of operational assets acquired under various methods. In general, all necessary and reasonable costs to ready the asset for its intended use are part of the cost of the asset. Assets can be acquired with cash, with debt, and/or with the company's stock (at market value).

McDonald's Corporation

SELF-STUDY **QUIZ**

It's your turn to apply these concepts by answering the following questions. In a recent year, McDonald's Corporation purchased property, plant, and equipment priced at $2.1 billion. Assume that the company also paid $168 million for sales tax; $20 million for transportation costs; $12 million for installation and preparation of the property, plant, and equipment before use; and $1 million in maintenance contracts to cover repairs to the property, plant, and equipment during use.

1. Compute the acquisition cost for the property, plant, and equipment:
2. How did you account for the sales tax, transportation costs, and installation costs? Explain.
3. Under the following assumptions, indicate the effects of the acquisition on the accounting equation. Use + for increase and − for decrease and indicate the accounts and amounts:

	ASSETS	LIABILITIES	STOCKHOLDERS' EQUITY
a. Paid 30 percent in cash and the rest by signing a note payable.			
b. Issued 10 million shares of common stock ($0.01 per share par value) at a market price of $63 per share and paid the balance in cash.			

After you have completed your answers, check them with the solutions at the bottom of the next page.

ORDINARY REPAIRS AND MAINTENANCE are expenditures for normal operating upkeep of long-lived assets.

REVENUE EXPENDITURES maintain the productive capacity of the asset during the current accounting period only and are recorded as expenses.

ADDITIONS AND IMPROVEMENTS are infrequent expenditures that increase an asset's economic usefulness in the future.

CAPITAL EXPENDITURES increase the productive life, operating efficiency, or capacity of the asset and are recorded as increases in asset accounts, not as expenses.

Repairs, Maintenance, and Additions

Most assets require substantial expenditures during their lives to maintain or enhance their productive capacity. These expenditures include cash outlays for ordinary repairs and maintenance, major repairs, replacements, and additions. Expenditures that are made after an asset has been acquired are classified as follows:

1. **Ordinary repairs and maintenance,** also called **revenue expenditures,** are expenditures for the normal maintenance and upkeep of long-lived assets. These expenditures are recurring in nature, involve relatively small amounts at each occurrence, and do not directly lengthen the useful life of the asset. These cash outlays are recorded as **expenses** in the current period.

   In the case of Southwest Airlines, examples of ordinary repairs would include changing the oil in the aircraft engines, replacing the lights in the control panels, and fixing torn fabric on passenger seats. Although the cost of individual ordinary repairs is relatively small, in the aggregate these expenditures can be substantial. In 2009, Southwest paid $719 million for aircraft maintenance and repairs. This amount was reported as an expense on its income statement.

2. **Additions and improvements** are expenditures that increase the productive life, operating efficiency, or capacity of the asset. These **capital expenditures** are added to the appropriate asset accounts. They occur infrequently, involve large amounts of money, and increase an asset's economic usefulness in the future through either increased efficiency or longer life. Examples include additions, major overhauls, complete reconditioning, and major replacements and improvements, such as the complete replacement of an engine on an aircraft.

In many cases, no clear line distinguishes improvements (assets) from ordinary repairs and maintenance (expenses). In these situations, managers must exercise professional judgment and make a subjective decision. Capitalizing expenses will increase assets and net income in the current year, lowering future years' income by the amount of the annual depreciation. On the other hand, for tax purposes, expensing the amount in the current

Solutions to SELF-STUDY QUIZ

1. **Property, Plant, and Equipment (PPE)**

Acquisition cost	$2,100,000,000
Sales tax	168,000,000
Transportation	20,000,000
Installation	12,000,000
Total	$2,300,000,000

   Because the maintenance contracts are not necessary to ready the assets for use, they are not included in the acquisition cost.

2. Sales tax and transportation and installation costs are capitalized because they are reasonable and necessary for getting the asset ready for its intended use.

3.

	Assets		Liabilities		Stockholders' Equity	
a.	PPE	+2,300,000,000	Note Payable	+1,610,000,000		
	Cash	−690,000,000				
b.	PPE	+2,300,000,000			Common Stock	+100,000
	Cash	−1,670,000,000			Additional Paid-In Capital	+629,900,000

period will lower taxes immediately. Because the decision to capitalize or expense is subjective, auditors review the items reported as capital and revenue expenditures closely.

To avoid spending too much time classifying additions and improvements (capital expenditures) and repair expenses (revenue expenditures), some companies develop simple policies to govern the accounting for these expenditures. For example, one large computer company expenses all individual items that cost less than $1,000. Such policies are acceptable because immaterial (relatively small dollar) amounts will not affect users' decisions when analyzing financial statements.

WorldCom: Hiding Billions in Expenses through Capitalization

FINANCIAL ANALYSIS

When expenditures that should be recorded as current period expenses are improperly capitalized as part of the cost of an asset, the effects on the financial statements can be enormous. In one of the largest accounting frauds in history, WorldCom (now part of Verizon) inflated its income and cash flows from operations by billions of dollars in just such a scheme. This fraud turned WorldCom's actual losses into large profits.

Over five quarters in 2001 and 2002, the company initially announced that it had capitalized $3.8 billion that should have been recorded as operating expenses. By early 2004, auditors discovered $74.4 billion in necessary restatements (reductions to previously reported pretax income) for 2000 and 2001.

Accounting for expenses as capital expenditures increases current income because it spreads a single period's operating expenses over many future periods as depreciation expense. It increases cash flows from operations by moving cash outflows from the operating section to the investing section of the cash flow statement.

PAUSE FOR FEEDBACK

Practice these applications for operational assets as they are used over time: repairing or maintaining (expensed in current period) and adding to or improving (capitalized as part of the cost of the asset).

SELF-STUDY QUIZ

A building that originally cost $400,000 has been used over the past 10 years and needs continual maintenance and repairs. For each of the following expenditures, indicate whether it should be expensed in the current period or capitalized as part of **the cost of the asset.**

	Expense or Capitalize?
1. Major replacement of electrical wiring throughout the building.	____________
2. Repairs to the front door of the building.	____________
3. Annual cleaning of the filters on the building's air conditioning system.	____________
4. Significant repairs due to damage from an unusual and infrequent flood.	____________

After you have completed your answers, check them with the solutions at the bottom of the page.

Solutions to SELF-STUDY QUIZ

1. Capitalize 2. Expense 3. Expense 4. Capitalize

LEARNING OBJECTIVE 3

Apply various cost allocation methods as assets are held and used over time.

USE, IMPAIRMENT, AND DISPOSAL OF PLANT AND EQUIPMENT

Depreciation Concepts

Except for land that is considered to have an unlimited life, a long-lived asset with a limited useful life, such as an airplane, represents the prepaid cost of a bundle of future services or benefits. The **matching principle** requires that a portion of an asset's cost be allocated as an expense in the same period that revenues are generated by its use. Southwest Airlines earns revenue when it provides air travel service and incurs an expense when using its aircraft to generate the revenue.

The term used to identify the matching of the cost of using buildings and equipment with the revenues they generate is **depreciation.** Thus, depreciation is **the process of allocating the cost of buildings and equipment over their productive lives using a systematic and rational method.**

DEPRECIATION is the process of allocating the cost of buildings and equipment over their productive lives using a systematic and rational method.

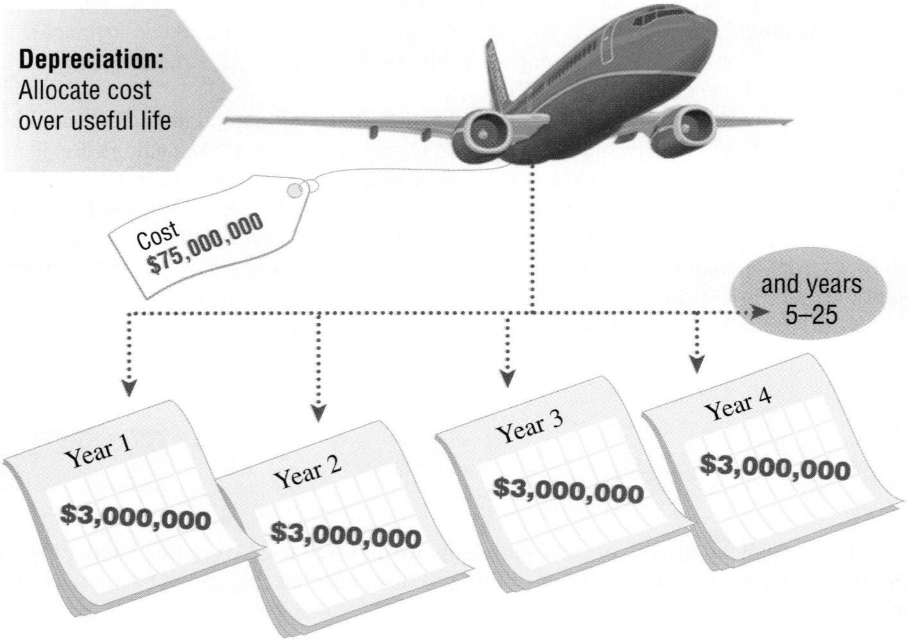

Using the asset→Depreciation Expense each year

Students often are confused by the concept of depreciation as accountants use it. In accounting, depreciation is a process of **cost allocation,** not a process of determining an asset's current market value or worth. When an asset is depreciated, the remaining balance sheet amount **probably does not represent its current market value.** On balance sheets subsequent to acquisition, the undepreciated cost is not measured on a market or fair value basis.

An adjusting journal entry is needed at the end of each period to reflect the use of buildings and equipment for the period:

	Debit	Credit
Depreciation Expense (+E, −SE)	x,xxx	
Accumulated Depreciation (+XA, −A)		x,xxx

Assets		=	Liabilities	+	Stockholders' Equity	
Accumulated Depreciation (+XA)	−x,xxx				Depreciation Expense (+E)	−x,xxx

The amount of depreciation recorded during each period is reported on the income statement as **Depreciation Expense.** The amount of depreciation expense accumulated since the acquisition date is reported on the balance sheet as a contra-account, **Accumulated Depreciation,** and deducted from the related asset's cost. The net amount on the balance sheet is called **net book value** or **carrying value.** The net book (or carrying) value of a long-lived asset is its acquisition cost less the accumulated depreciation from the acquisition date to the balance sheet date.

NET BOOK (or CARRYING) VALUE is the acquisition cost of an asset less accumulated depreciation.

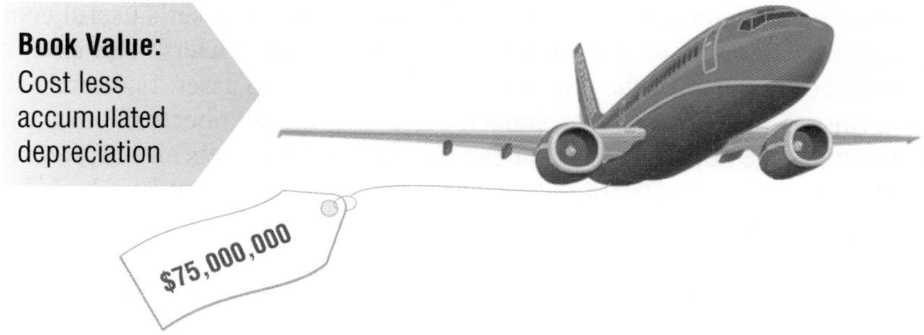

	Year 1	Year 2	Year 3	Year 25
Cost	$75,000,000	$75,000,000	$75,000,000	$75,000,000
−Accumulated depreciation	3,000,000	6,000,000	9,000,000	75,000,000
Net book value	$72,000,000	$69,000,000	$66,000,000	$ 0

Reported on Balance Sheet

From Exhibit 8.1 on page 390, we see that Southwest's acquisition cost for property and equipment is $15,888 million at the end of 2009. The accumulated depreciation and amortization on the property and equipment is $5,254 million. Thus, the book value is reported at $10,634 million. Southwest also reported depreciation and amortization expense of $616 million on its income statement for 2009.

Book Value as an Approximation of Remaining Life

FINANCIAL ANALYSIS

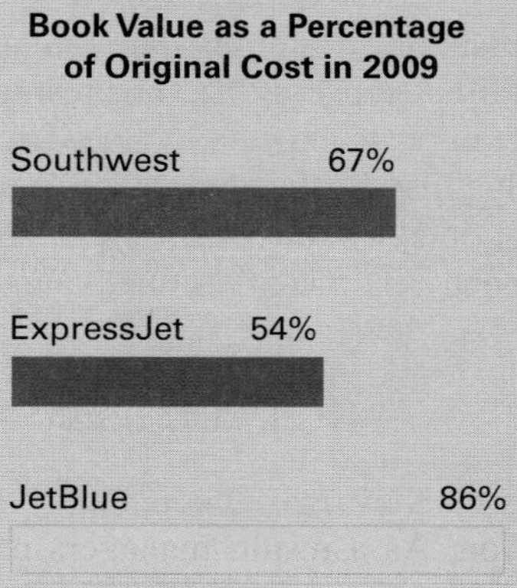

Some analysts compare the book value of assets to their original cost as an approximation of their remaining life. If the book value of an asset is 100 percent of its cost, it is a new asset; if the book value is 25 percent of its cost, the asset has about 25 percent of its estimated life remaining. In Southwest's case, the book value of its property and equipment is 67 percent of its original cost, compared to 54 percent for ExpressJet and 86 percent for JetBlue Airways.

This comparison suggests that Southwest's flight equipment may have more estimated life remaining than that of ExpressJet; however, its flight equipment is older than JetBlue's, which has been in operation only since 2000. This comparison is only a rough approximation and is influenced by some of the accounting issues discussed in the next section.

To calculate depreciation expense, three amounts are required for each asset:

1. Acquisition cost.
2. **Estimated** useful life to the company.
3. **Estimated** residual (or salvage) value at the end of the asset's useful life to the company.

Notice that the asset's useful life and residual value are estimates. Therefore, **depreciation expense is an estimate.**

ESTIMATED USEFUL LIFE is the expected service life of an asset to the present owner.

Estimated useful life represents management's estimate of the asset's useful **economic life** to the company rather than its total economic life to all potential users. The asset's expected physical life is often longer than the company intends to use the asset. Economic life may be expressed in terms of years or units of capacity, such as the number of hours a machine is expected to operate or the number of units it can produce. Southwest's aircraft fleet is expected to fly for more than 25 years, but Southwest wants to offer its customers a high level of service by replacing its older aircraft with modern equipment. For accounting purposes, Southwest uses a 23- to 25-year estimated useful life. The subsequent owner of the aircraft (likely a regional airline) would use an estimated useful life based on its own policies.

FINANCIAL ANALYSIS | Differences in Estimated Lives within a Single Industry

Notes to recent actual financial statements of various airline companies reveal the following estimates for the useful lives of flight equipment:

Company	Estimated Life (in years)
Southwest	23 to 25
United	27 to 30
US Airways	5 to 30
Singapore Airlines	15

The differences in the estimated lives may be attributed to a number of factors such as the type of aircraft used by each company, equipment replacement plans, operational differences, and the degree of management's conservatism. In addition, given the same type of aircraft, companies that plan to use the equipment over fewer years may estimate higher residual values than companies that plan to use the equipment longer. For example, Singapore Airlines uses a residual value of 10 percent over a relatively short useful life for its passenger aircraft, compared to 5 percent for Delta Air Lines over a 25-year useful life.

Differences in estimated lives and residual values of assets can have a significant impact on a comparison of the profitability of the competing companies. Analysts must be certain to identify the causes of differences in depreciable lives.

RESIDUAL (or SALVAGE) VALUE is the estimated amount to be recovered by the company at the end of the asset's estimated useful life.

Residual (or salvage) value represents management's estimate of the amount the company expects to recover upon disposal of the asset at the end of its estimated useful life. The residual value may be the estimated value of the asset as salvage or scrap or its expected value if sold to another user. In the case of Southwest's aircraft, residual value may be the amount it expects to receive when it sells the asset to a small regional airline that operates older equipment. The notes to Southwest's financial statements indicate that the company estimates residual value to be between 0 and 15 percent of the cost of the asset, depending on the asset.

Alternative Depreciation Methods

Because of significant differences among companies and the assets they own, accountants have not been able to agree on a single best method of depreciation. As a result, managers may

EXHIBIT 8.2

Data for Illustrating the Computation of Depreciation under Alternative Methods

SOUTHWEST AIRLINES
Acquisition of a New Service Vehicle

Cost, purchased on January 1, 2011	$62,500	
Estimated residual value	$ 2,500	
Estimated useful life		3 years **OR** 100,000 miles
Actual miles driven in:	Year 2011	30,000 miles
	Year 2012	50,000 miles
	Year 2013	20,000 miles

choose from several acceptable depreciation methods that match depreciation expense with the revenues generated in a period. Once selected, the method should be applied consistently over time to enhance comparability of financial information. We will discuss the three most common depreciation methods:

1. Straight-line (the most common, used by more than 95 percent of companies surveyed).
2. Units-of-production.
3. Declining-balance.

To illustrate each method, let's assume that Southwest Airlines acquired a new service vehicle (ground equipment) on January 1, 2011. The relevant information is shown in Exhibit 8.2.

Number of Companies Using Alternative Depreciation Methods*

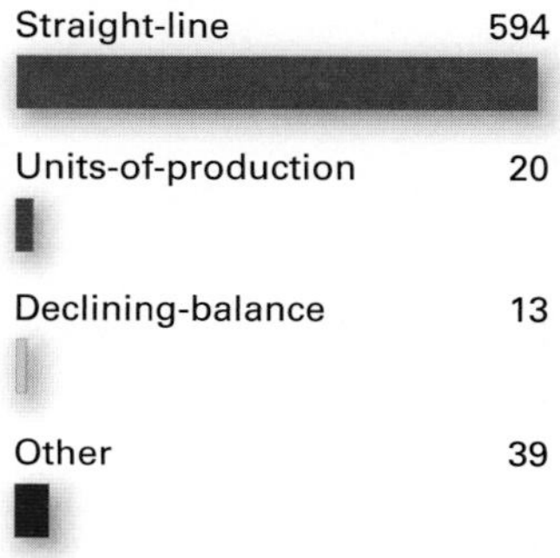

*Methods reported by companies sampled in *Accounting Trends & Techniques* (AICPA), 2009.

Straight-Line Method

More companies, including Southwest, use **straight-line depreciation** in their financial statements than all other methods combined. Under the straight-line method, an equal portion of an asset's depreciable cost is allocated to each accounting period over its estimated useful life. The formula to estimate annual depreciation expense follows:

The STRAIGHT-LINE DEPRECIATION method allocates the cost of an asset in equal periodic amounts over its useful life.

Straight-Line Formula:

$$\underbrace{(\text{Cost} - \text{Residual Value})}_{\text{Depreciable Cost}} \times \underbrace{\frac{1}{\text{Useful Life}}}_{\text{Straight-Line Rate}} = \text{Depreciation Expense}$$

$$(\$62{,}500 - \$2{,}500) \times \frac{1}{3\text{ years}} = \underline{\underline{\$20{,}000}}\text{ per year}$$

In this formula, "Cost minus Residual Value" is the amount to be depreciated, also called the **depreciable cost.** The formula "1 ÷ Useful Life" is the **straight-line rate.** Using the data provided in Exhibit 8.2, the depreciation expense for Southwest's new truck would be $20,000 per year.

Companies often create a **depreciation schedule** that shows the computed amount of depreciation expense each year over the entire useful life of the machine. You can use computerized spreadsheet programs, such as Excel, to create the depreciation schedule. Using the data in Exhibit 8.2 and the straight-line method, Southwest's depreciation schedule follows:

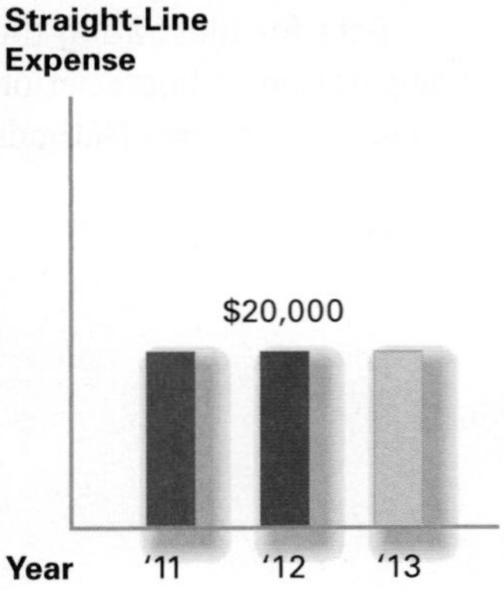

Amount for the adjusting entry: **Reported on the income statement (closed at year-end)** → Depreciation Expense

Balance in the contra-asset account after the adjusting entry → Accumulated Depreciation

Cost less accumulated depreciation: **Reported on the balance sheet** → Net Book Value

Straight-Line Method:

Year	Computation (Cost − Residual Value) × 1/Useful Life	Depreciation Expense	Accumulated Depreciation	Net Book Value
At acquisition				$62,500
2011	($62,500 − $2,500) × 1/3	$20,000	$20,000	42,500
2012	($62,500 − $2,500) × 1/3	20,000	40,000	22,500
2013	($62,500 − $2,500) × 1/3	20,000	60,000	2,500
	Total	$60,000		

Equal to estimated residual value at end of useful life

Notice that

- Depreciation expense is a constant amount each year.
- Accumulated depreciation increases by an equal amount each year.
- Net book value decreases by the same amount each year until it equals the estimated residual value.

This is the reason for the name **straight-line method.** Notice, too, that the adjusting entry can be prepared from this schedule, and the effect on the income statement and balance sheet are known. Southwest Airlines uses the straight-line method for all of its assets. The company reported depreciation expense in the amount of $616 million for 2009, equal to 6 percent of the airline's revenues for the year. Most companies in the airline industry use the straight-line method.

Units-of-Production Method

The UNITS-OF-PRODUCTION DEPRECIATION method allocates the cost of an asset over its useful life based on the relation of its periodic output to its total estimated output.

The **units-of-production depreciation** method relates depreciable cost to total estimated productive output. The formula to estimate annual depreciation expense under this method is as follows:

Units-of-Production Formula:

$$\frac{\text{(Cost} - \text{Residual Value)}}{\text{Estimated Total Production}} \times \text{Actual Production} = \text{Depreciation Expense}$$

$$\frac{(\$62{,}500 - \$2{,}500)}{100{,}000 \text{ miles}} = \$0.60 \text{ per mile depreciation rate}$$

$0.60 per mile × 30,000 actual miles in 2011 = $18,000 for 2011

Dividing the depreciable cost by the estimated total production yields the **depreciation rate per unit of production,** which is then multiplied by the actual production for the period to determine depreciation expense. In our illustration, for every mile that the new vehicle is driven, Southwest would record depreciation expense of $0.60. The depreciation schedule for the truck under the units-of-production method would appear as follows:

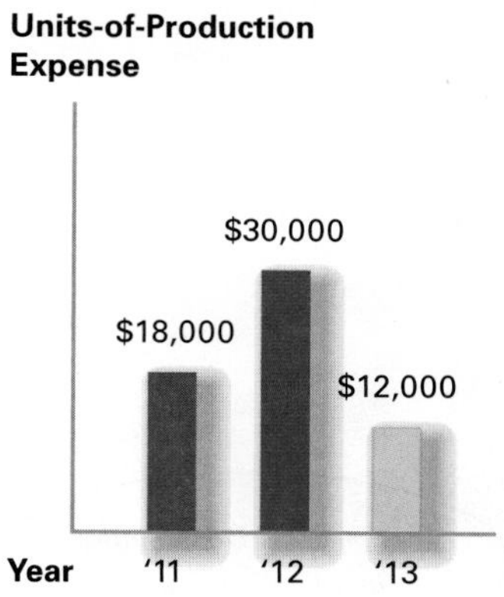

Units-of-Production Method:

Year	Computation [(Cost − Residual Value)/Total Estimated Production] × Actual Production	Depreciation Expense	Accumulated Depreciation	Net Book Value
At acquisition	RATE			$62,500
2011	$.60 per mile × 30,000 miles	$18,000	$18,000	44,500
2012	$.60 per mile × 50,000 miles	30,000	48,000	14,500
2013	$.60 per mile × 20,000 miles	12,000	60,000	2,500
	Total	$60,000		

Equal to estimated residual value at end of useful life

Notice that, from period to period, depreciation expense, accumulated depreciation, and book value vary directly with the units produced. In the units-of-production method, depreciation expense is a **variable expense** because it varies directly with production or use.

You might wonder what happens if the total estimated productive output differs from actual total output. Remember that the estimate is management's best guess of total output. If any difference occurs at the end of the asset's life, the final adjusting entry to depreciation expense should be for the amount needed to bring the asset's net book value equal to the asset's estimated residual value. For example, if, in 2013, Southwest's truck ran 25,000 actual miles, the same amount of depreciation expense, $12,000, would be recorded.

Although Southwest does not use the units-of-production method, the Exxon Mobil Corporation, a major energy company that explores, produces, transports, and sells crude oil and natural gas worldwide, does, as a note to the company's annual report explains.

ExxonMobil

REAL WORLD EXCERPT

2008 Annual Report

1. Summary of Accounting Policies

Property, Plant, and Equipment

Depreciation, depletion, and amortization, based on cost less estimated salvage value of the asset, are primarily determined under either the unit-of-production method or the straight-line method, which is based on estimated asset service life taking obsolescence into consideration . . . Unit-of-production rates are based on the amount of proved developed reserves of oil, gas, and other minerals that are estimated to be recoverable from existing facilities using current operating methods.

The units-of-production method is based on an estimate of an asset's total future productive capacity or output, which is difficult to determine. This is another example of the degree of subjectivity inherent in accounting.

Declining-Balance Method

If an asset is considered to be more efficient or productive when it is newer, managers might choose the **declining-balance depreciation** method to match a higher depreciation expense with higher revenues in the early years of an asset's life and a lower depreciation expense with lower revenues in the later years. We say, then, that this is an **accelerated depreciation** method. Although accelerated methods are seldom used for financial reporting purposes, the method that is used more frequently than others is the declining-balance method.

The DECLINING-BALANCE DEPRECIATION method allocates the cost of an asset over its useful life based on a multiple of the straight-line rate (often two times).

Declining-balance depreciation is based on applying a rate exceeding the straight-line rate to the asset's net book value over time. The rate is often double (two times) the straight-line rate and is termed the **double-declining-balance rate.** For example, if the straight-line rate is 10 percent (1 ÷ 10 years) for a 10-year estimated useful life, then the declining-balance rate is 20 percent (2 × the straight-line rate). Other typical acceleration rates are 1.5 times and 1.75 times. The double-declining-balance rate is adopted most frequently by companies employing an accelerated method, so we will use it in our illustration.

Accumulated Depreciation increases over time

Double-Declining-Balance Formula:

$$\text{(Cost} - \text{Accumulated Depreciation)} \times \frac{2}{\text{Useful Life}} = \text{Depreciation Expense}$$

$$(\$62{,}500 - \$0 \text{ in } 2011) \times \frac{2}{3 \text{ years}} = \$41{,}667 \text{ in the first year}$$

There are two important differences between this method and the others described previously:

1. Notice that accumulated depreciation, not residual value, is included in the formula. Since accumulated depreciation increases each year, net book value (Cost minus Accumulated Depreciation) decreases. The double-declining rate is applied to a lower net book value each year, resulting in a decline in depreciation expense over time.
2. An asset's book value cannot be depreciated below residual value. Therefore, if the annual computation reduces net book value below residual value, a lower amount of depreciation expense must be recorded so that net book value equals residual value. No additional depreciation expense is computed in subsequent years.

Computation of double-declining-balance depreciation expense is illustrated in the depreciation schedule:

Double-Declining-Balance Expense

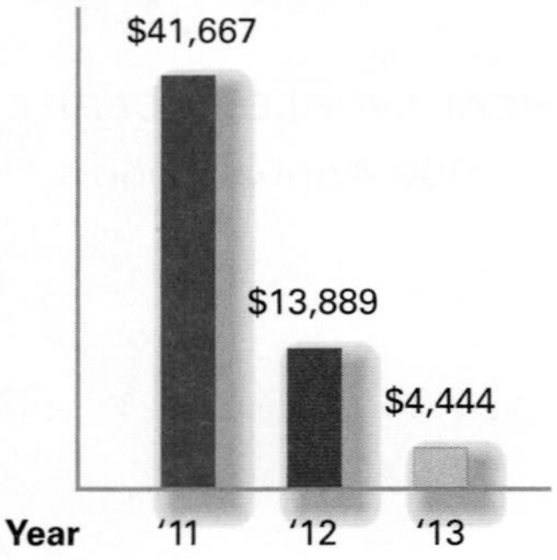

Year	Computation [(Cost − Accumulated Depreciation) × 2/Useful Life]	Depreciation Expense	Accumulated Depreciation	Net Book Value
At acquisition				$62,500
2011	($62,500 − $0) × 2/3	$41,667	$41,667	20,833
2012	($62,500 − $41,667) × 2/3	13,889	55,556	6,944
2013	($62,500 − $55,556) × 2/3	~~4,629~~	~~60,185~~	~~2,315~~
		4,444	60,000	2,500
	Total	$60,000		

Computed amount is too large.

Equal to estimated residual value at end of useful life

The calculated depreciation expense for 2013 ($4,629) is not the same as the amount actually reported on the income statement ($4,444). An asset should never be depreciated below the point at which net book value equals its residual value. The asset owned by Southwest has an estimated residual value of $2,500. If depreciation expense were recorded in the amount of $4,629, the book value of the asset would be less than $2,500. The correct depreciation expense for year 2013 is therefore $4,444, the amount that will reduce the book value to exactly $2,500. To determine the amount to record in 2013, indicate the amount needed for net book value

($2,500), determine what the balance in accumulated depreciation should be to yield the $60,000 ($62,500 cost − $2,500 residual value), and compute the amount of depreciation expense necessary to increase the balance in accumulated depreciation to $60,000 ($60,000 balance needed in accumulated depreciation − $55,556 prior balance in accumulated depreciation).

Companies in industries that expect fairly rapid obsolescence of their equipment use the declining-balance method. Sony is one of the companies that uses this method, as a note to its annual report shows.

2. Summary of Significant Accounting Policies:

Property, Plant, Equipment and Depreciation

Property, plant, and equipment are stated at cost. Depreciation of property, plant, and equipment is primarily computed on the declining-balance method for Sony Corporation and its Japanese subsidiaries, except for certain semiconductor manufacturing facilities and buildings whose depreciation is computed on the straight-line method over the estimated useful life of the assets. Property, plant, and equipment for foreign subsidiaries is also computed on the straight-line method. Useful lives for depreciation range from 15 to 50 years for buildings and from 2 to 10 years for machinery and equipment.

REAL WORLD EXCERPT
Sony Corporation
2008 Annual Report

As this note indicates, companies may use different depreciation methods for different classes of assets. Under the consistency principle, they are expected to apply the same methods to those assets over time.

In Summary

The three depreciation methods, computations, and the differences in depreciation expense over time for each method are summarized as follows:

Method	Computation	Depreciation Expense
Straight-line	(Cost − Residual Value) × 1/Useful Life	Equal amounts each year
Units-of-production	[(Cost − Residual Value)/Estimated Total Production] × Annual Production	Varying amounts based on production level
Double-declining-balance	(Cost − Accumulated Depreciation) × 2/Useful Life	Declining amounts over time

Impact of Alternative Depreciation Methods

FINANCIAL ANALYSIS

Assume that you are comparing two companies that are exactly the same, except that one uses accelerated depreciation and the other uses the straight-line method. Which company would you expect to report a higher net income? Actually, this question is a bit tricky. The answer is that you cannot say for certain which company's income would be higher.

The accelerated methods report higher depreciation and therefore lower net income during the early years of an asset's life. As the age of the asset increases, this effect reverses. Therefore, companies that use accelerated depreciation report lower depreciation expense and higher net income during the later years of an asset's life. The graph in the margin shows the pattern of depreciation over the life of an asset for the straight-line and declining-balance methods discussed in this chapter. When the curve for the accelerated method falls below the line for the straight-line method, the accelerated method produces a higher net income than the straight-line method. However, total depreciation expense by the end of the asset's life is the same for each method.

Users of financial statements must understand the impact of alternative depreciation methods used over time. Differences in depreciation methods rather than real economic differences can cause significant variation in reported net incomes.

Summary Depreciation Expense

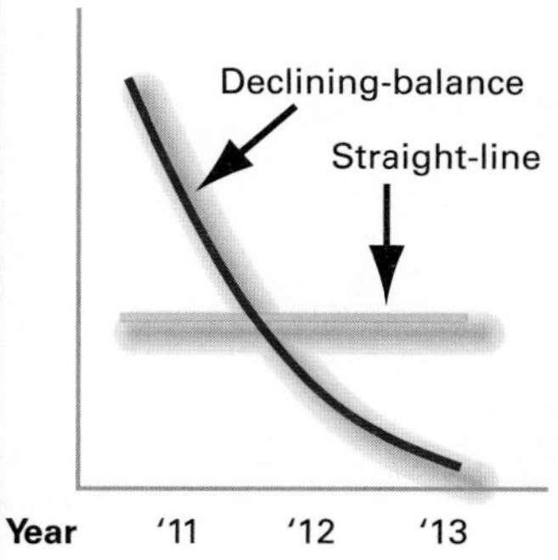

PAUSE FOR FEEDBACK

The three cost allocation methods discussed in this section are:

- Straight-line (Cost − Residual Value) × 1/Useful Life
- Units-of-production [(Cost − Residual Value)/Estimated Total Production] × Annual Production
- Double-declining-balance (Cost − Accumulated Depreciation) × 2/Useful Life

Practice these methods using the following information.

SELF-STUDY QUIZ

Assume that Southwest has acquired new computer equipment at a cost of $240,000. The equipment has an estimated life of six years, an estimated operating life of 50,000 hours, and an estimated residual value of $30,000. Determine depreciation expense for the first full year under each of the following methods:

1. Straight-line method.
2. Units-of-production method (assume the equipment ran for 8,000 hours in the first year).
3. Double-declining-balance method.

After you have completed your answers, check them with the solutions at the bottom of the page.

FINANCIAL ANALYSIS | Increased Profitability Due to an Accounting Adjustment? Reading the Notes

SINGAPORE AIRLINES
A great way to fly

Financial analysts are particularly interested in changes in accounting estimates because they can have a large impact on a company's before-tax operating income. In 2001, Singapore Airlines disclosed in its annual report that it had increased the estimated useful life of its aircraft from 10 to 15 years to reflect a change in its aircraft replacement policy. The change reduced depreciation expense for the year by $265 million and would reduce expenses by a similar amount each year over the remaining life of the aircraft. Analysts pay close attention to this number because it represents increased profitability due merely to an accounting adjustment.

How Managers Choose

Financial Reporting

For financial reporting purposes, corporate managers must determine which depreciation method provides the best matching of revenues and expenses for any given asset. If the asset is expected to provide benefits evenly over time, then the straight-line method is preferred. Managers also find this method to be easy to use and to explain. If no other method is more systematic or rational, then the straight-line method is selected. Also, during the early years of an asset's life, the straight-line method reports higher income than the accelerated methods do. For these reasons, the straight-line method is, by far and away, the most common.

On the other hand, certain assets produce more revenue in their early lives because they are more efficient than in later years. In this case, managers select an accelerated method to allocate cost.

Solutions to SELF-STUDY QUIZ

1. ($240,000 − $30,000) × 1/6 = $35,000
2. [($240,000 − $30,000) ÷ 50,000] × 8,000 = $33,600
3. ($240,000 − $0) × 2/6 = $80,000

Measurement Basis for Property, Plant, and Equipment

INTERNATIONAL PERSPECTIVE

One of the most important differences between U.S. GAAP and International Financial Reporting Standards (IFRS) relates to the measurement basis for property, plant, and equipment. IFRS permit companies to value property, plant, and equipment at historical cost or to revalue them to their fair value as of the balance sheet date. The primary argument in favor of revaluation is that the historical cost of an asset purchased 15 or 20 years ago is not meaningful because of the impact of inflation. For example, most people would not compare the original purchase price of a house acquired in 1978 to the purchase price for the identical house next door acquired in 2008 because the price of houses has changed dramatically between those years. However, revaluation to fair value is prohibited in the United States (under GAAP). A primary argument against the revaluation of property, plant, and equipment is the lack of objectivity involved in estimating an asset's current cost.

Tax Reporting

Southwest Airlines, like most public companies, maintains two sets of accounting records. Both sets of records reflect the same transactions, but the transactions are accounted for using two different sets of measurement rules. One set is prepared under GAAP for reporting to stockholders. The other set is prepared to determine the company's tax obligation under the Internal Revenue Code. The reason that the two sets of rules are different is simple: The objectives of GAAP and the Internal Revenue Code differ.

Financial Reporting (GAAP)	Tax Reporting (IRC)
The objective of financial reporting is to provide economic information about a business that is useful in projecting future cash flows of the business. Financial reporting rules follow generally accepted accounting principles.	The objective of the Internal Revenue Code is to raise sufficient revenues to pay for the expenditures of the federal government. Many of the Code's provisions are designed to encourage certain behaviors that are thought to benefit society (e.g., contributions to charities are made tax deductible to encourage people to support worthy programs).

In some cases, differences between the Internal Revenue Code and GAAP leave the manager no choice but to maintain separate records. In other cases, the differences are the result of management choice. When given a choice among acceptable tax accounting methods, managers apply what is called the **least and the latest rule.** All taxpayers want to pay the lowest amount of tax that is legally permitted and at the latest possible date. If you had the choice of paying $100,000 to the federal government at the end of this year or at the end of next year, you would choose the end of next year. By doing so, you could invest the money for an extra year and earn a significant return on the investment.

Two Sets of Books

A QUESTION OF ETHICS

When they first learn that companies maintain two sets of books, some people question the ethics or legality of the practice. In reality, **it is both legal and ethical to maintain separate records for tax and financial reporting purposes. However, these records must reflect the same transactions.** Understating revenues or overstating expenses on a tax return can result in financial penalties and/or imprisonment. Accountants who aid tax evaders also can be fined or imprisoned and lose their professional licenses.

Similarly, by maintaining two sets of books, corporations can defer (delay) paying millions and sometimes billions of dollars in taxes. The following companies reported significant gross deferred tax obligations in 2008. Much of these deferrals were due to differences in asset cost allocation methods:

Company	Deferred Tax Liabilities	Percentage Due to Applying Different Cost Allocation Methods
Southwest Airlines	$2,789 million	99%
PepsiCo	2,442 million	36
Hertz	2,220 million	53
Marriott International	135 million	30

Most corporations use the IRS-approved Modified Accelerated Cost Recovery System (MACRS) to calculate depreciation expense for their tax returns. MACRS is similar to the declining-balance method and is applied over relatively short asset lives to yield high depreciation expense in the early years. The high depreciation expense reported under MACRS reduces a corporation's taxable income and therefore the amount it must pay in taxes. MACRS provides an incentive for corporations to invest in modern property, plant, and equipment in order to be competitive in world markets. However, **it is not acceptable for financial reporting purposes.**

LEARNING OBJECTIVE 4

Explain the effect of asset impairment on the financial statements.

Measuring Asset Impairment

Corporations must review long-lived tangible and intangible assets for possible impairment. Two steps are necessary:

Step 1: Test for Impairment Impairment occurs when events or changed circumstances cause the estimated future cash flows (future benefits) of these assets to fall below their book value.

If net book value > Estimated future cash flows, then the asset is impaired.

Step 1: An asset is impaired if:
Book Value > Future Cash Flows
Step 2: Then, Impairment Loss =
Book Value − Fair Value

Step 2: Computation of Impairment Loss For any asset considered to be impaired, companies recognize a loss for the difference between the asset's book value and its **fair value** (a market concept).

Impairment Loss = Net Book Value − Fair Value

That is, the asset is **written down** to fair value.

To illustrate measuring impairment losses, let's assume that Southwest did a review for asset impairment and identified an aircraft with the following information:

Step 1: Test →	Net book value	$10,000,000	← **Step 2: If impaired, loss**
Step 1: Test →	Estimated future cash flows	8,000,000	
	Fair value	7,500,000	← **Step 2: If impaired, loss**

Step 1: Since the net book value of $10 million exceeds the estimated future cash flows of $8 million, then the asset is impaired because it is not expected to generate future benefits equal to its net book value. When impaired, proceed to Step 2.

Step 2: If impaired, the amount of the impairment loss is the difference between net book value and the asset's fair value. For Southwest, determining fair value includes using published sources and third-party bids to obtain the value of the asset. If the asset's fair value was $7,500,000, then the loss is calculated as $2,500,000 ($10,000,000 net book value less $7,500,000 fair value). The following journal entry would be recorded:

	Debit	Credit
Asset Impairment Loss (+Loss, −SE)	2,500,000	
Flight Equipment (−A)		2,500,000

Assets		=	Liabilities	+	Stockholders' Equity	
Flight Equipment	−2,500,000				Asset Impairment Loss	−2,500,000

Although Southwest did not report asset impairment losses in its recent annual report, it did report in notes to the financial statements that it follows the practice of reviewing assets for impairment:

> When appropriate, the Company evaluates its long-lived assets used in operations for impairment. Impairment losses would be recorded when events and circumstances indicate that an asset might be impaired and the undiscounted cash flows to be generated by that asset are less than the carrying amounts of the asset. Factors that would indicate potential impairment include, but are not limited to, significant decreases in the market value of the long-lived asset(s), a significant change in the long-lived asset's physical condition, and operating or cash flow losses associated with the use of the long-lived asset . . . There have been no impairments of long-lived assets recorded during 2009, 2008, or 2007.

SOUTHWEST.COM®
REAL WORLD EXCERPT
2009 Annual Report

Macy's, which owns and operates 840 department stores under the Macy's and Bloomingdale's names, did report large impairment losses in its annual report for the fiscal year ended January 31, 2009:

> **3. Asset Impairment Charges**
>
> Asset impairment charges in 2008 include $96 million related to properties held and used, $40 million related to store closings announced in January 2009, $63 million associated with acquired indefinite lived private brand tradenames, and $12 million associated with marketable securities . . .
>
> **4. Goodwill Impairment Charges**
>
> Based on the results of goodwill impairment testing as of January 31, 2009, the Company recorded an estimated pretax goodwill impairment charge of $5,382 million, $5,083 million after income taxes, in the fourth quarter of 2008 . . . after evaluating the results of the Christmas selling season, and in consideration of the continued deterioration in the general economic environment in recent periods (and the impact thereof on the Company's most recently completed annual business plan) and the resultant continued decline in the Company's market capitalization . . .

★macy's
REAL WORLD EXCERPT
2008 ANNUAL REPORT

By recording a total of $5.593 billion in impairment losses in 2008, Macy's reported a net loss of $4.803 billion, significantly below its $893 million in positive net income in 2007.

LEARNING OBJECTIVE 5

Analyze the disposal of property, plant, and equipment.

Disposal of Property, Plant, and Equipment

In some cases, a business may **voluntarily** decide not to hold a long-lived asset for its entire life. The company may drop a product from its line and no longer need the equipment that was used to produce it, or managers may want to replace a machine with a more efficient one. These disposals include sales, trade-ins, and retirements. When Southwest disposes of an old aircraft, the company may sell it to a cargo airline or regional airline. A business may also dispose of an asset **involuntarily,** as the result of a casualty such as a storm, fire, or accident.

Disposals of long-lived assets seldom occur on the last day of the accounting period. Therefore, depreciation must be recorded to the date of disposal. The disposal of a depreciable asset usually requires two journal entries:

1. An adjusting entry to update the depreciation expense and accumulated depreciation accounts.
2. An entry to record the disposal. The cost of the asset **and** any accumulated depreciation at the date of disposal must be removed from the accounts. The difference between any resources received on disposal of an asset and its book value at the date of disposal is treated as a gain or loss on the disposal of the asset. This gain (or loss) is reported on the income statement. It is not an operating revenue (or expense), however, because it arises from peripheral or incidental activities rather than from central operations. Gains and losses from disposals are usually shown as a separate item on the income statement.

Assume that at the end of year 17, Southwest sold an aircraft that was no longer needed because of the elimination of service to a small city. The aircraft was sold for $11 million cash. The original cost of the flight equipment of $30 million was depreciated using the straight-line method over 25 years with no residual value ($1.2 million depreciation expense per year). The last accounting for depreciation was at the end of year 16; thus, depreciation expense must be recorded for year 17. The computations are:

Cash received		$11,000,000
Original cost of flight equipment	$30,000,000	
Less: Accumulated depreciation ($1,200,000 × 17 years)	20,400,000	
Book value at date of sale		9,600,000
Gain on sale of flight equipment		$ 1,400,000

The entries and effects of the transaction on the date of the sale are as follows:

1. Update depreciation expense for year 17:

	Debit	Credit
Depreciation Expense (+E, −SE)	1,200,000	
Accumulated Depreciation (+XA, −A)		1,200,000

2. Record the sale:

	Debit	Credit
Cash (+A)	11,000,000	
Accumulated Depreciation (−XA, +A)	20,400,000	
Flight Equipment (−A)		30,000,000
Gain on Sale of Assets (+Gain, +SE)		1,400,000

Assets		= Liabilities	+ Stockholders' Equity	
(1) Accumulated Depreciation (+XA)	−1,200,000		Depreciation Expense (+E)	−1,200,000
(2) Cash	+11,000,000		Gain on Sale of Asset	+1,400,000
Flight Equipment	−30,000,000			
Accumulated Depreciation (−XA)	+20,400,000			

PAUSE FOR FEEDBACK

We learned that, when disposing of an operational asset, you must first record depreciation expense for usage of the asset since the last time it was recorded. Then eliminate the asset at cost and its related accumulated depreciation. The difference between the cash received, if any, and the net book value of the asset is either a gain or loss on disposal.

SELF-STUDY QUIZ

Now let's assume the same facts as illustrated above except that the asset was sold for $2,000,000 cash. Prepare the two entries on the date of the sale:

1. Update depreciation expense for year 17:

	Debit	Credit
____________________	______	
____________________		______

2. Record the sale:

	Debit	Credit
____________________	______	
____________________	______	
____________________	______	
____________________		______

	Assets	=	Liabilities	+	Stockholders' Equity
(1)					
(2)					

After you have completed your answers, check them with the solutions at the bottom of the page.

NATURAL RESOURCES AND INTANGIBLE ASSETS

Acquisition and Depletion of Natural Resources

LEARNING OBJECTIVE 6

Apply measurement and reporting concepts for natural resources and intangible assets.

You are probably most familiar with large companies that are involved in manufacturing (Ford, Black & Decker), distribution (Sears, Home Depot), or services (FedEx® Kinko's, Holiday Inn). A number of large companies, some of which are less well known, develop raw materials and products from **natural resources,** including mineral deposits such as gold or iron ore, oil wells, and timber tracts. These resources are often called **wasting assets** because they are depleted (i.e., physically used up). Companies that develop natural resources are critical to the

Solutions to SELF-STUDY QUIZ

		Debit	Credit
(1)	Depreciation Expense (+E, −SE)	1,200,000	
	Accumulated Depreciation (+XA, −A)......................		1,200,000
(2)	Cash (+A)...	2,000,000	
	Accumulated Depreciation (−XA, +A)........................	20,400,000	
	Loss on Sale of Flight Equipment (+Loss, −SE)	7,600,000	
	Flight Equipment (−A)...		30,000,000

	Assets		=	Liabilities	+	Stockholders' Equity	
(1)	Accumulated Depreciation	−1,200,000				Depreciation Expense	−1,200,000
(2)	Flight Equipment	−30,000,000				Loss on Sale of Asset	−7,600,000
	Accumulated Depreciation	+20,400,000					
	Cash	+2,000,000					

NATURAL RESOURCES are assets that occur in nature, such as mineral deposits, timber tracts, oil, and gas.

economy because they produce essential items such as lumber for construction, fuel for heating and transportation, and food for consumption. Because of the significant effect they can have on the environment, these companies attract considerable public attention. Concerned citizens often read the financial statements of companies involved in the exploration for oil, coal, and various ores to determine the amount of money they spend to protect the environment.

DEPLETION is the systematic and rational allocation of the cost of a natural resource over the period of its exploitation.

When natural resources are acquired or developed, they are recorded in conformity with the **cost principle.** As a natural resource is used up, its acquisition cost must be apportioned among the periods in which revenues are earned in conformity with the **matching principle.** The term **depletion** describes the process of allocating a natural resource's cost over the period of its exploitation.[1] The units-of-production method is often applied to compute depletion.

When a natural resource such as an oil well is depleted, the company obtains inventory (oil). Since depleting the natural resource is necessary to obtain the inventory, the depletion computed during a period is not expensed immediately, but is capitalized as part of the cost of the inventory. Only when the inventory is sold does the company record an expense (Cost of Goods Sold). Consider the following illustration:

A timber tract costing $530,000 is depleted over its estimated cutting period based on a "cutting" rate of approximately 20 percent per year:

Note that the amount of the natural resource that is depleted is capitalized as inventory, not expensed. When the inventory is sold, the cost of goods sold will be included as an expense on the income statement.

	Debit	Credit
Inventory (+A)	106,000	
Timber Tract (−A)		106,000
(or Accumulated Depletion +XA, −A)		

Assets		=	Liabilities	+	Stockholders' Equity
Inventory	+106,000				
Timber Tract	−106,000				
(or Accumulated Depletion +XA)					

Following is an excerpt from the asset section of International Paper's 2008 balance sheet, along with the related footnote describing the accounting policies for the company's natural resource, forestland:

REAL WORLD EXCERPT
International Paper
2008 ANNUAL REPORT

CONSOLIDATED BALANCE SHEET (DOLLARS IN MILLIONS)

	2008
Assets	
Cash	$1,144
. . .	
Forestlands	594

Notes to Consolidated Financial Statements:

Note 1. Summary of Business and Significant Accounting Policies

Forestlands

At December 31, 2008, International Paper and its subsidiaries owned or managed about 200,000 acres of forestlands in the United States, approximately 250,000 acres in Brazil, and through licenses and forest management agreements, had harvesting rights on government-owned forestlands in Russia. Costs attributable to timber are charged against income as trees are cut. The rate charged is determined annually based on the relationship of incurred costs to estimated current merchantable volume.

[1]Consistent with the procedure for recording depreciation, an accumulated depletion account may be used. In practice, however, most companies credit the asset account directly for periodic depletion. This procedure is also typically used for intangible assets, which are discussed in the next section.

Acquisition and Amortization of Intangible Assets

Intangible assets are increasingly important resources for organizations. An intangible asset, like any other asset, has value because of certain rights and privileges often conferred by law on its owner. Unlike tangible assets such as land and buildings, however, an intangible asset has no material or physical substance. Examples of intangible assets include patents, trademarks, and licenses. Most intangible assets usually are evidenced by a legal document. Accounting for intangible assets has become increasingly important due to the tremendous expansion in computer information systems and Web technologies and the frenzy in companies purchasing other companies at high prices, with the expectation that these intangible resources will provide significant future benefits to the company.

Intangible assets are recorded **at historical cost only if they have been purchased.** If these assets are developed internally by the company, they are expensed when incurred. Upon acquisition of intangible assets, managers determine whether the separate intangibles have definite or indefinite lives:

- **Definite Life.** The cost of an intangible asset with a definite life is allocated on a straight-line basis each period over its useful life in a process called **amortization** that is similar to depreciation and depletion. Most companies do not estimate a residual value for their intangible assets. Amortization expense is included on the income statement each period and the intangible assets are reported at cost less accumulated amortization on the balance sheet.

AMORTIZATION is the systematic and rational allocation of the acquisition cost of an intangible asset over its useful life.

Let's assume a company purchases a patent for $800,000 and intends to use it for 20 years. The adjusting entry to record $40,000 in patent amortization expense ($800,000 ÷ 20 years) is as follows:

	Debit	Credit
Patent Amortization Expense (+E, −SE)	40,000	
Patents (−A)		40,000
(or Accumulated Amortization +XA, −A)		

Assets		=	Liabilities	+	Stockholders' Equity	
Patents	−40,000				Patent Amortization Expense (+E)	−40,000
(or Accumulated Depletion +XA)						

- **Indefinite Life.** Intangible assets with indefinite lives are **not amortized.** Instead, these assets are to be tested at least annually for possible impairment, and the asset's book value is written down (decreased) to its fair value if impaired. The two-step process is similar to that used for assets discussed previously and summarized in the margin.

Asset Impairment Test and Loss Measurement:
Step 1: An asset is impaired if:
Book value > Future cash flows
Step 2: Then, Impairment Loss =
Book Value − Fair Value

The AICPA's 2009 **Accounting Trends & Techniques** summarizes intangible assets most frequently disclosed by the 600 companies surveyed:

	Number of Companies	Percentage of 600
Goodwill recognized in a business combination	542	90%
Trademarks, brand names, copyrights	330	55
Customer lists/relationships	320	53
Technology	162	27
Patents, patent rights	161	27
Licenses, franchises, memberships	114	19
Noncompete covenants	112	19
Contracts, agreements	104	17
Other—described in the annual report	65	11

Goodwill

For accounting purposes, GOODWILL (COST IN EXCESS OF NET ASSETS ACQUIRED) is the excess of the purchase price of a business over the fair value of the business's assets and liabilities.

By far the most frequently reported intangible asset is goodwill (cost in excess of net assets acquired). The term **goodwill,** as used by most businesspeople, means the favorable reputation that a company has with its customers. Goodwill arises from factors such as customer confidence, reputation for good service or quality goods, location, outstanding management team, and financial standing. From its first day of operations, a successful business continually builds goodwill. In this context, the goodwill is said to be **internally generated** and is not reported as an asset (i.e., it was not purchased).

The only way to report goodwill as an asset is to purchase another business. Often the purchase price of the business exceeds the fair value of all of its net assets (assets minus liabilities). Why would a company pay more for a business as a whole than it would pay if it bought the assets individually? The answer is to obtain its goodwill. You could easily buy modern bottling equipment to produce and sell a new cola drink, but you would not make as much money as you would if you acquired the goodwill associated with Coke or Pepsi brand names.

For accounting purposes, goodwill is defined as the difference between the purchase price of a company as a whole and the fair value of its net assets:

	Purchase price
−	Fair value of identifiable assets and liabilities
	Goodwill to be reported

In many acquisitions, the amount recorded as Goodwill can be very large. For example, Cisco Systems, which designs, manufactures, and sells Internet-based networking and other products and services, has completed several acquisitions since 2007. Of the $5.6 billion total cost of these acquisitions, $3.8 billion was reported as Goodwill, nearly 30 percent of the $12.925 billion in Goodwill reported on the July 25, 2009, balance sheet. Goodwill is considered to have an indefinite life and must be reviewed at least annually for possible impairment of value. Cisco reported the following:

REAL WORLD EXCERPT
Cisco Systems
2009 ANNUAL REPORT

2. Summary of Significant Accounting Policies

(g) Goodwill and Purchased Intangible Assets

Goodwill is tested for impairment on an annual basis in the fourth fiscal quarter and between annual tests in certain circumstances, and written down when impaired. Based on the impairment tests performed, there was no impairment of goodwill in fiscal 2009, 2008, or 2007 . . .

Trademarks

A TRADEMARK is an exclusive legal right to use a special name, image, or slogan.

A trademark is a special name, image, or slogan identified with a product or a company; it is protected by law. Trademarks are among the most valuable assets a company can own. For example, most of us cannot imagine the Walt Disney Company without Mickey Mouse. Similarly, you probably enjoy your favorite soft drink more because of the image that has been built up around its name than because of its taste. Many people can identify the shape of a corporate logo as quickly as they can recognize the shape of a stop sign. Although trademarks are valuable assets, they are rarely seen on balance sheets. The reason is simple; intangible assets are not recorded unless they are purchased. Companies often spend millions of dollars developing trademarks, but most of those expenditures are recorded as expenses rather than being capitalized as an intangible asset.

Copyrights

A **copyright** gives the owner the exclusive right to publish, use, and sell a literary, musical, or artistic piece for a period not exceeding 70 years after the author's death.[2] The book you are reading has a copyright to protect the publisher and authors. It is against the law, for example, for an instructor to copy several chapters from this book and hand them out in class. A copyright that is purchased is recorded at cost.

A COPYRIGHT is the exclusive right to publish, use, and sell a literary, musical, or artistic work.

Technology

The number of companies reporting a **technology** intangible asset continues to rise. Computer software and Web development costs are becoming increasingly significant. In 2008, IBM Corporation reported $1,022 million in software on its balance sheet and disclosed the following in the notes to the financial statements:

TECHNOLOGY includes costs for computer software and Web development.

> The company capitalizes certain costs that are incurred to purchase or to create and implement internal-use computer software, which includes software coding, installation, testing, and certain data conversion. These capitalized costs are amortized on a straight-line basis over two years and are recorded in selling, general, and administrative expense.

REAL WORLD EXCERPT
International Business Machines Corporation
2008 ANNUAL REPORT

Patents

A **patent** is an exclusive right granted by the federal government for a period of 20 years, typically granted to a person who invents a new product or discovers a new process.[3] The patent enables the owner to use, manufacture, and sell both the subject of the patent and the patent itself. It prevents a competitor from simply copying a new invention or discovery until the inventor has had time to earn an economic return on the new product. Without the protection of a patent, inventors likely would be unwilling to search for new products. Patents are recorded at their purchase price or, if **developed internally,** at only their registration and legal costs because GAAP requires the immediate expensing of research and development costs.

A PATENT is granted by the federal government for an invention; it is an exclusive right given to the owner to use, manufacture, and sell the subject of the patent.

Franchises

Franchises may be granted by the government or a business for a specified period and purpose. A city may grant one company a franchise to distribute gas to homes for heating purposes, or a company may sell franchises, such as the right to operate a KFC restaurant (owned by Yum Brands!). Franchise agreements are contracts that can have a variety of provisions. They usually require an investment by the franchisee; therefore, they should be accounted for as intangible assets. The life of the franchise agreement depends on the contract. It may be a single year or an indefinite period. Blockbuster, Inc.'s franchise agreement covers a period of 20 years. Blockbuster has more than 1,800 stores in the United States and internationally under franchise agreements.

A FRANCHISE is a contractual right to sell certain products or services, use certain trademarks, or perform activities in a geographical region.

Licenses and Operating Rights

Southwest Airlines's intangible assets are included on the balance sheet presented in Exhibit 8.1 as *other assets*. They primarily represent leasehold rights to airport-owned gates. Others include operating rights, which are authorized landing slots regulated by the government that are in limited supply at many airports. They are intangible assets that can be bought and sold by the airlines. Other types of **licenses and operating rights** that grant permission to companies include using airwaves for radio and television broadcasts and land for cable and telephone lines.

LICENSES AND OPERATING RIGHTS, obtained through agreements with governmental units or agencies, permit owners to use public property in performing their services.

[2]In general, the limit is 70 years beyond the death of an author. For anonymous authors, the limit is 95 years from the first publication date. For more detail, go to **lcweb.loc.gov/copyright**.
[3]For more details, go to **http://www.uspto.gov/web/offices/pac/doc/general/index.html#patent**.

Research and Development Expense—Not an Intangible Asset under U.S. GAAP

If an intangible asset is developed internally, the cost of development normally is recorded as **research and development expense.** For example, Abbott Laboratories (a manufacturer of pharmaceutical and nutritional products) recently spent more than $2,688 million on research to discover new products. This amount was reported as an expense, not an asset, because research and development expenditures typically do not possess sufficient probability of resulting in measurable future cash flows. If Abbott Labs had spent an equivalent amount to purchase patents for new products from other drug companies, it would have recorded the expenditure as an asset.

INTERNATIONAL PERSPECTIVE

Standards in Process

While all research and development costs must be reported as an expense under U.S. GAAP, International Financial Reporting Standards (IFRS) require that research expenditures be reported as an expense, but development costs be capitalized as an asset after technical and commercial feasibility of the resulting product or service have been established. The FASB is currently working on a new accounting standard aimed at eliminating this difference.

FOCUS ON CASH FLOWS

Productive Assets and Depreciation

LEARNING OBJECTIVE 7

Explain how the acquisition, use, and disposal of long-lived assets impact cash flows.

Effect on Statement of Cash Flows

The indirect method for preparing the operating activities section of the statement of cash flows involves reconciling net income on the accrual basis (reported on the income statement) to cash flows from operations. This means that, among other adjustments, (1) revenues and expenses that do not involve cash and (2) gains and losses that relate to investing or financing activities (not operations) should be eliminated.

When depreciation is recorded, no cash payment is made (i.e., there is no credit to Cash). Since depreciation expense (a noncash expense) is subtracted in calculating net income on the income statement, it must be added back to net income to eliminate its effect. Likewise, since any gain (or loss) on the sale of long-lived assets (an investing activity) is added (or subtracted) to determine net income, it must be subtracted from (or added to) net income to eliminate its effect.

In General The acquisition, sale, and depreciation of long-term assets are reflected on a company's cash flow statement as indicated in the following table:

	Effect on Cash Flows
Operating activities (indirect method)	
Net income	$xxx
Adjusted for: Depreciation and amortization expense	+
Gains on sale of long-lived assets	−
Losses on sale of long-lived assets	+
Losses due to asset impairment write-downs	+
Investing activities	
Purchase of long-lived assets	−
Sale of long-lived assets	+

Focus Company Analysis The following is a condensed version of Southwest's statement of cash flows for 2009. Buying and selling long-lived assets are investing activities. In 2009, Southwest used $585 million in cash to purchase flight equipment and ground property and equipment. Southwest did not sell any flight or ground equipment during the year. Selling long-lived assets is not an operating activity. Therefore, any gains (losses) on sales of long-term assets that were included in net income must be deducted from (added to) net income in the operating activities section to eliminate the effect of the sale. Unless they are large, these gain and loss adjustments normally are not specifically highlighted on the statement of cash flows. Southwest did not list any gains or losses as adjustments in 2009.

In capital-intensive industries such as airlines, depreciation is a significant noncash expense. In Southwest's case, depreciation and amortization expense is usually the single largest adjustment to net income in determining cash flows from operations. For example, in 2009, the adjustment for depreciation and amortization expense was 63 percent of operating cash flows.

SOUTHWEST AIRLINES CO.
Consolidated Statement of Cash Flows (partial)
For the Year Ended December 31, 2009
(In millions)

	2009
Cash Flows from Operating Activities:	
Net income	$ 99
Adjustments to reconcile net income to cash provided by operating activities:	
Depreciation and amortization	616
Other (*summarized*)	270
Net cash provided by (used in) operating activities	985
Cash Flows from Investing Activities:	
Purchases of property and equipment, net	(585)
Other (*summarized*)	(984)
Net cash used in investing activities	(1,569)

A Misinterpretation

FINANCIAL ANALYSIS

Some analysts misinterpret the meaning of a noncash expense, saying that "cash is provided by depreciation." Although depreciation is added in the operating section of the statement of cash flows, **depreciation is not a source of cash.** Cash from operations can be provided only by selling goods and services. A company with a large amount of depreciation expense does not generate more cash compared with a company that reports a small amount of depreciation expense, assuming that they are exactly the same in every other respect. While depreciation expense reduces the amount of reported net income for a company, it does not reduce the amount of cash generated by the company because it is a noncash expense. Remember that the effects of recording depreciation are a reduction in stockholders' equity and a reduction in fixed assets, not in cash. That is why, on the statement of cash flows, depreciation expense is added back to net income on an accrual basis to compute cash flows from operations (on a cash basis).

Although depreciation is a noncash expense, the **depreciation for tax purposes can affect a company's cash flows.** Depreciation is a deductible expense for income tax purposes. The higher the amount of depreciation recorded by a company for tax purposes, the lower the company's taxable income and the taxes it must pay. Because taxes must be paid in cash, a reduction in a company's results reduces the company's cash outflows (that is, lower net income leads to lower tax payments).

DEMONSTRATION CASE

(Resolve the requirements before proceeding to the suggested solution that follows.) Diversified Industries started as a residential construction company. In recent years, it has expanded into heavy construction, ready-mix concrete, sand and gravel, construction supplies, and earth-moving services. The company completed the following transactions during 2010. Amounts have been simplified.

2010

Jan. 1	The management decided to buy a 10-year-old building for $175,000 and the land on which it was situated for $130,000. It paid $100,000 in cash and signed a mortgage note payable for the rest.
Jan. 12	Paid $38,000 in renovation costs on the building prior to use.
June 19	Bought a third location for a gravel pit (designated Gravel Pit No. 3) for $50,000 cash. It was estimated that 100,000 cubic yards of gravel could be removed.
July 10	Paid $1,200 for ordinary repairs on the building.
Aug. 1	Paid $10,000 for costs of preparing the new gravel pit for exploitation.
Dec. 31	Year-end adjustments:

a. The building will be depreciated on a straight-line basis over an estimated useful life of 30 years. The estimated residual value is $33,000.

b. During 2010, 12,000 cubic yards of gravel were removed from Gravel Pit No. 3.

c. Diversified purchased another company several years ago at $100,000 over the fair value of the net assets acquired. The goodwill has an indefinite life.

d. At the beginning of the year, the company owned equipment with a cost of $650,000 and accumulated depreciation of $150,000. The equipment is being depreciated using the double-declining-balance method, with a useful life of 20 years and no residual value.

e. At year-end, the company tested its long-lived assets for possible impairment of their value. It identified a piece of old excavation equipment with a cost of $156,000 and remaining book value of $120,000. Due to its smaller size and lack of safety features, the old equipment has limited use. The future cash flows are expected to be $40,000 and the fair value is determined to be $35,000. Goodwill was found not to be impaired.

December 31, 2010, is the end of the annual accounting period.

Required:

1. Indicate the accounts affected and the amount and direction (+ for increase and − for decrease) of the effect of each of the preceding events (Jan. 1, Jan. 12, June 19, July 10, Aug. 1, and adjustments *a* through *e*) on the financial statement categories at the end of the year. Use the following headings:

Date	Assets	=	Liabilities	+	Stockholders' Equity

2. Record the December 31 adjusting journal entries (*a*) and (*b*) only.

3. Show the December 31, 2010, balance sheet classification and amount reported for each of the following items:

Fixed assets—land, building, equipment, and gravel pit

Intangible asset—goodwill

4. Assuming that the company had sales of $1,000,000 for the year and a net book value of $500,000 for fixed assets at the beginning of the year, compute the fixed asset turnover ratio. Explain its meaning.

SUGGESTED SOLUTION

1. Effects of events (with computations):

Date	Assets		=	Liabilities		+	Stockholders' Equity	
Jan. 1	Cash Land Building	−100,000 +130,000 +175,000		Note Payable	+205,000			
Jan. 12 (1)	Cash Building	−38,000 +38,000						
June 19 (2)	Cash Gravel Pit No. 3	−50,000 +50,000						
July 10 (3)	Cash	−1,200					Repairs Expense	−1,200
Aug. 1 (4)	Cash Gravel Pit No. 3	−10,000 +10,000						
Dec. 31 *a* (5)	Accumulated Depreciation (+XA)	−6,000					Depreciation Expense	−6,000
Dec. 31 *b* (6)	Gravel Pit No. 3 Gravel Inventory	−7,200 +7,200						
Dec. 31 *c* (7)	No entry							
Dec. 31 *d* (8)	Accumulated Depreciation	−50,000					Depreciation Expense	−50,000
Dec. 31 *e* (9)	Equipment	−85,000					Loss Due to Asset Impairment	−85,000

(1) Capitalize the $38,000 expenditure because it is necessary to prepare the asset for use.

(2) This is a natural resource.

(3) This is an ordinary repair (revenue expenditure) and should be expensed.

(4) Capitalize the $10,000 expenditure because it is necessary to prepare the asset for use.

(5)

Cost of Building		Straight-Line Depreciation
Initial purchase price	$175,000	($213,000 cost − $33,000 residual value) ×
Repairs prior to use	38,000	1/30 years = **$6,000** annual depreciation
Acquisition cost	$213,000	

(6)

Cost of Gravel Pit		Units-of-Production Depletion
Initial payment	$50,000	($60,000 cost ÷ 100,000 estimated production) ×
Preparation costs	10,000	12,000 actual cubic yards = **$7,200** depletion for 2010
Acquisition cost	$60,000	Capitalize the depletion to gravel inventory.

(7) Goodwill has an indefinite life and is therefore not amortized. We will test for impairment later.

(8) **Double-declining-balance depreciation**

($650,000 cost − $150,000 accumulated depreciation) × 2/20 years = **$50,000** depreciation for 2010.

(9) **Asset impairment**

Impairment Test: The book value of old equipment, $120,000, exceeds expected future cash flows, $40,000. The asset is impaired.

Impairment Loss	
Book value	$120,000
Less: Fair value	−35,000
Loss due to impairment	$ 85,000

2. Adjusting entries at December 31, 2010:

a. Depreciation Expense (+E, −SE)	6,000	
Accumulated Depreciation (+XA, −A)		6,000
b. Gravel Inventory (+A)	7,200	
Gravel Pit No. 3 (−A)		7,200

3. Partial balance sheet, December 31, 2010:

Assets		
Fixed assets		
Land		$130,000
Building	$213,000	
Less: Accumulated depreciation	6,000	207,000
Equipment ($650,000 − $85,000)	565,000	
Less: Accumulated depreciation ($150,000 + $50,000)	200,000	365,000
Gravel pit		52,800
Total fixed assets		754,800
Intangible asset		
Goodwill		100,000

4. Fixed asset turnover ratio:

$$\frac{\textbf{Sales}}{\textbf{(Beginning Net Fixed Asset Balance + Ending Net Fixed Asset Balance)} \div 2} = \frac{\textbf{\$1,000,000}}{\textbf{(\$500,000 + \$754,800)} \div 2} = \textbf{1.59}$$

This construction company is capital intensive. The fixed asset turnover ratio measures the company's efficiency at using its investment in property, plant, and equipment to generate sales.

Chapter Supplement

Changes in Depreciation Estimates

Depreciation is based on two estimates: useful life and residual value. These estimates are made at the time a depreciable asset is acquired. As experience with the asset accumulates, one or both of these initial estimates may need to be revised. In addition, extraordinary repairs and additions may be added to the original acquisition cost at some time during the asset's use. When it is clear that either estimate should be revised to a material degree or that the asset's cost has changed, the undepreciated asset balance (less any residual value at that date) should be apportioned over the remaining estimated life from the current year into the future. This is called a prospective **change in estimate.**

To compute the new depreciation expense due to a change in estimate for any of the depreciation methods described here, substitute the net book value for the original acquisition cost, the new residual value for the original amount, and the estimated remaining life in place of the original estimated life. As an illustration, the formula using the straight-line method follows.

Original Straight-Line Formula Modified for a Change in Estimate:

$$\text{(Cost} - \text{Residual Value)} \times \frac{1}{\text{Useful Life}} = \text{Original Depreciation Expense}$$

$$\text{(Net Book Value} - \text{New Residual Value)} \times \frac{1}{\text{Remaining Life}} = \text{Revised Depreciation Expense}$$

Assume Southwest purchased an aircraft for $60,000,000 with an estimated useful life of 20 years and estimated residual value of $3,000,000. Shortly after the start of year 5, Southwest changed the initial estimated life to 25 years and lowered the estimated residual value to $2,400,000. At the end of year 5, the computation of the new amount for depreciation expense is as follows:

Straight-Line Depreciation Expense with a Change in Estimate

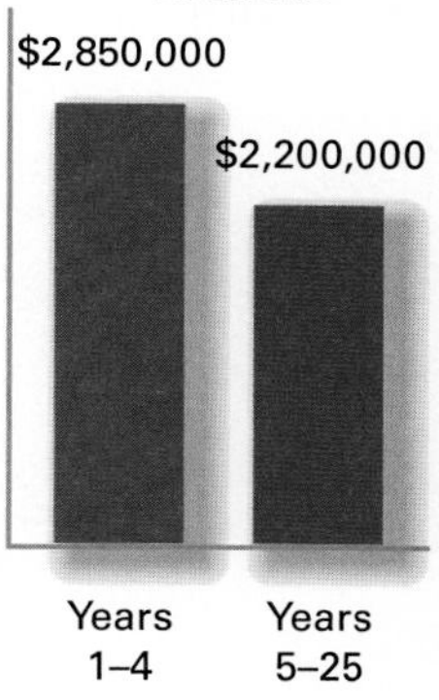

Original depreciation expense

($60,000,000 − $3,000,000) × 1/20 = $ 2,850,000 per year
× 4 years
Accumulated depreciation at the end of year 4: $11,400,000

Net book value at the end of year 4

Acquisition cost	$60,000,000
Less: Accumulated depreciation	11,400,000
Net book value	$48,600,000

Depreciation in years 5 through 25 based on changes in estimates

(Net Book Value − New Residual Value) × 1/Remaining Years = New Depreciation expense

($48,600,000 − $2,400,000) × 1/21 (25 − 4 years) = $2,200,000 per year

Companies may also change depreciation methods (for example, from declining balance to straight line). Such a change requires significantly more disclosure since it violates the consistency principle which requires that accounting information reported in the financial statements should be comparable across accounting periods. Under GAAP, changes in accounting estimates and depreciation methods should be made only when a new estimate or accounting method "better measures" the periodic income of the business.

PAUSE FOR FEEDBACK

When management changes an estimate used in a depreciation computation, the net book value at the time of the change minus any expected residual value is allocated over the remaining life of the asset.

SELF-STUDY QUIZ

Assume that Southwest Airlines owned a service truck that originally cost $100,000. When purchased at the beginning of 2006, the truck had an estimated useful life of 10 years with no residual value.

(continued)

At the beginning of 2011, after operating the truck for five years, Southwest determined that the remaining life was only two more years. Southwest uses the straight-line method.

1. What is the truck's net book value at the beginning of 2011?
2. Based on this change in estimate, what amount of depreciation should be recorded each year over the remaining life of the asset?

After you have completed your answers, check them with the solutions at the bottom of the page.

CHAPTER TAKE-AWAYS

1. **Define, classify, and explain the nature of long-lived productive assets and interpret the fixed asset turnover ratio.** p. 389
   a. Noncurrent assets are those that a business retains for long periods of time for use in the course of normal operations rather than for sale. They may be divided into tangible assets (land, buildings, equipment, natural resources) and intangible assets (including goodwill, patents, and franchises).
   b. The cost allocation method utilized affects the amount of net property, plant, and equipment that is used in the computation of the fixed asset turnover ratio. Accelerated methods reduce book value and increase the turnover ratio.
2. **Apply the cost principle to measure the acquisition and maintenance of property, plant, and equipment.** p. 391
   The acquisition cost of property, plant, and equipment is the cash-equivalent purchase price plus all reasonable and necessary expenditures made to acquire and prepare the asset for its intended use. These assets may be acquired using cash, debt, stock, or through self-construction. Expenditures made after the asset is in use are either additions and improvements (capital expenditures) or ordinary repairs (revenue expenditures):
   a. **Revenue expenditures (ordinary repairs and maintenance)** provide benefits during the current accounting period only. Amounts are debited to appropriate current expense accounts when the expenses are incurred.
   b. **Capital expenditures (additions and improvements)** provide benefits for one or more accounting periods beyond the current period. Amounts are debited to the appropriate asset accounts and depreciated, depleted, or amortized over their useful lives.
3. **Apply various cost allocation methods as assets are held and used over time.** p. 396
   Cost allocation methods: In conformity with the matching principle, cost less any estimated residual value is allocated to periodic expense over the periods benefited. Because of depreciation, the net book value of an asset declines over time and net income is reduced by the amount of the expense. Common depreciation methods include straight-line (a constant amount over time), units-of-production (a variable amount over time), and double-declining-balance (a decreasing amount over time).
   a. Depreciation—buildings and equipment.
   b. Depletion—natural resources.
   c. Amortization— intangibles.
4. **Explain the effect of asset impairment on the financial statements.** p. 406
   When events or changes in circumstances reduce the estimated future cash flows of long-lived assets below their book value, the book values should be written down (by recording a loss) to the fair value of the assets.

Solutions to SELF-STUDY QUIZ

1. (Cost \$100,000 − Residual Value \$0) × 1/10 = \$10,000 Original Annual Depreciation
   \$10,000 Annual Depreciation Expense × 5 years = \$50,000 Accumulated Depreciation.
   Net Book Value After 5 Years = Cost \$100,000 − Accumulated Depreciation \$50,000 = \$50,000.
2. (Net Book Value \$50,000 − Residual Value \$0) ×1/2 (remaining life) = \$25,000 Depreciation Expense per Year.

5. **Analyze the disposal of property, plant, and equipment.** p. 408

   When assets are disposed of through sale or abandonment,

   a. Record additional depreciation since the last adjustment was made.
   b. Remove the cost of the old asset and its related accumulated depreciation, depletion, or amortization.
   c. Recognize the cash proceeds.
   d. Recognize any gain or loss when the asset's net book value is not equal to the cash received.

6. **Apply measurement and reporting concepts for natural resources and intangible assets.** p. 409

   The cost principle should be applied in recording the acquisition of natural resources and intangible assets. Natural resources should be depleted (usually by the units-of-production method) usually with the amount of the depletion expense capitalized to an inventory account. Intangibles with definite useful lives are amortized using the straight-line method. Intangibles with indefinite useful lives, including goodwill, are not amortized, but are reviewed at least annually for impairment. Report intangibles at net book value on the balance sheet.

7. **Explain how the acquisition, use, and disposal of long-lived assets impact cash flows.** p. 414

   Depreciation expense is a noncash expense that has no effect on cash. It is added back to net income on the statement of cash flows to determine cash from operations. Acquiring and disposing of long-lived assets are investing activities.

In previous chapters, we discussed business and accounting issues related to the assets that a company holds. In Chapters 9, 10, and 11, we shift our focus to the other side of the balance sheet to see how managers finance business operations and the acquisition of productive assets. We discuss various types of liabilities in Chapters 9 and 10 and examine stockholders' equity in Chapter 11.

KEY RATIO

The **fixed asset turnover ratio** measures how efficiently a company utilizes its investment in property, plant, and equipment over time. Its ratio can then be compared to competitors' ratios. The fixed asset turnover ratio is computed as follows (p. 390):

$$\text{Fixed Asset Turnover} = \frac{\text{Net Sales (or Operating Revenues)}}{\text{Average Net Fixed Assets}}$$

FINDING FINANCIAL INFORMATION

Balance Sheet

Under Noncurrent Assets

Property, plant, and equipment (net of accumulated depreciation)
Natural resources (net of accumulated depletion)
Intangibles (net of accumulated amortization, if any)

Income Statement

Under Operating Expenses

Depreciation, depletion, and amortization expense **or** included in
Selling, general, and administrative expenses and
Cost of goods sold (with the amount for depreciation expense disclosed in a note)

Statement of Cash Flows

Under Operating Activities (indirect method)

Net income
\+ Depreciation and amortization expense
− Gains on sales of assets
\+ Losses on sales of assets

Under Investing Activities

\+ Sales of assets for cash
− Purchases of assets for cash

Notes

Under Summary of Significant Accounting Policies

Description of management's choice for depreciation and amortization methods, including useful lives, and the amount of annual depreciation expense, if not listed on the income statement.

Under a Separate Footnote

If not specified on the balance sheet, a listing of the major classifications of long-lived assets at cost and the balance in accumulated depreciation, depletion, and amortization.

KEY TERMS

Acquisition Cost p. 391
Additions and Improvements p. 394
Amortization p. 411
Capital Expenditures p. 394
Capitalized Interest p. 392
Copyright p. 413
Declining-Balance Depreciation p. 401
Depletion p. 410
Depreciation p. 396
Estimated Useful Life p. 398
Franchise p. 413
Goodwill (Cost in Excess of Net Assets Acquired) p. 412
Intangible Assets p. 389
Licenses and Operating Rights p. 413
Long-Lived Assets p. 389
Natural Resources p. 409
Net Book (or Carrying) Value p. 397
Ordinary Repairs and Maintenance p. 394
Patent p. 413
Residual (or Salvage) Value p. 398
Revenue Expenditures p. 394
Straight-Line Depreciation p. 399
Tangible Assets p. 389
Technology p. 413
Trademark p. 412
Units-of-Production Depreciation p. 400

QUESTIONS

1. Define **long-lived assets.** Why are they considered to be a "bundle of future services"?
2. How is the fixed asset turnover ratio computed? Explain its meaning.
3. What are the classifications of long-lived assets? Explain each.
4. Under the cost principle, what amounts should be included in the acquisition cost of a long-lived asset?
5. Describe the relationship between the matching principle and accounting for long-lived assets.
6. Distinguish between
   a. Capital expenditures and revenue expenditures. How is each accounted for?
   b. Ordinary repairs and improvements. How is each accounted for?
7. Distinguish among depreciation, depletion, and amortization.
8. In computing depreciation, three values must be known or estimated; identify and explain the nature of each.
9. The estimated useful life and residual value of a long-lived asset relate to the current owner or user rather than all potential users. Explain this statement.
10. What type of depreciation expense pattern is used under each of the following methods and when is its use appropriate?
    a. The straight-line method.
    b. The units-of-production method.
    c. The double-declining-balance method.
11. Over what period should an addition to an existing long-lived asset be depreciated? Explain.
12. What is **asset impairment**? How is it accounted for?
13. When equipment is sold for more than net book value, how is the transaction recorded? For less than net book value? What is **net book value**?
14. Define **intangible asset.** What period should be used to amortize an intangible asset with a definite life?
15. Define **goodwill.** When is it appropriate to record goodwill as an intangible asset?
16. Why is depreciation expense added to net income (indirect method) on the statement of cash flows?

MULTIPLE-CHOICE QUESTIONS

1. Miga Company and Porter Company both bought a new delivery truck on January 1, 2008. Both companies paid exactly the same cost, $30,000, for their respective vehicles. As of December 31, 2011, the net book value of Miga's truck was less than Porter Company's net book value for the same vehicle. Which of the following is an acceptable explanation for the difference in net book value?
   a. Miga Company estimated a lower residual value, but both estimated the same useful life and both elected straight-line depreciation.
   b. Both companies elected straight-line depreciation, but Miga Company used a longer estimated life.

c. Because GAAP specifies rigid guidelines regarding the calculation of depreciation, this situation is not possible.
d. Miga Company is using the straight-line method of depreciation, and Porter Company is using the double-declining-balance method of depreciation.

2. Barber, Inc., followed the practice of depreciating its building on a straight-line basis. A building was purchased in 2011 and had an estimated useful life of 25 years and a residual value of $20,000. The company's depreciation expense for 2011 was $20,000 on the building. What was the original cost of the building?
a. $480,000
b. $500,000
c. $520,000
d. Cannot be determined from the information given.

3. Ryan, Inc., uses straight-line depreciation for all of its depreciable assets. Ryan sold a used piece of machinery on December 31, 2012, that it purchased on January 1, 2011, for $10,000. The asset had a five-year life, zero residual value, and $2,000 accumulated depreciation as of December 31, 2011. If the sales price of the used machine was $6,500, the resulting gain or loss upon the sale was which of the following amounts?
a. Loss of $500
b. Gain of $500
c. Loss of $1,500
d. Gain of $1,500
e. No gain or loss upon the sale.

4. Under what method(s) of depreciation is an asset's **net book value** the depreciable base (the amount to be depreciated)?
a. Straight-line method
b. Declining-balance method
c. Units-of-production method
d. All of the above

5. What assets should be amortized using the straight-line method?
a. Intangible assets with definite lives
b. Intangible assets with indefinite lives
c. Natural resources
d. All of the above

6. A company wishes to report the highest earnings possible for financial reporting purposes. Therefore, when calculating depreciation,
a. It will follow the MACRS depreciation tables prescribed by the IRS.
b. It will select the shortest lives possible for its assets.
c. It will select the lowest residual values for its assets.
d. It will estimate higher residual values for its assets.

7. How many of the following statements regarding goodwill are true?
- Goodwill is not reported unless purchased in an exchange.
- Goodwill must be reviewed annually for possible impairment.
- Impairment of goodwill results in a decrease in net income.

a. Three
b. Two
c. One
d. None

8. Company X is going to retire equipment that is fully depreciated with no residual value. The equipment will simply be disposed of, not sold. Which of the following statements is *false*?
a. Total assets will not change as a result of this transaction.
b. Net income will not be impacted as a result of this transaction.
c. This transaction will not impact cash flow.
d. All of the above statements are true.

9. When recording depreciation, which of the following statements is *true*?
a. Total assets increase and stockholders' equity increases.
b. Total assets decrease and total liabilities increase.
c. Total assets decrease and stockholders' equity increases.
d. None of the above are true.

10. (Supplement) Thornton Industries purchased a machine for $45,000 and is depreciating it with the straight-line method over a life of 10 years, using a residual value of $3,000. At the beginning of the sixth year, a major overhaul was made costing $5,000, and the total estimated useful life was extended to 13 years. Depreciation expense for year 6 is:
a. $1,885
b. $2,000
c. $3,250
d. $3,625
e. $4,200

For more practice with multiple-choice questions, go to the text website at **www.mhhe.com/libby7e**.

MINI-EXERCISES

connect ACCOUNTING

M8-1 Classifying Long-Lived Assets and Related Cost Allocation Concepts
LO1, 3, 6

For each of the following long-lived assets, indicate its nature and the related cost allocation concept. Use the following symbols:

Nature		Cost Allocation Concept	
L	Land	DR	Depreciation
B	Building	DP	Depletion
E	Equipment	A	Amortization
NR	Natural resource	NO	No cost allocation
I	Intangible	O	Other
O	Other		

Asset	Nature	Cost Allocation	Asset	Nature	Cost Allocation
(1) Tractors	_____	_____	(6) Operating license	_____	_____
(2) Land in use	_____	_____	(7) Production plant	_____	_____
(3) Timber tract	_____	_____	(8) Trademark	_____	_____
(4) Warehouse	_____	_____	(9) Silver mine	_____	_____
(5) New engine for old machine	_____	_____	(10) Land held for sale	_____	_____

M8-2 Computing and Evaluating the Fixed Asset Turnover Ratio
LO1

The following information was reported by Kramer's Air Cargo Service for 2008:

Net fixed assets (beginning of year)	$1,900,000
Net fixed assets (end of year)	2,300,000
Net sales for the year	3,300,000
Net income for the year	1,600,000

Compute the company's fixed asset turnover ratio for the year. What can you say about Kramer's ratio when compared to Southwest's 2008 ratio?

M8-3 Identifying Capital and Revenue Expenditures
LO2

For each of the following items, enter the correct letter to the left to show the type of expenditure. Use the following:

Type of Expenditure	
C	Capital expenditure
R	Revenue expenditure
N	Neither

Transactions

_____ (1) Purchased a patent, $4,300 cash.
_____ (2) Paid $10,000 for monthly salaries.
_____ (3) Paid cash dividends, $20,000.
_____ (4) Purchased a machine, $7,000; gave a long-term note.
_____ (5) Paid three-year insurance premium, $900.
_____ (6) Paid for routine maintenance, $200, on credit.
_____ (7) Paid $400 for ordinary repairs.
_____ (8) Paid $6,000 for extraordinary repairs.
_____ (9) Paid $20,000 cash for addition to old building.

Computing Book Value (Straight-Line Depreciation) M8-4 LO3

Calculate the book value of a three-year-old machine that has a cost of $31,000, an estimated residual value of $1,000, and an estimated useful life of five years. The company uses straight-line depreciation.

Computing Book Value (Double-Declining-Balance Depreciation) M8-5 LO3

Calculate the book value of a three-year-old machine that has a cost of $45,000, an estimated residual value of $5,000, and an estimated useful life of four years. The company uses double-declining-balance depreciation. Round to the nearest dollar.

Computing Book Value (Units-of-Production Depreciation) M8-6 LO3

Calculate the book value of a three-year-old machine that has a cost of $21,000, has an estimated residual value of $1,000 and an estimated useful life of 40,000 machine hours. The company uses units-of-production depreciation and ran the machine 3,200 hours in year 1; 7,050 hours in year 2; and 7,500 hours in year 3.

Identifying Asset Impairment M8-7 LO4

For each of the following scenarios, indicate whether an asset has been impaired (Y for yes and N for no) and, if so, the amount of loss that should be recorded.

	Book Value	Estimated Future Cash Flows	Fair Value	Is Asset Impaired?	Amount of Loss
a. Machine	$ 15,500	$ 10,000	$ 9,500		
b. Copyright	31,000	41,000	37,900		
c. Factory building	58,000	29,000	27,000		
d. Building	227,000	227,000	200,000		

Recording the Disposal of a Long-Lived Asset (Straight-Line Depreciation) M8-8 LO5

As part of a major renovation at the beginning of the year, Scheffer's Pharmacy, Inc., sold shelving units (store fixtures) that were 10 years old for $1,800 cash. The original cost of the shelves was $6,000 and they had been depreciated on a straight-line basis over an estimated useful life of 13 years with an estimated residual value of $800. Record the sale of the shelving units.

Computing Goodwill and Patents M8-9 LO6

Elizabeth Pie Company has been in business for 50 years and has developed a large group of loyal restaurant customers. Giant Bakery Inc. has made an offer to buy Elizabeth Pie Company for $5,000,000. The book value of Elizabeth Pie's recorded assets and liabilities on the date of the offer is $4,300,000 with a fair value of $4,500,000. Elizabeth Pie also (1) holds a patent for a pie crust fluting machine that the company invented (the patent with a fair value of $300,000 was never recorded by Elizabeth Pie because it was developed internally) and (2) estimates goodwill from loyal customers to be $310,000 (also never recorded by the company). Should Elizabeth Pie Company management accept Giant Bakery's offer of $5,000,000? If so, compute the amount of goodwill that Giant Bakery should record on the date of the purchase.

Preparing the Statement of Cash Flows M8-10 LO7

Wexler Company had the following activities for the year ended December 31, 2012: Sold land that cost $18,000 for $18,000 cash; purchased $181,000 of equipment, paying $156,000 in cash and signing a note payable for the rest; and recorded $5,500 in depreciation expense for the year. Net income for the year was $13,000. Prepare the operating and investing sections of a statement of cash flows for the year based on the data provided.

EXERCISES

connect ACCOUNTING

E8-1 LO1 Hasbro, Inc.

Preparing a Classified Balance Sheet

The following is a list of account titles and amounts (dollars in millions) from a recent annual report of Hasbro, Inc., a leading manufacturer of games, toys, and interactive entertainment software for children and families:

Buildings and improvements	$196	Goodwill	$ 474
Prepaid expenses and other current assets	171	Machinery and equipment	413
Allowance for doubtful accounts	32	Accumulated depreciation	403
Other noncurrent assets	200	Inventories	300
Accumulated amortization (other intangibles)	800	Other intangibles	1,368
Cash and cash equivalents	630	Land and improvements	7
		Accounts receivable	644

Required:
Prepare the asset section of the balance sheet for Hasbro, Inc., classifying the assets into Current Assets, Property, Plant, and Equipment (net), and Other Assets.

E8-2 LO1 Apple Inc.

Computing and Interpreting the Fixed Asset Turnover Ratio from a Financial Analyst's Perspective

The following data were included in a recent Apple Inc. annual report ($ in millions):

In millions	2006	2007	2008	2009
Net sales	$19,315	$24,006	$32,479	$36,537
Net property, plant, and equipment	1,281	1,832	2,954	2,455

Required:
1. Compute Apple's fixed asset turnover ratio for 2007, 2008, and 2009.
2. How might a financial analyst interpret the results?

E8-3 LO2, 3

Computing and Recording Cost and Depreciation of Assets (Straight-Line Depreciation)

K-Delta Company bought a building for $71,000 cash and the land on which it was located for $107,000 cash. The company paid transfer costs of $9,000 ($3,000 for the building and $6,000 for the land). Renovation costs on the building were $23,000.

Required:
1. Give the journal entry to record the purchase of the property, including all expenditures. Assume that all transactions were for cash and that all purchases occurred at the start of the year.
2. Compute straight-line depreciation at the end of one year, assuming an estimated 10-year useful life and a $15,000 estimated residual value.
3. What would be the net book value of the property (land and building) at the end of year 2?

E8-4 LO2, 3

Determining Financial Statement Effects of an Asset Acquisition and Depreciation (Straight-Line Depreciation)

Ashkar Company ordered a machine on January 1, 2012, at an invoice price of $21,000. On the date of delivery, January 2, 2012, the company paid $6,000 on the machine, with the balance on credit at

10 percent interest. On January 3, 2012, it paid $1,000 for freight on the machine. On January 5, Ashkar paid installation costs relating to the machine amounting to $2,500. On July 1, 2012, the company paid the balance due on the machine plus the interest. On December 31, 2012 (the end of the accounting period), Ashkar recorded depreciation on the machine using the straight-line method with an estimated useful life of 10 years and an estimated residual value of $4,000.

Required (round all amounts to the nearest dollar):

1. Indicate the effects (accounts, amounts, and + or −) of each transaction (on January 1, 2, 3, and 5 and July 1) on the accounting equation. Use the following schedule:

Date	Assets	=	Liabilities	+	Stockholders' Equity

2. Compute the acquisition cost of the machine.
3. Compute the depreciation expense to be reported for 2012.
4. What impact does the interest paid on the 10 percent note have on the cost of the machine? Under what circumstances can interest expense be included in acquisition cost?
5. What would be the net book value of the machine at the end of 2013?

Recording Depreciation and Repairs (Straight-Line Depreciation)

E8-5
LO2, 3

Nasoff Company operates a small manufacturing facility as a supplement to its regular service activities. At the beginning of 2011, an asset account for the company showed the following balances:

Manufacturing equipment	$100,000
Accumulated depreciation through 2010	54,000

During 2011, the following expenditures were incurred for the equipment:

Routine maintenance and repairs on the equipment	$ 1,000
Major overhaul of the equipment that improved efficiency on January 2, 2011	12,000

The equipment is being depreciated on a straight-line basis over an estimated life of 15 years with a $10,000 estimated residual value. The annual accounting period ends on December 31.

Required:

1. Give the adjusting entry that was made at the end of **2010** for depreciation on the manufacturing equipment.
2. Starting at the beginning of **2011,** what is the remaining estimated life?
3. Give the journal entries to record the two expenditures during **2011.**

Determining Financial Statement Effects of Depreciation and Repairs (Straight-Line Depreciation)

E8-6
LO2, 3

Refer to the information in E8-5.

Required:

Indicate the effects (accounts, amounts, and + or −) of the following on the accounting equation.

Date	Assets	=	Liabilities	+	Stockholders' Equity

1. The adjustment for depreciation at the end of **2010.**
2. The two expenditures during **2011.**

Computing Depreciation under Alternative Methods

E8-7
LO3

Purity Ice Cream Company bought a new ice cream maker at the beginning of the year at a cost of $10,000. The estimated useful life was four years, and the residual value was $1,000. Assume that the estimated productive life of the machine was 9,000 hours. Actual annual usage was 3,600 hours in year 1; 2,700 hours in year 2; 1,800 hours in year 3; and 900 hours in year 4.

Required:

1. Complete a separate depreciation schedule for each of the alternative methods. Round your answers to the nearest dollar.
   a. Straight-line.
   b. Units-of-production (use four decimal places for the per unit output factor).
   c. Double-declining-balance.

Method: ________				
Year	**Computation**	**Depreciation Expense**	**Accumulated Depreciation**	**Net Book Value**
At acquisition				
1				
2				
etc.				

2. Assuming that the machine was used directly in the production of one of the products that the company manufactures and sells, what factors might management consider in selecting a preferable depreciation method in conformity with the matching principle?

E8-8
LO3

Computing Depreciation under Alternative Methods

Sterling Steel Inc. purchased a new stamping machine at the beginning of the year at a cost of $580,000. The estimated residual value was $60,000. Assume that the estimated useful life was five years, and the estimated productive life of the machine was 260,000 units. Actual annual production was as follows:

Year	Units
1	73,000
2	62,000
3	30,000
4	53,000
5	42,000

Required:

1. Complete a separate depreciation schedule for each of the alternative methods. Round your answers to the nearest dollar.
   a. Straight-line.
   b. Units-of-production.
   c. Double-declining-balance.

Method: ________				
Year	**Computation**	**Depreciation Expense**	**Accumulated Depreciation**	**Net Book Value**
At acquisition				
1				
2				
etc.				

2. Assuming that the machine was used directly in the production of one of the products that the company manufactures and sells, what factors might management consider in selecting a preferable depreciation method in conformity with the matching principle?

Explaining Depreciation Policy

E8-9
LO3

A recent annual report for General Motors Corporation contained the following note:

> **Note 3. Significant Accounting Policies**
>
> ***Property, Net***
>
> Property, plant, and equipment, including internal use software, is recorded at cost. Major improvements that extend the useful life of property are capitalized. Expenditures for repairs and maintenance are charged to expense as incurred. At January 1, 2001, we adopted the straight-line method of depreciation for real estate, facilities, and equipment placed in service after that date. Assets placed in service before January 1, 2001, continue to be depreciated using accelerated methods. The accelerated methods accumulate depreciation of approximately two-thirds of the depreciable cost in the first half of the estimated useful lives of property groups as compared to the straight-line method, which allocates depreciable costs equally over the estimated useful lives of property groups.

Required:
Why do you think the company changed its depreciation method for real estate, facilities, and equipment placed in service after January 1, 2001, and subsequent years?

Interpreting Management's Choice of Different Depreciation Methods for Tax and Financial Reporting

E8-10
LO3

FedEx

A recent annual report for FedEx includes the following information:

> For financial reporting purposes, we record depreciation and amortization of property and equipment on a straight-line basis over the asset's service life or related lease term if shorter. For income tax purposes, depreciation is computed using accelerated methods when applicable.

Required:
Explain why FedEx uses different methods of depreciation for financial reporting and tax purposes.

Computing Depreciation and Book Value for Two Years Using Alternative Depreciation Methods and Interpreting the Impact on Cash Flows

E8-11
LO3, 7

Schrade Company bought a machine for $96,000 cash. The estimated useful life was four years, and the estimated residual value was $6,000. Assume that the estimated useful life in productive units is 120,000. Units actually produced were 43,000 in year 1 and 45,000 in year 2.

Required:

1. Determine the appropriate amounts to complete the following schedule. Show computations, and round to the nearest dollar.

	Depreciation Expense for		Net Book Value at the End of	
Method of Depreciation	**Year 1**	**Year 2**	**Year 1**	**Year 2**
Straight-line				
Units-of-production				
Double-declining-balance				

2. Which method would result in the lowest EPS for year 1? For year 2?
3. Which method would result in the highest amount of cash outflows in year 1? Why?
4. Indicate the effects of (*a*) acquiring the machine and (*b*) recording annual depreciation on the operating and investing activities sections of the statement of cash flows (indirect method) for year 1 (assume the straight-line method).

E8-12
LO4, 5
United Parcel Service Inc.

Inferring Asset Impairment and Recording Disposal of an Asset

In a recent 10-K report, United Parcel Service states it "is the world's largest package delivery company, a leader in the U.S. less-than-truckload industry, and a global leader in supply chain management." The following note and data were reported:

Note 1—Summary of Accounting Policies

Impairment of Long-Lived Assets

. . . we review long-lived assets for impairment when circumstances indicate the carrying amount of an asset may not be recoverable based on the undiscounted future cash flows of the asset. . . .

	Dollars in Millions
Cost of property and equipment (beginning of year)	$33,611
Cost of property and equipment (end of year)	35,098
Capital expenditures during the year	2,636
Accumulated depreciation (beginning of year)	15,948
Accumulated depreciation (end of year)	16,833
Depreciation expense during the year	1,814
Cost of property and equipment sold during the year	1,040
Accumulated depreciation on property sold	929
Cash received on property sold	147

Required:
1. Reconstruct the journal entry for the disposal of property and equipment during the year.
2. Compute the amount of property and equipment that United Parcel wrote off as impaired during the year. (**Hint:** Set up T-accounts.)

E8-13
LO5
FedEx

Recording the Disposal of an Asset at Three Different Sale Prices

FedEx is the world's leading express-distribution company. In addition to the world's largest fleet of all-cargo aircraft, the company has more than 654 aircraft and 51,000 vehicles and trailers that pick up and deliver packages. Assume that FedEx sold a delivery truck that had been used in the business for three years. The records of the company reflected the following:

Delivery truck cost	$38,000
Accumulated depreciation	23,000

Required:
1. Give the journal entry for the disposal of the truck, assuming that the truck sold for
   a. $15,000 cash
   b. $15,600 cash
   c. $14,600 cash
2. Based on the three preceding situations, explain the effects of the disposal of an asset.

E8-14
LO5
Marriott International, Inc.

Recording the Disposal of an Asset at Three Different Sale Prices

Marriott International is a worldwide operator and franchisor of hotels and related lodging facilities totaling over $1.4 billion in property and equipment. It also develops, operates, and markets time-share properties totaling nearly $2 billion. Assume that Marriott replaced furniture that had been used in the business for five years. The records of the company reflected the following regarding the sale of the existing furniture:

Furniture (cost)	$6,000,000
Accumulated depreciation	5,500,000

Required:

1. Give the journal entry for the disposal of the furniture, assuming that it was sold for
   a. $500,000 cash
   b. $1,600,000 cash
   c. $400,000 cash
2. Based on the three preceding situations, explain the effects of the disposal of an asset.

Inferring Asset Age and Recording Accidental Loss on a Long-Lived Asset (Straight-Line Depreciation)

E8-15
LO3, 5

On January 1, 2012, the records of Seward Corporation showed the following regarding a truck:

Equipment (estimated residual value, $8,000)	$18,000
Accumulated depreciation (straight-line, three years)	6,000

On December 31, 2012, the delivery truck was a total loss as the result of an accident.

Required:

1. Based on the data given, compute the estimated useful life of the truck.
2. Give all journal entries with respect to the truck on December 31, 2012. Show computations.

Computing the Acquisition and Depletion of a Natural Resource

E8-16
LO6

FREEPORT-MCMORAN COPPER & GOLD

Freeport-McMoRan Copper & Gold Inc., headquartered in Phoenix, Arizona, is one of the world's largest copper, gold, and molybdenum mining and production companies, with its principal asset in natural resource reserves (approximately 102.0 billion pounds of copper, 40.0 million ounces of gold, 2.48 billion pounds of molybdenum, 266.6 million ounces of silver, and 0.7 billion pounds of cobalt, as of the end of 2008). Its annual revenues exceed $17.7 billion.

Assume that in February 2012, Freeport-McMoRan paid $700,000 for a mineral deposit in Indonesia. During March, it spent $74,000 in preparing the deposit for exploitation. It was estimated that 900,000 total cubic yards could be extracted economically. During 2012, 60,000 cubic yards were extracted. During January 2013, the company spent another $6,000 for additional developmental work that increased the estimated productive capacity of the mineral deposit.

Required:

1. Compute the acquisition cost of the deposit in 2012.
2. Compute depletion for 2012.
3. Compute the net book value of the deposit after payment of the January 2013 developmental costs.

Computing and Reporting the Acquisition and Amortization of Three Different Intangible Assets

E8-17
LO6

Trotman Company had three intangible assets at the end of 2012 (end of the accounting year):

a. Computer software and Web development technology purchased on January 1, 2011, for $70,000. The technology is expected to have a four-year useful life to the company.
b. A patent purchased from Ian Zimmer on January 1, 2012, for a cash cost of $6,000. Zimmer had registered the patent with the U.S. Patent Office five years ago.
c. An internally developed trademark registered with the federal government for $13,000 on November 1, 2012. Management decided the trademark has an indefinite life.

Required:

1. Compute the acquisition cost of each intangible asset.
2. Compute the amortization of each intangible at December 31, 2012. The company does not use contra-accounts.

3. Show how these assets and any related expenses should be reported on the balance sheet and income statement for 2012.

E8-18
LO6

Computing and Reporting the Acquisition and Amortization of Three Different Intangible Assets

Cheshire Company had three intangible assets at the end of 2011 (end of the accounting year):

a. A copyright purchased on January 1, 2011, for a cash cost of $12,300. The copyright is expected to have a 10-year useful life to Cheshire.
b. Goodwill of $65,000 from the purchase of the Hartford Company on July 1, 2010.
c. A patent purchased on January 1, 2010, for $39,200. The inventor had registered the patent with the U.S. Patent Office on January 1, 2006.

Required:

1. Compute the acquisition cost of each intangible asset.
2. Compute the amortization of each intangible at December 31, 2011. The company does not use contra-accounts.
3. Show how these assets and any related expenses should be reported on the balance sheet and income statement for 2011. (Assume there has been no impairment of goodwill.)

E8-19
LO6
Starbucks Corporation

Recording Leasehold Improvements and Related Amortization

Starbucks Corporation is the leading roaster and retailer of specialty coffee, with nearly 17,000 company-operated and licensed stores worldwide. Assume that Starbucks planned to open a new store on Commonwealth Avenue near Boston University and obtained a 10-year lease starting January 1, 2012. The company had to renovate the facility by installing an elevator costing $375,000. Amounts spent to enhance leased property are capitalized as intangible assets called Leasehold Improvements. The elevator will be amortized over the useful life of the lease.

Required:

1. Give the journal entry to record the installation of the new elevator.
2. Give any adjusting entries required at the end of the annual accounting period on December 31, 2012, related to the new elevator. Show computations.

E8-20
LO1, 2, 3, 4, 5, 6, 7

Finding Financial Information as a Potential Investor

You are considering investing the cash gifts you received for graduation in various stocks. You have received several annual reports of major companies.

Required:

For each of the following, indicate where you would locate the information in an annual report. (**Hint:** The information may be in more than one location.)

1. Depreciation expense.
2. The detail on major classifications of long-lived assets.
3. Prior year's accumulated depreciation.
4. The accounting method(s) used for financial reporting purposes.
5. Net amount of property, plant, and equipment.
6. Whether the company has had any capital expenditures for the year.
7. Policies on amortizing intangibles.
8. Any significant gains or losses on disposals of fixed assets.
9. The amount of assets written off as impaired during the year.

E8-21
LO3

(Supplement) Recording a Change in Estimate

Refer to E8-5.

Required:

Give the adjusting entry that should be made by Nasoff Company at the end of 2011 for depreciation of the manufacturing equipment, assuming no change in the original estimated life or residual value. Show computations.

(Supplement) Recording and Explaining Depreciation, Extraordinary Repairs, and Changes in Estimated Useful Life and Residual Value (Straight-Line Depreciation)

E8-22
LO2, 3

At the end of the annual accounting period, December 31, 2012, O'Connor Company's records reflected the following for Machine A:

Cost when acquired	$30,000
Accumulated depreciation	10,200

During January 2013, the machine was renovated at a cost of $15,500. As a result, the estimated life increased from five years to eight years, and the residual value increased from $4,500 to $6,500. The company uses straight-line depreciation.

Required:

1. Give the journal entry to record the renovation.
2. How old was the machine at the end of 2012?
3. Give the adjusting entry at the end of 2013 to record straight-line depreciation for the year.
4. Explain the rationale for your entries in requirements 1 and 3.

(Supplement) Computing the Effect of a Change in Useful Life and Residual Value on Financial Statements and Cash Flows (Straight-Line Depreciation)

E8-23
LO3, 7

Burbank Company owns the building occupied by its administrative office. The office building was reflected in the accounts at the end of last year as follows:

Cost when acquired	$330,000
Accumulated depreciation (based on straight-line depreciation, an estimated life of 50 years, and a $30,000 residual value)	78,000

During January of this year, on the basis of a careful study, management decided that the total estimated useful life should be changed to 30 years (instead of 50) and the residual value reduced to $22,500 (from $30,000). The depreciation method will not change.

Required:

1. Compute the annual depreciation expense prior to the change in estimates.
2. Compute the annual depreciation expense after the change in estimates.
3. What will be the net effect of changing estimates on the balance sheet, net income, and cash flows for the year?

To practice with more exercises, go to the text website at **www.mhhe.com/libby7e**.

connect ACCOUNTING

PROBLEMS

Explaining the Nature of a Long-Lived Asset and Determining and Recording the Financial Statement Effects of Its Purchase (AP8-1)

P8-1
LO1, 2

On January 2, 2012, Cruz Company bought a machine for use in operations. The machine has an estimated useful life of eight years and an estimated residual value of $2,600. The company provided the following expenditures:

a. Invoice price of the machine, $85,000.
b. Freight paid by the vendor per sales agreement, $1,000.
c. Installation costs, $2,400 paid in cash.
d. Payment was made as follows:

On January 2:

- The installation costs were paid in cash.
- Cruz Company common stock, par $1; 2,000 shares (market value, $3.50 per share).
- Note payable, $45,000; 11.5 percent due April 16, 2012 (principal plus interest).
- Balance of invoice price to be paid in cash. The invoice allows for a 3 percent discount for cash paid by January 12.

On January 15:

- Cruz Company paid the balance due.

Required:

1. What are the classifications of long-lived assets? Explain their differences.
2. Record the purchase on January 2 and the subsequent payment on January 15. Show computations.
3. Indicate the accounts, amounts, and effects (+ for increase and − for decrease) of the purchase and subsequent cash payment on the accounting equation. Use the following structure:

Date	Assets	=	Liabilities	+	Stockholders' Equity

4. Explain the basis you used for any questionable items.

P8-2
LO2, 3
FedEx

Analyzing the Effects of Repairs, an Addition, and Depreciation (AP8-2)

A recent annual report for FedEx included the following note:

> **Property and Equipment**
> Expenditures for major additions, improvements, flight equipment modifications, and certain equipment overhaul costs are capitalized when such costs are determined to extend the useful life of the asset or are part of the cost of acquiring the asset. Maintenance and repairs are charged to expense as incurred. . .

Assume that FedEx made extensive repairs on an existing building and added a new wing. The building is a garage and repair facility for delivery trucks that serve the Denver area. The existing building originally cost $820,000, and by the end of 2010 (10 years), it was half depreciated on the basis of a 20-year estimated useful life and no residual value. Assume straight-line depreciation was used. During 2011, the following expenditures related to the building were made:

a. Ordinary repairs and maintenance expenditures for the year, $7,000 cash.
b. Extensive and major repairs to the roof of the building, $122,000 cash. These repairs were completed on December 31, 2011.
c. The new wing was completed on December 31, 2011, at a cash cost of $230,000.

Required:

1. Applying the policies of FedEx, complete the following, indicating the effects for the preceding expenditures. If there is no effect on an account, write NE on the line.

	Building	Accumulated Depreciation	Depreciation Expense	Repairs Expense	Cash
Balance January 1, 2011	$820,000	$410,000			
Depreciation for 2011		_____	_____		_____
Balance prior to expenditures	820,000	_____	_____		
Expenditure (*a*)	_____	_____	_____	_____	_____
Expenditure (*b*)	_____	_____	_____	_____	_____
Expenditure (*c*)	_____	_____	_____	_____	_____
Balance December 31, 2011	_____	_____	_____	_____	

2. What was the book value of the building on December 31, 2011?
3. Explain the effect of depreciation on cash flows.

P8-3
LO2, 3
excel
www.mhhe.com/libby7e

Computing the Acquisition Cost and Recording Depreciation under Three Alternative Methods (AP8-3)

At the beginning of the year, Plummer's Sports Center bought three used fitness machines from Advantage, Inc. The machines immediately were overhauled, installed, and started operating. The machines were different; therefore, each had to be recorded separately in the accounts.

	Machine A	Machine B	Machine C
Amount paid for asset	$11,000	$30,000	$8,000
Installation costs	500	1,000	500
Renovation costs prior to use	2,500	1,000	1,500

By the end of the first year, each machine had been operating 4,800 hours.

Required:

1. Compute the cost of each machine.
2. Give the entry to record depreciation expense at the end of year 1, assuming the following:

	ESTIMATES		
Machine	Life	Residual Value	Depreciation Method
A	5 years	$1,000	Straight-line
B	60,000 hours	2,000	Units-of-production
C	4 years	1,500	Double-declining-balance

Inferring Depreciation Amounts and Determining the Effects of a Depreciation Error on Key Ratios (AP8-4)

P8-4
LO1, 3
Best Buy

eXcel
www.mhhe.com/libby7e

Best Buy Co., Inc., headquartered in Richfield, Minnesota, is one of the leading consumer electronics retailers, operating more than 1,000 stores in the United States, Europe, Canada, China, and Mexico. The following was reported in a recent annual report:

CONSOLIDATED BALANCE SHEETS

($ in millions)	February 28, 2009	March 1, 2008
ASSETS		
Property and Equipment		
Land and buildings	$ 755	$ 732
Leasehold improvements	2,013	1,752
Fixtures and equipment	4,060	3,057
Property under capital lease	112	67
	6,940	5,608
Less accumulated depreciation	2,766	2,302
Net property and equipment	4,174	3,306

Required:

1. Assuming that Best Buy did not sell any property, plant, and equipment in the current year, what was the amount of depreciation expense recorded during the current year?
2. Assume that Best Buy failed to record depreciation during the current year. Indicate the effect of the error (i.e., overstated or understated) on the following ratios:
   a. Earnings per share.
   b. Fixed asset turnover.
   c. Current ratio.
   d. Return on assets.

P8-5 LO1, 3 Evaluating the Effect of Alternative Depreciation Methods on Key Ratios from an Analyst's Perspective

excel
www.mhhe.com/libby7e

You are a financial analyst for Ford Motor Company and have been asked to determine the impact of alternative depreciation methods. For your analysis, you have been asked to compare methods based on a machine that cost $106,000. The estimated useful life is 13 years, and the estimated residual value is $2,000. The machine has an estimated useful life in productive output of 200,000 units. Actual output was 20,000 in year 1 and 16,000 in year 2. (Round results to the nearest dollar.)

Required:

1. For years 1 and 2 only, prepare separate depreciation schedules assuming:
   a. Straight-line method.
   b. Units-of-production method.
   c. Double-declining-balance method.

Method: ____________________

Year	Computation	Depreciation Expense	Accumulated Depreciation	Net Book Value
At acquisition				
1				
2				

2. Evaluate each method in terms of its effect on cash flow, fixed asset turnover, and EPS. Assuming that Ford Motor Company is most interested in reducing taxes and maintaining a high EPS for year 1, what would you recommend to management? Would your recommendation change for year 2? Why or why not?

P8-6 LO3, 5 Recording and Interpreting the Disposal of Three Long-Lived Assets (AP8-5)

excel
www.mhhe.com/libby7e

During 2012, Jensen Company disposed of three different assets. On January 1, 2012, prior to their disposal, the accounts reflected the following:

Asset	Original Cost	Residual Value	Estimated Life	Accumulated Depreciation (straight line)
Machine A	$21,000	$3,000	8 years	$13,500 (6 years)
Machine B	41,000	4,000	10 years	29,600 (8 years)
Machine C	75,000	5,000	15 years	56,000 (12 years)

The machines were disposed of in the following ways:

a. Machine A: Sold on January 1, 2012, for $7,200 cash.
b. Machine B: Sold on December 31, 2012, for $8,500; received cash, $2,500, and a $6,000 interest-bearing (12 percent) note receivable due at the end of 12 months.
c. Machine C: On January 1, 2012, this machine suffered irreparable damage from an accident. On January 10, 2012, a salvage company removed the machine at no cost.

Required:

1. Give all journal entries related to the disposal of each machine in 2012.
2. Explain the accounting rationale for the way that you recorded each disposal.

Inferring Activities Affecting Fixed Assets from Notes to the Financial Statements and Analyzing the Impact of Depreciation on Cash Flows

P8-7
LO5, 7

SINGAPORE AIRLINES
A great way to fly

Singapore Airlines reported the following information in the notes to a recent annual report (in Singapore dollars):

SINGAPORE AIRLINES

Notes to the Accounts

19. Property, Plant and Equipment (in $ millions)
The Company

	Beginning of Year	Additions	Disposals/ Transfers	End of Year
Cost				
Aircraft	18,180.1	2,257.2	1,730.3	18,707.0
Other fixed assets (summarized)	6,659.1	2,160.8	2,399.0	6,420.9
	24,839.2	4,418.0	4,129.3	25,127.9

	Beginning of Year	Depreciation	Impairment Loss	Disposals/ Transfers	End of Year
Accumulated depreciation					
Aircraft	5,634.2	1,427.1	41.4	843.9	6,258.8
Other fixed assets (summarized)	2,730.9	385.2	—	239.4	2,876.7
	8,365.1	1,812.3	41.4	1,083.3	9,135.5

Singapore Airlines also reported the following cash flow details:

Cash Flow from Operating Activities (in $ millions)

	Current Year	Prior Year
Profit before taxation	1,198.6	2,547.2
Adjustments for		
Depreciation	1,812.3	1,488.8
Impairment loss	41.4	
Surplus (gain) on disposal of fixed assets	(62.7)	(49.1)
Other adjustments (summarized)	(1,544.2)	414.9
Cash generated from operations	1,445.4	4,401.8

Required:

1. Reconstruct the information in Note 19 using T-accounts for Fixed Assets and Accumulated Depreciation:

Fixed Assets	
Beg. balance Acquisitions	Disposals/transfers
End. balance	

Accumulated Depreciation	
Disposals/transfers	Beg. balance Depreciation expense Impairment loss
	End. balance

2. Compute the amount of cash the company received for disposals and transfers for the current year. Show computations.
3. Compute the percentage of depreciation expense to cash flows from operations for the current year. What do you interpret from the result?

P8-8
LO2, 3, 6

Determining Financial Statement Effects of Activities Related to Various Long-Lived Assets (AP8-6)

During the 2011 annual accounting period, BSP Company completed the following transactions:

a. On January 1, 2011, purchased a patent for $28,000 cash (estimated useful life, seven years).
b. On January 1, 2011, purchased the assets (not detailed) of another business for $164,000 cash, including $10,000 for goodwill. The company assumed no liabilities. Goodwill has an indefinite life.
c. On December 31, 2011, constructed a storage shed on land leased from D. Heald. The cost was $15,600. The company uses straight-line depreciation. The lease will expire in three years. (Amounts spent to enhance leased property are capitalized as intangible assets called Leasehold Improvements.)
d. Total expenditures during 2011 for ordinary repairs and maintenance were $5,500.
e. On December 31, 2011, sold Machine A for $6,000 cash. Original cost on January 1, 2010, was $25,000; accumulated depreciation (straight line) to December 31, 2010, was $16,000 ($5,000 residual value and five-year useful life).
f. On December 31, 2011, paid $5,000 for a complete reconditioning of Machine B acquired on January 1, 2010. Original cost, $31,000; accumulated depreciation (straight line) to December 31, 2010, $1,600 ($7,000 residual value and 15-year useful life).

Required:

1. For each of these transactions, indicate the accounts, amounts, and effects (+ for increase and − for decrease) on the accounting equation. Use the following structure:

Date	Assets	=	Liabilities	+	Stockholders' Equity

2. For each of these assets, except the assets not detailed in (*b*), compute depreciation and amortization to be recorded at the end of the year on December 31, 2011.

P8-9
LO3, 6

Computing Goodwill from the Purchase of a Business and Related Depreciation and Amortization

The notes to a recent annual report from Weebok Corporation included the following:

> **Business Acquisitions**
> During the current year, the Company acquired the assets of Sport Shoes, Inc. . . .

Assume that Weebok acquired Sport Shoes on January 5, 2010. Weebok acquired the name of the company and all of its assets for $500,000 cash. Weebok did not assume the liabilities. The transaction was closed on January 5, 2010, at which time the balance sheet of Sport Shoes reflected the following book values and an independent appraiser estimated the following market values for the assets:

Sport Shoes, Inc.

January 5, 2010	Book Value	Market Value*
Accounts receivable (net)	$ 41,000	$ 41,000
Inventory	215,000	200,000
Fixed assets (net)	33,000	50,000
Other assets	4,000	10,000
Total assets	$293,000	
Liabilities	$ 55,000	
Stockholders' equity	238,000	
Total liabilities and stockholders' equity	$293,000	

**These values for the purchased assets were provided to Weebok by an independent appraiser.*

Required:

1. Compute the amount of goodwill resulting from the purchase. (**Hint:** Assets are purchased at market value in conformity with the cost principle.)
2. Compute the adjustments that Weebok would make at the end of the annual accounting period, December 31, 2010, for the following:
   a. Depreciation of the fixed assets (straight line), assuming an estimated remaining useful life of 10 years and no residual value.
   b. Goodwill (an intangible asset with an indefinite life).

Computing Amortization, Book Value, and Asset Impairment Related to Different Intangible Assets (AP8-7)

P8-10
LO3, 4, 6

Starn Tool Company has five different intangible assets to be accounted for and reported on the financial statements. The management is concerned about the amortization of the cost of each of these intangibles. Facts about each intangible follow:

a. **Patent.** The company purchased a patent at a cash cost of $55,900 on January 1, 2011. The patent has an estimated useful life of 13 years.
b. **Copyright.** On January 1, 2011, the company purchased a copyright for $22,500 cash. It is estimated that the copyrighted item will have no value by the end of 10 years.
c. **Franchise.** The company obtained a franchise from McKenna Company to make and distribute a special item. It obtained the franchise on January 1, 2011, at a cash cost of $14,400 for a 10-year period.
d. **License.** On January 1, 2010, the company secured a license from the city to operate a special service for a period of five years. Total cash expended to obtain the license was $14,000.
e. **Goodwill.** The company started business in January 2008 by purchasing another business for a cash lump sum of $400,000. Included in the purchase price was "Goodwill, $40,000." Company executives stated that "the goodwill is an important long-lived asset to us." It has an indefinite life.

Required:

1. Compute the amount of amortization that should be recorded for each intangible asset at the end of the annual accounting period, December 31, 2011.
2. Give the book value of each intangible asset on December 31, 2012.
3. Assume that on January 2, 2013, the copyrighted item was impaired in its ability to continue to produce strong revenues. The other intangible assets were not affected. Starn estimated that the copyright would be able to produce future cash flows of $17,000. The fair value of the copyright was determined to be $16,000. Compute the amount, if any, of the impairment loss to be recorded.

(Supplement) Analyzing and Recording Entries Related to a Change in Estimated Life and Residual Value

P8-11
LO3

Rungano Corporation is a global publisher of magazines, books, and music and video collections and is a leading direct mail marketer. Many direct mail marketers use high-speed Didde press equipment to print their advertisements. These presses can cost more than $1 million. Assume that Rungano owns a Didde press acquired at an original cost of $400,000. It is being depreciated on a straight-line basis over a 20-year estimated useful life and has a $50,000 estimated residual value. At the end of 2010, the press had been depreciated for a full six years. In January 2011, a decision was made, on the basis of improved maintenance procedures, that a total estimated useful life of 25 years and a residual value of $73,000 would be more realistic. The accounting period ends December 31.

Required:

1. Compute (*a*) the amount of depreciation expense recorded in 2010 and (*b*) the book value of the printing press at the end of 2010.
2. Compute the amount of depreciation that should be recorded in 2011. Show computations (round amount to the nearest dollar).
3. Give the adjusting entry for depreciation at December 31, 2011.

ALTERNATE PROBLEMS

AP8-1
LO1, 2

Explaining the Nature of a Long-Lived Asset and Determining and Recording the Financial Statement Effects of Its Purchase (P8-1)

On June 1, 2012, the Wallace Corp. bought a machine for use in operations. The machine has an estimated useful life of six years and an estimated residual value of $2,000. The company provided the following expenditures:

a. Invoice price of the machine, $60,000.
b. Freight paid by the vendor per sales agreement, $650.
c. Installation costs, $1,500.
d. Payment was made as follows:

On June 1:

- The installation costs were paid in cash.
- Wallace Corp. common stock, par $2; 2,000 shares (market value, $6 per share).
- Balance of the invoice price on a note payable, 12 percent due September 2, 2012 (principal plus interest).

On September 2:

- Wallace Corp. paid the balance and interest due on the note payable.

Required:

1. What are the classifications of long-lived assets? Explain their differences.
2. Record the purchase on June 1 and the subsequent payment on September 2. Show computations.
3. Indicate the accounts, amounts, and effects (+ for increase and − for decrease) of the purchase and subsequent cash payment on the accounting equation. Use the following structure:

Date	Assets	=	Liabilities	+	Stockholders' Equity

4. Explain the basis you used for any questionable items.

AP8-2
LO2, 3
AMERCO

Analyzing the Effects of Repairs, an Addition, and Depreciation (P8-2)

A recent annual report for AMERCO, the holding company for U-Haul International, Inc., included the following note:

> **Note 3: Accounting Policies**
>
> ***Property, Plant, and Equipment***
>
> Property, plant, and equipment are stated at cost. Interest expense incurred during the initial construction of buildings and rental equipment is considered part of cost. Depreciation is computed for financial reporting purposes using the straight-line or an accelerated method based on a declining balances formula over the following estimated useful lives: rental equipment 2–20 years and buildings and nonrental equipment 3–55 years. The Company follows the deferral method of accounting based in the AICPA's Airline Audit Guide for major overhauls in which engine overhauls are capitalized and amortized over five years and transmission overhauls are capitalized and amortized over three years. Routine maintenance costs are charged to operating expense as they are incurred.

AMERCO subsidiaries own property, plant, and equipment that are utilized in the manufacture, repair, and rental of U-Haul equipment and that provide offices for U-Haul. Assume that AMERCO made extensive repairs on an existing building and added a new wing. The building is a garage and repair facility for rental trucks that serve the Seattle area. The existing building originally cost $330,000, and by the end of 2012 (its fifth year), the building was one-quarter depreciated on the basis of a 20-year estimated useful life and no residual value. Assume straight-line depreciation. During 2013, the following expenditures related to the building were made:

a. Ordinary repairs and maintenance expenditures for the year, $5,000 cash.
b. Extensive and major repairs to the roof of the building, $17,000 cash. These repairs were completed on December 31, 2013.
c. The new wing was completed on December 31, 2013, at a cash cost of $70,000.

Required:

1. Applying the policies of AMERCO, complete the following, indicating the effects for the preceding expenditures. If there is no effect on an account, write NE on the line.

	Building	Accumulated Depreciation	Depreciation Expense	Repairs Expense	Cash
Balance January 1, 2013	$330,000	$82,500			
Depreciation for 2013		______	______		______
Balance prior to expenditures	330,000	______	______		
Expenditure (*a*)	______	______	______	______	______
Expenditure (*b*)	______	______	______	______	______
Expenditure (*c*)	______	______	______	______	______
Balance December 31, 2013	______	______	______	______	

2. What was the book value of the building on December 31, 2013?
3. Explain the effect of depreciation on cash flows.

Computing the Acquisition Cost and Recording Depreciation under Three Alternative Methods (P8-3)

AP8-3
LO2, 3

At the beginning of the year, Ramos Inc. bought three used machines from Santaro Corporation. The machines immediately were overhauled, installed, and started operating. The machines were different; therefore, each had to be recorded separately in the accounts.

	Machine A	Machine B	Machine C
Cost of the asset	$12,200	$32,500	$21,700
Installation costs	800	1,100	1,100
Renovation costs prior to use	600	1,400	1,600

By the end of the first year, each machine had been operating 7,000 hours.

Required:

1. Compute the cost of each machine.
2. Give the entry to record depreciation expense at the end of year 1, assuming the following:

	ESTIMATES		
Machine	Life	Residual Value	Depreciation Method
A	8 years	$1,000	Straight-line
B	33,000 hours	2,000	Units-of-production
C	5 years	1,400	Double-declining-balance

Inferring Depreciation Amounts and Determining the Effects of a Depreciation Error on Key Ratios (P8-4)

AP8-4
LO1, 3
The Gap, Inc.

The Gap, Inc., is a global specialty retailer of casual wear and personal products for women, men, children, and babies under the Gap, Banana Republic, Old Navy, Athleta, and Piperlime brands. As of

January 31, 2009, the Company operated 3,149 stores across the globe, as well as online. The following is a note from a recent annual report:

Note 1. Summary of Significant Accounting Policies:

Property and Equipment

Depreciation is computed using the straight-line method over the estimated useful lives of the related assets . . .

The cost of assets sold or retired and the related accumulated depreciation are removed from the accounts with any resulting gain or loss included in operating expenses in the Consolidated Statements of Earnings. Maintenance and repairs are expensed as incurred.

Interest related to assets under construction is capitalized during the construction period up to the amount of interest expense actually incurred.

Note 2. Additional Financial Statement Information

Property and Equipment

Property and equipment are stated at cost less accumulated depreciation and consist of the following:

($ in millions)	January 31, 2009	February 2, 2008
Leasehold improvements	$3,026	$3,077
Furniture and equipment	2,377	2,401
Land and buildings	988	1,022
Software	774	655
Construction-in-progress	80	165
Property and equipment, at cost	7,245	7,320
Less: Accumulated depreciation	(4,312)	(4,053)
Property and equipment, net of accumulated depreciation	$2,933	$3,267

Required:

1. Assuming that The Gap, Inc., did not have any asset impairment write-offs but did sell property, plant, and equipment in the most recent year with a cost of $501 million and an accumulated depreciation of $384 million, what was the amount of depreciation expense recorded in the current year?
2. Assume that The Gap, Inc., failed to record depreciation in the current year. Indicate the effect of the error (i.e., overstated or understated) on the following ratios:
   a. Earnings per share
   b. Fixed asset turnover
   c. Current ratio
   d. Return on assets

AP8-5 **Recording and Interpreting the Disposal of Three Long-Lived Assets** (P8-6)
LO3, 5

During 2011, Rank Company disposed of three different assets. On January 1, 2011, prior to their disposal, the accounts reflected the following:

Asset	Original Cost	Residual Value	Estimated Life	Accumulated Depreciation (straight line)
Machine A	$24,000	$2,000	5 years	$17,600 (4 years)
Machine B	16,500	5,000	10 years	8,050 (7 years)
Machine C	59,200	3,200	14 years	48,000 (12 years)

The machines were disposed of in the following ways:

a. Machine A: Sold on January 1, 2011, for $6,750 cash.
b. Machine B: Sold on December 31, 2011, for $7,000; received cash, $2,000, and a $5,000 interest-bearing (10 percent) note receivable due at the end of 12 months.
c. Machine C: On January 1, 2011, this machine suffered irreparable damage from an accident and was scrapped.

Required:

1. Give all journal entries related to the disposal of each machine.
2. Explain the accounting rationale for the way in which you recorded each disposal.

Determining Financial Statement Effects of Activities Related to Various Long-Lived Assets (P8-8)

AP8-6
LO2, 3, 6

During the 2012 annual accounting period, Nguyen Corporation completed the following transactions:

a. On January 1, 2012, purchased a license for $7,200 cash (estimated useful life, four years).
b. On January 1, 2012, repaved the parking lot of the building leased from H. Lane. The cost was $17,800; the estimated useful life was five years with no residual value. The lease will expire in 10 years. (Amounts spent to enhance leased property are capitalized as intangible assets called Leasehold Improvements.)
c. On July 1, 2012, purchased another business for $120,000 cash. The transaction included $115,000 for the assets and $24,000 for the liabilities assumed by Nguyen. The remainder was goodwill with an indefinite life.
d. On December 31, 2012, sold Machine A for $6,000 cash. Original cost, $21,500; accumulated depreciation (straight line) to December 31, 2011, $13,500 ($3,500 residual value and four-year life).
e. Total expenditures during 2012 for ordinary repairs and maintenance were $6,700.
f. On December 31, 2012, paid $8,000 for a complete reconditioning of Machine B acquired on January 1, 2009. Original cost, $18,000; accumulated depreciation (straight line) to December 31, 2011, $12,000 ($2,000 residual value and four-year life).

Required:

1. For each of these transactions, indicate the accounts, amounts, and effects (+ for increase and − for decrease) on the accounting equation. Use the following structure:

Date	Assets	=	Liabilities	+	Stockholders' Equity

2. For each of these assets, except the assets not detailed in (*c*), compute depreciation and amortization to be recorded at the end of the year on December 31, 2012.

Computing Amortization, Book Value, and Asset Impairment Related to Different Intangible Assets (P8-10)

AP8-7
LO3, 4, 6

Carey Corporation has five different intangible assets to be accounted for and reported on the financial statements. The management is concerned about the amortization of the cost of each of these intangibles. Facts about each intangible follow:

a. **Patent.** The company purchased a patent at a cash cost of $18,600 on January 1, 2012. It is amortized over its expected useful life of 10 years.
b. **Copyright.** On January 1, 2012, the company purchased a copyright for $24,750 cash. It is estimated that the copyrighted item will have no value by the end of 30 years.
c. **Franchise.** The company obtained a franchise from Cirba Company to make and distribute a special item. It obtained the franchise on January 1, 2012, at a cash cost of $19,200 for a 12-year period.
d. **License.** On January 1, 2011, the company secured a license from the city to operate a special service for a period of seven years. Total cash expended to obtain the license was $21,700.
e. **Goodwill.** The company started business in January 2013 by purchasing another business for a cash lump sum of $650,000. Included in the purchase price was "Goodwill, $75,000." Company executives stated that "the goodwill is an important long-lived asset to us." It has an indefinite life.

Required:

1. Compute the amount of amortization that should be recorded for each intangible asset at the end of the annual accounting period, December 31, 2012.
2. Give the book value of each intangible asset on January 1, 2015.

3. Assume that on January 2, 2015, the franchise was impaired in its ability to continue to produce strong revenues. The other intangible assets were not affected. Carey estimated that the franchise would be able to produce future cash flows of $13,500. The fair value of the franchise was determined to be $12,000. Compute the amount, if any, of the impairment loss to be recorded.

COMPREHENSIVE PROBLEM (CHAPTERS 6–8)

COMP8-1

DR PEPPER SNAPPLE GROUP

Complete the requirements for each of the following independent cases:

Case A. Dr Pepper Snapple Group, Inc., is a leading integrated brand owner, bottler, and distributor of nonalcoholic beverages in the United States, Canada, and Mexico. Key brands include Dr. Pepper, Snapple, 7-UP, Mott's juices, A&W root beer, Canada Dry ginger ale, Schweppes ginger ale, and Hawaiian Punch, among others.

The following represents selected data from recent financial statements of Dr Pepper Snapple Group (dollars in millions):

DR PEPPER SNAPPLE GROUP, INC.
Consolidated Balance Sheets (partial)

(in millions)	December 31, 2008	December 31, 2007
Assets		
Current assets:		
Cash and cash equivalents	$214	$ 67
Accounts receivable (net of allowances of $13 and $20, respectively)	532	538

Consolidated Statements of Operations (partial)

	For the Year Ended December 31		
(in millions)	2008	2007	2006
Net sales	$ 5,710	$ 5,695	$4,700
...			
Net (loss) income	$ (312)	$ 497	$ 510

The company also reported bad debt expense of $5 million in 2008, $11 million in 2007, and $7 million in 2006.

1. Record the company's write-offs of uncollectible accounts for 2008.
2. Assuming all sales were on credit, what amount of cash did Dr Pepper Snapple Group collect from customers in 2008?
3. Compute the company's net profit margin for the three years presented. What does the trend suggest to you about Dr Pepper Snapple Group?

Case B. Samuda Enterprises uses the aging approach to estimate bad debt expense. At the end of 2011, Samuda reported a balance in accounts receivable of $620,000 and estimated that $12,400 of its accounts receivable would likely be uncollectible. The allowance for doubtful accounts has a $1,500 debit balance at year-end (that is, more was written off during the year than the balance in the account).

1. What amount of bad debt expense should be recorded for 2011?
2. What amount will be reported on the 2011 balance sheet for accounts receivable?

Case C. At the end of 2012, the unadjusted trial balance of Territo, Inc., indicated $5,840,000 in Accounts Receivable, a credit balance of $9,200 in Allowance for Doubtful Accounts, and Sales Revenue (all on credit) of $160,450,000. Based on knowledge that the current economy is in distress, Territo increased its bad debt rate estimate to 0.3 percent on credit sales.

1. What amount of bad debt expense should be recorded for 2012?
2. What amount will be reported on the 2012 balance sheet for accounts receivable?

Case D. Stewart Company reports the following inventory records for November 2010:

INVENTORY			
Date	Activity	# of Units	Cost/Unit
November 1	Beginning balance	100	$18
November 4	Purchase	300	19
November 7	Sale (@ $50 per unit)	200	
November 13	Purchase	500	21
November 22	Sale (@ $50 per unit)	500	

Selling, administrative, and depreciation expenses for the month were $16,000. Stewart's tax rate is 30 percent.

1. Calculate the cost of ending inventory and the cost of goods sold under each of the following methods:
   a. First-in, first-out.
   b. Last-in, first out.
   c. Weighted average.
2. Based on your answers in requirement (1)
   a. What is the gross profit percentage under the FIFO method?
   b. What is net income under the LIFO method?
   c. Which method would you recommend to Stewart for tax and financial reporting purposes? Explain your recommendation.
3. Stewart applied the lower of cost or market method to value its inventory for reporting purposes at the end of the month. Assuming Stewart used the FIFO method and that inventory had a market replacement value of $19.50 per unit, what would Stewart report on the balance sheet for inventory? Why?

Case E. Matson Company purchased the following on January 1, 2011:

- Office equipment at a cost of $50,000 with an estimated useful life to the company of three years and a residual value of $15,000. The company uses the double-declining-balance method of depreciation for the equipment.
- Factory equipment at an invoice price of $820,000 plus shipping costs of $20,000. The equipment has an estimated useful life of 100,000 hours and no residual value. The company uses the units-of-production method of depreciation for the equipment.
- A patent at a cost of $300,000 with an estimated useful life of 15 years. The company uses the straight-line method of amortization for intangible assets with no residual value.

1. Prepare a partial depreciation schedule for 2011, 2012, and 2013 for the following assets (round your answers to the nearest dollar):
   a. Office equipment.
   b. Factory equipment. The company used the equipment for 8,000 hours in 2011, 9,200 hours in 2012, and 8,900 hours in 2013.
2. On January 1, 2014, Matson altered its corporate strategy dramatically. The company sold the factory equipment for $700,000 in cash. Record the entry related to the sale of the factory equipment.
3. On January 1, 2014, when the company changed its corporate strategy, its patent had estimated future cash flows of $210,000 and a fair value of $190,000. What would the company report on the income statement (account and amount) regarding the patent on January 2, 2014? Explain your answer.

CASES AND PROJECTS

Annual Report Cases

CP8-1
LO1, 2, 4, 6

AMERICAN EAGLE OUTFITTERS, INC.

Finding Financial Information

Refer to the financial statements of American Eagle Outfitters in Appendix B at the end of this book.

Required:

For each question, answer it and indicate where you located the information to answer the question. (**Hint:** Use the notes to the financial statements for some of these questions.)

1. How much did the company spend on property and equipment (capital expenditures) in fiscal 2008 (the year ended January 31, 2009)?
2. What is the typical estimated useful life of leasehold improvements for amortization purposes?
3. What was the original cost of fixtures and equipment held by the company at the end of the most recent reporting year?
4. What was the amount of depreciation and amortization reported as an expense for the current year? Compare this amount to the change in accumulated amortization and depreciation from fiscal 2007 to fiscal 2008. Why would these numbers be different?
5. What is the company's fixed asset turnover ratio for fiscal 2008?

CP8-2
LO1, 2, 6

URBAN OUTFITTERS INC.

Finding Financial Information

Refer to the financial statements of Urban Outfitters given in Appendix C at the end of this book.

Required:

For each question, answer it and indicate where you located the information to answer the question. (**Hint:** Use the notes to the financial statements for many of these questions.)

1. What method of depreciation does the company use?
2. What is the amount of accumulated depreciation and amortization at the end of the most recent reporting year?
3. For depreciation purposes, what is the estimated useful life of furniture and fixtures?
4. What was the original cost of leasehold improvements owned by the company at the end of the most recent reporting year?
5. What amount of depreciation and amortization was reported as expense for the most recent reporting year?
6. What is the company's fixed asset turnover ratio for the most recent year? What does it suggest?

CP8-3
LO1, 3

AMERICAN EAGLE OUTFITTERS, INC.

URBAN OUTFITTERS INC.

excel

www.mhhe.com/libby7e

Comparing Companies within an Industry

Refer to the financial statements of American Eagle Outfitters (Appendix B) and Urban Outfitters (Appendix C) and the Industry Ratio Report (Appendix D) at the end of this book.

Required:

1. Compute the percentage of net fixed assets to total assets for both companies for the most recent year. Why do the companies differ?
2. Compute the percentage of gross fixed assets that has been depreciated for both companies for the most recent year. Why do you think the percentages differ?
3. Compute the fixed asset turnover ratio for the most recent year presented for both companies. Which company has higher asset efficiency? Why?

4. Compare the fixed asset turnover ratio for both companies to the industry average. Are these companies doing better or worse than the industry average in asset efficiency?

Financial Reporting and Analysis Cases

Broadening Financial Research Skills: Identifying Competitors in an Industry

CP8-4

Reuters provides lists of industries and the competitors in each at www.reuters.com. Click on "Sectors and Industries," then "All Industries," then one of the industries listed, then "Company Ranks." When you skim down the page, you will find an alphabetical listing of companies in the industry.

Required:
Using your Web browser, go to the *Reuters* website and identify three competitors for the following industries:

1. Airline.
2. Hotels, motels, and cruise lines.
3. Footwear.
4. Computer hardware.

Using Financial Reports: Analyzing the Age of Assets

CP8-5
LO3
Sysco Corporation

In its recent annual report, Sysco Corporation noted it "is the largest North American distributor of food and related products primarily to the foodservice 'food-away-from-home' industry. We provide products and related services to approximately 400,000 customers, including restaurants, healthcare, and educational facilities, lodging establishments, and other foodservice customers." A note to a recent annual report for Sysco contained the following information:

(in thousands)	Current Year
Land	$ 307,328
Buildings and improvements	2,818,300
Fleet and equipment	2,072,116
Computer hardware and software	569,669
	5,767,413
Less accumulated depreciation	2,788,213
	$2,979,200

Depreciation expense (in thousands of dollars) charged to operations was $361,062 in the current year. Depreciation generally is computed using the straight-line method for financial reporting purposes.

Required:

1. What is your best estimate of the average expected life for Sysco's depreciable assets?
2. What is your best estimate of the average age of Sysco's depreciable assets?

Using Financial Reports: Analyzing Fixed Asset Turnover Ratio and Cash Flows

CP8-6
LO1, 6, 7

Cain Company operates in both the beverage and entertainment industries. In June 2006, Cain purchased Good Time, Inc., which produces and distributes motion picture, television, and home video products and recorded music; publishes books; and operates theme parks and retail stores. The purchase resulted in $2.7 billion in goodwill. Since 2006, Cain has undertaken a number of business acquisitions and divestitures (sales of businesses) as the company expands into the entertainment industry. Selected data from a recent annual report are as follows (amounts are in U.S. dollars in millions):

Property, Plant, Equipment, and Intangibles From the Consolidated Balance Sheet	Current Year	Prior Year
Film costs, net of amortization	$1,272	$ 991
Artists' contracts, advances, and other entertainment assets	761	645
Property, plant, and equipment, net	2,733	2,559
Excess of cost over fair value of assets acquired	3,076	3,355
From the Consolidated Statement of Income		
Total revenues	$9,714	$10,644
From the Consolidated Statement of Cash Flows		
Income from continuing operations	$ 880	$ 445
Adjustments:		
Depreciation	289	265
Amortization	208	190
Other adjustments (summarized)	(1,618)	(256)
Net cash provided by continuing operations	(241)	644
From the Notes to the Financial Statements		
Accumulated depreciation on property, plant, and equipment	$1,178	$ 1,023

Required:

1. Compute the cost of the property, plant, and equipment at the end of the current year. Explain your answer.
2. What was the approximate age of the property, plant, and equipment at the end of the current year?
3. Compute the fixed asset turnover ratio for the current year. Explain your results.
4. What is "excess of cost over fair value of assets acquired"?
5. On the consolidated statement of cash flows, why are the depreciation and amortization amounts added to income from continuing operations?

CP8-7
LO1, 5, 7
Eastman Kodak

Using Financial Reports: Inferring the Sale of Assets

A recent annual report for Eastman Kodak reported that the cost of property, plant, and equipment at the end of the current year was $6,805 million. At the end of the previous year, it had been $7,327 million. During the current year, the company bought $254 million worth of new equipment. The balance of accumulated depreciation at the end of the current year was $5,254 million; at the end of the previous year it was $5,516 million. Depreciation expense for the current year was $420 million. The company reported a $14 million gain on the disposition of property, plant, and equipment.

Required:

What amount of proceeds did Eastman Kodak receive when it sold property, plant, and equipment during the current year? (**Hint:** Set up T-accounts.)

Critical Thinking Cases

CP8-8
LO2
Hess Corporation

Making a Decision as a Financial Analyst: Interpreting the Impact of the Capitalization of Interest on an Accounting Ratio

Hess Corporation is a global energy company that explores, produces, refines, and markets crude oil and natural gas. The capitalization of interest associated with self-constructed assets was discussed in this chapter. A recent annual report for Hess Corporation disclosed the following information concerning capitalization of interest:

In Note 1:

> ***Capitalized Interest:*** Interest from external borrowings is capitalized on material projects using the weighted average cost of outstanding borrowings until the project is substantially complete and ready for its intended use, which for oil and gas assets is at first production from the field.

In Note 7:

> The Corporation capitalized interest of $7 million, $50 million, and $100 million in 2008, 2007, and 2006, respectively.

The company reported $267 million in Interest Expense on the 2008 income statement. A popular accounting ratio used by some analysts is the interest coverage ratio (Income ÷ Interest Expense).

Required:

1. Explain why an analyst would calculate the interest coverage ratio.
2. Did Hess include the $7 million capitalized interest in the reported interest expense of $267 million? If not, should an analyst include it when calculating the interest coverage ratio? Explain.

Evaluating an Ethical Dilemma: A Real-Life Example

CP8-9
LO1, 2

Assume you work as a staff member in a large accounting department for a multinational public company. Your job requires you to review documents relating to the company's equipment purchases. Upon verifying that purchases are properly approved, you prepare journal entries to record the equipment purchases in the accounting system. Typically, you handle equipment purchases costing $100,000 or less.

This morning, you were contacted by the executive assistant to the chief financial officer (CFO). She says that the CFO has asked to see you immediately in his office. Although your boss's boss has attended a few meetings where the CFO was present, you have never met the CFO during your three years with the company. Needless to say, you are anxious about the meeting.

Upon entering the CFO's office, you are warmly greeted with a smile and friendly handshake. The CFO compliments you on the great work that you've been doing for the company. You soon feel a little more comfortable, particularly when the CFO mentions that he has a special project for you. He states that he and the CEO have negotiated significant new arrangements with the company's equipment suppliers, which require the company to make advance payments for equipment to be purchased in the future. The CFO says that, for various reasons that he didn't want to discuss, he will be processing the payments through the operating division of the company rather than the equipment accounting group. Given that the payments will be made through the operating division, they will initially be classified as operating expenses of the company. He indicates that clearly these advance payments for property and equipment should be recorded as assets, so he will be contacting you at the end of every quarter to make an adjusting journal entry to capitalize the amounts inappropriately classified as operating expenses. He advises you that a new account, called Prepaid Equipment, has been established for this purpose. He quickly wraps up the meeting by telling you that it is important that you not talk about the special project with anyone. You assume he doesn't want others to become jealous of your new important responsibility.

A few weeks later, at the end of the first quarter, you receive a voicemail from the CFO stating, "The adjustment that we discussed is $771,000,000 for this quarter." Before deleting the message, you replay it to make sure you heard it right. Your company generates over $8 billion in revenues and incurs $6 billion in operating expenses every quarter, but you've never made a journal entry for that much money. So, just to be sure there's not a mistake, you send an e-mail to the CFO confirming the amount. He phones you back immediately to abruptly inform you, "There's no mistake. That's the number." Feeling embarrassed that you may have annoyed the CFO, you quietly make the adjusting journal entry.

For each of the remaining three quarters in that year and for the first quarter in the following year, you continue to make these end-of-quarter adjustments. The "magic number," as the CFO liked to call it, was $560,000,000 for Q2, $742,745,000 for Q3, $941,000,000 for Q4, and $818,204,000 for Q1 of the following year. During this time, you've had several meetings and lunches with the CFO where he provides you the magic number, sometimes supported with nothing more than a Post-it note with the number written on it. He frequently compliments you on your good work and promises that you'll soon be in line for a big promotion.

Despite the CFO's compliments and promises, you are growing increasingly uncomfortable with the journal entries that you've been making. Typically, whenever an ordinary equipment purchase involves an advance payment, the purchase is completed a few weeks later. At that time, the amount of the advance is removed from an Equipment Deposit account and transferred to the appropriate equipment account. This hasn't been the case with the CFO's special project. Instead, the Prepaid Equipment account has continued to grow, now standing at over $3.8 billion. There's been no discussion about how or when this balance will be reduced, and no depreciation has been recorded for it.

Just as you begin to reflect on the effect the adjustments have had on your company's fixed assets, operating expenses, and operating income, you receive a call from the vice president for internal audit. She needs to talk with you this afternoon about "a peculiar trend in the company's fixed asset turnover ratio and some suspicious journal entries that you've been making."

Required:

1. Complete the following table to determine what the company's accounting records would have looked like had you not made the journal entries as part of the CFO's special project. Comment on how the decision to capitalize amounts, which were initially recorded as operating expenses, has affected the level of income from operations in each quarter.

	Q1 Year 1 (March 31)		Q2 Year 1 (June 30)		Q3 Year 1 (September 30)		Q4 Year 1 (December 31)		Q1 Year 2 (March 31)	
(amounts in millions of U.S. dollars)	With the Entries	Without the Entries	With the Entries	Without the Entries	With the Entries	Without the Entries	With the Entries	Without the Entries	With the Entries	Without the Entries
Property and equipment, net	$38,614	$	$35,982	$	$38,151	$	$38,809	$	$39,155	$
Sales revenues	8,825	8,825	8,910	8,910	8,966	8,966	8,478	8,478	8,120	8,120
Operating expenses	7,628		8,526		7,786		7,725		7,277	
Income from operations	1,197		384		1,180		753		843	

2. Using the publicly reported numbers (which include the special journal entries that you recorded), compute the fixed asset turnover ratio (rounded to two decimal places) for the periods ended Q2–Q4 of year 1 and Q1 of year 2. What does the trend in this ratio suggest to you? Is this consistent with the changes in operating income reported by the company?
3. Before your meeting with the vice president for internal audit, you think about the above computations and the variety of peculiar circumstances surrounding the "special project" for the CFO. What in particular might have raised your suspicion about the real nature of your work?
4. Your meeting with internal audit was short and unpleasant. The vice president indicated that she had discussed her findings with the CFO before meeting with you. The CFO claimed that he too had noticed the peculiar trend in the fixed asset turnover ratio, but that he hadn't had a chance to investigate it further. He urged internal audit to get to the bottom of things, suggesting that perhaps someone might be making unapproved journal entries. Internal audit had identified you as the source of the journal entries and had been unable to find any documents that approved or substantiated the entries. She ended the meeting by advising you to find a good lawyer. Given your current circumstances, describe how you would have acted earlier had you been able to foresee where it might lead you.
5. In the real case on which this one is based, the internal auditors agonized over the question of whether they had actually uncovered a fraud or whether they were jumping to the wrong conclusion. *The Wall Street Journal* mentioned this on October 30, 2002, by stating, "it was clear . . . that their findings would be devastating for the company. They worried about whether their revelations would result in layoffs. Plus, they feared that they would somehow end up being blamed

for the mess." Beyond the personal consequences mentioned in this quote, describe other potential ways in which the findings of the internal auditors would likely be devastating for the publicly traded company and those associated with it.

WorldCom Verizon

Epilogue: This case is based on a fraud committed at WorldCom (now called Verizon). The case draws its numbers, the nature of the unsupported journal entries, and the CFO's role in carrying out the fraud from a report issued by WorldCom's bankruptcy examiner. Year 1 in this case was actually 2001 and year 2 was 2002. This case excludes other fraudulent activities that contributed to WorldCom's $11 billion fraud. The 63-year-old CEO was sentenced to 25 years in prison for planning and executing the biggest fraud in the history of American business. The CFO, who cooperated in the investigation of the CEO, was sentenced to five years in prison.

CP8-10
LO1, 2, 7
Marriott International

Evaluating the Impact of Capitalized Interest on Cash Flows and Fixed Asset Turnover from an Analyst's Perspective

You are a financial analyst charged with evaluating the asset efficiency of companies in the hotel industry. Recent financial statements for Marriott include the following note:

> **8. Property and Equipment**
>
> We record property and equipment at cost, including interest and real estate taxes incurred during development and construction. Interest capitalized as a cost of property and equipment totaled $55 million in 2008, $49 million in 2007, and $32 million in 2006. We capitalize the cost of improvements that extend the useful life of property and equipment when incurred.

Required:

1. Assume that Marriott followed this policy for a major construction project this year. How does Marriott's policy affect the following (use + for increase, − for decrease, and NE for no effect)?
   a. Cash flows.
   b. Fixed asset turnover ratio.
2. Normally, how would your answer to requirement (1*b*) affect your evaluation of Marriott's effectiveness in utilizing fixed assets?
3. If the fixed asset turnover ratio decreases due to interest capitalization, does this change indicate a real decrease in efficiency? Why or why not?

Financial Reporting and Analysis Team Project

CP8-11
LO1, 2, 3, 4, 6, 7

Team Project: Analysis of Long-Lived Assets

As a team, select an industry to analyze. *Reuters* provides lists of industries under Sectors and Industries at www.reuters.com. (Click on an industry and then select Company Rankings for a list of members of that industry.) Each team member should acquire the annual report or 10-K for one publicly traded company in the industry, with each member selecting a different company. (Library files, the SEC EDGAR service at www.sec.gov, or the company itself are good sources.)

Required:

1. List the accounts and amounts of the company's long-lived assets (land, buildings, equipment, intangible assets, natural resources, and/or other) for the last three years.
   a. What is the percentage of each to total assets?
   b. What do the results of your analysis suggest about the strategy your company has followed with respect to investing in long-lived assets?
2. What cost allocation method(s) and estimates does the company use for each type of long-lived asset?
3. What percentage of the property, plant, and equipment has been used as of the end of the most recent year? (Accumulated Depreciation ÷ Cost)

4. What does the company disclose regarding asset impairment? What was its impairment loss, if any, in the most recent year?
5. Ratio analysis:
   a. What does the fixed asset turnover ratio measure in general?
   b. Compute the ratio for the last three years.
   c. What do your results suggest about the company?
   d. If available, find the industry ratio for the most recent year, compare it to your results, and discuss why you believe your company differs or is similar to the industry ratio.
6. What was the effect of depreciation expense on cash flows from operating activities? Compute the percentage of depreciation expense to cash flows from operating activities for each of the past three years.
7. From the statement of cash flows, what were capital expenditures over the last three years? Did the company sell any long-lived assets?

LEARNING OBJECTIVES

After studying this chapter, you should be able to:

Lecture Presentation LP-9
www.mhhe.com/libby7e

1. Define, measure, and report current liabilities. p. 457
2. Use the quick ratio. p. 458
3. Analyze the accounts payable turnover ratio. p. 460
4. Report notes payable and explain the time value of money. p. 463
5. Report contingent liabilities. p. 465
6. Explain the importance of working capital and its impact on cash flows. p. 467
7. Report long-term liabilities. p. 469
8. Compute present values. p. 471
9. Apply present value concepts to liabilities. p. 475

CHAPTER NINE

REPORTING AND INTERPRETING LIABILITIES

Each week, Starbucks serves customers more than 50 million times. The company, founded in 1985, has 16,680 coffeehouses and does business in 49 international markets. The mission statement for the company is "to establish Starbucks as the premier purveyor of the finest coffees in the world." After 16 years of continuous growth, for the first time the company is experiencing slower growth, store closures, and cost reductions. Despite challenges, management remains confident that the Starbucks brand is strong and that the company can return to growth by staying true to its core values.

FOCUS COMPANY:

Starbucks

MANAGING FINANCING ACTIVITIES

www.starbucks.com

To achieve its goals, Starbucks must focus on a number of activities. The annual report identifies several of them:

- Serve the finest cup of coffee in the world.
- Grow the company one customer at a time based on exceptional customer service.
- Make someone's day with a relaxing in-store experience including music, art, and high-speed wireless Internet access.

In addition to these operating activities, management must focus on a number of critical financing activities to ensure that the company remains profitable and is able to generate sufficient resources to maintain liquidity and eventually open new coffeehouses. The financing activities for Starbucks serve two important purposes. They generate funds to (1) finance the current operating activities of the business and (2) acquire long-term assets that will permit the company to grow in the future.

UNDERSTANDING THE BUSINESS

Businesses finance the acquisition of their assets from two external sources: funds supplied by creditors (debt) and funds provided by owners (equity). The mixture of debt and equity a business uses is called its *capital structure*. In addition to selecting a capital structure, management can select from a variety of sources from which to borrow money, as illustrated by the liability section of the balance sheet from Starbucks shown in Exhibit 9.1.

EXHIBIT 9.1

Starbucks Consolidated Balance Sheets

STARBUCKS

REAL WORLD EXCERPT

Annual Report

STARBUCKS CORPORATION
Consolidated Balance Sheets
(in millions)

	Sep. 28, 2008	Sep. 30, 2007
Liabilities		
Current liabilities:		
Commercial paper and short-term borrowings	$ 713.0	$ 710.3
Accounts payable	324.9	390.8
Accrued compensation and related costs	253.6	292.4
Accrued occupancy costs	136.1	74.6
Accrued taxes	76.1	92.5
Insurance reserves	152.5	137.0
Other accrued expenses	164.4	160.3
Deferred revenue	368.4	296.9
Current portion of long-term debt	0.7	0.8
Total current liabilities	2,189.7	2,155.6
Long-term debt	549.6	550.1
Other long-term liabilities	442.4	354.1
Total liabilities	$3,181.7	$3,059.8

What factors do managers consider when they borrow money? Two key factors are risk and cost. From the firm's perspective, debt capital is more risky than equity because payments associated with debt are a company's legal obligation. If a company cannot meet a required debt payment (either principal or interest) because of a temporary cash shortage, creditors may force the company into bankruptcy and require the sale of assets to satisfy the debt. As with any business transaction, borrowers and lenders attempt to negotiate the most favorable terms possible. Managers devote considerable effort to analyzing alternative borrowing arrangements.

Companies that include debt in their capital structure must also make strategic decisions concerning the balance between short-term and long-term debt. To evaluate a company's capital structure, financial analysts calculate a number of accounting ratios. In this chapter, we will discuss both short-term and long-term debt, as well as some important accounting ratios. We will also introduce present value concepts. In the next chapter, we discuss a special category of long-term debt, bonds payable.

ORGANIZATION of the Chapter

Liabilities Defined and Classified
- Quick Ratio

Current Liabilities
- Accounts Payable
- Accounts Payable Turnover Ratio
- Accrued Liabilities
- Notes Payable
- Current Portion of Long-Term Debt
- Deferred Revenues
- Estimated Liabilities Reported on the Balance Sheet
- Estimated Liabilities Reported in the Notes
- Working Capital Management

Long-Term Liabilities
- Long-Term Notes Payable and Bonds
- Lease Liabilities

Present Value Concepts
- Present Value of a Single Amount
- Present Value of an Annuity
- Accounting Applications of Present Values

LIABILITIES DEFINED AND CLASSIFIED

LEARNING OBJECTIVE 1
Define, measure, and report current liabilities.

Most people have a reasonable understanding of the definition of the word *liability.* Accountants formally define **liabilities** as probable debts or obligations of the entity that result from past transactions, which will be paid with assets or services. As Exhibit 9.1 shows, as of September 28, 2008, Starbucks had borrowed on a long-term basis $549.6 million. The company has a current obligation to pay cash to its creditors at some time in the future based on the borrowing agreements. Because of this obligation, Starbucks must record long-term debt.

LIABILITIES are probable debts or obligations that result from past transactions, which will be paid with assets or services.

When a liability is first recorded, it is measured in terms of its current cash equivalent, which is the cash amount a creditor would accept to settle the liability immediately. Although Starbucks borrowed $549.6 million, it will repay much more than that because the company must also pay interest on the debt. Interest that will be paid in the future is not included in the reported amount of the liability because it accrues and becomes a liability with the passage of time.

Like most businesses, Starbucks has several kinds of liabilities as well as a wide range of creditors. The list of liabilities on the balance sheet differs from one company to the next because different operating activities result in different types of liabilities. The liability section of the Starbucks report begins with the caption Current Liabilities. **Current liabilities** are defined as short-term obligations that will be paid within the current operating cycle of the business or within one year of the balance sheet date, whichever is longer. Because most companies have an operating cycle that is shorter than one year, current liabilities usually can be defined simply as liabilities that are due within one year. Noncurrent liabilities include all other liabilities.

CURRENT LIABILITIES are short-term obligations that will be paid within the current operating cycle or one year, whichever is longer.

LIQUIDITY is the ability to pay current obligations.

Information about current liabilities is very important to managers and analysts because these obligations must be paid in the near future. Analysts say that a company has **liquidity** if it has the ability to meet its current obligations. A number of financial ratios are useful in evaluating liquidity, including the current ratio (discussed in Chapter 2) and the quick ratio. The quick ratio is a conservative measure of liquidity, comparing only the most liquid assets (cash, marketable securities, and receivables) to current liabilities. In contrast, the current ratio includes all current assets in the numerator of the ratio.

KEY RATIO ANALYSIS | Quick Ratio

ANALYTICAL QUESTION

Does a company currently have the resources to pay its short-term debt?

RATIO AND COMPARISONS

The quick ratio is computed as follows (quick assets are defined as including cash, marketable securities, and accounts receivable):

Quick Ratio = Quick Assets ÷ Current Liabilities

The 2008 quick ratio for Starbucks is:

$651.8 ÷ 2,189.7 = 0.30

COMPARISONS OVER TIME		
Starbucks		
2006	2007	2008
0.32	0.33	0.30

COMPARISONS WITH COMPETITORS	
Peet's Coffee	Caribou Coffee
2008	2008
1.00	0.40

INTERPRETATIONS

LEARNING OBJECTIVE 2

Use the quick ratio.

In General While a high quick ratio normally suggests good liquidity, too high a ratio suggests inefficient use of resources. Many strong companies use sophisticated management techniques to minimize funds invested in current assets and, as a result, have quick ratios that are very low.

Focus Company Analysis The quick ratio for Starbucks shows unusual stability in its level of liquidity. As the company experiences a slowdown in its business, management is probably carefully controlling the company's working capital (current assets minus current liabilities). The level of the ratio is similar to Caribou Coffee but both are much lower than Peet's Coffee. Analysts would not be concerned about the level of the Starbucks ratio because the company has nearly $270 million in cash and was able to generate over $1.2 billion in cash provided by operating activities. The high quick ratio reported by Peet's is the result of the company employing less debt, both long-term and short-term, in its capital structure.

A Few Cautions The quick ratio may be a misleading measure of liquidity because it can be influenced by small variations in the flow of transactions. The repayment of a large bank loan could have a big impact on the ratio. Also, customers not paying on their accounts would increase the ratio but in fact would be cause for concern. Analysts recognize that managers can manipulate the quick ratio by engaging in certain transactions just before the close of the fiscal year. For example, the quick ratio can be improved by adjusting the timing of some payments around the date the financial statements are prepared.

CURRENT LIABILITIES

Many current liabilities have a direct relationship to the operating activities of a business. In other words, specific operating activities are financed, in part, by a related current liability. Some examples from the Starbucks annual report (Exhibit 9.1) are:

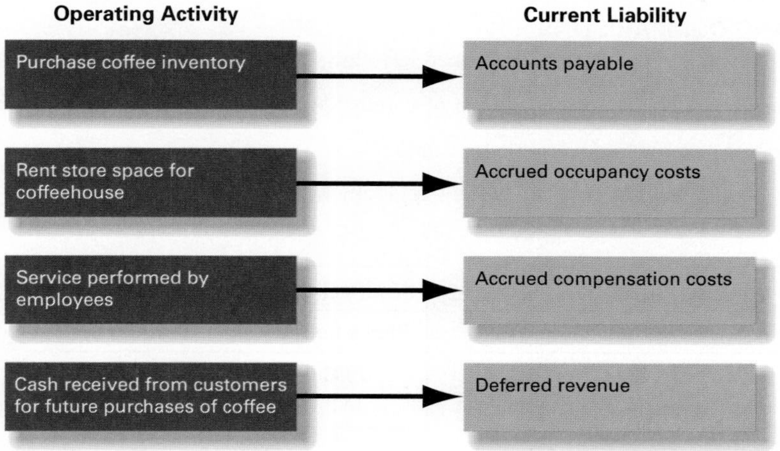

Early in this chapter, we mentioned that Starbucks is aggressively opening new stores each year. As a result, it must buy more inventory, rent more store space, and hire more employees. By understanding the relationship between operating activities and current liabilities, an analyst can easily explain changes in the various current liability accounts.

We will now discuss the current liability accounts that are found on most balance sheets.

Accounts Payable

Most companies do not produce all the goods and services that they use in their basic operating activities. Instead, they purchase some goods and services from other businesses. Typically, these transactions are made on credit with cash payments made after the goods and services have been provided. As a result, these transactions create accounts payable, also called **trade accounts payable.** *Accounting Trends & Techniques* (published by the AICPA) examined the reporting practices of 600 companies and found that most companies use the term **accounts payable.**[1]

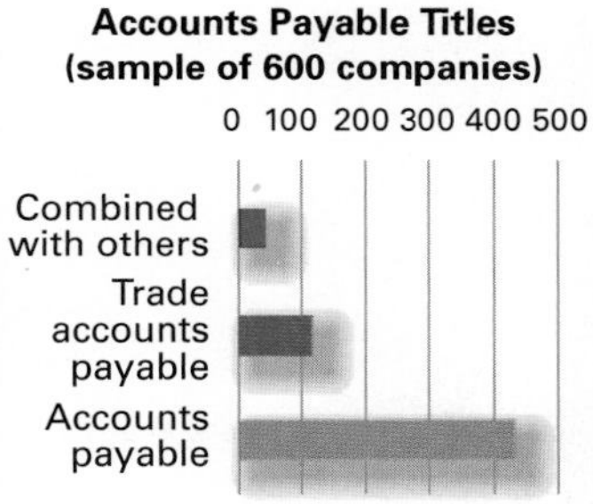

For many companies, trade credit is a relatively inexpensive way to finance the purchase of inventory because interest does not normally accrue on accounts payable. As an incentive to encourage more sales, some vendors offer generous credit terms that may allow the buyer to resell merchandise and collect cash before payment must be made to the original vendor.

Some managers may be tempted to delay payment to suppliers as long as possible to conserve cash. This strategy normally is not advisable. Most successful companies develop positive working relationships with suppliers to ensure that they receive quality goods and services. A positive relationship can be destroyed by slow payment of debt. In addition, financial analysts become concerned if a business does not meet its obligations to trade creditors on a timely basis because such slowness often indicates that a company is experiencing financial difficulties. Both managers and analysts use the accounts payable turnover ratio to evaluate effectiveness in managing payables.

[1]Reprinted with permission from *Accounting Trends & Techniques.* Copyright © 2008 by the American Institute of Certified Public Accountants, Inc.

KEY RATIO ANALYSIS

Accounts Payable Turnover

LEARNING OBJECTIVE 3

Analyze the accounts payable turnover ratio.

ANALYTICAL QUESTION

How efficient is management in meeting its obligations to suppliers?

RATIO AND COMPARISONS

The accounts payable turnover ratio is computed as follows:

Accounts Payable Turnover = Cost of Goods Sold ÷ Average Accounts Payable

The 2008 accounts payable turnover ratio for Starbucks was:

$4,645.3 ÷ $357.9* = 13.0

***($324.9 + $390.8) ÷ 2 = $357.9**

COMPARISONS OVER TIME		
Starbucks		
2006	**2007**	**2008**
11.3	11.0	13.0

COMPARISONS WITH COMPETITORS	
Peet's Coffee	**Caribou Coffee**
2008	**2008**
13.3	12.1

INTERPRETATIONS

In General The accounts payable turnover ratio measures how quickly management is paying trade accounts. A high accounts payable ratio normally suggests that a company is paying its suppliers in a timely manner. The ratio can be stated more intuitively by dividing it into the number of days in a year:

Average Age of Payables = 365 Days ÷ Turnover Ratio

The 2008 average age of payables for Starbucks was:

365 Days ÷ 13.0 = 28.1 Days

Focus Company Analysis The accounts payable turnover for Starbucks is similar to both of its competitors and is fairly stable over time. Usually, a low ratio would raise questions concerning a company's liquidity. Starbucks, on average, pays its creditors within approximately 30 days, which represents normal credit terms. Analysts would consider this ratio to be strong.

A Few Cautions The accounts payable turnover ratio is an average based on all accounts payable. The ratio might not reflect reality if a company pays some creditors on time but is late with others. The ratio is also subject to manipulation. Managers could be late in paying creditors during the entire year but catch up at year-end so that the ratio is at an acceptable level. As our focus company analysis indicates, a low turnover ratio can indicate either liquidity problems (i.e., the company is not able to generate sufficient cash to meet its obligations) or aggressive cash management (i.e., the company maintains only the minimum amount of cash necessary to support its operating activities). The first is a problem; the second is a strength. Analysts need to study other factors (such as the quick ratio and the amount of cash generated from operating activities) to determine which is the case.

Accrued Liabilities

ACCRUED LIABILITIES are expenses that have been incurred but have not been paid at the end of the accounting period.

In many situations, a business incurs an expense in one accounting period and makes the cash payment in another period. **Accrued liabilities** are expenses that have been incurred before the end of an accounting period but have not been paid. These expenses include items such as property taxes, electricity, and salaries. The balance sheet for Starbucks lists four of these items: accrued compensation and related costs, accrued occupancy costs (rent), accrued taxes, and other accrued expenses. Accrued liabilities are recorded as adjusting entries at year-end.

Accrued Taxes Payable

Like individuals, corporations must pay taxes on the income they earn. Corporate tax rates are graduated with large corporations paying a top federal tax rate of 35 percent. Corporations may also pay state and local income taxes and, in some cases, foreign income taxes. The notes to the Starbucks annual report include the following information pertaining to taxes:

STARBUCKS

REAL WORLD EXCERPT

Annual Report

INCOME TAXES

Note 15:

The provision for income taxes consisted of the following (*in millions*):

Fiscal Year Ended	Sep. 28, 2008	Sep. 30, 2007	Oct. 1, 2006
Current taxes:			
Federal	$180.4	$326.7	$332.2
State	34.3	65.3	57.8
Foreign	40.4	31.2	12.4
Deferred taxes, net	(111.1)	(39.5)	(77.6)
Total	$144.0	$383.7	$324.8

The 2008 federal income tax for Starbucks ($180.4 million) was approximately 57 percent of its reported earnings. For most corporations, federal income taxes represent a major cost.

Accrued Compensation and Related Costs

At the end of each accounting period, employees usually have earned salaries that have not yet been paid. Unpaid salaries may be reported as part of accrued liabilities or as a separate item, as is the case with Starbucks (the amount shown on the balance sheet is $253.6 million). In addition to reporting salaries that have been earned but not paid, companies must report the cost of unpaid benefits, including retirement programs, vacation time, and health insurance.

Let's look at vacation time as an example. Typically, a business grants employees paid vacation time based on the number of months they have worked. Under the matching concept, the cost of vacation time must be recorded in the year employees perform a service rather than the year they actually take vacation. If Starbucks estimates the cost of accrued vacation time to be $125,000, accountants make the following adjusting entry at the end of the fiscal year:

Compensation expense (+E, −SE)	125,000	
Accrued vacation liability (+L)		125,000

Assets		=	Liabilities		+	Stockholders' Equity	
			Accrued vacation liability	+125,000		Compensation expense (+E)	−125,000

When the vacations are taken (during the next summer), the accountants record the following:

Accrued vacation liability (−L)	125,000	
Cash (−A)		125,000

Assets		=	Liabilities		+	Stockholders' Equity
Cash	−125,000		Accrued vacation liability	−125,000		

Starbucks does not separately disclose the amount of accrued vacation liability. Instead, the company reports this liability as part of accrued compensation. Apparently, the amount of accrued vacation liability is not material in management's opinion. Most analysts would probably agree.

Payroll Taxes

All payrolls are subject to a variety of taxes, including federal, state, and local income taxes, Social Security taxes, and federal and state unemployment taxes. Employees pay some of these taxes and employers pay others. While we will look at only the three largest deductions for most people, reporting is similar for each type of payroll tax.

Employee Income Taxes Employers are required to withhold income taxes for each employee. The amount of income tax withheld is recorded by the employer as a current liability between the date of the deduction and the date the amount is remitted to the government. Federal Income Tax Withheld is often referred to as **FITW.**

Employee and Employer FICA Taxes The Social Security taxes often are called **FICA taxes** because they are required by the Federal Insurance Contributions Act. These taxes are imposed in equal amounts on both the employee and the employer. Effective January 1, 2010, the Social Security tax rate was 6.2 percent on the first $106,800 paid to each employee during the year. In addition, a separate 1.45 percent Medicare tax applies to all income. Therefore, the FICA tax rate is 7.65 percent on income up to $106,800 and 1.45 percent on all income above $106,800.

Employer Unemployment Taxes Employers are charged unemployment taxes through the Federal Unemployment Tax Act (FUTA) and State Unemployment Tax Acts (SUTA). These programs provide limited financial support to employees who lose their jobs through no fault of their own. Because the rate and specified amount of wages vary by state, we will focus on federal unemployment taxes. The FUTA specifies a federal tax rate of 6.2 percent on taxable wages up to the first $7,000 for each employee. Employers with a good payment history may receive a credit for taxes paid at the state level, up to 5.4 percent of taxable wages. For most large employers, the FUTA taxes are .8 percent of wages up to $7,000 for each employee.

Employee compensation expense includes all funds earned by employees as well as funds paid to others on behalf of employees. As a result, the cost of hiring employees is much more than the amount that those employees actually receive in cash.

To illustrate a payroll, let's assume that Starbucks accumulated the following information in its records for the first two weeks of June 2011:

Salaries and wages earned	$1,800,000
Income taxes withheld	275,000
FICA taxes (employees' share)	105,000
FUTA taxes	2,300

The entry to record the payroll is normally made with two entries. The first entry records amounts paid to employees or withheld from amounts they have earned:

Compensation expense (+E, −SE)	1,800,000	
Liability for income taxes withheld (+L)		275,000
FICA payable (+L)		105,000
Cash (−A)		1,420,000

Assets		=	Liabilities		+	Stockholders' Equity	
Cash	−1,420,000		FICA payable	+105,000		Compensation expense (+E)	−1,800,000
			Liability for income taxes withheld	+275,000			

The second entry records the taxes that employers must pay from their own funds. These additional tax payments are required by federal and state law. The FICA tax amount is equal to the amount that is paid by employees:

Compensation expense (+E, −SE)	107,300	
FICA payable (+L)		105,000
FUTA payable (+L).		2,300

Assets		=	Liabilities		+	Stockholders' Equity	
			FICA payable	+105,000		Compensation expense (+E)	−107,300
			FUTA payable	+2,300			

Types of Employee-Related Liabilities (sample of 600 companies)

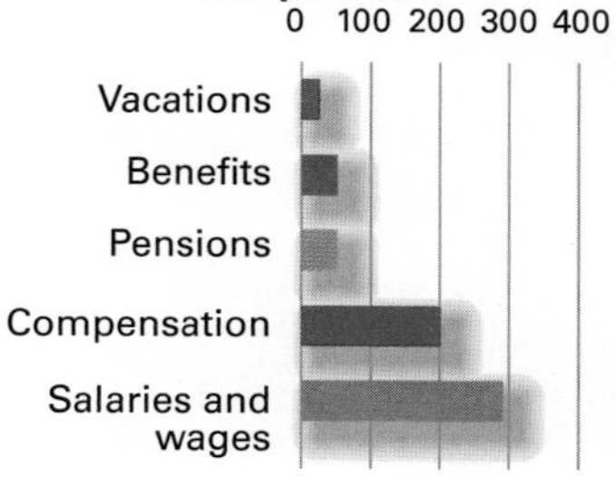

Accounting Trends & Techniques found that most companies in its sample of 600 companies report employee-related liabilities.[2]

Notes Payable

LEARNING OBJECTIVE 4

Report notes payable and explain the time value of money.

When a company borrows money, a formal written contract is usually prepared. Obligations supported by these contracts are called *notes payable.* A note payable specifies the amount borrowed, the date by which it must be repaid, and the interest rate associated with the borrowing.

Creditors are willing to lend cash because they will earn interest in return for giving up the use of their money for a period. This simple concept is called the **time value of money.** The longer borrowed money is held, the larger is the total dollar amount of interest expense. Interest at a given interest rate on a two-year loan is more than interest on a one-year loan. To the borrower, interest is an expense; to the creditor, it is revenue.

The TIME VALUE OF MONEY is interest that is associated with the use of money over time.

To calculate interest, three variables must be considered: (1) the principal (i.e., the cash that was borrowed), (2) the annual interest rate, and (3) the time period for the loan. The interest formula is:

Interest = Principal × Interest Rate × Time

To illustrate, assume that on November 1, 2011, Starbucks borrows $100,000 cash on a one-year, 12 percent note payable. The interest is payable on March 31, 2012, and October 31, 2012. The principal is payable at the maturity date, October 31, 2012. The note is recorded in the accounts as follows:

Cash (+A).	100,000	
Notes payable, short-term (+L)		100,000

Assets		=	Liabilities		+	Stockholders' Equity
Cash	+100,000		Notes payable	+100,000		

Interest is an expense of the period in which the money is used. Under the matching concept, interest expense is recorded when it is incurred rather than when the cash actually is paid. Because Starbucks uses the money for two months during 2011, it records interest expense in 2011 for two months, even though cash is not paid until March 31.

The computation of interest expense for 2011 is as follows:

Interest	**=**	**Principal**	**×**	**Interest Rate**	**×**	**Time**
$2,000	**=**	**$100,000**	**×**	**12%**	**×**	**2/12**

[2]Reprinted with permission from *Accounting Trends & Techniques.* Copyright © 2008 by the American Institute of Certified Public Accountants, Inc.

The entry to record interest expense on December 31, 2011 is:

Interest expense (+E, −SE)	2,000	
Interest payable (+L)		2,000

Assets		=	Liabilities		+	Stockholders' Equity	
			Interest payable	+2,000		Interest expense (+E)	−2,000

On March 31, 2012, Starbucks would pay $5,000 in interest, which includes the $2,000 accrued and reported in 2011 plus the $3,000 interest accrued in the first three months of 2012. The following journal entry would be made:

Interest expense (+E, −SE)	3,000	
Interest payable (−L)	2,000	
Cash (−A)		5,000

Assets		=	Liabilities		+	Stockholders' Equity	
Cash	−5,000		Interest payable	−2,000		Interest expense (+E)	−3,000

Current Portion of Long-Term Debt

The distinction between current and long-term debt is important for both managers and analysts. Because current debt must be paid within the next year, companies must have sufficient cash to repay it. To provide accurate information on its current liabilities, a company must reclassify its long-term debt as a current liability within a year of its maturity date. Assume that Starbucks signed a note payable of $5 million on January 1, 2011. Repayment is required on December 1, 2013. The December 31, 2011 and 2012, balance sheets would report the following:

December 31, 2011	
Long-term liabilities:	
Note payable	$5,000,000

December 31, 2012	
Current liabilities:	
Current portion of long-term note	$5,000,000

An example of this type of disclosure can be seen in Exhibit 9.1. Notice that in 2008, Starbucks reported $0.7 million as the current portion of long-term debt to be paid in full during the following accounting period. In some cases, companies will refinance debt when it comes due rather than pay out cash currently on hand.

FINANCIAL ANALYSIS

Refinanced Debt: Current or Noncurrent?

IFRS

Instead of repaying a debt from current cash, a company may refinance it either by negotiating a new loan agreement with a new maturity date or by borrowing money from a new creditor and repaying the original creditor. If a company intends to refinance a currently maturing debt and has the ability to do so, should the debt be classified as a current or a long-term liability? Remember that analysts are interested in a company's current liabilities because those liabilities will generate cash outflows in the next accounting period. If a liability will not generate a cash outflow in the next accounting period, GAAP requires that it not be classified as current. This rule is illustrated by a note from the General Mills annual report.

GENERAL MILLS

REAL WORLD EXCERPT

Annual Report

> We have a revolving credit agreement that provides us with the ability to refinance short-term borrowing on a long-term basis. Therefore we have reclassified a portion of our notes payable to long-term debt.

U.S. GAAP and IFRS differ with respect to the timing of the refinancing. In the case of IFRS, the actual refinancing must take place by the balance sheet date. Under GAAP, the ability to refinance must be in place before the financial statements are issued.

Deferred Revenues

In most business transactions, cash is paid after the product or service has been delivered. In some cases, cash is paid before delivery. You have probably paid for magazines that you will receive at some time in the future. The publisher collects money for your subscription in advance, before the magazine is published. When a company collects cash before the related revenue has been earned, the cash is called **deferred revenues.** The popular Starbucks card permits customers to pay in advance for their coffee. The advantage for the customer is convenience at the point of sale. The advantage for the company is that Starbucks is able to collect and use cash before customers actually buy the product. The Starbucks report shows that the company has collected $368.4 million from customers prior to providing them with coffee and explains the amount with the following note:

DEFERRED REVENUES are revenues that have been collected but not earned; they are liabilities until the goods or services have been provided.

STARBUCKS

REAL WORLD EXCERPT

Annual Report

> Revenues from the Company's stored value cards, such as the Starbucks Card, and gift certificates are recognized when tendered for payment, or upon redemption. Outstanding customer balances are included in "Deferred revenue" on the consolidated balance sheet.

Under the revenue principle, revenue cannot be recorded until it has been earned. Deferred revenues are reported as a liability because cash has been collected but the related revenue has not been earned by the end of the accounting period. The obligation to provide services or goods in the future still exists. These obligations are classified as current or long-term, depending on when they must be satisfied.

Estimated Liabilities Reported on the Balance Sheet

Some recorded liabilities are based on estimates because the exact amount will not be known until a future date. For example, an estimated liability is created when a company offers a warranty with the products it sells. The cost of providing future repair work must be estimated and recorded as a liability (and expense) in the period in which the product is sold.

Starbucks offers a warranty on coffee brewing and espresso equipment sold in its stores but does not record an estimated warranty liability at the time of sale. Rather than repairing brewing machines, the company gives the customer the right to return any defective product for a period of up to 24 months. The estimated amount of product that will be returned is reported as a reduction from sales revenue in the year the sales are recorded.

Estimated Liabilities Reported in the Notes

LEARNING OBJECTIVE 5
Report contingent liabilities.

Each of the liabilities that we have discussed is reported on the balance sheet at a specific dollar amount because each involves the probable future sacrifice of economic benefits.

A CONTINGENT LIABILITY is a potential liability that has arisen as the result of a past event; it is not an effective liability until some future event occurs.

Some transactions or events create only a reasonably possible (but not probable) future sacrifice of economic benefits. These situations create **contingent liabilities,** which are potential liabilities that are created as a result of a past event. A contingent liability may or may not become a recorded liability depending on future events. A situation that produces a contingent liability also causes a contingent loss.

Contingent Liability Examples

Whether a situation produces a recorded or a contingent liability depends on two factors: the probability of a future economic sacrifice and the ability of management to estimate the amount of the liability. The following table illustrates the possibilities:

	Probable	Reasonably Possible	Remote
Subject to estimate	Record as liability	Disclose in note	Disclosure not required
Not subject to estimate	Disclose in note	Disclose in note	Disclosure not required

Video 9-1
www.mhhe.com/libby7e

The probabilities of occurrence are defined in the following manner:

1. Probable—the chance that the future event or events will occur is high.
2. Reasonably possible—the chance that the future event or events will occur is more than remote but less than likely.
3. Remote—the chance that the future event or events will occur is slight.

INTERNATIONAL PERSPECTIVE

It's a Matter of Degree

The assessment of future probabilities is inherently subjective but both U.S. GAAP and IFRS provide some guidance. Under GAAP, "probable" has been defined as *likely,* which is interpreted as having a greater than 70 percent chance of occurring. In the case of IFRS, "probable" is defined as *more likely than not,* which would imply more than a 50 percent chance of occurring. This difference means that companies reporting under IFRS would record a liability when other companies reporting under GAAP would report the same event as a contingency.

In summary, (1) a liability that is both probable and capable of being reasonably estimated must be recorded and reported on the balance sheet, (2) a liability that is reasonably possible must be disclosed in a note in the financial statements whether it can be estimated or not, and (3) remote contingencies are not disclosed.

The notes to Starbucks's annual report include the following information about a lawsuit:

> **Note 17: Commitments and Contingencies**
>
> On March 20, 2008, the court ordered the company to pay approximately $87 million in restitution. On July 31, 2008, the company filed a notice of appeal. Starbucks believes that while the adverse ruling by the trial judge in this case makes the possibility of loss somewhat more likely, the company is only at the very beginning of the appellate process. Starbucks believes that the likelihood that the company will ultimately incur a loss in connection with this litigation is reasonably possible rather than probable. The company has not accrued any loss related to this litigation.

STARBUCKS

REAL WORLD EXCERPT

Annual Report

Contingent Liabilities (sample of 600 companies)

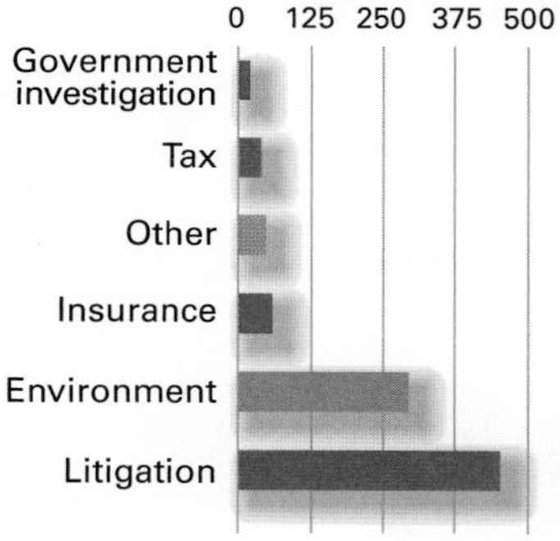

Consistent with the chart shown earlier, Starbucks did not record a liability because the likelihood of a loss did not meet the threshold of "probable." Therefore, disclosure in a footnote was sufficient.

Accounting Trends & Techniques studied the financial statements of 600 companies and found that litigation was the most common type of contingent liability.[3]

Working Capital Management

LEARNING OBJECTIVE 6

Explain the importance of working capital and its impact on cash flows.

Working capital is defined as the dollar difference between current assets and current liabilities. Working capital is important to both managers and financial analysts because it has a significant impact on the health and profitability of a company.

The working capital accounts are actively managed to achieve a balance between costs and benefits. If a business has too little working capital, it runs the risk of not being able to meet its obligations to creditors. On the other hand, too much working capital may tie up resources in unproductive assets and incur additional costs. Excess inventory, for example, ties up dollars that could be invested more profitably elsewhere in the business and incurs additional costs associated with storage and deterioration.

WORKING CAPITAL is the dollar difference between total current assets and total current liabilities.

Changes in working capital accounts are also important to managers and analysts because they have a direct impact on the cash flows from operating activities reported on the statement of cash flows.

Working Capital and Cash Flows

FOCUS ON CASH FLOWS

Many working capital accounts have a direct relationship to income-producing activities. Accounts receivable, for example, are related to sales revenue: Accounts receivable increase when sales are made on credit. Cash is collected when the customer pays the bill. Similarly, accounts payable increase when an expense is incurred without a cash payment. A cash outflow occurs when the account is paid. Changes in working capital accounts that are related to income-producing activities must be considered when computing cash flows from operating activities.

(continued)

[3]Reprinted with permission form *Accounting Trends & Techniques*. Copyright © 2008 by the American Institute of Certified Public Accountants, Inc.

EFFECT ON STATEMENT OF CASH FLOWS

In General On the statement of cash flows, net income is adjusted (under the indirect method) to compute cash flows from operating activities. Changes in working capital accounts have the impact shown in the following table:

	Effect on Cash Flows
Operating activities (indirect method)	
Net income	$xxx
Adjusted for: Decreases in current assets* or increases in current liabilities	+
Adjusted for: Increases in current assets* or decreases in current liabilities	−

*Other than cash.

Focus Company Analysis A segment of the Starbucks Consolidated Statements of Cash Flows, prepared using the indirect method, follows. Notice the significant amount of cash flows from operating activities from 2006 to 2008 (compared to the net earnings). These substantial cash flows are important for a company with the growth strategy that Starbucks is following.

STARBUCKS CORPORATION
Consolidated Statements of Cash Flows
(in millions)

Fiscal Year Ended	Sep. 28, 2008	Sep. 30, 2007	Oct. 1, 2006
OPERATING ACTIVITIES:			
Net earnings	$ 315.5	$ 672.6	$ 564.3
Adjustments to reconcile net earnings to net cash provided by operating activities:			
Cumulative effect of accounting change for FIN 47, net of taxes	—	—	17.2
Depreciation and amortization	604.5	491.2	412.6
Provision for impairments and asset disposals	325.0	26.0	19.6
Deferred income taxes, net	(117.1)	(37.3)	(84.3)
Equity in income of investees	(61.3)	(65.7)	(60.6)
Distributions of income from equity investees	52.6	65.9	49.2
Stock-based compensation	75.0	103.9	105.7
Tax benefit from exercise of stock options	3.8	7.7	1.3
Excess tax benefit from exercise of stock options	(14.7)	(93.1)	(117.4)
Other	(0.1)	0.7	2.0
Cash provided (used) by changes in operating assets and liabilities:			
Inventories	(0.6)	(48.6)	(85.5)
Accounts payable	(63.9)	36.1	105.0
Accrued taxes	7.3	86.4	132.7
Deferred revenue	72.4	63.2	56.6
Other operating assets and liabilities	60.3	22.2	13.2
Net cash provided by operating activities	1,258.7	1,331.2	1,131.6

PAUSE FOR FEEDBACK

Companies report two classifications of liabilities. We have discussed current liabilities and in the next section we will discuss long-term liabilities. Before you move on, complete the following questions to test your understanding of these concepts.

SELF-STUDY QUIZ

Assume that the quick ratio for Starbucks is 0.5. For each of the following events, state whether the quick ratio and working capital will increase or decrease:

1. Starbucks incurs an account payable of $250,000 with no change in quick assets.
2. The company borrows $1,000,000 in long-term debt.
3. The company pays taxes payable in the amount of $750,000.
4. The company finances a new building with long-term debt.

After you have completed your answers, check them with the solutions at the bottom of the page.

LONG-TERM LIABILITIES

LEARNING OBJECTIVE 7
Report long-term liabilities.

Long-term liabilities include all obligations that are not classified as current liabilities, such as long-term notes payable and bonds payable. Typically, a long-term liability will require payment more than one year in the future. These obligations may be created by borrowing money, or they may result from other activities.

LONG-TERM LIABILITIES are all of the entity's obligations not classified as current liabilities.

Most companies borrow money on a long-term basis in order to purchase operational assets. To reduce risk for creditors, some companies agree to use specific assets as security. If the liability is not satisfied, the creditor may take ownership of the asset. A liability supported by this type of agreement is called a **secured debt.** An unsecured debt is one for which the creditor relies primarily on the borrower's integrity and general earning power.

Long-Term Notes Payable and Bonds

Companies can raise long-term debt capital directly from a number of financial service organizations including banks, insurance companies, and pension plans. Raising debt from one of these organizations is known as **private placement.** This type of debt is often called a **note payable,** which is a written promise to pay a stated sum at one or more specified future dates called the **maturity date(s).**

In many cases, a company's need for debt capital exceeds the financial ability of any single creditor. In these situations, the company may issue publicly traded debt called **bonds.** The opportunity to sell a bond in established markets provides bondholders with an important benefit. They can sell their bonds to other investors prior to maturity if they have an immediate need for cash. Because bonds provide liquidity to investors, they are more likely to lend money to a company. Bonds will be discussed in detail in the next chapter.

Accounting for long-term debt is based on the same concepts used in accounting for short-term notes payable. A liability is recorded when the debt is incurred and interest expense is recorded with the passage of time.

Business operations are global in nature. Successful corporations market their products in many countries and locate manufacturing facilities around the world based on cost and

Solutions to SELF-STUDY QUIZ

Quick ratio	Working capital
1. Decrease	Decrease
2. Increase	Increase
3. Decrease	No change
4. No change	No change

productivity. The financing of corporations also has become international, even for companies that do not have international operations. Borrowing money in a foreign currency raises some interesting accounting and management issues.

INTERNATIONAL PERSPECTIVE

Borrowing in Foreign Currencies

Many corporations with foreign operations elect to finance those operations with foreign debt to lessen exchange rate risk. This type of risk exists because the relative value of each nation's currency varies on virtually a daily basis. As this book was being written, the British pound was worth approximately $1.50.

A U.S. corporation that conducts business operations in England might decide to borrow pounds to finance its operations there. The profits from the business, which will be in pounds, can be used to pay off the debt, which is in pounds. If this business earned profits in pounds but paid off debt in dollars, it would be exposed to exchange rate risk because the relative value of the dollar and the pound fluctuates.

Foreign corporations face this same problem. A note to a recent annual report from Toyota, a Japanese company that does significant business in the United States, stated:

TOYOTA

REAL WORLD EXCERPT

Annual Report

> Earnings declined in the current year ended, as the appreciation of the yen aggravated the adverse effects of sluggish demand. . . . The movement in exchange rates reduced operating income of the company. Losses on currency exchange thus offset most of the cost savings we achieved.

Toyota has borrowed a large amount of money in the United States to lessen the exchange rate risk it faces. The company also owns and operates many factories in the United States.

Even if a company does not have international operations, it may elect to borrow in foreign markets. Interest rates often are low in countries experiencing a recession. These situations give corporations the opportunity to borrow at a lower cost.

For reporting purposes, accountants must convert, or translate, foreign debt into U.S. dollars. Conversion rates for all major currencies are published in most newspapers. To illustrate foreign currency translation, assume that Starbucks borrowed 1 million pounds (£). For the Starbucks annual report, the accountant must use the conversion rate as of the balance sheet date, which we assume was £1.00 to $1.50. The dollar equivalent of the debt is $1,500,000 (£1,000,000 × 1.50). The dollar equivalent of foreign debt may change if the conversion rate changes even without any additional borrowings or repayments.

The notes to the balance sheet for Starbucks indicate that the company has borrowed money only in the United States. In contrast, many companies with international operations borrow in the local currency of the countries in which they operate. These companies often repay the foreign currency debt with earnings (in the same currency) from operations in the foreign country.

Lease Liabilities

An OPERATING LEASE does not meet any of the four criteria (shown below) established by GAAP and does not cause the recording of an asset and liability.

Companies often lease assets rather than purchase them. For example, renting extra delivery trucks during a busy period is more economical than owning them if they are not needed during the rest of the year. When a company leases an asset on a short-term basis, the agreement is called an **operating lease.** No liability is recorded when an operating lease is created. Instead, a company records rent expense as it uses the asset. Assume that on December 15, 2011, Starbucks signed an operating lease contract to rent five large trucks during January 2012. No liability is recorded in 2011. Rent expense is recorded during January 2012 as the trucks are actually used.

For a number of reasons, a company may prefer to lease an asset on a long-term basis rather than purchase it. This type of lease is called a **capital lease.** In essence, a capital lease contract represents the purchase and financing of an asset even though it is legally a lease agreement. Unlike an operating lease, capital leases are accounted for as if an asset had been purchased by recording an asset and a liability. Because of the significant differences between operating and capital leases, GAAP specifies criteria to distinguish between them. If a lease meets any of the following four criteria, it is considered a capital lease:

A CAPITAL LEASE meets at least one of the four criteria established by GAAP and results in the recording of an asset and liability.

- The lease term is 75 percent or more of the asset's expected economic life.
- Ownership of the asset is transferred to the lessee at the end of the lease term.
- The lease contract permits the lessee to purchase the asset at a price that is lower than its fair market value.
- The present value of the lease payments is 90 percent or more of the fair market value of the asset when the lease is signed.

If managers have a choice of recording a lease as an operating or a capital lease, most would prefer to record it as an operating lease. By doing so, the company is able to report less debt on its balance sheet. In the notes to its financial statements, Starbucks reports capital lease obligations of $4.1 million, which are included on the balance sheet under the category "other long-term liabilities." Many financial analysts are concerned that companies can avoid reporting debt associated with capital leases by structuring the lease agreement in a manner that meets the requirements for recording it as an operating lease.

To record a capital lease, it is necessary to determine the current cash equivalent of the required lease payments. Assume that Starbucks signs a lease for new delivery trucks. The accountant has determined that the lease is a capital lease with a current cash equivalent of $250,000. Once the lease is signed, the transaction would be recorded in a manner similar to the actual purchase of delivery trucks:

Leased equipment (+A)	250,000	
Lease payable (+L)		250,000

Assets		=	Liabilities		+	Stockholders' Equity
Leased equipment	+250,000		Lease Payable	+250,000		

In this example, you were given the current cash equivalent of the lease. In the next section, on present value concepts, we will show you how this amount is computed.

PRESENT VALUE CONCEPTS

LEARNING OBJECTIVE 8
Compute present values.

Our discussion of capital leases raises an interesting question about liabilities: Is the recorded amount of the liability the actual amount of cash that will be paid in the future? For example, if I agree to pay you $10,000 five years from now, should I report a liability of $10,000 on my personal balance sheet? To answer such questions, we will now introduce some relatively simple mathematics called **present value concepts.** These concepts will provide a foundation for our discussion of bond liabilities in the next chapter.

The concept of **present value** (PV) is based on the time value of money. Quite simply, money received today is worth more than money to be received one year from today (or at any other future date) because it can be used to earn interest. If you invest $1,000 today at 10 percent, you will have $1,100 in one year. In contrast, if you receive $1,000 one year from today, you will lose the opportunity to earn the $100 in interest revenue. The difference between the $1,000 and the $1,100 is the interest that can be earned during the year.

PRESENT VALUE is the current value of an amount to be received in the future; a future amount discounted for compound interest.

In one of your math classes, you have probably already solved some problems involving the time value of money. In the typical problem, you are told a certain dollar amount has been deposited in a savings account earning a specified rate of interest. You are asked to determine the dollar amount in the savings account after a certain number of years. In contrast, in this chapter we show you how to solve the opposite problem. In present value problems, you are told a dollar amount to be received in the future (such as the balance of a savings account after five years) and are asked to determine the present value of the amount (which is the amount that must be deposited in the savings account today).

The value of money changes over time because money can earn interest. In a present value problem, you know the dollar amount of a cash flow that will occur in the future and need to determine its value now. The opposite situation occurs when you know the dollar amount of a cash flow that occurs today and need to determine its value at some point in the future. These problems are called future value problems. Future value concepts are discussed in a supplement to this chapter.

Present Value of a Single Amount

The present value of a single amount is the worth to you today of receiving that amount some time in the future. For instance, you might be offered an opportunity to invest in a debt instrument that would pay you $10,000 in three years. Before you decided whether to invest, you would want to determine the present value of the instrument. Graphically, the present value of $1 due at the end of the third period with an interest rate of 10 percent can be represented as follows:

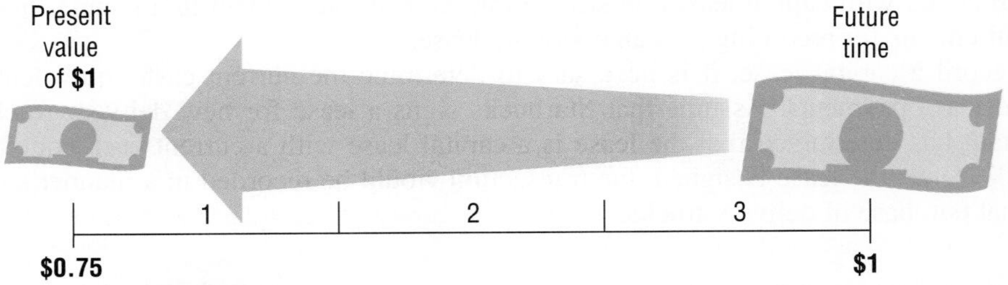

To compute the present value of an amount to be received in the future, we will subtract interest that is earned over time from the amount to be received in the future. For example, if you place $100 in a savings account that earns 5 percent, you will have $105 at the end of a year. In a present value problem, you will be told that you have $105 at the end of the year and must compute the amount to be deposited at the beginning of the year. To solve this type of problem, you must discount the amount to be received in the future at i interest rate for n periods. The formula to compute the present value of a single amount is

$$\textbf{Present value} = \frac{1}{(1+i)^n} \times \textbf{Amount}$$

While the formula is not difficult to use, most analysts use present value tables, calculators, or Excel. We will illustrate how to use present value tables (an explanation of how to use Excel to compute present values is presented in a supplement to this chapter). Assume that today is January 1, 2011, and you have the opportunity to receive $1,000 cash on December 31, 2013. At an interest rate of 10 percent per year, how much is the $1,000 payment worth to you on January 1, 2011? You could discount the amount year by year[4] but it is easier to use Table A.1,

[4]The detailed discounting is as follows:

Periods	Interest for the Year	Present Value*
1	$1,000 − ($1,000 × 1/1.10) = $90.91	$1,000 − $90.91 = $909.09
2	$909.09 − ($909.09 × 1/1.10) = $82.64	$909.09 − $82.64 = $826.45
3	$826.45 − ($826.45 × 1/1.10) = $75.15†	$826.45 − $75.15 = $751.30

*Verifiable in Table A.1. †Adjusted for rounding.

Appendix A, Present Value of $1. For $i = 10\%$, $n = 3$, we find that the present value of $1 is 0.7513. The present value of $1,000 to be received at the end of three years can be computed as follows:

$1,000 × 0.7513 = $751.30

From Table A.1
Interest rate = 10%,
$n = 3$

Learning how to compute a present value amount is not difficult, but it is more important that you understand what it means. The $751.30 is the amount you would pay now to have the right to receive $1,000 at the end of three years, assuming an interest rate of 10 percent. Conceptually, you should be indifferent between having $751.30 today and receiving $1,000 in three years, because you can use financial institutions to convert dollars from the present value to the future value and vice versa. If you had $751.30 today but preferred $1,000 in three years, you could simply deposit the money in a savings account and it would grow to $1,000 in three years. Alternatively, if you had a contract that promised you $1,000 in three years, you could sell it to an investor for $751.30 in cash today because it would permit the investor to earn the difference in interest.

To compute the present value using Excel, enter: = 1000/(1.10)^3

PAUSE FOR **FEEDBACK**

SELF-STUDY **QUIZ**

There are two types of payments when you compute present values. So far, we have discussed single payments. In the next section, we will discuss annuities. Before you move on, complete the following questions to test your understanding of these concepts.

1. If the interest rate in a present value problem increases from 8 percent to 10 percent, will the present value increase or decrease?
2. What is the present value of $10,000 to be received 10 years from now if the interest rate is 5 percent, compounded annually?

After you have completed your answers, check them with the solutions at the bottom of this page.

Present Value of an Annuity

Instead of a single payment, many business problems involve multiple cash payments over a number of periods. An **annuity** is a series of consecutive payments characterized by

An ANNUITY is a series of periodic cash receipts or payments that are equal in amount each interest period.

1. An equal dollar amount each interest period.
2. Interest periods of equal length (year, half a year, quarter, or month).
3. An equal interest rate each interest period.

Examples of annuities include monthly payments on an automobile or home, yearly contributions to a savings account, and monthly pension benefits.

The present value of an annuity is the value now of a series of equal amounts to be received (or paid out) for some specified number of periods in the future. It is computed by discounting each of the equal periodic amounts. A good example of this type of problem is a retirement

---

1. The present value will decrease.
2. $10,000 × 0.6139 = $6,139

Solutions to SELF-STUDY QUIZ

program that offers employees a monthly income after retirement. The present value of an annuity of $1 for three periods at 10 percent may be represented graphically as follows:

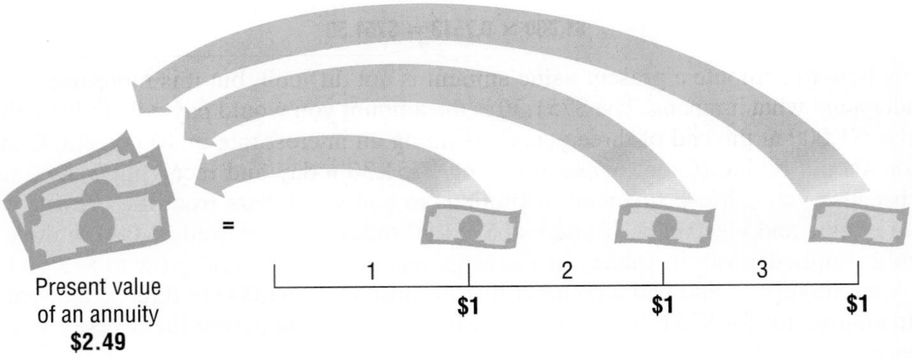

Assume you are to receive $1,000 cash on each December 31, 2011, 2012, and 2013. How much would the sum of these three $1,000 future amounts be worth on January 1, 2011, assuming an interest rate of 10 percent per year? We could use Table A.1, Appendix A, to calculate the present value as follows:

Year	Amount		Factor from Table A.1, Appendix A, $i = 10\%$		Present Value
1	$1,000	×	0.9091 ($n = 1$)	=	$ 909.10
2	$1,000	×	0.8264 ($n = 2$)	=	826.40
3	$1,000	×	0.7513 ($n = 3$)	=	751.30
			Total present value	=	$2,486.80

We can compute the present value of this annuity more easily however, by using Table A.2, Appendix A, as follows:

From Table A.2, Interest rate = 10%, n = 3

$1,000 × 2.4869 = $2,487 (rounded)

To compute the present value using Excel, enter: f_x = PV(0.10,3,−1000)

Interest Rates and Interest Periods

The preceding illustrations assumed annual periods for compounding and discounting. Although interest rates are almost always quoted on an annual basis, most compounding periods encountered in business are less than one year. When interest periods are less than a year, the values of n and i must be restated to be consistent with the length of the interest period.

To illustrate, 12 percent interest compounded annually for five years requires the use of $n = 5$ and $i = 12\%$. If compounding is quarterly, however, the interest period is one quarter of a year (i.e., four periods per year), and the quarterly interest rate is one quarter of the annual rate (i.e., 3 percent per quarter). Therefore, 12 percent interest compounded quarterly for five years requires use of $n = 20$ and $i = 3\%$.

A QUESTION OF ETHICS

Truth in Advertising

Newspaper, magazine, and television advertisements are easy to misinterpret if the consumer does not understand present value concepts. For example, most car companies offer seasonal promotions with special financing incentives. A car dealer may advertise 4 percent interest on car loans when banks are charging 10 percent. Typically, the lower interest rate is not really an incentive because the dealer simply charges a higher price for cars the dealership finances. Borrowing from the bank and paying cash at the dealership may help the buyer to negotiate a lower price. Customers should use the present value concepts illustrated in this chapter to compare financing alternatives.

Another misleading advertisement, seen every January, promises magazine subscribers a chance to become an instant millionaire. The fine print discloses that the winner will receive $25,000 for 40 years, which amounts to $1,000,000 (40 × $25,000), but the present value of this annuity at 8 percent is only $298,000. While most winners are happy to get the money, they are not really millionaires.

Some consumer advocates argue that consumers should not have to study present value concepts to understand such advertisements. While some of these criticisms may be valid, the quality of information contained in advertisements that include interest rates has improved over time.

Accounting Applications of Present Values

LEARNING OBJECTIVE 9

Apply present value concepts to liabilities.

Many business transactions require the use of future and present value concepts. So that you can enhance your understanding of these concepts, we provide three examples.

Computing the Amount of a Liability with a Single Payment

On January 1, 2011, Starbucks bought some new delivery trucks. The company signed a note and agreed to pay $200,000 on December 31, 2012, an amount representing the cash equivalent price of the trucks plus interest for two years. The market interest rate for this note was 12 percent.

To record this transaction, the accountant must first compute the present value of a single amount paid in the future. In conformity with the cost principle, the cost of the trucks is their current cash equivalent price, which is the present value of the future payment. The problem can be shown graphically as follows:

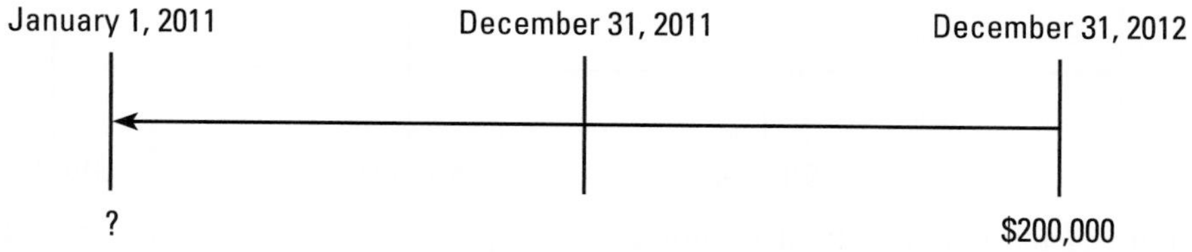

The present value of the $200,000 is computed as follows:

$200,000 × 0.7972 = $159,440

From Table A.1, Interest rate = 12%, n = 2

Therefore, the journal entry is as follows:

Delivery trucks (+A)	159,440	
Note payable (+L)		159,440

Assets		=	Liabilities		+	Stockholders' Equity	
Delivery trucks	+159,440		Note payable	+159,440			

To compute the present value using Excel, enter:
= 200000/(1.12)^2

After the initial transaction is recorded, each year's interest expense is recorded in an adjusting entry as follows:

December 31, 2011	Interest expense (+E, −SE) . . .	19,133*	
	Note payable (+L).		19,133

*$159,440 × 12% = $19,133

Assets		=	Liabilities		+	Stockholders' Equity	
			Note payable	+19,133		Interest expense (+E)	−19,133

December 31, 2012	Interest expense (+E, −SE) . . .	21,429*	
	Note payable (+L)		21,429

*($159,440 + $19,133) × 12% = 21,429

Assets		=	Liabilities		+	Stockholders' Equity	
			Note payable	+21,429		Interest expense (+E)	−21,429

At the end of two years, the loan amount must be repaid. The amount owed is the balance of Note Payable, which is the same as the maturity amount on the due date. The journal entry to record full payment of the debt follows:

Note payable (−L)	200,000	
Cash (−A)		200,000

Assets		=	Liabilities		+	Stockholders' Equity
Cash	−200,000		Note payable	−200,000		

Computing the Amount of a Liability with an Annuity

On January 1, 2011, Starbucks bought new printing equipment. The company elected to finance the purchase with a note payable to be paid off in three years in annual installments of $163,686. Each installment includes principal plus interest on the unpaid balance at 11 percent per year. The annual installments are due on December 31, 2011, 2012, and 2013. This problem can be shown graphically as follows:

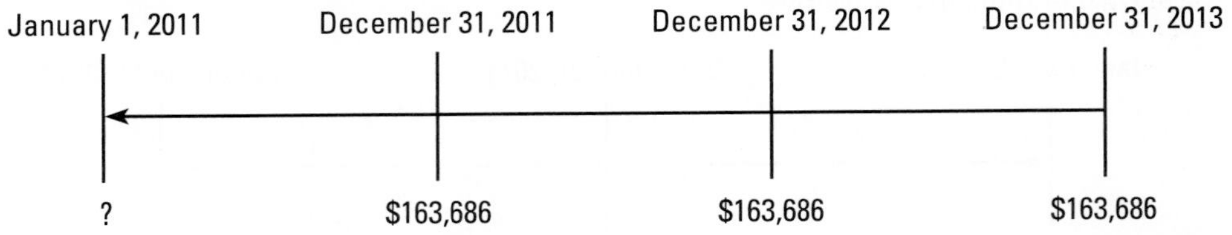

The amount of the note can be determined by computing the present value of each installment payment, $i = 11\%$ and $n = 3$. This is an annuity because payment is made in three equal installments. The amount of the note is computed as follows:

From Table A.2, Interest rate = 11%, n = 3

$163,686 × 2.4437 = $400,000

The acquisition on January 1, 2011, is recorded as follows:

To compute the present value using Excel, enter: f_x = PV(0.11,3,−163686)

Printing equipment (+A).	400,000	
Note payable (+L)		400,000

Assets		=	Liabilities		+	Stockholders' Equity
Printing equipment	+400,000		Note payable	+400,000		

Each year, the accountant must record the payments on this note as follows:

December 31, 2011	Note payable (−L)	119,686	
	Interest expense (+E, −SE) ($400,000 × 11%)	44,000	
	Cash (−A)		163,686

Assets		=	Liabilities		+	Stockholders' Equity	
Cash	−163,686		Note payable	−119,686		Interest expense (+E)	−44,000

December 31, 2012	Note payable (−L)	132,851	
	Interest expense (+E, −SE)		
	[($400,000 − 119,686) × 11%] . .	30,835	
	Cash (−A)		163,686

Assets		=	Liabilities		+	Stockholders' Equity	
Cash	−163,686		Note payable	−132,851		Interest expense (+E)	−30,835

December 31, 2013	Note payable (−L)	147,463	
	Interest expense (+E, −SE)	16,223*	
	Cash (−A)		163,686

*Interest: ($400,000 − $119,686 − $132,851) × 11% = $16,223 (rounded to accommodate rounding errors).

Assets		=	Liabilities		+	Stockholders' Equity	
Cash	−163,686		Note payable	−147,463		Interest expense (+E)	−16,223

Computing the Amount of a Lease Liability

On January 1, 2011, Starbucks signed a 20-year lease for coffee roasting equipment. The lease is based on an effective interest rate of 8 percent and requires annual payments of $10,000 on December 31 of each year. The term is 100 percent of the expected life of the equipment. As a result, this lease should be recorded as a capital lease. The amount of the liability is the present value of the lease payments, computed as follows:

$10,000 × 9.8181 = $98,181

From Table A.2
Interest rate = 8%,
n = 20

The signing of the lease on January 1, 2011, is recorded as follows:

Roasting equipment (+A)	98,181	
Lease payable (+L)		98,181

Assets		=	Liabilities		+	Stockholders' Equity
Roasting equipment	+98,181		Lease payable	+98,181		

To compute the present value using Excel, enter:
f_x = PV(0.08,20,−10,000)

In the next chapter, we will use the present value techniques you have just learned to understand how to account for bonds.

DEMONSTRATION CASE

(Try to answer the questions before proceeding to the suggested solution that follows.) Muller Construction completed several transactions during the year. In each case, decide if a liability should be recorded and, if so, determine the amount. Assume the current date is December 31, 2011.

1. Employees earned salaries of $100,000 which have not been paid at year-end. The employer share of FICA is $7,000.
2. The Company borrowed $100,000 on June 30th at 7 percent interest. No payments associated with this loan have been made.
3. A customer made a $75,000 down payment on a construction project. Work will begin next month.
4. The Company lost a lawsuit for $250,000 but plans to appeal.

5. A new truck was leased for a period equal to 85 percent of the expected life of the truck.
6. On December 31, 2011, a bank lent money to Muller. The Company agreed to repay the bank \$100,000 on December 31, 2012. The bank charges 5 percent interest.
7. The Company signed a loan agreement that requires it to pay \$50,000 per year for 20 years. The interest rate is 8 percent.

SUGGESTED SOLUTION

1. A liability of \$107,000 should be recorded.
2. The amount borrowed (\$100,000) should be recorded as a liability on June 30th. In addition, interest accrued but not paid should be recorded as a liability at year-end. This amount is \$100,000 × 7% × 6/12 = \$3,500.
3. The customer deposit (\$75,000) is a liability until work is performed and the related revenue earned.
4. Most likely, the \$250,000 should be recorded as a liability, unless the grounds for appeal significantly reduce the probability that the \$250,000 will eventually be paid.
5. Because the lease covers more than 75 percent of the estimated life of the truck, a liability should be recorded. The amount is the present value of the lease payments (which were not given in the problem).
6. A liability should be recorded for the present value of the obligation. The amount is determined by using the factor from Table A.1 for $n = 1$, $i = 5\%$: \$100,000 × 0.9524 = \$95,240.
7. A liability should be recorded for the present value of the obligation. The amount is determined by using the factor from Table A.2 for $n = 20$, $i = 8\%$: \$50,000 × 9.8181 = \$490,905.

Chapter Supplement A

Present Value Computations Using Excel

While the present value tables at the end of this book are useful for educational purposes, most present value problems in business are solved with calculators or Excel spreadsheets. Because of the widespread availability of Excel, we will show you how to solve present value problems using Excel. There are slightly different versions of Excel available, depending on the age of the computer.

Present Value of a Single Payment

The calculation of a present value amount is based on a fairly simple mathematical formula:

$$\text{PV} = \text{Payment}/(1 + i)^n$$

In this formula, *payment* is the cash payment made at some point in the future, i is the interest rate each period, and n is the number of periods in the problem. We could use this formula to solve all problems involving the present value of a single payment. It is, of course, easier to use a present value table (like the one at the end of this book) which is derived by solving the present value formula for various interest rates and numbers of periods. Unfortunately, a table that included all interest rates and numbers of periods actually encountered in business would be too large to work with. As a result, most accountants and analysts use Excel to compute a present value.

To compute the present value of a single payment in Excel, you enter the present value formula in a cell, using the format required by Excel. You should select a cell and enter the following formula:

$$= \text{Payment}/(1 + i)\text{^}n$$

To illustrate, if you wanted to solve for the present value of a \$100,000 payment to be made in five years with an interest rate of 10 percent, you would enter the following in the function field:

$$= 100000/(1.10)\text{^}5$$

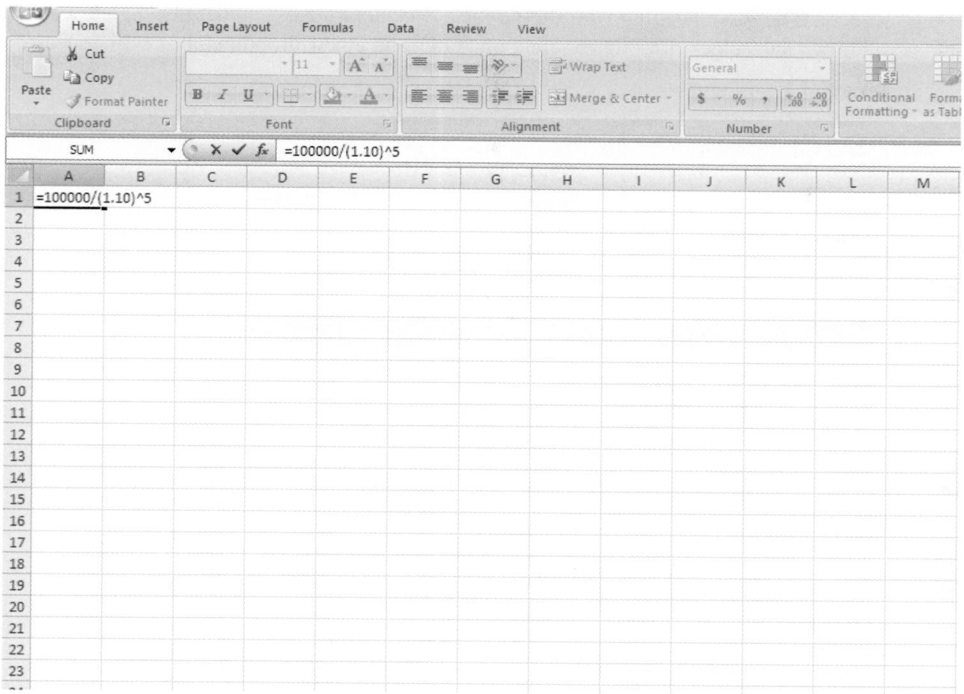

Based on this entry, Excel would compute a present value of $62,092.13. This answer is slightly different than the answer you would have if you used the present value tables at the end of the book. The tables in the book are rounded based on four digits. Excel does not round and, therefore, provides a more accurate computation.

Present Value of an Annuity

The formula for computing the present value of an annuity is a little more complicated than the present value of a single payment. As a result, Excel has been programmed to include the formula so that you do not have to enter it yourself.

To compute the present value of an annuity in Excel, select a cell and click on the insert function button (f_x). The following dropdown box will appear:

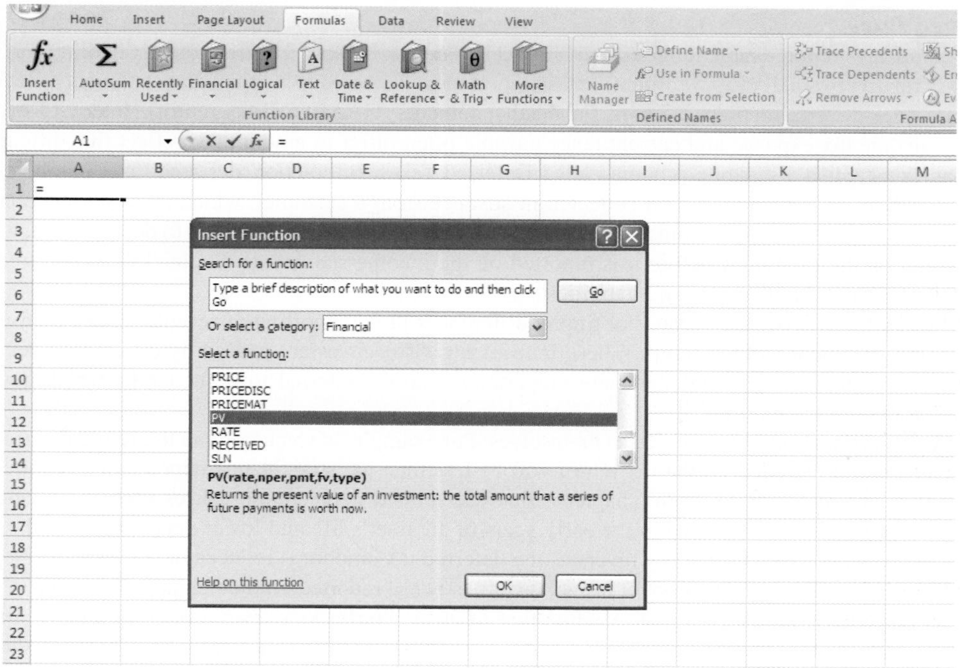

Under the "Select a Category" heading, you should pick "Financial." Next, under the "Select a Function" heading, scroll down and select "PV." Then, click on "OK" and a new dropdown box will appear:

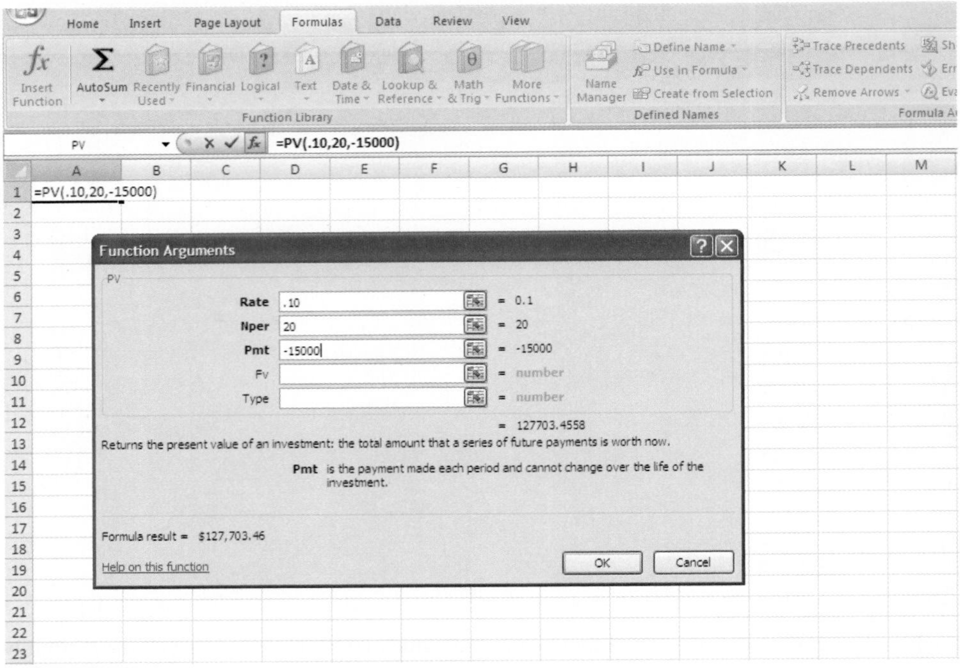

In this box, you should enter the interest rate, 10 percent in this example, under Rate. Notice that the rate must be entered as a decimal (i.e., 0.10) Enter the number of periods (20) under Nper. Excel has an unusual convention associated with the payment. It must be entered as a negative amount (−15000) under Pmt. Notice also that a comma should not be included in the amount you enter. When you click on OK, Excel will enter the present value in the cell you selected. In this example, the value determined by Excel is $127,703.46.

Chapter Supplement B

Deferred Taxes

Most companies report a large long-term liability called *deferred taxes*. The deferred tax liability for Starbucks is relatively small ($39.5 million) and is reported in the notes to its financial statements. Because separate rules govern the preparation of financial statements (GAAP) and tax returns (Internal Revenue Code), income tax expense and current taxes payable often differ in amount. To reflect this difference, companies establish a separate account called Deferred Taxes. In practice, deferred taxes can be either assets (such as taxes related to cash collected in advance from a customer, which is taxable before it is reported as a revenue on the income statement) or liabilities (such as taxes related to depreciation, which is reported on the tax return before it is reported on the income statement). Starbucks has deferred tax amounts reported as both assets and liabilities.

DEFERRED TAX ITEMS exist because of timing differences caused by reporting revenues and expenses according to GAAP on a company's income statement and according to the Internal Revenue Code on the tax return.

Deferred tax items exist because of timing differences in the reporting of revenues and expenses on the income statement and tax return. These **temporary differences** are caused by differences between GAAP, which governs financial statement preparation, and the Internal Revenue Code, which governs the preparation of tax returns.

TEMPORARY DIFFERENCES are timing differences that cause deferred income taxes and will reverse, or turn around, in the future.

Deferred tax amounts always reverse themselves. For example, at some point in the future the accelerated depreciation recorded on the tax return will be less than the straight-line depreciation reported on the income statement (recall from Chapter 8 that accelerated depreciation causes higher depreciation expense compared to straight line in the early years of an asset's life and lower depreciation in the later years). When a deferred tax liability reverses, the deferred tax amount is reduced, and the company pays more taxes to the IRS than the amount of income tax expense reported on the income statement.

Let's consider a simple example. Assume that in 2011, Starbucks owned a building that originally cost $10 million. The current book value (cost less accumulated depreciation) on the balance sheet is

$8.5 million. For tax purposes, the book value is $6.5 million. The $2 million difference is caused by using straight-line depreciation for financial reporting and accelerated depreciation for tax purposes. Starbucks has been able to delay or defer paying federal income taxes by reporting more depreciation on its tax return than it did on its income statement. The amount of deferred tax liability is computed by multiplying the timing difference by the corporate tax rate (34%):

Deferred Tax Liability = $2 million × 34% = $680,000

If there were no other deferred tax items, Starbucks would report a deferred tax liability on its balance sheet of $680,000.

At the end of the following year, 2012, Starbucks would again compare the tax book value and the GAAP book value of the building. Assume that the tax book value of the building was $6 million and the GAAP book value was $8.2 million. The timing difference would be $2.2 million, resulting in a deferred tax liability of $748,000 ($2.2 million × 34%).

The income tax expense reported under GAAP is the amount needed to complete a journal entry once the company has computed its income tax payment for the year and the change in its deferred taxes. Based on our example, the change in the deferred tax liability for Starbucks in 2012 was $68,000 ($748,000 − $680,000). Assume the company completed its tax return and determined it owed the IRS $550,000 for the year. The company would record the following:

Income tax expense (+E, −SE)	618,000	
Deferred taxes (+L)		68,000
Income taxes payable (+L)		550,000

Assets	=	Liabilities		+	Stockholders' Equity	
		Deferred taxes	+68,000		Income tax expense (+E)	−618,000
		Income taxes payable	+550,000			

The computation of deferred taxes involves some complexities that are discussed in advanced accounting courses. At this point, you need to understand only that deferred tax assets and liabilities are caused by temporary differences between the income statement and tax return. Each temporary difference has an impact on the income statement in one accounting period and on the tax return in another.

Chapter Supplement C

Future Value Concepts

Future value problems are similar to present value problems in the sense that they are both based on the time value of money. As we saw earlier, a present value problem determines the current cash equivalent of an amount to be received in the future. In comparison, a **future value** is the sum to which an amount will increase as the result of compound interest. The following table illustrates the basic difference between present value and future value problems:

The FUTURE VALUE is the sum to which an amount will increase as the result of compound interest.

	Now	Future
Present value	?	$1,000
Future value	$1,000	?

Future Value of a Single Amount

In future value of a single amount problems, you are asked to calculate how much money you will have in the future as the result of investing a certain amount in the present. If you were to receive a gift of $10,000, for instance, you might decide to put it in a savings account and use the money as a down payment on a house after you graduate. The future value computation would tell you how much money would be available when you graduate.

To solve a future value problem, you need to know three items:

1. Amount to be invested.
2. Interest rate (i) the amount will earn.
3. Number of periods (n) in which the amount will earn interest.

Since the future value concept is based on compound interest, the amount of interest for each period is calculated by multiplying the principal plus any interest not paid out in prior periods. Graphically, the calculation of the future value of $1 for three periods and an interest rate of 10 percent may be represented as follows:

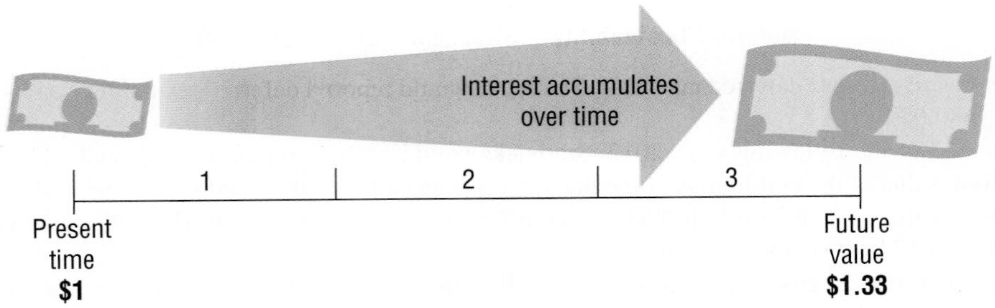

Assume that on January 1, 2011, you deposit $1,000 in a savings account at 10 percent annual interest, compounded annually. At the end of three years, the $1,000 will have increased to $1,331 as follows:

Year	Amount at Start of Year	+	Interest During the Year	=	Amount at End of Year
1	$1,000	+	$1,000 × 10% = $100	=	$1,100
2	1,100	+	1,100 × 10% = $110	=	1,210
3	1,210	+	1,210 × 10% = $121	=	1,331

We can avoid the detailed arithmetic by referring to Table A.3, Future Value of $1. For $i = 10\%$, $n = 3$, we find the value 1.331. We then compute the balance at the end of year 3 as follows:

$1,000 × 1.3310 = $1,331

From Table A.3, Interest rate = 10%, n = 3

Note that the increase of $331 is due to the time value of money. It is interest revenue to the owner of the savings account and interest expense to the savings institution.

Future Value of an Annuity

If you are saving money for some purpose, such as to finance a new car or a trip to Europe, you might decide to deposit a fixed amount of money in a savings account each month. The future value of an annuity computation will tell you how much money will be in your savings account at some point in the future.

The future value of an annuity includes compound interest on each payment from the date of payment to the end of the term of the annuity. Each new payment accumulates less interest than prior payments, only because the number of periods remaining in which to accumulate interest decreases. The future value of an annuity of $1 for three periods at 10 percent may be represented graphically as:

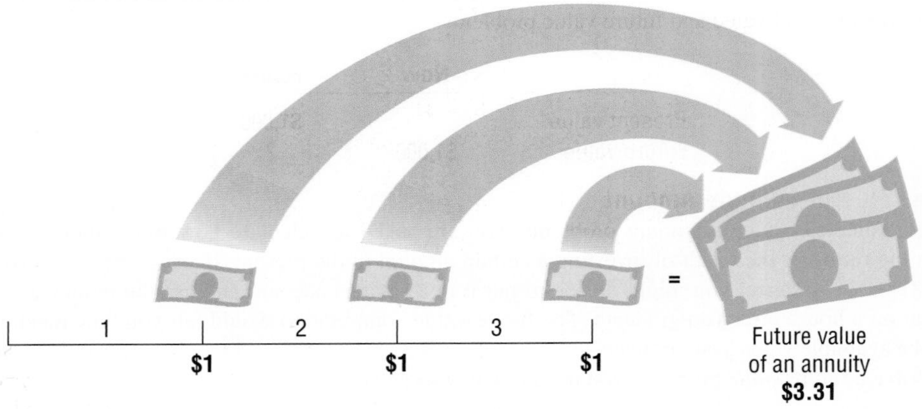

Assume that each year for three years, you deposit $1,000 cash in a savings account at 10 percent interest per year. You make the first $1,000 deposit on December 31, 2011, the second one on December 31, 2012, and the third and last one on December 31, 2013. The first $1,000 deposit earns compound interest for two years (for a total principal and interest of \$1,210); the second deposit earns interest for one year (for a total principal and interest of \$1,100). The third deposit earns no interest because it was made on the day that the balance is computed. Thus, the total amount in the savings account at the end of three years is \$3,310 (\$1,210 + \$1,100 + \$1,000).

To derive the future value of this annuity, we could compute the interest on each deposit. However, we can refer to Table A.4, Appendix A, Future Value of an Annuity of \$1 for $i = 10\%$, $n = 3$ to find the value 3.3100. The future value of your three deposits of \$1,000 each can be computed as follows:

$$\$1{,}000 \times 3.3100 = \$3{,}310$$

From Table A.4, Interest rate = 10%, $n = 3$

The Power of Compounding

Compound interest is a remarkably powerful economic force. Indeed, the ability to earn interest on interest is the key to building economic wealth. If you save \$1,000 per year for the first 10 years of your career, you will have more money when you retire than you would if you had saved \$15,000 per year for the last 10 years of your career. This surprising outcome occurs because the money you save early in your career will earn more interest than the money you save at the end of your career. If you start saving money now, the majority of your wealth will not be the money you saved but the interest your money was able to earn.

The chart in the margin illustrates the power of compounding over a brief 10-year period. If you deposit \$1 each year in an account earning 10 percent interest, at the end of just 10 years, only 64 percent of your balance will be made up of money you have saved; the rest will be interest you have earned. After 20 years, only 35 percent of your balance will be from saved money. The lesson associated with compound interest is clear: Even though saving money is difficult, you should start now.

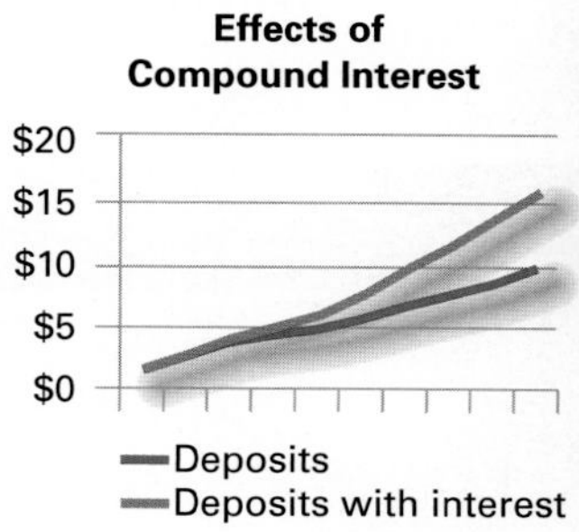

CHAPTER TAKE-AWAYS

1. **Define, measure, and report current liabilities.** p. 457

   Strictly speaking, accountants define liabilities as probable future sacrifices of economic benefits that arise from past transactions. They are classified on the balance sheet as either current or long term. Current liabilities are short-term obligations that will be paid within the current operating cycle of the business or within one year of the balance sheet date, whichever is longer. Long-term liabilities are all obligations not classified as current.

2. **Use the quick ratio.** p. 458

   The quick ratio is a comparison of quick assets and current liabilities. Analysts use this ratio to assess the liquidity of a company.

3. **Analyze the accounts payable turnover ratio.** p. 460

   This ratio is computed by dividing cost of goods sold by average accounts payable. It shows how quickly management is paying its trade creditors and is considered to be a measure of liquidity.

4. **Report notes payable and explain the time value of money.** p. 463

   A note payable specifies the amount borrowed, when it must be repaid, and the interest rate associated with the debt. Accountants must report the debt and the interest as it accrues. The time value of money refers to the fact that interest accrues on borrowed money with the passage of time.

5. **Report contingent liabilities.** p. 465

   A contingent liability is a potential liability that has arisen as the result of a past event. Such liabilities are disclosed in a note if the obligation is reasonably possible.

6. **Explain the importance of working capital and its impact on cash flows.** p. 467

   Working capital is used to fund the operating activities of a business. Changes in working capital accounts affect the statement of cash flows. Cash flows from operating activities are increased by decreases in current assets (other than cash) or increases in current liabilities. Cash flows from operating activities are decreased by increases in current assets (other than cash) or decreases in current liabilities.

7. **Report long-term liabilities.** p. 469

   Usually, long-term liabilities will be paid in more than one year in the future. Accounting for long-term debt is based on the same concepts used in accounting for short-term debt.

8. Compute present values. p. 471

The present value concept is based on the time value of money. Simply stated, a dollar to be received in the future is worth less than a dollar available today (present value). This concept can be applied either to a single payment or multiple payments called *annuities*. Either present value tables or Excel can be used to determine present values.

9. Apply present value concepts to liabilities. p. 475

Accountants use present value concepts to determine the reported amounts of liabilities. A liability involves the payment of some amount at a future date. The reported liability is not the amount of the future payment. Instead, the liability is reported at the amount of the present value of the future payment.

In this chapter, we focused on current liabilities and introduced you to present value concepts. In the next chapter, we will use present value concepts to measure long-term liabilities. We will also discuss long-term liabilities in the context of the capital structure of the company.

KEY RATIOS

Quick ratio measures the ability of a company to pay its current obligations. It is computed as follows (p. 458):

$$\text{Quick Ratio} = \frac{\text{Quick Assets}}{\text{Current Liabilities}}$$

Accounts payable turnover is a measure of how quickly a company pays its creditors. It is computed as follows (p. 460):

$$\text{Accounts Payable Turnover} = \frac{\text{Costs of Goods Sold}}{\text{Average Accounts Payable}}$$

FINDING FINANCIAL INFORMATION

Balance Sheet

Under Current Liabilities
Liabilities listed by account title, such as
- Accounts payable
- Accrued liabilities
- Notes payable

Current portion of long-term debt

Under Noncurrent Liabilities
Liabilities listed by account title, such as
- Long-term debt
- Deferred taxes
- Bonds

Income Statement

Liabilities are shown only on the balance sheet, never on the income statement. Transactions affecting liabilities often affect an income statement account. For example, accrued salary compensation affects an income statement account (compensation expense) and a balance sheet account (salaries payable).

Statement of Cash Flows

Under Operating Activities (indirect method)
Net income
+ Increases in most current liabilities
− Decreases in most current liabilities

Under Financing Activities
+ Increases in long-term liabilities
− Decreases in long-term liabilities

Notes

Under Summary of Significant Accounting Policies
Description of pertinent information concerning accounting treatment of liabilities. Normally, there is minimal information.

Under a Separate Note
If not listed on the balance sheet, a listing of the major classifications of liabilities with information about maturities and interest rates. Information about contingent liabilities is reported in the notes.

KEY TERMS

Accrued Liabilities p. 460
Annuity p. 473
Capital Lease p. 471
Contingent Liability p. 466
Current Liabilities p. 457
Deferred Revenues p. 465
Deferred Tax Items p. 480
Future Value p. 481
Liabilities p. 457
Liquidity p. 458
Long-Term Liabilities p. 469
Operating Lease p. 470
Present Value p. 471
Temporary Differences p. 480
Time Value of Money p. 463
Working Capital p. 467

QUESTIONS

1. Define *liability.* Differentiate between a current liability and a long-term liability.
2. How can external parties be informed about the liabilities of a business?
3. Liabilities are measured and reported at their current cash equivalent amount. Explain.
4. A *liability* is a known obligation of either a definite or an estimated amount. Explain.
5. Define *working capital.* How is it computed?
6. What is the quick ratio? How is it related to the classification of liabilities?
7. Define *accrued liability.* What type of entry usually reflects an accrued liability?
8. Define *deferred revenue.* Why is it a liability?
9. Define *note payable.* Differentiate between a secured and an unsecured note.
10. What is a contingent liability? How is a contingent liability reported?
11. Compute 2011 interest expense for the following note: face, \$4,000; 12 percent interest; date of note, April 1, 2011.
12. Explain the concept of the time value of money.
13. Explain the basic difference between future value and present value.
14. If you hold a valid contract that will pay you \$8,000 cash in 10 years and the going rate of interest is 10 percent, what is its present value? Show your computations.
15. What is an annuity?
16. Complete the following schedule:

	Table Values
Concept	$i = 5\%, n = 4; i = 10\%, n = 7;\ i = 14\%, n = 10$
PV of \$1	
PV of annuity of \$1	

17. You purchased an XIT auto for \$18,000 by making a \$3,000 cash payment and six semiannual installment payments for the balance at 12 percent interest. Determine the amount of each payment.

MULTIPLE-CHOICE QUESTIONS

1. What is the present value factor for an annuity of five periods and an interest rate of 10 percent?
   a. 1.6105
   b. 6.1051
   c. 3.7908
   d. 7.7217
2. The university spirit organization needs to buy a car to travel to football games. A dealership in Lockhart has agreed to the following terms: \$4,000 down plus 20 monthly payments of \$750. A dealership in Leander will agree to a \$1,000 down payment plus 20 monthly payments of \$850. The local bank is currently charging an annual interest rate of 12 percent for car loans. Which is the better deal, *and why*?

a. The Leander offer is better because the total payments of $18,000 are less than the total payments of $19,000 to be made to the Lockhart dealership.
b. The Lockhart offer is better because the cost in terms of present value is less than the present value cost of the Leander offer.
c. The Lockhart offer is better because the monthly payments are less.
d. The Leander offer is better because the cash down payment is less.
e. The Leander offer is better because the cost in terms of present value is less than the present value cost of the Lockhart offer.

3. Which of the following best describes *accrued liabilities*?
a. Long-term liabilities.
b. Current amounts owed to suppliers of inventory.
c. Current liabilities to be recognized as revenue in a future period.
d. Current amounts owed to various parties excluding suppliers of inventory.

4. Company X has borrowed $100,000 from the bank to be repaid over the next five years, with payments beginning next month. Which of the following best describes the presentation of this debt in the balance sheet as of today (the date of borrowing)?
a. $100,000 in the Long-Term Liability section.
b. $100,000 plus the interest to be paid over the five-year period in the Long-Term Liability section.
c. A portion of the $100,000 in the Current Liability section and the remainder of the principal in the Long-Term Liability section.
d. A portion of the $100,000 plus interest in the Current Liability section and the remainder of the principal plus interest in the Long-Term Liability section.

5. A company is facing a class-action lawsuit in the upcoming year. It is possible, but not probable, that the company will have to pay a settlement of approximately $2,000,000. How would this fact be reported in the financial statements to be issued at the end of the current month?
a. $2,000,000 in the Current Liability section.
b. $2,000,000 in the Long-Term Liability section.
c. In a descriptive narrative in the footnote section.
d. None because disclosure is not required.

6. Which of the following transactions would usually cause accounts payable turnover to increase?
a. Payment of cash to a supplier for merchandise previously purchased on credit.
b. Collection of cash from a customer.
c. Purchase of merchandise on credit.
d. None of the above.

7. How is working capital calculated?
a. Current assets multiplied by current liabilities.
b. Current assets plus current liabilities.
c. Current assets minus current liabilities.
d. Current assets divided by current liabilities.

8. The present value of an annuity of $10,000 per year for 10 years discounted at 8 percent is what amount?
a. $5,002
b. $67,101
c. $53,349
d. $80,000

9. Jacobs Company borrowed 100,000 at 8 percent interest for three months. How much interest does the company owe at the end of three months?
a. $8,000
b. $2,000
c. $800
d. $200

10. Fred wants to save enough money each year so that he can purchase a sports car in January 2013. Fred receives a large bonus from his employer every December 31. He anticipates that the car will cost $54,000 on January 1, 2013. Which of the following will Fred need to calculate how much he must save each December 31?
a. The anticipated interest rate and the present value of $1 table.
b. The anticipated interest rate and the future value of $1 table.
c. The anticipated interest rate and the present value table for annuities.
d. The anticipated interest rate and the future value table for annuities.

For more practice with multiple-choice questions, go to the text website at **www.mhhe.com/libby7e**.

connect ACCOUNTING

MINI-EXERCISES

Computing Interest Expense

M9-1
LO4

Kieso Company borrowed $600,000 on a 90-day note at 11 percent interest. The money was borrowed for 30 days in 2011 and 60 days in 2012; the note and interest were to be paid upon maturity in 2012. How much interest expense, if any, would be reported in 2011 and in 2012?

Recording a Note Payable

M9-2
LO4

Wygant Corporation borrowed $290,000 on October 1, 2011. The note carried a 10 percent interest rate with the principal and interest payable on May 1, 2012. Prepare the journal entry to record the note on October 1. Prepare the adjusting entry to record accrued interest on December 31.

Finding Financial Information

M9-3
LO1, 3, 6

For each of the following items, specify whether the information would be found in the balance sheet, the income statement, the statement of cash flows, the notes to the statements, or not at all.

1. The amount of working capital.
2. The total amount of current liabilities.
3. Information concerning company pension plans.
4. The accounts payable turnover ratio.
5. Information concerning the impact of changes in working capital on cash flows for the period.

Computing Measures of Liquidity

M9-4
LO2

The balance sheet for Stevenson Corporation reported the following: quick assets, $20,000; noncurrent assets, $240,000; total assets, $360,000; noncurrent liabilities, $176,000; total stockholders' equity, $94,000. Compute Stevenson's quick ratio and working capital.

Analyzing the Impact of Transactions on Liquidity

M9-5
LO2

Ospry, Inc., has a quick ratio of 0.50 and working capital in the amount of $1,240,000. For each of the following transactions, determine whether the quick ratio and working capital will increase, decrease, or remain the same.

a. Paid accounts payable in the amount of $50,000.
b. Recorded accrued salaries in the amount of $100,000.
c. Borrowed $250,000 from a local bank, to be repaid in 90 days.
d. Purchased $20,000 of new inventory on credit.

Reporting Contingent Liabilities

M9-6
LO5

Buzz Coffee Shops is famous for its large servings of hot coffee. After a famous case involving McDonald's, the lawyer for Buzz warned management (during 2011) that it could be sued if someone were to spill hot coffee and be burned: "With the temperature of your coffee, I can guarantee it's just a matter of time before you're sued for $1,000,000." Unfortunately, in 2012 the prediction came true when a customer filed suit. The case went to trial in 2013, and the jury awarded the customer $400,000 in damages, which the company immediately appealed. During 2014 the customer and the company settled their dispute for $150,000. What is the proper reporting of this liability each year?

Computing the Present Value of a Single Payment

M9-7
LO8

What is the present value of $500,000 to be paid in 10 years with an interest rate of 8 percent?

Computing the Present Value of an Annuity

M9-8
LO8

What is the present value of 10 equal payments of $15,000 with an interest rate of 10 percent?

M9-9
LO8

Computing the Present Value of a Complex Contract

As a result of a slowdown in operations, Global Stores is offering employees who have been terminated a severance package of $118,000 cash, another $129,000 to be paid in one year, and an annuity of $27,500 to be paid each year for six years beginning in one year. What is the present value of the package, assuming an interest rate of 5 percent?

M9-10

Computing the Future Value of an Annuity (Supplement C)

You plan to retire in 10 years. Would it be better for you to save $27,500 a year for the last five years before retirement or $16,250 for each of the 10 years? You are able to earn 9 percent interest on your investments.

M9-11

Making a Complex Computation of a Future Value (Supplement C)

You want a retirement fund of $125,000 when you retire in six years. You are able to earn 8 percent on your investments. How much should you deposit each year to build the retirement fund that you want?

EXERCISES

E9-1
LO1, 2, 5, 6

Computing Working Capital; Explaining the Quick Ratio and Working Capital

Diane Corporation is preparing its 2012 balance sheet. The company records show the following selected amounts at the end of the accounting period, December 31, 2012:

Total assets	$530,000
Total noncurrent assets	362,000
Liabilities:	
Notes payable (8%, due in 5 years)	15,000
Accounts payable	56,000
Income taxes payable	14,000
Liability for withholding taxes	3,000
Rent revenue collected in advance	7,000
Bonds payable (due in 15 years)	90,000
Wages payable	7,000
Property taxes payable	3,000
Note payable (10%, due in 6 months)	12,000
Interest payable	400
Common stock	100,000

Required:

1. Compute (*a*) working capital and (*b*) the quick ratio (quick assets are $70,000). Why is working capital important to management? How do financial analysts use the quick ratio?
2. Would your computations be different if the company reported $250,000 worth of contingent liabilities in the notes to the statements? Explain.

E9-2
LO1

Recording Payroll Costs

Paul Company completed the salary and wage payroll for March 2011. The payroll provided the following details:

Salaries and wages earned	$200,000
Employee income taxes withheld	40,000
Insurance premiums withheld	1,000
FICA payroll taxes*	15,000

**$15,000 each for employer and employees.*

Required:

1. Give the journal entry to record the payroll for March, including employee deductions.
2. Give the journal entry to record the employer's payroll taxes.
3. Give a combined journal entry to show the payment of amounts owed to governmental agencies.

Computing Payroll Costs; Discussion of Labor Costs

E9-3
LO1

Oaks Company has completed the payroll for January 2012, reflecting the following data:

Salaries and wages earned	\$86,000
Employee income taxes withheld	10,000
FICA payroll taxes*	6,000

**Assessed on both employer and employee (i.e., \$6,000 each).*

Required:

1. What amount of additional labor expense to the company was due to tax laws? What was the amount of the employees' take-home pay?
2. List the liabilities and their amounts reported on the company's January 31, 2012, balance sheet, assuming the employees have been paid.
3. Would employers react differently to a 10 percent increase in the employer's share of FICA than to a 10 percent increase in the basic level of salaries? Would financial analysts react differently?

Recording a Note Payable through Its Time to Maturity with Discussion of Management Strategy

E9-4
LO1, 4

Many businesses borrow money during periods of increased business activity to finance inventory and accounts receivable. Neiman Marcus is one of America's most prestigious retailers. Each Christmas season, Neiman Marcus builds up its inventory to meet the needs of Christmas shoppers. A large portion of these Christmas sales are on credit. As a result, Neiman Marcus often collects cash from the sales several months after Christmas. Assume that on November 1, 2011, Neiman Marcus borrowed \$4.8 million cash from Texas Capital Bank for working capital purposes and signed an interest-bearing note due in six months. The interest rate was 8 percent per annum payable at maturity. The accounting period ends December 31.

Required:

1. Give the journal entry to record the note on November 1.
2. Give any adjusting entry required at the end of the annual accounting period.
3. Give the journal entry to record payment of the note and interest on the maturity date, April 30, 2012.
4. If Neiman Marcus needs extra cash during every Christmas season, should management borrow money on a long-term basis to avoid the necessity of negotiating a new short-term loan each year?

Determining Financial Statement Effects of Transactions Involving Notes Payable

E9-5
LO1, 4

Using the data from the previous exercise, complete the following requirements.

Required:

1. Determine the financial statement effects for each of the following: (*a*) issuance of the note on November 1, (*b*) the impact of the adjusting entry at the end of the accounting period, and (*c*) payment of the note and interest on April 30, 2012. Indicate the effects (e.g., cash + or −) using the following schedule:
2. If Neiman Marcus needs extra cash during every Christmas season, should management borrow money on a long-term basis to avoid the necessity of negotiating a new short-term loan each year?

Date	Assets	Liabilities	Stockholders' Equity

Reporting Short-Term Borrowings

E9-6
LO1

PepsiCo, Inc., manufactures a number of products that are part of our daily lives. Its businesses include Pepsi, Frito-Lay, Tropicana, Quaker, and Gatorade. The company's annual revenues exceed \$22 billion. A recent PepsiCo annual report contained the following information:

At the end of the current year, \$3.6 billion of short-term borrowings were classified as long-term, reflecting PepsiCo's intent and ability to refinance these borrowings on a long-term basis, through either long-term debt issuances or rollover of existing short-term borrowings. The significant amount of short-term borrowings classified as long-term, as compared to the end of the previous year when no such amounts were reclassified, primarily reflects the large commercial paper issuances in the current year but also resulted from a refined analysis of amounts expected to be refinanced beyond one year.

Required:
As an analyst, comment on the company's classification of short-term borrowings as long-term liabilities. What conditions should exist to permit a company to make this type of classification?

E9-7 LO2 Using the Quick Ratio

Super Savers Department Store reported a quick ratio of 0.6. A review of its balance sheet revealed the following information:

Quick assets	$120,000
Current assets	750,000
Noncurrent assets	450,000
Noncurrent liabilities	300,000

Determine the amount of current liabilities reported in the balance sheet.

E9-8 LO1, 4, 6 Determining the Impact of Transactions, Including Analysis of Cash Flows

Vernon Company sells a wide range of goods through two retail stores operated in adjoining cities. Most purchases of goods for resale are on invoices. Occasionally, a short-term note payable is used to obtain cash for current use. The following transactions were selected from those occurring during 2012:

a. Purchased merchandise on credit, $18,000 on January 10, 2012; the company uses a periodic inventory system.
b. Borrowed $45,000 cash on March 1, 2012, from City Bank and gave an interest-bearing note payable: face amount, $45,000, due at the end of six months, with an annual interest rate of 10 percent payable at maturity.

Required:
1. Describe the impact of each transaction on the balance sheet equation. Indicate the effects (e.g., cash + or −), using the following schedule:

Date	Assets	Liabilities	Stockholders' Equity

2. What amount of cash is paid on the maturity date of the note?
3. Discuss the impact of each transaction on Vernon's cash flows.

E9-9 LO7 McDonald's Reporting a Liability

McDonald's is one of the world's most popular fast-food restaurants, offering good food and convenient locations. Effective management of its properties is a key to its success. As the following note in its current annual report indicates, McDonald's both owns and leases property:

The Company owns and leases real estate primarily in connection with its restaurant business. The Company identifies and develops sites that offer convenience to customers and long-term sales and profit potential to the Company. The Company generally owns the land and building or secures long-term leases for restaurant sites, which ensures long-term occupancy rights and helps control related costs.

Required:
Should McDonald's report lease obligations on its balance sheet? Explain. If the obligation should be reported as a liability, how should the amount be measured?

E9-10 LO7 Evaluating Lease Alternatives

As the new vice president for consumer products at Heffner Manufacturing, you are attending a meeting to discuss a serious problem associated with delivering merchandise to customers. Bob Smith, director of logistics, summarized the problem: "It's easy to understand, we just don't have enough delivery trucks given our recent growth." Barb Bader from the accounting department responded: "Maybe it's easy to understand but it's impossible to do anything. Because of Wall Street's concern about the amount of debt on our balance sheet, we're under a freeze and can't borrow money to acquire new assets. There's nothing we can do."

On the way back to your office after the meeting, your assistant offers a suggestion: "Why don't we just lease the trucks we need? That way we can get the assets we want without having to record a liability on the balance sheet."

How would you respond to this suggestion?

Reporting a Liability, with Discussion

E9-11
LO7

American Airlines

The annual report for American Airlines contained the following information:

In addition to pension benefits, other postretirement benefits, including certain health care and life insurance benefits (which provide secondary coverage to Medicare), are provided to retired employees. The amount of health care benefits is limited to lifetime maximums as outlined in the plan. Substantially all regular employees of American and employees of certain other subsidiaries may become eligible for these benefits if they satisfy eligibility requirements during their working lives.

Required:
Should American report a liability for these benefits on its balance sheet? Explain.

Computing Deferred Income Tax (Supplement B)

E9-12

The following information pertains to the Lewis Corporation.

	Year 2011	Year 2012
Income taxes payable	$250,000	$290,000
Increase in deferred tax liability	54,000	58,000

Required:
1. For each year, compute income tax expense (assume that no taxes have been paid).
2. Explain why tax expense is not simply the amount of cash paid during the year.

Recording Deferred Income Tax (Supplement B)

E9-13

The balance sheet for Nair Corporation provided the following summarized pretax data:

	Year 2011	Year 2012
Deferred tax liability	$355,000	$463,000

The income statement reported tax expense for 2012 in the amount of $580,000.

Required:
1. What was the amount of income taxes payable for 2012?
2. Why would management want to incur the cost of maintaining separate tax and financial accounting records?

Reporting Deferred Income Taxes (Supplement B)

E9-14

Starbucks

The annual report for Starbucks contains the following information (in millions):

Income Taxes
The provision for income taxes consisted of the following (in millions):

	2008	2007	2006
Current income taxes	$255.1	$423.2	$402.4
Deferred Taxes	(111.1)	(39.5)	(77.6)
Total	$144.0	$383.7	$324.8

Required:

1. Determine whether tax expense is higher or lower than taxes payable for each year.
2. Is the deferred tax liability reported on the 2008 balance sheet $111.1 million? Explain.

E9-15 **Computing Four Present Value Problems**
LO8

On January 1, 2011, Shannon Company completed the following transactions (assume a 10 percent annual interest rate):

a. Bought a delivery truck and agreed to pay $50,000 at the end of three years.
b. Rented an office building and was given the option of paying $10,000 at the end of each of the next three years or paying $28,000 immediately.
c. Established a savings account by depositing a single amount that will increase to $40,000 at the end of seven years.
d. Decided to deposit a single sum in the bank that will provide 10 equal annual year-end payments of $15,000 to a retired employee (payments starting December 31, 2011).

Required (show computations and round to the nearest dollar):

1. In (*a*), what is the cost of the truck that should be recorded at the time of purchase?
2. In (*b*), which option for the office building should the company select?
3. In (*c*), what single amount must be deposited in this account on January 1, 2011?
4. In (*d*), what single sum must be deposited in the bank on January 1, 2011?

E9-16 **Using Present Value Concepts for Decision Making**
LO8

You have just won the state lottery and have two choices for collecting your winnings. You can collect $50,000 today or receive $10,100 per year for the next seven years. A financial analyst has told you that you can earn 10 percent on your investments. Which alternative should you select?

E9-17 **Calculating a Retirement Fund**
LO8

You are a financial adviser working with a client who wants to retire in eight years. The client has a savings account with a local bank that pays 9 percent and she wants to deposit an amount that will provide her with $900,000 when she retires. Currently, she has $200,000 in the account. How much additional money should she deposit now to provide her with $900,000 when she retires?

E9-18 **Determining an Educational Fund**
LO8

Judge Drago has decided to set up an educational fund for his favorite granddaughter, Emma, who will start college in one year. The judge plans to deposit an amount in a savings account that pays 9 percent interest. He wants to deposit an amount that is sufficient to permit Emma to withdraw $13,000 starting in one year and continuing each year for a total of four years. How much should he deposit today to provide Emma with a fund to pay for her college tuition?

E9-19 **Computing a Present Value**
LO8

An investment will pay $11,000 at the end of the first year, $30,000 at the end of the second year, and $50,000 at the end of the third year. Determine the present value of this investment using a 10 percent interest rate.

E9-20 **Computing a Present Value**
LO8

An investment will pay $15,000 at the end of each year for eight years and a one-time payment of $120,000 at the end of the eighth year. Determine the present value of this investment using a 7 percent interest rate.

E9-21 **Determining the Value of an Asset**
LO8

Smith Company has purchased a new office building. The company has agreed to pay the developer $55,000 annually for 9 years. Using present value techniques, determine the value that should be recorded for the building when it is purchased. Assume a 6 percent annual interest rate.

Computing the Value of an Asset Based on Present Value

E9-22
L08

You have the chance to purchase the royalty interest in a gas well in the Barnett Shale. Your best estimate is that the net royalty income will average $25,000 per year for seven years. There will be no residual value at that time. Considering the uncertainty in your estimates, you expect to earn 9 percent per year on the investment. What should you be willing to pay for this investment now?

Computing Growth in a Savings Account: A Single Amount (Supplement C)

E9-23

On January 1, 2011, you deposited $6,000 in a savings account. The account will earn 10 percent annual compound interest, which will be added to the fund balance at the end of each year.

Required (round to the nearest dollar):

1. What will be the balance in the savings account at the end of 10 years?
2. What is the amount of interest earned during the 10 years?
3. How much interest revenue did the fund earn in 2011? 2012?

Computing Deposit Required and Accounting for a Single-Sum Savings Account (Supplement C)

E9-24

On January 1, 2011, Alan King decided to deposit $58,800 in a savings account that will provide funds four years later to send his son to college. The savings account will earn 8 percent, which will be added to the fund each year-end.

Required (show computations and round to the nearest dollar):

1. How much will be available in four years?
2. Give the journal entry that Alan should make on January 1, 2011.
3. What is the interest for the four years?
4. Give the journal entry that Alan should make on (*a*) December 31, 2011, and (*b*) December 31, 2012.

Recording Growth in a Savings Account with Equal Periodic Payments (Supplement C)

E9-25

On each December 31, you plan to deposit $2,000 in a savings account. The account will earn 9 percent annual interest, which will be added to the fund balance at year-end. The first deposit will be made December 31, 2011 (end of period).

Required (show computations and round to the nearest dollar):

1. Give the required journal entry on December 31, 2011.
2. What will be the balance in the savings account at the end of the 10th year (i.e., after 10 deposits)?
3. What is the interest earned on the 10 deposits?
4. How much interest revenue did the fund earn in 2012? 2013?
5. Give all required journal entries at the end of 2012 and 2013.

Computing Growth for a Savings Fund with Periodic Deposits (Supplement C)

E9-26

On January 1, 2011, you plan to take a trip around the world upon graduation four years from now. Your grandmother wants to deposit sufficient funds for this trip in a savings account for you. On the basis of a budget, you estimate that the trip currently would cost $15,000. To be generous, your grandmother decides to deposit $3,500 in the fund at the end of each of the next four years, starting on December 31, 2011. The savings account will earn 6 percent annual interest, which will be added to the savings account at each year-end.

Required (show computations and round to the nearest dollar):

1. How much money will you have for the trip at the end of year 4 (i.e., after four deposits)?
2. What is the interest for the four years?
3. How much interest revenue did the fund earn in 2011, 2012, 2013, and 2014?

For more practice with exercises, go to the text website at **www.mhhe.com/libby7e**.

PROBLEMS

connect ACCOUNTING

P9-1 Recording and Reporting Current Liabilities
LO1

Vigeland Company completed the following transactions during 2011. The annual accounting period ends December 31, 2011.

Jan.	15	Purchased and paid for merchandise for resale at an invoice cost of $14,200; periodic inventory system.
Apr.	1	Borrowed $700,000 from Summit Bank for general use; executed a 10-month, 8 percent interest-bearing note payable.
June	14	Received a $15,000 customer deposit from Mark Muller for services to be performed in the future.
July	15	Performed $3,750 of the services paid for by Mr. Muller.
Dec.	12	Received electric bill for $27,860. The company will pay it in early January.
	31	Determined wages of $15,000 earned but not yet paid on December 31 (disregard payroll taxes).

Required:
1. Prepare journal entries for each of these transactions.
2. Prepare all adjusting entries required on December 31, 2011.

P9-2 Recording and Reporting Current Liabilities with Discussion of Cash Flow Effects
LO1, 6

Rogers Company completed the following transactions during 2011. The annual accounting period ends December 31, 2011. (AP9-1)

Jan.	8	Purchased merchandise for resale on account at an invoice cost of $14,860; assume a periodic inventory system.
	17	Paid January 8 invoice.
Apr.	1	Borrowed $35,000 from National Bank for general use; executed a 12-month, 12 percent interest-bearing note payable.
June	3	Purchased merchandise for resale on account at an invoice cost of $17,420.
July	5	Paid June 3 invoice.
Aug.	1	Rented a small office in a building owned by the company and collected six months' rent in advance amounting to $6,000. (Record the collection in a way that will not require an adjusting entry at year-end.)
Dec.	20	Received a $100 deposit from a customer as a guarantee to return a large trailer "borrowed" for 30 days.
	31	Determined wages of $9,500 earned but not yet paid on December 31 (disregard payroll taxes).

Required:
1. Prepare journal entries for each of these transactions.
2. Prepare all adjusting entries required on December 31, 2011.
3. Show how all of the liabilities arising from these transactions are reported on the balance sheet at December 31, 2011.
4. For each transaction, state whether cash flow from operating activities is increased or decreased or whether there is no effect.

P9-3 Determining Financial Effects of Transactions Affecting Current Liabilities with Discussion of Cash Flow Effects (AP9-2)
LO1, 6

Using data from the previous problem, complete the following requirements.

Required:

1. For each transaction (including adjusting entries) listed in the previous problem, indicate the effects (e.g., cash + or −), using the following schedule:

Date	Assets	Liabilities	Stockholders' Equity

2. For each transaction, state whether cash flow from operating activities is increased, decreased, or remains the same.

Recording and Reporting Accrued Liabilities and Deferred Revenue with Discussion

P9-4
LO1

During 2012, Walnut Company completed the following two transactions. The annual accounting period ends December 31.

a. Paid and recorded wages of $130,000 during 2012; however, at the end of December 2012, three days' wages are unpaid and unrecorded because the weekly payroll will not be paid until January 6, 2013. Wages for the three days are $4,000.

b. Collected rent revenue on December 10, 2012, of $2,400 for office space that Walnut rented to another party. The rent collected was for 30 days from December 10, 2012, to January 10, 2013, and was credited in full to Rent Revenue.

Required:

1. Give (*a*) the adjusting entry required on December 31, 2012, and (*b*) the January 6, 2013, journal entry for payment of any unpaid wages from December 2012.
2. Give (*a*) the journal entry for the collection of rent on December 10, 2012, and (*b*) the adjusting entry on December 31, 2012.
3. Show how any liabilities related to these transactions should be reported on the company's balance sheet at December 31, 2012.
4. Explain why the accrual method of accounting provides more relevant information to financial analysts than the cash method.

Determining Financial Statement Effects of Transactions Involving Accrued Liabilities and Deferred Revenue

P9-5
LO1

Using the data from the previous exercise, complete the following requirements.

Required:

1. Determine the financial statement effects for each of the following: (*a*) the adjusting entry for accrued wages required on December 31, 2012, (*b*) the January 6, 2013, journal entry for payment of any unpaid wages from December 2012, (*c*) the journal entry for the collection of rent on December 10, 2012, and (*d*) the adjusting entry for rent on December 31, 2012. Indicate the effects (e.g., cash + or −) using the following schedule:

Date	Assets	Liabilities	Stockholders' Equity

2. Explain why the accrual method of accounting provides more relevant information to financial analysts than the cash method.

Determining Financial Statement Effects of Various Liabilities (AP9-3)

P9-6
LO1, 5

Dell Computers is a leader in the industry with over $56 billion in sales each year. A recent annual report for Dell contained the following note:

Warranty

We record warranty liabilities at the time of sale for the estimated costs that may be incurred under its limited warranty. Factors that affect our warranty liability include the number of installed units currently under warranty, historical and anticipated rates of warranty claims on those units, and cost per claim to satisfy our warranty obligation.

1. Assume that estimated warranty costs for 2011 were $500 million and that the warranty work was performed during 2012. Describe the financial statement effects for each year.

The Walt Disney Company

Walt Disney is a well-recognized brand in the entertainment industry with products ranging from broadcast media to parks and resorts. The following note is from a recent annual report:

Revenue Recognition

For non-expiring, multi-day tickets to our theme parks, we recognize revenue over a three-year period based on estimated usage patterns which are derived from historical usage patterns.

2. Assume that Disney collected $90 million in 2011 multi-day tickets that will be used in future years. For 2012, the company estimates that 60 percent of the tickets will be used. Describe the financial statement effects for each year.

Brunswick Corporation

Brunswick Corporation is a multinational company that manufactures and sells marine and recreational products. A recent annual report for Brunswick contained the following information:

Litigation

A jury awarded $44.4 million in damages in a suit brought by Independent Boat Builders, Inc., a buying group of boat manufacturers and its 22 members. Under the antitrust laws, the damage award has been trebled, and the plaintiffs will be entitled to their attorney's fees and interest.

The Company has filed an appeal contending the verdict was erroneous as a matter of law, both as to liability and damages.

3. How should Brunswick account for this litigation?
4. A recent annual report for The Walt Disney Company reported quick assets of $3,562,000,000 and current liabilities of $10,210,000,000. Based on the quick ratio, do you think that Disney is experiencing financial difficulty?

Halliburton

Halliburton is a major corporation involved in the entire life cycle of oil and gas reserves, starting with exploration and development, moving through production, operations, maintenance, conversion, and refining to infrastructure and abandonment. A recent annual report for the company stated the following:

Environmental Expenditures

Our accrued liabilities from environmental matters were $50 million for the current year and $41 million for the previous year.

5. In your own words, explain Halliburton's accounting policy for environmental expenditures. What is the justification for this policy?

P9-7 LO5 Making a Decision as Chief Financial Officer: Contingent Liabilities

For each of the following situations, determine whether the company should (*a*) report a liability on the balance sheet, (*b*) disclose a contingent liability, or (*c*) not report the situation. Justify and explain your conclusions.

1. An automobile company introduces a new car. Past experience demonstrates that lawsuits will be filed as soon as the new model is involved in any accidents. The company can be certain that at least one jury will award damages to people injured in an accident.
2. A research scientist determines that the company's best-selling product may infringe on another company's patent. If the other company discovers the infringement and files suit, your company could lose millions.
3. As part of land development for a new housing project, your company has polluted a natural lake. Under state law, you must clean up the lake once you complete development. The development project will take five to eight years to complete. Current estimates indicate that it will cost $2 to $3 million to clean up the lake.

4. Your company has just been notified that it lost a product liability lawsuit for $1 million that it plans to appeal. Management is confident that the company will win on appeal, but the lawyers believe that it will lose.
5. A key customer is unhappy with the quality of a major construction project. The company believes that the customer is being unreasonable but, to maintain goodwill, has decided to do $250,000 in repairs next year.

Determining Cash Flow Effects (AP9-4)

P9-8
LO6

For each of the following transactions, determine whether cash flows from operating activities will increase, decrease, or remain the same:

a. Purchased merchandise on credit.
b. Paid an account payable in cash.
c. Accrued payroll for the month but did not pay it.
d. Borrowed money from the bank. The term of the note is 90 days.
e. Reclassified a long-term note as a current liability.
f. Paid accrued interest expense.
g. Disclosed a contingent liability based on a pending lawsuit.
h. Paid back the bank for money borrowed in (*d*). Ignore interest.
i. Collected cash from a customer for services that will be performed in the next accounting period (i.e., deferred revenues are recorded).

Analyzing the Reclassification of Debt (AP9-5)

P9-9
LO2, 4

PepsiCo, Inc., is a $25 billion company in the beverage, snack food, and restaurant businesses. PepsiCo's annual report included the following note:

At year-end, $3.5 billion of short-term borrowings were reclassified as long-term, reflecting PepsiCo's intent and ability to refinance these borrowings on a long-term basis, through either long-term debt issuances or rollover of existing short-term borrowings.

As a result of this reclassification, PepsiCo's quick ratio improved from 0.21 to 0.59. Do you think the reclassification was appropriate? Why do you think management made the reclassification? As a financial analyst, would you use the quick ratio before the reclassification or after the reclassification to evaluate PepsiCo's liquidity?

Recording and Reporting Deferred Income Tax: Depreciation (Supplement B)

P9-10
LO7

www.mhhe.com/libby7e

Mansfield Corporation purchased a new warehouse at the beginning of 2011 for $1,000,000. The expected life of the asset is 20 years with no residual value. The company uses straight-line depreciation for financial reporting purposes and accelerated depreciation for tax purposes (assume 10 percent of original cost for this problem). The company's marginal federal income tax rate is 34 percent. The company determined its income tax obligation was as follows: 2011, $400,000; 2012, $625,000.

Required:

1. Compute the deferred income tax amount reported on the balance sheet for each year. Is the deferred income tax a liability or an asset? Explain.
2. Compute income tax expense for each year.

Computing Present Values (AP9-6)

P9-11
LO8, 9

www.mhhe.com/libby7e

On January 1, 2011, Boston Company completed the following transactions (use a 7 percent annual interest rate for all transactions):

a. Borrowed $115,000 for seven years. Will pay $8,050 interest at the end of each year and repay the $115,000 at the end of the 7th year.
b. Established a plant addition fund of $490,000 to be available at the end of year 8. A single sum that will grow to $490,000 will be deposited on January 1, 2011.

c. Agreed to pay a severance package to a discharged employee. The company will pay $75,000 at the end of the first year, $112,500 at the end of the second year, and $150,000 at the end of the third year.

d. Purchased a $170,000 machine on January 1, 2011, and paid cash, $40,000. A five-year note payable is signed for the balance. The note will be paid in five equal year-end payments starting on December 31, 2011.

Required (show computations and round to the nearest dollar):

1. In transaction (*a*), determine the present value of the debt.
2. In transaction (*b*), what single sum amount must the company deposit on January 1, 2011? What is the total amount of interest revenue that will be earned?
3. In transaction (*c*), determine the present value of this obligation.
4. In transaction (*d*), what is the amount of each of the equal annual payments that will be paid on the note? What is the total amount of interest expense that will be incurred?

P9-12 Comparing Options Using Present Value Concepts (AP9-7)

LO8

eXcel

www.mhhe.com/libby7e

After hearing a knock at your front door, you are surprised to see the Prize Patrol from a large, well-known magazine subscription company. It has arrived with the good news that you are the big winner, having won $12.5 million. You discover that you have three options: (1) you can receive $1.25 million per year for the next 10 years, (2) you can have $10 million today, or (3) you can have $2 million today and receive $1 million for each of the next 10 years. Your lawyer tells you that it is reasonable to expect to earn 10 percent on investments. Which option do you prefer? What factors influence your decision?

P9-13 Computing Future Values (Supplement C) (AP9-8)

eXcel

www.mhhe.com/libby7e

On December 31, 2011, Mercury Company created a fund that will be used to pay the principal amount of a $120,000 debt due on December 31, 2014. The company will make four equal annual deposits on each December 31 in 2011, 2012, 2013, and 2014. The fund will earn 7 percent annual interest, which will be added to the balance at each year-end. The fund trustee will pay the loan principal (to the creditor) upon receipt of the last fund deposit. The company's accounting period ends December 31.

Required (show computations and round to the nearest dollar):

1. How much must be deposited each December 31?
2. What amount of interest will be earned?
3. How much interest revenue will the fund earn in 2011, 2012, 2013, and 2014?

P9-14 Computing Future Values (Supplement C)

On January 1, 2011, Spearfish Company completed the following transactions (use an 8 percent annual interest rate for all transactions):

a. Deposited $50,000 in a debt retirement fund. Interest will be computed at six-month intervals and added to the fund at those times (i.e., semiannual compounding). (*Hint:* Think carefully about *n* and *i*.)

b. Established a pension retirement fund to be available by the end of year 6 by making six annual deposits of $130,000 at year-end, starting on December 31, 2011.

c. Deposited $250,000 in a debt retirement fund. Interest will be computed annually and added to the fund at those times.

Required:

1. In transaction (*a*), what will be the balance in the fund at the end of year 3? What is the total amount of interest revenue that will be earned?
2. In transaction (*b*), what is the amount of the retirement fund at the end of year 6? What is the total amount of interest revenue that will be earned?
3. In transaction (*c*), what will be the balance in the fund at the end of year 6? What is the total amount of interest revenue that will be earned?

ALTERNATE PROBLEMS

Recording and Reporting Current Liabilities with Discussion of Cash Flow Effects (P9-2)

AP9-1
LO1, 6

Sturgis Company completed the following transactions during 2012. The annual accounting period ends December 31, 2012.

Jan.	15	Recorded tax expense for the year in the amount of $125,000. Current taxes payable were $93,000.
	31	Paid accrued interest expense in the amount of $52,000.
Apr.	30	Borrowed $550,000 from Commerce Bank; executed a 12-month, 12 percent interest-bearing note payable.
June	3	Purchased merchandise for resale at an invoice cost of $75,820, on account.
July	5	Paid June 3 invoice.
Aug.	31	Signed contract to provide security service to a small apartment complex and collected six months' fees in advance amounting to $12,000. (Record the collection in a way that will not require an adjusting entry at year-end.)
Dec.	31	Reclassified a long-term liability in the amount of $100,000 as a current liability.
	31	Determined salary and wages of $85,000 earned but not yet paid December 31 (disregard payroll taxes).

Required:

1. Prepare journal entries for each of these transactions.
2. Prepare all adjusting entries required on December 31, 2012.
3. Show how all of the liabilities arising from these transactions are reported on the balance sheet at December 31, 2012.
4. For each transaction, state whether cash flow from operating activities is increased or decreased or whether there is no effect.

Determining Financial Effects of Transactions Affecting Current Liabilities with Discussion of Cash Flow Effects (P9-3)

AP9-2
LO1, 6

Using data from problem AP9-1, complete the following requirements.

Required:

1. For each transaction (including adjusting entries) listed in the previous problem, indicate the effects (e.g., cash + or −) using the following schedule:

Date	Assets	Liabilities	Stockholders' Equity

2. For each transaction, state whether cash flow from operating activities is increased or decreased or whether there is no effect.

Determining Financial Statement Effects of Various Liabilities (P9-6)

AP9-3
LO1, 2, 5

Ford

Ford Motor Company is one of the world's largest companies with annual sales of cars and trucks in excess of $170 billion. A recent annual report for Ford contained the following note:

Warranties

Estimated warranty costs are accrued for at the time the vehicle is sold to a dealer. Estimates for warranty cost are made based primarily on historical warranty claim experience.

1. This year, Ford reported claims amounting to $4.0 billion and accrued expenses for warranties in the amount of $3.9 billion. Describe the financial statement effects for this year.

Bally

Bally Total Fitness Holding Corporation is the largest publicly traded commercial operator of fitness centers in North America in terms of members, revenues, and square footage of its facilities.

The company operates 409 fitness centers primarily under the Bally Total Fitness name. The following note was contained in a recent annual report for Bally.

Revenue Recognition

As a general principle, revenue is recognized when the following criteria are met: (i) persuasive evidence of an arrangement exists, (ii) delivery has occurred and services have been rendered, (iii) the price to the buyer is fixed or determinable and, (iv) collectability is reasonably assured. Membership revenue is earned on a straight-line basis over the longer of the contractual term or the estimated membership term. The weighted average membership life is 39 months.

2. In your own words, explain how unearned revenue is reported in the balance sheet for Bally. Assume that the company collected $23 million in December 2011 for "New Year's Resolution" memberships starting January 1, 2012. What is the amount of unearned revenue that should be reported on the 2011 and 2012 balance sheets?

ExxonMobil

3. A recent annual report for ExxonMobil reported a quick ratio of 0.20. For the previous year, the ratio was 0.45. Based on this information, do you think that Exxon is experiencing financial difficulty? What other information would you want to consider in making this evaluation?

Brunswick

Brunswick Corporation is a multinational company that manufactures and sells marine and recreational products. A recent annual report for Brunswick contained the following information:

Legal and Environmental

The company is involved in numerous environmental remediation and clean-up projects with an aggregate estimated exposure of approximately $21 million to $42 million. The Company accrues for environmental remediation-related activities for which commitments or clean-up plans have been developed and for which costs can be reasonably estimated.

4. In your own words, explain Brunswick's accounting policy for environmental expenditures. What is the justification for this policy?

AP9-4 LO6 Determining Cash Flow Effects (P9-8)

For each of the following transactions, determine whether cash flows from operating activities will increase, decrease, or remain the same:

a. Purchased merchandise for cash.
b. Paid salaries and wages for the last month of the previous accounting period.
c. Paid taxes to the federal government.
d. Borrowed money from the bank. The term of the note is two years.
e. Withheld FICA taxes from employees' paychecks and immediately paid to the government.
f. Recorded accrued interest expense.
g. Paid cash as the result of losing a lawsuit. A contingent liability associated with the liability had been recorded.
h. Paid salaries and wages for the current month in cash.
i. Performed services for a customer who had paid for them in the previous accounting period (i.e., deferred revenue is earned).

AP9-5 LO4 Analyzing the Reclassification of Debt (P9-9)

GENERAL MILLS

General Mills is a multibillion-dollar company that makes and sells products used in the kitchens of most American homes. The Company's annual report included the following note:

We have a revolving credit agreement expiring in two years that provides for a credit line (which permits us to borrow money when needed). This agreement provides us with the opportunity to refinance short-term borrowings on a long-term basis.

Should General Mills classify the short-term borrowings as current or noncurrent debt based on this ability to borrow money to refinance the debt if needed? If you were a member of the management team, explain what you would want to do and why. If you were a financial analyst, would your answer be different?

AP9-6 LO8, 9 Computing Present Values (P9-11)

On January 1, 2011, Ellsworth Company completed the following transactions (use an 8 percent annual interest rate for all transactions):

a. Borrowed $2,000,000 to be repaid in five years. Agreed to pay $150,000 interest each year for the five years.

b. Established a plant addition fund of $1,000,000 to be available at the end of year 10. A single sum that will grow to $1,000,000 will be deposited on January 1, 2011.

c. Purchased a $750,000 machine on January 1, 2011, and paid cash, $400,000. A four-year note payable is signed for the balance. The note will be paid in four equal year-end payments starting on December 31, 2011.

Required (show computations and round to the nearest dollar):

1. In transaction (*a*), determine the present value of the obligation.
2. In transaction (*b*), what single amount must the company deposit on January 1, 2011? What is the total amount of interest revenue that will be earned?
3. In transaction (*c*), what is the amount of each of the equal annual payments that will be paid on the note? What is the total amount of interest expense that will be incurred?

Comparing Options Using Present Value Concepts (P9-12)

AP9-7
LO8

After completing a long and successful career as senior vice president for a large bank, you are preparing for retirement. Visiting the human resources office, you find that you have several retirement options: (1) you can receive an immediate cash payment of $750,000, (2) you can receive $60,000 per year for life (you have a life expectancy of 20 years), or (3) you can receive $50,000 per year for 10 years and then $80,000 per year for life (this option is intended to give you some protection against inflation). You have determined that you can earn 6 percent on your investments. Which option do you prefer and why?

Computing Future Values (Supplement C) (P9-13)

AP9-8

On January 1, 2011, Austin Auto Company decided to accumulate a fund to build an addition to its plant. The company will deposit $320,000 in the fund at each year-end, starting on December 31, 2011. The fund will earn 9 percent interest, which will be added to the balance at each year-end. The accounting period ends December 31.

Required:

1. What will be the balance in the fund immediately after the December 31, 2013, deposit?
2. Complete the following fund accumulation schedule:

Date	Cash Payment	Interest Revenue	Fund Increase	Fund Balance
12/31/2011				
12/31/2012				
12/31/2013				
Total				

CASES AND PROJECTS

Annual Report Cases

Finding Financial Information

CP9-1
LO1, 6, 7

AMERICAN EAGLE OUTFITTERS, INC.

Refer to the financial statements of American Eagle given in Appendix B at the end of this book.

Required:

1. What is the amount of accrued compensation and payroll taxes at the end of the most recent reporting year?
2. By what amount did accounts payable change over the most recent reporting year? How did this change in accounts payable affect cash flows from operating activities during the most recent reporting year?
3. What is the amount of long-term liabilities at the end of the most recent reporting year?
4. Describe the company's policy if gift cards are not redeemed.

CP9-2
LO1, 6, 7

URBAN OUTFITTERS INC.

Finding Financial Information

Refer to the financial statements of Urban Outfitters given in Appendix C at the end of this book.

Required:

1. What is the amount of accrued compensation at the end of the most recent reporting year?
2. By what amount did accounts payable change over the most recent reporting year? How did this change in accounts payable affect cash flows from operating activities during the most recent reporting year?
3. What is the amount of long-term liabilities at the end of the most recent reporting year?
4. Does the company have any liabilities associated with gift cards and merchandise credits?

CP9-3
LO2, 3

AMERICAN EAGLE OUTFITTERS, INC.

URBAN OUTFITTERS INC.

excel

www.mhhe.com/libby7e

Comparing Companies within an Industry

Refer to the financial statements of American Eagle (Appendix B) and Urban Outfitters (Appendix C) and the Industry Ratio Report (Appendix D) at the end of this book.

Required:

1. Compute the quick ratio for each company for the current year.
2. Compare the most recent quick ratio for each company to the industry average from the Industry Ratio Report. Based solely on the quick ratio, are these companies more or less liquid than the average company in their industry?
3. Compute the payable turnover ratio for each company for the most recent reporting year.
4. Compare the latest year payable turnover ratio for each company to the industry average from the Industry Ratio Report. Are these companies doing better or worse than the average company in their industry at paying trade creditors?
5. Using this information and any other data from the annual report, write a brief assessment of the liquidity for the two companies.

Financial Reporting and Analysis Case

CP9-4
LO8

Analyzing Hidden Interest in a Real Estate Deal: Present Value

Many advertisements contain offers that seem too good to be true. A few years ago, an actual newspaper ad offered "a $150,000 house with a zero interest rate mortgage" for sale. If the purchaser made monthly payments of $3,125 for four years ($150,000 ÷ 48 months), no interest would be charged. When the offer was made, mortgage interest rates were 12 percent. Present value for n = 48, and i = 1% is 37.9740.

Required:

1. Did the builder actually provide a mortgage at zero interest?
2. Estimate the true price of the home that was advertised. Assume that the monthly payment was based on an implicit interest rate of 12 percent.

Critical Thinking Cases

CP9-5
LO1, 2

Making Decisions as a Manager: Liquidity

In some cases, a manager can engage in transactions that improve the appearance of financial reports without affecting the underlying economic reality. In this chapter, we discussed the importance of liquidity as measured by the quick ratio and working capital. For each of the following transactions, (*a*) determine whether reported liquidity is improved and (*b*) state whether you believe that the fundamental liquidity of the company has been improved. Assume that the company has positive working capital and a quick ratio of 0.5.

a. Borrowed $1 million from the bank, payable in 90 days.
b. Borrowed $10 million with a long-term note, payable in five years.
c. Reclassified current portion of long-term debt as long term as the result of a new agreement with the bank that guarantees the company's ability to refinance the debt when it matures.
d. Paid $100,000 of the company's accounts payable.

e. Entered a borrowing agreement that guarantees the ability to borrow up to $10 million when needed.

CP9-6
LO2

Evaluating an Ethical Dilemma: Managing Reported Results

The president of a regional wholesale distribution company planned to borrow a significant amount of money from a local bank at the beginning of the next fiscal year. He knew that the bank placed a heavy emphasis on the liquidity of potential borrowers. To improve the company's quick ratio, the president told his employees to stop shipping new merchandise to customers and to stop accepting merchandise from suppliers for the last three weeks of the fiscal year. Is this behavior ethical? Would your answer be different if the president had been concerned about reported profits and asked all of the employees to work overtime to ship out merchandise that had been ordered at the end of the year?

CP9-7
LO8

Evaluating an Ethical Dilemma: Fair Advertising

The New York State Lottery Commission ran the following advertisement in a number of New York newspapers:

The Lotto jackpot for Wednesday, August 25, 1999, will be $3 million including interest earned over a 20-year payment period. Constant payments will be made each year.

Explain the meaning of this advertisement in your own words. Evaluate the "fairness" of this advertisement. Could anyone be misled? Do you agree that the lottery winner has won $3 million? If not, what amount is more accurate? State any assumptions you make.

Financial Reporting and Analysis Team Project

CP9-8
LO1, 2, 3, 5, 6, 7

Team Project: Examining an Annual Report

As a team, select an industry to analyze. *Reuters* provides lists of industries and their makeup at www.reuters.com. Each team member should acquire the annual report or 10-K for one publicly traded company in the industry, with each member selecting a different company. (Library files, the SEC EDGAR service at www.sec.gov, Compustat CD, or the company itself are good sources.)

Required:

On an individual basis, each team member should write a short report answering the following questions about the selected company. Discuss any patterns across the companies that you as a team observe. Then, as a team, write a short report comparing and contrasting your companies.

1. List the accounts and amounts of the company's liabilities for the last three years.
   a. What is the percentage of each to the respective year's total liabilities?
   b. What do the results of your analysis suggest about the strategy your company has followed with respect to borrowed funds overall and over time?
   c. Does the company disclose any lease liabilities in the footnotes? If so, compute the percentage of lease commitments to total liabilities.
2. What, if any, contingent liabilities are reported by the company for the most recent year and what is your assessment of the risk of each after reading the footnote(s)?
3. Ratio Analysis:
   a. What does the quick ratio measure in general?
   b. Compute the ratio for the last three years.
   c. What do your results suggest about the company?
   d. If available, find the industry ratio for the most recent year, compare it to your results, and discuss why you believe your company differs or is similar to the industry ratio.
4. Ratio Analysis:
   a. What does the accounts payable turnover ratio measure in general?
   b. Compute the ratio for the last three years.
   c. What do your results suggest about the company?
   d. If available, find the industry ratio for the most recent year, compare it to your results, and discuss why you believe your company differs from or is similar to the industry ratio.
5. What is the effect of the change in accounts payable on cash flows from operating activities for the most recent year (that is, did the change increase or decrease operating cash flows)? Explain your answer.

LEARNING OBJECTIVES

After studying this chapter, you should be able to:

Lecture Presentation LP-10
www.mhhe.com/libby7e

1. Describe the characteristics of bonds. p. 507

2. Report bonds payable and interest expense for bonds sold at par and analyze the times interest earned ratio. p. 511

3. Report bonds payable and interest expense for bonds sold at a discount. p. 514

4. Report bonds payable and interest expense for bonds sold at a premium. p. 519

5. Analyze the debt-to-equity ratio. p. 522

6. Report the early retirement of bonds. p. 523

7. Explain how financing activities are reported on the statement of cash flows. p. 524

REPORTING AND INTERPRETING BONDS

Many businesses are not household names but nevertheless play an important role in our daily lives. More than 40 percent of the nation's freight is moved by railroad. A leader in this industry is Burlington Northern Santa Fe (BNSF). Last year, the company moved 23 million tons of wheat, 8 million tons of lumber, 14.5 million tons of steel, and 13 million tons of plastic. Most likely, you have consumed or used a product today that moved by rail.

BNSF is in a capital-intensive industry. It has invested in very expensive equipment, including 6,500 locomotives and over 82,000 freight cars. The company owns 23,000 miles of rail tracks and spent over $2 billion last year on capital investments. Management of capital-intensive businesses face a number of challenges. Large investments must be made based on estimates of customer demand many years into the future. If management underinvests, customers will be lost to other companies. If an overinvestment is made, money will be tied up in assets that do not generate revenue and profits will suffer.

In addition to deciding upon the proper level of investment in long-term assets, management must pick the optimal balance of financing for those assets. BNSF finances its capital investments from three sources: internally generated funds, investments by owners, and borrowings from long-term creditors.

In this chapter, we will discuss bonds and long-term debt. BNSF has disclosed information about its long-term borrowing in the note shown in Exhibit 10.1. Much of the terminology in this note will be new to you. After studying this chapter, you will understand each of the terms used in the note.

FOCUS COMPANY:

Burlington Northern Santa Fe

FINANCING GROWTH WITH BONDS PAYABLE

www.bnsf.com

UNDERSTANDING THE BUSINESS

Capital structure is the mixture of debt and equity a company uses to finance its operations. Almost all companies employ some debt in their capital structure. Indeed, large corporations need to borrow billions of dollars, which makes borrowing from individual creditors impractical. Instead, these corporations issue bonds to raise debt capital.

Bonds are securities that corporations and governmental units issue when they borrow large amounts of money. After bonds have been issued, they can be traded on established

EXHIBIT 10.1

Note from BNSF Annual Report

9. Debt

Debt outstanding was as follows (in millions):

December 31,	2008		2007	
Notes and debentures, due 2009 to 2097	$7,593	6.3%	$6,376	6.6%
Equipment obligations, due 2009 to 2016	244	6.7	297	6.7
Capitalized lease obligations, due 2009 to 2028	1,281	5.3	938	6.3
Mortgage bonds, due 2009 to 2047	97	6.0	102	6.1
Financing obligations, due 2009 to 2028	278	6.2	211	6.3
Commercial paper	100	4.7	261	5.5
Unamortized discount and other, net	(38)		(39)	
Total	9,555		8,146	
Current portion of long-term debt	(456)	4.8%	(411)	7.2%
Long-term debt	$9,099		$7,735	

exchanges such as the New York Bond Exchange. The ability to sell a bond on the bond exchange is a significant advantage for creditors because it provides them with liquidity, or the ability to convert their investments into cash. If you lend money directly to a corporation for 20 years, you must wait that long before your cash investment is repaid. If you lend money by purchasing a bond, you can always sell it to another creditor if you need cash before it matures.

The liquidity of publicly traded bonds offers an important advantage to corporations. Because most creditors are reluctant to lend money for long periods with no opportunity to receive cash prior to maturity, they demand a higher interest rate for long-term loans. By issuing more liquid debt, corporations can reduce the cost of long-term borrowing.

This chapter provides a basic understanding of the management, accounting, and financial issues associated with bonds. We begin with a description of bonds payable. Then we see how bond transactions are analyzed and recorded. The chapter closes with a discussion of the early retirement of debt.

ORGANIZATION of the Chapter

Characteristics of Bonds Payable

- Bonds Issued at Par
- Times Interest Earned Ratio

Reporting Bond Transactions

- Bonds Issued at a Discount
- Reporting Interest Expense Using Straight-Line Amortization
- Reporting Interest Expense Using Effective-Interest Amortization

- Bonds Issued at a Premium
- Reporting Interest Expense Using Straight-Line Amortization
- Reporting Interest Expense Using Effective-Interest Amortization
- Debt-to-Equity Ratio

Early Retirement of Debt

CHARACTERISTICS OF BONDS PAYABLE

LEARNING OBJECTIVE 1

Describe the characteristics of bonds.

Both stock and bonds are issued by corporations to raise money for long-term purposes. Several reasons why a corporation would want to issue bonds instead of stock are:

1. **Stockholders maintain control.** Bondholders do not vote or share in the company's earnings.
2. **Interest expense is tax-deductible.** The tax deductibility of interest expense reduces the net cost of borrowing. In contrast, dividends paid on stock are not tax deductible.
3. **The impact on earnings is positive.** Money can often be borrowed at a low interest rate and invested at a higher rate. Assume that Home Video, Inc., owns a video rental store. The company has stockholders' equity of $100,000 invested in the store and earns net income of $20,000 per year. Management plans to open a new store that will also cost $100,000 and earn $20,000 per year. Should management issue new stock or borrow the money at an interest rate of 8 percent? The following analysis shows that the use of debt will increase the return to the owners:

	Option 1 Stock	Option 2 Debt
Income before interest and taxes	$ 40,000	$ 40,000
Interest (8% × $100,000)		8,000
Income before taxes	40,000	32,000
Income taxes (35%)	14,000	11,200
Net income	$ 26,000	$ 20,800
Stockholders' equity	$200,000	$100,000
Return on equity	13%	20.8%

Unfortunately, bonds carry higher risk than equity. The following are the major disadvantages associated with issuing bonds:

1. **Risk of bankruptcy.** Interest payments to bondholders are fixed charges that must be paid each period whether the corporation earns income or incurs a loss.
2. **Negative impact on cash flows.** Debt must be repaid at a specified time in the future. Management must be able to generate sufficient cash to repay the debt or have the ability to refinance it.

A bond usually requires the payment of interest over its life with repayment of principal on the maturity date. The **bond principal** is the amount (1) that is payable at the maturity date and (2) on which the periodic cash interest payments are computed. The principal is also called the **par value, face amount,** and maturity value. All bonds have a par value, which is the amount that will be paid when the bond matures. For most individual bonds, the par value is $1,000, but it can be any amount.

The BOND PRINCIPAL is the amount (*a*) payable at the maturity of the bond and (*b*) on which the periodic cash interest payments are computed.

A bond always specifies a **stated rate** of interest and the timing of periodic cash interest payments, usually annually or semiannually. Each periodic interest payment is computed as principal times the stated interest rate. The selling price of a bond does not affect the periodic cash payment of interest. For example, a $1,000, 8 percent bond always pays cash interest of (1) $80 on an annual basis or (2) $40 on a semiannual basis.

PAR VALUE is another name for bond principal, or the maturity amount of a bond.

FACE AMOUNT is another name for bond principal, or the maturity amount of the bond.

Different types of bonds have different characteristics for good economic reasons. Individual creditors have different risk and return preferences. A retired person may be willing to receive a lower interest rate in return for greater security. This type of creditor might want a mortgage bond that pledges a specific asset as security in case the company cannot repay the bond. Another type of creditor might be willing to accept a low interest rate and an unsecured status in return for the opportunity to convert the bond into common stock at some point in the future. Companies try to design bond features that are attractive to different groups of

The STATED RATE is the rate of cash interest per period stated in the bond contract.

creditors just as automobile manufacturers try to design cars that appeal to different groups of consumers. Some key types of bonds are shown in the illustration below.

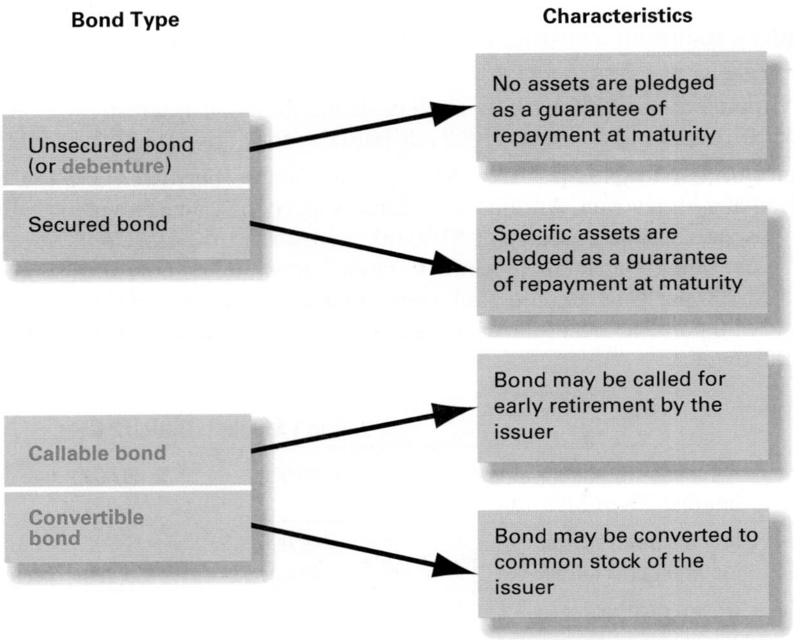

A DEBENTURE is an unsecured bond; no assets are specifically pledged to guarantee repayment.

A CALLABLE BOND may be called for early retirement at the option of the issuer.

A CONVERTIBLE BOND may be converted to other securities of the issuer (usually common stock).

An INDENTURE is a bond contract that specifies the legal provisions of a bond issue.

When BNSF decides to issue new bonds, it prepares a bond **indenture** (bond contract) that specifies the legal provisions of the bonds. These provisions include the maturity date, the rate of interest to be paid, the date of each interest payment, and any conversion privileges. The indenture also contains covenants designed to protect the creditors. Typical indentures include limitations on new debt that the company might issue in the future, limitations on the payment of dividends, or requirements for minimums of certain accounting ratios, such as the current ratio. Because covenants may limit the company's future actions, management prefers those that are least restrictive. Creditors, however, prefer more restrictive covenants, which lessen the risk of the investment. As with any business transaction, the final result is achieved through negotiation.

Disclosure of Debt Covenants (sample of 600 companies)

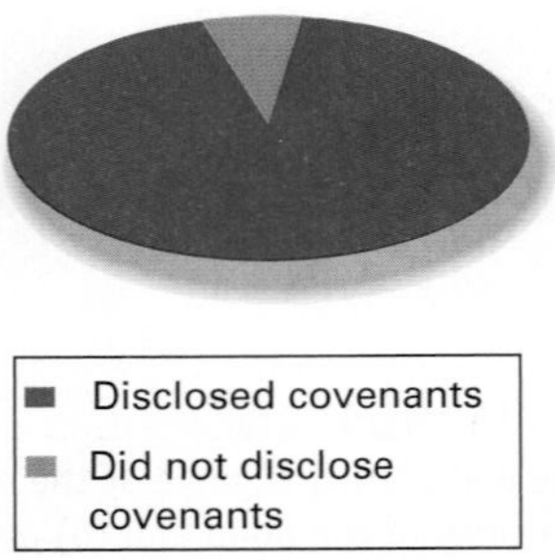

Bond covenants are typically reported in the notes to the financial statements. *Accounting Trends & Techniques* (published by the AICPA) has reviewed the reporting practices of 600 companies.[1] The graph in the margin shows the percentage of companies that disclosed debt covenants. BNSF reported the following information about its debt covenants.

BNSF

REAL WORLD EXCERPT
Annual Report

Credit Agreement

Our debt agreement includes covenants, including a maximum debt-to-capital test. The Company was in compliance with its debt covenants.

[1]Reprinted with permission from *Accounting Trends & Techniques*. Copyright © 2008 by the American Institute of Certified Public Accountants, Inc.

The bond issuer also prepares a prospectus, which is a legal document that is given to potential bond investors. The prospectus describes the company, the bonds, and how the proceeds of the bonds will be used. BNSF used the money it borrowed to increase working capital, make capital expenditures, and repurchase common stock.

When a bond is issued to an investor, the person receives a **bond certificate.** All bond certificates for a single bond issue are identical. The face of each certificate shows the same maturity date, interest rate, interest dates, and other provisions. An independent party, called the **trustee,** is usually appointed to represent the bondholders. A trustee's duties are to ascertain whether the issuing company has fulfilled all provisions of the bond indenture.

A BOND CERTIFICATE is the bond document that each bondholder receives.

A TRUSTEE is an independent party appointed to represent the bondholders.

Because of the complexities associated with bonds, several agencies exist to evaluate the probability that a bond issuer will not be able to meet the requirements specified in the indenture. This risk is called *default risk.* Moody's and Standard & Poor's use letter ratings to specify the quality of a bond. Bonds with ratings above Baa/BBB are investment grade; bonds with ratings below that level are speculative and are often called *junk bonds.* Many banks, mutual funds, and trusts are permitted to invest only in investment-grade bonds. In addition to evaluating the risk of a specific bond, analysts also assess the overall risk of the issuer.

Bond Information from the Business Press

FINANCIAL ANALYSIS

Bond prices are reported each day in the business press based on transactions that have occurred on the bond exchange. The following is typical of the information you will find:

Bond	Yield	Volume	Close	Change
Safeway 6.0 13	6.8	58	97.2	−1/4
Sears 6.5 17	6.77	25	98.1	−3/8
BNSF 7.375 29	6.08	121	114.71	−1/8

This listing states that the BNSF bond has a coupon interest rate of 7.375 percent and will mature in the year 2029. The bond currently provides an effective interest yield of 6.08 percent and has a selling price of 114.71 percent of par, or $1147.10. On this date, 121 bonds were sold, and the price fell 1/8 point from the closing price on the previous trading day (a point is 1 percent).

It is important to remember that these changes do not affect the company's financial statements. For financial reporting purposes, the company uses the interest rates that existed when the bonds were first sold to the public.

REPORTING BOND TRANSACTIONS

When BNSF issued its bonds, it specified two types of cash payment in the bond contract:

1. **Principal.** This amount is usually a single payment that is made when the bond matures. It is also called the **par value** or **face value.**
2. **Cash interest payments.** These payments, which represent an annuity, are computed by multiplying the principal amount times the interest rate stated in the bond contract. This interest is called the **contract, stated,** or **coupon rate** of interest. The bond contract specifies whether the interest payments are made quarterly, semiannually, or annually. When you are asked to work problems in which interest payments are made more frequently than once a year, you must adjust both the periodic interest rate and the number of periods. For example, a $1,000 (face value) bond with an annual interest rate of 6 percent and a life of 10 years would pay interest of $30 ($1,000 × 6% × 1/2) for 20 periods (every six months for 10 years, or 10 × 2).

The COUPON RATE is the stated rate of interest on bonds.

The issuing company does not determine the price at which the bonds sell. Instead, the market determines the price using the present value concepts introduced in the last chapter. To determine the present value of the bond, you compute the present value of the principal (a single payment) and the present value of the interest payments (an annuity) and add the two amounts.

Creditors demand a certain rate of interest to compensate them for the risks related to bonds, called the **market interest rate** (also known as the **yield** or **effective-interest rate**). Because the market rate is the interest rate on debt when it is incurred, it is the rate that should be used in computing the present value of a bond.

The **MARKET INTEREST RATE** (or **YIELD** or **EFFECTIVE-INTEREST RATE**) is the current rate of interest on a debt when incurred.

BOND PREMIUM is the difference between the selling price and par when the bond is sold for more than par.

BOND DISCOUNT is the difference between the selling price and par when the bond is sold for less than par.

The present value of a bond may be the same as par, above par (**bond premium**), or below par (**bond discount**). If the stated and the market interest rates are the same, a bond sells at par; if the market rate is higher than the stated rate, a bond sells at a discount; and if the market rate is lower than the stated rate, the bond sells at a premium. This relationship can be shown graphically as follows:

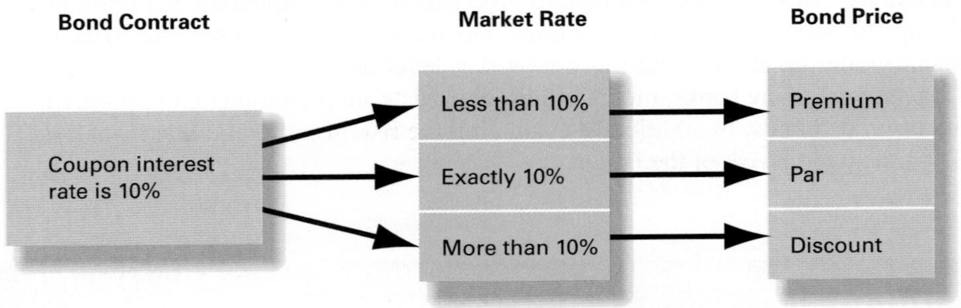

In commonsense terms, when a bond pays an interest rate that is less than the rate creditors demand, they will not buy it unless its price is reduced (i.e., a discount must be provided). When a bond pays more than creditors demand, they will be willing to pay a premium to buy it.

When a bond is issued at par, the issuer receives cash equal to its par value. When a bond is issued at a discount, the issuer receives less cash than the par value. When a bond is issued at a premium, the issuer receives more cash than the par value. Corporations and creditors do not care whether a bond is issued at par, at a discount, or at a premium because bonds are always priced to provide the market rate of interest. To illustrate, consider a corporation that issues three separate bonds on the same day. The bonds are the same except that one has a stated interest rate of 8 percent, another a rate of 10 percent, and a third a rate of 12 percent. If the market rate of interest were 10 percent, the first would be issued at a discount, the second at par, and the third at a premium. As a result, a creditor who bought any one of the bonds would earn the market interest rate of 10 percent.

During the life of the bond, its market price will change as market interest rates change. While this information is reported in the financial press, it does not affect the company's financial statements and the way its interest payments are accounted for from one period to the next.

In the next section of this chapter, we will see how to account for bonds issued at par, at a discount, and at a premium.

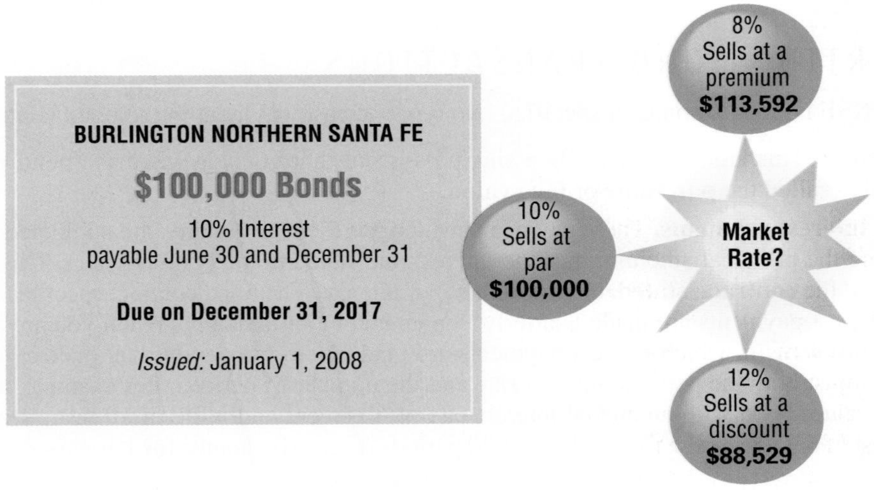

PAUSE FOR FEEDBACK

SELF-STUDY QUIZ

Your study of bonds will be easier if you understand the new terminology that has been introduced in this chapter. Let's review some of those terms. Define the following:

1. Market interest rate.
2. Coupon interest rate.
3. Synonyms for *coupon interest rate.*
4. Bond discount.
5. Bond premium.
6. Synonyms for *market interest rate.*

After you have completed your answers, check them with the solutions at the bottom of the page.

Bonds Issued at Par

LEARNING OBJECTIVE 2

Report bonds payable and interest expense for bonds sold at par and analyze the times interest earned ratio.

Bonds sell at their par value when buyers are willing to invest in them at the interest rate stated in the bond contract. To illustrate, let's assume that on January 1, 2011, BNSF issued 10 percent bonds with a par value of $100,000 and received $100,000 in cash (which means that the bonds sold at par). The bonds were dated to start earning interest on January 1, 2011, and will pay interest each June 30 and December 31. The bonds mature in two years on December 31, 2012.

The amount of money a corporation receives when it sells bonds is the present value of the future cash flows associated with them. When BNSF issued its bonds, it agreed to make two types of payments in the future: a single payment of $100,000 when the bond matures in two years, and an annuity of $5,000 payable twice a year for two years. The bond payments can be shown graphically as follows:

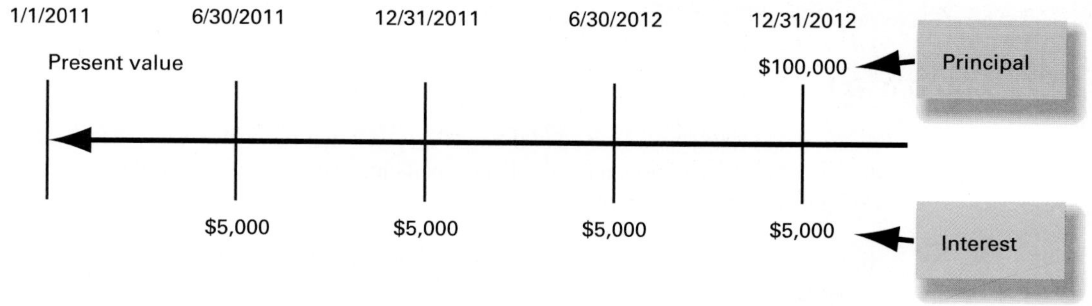

Solutions to SELF-STUDY QUIZ

1. The market interest rate is the interest rate demanded by creditors. It is the rate used in the present value computations to discount future cash flows.
2. Coupon interest rate is the stated rate on the bonds.
3. Coupon interest rate is also called stated rate and contract rate.
4. A bond that sells for less than par is sold at a discount. This occurs when the coupon rate is lower than the market rate.
5. A bond that sells for more than par is sold at a premium. This occurs when the coupon rate is higher than the market rate.
6. Market interest rate is also called yield or effective-interest rate.

To compute the present value using Excel, enter: f_x =PV(0.05,4,−5000,−100000)

The present value of the bond payments can be computed with the tables contained in Appendix A using the factor for four periods and an interest rate of 5 percent per period:

	Present Value
a. Single payment: \$100,000 × 0.8227	\$ 82,270
b. Annuity: \$5,000 × 3.5460	17,730
Issue (sale) price of BNSF bonds	\$100,000

When the effective rate of interest equals the stated rate of interest, the present value of the future cash flows associated with a bond always equals the bond's par value amount. Remember a bond's selling price is determined by the present value of its future cash flows, not the par value. On date of issue, bond liabilities are recorded at the present value of future cash flows on the date of issue, not the par value, as follows:

Cash (+A)	100,000	
Bonds payable (+L)		100,000

Assets		=	Liabilities		+	Stockholders' Equity
Cash	+100,000		Bonds payable	+100,000		

Bonds may pay interest each month, each quarter, each half-year, or each year. In all cases, the present value of the bond is determined using the interest rate factor for the number of interest periods and the interest rate for each period.

STOP

PAUSE FOR **FEEDBACK**

SELF-STUDY **QUIZ**

Assume that BNSF issues \$500,000 bonds that will mature in five years. The bonds pay interest at the end of each year at an annual rate of 8 percent. They are sold when the market rate is 8 percent. Compute the selling price of the bonds.

After you have completed your answer, check it with the solution at the bottom of the page.

Reporting Interest Expense on Bonds Issued at Par

Continuing with our example, the creditors who bought the BNSF bonds did so with the expectation that they would earn interest over the life of the bond. BNSF will pay interest at 10 percent per year on the par value of the bonds each June 30 and December 31 until the bond's maturity date.

Solutions to SELF-STUDY QUIZ

1. \$500,000 × 0.6806 = \$340,300
(\$500,000 × 8%) × 3.9927 = 159,708
\$500,000 (rounded)

The amount of interest each period will be \$5,000 (10% × \$100,000 × 1/2). The entry to record each interest payment is as follows:

Interest expense (+E, −SE)	5,000	
Cash (−A)		5,000

Assets		=	Liabilities	+	Stockholders' Equity	
Cash	−5,000				Interest expense (+E)	−5,000

Interest expense is reported on the income statement. Because interest is related to financing activities rather than operating activities, it is normally not included in operating expenses on the income statement. Instead, interest expense is reported as a deduction from "operating income." The income statement for BNSF shows how interest expense is usually reported.

Consolidated Statements of Income
In millions, except per share data

Year ended December 31,	2008	2007	2006
Operating income	\$3,912	\$3,486	\$3,521
Interest expense	533	511	485
Other expense, net	11	18	40
Income before income taxes	3,368	2,957	2,996
Income tax expense	1,253	1,128	1,107
Net income	\$2,115	\$1,829	\$1,889

BNSF

REAL WORLD EXCERPT
Annual Report

Bond interest payment dates rarely coincide with the last day of a company's fiscal year. Under the matching concept, interest expense that has been incurred but not paid must be accrued with an adjusting entry. If BNSF's fiscal year ended on May 31, the company would accrue interest for five months and record interest expense and interest payable.

Because interest payments are a legal obligation for the borrower, financial analysts want to be certain that a business is generating sufficient resources to meet its obligations. The times interest earned ratio is useful when making this assessment.

Times Interest Earned

KEY RATIO ANALYSIS

ANALYTICAL QUESTION

Is the company generating sufficient resources from its profit-making activities to meet its current interest obligations?

RATIO AND COMPARISONS

The times interest earned ratio is computed as follows:

$$\textbf{Times Interest Earned} = \frac{\textbf{Net Income + Interest Expense + Income Tax Expense}}{\textbf{Interest Expense}}$$

(Continued)

The 2008 ratio for BNSF:

$$(\$2{,}115 + \$533 + \$1{,}253) \div \$533 = 7.3$$

COMPARISONS OVER TIME		
BNSF		
2006	2007	2008
7.2	6.8	7.3

COMPARISONS WITH COMPETITORS	
CSX Rail	Union Pacific
2008	2008
5.1	8.2

INTERPRETATIONS

In General A high times interest earned ratio is viewed more favorably than a low one. The ratio shows the amount of resources generated for each dollar of interest expense. A high ratio indicates an extra margin of protection in case profitability deteriorates. Analysts are particularly interested in a company's ability to meet its required interest payments because failure to do so could result in bankruptcy.

Focus Company Analysis In 2008, profit-making activities for BNSF generated $7.30 for each dollar of interest, a very comfortable safety margin. In addition, the ratio has been fairly constant over recent years. BNSF is able to generate significant cash flows from its operating activities. Also, the ratio is in line with other companies in the industry. Required interest payments do not appear to be at risk.

A Few Cautions The times interest earned ratio is often misleading for new or rapidly growing companies, which tend to invest considerable resources to build their capacity for future operations. In such cases, the times interest earned ratio will reflect significant amounts of interest expense associated with the new capacity but not the income that will be earned with the new capacity. Analysts should consider the company's long-term strategy when using this ratio. Some analysts prefer to compare interest expense to the amount of cash a company can generate. Because creditors cannot be paid with "income" that is generated, they must be paid with cash.

LEARNING OBJECTIVE 3

Report bonds payable and interest expense for bonds sold at a discount.

Bonds Issued at a Discount

Bonds sell at a discount when the market rate of interest is higher than the stated interest rate on them. Let's assume that the market rate of interest was 12 percent when BNSF sold its bonds (which have a par value of $100,000). The bonds have a stated rate of 10 percent, payable twice a year on June 30 and December 31. Because the stated rate of interest was less than the market rate on the date of issue, the bonds sold at a discount.

To compute the cash issue price of the bonds, we can use the tables in Appendix A. As in the previous example, the number of periods is four and we use an interest rate of 6 percent per period, which is the market rate of interest. The cash issue price of the BNSF bonds is computed as follows:

To compute the present value using Excel, enter: f_x = PV(0.06,4,−5000,−100000)

	Present Value
a. Single payment: $100,000 × 0.7921	$79,210
b. Annuity: $5,000 × 3.4651	17,326
Issue (sale) price of BNSF bonds	$96,536*

**The amount of the discount: $100,000 − $96,536 = $3,464.*

The cash price of the bonds issued by BNSF is $96,536. Some people refer to this price as 96.5, which means that the bonds were sold at 96.5 percent of their par value ($96,536 ÷ $100,000).

When a bond is sold at a discount, the Bonds Payable account is credited for the par amount, and the discount is recorded as a debit to Discount on Bonds Payable. The issuance of the BNSF bonds at a discount is recorded as follows:

Cash (+A)	96,536	
Discount on bonds payable (+XL, −L)	3,464	
Bonds payable (+L)		100,000

Assets		=	Liabilities		+	Stockholders' Equity
Cash	+96,536		Bonds payable	+100,000		
			Discount on bonds	−3,464		

Note that the discount is recorded in a separate contra-liability account (Discount on Bonds Payable) as a debit. The balance sheet reports the bonds payable at their book value, which is their maturity amount less any unamortized discount. BNSF, like most companies, does not separately disclose the amount of unamortized discount or premium when the amount is small relative to other balance sheet amounts.

While BNSF received only $96,536 when it sold the bonds, it must repay $100,000 when the bonds mature. The extra cash that must be paid is an adjustment of interest expense to ensure that creditors earn the market rate of interest. To adjust interest expense, the borrower apportions or amortizes the bond discount to each interest period as an increase in interest expense. Therefore, the amortization of bond discount results in an increase in interest expense. Two amortization methods are often used by companies: (1) straight line and (2) effective interest. Many companies use straight-line amortization because it is easy to compute the required numbers. However, the effective-interest method is the method required by GAAP. You may wonder why companies are permitted to use a method that is not the one required by accounting rules. The answer is materiality. Companies are permitted to use the straight-line method because the results are normally not materially different than those computed using the effective-interest method. We will first discuss the straight-line method and then the effective-interest method.

Part A: Reporting Interest Expense on Bonds Issued at a Discount Using Straight-Line Amortization

To amortize the $3,464 bond discount over the life of BNSF bonds using **straight-line amortization,** we allocate an equal dollar amount to each interest period. BNSF bonds have four interest periods. The amortization of discount each period is: $3,464 ÷ 4 periods = $866. We add this amount to the cash payment of interest ($5,000) to compute interest expense for the period ($5,866). The interest payments on BNSF bonds each period are as follows:

STRAIGHT-LINE AMORTIZATION is a simplified method of amortizing a bond discount or premium that allocates an equal dollar amount to each interest period.

Interest expense (+E, −SE)	5,866	
Discount on bonds payable (−XL, +L)		866
Cash (−A)		5,000

Assets		=	Liabilities		+	Stockholders' Equity	
Cash	−5,000		Discount on bonds	+866		Interest expense(+E)	−5,866

Bonds payable are reported on the balance sheet at their book value. At the end of the first interest period (June 30, 2011), the book value of BNSF bonds is more than the original issue price. The book value increases to $97,402 ($96,536 + $866) because of the amortization of the discount. In each interest period, the book value of the bonds increases by $866 because the unamortized discount decreases by $866. At the maturity date of the bonds, the unamortized discount (i.e., the balance in the Discount on Bonds Payable account) is zero. At that time, the maturity amount of the bonds and the book value are the same (i.e., \$100,000). This process can be seen in the following amortization schedule:

	AMORTIZATION SCHEDULE: BOND DISCOUNT (STRAIGHT-LINE)			
Date	(a) Interest to Be Paid (10% × \$100,000 × 1/2)	(b) Interest Expense (a + c)	(c) Amortization (\$3,464 ÷ 4 periods)	(d) Book Value Beginning Book Value + (c)
1/1/2011				\$96,536
6/30/2011	\$5,000	\$5,866	\$866	97,402
12/31/2011	5,000	5,866	866	98,268
6/30/2012	5,000	5,866	866	99,134
12/31/2012	5,000	5,866	866	100,000

STOP

PAUSE FOR **FEEDBACK**

SELF-STUDY **QUIZ**

Assume that BNSF issued \$100,000 bonds that will mature in 10 years. The bonds pay interest at the end of each year at an annual rate of 5 percent. They were sold when the market rate was 6 percent at a price of \$92,641. What amount of interest was paid at the end of the first year? What amount of interest expense would be reported at the end of the first year using straight-line amortization?

After you have completed your answers, check them with the solutions at the bottom of the page.

Part B: Reporting Interest Expense on Bonds Issued at a Discount Using Effective-Interest Amortization

EFFECTIVE–INTEREST AMORTIZATION is a method of amortizing a bond discount or premium on the basis of the effective-interest rate; it is the theoretically preferred method.

Under the **effective-interest amortization** method, interest expense for a bond is computed by multiplying the current unpaid balance times the market rate of interest that existed on the date the bonds were sold. The periodic amortization of a bond premium or discount is then calculated as the difference between interest expense and the amount of cash paid or accrued. This process can be summarized as follows:

Step 1: Compute interest expense

Unpaid Balance × Effective - Interest Rate × n/12

n = Number of Months in Each Interest Period

Step 2: Compute amortization amount

Interest Expense − Cash Interest

The first interest payment on BNSF bonds is made on June 30, 2011. Interest expense at the end of the first interest period (June 30, 2011) is calculated by multiplying the unpaid balance of the debt by the market rate of interest (\$96,536 × 12% × 1/2 = \$5,792).

Solutions to SELF-STUDY QUIZ

1. \$5,000 (5% × \$100,000)
2. \$5,736 [\$5,000 + (\$7,359 ÷ 10)]

The amount of cash paid is calculated by multiplying the principal by the stated rate of interest ($100,000 × 10% × 1/2 = $5,000). The difference between the interest expense and the cash paid (or accrued) is the amount of discount that has been amortized ($5,792 − $5,000 = $792).

Effective-interest amortization causes these amounts to change each period.

Interest expense (+E, −SE)	5,792	
Discount on bonds payable (−XL, +L)		792
Cash (−A)		5,000

Assets		=	Liabilities		+	Stockholders' Equity	
Cash	−5,000		Discount on bonds	+792		Interest expense (+E)	−5,792

Each period, the amortization of the bond discount increases the bond's book value (or unpaid balance). The amortization of bond discount can be thought of as interest earned by the bondholders but not paid to them. During the first interest period, the bondholders earned interest of $5,792 but received only $5,000 in cash. The additional $792 was added to the principal of the bond and will be paid to bondholders when the bond matures.

Interest expense for the next interest period must reflect the change in the unpaid balance of bonds payable that occurred with amortization of the bond discount. The interest expense for the second half of 2011 is calculated by multiplying the unpaid balance ($96,536 + $792 = $97,328) on June 30, 2011, by the market rate of interest ($97,328 × 12% × 1/2 = $5,840). Thus amortization of the bond discount on December 31, 2011, is $840.

Interest expense (+E, −SE)	5,840	
Discount on bonds payable (−XL, +L)		840
Cash (−A)		5,000

Assets		=	Liabilities		+	Stockholders' Equity	
Cash	−5,000		Discount on bonds	+840		Interest expense (+E)	−5,840

Notice that interest expense for December 31, 2011, is more than interest expense for June 30, 2011. BNSF effectively borrowed more money during the second half of the year because of the unpaid interest. Because of the amortization of the bond discount, interest expense increases each year during the life of the bond. This process can be illustrated with the amortization schedule shown below:

	AMORTIZATION SCHEDULE: BOND DISCOUNT (EFFECTIVE-INTEREST)			
Date	(a) Interest to Be Paid (10% × $100,000 × 1/2)	(b) Interest expense (12% × Beginning of Period Book Value × 1/2)	(c) Amortization (b) − (a)	(d) Book Value Beginning Book Value + (c)
1/1/2011				$ 96,536
6/30/2011	$5,000	$5,792	$792	97,328
12/31/2011	5,000	5,840	840	98,168
6/30/2012	5,000	5,890	890	99,058
12/31/2012	5,000	5,943	943	100,001*

**This amount should be exactly $100,000. The $1 error is due to rounding.*

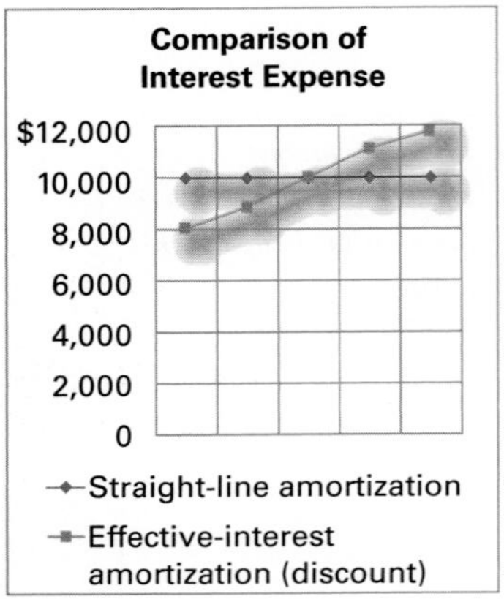

Interest expense (column b) is computed by multiplying the market rate of interest by the book value of the bonds at the beginning of the period (column d). Amortization is computed by subtracting cash interest (column a) from interest expense (column b). The book value of the bonds (column d) is computed by adding amortization (column c) to the book value at the beginning of the period. In summary, under the effective-interest amortization method, interest expense changes each accounting period as the effective amount of the liability changes. Under the straight-line amortization method, interest expense remains constant over the life of the bond. The chart in the margin illustrates these differences.

PAUSE FOR **FEEDBACK**

SELF-STUDY **QUIZ**

Assume that BNSF issued $100,000 bonds that will mature in 10 years. The bonds pay interest at the end of each year at an annual rate of 5 percent. They were sold when the market rate was 6 percent at a price of $92,641. What amount of interest was paid at the end of the first year? What amount of interest expense would be reported at the end of the first year using effective-interest amortization?

After you have completed your answers, check them with the solutions at the bottom of the page.

FINANCIAL ANALYSIS | Zero Coupon Bonds

So far, we have discussed common bonds, which are issued by many corporations. For a number of reasons, corporations also may issue bonds with unusual features. The concepts you have learned will help you understand these bonds. For example, a corporation might issue a bond that does not pay periodic cash interest. These bonds are often called *zero coupon bonds.* Why would an investor buy a bond that did not pay interest? Our discussion of bond discounts has probably given you a good idea of the answer. The coupon interest rate on a bond can be virtually any amount and the price of the bond will be adjusted so that investors earn the market rate of interest. A bond with a zero coupon interest rate is simply a deeply discounted bond that will sell for substantially less than its maturity value.

Let's use the $100,000 BNSF bond to illustrate a zero coupon rate. Assume that the market rate is 10 percent and the bond pays no cash interest. The bond matures in five years. The selling price of the bond is the present value of the maturity amount because no other cash payments will be made over the life of the bond. We can compute the present value with the tables contained in Appendix A, using the factor for five periods and an interest rate of 10 percent:

To compute the present value using Excel, enter: = 100000/(1.10)^5

	Present Value
Single payment: $100,000 × 0.6209	$62,090

Solutions to SELF-STUDY QUIZ

1. $5,000 (5% × $100,000)
2. $5,558 (6% × $92,641)

Accounting for a zero coupon bond is no different from accounting for other bonds sold at a discount. However, the amount of the discount is much larger. For example, the annual report for General Mills contained the following information concerning the company's zero coupon bonds:

Note 9: Long-Term Debt

(in millions)	2003	2002
Zero Coupon notes, yield 11.1% $261 due 2013	$87	$78

GENERAL MILLS

REAL WORLD EXCERPT
Annual Report

While these bonds do not pay cash interest, they have been priced to provide the investor with an effective interest rate of 11.1 percent. Notice that the amount of the obligation increases from 2002 to 2003. This increase is the result of the amortization of the bond discount.

Bonds Issued at a Premium

LEARNING OBJECTIVE 4

Report bonds payable and interest expense for bonds sold at a premium.

Bonds sell at a premium when the market rate of interest is lower than their stated interest rate. Let's assume that the market rate of interest is 8 percent while the BNSF bonds pay cash interest of 10 percent. The bonds pay interest semiannually and mature in two years. They are issued on January 1, 2011.

The present value of BNSF 10 percent bonds can be computed from the tables contained in Appendix A using the factor for four periods and an interest rate of 4 percent per period:

To compute the present value using Excel, enter: f_x=PV(0.04,4,−5000,−100000)

	Present Value
a. Single payment: $100,000 × 0.8548	$ 85,480
b. Annuity: $5,000 × 3.6299	18,150
Issue (sale) price of BNSF bonds	$103,630*

**The amount of the premium: $103,630 − $100,000 = $3,630.*

When a bond is sold at a premium, the Bonds Payable account is credited for the par amount, and the premium is recorded as a credit to Premium on Bonds Payable. The January 1, 2011, issuance of BNSF bonds at a premium would be recorded as follows:

Cash (+A)	103,630	
Premium on bonds payable (+L)		3,630
Bonds payable (+L)		100,000

Assets		=	Liabilities		+	Stockholders' Equity
Cash	+103,630		Premium on bonds	+3,630		
			Bonds payable	+100,000		

The book value of the bond is the sum of the two accounts, Premium on Bonds Payable and Bonds Payable, or $103,630.

Part A: Reporting Interest Expense on Bonds Issued at a Premium Using Straight-Line Amortization

As with a discount, the recorded premium of $3,630 must be apportioned to each interest period. Using the straight-line method, the amortization of premium each annual interest period is

\$908 (\$3,630 ÷ 4 periods). This amount is subtracted from the cash interest payment (\$5,000) to calculate interest expense (\$4,092). Thus, amortization of a bond premium decreases interest expense.

The payment of interest on the bonds is recorded as follows:

Interest expense (+E, −SE)	4,092	
Premium on bonds payable (−L)	908	
Cash (−A)		5,000

Assets		=	Liabilities		+	Stockholders' Equity	
Cash	−5,000		Premium on bonds	−908		Interest expense (+E)	−4,092

Notice that the \$5,000 cash paid each period includes \$4,092 interest expense and \$908 premium amortization. Thus, the cash payment to investors includes the current interest they have earned plus a return of part of the premium they paid when they bought the bonds.

The book value of the bonds is the amount in the Bonds Payable account plus any unamortized premium. On June 30, 2011, the book value of the bonds is \$102,722 (\$100,000 + \$3,630 − \$908). A complete amortization schedule follows:

	AMORTIZATION SCHEDULE: BOND PREMIUM (STRAIGHT-LINE)			
Date	(a) Interest to Be Paid (10% × \$100,000 × 1/2)	(b) Interest expense (a − c)	(c) Amortization (\$3,630 ÷ 4 periods)	(d) Book Value Beginning Book Value − (c)
1/1/2011				\$103,630
6/30/2011	\$5,000	\$4,092	\$908	102,722
12/31/2011	5,000	4,092	908	101,814
6/30/2012	5,000	4,092	908	100,906
12/31/2012	5,000	4,092	908	99,998*

**This amount should be exactly \$100,000. The \$2 error is due to rounding.*

At maturity, after the last interest payment, the bond premium is fully amortized and the maturity amount equals the book value of the bonds. When the bonds are paid off in full, the same entry will be made whether the bond was originally sold at par, at a discount, or at a premium. Exhibit 10.2 compares the effects of the amortization of a bond discount and a bond premium on a \$1,000 bond.

STOP

PAUSE FOR **FEEDBACK**

SELF-STUDY **QUIZ**

Assume that BNSF issued \$100,000 bonds that will mature in 10 years. The bonds pay interest at the end of each year at an annual rate of 9 percent. They were sold when the market rate was 8 percent at a price of \$106,711. What amount of interest was paid at the end of the first year? What amount of interest expense would be reported at the end of the first year using straight-line amortization?

After you have completed your answers, check them with the solutions at the bottom of the page.

Solutions to SELF-STUDY QUIZ

1. \$9,000 (9% × \$100,000)
2. \$8,329 [\$9,000 − (\$6,711 ÷10)]

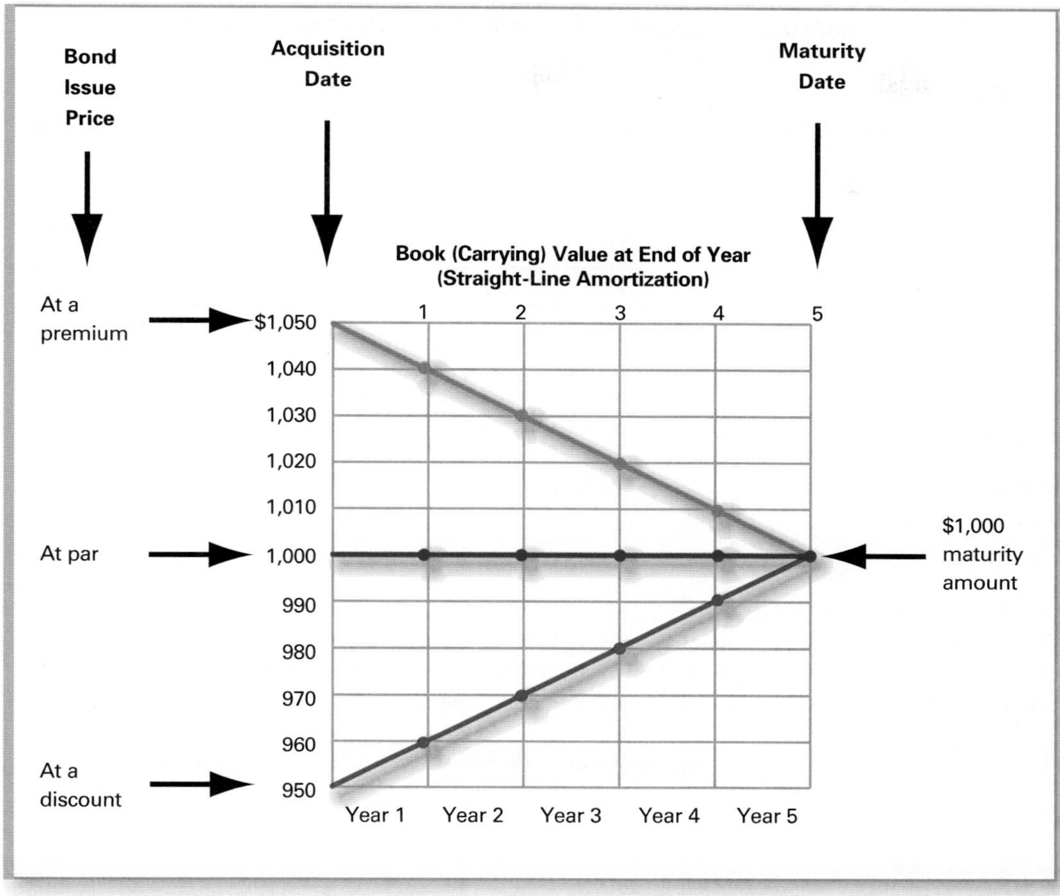

EXHIBIT 10.2

Amortization of Bond Discount and Premium Compared

Part B: Reporting Interest Expense on Bonds Issued at a Premium Using Effective-Interest Amortization

The effective-interest amortization method is basically the same for a discount or a premium. In either case, interest expense for a bond is computed by multiplying the current unpaid balance by the market rate of interest on the date the bonds were sold. The periodic amortization of a bond premium or discount is then calculated as the difference between interest expense and the amount of cash paid or accrued.

The first interest payment on BNSF bonds is made on June 30, 2011. The interest expense on that date is calculated by multiplying the unpaid balance of the debt by the market rate of interest ($103,630 × 8% × 1/2 = $4,145). The amount of cash paid is calculated by multiplying the principal by the stated rate of interest ($100,000 × 10% × 1/2 = $5,000). The difference between the interest expense and the cash paid (or accrued) is the amount of premium that has been amortized ($5,000 − $4,145 = $855).

Interest expense (+E, −SE)	4,145	
Premium of bonds payable (−L)	855	
Cash (−A)		5,000

Assets		=	Liabilities		+	Stockholders' Equity	
Cash	−5,000		Premium on bonds	−855		Interest expense (+E)	−4,145

The basic difference between effective-interest amortization of a bond discount and a bond premium is that the amortization of a discount increases the book value of the liability and the amortization of a premium reduces it. The following schedule illustrates the amortization of a premium over the life of a bond.

	AMORTIZATION SCHEDULE: BOND PREMIUM (EFFECTIVE-INTEREST)			
Date	(a) Interest to Be Paid (10% × $100,000 × 1/2)	(b) Interest expense (8% × Beginning of Period Book Value × 1/2)	(c) Amortization (b) − (a)	(d) Book Value Beginning Book Value − (c)
1/1/2011				$103,630
6/30/2011	$5,000	$4,145	$855	102,775
12/31/2011	5,000	4,111	889	101,886
6/30/2012	5,000	4,075	925	100,961
12/31/2012	5,000	4,039*	961	100,000

**Rounded.*

STOP

PAUSE FOR **FEEDBACK**

SELF-STUDY **QUIZ**

Assume that BNSF issued $100,000 bonds that will mature in 10 years. The bonds pay interest at the end of each year at an annual rate of 9 percent. They were sold when the market rate was 8 percent at a price of $106,711. What amount of interest was paid at the end of the first year? What amount of interest expense would be reported at the end of the first year using effective-interest amortization?

After you have completed your answers, check them with the solutions at the bottom of the page.

KEY RATIO ANALYSIS | Debt-to-Equity

LEARNING OBJECTIVE 5

Analyze the debt-to-equity ratio.

ANALYTICAL QUESTION

What is the relationship between the amount of capital provided by owners and the amount provided by creditors?

% RATIO AND COMPARISONS

The debt-to-equity ratio is computed as follows:

Debt-to-Equity = Total Liabilities ÷ Stockholders' Equity

The 2008 ratio for BNSF is:

$25,272 ÷ $11,134 = 2.3

COMPARISONS OVER TIME		
BNSF		
2006	2007	2008
2.0	2.0	2.3

COMPARISONS WITH COMPETITORS	
CSX Rail	Union Pacific
2008	2008
2.3	1.6

Solutions to SELF-STUDY QUIZ

1. $9,000 (9% × $100,000)
2. $8,537 (8% × $106,711)

INTERPRETATIONS

In General A high ratio suggests that a company relies heavily on funds provided by creditors. Heavy reliance on creditors increases the risk that a company may not be able to meet its contractual financial obligations during a business downturn.

Focus Company Analysis The debt-to-equity ratio for BNSF has increased slightly over the past few years. The company has invested heavily in the expansion of productive assets and has issued over $2.5 billion in new debt to finance this expansion. Most analysts would see this as a positive situation. They would be more concerned if the new debt was used to finance continuing operations. It is also important to note that the ratio is in line with others in the industry.

A Few Cautions The debt-to-equity ratio tells only part of the story with respect to the risks associated with debt. It does not help the analyst understand whether the company's operations can support its debt. Remember that debt carries an obligation to make cash payments for interest and principal. As a result, most analysts would evaluate the debt-to-equity ratio within the context of the amount of cash the company can generate from operating activities.

EARLY RETIREMENT OF DEBT

LEARNING OBJECTIVE 6

Report the early retirement of bonds.

Bonds are normally issued for long periods, such as 20 or 30 years. As mentioned earlier, bondholders who need cash prior to the maturity date can simply sell the bonds to another investor. This transaction does not affect the books of the company that issued the bonds. In several situations, a corporation may decide to retire bonds before their maturity date. A bond with a call feature may be called in for early retirement at the issuer's option. Typically, the bond indenture includes a call premium for bonds retired before the maturity date, which often is stated as a percentage of par value.

Assume that several years ago, BNSF issued bonds in the amount of $1 million and that the bonds sold at par. If BNSF called the bonds in 2011 at 102 percent of par, the company's accountants would make the following journal entry:

Bonds payable (−L)	1,000,000	
Loss on bond call (+Loss, −SE)		20,000
Cash (−A)		1,020,000

Assets		=	Liabilities		+	Stockholders' Equity	
Cash	−1,020,000		Bonds payable	−1,000,000		Loss	−20,000

The loss on the bond call is the amount over par that must be paid according to the bond indenture. This loss on the bond call would be reported on the income statement.

In some cases, a company may elect to retire debt early by purchasing it on the open market, just as an investor would. This approach is necessary when the bonds do not have a call feature. It might also be an attractive approach if the price of the bonds were to fall after the date of issue. What could cause the price of a bond to fall? The most common cause is a rise in interest rates. As you may have noticed during our discussion of present value concepts, bond prices move in the opposite direction of interest rates. If interest rates go up, bond prices fall, and vice versa. When interest rates have gone up, a company that wants to retire a bond before maturity may find buying the bond on the open market is less expensive than paying a call premium.

PAUSE FOR FEEDBACK

SELF-STUDY QUIZ

Which company has a higher level of risk: a company with a high debt-to-equity ratio and a high interest coverage ratio or a company with a low debt-to-equity ratio and a low interest coverage ratio?

After you have completed your answer, check it with the solution at the bottom of the page.

FOCUS ON CASH FLOWS | Bonds Payable

LEARNING OBJECTIVE 7

Explain how financing activities are reported on the statement of cash flows.

The issuance of a bond payable is reported as a cash inflow from financing activities on the statement of cash flows. The repayment of principal is reported as a cash outflow from financing activities. Many students are surprised to learn that the payment of interest is not reported in the Financing Activities section of the statement of cash flows. Interest expense is reported on the income statement and is related directly to the computation of net income. As a result, U.S. GAAP requires that interest payments be reported in the Cash Flows from Operating Activities section of the statement. Companies are also required to report the amount of cash paid for interest expense each accounting period. *Accounting Trends & Techniques* reports that companies disclose this information in a variety of locations.

Disclosure of Cash Interest Payments (sample of 600 companies)

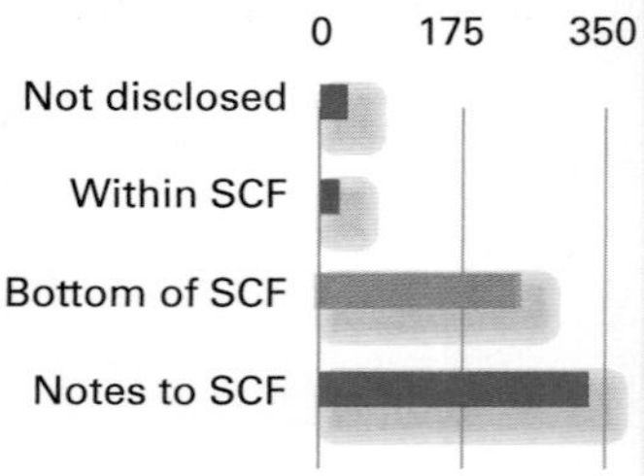

EFFECT ON STATEMENT OF CASH FLOWS

In General As we saw in Chapter 9, transactions involving short-term creditors (e.g., accounts payable) affect working capital and are therefore reported in the Operating Activities section of the statement of cash flows. Cash received from long-term creditors is reported as an inflow from financing activities. Cash payments made to long-term creditors (with the exception of interest expense) are reported as outflows from financing activities. Examples are shown in the following table:

	Effect on Cash Flows
Financing activities	
Issuance of bonds	+
Debt retirement	−
Repayment of bond principal upon maturity	−

Selected Focus Company Comparisons: Cash Flows from Financing Activities (in millions)

General Mills	($102.3)
Outback	(54.7)
Home Depot	737.0

Focus Company Analysis A segment of BNSF's statement of cash flows follows. Several items pertain to issues discussed in this chapter. The remaining items will be discussed in other chapters. Notice that BNSF reports both payments on long-term debt and new borrowings. Although businesses normally borrow money to finance the acquisition of long-lived assets, they also borrow to rearrange their capital structure. In the case of BNSF, the company had outstanding debt with an interest rate of 9.25 percent. The company was able to retire this debt by borrowing at an interest rate of 7.875 percent, saving the company nearly $8 million in annual interest cost.

Analysts are particularly interested in the Financing Activities section of the statement of cash flows because it provides important insights about the future capital structure for a company. Rapidly growing companies typically report significant amounts of funds in this section of the statement.

Solution to SELF-STUDY QUIZ

A company can be forced into bankruptcy if it does not meet its interest obligations to creditors. Many successful companies borrow very large amounts of money without creating unreasonable risk because they generate sufficient funds from normal operations to meet their obligations. Even a small amount of debt can be a problem if a company does not generate funds to meet current interest obligations. Usually, the company with a high interest coverage ratio (even if it has a high debt-to-equity ratio) is viewed as being less risky than one with a low interest coverage ratio.

BNSF
Consolidated Statements of Cash Flows
(in millions)

Year ended December 31,	2008	2007	2006
Financing Activities			
Net (decrease) increase in commercial paper and bank borrowings	(161)	(584)	283
Proceeds from issuance of long-term debt	1,150	1,300	300
Payments on long-term debt	(217)	(482)	(467)
Dividends paid	(471)	(380)	(310)
Proceeds from stock options exercised	91	142	116
Purchase of BNSF common stock	(1,147)	(1,265)	(730)
Excess tax benefits from equity compensation plans	96	121	95
Proceeds from facility financing obligation	68	41	—
Other, net	(10)	(15)	(9)
Net cash used for financing activities	(601)	(1,122)	(722)

DEMONSTRATION CASE

(Try to answer the questions before proceeding to the suggested solution that follows.) To raise funds to build a new plant, Reed Company's management issued bonds. The bond indenture specified the following:

Par value of the bonds: $100,000.
Date of issue: January 1, 2011; due in 10 years.
Interest rate: 12 percent per annum, payable semiannually on June 30 and December 31.

All the bonds were sold on January 1, 2011, at 106. The market rate of interest on the date of issue was 11 percent.

Required:

1. How much cash did Reed Company receive from the sale of the bonds payable? Show computations.
2. What was the amount of premium on the bonds payable?
3. Give the journal entry to record the sale and issuance of the bonds payable.
4. Give the journal entry for payment of interest and amortization of premium for the first interest payment.

SUGGESTED SOLUTION

1. Sale price of the bonds: $100,000 × 106% = $106,000.
2. Premium on the bonds payable: $106,000 − $100,000 = $6,000.
3. January 1, 2011 (issuance date):

Cash (+A)	106,000	
Premium on bonds payable (+L)		6,000
Bonds payable (+L)		100,000
To record sale of bonds payable at 106.		

4. Part A: straight-line amortization

June 30, 2011		
Interest expense (+E, −SE) ($6,000 − $300)	5,700	
Premium on bonds payable* (−L)	300	
Cash (−A) ($100,000 × 12% × 1/2)		6,000
To record payment of interest.		

*$6,000 ÷ 20 periods = $300

Part B: effective-interest amortization

June 30, 2011		
Interest expense* (+E, −SE)	5,830	
Premium on bonds payable (−L)	170	
Cash (−A) ($100,000 × 12% × 1/2)		6,000
To record payment of interest.		

*$106,000 × 11% × 1/2 = 5,830

Chapter Supplement A

Bond Calculations Using Excel

Instead of using the present value tables in Appendix A, most analysts and accountants use Excel to do the financial computations that are necessary when working with bonds. In Chapter 9, we showed you how to use Excel to compute the present value of both single payment and annuity problems. Because a bond involves both types of payments, you can use that process to compute the present value of each type of payment and add them together. Alternatively, you can use a single Excel process to compute the present value of a bond. We will illustrate the Excel process by using the bond example from this chapter. Assume that BNSF issued a $100,000 bond that matured in two years and paid $10,000 interest twice per year (4 payments of $5,000 each.) When the bond was issued, the market rate of interest was 12 percent. The present value of this bond can be computed as follows:

- **Determine the present value of a bond.** The present value of a bond can be computed using an Excel function (you don't have to enter the formula yourself). On the toolbar, click on the insert function button (f_x). A dropdown box called "insert function" will appear. You will be asked to "type a brief description of what you want to do and click 'go.'" You should enter "present value" and click the go button. A new screen will appear and you should highlight "PV," and click on the "ok" button. A new dropdown box will appear. Enter the amounts from the problem in this box: "Rate" is the market rate of interest per period. For this problem, enter 0.06. "NPER" is the number of periods. You should enter 4. "PMT" is the cash interest payment per period which is −5000 for this problem. "Fv" is the maturity value of the bond or −100000 in this case. Notice that when using Excel, amounts must be entered as negative numbers because they represent payments. Also, you should not enter a comma between the numbers. The final box is "type," which permits you to do problems involving payments at either the beginning or end of the period. Most problems involve payments at the end of the period, so you do not need to enter anything in this box because the default is for end-of-period problems. Once you have entered the required data, click on "ok" and Excel will compute this value as $96,534.89 and show it on your spreadsheet. Notice that this amount is slightly different than the amount computed using present value tables because the table numbers have been rounded. An Excel screen with the data entered follows:

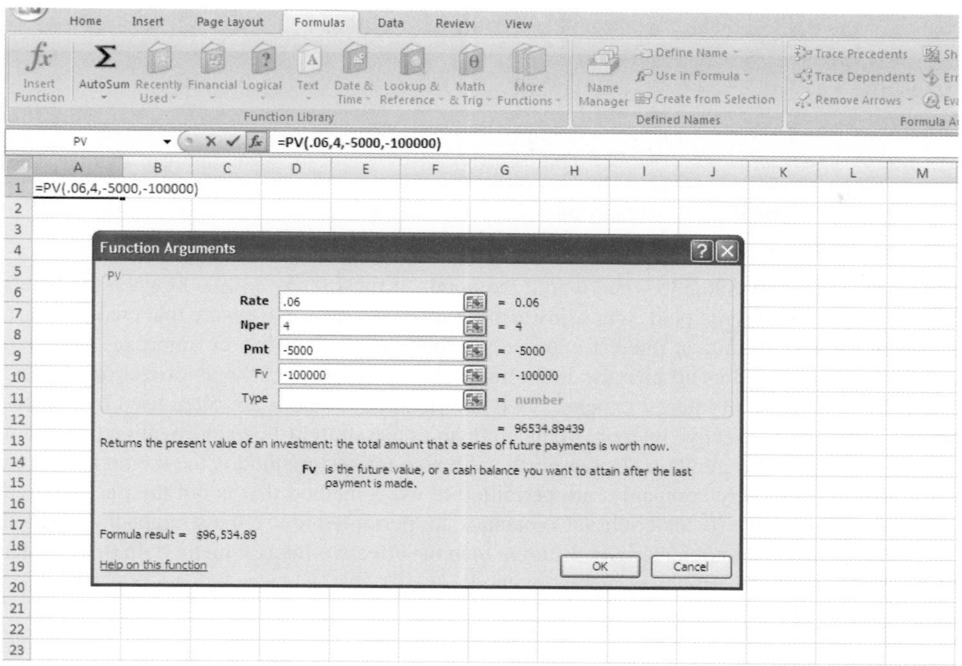

Chapter Supplement B

For financial reporting purposes, it is not necessary to use a discount or premium account when recording bonds sold at a discount or premium. This supplement is intended for use as an alternative to the discussion in the chapter, which shows the use of discount and premium accounts.

Bonds Issued at a Discount (Without Discount Account)

Bonds sell at a discount when the market rate of interest is higher than the stated interest rate on them. Let's assume that the market rate of interest was 12 percent when BNSF sold its bonds (which have a par value of $100,000). The bonds have a stated rate of 10 percent, payable twice a year on June 30 and December 31. Because the stated rate of interest was less than the market rate on the date of issue, the bonds sold at a discount.

To compute the cash issue price of the bonds, we can use the tables in Appendix A. As in the chapter example, the number of periods is four and we use an interest rate of 6 percent per period, which is the market rate of interest. The cash issue price of the BNSF bonds is computed as follows:

	Present Value
a. Single payment: $100,000 × 0.7921	$79,210
b. Annuity: $5,000 × 3.4651	17,326
Issue (sale) price of BNSF bonds	$96,536*

**The amount of the discount: $100,000 − $96,536 = $3,464.*

To compute the present value using Excel, enter: f_x =PV(0.06,4,–5000,–100000)

The cash price of the bonds issued by BNSF is $96,536. Some people refer to this price as 96.5, which means that the bonds were sold at 96.5 percent of their par value ($96,536 ÷ $100,000).

The issuance of the BNSF bonds at a discount is recorded as follows:

Cash (+A)		96,536	
Bonds payable (+L)			96,536

Assets		=	Liabilities		+	Stockholders' Equity	
Cash	+96,536		Bonds payable	+96,536			

While BNSF received only $96,536 when it sold the bonds, it must repay $100,000 when the bonds mature. The extra cash that must be paid is an adjustment of interest expense to ensure that creditors earn the market rate of interest. To adjust interest expense, the borrower apportions or amortizes the bond discount to each interest period as an increase in interest expense. Therefore, the amortization of bond discount results in an increase in interest expense. Two amortization methods are often used by companies: (1) straight line and (2) effective interest. Many companies use straight-line amortization because it is easy to compute the required numbers. However, the effective-interest method is the method required by GAAP. You may wonder why companies are permitted to use a method that is not the one required by accounting rules. The answer is materiality. Companies are permitted to use the straight-line method because the results are normally not materially different than the effective-interest method. In this chapter supplement, we discuss only the effective-interest method.

Reporting Interest Expense on Bonds Issued at a Discount Using Effective-Interest Amortization

Under the effective-interest amortization method, interest expense for a bond is computed by multiplying the current unpaid balance times the market rate of interest that existed on the date the bonds were sold. The periodic amortization of a bond premium or discount is then calculated as the difference between interest expense and the amount of cash paid or accrued. This process can be summarized as follows:

Step 1: Compute interest expense

Unpaid Balance × Effective-Interest Rate × n/12

n = Number of Months in Each Interest Period

Step 2: Compute amortization amount

Interest Expense − Cash Interest

The first interest payment on BNSF bonds is made on June 30, 2011. Interest expense at the end of the first interest period (June 30, 2011) is calculated by multiplying the unpaid balance of the debt by the market rate of interest ($96,536 × 12% × 1/2 = $5,792). The amount of cash paid is calculated by multiplying the principal by the stated rate of interest ($100,000 × 10% × 1/2 = $5,000). The difference between the interest expense and the cash paid (or accrued) is the amount of discount that has been amortized ($5,792 = $5,000 = $792).

Effective-interest amortization causes these amounts to change each period.

Interest expense (+E, −SE)		5,792	
Bonds payable (+L)			792
Cash (−A)			5,000

Assets		=	Liabilities		+	Stockholders' Equity	
Cash	−5,000		Bonds payable	+792		Interest expense (+E)	−5,792

Each period, the amortization of the bond discount increases the bond's book value (or unpaid balance). The amortization of bond discount can be thought of as interest earned by the bondholders but not paid to them. During the first interest period, the bondholders earned interest of $5,792 but received only $5,000 in cash. The additional $792 was added to the principal of the bond and will be paid to bondholders when the bond matures.

Interest expense for the next interest period must reflect the change in the unpaid balance of bonds payable that occurred with amortization of the bond discount. The interest expense for the second half of 2011 is calculated by multiplying the unpaid balance ($96,536 + $792 = $97,328) on June 30, 2011, by the market rate of interest ($97,328 × 12% × 1/2 = $5,840). Thus amortization of the bond discount on December 31, 2011, is $840.

Interest expense (+E, −SE)	5,840	
Bonds payable (+L)		840
Cash (−A).		5,000

Assets		=	Liabilities		+	Stockholders' Equity	
Cash	−5,000		Bonds payable	+840		Interest expense (+E)	−5,840

Notice that interest expense for December 31, 2011, is more than interest expense for June 30, 2011. BNSF effectively borrowed more money during the second half of the year because of the unpaid interest. Because of the amortization of the bond discount, interest expense increases each year during the life of the bond. This process can be illustrated with the amortization schedule shown below:

	AMORTIZATION SCHEDULE: BOND DISCOUNT (EFFECTIVE-INTEREST)			
Date	(a) Interest to Be Paid (10% × $100,000 × 1/2)	(b) Interest expense (12% × Beginning of Period Book Value × 1/2)	(c) Amortization (b) − (a)	(d) Book Value Beginning Book Value + (c)
1/1/2011				$ 96,536
6/30/2011	$5,000	$5,792	$792	97,328
12/31/2011	5,000	5,840	840	98,168
6/31/2012	5,000	5,890	890	99,058
12/31/2012	5,000	5,943	943	100,001*

**This amount should be exactly $100,000. The $1 error is due to rounding.*

Interest expense (column b) is computed by multiplying the market rate of interest by the book value of the bonds at the beginning of the period (column d). Amortization is computed by subtracting cash interest (column a) from interest expense (column b). The book value of the bonds (column d) is computed by adding amortization (column c) to the book value at the beginning of the period. In summary, under the effective-interest amortization method, interest expense changes each accounting period as the effective amount of the liability changes.

PAUSE FOR **FEEDBACK**

STOP

SELF-STUDY **QUIZ**

Assume that BNSF issued $100,000 bonds that will mature in 10 years. The bonds pay interest at the end of each year at an annual rate of 5 percent. They were sold when the market rate was 6 percent at a price of $92,641. What amount of interest was paid at the end of the first year? What amount of interest expense would be reported at the end of the first year using effective-interest amortization?

After you have completed your answers, check them with the solutions at the bottom of the page.

Solutions to SELF-STUDY QUIZ

1. $5,000 (5% × $100,000)
2. $5,558 (6% × $92,641)

FINANCIAL ANALYSIS

Zero Coupon Bonds

So far, we have discussed common bonds that are issued by many corporations. For a number of reasons, corporations may issue bonds with unusual features. The concepts you have learned will help you understand these bonds. For example, a corporation might issue a bond that does not pay periodic cash interest. These bonds are often called zero coupon bonds. Why would an investor buy a bond that did not pay interest? Our discussion of bond discounts has probably given you a good idea of the answer. The coupon interest rate on a bond can be virtually any amount and the price of the bond will be adjusted so that investors earn the market rate of interest. A bond with a zero coupon interest rate is simply a deeply discounted bond that will sell for substantially less than its maturity value.

Let's use the $100,000 BNSF bond to illustrate a zero coupon rate. Assume that market rate is 10 percent and the bond pays no cash interest. The bond matures in five years. The selling price of the bond is the present value of the maturity amount because no other cash payments will be made over the life of the bond. We can compute the present value with the tables contained in Appendix A, using the factor for five periods and an interest rate of 10%:

To compute the present value using Excel, enter: = 100000/(1.10)^5

	Present Value
Single payment: $100,000 × 0.6209	$62,090

Accounting for a zero coupon bond is no different from accounting for other bonds sold at a discount. However, the amount of the discount is much larger. The annual report for General Mills contained the following information concerning the company's zero coupon bonds:

GENERAL MILLS
REAL WORLD EXCERPT
Annual Report

Note 9: Long-Term Debt

(in millions)	2003	2002
Zero Coupon notes, yield 11.1% $261 due 2013	$87	$78

While these bonds do not pay cash interest, they have been priced to provide the investor with an effective interest rate of 11.1 percent. Notice that the amount of the obligation increases from 2002 to 2003. This increase is the result of the amortization of the bond discount.

Bonds Issued at a Premium (Without Premium Account)

Bonds sell at a premium when the market rate of interest is lower than their stated interest rate. Let's assume that the market rate of interest is 8 percent while the BNSF bonds pay cash interest of 10 percent. The bonds pay interest semiannually and mature in two years. They are issued on January 1, 2011.

The present value of BNSF 10 percent bonds can be computed from the tables contained in Appendix A using the factor for four periods and an interest rate of 4 percent per period:

To compute the present value using Excel, enter: f_x = PV(0.04,4,–5000, –100000)

	Present Value
a. Single payment: $100,000 × 0.8548	$ 85,480
b. Annuity: $5,000 × 3.6299	18,150
Issue (sale) price of BNSF bonds	$103,630*

**The amount of the premium: $103,630 − $100,000 = $3,630.*

When a bond is sold at a premium, the Bonds Payable account is credited for the present value of the bonds. The January 1, 2011, issuance of BNSF bonds at a premium would be recorded as follows:

Cash (+A)	103,630	
Bonds payable (+L)		103,630

Assets		=	Liabilities		+	Stockholders' Equity	
Cash	+103,630		Bonds payable	+103,630			

Reporting Interest Expense on Bonds Issued at a Premium Using Effective-Interest Amortization

The effective-interest amortization method is basically the same for a discount or a premium. In either case, interest expense for a bond is computed by multiplying the current unpaid balance by the market rate of interest on the date the bonds were sold. The periodic amortization of a bond premium or discount is then calculated as the difference between interest expense and the amount of cash paid or accrued.

The first interest payment on BNSF bonds is made on June 30, 2011. The interest expense on that date is calculated by multiplying the unpaid balance of the debt by the market rate of interest ($103,630 × 8% × 1/2 = $4,145). The amount of cash paid is calculated by multiplying the principal by the stated rate of interest ($100,000 × 10% × 1/2 = $5,000). The difference between the interest expense and the cash paid (or accrued) is the amount of premium that has been amortized ($5,000 − $4,145 = $855).

Interest expense (+E, −SE)	4,145	
Bonds payable (−L)	855	
Cash (−A)		5,000

Assets		=	Liabilities		+	Stockholders' Equity	
Cash	−5,000		Bonds payable	−855		Interest expense (+E)	−4,145

The basic difference between effective-interest amortization of a bond discount and a bond premium is that the amortization of a discount increases the book value of the liability and the amortization of a premium reduces it. The following schedule illustrates the amortization of a premium over the life of a bond.

	AMORTIZATION SCHEDULE: BOND PREMIUM (EFFECTIVE-INTEREST)			
Date	(a) Interest to Be Paid (10% × $100,000 × 1/2)	(b) Interest expense (8% × Beginning Book Value × 1/2)	(c) Amortization (b) − (a)	(d) Book Value Beginning Book Value − (c)
1/1/2011				$103,630
6/30/2011	$5,000	$4,145	$855	102,775
12/31/2011	5,000	4,111	889	101,886
6/30/2012	5,000	4,075	925	100,961
12/31/2012	5,000	4,039*	961	100,000

*Rounded.

PAUSE FOR **FEEDBACK**

SELF-STUDY **QUIZ**

Assume that BNSF issued $100,000 bonds that will mature in 10 years. The bonds pay interest at the end of each year at an annual rate of 9 percent. They were sold when the market rate was 8 percent. The bonds were sold at a price of $106,711. What amount of interest was paid at the end of the first year? What amount of interest expense would be reported at the end of the first year using effective-interest amortization?

After you have completed your answers, check them with the solutions at the bottom of the page.

CHAPTER **TAKE-AWAYS**

1. **Describe the characteristics of bonds.** p. 507

   Bonds have a number of characteristics designed to meet the needs of both the issuing corporation and the creditor. A complete listing of bond characteristics is discussed in the chapter.

   Corporations use bonds to raise long-term capital. Bonds offer a number of advantages compared to stock, including the ability to earn a higher return for stockholders, the tax deductibility of interest, and the fact that control of the company is not diluted. Bonds do carry additional risk, however, because interest and principal payments are not discretionary.

2. **Report bonds payable and interest expense for bonds sold at par and analyze the times interest earned ratio.** p. 511

   Three types of events must be recorded over the life of a typical bond: (1) the receipt of cash when the bond is first sold, (2) the periodic payment of cash interest, and (3) the repayment of principal at the maturity of the bond. Bonds are reported at the present value of the future cash flows specified in the bond contract. When the market interest rate and the coupon interest rate are the same, the bond will sell at par, which is the same as the maturity value of the bond.

   The times interest earned ratio measures a company's ability to meet its interest obligations with resources from its profit-making activities. It is computed by comparing interest expense to earnings (including net income, interest expense, and income tax expense).

3. **Report bonds payable and interest expense for bonds sold at a discount.** p. 514

   Bonds are sold at a discount whenever the coupon interest rate is less than the market rate of interest. A discount is the dollar amount of the difference between the par value of the bond and its selling price. The discount is recorded as a contra-liability when the bond is sold and is amortized over the life of the bond as an adjustment to interest expense.

4. **Report bonds payable and interest expense for bonds sold at a premium.** p. 519

   Bonds are sold at a premium whenever the coupon interest rate is more than the market rate of interest. A premium is the dollar amount of the difference between the selling price of the bond and its par value. The premium is recorded as a liability when the bond is sold and is amortized over the life of the bond as an adjustment to interest expense.

5. **Analyze the debt-to-equity ratio.** p. 522

   The debt-to-equity ratio compares the amount of capital supplied by creditors to the amount supplied by owners. It is a measure of a company's debt capacity. It is an important ratio because of the high risk associated with debt capital that requires interest and principal payments.

6. **Report the early retirement of bonds.** p. 523

   A corporation may retire bonds before their maturity date. The difference between the book value and the amount paid to retire the bonds is reported as a gain or loss, depending on the circumstances.

Solutions to SELF-STUDY QUIZ

1. $9,000 (9% × $100,000)
2. $8,537 (8% × $106,711)

7. Explain how financing activities are reported on the statement of cash flows. **p. 524**

Cash flows associated with transactions involving long-term creditors are reported in the Financing Activities section of the statement of cash flows. Interest expense is reported in the Operating Activities section.

KEY **RATIOS**

Times interest earned ratio measures a company's ability to generate resources from current operations to meet its interest obligations. The ratio is computed as follows (p. 513):

$$\text{Times Interest Earned} = \frac{\text{Net Income} + \text{Interest Expense} + \text{Income Tax Expense}}{\text{Interest Expense}}$$

Debt-to-equity ratio measures the balance between debt and equity. Debt funds are viewed as being riskier than equity funds. The ratio is computed as follows (p. 522):

$$\text{Debt-to-Equity} = \frac{\text{Total Liabilities}}{\text{Stockholders' Equity}}$$

FINDING **FINANCIAL INFORMATION**

Balance Sheet

Under Current Liabilities

Bonds are normally listed as long-term liabilities. An exception occurs when the bonds are within one year of maturity. Such bonds are reported as current liabilities with the following title: Current Portion of Long-Term Debt

Under Noncurrent Liabilities

Bonds are listed under a variety of titles, depending on the characteristics of the bond. Titles include:

Bonds Payable
Debentures
Convertible Bonds

Income Statement

Bonds are shown only on the balance sheet, never on the income statement. Interest expense associated with bonds is reported on the income statement. Most companies report interest expense in a separate category on the income statement.

Statement of Cash Flows

Under Financing Activities

\+ Cash inflows from long-term creditors
− Cash outflows to long-term creditors

Under Operating Activities

The cash outflow associated with interest expense is reported as an operating activity.

Notes

Under Summary of Significant Accounting Policies

Description of pertinent information concerning accounting treatment of liabilities. Normally, there is minimal information. Some companies report the method used to amortize bond discounts and premiums.

Under a Separate Note

Most companies include a separate note called "Long-Term Debt" that reports information about each major debt issue, including amount and interest rate. The note also provides detail concerning debt covenants.

KEY TERMS

Bond Certificate p. 509
Bond Discount p. 510
Bond Premium p. 510
Bond Principal p. 507
Callable Bonds p. 508
Convertible Bonds p. 508
Coupon Rate p. 509
Debenture p. 508
Effective-Interest Amortization p. 516
Effective-Interest Rate p. 510
Face Amount p. 507
Indenture p. 508
Market Interest Rate p. 510
Par Value p. 507
Stated Rate p. 507
Straight-Line Amortization p. 515
Trustee p. 509
Yield p. 510

QUESTIONS

1. What are the primary characteristics of a bond? For what purposes are bonds usually issued?
2. What is the difference between a bond indenture and a bond certificate?
3. Differentiate secured bonds from unsecured bonds.
4. Differentiate between callable and convertible bonds.
5. From the perspective of the issuer, what are some advantages of issuing bonds instead of capital stock?
6. As the tax rate increases, the net cost of borrowing money decreases. Explain.
7. At the date of issuance, bonds are recorded at their current cash equivalent amount. Explain.
8. Explain the nature of the discount and premium on bonds payable.
9. What is the difference between the stated interest rate and the effective-interest rate on a bond?
10. Differentiate among the stated and effective rates of interest on a bond (*a*) sold at par, (*b*) sold at a discount, and (*c*) sold at a premium.
11. What is the book value of a bond payable?
12. Explain the basic difference between the straight-line and the effective-interest methods of amortizing a bond discount or premium. Explain when each method should or may be used.

MULTIPLE-CHOICE QUESTIONS

1. Annual interest expense for a single bond issue continues to increase over the life of the bonds. Which of the following explains this?
a. The market rate of interest has increased since the bonds were sold.
b. The coupon rate of interest has increased since the bonds were sold.
c. The bonds were sold at a discount.
d. The bonds were sold at a premium.

2. Which of the following is **not** an advantage of issuing bonds when compared to issuing additional shares of stock in order to obtain additional capital?
a. Stockholders maintain proportionate ownership percentages.
b. Interest expense reduces taxable income.
c. Timing flexibility associated with the payment of interest.
d. All of the above are advantages associated with bonds.

3. A bond with a maturity value of $100,000 has a stated interest rate of 8 percent. The bond matures in 10 years. When the bond is issued, the market rate of interest is 10 percent. What amount should be reported when the bond is issued?
a. $100,000
b. $87,707
c. $49,157
d. $113,421

4. Which account would not be included in the debt-to-equity ratio calculation?
a. Unearned Revenue.
b. Retained Earnings.
c. Income Taxes Payable.
d. All of the above are included.

5. Which of the following is false when a bond is issued at a premium?
   a. The bond will issue for an amount above its par value.
   b. Bonds payable will be credited for the par value of the bond.
   c. Interest expense will exceed the cash interest payments.
   d. All of the above are false.
6. A bond with a face value of $100,000 was issued for $93,500 on January 1, 2011. The stated rate of interest was 8 percent and the market rate of interest was 10 percent when the bond was sold. Interest is paid annually. How much interest will be paid on December 31, 2011?
   a. $10,000
   b. $8,000
   c. $7,480
   d. $9,350
7. To determine whether a bond will be sold at a premium, discount, or at face value, one must know which of the following pairs of information?
   a. Par value and the coupon rate on the date the bond was issued.
   b. Par value and the market rate on the date the bond was issued.
   c. Coupon rate and the market rate on the date the bond was issued.
   d. Coupon rate and the stated rate on the date the bond was issued.
8. When using the effective-interest method of amortization, interest expense reported in the income statement is impacted by the
   a. Par value of the bonds.
   b. Coupon rate of interest stated in the bond certificate.
   c. Market rate of interest on the date the bonds were issued.
   d. Both (a) and (b).
9. A bond with a face value of $100,000 is sold on January 1. The bond has a stated interest rate of 10 percent and matures in 10 years. When the bond was issued the market rate of interest was 10 percent. On December 31, the market rate of interest increased to 11 percent. What amount should be reported on December 31 as the bond liability?
   a. $100,000
   b. $94,112
   c. $94,460
   d. $87,562
10. When using the effective-interest method of amortization, the book value of the bonds changes by what amount on each interest payment date?
   a. Interest expense
   b. Cash interest payment
   c. Amortization
   d. None of the above

For more practice with multiple-choice questions, go to the text website at **www.mhhe.com/libby7e**.

MINI-EXERCISES

Finding Financial Information

M10-1
L01, 2

For each of the following items, specify whether the information would be found in the balance sheet, the income statement, the statement of cash flows, the notes to the statements, or not at all.

1. The amount of a bond liability.
2. Interest expense for the period.
3. Cash interest paid for the period.
4. Interest rates for specific bond issues.
5. The names of major holders of bonds.
6. The maturity date of specific bond issues.

Computing Bond Issuance Price

M10-2
L02

Willams Company plans to issue $600,000, 10-year bonds that pay 8 percent payable semiannually on June 30 and December 31. All of the bonds will be sold on January 1, 2011. Determine the issuance price of the bonds assuming a market yield of 8 percent.

M10-3
LO3

Computing Bond Issuance Price

Trew Company plans to issue $900,000, 10-year, 6 percent bonds. Interest is payable semiannually on June 30 and December 31. All of the bonds will be sold on January 1, 2011. Determine the issuance price of the bonds assuming a market yield of 8.5 percent.

M10-4
LO3

Recording the Issuance of a New Bond and the Payment of Interest (Effective-Interest Amortization)

Coffman Company issued $1,000,000, 10-year, 10 percent bonds on January 1, 2011. The bonds sold for $940,000. Interest is payable semiannually each June 30 and December 31. Record the sale of the bonds on January 1, 2011, and the payment of interest on June 30, 2011, using effective-interest amortization. The yield on the bonds is 11 percent.

M10-5
LO3

Recording the Issuance of a New Bond and the Payment of Interest (Straight-Line Amortization)

Wefald Company issued $600,000, 10-year, 10 percent bonds on January 1, 2011. The bonds sold for $580,000. Interest is payable semiannually each June 30 and December 31. Record the sale of the bonds on January 1, 2011, and the payment of interest on June 30, 2011, using straight-line amortization.

M10-6
LO4

Computing Bond Issuance Price

Waterhouse Company plans to issue $500,000, 10-year, 10 percent bonds. Interest is paid semiannually on June 30 and December 31. All of the bonds will be sold on January 1, 2011. Determine the issuance price of the bonds, assuming a market yield of 8 percent.

M10-7
LO4

Recording the Issuance of a New Bond and the Payment of Interest (Straight-Line Amortization)

Ernst Company issued $600,000, 10-year, 9 percent bonds on January 1, 2011. The bonds sold for $620,000. Interest is payable annually each December 31. Record the sale of the bonds on January 1, 2011, and the payment of interest on December 31, 2011, using straight-line amortization.

M10-8
LO4

Recording the Issuance of a New Bond and the Payment of Interest (Effective-Interest Amortization)

RKO Company issued $850,000, 10-year, 8 percent bonds on January 1, 2011. The bonds sold for $910,000. Interest is payable annually each December 31. Record the sale of the bonds on January 1, 2011, and the payment of interest on December 31, 2011, using the effective-interest method of amortization. The yield on the bonds is 7 percent.

M10-9
LO2, 5

Understanding Financial Ratios

The debt-to-equity and times interest earned ratios were discussed in this chapter. Which is a better indicator of a company's ability to meet its required interest payment? Explain.

M10-10
LO6

Determining Financial Statement Effects of an Early Retirement of Debt

If interest rates fell after the issuance of a bond and the company decided to retire the debt, would you expect the company to report a gain or loss on debt retirement? Describe the financial statement effects of a debt retirement under these circumstances.

M10-11
LO7

Determining Cash Flow Effects

If a company issues a bond at a discount, will interest expense each period be more or less than the cash payment for interest? If another company issues a bond at a premium, will interest expense be more or less than the cash payment for interest? Is your answer to either question affected by the method used to amortize the discount or premium?

M10-12
LO7

Reporting Cash Flow Effects

In what section of the statement of cash flows would you find cash paid to retire bonds? In what section would you find cash paid for interest?

connect ACCOUNTING

EXERCISES

Bond Terminology: Fill in the Missing Blanks

E10-1
LO1

1. The __________ is the amount (*a*) payable at the maturity of the bond and (*b*) on which the periodic cash interest payments are computed.
2. __________ is another name for bond principal, or the maturity amount of a bond.
3. __________ is another name for principal, or the principal amount of the bond.
4. The __________ is the rate of cash interest per period stated in the bond contract.
5. A __________ is an unsecured bond; no assets are specifically pledged to guarantee repayment.
6. __________ bonds may be called for early retirement at the option of the issuer.
7. __________ bonds may be converted to other securities of the issuer (usually common stock).

Interpreting Information Reported in the Business Press

E10-2
LO1
AT&T

As this book was being written, the business press reported the following information concerning bonds issued by AT&T:

Bonds	Yield	Close
AT&T 6.5	7.3	89.5

Explain the meaning of the reported information. If you bought AT&T bonds with $10,000 face value, how much would you pay (based on the preceding information reported)? Assume that the bonds were originally sold at par. What impact would the decline in value have on the financial statements for AT&T?

Analyzing a Conversion Feature

E10-3
LO1
Wynn Resorts

Wynn Resorts owns a variety of popular gaming resorts. Its annual report contained the following information:

Debenture Conversions

Our convertible debentures are currently convertible at each holder's option into shares of the Company's common stock at a conversion price of $23.00 per share (equivalent to 43.4782 shares per $1,000 principal amount). During the fourth quarter of 2006, we issued 1,434 shares of common stock upon the conversion of $33,000 of convertible debentures.

The current selling price for Wynn stock is $90. Explain why some bondholders have not converted the bonds to common stock, given that they can do so at $23 per share.

Computing Issue Prices of Bonds for Three Cases

E10-4
LO2, 3, 4

LaTanya Corporation is planning to issue $100,000, seven-year, 8 percent bonds. Interest is payable each December 31. All of the bonds will be sold on January 1, 2011.

Required:
Compute the issue (sale) price on January 1, 2011, for each of the following independent cases (show computations):
a. **Case A:** Market (yield) rate, 8 percent.
b. **Case B:** Market (yield) rate, 6 percent.
c. **Case C:** Market (yield) rate, 10 percent.

Computing Issue Prices of Bonds for Three Cases

E10-5
LO2, 3, 4

James Corporation is planning to issue $500,000 worth of bonds that mature in 10 years and pay 6 percent interest each June 30 and December 31. All of the bonds will be sold on January 1, 2011.

Required:
Compute the issue (sale) price on January 1, 2011, for each of the following independent cases (show computations):
a. **Case A:** Market (yield) rate, 4 percent.
b. **Case B:** Market (yield) rate, 6 percent.
c. **Case C:** Market (yield) rate, 8 percent.

E10-6
LO2, 5

Analyzing Financial Ratios

You have just started your first job as a financial analyst for a large stock brokerage company. Your boss, a senior analyst, has finished a detailed report evaluating bonds issued by two different companies. She stopped by your desk and asked for help: "I have compared two ratios for the companies and found something interesting." She went on to explain that the debt-to-equity ratio for Applied Technologies, Inc., is much lower than the industry average and that the one for Innovative Solutions, Inc., is much higher. On the other hand, the times interest earned ratio for Applied Technologies is much higher than the industry average, and the ratio for Innovative Solutions is much lower. Your boss then asked you to think about what the ratios indicate about the two companies so that she could include the explanation in her report. How would you respond to your boss?

E10-7
LO3

Computing the Issue Price of a Bond

GMAC Corporation issued a $100,000 bond that matures in five years. The bond has a stated interest rate of 6 percent. On January 1, 2011, when the bond was issued, the market rate was 8 percent. The bond pays interest twice per year, on June 30 and December 31. At what price was the bond issued?

E10-8
LO3

Recording Bond Issue and First Interest Payment with Discount (Straight-Line Amortization)

On January 1, 2011, Clearwater Corporation sold a $750,000, 8 percent bond issue (9 percent market rate). The bonds were dated January 1, 2011, pay interest each December 31, and mature in 10 years.

Required:
1. Give the journal entry to record the issuance of the bonds.
2. Give the journal entry to record the interest payment on December 31, 2011. Use straight-line amortization.
3. Show how the interest expense and the bonds payable should be reported on the December 31, 2011, annual financial statements.

E10-9
LO3

Recording Bond Issue and First Interest Payment with Discount (Effective-Interest Amortization)

On January 1, 2011, Park Corporation sold a $600,000, 7.5 percent bond issue (8.5 percent market rate). The bonds were dated January 1, 2011, pay interest each June 30 and December 31, and mature in four years.

Required:
1. Give the journal entry to record the issuance of the bonds.
2. Give the journal entry to record the interest payment on June 30, 2011. Use effective-interest amortization.
3. Show how the bond interest expense and the bonds payable should be reported on the June 30, 2011, income statement and balance sheet.

E10-10

(Supplement B) Recording Bond Issue and First Interest Payment with Discount (Effective-Interest Amortization with No Discount Account)

Using data from the previous exercise, complete each of the requirements in Exercise 10-9 without using a discount account.

E10-11
LO3

Recording Bond Issue: Entries for Issuance and Interest (Straight-Line Amortization)

Westover Corporation had $300,000, 10-year bonds outstanding on December 31, 2011 (end of the accounting period). Interest is payable each December 31. The bonds were issued on January 1, 2011. The company uses the straight-line method to amortize any premium or discount. The December 31, 2011, annual financial statements showed the following:

Income statement	
Bond interest expense	$ 23,100
Balance sheet	
Bonds payable (net liability)	281,100

Required (show computations):

1. What was the issue price of the bonds? Give the journal entry to record the issuance of the bonds.
2. Give the entry to record 2011 interest.

Analyzing a Bond Amortization Schedule: Reporting Bonds Payable

E10-12
LO3

Santa Corporation sold a $1,000 bond on January 1, 2011. The bond specified an interest rate of 6 percent payable at the end of each year. The bond matures at the end of 2013. It was sold at a market rate of 8 percent per year. The following spreadsheet was completed:

	Cash Paid	Interest Expense	Amortization	Balance
January 1, 2011				$ 948
End of year 2011	$60	$76	$16	964
End of year 2012	60	77	17	981
End of year 2013	60	79	19	1,000

Required:

1. What was the bond's issue price?
2. Did the bond sell at a discount or a premium? How much was the premium or discount?
3. What amount of cash was paid each year for bond interest?
4. What amount of interest expense should be shown each year on the income statement?
5. What amount(s) should be shown on the balance sheet for bonds payable at each year-end? (For year 2013, show the balance just before retirement of the bond.)
6. What method of amortization was used?
7. Show how the following amounts were computed for year 2012: (*a*) $60, (*b*) $77, (*c*) $17, and (*d*) $981.
8. Is the method of amortization that was used preferable? Explain.

Explaining Why Debt Is Sold at a Discount

E10-13
LO3
American Airlines

The annual report of American Airlines contained the following note:

The Company recorded the issuance of $775 million in bonds (net of $25 million discount) as long-term debt on the consolidated balance sheet. The bonds bear interest at fixed rates, with an average effective rate of 8.06 percent, and mature over various periods of time, with a final maturity in 2031.

After reading this note, an investor asked her financial advisor why the company didn't simply sell the notes for an effective yield of more than 8.06 percent and avoid having to account for a small discount over the next 20 years. Prepare a written response to this question.

Explaining Bond Features

E10-14
LO1, 3
The Walt Disney Co.

The annual report for Walt Disney Company contained the following note:

The Company has outstanding $1.3 billion of convertible senior notes due on April 15, 2023. The notes bear interest at a fixed annual rate of 2.13%. The notes are convertible into common stock, under certain circumstances, at a conversion rate of 33.9443 shares of common stock per $1,000 principal amount of notes. This is equivalent to a conversion price of $29.46.

When the notes were issued, interest rates were much higher than the 2.13 percent offered by Disney. Why would an investor accept such a low interest rate?

Evaluating Bond Features

E10-15
LO1, 3
PEPSICO

You are a personal financial planner working with a married couple in their early 40s who have decided to invest $100,000 in corporate bonds. You have found two bonds that you think will interest your clients. One is a zero coupon bond issued by PepsiCo with an effective interest rate of 9 percent and a maturity date of 2020. It is callable at par. The other is a Walt Disney bond that matures in 2093. It has an effective interest rate of 9.5 percent and is callable at 105 percent of par. Which bond would you recommend and why? Would your answer be different if you expected interest rates to fall significantly over the next few years? Would you prefer a different bond if the couple were in their late 60s and retired?

E10-16
LO4

Recording Bond Issue and First Interest Payment with Premium (Straight-Line Amortization)

On January 1, 2011, Victor Corporation sold a $1,400,000, 8 percent bond issue (6 percent market rate). The bonds were dated January 1, 2011, pay interest each June 30 and December 31, and mature in four years.

Required:

1. Give the journal entry to record the issuance of the bonds.
2. Give the journal entry to record the interest payment on June 30, 2011. Use straight-line amortization.
3. Show how the bond interest expense and the bonds payable should be reported on the June 30, 2011, balance sheet and income statement.

E10-17
LO4

Recording Bond Issue and First Interest Payment with Premium (Effective-Interest Amortization)

On January 1, 2011, Frog Corporation sold a $2,000,000, 10 percent bond issue (8.5 percent market rate). The bonds were dated January 1, 2011, pay interest each June 30 and December 31, and mature in 10 years.

Required:

1. Give the journal entry to record the issuance of the bonds.
2. Give the journal entry to record the interest payment on June 30, 2011. Use effective-interest amortization.
3. Show how the bond interest expense and the bonds payable should be reported on the June 30, 2011, financial statements.

E10-18

(Supplement B) Recording Bond Issue and First Interest Payment with Premium (Effective-Interest Amortization with No Premium Account)

Using data from the previous exercise, complete each of the requirements in Exercise 10-17 without using a premium account.

E10-19
LO4

Preparing a Debt Payment Schedule with Effective-Interest Method of Amortization and Determining Reported Amounts

Houston Company issued a $10,000, three-year, 5 percent bond on January 1, 2011. The bond interest is paid each December 31. The bond was sold to yield 4 percent.

Required:

1. Complete a bond amortization schedule. Use the effective-interest method.
2. What amounts will be reported on the income statement and balance sheet at the end of 2011, 2012, and 2013?

E10-20
LO2, 4, 5, 7

Determining Financial Statement Effects for Bond Issue and First Interest Payment with Premium (Straight-Line Amortization)

Denver Corporation sold a $300,000, 6 percent bond issue on January 1, 2011, at a market rate of 3 percent. The bonds were dated January 1, 2011, with interest to be paid each December 31; they mature in 10 years. The company uses the straight-line method to amortize any discount or premium.

Required:

1. How are the financial statements affected by the issuance of the bonds? Describe the impact on the debt-to-equity and times interest earned ratios, if any.
2. How are the financial statements affected by the payment of interest on December 31? Describe the impact on the debt-to-equity and times interest earned ratios, if any.
3. Show how the bond interest expense and the bonds payable should be reported on the December 31, 2011, annual financial statements.

E10-21
LO4, 7

Computing the Issue Price of a Bond with Analysis of Income and Cash Flow Effects

Gateway Company issued a $1 million bond that matures in 10 years. The bond has a 10 percent stated rate of interest. When the bond was issued, the market rate was 8 percent. The bond pays interest each six months. Record the issuance of the bond on June 30. Notice that the company received more than $1 million when it issued the bond. How will this premium affect future income and future cash flows?

Reporting the Early Retirement of a Bond

E10-22
L06

Several years ago, Walters Company issued a $600,000 bond at par value. As a result of declining interest rates, the company has decided to call the bond at a call premium of 5 percent. Record the retirement of the bonds.

Reporting the Early Retirement of a Bond with a Discount

E10-23
L06

The Mira Vista Company issued $500,000 in bonds at a discount five years ago. The current book value of the bonds is $475,000. The company now has excess cash on hand and plans to retire the bonds. The company must pay a 7 percent (of par) call premium to retire the bonds. Record the retirement of the bonds.

Determining Effects on the Statement of Cash Flows

E10-24
L07

A number of events over the life of a bond have effects that are reported on the statement of cash flows. For each of the following events, determine whether the event affects the statement of cash flows. If so, describe the impact and specify where on the statement the effect is reported.

Required:

1. A $1,000,000 bond is issued at a discount. The reported amount of the bond on the balance sheet is $960,000.
2. At year-end, $45,000 accrued interest is reported and $1,000 of the bond discount is amortized using the straight-line method.
3. Early in the second year, accrued interest is paid. At the same time, $9,000 interest that accrued in the second year is paid.
4. The company elects to retire the debt in the fifth year. At that time, the reported carrying value of the bonds is $960,000 and the company reports a $20,000 gain on the early retirement of debt.

For more practice with exercises, go to the text website at **www.mhhe.com/libby7e**.

connect ACCOUNTING

PROBLEMS

Analyzing the Use of Debt

P10-1
L01

Arbor Corporation's financial statements for 2011 showed the following:

Income Statement	
Revenues	$300,000
Expenses	(196,000)
Interest expense	(4,000)
Pretax income	100,000
Income tax (40%)	(40,000)
Net income	$ 60,000

Balance Sheet	
Assets	$360,000
Liabilities (average interest rate, 10%)	$ 40,000
Common stock, par $10	230,000
Retained earnings	90,000
	$360,000

Notice in these data that the company had a debt of only $40,000 compared with common stock outstanding of $230,000. A consultant recommended the following: debt, $90,000 (at 10 percent) and common stock outstanding of $180,000 (18,000 shares) . That is, the company should finance the business with more debt and less owner contribution.

Required (round to nearest percent):

1. You have been asked to develop a comparison between (*a*) the actual results and (*b*) the results had the consultant's recommendation been followed. To do this, you develop the following schedule:

Item	Actual Results for 2011	Results with an Increase in Debt and Reduction in Equity
a. Total debt		
b. Total assets		
c. Total stockholders' equity		
d. Interest expense (total at 10 percent)		
e. Net income		
f. Return on total assets		
g. Earnings available to stockholders:		
(1) Amount		
(2) Per share		
(3) Return on stockholders' equity		

2. Based on the completed schedule in requirement (1), provide a comparative analysis and interpretation of the actual results and the consultant's recommendation.

P10-2 LO2 Reporting Bonds Issued at Par (AP10-1)

On January 1, 2011, Nowell Company issued $300,000 in bonds that mature in five years. The bonds have a stated interest rate of 8 percent and pay interest on June 30 and December 31 each year. When the bonds were sold, the market rate of interest was 8 percent.

Required:

1. What was the issue price on January 1, 2011?
2. What amount of interest expense should be recorded on (*a*) June 30, 2011? and (*b*) December 31, 2011?
3. What amount of cash interest should be paid on (*a*) June 30, 2011? and (*b*) December 31, 2011?
4. What is the book value of the bonds on (*a*) December 31, 2011? and (*b*) December 31, 2012?

P10-3 LO2, 3, 4 Completing Schedule Comparing Bonds Issued at Par, Discount, and Premium (Straight-Line Amortization) (AP10-2)

Barnett Corporation sold a $500,000, 7 percent bond issue on January 1, 2011. The bonds pay interest each June 30 and December 31 and mature 10 years from January 1, 2011. For comparative study and analysis, assume three separate cases. Use straight-line amortization and disregard income tax unless specifically required. Assume three independent selling scenarios:

Required:

Complete the following schedule as of December 31, 2011, to analyze the differences among the three cases.

	Case A (Par)	Case B (at 95)	Case C (at 103)
a. Cash received at issue			
b. Bond interest expense, pretax for 2011			
c. Bonds payable, 7 percent			
d. Unamortized discount			
e. Unamortized premium			
f. Net liability			
g. Stated interest rate			

Comparing Bonds Issued at Par, Discount, and Premium (Straight-Line Amortization)

P10-4
LO2, 3, 4

Akron Corporation, whose annual accounting period ends on December 31, issued the following bonds:

Date of bonds: January 1, 2011
Maturity amount and date: $100,000 due in 10 years
Interest: 10 percent per annum payable each June 30 and December 31
Date sold: January 1, 2011
Straight-line amortization is used.

Required:

1. Provide the following amounts to be reported on the December 31, 2011, financial statements:

	Issued at Par Case A	at 99 Case B	at 104 Case C
a. Interest expense	$	$	$
b. Bonds payable			
c. Unamortized premium or discount			
d. Net liability			
e. Stated rate of interest			
f. Cash interest paid			

2. Explain why items (*a*) and (*f*) in requirement (1) are different.
3. Assume that you are an investment adviser and a retired person has written to you asking, "Why should I buy a bond at a premium when I can find one at a discount? Isn't that stupid? It's like paying list price for a car instead of negotiating a discount." Write a brief letter in response to the question.

Determining Reported Amounts with Discussion of Management Strategy (Effective-Interest Amortization)

P10-5
LO2, 3, 5

On January 1, 2011, Cunningham Corporation issued $200,000 in bonds that mature in 10 years. The bonds have a stated interest rate of 6 percent and pay interest on December 31. When the bonds were sold, the market rate of interest was 8 percent. The company uses the effective-interest method. By December 31, 2011, the market rate of interest had increased to 10 percent.

Required:

1. What amount of bond liability is recorded on January 1, 2011?
2. What amount of interest expense is recorded on December 31, 2011?
3. As a manager of a company, would you prefer the straight-line or effective-interest method of amortization?
4. Determine the impact of these transactions at year-end on the debt-to-equity ratio and times interest earned ratio.

Reporting Bonds Issued at a Discount (Straight-Line Amortization) (AP10-3)

P10-6
LO3

On January 1, 2011, Antonio Company issued $700,000 in bonds that mature in 10 years. The bonds have a stated interest rate of 8 percent and pay interest on June 30 and December 31 each year. When the bonds were sold, the market rate of interest was 10 percent. The company uses the straight-line amortization method.

Required:

1. What was the issue price on January 1, 2011?
2. What amount of interest expense should be recorded on (*a*) June 30, 2011? and (*b*) December 31, 2011?
3. What amount of cash interest should be paid on (*a*) June 30, 2011? and (*b*) December 31, 2011?
4. What is the book value of the bonds on (*a*) June 30, 2011? and (*b*) December 31, 2011?

Reporting Bonds Issued at a Discount (Effective-Interest Amortization) (AP10-4)

P10-7
LO3

On January 1, 2011, TCU Utilities issued $1,000,000 in bonds that mature in 10 years. The bonds have a stated interest rate of 10 percent and pay interest on June 30 and December 31 each year. When the bonds were sold, the market rate of interest was 12 percent. The company uses the effective-interest amortization method.

Required:

1. What was the issue price on January 1, 2011?
2. What amount of interest expense should be recorded on (*a*) June 30, 2011? and (*b*) December 31, 2011?
3. What amount of cash interest should be paid on (*a*) June 30, 2011? and (*b*) December 31, 2011?
4. What is the book value of the bonds on (*a*) June 30, 2011? and (*b*) December 31, 2011?

P10-8
L03, 5
eXcel
www.mhhe.com/libby7e

Computing Amounts for Bond Issue and Comparing Amortization Methods

Electrolux Corporation manufactures electrical test equipment. The company's board of directors authorized a bond issue on January 1, 2011, with the following terms:

Maturity (par) value: $800,000
Interest: 8 percent per annum payable each December 31
Maturity date: December 31, 2015
Effective-interest rate when sold: 12 percent

Required:

1. Compute the bond issue price. Explain why both the stated and effective-interest rates are used in this computation.
2. Assume that the company used the straight-line method to amortize the discount on the bond issue. Compute the following amounts for each year (2011–2015):
   a. Cash payment for bond interest.
   b. Amortization of bond discount or premium.
   c. Bond interest expense.
3. Assume instead that the company used the effective-interest method to amortize the discount. Prepare an effective-interest bond amortization schedule similar to the one in the text. The effective-interest method provides a constant interest rate when interest expense is related to the net liability. Explain by referring to the bond amortization schedule.
4. Which method should the company use to amortize the bond discount? As a financial analyst, would you prefer one method over the other? If so, why?

P10-9
L04
eXcel
www.mhhe.com/libby7e

Reporting Bonds Issued at a Premium (Straight-Line Amortization) (AP10-5)

On January 1, 2011, Vigeland Corporation issued $2,000,000 in bonds that mature in 10 years. The bonds have a stated interest rate of 10 percent and pay interest on June 30 and December 31 each year. When the bonds were sold, the market rate of interest was 8 percent. The company uses the straight-line amortization method.

Required:

1. What was the issue price on January 1, 2011?
2. What amount of interest expense should be recorded on (*a*) June 30, 2011? and (*b*) December 31, 2011?
3. What amount of cash interest should be paid on (*a*) June 30, 2011? and (*b*) December 31, 2011?
4. What is the book value of the bonds on (*a*) June 30, 2011? and (*b*) December 31, 2011?

P10-10
L04

Reporting Bonds Issued at a Premium (Effective-Interest Amortization) (AP10-6)

On January 1, 2011, Cron Corporation issued $700,000 in bonds that mature in five years. The bonds have a stated interest rate of 13 percent and pay interest on June 30 and December 31 each year. When the bonds were sold, the market rate of interest was 12 percent. The company uses the effective-interest amortization method.

Required:

1. What was the issue price on January 1, 2011?
2. What amount of interest expense should be recorded on (*a*) June 30, 2011? and (*b*) December 31, 2011?
3. What amount of cash interest should be paid on (*a*) June 30, 2011? and (*b*) December 31, 2011?
4. What is the book value of the bonds on (*a*) June 30, 2011? and (*b*) December 31, 2011?

P10-11
LO4

Recording Bond Issuance and Interest Payments (Straight-Line Amortization)

Commonwealth Company issued bonds with the following provisions:

Maturity value: $300,000
Interest: 11 percent per annum payable annually each December 31
Terms: Bonds dated January 1, 2011, due five years from that date

The annual accounting period ends December 31. The bonds were sold on January 1, 2011, at a 10 percent market rate.

Required:

1. Compute the issue (sale) price of the bonds (show computations).
2. Give the journal entry to record the issuance of the bonds.
3. Give the journal entries at the following date (use straight-line amortization): December 31, 2011.
4. How much interest expense would be reported on the income statement for 2011? Show how the liability related to the bonds should be reported on the December 31, 2011, balance sheet.

P10-12
LO4
eXcel
www.mhhe.com/libby7e

Completing an Amortization Schedule (Effective-Interest Amortization)

MBTA Corporation issued bonds and received cash in full for the issue price. The bonds were dated and issued on January 1, 2011. The stated interest rate was payable at the end of each year. The bonds mature at the end of four years. The following schedule has been completed (amounts in thousands):

Date	Cash	Interest	Amortization	Balance
January 1, 2011				$48,808
End of year 2011	$3,600	$3,417	$183	48,625
End of year 2012	3,600	?	?	48,429
End of year 2013	3,600	?	?	?
End of year 2014	3,600	?	?	48,000

Required:

1. Complete the amortization schedule.
2. What was the maturity amount of the bonds?
3. How much cash was received at the date of issuance (sale) of the bonds?
4. Was there a premium or a discount? If so, which and how much?
5. How much cash will be disbursed for interest each period and in total for the full life of the bond issue?
6. What method of amortization is being used? Explain.
7. What is the stated rate of interest?
8. What is the effective rate of interest?
9. What amount of interest expense should be reported on the income statement each year?
10. Show how the bonds should be reported on the balance sheet at the end of each year (show the last year immediately before retirement of the bonds).

P10-13
LO4
DirectTV

Comparing Carrying Value and Market Value

DirectTV is the largest provider of direct-to-home digital television services and the second largest provider in the multichannel video programming distribution industry in the United States. It provides over 16 million subscribers with access to hundreds of channels of digital-quality video pictures and CD-quality audio programming that it transmits directly to subscribers' homes via high-powered geosynchronous satellites. The company's annual report contained the following note:

Long-Term Debt

The unamortized bond premium included in total debt for the current year was $2.8 million and $3.1 million for the prior year.

Required:

Explain why the unamortized premium is included in total debt and why the premium decreased in amount from one year to the next.

P10-14 **LO6**

McDermott International

Explaining Note to a Financial Statement (AP10-7)

McDermott International is an engineering and construction company with significant oil and gas operations. The annual report for McDermott contains the following note:

The company used cash on hand to purchase the entire $200 million in aggregate principal amount of its Secured Notes outstanding for approximately $249.0 million, including accrued interest of approximately $10.9 million. As a result of this early retirement of debt, we recognized $49.0 million of expense during the year ended December 31.

Required:

1. In your own words, explain the meaning of this note.
2. Why did management incur an expense on the early retirement of this debt?

P10-15 **LO7**

Reporting Bond Transactions on the Statement of Cash Flows

Determine whether each of the following would be reported in the financing activities section of the statement of cash flows and, if so, specify whether it is a cash inflow or outflow.

1. Sale of bonds at a discount.
2. Payment of interest on a bond.
3. Early retirement of a bond with a 5 percent call premium.
4. Amortization of a bond discount.
5. Payment of bond principal upon maturity.
6. Sale of bond from one investor to another. Transaction was in cash.

ALTERNATE PROBLEMS

AP10-1 **LO2**

Reporting Bonds Issued at Par (P10-2)

On January 1, 2011, Trucks R Us Corporation issued $2,000,000 in bonds that mature in five years. The bonds have a stated interest rate of 10 percent and pay interest on June 30 and December 31 each year. When the bonds were sold, the market rate of interest was 10 percent.

Required:

1. What was the issue price on January 1, 2011?
2. What amount of interest expense should be recorded on (*a*) June 30, 2011? and (*b*) December 31, 2011?
3. What amount of cash interest should be paid on (*a*) June 30, 2011? and (*b*) December 31, 2011?
4. What is the book value of the bonds on (*a*) December 31, 2011? and (*b*) December 31, 2012?

AP10-2 **LO2, 3, 4**

Completing Schedule Comparing Bonds Issued at Par, Discount, and Premium (Straight-Line Amortization) (P10-3)

On January 1, 2011, Bidden Corporation sold and issued $100,000, five-year, 10 percent bonds. The bond interest is payable each June 30 and December 31. Assume three separate and independent selling scenarios: Case A, at par; Case B, at 95; and Case C, at 110.

Required:

Complete a schedule similar to the following for each separate case assuming straight-line amortization of discount and premium. Disregard income tax. Give all dollar amounts in thousands.

	At End of 2011	At End of 2012	At End of 2013	At End of 2014
Case A: Sold at par	$	$	$	$
Interest expense on income statement				
Net liability on balance sheet				
Case B: Sold at a discount				
Interest expense on income statement				
Net liability on balance sheet				
Case C: Sold at a premium				
Interest expense on income statement				
Net liability on balance sheet				

Reporting Bonds Issued at a Discount (Straight-Line Amortization) (P10-6)

AP10-3
LO3

On January 1, 2011, Kennedy Corporation issued $1,000,000 in bonds that mature in five years. The bonds have a stated interest rate of 7 percent and pay interest on December 31 each year. When the bonds were sold, the market rate of interest was 9 percent. The company uses the straight-line amortization method.

Required:

1. What was the issue price on January 1, 2011?
2. What amount of interest expense should be recorded on (*a*) December 31, 2011? and (*b*) December 31, 2012?
3. What amount of cash interest should be paid on (*a*) December 31, 2011? and (*b*) December 31, 2012?
4. What is the book value of the bonds on (*a*) December 31, 2011? and (*b*) December 31, 2012?

Reporting Bonds Issued at a Discount (Effective-Interest Amortization) (P10-7)

AP10-4
LO3

On January 1, 2011, Avaya Corporation issued $2,000,000 in bonds that mature in five years. The bonds have a stated interest rate of 6 percent and pay interest on December 31 each year. When the bonds were sold, the market rate of interest was 7 percent. The company uses the effective-interest amortization method.

Required:

1. What was the issue price on January 1, 2011?
2. What amount of interest expense should be recorded on (*a*) December 31, 2011? and (*b*) December 31, 2012?
3. What amount of cash interest should be paid on (*a*) December 31, 2011? and (*b*) December 31, 2012?
4. What is the book value of the bonds on (*a*) December 31, 2011? and (*b*) December 31, 2012?

Reporting Bonds Issued at a Premium (Straight-Line Amortization) (P10-9)

AP10-5
LO4

On January 1, 2011, Grand Isle Corporation issued $900,000 in bonds that mature in five years. The bonds have a stated interest rate of 10 percent and pay interest on December 31 each year. When the bonds were sold, the market rate of interest was 9 percent. The company uses the straight-line amortization method.

Required:

1. What was the issue price on January 1, 2011?
2. What amount of interest expense should be recorded on (*a*) December 31, 2011? and (*b*) December 31, 2012?
3. What amount of cash interest should be paid on (*a*) December 31, 2011? and (*b*) December 31, 2012?
4. What is the book value of the bonds on (*a*) December 31, 2011? and (*b*) December 31, 2012?

Reporting Bonds Issued at a Premium (Effective-Interest Amortization) (P10-10)

AP10-6
LO4

On January 1, 2011, Thomas Insurance Corporation issued $4,000,000 in bonds that mature in five years. The bonds have a stated interest rate of 9 percent and pay interest on December 31 each year. When the bonds were sold, the market rate of interest was 6 percent. The company uses the effective-interest amortization method.

Required:

1. What was the issue price on January 1, 2011?
2. What amount of interest expense should be recorded on (*a*) December 31, 2011? and (*b*) December 31, 2012?
3. What amount of cash interest should be paid on (*a*) December 31, 2011? and (*b*) December 31, 2012?
4. What is the book value of the bonds on (*a*) December 31, 2011? and (*b*) December 31, 2012?

Understanding the Early Retirement of Debt (P10-14)

AP10-7
LO6
AMC Entertainment

AMC Entertainment, Inc., owns and operates 243 movie theaters with 1,617 screens in 22 states. The company sold 11 7/8 percent bonds in the amount of $52,720,000 and used the cash proceeds to retire bonds with a coupon rate of 13.6 percent. At that time, the 13.6 percent bonds had a book value of $50,000,000.

Required:

1. Prepare the journal entry to record the early retirement of the 13.6 percent bonds.
2. How should AMC report any gain or loss on this transaction?
3. Why did the company issue new bonds in order to retire the old bonds?

CASES AND PROJECTS

Annual Reporting Cases

CP10-1
LO1, 2

Finding Financial Information

Refer to the financial statements of American Eagle Outfitters given in Appendix B at the end of this book.

Required:

1. How much interest was paid in cash during the most recent reporting year?
2. Explain why the company does not report bonds payable on its balance sheet.
3. Describe the company's established arrangements, if any, that permit it to borrow money if needed.

CP10-2
LO1, 2

Finding Financial Information

Refer to the financial statements of Urban Outfitters given in Appendix C at the end of this book.

Required:

1. Unlike most companies, Urban Outfitters does not report the amount of interest paid in cash during the most recent reporting year. Explain why you think the company has omitted this information.
2. Explain why the company does not report bonds payable on its balance sheet.
3. Describe the company's established arrangements, if any, that permit it to borrow money if needed.

CP10-3
LO2, 5, 7

www.mhhe.com/libby7e

Comparing Companies within an Industry

Refer to the financial statements of American Eagle (Appendix B) and Urban Outfitters (Appendix C) and the Industry Ratio Report (Appendix D) at the end of this book. Most companies report some amounts of bonds payable on their balance sheets. It is somewhat surprising, therefore, that neither company reports any bond liabilities.

Required:

1. Examine the statements of cash flow for both companies. What is the primary source for cash flow for both companies?
2. Two financial ratios (the debt-to-equity ratio and the times interest earned ratio) are discussed in this chapter. Are they relevant for these companies? Explain.

CP10-4
LO3

Analyzing Zero Coupon Bonds from an Actual Company

JCPenney Company was one of the first companies to issue zero coupon bonds. It issued bonds with a face (maturity) value of $400 million due eight years after issuance. When the bonds were sold to the public, similar bonds paid 15 percent effective interest. An article in *Forbes* magazine discussed the JCPenney bonds and stated: "It's easy to see why corporations like to sell bonds that don't pay interest. But why would anybody want to buy that kind of paper [bond]?"

Required:

1. Explain why an investor would buy a JCPenney bond with a zero interest rate.
2. If investors could earn 15 percent on similar investments, how much did JCPenney receive when it issued the bonds with a face value of $400 million?

Critical Thinking Cases

CP10-5
LO1

Evaluating an Ethical Dilemma

You work for a small company considering investing in a new Internet business. Financial projections suggest that the company will be able to earn in excess of $40 million per year on an investment of $100 million. The company president suggests borrowing the money by issuing bonds that will carry a 7 percent interest rate. He says, "This is better than printing money! We won't have to invest a penny of our own money, and we get to keep $33 million per year after we pay interest to the bondholders." As you think about the proposed transaction, you feel a little uncomfortable about taking advantage of the creditors in this fashion. You feel that it must be wrong to earn such a high return by using money that belongs to other people. Is this an ethical business transaction?

Evaluating an Ethical Dilemma

CP10-6
LO1

Assume that you are a portfolio manager for a large insurance company. The majority of the money you manage is from retired school teachers who depend on the income you earn on their investments. You have invested a significant amount of money in the bonds of a large corporation and have just received a call from the company's president explaining that it is unable to meet its current interest obligations because of deteriorating business operations related to increased international competition. The president has a recovery plan that will take at least two years. During that time, the company will not be able to pay interest on the bonds and, she admits, if the plan does not work, bondholders will probably lose more than half of their money. As a creditor, you can force the company into immediate bankruptcy and probably get back at least 90 percent of the bondholders' money. You also know that your decision will cause at least 10,000 people to lose their jobs if the company ceases operations. Given only these two options, what should you do?

Financial Reporting and Analysis Team Project

Team Project: Examining an Annual Report

CP10-7
LO1, 2, 3, 4, 5, 7

As a team, select an industry to analyze. *Reuters* provides lists of industries and their makeup at www.reuters.com. Each team member should acquire the annual report or 10-K for one publicly traded company in the industry, with each member selecting a different company. (Library files, the SEC EDGAR service at www.sec.gov, Compustat CD, or the company itself are good sources.)

Required:

On an individual basis, each team member should write a short report answering the following questions about the selected company. Discuss any patterns across the companies that you as a team observe. Then, as a team, write a short report comparing and contrasting your companies.

1. Has your company issued any long-term bonds or notes? If so, read the footnote and list any unusual features (e.g., callable, convertible, secured by specific collateral).
2. If your company issued any bonds, were they issued at either a premium or a discount? If so, does the company use the straight-line or effective-interest amortization method?
3. Ratio analysis:
   a. What does the debt-to-equity ratio measure in general?
   b. Compute the ratio for the last three years.
   c. What do your results suggest about the company?
   d. If available, find the industry ratio for the most recent year, compare it to your results, and discuss why you believe your company differs from or is similar to the industry ratio.
4. Ratio analysis:
   a. What does the times interest earned ratio measure in general?
   b. Compute the ratio for the last three years. If interest expense is not separately disclosed, you will not be able to compute the ratio. If so, state why you think it is not separately disclosed.
   c. What do your results suggest about the company?
   d. If available, find the industry ratio for the most recent year, compare it to your results, and discuss why you believe your company differs from or is similar to the industry ratio.
5. During the recent year, how much cash did the company receive on issuing debt? How much did it pay on debt principal? What does management suggest were the reasons for issuing and/or repaying debt during the year?

LEARNING OBJECTIVES

After studying this chapter, you should be able to:

Lecture presentation LP-11
www.mhhe.com/libby7e

1. Explain the role of stock in the capital structure of a corporation. p. 553
2. Analyze the earnings per share ratio. p. 556
3. Describe the characteristics of common stock and analyze transactions affecting common stock. p. 556
4. Discuss dividends and analyze transactions. p. 560
5. Analyze the dividend yield ratio. p. 560
6. Discuss the purpose of stock dividends and stock splits, and report transactions. p. 563
7. Describe the characteristics of preferred stock and analyze transactions affecting preferred stock. p. 565
8. Discuss the impact of capital stock transactions on cash flows. p. 567

REPORTING AND INTERPRETING OWNERS' EQUITY

The Kroger Co. (Kroger) is a familiar name for U.S. consumers. The popular supermarket chain was founded in 1883 and now operates 2,481 supermarkets, 771 convenience stores, and 385 fine jewelry stores. The company is one of the largest retailers in the United States based on annual sales, ranking in the top 25 of the Fortune 100 list. The typical Kroger supermarket stocks approximately 14,000 individual items with 27 percent of its sales volume coming from private label merchandise, many of which are manufactured by Kroger. The Kroger Co.'s growth strategy is based on increasing sales by improving its existing store base through remodels. The company currently makes about \$2 billion in capital expenditures each year. Through this strategy, management seeks to provide short-term results for shareholders while continuing to invest in the long-term growth of the company.

In this chapter, we study the role that stockholders' equity plays in building a successful business and strategies that managers use to maximize stockholders' wealth.

FOCUS COMPANY:

The Kroger Co.

FINANCING CORPORATE GROWTH WITH CAPITAL SUPPLIED BY OWNERS

www.kroger.com

UNDERSTANDING THE BUSINESS

To some people, the words *corporation* and *business* are almost synonymous. You've probably heard friends refer to a career in business as "the corporate world." Equating business with corporations is understandable because corporations are the dominant form of business organization in terms of volume of operations. If you were to write the names of 50 familiar businesses on a piece of paper, probably all of them would be corporations.

The popularity of the corporate form can be attributed to a critical advantage that corporations have over sole proprietorships and partnerships: They can raise large amounts of capital because both large and small investors can easily participate in their ownership. This ease of participation is related to several factors.

EXHIBIT 11.1

Excerpt from Consolidated Balance Sheets for The Kroger Co.

REAL WORLD EXCERPT

Annual Report

(Amounts in Millions)	January 31, 2009	February 2, 2008
Shareowners' Equity		
Preferred stock, $100 par, 5 shares authorized and unissued	—	—
Common stock, $1 par, 1,000 shares authorized: 955 shares issued in 2008 and 947 shares issued in 2007	**955**	947
Additional paid-in capital	**3,266**	3,031
Accumulated other comprehensive loss	**(495)**	(122)
Accumulated earnings	**7,489**	6,480
Common stock in treasury, at cost, 306 shares in 2008 and 284 shares in 2007	**(6,039)**	(5,422)
Total shareowners' equity	**5,176**	4,914
Total liabilities and shareowners' equity	**$23,211**	$22,293

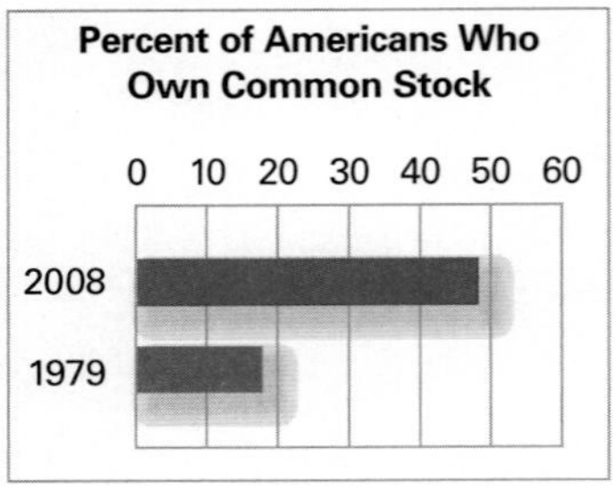

- Shares of stock can be purchased in small amounts. You could buy a single share of Kroger Co. stock for about $22 and become one of the owners of this successful company.
- Ownership interests can be easily transferred through the sale of shares on established markets such as the New York Stock Exchange.
- Stock ownership provides investors with limited liability. In the event of bankruptcy, creditors have claims against only the corporation's assets, not the assets of the individual owners.

Many Americans own stock either directly or indirectly through a mutual fund or pension program. Stock ownership offers them the opportunity to earn higher returns than they could on deposits to bank accounts or investments in corporate bonds. Unfortunately, stock ownership also involves higher risk. The proper balance between risk and the expected return on an investment depends on individual preferences.

Exhibit 11.1 presents financial information from The Kroger Co.'s annual report. Notice that the stockholders' equity section of the balance sheet lists two primary sources of stockholders' equity:

1. Contributed capital from the sale of stock. This is the amount of money stockholders invested through the purchase of shares. For Kroger, contributed capital is the sum of common stock ($955 million) plus additional paid-in capital ($3,266 million).
2. Retained earnings (sometimes called accumulated earnings) generated by the company's profit-making activities. This is the cumulative amount of net income the corporation has earned since its organization less the cumulative amount of dividends paid since organization. While most companies call this amount retained earnings, Kroger uses the name accumulated earnings.

Most companies generate a significant portion of their stockholders' equity from retained earnings. In the case of The Kroger Co., retained earnings is actually more than the original capital invested by shareholders.

ORGANIZATION of the Chapter

Ownership of a Corporation
- Benefits of Stock Ownership
- Authorized, Issued, and Outstanding Shares
- Earnings per Share (EPS) Ratio

Common Stock Transactions
- Initial Sale of Stock
- Sale of Stock in Secondary Markets
- Stock Issued for Employee Compensation
- Repurchase of Stock

Dividends on Common Stock
- Dividend Yield Ratio

Stock Dividends and Stock Splits
- Stock Dividends
- Stock Splits

Preferred Stock
- Dividends on Preferred Stock

OWNERSHIP OF A CORPORATION

The corporation is the only business form the law recognizes as a separate entity. As a distinct entity, the corporation enjoys a continuous existence separate and apart from its owners. It may own assets, incur liabilities, expand and contract in size, sue others, be sued, and enter into contracts independently of its stockholder owners.

Video 11-1
www.mhhe.com/libby7e

To protect everyone's rights, the creation and governance of corporations are tightly regulated by law. Corporations are created by application to a state government (not the federal government). On approval of the application, the state issues a charter, sometimes called the articles of incorporation. Corporations are governed by a board of directors elected by the stockholders.

Each state has different laws governing the organization of corporations created within its boundaries. The Kroger Co. has its headquarters in Ohio and it has elected to incorporate in the state of Ohio. You will find that an unusually large number of corporations are incorporated in Delaware even though their headquarters are located in a different state. Companies choose Delaware for incorporation because the state has some of the most favorable laws for establishing corporations.

Benefits of Stock Ownership

LEARNING OBJECTIVE 1
Explain the role of stock in the capital structure of a corporation.

When you invest in a corporation, you are known as a stockholder or shareholder. As a stockholder, you receive shares of stock that you subsequently can sell on established stock exchanges. Owners of common stock receive a number of benefits:

- **A voice in management.** You may vote in the stockholders' meeting on major issues concerning management of the corporation.
- **Dividends.** You receive a proportional share of the distribution of profits.
- **Residual claim.** You will receive a proportional share of the distribution of remaining assets upon the liquidation of the company.

Owners, unlike creditors, are able to vote at the annual stockholders' meeting with a number of votes equal to the number of shares owned. The following notice of the annual meeting of shareholders was recently sent to all owners of Kroger Co. stock:

REAL WORLD EXCERPT

Notice of Shareholders' Meeting

NOTICE OF ANNUAL MEETING OF SHAREHOLDERS

Cincinnati, Ohio,
May 15, 2009

To All Shareholders of The Kroger Co.:

The annual meeting of shareholders of The Kroger Co. will be held at the MUSIC HALL BALLROOM, MUSIC HALL, 1241 Elm Street, Cincinnati, Ohio, 45202, on June 25, 2009, at 11 a.m., eastern time, for the following purposes:

1. *To elect the directors for the ensuing year;*
2. *To consider and act upon a proposal to ratify the selection of independent auditors for the year 2009;*
3. *To act upon two shareholder proposals, if properly presented at the annual meeting; and*
4. *To transact such other business as may properly be brought before the meeting;*

all as set forth in the Proxy Statement accompanying this Notice. Holders of common shares of record at the close of business on April 27, 2009, will be entitled to vote at the meeting.

This notice also contained several pages of information concerning the people who were nominated to be members of the board of directors as well as a variety of financial information. Since most owners do not actually attend the annual meeting, the notice included a proxy card, which is similar to an absentee ballot. Owners may complete the proxy and mail it to the company, which includes it in the votes at the annual meeting.

As shown in Exhibit 11.2, stockholders have ultimate authority in a corporation. The board of directors and, indirectly, all employees are accountable to the stockholders. The organizational structure shown is typical of most corporations, but the specific structure depends on the nature of the company's business.

Authorized, Issued, and Outstanding Shares

The corporate charter specifies the maximum number of shares that can be sold to the public. The financial statements must report information concerning the number of shares that have been sold to date. Let's look at the share information reported by The Kroger Co. as of January 31, 2009, shown in Exhibit 11.1. For Kroger, the maximum number of common shares that can be sold, called the **authorized number of shares,** is 1,000,000,000. As of January 31, 2009, the company had sold 955,000,000 shares. Stock that has been sold to the public is called **issued shares.**

The AUTHORIZED NUMBER OF SHARES is the maximum number of shares of a corporation's capital stock that can be issued as specified in the charter.

ISSUED SHARES represent the total number of shares of stock that have been sold.

OUTSTANDING SHARES refer to the total number of shares of stock that are owned by stockholders on any particular date.

For a number of reasons, a company might want to buy back stock that has already been sold to the public. Stock that has been bought back is called *treasury stock.* When a company buys back its stock, a difference is created between the number of issued shares and the number of **outstanding shares,** or shares currently held by individual stockholders. We can compute outstanding shares for The Kroger Co. using data from the January 31, 2009, balance sheet shown in Exhibit 11.1:

Issued shares	955,000,000
Less: Treasury stock	(306,000,000)
Outstanding shares	649,000,000

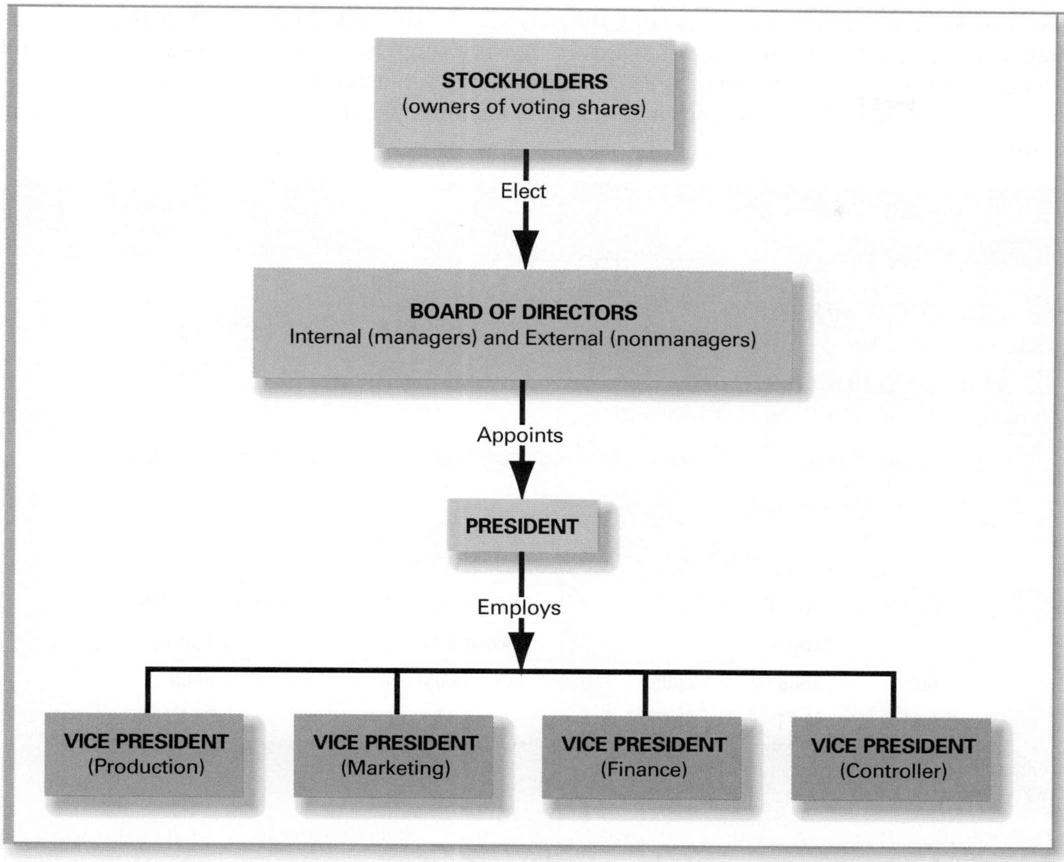

EXHIBIT 11.2

Typical Organizational Structure of a Corporation

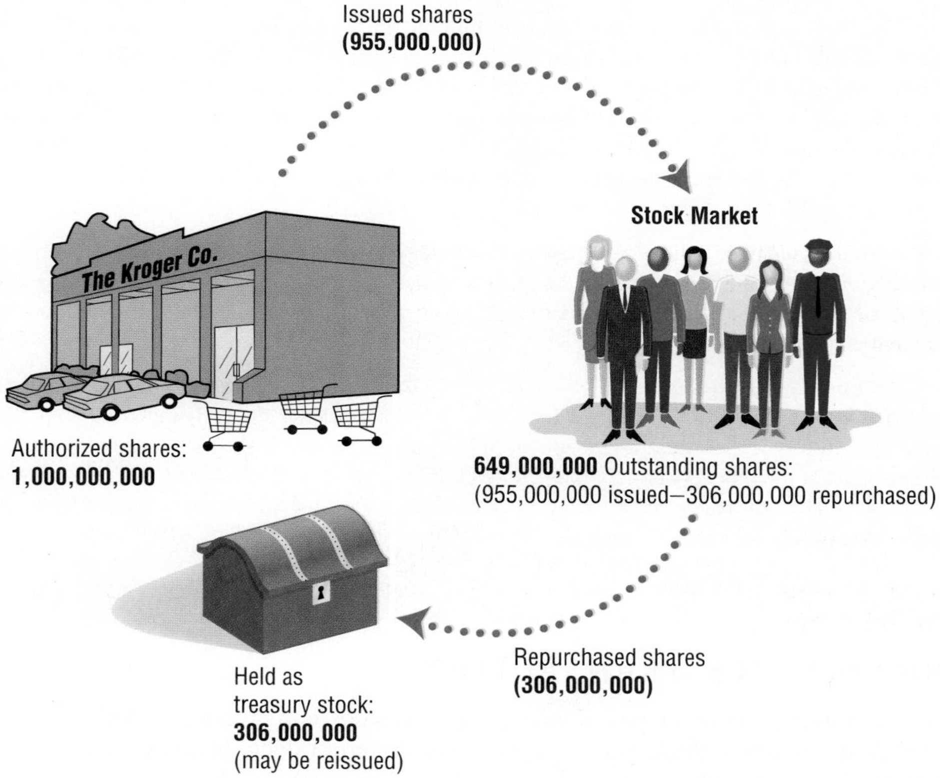

Notice that when treasury stock is held, the number of shares issued and the number of shares outstanding differ by the number of shares of treasury stock held (treasury stock is included in "issued" but not in "outstanding"). The number of shares outstanding is important to financial analysts who need to express certain dollar amounts on a per share basis. One example is the earnings per share ratio.

KEY RATIO ANALYSIS

Earnings Per Share (EPS)

LEARNING OBJECTIVE 2
Analyze the earnings per share ratio.

ANALYTICAL QUESTION

How well is a company performing?

RATIO AND COMPARISONS

Earnings per share is computed as follows:

Earnings per Share = Net Income ÷ Average Number of Common Shares Outstanding

The 2009 ratio for The Kroger Co.:

$1,249 ÷ 652 (million) shares* = $1.92

COMPARISONS OVER TIME		
Kroger		
2007	2008	2009
$1.56	$1.71	$1.92

COMPARISONS WITH COMPETITORS	
Whole Foods	Safeway
2009	2009
$0.82	$2.15

INTERPRETATIONS

In General All analysts and investors are interested in a company's earnings. You have probably seen newspaper headlines announcing a company's earnings. Notice that those news stories normally report earnings on an earnings per share (EPS) basis. EPS is a popular measure because income numbers are much easier to compare on a per share basis. For example, in 2009, The Kroger Co. earned income of $1,249 (million) compared to $1,181 (million) in the previous year, nearly a 6 percent increase. If we make that comparison on a per share basis, we can say that EPS increased from $1.71 to $1.92, a 12 percent increase. The difference in the percent increase is the result of Kroger having fewer shares outstanding. EPS is also useful in comparing companies of different sizes. Whole Foods is a smaller company than Kroger, with income of $114.5 (million) in 2009. While net income for Whole Foods was less than 10 percent of the net income earned by The Kroger Co., EPS for Whole Foods was 42 percent of the EPS for Kroger.

Focus Company Analysis The Kroger Co. has a strategy of growth and reinvestment of earnings. Analysts are watching EPS to be sure the company will achieve its strategy. Kroger's EPS increased by 23 percent between 2007 and 2009, a strong level of growth considering the difficult economic environment during that period.

A Few Cautions While EPS is an effective and widely used measure of profitability, it can be misleading if there are significant differences in the market values of the shares being compared. Two companies earning $1.50 per share might appear to be comparable, but if shares in one company cost $10 while shares of the other cost $175, they are not comparable. The stock price for Whole Foods is nearly $30 per share while the price for Kroger stock is $22. Obviously, investors expect a large EPS number for companies with higher stock prices.

*As reported in the notes to the financial statements.

LEARNING OBJECTIVE 3
Describe the characteristics of common stock and analyze transactions affecting common stock.

COMMON STOCK TRANSACTIONS

Most corporations issue two types of stock, common stock and preferred stock. All corporations must issue common stock, but only some issue preferred stock. In this section, we discuss common stock and in a subsequent section, we discuss preferred stock.

Common stock is held by individuals who are often thought of as the "owners" of the corporation because they have the right to vote and share in the profitability of the business through dividends. Periodically, the board of directors declares dividends based on the company's profitability.

The fact that common stock dividends may increase with increases in the company's profitability helps to explain why investors can make money in the stock market. Basically, you can think of the price of a share of stock as the present value of all its future dividends. If a company's profitability improves so that it can pay higher dividends, the present value of its common stock will increase.

Common stock normally has a **par value,** a nominal value per share established in the corporate charter. Par value has no relationship to the market value of a stock. The annual report for The Kroger Co. states that the common stock has a par value of $1, while its market value is more than $20 per share.

Most states require stock to have a par value. The original purpose of this requirement was to protect creditors by specifying a permanent amount of capital that owners could not withdraw before a bankruptcy, which would leave creditors with an empty corporate shell. This permanent amount of capital is called **legal capital.** Today, this requirement has little importance because of other contractual protections for creditors.

Some states require the issuance of **no-par value stock,** which does not have a specified amount per share. When a corporation issues no-par stock, legal capital is as defined by the state law.

COMMON STOCK is the basic voting stock issued by a corporation.

PAR VALUE is the nominal value per share of capital stock specified in the charter; serves as the basis for legal capital.

LEGAL CAPITAL is the permanent amount of capital defined by state law that must remain invested in the business; serves as a cushion for creditors.

NO-PAR VALUE STOCK is capital stock that has no par value specified in the corporate charter.

Initial Sale of Stock

Two names are applied to transactions involving the initial sale of a company's stock to the public. An **initial public offering,** or IPO, involves the very first sale of a company's stock to the public (i.e., when the company first "goes public"). You have probably heard stories of Internet stocks that have increased dramatically in value the day of the IPO. While investors sometimes earn significant returns on IPOs, they also take significant risks. Once a company's stock has been traded on established markets, additional sales of new stock to the public are called **seasoned new issues.**

Most sales of stock to the public are cash transactions. To illustrate the accounting for an initial sale of stock, assume that The Kroger Co. sold 100,000 shares of its $1 par value stock for $20 per share. The company would record the following journal entry:

Cash (+A) (100,000 × $20)	2,000,000	
Common stock (+SE) (100,000 × $1)		100,000
Capital in excess of par (+SE)		1,900,000

Assets		=	Liabilities	+	Stockholders' Equity	
Cash	+2,000,000				Common stock	+100,000
					Capital in excess of par	+1,900,000

Notice that the Common Stock account is credited for the number of shares sold times the par value per share, and the Capital in Excess of Par account is credited for the remainder. If the corporate charter does not specify a par value for the stock, the stated value is used in the same manner that par value is used. If there is no par or stated value, the entire proceeds from the sale will be entered in the common stock account.

Sale of Stock in Secondary Markets

When a company sells stock to the public, the transaction is between the issuing corporation and the buyer. Subsequent to the initial sale, investors can sell shares to other investors without directly affecting the corporation. For example, if investor Jon Drago sold 1,000 shares of The Kroger Co. stock to Jennifer Lea, The Kroger Co. would not record a journal entry on its books. Mr. Drago received cash for the shares he sold, and Ms. Lea received stock for the cash she paid. The Kroger Co. did not receive or pay anything.

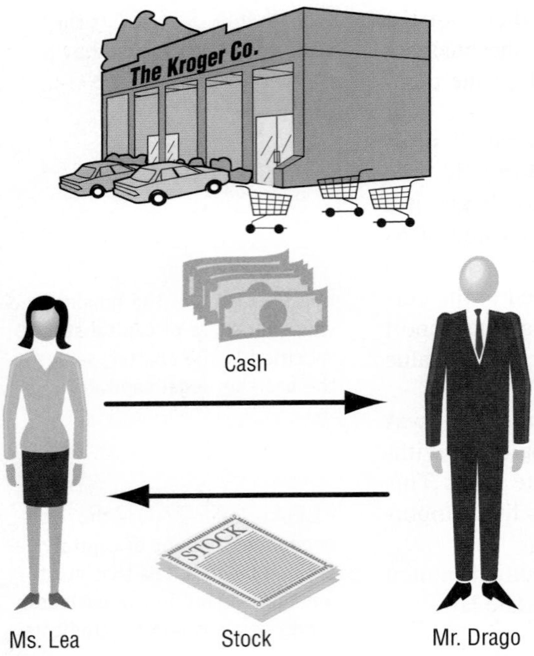

Each business day, *The Wall Street Journal* reports the results of thousands of transactions between investors in secondary markets, such as the New York Stock Exchange (NYSE), the American Stock Exchange (AMEX), and the NASDAQ market. Managers of corporations closely follow the price movements of their company's stock. Stockholders expect to earn money on their investments through both dividends and increases in the stock price. In many instances, senior management has been replaced because of a stock's poor performance in the stock market. While managers watch the stock price on a daily basis, transactions between investors do not directly affect the company's financial statements.

Stock Issued for Employee Compensation

One of the advantages of the corporate form is the ability to separate the management of a business from its ownership. Separation can also be a disadvantage because some managers may not act in the owners' best interests. This problem can be overcome in a number of ways. Compensation packages can be developed to reward managers for meeting goals that are important to stockholders. Another strategy is to offer managers stock options, which permit them to buy stock at a fixed price.

The holder of a stock option has an interest in a company's performance just as an owner does. Stock option plans have become an increasingly common form of compensation over the past few years. Indeed, 98 percent of the companies surveyed by *Accounting Trends & Techniques* now offer stock option plans to their employees.

The Kroger Co. offers employees stock options as part of their compensation. The options specify that shares could be bought at the then-current market price. Granting a stock option is a form of compensation, even if the grant price and the current stock price are the same. You can think of a stock option as a risk-free investment. If you hold a stock option and the stock price declines, you have lost nothing. If the stock price increases, you can exercise your option at the low grant price and sell the stock at the higher price for a profit.

Companies must estimate and report compensation expense associated with stock options. These procedures are discussed in more detail in intermediate accounting courses.

Repurchase of Stock

TREASURY STOCK is a corporation's own stock that has been issued but subsequently reacquired and is still being held by that corporation.

A corporation may want to repurchase its stock from existing stockholders for a number of reasons. One common reason is the existence of an employee bonus plan that provides workers with shares of the company's stock as part of their compensation. Because of Securities and Exchange Commission regulations concerning newly issued shares, most companies find it less costly to give employees repurchased shares than to issue new ones. Stock that has been reacquired and is held by the issuing corporation is called **treasury stock.** These shares have no voting, dividend, or other stockholder rights while they are held as treasury stock.

Most companies record the purchase of treasury stock based on the cost of the shares that were purchased. Assume that The Kroger Co. bought 100,000 shares of its stock in the open market when it was selling for $20 per share. Using the cost method, the company would record the following journal entry:

Treasury stock (+XSE, −SE) (100,000 × $20)	2,000,000	
Cash (−A)		2,000,000

Assets		=	Liabilities	+	Stockholders' Equity	
Cash	−2,000,000				Treasury stock	−2,000,000

Intuitively, many students expect the Treasury Stock account to be reported as an asset. Such is not the case because a company cannot create an asset by investing in itself. The Treasury Stock account is actually a contra-equity account, which means that it is subtracted from total stockholders' equity. This practice makes sense because treasury stock is stock that is no longer outstanding and therefore should not be included in stockholders' equity.

As the information in Exhibit 11.1 indicates, The Kroger Co. reported treasury stock in the amount of $6,039 (million) on its balance sheet as of January 31, 2009. The statement of stockholders' equity reports the same amount plus additional information.

When a company sells its treasury stock, it does not report an accounting profit or loss on the transaction, even if it sells the stock for more or less than it paid. GAAP does not permit a corporation to report income or losses from investments in its own stock because transactions with the owners are not considered normal profit-making activities. Based on the previous example, assume that The Kroger Co. re-sold 10,000 shares of treasury stock for $30 per share. Remember that the company had purchased the stock for $20 per share. Kroger would record the following journal entry:

Cash (+A) (10,000 × $30)	300,000	
Treasury stock (−XSE, +SE) (10,000 × $20)		200,000
Capital in excess of par (+SE).		100,000

Assets		=	Liabilities	+	Stockholders' Equity	
Cash	+300,000				Treasury stock	+200,000
					Capital in excess of par	+100,000

If treasury stock were sold at a price below its purchase price (i.e., at an economic loss), stockholders' equity would be reduced by the amount of the difference between the purchase price and the sale price. Assume that Kroger had sold the stock in the previous illustration for only $15 per share:

Cash (+A) (100,000 × $15)	150,000	
Capital in excess of par (−SE) (10,000 × $5).	50,000	
Treasury stock (−XSE, +SE) (10,000 × $20)		200,000

Assets		=	Liabilities	+	Stockholders' Equity	
Cash	+150,000				Treasury stock	+200,000
					Capital in excess of par	−50,000

Companies Reporting Treasury Stock (sample of 600 companies)

PAUSE FOR **FEEDBACK**

We have looked at several transactions involving the sale and repurchase of common stock. In the next section, we will discuss dividends. Before you move on, complete the following questions to test your understanding of these concepts.

SELF-STUDY **QUIZ**

1. Assume that Applied Technology Corporation issued 10,000 shares of its common stock, par value $2, for $150,000 cash. Prepare the journal entry to record this transaction.
2. Assume that Applied Technology repurchased 5,000 shares of its stock in the open market when the stock was selling for $12 per share. Record this transaction.

After you have completed your answers, check them with the solutions at the bottom of the page.

Solutions to SELF-STUDY QUIZ

1. Cash (+A)	150,000	
Common stock (+SE)		20,000
Capital in excess of par (+SE)		130,000
2. Treasury stock (+XSE, −SE)	60,000	
Cash (−A)		60,000

LEARNING OBJECTIVE 4

Discuss dividends and analyze transactions.

DIVIDENDS ON COMMON STOCK

Investors buy common stock because they expect a return on their investment. This return can come in two forms: stock price appreciation and dividends. Some investors prefer to buy stocks that pay little or no dividends because companies that reinvest the majority of their earnings tend to increase their future earnings potential, along with their stock price. Wealthy investors in high tax brackets prefer to receive their return in the form of higher stock prices because capital gains may be taxed at a lower rate than dividend income. Other investors, such as retired people who need a steady income, prefer to receive their return in the form of dividends. These people often seek stocks that will pay very high dividends, such as utility stocks. Because of the importance of dividends to many investors, analysts often compute the dividend yield ratio to evaluate a corporation's dividend policy.

KEY RATIO ANALYSIS

Dividend Yield

LEARNING OBJECTIVE 5

Analyze the dividend yield ratio.

ANALYTICAL QUESTION

What is return on investment based on dividends?

RATIO AND COMPARISONS

The dividend yield ratio is computed as follows:

Dividend Yield = Dividends per Share ÷ Market Price per Share

The 2009 ratio for The Kroger Co.:

$0.36 ÷ $22 = 1.6%

COMPARISONS OVER TIME		
Kroger		
2007	**2008**	**2009**
1.0%	1.0%	1.6%

COMPARISONS WITH COMPETITORS	
Whole Foods	**Safeway**
2009	**2009**
2.1%	2.1%

INTERPRETATIONS

In General Investors in common stock earn a return from both dividends and capital appreciation (increases in the market price of the stock). Growth-oriented companies often rely mainly on increases in their market price to provide a return to investors. Others pay large dividends but have more stable market prices. Each type of stock appeals to different types of investors with different risk and return preferences.

Focus Company Analysis Like many companies, The Kroger Co. pays a modest dividend and reinvests the majority of its earnings in the company. The Kroger Co. also repurchases a significant amount of stock each year from current stockholders. Clearly, investors in The Kroger Co. hope to earn a significant return on the increased value of the company.

A Few Cautions Remember that the dividend yield ratio tells only part of the return on investment story. Often potential capital appreciation is a much more important consideration. The Kroger Co. is currently reinvesting a large portion of its earnings. Analysts should assess the future earnings potential of the company, not just its current dividend yield.

The declaration and payment of a dividend involve several significant events. Let's review these events based on a dividend announcement reported by *Barron's*.

> CINCINNATI, June 25 /PRNewswire-FirstCall/—The Kroger Co. (NYSE: KR) announced today that its Board of Directors declared a quarterly dividend of $0.09 per share to be paid on September 1, 2009, to shareholders of record as of the close of business on August 14, 2009.

REAL WORLD EXCERPT

Dividend Announcement

This announcement contains three important dates:

1. **Declaration date—June 25, 2009.** The **declaration date** is the date on which the board of directors officially approves the dividend. As soon as it makes the declaration, it creates a dividend liability.
2. **Date of record—August 14, 2009.** The **record date** follows the declaration; it is the date on which the corporation prepares the list of current stockholders based on its records. The dividend is payable only to those names listed on the record date. No journal entry is made on this date.
3. **Date of payment—September 1, 2009.** The **payment date** is the date on which the cash is disbursed to pay the dividend liability. It follows the date of record, as specified in the dividend announcement.

The DECLARATION DATE is the date on which the board of directors officially approves a dividend.

The RECORD DATE is the date on which the corporation prepares the list of current stockholders as shown on its records; dividends can be paid only to the stockholders who own stock on that date.

The PAYMENT DATE is the date on which a cash dividend is paid to the stockholders of record.

These three dates apply for all cash dividends and can be shown graphically as follows:

Declaration Date —— Date of Record —— Date of Payment

On the declaration date, a company records a liability related to the dividend. To illustrate, on June 25, The Kroger Co. records the following journal entry. Assuming 649 million shares are outstanding, the dividend amounts to $58,410,000 ($0.09 × 649,000,000):

Retained earnings (−SE)	58,410,000	
Dividends payable (+L)		58,410,000

Assets	=	Liabilities		+	Stockholders' Equity	
		Dividends payable	+58,410,000		Retained earnings	−58,410,000

The payment of the liability on September 1 is recorded as follows:

Dividends payable (−L)	58,410,000	
Cash (−A)		58,410,000

Assets		=	Liabilities		+	Stockholders' Equity
Cash	−58,410,000		Dividends payable	−58,410,000		

Notice that the declaration and payment of a cash dividend reduce assets (cash) and stockholders' equity (retained earnings) by the same amount. This observation explains the two fundamental requirements for payment of a cash dividend:

1. **Sufficient retained earnings.** The corporation must have accumulated a sufficient amount of retained earnings to cover the amount of the dividend. State incorporation laws often limit cash dividends to the balance in the Retained Earnings account.

2. **Sufficient cash.** The corporation must have sufficient cash to pay the dividend and meet the operating needs of the business. The mere fact that the Retained Earnings account has a large credit balance does not mean that the board of directors can declare and pay a cash dividend. The cash generated in the past by earnings represented in the Retained Earnings account may have been expended to acquire inventory, buy operational assets, and pay liabilities. Consequently, no necessary relationship exists between the balance of retained earnings and the balance of cash on any particular date. Quite simply, retained earnings is not cash.

FINANCIAL ANALYSIS | Impact of Dividends on Stock Price

Another date that is important in understanding dividends has no accounting implications. The date two business days before the date of record is known as the *ex-dividend date.* This date is established by the stock exchanges to make certain that dividend checks are sent to the right people. If you buy stock before the ex-dividend date, you will receive the dividend. If you buy stock on the ex-dividend date or later, the previous owner will receive the dividend.

If you follow stock prices, you will notice that they often fall on the ex-dividend date. The stock is worth less on that date because it no longer includes the right to receive the next dividend.

PAUSE FOR FEEDBACK

One of the reasons that investors buy common stock is to earn dividends. We have looked at dividends paid in cash. In the next section, we will look at dividends paid in stock. Before you move on, complete the following questions to test your understanding of these concepts.

SELF-STUDY QUIZ

1. On which dividend date is a liability created?
2. A cash outflow occurs on which dividend date?
3. What are the two fundamental requirements for the payment of a dividend?

After you have completed your answers, check them with the solutions at the bottom of the page.

Solutions to SELF-STUDY QUIZ

1. Declaration date.
2. Date of payment.
3. Dividends can be paid only if sufficient retained earnings and sufficient cash are both available.

STOCK DIVIDENDS AND STOCK SPLITS

Stock Dividends

LEARNING OBJECTIVE 6

Discuss the purpose of stock dividends and stock splits, and report transactions.

Without a qualifier, the term *dividend* means a cash dividend, but dividends can also be paid with additional shares of stock. A **stock dividend** is a distribution of additional shares of a corporation's own stock to its stockholders on a pro rata basis at no cost to the stockholder. The phrase *pro rata basis* means that each stockholder receives additional shares equal to the percentage of shares held. A stockholder with 10 percent of the outstanding shares would receive 10 percent of any additional shares issued as a stock dividend.

A STOCK DIVIDEND is a distribution of additional shares of a corporation's own stock.

The term *stock dividend* is sometimes misused in annual reports and news articles. A recent *Wall Street Journal* headline announced that a particular company had just declared a "stock dividend." A close reading of the article revealed that the company had actually declared a cash dividend on the stock.

The value of a stock dividend is the subject of much debate. In reality, a stock dividend by itself has no economic value. All stockholders receive a pro rata distribution of shares, which means that each stockholder owns exactly the same portion of the company as before. The value of an investment is determined by the percentage of the company that is owned, not the number of shares held. If you get change for a dollar, you do not have more wealth because you hold four quarters instead of only one dollar. Similarly, if you own 10 percent of a company, you are not wealthier simply because the company declares a stock dividend and gives you (and all other stockholders) more shares of stock.

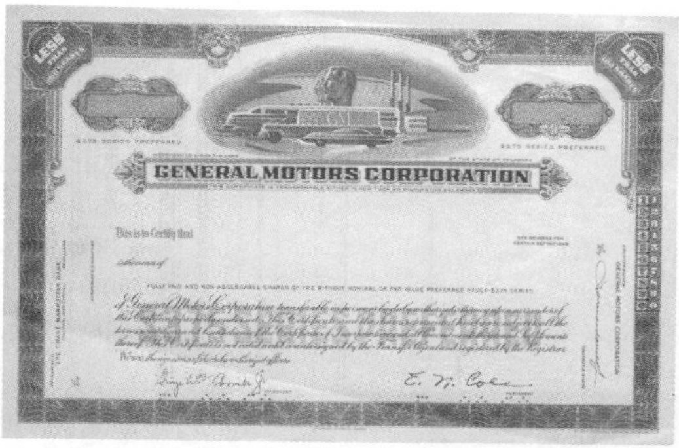

The stock market reacts immediately when a stock dividend is issued, and the stock price falls proportionally. Theoretically, if the stock price was \$60 before a stock dividend and the number of shares is doubled, in the absence of events affecting the company, the price would fall to \$30. Thus, an investor would own 100 shares worth \$6,000 before the stock dividend (100 × \$60) and 200 shares worth \$6,000 after the stock dividend (200 × \$30).

In reality, the fall in price is not exactly proportional to the number of new shares issued. In some cases, the stock dividend makes the stock more attractive to new investors. Many investors prefer to buy stock in round lots, which are multiples of 100 shares. An investor with \$10,000 might not buy a stock selling for \$150, for instance, because she cannot afford to buy 100 shares. She might buy the stock if the price were less than \$100 as the result of a stock dividend. In other cases, stock dividends are associated with increases in cash dividends, which are attractive to some investors.

Size of Stock Dividends (sample of 600 companies)

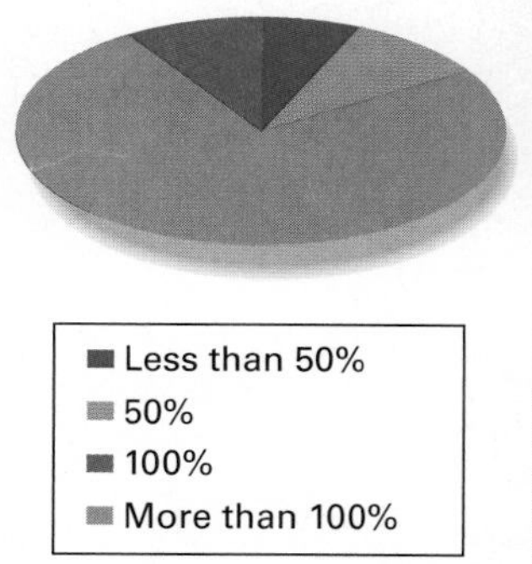

When a stock dividend occurs, the company must transfer an additional amount from the Retained Earnings account (or Capital in Excess of Par Value account, if there is not a sufficient balance in Retained Earnings) into the Common Stock account to reflect the additional shares issued. The amount transferred depends on whether the stock dividend is classified as large or small. Most stock dividends are classified as large. A large stock dividend involves the distribution of additional shares that amount to more than 20–25 percent of currently outstanding shares. A small stock dividend involves the distribution of shares that amount to less than 20–25 percent of the outstanding shares. If the stock dividend is classified as large, the amount transferred to the Common Stock account is based on the par value of the additional shares issued. If the stock dividend is small (i.e., less than 20–25 percent), the amount transferred should be the total market value of the shares issued, with the par value of the stock transferred to the Common Stock account and the excess transferred to the Capital in Excess of Par Value account.

Assume The Kroger Co. issued a large stock dividend. The company issued 400,000,000 shares and made the following journal entry:

Retained earnings (−SE) (\$1 × 400,000,000)	400,000,000	
Common stock (+SE)		400,000,000

Assets	=	Liabilities		+	Stockholders' Equity
		Retained earnings	400,000,000		
		Common stock	400,000,000		

This journal entry moves an amount from Retained Earnings to the company's Common Stock account. Notice that the stock dividend did not change total stockholders' equity. It changed only the balances of some of the accounts that constitute stockholders' equity.

Stock Splits

A STOCK SPLIT is an increase in the total number of authorized shares by a specified ratio; it does not decrease retained earnings.

Stock splits are not dividends. While they are similar to a stock dividend, they are quite different in terms of their impact on the stockholders' equity accounts. In a **stock split,** the total number of authorized shares is increased by a specified amount, such as 2-for-1. In this instance, each share held is called in and two new shares are issued in its place. Typically, a stock split is accomplished by reducing the par or stated value per share of all authorized shares, so that their total par value is unchanged. For instance, if The Kroger Co. executes a 2-for-1 stock split, it reduces the par value of its stock from $1 to $0.50 and doubles the number of shares outstanding. In contrast to a stock dividend, a stock split does not result in the transfer of a dollar amount to the Common Stock account. The reduction in the par value per share compensates for the increase in the number of shares, so that no transfer is needed.

In both a stock dividend and a stock split, the stockholder receives more shares of stock without having to invest additional resources to acquire the shares. A stock dividend requires a journal entry; a stock split does not but is disclosed in the notes to the financial statements. The comparative effects of a large stock dividend versus a stock split may be summarized as follows:

STOCKHOLDERS' EQUITY

	Before	After a 100% Stock Dividend	After a Two-for-One Stock Split
Number of shares outstanding	30,000	60,000	60,000
Par value per share	$ 10	$ 10	$ 5
Total par value outstanding	300,000	600,000	300,000
Retained earnings	650,000	350,000	650,000
Total stockholders' equity	950,000	950,000	950,000

STOP PAUSE FOR **FEEDBACK**

We have concluded our discussion of common stock by looking at stock dividends and stock splits. In the next section, we will examine preferred stock. Before you move on, complete the following questions to test your understanding of these concepts.

SELF-STUDY **QUIZ**

Barton Corporation issued 100,000 new shares of common stock (par value $10) in a stock dividend when the market value was $30 per share.

1. Record this transaction, assuming that it was a small stock dividend.
2. Record this transaction, assuming that it was a large stock dividend.
3. What journal entry would be required if the transaction were a stock split?

After you have completed your answers, check them with the solutions at the bottom of the page.

Solutions to SELF-STUDY QUIZ

1. Retained earnings	3,000,000	
Common stock		1,000,000
Capital in excess of par		2,000,000
2. Retained earnings	1,000,000	
Common stock		1,000,000

3. No journal entry is required in the case of a stock split.

PREFERRED STOCK

LEARNING OBJECTIVE 7
Describe the characteristics of preferred stock and analyze transactions affecting preferred stock.

In addition to common stock, some corporations issue **preferred stock.** Notice in Exhibit 11.1 that The Kroger Co. is authorized to issue 5 (million) shares of preferred stock but has not done so. Kroger included this amount in its corporate charter so that it could raise additional funds, if needed, without having to amend its charter.

Preferred stock differs from common stock based on a number of rights granted to the stockholders. The most significant differences are:

PREFERRED STOCK is stock that has specified rights over common stock.

- **Preferred stock does not grant voting rights.** As a result, preferred stock does not appeal to investors who want some control over the operations of a corporation. Indeed, this is one of the main reasons some corporations issue preferred stock to raise their equity capital: Preferred stock permits them to raise funds without diluting common stockholders' control. The chart in the margin shows the percentage of companies surveyed by *Accounting Trends & Techniques* that include preferred stock in their capital structure.
- **Preferred stock is less risky.** Generally, preferred stock is less risky than common stock because holders receive priority payment of dividends and distribution of assets if the corporation goes out of business. Usually a specified amount per share must be paid to preferred stockholders upon dissolution, before any remaining assets can be distributed to the common stockholders.
- **Preferred stock typically has a fixed dividend rate.** For example, "6 percent preferred stock, par value $10 per share" pays an annual dividend of 6 percent of par, or $0.60 per share. If preferred stock had no par value, the preferred dividend would be specified as $0.60 per share. The fixed dividend is attractive to certain investors who want a stable income from their investments.

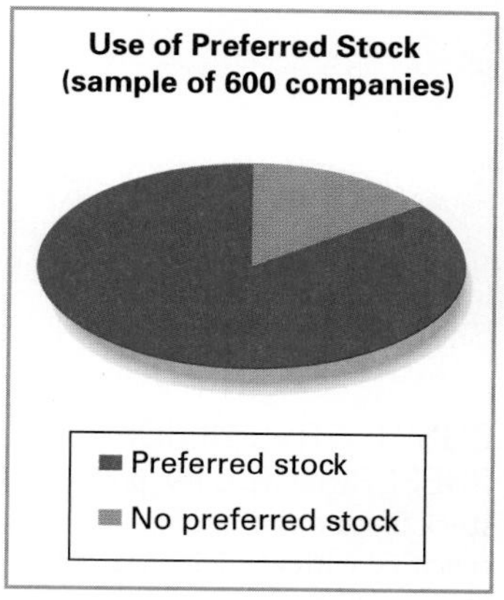

What's in a Name?

INTERNATIONAL PERSPECTIVE

It is often confusing when different words are used to describe exactly the same thing. Such is the case with International Financial Accounting Standards (IFRS) and U.S. GAAP. The following table serves as a translation guide. Remember the actual elements are exactly the same. It is only their names that differ:

GAAP		IFRS
Capital stock	=	Issued capital or share capital
Paid-in capital	=	Share premium
Treasury stock	=	Treasury shares
Preferred stock	=	Preference shares

Dividends on Preferred Stock

Because investors who purchase preferred stock give up certain advantages that are available to investors in common stock, preferred stock offers a dividend preference. The two most common dividend preferences are current and cumulative.

Current Dividend Preference

The **current dividend preference** requires the current preferred dividend to be paid before any dividends are paid on the common stock. This preference is always a feature of preferred stock. After the current dividend preference has been met and if no other preference is operative, dividends can be paid to the common stockholders.

CURRENT DIVIDEND PREFERENCE is the feature of preferred stock that grants priority on preferred dividends over common dividends.

Declared dividends must be allocated between preferred stock and common stock. First, the preferred stock preference must be met; then the remainder of the total dividend can be allocated to the common stock. To illustrate, assume the Sophia Company has the following stock outstanding:

SOPHIA COMPANY
Preferred stock outstanding, 6%, par $20; 2,000 shares = $40,000 par
Common stock outstanding, par $10; 5,000 shares = $50,000 par

Assuming a current dividend preference only, dividends would be allocated as follows:

Example	Total Dividends	6% Preferred Stock*	Common Stock
No. 1	$ 3,000	$2,400	$ 600
No. 2	18,000	2,400	15,600

**Preferred dividend preference, $40,000 × 6% = $2,400.*

Cumulative Dividend Preference

CUMULATIVE DIVIDEND PREFERENCE is the preferred stock feature that requires specified current dividends not paid in full to accumulate for every year in which they are not paid. These cumulative preferred dividends must be paid before any common dividends can be paid.

DIVIDENDS IN ARREARS are dividends on cumulative preferred stock that have not been declared in prior years.

The **cumulative dividend preference** states that if all or a part of the current dividend is not paid in full, the cumulative unpaid amount, known as **dividends in arrears,** must be paid before any common dividends can be paid. Of course, if the preferred stock is noncumulative, dividends can never be in arrears; any preferred dividends that are not declared are permanently lost. Because preferred stockholders are unwilling to accept this unfavorable feature, preferred stock is usually cumulative.

To illustrate the cumulative preference, assume that Sophia Company has the same amount of stock outstanding as in the last example. In this case, dividends have been in arrears for two years.

Example	Total Dividends	6% Preferred Stock*	Common Stock
No. 1	$ 8,000	$7,200	$ 800
No. 2	30,000	7,200	22,800

**Current dividend preference, $40,000 × 6% = $2,400; dividends in arrears preference, $2,400 × 2 years = $4,800; current dividend preference plus dividends in arrears = $7,200.*

FINANCIAL ANALYSIS | Restrictions on the Payment of Dividends

Two common constraints on the ability of a corporation to pay dividends are the existence of loan covenants and preferred stock dividends in arrears. For additional security, some creditors include a loan covenant that limits the amount of dividends a corporation can pay. These debt covenants often also include a limit on borrowing and require a minimum balance of cash or working capital. If debt covenants are violated, the creditor can demand immediate repayment of the debt. The full-disclosure principle requires the disclosure of loan covenants, typically in a separate note to the financial statements.

The existence of dividends in arrears on preferred stock can also limit a company's ability to pay dividends to common stockholders and can affect a company's future cash flows. Because dividends are never an actual liability until the board of directors declares them, dividends in arrears are not reported on the balance sheet. Instead, they are disclosed in the notes to the statements. The following note from Lone Star Industries is typical:

The total of dividends in arrears on the $13.50 preferred stock at the end of the year was $11,670,000. The aggregate amount of such dividend must be paid before any dividends are paid on common stock.

LONE STAR INDUSTRIES

REAL WORLD EXCERPT

Annual Report

Analysts are particularly interested in information concerning these restrictions because of the impact they have on the company's dividend policy and future cash flows.

Financing Activities

FOCUS ON CASH FLOWS

Transactions involving capital stock have a direct impact on the capital structure of a business. Because of the importance of these transactions, they are reported in the section of the statement of cash flows called Cash Flows from Financing Activities. Examples of cash flows associated with capital stock are included in the statement of cash flows for The Kroger Co. shown in Exhibit 11.3.

LEARNING OBJECTIVE 8

Discuss the impact of capital stock transactions on cash flows.

EFFECT ON STATEMENT OF CASH FLOWS

In General Cash received from owners is reported as an inflow; cash payments made to owners are reported as outflows. See the following example:

	Effect on Cash Flows
Financing activities	
Issuance of capital stock	+
Purchase of treasury stock	−
Sale of treasury stock	+
Payment of cash dividends	−

Selected Focus Company Comparisons: Dividends Paid (in millions)

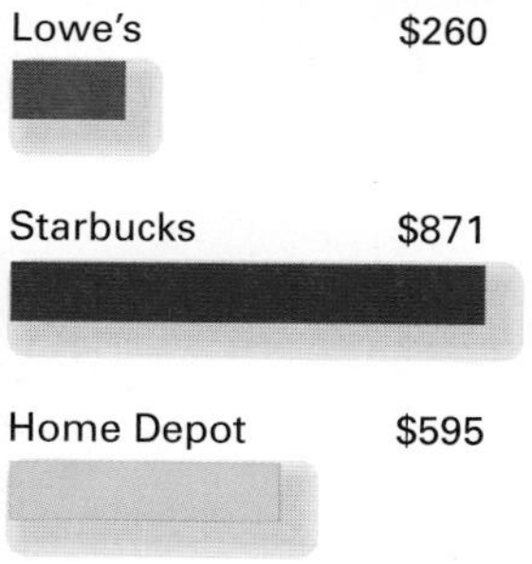

Focus Company Analysis Notice that for each of the last three years, The Kroger Co. has paid out a significant amount of cash for purchases of treasury stock and has increased the cash paid out for dividends each year (see Exhibit 11.3).

EXHIBIT 11.3

Excerpt from Statement of Cash Flows for The Kroger Co.

CONSOLIDATED STATEMENTS OF CASH FLOWS
(in millions)

	2008	2007	2006
Cash flows from financing activities:			
Proceeds from issuance of long-term debt	**$1,377**	$1,372	$ 10
Payments on long-term debt	**(1,048)**	(560)	(556)
Borrowings (payments) on bank revolver	**(441)**	218	352
Excess tax benefits on stock-based awards	**15**	36	38
Proceeds from issuance of capital stock	**172**	188	168
Treasury stock purchases	**(637)**	(1,421)	(633)
Dividends paid	**(227)**	(202)	(140)
Increase in book overdrafts	**2**	61	1
Other	**18**	(2)	(25)
Net cash used by financing activities	**(769)**	(310)	(785)

REAL WORLD EXCERPT

Annual Report

DEMONSTRATION CASE

(Try to resolve the requirements before proceeding to the suggested solution that follows.)

This case focuses on the organization and operations for the first year of Shelly Corporation, which was organized by 10 local entrepreneurs on January 1, 2011, for the purpose of operating a business to sell various supplies to hotels. The charter authorized the following capital stock:

Common stock, no-par value, 20,000 shares
Preferred stock, 5 percent, $100 par value, 5,000 shares

The laws of the state specify that the legal capital for no-par stock is the full sale amount.

The following summarized transactions, selected from 2011, were completed on the dates indicated:

a. Jan. Sold a total of 8,000 shares of common stock to the 10 entrepreneurs for cash at $50 per share. Credit the Common Stock account for the total issue amount.

b. Feb. Sold 2,000 shares of preferred stock at $102 per share; cash collected in full.

c. Mar. Declared cash dividend of $1 on common stock.

d. July Purchased 100 shares of preferred stock that had been sold and issued earlier. Shelly Corporation paid the stockholder $104 per share.

e. Aug. Sold 20 shares of the preferred treasury stock at $105 per share.

Required:

1. Give the appropriate journal entries with a brief explanation for each transaction.

2. Prepare the Stockholders' Equity section of the balance sheet for Shelly Corporation at December 31, 2011. Assume retained earnings is $23,000.

SUGGESTED SOLUTION

1. Journal entries:

a. Jan. 2011	Cash (+A)	400,000	
	Common stock (+SE)		400,000
	Sale of no-par common stock ($50 × 8,000 shares = $400,000).		
b. Feb. 2011	Cash (+A)	204,000	
	Preferred stock (+SE)		200,000
	Capital in excess of par, preferred stock (+SE) . . .		4,000
	Sale of preferred stock ($102 × 2,000 shares = $204,000).		
c. March 2011	Retained earnings (−SE)	8,000	
	Dividend payable (+L)		8,000
	Declared cash dividend.		
d. July 2011	Treasury stock (+XSE, −SE)	10,400	
	Cash (−A)		10,400
	Purchased 100 shares of preferred stock ($104 × 100 shares = $10,400).		
e. Aug. 2011	Cash (+A)	2,100	
	Treasury stock (−XSE, +SE)		2,080
	Capital in excess of par, preferred stock (+SE) . . .		20
	Sold 20 shares of the preferred treasury stock at $105.		

2. Stockholders' equity section of the balance sheet:

SHELLY CORPORATION
Partial Balance Sheet
At December 31, 2011

Stockholders' Equity		
Contributed capital		
Preferred stock, 5% (par value $100; authorized 5,000 shares, issued 2,000 shares of which 80 shares are held as treasury stock)	$200,000	
Capital in excess of par, preferred stock	4,020	
Common stock (no-par value; authorized 20,000 shares, issued and outstanding 8,000 shares)	400,000	
Total contributed capital	$604,020	
Retained earnings	23,000	
Total contributed capital and retained earnings	$627,020	
Less cost of preferred treasury stock held (80 shares)	(8,320)	
Total stockholders' equity		$618,700

Chapter Supplement

Accounting for Owners' Equity for Sole Proprietorships and Partnerships

Owners' Equity for a Sole Proprietorship

A *sole proprietorship* is an unincorporated business owned by one person. Only two owners' equity accounts are needed: (1) a capital account for the proprietor (J. Doe, Capital) and (2) a drawing (or withdrawal) account for the proprietor (J. Doe, Drawings).

The capital account of a sole proprietorship serves two purposes: to record investments by the owner and to accumulate periodic income or loss. The drawing account is used to record the owner's withdrawals of cash or other assets from the business. The drawing account is closed to the capital account at the end of each accounting period. Thus, the capital account reflects the cumulative total of all investments by the owner and all earnings of the entity less all withdrawals from the entity by the owner.

In most respects, the accounting for a sole proprietorship is the same as for a corporation. Exhibit 11.4 presents the recording of selected transactions of Doe Retail Store and the statement of owners' equity.

Because a sole proprietorship does not pay income taxes, its financial statements do not reflect income tax expense or income taxes payable. Instead, the net income of a sole proprietorship is taxed when it is included on the owner's personal income tax return. Likewise, the owner's salary is not recognized as an expense in a sole proprietorship because an employer/employee contractual relationship cannot exist with only one party involved. The owner's salary is therefore accounted for as a distribution of profits (i.e., a withdrawal).

Owners' Equity for a Partnership

The Uniform Partnership Act, which most states have adopted, defines a partnership as "an association of two or more persons to carry on as co-owners of a business for profit." Small businesses and professionals such as accountants, doctors, and lawyers often use the partnership form of business.

A partnership is formed by two or more persons reaching mutual agreement about the terms of the relationship. The law does not require an application for a charter as in the case of a corporation. Instead, the agreement between the partners constitutes a partnership contract. This agreement should specify matters such as division of periodic income, management responsibilities, transfer or sale of partnership

EXHIBIT 11.4

Accounting for Owners' Equity for a Sole Proprietorship

Selected Entries during 2011
January 1, 2011
J. Doe started a retail store by investing $150,000 of personal savings. The journal entry follows:

Cash (+A)	150,000	
J. Doe, capital (+OE)		150,000

Assets		=	Liabilities	+	Owners' Equity	
Cash	+150,000				J. Doe, capital	+150,000

During 2011
Each month during the year, Doe withdrew $1,000 cash from the business for personal living costs. Accordingly, each month the following journal entry was made:

J. Doe, drawings (−OE).	1,000	
Cash (−A)		1,000

Assets		=	Liabilities	+	Owners' Equity	
Cash	−1,000				J. Doe, drawings	−1,000

Note: At December 31, 2011, after the last withdrawal, the drawings account reflected a debit balance of $12,000.

December 31, 2011
The usual journal entries for the year, including adjusting and closing entries for the revenue and expense accounts, resulted in an $18,000 net income, which was closed to the capital account as follows:

Individual revenue and expense accounts (−R&E)	18,000	
J. Doe, capital (+OE)		18,000

Assets	=	Liabilities	+	Owners' Equity	
				Revenues and expenses	−18,000
				J. Doe, capital	+18,000

December 31, 2011
The drawings account was closed as follows:

J. Doe, capital (−OE).	12,000	
J. Doe, drawings (+OE).		12,000

Assets	=	Liabilities	+	Owners' Equity	
				J. Doe, capital	−12,000
				J. Doe, drawings	+12,000

Balance Sheet December 31, 2011 (partial)

Owners' equity	
J. Doe, capital, January 1, 2011	$150,000
Add: Net income for 2011	18,000
Total	168,000
Less: Withdrawals for 2011	(12,000)
J. Doe, capital, December 31, 2011	$156,000

interests, disposition of assets upon liquidation, and procedures to be followed in case of the death of a partner. If the partnership agreement does not specify these matters, the laws of the resident state are binding.

The primary advantages of a partnership are (1) ease of formation, (2) complete control by the partners, and (3) lack of income taxes on the business itself. The primary disadvantage is the unlimited liability of each partner for the partnership's debts. If the partnership does not have sufficient assets to satisfy outstanding debt, creditors of the partnership can seize the partners' personal assets.

As with a sole proprietorship, accounting for a partnership follows the same underlying principles as any other form of business organization, except for those entries that directly affect owners' equity. Accounting for partners' equity follows the same pattern as for a sole proprietorship, except that separate capital and drawing accounts must be established for each partner. Investments by each partner are credited to that partner's capital account; withdrawals are debited to the respective partner's drawing account. The net income of a partnership is divided among the partners in accordance with the partnership agreement and credited to each account. The respective drawing accounts are closed to the partner capital accounts. After the closing process, each partner's capital account reflects the cumulative total of all of that partner's investments plus that partner's share of the partnership earnings less all that partner's withdrawals.

Exhibit 11.5 presents selected journal entries and partial financial statements for AB Partnership to illustrate the accounting for the distribution of income and partners' equity.

The financial statements of a partnership follow the same format as those for a corporation except that (1) the income statement includes an additional section entitled Distribution of Net Income, (2) the partners' equity section of the balance sheet is detailed for each partner, (3) the partnership has no income tax expense because partnerships do not pay income tax (partners must report their share of the partnership profits on their individual tax returns), and (4) salaries paid to the partners are not recorded as expenses but are treated as distributions of earnings.

EXHIBIT 11.5

Accounting for Partners' Equity

Selected Entries during 2011
January 1, 2011
A. Able and B. Baker organized AB Partnership on this date. Able contributed $60,000 and Baker $40,000 cash to the partnership and agreed to divide net income (and net loss) 60 percent and 40 percent, respectively. The journal entry for the business to record the investment was as follows:

Cash (+A)	100,000	
A. Able, capital (+OE)		60,000
B. Baker, capital (+OE)		40,000

Assets		=	Liabilities	+	Owners' Equity	
Cash	+100,000				A. Able, capital	+60,000
					B. Baker, capital	+40,000

During 2011
The partners agreed that Able would withdraw $1,000 and Baker $650 per month in cash. Accordingly, each month the following journal entry was made:

A. Able, drawings (−OE)	1,000	
B. Baker, drawings (−OE)	650	
Cash (−A)		1,650

Assets		=	Liabilities	+	Owners' Equity	
Cash	−1,650				A. Able, drawings	−1,000
					B. Baker, drawings	−650

EXHIBIT 11.5

Concluded

December 31, 2011

Assume that the normal closing entries for the revenue and expense accounts resulted in a net income of $30,000. The partnership agreement specified Able would receive 60 percent of earnings and Baker would receive 40 percent. The closing entry was as follows:

Individual revenue and expense accounts (−R&E) . . .	30,000	
A. Able, capital (+OE)		18,000
B. Baker, capital (+OE)		12,000

Assets	=	Liabilities	+	Owners' Equity	
				Revenues and expenses	−30,000
				A. Able, capital	+18,000
				B. Baker, capital	+12,000

December 31, 2011

The journal entry required to close the drawing accounts follows:

A. Able, capital (−OE)	12,000	
B. Baker, capital (−OE)	7,800	
A. Able, drawings (+OE)		12,000
B. Baker, drawings (+OE)		7,800

Assets	=	Liabilities	+	Owners' Equity	
				A. Able, capital	−12,000
				B. Baker, capital	−7,800
				A. Able, drawings	+12,000
				B. Baker, drawings	+7,800

A separate statement of partners' capital, similar to the following, is customarily prepared to supplement the balance sheet:

AB PARTNERSHIP
Statement of Partners' Capital
For the Year Ended December 31, 2011

	A. Able	B. Baker	Total
Investment, January 1, 2011	$60,000	$40,000	$100,000
Add: Additional investments during the year	0	0	0
Net income for the year	18,000	12,000	30,000
Totals	78,000	52,000	130,000
Less: Drawings during the year	(12,000)	(7,800)	(19,800)
Partners' equity, December 31, 2011	$66,000	$44,200	$110,200

CHAPTER TAKE-AWAYS

1. Explain the role of stock in the capital structure of a corporation. p. 553

The law recognizes corporations as separate legal entities. Owners invest in a corporation and receive capital stock that can be traded on established stock exchanges. Stock provides a number of rights, including the right to receive dividends.

2. **Analyze the earnings per share ratio.** p. 556

The earnings per share ratio facilitates the comparison of a company's earnings over time or with other companies' earnings at a single point in time. By expressing earnings on a per share basis, differences in the size of companies become less important.

3. **Describe the characteristics of common stock and analyze transactions affecting common stock.** p. 556

Common stock is the basic voting stock issued by a corporation. Usually it has a par value, but no-par stock also can be issued. Common stock offers some special rights that appeal to certain investors.

A number of key transactions involve capital stock: (1) initial sale of stock, (2) treasury stock transactions, (3) cash dividends, and (4) stock dividends and stock splits. Each is illustrated in this chapter.

4. **Discuss dividends and analyze transactions.** p. 560

The return associated with an investment in capital stock comes from two sources: appreciation and dividends. Dividends are recorded as a liability when they are declared by the board of directors (i.e., on the date of declaration). The liability is satisfied when the dividends are paid (i.e., on the date of payment).

5. **Analyze the dividend yield ratio.** p. 560

The dividend yield ratio measures the percentage of return on an investment from dividends. For most companies, the return associated with dividends is very small.

6. **Discuss the purpose of stock dividends and stock splits, and report transactions.** p. 563

Stock dividends are pro rata distributions of a company's stock to existing owners. The transaction involves transferring an additional amount into the common stock account. A stock split also involves the distribution of additional shares to owners but no additional amount is transferred into the common stock account. Instead, the par value of the stock is reduced.

7. **Describe the characteristics of preferred stock and analyze transactions affecting preferred stock.** p. 565

Preferred stock provides investors certain advantages, including dividend preferences and a preference on asset distributions in the event the corporation is liquidated.

8. **Discuss the impact of capital stock transactions on cash flows.** p. 567

Both inflows (e.g., the issuance of capital stock) and outflows (e.g., the purchase of treasury stock) are reported in the Financing Activities section of the statement of cash flows. The payment of dividends is reported as an outflow in this section.

This chapter concludes a major section of the book. In the previous several chapters, we have discussed individual sections of the balance sheet. We will now shift our focus to a common business transaction that affects many accounts on each of the financial statements. For a number of strategic reasons, businesses often invest in other businesses. In the next chapter, you will see why companies invest in other companies and how those investments affect their financial statements.

KEY RATIOS

The **earnings per share ratio** states the net income of a corporation on a per share of common stock basis. The ratio is computed as follows (p. 556):

$$\textbf{Earnings per Share} = \frac{\textbf{Net Income}}{\textbf{Average Number of Shares of Common Stock Outstanding}}$$

The **dividend yield ratio** measures the dividend return on the current price of the stock. The ratio is computed as follows (p. 560):

$$\textbf{Dividend Yield Ratio} = \frac{\textbf{Dividends per Share}}{\textbf{Market Price per Share}}$$

FINDING FINANCIAL INFORMATION

Balance Sheet

Under Current Liabilities

Dividends, once declared by the board of directors, are reported as a liability (usually current).

Under Noncurrent Liabilities

Transactions involving capital stock do not generate noncurrent liabilities.

Under Stockholders' Equity

Typical accounts include
- Preferred stock
- Common stock
- Capital in excess of par
- Retained earnings
- Treasury stock

Statement of Stockholders' Equity

This statement reports detailed information concerning stockholders' equity, including
(1) amounts in each equity account,
(2) number of shares outstanding,
(3) impact of transactions such as earning income, payment of dividends, and purchase of treasury stock.

Income Statement

Capital stock is never shown on the income statement. Dividends paid are not an expense. They are a distribution of income and are, therefore, not reported on the income statement.

Statement of Cash Flows

Under Financing Activities

+ Cash inflows from initial sale of stock
+ Cash inflows from sale of treasury stock
− Cash outflows for dividends
− Cash outflows for purchase of treasury stock

Notes

Under Summary of Significant Accounting Policies

Usually, very little information concerning capital stock is provided in this summary.

Under a Separate Note

Most companies report information about their stock option plans and information about major transactions such as stock dividends or significant treasury stock transactions. A historical summary of dividends paid per share is typically provided. Also, dividends in arrears on preferred stock, if any, would be reported as a note.

KEY TERMS

Authorized Number of Shares p. 554
Common Stock p. 557
Cumulative Dividend Preference p. 566
Current Dividend Preference p. 565
Declaration Date p. 561
Dividends in Arrears p. 566
Issued Shares p. 554
Legal Capital p. 557
No-Par Value Stock p. 557
Outstanding Shares p. 554
Par Value p. 557
Payment Date p. 561
Preferred Stock p. 565
Record Date p. 561
Stock Dividend p. 563
Stock Split p. 564
Treasury Stock p. 558

QUESTIONS

1. Define the term *corporation* and identify the primary advantages of this form of business organization.
2. What is the charter of a corporation?
3. Explain each of the following terms: (*a*) authorized capital stock, (*b*) issued capital stock, and (*c*) outstanding capital stock.

4. Differentiate between common stock and preferred stock.
5. Explain the distinction between par value and no-par value capital stock.
6. What are the usual characteristics of preferred stock?
7. What are the two basic sources of stockholders' equity? Explain each.
8. Owners' equity is accounted for by source. What does source mean?
9. Define treasury stock. Why do corporations acquire treasury stock?
10. How is treasury stock reported on the balance sheet? How is the "gain or loss" on treasury stock that has been sold reported on the financial statements?
11. What are the two basic requirements to support the declaration of a cash dividend? What are the effects of a cash dividend on assets and stockholders' equity?
12. Differentiate between cumulative and noncumulative preferred stock.
13. Define *stock dividend.* How does a stock dividend differ from a cash dividend?
14. What are the primary reasons for issuing a stock dividend?
15. Identify and explain the three important dates with respect to dividends.
16. Define *retained earnings.* What are the primary components of retained earnings at the end of each period?

MULTIPLE-CHOICE QUESTIONS

1. Katz Corporation has issued 400,000 shares of common stock and holds 20,000 shares in treasury. The charter authorized the issuance of 500,000 shares. The company has declared and paid a dividend of $1 per share. What is the total amount of the dividend?
   a. $400,000
   b. $20,000
   c. $380,000
   d. $500,000
2. Which statement regarding treasury stock is false?
   a. Treasury stock is considered to be issued but not outstanding.
   b. Treasury stock has no voting, dividend, or liquidation rights.
   c. Treasury stock reduces total equity on the balance sheet.
   d. None of the above are false.
3. Which of the following statements about stock dividends is true?
   a. Stock dividends are reported on the statement of cash flows.
   b. Stock dividends are reported on the statement of retained earnings.
   c. Stock dividends increase total equity.
   d. Stock dividends decrease total equity.
4. Which order best describes the largest number of shares to the smallest number of shares?
   a. Shares authorized, shares issued, shares outstanding.
   b. Shares issued, shares outstanding, shares authorized.
   c. Shares outstanding, shares issued, shares authorized.
   d. Shares in the treasury, shares outstanding, shares issued.
5. A company issued 100,000 shares of common stock with a par value of $1 per share. The stock sold for $20 per share. By what amount does stockholders' equity increase?
   a. $100,000
   b. $1,900,000
   c. $2,000,000
   d. No change in stockholders' equity
6. A journal entry is not recorded on what date?
   a. Date of declaration.
   b. Date of record.
   c. Date of payment.
   d. A journal entry is recorded on all of these dates.
7. A company has net income of $225,000 and declares and pays dividends in the amount of $75,000. What is the net impact on retained earnings?
   a. Increase of $225,000
   b. Decrease of $75,000
   c. Increase of $150,000
   d. Decrease of $150,000

8. Which statement regarding dividends is false?
   a. Dividends represent a sharing of corporate profits with owners.
   b. Both stock and cash dividends reduce retained earnings.
   c. Cash dividends paid to stockholders reduce net income.
   d. None of the above statements are false.

9. When treasury stock is purchased with cash, what is the impact on the balance sheet equation?
   a. No change: the reduction of the asset cash is offset with the addition of the asset treasury stock.
   b. Assets decrease and stockholders' equity increases.
   c. Assets increase and stockholders' equity decreases.
   d. Assets decrease and stockholders' equity decreases.

10. Does a stock dividend increase an investor's personal wealth immediately?
   a. No, because the stock price falls when a stock dividend is issued.
   b. Yes, because the investor has more shares.
   c. Yes, because the investor acquired additional shares without paying a brokerage fee.
   d. Yes, because the investor will receive more in cash dividends by owning more shares.

For more practice with multiple-choice questions, go to the text website at **www.mhhe.com/libby7e.**

MINI-EXERCISES

connect ACCOUNTING

M11-1 LO1

Evaluating Stockholders' Rights

Name three rights of common stockholders. Which of these is most important in your opinion? Why?

M11-2 LO1

Computing the Number of Unissued Shares

The balance sheet for Ronlad Corporation reported 168,000 shares outstanding, 268,000 shares authorized, and 10,000 shares in treasury stock. Compute the maximum number of new shares that the company could issue.

M11-3 LO3

Recording the Sale of Common Stock

To expand operations, Aragon Consulting issued 170,000 shares of previously unissued stock with a par value of $1. The selling price for the stock was $21 per share. Record the sale of this stock. Would your answer be different if the par value was $2 per share? If so, record the sale of stock with a par value of $2.

M11-4 LO3, 7

Comparing Common Stock and Preferred Stock

Your parents have just retired and have asked you for some financial advice. They have decided to invest $100,000 in a company very similar to Kroger. The company has issued both common and preferred stock. What factors would you consider in giving them advice? Which type of stock would you recommend?

M11-5 LO3

Determining the Effects of Treasury Stock Transactions

Carbide Corporation purchased 20,000 shares of its own stock for $45 per share. The next year, the company sold 5,000 shares for $50 per share and the following year, it sold 10,000 shares for $37 per share. Determine the impact (increase, decrease, or no change) of each of these transactions on the following classifications:

1. Total assets
2. Total liabilities
3. Total stockholders' equity
4. Net income

Determining the Amount of a Dividend **M11-6** L04

Cole Company has 288,000 shares of common stock authorized, 260,000 shares issued, and 60,000 shares of treasury stock. The company's board of directors has declared a dividend of 65 cents per share. What is the total amount of the dividend that will be paid?

Recording Dividends **M11-7** L04

On April 15, 2011, the board of directors for Auction.com declared a cash dividend of 65 cents per share payable to stockholders of record on May 20. The dividends will be paid on June 14. The company has 100,000 shares of stock outstanding. Prepare any necessary journal entries for each date.

Determining the Amount of a Preferred Dividend **M11-8** L07

Lipscomb, Inc., has 200,000 shares of cumulative preferred stock outstanding. The preferred stock pays dividends in the amount of $2 per share but because of cash flow problems, the company did not pay any dividends last year. The board of directors plans to pay dividends in the amount of $1.4 million this year. What amount will go to the preferred stockholders?

Determining the Impact of Stock Dividends and Stock Splits **M11-9** L06

Reliable Tools, Inc., announced a 100 percent stock dividend. Determine the impact (increase, decrease, no change) of this dividend on the following:

1. Total assets
2. Total liabilities
3. Common stock
4. Total stockholders' equity
5. Market value per share of common stock

Assume that the company announced a 2-for-1 stock split. Determine the impact of the stock split.

Recording a Stock Dividend **M11-10** L06

University Food Systems, Inc., has issued a 40 percent stock dividend. The company has 752,000 shares authorized and 200,000 shares outstanding. The par value of the stock is $10 per share, and the market value is $130 per share. Record the payment of this stock dividend.

connect ACCOUNTING

EXERCISES

Computing Shares Outstanding **E11-1** L01 Philip Morris

The annual report for Philip Morris Companies, Inc., disclosed that 4 billion shares of common stock have been authorized. At the end of last year, 2,805,961,317 shares had been issued and the number of shares in treasury stock was 380,474,028. During the current year, no additional shares were issued, but additional shares were purchased for treasury stock and shares were sold from treasury stock. The net change was a decrease of 5,047,286 shares of treasury stock. Determine the number of shares outstanding at the end of the current year.

Computing Number of Shares **E11-2** L01, 3

The charter of Vista West Corporation specifies that it may issue 200,000 shares of common stock. Since the company was incorporated, it has sold a total of 160,000 shares to the public but bought back a total of 20,000. The par value of the stock is $3 and the stock was sold at an average price of $16. When the stock was bought back from the public, the market price was $20.

Required:

1. Determine the authorized shares.
2. Determine the issued shares.
3. Determine the outstanding shares.

E11-3
LO1, 3, 7

Determining the Effects of the Issuance of Common and Preferred Stock

Tandy, Incorporated, was issued a charter on January 15, 2011, that authorized the following capital stock:

Common stock, no-par, 103,000 shares

Preferred stock, 9 percent, par value $8 per share, 4,000 shares

The board of directors established a stated value on the no-par common stock of $10 per share. During 2011, the following selected transactions were completed in the order given:

a. Sold and issued 20,000 shares of the no-par common stock at $16 cash per share.
b. Sold and issued 3,000 shares of preferred stock at $20 cash per share.
c. At the end of 2011, the accounts showed net income of $40,000.

Required:
1. Prepare the stockholders' equity section of the balance sheet at December 31, 2011.
2. Assume that you are a common stockholder. If Tandy needed additional capital, would you prefer to have it issue additional common stock or additional preferred stock? Explain.

E11-4
LO1, 2, 3

Reporting Stockholders' Equity

The financial statements for Highland Publications Corporation included the following selected information:

Common stock	$1,600,000
Retained earnings	$900,000
Net income	$1,000,000
Shares issued	90,000
Shares outstanding	80,000
Dividends declared and paid	$800,000

The common stock was sold at a price of $20 per share.

Required:
1. What is the amount of capital in excess of par?
2. What was the amount of retained earnings at the beginning of the year?
3. How many shares are in treasury stock?
4. Compute earnings per share.

E11-5
LO1, 3, 4

Reporting Stockholders' Equity and Determining Dividend Policy

Tarrant Corporation was organized in 2011 to operate a financial consulting business. The charter authorized the following capital stock: common stock, par value $10 per share, 11,500 shares. During the first year, the following selected transactions were completed:

a. Sold and issued 5,600 shares of common stock for cash at $20 per share.
b. Sold and issued 1,000 shares of common stock for cash at $25 per share.
c. At year-end, the accounts reflected a $6,000 loss. Because a loss was incurred, no income tax expense was recorded.

Required:
1. Give the journal entry required for each of these transactions.
2. Prepare the stockholders' equity section as it should be reported on the year-end balance sheet.
3. Can the company pay dividends at this time? Explain.

E11-6
LO1, 3

Finding Amounts Missing from the Stockholders' Equity Section

Dillard's

The stockholders' equity section on the balance sheet of Dillard's, a popular department store, is shown below. The company reported a net loss of $241,065,000 and declared and paid dividends of $11,898,000 in 2009.

Stockholders' Equity (in thousands):	2009	2008
Common stock, Class A—116,560,308 and 116,445,495 shares issued; ? and ? shares outstanding	?	1,165
Common stock, Class B (convertible)—4,010,929 shares issued and outstanding	40	40
Additional paid-in capital	781,055	778,987
Retained earnings	2,427,727	?
Less treasury stock, at cost, Class A—47,116,748 and 45,290,148 shares	(942,001)	(924,560)

Required:

Complete the following statements and show your computations.

1. Common stock, class A at par value for 2009 was ________.
2. The number of shares of common stock outstanding was ________ in 2008 and ________ in 2009.
3. Retained earnings for 2008 was ________.
4. At the end of 2009, have the treasury stock transactions (*a*) increased corporate resources or (*b*) decreased resources? ________ By how much? ________.
5. During 2009, the treasury stock transactions increased (decreased) stockholders' equity by________.
6. How much did the treasury stock cost per share? $________.

Reporting Stockholders' Equity

E11-7
LO1, 3

Williamson Corporation was organized in 2011 to operate a tax preparation business. The charter authorized the following capital stock: common stock, par value $2 per share, 80,000 shares. During the first year, the following selected transactions were completed:

a. Sold and issued 50,000 shares of common stock for cash at $50 per share.
b. Bought 1,000 shares from a stockholder for cash at $52 per share.

Required:

1. Give the journal entry required for each of these transactions.
2. Prepare the stockholders' equity section as it should be reported on the year-end balance sheet.

Reporting Stockholders' Equity

E11-8
LO1, 3
Ruth's Chris Steakhouse

Ruth's Chris Steakhouse is the largest upscale steakhouse company in the United States, based on total company- and franchisee-owned restaurants. The company's menu features a broad selection of high-quality USDA prime grade steaks and other premium offerings. Currently, there are 100 Ruth's Chris restaurants, of which 50 are company-owned and 50 are franchisee-owned, including 10 international franchisee-owned restaurants in Mexico, Hong Kong, Taiwan, and Canada. Information from the company's annual report is shown below (dollar amounts in thousands, except per share data):

a. Common stock, par value $0.01, 100,000,000 shares authorized, 23,215,356 issued and outstanding at December 31, 2007; 23,337,986 issued and outstanding at December 31, 2008.
b. Additional paid-in capital $168,431 in 2007 and $171,389 in 2008.
c. Accumulated deficit $80,597 in 2007.
d. Net loss in 2008 was $53,883. No dividends were paid.

Required:

Prepare the stockholders' equity section of the balance sheet at December 31, 2008.

Determining the Effects of Transactions on Stockholders' Equity

E11-9
LO1, 3, 7

Quick Fix-it Corporation was organized in January 2011 to operate several car repair businesses in a large metropolitan area. The charter issued by the state authorized the following capital stock:

Common stock, $10 par value, 98,000 shares

Preferred stock, $50 par value, 8 percent, 59,000 shares

During January and February 2011, the following stock transactions were completed:

a. Sold 78,000 shares of common stock at $20 per share and collected cash.
b. Sold 20,000 shares of preferred stock at $80 per share; collected the cash and immediately issued the stock.
c. Bought 4,000 shares of common stock from a current stockholder for $20 per share.

Required:
Net income for 2011 was $90,000; cash dividends declared and paid at year-end were $30,000. Prepare the stockholders' equity section of the balance sheet at December 31, 2011.

E11-10 **Recording Stockholders' Equity Transactions**
LO3, 7

On-line Learning Corporation obtained a charter at the start of 2011 that authorized 52,000 shares of no-par common stock and 23,000 shares of preferred stock, par value $10. The corporation was organized by four individuals who purchased 16,000 shares of the common stock. The remaining shares were to be sold to other individuals at $37 per share on a cash basis. During 2011, the following selected transactions occurred:

a. Collected $20 per share cash from the four organizers and issued 5,000 shares of common stock to each of them.
b. Sold and issued 6,000 shares of common stock to an outsider at $40 cash per share.
c. Sold and issued 7,000 shares of preferred stock at $30 cash per share.

Required:
1. Give the journal entries indicated for each of these transactions.
2. Is it ethical to sell stock to outsiders at a higher price than the amount paid by the organizers?

E11-11 **Finding Amounts Missing from the Stockholders' Equity Section**
LO3, 7

The stockholders' equity section on the December 31, 2011, balance sheet of American Corporation follows:

Stockholders' Equity	
Contributed capital	
Preferred stock (par $20; authorized 10,000 shares, ? issued, of which 500 shares are held as treasury stock)	$100,000
Common stock (no-par; authorized 20,000 shares, issued and outstanding 8,000 shares)	600,000
Contributed capital (includes $1,500 from treasury stock transactions)	16,500
Retained earnings	34,000
Cost of treasury stock, preferred	(9,500)

Required:
Complete the following statements and show your computations.
1. The number of shares of preferred stock issued was ________.
2. The number of shares of preferred stock outstanding was ________.
3. The average sale price of the preferred stock when issued was $________ per share.
4. Have the treasury stock transactions (*a*) increased corporate resources or (*b*) decreased resources? ________ By how much? ________.
5. The treasury stock transactions increased (decreased) stockholders' equity by ________.
6. How much did the treasury stock held cost per share? $________.
7. Total stockholders' equity is $________.
8. The average issue price of the common stock was $________.

E11-12 **Finding Information Missing from an Annual Report**
LO1, 3, 4

Procter & Gamble is a $77 billion company that sells products that are part of most of our daily lives, including Mr. Clean, Cheer, Crest, Vicks, Scope, Pringles, Folgers, Vidal Sassoon, Zest, and Charmin. The annual report for P&G contained the following information:

a. Retained earnings at the end of 2007 totaled $41,797 million.
b. Net income for 2008 was $12,075 million.
c. Par value of the stock is $1 per share.
d. Cash dividends declared in 2008 were $1.45 per share.
e. The Common Stock, Par Value account totaled $4,002 million at the end of 2008 and $3,990 at the end of 2007.

P&G

Required *(assume that no other information concerning stockholders' equity is relevant):*
1. Estimate the number of shares outstanding at the end of 2008.
2. Estimate the amount of retained earnings at the end of 2008.

Analyzing the Repurchase of Stock

E11-13
LO3, 4

FREEPORT-McMoRAN COPPER & GOLD

The business section of *The New York Times* recently contained the following article:

> Freeport-McMoRan Copper & Gold Inc., one of the world's largest copper producers, said yesterday that it would repurchase up to five million shares of its common stock in the open market and through private transactions. The company, based in Phoenix, said it recently completed a program announced last September to buy back 2.5 million shares. Freeport-McMoRan said the purchases were being made to enhance shareholders' value. The company has about 70.7 million shares outstanding. Shares of Freeport-McMoRan fell to $53.50 on the New York Stock Exchange yesterday.

Required:
1. Determine the impact of the stock repurchase on the financial statements.
2. Why do you think the board decided to repurchase the stock?
3. What impact will this purchase have on the company's future dividend obligations?

Preparing a Statement of Stockholders' Equity and Evaluating Dividend Policy

E11-14
LO1, 3, 4, 5

The following account balances were selected from the records of TEAC Corporation at December 31, 2011, after all adjusting entries were completed:

Common stock (par $20; authorized 100,000 shares, issued 34,000 shares, of which 2,000 shares are held as treasury stock)	$680,000
Capital in excess of par	163,000
Dividends declared and paid in 2011	16,000
Retained earnings, January 1, 2011	75,000
Treasury stock at cost (2,000 shares)	25,000

Net income for the year was $30,000. Restriction on retained earnings equal to the cost of treasury stock held is required by law in this state. The stock price is currently $22.29 per share.

Required:
1. Prepare the Stockholders' Equity section of the balance sheet at December 31, 2011.
2. Compute and evaluate the dividend yield ratio. Determine the number of shares of stock that received dividends.

Recording Treasury Stock Transactions and Analyzing Their Impact

E11-15
LO3

During 2011 the following selected transactions affecting stockholders' equity occurred for Orlando Corporation:

a. Apr.	1	Purchased in the market 200 shares of the company's own common stock at $20 per share.
b. Jun.	14	Sold 40 shares of treasury stock for $25 cash per share.
c. Sept.	1	Sold 30 shares of treasury stock for $15 cash per share.

Required:
1. Give journal entries for each of these transactions.
2. Describe the impact, if any, that these transactions have on the income statement.

E11-16 LO3, 4, 8

Recording Treasury Stock Transactions and Analyzing Their Impact

During 2011 the following selected transactions affecting stockholders' equity occurred for TARP Corporation:

a.	Feb. 1	Purchased in the open market 160 shares of the company's own common stock at $20 cash per share.
b.	Jul. 15	Sold 80 of the shares purchased on February 1 for $21 cash per share.
c.	Sept. 1	Sold 50 more of the shares purchased on February 1 for $19 cash per share.

Required:

1. Give the indicated journal entries for each of the transactions.
2. What impact does the purchase of treasury stock have on dividends paid?
3. What impact does the sale of treasury stock for an amount higher than the purchase price have on net income and the statement of cash flows?

E11-17 LO4, 6

Analyzing the Impact of Dividend Policy

Peters and Associates is a small manufacturer of electronic connections for local area networks. Consider three independent situations.

Case 1: Peters increases its cash dividends by 50 percent, but no other changes occur in the company's operations.

Case 2: The company's income and cash flows increase by 50 percent, but this does not change its dividends.

Case 3: Peters issues a 50 percent stock dividend, but no other changes occur.

Required:

1. How do you think each situation would affect the company's stock price?
2. If the company changed its accounting policies and reported higher net income, would the change have an impact on the stock price?

E11-18 LO4, 7

Computing Dividends on Preferred Stock and Analyzing Differences

The records of Hollywood Company reflected the following balances in the stockholders' equity accounts at December 31, 2010:

Common stock, par $12 per share, 30,000 shares outstanding

Preferred stock, 10 percent, par $10 per share, 5,000 shares outstanding

Retained earnings, $216,000

On September 1, 2011, the board of directors was considering the distribution of a $65,000 cash dividend. No dividends were paid during the previous two years. You have been asked to determine dividend amounts under two independent assumptions (show computations):

a. The preferred stock is noncumulative.
b. The preferred stock is cumulative.

Required:

1. Determine the total and per share amounts that would be paid to the common stockholders and to the preferred stockholders under the two independent assumptions.
2. Write a brief memo to explain why the dividends per share of common stock were less for the second assumption.
3. What factor would cause a more favorable per share result to the common stockholders?

E11-19 LO4, 6, 7

Determining the Impact of Dividends

Service Corporation has the following capital stock outstanding at the end of 2011:

Preferred stock, 6 percent, par $15, outstanding shares, 8,000

Common stock, par $8, outstanding shares, 30,000

On October 1, 2011, the board of directors declared dividends as follows:

Preferred stock: Full cash preference amount, payable December 20, 2011

Common stock: 50 percent common stock dividend issuable December 20, 2011

On December 20, 2011, the market prices were preferred stock, $40, and common stock, $32.

Required:
Explain the overall effect of each of the dividends on the assets, liabilities, and stockholders' equity of the company.

E11-20
LO4, 7
Sears, Roebuck and Company

Recording the Payment of Dividends

A recent annual report for Sears, Roebuck and Co. disclosed that the company paid preferred dividends in the amount of $119.9 million. It declared and paid dividends on common stock in the amount of $2 per share. During the year, Sears had 1,000,000,000 shares of common authorized; 387,514,300 shares had been issued; 41,670,000 shares were in treasury stock. Assume that the transaction occurred on July 15.

Required:
Prepare a journal entry to record the declaration and payment of dividends.

E11-21
LO5

Evaluating the Dividend Yield Ratio

Duke Energy is a utility company that provides gas and electric service in North Carolina, South Carolina, Ohio, Kentucky, and Indiana. The company's dividend yield is 6.6 percent. Starbucks, a well-known retailer of coffee products, does not pay dividends, resulting in a dividend yield of 0.0 percent. Both companies are approximately the same size, with market values of $5 billion.

Required:
1. Based on this limited information, why do you think the dividend policies of the two companies are so different?
2. Will the two companies attract different types of investors? Explain.

E11-22
LO6

Analyzing Stock Dividends

At the beginning of the year, the stockholders' equity section of the balance sheet of Solutions Corporation reflected the following:

Common stock (par $12; authorized 65,000 shares, outstanding 30,000 shares)	$360,000
Capital in excess of par	120,000
Retained earnings	736,000

On February 1, 2011, the board of directors declared a 60 percent stock dividend to be issued April 30, 2011. The market value of the stock on February 1, 2011, was $15 per share.

Required:
1. For comparative purposes, prepare the Stockholders' Equity section of the balance sheet (*a*) immediately before the stock dividend and (*b*) immediately after the stock dividend. (*Hint:* Use two amount columns for this requirement.)
2. Explain the effects of this stock dividend on assets, liabilities, and stockholders' equity.

E11-23
LO3

Recording Dividends

Two billion times a day, Proctor & Gamble (P&G) brands touch the lives of people around the world. The company has one of the largest and strongest portfolios of trusted, quality brands, including Pampers, Tide, Bounty, Pringles, Folgers, Charmin, Downy, Crest, and Clairol Nice 'n Easy. The P&G community consists of nearly 98,000 employees working in almost 80 countries worldwide. The company has 5,000 million shares of common stock authorized and 3,000 million shares issued and outstanding. Par value is $1 per share. In 2009, the company issued the following press release:

CINCINNATI, July 13, 2009 /PRNewswire-FirstCall/—The Board of Directors of The Procter & Gamble Company declared a quarterly dividend of forty-four cents ($0.44) per share on the Common Stock of the Company, payable on or after August 17, 2009, to shareholders of record at the close of business on July 24, 2009.

Required:
Prepare journal entries as appropriate for each date mentioned in the press release.

E11-24 **Comparing Stock Dividends and Splits**
LO6

On July 1, 2011, Davidson Corporation had the following capital structure:

Common stock (par $3)	$600,000
Capital in excess of par	900,000
Retained earnings	700,000
Treasury stock	–0–

Required:
Complete the following comparative tabulation based on two independent cases:

Case 1: The board of directors declared and issued a 50 percent stock dividend when the stock was selling at $5 per share.

Case 2: The board of directors voted a 6-to-5 stock split (i.e., a 20 percent increase in the number of shares). The market price prior to the split was $5 per share.

Items	Before Dividend and Split	After Stock Dividend	After Stock Split
Common stock account	$	$	$
Par per share	$3	$	$
Shares outstanding	#	#	#
Capital in excess of par	$900,000	$	$
Retained earnings	$700,000	$	$
Total stockholders' equity	$	$	$

E11-25 **Recording a Stock Dividend**
LO6
GameStop

GameStop issued the following press release when the company's stock was selling for $27 per share:

GRAPEVINE, Texas—(BUSINESS WIRE)—Feb. 12, 2007—GameStop Corp. (NYSE: GME), the world's largest video game and entertainment software retailer, today announced that its Board of Directors approved a two-for-one stock split of the Company's common stock to be effected in the form of a stock dividend.

Each shareholder of record at the close of business on February 20, 2007, will receive one additional share of GameStop common stock for every outstanding share held on the record date. The additional shares will be distributed on March 16, 2007.

"As GameStop continues to rapidly grow, we wanted to make our stock more attractive to a broader range of potential investors. This stock split also reinforces the confidence that the Board and I have in the GameStop buy, sell, trade strategy and the future of video game growth worldwide," indicated R. Richard Fontaine, Chairman and Chief Executive Officer.

The stock split is GameStop's first since becoming a publicly traded company in February 2002. GameStop had approximately 76 million common shares outstanding as of February 3, 2007. Upon completion of the split, the outstanding shares of GameStop's common stock (par value $0.01) will increase to approximately 152 million.

Required:
1. Give any journal entries that would be required.
2. Describe the impact that this transaction will have on future cash dividends.

E11-26 **Comparing Stock Dividends and Splits**
LO6

Weil Corporation has 80,000 shares of common stock (par value $8) outstanding.

Required:

Complete the following comparative tabulation based on two independent cases:

Case 1: The board of directors declared and issued a 40 percent stock dividend when the stock was selling at $15 per share. The dividend will be accounted for as a large stock dividend.

Case 2: The board of directors voted a 5-to-3 stock split (i.e., a 66.67 percent increase in the number of shares). The market price prior to the split was $15 per share.

Items	Before Dividend and Split	After Stock Dividend	After Stock Split
Common stock account	$	$	$
Par per share	$8	$	$
Shares outstanding	#	#	#
Capital in excess of par	$ 280,000	$	$
Retained earnings	$1,300,000	$	$
Total stockholders' equity	$	$	$

Evaluating Dividend Policy

E11-27
LO4

Ford Motor Company is an internationally known manufacturer of automobiles and trucks. The company recently lost over $12 billion in a single year of operations. Despite that staggering loss, the company issued the following press release:

DEARBORN, Mich., July 13 /PRNewswire-FirstCall/—The Board of Directors of Ford Motor Company (NYSE: F) today declared a third quarter dividend of 5 cents per share on the company's common stock. The dividend, which is payable on Sept. 1 to shareholders of record on Aug. 2 is a reduction of 5 cents per share from the dividend paid in the second quarter.

Required:

1. Explain why Ford can pay dividends despite its loss.
2. What factors did the board of directors consider when it declared the dividends?

Analyzing Dividends in Arrears

E11-28
LO7
Archon Corporation

Archon Corporation operates the Pioneer Hotel & Gambling Hall in Nevada. In addition, the Company owns real estate on Las Vegas Boulevard South (the "Strip") in Las Vegas, Nevada, and investment properties in Dorchester, Massachusetts, and Gaithersburg, Maryland. An investor found the following note contained in the Archon annual report:

The Company has not declared dividends on its preferred stock since fiscal 1996. Dividends of approximately $1.5 million, $1.5 million, $1.6 million, $1.5 million, and $1.6 million for fiscal 2006, 2005, 2004, 2003, and 2002, respectively, have not been declared and are in arrears. Total accumulated preferred stock dividends in arrears for the five preceding years ended on September 30, 2006, are $12.3 million, $10.8 million, $9.5 million, $8.2 million, and $7.3 million, respectively.

The investor who read the note suggested that the Archon preferred stock would be a good investment because of the large amount of dividend income that would be earned when the company started paying dividends again: "As the owner of the stock, I'll get dividends for the period I hold the stock plus some previous periods when I didn't even own the stock." Do you agree? Explain.

For more practice with exercises, go to the text website at **www.mhhe.com/libby7e**.

PROBLEMS

Finding Missing Amounts (AP11-1)

P11-1
LO2, 3, 4, 6

At December 31, 2011, the records of NCIS Corporation provided the following selected and incomplete data:

Common stock (par $10; no changes during the year).
Shares authorized, 200,000.
Shares issued, ____?____; issue price $17 per share; cash collected in full, $2,125,000.

Shares held as treasury stock, 3,000 shares, cost $20 per share.
Net income, $118,000.
Dividends declared and paid, $73,200.
Retained earnings balance, January 1, 2011, $555,000.
The treasury stock was acquired after a stock split was issued.

Required:

1. Complete the following tabulation:
   Shares authorized ________.
   Shares issued ________.
   Shares outstanding ________.
2. The balance in the Capital in Excess of Par account appears to be $________.
3. Earnings per share is $________.
4. Dividend paid per share of common stock is $________.
5. Treasury stock should be reported on the balance sheet under the major caption ________ in the amount of $________.
6. Assume that the board of directors voted a 100 percent stock split (the number of shares will double). After the stock split, the par value per share will be $________, and the number of outstanding shares will be ________.
7. Assuming the stock split mentioned above, give any journal entry that should be made. If none, explain why.
8. Disregard the stock split (assumed above). Assume instead that a 10 percent stock dividend was declared and issued when the market price of the common stock was $21. Give any journal entry that should be made.

P11-2
LO3, 7
eXcel
www.mhhe.com/libby7e

Preparing the Stockholders' Equity Section of the Balance Sheet

Witt Corporation received its charter during January 2011. The charter authorized the following capital stock:

Preferred stock: 10 percent, par $10, authorized 21,000 shares

Common stock: par $8, authorized 50,000 shares

During 2011, the following transactions occurred in the order given:

a. Issued a total of 40,000 shares of the common stock to the four organizers at $12 per share.
b. Sold 5,500 shares of the preferred stock at $16 per share.
c. Sold 3,000 shares of the common stock at $15 per share and 1,000 shares of the preferred stock at $26.
d. Net income for the year was $51,000.

Required:
Prepare the Stockholders' Equity section of the balance sheet at December 31, 2011.

P11-3
LO3, 7

Recording Transactions Affecting Stockholders' Equity (AP11-2)

King Corporation began operations in January 2011. The charter authorized the following capital stock:

Preferred stock: 10 percent, $10 par, authorized 40,000 shares

Common stock: $5 par, authorized 85,000 shares

During 2011, the following transactions occurred in the order given:

a. Issued 22,000 shares of common stock to each of the three organizers and collected $9 cash per share from each of them.
b. Sold 9,000 shares of the preferred stock at $20 per share.
c. Sold 1,000 shares of the preferred stock at $20 and 1,500 shares of common stock at $10 per share.

Required:
Give the journal entries indicated for each of these transactions.

P11-4
LO1, 3

Recording Transactions and Comparing Par and No-Par Stock

The following press release was issued by Haynes International:

HAYNES International

NEW YORK, March 19 (Reuters)—Haynes International Inc., a producer of high-performance nickel and cobalt-based alloys, on Monday raised $136.5 million with a U.S. initial public offering that was priced above the forecast range.

The 2.1-million-share offering was sold for $65 per share, compared with a $61 to $64 forecast range.

Required:

1. Record the issuance of stock, assuming the stock was no-par value common stock.
2. Record the issuance of stock, assuming the common stock had a par value of $1 per share.
3. Should a stockholder care whether a company issues par or no-par value stock? Explain.

Preparing the Stockholders' Equity Section after Selected Transactions (AP11-3)

P11-5
L01, 3

United Resources Company obtained a charter from the state in January 2011, which authorized 200,000 shares of common stock, $1 par value. During the first year, the company earned $475,000 and the following selected transactions occurred in the order given:

a. Sold 100,000 shares of the common stock in an initial public offering at $12 per share.
b. Repurchased 20,000 shares of the previously issued shares at $15 cash per share for treasury stock.
c. Resold 5,000 of the shares of the treasury stock at $18 cash per share.

Required:

Prepare the stockholders' equity section of the balance sheet at December 31, 2011.

Recording Stockholders' Equity Transactions (AP11-4)

P11-6
L01, 3
Tim Hortons

Tim Hortons restaurants operate in a variety of formats. A standard Tim Hortons restaurant is a free-standing building typically ranging in size from 1,400 to 3,090 square feet with a dining room and single or double drive-thru window. The Company also has nonstandard restaurants designed to fit anywhere, consisting of kiosks in offices, hospitals, colleges, airports, gas station convenience stores, and drive-thru-only units on smaller pieces of property. The company's annual report included the following information:

	2008	2007	2006
Cash flows (used in) provided from financing activities			
Purchase of treasury stock (note 19)	(165,258)	(170,604)	(64,971)
Purchase of common stock held in trust (note 19)	(3,842)	(7,202)	(9,171)
Purchase of common stock for settlement of stock-based compensation (note 20)	(226)	(110)	(5,489)
Dividend payments	(66,086)	(52,865)	(27,046)
Proceeds from share issuance	—	—	903,825
Share issuance costs	—	—	(61,918)
Proceeds from issuance of debt, net of issuance costs	3,796	2,588	501,263
Tax sharing payment from Wendy's (note 7)	—	9,116	—
Repayment of borrowings from Wendy's	—	—	(1,087,968)
Principal payments on other long-term debt obligations	(7,376)	(4,060)	(206,750)
Net cash used in financing activities	(238,992)	(223,137)	(58,225)

For 2008, prepare journal entries to record the purchase of treasury stock and the declaration and payment of dividends. For 2006, prepare the journal entry to record the sale of common stock. The common stock has a par value of $0.001 and 50,000,000 shares were issued during 2006.

Analyzing Stockholders' Equity Transactions, Including Treasury Stock

P11-7
L03, 4, 6

1. Compare a stock dividend with a cash dividend.
2. Compare a large stock dividend with a small stock dividend.
3. Describe the impact of the sale of treasury stock for more than cost on the income statement and the statement of cash flows.
4. Explain why a company might purchase treasury stock.

P11-8
LO3, 8
RadioShack Corporation

Analyzing Treasury Stock Transactions

RadioShack Corporation primarily engages in the retail sale of consumer electronics goods and services through 4,467 company-operated stores under the RadioShack brand, located throughout the United States, as well as in Puerto Rico and the U.S. Virgin Islands. These stores are located in major shopping malls and strip centers, as well as individual storefronts. The company's statement of cash flows contained the following information (in millions):

	2006	2005	2004
Cash flows from financing activities:			
Purchases of treasury stock	—	(625.8)	(251.1)
Sale of treasury stock	10.5	30.1	35.4

Required:
1. Record the purchase of treasury stock in 2005.
2. Record the sale of treasury stock in 2006. Assume the stock had been purchased at a cost of $9 million.
3. Would RadioShack have reported a loss if the stock sold in 2006 had been purchased originally for $13 million?

P11-9
LO4, 6, 7

Comparing Stock and Cash Dividends (AP11-5)

Chicago Company had the following stock outstanding and retained earnings at December 31, 2011:

Common stock (par $8; outstanding, 35,000 shares)	$280,000
Preferred stock, 10% (par $15; outstanding, 8,000 shares)	120,000
Retained earnings	281,000

The board of directors is considering the distribution of a cash dividend to the two groups of stockholders. No dividends were declared during the previous two years. Three independent cases are assumed:

Case A: The preferred stock is noncumulative; the total amount of dividends is $31,000.

Case B: The preferred stock is cumulative; the total amount of dividends is $25,000.

Case C: Same as Case B, except the amount is $67,000.

Required:
1. Compute the amount of dividends, in total and per share, that would be payable to each class of stockholders for each case. Show computations.
2. Assume the company issued a 30 percent common stock dividend on the outstanding shares when the market value per share was $24. Complete the following comparative schedule including explanation of the comparative differences.

	AMOUNT OF DOLLAR INCREASE (DECREASE)	
Item	Cash Dividend—Case C	Stock Dividend
Assets	$	$
Liabilities	$	$
Stockholders' equity	$	$

P11-10
LO4, 8
DELL

Analyzing Dividend Policy

Heather and Scott, two young financial analysts, were reviewing financial statements for Dell, one of the world's largest manufacturers of personal computers. Scott noted that the company did not report any dividends in the Financing Activity section of the statement of cash flows and said, "I have heard that Dell is one of the best performing companies. If it's so good, I wonder why it isn't paying any dividends." Heather wasn't convinced that Scott was looking in the right place for dividends but didn't say anything.

Scott continued the discussion by noting, "Sales for Dell are up nearly 35 percent over the previous two years. While net income is up over $500 million compared to last year, cash flow from operating activities declined by nearly $500 million compared to the previous year."

At that point, Heather noted that the statement of cash flows reported that Dell had repurchased nearly $3 billion in common stock. She also was surprised to see that inventory and accounts receivable had decreased by nearly $2 billion in the previous year. "No wonder it can't pay dividends. With cash flows declining by $500 million, the Board is probably reluctant to obligate itself to dividends."

Required:

1. Correct any misstatements that either Heather or Scott made. Explain.
2. Which of the factors presented in the case help you understand Dell's dividend policy?

Determining the Financial Statement Effects of Dividends

P11-11
LO4, 6, 7

Uno Company has outstanding 52,000 shares of $10 par value common stock and 25,000 shares of $20 par value preferred stock (8 percent). On December 1, 2011, the board of directors voted an 8 percent cash dividend on the preferred stock and a 30 percent stock dividend on the common stock. At the date of declaration, the common stock was selling at $35 and the preferred at $20 per share. The dividends are to be paid, or issued, on February 15, 2012. The annual accounting period ends December 31.

Required:

Explain the comparative effects of the two dividends on the assets, liabilities, and stockholders' equity (*a*) through December 31, 2011, (*b*) on February 15, 2012, and (*c*) overall, from December 1, 2011, through February 15, 2012. A schedule similar to the following might be helpful:

	COMPARATIVE EFFECTS EXPLAINED	
Item	Cash Dividend on Preferred	Stock Dividend on Common
1. Through December 31, 2011:		
Assets, etc.		

Recording Dividends

P11-12
LO4, 6

Procter & Gamble is a well-known consumer products company that owns a variety of popular brands. A recent news article contained the following information:

CINCINNATI, March 9 /PRNewswire-FirstCall/—The Procter & Gamble Company (NYSE: PG) today said that earnings per share for the January through March quarter as well as the fiscal year is expected to exceed current consensus estimates by $0.01 to $0.02. The increased earnings are being driven by continued strong organic volume growth.

Stock Dividend

The company also announced today that its board of directors approved a 10% stock dividend to shareholders of record on May 21. This move does not change the proportionate interest a shareholder maintains in the company. The additional shares will be distributed on June 18. In a separate action, the board declared an increase in the annual rate of its common stock dividend from $1.82 to $2.00 per share.

Required:

1. Prepare any journal entries that P&G should make as the result of information in the preceding report. Assume that the company has 2,500 million shares outstanding, the par value is $1.00 per share, and the market value is $50 per share.
2. What do you think happened to the company's stock price after the announcement?
3. What factors did the board of directors consider in making this decision?

(Chapter Supplement) Comparing Stockholders' Equity Sections for Alternative Forms of Organization

P11-13

Assume for each of the following independent cases that the annual accounting period ends on December 31, 2011, and that the revenue and expense accounts at that date reflect a loss of $20,000.

Case A: Assume that the company is a *sole proprietorship* owned by Proprietor A. Prior to the closing entries, the capital account reflects a credit balance of $52,000 and the drawing account shows a balance of $9,000.

Case B: Assume that the company is a *partnership* owned by Partner A and Partner B. Prior to the closing entries, the owners' equity accounts reflect the following balances: A, Capital, $43,000;

B, Capital, $43,000; A, Drawings, $5,000; and B, Drawings, $7,000. Profits and losses are divided equally.

Case C: Assume that the company is a *corporation.* Prior to the closing entries, the stockholders' equity accounts show the following: Common Stock, par $10, authorized 30,000 shares, outstanding 14,000 shares; Capital in Excess of Par, $9,000; Retained Earnings, $62,000.

Required:

1. Give all the closing entries indicated at December 31, 2011, for each of the separate cases.
2. Show how the owners' equity section of the balance sheet would appear at December 31, 2011, for each case.

ALTERNATE PROBLEMS

AP11-1 Finding Missing Amounts (P11-1)
LO2, 3, 4, 6

At December 31, 2011, the records of Duo Corporation provided the following selected and incomplete data:

Common stock (par $1; no changes during the year).
Shares authorized, 5,000,000.
Shares issued, ____?____; issue price $80 per share.
Shares held as treasury stock, 100,000 shares, cost $60 per share.
Net income, $4,800,000.
Common stock account, $1,500,000.
Dividends declared and paid, $2 per share.
Retained earnings balance, January 1, 2011, $82,900,000.

Required:

1. Complete the following tabulation:
   Shares issued ________.
   Shares outstanding ________.
2. The balance in the Capital in Excess of Par account appears to be $________.
3. EPS on net income is $________.
4. Total dividends paid on common stock during 2011 is $________.
5. Treasury stock should be reported on the balance sheet under the major caption ________ in the amount of $________.

AP11-2 Recording Transactions Affecting Stockholders' Equity (P11-3)
LO3, 7

Granderson Company was granted a charter that authorized the following capital stock:

Common stock: 100,000 shares, par value per share is $40

Preferred stock: 8 percent; par $5; 20,000 shares

During the first year, 2011, the following selected transactions occurred in the order given:

a. Sold 30,000 shares of the common stock at $40 cash per share and 5,000 shares of the preferred stock at $26 cash per share.
b. Issued 2,000 shares of preferred stock when the stock was selling at $32.
c. Repurchased 3,000 shares of the common stock sold earlier; paid cash, $38 per share.

Required:
Give journal entries for each of these transactions.

AP11-3 Preparing the Stockholders' Equity Section After Selected Transactions (P11-5)
LO1, 3

Luther Company obtained a charter from the state in January 2011 which authorized 1,000,000 shares of common stock, $5 par value. During the first year, the company earned $429,000, and the following selected transactions occurred in the order given:

a. Sold 700,000 shares of the common stock at $54 per share. Collected the cash and issued the stock.
b. Purchased 25,000 shares at $50 cash per share to use as stock incentives for senior management.

Required:
Prepare the Stockholders' Equity section of the balance sheet at December 31, 2011.

Recording Stockholders' Equity Transactions (P11-6)

AP11-4
LO1, 3, 4
Whole Foods Market

Whole Foods Market, Inc., is the world's leading natural and organic foods supermarket. The company is based in Austin, Texas, and conducts business through various wholly-owned subsidiaries. The following information was contained in the company's balance sheet (amounts in thousands):

	Current Year	Prior Year
Shareholders' equity:		
Common stock, no par value	1,147,872	874,972
Common stock in treasury, at cost	(99,964)	—
Retained earnings	349,260	486,299

Required:
Prepare journal entries to record the issuance of common stock and the purchase of treasury stock in the current year. During the current year, the company earned net income of $203.828 million. Record the declaration and payment of dividends, if any, during the current year.

Comparing Stock and Cash Dividends (P11-9)

AP11-5
LO4, 6, 7

Carlton Company had the following stock outstanding and retained earnings at December 31, 2011:

Common stock (par $1; outstanding, 500,000 shares)	$500,000
Preferred stock, 8% (par $10; outstanding, 21,000 shares)	210,000
Retained earnings	900,000

The board of directors is considering the distribution of a cash dividend to the two groups of stockholders. No dividends were declared during the previous two years. Three independent cases are assumed:

Case A: The preferred stock is noncumulative; the total amount of dividends is $25,000.

Case B: The preferred stock is cumulative; the total amount of dividends is $25,000.

Case C: Same as Case B, except the amount is $75,000.

Required:
1. Compute the amount of dividends, in total and per share, payable to each class of stockholders for each case. Show computations.
2. Assume that the company issued a 40 percent common stock dividend on the outstanding shares when the market value per share was $50. Complete the following comparative schedule, including an explanation of the comparative differences.

	AMOUNT OF DOLLAR INCREASE (DECREASE)	
Item	Cash Dividend—Case C	Stock Dividend
Assets	$	$
Liabilities	$	$
Stockholders' equity	$	$

COMPREHENSIVE PROBLEM (CHAPTERS 9–11)

Complete the following requirements for each independent case.

Case A: The charter for Rogers, Incorporated, authorized the following capital stock:

Common stock, par $10, 103,000 shares

Preferred stock, 9 percent, par value $8 per share, 4,000 shares

The company sold 40,000 shares of common stock and 3,000 shares of preferred stock. During 2011, the following selected transactions were completed in the order given:

1. Rogers declared and paid dividends in the amount of $10,000. How much was paid to the holders of preferred stock? How much was paid to the common stockholders?
2. Rogers purchased 5,000 shares for treasury stock. After this transaction, how many shares of common stock were outstanding?
3. Describe the financial statement effects if Rogers sold 1,000 shares of treasury stock for $5 more than it paid.
4. Describe the financial statement effects if Rogers declared and issued a 2-for-1 stock split.

Case B: Ospry, Inc., has a quick ratio of 0.50 and working capital in the amount of $960,000. For each of the following transactions, determine whether the quick ratio and working capital will increase, decrease, or remain the same.

1. Paid accounts payable in the amount of $10,000.
2. Recorded rent payable in the amount of $22,000.
3. Collected $5,000 in accounts receivable.
4. Purchased $20,000 of new inventory for cash.

Case C: James Corporation is planning to issue $1,000,000 worth of bonds that mature in 10 years and pay 5 percent interest each December 31. All of the bonds will be sold on January 1, 2011.

Required:
Compute the issue (sale) price on January 1, 2011, for each of the following independent cases (show computations):

1. Market (yield) rate, 5 percent.
2. Market (yield) rate, 4 percent.
3. Market (yield) rate, 6 percent.

Case D: Miller Enterprises is a national chain of upscale bicycle shops. The company has followed a successful strategy of locating near major universities. Miller has the opportunity to expand into several new markets but must raise additional capital. The company has engaged in the following transactions:

- Issued 45,000 additional shares of common stock. The stock has a par value of $1 and sells in the market for $25 per share.
- Issued bonds. These bonds have a face value of $1,000,000 and mature in 10 years. The bonds pay 10 percent interest, semiannually. The current market rate of interest is 8 percent.

Required:
1. Record the sale of the bonds.
2. Record the issuance of the stock.

CASES AND PROJECTS

Annual Report Cases

CP11-1
LO1, 3, 4

AMERICAN EAGLE OUTFITTERS, INC.

Finding Financial Information

Refer to the financial statements of American Eagle Outfitters given in Appendix B at the end of this book.

Required:
1. Does the company have any treasury stock? If so, how much?
2. Does the company pay dividends? If so, how much per share?
3. Did the company buy or sell treasury stock during the current year?
4. What is the par value of the common stock?

CP11-2
LO1, 3, 4, 6

URBAN OUTFITTERS INC.

Finding Financial Information

Refer to the financial statements of Urban Outfitters given in Appendix C at the end of this book.

Required:

1. How many shares of common stock are authorized at the end of the current year? How many shares are issued and outstanding at the end of the current year?
2. Did the company pay dividends during the most recent reporting year? If so, what was the total amount of dividends paid and how much were they per share?
3. Does the company have any treasury stock? If so, how much?
4. Has the company issued a stock dividend or a stock split over the past three reporting years? If so, describe.
5. Does the company's common stock have a par value? If it does, what is the par value?

CP11-3
LO4, 5, 6

AMERICAN EAGLE OUTFITTERS, INC.

URBAN OUTFITTERS INC.

excel
www.mhhe.com/libby7e

Comparing Companies within an Industry

Refer to the financial statements of American Eagle (Appendix B) and Urban Outfitters (Appendix C).

Required:

1. A few years ago, American Eagle Outfitters split its stock. Describe the impact that the split would have on the market value of the stock compared to a company that did not split its stock. Why do some companies elect to split their stock?
2. Calculate the dividend yield ratios for Urban Outfitters (assume the market price of the stock is $28) and American Eagle (assume the market price of the stock is $15) for the most recent reporting year.
3. Why would an investor choose to invest in a stock that does not pay dividends?
4. Using the information from the following table, compare the dividend-related industry average ratios for the retail apparel industry to the pharmaceutical industry and the electric utility industry. What type of investor would be interested in buying stock in a utility instead of a retail store? Why?

DIVIDEND RATIOS FOR VARIOUS INDUSTRIES

	Retail Apparel	Pharmaceuticals	Electric Utilities
Dividend yield	1.1%	2.6%	3.8%
Example company	The GAP	Eli Lilly	American Electric Power

Financial Reporting and Analysis Case

CP11-4
LO4

Halliburton

Computing Dividends for an Actual Company

A recent annual report for Halliburton Company contained the following information (in millions of dollars):

Stockholders' Equity	Current Year	Previous Year
Common stock, par value $2.50, authorized 2,000 shares	$ 298.3	$ 298.4
Paid-in capital in excess of par	130.5	129.9
Retained earnings	2,080.8	2,052.3
Less 12.8 and 13.0 treasury stock, at cost	382.2	384.7

In the current year, Halliburton declared and paid cash dividends of $1 per share. What would be the total amount of dividends declared and paid if they had been based on the amount of stock outstanding at the end of the year?

Critical Thinking Cases

CP11-5
LO4, 6

Evaluating an Ethical Dilemma

You are a member of the board of directors of a large company that has been in business for more than 100 years. The company is proud of the fact that it has paid dividends every year it has been in business. Because of this stability, many retired people have invested large portions of their savings in your common stock. Unfortunately, the company has struggled for the past few years as it tries to introduce new products and is considering not paying a dividend this year. The president wants to skip the dividend in order to have more cash to invest in product development: "If we don't invest this money now, we won't get these products to market in time to save the company. I don't want to risk thousands of jobs." One of the most senior board members speaks next: "If we don't pay the dividend, thousands of retirees will be thrown into financial distress. Even if you don't care about them, you have to recognize our stock price will crash when they all sell." The company treasurer proposes an alternative: "Let's skip the cash dividend and pay a stock dividend. We can still say we've had a dividend every year." The entire board now turns to you for your opinion. What should the company do?

CP11-6
LO4

Evaluating an Ethical Dilemma

You are the president of a very successful Internet company that has had a remarkably profitable year. You have determined that the company has more than $10 million in cash generated by operating activities not needed in the business. You are thinking about paying it out to stockholders as a special dividend. You discuss the idea with your vice president, who reacts angrily to your suggestion:

"Our stock price has gone up by 200 percent in the last year alone. What more do we have to do for the owners? The people who really earned that money are the employees who have been working 12 hours a day, six or seven days a week, to make the company successful. Most of them didn't even take vacations last year. I say we have to pay out bonuses and nothing extra for the stockholders."

As president, you know that you are hired by the board of directors, which is elected by the stockholders. What is your responsibility to both groups? To which group would you give the $10 million?

Financial Reporting and Analysis Team Project

CP11-7
LO1, 3, 4, 6, 7

Team Project: Examining an Annual Report

As a team, select an industry to analyze. *Reuters* provides lists of industries and their makeup at www.reuters.com. Each team member should acquire the annual report or 10-K for one publicly traded company in the industry, with each member selecting a different company. (Library files, the SEC EDGAR service at www.sec.gov, Compustat CD, or the company itself are good sources.)

Required:

On an individual basis, each team member should write a short report answering the following questions about the selected company. Discuss any patterns across the companies that you as a team observe. Then, as a team, write a short report comparing and contrasting your companies.

1. *a.* List the accounts and amounts of the company's stockholders' equity.
   b. From the footnotes, identify any unusual features in its contributed capital accounts (e.g., convertible preferred, nonvoting common, no par value), if any.
2. What amount of stock was issued in the most recent year? (You will need to refer to the statement of cash flows for the cash proceeds and the statement of stockholders' equity for the amounts in the capital accounts.)
   a. What was the average market value per share of the issuance?
   b. Recreate the journal entry for the issuance.
3. What amount of treasury stock, if any, did the company purchase during the year?
4. What types of dividends, if any, did the company declare during the year? How much was paid in cash?

LEARNING OBJECTIVES

After studying this chapter, you should be able to:

Lecture Presentation LP-13
www.mhhe.com/libby7e

1. Classify cash flow statement items as part of net cash flows from operating, investing, and financing activities. p. 638
2. Report and interpret cash flows from operating activities using the indirect method. p. 645
3. Analyze and interpret the quality of income ratio. p. 651
4. Report and interpret cash flows from investing activities. p. 652
5. Analyze and interpret the capital acquisitions ratio. p. 654
6. Report and interpret cash flows from financing activities. p. 655
7. Understand the format of the cash flow statement and additional cash flow disclosures. p. 657

STATEMENT OF CASH FLOWS

In the highly competitive beverage market dominated by giants Coca-Cola and PepsiCo, National Beverage aims at value-conscious consumers seeking flavor variety. With over 50 different flavors available in its well-known Shasta and Faygo carbonated soft drinks, combined with Everfresh juices, LaCroix waters, and Rip It energy products, National Beverage can meet all of the beverage needs of a wide variety of consumers and retailers. For its value strategy to earn profits for shareholders, National Beverage must also be a cost-effective producer. It maintains product quality and cost discipline through centralized purchasing and by owning and operating all of its production and bottling facilities. Its 12 plants, strategically located near customer distribution centers in different markets, reduce distribution costs and allow National Beverage to tailor its products and media promotions to regional tastes. Through these difficult economic times, sales and profits at National Beverage continue to grow. As Nick Caporella, Chairman and CEO of the company since its founding, said in its latest annual report, the keys to the company's strong performance in tough times are:

Brands that sparkle in tough times
Fortress balance sheet
Investor focus that yields appreciation
Investor cash—returned appropriately
No debt and ***hordes of cash***

FOCUS COMPANY:

National Beverage Corp.

PRODUCING VALUE FOR CUSTOMERS AND CASH FLOWS FOR SHAREHOLDERS IN TOUGH TIMES

www.nationalbeverage.com

Although it may seem puzzling, growing profitable operations do not always ensure positive cash flow. As we have seen in earlier chapters, this occurs because the timing of revenues and expenses does not always match cash inflows and outflows. As a consequence, National Beverage must carefully manage cash flows as well as profits. For the same reasons, financial analysts must consider the information provided in National Beverage's cash flow statement in addition to its income statement and balance sheet.

UNDERSTANDING THE BUSINESS

Clearly, net income is important, but cash flow is also critical to a company's success. Cash flow permits a company to expand operations, replace worn assets, take advantage of new investment opportunities, and pay dividends to its owners. Some Wall Street analysts go so far as to say "Cash flow is king." Both managers and analysts need to understand the various sources and uses of cash that are associated with business activity.

The cash flow statement focuses attention on a firm's ability to generate cash internally, its management of current assets and current liabilities, and the details of its investments and its external financing. It is designed to help both managers and analysts answer important cash-related questions such as these:

- Will the company have enough cash to pay its short-term debts to suppliers and other creditors without additional borrowing?
- Is the company adequately managing its accounts receivable and inventory?
- Has the company made necessary investments in new productive capacity?
- Did the company generate enough cash flow internally to finance necessary investments, or did it rely on external financing?
- Is the company changing the makeup of its external financing?

We begin our discussion with an overview of the statement of cash flows. Then we examine the information reported in each section of the statement in depth. The chapter ends with a discussion of additional cash flow disclosures.

ORGANIZATION of the Chapter

Classifications of the Statement of Cash Flows

- Cash Flows from Operating Activities
- Cash Flows from Investing Activities
- Cash Flows from Financing Activities
- Net Increase (Decrease) in Cash
- Relationships to the Balance Sheet and Income Statement

Reporting and Interpreting Cash Flows from Operating Activities

- Reporting Cash Flows from Operating Activities—Indirect Method
- Interpreting Cash Flows from Operating Activities
- Quality of Income Ratio

Reporting and Interpreting Cash Flows from Investing Activities

- Reporting Cash Flows from Investing Activities
- Interpreting Cash Flows from Investing Activities
- Capital Acquisitions Ratio

Reporting and Interpreting Cash Flows from Financing Activities

- Reporting Cash Flows from Financing Activities
- Interpreting Cash Flows from Financing Activities

Completing the Statement and Additional Disclosures

- Statement Structure
- Noncash Investing and Financing Activities
- Supplemental Cash Flow Information

LEARNING OBJECTIVE 1

Classify cash flow statement items as part of net cash flows from operating, investing, and financing activities.

CLASSIFICATIONS OF THE STATEMENT OF CASH FLOWS

Basically, the statement of cash flows explains how the amount of cash on the balance sheet at the beginning of the period has become the amount of cash reported at the end of the period. For purposes of this statement, the definition of cash includes cash and cash equivalents. **Cash equivalents** are short-term, highly liquid investments that are both

1. Readily convertible to known amounts of cash.
2. So near to maturity there is little risk that their value will change if interest rates change.

EXHIBIT 13.1

Consolidated Statement of Cash Flows

REAL WORLD EXCERPT

Annual Report

NATIONAL BEVERAGE CORP.
Consolidated Statement of Cash Flows
Year Ended April 30, 2009
(amounts in thousands)

Cash flows from operating activities:	
Net income	$ 24,742
Adjustments to reconcile net income to cash flow from operating activities:	
Depreciation and amortization	8,891
Changes in assets and liabilities:	
Accounts receivable	(4,549)
Inventory	(858)
Prepaid expenses	6,457
Accounts payable	(1,798)
Accrued expenses	2,604
Net cash provided by operating activities	35,489
Cash flows from investing activities:	
Purchases of property, plant, and equipment	(6,658)
Proceeds from disposal of property, plant, and equipment	167
Purchase of short-term investments	(109,450)
Proceeds from sale of short-term investments	112,450
Net cash used in investing activities	(3,491)
Cash flows from financing activities:	
Purchase of treasury stock	(305)
Proceeds from issuance of stock	950
Net cash provided by financing activities	645
Net increase in cash and cash equivalents:	32,643
Cash and cash equivalents at beginning of period	51,497
Cash and cash equivalents at end of period	$ 84,140

**Certain amounts have been adjusted to simplify the presentation.*

Generally, only investments with original maturities of three months or less qualify as a cash equivalent under this definition.[1] Examples of cash equivalents are Treasury bills (a form of short-term U.S. government debt), money market funds, and commercial paper (short-term notes payable issued by large corporations).

A CASH EQUIVALENT is a short-term, highly liquid investment with an original maturity of less than three months.

As you can see in Exhibit 13.1, the statement of cash flows reports cash inflows and outflows in three broad categories: (1) operating activities, (2) investing activities, and (3) financing activities. Together, these three cash flow categories explain the change in cash from the beginning balance to the ending balance on the balance sheet.

Video 13-1
www.mhhe.com/libby7e

Cash Flows from Operating Activities

Cash flows from operating activities (cash flows from operations) are the cash inflows and outflows that relate directly to revenues and expenses reported on the income statement.

CASH FLOWS FROM OPERATING ACTIVITIES (cash flows from operations) are cash inflows and outflows directly related to earnings from normal operations.

[1]**Original maturity** means original maturity to the entity holding the investment. For example, both a three-month Treasury bill and a three-year Treasury note purchased three months from maturity qualify as cash equivalents. A Treasury note purchased three years ago, however, does not become a cash equivalent when its remaining maturity is three months.

There are two alternative approaches for presenting the operating activities section of the statement:

The DIRECT METHOD of presenting the operating activities section of the cash flow statement reports components of cash flows from operating activities as gross receipts and gross payments.

1. The **direct method** reports the components of cash flows from operating activities as gross receipts and gross payments.

Inflows	Outflows
Cash received from	**Cash paid for**
Customers	Purchase of services (electricity, etc.) and goods for resale
Dividends and interest on investments	Salaries and wages
	Income taxes
	Interest on liabilities

The difference between the inflows and outflows is called **net cash inflow (outflow) from operating activities.** National Beverage experienced a net cash inflow of $35,489 (all amounts in thousands) from its operations for the fiscal year ended April 30, 2009 (hereafter 2009). Though the FASB recommends the direct method, it is rarely used in the United States. Many financial executives have reported that they do not use it because it is more expensive to implement than the indirect method. Both the FASB and the IASB are considering a proposal to require this method, but intense opposition from the preparer community continues.

The INDIRECT METHOD of presenting the operating activities section of the cash flow statement adjusts net income to compute cash flows from operating activities.

2. The **indirect method** starts with net income from the income statement and then eliminates noncash items to arrive at net cash inflow (outflow) from operating activities.

Net income
+/− Adjustments for noncash items
Net cash inflow (outflow) from operating activities

Use of Direct and Indirect Method by U.S. Companies

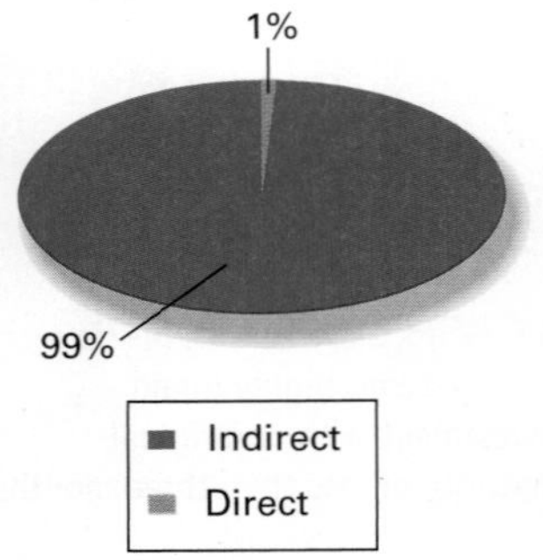

Almost 99 percent of large U.S. companies, including National Beverage, use the indirect method.[2] Notice in Exhibit 13.1 that in the year 2009, National Beverage reported positive net income of $24,742 but generated positive cash flows from operating activities of $35,489. Why should income and cash flows from operating activities differ? Remember that on the income statement, revenues are recorded when they are earned, without regard to when the related cash inflows occur. Similarly, expenses are matched with revenues and recorded without regard to when the related cash outflows occur.

For now, the most important thing to remember about the two methods is that they are simply alternative ways to arrive at the same number. The total amount of **cash flows from operating activities is always the same** (an inflow of $35,489 in National Beverage's case), **regardless of whether it is computed using the direct or indirect method,** as illustrated below.

Direct		Indirect	
Cash collected from customers	$ 570,628	Net income	$24,742
Cash collected for interest	860	Depreciation	8,891
Cash payments to suppliers	(407,978)	Changes in assets and liabilities	1,856
Cash payments for other expenses	(113,966)		
Cash payments for income taxes	(14,055)		
Net cash provided by operating activities	$ 35,489	Net cash provided by operating activities	$35,489

[2]*Accounting Trends & Techniques* (New York: American Institute of CPAs, 2008).

Cash Flows from Investing Activities

Cash flows from investing activities are cash inflows and outflows related to the purchase and disposal of long-lived productive assets and investments in the securities of other companies. Typical cash flows from investing activities include:

CASH FLOWS FROM INVESTING ACTIVITIES are cash inflows and outflows related to the acquisition or sale of productive facilities and investments in the securities of other companies.

Inflows	Outflows
Cash received from	**Cash paid for**
Sale or disposal of property, plant, and equipment	Purchase of property, plant, and equipment
Sale or maturity of investments in securities	Purchase of investments in securities

The difference between these cash inflows and outflows is called **net cash inflow (outflow) from investing activities.**

For National Beverage, this amount was an outflow of $3,491 for the year 2009. Most of the activity was related to purchases and sales of short-term investments, and a smaller amount was related to the purchase and sale of property, plant, and equipment. Since total purchases exceeded cash collected from sales, there was a net cash outflow.

Cash Flows from Financing Activities

Cash flows from financing activities include exchanges of cash with creditors (debtholders) and owners (stockholders). Usual cash flows from financing activities include the following:

CASH FLOWS FROM FINANCING ACTIVITIES are cash inflows and outflows related to external sources of financing (owners and creditors) for the enterprise.

Inflows	Outflows
Cash received from	**Cash paid for**
Borrowing on notes, mortgages, bonds, etc., from creditors	Repayment of principal to creditors (excluding interest, which is an operating activity)
Issuing stock to owners	Repurchasing stock from owners
	Dividends to owners

The difference between these cash inflows and outflows is called **net cash inflow (outflow) from financing activities.**

National Beverage experienced a net cash inflow from financing activities of $645 for the year 2009. The Financing Activities section of its statement shows that National Beverage paid $305 to repurchase its stock from owners and received $950 for new stock issuances.[3] No dividends were paid and no cash was borrowed or repaid.

Net Increase (Decrease) in Cash

The combination of **the net cash flows from operating activities, investing activities, and financing activities must equal the net increase (decrease) in cash** for the reporting period. For the year 2009, National Beverage reported a net increase in cash of $32,643, which explains the change in cash on the balance sheet from the beginning balance of $51,497 to the ending balance of $84,140.

Net cash provided by operating activities	$35,489	
Net cash used in investing activities	(3,491)	
Net cash provided by financing activities	645	
Net increase in cash and cash equivalents	32,643	
Cash and cash equivalents at beginning of period	51,497	*Beginning and ending balances from the balance sheet*
Cash and cash equivalents at end of period	$84,140	

[3]This description was simplified to eliminate discussion of stock options.

PAUSE FOR FEEDBACK

We just discussed the three main sections of the cash flow statement: Cash Flows from Operating Activities, which are related to earning income from normal operations; Cash Flows from Investing Activities, which are related to the acquisition and sale of productive assets; and Cash Flows from Financing Activities, which are related to external financing of the enterprise. The net cash inflow or outflow for the year is the same amount as the increase or decrease in cash and cash equivalents for the year on the balance sheet. To make sure you understand the appropriate classifications of the different cash flows, answer the following questions before you move on.

SELF-STUDY QUIZ

Dr Pepper Snapple Group is the third largest nonalcoholic beverage company in the world. A listing of some of its cash flows follows. Indicate whether each item is disclosed in the Operating Activities (O), Investing Activities (I), or Financing Activities (F) section of the statement of cash flows.

___ 1. Proceeds from issuance of long-term debt.
___ 2. Collections from customers.
___ 3. Payment of interest on debt.
___ 4. Purchase of property, plant, and equipment.
___ 5. Proceeds from disposal of investment securities.

After you have completed your answers, check them with the solutions at the bottom of the page.

To give you a better understanding of the statement of cash flows, we now discuss National Beverage's statement in more detail, including the way in which it relates to the balance sheet and income statement. Then we examine how each section of the statement describes a set of important decisions made by National Beverage's management. Last, we examine how financial analysts use each section to evaluate the company's performance.

Relationships to the Balance Sheet and Income Statement

Preparing and interpreting the cash flow statement requires an analysis of the balance sheet and income statement accounts that relate to the three sections of the cash flow statement. In previous chapters, we emphasized that companies record transactions as journal entries that are posted to T-accounts, which are used to prepare the income statement and the balance sheet. But companies cannot prepare the statement of cash flows using the amounts recorded in the T-accounts because those amounts are based on accrual accounting. Instead, they must analyze the numbers recorded under the accrual method and adjust them to a cash basis. To prepare the statement of cash flows, they need the following data:

1. **Comparative balance sheets** used in calculating the cash flows from all activities (operating, investing, and financing).
2. A **complete income statement** used primarily in calculating cash flows from operating activities.
3. **Additional details** concerning selected accounts where the total change amount in an account balance during the year does not reveal the underlying nature of the cash flows.

Our approach to preparing and understanding the cash flow statement focuses on the changes in the balance sheet accounts. It relies on a simple manipulation of the balance sheet equation:

Assets = Liabilities + Stockholders' Equity

Solutions to SELF-STUDY QUIZ

1. F, 2. O, 3. O, 4. I, 5. I

EXHIBIT 13.2

Selected Cash Transactions and Their Effects on Other Balance Sheet Accounts

Category	Transaction	Cash Effect	Other Account Affected
Operating	Collect accounts receivable	+Cash	−Accounts Receivable (A)
	Pay accounts payable	−Cash	−Accounts Payable (L)
	Prepay rent	−Cash	+Prepaid Rent (A)
	Pay interest	−Cash	−Retained Earnings (SE)
	Sale for cash	+Cash	+Retained Earnings (SE)
Investing	Purchase equipment for cash	−Cash	+Equipment (A)
	Sell investment securities for cash	+Cash	−Investments (A)
Financing	Pay back debt to bank	−Cash	−Notes Payable—Bank (L)
	Issue stock for cash	+Cash	+Common Stock and Additional Paid-in-Capital (SE)

First, assets can be split into cash and noncash assets:

Cash + Noncash Assets = Liabilities + Stockholders' Equity

If we move the noncash assets to the right side of the equation, then:

Cash = Liabilities + Stockholders' Equity − Noncash Assets

Given this relationship, the changes (Δ) in cash between the beginning and the end of the period must equal the changes (Δ) in the amounts on the right side of the equation between the beginning and the end of the period:

Δ Cash = Δ Liabilities + Δ Stockholders' Equity − Δ Noncash Assets

Thus, **any transaction that changes cash must be accompanied by a change in liabilities, stockholders' equity, or noncash assets.** Exhibit 13.2 illustrates this concept for selected cash transactions.

Next, we compute the change in each balance sheet account (Ending Balance − Beginning Balance) and classify each change as relating to operating (O), investing (I), or financing (F) activities by marking it with the corresponding letter. **The balance sheet accounts related to earning income (operating items) should be marked with an O.** These accounts are often called **operating assets and liabilities.** The accounts that should be marked with an O include the following:

- Most current assets (other than short-term investments, which relate to investing activities, and cash).[4]
- Most current liabilities (other than amounts owed to investors and financial institutions,[5] all of which relate to financing activities).
- Retained Earnings because it increases by the amount of net income, which is the starting point for the operating section. (Retained Earnings also decreases by dividends declared and paid, which is a financing outflow noted by an F.)

In Exhibit 13.3, all of the relevant current assets and liabilities have been marked with an O. These items include:

- Accounts Receivable
- Inventories
- Prepaid Expenses
- Accounts Payable
- Accrued Expenses

[4]Certain noncurrent assets such as long-term receivables from customers and noncurrent liabilities such as postretirement obligations to employees are considered to be operating items. These items are covered in more advanced accounting classes.

[5]Examples of the accounts excluded are Dividends Payable, Short-Term Debt to Financial Institutions, and Current Maturities of Long-Term Debt. Current maturities of long-term debt are amounts of debt with an original term of more than one year that are due within one year of the statement date. Certain noncurrent liabilities involving payables to suppliers, employees, or for taxes are also considered to be operating liabilities. These items are covered in more advanced accounting classes.

EXHIBIT 13.3

Comparative Balance Sheet and Current Income Statement

REAL WORLD EXCERPT

Annual Report

NATIONAL BEVERAGE CORP.
Consolidated Balance Sheet
(dollars in thousands)

Related Cash Flow Section		**April 30, 2009**	**April 30, 2008**	*Change*
	Assets			
	Current assets:			
Change in Cas	Cash and cash equivalents	$ 84,140	$ 51,497	+32,643
I	Short-term investments	—	3,000	−3,000
O	Accounts receivable	53,735	49,186	+4,549
O	Inventories	39,612	38,754	+858
O	Prepaid expenses	5,552	12,009	−6,457
	Total current assets	183,039	154,446	
I†	Property, Plant, and Equipment, net	79,381	81,781	−2,400
	Total assets	$262,420	$236,227	
	Liabilities and Stockholders' Equity			
	Current liabilities:			
O	Accounts payable	$ 48,005	$ 49,803	−1,798
O	Accrued expenses	44,403	41,799	+2,604
	Total current liabilities	92,408	91,602	
	Stockholders' equity:			
F	Contributed capital	9,803	9,158	+645
O and F	Retained earnings	160,209	135,467	+24,742
	Total stockholders' equity	170,012	144,625	
	Total liabilities and stockholders' equity	$262,420	$236,227	

NATIONAL BEVERAGE CORP.
Consolidated Statement of Income
For the Fiscal Year Ended April 30, 2009
(dollars in thousands)

Net sales	$575,177
Cost of sales	405,322
Gross profit	169,855
Operating expenses:	
Selling, general, and administrative expense	123,027
Depreciation and amortization expense	8,891
Total operating expenses	131,918
Operating income	37,937
Interest income	860
Income before provision for income taxes	38,797
Provision for income taxes	14,055
Net income	$ 24,742

**Certain balances have been adjusted to simplify the presentation.*

†The Accumulated Depreciation account is also related to operations because it relates to depreciation.

As we have noted, retained earnings is also relevant to operations.

The balance sheet accounts related to investing activities should be marked with an I. These include all of the remaining assets on the balance sheet. In Exhibit 13.3 these items include:

- Short-Term Investments
- Property, Plant, and Equipment, net

The balance sheet accounts related to financing activities should be marked with an F. These include all of the remaining liability and stockholders' equity accounts on the balance sheet. In Exhibit 13.3 these items include:

- Contributed Capital
- Retained Earnings (for decreases resulting from dividends declared and paid)

Next, we use this information to prepare each section of the statement of cash flows.

REPORTING AND INTERPRETING CASH FLOWS FROM OPERATING ACTIVITIES

As noted above, the operating section can be prepared in two formats, and virtually all U.S. companies choose the indirect method. As a result, we discuss the indirect method here and the direct method in Supplement A at the end of the chapter.

Recall that:

1. Cash flow from operating activities is always the **same** regardless of whether it is computed using the direct or indirect method.
2. The investing and financing sections are always presented in the **same** manner regardless of the format of the operating section.

Reporting Cash Flows from Operating Activities—Indirect Method

LEARNING OBJECTIVE 2

Report and interpret cash flows from operating activities using the indirect method.

Exhibit 13.3 shows National Beverage's comparative balance sheet and income statement. Remember that the indirect method starts with net income and converts it to cash flows from operating activities. This involves adjusting net income for the differences in the timing of accrual basis net income and cash flows. The general structure of the operating activities section is:

Operating Activities
Net income
Adjustments to reconcile net income to cash flow from operating activities:
+Depreciation and amortization expense
−Gain on sale of long-term asset
+Loss on sale of long-term asset
+Decreases in operating assets
+Increases in operating liabilities
−Increases in operating assets
−Decreases in operating liabilities
Net Cash Flow from Operating Activities

To keep track of all the additions and subtractions made to convert net income to cash flows from operating activities, it is helpful to set up a schedule to record the computations. We will construct a schedule for National Beverage in Exhibit 13.4.

EXHIBIT 13.4

National Beverage Corp.: Schedule for Net Cash Flow from Operating Activities, Indirect Method (dollars in thousands)

CONVERSION OF NET INCOME TO NET CASH FLOW FROM OPERATING ACTIVITIES

Items	Amount	Explanation
Net income, accrual basis	$24,742	From income statement.
Add (subtract) to convert to cash basis:		
Depreciation and amortization	+8,891	Add back because depreciation and amortization expense does not affect cash.
Accounts receivable increase	−4,549	Subtract because cash collected from customers is less than accrual basis revenues.
Inventory increase	−858	Subtract because purchases are more than cost of goods sold expense.
Prepaid expense decrease	+6,457	Add because cash prepayments for expenses are less than accrual basis expenses.
Accounts payable decrease	−1,798	Subtract because cash payments to suppliers are more than amounts purchased on account (borrowed from suppliers).
Accrued expenses increase	+2,604	Add because cash payments for expenses are less than accrual basis expenses.
Net cash used in operating activities	$35,489	Reported on the statement of cash flows.

We begin our schedule presented in Exhibit 13.4 with net income of $24,742 taken from National Beverage's income statement (Exhibit 13.3). Completing the operating section using the indirect method involves two steps:

Step 1: **Adjust net income for depreciation and amortization expense and gains and losses on sale of investing assets such as property, plant, and equipment and investments.** Recording depreciation and amortization expense does not affect the cash account (or any other operating asset or liability). It affects a noncurrent investing asset (Property, plant, and equipment, net). **Since depreciation and amortization expense are subtracted in computing net income but do not affect cash, we always add each back** to convert net income to cash flow from operating activities. In the case of National Beverage, we need to remove the effect of depreciation and amortization expense by adding back $8,891 to net income (see Exhibit 13.4).

If National Beverage had sold property, plant, and equipment at a gain or loss, the amount of cash received would be classified as an investing cash inflow. Since all of the cash received is an investing cash flow, an adjustment must also be made in the operating activities section to avoid double counting the gain or loss. **Gains on sales of property, plant, and equipment are subtracted and losses on such sales are added** to convert net income to cash flow from operating activities. We illustrate the relevant computations and adjustments for gains and losses on the sale of long-term assets in Supplement B at the end of the chapter.[6]

Step 2: **Adjust net income for changes in assets and liabilities marked as operating (O).** Each **change** in operating assets (other than cash and short-term investments) and liabilities (other than amounts owed to owners and financial institutions) causes a difference between net income and cash flow from operating activities.[7] When converting net income to cash flow from operating activities, apply the following general rules:

[6]Other similar additions and subtractions are discussed in more advanced accounting courses.

[7]As noted earlier, certain noncurrent assets, such as long-term receivables from customers, and noncurrent liabilities, such as postretirement obligations to employees, are considered to be operating items. These items are covered in more advanced accounting classes.

- Add the change when an operating asset decreases or an operating liability increases.
- Subtract the change when an operating asset increases or an operating liability decreases.

Understanding what makes these assets and liabilities increase and decrease is the key to understanding the logic of these additions and subtractions.

Change in Accounts Receivable

We illustrate this logic with the first operating item (O) listed on National Beverage's balance sheet (Exhibit 13.3), accounts receivable. Remember that the income statement reflects sales revenue, but the cash flow statement must reflect cash collections from customers. As the following accounts receivable T-account illustrates, when sales revenues are recorded, accounts receivable increases, and when cash is collected from customers, accounts receivable decreases.

	Accounts Receivable (A)			
Change $4,549	Beginning balance	49,186		
	Sales revenue (on account)	575,177	Collections from customers	570,628
	Ending balance	53,735		

In the National Beverage example, sales revenue reported on the income statement is greater than cash collections from customers by $575,177 − $570,628 = $4,549. Since less money was collected from customers, this amount must be subtracted from net income to convert to cash flows from operating activities. Note that this amount is also the same as the **change** in the accounts receivable account:

Ending balance	$53,735
− Beginning balance	49,186
Change	$ 4,549

This same underlying logic is used to determine adjustments for the other current assets and liabilities.

To summarize, the income statement reflects revenues of the period, but cash flow from operating activities must reflect cash collections from customers. Sales on account increase the balance in accounts receivable, and collections from customers decrease the balance.

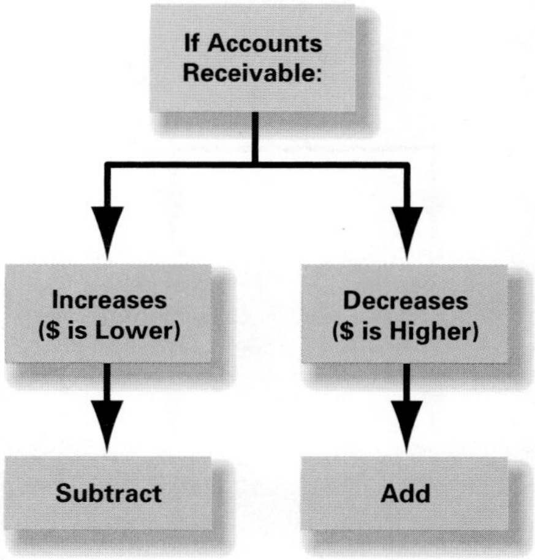

Accounts Receivable (A)		
Beg.	49,186	
Increase	4,549	
End.	53,735	

The balance sheet for National Beverage Corp. (Exhibit 13.3) indicates an **increase** in accounts receivable of $4,549 for the period, which means that cash collected from customers is lower than revenue. To convert to cash flows from operating activities, the amount of the increase (the reduced collections) must be **subtracted** in Exhibit 13.4. (A decrease is added.)

Change in Inventory

The income statement reflects merchandise sold for the period, whereas cash flow from operating activities must reflect cash purchases. As shown in the Inventories T-account, purchases of goods increase the balance in inventory, and recording merchandise sold decreases the balance in inventory.

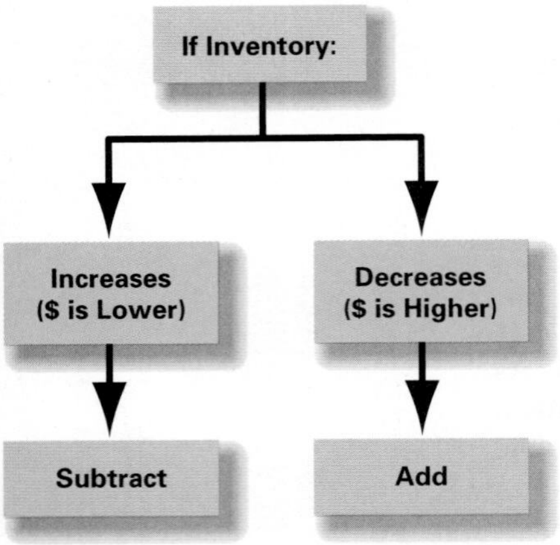

Inventories (A)	
Beg. bal. Purchases	Cost of goods sold
End. bal.	

Inventories (A)		
Beg.	38,754	
Increase	858	
End.	39,612	

National Beverage's balance sheet (Exhibit 13.3) indicates that inventory **increased** by $858, which means that the amount of purchases is more than the amount of merchandise sold. The increase (the extra purchases) must be **subtracted** from net income to convert to cash flow from operating activities in Exhibit 13.4. (A decrease is added.)

Change in Prepaid Expenses

The income statement reflects expenses of the period, but cash flow from operating activities must reflect the cash payments. Cash prepayments increase the balance in prepaid expenses, and recording of expenses decreases the balance in prepaid expenses.

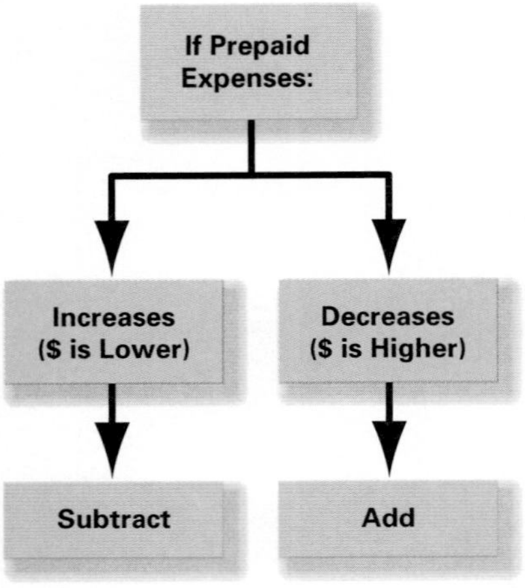

Prepaid Expenses (A)	
Beg. bal. Cash prepayments	Services used (expense)
End. bal.	

Prepaid Expenses (A)			
Beg.	12,009		
		Decrease	6,457
End.	5,552		

The National Beverage balance sheet (Exhibit 13.3) indicates a $6,457 **decrease** in prepaid expenses, which means that new cash prepayments are less than the amount of expenses. The decrease (the lower prepayments) must be **added** to net income in Exhibit 13.4. (An increase is subtracted.)

Change in Accounts Payable

Cash flow from operations must reflect cash purchases, but not all purchases are for cash. Purchases on account increase accounts payable and cash paid to suppliers decreases accounts payable.

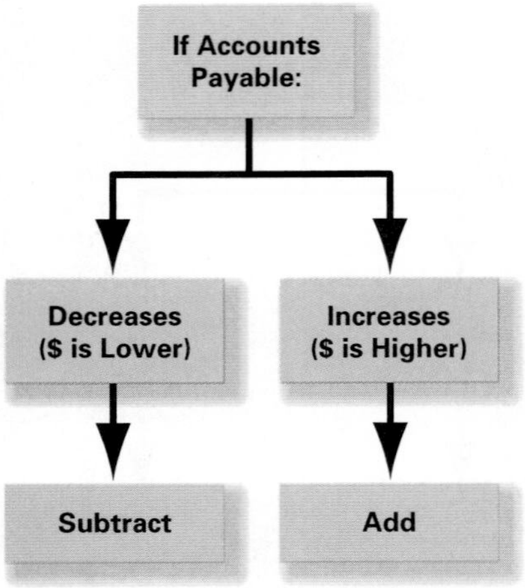

Accounts Payable (L)	
Cash payments	Beg. bal. Purchases on account
	End. bal.

Accounts Payable (L)			
		Beg.	49,803
Decrease	1,798		
		End.	48,005

National Beverage's accounts payable **decreased** by $1,798, which means that cash payments were more than purchases on account. This decrease (the extra payments) must be **subtracted** in Exhibit 13.4. (An increase is added.)

Change in Accrued Expenses

The income statement reflects all accrued expenses, but the cash flow statement must reflect actual payments for those expenses. Recording accrued expenses increases the balance in the liability accrued expenses and cash payments for the expenses decrease accrued expenses.

Accrued Expenses (L)	
Pay off accruals	Beg. bal. Accrued expenses
	End. bal.

Accrued Expenses (L)			
		Beg.	41,799
		Increase	2,604
		End.	44,403

National Beverage's accrued expenses (Exhibit 13.3) **increased** by $2,604, which indicates that cash paid for the expenses is less than accrual basis expenses. The increase (the lower cash paid) must be **added** in Exhibit 13.4. (A decrease is subtracted.)

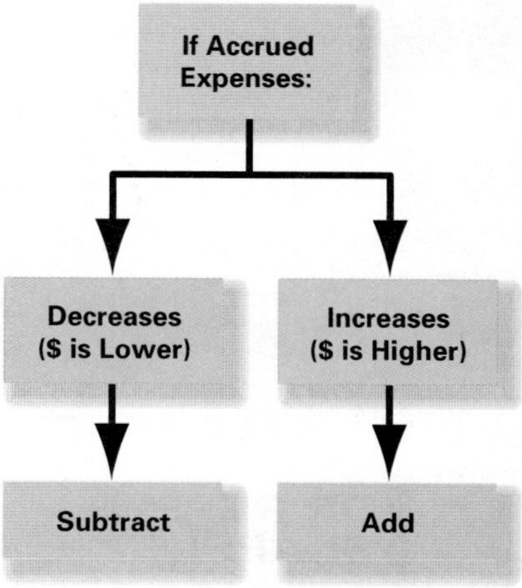

Summary

We can summarize the typical additions and subtractions that are required to reconcile net income with cash flow from operating activities as follows:

ADDITIONS AND SUBTRACTIONS TO RECONCILE NET INCOME TO CASH FLOW FROM OPERATING ACTIVITIES

Item	When Item Increases	When Item Decreases
Depreciation and amortization	+	NA
Gain on sale of long-term asset	−	NA
Loss on sale of long-term asset	+	NA
Accounts receivable	−	+
Inventory	−	+
Prepaid expenses	−	+
Accounts payable	+	−
Accrued expense liabilities	+	−

Notice again in this table that to reconcile net income to cash flows from operating activities, you must:

- **Add the change when an operating asset decreases or operating liability increases.**
- **Subtract the change when an operating asset increases or operating liability decreases.**

The cash flow statement for National Beverage (Exhibit 13.1) shows the same additions and subtractions to reconcile net income to cash flows from operating activities described in Exhibit 13.4.

Classification of Interest on the Cash Flow Statement

INTERNATIONAL PERSPECTIVE

U.S. GAAP and IFRS differ in the cash flow statement treatment of interest received and interest paid as follows:

	Interest Received	Interest Paid
U.S. GAAP	Operating	Operating
IFRS	Operating or Investing	Operating or Financing

Under U.S. GAAP, interest paid and received are both classified as operating cash flows, because the related revenue and expense enter into the computation of net income. This makes it easier to compare net income to cash flow from operations. It also benefits the financial statement user by ensuring comparability across companies. IFRS, on the other hand, allows interest received to be classified as either operating or investing and interest paid to be classified as either operating or financing. This recognizes that interest received results from investing activities and interest paid, like dividends paid, are payments to providers of financing. However, the alternative classifications may be confusing to financial statement readers. These differences are currently on the agenda of the joint FASB/IASB financial statement presentation project.

PAUSE FOR FEEDBACK

The indirect method for reporting cash flows from operating activities reports a conversion of net income to net cash flow from operating activities. The conversion involves additions and subtractions for (1) expenses (such as depreciation expense) and revenues that do not affect current assets or current liabilities and (2) changes in each of the individual current assets (other than cash and short-term investments) and current liabilities (other than short-term debt to financial institutions and current maturities of long-term debt, which relate to financing), which reflect differences in the timing of accrual basis net income and cash flows. To test whether you understand these concepts, answer the following questions before you move on.

SELF-STUDY QUIZ

DR PEPPER SNAPPLE GROUP

Indicate which of the following items taken from Dr Pepper Snapple Group's cash flow statement would be added (+), subtracted (−), or not included (NA) in the reconciliation of net income to cash flow from operations.

_____ 1. Increase in inventories.

_____ 2. Proceeds from issuance of notes payable.

_____ 3. Amortization expense.

_____ 4. Decrease in accounts receivable.

_____ 5. Increase in accounts payable.

_____ 6. Increase in prepaid expenses.

After you have completed your answers, check them with the solutions at the bottom of the page.

Interpreting Cash Flows from Operating Activities

The operating activities section of the cash flow statement focuses attention on the firm's ability to generate cash internally through operations and its management of current assets and current liabilities (also called **working capital**). Most analysts believe that this is the most important section of the statement because, in the long run, operations are the only source of cash. That is, investors will not invest in a company if they do not believe that cash generated from operations will be available to pay them dividends or expand the company. Similarly, creditors will not lend money if they do not believe that cash generated from operations will be available to pay back the loan. For example, many dot-com companies crashed when investors lost faith in their ability to turn business ideas into cash flows from operations.

A common rule of thumb followed by financial and credit analysts is to avoid firms with rising net income but falling cash flow from operations. Rapidly rising inventories or receivables often predict a slump in profits and the need for external financing. A true understanding of the meaning of the difference requires a detailed understanding of its causes.

In the year 2009, National Beverage reported that cash flow from operations was higher than net income. What caused this relationship? To answer these questions, we must carefully analyze how National Beverage's operating activities are reported in its cash flow statement. To properly interpret this information, we also must learn more about the beverage industry. National Beverage normally reports higher cash flow from operations than net income because of the effect of depreciation and amortization, which reduces income but is not a cash outflow. At the same time, it carefully manages the assets and liabilities that enter into the operating cash flow calculation, keeping those total changes to a minimum. Many analysts compute the quality of income ratio as a general sign of the ability to generate cash through operations.

Solutions to SELF-STUDY QUIZ

1. −, 2. NA, 3. +, 4. +, 5. +, 6. −.

Quality of Income Ratio

KEY RATIO ANALYSIS

ANALYTICAL QUESTION

How much cash does each dollar of net income generate?

RATIO AND COMPARISONS

LEARNING OBJECTIVE 3

Analyze and interpret the quality of income ratio.

$$\textbf{Quality of Income Ratio} = \frac{\textbf{Cash Flow from Operating Activities}}{\textbf{Net Income}}$$

National Beverage Corp.'s ratio for the year 2009 was:

$$\frac{\$35{,}489}{\$24{,}742} = 1.43\ (143\%)$$

COMPARISONS OVER TIME		
National Beverage		
2007	**2008**	**2009**
1.33	1.51	1.43

COMPARISONS WITH COMPETITORS	
Coca-Cola	**PepsiCo**
2008	**2008**
1.30	1.36

Selected Focus Company Comparisons

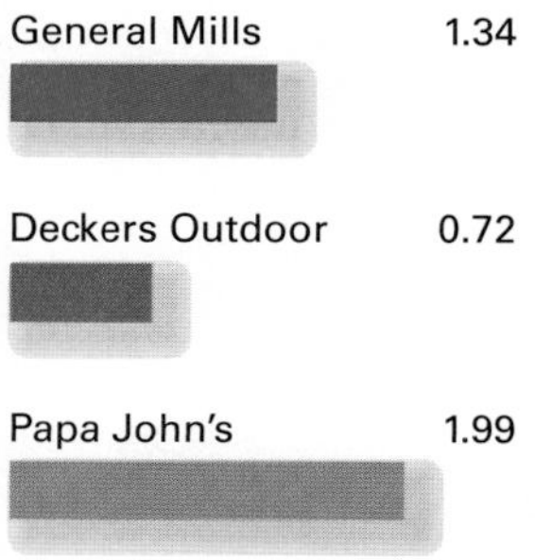

INTERPRETATIONS

In General The quality of income ratio measures the portion of income that was generated in cash. All other things equal, a higher quality of income ratio indicates greater ability to finance operating and other cash needs from operating cash inflows. A higher ratio also indicates that it is less likely that the company is using aggressive revenue recognition policies to increase net income, and therefore is less likely to experience a decline in earnings in the future. When this ratio does not equal 1.0, analysts must establish the sources of the difference to determine the significance of the findings. There are four potential causes of any difference:

1. **The corporate lifecycle (growth or decline in sales).** When sales are increasing, receivables and inventory normally increase faster than accounts payable. This often reduces operating cash flows below income, which, in turn, reduces the ratio. When sales are declining, the opposite occurs, and the ratio increases.
2. **Seasonality.** Seasonal (from quarter to quarter) variations in sales and purchases of inventory can cause the ratio to deviate from 1.0 during particular quarters.
3. **Changes in revenue and expense recognition.** Aggressive revenue recognition or failure to accrue appropriate expenses will inflate net income and reduce the ratio.
4. **Changes in management of operating assets and liabilities.** Inefficient management will increase operating assets and decrease liabilities, reducing operating cash flows and the quality of income ratio. More efficient management, such as shortening of payment terms, will have the opposite effect.

Focus Company Analysis During the past three years, National Beverage's quality of income ratio has ranged from 1.33 to 1.51. Its ratio is above those for Coca-Cola and PepsiCo. National Beverage's high ratio would generally be viewed positively by analysts and would prompt them to read the management's discussion and analysis section of the annual report to determine its causes.

A Few Cautions The quality of income ratio can be interpreted only based on an understanding of the company's business operations and strategy. For example, a low ratio for a quarter can be due simply to normal seasonal changes. However, it also can indicate obsolete inventory, slowing sales, or failed expansion plans. To test for these possibilities, analysts often analyze this ratio in tandem with the accounts receivable turnover and inventory turnover ratios.

A QUESTION OF ETHICS

Fraud and Cash Flows from Operations

The cash flow statement often gives outsiders the first hint that financial statements may contain errors and irregularities. The importance of this indicator as a predictor is receiving more attention in the United States and internationally. *Investors Chronicle* recently reported on an accounting fraud at a commercial credit company, suggesting that

REAL WORLD EXCERPT
Investors Chronicle

> . . . a look at Versailles's cash flow statement—an invaluable tool in spotting creative accounting—should have triggered misgivings. In the company's last filed accounts . . . Versailles reported operating profits of . . . $25 million but a cash outflow from operating activities of $24 million . . . such figures should . . . have served as a warning. After all, what use is a company to anyone if it reports only accounting profits which are never translated into cash?

As noted in earlier chapters, unethical managers sometimes attempt to reach earnings targets by manipulating accruals and deferrals of revenues and expenses to inflate income. Since these adjusting entries do not affect the cash account, they have no effect on the cash flow statement. A growing difference between net income and cash flow from operations can be a sign of such manipulations. This early warning sign has signaled some famous bankruptcies, such as that of W. T. Grant in 1975. The company had inflated income by failing to make adequate accruals of expenses for uncollectible accounts receivable and obsolete inventory. The more astute analysts noted the growing difference between net income and cash flow from operations and recommended selling the stock long before the bankruptcy.

Source: James Chapman, "Creative Accounting: Exposed!" *Investors Chronicle*.

LEARNING OBJECTIVE 4
Report and interpret cash flows from investing activities.

REPORTING AND INTERPRETING CASH FLOWS FROM INVESTING ACTIVITIES

Reporting Cash Flows from Investing Activities

Preparing this section of the cash flow statement requires an analysis of the accounts related to property, plant, and equipment; intangible assets; and investments in the securities of other companies. Normally, the relevant balance sheet accounts include Short-Term Investments and long-term asset accounts such as Long-Term Investments and Property, Plant, and Equipment. The following relationships are the ones that you will encounter most frequently:

Related Balance Sheet Account(s)	Investing Activity	Cash Flow Effect
Property, plant, and equipment and intangible assets (patents, etc.)	Purchase of property, plant, and equipment or intangible assets for cash	Outflow
	Sale of property, plant, and equipment or intangible assets for cash	Inflow
Short- or long-term investments (stocks and bonds of other companies)	Purchase of investment securities for cash	Outflow
	Sale (maturity) of investment securities for cash	Inflow

Remember this:

- **Only purchases paid for with cash or cash equivalents are included.**
- **The amount of cash that is received from the sale of assets is included, regardless of whether the assets are sold at a gain or loss.**

EXHIBIT 13.5

National Beverage Corp.: Schedule for Net Cash Flow from Investing Activities (dollars in thousands)

Items	Cash Inflows (Outflows)	Explanation
Purchase of property, plant, and equipment	$ (6,658)	Payment in cash for equipment
Proceeds from disposal of property, plant, and equipment	167	Receipt of cash from sale of equipment
Purchase of short-term investments	(109,450)	Payment in cash for new investments
Proceeds from sale of short-term investments	112,450	Receipt of cash from sale of investments
Net cash inflow (outflow) from investing activities	$ (3,491)	Reported on the statement of cash flows

In National Beverage's case, the balance sheet (Exhibit 13.3) shows two investing assets (noted with an I) that have changed during the period: Equipment, net, and Short-term investments. To determine the causes of these changes, accountants need to search the related company records.

Property, Plant, and Equipment, Net

Analysis of National Beverage Corp.'s records reveals that the company purchased new property, plant, and equipment for $6,658 in cash, which is a cash outflow. The company also sold old equipment for $167 in cash, an amount equal to its net book value. This is a cash inflow. These investing items are listed in the schedule of investing activities in Exhibit 13.5. These items, less the amount of depreciation expense added back in the Operations section ($8,891), explain the decrease in property, plant, and equipment, net, of $2,400.

Property, Plant, and Equipment, Net (A)			
Beg.	81,781	Sold	167
Purchased	6,658	Depreciation	8,891
End.	79,381		

Investments

National Beverage's records also indicate that it purchased $109,450 in short-term investments during the year for cash, which is an investing cash outflow. The company also sold short-term investments for $112,450, an amount equal to their net book value. These investing items are listed in the schedule of investing activities in Exhibit 13.5. They explain the $3,000 decrease in short-term investments reported on the balance sheet.

Short-Term Investments (A)			
Beg.	3,000		
Purchased	109,450	Sold	112,450
End.	0		

The net cash flow from investing activities resulting from these four items is a $3,491 outflow (see Exhibit 13.5).

Interpreting Cash Flows from Investing Activities

Two common ways to assess a company's ability to internally finance its expansion needs are the capital acquisitions ratio and free cash flow.

KEY RATIO ANALYSIS | Capital Acquisitions Ratio

LEARNING OBJECTIVE 5

Analyze and interpret the capital acquisitions ratio.

ANALYTICAL QUESTION

To what degree was the company able to finance purchases of property, plant, and equipment with cash provided by operating activities?

RATIO AND COMPARISONS

$$\textbf{Capital Acquisitions Ratio} = \frac{\textbf{Cash Flow from Operating Activities}}{\textbf{Cash Paid for Property, Plant, and Equipment}}$$

National Beverage's ratio for 2009 was

$$\frac{\$35{,}489}{\$6{,}658} = 5.33$$

Examine the ratio using two techniques:

COMPARISONS OVER TIME		
National Beverage		
2007	**2008**	**2009**
2.99	3.49	5.33

COMPARISONS WITH COMPETITORS	
Coca-Cola	**PepsiCo**
2008	**2008**
3.85	2.86

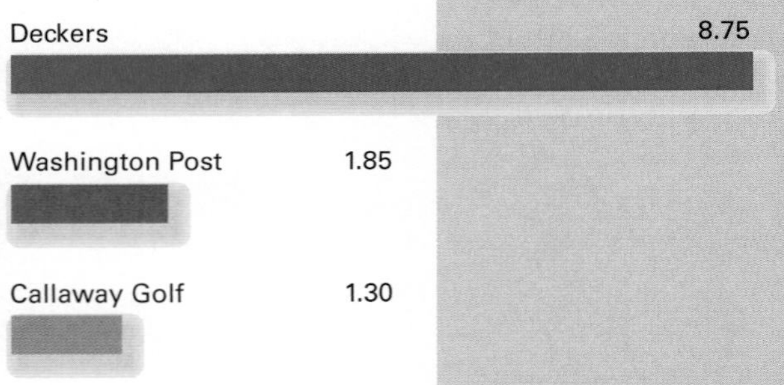

INTERPRETATIONS

In General The capital acquisitions ratio reflects the portion of purchases of property, plant, and equipment financed from operating activities (without the need for outside debt or equity financing or the sale of other investments or fixed assets). A high ratio indicates less need for outside financing for current and future expansion. It benefits the company because it provides the company opportunities for strategic acquisitions, avoids the cost of additional debt, and reduces the risk of bankruptcy that comes with additional leverage (see Chapter 10).

Focus Company Analysis National Beverage's capital acquisitions ratio has increased from 2.99 to 5.33 in recent years. It generates more than sufficient cash to meet its investing needs. This is all part of the company's strategy discussed at the beginning of the chapter: To maintain a "fortress balance sheet, no debt, and hordes of cash." As a consequence, when credit markets tightened during the recent financial meltdown, National Beverage's investment plans were unaffected. National Beverage has even maintained a ratio that is higher than its larger competitors, Coca-Cola and PepsiCo.

A Few Cautions Since the needs for investment in plant and equipment differ dramatically across industries (for example, airlines versus pizza delivery restaurants), a particular firm's ratio should be compared only with its prior years' figures or with other firms in the same industry. Also, a high ratio may indicate a failure to update plant and equipment, which can limit a company's ability to compete in the future.

FINANCIAL ANALYSIS | Free Cash Flow

FREE CASH FLOW equals Cash Flows from Operating Activities − Dividends − Capital Expenditures.

Managers and analysts often calculate **free cash flow**[8] as a measure of a firm's ability to pursue long-term investment opportunities. Free cash flow is normally calculated as follows:

Free Cash Flow = Cash Flow from Operating Activities − Dividends − Capital Expenditures

[8] An alternative definition that does not subtract dividends and interest is often called the **total cash flow of the firm** in finance.

Any positive free cash flow is available for additional capital expenditures, investments in other companies, and mergers and acquisitions without the need for external financing or reductions in dividends to shareholders. While free cash flow is considered a positive sign of financial flexibility, it also can represent a hidden cost to shareholders. Sometimes managers use free cash flow to pursue unprofitable investments just for the sake of growth or to obtain perquisites (such as fancy offices and corporate jets) that do not benefit the shareholders. In these cases, the shareholders would be better off if free cash flow were paid as additional dividends or used to repurchase the company's stock on the open market.

REPORTING AND INTERPRETING CASH FLOWS FROM FINANCING ACTIVITIES

LEARNING OBJECTIVE 6

Report and interpret cash flows from financing activities.

Reporting Cash Flows from Financing Activities

Financing activities are associated with generating capital from creditors and owners. This section of the cash flow statement reflects changes in two current liabilities, Notes Payable to Financial Institutions (often called short-term debt) and Current Maturities of Long-Term Debt, as well as changes in long-term liabilities and stockholders' equity accounts. These balance sheet accounts relate to the issuance and retirement of debt and stock and the payment of dividends. The following relationships are the ones that you will encounter most frequently:

Related Balance Sheet Account(s)	Financing Activity	Cash Flow Effect
Short-term debt (notes payable)	Borrowing cash from banks or other financial institutions	Inflow
	Repayment of loan principal	Outflow
Long-term debt	Issuance of bonds for cash	Inflow
	Repayment of bond principal	Outflow
Common stock and additional paid-in capital	Issuance of stock for cash	Inflow
	Repurchase (retirement) of stock with cash	Outflow
Retained earnings	Payment of cash dividends	Outflow

Remember this:

- **Cash repayments of principal are cash flows from financing activities.**
- **Interest payments are cash flows from operating activities.** Since interest expense is reported on the income statement, the related cash flow is shown in the operating section.
- **Dividend payments are cash flows from financing activities.** Dividend payments are not reported on the income statement because they represent a distribution of income to owners. Therefore, they are shown in the financing section.
- **If debt or stock is issued for other than cash, it is not included in this section.**

To compute cash flows from financing activities, you should review changes in debt and stockholders' equity accounts. In the case of National Beverage Corp., the analysis of changes in the balance sheet (Exhibit 13.3) finds that only contributed capital changed during the period (noted with an F).

EXHIBIT 13.6

National Beverage Corp.: Schedule for Net Cash Flow from Financing Activities (dollars in thousands)

Items	Cash Inflows (Outflows)	Explanation
Repurchase of stock (treasury stock)	$(305)	Cash payments to repurchase outstanding stock
Net proceeds from stock issuance	950	Cash proceeds from issue of common stock
Net cash inflow (outflow) from financing activities	$ 645	Reported on the statement of cash flows

Contributed Capital

National Beverage's change in contributed capital resulted from two decisions. First, National Beverage repurchased outstanding stock for $305 cash, which is a cash outflow. The company also issued common stock to employees for $950 in cash, which is a cash inflow.[9] Together, these two amounts account for the $645 increase in contributed capital (the sum of common stock and additional paid-in capital). They are listed in the schedule of financing activities in Exhibit 13.6, which shows a net cash inflow of $645.

Contributed Capital (SE)			
		Beg.	9,158
Repurchased	305	Issue	950
		End.	9,803

Short- and Long-Term Debt

If National Beverage had borrowed or repaid principal on short- or long-term debt during the period, these also would be listed in this section. The appropriate amounts would be determined by analyzing the short- and long-term debt accounts.

Short- or Long-Term Debt (L)	
	Beginning
Retire (repay)	Issue (borrow)
	Ending

Retained Earnings

Finally, retained earnings should be analyzed. Retained earnings rise when income is earned and fall when dividends are declared and paid. National Beverage's retained earnings rose by an amount equal to its net income, so no dividends were declared and paid. Should National Beverage decide to pay dividends, as it did in 2008, it would also list them as financing cash outflows.

Retained Earnings (SE)			
		Beg.	135,467
Dividends	0	Net Income	24,742
		End.	160,209

Interpreting Cash Flows from Financing Activities

The long-term growth of a company is normally financed from three sources: internally generated funds (cash from operating activities), the issuance of stock, and money borrowed on a

[9]This description was simplified to eliminate discussion of stock options.

long-term basis. As we discussed in Chapter 10, companies can adopt a number of different capital structures (the balance of debt and equity). The financing sources that management uses to fund growth will have an important impact on the firm's risk and return characteristics. The statement of cash flows shows how management has elected to fund its growth. This information is used by analysts who wish to evaluate the capital structure and growth potential of a business.

PAUSE FOR **FEEDBACK**

As we just discussed, the investing section of the statement of cash flows includes cash payments to acquire fixed assets and short- and long-term investments and cash proceeds from the sale of fixed assets and short- and long-term investments. Cash inflows from financing activities include cash proceeds from the issuance of short- and long-term debt and common stock. Cash outflows include cash principal payments on short- and long-term debt, cash paid for the repurchase of the company's stock, and cash dividend payments. Check your understanding of these concepts by answering the following questions before you move on.

SELF-STUDY **QUIZ**

Indicate which of the following items taken from the cash flow statement of Dr Pepper Snapple Group would be reported in the Investing section (I) or the Financing section (F) and whether the amount would be an inflow (+) or an outflow (−).

_____ 1. Purchases of short-term investments.

_____ 2. Proceeds from issuance of note payable (to bank).

_____ 3. Cash dividends paid.

_____ 4. Proceeds from issuance of common stock.

_____ 5. Proceeds from sale of property, plant, and equipment.

After you have completed your answers, check them with the solutions at the bottom of the page.

COMPLETING THE STATEMENT AND ADDITIONAL DISCLOSURES

LEARNING OBJECTIVE 7

Understand the format of the cash flow statement and additional cash flow disclosures.

Statement Structure

Refer to the formal statement of cash flows for National Beverage Corp. shown in Exhibit 13.1. As you can see, it is a simple matter to construct the statement after the detailed analysis of the accounts and transactions has been completed (shown in Exhibits 13.4, 13.5, and 13.6). Exhibit 13.7 summarizes the general structure of the statement for companies that use the indirect method. As you can see, when the **net increase or decrease in cash and cash equivalents** is added to the cash and cash equivalents taken from the beginning of the period balance sheet, it equals the cash and cash equivalents amount reported on the end of the period balance sheet. Companies also must provide two other disclosures related to the cash flow statement.

---

1. I−, 2. F+, 3. F−, 4. F+, 5. I+.

Solutions to SELF-STUDY QUIZ

EXHIBIT 13.7

Structure of the Statement of Cash Flows (Indirect Method)

Statement of Cash Flows (Indirect Method)

Operating Activities:
Net Income
+Depreciation and amortization expense
−Gain on sale of long-term asset
+Loss on sale of long-term asset
+Decreases in operating assets
+Increases in operating liabilities
−Increases in operating assets
−Decreases in operating liabilities
Net Cash Flow from Operating Activities

Investing Activities:
−Purchase of property, plant, and equipment or intangible assets
+Sale of property, plant, and equipment or intangible assets
−Purchase of investment securities
+Sale (maturity) of investment securities
Net Cash Flow from Investing Activities

Financing Activities:
+Borrowing from bank or other financial institution
−Repayment of loan principal
+Issuance of bonds for cash
−Repayment of bond principal
+Issuance of stock
−Repurchase (retirement) of stock
−Payment of (cash) dividends
Net Cash Flow from Financing Activities

Net increase or decrease in cash and cash equivalents
Cash and cash equivalents at beginning of period
Cash and cash equivalents at end of period

Noncash Investing and Financing Activities

NONCASH INVESTING AND FINANCING ACTIVITIES are transactions that do not have direct cash flow effects; they are reported as a supplement to the statement of cash flows in narrative or schedule form.

Certain transactions are important investing and financing activities but have no cash flow effects. These are called **noncash investing and financing activities.** For example, the purchase of a $100,000 building with a $100,000 mortgage given by the former owner does not cause either an inflow or an outflow of cash. As a result, these noncash activities are not listed in the three main sections of the cash flow statement. However, supplemental disclosure of these transactions is required, in either narrative or schedule form. National Beverage's statement of cash flows does not list any noncash investing and financing activities. However, when Continental Airlines purchases airplanes, the manufacturer provides some of the financing for those purchases. These amounts are disclosed as follows at the bottom of its cash flow statement:

REAL WORLD EXCERPT
Continental Airlines
Annual Report

CONTINENTAL AIRLINES

(in millions)	YEAR ENDED DECEMBER 31,		
Investing and Financing Activities Not Affecting Cash:	**2008**	**2007**	**2006**
Property and equipment acquired through issuance of debt	$1,014	$190	$192

Supplemental Cash Flow Information

Companies that use the indirect method of presenting cash flows from operations also must provide two other figures: **cash paid for interest** and **cash paid for income taxes.** These are normally listed at the bottom of the statement or in the notes.

Epilogue

Our more detailed analysis of National Beverage's cash flow indicates the causes of the difference between net income and cash flows. In fact, it was a normal consequence of depreciation and amortization as well as careful management of operating assets and liabilities. Our further analysis of National Beverage's investing and financing activities indicates that the cash needed to continue its investment strategy should continue to be more than met by operations. The continuing success of its product value and strong balance sheet strategy is evident in its continued success in the first quarter of fiscal 2010. Check the company's latest quarterly reports to update this information.

DEMONSTRATION CASE

Redhook Ale Brewery

(Complete the following requirements before proceeding to the suggested solution.) During a recent year (ended December 31), Redhook Ale Brewery, a Seattle-based craft brewer, reported net income of $3,182 (all numbers in thousands of dollars) and cash and cash equivalents at the beginning of the year of $472. It also engaged in the following activities:

a. Paid $18,752 in principal on debt.
b. Received $46,202 in cash from initial public offering of common stock.
c. Incurred other noncurrent accrued operating expenses of $857.
d. Paid $18,193 in cash for purchase of fixed assets.
e. Accounts receivable increased by $881.
f. Borrowed $16,789 from various lenders.
g. Refundable deposits payable increased by $457.
h. Inventories increased by $574.
i. Made cash deposits on equipment of $5,830.
j. Income tax refund receivable decreased by $326.
k. Sold (issued) stock to employees for $13 in cash.
l. Accounts payable decreased by $391.
m. Received $4 from other investing activities.
n. Accrued expenses increased by $241.
o. Prepaid expenses increased by $565.
p. Recorded depreciation of $1,324.
q. Paid $5 cash in other financing activities.

Required:

Based on this information, prepare the cash flow statement using the indirect method.

SUGGESTED SOLUTION

REDHOOK ALE BREWERY
Statement of Cash Flows
For the Year Ended December 31
(dollars in thousands)

Operating activities	
Net Income	$ 3,182
Adjustments:	
Depreciation	1,324
Other noncurrent accrued expenses	857
Change in accounts receivable	(881)
Change in inventories	(574)
Change in income taxes receivable	326
Change in prepaid expenses	(565)
Change in accounts payable	(391)
Change in accrued expenses	241
Change in refundable deposits payable	457
Net cash flow from operating activities	3,976
Investing activities	
Expenditures for fixed assets	(18,193)
Deposits on equipment	(5,830)
Other	4
Net cash flow from investing activities	(24,019)
Financing activities	
Proceeds from debt	16,789
Repayment of debt	(18,752)
Proceeds from sale of stock (IPO)	46,202
Proceeds from sale of stock (employees)	13
Other	(5)
Net cash flow from financing activities	44,247
Increase in cash and cash equivalents	24,204
Cash and cash equivalents:	
Beginning of year	472
End of year	$24,676

Chapter Supplement A

Reporting Cash Flows from Operating Activities—Direct Method

The **direct method** presents a summary of all operating transactions that result in either a debit or a credit to cash. It is prepared by adjusting each item on the income statement from an accrual basis to a cash basis. We will complete this process for all of the revenues and expenses reported in National Beverage's income statement in Exhibit 13.3 and accumulate them in a new schedule in Exhibit 13.8.

Converting Revenues to Cash Inflows

When sales are recorded, accounts receivable increases, and when cash is collected, accounts receivable decreases. Thus, the following formula will convert sales revenue amounts from the accrual basis to the cash basis:

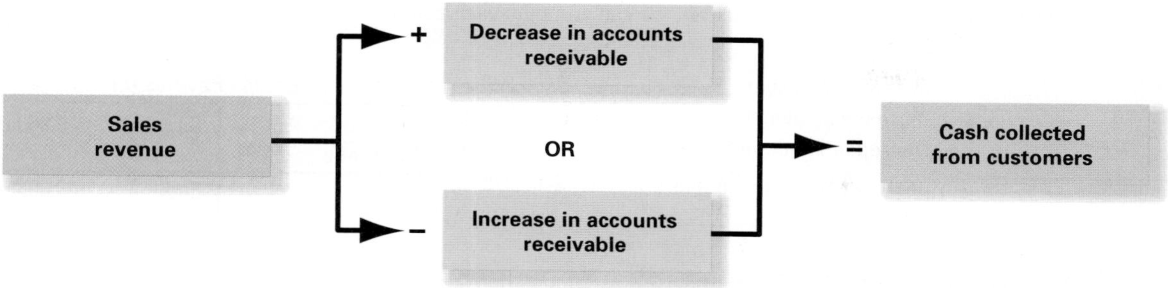

Using information from National Beverage's income statement and balance sheet presented in Exhibit 13.3, we can compute cash collected from customers as follows:

			Accounts Receivable (A)	
Net sales	$575,177			
– Increase in accounts receivable	4,549	Beg.	49,186	
	←	Increase	4,549	
Cash collected from customers	$570,628	End.	53,735	

National Beverage's second revenue is interest income.[10] Since there is no interest receivable balance, using the same logic, we can see that interest income must be equal to cash collected for interest.

Interest income	$860
No change in interest receivable	0
Cash collected for interest	$860

Converting Cost of Goods Sold to Cash Paid to Suppliers

Cost of goods sold represents the cost of merchandise sold during the accounting period. It may be more or less than the amount of cash paid to suppliers during the period. In National Beverage's case, inventory increased during the year because the company bought more merchandise from suppliers than it sold to customers. If the company paid cash to suppliers of inventory, it must have paid more cash to suppliers than the amount of cost of goods sold, so the increase in inventory must be added to compute cash paid to suppliers.

Typically, companies owe their suppliers money (an accounts payable balance will appear on the balance sheet). To convert cost of goods sold to cash paid to suppliers, the borrowing and repayments represented by the accounts payable must also be considered. Borrowing increases cash and accounts payable and repayment decreases cash and accounts payable, so National Beverage's decrease in accounts payable must also be added in the computation. Cost of goods sold can therefore be converted to a cash basis in the following manner:

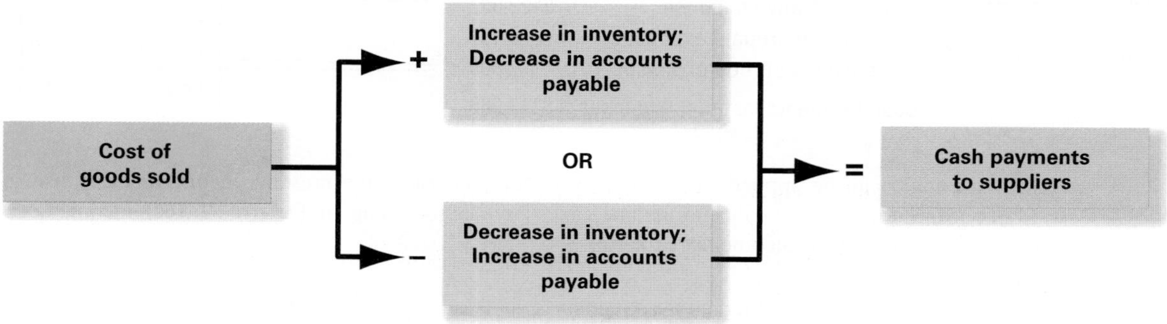

[10] Certain amounts have been adjusted to simplify the presentation.

Using information from Exhibit 13.3, we can compute cash paid to suppliers as follows:

Inventories (A)			
Beg.	38,754		
Increase	858		
End.	39,612		

Cost of goods sold	$405,322
+ Increase in inventory	858
+ Decrease in accounts payable	1,798
Cash payments to suppliers	$407,978

Accounts Payable (L)			
		Beg.	49,803
Decrease	1,798		
		End.	48,005

Converting Operating Expenses to a Cash Outflow

The total amount of an expense on the income statement may differ from the cash outflow associated with that activity. Some expenses are paid before they are recognized as expenses (e.g., prepaid rent). When prepayments are made, the balance in the asset prepaid expenses increases; when expenses are recorded, prepaid expenses decreases. When National Beverage's prepaid expenses decreased by $6,457 during the period, it paid less cash than it recorded as operating expenses. The decrease must be subtracted in computing cash paid for expenses.

Some other expenses are paid for after they are recognized (e.g., accrued expenses). In this case, when expenses are recorded, the balance in the liability accrued expenses increases; when payments are made, accrued expenses decreases. When National Beverage's accrued expenses increased by $2,604, it paid less cash than it recorded as operating expenses. The increase must also be subtracted in computing cash paid for expenses.

Generally, other expenses can be converted from the accrual basis to the cash basis in the following manner:

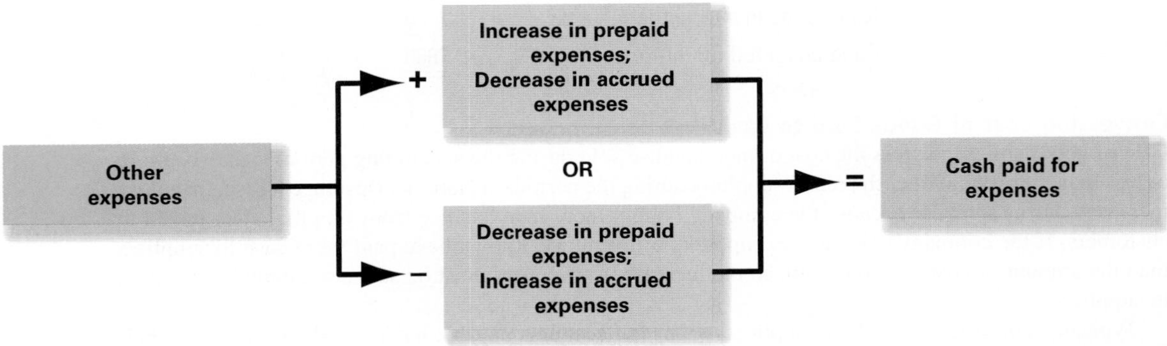

Using information from Exhibit 13.3, we can compute cash paid for expenses for National Beverage as follows:

Prepaid Expenses (A)			
Beg.	12,009		
		Decrease	6,457
End.	5,552		

Selling, general, and administrative expense	$123,027
− Decrease in prepaid expenses	6,457
− Increase in accrued expenses	2,604
Cash payments for other expenses	$113,966

Accrued Expenses (L)			
		Beg.	41,799
		Increase	2,604
		End.	44,403

The same logic can be applied to income taxes. National Beverage presents income tax expense of $14,055. Since there is no balance in Income Taxes Payable (or change in Deferred Taxes), income taxes paid must be the same as income tax expense.

Income tax expense	$14,055
No change in taxes payable	0
Cash payments for income taxes	$14,055

These amounts of the operating cash inflows and outflows are accumulated in Exhibit 13.8.

Cash flows from operating activities	
Cash collected from customers	$ 570,628
Cash collected for interest	860
Cash payments to suppliers	(407,978)
Cash payments for other expenses	(113,966)
Cash payments for income taxes	(14,055)
Net cash provided by operating activities	$ 35,489

EXHIBIT 13.8

National Beverage Corp.: Schedule for Net Cash Flow from Operating Activities, Direct Method (dollars in thousands)

To summarize, the following adjustments must commonly be made to convert income statement items to the related operating cash flow amounts:

Income Statement Account	+/− Change in Balance Sheet Account(s)	= Operating Cash Flow
Sales revenue	+Decrease in Accounts Receivable (A) −Increase in Accounts Receivable (A)	= Collections from customers
Interest/Dividend revenue	+Decrease in Interest/Dividends Receivable (A) −Increase in Interest/Dividends Receivable (A)	= Collections of interest/ dividends on investments
Cost of goods sold	+Increase in Inventory (A) −Decrease in Inventory (A) −Increase in Accounts Payable (L) +Decrease in Accounts Payable (L)	= Payments to suppliers of inventory
Other expenses	+Increase in Prepaid Expenses (A) −Decrease in Prepaid Expenses (A) −Increase in Accrued Expenses (L) +Decrease in Accrued Expenses (L)	= Payments to suppliers of services (e.g., rent, utilities, wages, interest)
Income tax expense	+Increase in Prepaid Income Taxes (Deferred Taxes) (A) −Decrease in Prepaid Income Taxes (Deferred Taxes) (A) −Increase in Income Taxes Payable (Deferred Taxes) (L) +Decrease in Income Taxes Payable (Deferred Taxes) (L)	= Payments of income taxes

It is important to note again that the net cash inflow or outflow is the same regardless of whether the direct or indirect method of presentation is used (in National Beverage's case, an inflow of $35,489). The two methods differ only in terms of the details reported on the statement.

PAUSE FOR **FEEDBACK**

STOP

SELF-STUDY **QUIZ**

Indicate which of the following line items taken from the cash flow statement would be added (+), subtracted (−), or not included (NA) in the cash flow from operations section when the **direct method** is used.

_____ 1. Increase in inventories.
_____ 2. Payment of dividends to stockholders.
_____ 3. Cash collections from customers.
_____ 4. Purchase of plant and equipment for cash.
_____ 5. Payments of interest to debtholders.
_____ 6. Payment of taxes to the government.

After you have completed your answers, check them with the solutions at the bottom of the page.

1. NA, 2. NA, 3. +, 4. NA, 5. −, 6. −.

Solutions to SELF-STUDY QUIZ

Chapter Supplement B

Adjustment for Gains and Losses on Sale of Long-Term Assets—Indirect Method

As noted earlier, the Operating Activities section of the cash flow statement prepared using the indirect method may include an adjustment for gains and losses on the sale of long-term assets reported on the income statement. As discussed in Chapter 8, when property, plant, and equipment with an original cost of $10,000 and accumulated depreciation of $4,000 is sold for $8,000 cash, the following entry is made.

$8,000 Investing cash inflow

$2,000 subtraction in the Operating section

Cash (+A)	8,000	
Accumulated depreciation (−XA, +A)	4,000	
Property, plant, and equipment (−A)		10,000
Gain on disposal (+Gain, +SE) ($8,000 − $6,000)		2,000

Assets		=	Liabilities	+	Stockholders' Equity	
Cash	+8,000				Gain on disposal	+2,000
Accumulated depreciation	+4,000					
Property, plant, and equipment	−10,000					

The $8,000 inflow of cash is an investing cash inflow, but the reported gain of $2,000 is also shown on the income statement. Because the gain is included in the computation of income, it is necessary to remove (subtract) the $2,000 gain from the Operating Activities section of the statement to avoid double counting.

Cash flows from operating activities	
Net income	$24,742
Adjustments to reconcile net income to cash flow from operating activities:	
. . .	. . .
Gain on disposal of property, plant, and equipment	(2,000)
. . .	. . .
Net cash flow provided by operating activities	. . .
Cash flows from investing activities	
Purchases of property, plant, and equipment	. . .
Proceeds from disposal of property, plant, and equipment	8,000
. . .	. . .
Net cash used in investing activities	. . .

If the company had sold the same asset for $5,000 cash, the following entry would be made:

$5,000 Investing cash inflow

$1,000 addition in the Operating section

Cash (+A)	5,000	
Accumulated depreciation (−XA, +A)	4,000	
Loss on disposal (−Loss, −SE) ($5,000 − $6,000)	1,000	
Property, plant, and equipment (−A)		10,000

Assets		=	Liabilities	+	Stockholders' Equity	
Cash	+5,000				Loss on disposal	−1,000
Accumulated depreciation	+4,000					
Property, plant, and equipment	−10,000					

On the cash flow statement, the loss of $1,000 must be removed (added back) in the computation of cash from operating activities, and the total cash collected of $5,000 must be shown in the investing activities section of the statement.

Cash flows from operating activities	
Net income	$24,742
Adjustments to reconcile net income to cash flow from operating activities:	
...	...
Loss on disposal of property, plant, and equipment	1,000
...	...
Net cash flow provided by operating activities	...
Cash flows from investing activities	
Purchases of property, plant, and equipment	...
Proceeds from disposal of property, plant, and equipment	5,000
...	...
Net cash used in investing activities	...

Chapter Supplement C

Using a Spreadsheet to Prepare the Statement of Cash Flows—Indirect Method

As situations become more complex, the analytical approach that we used to prepare the statement of cash flows for National Beverage Corp. becomes cumbersome and inefficient. In actual practice, many companies use a spreadsheet approach to prepare the statement of cash flows. The spreadsheet is based on the same logic that we used in our previous illustration. The spreadsheet's primary advantage is that it offers a more systematic way to keep track of data. You may find it useful even in simple situations.

Exhibit 13.9 shows National Beverage Corp.'s spreadsheet, which is organized as follows:

1. Four columns to record dollar amounts are established. The first column is for the beginning balances for items reported on the balance sheet; the next two columns reflect debit and credit changes to those balances; and the final column contains the ending balances for the balance sheet accounts.
2. On the far left of the top half of the spreadsheet, each account name from the balance sheet is entered.
3. On the far left of the bottom half of the spreadsheet, the name of each item that will be reported on the statement of cash flows is entered.

Changes in the various balance sheet accounts are analyzed in terms of debits and credits in the top half of the spreadsheet with the offsetting debits and credits being recorded in the bottom half of the spreadsheet in terms of their impact on cash flows. Each change in the noncash balance sheet accounts explains part of the change in the Cash account. To illustrate, let's examine each of the entries on the spreadsheet for National Beverage Corp. shown in Exhibit 13.9. You will note that they follow each of the items presented in the schedules to prepare the cash flow statement shown in Exhibits 13.4, 13.5, and 13.6.

a. This entry is used to start the reconciliation; net income of $24,742 is shown as an inflow in the operating activities section to be adjusted by the noncash reconciling entries. The credit to Retained Earnings reflects the effects of the original closing entry. This is the starting point for the reconciliation.

b. Depreciation and amortization expense of $8,891 is a noncurrent expense. It is added back to net income because this type of expense does not cause a cash outflow when it is recorded. The credit to Accumulated Depreciation reflects the effects of the original entry to record depreciation.

c. When an asset that was classified as part of fixed assets is sold, the actual cash proceeds of $167 appear in the Investing section of the statement of cash flows.

d. This entry reconciles the change in accounts receivable during the period with net income. It is subtracted from net income because cash collections from customers totaled $4,549 less than sales revenue.

e. This entry reconciles the purchases of inventory with cost of goods sold. It is subtracted from net income because $858 more inventory was purchased than was sold.

f. This entry reconciles the prepayment of expenses with their expiration. It is added to net income because cash payments for new prepayments are $6,457 less than the amounts that expired and were recorded on the income statement during the period.

EXHIBIT 13.9 Spreadsheet to Prepare Statement of Cash Flows, Indirect Method (dollars in thousands)

	Beginning Balances, 4/30/2008	Analysis of Change: Debit	Analysis of Change: Credit	Ending Balances, 4/30/2009
Items from Balance Sheet				
Cash and cash equivalents	51,497	(*n*) 32,643		84,140
Short-term investments	3,000	(*k*) 109,450	(*j*) 112,450	—
Accounts receivable	49,186	(*d*) 4,549		53,735
Inventories	38,754	(*e*) 858		39,612
Prepaid expenses	12,009		(*f*) 6,457	5,552
Equipment, net	81,781	(*i*) 6,658	(*b*) 8,891	79,381
			(*c*) 167	
Accounts payable	49,803	(*g*) 1,798		48,005
Accrued expenses	41,799		(*h*) 2,604	44,403
Contributed capital	9,158	(*l*) 305	(*m*) 950	9,803
Retained earnings	135,467		(*a*) 24,742	160,209
		Inflows	**Outflows**	**Subtotals**
Statement of Cash Flows				
Cash flows from operating activities:				
Net income		(*a*) 24,742		
Adjustments to reconcile net income to cash provided by operating activities:				
Depreciation and amortization		(*b*) 8,891		
Changes in assets and liabilities:				
Accounts receivable			(*d*) 4,549	
Inventories			(*e*) 858	
Prepaid expenses		(*f*) 6,457		
Accounts payable			(*g*) 1,798	
Accrued expenses		(*h*) 2,604		
				35,489
Cash flows from investing activities:				
Proceeds from sale of equipment		(*c*) 167		
Purchases of equipment			(*i*) 6,658	
Maturities (sale) of short-term investments		(*j*) 112,450		
Purchase of short-term investments			(*k*) 109,450	
				(3,491)
Cash flows from financing activities:				
Purchase of treasury stock			(*l*) 305	
Net proceeds from stock issuance		(*m*) 950		
				645
Net increase in cash and cash equivalents			(*n*) 32,643	
		312,522	312,522	32,643

g. This entry reconciles cash paid to suppliers with purchases on account. It is subtracted because $1,798 more cash was paid than was borrowed during the period.

h. This entry reconciles the accrual of expenses with payments for these expenses. It is added because cash payments for expenses are $2,604 less than new accruals.

i. This entry records the purchases of new plant and equipment (fixed assets) for $6,658 cash.

j. This entry records the receipt of $112,450 cash on maturity of some short-term investments.
k. This entry records the purchases of short-term investments for $109,450 cash.
l. This entry records $305 cash paid to repurchase some of National Beverage's own stock from shareholders.
m. This entry records the $950 cash received from the issuance of stock.
n. This entry shows that the $32,643 net increase reported on the statement of cash flows ($35,489 − $3,491 + $645) is the same as the change in the cash balance on the balance sheet during the period.

The preceding entries complete the spreadsheet analysis because all accounts are reconciled. The accuracy of the analysis can be checked by adding the two analysis columns to verify that debits = credits. You should also note that the debits and credits in the balance sheet accounts directly match those recorded in the T-accounts presented in the body of the chapter. The formal statement of cash flows can be prepared directly from the spreadsheet.

The analytical technique that you have learned for preparing the statement of cash flows will help you deal with other significant business problems. For example, this type of analysis is useful for developing cash budgets for a business. Many small businesses that experience rapid sales growth get into serious financial difficulties because they did not forecast the cash flow effects associated with credit sales and large increases in inventory.

CHAPTER TAKE-AWAYS

1. **Classify cash flow statement items as part of net cash flows from operating, investing, and financing activities.** p. 638

   The statement has three main sections: Cash Flows from Operating Activities, which are related to earning income from normal operations; Cash Flows from Investing Activities, which are related to the acquisition and sale of productive assets; and Cash Flows from Financing Activities, which are related to external financing of the enterprise. The net cash inflow or outflow for the year is the same amount as the increase or decrease in cash and cash equivalents for the year on the balance sheet. Cash equivalents are highly liquid investments with original maturities of three months or less.

2. **Report and interpret cash flows from operating activities using the indirect method.** p. 645

   The indirect method for reporting cash flows from operating activities reports a conversion of net income to net cash flow from operating activities. The conversion involves additions and subtractions for (1) noncurrent accruals including expenses (such as depreciation expense) and revenues that do not affect current assets or current liabilities and (2) changes in each of the individual current assets (other than cash and short-term investments) and current liabilities (other than short-term debt to financial institutions and current maturities of long-term debt, which relate to financing), which reflect differences in the timing of accrual basis net income and cash flows.

3. **Analyze and interpret the quality of income ratio.** p. 651

   Quality of income ratio (Cash Flow from Operating Activities ÷ Net Income) measures the portion of income that was generated in cash. A higher quality of income ratio indicates greater ability to finance operating and other cash needs from operating cash inflows. A higher ratio also indicates that it is less likely that the company is using aggressive revenue recognition policies to increase net income.

4. **Report and interpret cash flows from investing activities.** p. 652

   Investing activities reported on the cash flow statement include cash payments to acquire fixed assets and short- and long-term investments and cash proceeds from the sale of fixed assets and short- and long-term investments.

5. **Analyze and interpret the capital acquisitions ratio.** p. 654

   The capital acquisitions ratio (Cash Flow from Operating Activities ÷ Cash Paid for Property, Plant, and Equipment) reflects the portion of purchases of property, plant, and equipment financed from operating activities without the need for outside debt or equity financing or the sale of other investments or fixed assets. A high ratio benefits the company because it provides the company with opportunities for strategic acquisitions.

6. **Report and interpret cash flows from financing activities.** p. 655

   Cash inflows from financing activities include cash proceeds from issuance of short- and long-term debt and common stock. Cash outflows include cash principal payments on short- and long-term debt, cash paid for the repurchase of the company's stock, and cash dividend payments. Cash payments associated with interest are a cash flow from operating activities.

7. **Understand the format of the cash flow statement and additional cash flow disclosures.** p. 657

   The statement of cash flows splits transactions that affect cash into three categories: Operating, Investing, and Financing Activities. The operating section is most often prepared using the indirect method that begins with Net Income and adjusts the amount to eliminate noncash transactions. Noncash investing and financing activities are investing and financing activities that do not involve cash. They include, for example, purchases of fixed assets with long-term debt or stock, exchanges of fixed assets, and exchanges of debt for stock. These transactions are disclosed only as supplemental disclosures to the cash flow statement along with cash paid for taxes and interest under the indirect method.

Throughout the preceding chapters, we emphasized the conceptual basis of accounting. An understanding of the rationale underlying accounting is important for both preparers and users of financial statements. In Chapter 14, we bring together our discussion of the major users of financial statements and how they analyze and use them. We discuss and illustrate many widely used analytical techniques discussed in earlier chapters, as well as additional techniques. As you study Chapter 14, you will see that an understanding of accounting rules and concepts is essential for effective analysis of financial statements.

KEY RATIOS

The **quality of income ratio** indicates what portion of income was generated in cash. It is computed as follows (p. 651):

$$\textbf{Quality of Income Ratio} = \frac{\textbf{Cash Flow from Operating Activities}}{\textbf{Net Income}}$$

The **capital acquisitions ratio** measures the ability to finance purchases of plant and equipment from operations. It is computed as follows (p. 654):

$$\textbf{Capital Acquisitions Ratio} = \frac{\textbf{Cash Flow from Operating Activities}}{\textbf{Cash Paid for Property, Plant, and Equipment}}$$

FINDING FINANCIAL INFORMATION

Balance Sheet

Changes in Assets, Liabilities, and Stockholders' Equity

Income Statement

Net Income and Noncurrent Accruals

Statement of Cash Flows

Cash Flows from Operating Activities

Cash Flows from Investing Activities

Cash Flows from Financing Activities

Separate Schedule (or note)
Noncash investing and financing activities
Interest and taxes paid

Notes

Under Summary of Significant Accounting Policies
Definition of cash equivalents

Under Separate Note
If not listed on cash flow statement:
Noncash investing and financing activities
Interest and taxes paid

KEY TERMS

Cash Equivalent p. 638
Cash Flows from Financing Activities p. 641
Cash Flows from Investing Activities p. 641
Cash Flows from Operating Activities (Cash Flows from Operations) p. 639
Direct Method p. 640
Free Cash Flow p. 654
Indirect Method p. 640
Noncash Investing and Financing Activities p. 658

QUESTIONS

1. Compare the purposes of the income statement, the balance sheet, and the statement of cash flows.
2. What information does the statement of cash flows report that is not reported on the other required financial statements?
3. What are cash equivalents? How are purchases and sales of cash equivalents reported on the statement of cash flows?
4. What are the major categories of business activities reported on the statement of cash flows? Define each of these activities.
5. What are the typical cash inflows from operating activities? What are the typical cash outflows from operating activities?
6. Under the indirect method, depreciation expense is added to net income to report cash flows from operating activities. Does depreciation cause an inflow of cash?
7. Explain why cash paid during the period for purchases and for salaries is not specifically reported on the statement of cash flows, indirect method, as cash outflows.
8. Explain why a $50,000 increase in inventory during the year must be included in developing cash flows from operating activities under both the direct and indirect methods.
9. Compare the two methods of reporting cash flows from operating activities in the statement of cash flows.
10. What are the typical cash inflows from investing activities? What are the typical cash outflows from investing activities?
11. What are the typical cash inflows from financing activities? What are the typical cash outflows from financing activities?
12. What are noncash investing and financing activities? Give two examples. How are they reported on the statement of cash flows?
13. How is the sale of equipment reported on the statement of cash flows using the indirect method?

MULTIPLE-CHOICE QUESTIONS

1. In what order do the three sections of the statement of cash flows usually appear when reading from top to bottom?
   a. Financing, Investing, Operating
   b. Investing, Operating, Financing
   c. Operating, Financing, Investing
   d. Operating, Investing, Financing
2. Total cash inflow in the operating section of the statement of cash flows should include which of the following?
   a. Cash received from customers at the point of sale.
   b. Cash collections from customer accounts receivable.
   c. Cash received in advance of revenue recognition (unearned revenue).
   d. All of the above.
3. If the balance in prepaid expenses has increased during the year, what action should be taken on the statement of cash flows when following the indirect method, and why?
   a. The change in the account balance should be subtracted from net income because the net increase in prepaid expenses did not impact net income but did reduce the cash balance.
   b. The change in the account balance should be added to net income because the net increase in prepaid expenses did not impact net income but did increase the cash balance.

c. The net change in prepaid expenses should be subtracted from net income to reverse the income statement effect that had no impact on cash.
d. The net change in prepaid expenses should be added to net income to reverse the income statement effect that had no impact on cash.

4. Consider the following: Net income = $10,000, depreciation expense = $2,000, accounts receivable increased by $700, inventory decreased by $400, and accounts payable increased by $300. Based on this information alone, what is cash flow from operating activities?
a. $12,000 c. $11,700
b. $8,000 d. $10,000

5. Which of the following would **not** appear in the investing section of the statement of cash flows?
a. Purchase of inventory.
b. Sale of obsolete equipment used in the factory.
c. Purchase of land for a new office building.
d. All of the above would appear.

6. Which of the following items would **not** appear in the financing section of the statement of cash flows?
a. The repurchase of the company's own stock. c. The repayment of debt.
b. The receipt of dividends. d. The payment of dividends.

7. Which of the following is **not** added to net income when computing cash flows from operations under the indirect method?
a. The net increase in accounts payable.
b. The net decrease in accounts receivable.
c. Depreciation expense reported on the income statement.
d. All of the above are added to net income.

8. Consider the following: Issued common stock for $25,000, sold office equipment for $1,200, paid cash dividends $6,000, purchased investments for $2,000, paid accounts payable of $4,000. What was the net cash inflow (outflow) from financing activities?
a. $19,000 c. ($19,000)
b. $14,000 d. ($14,000)

9. Consider the following: Issued common stock for $25,000, sold office equipment for $1,200, paid cash dividends $6,000, purchased investments for $2,000, purchased new equipment for $4,000. What was the net cash inflow (outflow) from investing activities?
a. $20,200 c. ($10,800)
b. ($2,800) d. ($4,800)

10. The **total** change in cash as shown near the bottom of the statement of cash flows for the year should agree with which of the following?
a. The difference in retained earnings when reviewing the comparative balance sheet.
b. Net income or net loss as found on the income statement.
c. The difference in cash when reviewing the comparative balance sheet.
d. None of the above.

For more practice with multiple-choice questions, go to the text website at **www.mhhe.com/libby7e**.

MINI-EXERCISES

Mc Graw Hill connect ACCOUNTING

M13-1
LO1

MillerCoors

Matching Items Reported to Cash Flow Statement Categories (Indirect Method)

MillerCoors Brewing Company is the world's fifth largest brewer. In the United States, its tie to the magical appeal of the Rocky Mountains is one of its most powerful trademarks. Some of the items included in its recent annual consolidated statement of cash flows presented using the **indirect method** are listed here. Indicate whether each item is disclosed in the Operating Activities (O), Investing Activities (I), or Financing Activities (F) section of the statement or use (NA) if the item does not appear on the statement. (**Note:** This is the exact wording used on the actual statement.)

_______ 1. Purchase of stock. [This involves repurchase of the company's own stock.]
_______ 2. Principal payment on long-term debt.

_______ 3. Proceeds from sale of properties.
_______ 4. Inventories (decrease).
_______ 5. Accounts payable (decrease).
_______ 6. Depreciation, depletion, and amortization.

Determining the Effects of Account Changes on Cash Flow from Operating Activities (Indirect Method)

M13-2
LO2

Indicate whether each item would be added (+) or subtracted (−) in the computation of cash flow from operating activities using the indirect method.

_______ 1. Accrued expenses (increase).
_______ 2. Inventories (increase).
_______ 3. Accounts receivable (decrease).
_______ 4. Accounts payable (decrease).
_______ 5. Depreciation, depletion, and amortization.

Matching Items Reported to Cash Flow Statement Categories (Direct Method)

M13-3
LO1

Lion Nathan, brewer of XXXX, Toohey's, and other well-known Australian brands, has net revenue of more than $2 billion (Australian). Some of the items included in its recent annual consolidated statement of cash flows presented using the **direct method** are listed here. Indicate whether each item is disclosed in the Operating Activities (O), Investing Activities (I), or Financing Activities (F) section of the statement or use (NA) if the item does not appear on the statement. (**Note:** This is the exact wording used on the actual statement.)

LION NATHAN

_______ 1. Receipts from customers.
_______ 2. Dividends paid.
_______ 3. Payment for share buy-back.
_______ 4. Proceeds from sale of property, plant, and equipment.
_______ 5. Repayments of borrowings (bank debt).
_______ 6. Net interest paid.

Analyzing the Quality of Income Ratio

M13-4
LO3

Lisa K. Corporation reported net income of $86,000, depreciation expense of $2,000, and cash flow from operations of $52,500. Compute the quality of income ratio. What does the ratio tell you about the company's ability to finance operating and other cash needs from operating cash inflows?

Computing Cash Flows from Investing Activities

M13-5
LO4

Based on the following information, compute cash flows from investing activities.

Cash collections from customers	$550
Sale of used equipment	250
Depreciation expense	200
Purchase of short-term investments	285

Computing Cash Flows from Financing Activities

M13-6
LO6

Based on the following information, compute cash flows from financing activities.

Purchase of short-term investments	$500
Dividends paid	900
Interest paid	300
Additional short-term borrowing from bank	950

Reporting Noncash Investing and Financing Activities

M13-7
LO7

Which of the following transactions qualify as noncash investing and financing activities?

_______ Purchase of building with mortgage payable.
_______ Additional short-term borrowing from bank.
_______ Dividends paid in cash.
_______ Purchase of equipment with short-term investments.

EXERCISES

E13-1
LO1
Reebok

Matching Items Reported to Cash Flow Statement Categories (Indirect Method)

Reebok International Ltd. is a global company that designs and markets sports and fitness products, including footwear, apparel, and accessories. Some of the items included in its recent annual consolidated statement of cash flows presented using the **indirect method** are listed here.

Indicate whether each item is disclosed in the Operating Activities (O), Investing Activities (I), or Financing Activities (F) section of the statement or (NA) if the item does not appear on the statement. (**Note:** This is the exact wording used on the actual statement.)

______ 1. Dividends paid.
______ 2. Repayments of long-term debt.
______ 3. Depreciation and amortization.
______ 4. Proceeds from issuance of common stock to employees.
______ 5. [Change in] Accounts payable and accrued expenses.
______ 6. Cash collections from customers.
______ 7. Net repayments of notes payable to banks.
______ 8. Net income.
______ 9. Payments to acquire property and equipment.
______ 10. [Change in] Inventory.

E13-2
LO1
BHP Billiton

Matching Items Reported to Cash Flow Statement Categories (Direct Method)

The Australian company BHP Billiton is the world's biggest mining company. Some of the items included in its recent annual consolidated statement of cash flows presented using the **direct method** are listed here.

Indicate whether each item is disclosed in the Operating Activities (O), Investing Activities (I), or Financing Activities (F) section of the statement or (NA) if the item does not appear on the statement. (**Note:** This is the exact wording used on the actual statement.)

______ 1. Proceeds from sale of property, plant, and equipment.
______ 2. Interest received.
______ 3. Repayments of loans.
______ 4. Income taxes paid.
______ 5. Proceeds from ordinary share [stock] issues.
______ 6. Dividends paid.
______ 7. Payments in the course of operations.
______ 8. Receipts from customers.
______ 9. Payments for property, plant, and equipment.
______ 10. Net income.

E13-3
LO1

Determining Cash Flow Statement Effects of Transactions

Stanley Furniture Company is a Virginia-based furniture manufacturer. For each of the following first-year transactions, indicate whether **net cash inflows (outflows)** from operating activities (NCFO), investing activities (NCFI), or financing activities (NCFF) are affected and whether the effect is an inflow (+) or outflow (−), or (NE) if the transaction has no effect on cash. (**Hint:** Determine the journal entry recorded for the transaction. The transaction affects net cash flows *if and only if* the account Cash is affected.)

______ 1. Recorded an adjusting entry to record accrued salaries expense.
______ 2. Paid cash to purchase new equipment.
______ 3. Collected payments on account from customers.
______ 4. Recorded and paid interest on debt to creditors.
______ 5. Declared and paid cash dividends to shareholders.
______ 6. Sold used equipment for cash at book value.
______ 7. Prepaid rent for the following period.
______ 8. Repaid principal on revolving credit loan from bank.
______ 9. Purchased raw materials inventory on account.
______ 10. Made payment to suppliers on account.

Determining Cash Flow Statement Effects of Transactions

E13-4
LO1

Hewlett-Packard

Hewlett-Packard is a leading manufacturer of computer equipment for the business and home markets. For each of the following recent transactions, indicate whether **net cash inflows (outflows)** from operating activities (NCFO), investing activities (NCFI), or financing activities (NCFF) are affected and whether the effect is an inflow (+) or outflow (−), or (NE) if the transaction has no effect on cash. (**Hint:** Determine the journal entry recorded for the transaction. The transaction affects net cash flows *if and only if* the account Cash is affected.)

_____ 1. Purchased raw materials inventory on account.
_____ 2. Prepaid rent for the following period.
_____ 3. Purchased new equipment by signing a three-year note.
_____ 4. Recorded an adjusting entry for expiration of a prepaid expense.
_____ 5. Recorded and paid income taxes to the federal government.
_____ 6. Purchased investment securities for cash.
_____ 7. Issued common stock for cash.
_____ 8. Collected payments on account from customers.
_____ 9. Sold equipment for cash equal to its net book value.
_____ 10. Issued long-term debt for cash.

Comparing the Direct and Indirect Methods

E13-5
LO1

To compare statement of cash flows reporting under the direct and indirect methods, enter check marks to indicate which items are used with each method.

	STATEMENT OF CASH FLOWS METHOD	
Cash Flows (and Related Changes)	Direct	Indirect
1. Accounts payable increase or decrease		
2. Payments to employees		
3. Cash collections from customers		
4. Accounts receivable increase or decrease		
5. Payments to suppliers		
6. Inventory increase or decrease		
7. Wages payable, increase or decrease		
8. Depreciation expense		
9. Net income		
10. Cash flows from operating activities		
11. Cash flows from investing activities		
12. Cash flows from financing activities		
13. Net increase or decrease in cash during the period		

Reporting Cash Flows from Operating Activities (Indirect Method)

E13-6
LO2

The following information pertains to Satellite Company:

Income Statement for 2012		
Sales		$85,000
Expenses		
Cost of goods sold	$51,875	
Depreciation expense	8,500	
Salaries expense	12,000	72,375
Net income		$12,625
Partial Balance Sheet	**2012**	**2011**
Accounts receivable	$10,500	$12,000
Inventory	14,000	8,000
Salaries payable	1,750	800

Required:
Present the operating activities section of the statement of cash flows for Satellite Company using the indirect method.

E13-7 **LO2** **Reporting and Interpreting Cash Flows from Operating Activities from an Analyst's Perspective (Indirect Method)**

Capaz Company completed its income statement and balance sheet for 2012 and provided the following information:

Income Statement for 2012		
Service revenue		$53,000
Expenses		
Salaries	$41,000	
Depreciation	7,000	
Amortization of copyrights	200	
Other expenses	9,700	57,900
Net loss		$ (4,900)
Partial Balance Sheet	**2012**	**2011**
Accounts receivable	$ 8,000	$15,000
Salaries payable	15,000	1,000
Other accrued liabilities	1,000	5,100

In addition, Capaz bought a small service machine for $5,000.

Required:
1. Present the operating activities section of the statement of cash flows for Capaz Company using the indirect method.
2. What were the major reasons that Capaz was able to report a net loss but positive cash flow from operations? Why are the reasons for the difference between cash flow from operations and net income important to financial analysts?

E13-8 **LO2** **Reporting and Interpreting Cash Flows from Operating Activities with Loss on Sale of Equipment (Indirect Method)**

New Vision Company completed its income statement and balance sheet for 2011 and provided the following information:

Service revenue		$66,000
Expenses:		
Salaries	$42,000	
Depreciation	7,300	
Utilities	7,000	
Loss on sale of equipment	1,700	58,000
Net income		$ 8,000
Partial Balance Sheet	**2011**	**2010**
Accounts receivable	$12,000	$24,000
Salaries payable	19,000	10,000
Other accrued liabilities	5,000	9,000
Land	52,000	57,000

Required:
Present the operating activities section of the statement of cash flows for New Vision Company using the indirect method.

Reporting and Interpreting Cash Flows from Operating Activities from an Analyst's Perspective (Indirect Method)

E13-9
LO2

TimeWarner

Time Warner Inc. is a leading media and entertainment company with businesses in television networks, filmed entertainment, and publishing. The company's 2008 annual report contained the following information (dollars in millions):

Net loss	$(13,402)
Depreciation, amortization, and impairments	34,790
Decrease in receivables	1,245
Increase in inventories	5,766
Decrease in accounts payable	445
Additions to equipment	4,377

Required:

1. Based on this information, compute cash flow from operating activities using the indirect method.
2. What were the major reasons that Time Warner was able to report a net loss but positive cash flow from operations? Why are the reasons for the difference between cash flow from operations and net income important to financial analysts?

Inferring Balance Sheet Changes from the Cash Flow Statement (Indirect Method)

E13-10
LO2

Colgate-Palmolive

A recent statement of cash flows for Colgate-Palmolive reported the following information (dollars in millions):

Operating Activities	
Net income	$1,957.2
Depreciation	347.6
Cash effect of changes in	
Receivables	(69.8)
Inventories	(134.7)
Other current assets	(31.0)
Payables	125.2
Other	43.8
Net cash provided by operations	$2,238.3

Required:

Based on the information reported on the statement of cash flows for Colgate-Palmolive, determine whether the following accounts increased or decreased during the period: Receivables, Inventories, Other Current Assets, and Payables.

Inferring Balance Sheet Changes from the Cash Flow Statement (Indirect Method)

E13-11
LO2

Apple, Inc.

A recent statement of cash flows for Apple contained the following information (dollars in millions):

Operations	
Net income	$11,875
Depreciation	703
Changes in assets and liabilities	
Accounts receivable	(939)
Inventories	54
Other current assets	(1,050)
Accounts payable	92
Deferred revenue	6,908
Other current liabilities	(184)
Other adjustments	(7,300)
Cash generated by operations	$10,159

Required:
For each of the asset and liability accounts listed on the statement of cash flows, determine whether the account balances increased or decreased during the period.

E13-12 (Supplement B) Computing and Reporting Cash Flow Effects of Sale of Plant and Equipment

During two recent years Perez Construction, Inc., disposed of the following plant and equipment:

	Year 1	Year 2
Plant and equipment (at cost)	$ 75,000	$13,500
Accumulated depreciation on equipment disposed of	40,385	3,773
Cash received	17,864	12,163
Gain (loss) on sale	(16,751)	2,436

Required:
1. Determine the cash flow from the sale of property for each year that would be reported in the investing activities section of the cash flow statement.
2. Perez uses the indirect method for the operating activities section of the cash flow statement. What amounts related to the sales would be added or subtracted in the computation of Net Cash Flows from Operating Activities for each year?

E13-13 (Supplement B) Computing and Reporting Cash Flow Effects of the Sale of Equipment

During the period, Wong Company sold some excess equipment at a loss. The following information was collected from the company's accounting records:

From the Income Statement	
Depreciation expense	$ 820
Loss on sale of equipment	4,400
From the Balance Sheet	
Beginning equipment	19,000
Ending equipment	12,100
Beginning accumulated depreciation	1,800
Ending accumulated depreciation	1,900

No new equipment was bought during the period.

Required:
1. For the equipment that was sold, determine its original cost, its accumulated depreciation, and the cash received from the sale. (Use the equipment and accumulated depreciation T-accounts to infer the book value of the equipment sold.)
2. Wong Company uses the indirect method for the Operating Activities section of the cash flow statement. What amount related to the sale would be added or subtracted in the computation of Net Cash Flows from Operating Activities?
3. What amount related to the sales would be added or subtracted in the computation of Net Cash Flows from Investing Activities?

E13-14 Analyzing Cash Flows from Operating Activities; Interpreting the Quality of Income Ratio
LO2, 3

A recent annual report for PepsiCo contained the following information for the period (dollars in millions):

Net income	$5,142
Depreciation and amortization	1,543
Increase in accounts receivable	549
Increase in inventory	345
Increase in prepaid expense	68
Increase in accounts payable	718
Decrease in taxes payable	180
Increase in other current liabilities	738
Cash dividends paid	2,541
Treasury stock purchased	4,720

Required:

1. Compute cash flows from operating activities for PepsiCo using the indirect method.
2. Compute the quality of income ratio.
3. What were the major reasons that PepsiCo's quality of income ratio did not equal 1.0?

Reporting Cash Flows from Investing and Financing Activities

E13-15
LO4, 6

Oering's Furniture Corporation is a Virginia-based manufacturer of furniture. In a recent year, it reported the following activities:

Net income	$ 5,135
Purchase of property, plant, and equipment	1,071
Borrowings under line of credit (bank)	1,117
Proceeds from issuance of stock	11
Cash received from customers	37,164
Payments to reduce long-term debt	46
Sale of marketable securities	219
Proceeds from sale of property and equipment	6,894
Dividends paid	277
Interest paid	90
Purchase of treasury stock (stock repurchase)	2,583

Required:

Based on this information, present the cash flows from investing and financing activities sections of the cash flow statement.

Preparing a Statement of Cash Flows (Indirect Method)

E13-16
LO2, 4, 6

Deep Waters Company was started several years ago by two diving instructors. The company's comparative balance sheets and income statement are presented below, along with additional information.

	2012	2011
Balance Sheet at December 31		
Cash	$ 3,700	$4,000
Accounts receivable	900	800
Prepaid expenses	100	50
Equipment	400	0
	$ 5,100	$4,850
Wages payable	$ 450	$1,100
Contributed capital	1,600	1,000
Retained earnings	3,050	2,750
	$ 5,100	$4,850
Income Statement for 2012		
Lessons revenue	$33,950	
Wages expense	30,000	
Other expenses	3,650	
Net income	$ 300	

Additional Data:

a. Prepaid expenses relate to rent paid in advance.
b. Other expenses were paid in cash.
c. Purchased equipment for $400 cash at the end of 2012 to be used starting in 2013.
d. An owner contributed capital by paying $600 cash in exchange for the company's stock.

Required:
Prepare the statement of cash flows for the year ended December 31, 2012, using the indirect method.

E13-17 LO4, 5, 6 Reporting and Interpreting Cash Flows from Investing and Financing Activities with Discussion of Management Strategy

GIBRALTAR INDUSTRIES

Gibraltar Industries is a Buffalo, New York–based manufacturer of high-value-added steel products. In a recent year, it reported the following activities:

Acquisitions (investments in other companies)	$ (8,724)
Decrease in inventories	1,770
Depreciation and amortization	33,907
Long-term debt reduction	(185,567)
Net cash provided by operating activities	107,874
Net income	24,068
Net proceeds from issuance of common stock	250
Net proceeds from sale of property and equipment	2,692
Payment of dividends	(5,985)
Proceeds from long-term debt	53,439
Proceeds from sale of other equity investments	34,701
Purchases of property, plant, and equipment	(21,595)

Required:
1. Based on this information, present the cash flows from investing and financing activities sections of the cash flow statement.
2. Compute the capital acquisitions ratio. What does the ratio tell you about Gibraltar's ability to finance purchases of property, plant, and equipment with cash provided by operating activities?
3. What do you think was Gibraltar management's plan for the use of the cash generated by selling other equity investments?

E13-18 LO5, 7 Reporting Noncash Transactions on the Statement of Cash Flows; Interpreting the Effect on the Capital Acquisitions Ratio

An analysis of Courtney Corporation's operational asset accounts provided the following information:

a. Acquired a large machine that cost $36,000, paying for it by giving a $15,000, 12 percent interest-bearing note due at the end of two years and 500 shares of its common stock, with a par value of $10 per share and a market value of $42 per share.
b. Acquired a small machine that cost $12,700. Full payment was made by transferring a tract of land that had a book value of $12,700.

Required:
1. Show how this information should be reported on the statement of cash flows.
2. What would be the effect of these transactions on the capital acquisitions ratio? How might these transactions distort one's interpretation of the ratio?

E13-19 (Supplement A) Reporting Cash Flows from Operating Activities from an Analyst's Perspective (Direct Method)

Refer to the information for Satellite Company in Exercise 13-6.

Required:
Present the operating activities section of the statement of cash flows for Satellite Company using the direct method.

(Supplement A) Reporting and Interpreting Cash Flows from Operating Activities from an Analyst's Perspective (Direct Method) — E13-20

Refer to the information for Capaz Company in Exercise 13-7.

Required:

1. Present the operating activities section of the statement of cash flows for Capaz Company using the direct method. Assume that other accrued liabilities relate to other expenses on the income statement.
2. What were the major reasons that Capaz was able to report a net loss but positive cash flow from operations? Why are the reasons for the difference between cash flow from operations and net income important to financial analysts?

(Supplement A) Reporting and Interpreting Cash Flows from Operating Activities from an Analyst's Perspective (Direct Method) — E13-21

Refer to the following summarized income statement and additional selected information for Huanca, Inc.:

Income Statement	
Revenues	$146,500
Cost of sales	55,500
Gross margin	91,000
Salary expense	56,835
Depreciation and amortization	33,305
Other expense	7,781
Net loss before tax	(6,921)
Income tax expense	2,561
Net loss	$ (9,482)
Other information:	
Decrease in receivables	$ 170
Decrease in inventories	643
Increase in prepaid expenses	664
Increase in accounts payable	2,282
Decrease in accrued liabilities	719
Increase in income taxes payable	1,861

Required:

1. Based on this information, compute cash flow from operating activities using the direct method. Assume that prepaid expenses and accrued liabilities relate to other expense.
2. What were the major reasons that Huanca's was able to report a net loss but positive cash flow from operations? Why are the reasons for the difference between cash flows from operations and net income important to financial analysts?

(Supplement C) Preparing a Statement of Cash Flows, Indirect Method: Complete Spreadsheet — E13-22

An analysis of accounts follows:

a. Purchased equipment, $19,000, and issued capital stock in full payment.
b. Purchased a long-term investment for cash, $15,000.
c. Paid cash dividend, $10,000.
d. Sold operational asset for $6,000 cash (cost, $21,000, accumulated depreciation, $15,000).
e. Sold capital stock, 300 shares at $12 per share cash.

Items from Financial Statements	Beginning Balances, 12/31/2012	ANALYSIS OF CHANGES Debit	Credit	Ending Balances, 12/31/2013
Income statement items				
Sales			$140,000	
Cost of goods sold		$59,000		
Depreciation		5,000		
Wage expense		28,000		
Income tax expense		9,000		
Interest expense		5,000		
Remaining expenses		15,800		
Net income		18,200		
Balance sheet items				
Cash	$ 20,500			$ 18,800
Accounts receivable	22,000			22,000
Merchandise inventory	68,000			75,000
Investments, long-term	—			15,000
Equipment	114,500			112,500
Total debits	$225,000			$243,300
Accumulated depreciation	$ 32,000			$ 22,000
Accounts payable	17,000			14,000
Wages payable	2,500			1,500
Income taxes payable	3,000			4,500
Bonds payable	54,000			54,000
Common stock, no par	100,000			122,600
Retained earnings	16,500			24,700
Total credits	$225,000			$243,300
		Inflows	Outflows	
Statement of cash flows				
Cash flows from operating activities:				
Cash flows from investing activities:				
Cash flows from financing activities:				
Net increase (decrease) in cash				
Totals				

Required:

Complete the spreadsheet for the statement of cash flows using the indirect method.

For more practice with exercises, go to the text website at **www.mhhe.com/libby7e**.

PROBLEMS

P13-1
LO1, 2, 4, 6
eXcel
www.mhhe.com/libby7e

Preparing a Statement of Cash Flows (Indirect Method) (AP13-1)

HiDef Films, Inc., is developing its annual financial statements at December 31, 2012. The statements are complete except for the statement of cash flows. The completed comparative balance sheets and income statement are summarized as follows:

	2012	2011
Balance sheet at December 31		
Cash	$ 68,250	$ 63,500
Accounts receivable	15,250	22,250
Merchandise inventory	22,250	18,000
Property and equipment	209,250	150,000
Less: Accumulated depreciation	(59,000)	(45,750)
	$256,000	$208,000

Accounts payable	$ 9,000	$ 19,000
Wages payable	4,000	1,200
Note payable, long-term	59,500	71,000
Contributed capital	98,500	65,900
Retained earnings	85,000	50,900
	$256,000	$208,000
Income statement for 2012		
Sales	$195,000	
Cost of goods sold	92,000	
Depreciation expense	13,250	
Other expenses	43,000	
Net income	$ 46,750	

Additional Data:

a. Bought equipment for cash, $59,250.
b. Paid $11,500 on the long-term note payable.
c. Issued new shares of stock for $32,600 cash.
d. Dividends of $12,650 were declared and paid.
e. Other expenses all relate to wages.
f. Accounts payable includes only inventory purchases made on credit.

Required:

1. Prepare the statement of cash flows using the indirect method for the year ended December 31, 2012.
2. Based on the cash flow statement, write a short paragraph explaining the major sources and uses of cash by HiDef Films during 2012.

Preparing a Statement of Cash Flows (Indirect Method) (AP13-2)

P13-2
LO1, 2, 4, 6

BG Wholesalers is developing its annual financial statements at December 31, 2013. The statements are complete except for the statement of cash flows. The completed comparative balance sheets and income statement are summarized:

	2013	2012
Balance sheet at December 31		
Cash	$ 37,000	$ 29,000
Accounts receivable	32,000	28,000
Merchandise inventory	41,000	38,000
Property and equipment	132,000	111,000
Less: Accumulated depreciation	(41,000)	(36,000)
	$201,000	$170,000
Accounts payable	$ 36,000	$ 27,000
Accrued wage expense	1,200	1,400
Note payable, long-term	38,000	44,000
Contributed capital	88,600	72,600
Retained earnings	37,200	25,000
	$201,000	$170,000
Income statement for 2013		
Sales	$120,000	
Cost of goods sold	70,000	
Other expenses	37,800	
Net income	$ 12,200	

Additional Data:

a. Bought equipment for cash, $21,000.
b. Paid $6,000 on the long-term note payable.
c. Issued new shares of stock for $16,000 cash.
d. No dividends were declared or paid.
e. Other expenses included depreciation, $5,000; wages, $20,000; taxes, $6,000; other, $6,800.
f. Accounts payable includes only inventory purchases made on credit. Because there are no liability accounts relating to taxes or other expenses, assume that these expenses were fully paid in cash.

Required:

1. Prepare the statement of cash flows for the year ended December 31, 2013, using the indirect method.
2. Based on the cash flow statement, write a short paragraph explaining the major sources and uses of cash during 2013.

P13-3 (Supplement A) Preparing a Statement of Cash Flows (Direct Method) (AP13-3)

Use the information concerning HiDef Films, Inc., provided in Problem 13-1 to fulfill the following requirements.

Required:

1. Prepare the statement of cash flows using the direct method for the year ended December 31, 2012.
2. Based on the cash flow statement, write a short paragraph explaining the major sources and uses of cash by HiDef Films during 2012.

P13-4 (Supplement A) Comparing Cash Flows from Operating Activities (Direct and Indirect Methods)

Alpha Company's accountants have just completed the income statement and balance sheet for the year and have provided the following information (dollars in thousands):

INCOME STATEMENT		
Sales revenue		$20,800
Expenses		
Cost of goods sold	$9,030	
Depreciation expense	2,900	
Salaries expense	4,070	
Rent expense	2,800	
Insurance expense	900	
Utilities expense	720	
Interest expense on bonds	600	
Loss on sale of investments	650	21,670
Net loss		$ (870)

SELECTED BALANCE SHEET ACCOUNTS	2012	2013
Merchandise inventory	$ 65	$ 84
Accounts receivable	530	440
Accounts payable	212	245
Salaries payable	23	31
Rent payable	8	4
Prepaid rent	7	4
Prepaid insurance	7	17

Other Data:
The company issued $20,000, 8 percent bonds payable during the year.

Required:
1. Prepare the cash flows from operating activities section of the statement of cash flows using the direct method.
2. Prepare the cash flows from operating activities section of the statement of cash flows using the indirect method.

(Supplement B) Preparing a Statement of Cash Flows with Gain on Sale of Equipment (Indirect Method)

P13-5
LO2, 4, 6

XS Supply Company is developing its annual financial statements at December 31, 2011. The statements are complete except for the statement of cash flows. The completed comparative balance sheets and income statement are summarized:

	2011	2010
Balance sheet at December 31		
Cash	$ 34,000	$ 29,000
Accounts receivable	35,000	28,000
Merchandise inventory	41,000	38,000
Property and equipment	121,000	100,000
Less: Accumulated depreciation	(30,000)	(25,000)
	$201,000	$170,000
Accounts payable	$ 36,000	$ 27,000
Wages payable	1,200	1,400
Note payable, long-term	38,000	44,000
Contributed capital	88,600	72,600
Retained earnings	37,200	25,000
	$201,000	$170,000
Income statement for 2011		
Sales	$120,000	
Gain on sale of equipment	1,000	
Cost of goods sold	70,000	
Other expenses	38,800	
Net income	$ 12,200	

Additional Data:

a. Bought equipment for cash, $31,000.
Sold equipment with original cost of $10,000, accumulated depreciation of $7,000, for $4,000 cash.
b. Paid $6,000 on the long-term note payable.
c. Issued new shares of stock for $16,000 cash.
d. No dividends were declared or paid.
e. Other expenses included depreciation, $12,000; wages, $13,000; taxes, $6,000; and other, $7,800.
f. Accounts payable includes only inventory purchases made on credit. Because there are no liability accounts relating to taxes or other expenses, assume that these expenses were fully paid in cash.

Required:
1. Prepare the statement of cash flows for the year ended December 31, 2011, using the indirect method.
2. Evaluate the statement of cash flows.

P13-6 (Supplement C) Preparing Statement of Cash Flows Spreadsheet, Statement of Cash Flows, and Schedules Using Indirect Method

excel
www.mhhe.com/libby7e

Forrest Company is developing its annual financial statements at December 31, 2013. The statements are complete except for the statement of cash flows. The completed comparative balance sheets and income statement are summarized as follows:

	2013	2012
Balance sheet at December 31		
Cash	$ 44,000	$ 18,000
Accounts receivable	26,000	29,000
Merchandise inventory	30,000	36,000
Fixed assets (net)	76,000	72,000
	$176,000	$155,000
Accounts payable	$ 25,000	$ 22,000
Wages payable	800	1,000
Note payable, long-term	38,000	48,000
Common stock, no par	80,000	60,000
Retained earnings	32,200	24,000
	$176,000	$155,000
Income statement for 2013		
Sales	$100,000	
Cost of goods sold	(61,000)	
Expenses	(27,000)	
Net income	$ 12,000	

Additional Data:

a. Bought fixed assets for cash, $10,000.
b. Paid $10,000 on the long-term note payable.
c. Sold unissued common stock for $20,000 cash.
d. Declared and paid a $3,800 cash dividend.
e. Incurred expenses that included depreciation, $6,000; wages, $10,000; taxes, $3,000; and other, $8,000.

Required:

1. Prepare a statement of cash flows spreadsheet using the indirect method to report cash flows from operating activities.
2. Prepare the statement of cash flows.
3. Prepare a schedule of noncash investing and financing activities if necessary.

ALTERNATE PROBLEMS

AP13-1 Preparing a Statement of Cash Flows (Indirect Method) (P13-1)

LO1, 2, 4, 6

Ingersol Construction Supply Company is developing its annual financial statements at December 31, 2012. The statements are complete except for the statement of cash flows. The completed comparative balance sheets and income statement are summarized as follows:

	2012	2011
Balance sheet at December 31		
Cash	$ 34,000	$ 29,000
Accounts receivable	45,000	28,000
Merchandise inventory	32,000	38,000
Property and equipment	121,000	100,000
Less: Accumulated depreciation	(30,000)	(25,000)
	$202,000	$170,000

Accounts payable	$ 36,000	$ 27,000
Wages payable	2,200	1,400
Note payable, long-term	40,000	46,000
Contributed capital	86,600	70,600
Retained earnings	37,200	25,000
	$202,000	$170,000
Income statement for 2012		
Sales	$135,000	
Cost of goods sold	70,000	
Other expenses	37,800	
Net income	$ 27,200	

Additional Data:

a. Bought equipment for cash, $21,000.
b. Paid $6,000 on the long-term note payable.
c. Issued new shares of stock for $16,000 cash.
d. Dividends of $15,000 were declared and paid in cash.
e. Other expenses included depreciation, $5,000; wages, $20,000; taxes, $6,000; and other, $6,800.
f. Accounts payable includes only inventory purchases made on credit. Because there are no liability accounts relating to taxes or other expenses, assume that these expenses were fully paid in cash.

Required:

1. Prepare the statement of cash flows using the indirect method for the year ended December 31, 2012.
2. Evaluate the statement of cash flows.

Preparing a Statement of Cash Flows (Indirect Method) (P13-2)

AP13-2
LO1, 2, 4, 6

Audio House, Inc., is developing its annual financial statements at December 31, 2013. The statements are complete except for the statement of cash flows. The completed comparative balance sheets and income statement are summarized as follows:

	2013	2012
Balance sheet at December 31		
Cash	$ 64,000	$ 65,000
Accounts receivable	15,000	20,000
Inventory	22,000	20,000
Property and equipment	210,000	150,000
Less: Accumulated depreciation	(60,000)	(45,000)
	$251,000	$210,000
Accounts payable	$ 8,000	$ 19,000
Taxes payable	2,000	1,000
Note payable, long-term	86,000	75,000
Contributed capital	75,000	70,000
Retained earnings	80,000	45,000
	$251,000	$210,000
Income statement for 2013		
Sales	$190,000	
Cost of goods sold	90,000	
Other expenses	60,000	
Net income	$ 40,000	

Additional Data:

a. Bought equipment for cash, $60,000.
b. Borrowed an additional $11,000 and signed an additional long-term note payable.
c. Issued new shares of stock for $5,000 cash.
d. Dividends of $5,000 were declared and paid in cash.
e. Other expenses included depreciation, $15,000; wages, $20,000; and taxes, $25,000.
f. Accounts payable includes only inventory purchases made on credit.

Required:

1. Prepare the statement of cash flows for the year ended December 31, 2013, using the indirect method.
2. Based on the cash flow statement, write a short paragraph explaining the major sources and uses of cash during 2013.

AP13-3 **(Supplement A) Preparing a Statement of Cash Flows (Direct Method)** (P13-3)

Use the information concerning Ingersol Construction Supply Company provided in Alternate Problem 13-1 to fulfill the following requirements.

Required:

1. Prepare the statement of cash flows using the direct method for the year ended December 31, 2012.
2. Evaluate the statement of cash flows.

CASES AND PROJECTS

Annual Report Cases

CP13-1 LO2, 4, 6

AMERICAN EAGLE OUTFITTERS, INC.

Finding Financial Information

Refer to the financial statements of American Eagle Outfitters given in Appendix B at the end of this book.

Required:

1. On the statement of cash flows, what was the largest item (in absolute value) listed under "Adjustments to reconcile net income to net cash provided by operating activities"? What was the largest "Changes in assets and liabilities" in the operating section of the cash flow statement? Explain the direction of the effect of each in the reconciliation.
2. Examine American Eagle Outfitters's investing and financing activities. List the company's three largest uses of cash over the past three years. List two major sources of cash for these activities.
3. What was free cash flow for the year ended January 31, 2009? What does this imply about the company's financial flexibility?

CP13-2 LO2, 4, 6

URBAN OUTFITTERS INC.

Finding Financial Information

Refer to the financial statements of Urban Outfitters given in Appendix C at the end of this book.

Required:

1. Does Urban Outfitters use the direct or indirect method to report cash flows from operating activities?
2. What amount of tax payments did the company make during the most recent reporting year? (**Hint:** The statement of cash flows may be helpful to answer this question.)
3. Explain why the "share-based compensation" and "depreciation and amortization" items were added in the reconciliation of net income to net cash provided by operating activities.
4. Has the company paid cash dividends during the last three years? How do you know?
5. What was free cash flow for the year ended January 31, 2009?

CP13-3 LO3, 5

AMERICAN EAGLE OUTFITTERS, INC.

URBAN OUTFITTERS INC.

www.mhhe.com/libby7e

Comparing Companies within an Industry

Refer to the financial statements of American Eagle Outfitters (Appendix B) and Urban Outfitters (Appendix C) and the Industry Ratio Report (Appendix D) at the end of this book.

Required:

1. Compute the quality of income ratio for both companies for the most recent reporting year. Which company has a better quality of income ratio?
2. Compare the quality of income ratio for both companies to the industry average. Are these companies producing more or less cash from operating activities relative to net income than the average company in the industry?
3. Compute the capital acquisitions ratio for both companies for the most recent reporting year. Compare their abilities to finance purchases of property, plant, and equipment with cash provided by operating activities.
4. Compare the capital acquisitions ratio for both companies to the industry average. How does each company's ability to finance the purchase of property, plant, and equipment with cash provided by operating activities compare with that of other companies in the industry?

Financial Reporting and Analysis Cases

Preparing a Complex Statement of Cash Flows (Indirect Method)

CP13-4
LO1, 2, 4, 6

Rocky Mountain Chocolate Factory

Rocky Mountain Chocolate Factory manufactures an extensive line of premium chocolate candies for sale at its franchised and company-owned stores in malls throughout the United States. Its balance sheet for the first quarter of a recent year is presented along with an analysis of selected accounts and transactions:

ROCKY MOUNTAIN CHOCOLATE FACTORY, INC.
Balance Sheets

Assets	**May 31 (Unaudited)**	**February 29**
Current assets		
Cash and cash equivalents	$ 921,505	$ 528,787
Accounts and notes receivable—trade, less allowance for doubtful accounts of $43,196 at May 31 and $28,196 at February 29	1,602,582	1,463,901
Inventories	2,748,788	2,504,908
Deferred tax asset	59,219	59,219
Other	581,508	224,001
Total current assets	5,913,602	4,780,816
Property and equipment—at cost	14,010,796	12,929,675
Less accumulated depreciation and amortization	−2,744,388	−2,468,084
	11,266,408	10,461,591
Other assets		
Notes and accounts receivable due after one year	100,206	111,588
Goodwill and other intangibles, net of accumulated amortization of $259,641 at May 31 and $253,740 at Feb. 29	330,359	336,260
Other	574,130	624,185
	1,004,695	1,072,033
	$18,184,705	$16,314,440
Liabilities and Equity		
Current liabilities		
Short-term debt	$ 0	$ 1,000,000
Current maturities of long-term debt	429,562	134,538
Accounts payable—trade	1,279,455	998,520
Accrued liabilities	714,473	550,386
Income taxes payable	11,198	54,229
Total current liabilities	2,434,688	2,737,673
Long-term debt, less current maturities	4,193,290	2,183,877
Deferred income taxes	275,508	275,508
Stockholders' Equity		
Common stock—authorized 7,250,000 shares, $.03 par value; issued 3,034,302 shares at May 31 and at Feb. 29	91,029	91,029
Additional paid-in capital	9,703,985	9,703,985
Retained earnings	2,502,104	2,338,267
	12,297,118	12,133,281
Less common stock held in treasury, at cost—129,153 shares at May 31 and at February 29	1,015,899	1,015,899
	11,281,219	11,117,382
	$18,184,705	$16,314,440

The accompanying notes are an integral part of these statements.

Analysis of Selected Accounts and Transactions:

a. Net income was $163,837. Notes and accounts receivable due after one year relate to operations.
b. Depreciation and amortization totaled $282,205.
c. No "other" noncurrent assets (which relate to investing activities) were purchased this period.
d. No property, plant, and equipment were sold during the period. No goodwill was acquired or sold.
e. Proceeds from issuance of long-term debt were $4,659,466, and principal payments were $2,355,029. (Combine the current maturities with the long-term debt in your analysis.)
f. No dividends were declared or paid.
g. Ignore the "deferred tax asset" and "deferred income taxes" accounts.

Required:
Prepare a statement of cash flows using the indirect method for the year.

CP13-5
LO2
Carlyle Golf, Inc.

Making a Decision as a Financial Analyst: Analyzing Cash Flow for a New Company

Carlyle Golf, Inc., was formed in September of last year. The company designs, contracts for the manufacture of, and markets a line of men's golf apparel. A portion of the statement of cash flows for Carlyle follows:

CURRENT YEAR	
Cash flows from operating activities	
Net income	$(460,089)
Depreciation	3,554
Noncash compensation (stock)	254,464
Deposits with suppliers	(404,934)
Increase in prepaid assets	(42,260)
Increase in accounts payable	81,765
Increase in accrued liabilities	24,495
Net cash flows	$(543,005)

Management expects a solid increase in sales in the near future. To support the increase in sales, it plans to add $2.2 million to inventory. The company did not disclose a sales forecast. At the end of the current year, Carlyle had less than $1,000 in cash. It is not unusual for a new company to experience a loss and negative cash flows during its start-up phase.

Required:
As a financial analyst recently hired by a major investment bank, you have been asked to write a short memo to your supervisor evaluating the problems facing Carlyle. Emphasize typical sources of financing that may or may not be available to support the expansion.

Critical Thinking Case

CP13-6
LO1, 2, 6

Enron

Ethical Decision-Making: A Real-Life Example

In a February 19, 2004, press release, the Securities and Exchange Commission described a number of fraudulent transactions that Enron executives concocted in an effort to meet the company's financial targets. One particularly well-known scheme is called the "Nigerian barge" transaction, which took place in the fourth quarter of 1999. According to court documents, Enron arranged to sell three electricity-generating power barges moored off the coast of Nigeria. The "buyer" was the investment banking firm of Merrill Lynch. Although Enron reported this transaction as a sale in its income statement, it turns out this was no ordinary sale. Merrill Lynch didn't really want the barges and had only agreed to buy them because Enron guaranteed, in a secret side deal, that it would arrange for the barges to be bought back from Merrill Lynch within six months of the initial transaction. In addition, Enron promised to pay Merrill Lynch a hefty fee for doing the deal. In an interview on National

Public Radio on August 17, 2002, Michigan Senator Carl Levin declared, "(T)he case of the Nigerian barge transaction was, by any definition, a loan."

Required:

1. Discuss whether the Nigerian barge transaction should have been considered a loan rather than a sale. As part of your discussion, consider the following questions. Doesn't the Merrill Lynch payment to Enron at the time of the initial transaction automatically make it a sale, not a loan? What aspects of the transaction are similar to a loan? Which aspects suggest that the four criteria for revenue recognition (summarized near the end of Chapter 3) were not fulfilled?
2. The income statement effect of recording the transaction as a sale rather than a loan is fairly clear: Enron was able to boost its revenues and net income. What is somewhat less obvious, but nearly as important, are the effects on the statement of cash flows. Describe how recording the transaction as a sale rather than as a loan would change the statement of cash flows.
3. How would the two different statements of cash flows (described in your response to requirement 2) affect financial statement users?

Financial Reporting and Analysis Team Project

Team Project: Analyzing Cash Flows

CP13-7
LO1, 2, 3, 4, 5, 6

As a team, select an industry to analyze. *Reuters* provides lists of industries under Sectors and Industries at www.reuters.com. (Click on an industry and then select Company Rankings for a list of members of that industry.) Each team member should acquire the annual report or 10-K for one publicly traded company in the industry, with each member selecting a different company. (Library files, the SEC EDGAR service at www.sec.gov, or the company itself are good sources.)

Required:

On an individual basis, each team member should write a short report answering the following questions about the selected company. Discuss any patterns across the companies that you as a team observe. Then, as a team, write a short report comparing and contrasting your companies.

1. Which of the two basic reporting approaches for cash flows from operating activities did the company adopt?
2. What is the quality of income ratio for the most current year? What were the major causes of differences between net income and cash flow from operations?
3. What is the capital acquisitions ratio for the three-year period presented in total? How is the company financing its capital acquisitions?
4. What portion of the cash from operations in the current year is being paid to stockholders in the form of dividends?

TABLE A.1

Present Value of $1

Periods	2%	3%	3.75%	4%	4.25%	5%	6%	7%	8%
1	0.9804	0.9709	0.9639	0.9615	0.9592	0.9524	0.9434	0.9346	0.9259
2	0.9612	0.9426	0.9290	0.9246	0.9201	0.9070	0.8900	0.8734	0.8573
3	0.9423	0.9151	0.8954	0.8890	0.8826	0.8638	0.8396	0.8163	0.7938
4	0.9238	0.8885	0.8631	0.8548	0.8466	0.8227	0.7921	0.7629	0.7350
5	0.9057	0.8626	0.8319	0.8219	0.8121	0.7835	0.7473	0.7130	0.6806
6	0.8880	0.8375	0.8018	0.7903	0.7790	0.7462	0.7050	0.6663	0.6302
7	0.8706	0.8131	0.7728	0.7599	0.7473	0.7107	0.6651	0.6227	0.5835
8	0.8535	0.7894	0.7449	0.7307	0.7168	0.6768	0.6274	0.5820	0.5403
9	0.8368	0.7664	0.7180	0.7026	0.6876	0.6446	0.5919	0.5439	0.5002
10	0.8203	0.7441	0.6920	0.6756	0.6595	0.6139	0.5584	0.5083	0.4632
20	0.6730	0.5537	0.4789	0.4564	0.4350	0.3769	0.3118	0.2584	0.2145

Periods	9%	10%	11%	12%	13%	14%	15%	20%	25%
1	0.9174	0.9091	0.9009	0.8929	0.8850	0.8772	0.8696	0.8333	0.8000
2	0.8417	0.8264	0.8116	0.7972	0.7831	0.7695	0.7561	0.6944	0.6400
3	0.7722	0.7513	0.7312	0.7118	0.6931	0.6750	0.6575	0.5787	0.5120
4	0.7084	0.6830	0.6587	0.6355	0.6133	0.5921	0.5718	0.4823	0.4096
5	0.6499	0.6209	0.5935	0.5674	0.5428	0.5194	0.4972	0.4019	0.3277
6	0.5963	0.5645	0.5346	0.5066	0.4803	0.4556	0.4323	0.3349	0.2621
7	0.5470	0.5132	0.4817	0.4523	0.4251	0.3996	0.3759	0.2791	0.2097
8	0.5019	0.4665	0.4339	0.4039	0.3762	0.3506	0.3269	0.2326	0.1678
9	0.4604	0.4241	0.3909	0.3606	0.3329	0.3075	0.2843	0.1938	0.1342
10	0.4224	0.3855	0.3522	0.3220	0.2946	0.2697	0.2472	0.1615	0.1074
20	0.1784	0.1486	0.1240	0.1037	0.0868	0.0728	0.0611	0.0261	0.0115

TABLE A.2

Present Value of Annuity of $1

Periods*	2%	3%	3.75%	4%	4.25%	5%	6%	7%	8%
1	0.9804	0.9709	0.9639	0.9615	0.9592	0.9524	0.9434	0.9346	0.9259
2	1.9416	1.9135	1.8929	1.8861	1.8794	1.8594	1.8334	1.8080	1.7833
3	2.8839	2.8286	2.7883	2.7751	2.7620	2.7232	2.6730	2.6243	2.5771
4	3.8077	3.7171	3.6514	3.6299	3.6086	3.5460	3.4651	3.3872	3.3121
5	4.7135	4.5797	4.4833	4.4518	4.4207	4.3295	4.2124	4.1002	3.9927
6	5.6014	5.4172	5.2851	5.2421	5.1997	5.0757	4.9173	4.7665	4.6229
7	6.4720	6.2303	6.0579	6.0021	5.9470	5.7864	5.5824	5.3893	5.2064
8	7.3255	7.0197	6.8028	6.7327	6.6638	6.4632	6.2098	5.9713	5.7466
9	8.1622	7.7861	7.5208	7.4353	7.3513	7.1078	6.8017	6.5152	6.2469
10	8.9826	8.5302	8.2128	8.1109	8.0109	7.7217	7.3601	7.0236	6.7101
20	16.3514	14.8775	13.8962	13.5903	13.2944	12.4622	11.4699	10.5940	9.8181

**There is one payment each period.*

TABLE A.2 ***(continued)***

Present Value of Annuity of $1

Periods*	9%	10%	11%	12%	13%	14%	15%	20%	25%
1	0.9174	0.9091	0.9009	0.8929	0.8550	0.8772	0.8696	0.8333	0.8000
2	1.7591	1.7355	1.7125	1.6901	1.6681	1.6467	1.6257	1.5278	1.4400
3	2.5313	2.4869	2.4437	2.4018	2.3612	2.3216	2.2832	2.1065	1.9520
4	3.2397	3.1699	3.1024	3.0373	2.9745	2.9137	2.8550	2.5887	2.3616
5	3.8897	3.7908	3.6959	3.6048	3.5172	3.4331	3.3522	2.9906	2.6893
6	4.4859	4.3553	4.2305	4.1114	3.9975	3.8887	3.7845	3.3255	2.9514
7	5.0330	4.8684	4.7122	4.5638	4.4226	4.2883	4.1604	3.6046	3.1611
8	5.5348	5.3349	5.1461	4.9676	4.7988	4.6389	4.4873	3.8372	3.3289
9	5.9952	5.7590	5.5370	5.3282	5.1317	4.9464	4.7716	4.0310	3.4631
10	6.4177	6.1446	5.8892	5.6502	5.4262	5.2161	5.0188	4.1925	3.5705
20	9.1285	8.5136	7.9633	7.4694	7.0248	6.6231	6.2593	4.8696	3.9539

**There is one payment each period.*

TABLE A.3

Future Value of $1

Periods	2%	3%	3.75%	4%	4.25%	5%	6%	7%	8%
0	1.	1.	1.	1.	1.	1.	1.	1.	1.
1	1.02	1.03	1.0375	1.04	1.0425	1.05	1.06	1.07	1.08
2	1.0404	1.0609	1.0764	1.0816	1.0868	1.1025	1.1236	1.1449	1.1664
3	1.0612	1.0927	1.1168	1.1249	1.1330	1.1576	1.1910	1.2250	1.2597
4	1.0824	1.1255	1.1587	1.1699	1.1811	1.2155	1.2625	1.3108	1.3605
5	1.1041	1.1593	1.2021	1.2167	1.2313	1.2763	1.3382	1.4026	1.4693
6	1.1262	1.1941	1.2472	1.2653	1.2837	1.3401	1.4185	1.5007	1.5869
7	1.1487	1.2299	1.2939	1.3159	1.3382	1.4071	1.5036	1.6058	1.7138
8	1.1717	1.2668	1.3425	1.3686	1.3951	1.4775	1.5938	1.7182	1.8509
9	1.1951	1.3048	1.3928	1.4233	1.4544	1.5513	1.6895	1.8385	1.9990
10	1.2190	1.3439	1.4450	1.4802	1.5162	1.6289	1.7908	1.9672	2.1589
20	1.4859	1.8061	2.0882	2.1911	2.2989	2.6533	3.2071	3.8697	4.6610

Periods	9%	10%	11%	12%	13%	14%	15%	20%	25%
0	1.	1.	1.	1.	1.	1.	1.	1.	1.
1	1.09	1.10	1.11	1.12	1.13	1.14	1.15	1.20	1.25
2	1.1881	1.2100	1.2321	1.2544	1.2769	1.2996	1.3225	1.4400	1.5625
3	1.2950	1.3310	1.3676	1.4049	1.4429	1.4815	1.5209	1.7280	1.9531
4	1.4116	1.4641	1.5181	1.5735	1.6305	1.6890	1.7490	2.0736	2.4414
5	1.5386	1.6105	1.6851	1.7623	1.8424	1.9254	2.0114	2.4883	3.0518
6	1.6771	1.7716	1.8704	1.9738	2.0820	2.1950	2.3131	2.9860	3.8147
7	1.8280	1.9487	2.0762	2.2107	2.3526	2.5023	2.6600	3.5832	4.7684
8	1.9926	2.1436	2.3045	2.4760	2.6584	2.8526	3.0590	4.2998	5.9605
9	2.1719	2.3579	2.5580	2.7731	3.0040	3.2519	3.5179	5.1598	7.4506
10	2.3674	2.5937	2.8394	3.1058	3.3946	3.7072	4.0456	6.1917	9.3132
20	5.6044	6.7275	8.0623	9.6463	11.5231	13.7435	16.3665	38.3376	86.7362

TABLE A.4

Future Value of Annuity of $1

Periods*	2%	3%	3.75%	4%	4.25%	5%	6%	7%	8%
1	1.	1.	1.	1.	1.	1.	1.	1.	1.
2	2.02	2.03	2.0375	2.04	2.0425	2.05	2.06	2.07	2.08
3	3.0604	3.0909	3.1139	3.1216	3.1293	3.1525	3.1836	3.2149	3.2464
4	4.1216	4.1836	4.2307	4.2465	4.2623	4.3101	4.3746	4.4399	4.5061
5	5.2040	5.3091	5.3893	5.4163	5.4434	5.5256	5.6371	5.7507	5.8666
6	6.3081	6.4684	6.5914	6.6330	6.6748	6.8019	6.9753	7.1533	7.3359
7	7.4343	7.6625	7.8386	7.8983	7.9585	8.1420	8.3938	8.6540	8.9228
8	8.5830	8.8923	9.1326	9.2142	9.2967	9.5491	9.8975	10.2598	10.6366
9	9.7546	10.1591	10.4750	10.5828	10.6918	11.0266	11.4913	11.9780	12.4876
10	10.9497	11.4639	11.8678	12.0061	12.1462	12.5779	13.1808	13.8164	14.4866
20	24.2974	26.8704	29.0174	29.7781	30.5625	33.0660	36.7856	40.9955	45.7620

Periods*	9%	10%	11%	12%	13%	14%	15%	20%	25%
1	1.	1.	1.	1.	1.	1.	1.	1.	1.
2	2.09	2.10	2.11	2.12	2.13	2.14	2.15	2.20	2.25
3	3.2781	3.3100	3.3421	3.3744	3.4069	3.4396	3.4725	3.6400	3.8125
4	4.5731	4.6410	4.7097	4.7793	4.8498	4.9211	4.9934	5.3680	5.7656
5	5.9847	6.1051	6.2278	6.3528	6.4803	6.6101	6.7424	7.4416	8.2070
6	7.5233	7.7156	7.9129	8.1152	8.3227	8.5355	8.7537	9.9299	11.2588
7	9.2004	9.4872	9.7833	10.0890	10.4047	10.7305	11.0668	12.9159	15.0735
8	11.0285	11.4359	11.8594	12.2997	12.7573	13.2328	13.7268	16.4991	19.8419
9	13.0210	13.5975	14.1640	14.7757	15.4157	16.0853	16.7858	20.7989	25.8023
10	15.1929	15.9374	16.7220	17.5487	18.4197	19.3373	20.3037	25.9587	33.2529
20	51.1601	57.2750	64.2028	72.0524	80.9468	91.0249	102.4436	186.6880	342.9447

**There is one payment each period.*

UNITED STATES SECURITIES AND EXCHANGE COMMISSION

Washington, D.C. 20549

Form 10-K

☑ **ANNUAL REPORT PURSUANT TO SECTION 13 OR 15(d) OF THE SECURITIES EXCHANGE ACT OF 1934**

For the Fiscal Year Ended January 31, 2009

OR

☐ **TRANSITION REPORT PURSUANT TO SECTION 13 OR 15(d) OF THE SECURITIES EXCHANGE ACT OF 1934**

Commission File Number: 1-33338

American Eagle Outfitters, Inc.

(Exact name of registrant as specified in its charter)

Delaware *(State or other jurisdiction of incorporation or organization)*	**No. 13-2721761** *(I.R.S. Employer Identification No.)*
77 Hot Metal Street, Pittsburgh, PA *(Address of principal executive offices)*	**15203-2329** *(Zip Code)*

Registrant's telephone number, including area code: (412) 432-3300

Securities registered pursuant to Section 12(b) of the Act:

Common Shares, $0.01 par value *(Title of class)*	New York Stock Exchange *(Name of each exchange on which registered)*

Securities registered pursuant to Section 12(g) of the Act:
None

Indicate by check mark if the registrant is a well-known seasoned issuer, as defined in Rule 405 of the Securities Act. YES ☑ NO ☐

Indicate by check mark if the registrant is not required to file reports pursuant to Section 13 or Sections 15(d) of the Act. YES ☐ NO ☑

Indicate by check mark whether the registrant (1) has filed all reports required to be filed by Section 13 or 15(d) of the Securities Exchange Act of 1934 during the preceding 12 months, and (2) has been subject to the filing requirements for at the past 90 days. YES ☑ NO ☐

Indicate by check mark if disclosure of delinquent filers pursuant to Item 405 of Regulation S-K is not contained herein, and will not be contained, to the best of registrant's knowledge, in definitive proxy or information statements incorporated by reference in Part III of this Form 10-K or any amendment to this Form 10-K. ☐

Indicate by check mark whether the registrant is a large accelerated filer, an accelerated filer, a non-accelerated filer, or a smaller reporting company. See the definitions of "large accelerated filer," "accelerated filer" and "smaller reporting company" in Rule 12b-2 of the Exchange Act. (Check one):

Large accelerated filer ☑ Accelerated filer ☐ Non-accelerated filer ☐ Smaller reporting company ☐
(Do not check if a smaller reporting company)

Indicate by check mark whether the registrant is a shell company (as defined in Rule 12b-2 of the Act). YES ☐ NO ☑

The aggregate market value of voting and non-voting common equity held by non-affiliates of the registrant as of August 2, 2008 was $2,443,983,683.

Indicate the number of shares outstanding of each of the registrant's classes of common stock, as of the latest practicable date: 206,380,486 Common Shares were outstanding at March 13, 2009.

DOCUMENTS INCORPORATED BY REFERENCE

Part III — Proxy Statement for 2009 Annual Meeting of Stockholders, in part, as indicated.

AMERICAN EAGLE OUTFITTERS, INC.

TABLE OF CONTENTS

PART I

ITEM 1. *BUSINESS.*

General

American Eagle Outfitters, Inc., a Delaware corporation, is a leading retailer that operates under the American Eagle Outfitters®, aerie® by American Eagle, 77kids™ by american eagle and MARTIN + OSA® brands.

American Eagle Outfitters designs, markets and sells its own brand of high quality, on-trend clothing, accessories and personal care products at affordable prices while targeting 15 to 25 year-old customers. We opened our first American Eagle Outfitters store in the United States in 1977 and expanded the brand into Canada in 2001. American Eagle Outfitters also operates ae.com®, which offers additional sizes, colors and styles of favorite AE® merchandise and ships to 62 countries around the world. The American Eagle Outfitters original collection includes standards like jeans and graphic Ts, as well as essentials like accessories, outerwear, footwear, basics and swimwear under our American Eagle Outfitters, American Eagle® and AE brand names.

During Fiscal 2006, American Eagle Outfitters launched its new intimates brand, aerie by American Eagle ("aerie"). The aerie collection is available in aerie stores, predominantly all American Eagle stores and at aerie.com. The collection offers Dormwear® and intimates collections for the AE® girl. Designed to be subtly sexy, comfortable and cozy, the aerie brand offers AE customers a new way to express their personal style everyday, from the dormroom to the coffee shop to the classroom.

We also introduced MARTIN + OSA® ("M+O") during Fiscal 2006, a concept targeting 28 to 40 year-old women and men, which offers Refined Casual™ clothing and accessories, designed to be valuable, irresistible, inspiring, authentic and adventurous. In Fiscal 2008, MARTIN + OSA began offering merchandise online at martinandosa.com.

In October 2008, we launched a new children's apparel brand, 77kids™ by american eagle ("77kids"). The 77kids brand offers "kid cool," durable clothing and accessories for kids ages two to 10. The brand debuted worldwide online at 77kids.com during Fiscal 2008, with future plans for stores in the U.S.

As used in this report, all references to "we," "our," and the "Company" refer to American Eagle Outfitters, Inc. and its wholly-owned subsidiaries. "American Eagle Outfitters," "American Eagle," "AE," and the "AE Brand" refer to our U.S. and Canadian American Eagle Outfitters stores. "AEO Direct" refers to our e-commerce operations, ae.com, aerie.com, martinandosa.com and 77kids.com. "NLS" refers to National Logistics Services which we operated in Canada prior to its disposition during Fiscal 2006. "Bluenotes" refers to the Bluenotes/Thriftys specialty apparel chain which we operated in Canada prior to its disposition during Fiscal 2004.

As of January 31, 2009, we operated 954 American Eagle Outfitters stores in the United States and Canada, 116 aerie stand-alone stores and 28 MARTIN + OSA stores.

Our financial year is a 52/53 week year that ends on the Saturday nearest to January 31. As used herein, "Fiscal 2010" and "Fiscal 2009" refer to the 52 week periods ending January 29, 2011 and January 30, 2010, respectively. "Fiscal 2008" and "Fiscal 2007" refer to the 52 week periods ended January 31, 2009 and February 2, 2008, respectively. "Fiscal 2006" refers to the 53 week period ended February 3, 2007. "Fiscal 2005" and "Fiscal 2004" refer to the 52 week periods ended January 28, 2006 and January 29, 2005, respectively.

Information concerning our segments and certain geographic information is contained in Note 2 of the Consolidated Financial Statements included in this Form 10-K and is incorporated herein by reference.

Growth Strategy

During Fiscal 2008, we continued to make significant progress on our key growth initiatives. As we enter Fiscal 2009, we are taking a more cautious stance on real estate growth in light of a slow-down in the economy. However, we remain focused on several well-defined strategies that we have in place to grow our business and strengthen our financial performance. Our primary growth strategies are focused on the following key areas of opportunity:

Real Estate

We are continuing the expansion of our brands throughout the United States. At the end of Fiscal 2008, we operated in all 50 states, the District of Columbia, Puerto Rico and Canada. During Fiscal 2008, we opened 122 new stores, consisting of 33 U.S. AE stores, two Canadian AE stores, 77 aerie stores (including eight Canadian aerie stores) and 10 MARTIN + OSA stores. These store openings, offset by 11 store closings, increased our total store base by approximately 11% to 1,098 stores.

Additionally, our gross square footage increased by approximately 11% during Fiscal 2008, with approximately 89% attributable to new store openings and the remaining 11% attributable to the incremental square footage from 30 AE store remodels.

In Fiscal 2009, we will continue to open AE and aerie by American Eagle stores. We plan to open 17 aerie stores, with an average size of 4,200 gross square feet. Additionally, we plan to open 11 new AE stores including a flagship location in the Times Square area of New York, New York. We also plan to remodel approximately 25 to 35 existing AE stores. Our square footage growth is expected to be approximately 3%. We believe that there are attractive retail locations where we can continue to open American Eagle stores and our other brands in enclosed regional malls, urban areas and lifestyle centers.

The tables below show certain information relating to our historical store growth in the U.S. and Canada:

	Fiscal 2008	Fiscal 2007	Fiscal 2006	Fiscal 2005	Fiscal 2004
Consolidated stores at beginning of period	987	911	869	846	805
Consolidated stores opened during the period	122	80	50	36	50
Consolidated stores closed during the period	(11)	(4)	(8)	(13)	(9)
Total consolidated stores at end of period	**1,098**	**987**	**911**	**869**	**846**

	Fiscal 2008	Fiscal 2007	Fiscal 2006	Fiscal 2005	Fiscal 2004
AE Brand stores at beginning of period	929	903	869	846	805
AE Brand stores opened during the period	35	30	42	36	50
AE Brand stores closed during the period	(10)	(4)	(8)	(13)	(9)
Total AE Brand stores at end of period	**954**	**929**	**903**	**869**	**846**

	Fiscal 2008	Fiscal 2007	Fiscal 2006	Fiscal 2005	Fiscal 2004
aerie stores at beginning of period	39	3	—	—	—
aerie stores opened during the period	77	36	3	—	—
aerie stores closed during the period	—	—	—	—	—
Total aerie stores at end of period	**116**	**39**	**3**	**—**	**—**

	Fiscal 2008	Fiscal 2007	Fiscal 2006	Fiscal 2005	Fiscal 2004
M+O stores at beginning of period	19	5	—	—	—
M+O stores opened during the period	10	14	5	—	—
M+O stores closed during the period	(1)	—	—	—	—
Total M+O stores at end of period	**28**	**19**	**5**	**—**	**—**

Remodeling of our AE stores into our current store format is important to enhance our customer's shopping experience. In order to maintain a balanced presentation and to accommodate additional product categories, we selectively enlarge our stores during the remodeling process to an average 7,000 gross square feet, either within their existing location or by upgrading the store location within the mall. We believe the larger format can better accommodate our expansion of merchandise categories. We select stores for expansion or relocation based on market demographics and store volume forecasts.

During Fiscal 2008, we remodeled 30 AE U.S. stores. Of the 30 remodeled stores, 18 stores were remodeled and expanded within their existing locations, 10 stores were relocated to a larger space within the mall and two stores were remodeled within their existing locations. Additionally, three stores were refurbished as discussed below.

We maintain a cost effective store refurbishment program targeted towards our lower volume stores, typically located in smaller markets. Stores selected as part of this program maintain their current location and size but are updated to include certain aspects of our current store format, including paint and certain new fixtures.

AE Brand

American Eagle is an established and leading brand for 15-25 year olds, with a long heritage of quality merchandise offered at a great value. We believe that we can leverage the success we have had in making American Eagle a destination brand and increase market-share in brand-defining key categories. In Fiscal 2009, we expect to strengthen categories such as knit tops, jeans, sweaters, dresses, shorts, fleece and accessories by offering AE classics combined with relevant fashion. We have reinforced our customer connection and increased our focus on identifying emerging fashion trends that are embraced by the AE customer. We will highlight AE value offerings by strengthening our everyday value pricing, as well as with promotional events planned throughout the year. Our customer loyalty program, the AE All-Access Pass® serves as a critical one-on-one connection point with our best customers and rewards brand loyalty.

aerie by American Eagle

In the fall of 2006, we launched our new intimates brand, aerie by American Eagle, which targets our core AE customers. The aerie collection offers Dormwear® and intimates collections for the AE® girl. It is intended to drive store productivity by expanding the product categories and building upon our experience. The aerie collection is offered in 116 stand-alone stores, predominantly all American Eagle stores and on aerie.com. aerie also offers its customers a loyalty program, the aerie a-list®. aerie rewards its a-list members with a free special gift on any Thursday of their choosing, once a month.

Based on the positive customer response to aerie, in Fiscal 2008, we accelerated our real estate strategy for this brand. Our accelerated strategy included opening 77 stores during Fiscal 2008. The aerie brand remains a focus in Fiscal 2009, with planned openings of approximately 17 stores.

AEO Direct

We sell merchandise via our e-commerce operations, ae.com and aerie.com, which are extensions of the lifestyle that we convey in our stores. In Fiscal 2008, we expanded AEO Direct through the addition of e-commerce operations for martinandosa.com and 77kids.com. During Fiscal 2008, we added 21 countries to our shipping destinations and currently ship to 62 countries. In addition to purchasing items online, customers can experience AEO Direct in-store. The Company has implemented a new program called Store-to-Door, which enables store associates to sell any item available online to an in-store customer in a single transaction, without placing a phone call. Customers are taking advantage of Store to Door by purchasing extended sizes that are not available in-store, as well as finding a certain size or color that happens to be sold out at the time of their visit. The ordered items are shipped to the customer's home free of charge. During Fiscal 2008, we began accepting PayPal as a means of payment from our ae.com, aerie.com and 77kids.com customers. We are continuing to focus on the growth of AEO Direct through various initiatives, including improved site efficiency and faster check-out, expansion of sizes and styles, unique online content and targeted marketing strategies.

MARTIN + OSA

In the fall of 2006, we launched MARTIN + OSA, a concept targeting 28 to 40 year-old women and men. MARTIN + OSA offers Refined Casual™ clothing and accessories designed to be valuable, irresistible, inspiring, authentic and adventurous. During Fiscal 2008, we opened 10 MARTIN + OSA stores. Additionally, in Fiscal 2008, MARTIN + OSA began offering merchandise online at martinandosa.com. At this time, our 2009 capital expenditures projection does not include new M+O stores. We will continue to strengthen our operating model with the 28 existing stores and look for ongoing progress in merchandising and building consumer awareness.

77kids by american eagle

In October 2008, we launched a new children's apparel brand, 77kids. The 77kids brand offers "kid cool," durable clothing and accessories for kids ages two to 10. The brand debuted worldwide online at 77kids.com during Fiscal 2008, with future plans for stores in the U.S.

Consolidated Store Locations

Our stores average approximately 5,800 gross square feet and approximately 4,600 on a selling square foot basis. As of January 31, 2009, we operated 1,098 stores in the United States and Canada under the American Eagle Outfitters, aerie and MARTIN + OSA brands as shown below:

United States, including the District of Columbia and the Commonwealth of Puerto Rico — 1,012 stores

Alabama	19	Illinois	36	Montana	2	Puerto Rico	2
Alaska	5	Indiana	21	Nebraska	8	Rhode Island	4
Arizona	17	Iowa	12	Nevada	7	South Carolina	15
Arkansas	8	Kansas	10	New Hampshire	8	South Dakota	3
California	92	Kentucky	13	New Jersey	28	Tennessee	24
Colorado	16	Louisiana	15	New Mexico	3	Texas	71
Connecticut	18	Maine	4	New York	58	Utah	12
Delaware	4	Maryland	21	North Carolina	30	Vermont	3
District of Columbia	1	Massachusetts	34	North Dakota	4	Virginia	30
Florida	52	Michigan	35	Ohio	41	Washington	20
Georgia	33	Minnesota	20	Oklahoma	12	West Virginia	9
Hawaii	4	Mississippi	8	Oregon	11	Wisconsin	18
Idaho	4	Missouri	18	Pennsylvania	67	Wyoming	2
Canada — 86 stores							
Alberta	10	New Brunswick	4	Ontario	43		
British Columbia	12	Newfoundland	2	Quebec	9		
Manitoba	2	Nova Scotia	2	Saskatchewan	2		

Purchasing

We purchase merchandise from suppliers who either manufacture their own merchandise, supply merchandise manufactured by others, or both. During Fiscal 2008, we purchased a majority of our merchandise from non-North American suppliers.

All of our merchandise suppliers receive a vendor compliance manual that describes our quality standards and shipping instructions. We maintain a quality control department at our distribution centers to inspect incoming merchandise shipments for uniformity of sizes and colors and for overall quality of manufacturing. Periodic inspections are also made by our employees and agents at manufacturing facilities to identify quality problems prior to shipment of merchandise.

Corporate Social Responsibility

We are firmly committed to the goal of using highly regarded and efficient suppliers throughout the world. We require our suppliers to provide a workplace environment that not only meets basic human rights standards, but also one that complies with local legal requirements and treats workers with dignity and respect.

For many years, we have had a policy to inspect factories throughout the world where goods are produced to our order. This inspection process is an important component of our comprehensive vendor compliance program that was developed with the assistance of an internationally recognized consulting firm. This program contractually requires all suppliers to meet our global workplace standards, including human rights standards, as set forth in our Vendor Code of Conduct. The Vendor Code of Conduct is required to be posted in all factories in the local language. The program utilizes third party inspectors to audit compliance by vendor factories with our workplace standards and Vendor Code of Conduct. A copy of the Vendor Code of Conduct is also posted on our website at www.ae.com. In Fiscal 2007, we opened a compliance office in Hong Kong. The key functions performed by the AE team there are to validate the inspection reporting of our third-party auditors, and to work with new and existing factories on remediation of issues. Also in Fiscal 2007, we instituted a process of pre-inspection for facilities being considered for AE production and expanded our annual re-audit program to strive to include all primary existing facilities.

Security Compliance

During recent years, there has been an increasing focus within the international trade community on concerns related to global terrorist activity. Various security issues and other terrorist threats have brought increased demands from the Bureau of Customs and Border Protection ("CBP") and other agencies within the Department of Homeland Security that importers take responsible action to secure their supply chains. In response, we became a certified member of the Customs — Trade Partnership Against Terrorism program ("C-TPAT") during 2004. C-TPAT is a voluntary program offered by CBP in which an importer agrees to work with CBP to strengthen overall supply chain security. Our internal security procedures were reviewed by CBP during February 2005 and a validation of processes with respect to our external partners was completed in June 2005 and then re-evaluated in June 2008. We received formal written validations of our security procedures from CBP during the first quarter of Fiscal 2006 and the second quarter of Fiscal 2008, each indicating the highest level of benefits afforded to C-TPAT members.

Additionally, we took significant steps to expand the scope of our security procedures during 2004, including, but not limited to: a significant increase in the number of factory audits performed; a revision of the factory audit format to include a review of all critical security issues as defined by CBP; a review of security procedures of our other international trading partners, including forwarders, consolidators, shippers and brokers; and a requirement that all of our international trading partners be members of C-TPAT. In Fiscal 2007, we further increased the scope of our inspection program to strive to include pre-inspections of all potential production facilities and re-audits of all primary existing facilities.

Trade Compliance

We act as the importer of record for substantially all of the merchandise we purchase overseas from foreign suppliers. Accordingly, we have an affirmative obligation to comply with the rules and regulations established for importers by the CBP regarding issues such as merchandise classification, valuation and country of origin. We have developed and implemented a comprehensive series of trade compliance procedures to assure that we adhere to all CBP requirements. In its most recent review and audit of our import operations and procedures, CBP found no unacceptable risks of non-compliance.

Merchandise Inventory, Replenishment and Distribution

Purchase orders are entered into the merchandise system at the time of order. Merchandise is normally shipped directly from vendors and routed to our two US distribution centers, one in Warrendale, Pennsylvania and the other in Ottawa, Kansas, or to our Canadian distribution center in Mississauga, Ontario.

Upon receipt, merchandise is entered into the merchandise system, then processed and prepared for shipment to the stores or forwarded to a warehouse holding area to be used as store replenishment goods. The allocation of merchandise among stores varies based upon a number of factors, including geographic location, customer demographics and store size. Merchandise is shipped to our stores two to five times per week depending upon the season and store requirements.

The expansion of our Kansas distribution center in Fiscal 2007 enabled us to bring fulfillment services for AEO Direct in-house. The second phase of this expansion was completed in Fiscal 2008 to enhance operating efficiency and support our future growth.

Customer Credit and Returns

In April 2008, we introduced a new co-branded credit card (the "AE Visa Card") and re-launched our private label credit card (the "AE Credit Card"). Both of these credit cards are issued by a third-party bank (the "Bank"), and we have no liability to the Bank for bad debt expense, provided that purchases are made in accordance with the Bank's procedures. Once a customer is approved to receive the AE Visa Card and the card is activated, the customer is eligible to participate in our credit card rewards program. Under the rewards program, points are earned on purchases made with the AE Visa Card at AE and aerie, and at other retailers where the card is accepted. Points earned under the credit cards reward program result in the issuance of an AE gift card when a certain point threshold is reached. The AE gift card does not expire, however points earned that have not been used towards the issuance of an AE gift card expire after 36 months of no purchase activity. AE Credit Card holders receive special promotional offers and advance notice of all American Eagle in-store sales events. The AE Visa Card is accepted in all of our stores and AEO Direct sites, while the AE Credit Card is accepted at American Eagle, aerie, ae.com, aerie.com and 77kids.com, only.

Our customers in the U.S. and Canada stores may also pay for their purchases with American Express®, Discover®, MasterCard®, Visa®, bank debit cards, cash or check. Our AEO Direct customers may pay for their purchases using American Express®, Discover®, MasterCard® and Visa®. In addition, our ae.com, aerie.com, and 77kids.com customers may pay for their purchases using PayPal®.

Customers may also use gift cards to pay for their purchases. AE and aerie gift cards can be purchased in our American Eagle and aerie stores, respectively, and can be used both in-store and online. In addition, AE, aerie and 77kids gift cards are available through ae.com, aerie.com or 77kids.com. MARTIN + OSA gift cards can be used both in-store and online and are available for purchase in our MARTIN + OSA stores and at martinandosa.com. When the recipient uses the gift card, the value of the purchase is electronically deducted from the card and any remaining value can be used for future purchases. Our gift cards do not expire and we do not charge a service fee on inactive gift cards.

We offer our retail customers a hassle-free return policy. We believe that certain of our competitors offer similar credit card and customer service policies.

Competition

The retail apparel industry, including retail stores and e-commerce, is highly competitive. We compete with various individual and chain specialty stores, as well as the casual apparel and footwear departments of department stores and discount retailers, primarily on the basis of quality, fashion, service, selection and price.

Trademarks and Service Marks

We have registered AMERICAN EAGLE OUTFITTERS®, AMERICAN EAGLE®, AE® and AEO® with the United States Patent and Trademark Office. We have also registered or have applied to register these trademarks with the registries of many of the foreign countries in which our manufacturers are located and/or where our product is shipped.

We have registered AMERICAN EAGLE OUTFITTERS® and have applied to register AMERICAN EAGLE™ with the Canadian Intellectual Property Office. In addition, we are exclusively licensed in Canada to use AE™ and AEO® in connection with the sale of a wide range of clothing products.

In the United States and around the world, we have also registered, or have applied to register, a number of other marks used in our business, including aerie®, MARTIN+OSA® and 77kids by american eagle™.

These trademarks are renewable indefinitely, as long as they are still in use and their registrations are properly maintained. We believe that the recognition associated with these trademarks makes them extremely valuable and, therefore, we intend to use and renew our trademarks in accordance with our business plans.

Employees

As of January 31, 2009, we had approximately 37,500 employees in the United States and Canada, of whom approximately 31,000 were part-time and seasonal hourly employees. We consider our relationship with our employees to be good.

Seasonality

Historically, our operations have been seasonal, with a large portion of net sales and operating income occurring in the third and fourth fiscal quarter, reflecting increased demand during the back-to-school and year-end holiday selling seasons, respectively. As a result of this seasonality, any factors negatively affecting us during the third and fourth fiscal quarters of any year, including adverse weather or unfavorable economic conditions, could have a material adverse effect on our financial condition and results of operations for the entire year. Our quarterly results of operations also may fluctuate based upon such factors as the timing of certain holiday seasons, the number and timing of new store openings, the acceptability of seasonal merchandise offerings, the timing and level of markdowns, store closings and remodels, competitive factors, weather and general economic conditions.

Available Information

Our Annual Reports on Form 10-K, Quarterly Reports on Form 10-Q, Current Reports on Form 8-K and amendments to those reports are available, free of charge, under the "About AE" section of our website at www.ae.com. These reports are available as soon as reasonably practicable after such material is electronically filed with the Securities and Exchange Commission (the "SEC").

Our corporate governance materials, including our corporate governance guidelines, the charters of our audit, compensation, and nominating and corporate governance committees, and our code of ethics may also be found under the "About AEO, Inc." section of our website at www.ae.com. Any amendments or waivers to our code of ethics will also be available on our website. A copy of the corporate governance materials is also available upon written request.

Additionally, our investor presentations are available under the "About AEO, Inc." section of our website at www.ae.com. These presentations are available as soon as reasonably practicable after they are presented at investor conferences.

Certifications

As required by New York Stock Exchange ("NYSE") Corporate Governance Standards Section 303A.12(a), on July 9, 2008 our Chief Executive Officer submitted to the NYSE a certification that he was not aware of any violation by the Company of NYSE corporate governance listing standards. Additionally, we filed with this Form 10-K, the Principal Executive Officer and Principal Financial Officer certifications required under Sections 302 and 906 of the Sarbanes-Oxley Act of 2002.

ITEM 6. *SELECTED CONSOLIDATED FINANCIAL DATA.*

The following Selected Consolidated Financial Data should be read in conjunction with "Management's Discussion and Analysis of Financial Condition and Results of Operations," included under Item 7 below and the Consolidated Financial Statements and Notes thereto, included in Item 8 below. Most of the selected data presented below is derived from our Consolidated Financial Statements, which are filed in response to Item 8 below. The selected Consolidated Statement of Operations data for the years ended January 28, 2006 and January 29, 2005 and the selected Consolidated Balance Sheet data as of February 3, 2007, January 28, 2006 and January 29, 2005 are derived from audited Consolidated Financial Statements not included herein.

	For the Years Ended(1)				
	January 31, 2009	February 2, 2008	February 3, 2007	January 28, 2006	January 29, 2005
	(In thousands, except per share amounts, ratios and other financial information)				
Summary of Operations(2)					
Net sales(3)	$2,988,866	$3,055,419	$2,794,409	$2,321,962	$1,889,647
Comparable store sales (decrease) increase(4)	(10)%	1%	12%	16%	21%
Gross profit	$1,174,101	$1,423,138	$1,340,429	$1,077,749	$ 881,188
Gross profit as a percentage of net sales	39.3%	46.6%	48.0%	46.4%	46.6%
Operating income(5)	$ 302,140	$ 598,755	$ 586,790	$ 458,689	$ 360,968
Operating income as a percentage of net sales	10.1%	19.6%	21.0%	19.8%	19.1%
Income from continuing operations(2)	$ 179,061	$ 400,019	$ 387,359	$ 293,711	$ 224,232
Income from continuing operations as a percentage of net sales(2)	6.0%	13.1%	13.9%	12.7%	11.9%
Per Share Results(6)					
Income from continuing operations per common share-basic(2)	$ 0.87	$ 1.85	$ 1.74	$ 1.29	$ 1.03
Income from continuing operations per common share-diluted(2)	$ 0.86	$ 1.82	$ 1.70	$ 1.26	$ 1.00
Weighted average common shares outstanding — basic	205,169	216,119	222,662	227,406	217,725
Weighted average common shares outstanding — diluted	207,582	220,280	228,384	233,031	225,366
Cash dividends per common share(7)	$ 0.40	$ 0.38	$ 0.28	$ 0.18	$ 0.04
Balance Sheet Information					
Total cash and short-term investments	$ 483,853	$ 619,939	$ 813,813	$ 751,518	$ 589,607
Long-term investments	$ 251,007	$ 165,810	$ 264,944	$ 145,744	$ 84,416
Total assets(8)	$1,963,676	$1,867,680	$1,979,558	$1,605,649	$1,328,926
Short-term debt	$ 75,000	$ —	$ —	$ —	$ —
Long-term debt	$ —	$ —	$ —	$ —	$ —
Stockholders' equity	$1,409,031	$1,340,464	$1,417,312	$1,155,552	$ 963,486
Working capital(8)	$ 523,596	$ 644,656	$ 724,490	$ 725,294	$ 582,739
Current ratio(8)	2.30	2.71	2.56	3.06	3.06
Average return on stockholders' equity	13.0%	29.0%	30.1%	27.8%	26.7%

	For the Years Ended(1)				
	January 31, 2009	February 2, 2008	February 3, 2007	January 28, 2006	January 29, 2005
	(In thousands, except per share amounts, ratios and other financial information)				
Other Financial Information(9)					
Total stores at year-end	1,098	987	911	869	846
Capital expenditures	$ 265,335	$ 250,407	$ 225,939	$ 81,545	$ 97,288
Net sales per average selling square foot(10)	$ 521	$ 638	$ 642	$ 577	$ 504
Total selling square feet at end of period	5,072,612	4,595,649	4,220,929	3,896,441	3,709,012
Net sales per average gross square foot(10)	$ 446	$ 517	$ 524	$ 471	$ 412
Total gross square feet at end of period	6,328,167	5,709,932	5,173,065	4,772,487	4,540,095
Number of employees at end of period	37,500	38,700	27,600	23,000	20,600

(1) Except for the fiscal year ended February 3, 2007, which includes 53 weeks, all fiscal years presented include 52 weeks.

(2) All amounts presented are from continuing operations and exclude Bluenotes' results of operations for all periods.

(3) Amount for the fiscal years ended January 31, 2009, February 2, 2008 and February 3, 2007 include proceeds from merchandise sell-offs. Refer to Note 2 to the accompanying Consolidated Financial Statements for additional information regarding the components of net sales.

(4) The comparable store sales increase for the period ended February 2, 2008 is compared to the corresponding 52 week period in Fiscal 2006. The comparable store sales increase for the period ended February 3, 2007 is compared to the corresponding 53 week period in Fiscal 2005.

(5) All amounts presented exclude gift card service fee income, which was reclassified to other income, net during Fiscal 2006. Refer to Note 2 to the accompanying Consolidated Financial Statements for additional information regarding gift cards.

(6) Per share results for all periods presented reflect the three-for-two stock split distributed on December 18, 2006. Refer to Note 2 to the accompanying Consolidated Financial Statements for additional information regarding the stock split.

(7) Amount for the fiscal year ended January 29, 2005 represents cash dividends paid for two quarters only. Note that the Company initiated quarterly dividend payments during the third quarter of Fiscal 2004.

(8) Amounts for the years ended January 28, 2006 and January 29, 2005 reflect certain assets of NLS as held-for-sale.

(9) All amounts exclude Bluenotes for all periods presented.

(10) Net sales per average square foot is calculated using retail store sales for the year divided by the straight average of the beginning and ending square footage for the year.

Report of Independent Registered Public Accounting Firm

To the Board of Directors and Stockholders of
American Eagle Outfitters, Inc.

We have audited the accompanying consolidated balance sheets of American Eagle Outfitters, Inc. (the Company) as of January 31, 2009 and February 2, 2008, and the related consolidated statements of operations, comprehensive income, stockholders' equity, and cash flows for each of the three years in the period ended January 31, 2009. These financial statements are the responsibility of the Company's management. Our responsibility is to express an opinion on these financial statements based on our audits.

We conducted our audits in accordance with the standards of the Public Company Accounting Oversight Board (United States). Those standards require that we plan and perform the audit to obtain reasonable assurance about whether the financial statements are free of material misstatement. An audit includes examining, on a test basis, evidence supporting the amounts and disclosures in the financial statements. An audit also includes assessing the accounting principles used and significant estimates made by management, as well as evaluating the overall financial statement presentation. We believe that our audits provide a reasonable basis for our opinion.

In our opinion, the financial statements referred to above present fairly, in all material respects, the consolidated financial position of American Eagle Outfitters, Inc. at January 31, 2009 and February 2, 2008, and the consolidated results of its operations and its cash flows for each of the three years in the period ended January 31, 2009, in conformity with U.S. generally accepted accounting principles.

As discussed in Note 12 to the consolidated financial statements, the Company adopted FASB Interpretation No. 48, "Accounting for Uncertainty in Income Taxes, an interpretation of FASB Statement No. 109," effective February 4, 2007.

We have also audited, in accordance with the standards of the Public Company Accounting Oversight Board (United States), American Eagle Outfitters, Inc.'s internal control over financial reporting as of January 31, 2009, based on criteria established in Internal Control — Integrated Framework issued by the Committee of Sponsoring Organizations of the Treadway Commission and our report dated March 25, 2009 expressed an unqualified opinion thereon.

/s/ Ernst & Young LLP

Pittsburgh, Pennsylvania
March 25, 2009

AMERICAN EAGLE OUTFITTERS, INC.

CONSOLIDATED BALANCE SHEETS

	January 31, 2009	February 2, 2008
	(In thousands, except per share amounts)	
ASSETS		
Current assets:		
Cash and cash equivalents	$ 473,342	$ 116,061
Short-term investments	10,511	503,878
Merchandise inventory	294,928	286,485
Accounts and note receivable	41,471	31,920
Prepaid expenses and other	59,660	35,486
Deferred income taxes	45,447	47,004
Total current assets	925,359	1,020,834
Property and equipment, at cost, net of accumulated depreciation and amortization	740,240	625,568
Goodwill	10,706	11,479
Long-term investments	251,007	165,810
Non-current deferred income taxes	15,001	24,238
Other assets, net	21,363	19,751
Total assets	$1,963,676	$1,867,680
LIABILITIES AND STOCKHOLDERS' EQUITY		
Current liabilities:		
Accounts payable	$ 152,068	$ 157,928
Notes Payable	75,000	—
Accrued compensation and payroll taxes	29,417	49,494
Accrued rent	64,695	62,161
Accrued income and other taxes	6,259	22,803
Unredeemed stored value cards and gift certificates	42,299	54,554
Current portion of deferred lease credits	13,726	12,953
Other liabilities and accrued expenses	18,299	16,285
Total current liabilities	401,763	376,178
Non-current liabilities:		
Deferred lease credits	88,314	70,355
Non-current accrued income taxes	39,898	44,837
Other non-current liabilities	24,670	35,846
Total non-current liabilities	152,882	151,038
Commitments and contingencies	—	—
Stockholders' equity:		
Preferred stock, $0.01 par value; 5,000 shares authorized; none issued and outstanding	—	—
Common stock, $0.01 par value; 600,000 shares authorized; 249,328 and 248,763 shares issued; 205,281 and 204,480 shares outstanding, respectively	2,485	2,481
Contributed capital	513,574	493,395
Accumulated other comprehensive (loss) income	(14,389)	35,485
Retained earnings	1,694,161	1,601,784
Treasury stock, 43,248 and 43,596 shares, respectively, at cost	(786,800)	(792,681)
Total stockholders' equity	1,409,031	1,340,464
Total liabilities and stockholders' equity	$1,963,676	$1,867,680

Refer to Notes to Consolidated Financial Statements

AMERICAN EAGLE OUTFITTERS, INC.
CONSOLIDATED STATEMENTS OF OPERATIONS

	For the Years Ended		
	January 31, 2009	February 2, 2008	February 3, 2007
	(In thousands, except per share amounts)		
Net sales	$2,988,866	$3,055,419	$2,794,409
Cost of sales, including certain buying, occupancy and warehousing expenses	1,814,765	1,632,281	1,453,980
Gross profit	1,174,101	1,423,138	1,340,429
Selling, general and administrative expenses	740,742	715,180	665,606
Depreciation and amortization expense	131,219	109,203	88,033
Operating income	302,140	598,755	586,790
Other income, net	17,790	37,626	42,277
Other-than-temporary impairment charge	22,889	—	—
Income before income taxes	297,041	636,381	629,067
Provision for income taxes	117,980	236,362	241,708
Net income	$ 179,061	$ 400,019	$ 387,359
Basic income per common share	$ 0.87	$ 1.85	$ 1.74
Diluted income per common share	$ 0.86	$ 1.82	$ 1.70
Weighted average common shares outstanding — basic	205,169	216,119	222,662
Weighted average common shares outstanding — diluted	207,582	220,280	228,384

Refer to Notes to Consolidated Financial Statements

AMERICAN EAGLE OUTFITTERS, INC.

CONSOLIDATED STATEMENTS OF COMPREHENSIVE INCOME

	For the Years Ended		
	January 31, 2009	February 2, 2008	February 3, 2007
		(In thousands)	
Net income	$179,061	$400,019	$387,359
Other comprehensive (loss) income:			
Temporary impairment related to investment securities, net of tax	(22,795)	—	—
Reclassification adjustment for OTTI charges realized in net income related to ARS	751		
Reclassification adjustment for losses realized in net income due to the sale of available-for-sale securities, net of tax	197	242	356
Unrealized (loss) gain on investments, net of tax	(378)	947	(191)
Reclassification adjustment for gain realized in net income related to the transfer of investment securities from available-for-sale classification to trading classification, net of tax	—	—	(177)
Foreign currency translation adjustment	(27,649)	12,582	(1,180)
Reclassification adjustment for foreign currency loss realized in net income related to the disposition of National Logistics Services	—	—	878
Other comprehensive (loss) income	(49,874)	13,771	(314)
Comprehensive income	$129,187	$413,790	$387,045

Refer to Notes to Consolidated Financial Statements

AMERICAN EAGLE OUTFITTERS, INC.

CONSOLIDATED STATEMENTS OF STOCKHOLDERS' EQUITY

	Shares Outstanding (1)	Common Stock	Contributed Capital	Retained Earnings	Treasury Stock(2)	Deferred Compensation Expense	Accumulated Other Comprehensive Income (Loss)	Stockholders' Equity
	(In thousands, except per share amounts)							
Balance at January 28, 2006	**221,897**	**2,416**	**369,807**	**978,855**	**(216,513)**	**(1,041)**	**22,028**	**1,155,552**
Stock awards	4,556	45	83,615	—	—	1,041	—	84,701
Repurchase of common stock as part of publicly announced programs	(5,250)	—	—	—	(146,485)	—	—	(146,485)
Repurchase of common stock from employees	(443)	—	—	—	(7,635)	—	—	(7,635)
Cash paid for fractional shares in three-for-two stock split	(4)	—	(113)	—	—	—	—	(113)
Reissuance of treasury stock	528	—	109	(2,348)	8,007	—	—	5,768
Net income	—	—	—	387,359	—	—	—	387,359
Other comprehensive loss, net of tax	—	—	—		—	—	(314)	(314)
Cash dividends ($0.28 per share)	—	—	—	(61,521)	—	—	—	(61,521)
Balance at February 3, 2007	**221,284**	**2,461**	**453,418**	**1,302,345**	**(362,626)**	—	**21,714**	**1,417,312**
Adoption of FIN 48	—	—	—	(13,304)				(13,304)
Balance at February 4, 2007	**221,284**	**2,461**	**453,418**	**1,289,041**	**(362,626)**	—	**21,714**	**1,404,008**
Stock awards	1,092	20	39,977	—	—	—	—	39,997
Repurchase of common stock as part of publicly announced programs	(18,750)	—	—	—	(438,291)	—	—	(438,291)
Repurchase of common stock from employees	(415)	—	—	—	(12,310)	—	—	(12,310)
Reissuance of treasury stock	1,269	—	—	(6,480)	20,546	—	—	14,066
Net income	—	—	—	400,019	—			400,019
Other comprehensive income, net of tax	—	—	—	—	—	—	13,771	13,771
Cash dividends ($0.38 per share)	—	—	—	(80,796)	—	—	—	(80,796)
Balance at February 2, 2008	**204,480**	**$2,481**	**$493,395**	**$1,601,784**	**$(792,681)**	$ —	**$ 35,485**	**$1,340,464**
Stock awards	453	4	20,179	420	—	—	—	20,603
Repurchase of common stock from employees	(164)	—	—	—	(3,432)	—	—	(3,432)
Reissuance of treasury stock	512	—	—	(4,710)	9,313	—	—	4,603
Net income	—	—	—	179,061	—	—	—	179,061
Other comprehensive loss, net of tax	—	—	—	—	—	—	(49,874)	(49,874)
Cash dividends ($0.40 per share)	—	—	—	(82,394)	—	—	—	(82,394)
Balance at January 31, 2009	**205,281**	**$2,485**	**$513,574**	**$1,694,161**	**$(786,800)**	$ —	**$(14,389)**	**$1,409,031**

All amounts presented reflect the December 18, 2006 three-for-two stock split.

(1) 600,000 authorized, 249,328 issued and 205,281 outstanding (excluding 799 shares of non-vested restricted stock), $0.01 par value common stock at January 31, 2009; 600,000 authorized, 248,763 issued and 204,480 outstanding (excluding 687 shares of non-vested restricted stock), $0.01 par value common stock at February 2, 2008; and 250,000 authorized, 248,155 issued and 221,284 outstanding (excluding 1,172 shares of non-vested restricted stock), at February 3, 2007; The Company has 5,000 authorized, with none issued or outstanding, $0.01 par value preferred stock at January 31, 2009, February 2, 2008 and February 3, 2007.

(2) 43,248 shares 43,596 shares, and 25,699 shares at January 31, 2009, February 2, 2008, and February 3, 2007, respectively. During Fiscal 2008 and Fiscal 2007, 512 shares and 1,269 shares, respectively, were reissued from treasury stock for the issuance of share-based payments.

Refer to Notes to Consolidated Financial Statements

AMERICAN EAGLE OUTFITTERS, INC.

CONSOLIDATED STATEMENTS OF CASH FLOWS

	For the Years Ended		
	January 31, 2009	February 2, 2008	February 3, 2007
		(In thousands)	
Operating activities:			
Net income	$ 179,061	$ 400,019	$ 387,359
Adjustments to reconcile net income to net cash provided by operating activities			
Depreciation and amortization	133,141	110,753	89,698
Stock-based compensation	20,296	33,670	36,556
Provision for deferred income taxes	24,469	(8,147)	(27,572)
Tax benefit from share-based payments	1,121	7,260	25,465
Excess tax benefit from share-based payments	(693)	(6,156)	(19,541)
Foreign currency transaction (gain) loss	(1,141)	1,221	687
Loss on impairment of assets	6,713	592	—
Other-than-temporary impairment charge	22,889	—	—
Proceeds from sale of trading securities	—	—	183,968
Changes in assets and liabilities:			
Merchandise inventory	(13,735)	(19,074)	(53,527)
Accounts receivable	(10,094)	(5,660)	7,448
Prepaid expenses and other	(24,781)	(1,334)	(4,204)
Other assets, net	390	(3,242)	(5,357)
Accounts payable	(3,053)	(15,559)	32,345
Unredeemed gift cards and gift certificates	(11,392)	(699)	11,623
Deferred lease credits	18,887	4,640	7,791
Accrued income and other taxes	(20,697)	(31,416)	43,482
Accrued liabilities	(19,188)	(2,598)	33,047
Total adjustments	123,132	64,251	361,909
Net cash provided by operating activities	**302,193**	**464,270**	**749,268**
Investing activities:			
Capital expenditures	(265,335)	(250,407)	(225,939)
Proceeds from sale of assets	—	—	12,345
Purchase of available-for-sale securities	(48,655)	(1,772,653)	(1,353,339)
Sale of available-for-sale securities	393,559	2,126,891	915,952
Other investing activities	(1,180)	(1,170)	(140)
Net cash provided by (used for) investing activities	**78,389**	**102,661**	**(651,121)**
Financing activities:			
Payments on note payable and capital leases	(2,177)	(1,912)	(3,020)
Proceeds from issuance of note payable	75,000	—	2,025
Repurchase of common stock as part of publicly announced programs	—	(438,291)	(146,485)
Repurchase of common stock from employees	(3,432)	(12,310)	(7,635)
Cash paid for fractional shares in connection with three-for-two stock split	—	—	(113)
Net proceeds from stock options exercised	3,799	13,183	28,447
Excess tax benefit from share-based payments	693	6,156	19,541
Cash dividends paid	(82,394)	(80,796)	(61,521)
Net cash used for financing activities	**(8,511)**	**(513,970)**	**(168,761)**
Effect of exchange rates on cash	(14,790)	3,363	(178)
Net increase (decrease) in cash and cash equivalents	**357,281**	**56,324**	**(70,792)**
Cash and cash equivalents — beginning of period	116,061	59,737	130,529
Cash and cash equivalents — end of period	$ 473,342	$ 116,061	$ 59,737

Refer to Notes to Consolidated Financial Statements

AMERICAN EAGLE OUTFITTERS, INC.

NOTES TO CONSOLIDATED FINANCIAL STATEMENTS FOR THE YEAR ENDED JANUARY 31, 2009

1. Business Operations

American Eagle Outfitters, Inc., a Delaware corporation, is a leading retailer that operates under the American Eagle Outfitters®, aerie® by American Eagle, 77kids™ by american eagle and MARTIN + OSA® brands.

American Eagle Outfitters designs, markets and sells its own brand of high quality, on-trend clothing, accessories and personal care products at affordable prices while targeting 15 to 25 year-old customers. The Company opened its first American Eagle Outfitters store in the United States in 1977 and expanded the brand into Canada in 2001. American Eagle Outfitters also operates ae.com®, which offers additional sizes, colors and styles of favorite AE® merchandise and ships to 62 countries around the world. AE's original collection includes standards like jeans and graphic Ts, as well as essentials like accessories, outerwear, footwear, basics and swimwear under our American Eagle Outfitters, American Eagle® and AE brand names.

During Fiscal 2006, American Eagle Outfitters launched its new intimates brand, aerie by American Eagle ("aerie"). The aerie collection is available in aerie stores, predominantly all American Eagle stores and at aerie.com. The collection offers Dormwear® and intimates collections for the AE® girl. Designed to be subtly sexy, comfortable and cozy, the aerie brand offers AE customers a new way to express their personal style everyday, from the dormroom to the coffee shop to the classroom.

The Company also introduced MARTIN + OSA® ("M+O") during Fiscal 2006, a concept targeting 28 to 40 year-old women and men, which offers Refined Casual™ clothing and accessories, designed to be valuable, irresistible, inspiring, authentic and adventurous. In Fiscal 2008, MARTIN + OSA began offering merchandise online at martinandosa.com.

In October 2008, the Company launched a new children's apparel brand, 77kids™ by american eagle ("77kids"). The 77kids brand offers "kid cool," durable clothing and accessories for kids ages two to 10. The brand debuted worldwide online at 77kids.com during Fiscal 2008, with future plans for stores in the U.S.

The following table sets forth the approximate consolidated percentage of net sales attributable to each merchandise group for each of the periods indicated:

	For the Years Ended		
	January 31, 2009	February 2, 2008	February 3, 2007
Men's apparel and accessories	42%	38%	37%
Women's apparel, accessories and intimates	58%	62%	63%
Total	100%	100%	100%

2. Summary of Significant Accounting Policies

Principles of Consolidation

The Consolidated Financial Statements include the accounts of the Company and its wholly-owned subsidiaries. All intercompany transactions and balances have been eliminated in consolidation. At January 31, 2009, the Company operated in one reportable segment.

Fiscal Year

The Company's financial year is a 52/53 week year that ends on the Saturday nearest to January 31. As used herein, "Fiscal 2010" and "Fiscal 2009" refer to the 52 week periods ending January 29, 2011 and January 30, 2010, respectively. "Fiscal 2008" and "Fiscal 2007" refer to the 52 week periods ended January 31, 2009 and February 2, 2008, respectively. "Fiscal 2006" refers to the 53 week period ended February 3, 2007. "Fiscal 2005" and "Fiscal 2004" refer to the 52 week periods ended January 28, 2006 and January 29, 2005, respectively.

AMERICAN EAGLE OUTFITTERS, INC.

NOTES TO CONSOLIDATED FINANCIAL STATEMENTS — (Continued)

Estimates

The preparation of financial statements in conformity with accounting principles generally accepted in the United States of America requires our management to make estimates and assumptions that affect the reported amounts of assets and liabilities and disclosure of contingent assets and liabilities at the date of the financial statements and the reported amounts of revenues and expenses during the reporting period. Actual results could differ from those estimates. On an ongoing basis, our management reviews its estimates based on currently available information. Changes in facts and circumstances may result in revised estimates.

Recent Accounting Pronouncements

In February 2008, the FASB issued Staff Position ("FSP") No. FAS 157-2, *Effective Date of FASB Statement No. 157* ("FSP No. FAS 157-2") which delays the effective date of SFAS No. 157 for nonfinancial assets and nonfinancial liabilities, except for items that are recognized or disclosed at fair value on a recurring basis (at least annually). For items within its scope, FSP No. FAS 157-2 defers the effective date to fiscal years beginning after November 15, 2008. The Company will adopt SFAS No. 157-2 for its financial assets and financial liabilities beginning in the first quarter of Fiscal 2009. The adoption of SFAS No. 157 for nonfinancial assets and nonfinancial liabilities will not have a material impact on the Company's Consolidated Financial Statements.

In June 2008, the FASB issued FSP Emerging Issues Task Force ("EITF") No. 03-6-1, *Determining Whether Instruments Granted in Share-Based Payment Transactions Are Participating Securities* ("FSP EITF No. 03-6-1"). FSP EITF No. 03-6-1 addresses whether awards granted in unvested share-based payment transactions that contain non-forfeitable rights to dividends or dividend equivalents (whether paid or unpaid) are participating securities and therefore need to be included in computing earnings per share under the two-class method, as described in SFAS No. 128, *Earnings Per Share* ("SFAS No. 128"). This FSP will be effective for the Company beginning in the first quarter of Fiscal 2009 and will be applied retrospectively in accordance with the FSP. The adoption of FSP EITF No. 03-6-1 will not have a material impact on the Company's Consolidated Financial Statements.

In October 2008, the FASB issued FSP FAS 157-3, *Determining the Fair Value of a Financial Asset in a Market That is Not Active* ("FSP FAS 157-3"). FSP FAS 157-3 clarifies the application of SFAS No. 157, when the market for a financial asset is not active, specifically regarding consideration of management's internal assumptions in measuring fair value when observable data are not present, how observable market information from an inactive market should be taken into account, and the use of broker quotes or pricing services in assessing the relevance of observable and unobservable data. This FSP was effective immediately. The Company initially considered the guidance provided by FSP FAS 157-3 in its determination of estimated fair values of its investment portfolio as of November 1, 2008. Refer to Note 4 to the Consolidated Financial Statements for additional information regarding the fair value measurement of our investment portfolio.

Foreign Currency Translation

The Canadian dollar is the functional currency for the Canadian business. In accordance with SFAS No. 52, *Foreign Currency Translation* ("SFAS No. 52"), assets and liabilities denominated in foreign currencies were translated into U.S. dollars (the reporting currency) at the exchange rate prevailing at the balance sheet date. Revenues and expenses denominated in foreign currencies were translated into U.S. dollars at the monthly average exchange rate for the period. Gains or losses resulting from foreign currency transactions are included in the results of operations, whereas, related translation adjustments are reported as an element of other comprehensive income (loss) in accordance with SFAS No. 130, *Reporting Comprehensive Income* (Refer to Note 9 to the Consolidated Financial Statements).

AMERICAN EAGLE OUTFITTERS, INC.

NOTES TO CONSOLIDATED FINANCIAL STATEMENTS — (Continued)

Fair Value of Financial Instruments

SFAS No. 107, *Disclosures about Fair Value of Financial Instruments* ("SFAS No. 107"), requires management to disclose the estimated fair value of certain assets and liabilities defined by SFAS No. 107 as financial instruments. At January 31, 2009, management believes that the carrying amounts of cash and cash equivalents, receivables and payables approximate fair value because of the short maturity of these financial instruments.

SFAS No. 157, *Fair Value Measurements* ("SFAS No. 157"), defines fair value, establishes a framework for measuring fair value in accordance with accounting principles generally accepted in the United States, and expands disclosures about fair value measurements. Fair value is defined under SFAS No. 157 as the exit price associated with the sale of an asset or transfer of a liability in an orderly transaction between market participants at the measurement date. The Company has adopted the provisions of SFAS No. 157 as of February 3, 2008, for its financial instruments, including its investment securities.

SFAS No. 107, which requires disclosures about the fair values of financial instruments for which it is practicable to estimate fair value, was amended to incorporate the SFAS No. 157 definition of fair value. SFAS No. 107 disclosure requirements apply to financial instruments that are measured at fair value on a recurring or non-recurring basis and, therefore, are subject to the disclosure requirements of SFAS No. 157, and other financial instruments that are not subject to those disclosure requirements.

Cash and Cash Equivalents, Short-term Investments and Long-term Investments

Cash includes cash equivalents. The Company considers all highly liquid investments purchased with a maturity of three months or less to be cash equivalents.

As of January 31, 2009, short-term investments included the preferred stock equity investments that the Company received as a result of the Lehman bankruptcy, which triggered the dissolution of the ARPS from their trusts. Additionally, short-term investments included ARPS which will be liquidated during the first quarter of 2009 as a result of the Lehman bankruptcy.

As of January 31, 2009, long-term investments included investments with remaining maturities of greater than 12 months and consisted of auction rate securities classified as available-for-sale that have experienced failed auctions or have long-term auction resets. In addition, long-term investments included ARS and ARPS that the Company currently intends to hold for greater than one year. The remaining contractual maturities of our ARS classified as long-term investments is two to 39 years. The weighted average contractual maturity for our long-term investments is approximately 25 years.

Unrealized gains and losses on the Company's available-for-sale securities are excluded from earnings and are reported as a separate component of stockholders' equity, within accumulated other comprehensive income (loss), until realized. When available-for-sale securities are sold, the cost of the securities is specifically identified and is used to determine any realized gain or loss.

The Company evaluates its investments for impairment in accordance with FSP FAS 115-1, *The Meaning of Other-Than-Temporary Impairment and Its Application to Certain Investments* ("FSP FAS 115-1"). FSP FAS 115-1 provides guidance for determining when an investment is considered impaired, whether impairment is other-than-temporary, and measurement of an impairment loss. If, after consideration of all available evidence to evaluate the realizable value of its investment, impairment is determined to be other-than-temporary, then an impairment loss is recognized in the Consolidated Statement of Operations equal to the difference between the investment's cost value and its fair value.

Refer to Note 3 to the Consolidated Financial Statements for information regarding cash and cash equivalents, short-term investments and long-term investments.

AMERICAN EAGLE OUTFITTERS, INC.

NOTES TO CONSOLIDATED FINANCIAL STATEMENTS — (Continued)

Merchandise Inventory

Merchandise inventory is valued at the lower of average cost or market, utilizing the retail method. Average cost includes merchandise design and sourcing costs and related expenses. The Company records merchandise receipts at the time merchandise is delivered to the foreign shipping port by the manufacturer (FOB port). This is the point at which title and risk of loss transfer to the Company.

The Company reviews its inventory levels to identify slow-moving merchandise and generally uses markdowns to clear merchandise. Additionally, the Company estimates a markdown reserve for future planned permanent markdowns related to current inventory. Markdowns may occur when inventory exceeds customer demand for reasons of style, seasonal adaptation, changes in customer preference, lack of consumer acceptance of fashion items, competition, or if it is determined that the inventory in stock will not sell at its currently ticketed price. Such markdowns may have a material adverse impact on earnings, depending on the extent and amount of inventory affected. The Company also estimates a shrinkage reserve for the period between the last physical count and the balance sheet date. The estimate for the shrinkage reserve can be affected by changes in merchandise mix and changes in actual shrinkage trends.

The Company sells end-of-season, overstock and irregular merchandise to a third party vendor. Below is a summary of merchandise sell-offs presented on a gross basis for Fiscal 2008, Fiscal 2007 and Fiscal 2006. Refer to the Revenue Recognition disclosure below for additional information regarding merchandise sell-offs.

	For the Years Ended		
	January 31, 2009	**February 2, 2008**	**February 3, 2007**
		(In thousands)	
Proceeds from sell-offs	$38,240	$23,775	$16,061
Marked-down cost of merchandise disposed of via sell-offs	$38,012	$25,805	$22,656

Property and Equipment

Property and equipment is recorded on the basis of cost with depreciation computed utilizing the straight-line method over the assets' estimated useful lives. The useful lives of our major classes of assets are as follows:

Buildings	25 years
Leasehold improvements	Lesser of 5 to 10 years or the term of the lease
Fixtures and equipment	3 to 5 years

In accordance with SFAS No. 144, *Accounting for the Impairment or Disposal of Long Lived Assets* ("SFAS No. 144"), our management evaluates the ongoing value of leasehold improvements and store fixtures associated with retail stores, which have been open longer than one year. The Company evaluates long-lived assets for impairment at the individual store level, which is the lowest level at which individual cash flows can be identified. Impairment losses are recorded on long-lived assets used in operations when events and circumstances indicate that the assets might be impaired and the undiscounted cash flows estimated to be generated by those assets are less than the carrying amounts of the assets. When events such as these occur, the impaired assets are adjusted to their estimated fair value and an impairment loss is recorded in selling, general and administrative expenses.

During Fiscal 2008, the Company recorded an asset impairment charge of $6.7 million related primarily to the impairment of five M+O stores. Based on the Company's review of the operating performance and projections of future performance of these stores, the Company determined that these stores would not be able to generate sufficient cash flow over the life of the related leases to recover the Company's initial investment in them. During Fiscal 2007, the Company recognized impairment losses of $0.6 million. The Company did not recognize any impairment losses during Fiscal 2006.

AMERICAN EAGLE OUTFITTERS, INC.

NOTES TO CONSOLIDATED FINANCIAL STATEMENTS — (Continued)

When the Company closes, remodels or relocates a store prior to the end of its lease term, the remaining net book value of the assets related to the store is recorded as a write-off of assets. During Fiscal 2008, Fiscal 2007 and Fiscal 2006, the Company recorded \$4.9 million, \$6.7 million and \$6.1 million related to asset write-offs within depreciation and amortization expense.

Goodwill

As of January 31, 2009, the Company had approximately \$10.7 million of goodwill compared to \$11.5 million as of February 2, 2008. The Company's goodwill is primarily related to the acquisition of our importing operations on January 31, 2000, as well as the acquisition of its Canadian business on November 29, 2000. The reduction in goodwill is due to the fluctuation in the foreign exchange spot rate at which the Canadian goodwill is translated. In accordance with SFAS No. 142, *Goodwill and Other Intangible Assets*, management evaluates goodwill for possible impairment on at least an annual basis.

Other Assets, Net

Other assets, net consist primarily of assets related to our deferred compensation plans and trademark costs, net of accumulated amortization. Trademark costs are amortized over five to 15 years.

Deferred Lease Credits

Deferred lease credits represent the unamortized portion of construction allowances received from landlords related to the Company's retail stores. Construction allowances are generally comprised of cash amounts received by the Company from its landlords as part of the negotiated lease terms. The Company records a receivable and a deferred lease credit liability at the lease commencement date (date of initial possession of the store). The deferred lease credit is amortized on a straight-line basis as a reduction of rent expense over the term of the lease (including the pre-opening build-out period) and the receivable is reduced as amounts are received from the landlord.

Self-Insurance Liability

The Company is self-insured for certain losses related to employee medical benefits and worker's compensation. Costs for self-insurance claims filed and claims incurred but not reported are accrued based on known claims and historical experience. Management believes that it has adequately reserved for its self-insurance liability, which is capped through the use of stop loss contracts with insurance companies. However, any significant variation of future claims from historical trends could cause actual results to differ from the accrued liability.

Co-branded Credit Card and Customer Loyalty Program

In April 2008, the Company introduced a new co-branded credit card (the "AE Visa Card") and re-launched its private label credit card (the "AE Credit Card"). Both of these credit cards are issued by a third-party bank (the "Bank"), and the Company has no liability to the Bank for bad debt expense, provided that purchases are made in accordance with the Bank's procedures. The Bank pays fees to the Company, which are recorded as revenue, based on the number of credit card accounts activated and on card usage volume. Once a customer is approved to receive the AE Visa Card and the card is activated, the customer is eligible to participate in the Company's credit card rewards program. Under the rewards program, points are earned on purchases made with the AE Visa Card at AE and aerie, and at other retailers where the card is accepted. Points earned under the credit cards reward program result in the issuance of an AE gift card when a certain point threshold is reached. The AE gift card does not expire, however points earned that have not been used towards the issuance of an AE gift card expire after 36 months of no purchase activity.

Points earned under the credit card rewards program on purchases at AE and aerie are accounted for in accordance with EITF Issue No. 00-21, *Revenue Arrangements with Multiple Deliverables* ("EITF 00-21"). Accordingly, the portion of the sales revenue attributed to the award points is deferred and recognized when the award gift card is redeemed or

AMERICAN EAGLE OUTFITTERS, INC.

NOTES TO CONSOLIDATED FINANCIAL STATEMENTS — (Continued)

when the points expire. Additionally, credit card reward points earned on non-AE or aerie purchases are accounted for in accordance with EITF Issue No. 01-09, *Accounting for Consideration Given by a Vendor to a Customer (Including a Reseller of the Vendor's Products)* ("EITF 01-09"). As the points are earned, a current liability is recorded for the estimated cost of the award gift card, and the impact of adjustments is recorded in cost of sales.

The Company also offers its customers the AE All-Access Pass® (the "Pass"), a customer loyalty program. Using the Pass, customers accumulate points based on purchase activity and earn rewards by reaching certain point thresholds during three-month earning periods. Rewards earned during these periods are valid through the stated expiration date, which is approximately one month from the mailing date. These rewards can be redeemed for a discount on a purchase of merchandise. Rewards not redeemed during the one-month redemption period are forfeited. The Company has historically accounted for the credits earned using the Pass in accordance with EITF 01-09. However, in connection with the launch of the credit card rewards program, the Company determined that these credits should be accounted for consistently in accordance with EITF 00-21. The effect of applying EITF 00-21 did not have a material impact on the Company's Consolidated Financial Statements. Accordingly, beginning in Fiscal 2008, the portion of the sales revenue attributed to the award credits is deferred and recognized when the award credits are redeemed or expire.

Stock Repurchases

During Fiscal 2007, the Company's Board authorized a total of 60.0 million shares of its common stock for repurchase under its share repurchase program with expiration dates extending into Fiscal 2010. During Fiscal 2007, the Company repurchased 18.7 million shares as part of its publicly announced repurchase programs for approximately $438.3 million, at a weighted average price of $23.38 per share. The Company did not repurchase any common stock as part of its publicly announced repurchase program during Fiscal 2008. As of March 25, 2009, the Company had 41.3 million shares remaining authorized for repurchase. These shares will be repurchased at the Company's discretion. Of the 41.3 million shares that may yet be purchased under the program, the authorization relating to 11.3 million shares expires at the end of Fiscal 2009 and the authorization relating to 30.0 million shares expires at the end of Fiscal 2010.

During Fiscal 2008 and Fiscal 2007, the Company repurchased 0.2 million and 0.4 million shares, respectively from certain employees at market prices totaling $3.4 million and $12.3 million, respectively. These shares were repurchased for the payment of taxes in connection with the vesting of share-based payments, as permitted under the 2005 Plan.

The aforementioned share repurchases have been recorded as treasury stock.

Stock Split

On November 13, 2006, the Company's Board approved a three-for-two stock split. This stock split was distributed on December 18, 2006, to stockholders of record on November 24, 2006. All share amounts and per share data presented herein reflect this stock split.

Income Taxes

Effective February 4, 2007, the Company adopted FIN 48. FIN 48 prescribes a comprehensive model for recognizing, measuring, presenting and disclosing in the financial statements tax positions taken or expected to be taken on a tax return, including a decision whether to file or not to file in a particular jurisdiction. Under FIN 48, a tax benefit from an uncertain position may be recognized only if it is "more likely than not" that the position is sustainable based on its technical merits. Refer to Note 12 to the Consolidated Financial Statements for further discussion of the adoption of FIN 48.

The Company calculates income taxes in accordance with SFAS No. 109, which requires the use of the asset and liability method. Under this method, deferred tax assets and liabilities are recognized based on the difference between the Consolidated Financial Statement carrying amounts of existing assets and liabilities and their respective tax bases as computed pursuant to FIN 48. Deferred tax assets and liabilities are measured using the

AMERICAN EAGLE OUTFITTERS, INC.

NOTES TO CONSOLIDATED FINANCIAL STATEMENTS — (Continued)

tax rates, based on certain judgments regarding enacted tax laws and published guidance, in effect in the years when those temporary differences are expected to reverse. A valuation allowance is established against the deferred tax assets when it is more likely than not that some portion or all of the deferred taxes may not be realized. Changes in our level and composition of earnings, tax laws or the deferred tax valuation allowance, as well as the results of tax audits may materially impact our effective tax rate.

The calculation of the deferred tax assets and liabilities, as well as the decision to recognize a tax benefit from an uncertain position and to establish a valuation allowance require management to make estimates and assumptions. We believe that our assumptions and estimates are reasonable, although actual results may have a positive or negative material impact on the balances of deferred tax assets and liabilities, valuation allowances, or net income.

Revenue Recognition

Revenue is recorded for store sales upon the purchase of merchandise by customers. The Company's e-commerce operation records revenue upon the estimated customer receipt date of the merchandise. Shipping and handling revenues are included in net sales. Sales tax collected from customers is excluded from revenue and is included as part of accrued income and other taxes on the Company's Consolidated Balance Sheets.

Revenue is recorded net of estimated and actual sales returns and deductions for coupon redemptions and other promotions. The Company records the impact of adjustments to its sales return reserve quarterly within net sales and cost of sales. The sales return reserve reflects an estimate of sales returns based on projected merchandise returns determined through the use of historical average return percentages. A summary of activity in the sales return reserve account follows:

	For the Years Ended	
	January 31, 2009	February 2, 2008
	(In thousands)	
Beginning balance	$ 4,683	$ 5,998
Returns	(81,704)	(83,082)
Provisions	81,113	81,767
Ending balance	$ 4,092	$ 4,683

Revenue is not recorded on the purchase of gift cards. A current liability is recorded upon purchase, and revenue is recognized when the gift card is redeemed for merchandise. Additionally, the Company recognizes revenue on unredeemed gift cards based on an estimate of the amounts that will not be redeemed ("gift card breakage"), determined through historical redemption trends. Gift card breakage revenue is recognized in proportion to actual gift card redemptions as a component of net sales. For further information on a change in the Company's gift card program, refer to the Gift Cards caption below.

The Company sells end-of-season, overstock and irregular merchandise to a third party vendor. For Fiscal 2008, the Company recorded $38.2 million of proceeds and $38.0 million of cost of sell-offs within net sales and cost of sales, respectively. For Fiscal 2007, the Company recorded $23.8 million of proceeds and $25.8 million of cost of sell-offs within net sales and cost of sales, respectively. For Fiscal 2006, the Company recorded $5.3 million of proceeds and $6.5 million of cost of sell-offs within net sales and cost of sales, respectively. During the three months ended October 28, 2006, the Company began classifying sell-offs on a gross basis, with proceeds and cost of sell-offs recorded in net sales and cost of sales, respectively. Prior to this time, the Company had presented the proceeds and cost of sell-offs on a net basis within cost of sales. Amounts for the six months ended July 29, 2006 were not adjusted to reflect this change as the amounts were determined to be immaterial.

Shipping and handling amounts billed to customers are recorded as revenue. During Fiscal 2008, Fiscal 2007 and Fiscal 2006, the Company recorded shipping and handling revenue of $16.9 million, $16.1 million and $17.7 million, respectively, in net sales.

AMERICAN EAGLE OUTFITTERS, INC.

NOTES TO CONSOLIDATED FINANCIAL STATEMENTS — (Continued)

Cost of Sales, Including Certain Buying, Occupancy and Warehousing Expenses

Cost of sales consists of merchandise costs, including design, sourcing, importing and inbound freight costs, as well as markdowns, shrinkage and certain promotional costs. Buying, occupancy and warehousing costs consist of: compensation, employee benefit expenses and travel for our buyers and certain senior merchandising executives; rent and utilities related to our stores, corporate headquarters, distribution centers and other office space; freight from our distribution centers to the stores; compensation and supplies for our distribution centers, including purchasing, receiving and inspection costs; and shipping and handling costs related to our e-commerce operation.

Selling, General and Administrative Expenses

Selling, general and administrative expenses consist of compensation and employee benefit expenses, including salaries, incentives and related benefits associated with our stores and corporate headquarters. Selling, general and administrative expenses also include advertising costs, supplies for our stores and home office, communication costs, travel and entertainment, leasing costs and professional services. Selling, general and administrative expenses do not include compensation, employee benefit expenses and travel for our design, sourcing and importing teams, our buyers and our distribution centers as these amounts are recorded in cost of sales.

Advertising Costs

Certain advertising costs, including direct mail, in-store photographs and other promotional costs are expensed when the marketing campaign commences. As of January 31, 2009 and February 2, 2008, the Company had prepaid advertising expense of $2.9 million and $4.5 million, respectively. All other advertising costs are expensed as incurred. The Company recognized $79.7 million, $74.9 million and $64.3 million in advertising expense during Fiscal 2008, Fiscal 2007 and Fiscal 2006, respectively.

Design Costs

The Company has certain design costs, including compensation, rent, depreciation, travel, supplies and samples, which are included in cost of sales as the respective inventory is sold.

Store Pre-Opening Costs

Store pre-opening costs consist primarily of rent, advertising, supplies and payroll expenses. These costs are expensed as incurred.

Other Income, Net

Other income, net consists primarily of interest income as well as foreign currency transaction gain/loss and interest expense.

Other-than-Temporary Impairment

The Company evaluates its investments for impairment in accordance with FSP FAS 115-1. FSP FAS 115-1 provides guidance for determining when an investment is considered impaired, whether impairment is other-than-temporary, and measurement of an impairment loss. An investment is considered impaired if the fair value of the investment is less than its carrying value. If, after consideration of all available evidence to evaluate the realizable value of its investment, impairment is determined to be other-than-temporary, then an impairment loss is recognized in the Consolidated Statement of Operations equal to the difference between the investment's carrying value and its fair value.

For Fiscal 2008, the Company recorded OTTI charges related to its investment securities of $22.9 million. Refer to Notes 3 and 4 to the Consolidated Financial Statements for additional information regarding our OTTI charges.

Gift Cards

The value of a gift card is recorded as a current liability upon purchase and revenue is recognized when the gift card is redeemed for merchandise. Prior to July 8, 2007, if a gift card remained inactive for greater than 24 months, the

AMERICAN EAGLE OUTFITTERS, INC.

NOTES TO CONSOLIDATED FINANCIAL STATEMENTS — (Continued)

Company assessed the recipient a one-dollar per month service fee, where allowed by law, which was automatically deducted from the remaining value of the card. For those jurisdictions where assessing a service fee was not allowable by law, the estimated breakage was recorded in a manner consistent with that described above, starting after 24 months of inactivity. Both gift card service fees and breakage estimates were recorded within other income, net.

On July 8, 2007, the Company discontinued assessing a service fee on active gift cards. As a result, the Company estimates gift card breakage and recognizes revenue in proportion to actual gift card redemptions as a component of net sales. The Company determines an estimated gift card breakage rate by continuously evaluating historical redemption data and the time when there is a remote likelihood that a gift card will be redeemed. The Company recorded $12.2 million of revenue related to gift card breakage during Fiscal 2008. The Company recorded $13.1 million of revenue related to gift card breakage during Fiscal 2007, which included cumulative breakage revenue related to gift cards issued since the Company introduced its gift card program. Prior to July 8, 2007, the Company recorded gift card service fee income in other income, net. The Company recorded gift card service fee income of $0.8 million and $2.3 million in Fiscal 2007 and Fiscal 2006, respectively.

Legal Proceedings and Claims

The Company is subject to certain legal proceedings and claims arising out of the conduct of its business. In accordance with SFAS No. 5, *Accounting for Contingencies*, management records a reserve for estimated losses when the loss is probable and the amount can be reasonably estimated. If a range of possible loss exists and no anticipated loss within the range is more likely than any other anticipated loss, the Company records the accrual at the low end of the range, in accordance with FASB Interpretation No. 14, *Reasonable Estimation of the Amount of a Loss — an interpretation of FASB Statement No. 5*. As the Company believes that it has provided adequate reserves, it anticipates that the ultimate outcome of any matter currently pending against the Company will not materially affect the financial position or results of operations of the Company.

Supplemental Disclosures of Cash Flow Information

The table below shows supplemental cash flow information for cash amounts paid during the respective periods:

	For the Years Ended		
	January 31, 2009	February 2, 2008	February 3, 2007
		(In thousands)	
Cash paid during the periods for:			
Income taxes	$132,234	$260,615	$204,179
Interest	$ 1,947	$ —	$ 19
Supplemental disclosure of non-cash transactions:			
Transfer of investment securities from available-for-sale to trading classification	$ —	$ —	$180,787

AMERICAN EAGLE OUTFITTERS, INC.

NOTES TO CONSOLIDATED FINANCIAL STATEMENTS — (Continued)

Earnings Per Share

The following table shows the amounts used in computing earnings per share and the effect on net income and the weighted average number of shares of potential dilutive common stock (stock options and restricted stock).

	For the Years Ended		
	January 31, 2009	February 2, 2008	February 3, 2007
		(In thousands)	
Net income	$179,061	$400,019	$387,359
Weighted average common shares outstanding:			
Basic shares	205,169	216,119	222,662
Dilutive effect of stock options and non-vested restricted stock	2,413	4,161	5,722
Diluted shares	207,582	220,280	228,384

Equity awards to purchase 7.6 million, 2.5 million and 1.1 million shares of common stock during Fiscal 2008, Fiscal 2007 and Fiscal 2006, respectively, were outstanding, but were not included in the computation of weighted average diluted common share amounts as the effect of doing so would have been anti-dilutive. Additionally, for Fiscal 2008, approximately 0.8 million shares of performance-based restricted stock were not included in the computation of weighted average diluted common share amounts. This was due to the Company not attaining the operating performance required for the shares to vest as compared to the pre-established annual performance goals.

Segment Information

In accordance with SFAS No. 131, *Disclosures about Segments of an Enterprise and Related Information* ("SFAS No. 131"), the Company has identified four operating segments (American Eagle Brand U.S. and Canadian retail stores, aerie by American Eagle retail stores, MARTIN + OSA retail stores and AEO Direct) that reflect the basis used internally to review performance and allocate resources. All of the operating segments have been aggregated and are presented as one reportable segment, as permitted by SFAS No. 131.

The following tables present summarized geographical information:

	For the Years Ended		
	January 31, 2009	February 2, 2008	February 3, 2007
		(In thousands)	
Net sales:			
United States	$2,707,261	$2,770,119	$2,562,831
Foreign(1)	281,605	285,300	231,578
Total net sales	$2,988,866	$3,055,419	$2,794,409

(1) Amounts represent sales from American Eagle and aerie Canadian retail stores, as well as AEO Direct sales, that are billed to and/or shipped to foreign countries.

	January 31, 2009	February 2, 2008
	(In thousands)	
Long-lived assets, net:		
United States	$708,180	$596,715
Foreign	42,766	40,332
Total long-lived assets, net	$750,946	$637,047

AMERICAN EAGLE OUTFITTERS, INC.

NOTES TO CONSOLIDATED FINANCIAL STATEMENTS — (Continued)

Reclassification

Certain reclassifications have been made to the Consolidated Financial Statements for prior periods in order to conform to the Fiscal 2007 presentation, including unaudited quarterly financial information. Refer to Note 13 to the Consolidated Financial Statements.

3. Cash and Cash Equivalents, Short-term Investments and Long-term Investments

The following table summarizes the fair market value of our cash and marketable securities, which are recorded as cash and cash equivalents on the Consolidated Balance Sheets, our short-term investments and our long-term investments:

	January 31, 2009		
	Balance	Unrealized Holding Gains	Unrealized Holding Losses
		(In thousands)	
Cash and cash equivalents:			
Cash	$ 61,355	$—	$ —
Money-market	411,987	—	—
Total cash and cash equivalents	$473,342	$—	$ —
Short-term investments:			
Preferred stock	$ 6,219	$—	$ —
Auction rate preferred securities	4,292	—	—
Total short-term investments	$ 10,511	$—	$ —
Long-term investments:			
Student-loan backed ARS	$169,254	$—	$(31,446)
State and local government ARS	69,970	—	(630)
Auction rate preferred securities	11,783	—	(3,217)
Total long-term investments	$251,007	$—	$(35,293)
Total	$734,860	$—	$(35,293)

	February 2, 2008		
	Balance	Unrealized Holding Gains	Unrealized Holding Losses
		(In thousands)	
Cash and cash equivalents:			
Cash	$ 45,422	$ —	$ —
Money-market	70,639	—	—
Total cash and cash equivalents	$116,061	$ —	$ —
Short-term investments:			
Student-loan backed ARS	$248,800	$ —	$ —
Treasury and agency ARS	20,172	107	—
State and local government ARS	136,161	52	—
Auction rate preferred securities	98,745	—	(27)
Total short-term investments	$503,878	$159	$ (27)
Long-term investments:			
Treasury and agency ARS	$122,811	$526	$ (61)
State and local government ARS	6,419	—	—
Auction rate preferred securities	36,580	65	(48)
Total long-term investments	$165,810	$591	$(109)
Total	$785,749	$750	$(136)

AMERICAN EAGLE OUTFITTERS, INC.

NOTES TO CONSOLIDATED FINANCIAL STATEMENTS — (Continued)

Proceeds from the sale of available-for-sale securities were $393.6 million, $2.127 billion and $916.0 million for Fiscal 2008, Fiscal 2007 and Fiscal 2006, respectively. These proceeds are offset against purchases of $48.7 million, $1.773 billion and $1.353 billion for Fiscal 2008, Fiscal 2007 and Fiscal 2006, respectively. In addition to the OTTI charge discussed below for Fiscal 2008, the Company recorded net realized losses related to the sale of available-for-sale securities of $1.1 million, $0.4 million and $0.6 million for Fiscal 2008, Fiscal 2007 and Fiscal 2006, respectively, in other income, net.

During Fiscal 2006, the Company transferred certain investment securities from available-for-sale classification to trading classification (the "trading securities"). As a result of this transfer, during Fiscal 2006 a reclassification adjustment of $(0.3) million was recorded in other comprehensive income related to the gain realized in net income at the time of transfer. As a result of trading classification, the Company realized $3.5 million of capital gains, which were recorded in other income, net during Fiscal 2006. The trading securities were sold during Fiscal 2006, at which time the Company received proceeds of $184.0 million. As of January 31, 2009, the Company had no investments classified as trading securities.

The following tables present the length of time available-for-sale securities were in continuous unrealized loss positions but were not deemed to be other-than-temporarily impaired:

	Less than 12 Months		Greater than or Equal to 12 Months	
	Gross Unrealized Holding Losses	Fair Value	Gross Unrealized Holding Losses	Fair Value
	(In thousands)			
January 31, 2009				
Student-loan backed ARS	$(31,446)	$169,254	$—	$—
State and local government ARS	(630)	69,970	—	—
Auction rate preferred securities	(3,217)	11,783	—	—
Total	$(35,293)	$251,007	$—	$—
February 2, 2008				
Auction rate preferred securities ("ARPS")	$ (75)	$ 19,136	$—	$—
Treasury and agency securities	(61)	18,377	—	—
Total	$ (136)	$ 37,513	$—	$—

As of January 31, 2009, we had a total of $734.9 million in cash and cash equivalents, short-term and long-term investments, which included $255.3 million of investments in ARS and $6.2 million of preferred securities, net of $35.3 million ($21.8 million net of tax) of temporary impairment and $22.9 million in OTTI. Our short-term and long-term investments consist of the following:

	No. of Issues	Par Value	Temporary Impairment	OTTI	Carrying Value as of January 31, 2009
		(In thousands, except no. of issues amount)			
Auction-rate securities ("ARS"):					
Closed-end municipal fund ARS	5	$ 41,750	$ (263)	$ —	$ 41,487
Municipal Bond ARS	5	28,850	(367)	—	28,483
Auction rate preferred securities	5	29,400	(3,217)	(10,108)	16,075
Federally-insured student loan ARS	17	166,700	(17,283)	—	149,417
Private-insured student loan ARS	4	34,000	(14,163)	—	19,837
Total Auction-rate securities	36	300,700	(35,293)	(10,108)	255,299
Preferred Stock	4	19,000	—	(12,781)	6,219
Total	40	$319,700	$(35,293)	$(22,889)	$261,518

AMERICAN EAGLE OUTFITTERS, INC.

NOTES TO CONSOLIDATED FINANCIAL STATEMENTS — (Continued)

Auction rate preferred securities ("ARPS") are a type of ARS that have an underlying asset of perpetual preferred stock. In the event of default or liquidation of the collateral by the ARS issuer or trustee, the Company is entitled to receive non-convertible preferred shares in the ARS issuer. Lehman Brothers Holdings, Inc. ("Lehman") (which filed for Chapter 11 bankruptcy protection during September 2008) acted as the broker and auction agent for all of the ARPS held by the Company. The Lehman bankruptcy resulted in the dissolution of the investment trusts for most of the Company's ARPS. As a result, during Fiscal 2008, the Company received a total of 760,000 preferred shares of four companies. For Fiscal 2008, the Company recorded an OTTI charge of $12.8 million based on the closing market price of the preferred shares on January 30, 2009.

Furthermore, as a result of the Lehman bankruptcy, it is probable that the trusts for three additional ARPS will dissolve in the first quarter of 2009. Since it is unlikely that these investments will recover in value in the near term, for Fiscal 2008 the Company recorded an OTTI charge related to these ARPS of $10.1 million based on the closing market price for the underlying preferred shares on January 30, 2009.

In addition to the OTTI recorded, as a result of the current market conditions, the Company recorded a net temporary impairment charge of $35.3 million in connection with the valuation of the remainder of its ARS portfolio at January 31, 2009.

For instruments deemed to be temporarily impaired, we believe that these ARS investments can be liquidated through successful auctions or redemptions at par or par plus accrued interest. We maintain our ability and intent to hold these investments until recovery of market value and believe that the current illiquidity and impairment of these investments is temporary. In addition, we believe that the current lack of liquidity relating to ARS investments will have no impact on our ability to fund our ongoing operations and growth initiatives.

We continue to monitor the market for ARS and consider the impact, if any, on the fair value of its investments. If current market conditions deteriorate further, or the anticipated recovery in market values does not occur, we may be required to record additional OTTI and/or temporary impairment.

Refer to Note 14 to the Consolidated Financial Statements for additional information regarding a subsequent event relating to our investment securities.

4. Fair Value Measurements

SFAS No. 157 defines fair value, establishes a framework for measuring fair value in accordance with accounting principles generally accepted in the United States, and expands disclosures about fair value measurements. Fair value is defined under SFAS No. 157 as the exit price associated with the sale of an asset or transfer of a liability in an orderly transaction between market participants at the measurement date. The Company has adopted the provisions of SFAS No. 157 as of February 3, 2008, for its financial instruments, including its investment securities.

Valuation techniques used to measure fair value under SFAS No. 157 must maximize the use of observable inputs and minimize the use of unobservable inputs. In addition, SFAS No. 157 establishes a three-tier fair value hierarchy, which prioritizes the inputs used in measuring fair value. These tiers include:

- *Level 1* — Quoted prices in active markets for identical assets or liabilities. Our short-term investments with active markets, which represent our preferred stock investments, as well as cash and cash equivalents are reported at fair value utilizing Level 1 inputs. For these items, quoted current market prices are readily available.
- *Level 2* — Inputs other than Level 1 that are observable, either directly or indirectly, such as quoted prices for similar assets or liabilities; quoted prices in markets that are not active; or other inputs that are observable or can be corroborated by observable market data for substantially the full term of the assets or liabilities. The Company has concluded that the ARPS with underlyings of publicly traded preferred stock that it has

AMERICAN EAGLE OUTFITTERS, INC.

NOTES TO CONSOLIDATED FINANCIAL STATEMENTS — (Continued)

classified as short term represent a Level 2 valuation and have been valued using the publicly available trading prices of the underlying preferred shares as the basis for its valuation.

- *Level 3* — Unobservable inputs (i.e. projections, estimates, interpretations, etc.) that are supported by little or no market activity and that are significant to the fair value of the assets or liabilities. The Company has concluded that the ARS that it has classified as long-term due to failed auctions or that have long-term auction resets, as well as ARPS with underlyings of non-publicly traded preferred stock, represent a Level 3 valuation and should be valued using a discounted cash flow analysis. The assumptions used in preparing the discounted cash flow model include estimates for interest rates, timing and amount of cash flows and expected recovery periods of the ARS.

As of January 31, 2009, the Company held certain assets that are required to be measured at fair value on a recurring basis. These include cash equivalents and short and long-term investments.

In accordance with SFAS No. 157, the following table represents the Company's fair value hierarchy for its financial assets (cash equivalents and investments) measured at fair value on a recurring basis as of January 31, 2009:

	Fair Value Measurements at January 31, 2009			
	Carrying Amount as of January 31, 2009	Quoted Market Prices in Active Markets for Identical Assets (Level 1)	Significant Other Observable Inputs (Level 2)	Significant Unobservable Inputs (Level 3)
	(In thousands)			
Cash and Cash Equivalents				
Cash	$ 61,355	$ 61,355	$ —	$ —
Money-market	411,987	411,987	—	—
Total cash and cash equivalents	$473,342	$473,342	$ —	$ —
Short-term Investments				
Preferred stock	$ 6,219	$ 6,219	$ —	$ —
Auction rate preferred securities	4,292	—	4,292	—
Total Short-term Investments	$ 10,511	$ 6,219	$4,292	$ —
Long-term Investments				
Student-loan backed ARS	$169,254	$ —	$ —	$169,254
State and local government ARS	69,970	—	—	69,970
Auction rate preferred securities	11,783	—	—	11,783
Total Long-term Investments	$251,007	$ —	$ —	$251,007
Total	$734,860	$479,561	$4,292	$251,007
Percent to total	100.0%	65.3%	0.6%	34.1%

The Company used a discounted cash flow ("DCF") model to value its Level 3 investments. The assumptions in the Company's model included different recovery periods depending on the type of security and varying discount factors for yield and illiquidity. These assumptions are subjective. They are based on the Company's current judgment and its view of current market conditions. The use of different assumptions would result in a different valuation and related charge.

AMERICAN EAGLE OUTFITTERS, INC.

NOTES TO CONSOLIDATED FINANCIAL STATEMENTS — (Continued)

As a result of the fair value analysis for Fiscal 2008, the Company recorded a net temporary impairment of $35.3 million ($21.8 million, net of tax). This amount was recorded in other comprehensive income ("OCI"). The Company also recorded OTTI of $22.9 million during Fiscal 2008. The reconciliation of our assets measured at fair value on a recurring basis using unobservable inputs (Level 3) is as follows:

	Level 3 (Unobservable Inputs)			
	Total	Auction-Rate Municipal Securities	Student Loan-Backed Auction-Rate Securities	Auction-Rate Preferred Securities
	(In thousands)			
Carrying Value at February 2, 2008	$ —	$ —	$ —	$ —
Additions to Level 3 upon adoption of SFAS No. 157(1)	340,475	84,575	212,000	43,900
Settlements	(29,875)	(18,575)	(11,300)	—
Additions to Level 3(2)	4,600	4,600	—	—
Transfer out of Level 3(3)	(28,900)	—	—	(28,900)
Gains and losses:				
Reported in earnings	—	—	—	—
Reported in OCI	(35,293)	(630)	(31,446)	(3,217)
Balance at January 31, 2009	$251,007	$ 69,970	$169,254	$ 11,783

(1) Represents amounts transferred upon the adoption of SFAS No. 157 during the first quarter of Fiscal 2008.

(2) Additions to Level 3 include securities previously classified as Level 2, which were securities that had experienced partial calls prior to the fourth quarter of 2008 and were previously valued at par.

(3) Transfers out of Level 3 include preferred securities (into Level 1) and ARPS (into Level 2). The transfers to Level 1 occurred due to the Company acquiring exchange traded preferred shares as a result of the ARPS trusts liquidating. The transfers to Level 2 occurred as a result of the company determining that it was more appropriate to value these investments using observable market prices of the underlying securities. Refer to Note 3 to the Consolidated Financial Statements. The OTTI charge of $22.9 million that was reported in earnings was taken on Level 1 and Level 2 securities transferred from Level 3.

5. Accounts and Note Receivable

Accounts and note receivable are comprised of the following:

	January 31, 2009	February 2, 2008
	(In thousands)	
Construction allowances	$11,139	$12,284
Merchandise sell-offs	17,057	11,101
Interest income	1,355	4,803
Marketing cost reimbursements	2,363	917
Credit card receivable	5,175	—
Merchandise vendor receivables	2,899	626
Other	1,483	2,189
Total	$41,471	$31,920

AMERICAN EAGLE OUTFITTERS, INC.

NOTES TO CONSOLIDATED FINANCIAL STATEMENTS — (Continued)

6. Property and Equipment

Property and equipment consists of the following:

	January 31, 2009	February 2, 2008
	(In thousands)	
Land	$ 6,364	$ 6,869
Buildings	122,414	106,632
Leasehold improvements	605,299	528,188
Fixtures and equipment	536,009	427,827
Construction in progress	28,543	21,794
	$1,298,629	$1,091,310
Less: Accumulated depreciation and amortization	(558,389)	(465,742)
Net property and equipment	$ 740,240	$ 625,568

Depreciation expense is summarized as follows:

	For the Years Ended		
	January 31, 2009	February 2, 2008	February 3, 2007
		(In thousands)	
Depreciation expense	$130,802	$108,919	$87,869

7. Note Payable and Other Credit Arrangements

The Company has borrowing agreements with two separate financial institutions under which it may borrow an aggregate of $350.0 million. Of this amount, $150.0 million can be used for demand letter of credit facilities and $100.0 million can be used for demand line borrowings. The remaining $100.0 million can be used for either letters of credit or demand line borrowings at the Company's discretion. As of January 31, 2009, the Company had outstanding demand letters of credit of $57.3 million and demand line borrowings of $75.0 million. The outstanding amounts on these facilities can be demanded for repayment by the financial institutions at any time. Additionally, the availability of any remaining borrowings is subject to acceptance by the respective financial institution. The average borrowing rate on the demand lines for Fiscal 2008 was 2.9% and the Company has incorporated the demand line proceeds into working capital. The demand line facilities comprising the $100.0 million borrowing capacity expire on April 22, 2009. The Company is currently working with its lenders to renew these facilities or to obtain committed credit lines of a comparable amount. If unable to renew both of its demand line facilities, the Company would be required to repay immediately the $75 million that it has drawn on those facilities. The Company believes that this would have no material impact on its ability to fund operations.

8. Leases

The Company leases all store premises, some of its office space and certain information technology and office equipment. The store leases generally have initial terms of ten years. Most of these store leases provide for base rentals and the payment of a percentage of sales as additional contingent rent when sales exceed specified levels. Additionally, most leases contain construction allowances and/or rent holidays. In recognizing landlord incentives and minimum rent expense, the Company amortizes the charges on a straight-line basis over the lease term (including the pre-opening build-out period). These leases are classified as operating leases.

AMERICAN EAGLE OUTFITTERS, INC.

NOTES TO CONSOLIDATED FINANCIAL STATEMENTS — (Continued)

A summary of fixed minimum and contingent rent expense for all operating leases follows:

	For the Years Ended		
	January 31, 2009	February 2, 2008	February 3, 2007
		(In thousands)	
Store rent:			
Fixed minimum	$197,820	$167,051	$145,519
Contingent	11,767	17,626	19,138
Total store rent, excluding common area maintenance charges, real estate taxes and certain other expenses	209,587	184,677	164,657
Offices, distribution facilities, equipment and other	18,260	17,250	12,540
Total rent expense	$227,847	$201,927	$177,197

In addition, the Company is typically responsible under its store, office and distribution center leases for tenant occupancy costs, including maintenance costs, common area charges, real estate taxes and certain other expenses.

The table below summarizes future minimum lease obligations, consisting of fixed minimum rent, under operating leases in effect at January 31, 2009:

Fiscal years:	Future Minimum Lease Obligations
	(In thousands)
2009	$ 234,095
2010	229,702
2011	212,901
2012	195,283
2013	178,133
Thereafter	720,253
Total	$1,770,367

AMERICAN EAGLE OUTFITTERS, INC.

NOTES TO CONSOLIDATED FINANCIAL STATEMENTS — (Continued)

9. Other Comprehensive Income

The accumulated balances of other comprehensive income included as part of the Consolidated Statements of Stockholders' Equity follow:

	Before Tax Amount	Tax (Expense) Benefit	Accumulated Other Comprehensive Income (Loss)
		(In thousands)	
Balance at January 28, 2006	**$ 21,488**	**$ 540**	**$ 22,028**
Unrealized loss on investments	(276)	85	(191)
Reclassification adjustment for net losses realized in net income related to sale of available-for-sale securities	578	(222)	356
Reclassification adjustment for gain realized in net income related to the transfer of investment securities from available-for-sale classification to trading classification	(287)	110	(177)
Foreign currency translation adjustment	(1,180)	—	(1,180)
Reclassification adjustment for loss realized in net income related to the disposition of National Logistics Services	878	—	878
Balance at February 3, 2007	**21,201**	**513**	**21,714**
Unrealized gain on investments	1,538	(591)	947
Reclassification adjustment for net losses realized in net income related to sale of available-for-sale securities	393	(151)	242
Foreign currency translation adjustment	12,582	—	12,582
Balance at February 2, 2008	**$ 35,714**	**$ (229)**	**$ 35,485**
Temporary impairment related to ARS	(36,825)	14,030	(22,795)
Reclassification adjustment for losses realized in net income related to sale of ARS	318	(121)	197
Reclassification adjustment for OTTI charges realized in net income related to ARS	1,214	(463)	751
Unrealized loss on investments	(607)	229	(378)
Foreign currency translation adjustment	(27,649)	—	(27,649)
Balance at January 31, 2009	**$(27,835)**	**$13,446**	**$(14,389)**

The components of accumulated other comprehensive income were as follows:

	For the Years Ended January 31, 2009	For the Years Ended February 2, 2008
	(In thousands)	
Net unrealized (loss) gain on available-for-sale securities, net of tax(1)	$(21,847)	$ 378
Foreign currency translation adjustment	7,458	35,107
Accumulated other comprehensive (loss) income	$(14,389)	$35,485

(1) Amounts are shown net of tax of $13.4 million and $(0.2) million for Fiscal 2008 and Fiscal 2007, respectively.

AMERICAN EAGLE OUTFITTERS, INC.

NOTES TO CONSOLIDATED FINANCIAL STATEMENTS — (Continued)

10. Share-Based Payments

At January 31, 2009, the Company had awards outstanding under three share-based compensation plans, which are described below.

At the beginning of Fiscal 2006, the Company adopted the fair value recognition provisions of SFAS No. 123(R), using the modified prospective transition method. Under this transition method, share-based compensation cost recognized includes: (a) compensation cost for all share-based payments granted prior to, but not yet vested as of January 29, 2006, based on the grant date fair value estimated in accordance with the original provisions of SFAS No. 123 and (b) compensation cost for all share-based payments granted subsequent to January 29, 2006, based on the grant date fair value estimated using the Black-Scholes option pricing model. The Company recognizes compensation expense for stock option awards and time-based restricted stock awards on a straight-line basis over the requisite service period of the award (or to an employee's eligible retirement date, if earlier). Performance-based restricted stock awards are recognized as compensation expense based on the fair value of the Company's common stock on the date of grant, the number of shares ultimately expected to vest and the vesting period. Total share-based compensation expense included in the Consolidated Statements of Operations for Fiscal 2008, Fiscal 2007 and Fiscal 2006 was $20.3 million ($12.5 million, net of tax), $33.7 million ($20.7 million, net of tax) and $36.6 million ($22.6 million, net of tax), respectively.

SFAS No. 123(R) requires recognition of compensation cost under a non-substantive vesting period approach. Accordingly, the Company recognizes compensation expense over the period from the grant date to the date retirement eligibility is achieved, if that is expected to occur during the nominal vesting period. Additionally, for awards granted to retirement eligible employees, the full compensation cost of an award must be recognized immediately upon grant.

Share-based compensation plans

1994 Stock Option Plan

On February 10, 1994, the Company's Board adopted the American Eagle Outfitters, Inc. 1994 Stock Option Plan (the "1994 Plan"). The 1994 Plan provided for the grant of 12.2 million incentive or non-qualified options to purchase common stock. The 1994 Plan was subsequently amended to increase the shares available for grant to 24.3 million shares. Additionally, the amendment provided that the maximum number of options that may be granted to any individual may not exceed 8.1 million shares. The options granted under the 1994 Plan were approved by the Compensation Committee of the Board, primarily vest over five years, and expire ten years from the date of grant. The 1994 Plan terminated on January 2, 2004 with all rights of the optionees and all unexpired options continuing in force and operation after the termination.

1999 Stock Incentive Plan

The 1999 Stock Option Plan (the "1999 Plan") was approved by the stockholders on June 8, 1999. The 1999 Plan authorized 18.0 million shares for issuance in the form of stock options, stock appreciation rights, restricted stock awards, performance units or performance shares. The 1999 Plan was subsequently amended to increase the shares available for grant to 33.0 million. Additionally, the 1999 Plan provided that the maximum number of shares awarded to any individual may not exceed 9.0 million shares. The 1999 Plan allowed the Compensation Committee to determine which employees and consultants received awards and the terms and conditions of these awards. The 1999 Plan provided for a grant of 1,875 stock options quarterly (not to be adjusted for stock splits) to each director who is not an officer or employee of the Company starting in August 2003. The Company ceased making these quarterly stock option grants in June 2005. Under this plan, 33.2 million non-qualified stock options and 6.7 million shares of restricted stock were granted to employees and certain non-employees (without considering cancellations to date of awards for 7.9 million shares). Approximately 33% of the options granted were to vest over eight years after the date of grant but were accelerated as the Company met annual performance goals. Approximately 34% of

AMERICAN EAGLE OUTFITTERS, INC.

NOTES TO CONSOLIDATED FINANCIAL STATEMENTS — (Continued)

the options granted under the 1999 Plan vest over three years, 23% vest over five years and the remaining grants vest over one year. All options expire after ten years. Performance-based restricted stock was earned if the Company met established performance goals. The 1999 Plan terminated on June 15, 2005 with all rights of the awardees and all unexpired awards continuing in force and operation after the termination.

2005 Stock Award and Incentive Plan

The 2005 Stock Award and Incentive Plan (the "2005 Plan") was approved by the stockholders on June 15, 2005. The 2005 Plan authorized 18.4 million shares for issuance, of which 6.4 million shares are available for full value awards in the form of restricted stock awards, restricted stock units or other full value stock awards and 12.0 million shares are available for stock options, stock appreciation rights, dividend equivalents, performance awards or other non-full value stock awards. The 2005 Plan provides that the maximum number of shares awarded to any individual may not exceed 6.0 million shares per year plus the amount of the unused annual limit of the previous year. The 2005 Plan allows the Compensation Committee to determine which employees receive awards and the terms and conditions of these awards. The 2005 Plan provides for grants to directors who are not officers or employees of the Company, which are not to exceed 20,000 shares per year (not to be adjusted for stock splits). Through January 31, 2009, 9.1 million non-qualified stock options, 2.9 million shares of restricted stock and 0.2 million shares of common stock had been granted under the 2005 Plan to employees and directors (without considering cancellations to date of awards for 2.9 million shares). Approximately 99% of the options granted under the 2005 Plan vest over three years and 1% vest over five years. Options were granted for ten and seven-year terms. Approximately 97% of the restricted stock awards are performance-based and are earned if the Company meets established performance goals. The remaining 3% of the restricted stock awards are time-based and vest over three years.

Stock Option Grants

A summary of the Company's stock option activity under all plans for Fiscal 2008 follows:

	For the Year Ended January 31, 2009(1)			
	Options	Weighted-Average Exercise Price	Weighted-Average Remaining Contractual Life (In years)	Aggregate Intrinsic Value (In thousands)
Outstanding — February 2, 2008	12,915,576	$14.41		
Granted	3,514,653	$20.95		
Exercised(2)	451,644	$ 8.44		
Cancelled	1,481,851	$23.51	—	—
Outstanding — January 31, 2009	14,496,734	$15.25	4.1	$14,219
Vested and expected to vest — January 31, 2009	14,160,412	$15.10	4.1	$14,217
Exercisable — January 31, 2009	6,261,165	$ 6.74	2.6	$14,208

(1) As of January 31, 2009, the Company had 5.5 million shares available for stock option grants.

(2) Options exercised during Fiscal 2008 ranged in price from $1.98 to $19.74.

The weighted-average grant date fair value of stock options granted during Fiscal 2008, Fiscal 2007 and Fiscal 2006 was $7.16, $10.64, and $7.59, respectively. The aggregate intrinsic value of options exercised during Fiscal 2008, Fiscal 2007 and Fiscal 2006 was $3.9 million, $22.5 million, and $73.4 million, respectively. Cash received from the exercise of stock options and the actual tax benefit realized from stock option exercises were $3.8 million

AMERICAN EAGLE OUTFITTERS, INC.

NOTES TO CONSOLIDATED FINANCIAL STATEMENTS — (Continued)

and $1.1 million, respectively, for Fiscal 2008. Cash received from the exercise of stock options and the actual tax benefit realized from stock option exercises were $13.2 million and $7.3 million, respectively, for Fiscal 2007. For Fiscal 2006, cash received from the exercise of stock options and the actual tax benefit realized from stock option exercises were $28.4 million and $25.5 million, respectively.

The fair value of stock options was estimated at the date of grant using a Black-Scholes option pricing model with the following weighted-average assumptions:

Black-Scholes Option Valuation Assumptions	For the Years Ended January 31, 2009	February 2, 2008	February 3, 2007
Risk-free interest rates(1)	2.5%	4.5%	4.9%
Dividend yield	1.7%	0.9%	1.0%
Volatility factors of the expected market price of the Company's common stock(2)	44.4%	39.2%	41.3%
Weighted-average expected term(3)	4.3 years	4.4 years	4.4 years

(1) Based on the U.S. Treasury yield curve in effect at the time of grant with a term consistent with the expected life of our stock options.

(2) Based on a combination of historical volatility of the Company's common stock and implied volatility.

(3) Represents the period of time options are expected to be outstanding. The weighted average expected option term for the year ended January 31, 2009 was determined based on historical experience. The weighted average expected option terms for the years ended February 2, 2008 and February 3, 2007 were determined using a combination of the "simplified method" for plain vanilla options as allowed by Staff Accounting Bulletin No. 107, *Share-Based Payments* ("SAB No. 107"), and past behavior. The "simplified method" calculates the expected term as the average of the vesting term and original contractual term of the options.

As of January 31, 2009, there was $20.6 million of unrecognized compensation expense related to nonvested stock option awards that is expected to be recognized over a weighted average period of 1.8 years.

Restricted Stock Grants

Under the 2005 Plan, the fair value of restricted stock awards is based on the closing market price of the Company's common stock on the date of grant. A summary of the activity of the Company's restricted stock is presented in the following tables.

Time-Based Restricted Stock	For the Year Ended January 31, 2009 Shares	Weighted-Average Grant Date Fair Value
Nonvested — February 2, 2008	74,500	$19.97
Granted	—	—
Vested	(18,500)	20.25
Cancelled	(15,000)	19.60
Nonvested — January 31, 2009	41,000	$19.97

AMERICAN EAGLE OUTFITTERS, INC.

NOTES TO CONSOLIDATED FINANCIAL STATEMENTS — (Continued)

	For the Year Ended January 31, 2009	
Performance-Based Restricted Stock	**Shares**	**Weighted-Average Grant Date Fair Value**
Nonvested — February 2, 2008	612,575	$29.73
Granted	878,415	21.24
Vested	(433,983)	29.72
Cancelled	(299,195)	26.33
Nonvested — January 31, 2009	757,812	$21.26

As of January 31, 2009, there was $0.2 million of unrecognized compensation expense related to nonvested restricted stock awards that is expected to be recognized over a weighted average period of four months. The total fair value of restricted stock awards vested during Fiscal 2008, Fiscal 2007 and Fiscal 2006 was $9.6 million, $32.6 million and $18.9 million, respectively.

As of January 31, 2009, the Company had 4.1 million shares available for restricted stock awards, restricted stock units or other full value stock awards.

11. Retirement Plan and Employee Stock Purchase Plan

The Company maintains a profit sharing and 401(k) plan (the "Retirement Plan"). Under the provisions of the Retirement Plan, full-time employees and part-time employees are automatically enrolled to contribute 3% of their salary if they have attained 20½ years of age and have completed 60 days of service. Individuals can decline enrollment or can contribute up to 30% of their salary to the 401(k) plan on a pretax basis, subject to IRS limitations. After one year of service, the Company will match 100% of the first 3% of pay plus an additional 50% of the next 3% of pay that is contributed to the plan. Contributions to the profit sharing plan, as determined by the Board, are discretionary. The Company recognized $6.3 million, $6.1 million and $6.9 million in expense during Fiscal 2008, Fiscal 2007 and Fiscal 2006, respectively, in connection with the Retirement Plan.

The Employee Stock Purchase Plan is a non-qualified plan that covers all full-time employees and part-time employees who are at least 18 years old and have completed 60 days of service. Contributions are determined by the employee, with the Company matching 15% of the investment up to a maximum investment of $100 per pay period. These contributions are used to purchase shares of Company stock in the open market.

12. Income Taxes

The components of income before income taxes were:

	For the Years Ended		
	January 31, 2009	**February 2, 2008**	**February 3, 2007**
		(In thousands)	
U.S.	$244,629	$568,519	$561,178
Foreign	52,412	67,862	67,889
Total	$297,041	$636,381	$629,067

AMERICAN EAGLE OUTFITTERS, INC.

NOTES TO CONSOLIDATED FINANCIAL STATEMENTS — (Continued)

The significant components of the Company's deferred tax assets and liabilities were as follows:

	January 31, 2009	February 2, 2008
	(In thousands)	
Deferred tax assets:		
Rent	$ 22,207	$ 19,307
Deferred compensation	21,492	27,448
Inventories	14,828	9,750
Temporary impairment of investment securities	13,446	—
Foreign and state income taxes	12,984	13,417
Other-than-temporary impairment of investment securities	8,721	—
Tax credits	4,217	2,450
Employee compensation and benefits	3,677	9,935
Other	10,158	9,040
Gross deferred tax assets	111,730	91,347
Valuation allowance	(12,933)	(2,450)
Total deferred tax assets	$ 98,797	$ 88,897
Deferred tax liabilities:		
Property and equipment	$ (36,641)	$(17,655)
Prepaid expenses	(1,708)	—
Deferred tax liabilities	$ (38,349)	$(17,655)
Total deferred tax assets, net	$ 60,448	$ 71,242
Classification in the Consolidated Balance Sheet		
Current deferred tax assets	$ 45,447	$ 47,004
Noncurrent deferred tax assets	15,001	24,238
Total net deferred tax assets	$ 60,448	$ 71,242

The net decrease in deferred tax assets and liabilities was primarily due to an increase in the deferred tax liability for property and equipment related to bonus depreciation partially offset by the increase in the deferred tax asset related to the temporary impairment of certain investment securities reflected in Other Comprehensive Income.

Significant components of the provision for income taxes were as follows:

	For the Years Ended		
	January 31, 2009	February 2, 2008	February 3, 2007
		(In thousands)	
Current:			
Federal	$ 69,592	$172,604	$213,001
Foreign taxes	16,341	24,030	22,665
State	7,578	27,987	33,614
Total current	93,511	224,621	269,280
Deferred:			
Federal	21,927	10,306	(26,141)
Foreign taxes	(340)	(2,077)	2,694
State	2,882	3,512	(4,125)
Total deferred	24,469	11,741	(27,572)
Provision for income taxes	$117,980	$236,362	$241,708

AMERICAN EAGLE OUTFITTERS, INC.

NOTES TO CONSOLIDATED FINANCIAL STATEMENTS — (Continued)

As a result of additional tax deductions related to share-based payments, tax benefits have been recognized as contributed capital for Fiscal 2008, Fiscal 2007, and Fiscal 2006 in the amounts of $1.1 million, $7.2 million and $25.5 million, respectively.

In December 2004, the FASB issued Staff Position No. FAS 109-2, *Accounting and Disclosure Guidance for the Foreign Earnings Repatriation Provision within the American Jobs Creation Act of 2004* ("FSP No. 109-2"). FSP No. 109-2 provides guidance to companies to determine how the American Jobs Creation Act of 2004 (the "Act") affects a company's accounting for the deferred tax liabilities on un-remitted foreign earnings. The Act provides for a special one-time deduction of 85% of certain foreign earnings that are repatriated and that meet certain requirements. During Fiscal 2006, the Company repatriated $83.4 million as extraordinary dividends from its Canadian subsidiaries. As a result of the repatriation, the Company recognized total income tax expense of $4.4 million, of which $0.6 million was recorded during Fiscal 2006 and $3.8 million was recorded during Fiscal 2005.

As of January 31, 2009, the Company had undistributed earnings from its Canadian subsidiaries. The Company does not anticipate any deferred tax liability associated with the repatriation of these earnings as the tax on the repatriated earnings would be offset by U.S. foreign income tax credits.

Effective February 4, 2007, the Company adopted FIN 48, which prescribes a comprehensive model for recognizing, measuring, presenting and disclosing in the financial statements tax positions taken or expected to be taken on a tax return, including a decision whether to file or not to file in a particular jurisdiction. Under FIN 48, a tax benefit from an uncertain position may be recognized only if it is "more likely than not" that the position is sustainable based on its technical merits.

As a result of adopting FIN 48, the Company recorded a net liability of approximately $13.3 million for unrecognized tax benefits, which was accounted for as a reduction to the beginning balance of retained earnings as of February 4, 2007. As of January 31, 2009, the gross amount of unrecognized tax benefits was $41.1 million, of which $23.1 million would affect the effective tax rate if recognized. The gross amount of unrecognized tax benefits as of February 2, 2008 was $43.0 million, of which $25.2 million would affect the effective tax rate if recognized.

The following table summarizes the activity related to our unrecognized tax benefits:

	For the Year Ended January 31, 2009	For the Year Ended February 2, 2008
	(In thousands)	
Unrecognized tax benefits, beginning of year balance	$42,953	$39,311
Increases in tax positions of prior periods	205	2,562
Decreases in tax positions of prior periods	(1,705)	(5,026)
Increases in current period tax positions	4,221	8,057
Settlements	(4,529)	(1,764)
Lapse of statute of limitations	(30)	(187)
Translation adjustment	(35)	—
Unrecognized tax benefits, end of the year balance	$41,080	$42,953

Over the next twelve months the Company believes that it is reasonably possible that unrecognized tax benefits may decrease by approximately $18 million due to settlements, expiration of the statute of limitations or other changes in unrecognized tax benefits.

The Company and its subsidiaries file income tax returns in the U.S. federal jurisdiction and various state and foreign jurisdictions. The examination of the Company's U.S. federal income tax returns for tax years ended July 2003 to July 2005 were substantially completed in January 2008. The Internal Revenue Service ("IRS") examination has

AMERICAN EAGLE OUTFITTERS, INC.

NOTES TO CONSOLIDATED FINANCIAL STATEMENTS — (Continued)

been resolved except for one unagreed item, which is currently under review with IRS Appeals. The Company believes its reserves are adequate to cover the ultimate resolution of this unagreed item. An examination of the July 2006 and 2007 federal tax returns started in the first quarter of Fiscal 2008 and remains in process. The Company does not anticipate that any adjustments will result in a material change to its financial position or results of operations. All years prior to July 2003 are no longer subject to U.S. federal income tax examinations by tax authorities. With respect to state and local jurisdictions and countries outside of the United States, with limited exceptions, generally, the Company and its subsidiaries are no longer subject to income tax audits for tax years before 2002. Although the outcome of tax audits is always uncertain, the Company believes that adequate amounts of tax, interest and penalties have been provided for any adjustments that are expected to result from these years.

The Company has been certified to qualify for nonrefundable incentive tax credits in Kansas for additional expenditures related to the Ottawa, Kansas distribution center. As a result, the Company has a deferred tax asset related to Kansas tax credit carryforwards of $4.2 million (net of federal income taxes). These tax credits can be utilized to offset future Kansas income taxes and will expire in 10 years. The use of these tax credits is dependent upon the level of income tax paid to Kansas and our meeting certain requirements in future periods. Due to the contingencies related to the future use of these tax credits, we believe it is more likely than not that the full benefit of this asset will not be realized within the carryforward period. Thus, a valuation allowance of $3.8 million (net of federal income taxes) has been recorded as of January 31, 2009, of which $1.3 million was recorded in Fiscal 2008 and $2.5 million was recorded in Fiscal 2007. The Company may earn additional tax credits or change its assessment of the valuation allowance if certain employment and training requirements are met.

During Fiscal 2008, the Company recorded a valuation allowance against deferred tax assets arising from the other than temporary impairment of certain investment securities. As of January 31, 2009, the valuation allowance related to the other than temporary impairment of certain investment securities totaled $8.7 million. The Company has not recorded a valuation allowance on the temporary impairment of the investment securities recorded in Other Comprehensive Income. The Company believes this treatment is consistent with the Company's intent and ability to hold the debt securities to recovery.

The Company records accrued interest and penalties related to unrecognized tax benefits in income tax expense. Accrued interest and penalties related to unrecognized tax benefits included in the Consolidated Balance Sheet were $11.4 million and $11.2 million as of January 31, 2009 and February 2, 2008, respectively. During Fiscal 2008 and 2007, the Company recognized an immaterial amount of interest and penalties in the provision for income taxes.

A reconciliation between the statutory federal income tax rate and the effective tax rate from continuing operations follows:

	For the Years Ended		
	January 31, 2009	February 2, 2008	February 3, 2007
Federal income tax rate	35%	35%	35%
State income taxes, net of federal income tax effect	3	3	4
Valuation allowance on investment security impairment	3	—	—
Tax impact of tax advantaged income	(1)	(1)	(1)
	40%	37%	38%

13. Quarterly Financial Information — Unaudited

The sum of the quarterly EPS amounts may not equal the full year amount as the computations of the weighted average shares outstanding for each quarter and the full year are calculated independently.

AMERICAN EAGLE OUTFITTERS, INC.

NOTES TO CONSOLIDATED FINANCIAL STATEMENTS — (Continued)

	Fiscal 2008 Quarters Ended			
	May 3, 2008	August 2, 2008	November 1, 2008	January 31, 2009
	(In thousands, except per share amounts)			
Net sales	$640,302	$688,815	$754,036	$905,713
Gross profit	263,667	289,384	309,412	311,638
Net income	43,895	59,831	42,604	32,731
Income per common share — basic	0.21	0.29	0.21	0.16
Income per common share — diluted	0.21	0.29	0.21	0.16

	Fiscal 2007 Quarters Ended			
	May 5, 2007	August 4, 2007	November 3, 2007	February 2, 2008
	(In thousands, except per share amounts)			
Net sales	$612,386	$703,189	$744,443	$995,401
Gross profit	298,459	316,447	352,917	455,315
Net income	78,770	81,344	99,426	140,479
Income per common share — basic	0.36	0.37	0.46	0.67
Income per common share — diluted	0.35	0.37	0.45	0.66

14. Subsequent Event — Unaudited

Subsequent to Fiscal 2008, the Company received an additional 0.6 million preferred shares from the dissolution of the trusts that held the ARPS. Since the end of Fiscal 2008, the Company liquidated approximately 1.1 million shares of its preferred stock investments for approximately $5.8 million. As a result of this liquidation, as of March 25, 2009, the Company recorded an incremental loss of $1.9 million during the first quarter of Fiscal 2009. As of March 25, 2009, the Company held 0.2 million preferred shares.

Refer to Notes 3 and 4 to the Consolidated Financial Statements for additional information on our investment securities, including a description of the securities and a discussion of the uncertainties relating to their liquidity.

UNITED STATES
SECURITIES AND EXCHANGE COMMISSION
Washington, DC 20549

FORM 10-K

FOR ANNUAL AND TRANSITION REPORTS PURSUANT TO SECTIONS 13 OR 15(d) OF THE SECURITIES EXCHANGE ACT OF 1934

☒ **ANNUAL REPORT PURSUANT TO SECTION 13 OR 15(d) OF THE SECURITIES EXCHANGE ACT OF 1934**

For the fiscal year ended January 31, 2009

☐ **TRANSITION REPORT PURSUANT TO SECTION 13 OR 15(d) OF THE SECURITIES EXCHANGE ACT OF 1934**

For the transition period from to

Commission File No. 000-22754

URBAN OUTFITTERS, INC.
(Exact Name of Registrant as Specified in Its Charter)

Pennsylvania **(State or Other Jurisdiction of Incorporation or Organization)**	**23-2003332** **(I.R.S. Employer Identification No.)**
5000 South Broad Street, Philadelphia, PA **(Address of Principal Executive Offices)**	**19112-1495** **(Zip Code)**

Registrant's telephone number, including area code: (215) 454-5500

Securities registered pursuant to Section 12(b) of the Act:

Title of Each Class	Name of Exchange on Which Registered
Common Shares, $.0001 par value	The NASDAQ Global Select Market LLC

Securities registered pursuant to Section 12(g) of the Act: None

Indicate by checkmark if the registrant is a well-known seasoned issuer, as defined in Rule 405 of the Securities Act. Yes ☒ No ☐

Indicate by checkmark if the registrant is not required to file reports pursuant to Section 13 or Section 15(d) of the Act. Yes ☐ No ☒

Indicate by checkmark whether the registrant (1) has filed all reports required to be filed by Section 13 or 15(d) of the Securities Exchange Act of 1934 during the preceding 12 months (or for such shorter period that the registrant was required to file such reports), and (2) has been subject to such filing requirements for the past 90 days. Yes ☒ No ☐

Indicate by checkmark if disclosure of delinquent filers pursuant to Item 405 of Regulation S-K is not contained herein, and will not be contained, to the best of Registrant's knowledge, in definitive proxy or information statements incorporated by reference in Part III of this Form 10-K or any amendment to this Form 10-K. ☐

Indicate by checkmark whether the registrant is a large accelerated filer, an accelerated filer, a non-accelerated filer, or a smaller reporting company. See the definitions of "large accelerated filer," "accelerated filer" and "smaller reporting company" in Rule 12b-2 of the Exchange Act.

Large accelerated filer ☒ Accelerated filer ☐
Non-accelerated filer ☐ (Do not check if a smaller reporting company) Smaller reporting company ☐

Indicate by a checkmark whether the registrant is a shell company (as defined in Rule 12b-2 of the Act). Yes ☐ No ☒

The aggregate market value of the voting and non-voting common equity held by non-affiliates computed by reference to the price at which the common equity was last sold, or the average bid and asked price of such common equity, as of the last business day of the registrant's most recently completed second fiscal quarter, was $4,219,837,641.

The number of shares outstanding of the registrant's common stock on March 26, 2009 was 167,729,688.

DOCUMENTS INCORPORATED BY REFERENCE

Certain information required by Items 10, 11, 12, 13 and 14 is incorporated by reference into Part III hereof from portions of the Proxy Statement for the registrant's 2009 Annual Meeting of Shareholders.

REPORT OF INDEPENDENT REGISTERED PUBLIC ACCOUNTING FIRM

To the Board of Directors and Shareholders of
Urban Outfitters, Inc.
Philadelphia, Pennsylvania

We have audited the accompanying consolidated balance sheets of Urban Outfitters, Inc. and subsidiaries (the "Company") as of January 31, 2009 and 2008, and the related consolidated statements of income, shareholders' equity, and cash flows for each of the three years in the period ended January 31, 2009. These financial statements are the responsibility of the Company's management. Our responsibility is to express an opinion on these financial statements based on our audits.

We conducted our audits in accordance with the standards of the Public Company Accounting Oversight Board (United States). Those standards require that we plan and perform the audit to obtain reasonable assurance about whether the financial statements are free of material misstatement. An audit includes examining, on a test basis, evidence supporting the amounts and disclosures in the financial statements. An audit also includes assessing the accounting principles used and significant estimates made by management, as well as evaluating the overall financial statement presentation. We believe that our audits provide a reasonable basis for our opinion.

In our opinion, such consolidated financial statements present fairly, in all material respects, the financial position of Urban Outfitters, Inc. and subsidiaries as of January 31, 2009 and 2008, and the results of their operations and their cash flows for each of the three years in the period ended January 31, 2009, in conformity with accounting principles generally accepted in the United States of America.

We have also audited, in accordance with the standards of the Public Company Accounting Oversight Board (United States), the Company's internal control over financial reporting as of January 31, 2009, based on the criteria established in *Internal Control—Integrated Framework* issued by the Committee of Sponsoring Organizations of the Treadway Commission and our report dated March 31, 2009 expressed an unqualified opinion on the Company's internal control over financial reporting.

/s/ DELOITTE & TOUCHE LLP

Philadelphia, Pennsylvania
March 31, 2009

URBAN OUTFITTERS, INC.

Consolidated Balance Sheets
(in thousands, except share and per share data)

	January 31, 2009	January 31, 2008
ASSETS		
Current assets:		
Cash and cash equivalents	$ 316,035	$ 105,271
Marketable securities	49,948	80,127
Accounts receivable, net of allowance for doubtful accounts of $1,229 and $966, respectively	36,390	26,365
Inventories	169,698	171,925
Prepaid expenses and other current assets	46,412	46,238
Deferred taxes	5,919	3,684
Total current assets	624,402	433,610
Property and equipment, net	505,407	488,889
Marketable securities	155,226	188,252
Deferred income taxes and other assets	43,974	32,040
Total Assets	$1,329,009	$1,142,791
LIABILITIES AND SHAREHOLDERS' EQUITY		
Current liabilities:		
Accounts payable	$ 62,955	$ 74,020
Accrued compensation	11,975	10,128
Accrued expenses and other current liabilities	66,220	83,230
Total current liabilities	141,150	167,378
Deferred rent and other liabilities	134,084	121,982
Total Liabilities	275,234	289,360
Commitments and contingencies (see Note 11)		
Shareholders' equity:		
Preferred shares; $.0001 par value, 10,000,000 shares authorized, none issued	—	—
Common shares; $.0001 par value, 200,000,000 shares authorized, 167,712,088 and 166,104,615 issued and outstanding, respectively	17	17
Additional paid-in capital	170,166	144,204
Retained earnings	901,339	701,975
Accumulated other comprehensive (loss) income	(17,747)	7,235
Total Shareholders' Equity	1,053,775	853,431
Total Liabilities and Shareholders' Equity	$1,329,009	$1,142,791

The accompanying notes are an integral part of these consolidated financial statements.

URBAN OUTFITTERS, INC.

Consolidated Statements of Income
(in thousands, except share and per share data)

	Fiscal Year Ended January 31, 2009	2008	2007
Net sales	$ 1,834,618	$ 1,507,724	$ 1,224,717
Cost of sales, including certain buying, distribution and occupancy costs	1,121,140	930,952	772,796
Gross profit	713,478	576,772	451,921
Selling, general and administrative expenses	414,043	351,827	287,932
Income from operations	299,435	224,945	163,989
Interest income	11,504	9,390	6,531
Other income	694	575	353
Other expenses	(2,143)	(515)	(715)
Income before income taxes	309,490	234,395	170,158
Income tax expense	110,126	74,164	53,952
Net income	$ 199,364	$ 160,231	$ 116,206
Net income per common share:			
Basic	$ 1.20	$ 0.97	$ 0.71
Diluted	$ 1.17	$ 0.94	$ 0.69
Weighted average common shares outstanding:			
Basic	166,793,062	165,305,207	164,679,786
Diluted	170,860,605	169,640,585	168,652,005

The accompanying notes are an integral part of these consolidated financial statements.

URBAN OUTFITTERS, INC.
Consolidated Statements of Shareholders' Equity
(in thousands, except share data)

	Comprehensive Income	Common Shares Number of Shares	Common Shares Par Value	Additional Paid-in Capital	Unearned Compensation	Retained Earnings	Accumulated Other Comprehensive Income (Loss)	Total
Balances as of February 1, 2006		164,831,477	$ 16	$138,050	$(3,905)	$426,190	$ 528	$ 560,880
Net income	$116,206	—	—	—	—	116,206	—	116,206
Foreign currency translation	3,614	—	—	—	—	—	3,614	3,614
Unrealized gains on marketable securities, net of tax	142	—	—	—	—	—	142	142
Comprehensive income	$119,962							
Share-based compensation		—	—	3,497	—	—	—	3,497
Unearned compensation reclass		—	—	(3,905)	3,905	—	—	—
Exercise of stock options		1,375,986	1	6,350	—	—	—	6,351
Tax effect of share exercises		—	—	5,394	—	—	—	5,394
Share Repurchase		(1,220,000)	—	(20,801)	—	—	—	(20,801)
Balances as of January 31, 2007		164,987,463	17	128,586	—	542,396	4,284	675,283
Net income	$160,231	—	—	—	—	160,231	—	160,231
Foreign currency translation	703	—	—	—	—	—	703	703
FIN48 adjustment	—	—	—	—	—	(652)	—	(652)
Unrealized gains on marketable securities, net of tax	2,248	—	—	—	—	—	2,248	2,248
Comprehensive income	$163,182							
Share-based compensation		—	—	3,277	—	—	—	3,277
Exercise of stock options		1,117,152	—	5,000	—	—	—	5,000
Tax effect of share exercises		—	—	7,341	—	—	—	7,341
Balances as of January 31, 2008		166,104,615	17	144,204	—	701,975	7,235	853,431
Net income	$199,364	—	—	—	—	199,364	—	199,364
Foreign currency translation	(19,866)	—	—	—	—	—	(19,866)	(19,866)
Unrealized losses on marketable securities, net of tax	(5,116)	—	—	—	—	—	(5,116)	(5,116)
Comprehensive income	$174,382							
Share-based compensation		—	—	3,637	—	—	—	3,637
Exercise of stock options		1,607,473	—	8,891	—	—	—	8,891
Tax effect of share exercises		—	—	13,434	—	—	—	13,434
Balances as of January 31, 2009		167,712,088	$ 17	$170,166	$ —	$901,339	$(17,747)	$1,053,775

The accompanying notes are an integral part of these consolidated financial statements.

URBAN OUTFITTERS, INC.
Consolidated Statements of Cash Flows
(in thousands)

	Fiscal Year Ended January 31,		
	2009	2008	2007
Cash flows from operating activities:			
Net income	$ 199,364	$ 160,231	$ 116,206
Adjustments to reconcile net income to net cash provided by operating activities:			
Depreciation and amortization	81,949	70,017	55,713
Provision for deferred income taxes	(9,351)	(2,782)	(4,959)
Excess tax benefit of share–based compensation	(13,434)	(7,341)	(5,394)
Share-based compensation expense	3,637	3,277	3,497
Loss on disposition of property and equipment, net	61	317	1,393
Changes in assets and liabilities:			
Receivables	(10,726)	(5,462)	(6,371)
Inventories	(272)	(17,430)	(13,416)
Prepaid expenses and other assets	9,210	(22,441)	6,848
Accounts payable, accrued expenses and other liabilities	(8,868)	75,967	33,600
Net cash provided by operating activities	251,570	254,353	187,117
Cash flows from investing activities:			
Cash paid for property and equipment	(112,553)	(115,370)	(212,029)
Cash paid for marketable securities	(809,039)	(293,633)	(182,653)
Sales and maturities of marketable securities	864,685	220,101	193,274
Net cash used in investing activities	(56,907)	(188,902)	(201,408)
Cash flows from financing activities:			
Exercise of stock options	8,891	5,000	6,351
Excess tax benefit of stock option exercises	13,434	7,341	5,394
Share repurchases	—	—	(20,801)
Net cash provided by (used in) financing activities	22,325	12,341	(9,056)
Effect of exchange rate changes on cash and cash equivalents	(6,224)	212	702
Increase (decrease) in cash and cash equivalents	210,764	78,004	(22,645)
Cash and cash equivalents at beginning of period	105,271	27,267	49,912
Cash and cash equivalents at end of period	$ 316,035	$ 105,271	$ 27,267
Supplemental cash flow information:			
Cash paid during the year for:			
Income taxes	$ 115,040	$ 70,765	$ 52,535
Non-cash investing activities—Accrued capital expenditures	$ 6,561	$ 6,645	$ 14,618

The accompanying notes are an integral part of these consolidated financial statements.

URBAN OUTFITTERS, INC.

NOTES TO CONSOLIDATED FINANCIAL STATEMENTS
(in thousands, except share and per share data)

1. Nature of Business

Urban Outfitters, Inc. (the "Company" or "Urban Outfitters"), which was founded in 1970 and originally operated by a predecessor partnership, was incorporated in the Commonwealth of Pennsylvania in 1976. The principal business activity of the Company is the operation of a general consumer product retail and wholesale business selling to customers through various channels including retail stores, three catalogs and four web sites. As of January 31, 2009 and 2008, the Company operated 294 and 245 stores, respectively. Stores located in the United States totaled 270 as of January 31, 2009 and 229 as of January 31, 2008. Operations in Europe and Canada included 17 stores and 7 stores as of January 31, 2009, respectively and 12 stores and 4 stores as of January 31, 2008, respectively. In addition, the Company's wholesale segment sold and distributed apparel to approximately 1,800 better specialty retailers worldwide.

2. Summary of Significant Accounting Policies

Fiscal Year-End

The Company operates on a fiscal year ending January 31 of each year. All references to fiscal years of the Company refer to the fiscal years ended on January 31 in those years. For example, the Company's fiscal 2009 ended on January 31, 2009.

Principles of Consolidation

The consolidated financial statements include the accounts of Urban Outfitters, Inc. and its wholly owned subsidiaries. All inter-company transactions and accounts have been eliminated in consolidation.

Use of Estimates

The preparation of financial statements in conformity with accounting principles generally accepted in the United States requires management to make estimates and assumptions that affect the reported amounts of assets and liabilities and disclosure of contingent assets and liabilities at the date of the financial statements and the reported amounts of net sales and expenses during the reporting period. Actual results could differ from those estimates.

Cash and Cash Equivalents

Cash and cash equivalents are defined as cash and highly liquid investments with maturities of less than three months at the time of purchase. As of January 31, 2009 and 2008, cash and cash equivalents included cash on hand, cash in banks and money market accounts. A significant portion of the Company's cash held in money market accounts is insured under the Federal Government's Troubled Assets Relief Program ("TARP").

URBAN OUTFITTERS, INC.

NOTES TO CONSOLIDATED FINANCIAL STATEMENTS—(Continued)

Marketable Securities

The Company's marketable securities may be classified as either held-to-maturity or available-for-sale. Held-to-maturity securities represent those securities that the Company has both the intent and ability to hold to maturity and are carried at amortized cost. Interest on these securities, as well as amortization of discounts and premiums, is included in interest income. Available-for-sale securities represent debt securities that do not meet the classification of held-to-maturity, are not actively traded and are carried at fair value, which approximates amortized cost. Unrealized gains and losses on these securities are excluded from earnings and are reported as a separate component of shareholders' equity until realized. When available-for-sale securities are sold, the cost of the securities is specifically identified and is used to determine the realized gain or loss. Securities classified as current have maturity dates of less than one year from the balance sheet date. Securities classified as long-term have maturity dates greater than one year from the balance sheet date. Available for sale securities such as ARS that fail at auction and do not liquidate under normal course are classified as long term assets, any successful auctions would be classified as current assets. Marketable securities as of January 31, 2009 and 2008 were classified as available-for-sale.

Approximately 7% of the Company's cash, cash equivalents and marketable securities are invested in "A" or better rated Auction Rate Securities ("ARS") that represent interests in municipal and student loan related collateralized debt obligations, all of which are guaranteed by either government agencies and/or insured by private insurance agencies at 97% or greater of par value. The Company's ARS had a fair value of $38.7 million as of January 31, 2009 and $95.2 million as of January 31, 2008. As of and subsequent to the end of the current fiscal year, all of the ARS held by the Company failed to liquidate at auction due to a lack of market demand. Liquidity for these ARS is typically provided by an auction process that resets the applicable interest rate at pre-determined intervals, usually 7, 28, 35 or 90 days. The principal associated with these failed auctions will not be available until a successful auction occurs, the bond is called by the issuer, a buyer is found from outside the auction process, or the debt obligation reaches its maturity. Based on review of credit quality, collateralization, final stated maturity, estimates of the probability of being called or becoming illiquid prior to final maturity, redemptions of similar ARS, previous market activity for same investment security, impact due to extended periods of maximum auction rates and valuation models, the Company has recorded $5.3 million of temporary impairment on its ARS as of January 31, 2009. To date the Company has collected all interest receivable on outstanding ARS when due and have not been informed by the issuers that accrued interest payments are currently at risk. The Company has the ability to hold the investments until their maturity. As a result of the current illiquidity, the Company has classified all ARS as long term assets under marketable securities. The Company continues to monitor the market for ARS and consider the impact, if any, on the fair value of its investments.

The Company also includes disclosure about its investments that are in an unrealized loss position for which other-than-temporary impairments have not been recognized in accordance with the Emerging Issues Task Force ("EITF") Issue No. 03-01, "The Meaning of Other-Than-Temporary Impairment and its Applications to Certain Investments".

URBAN OUTFITTERS, INC.

NOTES TO CONSOLIDATED FINANCIAL STATEMENTS—(Continued)

Accounts Receivable

Accounts receivable primarily consists of amounts due from our wholesale customers as well as credit card receivables. The activity of the allowance for doubtful accounts for the years ended January 31, 2009, 2008 and 2007 is as follows:

	Balance at beginning of year	Additions	Deductions	Balance at end of year
Year ended January 31, 2009	$966	$4,375	$(4,112)	$1,229
Year ended January 31, 2008	$849	$2,628	$(2,511)	$ 966
Year ended January 31, 2007	$445	$2,192	$(1,788)	$ 849

Inventories

Inventories, which consist primarily of general consumer merchandise held for sale, are valued at the lower of cost or market. Cost is determined on the first-in, first-out method and includes the cost of merchandise and import related costs, including freight, import taxes and agent commissions. A periodic review of inventory quantities on hand is performed in order to determine if inventory is properly stated at the lower of cost or market. Factors related to current inventories such as future consumer demand and fashion trends, current aging, current and anticipated retail markdowns or wholesale discounts, and class or type of inventory are analyzed to determine estimated net realizable value. Criteria utilized by the Company to quantify aging trends include factors such as average selling cycle and seasonality of merchandise, the historical rate at which merchandise has sold below cost during the average selling cycle, and the value and nature of merchandise currently priced below original cost. A provision is recorded to reduce the cost of inventories to the estimated net realizable values, if appropriate. The majority of inventory at January 31, 2009 and 2008 consisted of finished goods. Unfinished goods and work-in-process were not material to the overall net inventory value.

Property and Equipment

Property and equipment are stated at cost and primarily consist of store related leasehold improvements, buildings and furniture and fixtures. Depreciation is typically computed using the straight-line method over five years for furniture and fixtures, the lesser of the lease term or useful life for leasehold improvements, three to ten years for other operating equipment and 39 years for buildings. Major renovations or improvements that extend the service lives of our assets are capitalized over the extension period or life of the improvement, whichever is less.

The Company reviews long-lived assets for possible impairment whenever events or changes in circumstances indicate the carrying amount may not be recoverable. This determination includes evaluation of factors such as future asset utilization and future net undiscounted cash flows expected to result from the use of the assets. Management believes there has been no impairment of the Company's long-lived assets as of January 31, 2009.

URBAN OUTFITTERS, INC.

NOTES TO CONSOLIDATED FINANCIAL STATEMENTS—(Continued)

Deferred Rent

Rent expense from leases is recorded on a straight-line basis over the lease period. The net excess of rent expense over the actual cash paid is recorded as deferred rent. In addition, certain store leases provide for contingent rentals when sales exceed specified break-point levels that are weighted based upon historical cyclicality. For leases where achievement of these levels is considered probable based on cumulative lease year revenue versus the established breakpoint at any given point in time, contingent rent is accrued. This is expensed in addition to minimum rent which is recorded on a straight-line basis over the lease period.

Operating Leases

The Company leases its retail stores under operating leases. Many of the lease agreements contain rent holidays, rent escalation clauses and contingent rent provisions or some combination of these items. The Company recognizes rent expense on a straight-line basis over the accounting lease term.

The Company records rent expense on a straight-line basis over the lease period commencing on the date that the premise is available from the landlord. The lease period includes the construction period to make the leased space suitable for operating during which time the Company is not permitted to occupy the space. For purposes of calculating straight-line rent expense, the commencement date of the lease term reflects the date the Company takes possession of the building for initial construction and setup.

The Company classifies tenant improvement allowances on its consolidated financial statements within deferred rent that will be amortized as a reduction of rent expense over the straight-line period. Tenant improvement allowance activity is presented as part of cash flows from operating activities in the accompanying consolidated statements of cash flows.

Revenue Recognition

Revenue is recognized at the point-of-sale for retail store sales or when merchandise is shipped to customers for wholesale and direct-to-consumer sales, net of estimated customer returns. Revenue is recognized at the completion of a job or service for landscape sales. Revenue is presented on a net basis and does not include any tax assessed by a governmental or municipal authority. Payment for merchandise at stores and through the Company's direct-to-consumer business is tendered by cash, check, credit card, debit card or gift card. Therefore, the Company's need to collect outstanding accounts receivable for its retail and direct-to-consumer business is negligible and mainly results from returned checks or unauthorized credit card transactions. The Company maintains an allowance for doubtful accounts for its wholesale and landscape service accounts receivable, which management reviews on a regular basis and believes is sufficient to cover potential credit losses and billing adjustments. Deposits for custom orders are recorded as a liability and recognized as a sale upon delivery of the merchandise to the customer. These custom orders, typically for upholstered furniture, are not material. Deposits for landscape services are recorded as a liability and recognized as a sale upon completion of service. Landscape services and related deposits are not material.

URBAN OUTFITTERS, INC.

NOTES TO CONSOLIDATED FINANCIAL STATEMENTS—(Continued)

The Company accounts for a gift card transaction by recording a liability at the time the gift card is issued to the customer in exchange for consideration from the customer. A liability is established and remains on the Company's books until the card is redeemed by the customer, at which time the Company records the redemption of the card for merchandise as a sale or when it is determined the likelihood of redemption is remote. The Company determines the probability of the gift cards being redeemed to be remote based on historical redemption patterns. Revenues attributable to gift card liabilities relieved after the likelihood of redemption becomes remote are included in sales and are not material. The Company's gift cards do not expire.

Sales Return Reserve

The Company records a reserve for estimated product returns where the sale has occurred during the period reported, but the return is likely to occur subsequent to the period reported and may otherwise be considered in-transit. The reserve for estimated in-transit product returns is based on the Company's most recent historical return trends. If the actual return rate or experience is materially higher than the Company's estimate, additional sales returns would be recorded in the future. The activity of the sales returns reserve for the years ended January 31, 2009, 2008 and 2007 is as follows:

	Balance at beginning of year	Additions	Deductions	Balance at end of year
Year ended January 31, 2009	$6,776	$28,408	$(27,637)	$7,547
Year ended January 31, 2008	$8,916	$35,952	$(38,092)	$6,776
Year ended January 31, 2007	$6,390	$29,376	$(26,850)	$8,916

Cost of Sales, Including Certain Buying, Distribution and Occupancy Costs

Cost of sales, including certain buying, distribution and occupancy costs includes the following: the cost of merchandise; merchandise markdowns; obsolescence and shrink; store occupancy costs including rent and depreciation; customer shipping expense for direct-to-consumer orders; in-bound and outbound freight; U.S. Customs related taxes and duties; inventory acquisition and purchasing costs; warehousing and handling costs and other inventory acquisition related costs.

Selling, General and Administrative Expenses

Selling, general and administrative expenses includes expenses such as (i) direct selling and selling supervisory expenses; (ii) various corporate expenses such as information systems, finance, loss prevention, talent acquisition, and executive management expenses; and (iii) other associated general expenses.

Shipping and Handling Fees and Costs

The Company includes shipping and handling revenues in net sales and shipping and handling costs in cost of sales. The Company's shipping and handling revenues consist of amounts billed to customers for shipping and handling merchandise. Shipping and handling costs include shipping supplies, related labor costs and third-party shipping costs.

URBAN OUTFITTERS, INC.

NOTES TO CONSOLIDATED FINANCIAL STATEMENTS—(Continued)

Advertising

The Company expenses the costs of advertising when the advertising occurs, except for direct-to-consumer advertising, which is capitalized and amortized over its expected period of future benefit. Advertising costs primarily relate to our direct-to-consumer marketing expenses which are composed of catalog printing, paper, postage and other costs related to production of photographic images used in our catalogs and on our web sites. These costs are amortized over the period in which the customer responds to the marketing material determined based on historical customer response trends to a similar season's advertisement. Amortization rates are reviewed on a regular basis during the fiscal year and may be adjusted if the predicted customer response appears materially different than the historical response rate. The Company has the ability to measure the response rate to direct marketing early in the course of the advertisement based on its customers' reference to a specific catalog or by product placed and sold. The average amortization period for a catalog or web promotion is typically three months. If there is no expected future benefit, the cost of advertising is expensed when incurred. Advertising costs reported as prepaid expenses were $2,585 and $2,496 as of January 31, 2009 and 2008, respectively. Advertising expenses were $45,561, $40,828 and $35,882 for fiscal 2009, 2008 and 2007, respectively.

Start-up Costs

The Company expenses all start-up and organization costs as incurred, including travel, training, recruiting, salaries and other operating costs.

Web Site Development Costs

The Company capitalizes applicable costs incurred during the application and infrastructure development stage and expenses costs incurred during the planning and operating stage. During fiscal 2009, 2008 and 2007, the Company did not capitalize any internal-use software development costs because substantially all costs were incurred during the planning stage, and costs incurred during the application and infrastructure development stage were not material.

Income Taxes

The Company applies Statement of Financial Accounting Standards ("SFAS") No. 109, "Accounting for Income Taxes," which principally utilizes a balance sheet approach to provide for income taxes. Under this method, deferred tax assets and liabilities are recognized for the expected future tax consequences of net operating loss carryforwards and temporary differences between the carrying amounts and the tax bases of assets and liabilities. The Company files a consolidated United States federal income tax return (see Note 8).

The Company adopted the provisions of FIN 48, "Accounting for Uncertainty in Income Taxes – an Interpretation of FASB Statement No. 109" on February 1, 2007. FIN 48 prescribes the recognition threshold and measurement attribute for the financial statement recognition and measurement of uncertain tax positions taken or expected to be taken in a tax return (see Note 8).

URBAN OUTFITTERS, INC.

NOTES TO CONSOLIDATED FINANCIAL STATEMENTS—(Continued)

Net Income Per Common Share

Basic net income per common share is computed by dividing net income available to common shareholders by the weighted average number of common shares outstanding. Diluted net income per common share is computed by dividing net income available to common shareholders by the weighted average number of common shares outstanding, after giving effect to the potential dilution from the exercise of securities, such as stock options and non-vested shares, into shares of common stock as if those securities were exercised (see Note 10).

Accounting for Stock-Based Compensation

Effective February 1, 2006, the Company adopted SFAS No. 123R, "Share Based Payment", ("SFAS 123R"), using the modified prospective approach. Under the modified prospective approach, the amount of compensation cost recognized includes: (i) compensation cost for all share-based payments granted before but not yet vested as of January 31, 2006, based on the grant date fair value estimated in accordance with the provisions of SFAS No. 123, and (ii) compensation cost for all share-based payments granted or modified subsequent to January 31, 2006, based on the estimated fair value at the date of grant or subsequent modification date in accordance with the provisions of SFAS 123R.

SFAS 123R also required the Company to change the classification in our consolidated statement of cash flows, of any income tax benefits realized upon the exercise of stock options or issuance of restricted share unit awards in excess of that which is associated with the expense recognized for financial reporting purposes. These amounts are presented as financing inflows in our consolidated statement of cash flows.

Prior to February 1, 2006 the Company accounted for our share-based compensation plans in accordance with the provisions of Accounting Principles Board Opinion No. 25, "Accounting for Stock Issued to Employees", as permitted by SFAS 123, and accordingly did not recognize compensation expense for stock options with an exercise price equal to or greater than the market price of the underlying stock at the date of the grant (see Note 9).

Accumulated Other Comprehensive Income

Comprehensive income is comprised of two subsets—net income and other comprehensive income. Amounts in accumulated other comprehensive income relate to foreign currency translation adjustments and unrealized gains or losses on marketable securities. The foreign currency translation adjustments are not adjusted for income taxes because these adjustments relate to indefinite investments in non-U.S. subsidiaries. As of January 31, 2009, accumulated other comprehensive income consisted of a foreign currency translation loss of $14,496. As of January 31, 2008, accumulated other comprehensive income consisted of a foreign currency translation gain of $5,370. As of January 31, 2009, other comprehensive income included an unrealized loss, net of tax, on marketable securities of $3,251 and as of January 31, 2008, an unrealized gain of $1,865, net of tax, on marketable securities. Gross realized gains are included in other income and were not material to the Company's financial statements for all three years presented.

URBAN OUTFITTERS, INC.

NOTES TO CONSOLIDATED FINANCIAL STATEMENTS—(Continued)

Foreign Currency Translation

The financial statements of the Company's foreign operations are translated into U.S. dollars. Assets and liabilities are translated at current exchange rates while income and expense accounts are translated at the average rates in effect during the year. Translation adjustments are not included in determining net income, but are included in accumulated other comprehensive income within shareholders' equity. As of January 31, 2009, 2008 and 2007, foreign currency translation adjustments resulted in a loss of $14,496, and gains of $5,370 and $4,667, respectively.

Fair Value of Financial Instruments

Effective February 1, 2008, the Company adopted the provisions of SFAS No. 157, "Fair Value Measurements" ("SFAS No. 157") that relate to its financial assets and financial liabilities as discussed in Note 4. SFAS No. 157 establishes a hierarchy that prioritizes fair value measurements based on the types of inputs used for the various valuation techniques (market approach, income approach and cost approach).

Management's assessment of the significance of a particular input to the fair value measurement requires judgment and may affect the valuation of financial assets and liabilities and their placement within the fair value hierarchy.

Concentration of Credit Risk

Financial instruments that potentially subject the Company to concentrations of credit risk consist principally of cash, cash equivalents, marketable securities and accounts receivable. The Company manages the credit risk associated with cash, cash equivalents and marketable securities by investing high-quality securities held with reputable trustees and, by policy, limiting the amount of credit exposure to any one issue. The Company's investment policy requires that the majority of its cash, cash equivalents and marketable securities are invested in federally insured or guaranteed investment vehicles such as; money market accounts up to applicable TARP limits, FDIC insured corporate bonds, federal government agencies and irrevocable pre-refunded municipal bonds. Receivables from third-party credit cards are processed by financial institutions, which are monitored for financial stability. The Company periodically evaluates the financial condition of its wholesale segment customers. The Company's allowance for doubtful accounts reflects current market conditions and management's assessment regarding the likelihood of collecting its accounts receivable. The Company maintains cash accounts that, at times, may exceed federally insured limits. The Company has not experienced any losses from maintaining cash accounts in excess of such limits. Management believes that it is not exposed to any significant risks related to its cash accounts.

URBAN OUTFITTERS, INC.

NOTES TO CONSOLIDATED FINANCIAL STATEMENTS—(Continued)

Recently Issued Accounting Pronouncements

In November 2007, the Financial Accounting Standards Board ("FASB") issued SFAS No. 141R "Business Combinations" ("SFAS No 141R"), which requires that all business combinations be accounted for by applying the acquisition method. Under the acquisition method, the acquirer recognizes and measures the identifiable assets acquired, the liabilities assumed, and any contingent consideration and contractual contingencies, as a whole at their fair value as of the acquisition date. Under SFAS No. 141R, all transaction costs are expensed as incurred. SFAS No. 141R rescinds EITF 93-7. Under EITF 93-7, the effect of any subsequent adjustments to uncertain tax positions were generally applied to goodwill, except for post-acquisition interest on uncertain tax positions, which was recognized as an adjustment to income tax expense. Under SFAS No. 141R, all subsequent adjustments to these uncertain tax positions that otherwise would have impacted goodwill will be recognized in the income statement. The guidance in SFAS No. 141R will be applied prospectively to business combinations for which the acquisition date is on or after the beginning of the first annual reporting period beginning after December 15, 2008. The Company does not expect the application of SFAS No. 141R to have a material impact on our consolidated financial statements.

In February 2007, the FASB issued SFAS No. 159, "The Fair Value Option for Financial Assets and Financial Liabilities: Including an Amendment of FASB Statement No. 115" ("SFAS No. 159"). SFAS No. 159 provides companies with an option to report selected financial assets and liabilities at fair value and requires entities to display the fair value of those assets and liabilities for which the Company has chosen to use fair value on the face of the balance sheet. SFAS No. 159 is effective for financial statements issued for fiscal years beginning after November 15, 2007. Effective February 1, 2008, the Company adopted SFAS No. 159 and has elected not to apply the provisions of SFAS No. 159 to report certain of its assets and liabilities at fair value.

In September 2006, the FASB issued SFAS No. 157, "Fair Value Measurements." SFAS No. 157 defines fair value, establishes a framework for measuring fair value in U.S. Generally Accepted Accounting Principles, and expands disclosures about fair value measurements. SFAS No. 157 is effective for financial assets and financial liabilities in fiscal years beginning after November 15, 2007 and for certain nonfinancial assets and certain nonfinancial liabilities in fiscal years beginning after November 15, 2008. Effective February 1, 2008, we have adopted the provisions of SFAS No. 157 that relate to our financial assets and financial liabilities (see Note 4). We are currently evaluating the impact of the provisions of SFAS No. 157 that relate to our nonfinancial assets and nonfinancial liabilities, which are effective for us as of February 1, 2009.

URBAN OUTFITTERS, INC.

NOTES TO CONSOLIDATED FINANCIAL STATEMENTS—(Continued)

3. Marketable Securities

During all periods shown, marketable securities are classified as available-for-sale. The amortized cost, gross unrealized gains (losses) and fair values of available-for-sale securities by major security type and class of security as of January 31, 2009 and 2008 are as follows:

	Amortized Cost	Unrealized Gains	Unrealized (Losses)	Fair Value
As of January 31, 2009				
Short-term Investments:				
Municipal bonds	$ 15,814	$ 123	$ —	$ 15,937
Mutual funds	5,046	—	—	5,046
Federal government agencies	24,975	—	—	24,975
Demand notes and equities	4,840	2	(852)	3,990
	50,675	125	(852)	49,948
Long-term Investments:				
Municipal bonds	76,517	1,239	(10)	77,746
Auction rate instruments (1)	44,025	—	(5,283)	38,742
Federal government agencies	25,640	—	(141)	25,499
FDIC insured corporate bonds	13,318	—	(79)	13,239
	159,500	1,239	(5,513)	155,226
	$210,175	$1,364	$(6,365)	$205,174
As of January 31, 2008				
Short-term Investments:				
Municipal bonds	$ 24,675	$ 142	$ —	$ 24,817
Auction rate instruments	33,825	—	—	33,825
Demand notes	21,485	—	—	21,485
	79,985	142	—	80,127
Long-term Investments:				
Municipal bonds	124,148	2,729	—	126,877
Auction rate instruments (1)	61,375	—	—	61,375
	185,523	2,729	—	188,252
	$265,508	$2,871	—	$268,379

(1) ARS have been classified as long-term assets in marketable securities in the Company's Consolidated Balance Sheet as of January 31, 2009 and 2008 due to ARS failures.

Proceeds from the sale and maturities of available-for-sale securities were $864,685, $220,101 and $193,274 in fiscal 2009, 2008 and 2007, respectively. The Company included in other income, a net realized loss of $896 during fiscal 2009, a net realized gain of $1 during fiscal 2008 and a net realized loss of $8 during fiscal 2007. Amortization of discounts and premiums, net, resulted in charges of $2,444, $1,734 and $1,818 for fiscal years 2009, 2008, and 2007, respectively.

URBAN OUTFITTERS, INC.

NOTES TO CONSOLIDATED FINANCIAL STATEMENTS—(Continued)

As of January 31, 2009, there were a total of 50 issued securities with unrealized loss positions within the Company's portfolio with a total unrealized loss position of $6,365. The total unrealized loss position due to write-downs of ARS held by the Company that have experienced auction failures was $5,283. The Company deemed all of these securities as temporarily impaired. The unrealized loss positions were primarily due to auction failures of the ARS held and fluctuations in the market interest rates for remaining securities. The Company believes it has the ability to realize the full value of all of these investments upon maturity or redemption. At January 31, 2008, there were no issued securities with an unrealized loss position within the Company's portfolio.

As of January 31, 2009, the par value of our ARS was $44,025 and the estimated fair value was $38,742. Our ARS portfolio consists of "A" or better rated ARS that represent interests in municipal and student loan related collateralized debt obligations, all of which are guaranteed by either government agencies and/or insured by private insurance agencies at 97% or greater of par value. To date, we have collected all interest payable on outstanding ARS when due and have not been informed by the issuers that accrued interest payments are currently at risk. We have the ability to hold the underlying securities until their maturity.

4. Fair Value of Financial Assets and Financial Liabilities

Effective February 1, 2008, the Company adopted the provisions of SFAS No. 157 that relate to its financial assets and financial liabilities. SFAS No. 157 establishes a hierarchy that prioritizes fair value measurements based on the types of inputs used for the various valuation techniques (market approach, income approach and cost approach). The levels of the hierarchy are described as follows:

- Level 1: Observable inputs such as quoted prices in active markets for identical assets or liabilities.
- Level 2: Inputs other than quoted prices that are observable for the asset or liability, either directly or indirectly; these include quoted prices for similar assets or liabilities in active markets and quoted prices for identical or similar assets or liabilities in markets that are not active.
- Level 3: Unobservable inputs that reflect the reporting entity's own assumptions.

URBAN OUTFITTERS, INC.

NOTES TO CONSOLIDATED FINANCIAL STATEMENTS—(Continued)

Management's assessment of the significance of a particular input to the fair value measurement requires judgment and may affect the valuation of financial assets and liabilities and their placement within the fair value hierarchy. The Company's financial assets that are accounted for at fair value on a recurring basis are presented in the table below:

	Marketable Securities Fair Value as of January 31, 2009			
	Level 1	Level 2	Level 3	Total
Assets:				
Municipal bonds	$ —	$93,683	$ —	$ 93,683
Mutual funds	5,046	—	—	5,046
Auction rate securities	—	—	38,742	38,742
Federal government agencies	50,474	—	—	50,474
FDIC insured corporate bonds	13,239	—	—	13,239
Demand notes and equities	988	3,002	—	3,990
	$69,747	$96,685	$38,742	$205,174

Level 1 assets consist of financial instruments whose value has been based on quoted market prices for identical financial instruments in an active market.

Level 2 assets consist of financial instruments whose value has been based on quoted prices for similar assets and liabilities in active markets as well as quoted prices for identical or similar assets or liabilities in markets that are not active.

Level 3 consists of financial instruments where there was no active market as of January 31, 2009. As of January 31, 2009 all of the Company's level 3 financial instruments consisted of failed ARS of which there was insufficient observable market information to determine fair value. The Company estimated the fair values for these securities by incorporating assumptions that market participants would use in their estimates of fair value. Some of these assumptions included credit quality, collateralization, final stated maturity, estimates of the probability of being called or becoming liquid prior to final maturity, redemptions of similar ARS, previous market activity for the same investment security, impact due to extended periods of maximum auction rates and valuation models. As a result of this review, the Company determined its ARS to have a temporary impairment of $5,283 as of January 31, 2009. The estimated fair values could change significantly based on future market conditions. The Company will continue to assess the fair value of its ARS for substantive changes in relevant market conditions, changes in its financial condition or other changes that may alter its estimates described above. Failed ARS represent approximately 7.4% of the Company's total cash, cash equivalents and marketable securities.

URBAN OUTFITTERS, INC.

NOTES TO CONSOLIDATED FINANCIAL STATEMENTS—(Continued)

Below is a reconciliation of the beginning and ending ARS securities balances that the Company valued using a Level 3 valuation for the fiscal year ended January 31, 2009.

	Fiscal Year Ended January 31, 2009
Balance at beginning of period	$ 61,375
Total (losses) realized/unrealized:	
Included in earnings	(2,880)
Included in other comprehensive income	(5,283)
Purchases, issuances and settlements	(17,350)
Transfers in and/or out of Level 3	2,880
Ending Balance as of January 31, 2009	$ 38,742
Total (losses) for the period included in other comprehensive income attributable to the change in unrealized (losses) related to assets still held at reporting date	$ (5,283)

5. Property and Equipment

Property and equipment is summarized as follows:

	January 31, 2009	January 31, 2008
Land	$ 543	$ 543
Buildings	96,205	94,547
Furniture and fixtures	214,178	184,910
Leasehold improvements	486,959	432,831
Other operating equipment	48,021	38,433
Construction-in-progress	15,458	19,796
	861,364	771,060
Accumulated depreciation	(355,957)	(282,171)
Total	$ 505,407	$ 488,889

Depreciation expense for property and equipment for fiscal years ended 2009, 2008 and 2007 was \$79,505, \$68,282 and \$53,895, respectively.

URBAN OUTFITTERS, INC.

NOTES TO CONSOLIDATED FINANCIAL STATEMENTS—(Continued)

6. Accrued Expenses and Other Current Liabilities

Accrued expenses and other current liabilities consist of the following:

	January 31,	
	2009	2008
Accrued rents and estimated property taxes	$10,074	$ 8,707
Gift certificates and merchandise credits	22,307	19,518
Accrued construction	6,261	6,629
Accrued income taxes	301	20,569
Accrued sales taxes	5,174	4,024
Sales return reserve	7,547	6,018
Other current liabilities	14,556	17,765
Total	$66,220	$83,230

7. Line of Credit Facility

On December 11, 2007, the Company renewed and amended its line of credit facility with Wachovia Bank, National Association (the "Line"). The Line is a three-year revolving credit facility with an accordion feature allowing an increase in available credit up to $100 million at the Company's discretion, subject to a seven day request period. As of January 31, 2009, the credit limit under the Line was $60 million. The Line contains a sub-limit for borrowings by the Company's European subsidiaries that are guaranteed by the Company. Cash advances bear interest at LIBOR plus 0.50% to 1.60% based on the Company's achievement of prescribed adjusted debt ratios. The Line subjects the Company to various restrictive covenants, including maintenance of certain financial ratios and covenants such as fixed charge coverage and adjusted debt. The covenants also include limitations on the Company's capital expenditures, ability to repurchase shares and the payment of cash dividends. As of January 31, 2009, there were no borrowings under the Line. Outstanding letters of credit and stand-by letters of credit under the Line totaled approximately $35,139 as of January 31, 2009. The available credit, including the accordion feature under the Line was $64,861 as of January 31, 2009. The Company believes the renewed Line will satisfy its letter of credit needs through fiscal 2011. Wachovia Bank, National Association was acquired by Wells Fargo, effective January 1, 2009. The Wells Fargo acquisition does not affect the original line agreement.

URBAN OUTFITTERS, INC.

NOTES TO CONSOLIDATED FINANCIAL STATEMENTS—(Continued)

8. Income Taxes

The components of income before income taxes are as follows:

	Fiscal Year Ended January 31,		
	2009	2008	2007
Domestic	$297,747	$229,600	$161,985
Foreign	11,743	4,795	8,173
	$309,490	$234,395	$170,158

The components of the provision for income tax expense are as follows:

	Fiscal Year Ended January 31,		
	2009	2008	2007
Current:			
Federal	$103,907	$66,000	$48,893
State	15,037	9,936	8,442
Foreign	533	1,010	1,576
	119,477	76,946	58,911
Deferred:			
Federal	(7,917)	(2,189)	6
State	(462)	(2,499)	(2,333)
Foreign	(1,128)	891	284
	(9,507)	(3,797)	(2,043)
Change in valuation allowances	156	1,015	(2,916)
	$110,126	$74,164	$53,952

The Company's effective tax rate was different than the statutory U.S. federal income tax rate for the following reasons:

	Fiscal Year Ended January 31,		
	2009	2008	2007
Expected provision at statutory U.S. federal tax rate	35.0%	35.0%	35.0%
State and local income taxes, net of federal tax benefit	2.6	2.1	2.3
Foreign taxes	(1.5)	0.5	(2.3)
Federal rehabilitation tax credits	0	(5.0)	(2.8)
Other	(0.5)	(1.0)	(0.5)
Effective tax rate	35.6%	31.6%	31.7%

URBAN OUTFITTERS, INC.

NOTES TO CONSOLIDATED FINANCIAL STATEMENTS—(Continued)

The significant components of deferred tax assets and liabilities as of January 31, 2009 and 2008 are as follows:

	January 31, 2009	January 31, 2008
Deferred tax liabilities:		
Prepaid expenses	$ (1,407)	$ (1,977)
Depreciation	(17,762)	(17,399)
Gross deferred tax liabilities	(19,169)	(19,376)
Deferred tax assets:		
Deferred rent	47,945	42,620
Inventories	5,582	4,176
Accounts receivable	626	563
Net operating loss carryforwards	2,760	1,666
FIN 48	4,368	4,090
Accrued salaries and benefits, and other	5,586	2,553
Gross deferred tax assets, before valuation allowances	66,867	55,668
Valuation allowances	(1,402)	(1,246)
Net deferred tax assets	$ 46,296	$ 35,046

Net deferred tax assets are attributed to the jurisdictions in which the Company operates. As of January 31, 2009 and 2008, respectively, $32,923 and $23,187 were attributable to U.S. federal, $11,392 and $10,815 were attributed to state jurisdictions and $1,981 and $1,044 were attributed to foreign jurisdictions.

As of January 31, 2009, certain non-U.S. subsidiaries of the Company had net operating loss carryforwards for tax purposes of approximately $7,942 that do not expire and certain U.S. subsidiaries of the Company had state net operating loss carryforwards for tax purposes of approximately $5,462 that expire from 2014 through 2029. At January 31, 2009, The Company had a full valuation allowance for certain foreign net operating loss carryforwards where it was uncertain the carryforwards would be utilized. The Company had no valuation allowance for certain other foreign net operating loss carryforwards where management believes it is more likely than not the tax benefit of these carryforwards will be realized. As of January 31, 2009 and 2008, the non-current portion of net deferred tax assets aggregated $40,378 and $31,362, respectively.

The cumulative amount of the Company's share of undistributed earnings of non-U.S. subsidiaries for which no deferred taxes have been provided was $53,553 as of January 31, 2009. These earnings are deemed to be permanently re-invested to finance growth programs.

URBAN OUTFITTERS, INC.

NOTES TO CONSOLIDATED FINANCIAL STATEMENTS—(Continued)

A reconciliation of the beginning and ending balances of the total amounts of gross unrecognized tax benefits is as follows:

	January 31, 2009	January 31, 2008
Balance at the beginning of the period	$7,805	$ 8,717
Increases in tax positions for prior years	24	227
Decreases in tax positions for prior years	(380)	(1,414)
Increases in tax positions for current year	838	917
Settlements	(554)	(345)
Lapse in statute of limitations	(224)	(297)
Balance at the end of the period	$7,509	$ 7,805

The total amount of net unrecognized tax benefits that, if recognized, would impact the Company's effective tax rate were $6,389 and $6,036 at January 31, 2009 and 2008 respectively. The Company accrues interest and penalties related to unrecognized tax benefits in income tax expense in the Consolidated Statements of Income, which is consistent with the recognition of these items in prior reporting periods. During the years ended January 31, 2009 and 2008, the Company recognized $985 and $465 in interest and penalties. The Company had $3,609 and $2,625 for the payment of interest and penalty accrued at January 31, 2009 and 2008, respectively.

The Company files income tax returns in the U.S. federal jurisdiction and various state and foreign jurisdictions. The Company is currently under examination of its federal income tax return for the period ended January 31, 2005. The Company is not subject to U.S. federal tax examinations for years before fiscal 2004. State jurisdictions that remain subject to examination range from fiscal 2001 to 2008, with few exceptions. It is possible that these examinations may be resolved within twelve months. Due to the potential for resolution of Federal and state examinations, and the expiration of various statutes of limitation, it is reasonably possible that the Company's gross unrecognized tax benefits balance may change within the next twelve months by a range of zero to $2,096.

9. Share-Based Compensation

The Company's 2008, 2004 and 2000 Stock Incentive Plans each authorize up to 10,000,000 common shares, which can be granted as restricted shares, unrestricted shares, incentive stock options, nonqualified stock options, performance shares or as stock appreciation rights. Grants under these plans generally expire seven or ten years from the date of grant, thirty days after termination, or six months after the date of death or termination due to disability. Stock options generally vest over a period of three or five years, with options becoming exercisable in installments determined by the administrator over the vesting period. However, options granted to non-employee directors generally vest over a period of one year. The Company's 1997 Stock Option Plan (the "1997 Plan"), which replaced the previous 1987, 1992 and 1993 Stock Option Plans (the "Superseded Plans"), expired during the year ended January 31, 2004. Individual grants outstanding under the 1997 Plan and certain of the Superseded Plans have expiration dates, which extend into the year 2010. Grants under the 1997

URBAN OUTFITTERS, INC.

NOTES TO CONSOLIDATED FINANCIAL STATEMENTS—(Continued)

Plan and the Superseded Plans generally expire ten years from the date of grant, thirty days after termination, or six months after the date of death or termination due to disability. Stock options generally vest over a five year period, with options becoming exercisable in equal installments of twenty percent per year. As of January 31, 2009 there were 10,000,000, 1,194,700 and 24,450 common shares available for grant under the 2008, 2004 and 2000 Stock Incentive Plans, respectively.

Under the provisions of SFAS No. 123R, the Company recorded $2,481, $2,124 and $2,344 of stock compensation related to stock option awards as well as related tax benefits of $851, $644 and $499 in the Company's Consolidated Statements of Income for the fiscal years ended January 31, 2009, 2008 and 2007, respectively or less than $0.01 for both basic and diluted earnings per share. During fiscal 2009, the Company granted 1,235,800 stock options. The estimated fair value of the grants was calculated using a Lattice Binomial option pricing model for the options granted during the fiscal year ended January 31, 2009. For stock options granted during the fiscal year ended January 31, 2008, the fair value of these grants was calculated using the Black Scholes option pricing model. Both the Lattice Binomial and Black Scholes option pricing models incorporate certain economic assumptions to value these stock-based awards. The prevailing difference between the two models is the Lattice Binomial model's ability to enhance the simple assumptions that underlie the Black Scholes model. The Lattice Binomial model allows for assumptions such as the risk-free rate of interest, volatility and exercise rate to vary over time reflecting a more realistic pattern of economic and behavioral occurrences. The Company uses historical data on exercise timing to determine the expected life assumption. The decrease in the expected life in fiscal year 2009 is due to the fact that the majority of the grants issued in fiscal 2009 expire in seven years. The risk-free rate of interest for periods within the contractual life of the option is based on U.S. Government Securities Treasury Constant Maturities over the expected term of the equity instrument. In the current fiscal year, utilizing the Lattice Binomial option pricing model, the expected volatility is based on a weighted average of the implied volatility and the Company's most recent historical volatility. In previous fiscal years under the Black Scholes option pricing model, the expected volatility was based on the historical volatility of the Company's stock. The table below outlines the weighted average assumptions for these grants:

	Fiscal 2009	Fiscal 2008	Fiscal 2007
Expected life, in years	4.3	6.2	6.8
Risk-free interest rate	2.5%	4.5%	4.8%
Volatility	41.4%	49.8%	54.4%
Dividend rate	—	—	—

Based on the Company's historical experience, the Company has assumed an annualized forfeiture rate of 2% for its unvested options. Under the true-up provisions of SFAS No. 123R, the Company will record additional expense if the actual forfeiture rate is lower than it estimated, and will record a recovery of prior expense if the actual forfeiture is higher than estimated.

Total compensation cost of stock options granted but not yet vested, as of January 31, 2009, was $11,627, which is expected to be recognized over the weighted average period of 2.71 years.

URBAN OUTFITTERS, INC.

NOTES TO CONSOLIDATED FINANCIAL STATEMENTS—(Continued)

The following tables summarize activity under all stock option plans for the respective periods:

	Fiscal Year Ended January 31, 2009	2008	2007
	(In thousands, except per share data)		
Weighted-average fair value of options granted per share	$ 10.56	$ 12.76	$ 11.62
Intrinsic value of options exercised	$41,622	$23,610	$20,822
Cash received from option exercises	$ 8,891	$ 5,000	$ 6,351
Actual tax benefit realized for tax deductions from option exercises	$13,434	$ 7,341	$ 5,394

Information regarding options under these plans is as follows:

	Fiscal Year Ended January 31, 2009			
	Shares	Weighted Average Exercise Price	Weighted Average Remaining Contractual Term (years)	Aggregate Intrinsic Value (1)
Options outstanding at beginning of year	11,568,723	$16.04		
Options granted	1,235,800	36.12		
Options exercised	(1,607,473)	5.53		
Options forfeited	(62,300)	24.48		
Options expired	(80,500)	29.78		
Options outstanding at end of year	11,054,250	19.64	5.5	$217,119
Options outstanding expected to vest	10,833,165	19.64	5.5	$212,777
Options exercisable at end of year	9,698,950	17.53	5.3	$170,010
Weighted average fair value of options granted per share	$ 10.56			

URBAN OUTFITTERS, INC.

NOTES TO CONSOLIDATED FINANCIAL STATEMENTS—(Continued)

The following table summarizes information concerning currently outstanding and exercisable options as of January 31, 2009:

	Options Outstanding			Options Exercisable	
Range of Exercise Prices	Amount Outstanding	Wtd. Avg. Remaining Contractual Life	Wtd. Avg. Exercise Price	Amount Exercisable	Wtd. Avg. Exercise Price
\$ 0.00 - \$ 3.75	1,280,450	2.2	\$ 1.76	1,280,450	\$ 1.76
\$ 3.76 - \$ 7.50	1,513,050	4.2	4.46	1,513,050	4.46
\$ 7.51 - \$11.25	208,000	2.9	9.21	208,000	9.21
\$11.26 - \$15.00	2,548,700	5.4	14.26	2,536,700	14.27
\$15.01 - \$18.76	195,000	5.7	15.60	160,000	15.38
\$18.77 - \$22.51	146,500	7.7	20.22	80,000	19.77
\$22.52 - \$26.26	371,000	6.7	24.20	320,000	24.19
\$22.27 - \$30.01	308,000	6.5	28.15	298,000	28.11
\$30.02 - \$33.76 (1)	3,394,250	6.9	31.09	3,302,750	31.11
\$33.77 - \$37.51	1,089,300	6.6	37.33	—	—
	11,054,250	5.5	19.64	9,698,950	17.53

(1) Options included in this range contain certain restrictions on the sale of the stock which expire in November 2010.

Non-vested Shares

The Company may make non-vested share awards to employees, non-employee directors and consultants. A non-vested share award is an award of common shares that is subject to certain restrictions during a specified period, such as an employee's continued employment combined with the Company achieving certain financial goals. The Company holds the common shares during the restriction period, and the grantee cannot transfer the shares before the termination of that period. The grantee is, however, generally entitled to vote the common shares and receive any dividends declared and paid on the Company's common shares during the restriction period.

Restricted Shares

During the fiscal year ended January 31, 2005, the Company granted 400,000 shares of restricted common stock with a grant date fair value of \$5,766 or \$14.42 per share. Share-based compensation expense of \$1,156, \$1,153 and \$1,153 is included in the accompanying Consolidated Statements of Income for each fiscal year ended January 31, 2009, 2008 and 2007, respectively. Total unrecognized compensation expense of non-vested, non-performance shares granted, as of January 31, 2009 was \$442, which is expected to be recognized over the period of 0.4 years. As of January 31, 2009 this was the only grant of non-vested, non-performance shares.

URBAN OUTFITTERS, INC.

NOTES TO CONSOLIDATED FINANCIAL STATEMENTS—(Continued)

Performance Shares

On April 28, 2008, the Company granted two awards of 30,184 Performance Stock Units ("PSU's"). These PSU's are subject to a vesting period of two years for the first grant ("Grant A"), and three years for the second grant ("Grant B"). Each PSU grant is subject to various performance criteria. If any of these criteria are not met, the grants are forfeited. Each PSU is equal to one share of common stock with a total award value not to exceed 30% appreciation. Grant A had a grant date fair value of $21.55 per share and Grant B had a grant date fair value of $19.47 per share, with both grants having a total grant date fair value of $1,238. The grant date fair value was calculated using a Lattice Binomial Model. In accordance with FAS 123R, there was no compensation expense recognized in the Company's Consolidated Statements of Income during the year ended January 31, 2009 because vesting was deemed highly improbable due to the unlikely achievement of the performance criteria governing the grant. The performance criteria achievement is re-measured at each reporting period, and if it is deemed likely that the performance targets will be achieved, any unrecognized compensation expense will be recognized prospectively as of the end of the then current reporting.

10. Net Income Per Common Share

The following is a reconciliation of the weighted average shares outstanding used for the computation of basic and diluted net income per common share:

	Fiscal Year Ended January 31,		
	2009	2008	2007
Basic weighted average shares outstanding	166,793,062	165,305,207	164,679,786
Effect of dilutive options and restricted stock	4,067,543	4,335,378	3,972,219
Diluted weighted average shares outstanding	170,860,605	169,640,585	168,652,005

For the fiscal years ended January 31, 2009, 2008 and 2007, options to purchase 3,351,338 shares ranging in price from $16.58 to $37.51, options to purchase 4,063,875 shares ranging in price from $22.11 to $31.11 and options to purchase 4,763,375 shares ranging in price from $15.48 to $31.11, were excluded from the calculation of diluted net income per common share for the respective fiscal years because the effect was anti-dilutive.

URBAN OUTFITTERS, INC.

NOTES TO CONSOLIDATED FINANCIAL STATEMENTS—(Continued)

11. Commitments and Contingencies

Leases

The Company leases its stores under non-cancelable operating leases. The following is a schedule by year of the future minimum lease payments for operating leases with original terms in excess of one year:

Fiscal Year	
2010	$ 132,497
2011	133,527
2012	132,021
2013	127,000
2014	121,079
Thereafter	440,062
Total minimum lease payments	$1,086,186

Amounts noted above include commitments for 34 executed leases for stores not opened as of January 31, 2009. The majority of our leases allow for renewal options between five and ten years upon expiration of the initial lease term. The store leases generally provide for payment of direct operating costs including real estate taxes. Certain store leases provide for contingent rentals when sales exceed specified levels. Additionally, the Company has entered into store leases that require a percentage of total sales to be paid to landlords in lieu of minimum rent.

Rent expense consisted of the following:

	Fiscal Year Ended January 31,		
	2009	2008	2007
Minimum and percentage rentals	$112,907	$100,020	$73,058
Contingent rentals	1,993	3,282	1,991
Total	$114,900	$103,302	$75,049

The Company also has commitments for un-fulfilled purchase orders for merchandise ordered from our vendors in the normal course of business, which are liquidated within 12 months, of $302,961. The majority of the Company's merchandise commitments are cancellable with no or limited recourse available to the vendor until merchandise shipping date. The Company also has commitments related to contracts with store construction contractors, fully liquidated upon the completion of construction, which is typically within 12 months, of $1,684.

URBAN OUTFITTERS, INC.
NOTES TO CONSOLIDATED FINANCIAL STATEMENTS—(Continued)

Benefit Plan

Full and part-time U.S. based employees who are at least 18 years of age are eligible after six months of employment to participate in the Urban Outfitters 401(k) Savings Plan (the "Plan"). Under the Plan, employees can defer 1% to 25% of compensation as defined. The Company makes matching contributions in cash of $0.25 per employee contribution dollar on the first 6% of the employee contribution. The employees' contribution is 100% vested while the Company's matching contribution vests at 20% per year of employee service. The Company's contributions were $1,090, $969 and $812 for fiscal years 2009, 2008 and 2007, respectively.

Contingencies

The Company is party to various legal proceedings arising from normal business activities. Management believes that the ultimate resolution of these matters will not have a material adverse effect on the Company's financial position, results of operations or cash flows.

12. Related Party Transactions

Harry S. Cherken, Jr., a director of the Company, is a partner in the law firm of Drinker Biddle & Reath LLP ("DBR"), which provides general legal services to the Company. Fees paid to DBR during fiscal 2009, 2008 and 2007 were $2,670, $3,662 and $1,493, respectively. Fees due to DBR as of January 31, 2009 and January 31, 2008 for services rendered were approximately $442 and $556, respectively.

The McDevitt Company, a real estate company, acted as a broker in substantially all of the Company's new real estate transactions during fiscal 2009, 2008 and 2007. The Company has not paid any compensation to The McDevitt Company, but the Company has been advised that The McDevitt Company has received commissions from other parties to such transactions. Wade L. McDevitt is the president and the sole shareholder of The McDevitt Company and brother-in-law of Scott Belair, one of the Company's directors. There were no amounts due to The McDevitt Company as of January 31, 2009 and January 31, 2008.

The Addis Group ("Addis"), an insurance brokerage company, acted as the Company's commercial insurance broker for the years ended January 31, 2009, 2008 and 2007. The Company has not paid any compensation to Addis for such services, but has been advised that Addis has received commissions from other parties to such transactions, to serve as risk manager under one line of coverage. Scott Addis is the President of The Addis Group and the brother-in-law of Richard A. Hayne, Chairman of the Board of the Company. There were no amounts due to or from Addis as of January 31, 2009 and January 31, 2008.

URBAN OUTFITTERS, INC.

NOTES TO CONSOLIDATED FINANCIAL STATEMENTS—(Continued)

13. Segment Reporting

The Company is a national retailer of lifestyle-oriented general merchandise with two reporting segments—"Retail" and "Wholesale". The Company's Retail segment consists of the aggregation of its four brands operating through 294 stores under the retail names "Urban Outfitters," "Anthropologie," "Free People" and "Terrain" and includes their direct marketing campaigns which consist of three catalogs and four web sites as of January 31, 2009. Our Retail stores and their direct marketing campaigns are considered operating segments. Net sales from the Retail segment accounted for more than 93% of total consolidated net sales for the years ended January 31, 2009, 2008 and 2007. The remainder is derived from the Company's Wholesale segment that manufactures and distributes apparel to the retail segment and to approximately 1,800 better specialty retailers worldwide.

The Company has aggregated its retail stores and associated direct marketing campaigns into a Retail segment based upon their unique management, customer base and economic characteristics. Reporting in this format provides management with the financial information necessary to evaluate the success of the segments and the overall business. The Company evaluates the performance of the segments based on the net sales and pre-tax income from operations (excluding inter-company charges) of the segment. Corporate expenses include expenses incurred and directed by the corporate office that are not allocated to segments. The principal identifiable assets for each operating segment are inventories and property and equipment. Other assets are comprised primarily of general corporate assets, which principally consist of cash and cash equivalents, marketable securities, and other assets, and which are typically not allocated to the Company's segments. The Company accounts for inter-segment sales and transfers as if the sales and transfers were made to third parties making similar volume purchases.

URBAN OUTFITTERS, INC.

NOTES TO CONSOLIDATED FINANCIAL STATEMENTS—(Continued)

The accounting policies of the operating segments are the same as the policies described in Note 2, "Summary of Significant Accounting Policies." Both the retail and wholesale segments are highly diversified. No customer comprises more than 10% of sales. A summary of the information about the Company's operations by segment is as follows:

	Fiscal Year		
	2009	2008	2007
Net sales			
Retail operations	$1,724,558	$1,413,251	$1,150,511
Wholesale operations	120,364	102,479	79,687
Intersegment elimination	(10,304)	(8,006)	(5,481)
Total net sales	$1,834,618	$1,507,724	$1,224,717
Income from operations			
Retail operations	$ 297,572	$ 219,248	$ 159,338
Wholesale operations	28,170	21,438	18,319
Intersegment elimination	(11,209)	(1,325)	(1,504)
Total segment operating income	314,533	239,361	176,153
General corporate expenses	(15,098)	(14,416)	(12,164)
Total income from operations	$ 299,435	$ 224,945	$ 163,989
Depreciation expense for property and equipment			
Retail operations	$ 78,892	$ 68,123	$ 53,458
Wholesale operations	613	615	437
Total depreciation expense for property and equipment	$ 79,505	$ 68,738	$ 53,895
Inventories			
Retail operations	$ 157,030	$ 159,015	
Wholesale operations	12,668	12,910	
Total inventories	$ 169,698	$ 171,925	
Property and equipment, net			
Retail operations	$ 500,650	$ 486,031	
Wholesale operations	4,757	2,858	
Total property and equipment, net	$ 505,407	$ 488,889	
Cash paid for property and equipment			
Retail operations	$ 111,658	$ 113,914	$ 211,533
Wholesale operations	895	1,456	496
Total cash paid for property and equipment	$ 112,533	$ 115,370	$ 212,029

The Company has foreign operations in Europe and Canada. Revenues and long-lived assets, based upon our domestic and foreign operations, are as follows:

	Fiscal Year		
	2009	2008	2007
Net sales			
Domestic operations	$1,663,616	$1,373,162	$1,132,053
Foreign operations	171,002	134,562	92,664
Total net sales	$1,834,618	$1,507,724	$1,224,717
Property and equipment, net			
Domestic operations	$ 460,551	$ 434,776	
Foreign operations	44,856	54,113	
Total property and equipment, net	$ 505,407	$ 488,889	

APPENDIX D

INDUSTRY RATIO REPORT

Retail Family Clothing Stores

Liquidity	
Current Ratio	2.55
Quick Ratio	1.38

Activity	
Inventory Turnover	5.92
Days to Sell Inventory	70.897 days
Receivables Turnover	54.24
Average Collection Period	15.07 days
Fixed Asset Turnover	5.76
Total Asset Turnover	1.90
Accounts Payable Turnover	6.43

Profitability	
Gross Profit Margin	38.99%
Operating Profit Margin	6.24%
Net Profit Margin	3.77%
Return on Equity	13.11%
Return on Assets	7.17%
Quality of Income	0.72

Leverage	
Times Interest Earned	16.33
Interest Coverage Ratio	16.39
Total Debt/Total Equity	1.08
Total Assets/Total Equity	1.92

Dividends	
Dividend Payout	19.61%
Dividend Yield	2.22%

Other	
Advertising-to-Sales	2.39%
Sales Growth	2.39%
Capital Acquisitions Ratio	1.93
Price/Earnings	6.81

COMPANIES USED IN INDUSTRY ANALYSIS

Company Name	Ticker Symbol
Abercrombie & Fitch	ANF
Aeropostale Inc.	ARO
American Eagle Outfitters	AEO
Ann Taylor Stores	ANN
bebe stores Inc.	BEBE
Chico's FAS Inc.	CHS
Collective Brands Inc.	PSS
Dress Barn Inc.	DBRN
Foot Locker Inc.	FL
Gap Inc.	GPS
Guess? Inc.	GES
J. Crew Group Inc.	JCG
Limited Brands Inc.	LTD
Nordstrom Inc.	JWN
Pacific Sunwear of California Inc.	PSUN
Ross Stores Inc.	ROST
The Buckle Inc.	BKE
The Men's Wearhouse Inc.	MW
Urban Outfitters Inc.	URBN
Wet Seal Inc.	WTSLA

A

Account A standardized format that organizations use to accumulate the dollar effect of transactions on each financial statement item. (51)

Accounting A system that collects and processes (analyzes, measures, and records) financial information about an organization and reports that information to decision makers. (4)

Accounting Cycle The process used by entities to analyze and record transactions, adjust the records at the end of the period, prepare financial statements, and prepare the records for the next cycle. (165)

Accounting Entity The organization for which financial data are to be collected. (7)

Accounting Period The time period covered by the financial statements. (10)

Accounts Receivable (Trade Receivables, Receivables) Open accounts owed to the business by trade customers. (286)

Accrual Basis Accounting Records revenues when earned and expenses when incurred, regardless of the timing of cash receipts or payments. (108)

Accrued Expenses Previously unrecorded expenses that need to be adjusted at the end of the accounting period to reflect the amount incurred and its related payable account. (173)

Accrued Liabilities Expenses that have been incurred but have not been paid at the end of the accounting period. (460)

Accrued Revenues Previously unrecorded revenues that need to be adjusted at the end of the accounting period to reflect the amount earned and its related receivable account. (170)

Acquisition Cost The net cash equivalent amount paid or to be paid for an asset. (391)

Additional Paid-In Capital (Paid-In Capital, Contributed Capital in Excess of Par) The amount of contributed capital less the par value of the stock. (242)

Additions and Improvements Infrequent expenditures that increase an asset's economic usefulness in the future. (394)

Adjusting Entries Entries necessary at the end of the accounting period to measure all revenues and expenses of that period. (167)

Aging of Accounts Receivable Method Estimates uncollectible accounts based on the age of each account receivable. (291)

Allowance for Doubtful Accounts (Allowance for Bad Debts, Allowance for Uncollectible Accounts) Contra-asset account containing the estimated uncollectible accounts receivable. (287)

Allowance Method Bases bad debt expense on an estimate of uncollectible accounts. (287)

Amortization Systematic and rational allocation of the acquisition cost of an intangible asset over its useful life. (411)

Amortized Cost Method Reports investments in debt securities held to maturity at cost minus any premium or plus any discount. (600)

Annuity A series of periodic cash receipts or payments that are equal in amount each interest period. (473)

Assets Probable future economic benefits owned by the entity as a result of past transactions. (46)

Audit An examination of the financial reports to ensure that they represent what they claim and conform with generally accepted accounting principles. (20)

Authorized Number of Shares The maximum number of shares of a corporation's capital stock that can be issued as specified in the charter. (554)

Average Cost Method Uses the weighted average unit cost of the goods available for sale for both cost of goods sold and ending inventory. (341)

B

Bad Debt Expense (Doubtful Accounts Expense, Uncollectible Accounts Expense, Provision for Uncollectible Accounts) Expense associated with estimated uncollectible accounts receivable. (287)

Balance Sheet (Statement of Financial Position) Reports the amount of assets, liabilities, and stockholders' equity of an accounting entity at a point in time. (7)

Bank Reconciliation Process of verifying the accuracy of both the bank statement and the cash accounts of a business. (297)

Bank Statement A monthly report from a bank that shows deposits recorded, checks cleared, other debits and credits, and a running bank balance. (297)

Basic Accounting Equation (Balance Sheet Equation) Assets = Liabilities + Stockholders' Equity. (8)

Board of Directors Elected by the shareholders to represent their interests; is responsible for maintaining the integrity of the company's financial reports. (233)

Bond Certificate The bond document that each bondholder receives. (509)

Bond Discount The difference between the selling price and par when a bond is sold for less than par. (510)

Bond Premium The difference between the selling price and par when a bond is sold for more than par. (510)

Bond Principal The amount (a) payable at the maturity of the bond and (b) on which the periodic cash interest payments are computed. (507)

C

Callable Bonds Bonds that may be called for early retirement at the option of the issuer. (508)

Capital Expenditures Expenditures that increase the productive life, operating efficiency, or capacity of an asset and are recorded as increases in asset accounts, not as expenses. (394)

Capital Lease Meets at least one of the four criteria established by GAAP and results in the recording of an asset and liability. (471)

Capitalized Interest Interest expenditures included in the cost of a self-constructed asset. (392)

Cash Money or any instrument that banks will accept for deposit and immediate credit to a company's account, such as a check, money order, or bank draft. (295)

Cash Basis Accounting Records revenues when cash is received and expenses when cash is paid. (108)

Cash Equivalents Short-term investments with original maturities of three months or less that are readily convertible to cash an whose value is unlikely to change. (295, 6

Cash Flows from Financing Activities C inflows and outflows related to external sources of financing (owners and creditors) for the enterprise. (641)

Cash Flows from Investing Activities Cash inflows and outflows related to the acquisition or sale of productive facilities and investments in the securities of other companies. (641)

Cash Flows from Operating Activities (Cash Flows from Operations) Cash inflows and outflows directly related to earnings from normal operations. (639)

Closing Entries Made at the end of the accounting period to transfer balances in temporary accounts to Retained Earnings and to establish a zero balance in each of the temporary accounts. (183)

Common Stock The basic voting stock issued by a corporation. (557)

Comparable Information Information that can be compared across businesses because similar accounting methods have been applied. (236)

Component Percentage Expresses each item on a particular financial statement as a percentage of a single base amount. (700)

Conservatism Suggests that care should be taken not to overstate assets and revenues or understate liabilities and expenses. (50, 237)

Consistent Information Information that can be compared over time because similar accounting methods have been applied. (236)

Contingent Liability A potential liability that has arisen as the result of a past event; it is not an effective liability until some future event occurs. (466)

Continuity (Going-Concern) Assumption States that businesses are assumed to continue to operate into the foreseeable future. (46)

Contra-Account An account that is an offset . or reduction of, the primary account. (172)

tributed Capital Cash (and sometimes assets) provided from the owners to siness. (49)

ible Bonds Bonds that may be to other securities of the issuer mmon stock). (508)

clusive right to publish, use, and musical, or artistic work. (413)

rnance The procedures e that the company interests of the

Cost-Benefit Constraint Suggests that the benefits of accounting for and reporting of information should outweigh the costs. (236)

Cost of Goods Sold Equation BI + P − EI = CGS. (336)

Cost Principle See *historical cost principle.*

Coupon Rate The stated rate of interest on bonds. (509)

Credit The right side of an account. (58)

Credit Card Discount Fee charged by the credit card company for its services. (282)

Cumulative Dividend Preference The preferred stock feature that requires specified current dividends not paid in full to accumulate for every year in which they are not paid. These cumulative preferred dividends must be paid before any common dividends can be paid. (566)

Current Assets Assets that will be used or turned into cash within one year. Inventory is always considered a current asset regardless of the time needed to produce and sell it. (47)

Current Dividend Preference The feature of preferred stock that grants priority on preferred dividends over common dividends. (565)

Current Liabilities Short-term obligations that will be paid in cash (or other current assets) within the current operating cycle or one year, whichever is longer. (48, 457)

D

Debenture An unsecured bond; no assets are specifically pledged to guarantee repayment. (508)

Debit The left side of an account. (58)

Declaration Date The date on which the board of directors officially approves a dividend. (561)

Declining-Balance Depreciation Method that allocates the cost of an asset over its useful life based on a multiple of (often two times) the straight-line rate. (401)

Deferred Expenses Previously acquired assets that need to be adjusted at the end of the accounting period to reflect the amount of expense incurred in using the asset to generate revenue. (171)

Deferred (Unearned) Revenues Previously recorded liabilities that need to be adjusted at the end of the accounting period to reflect the amount of revenue earned; on the balance sheet, revenues that have been collected but not earned; liabilities until the goods or services have been provided. (169, 465)

Deferred Tax Items Timing differences caused by reporting revenues and expenses according to GAAP on a company's income statement and according to the Internal Revenue Code on the tax return. (480)

Depletion Systematic and rational allocation of the cost of a natural resource over the period of its exploitation. (410)

Depreciation The process of allocating the cost of buildings and equipment over their productive lives using a systematic and rational allocation of the cost of property, plant, and equipment (but not land) over their useful lives. (396)

Direct Labor The earnings of employees who work directly on the products being manufactured. (335)

Direct Method A method of presenting the operating activities section of the statement of cash flows that reports components of cash flows from operating activities as gross receipts and gross payments. (640)

Discontinued Operations Financial results from the disposal of a major component of the business, reported net of income tax effects. (255)

Dividends in Arrears Dividends on cumulative preferred stock that have not been paid in prior years. (566)

E

Earnings Forecasts Predictions of earnings for future accounting periods. (233)

Effective-Interest Amortization Amortizes a bond discount or premium on the basis of the effective-interest rate; it is the theoretically preferred method. (516)

Effective-Interest Rate (Yield) The current rate of interest on a debt when incurred; also called the *market interest rate.* (510)

Efficient Markets Securities markets in which prices fully reflect available information. (717)

Equity Method Used when an investor can exert significant influence over an affiliate; the method permits recording the investor's share of the affiliate's income. (610)

Estimated Useful Life The expected service life of an asset to the present owner. (398)

Expenses Decreases in assets or increases in liabilities from ongoing operations incurred to generate revenues during the period. (106)

Extraordinary Items Gains and losses that are both unusual in nature and infrequent in occurrence; they are reported net of tax on the income statement. (255)

F

Face Amount Another name for bond principal or the maturity amount of a bond. (507)

Factory Overhead Manufacturing costs that are not raw material or direct labor costs. (336)

Fair Value Method Reports securities at their current market value (the amount that would be received in an orderly sale). (601)

Financial Accounting Standards Board (FASB) The private sector body given the primary responsibility to work out the detailed rules that become generally accepted accounting principles. (19)

Finished Goods Inventory Manufactured goods that are complete and ready for sale. (334)

First-In, First-Out (FIFO) Method An inventory costing method that assumes that the first goods purchased (the first in) are the first goods sold. (339)

Form 8-K The report used by publicly traded companies to disclose any material event not previously reported that is important to investors. (240)

Form 10-K The annual report that publicly traded companies must file with the SEC. (240)

Form 10-Q The quarterly report that publicly traded companies must file with the SEC. (240)

Franchise A contractual right to sell certain products or services, use certain trademarks, or perform activities in a geographical region. (413)

Free Cash Flow Cash Flows from Operating Activities less Dividends less Capital Expenditures. (654)

Future Value The sum to which an amount will increase as the result of compound interest. (481)

G

Gains Increases in assets or decreases in liabilities from peripheral transactions. (106)

Generally Accepted Accounting Principles (GAAP) The measurement rules used to develop the information in financial statements. (18)

Goods Available for Sale The sum of beginning inventory and purchases (or transfers to finished goods) for the period. (336)

Goodwill (Cost in Excess of Net Assets Acquired) For accounting purposes, the excess of the purchase price of a business over the fair value of the acquired business's assets and liabilities. (412, 614)

Gross Profit (Gross Margin) Net sales less cost of goods sold. (243)

H

Held-to-Maturity Investments Investments in debt securities that management has the ability and intent to hold until maturity. (600)

Historical Cost Principle Requires assets to be recorded at the historical cash-equivalent cost, which on the date of the transaction is cash paid plus the current dollar value of all noncash considerations also given in the exchange. (46)

I

Income before Income Taxes (Pretax Earnings) Revenues minus all expenses except income tax expense. (243)

Income from Operations (Operating Income) Net sales less cost of goods sold and other operating expenses. (243)

Income Statement (Statement of Income, Statement of Earnings, Statement of Operations) Reports the revenues less the expenses of the accounting period. (10)

Indenture A bond contract that specifies the legal provisions of a bond issue. (508)

Indirect Method A method of presenting the operating activities section of the statement of cash flows that adjusts net income to compute cash flows from operating activities. (640)

Institutional Investors Managers of pension, mutual, endowment, and other funds that invest on the behalf of others. (236)

Intangible Assets Assets that have special rights but not physical substance. (389)

Internal Controls Processes by which a company provides reasonable assurance regarding the reliability of the company's financial reporting, the effectiveness and efficiency of its operations, and its compliance with applicable laws and regulations. (296)

Inventory Tangible property held for sale in the normal course of business or used in producing goods or services for sale. (333)

Investments in Affiliates (or Associated Companies) Investments in stock held for the purpose of influencing the operating and financing strategies of the entity for the long term. (610)

Issued Shares The total number of shares of stock that have been sold; shares outstanding plus treasury shares held. (554)

J

Journal Entry An accounting method for expressing the effects of a transaction on accounts in a debits-equal-credits format. (59)

L

Last-In, First-Out (LIFO) Method An inventory costing method that assumes that the most recently purchased units (the last in) are sold first. (340)

Legal Capital The permanent amount of capital defined by state law that must remain invested in the business; serves as a cushion for creditors. (557)

Lenders (Creditors) Suppliers and financial institutions that lend money to companies. (236)

Liabilities Probable debts or obligations of the entity that result from past transactions, which will be paid with assets or services. (47, 457)

Licenses and Operating Rights Obtained through agreements with governmental units or agencies; permit owners to use public property in performing their services. (413)

LIFO Liquidation A sale of a lower-cost inventory item from beginning LIFO inventory. (357)

LIFO Reserve A contra-asset for the excess of FIFO over LIFO inventory. (351)

Liquidity The ability to pay current obligations. (458)

Long-Lived Assets Tangible and intangible resources owned by a business and used in its operations over several years. (389)

Long-Term Liabilities All of the entity's obligations that are not classified as current liabilities. (469)

Losses Decreases in assets or increases in liabilities from peripheral transactions. (106)

Lower of Cost or Market (LCM) Valuation method departing from the cost principle; it serves to recognize a loss when replacement cost or net realizable value drops below cost. (346)

M

Market Interest Rate The current rate of interest on a debt when incurred; also called *yield* or *effective-interest rate.* (510)

Market Tests Ratios that tend to measure the market worth of a share of stock. (713)

Matching Principle Requires that expenses be recorded when incurred in earning revenue. (111)

Material Amounts Amounts that are large enough to influence a user's decision. (237)

Materiality Exception suggests that small amounts that are not likely to influence a user's decision can be accounted for in the most cost-beneficial manner. (50)

Merchandise Inventory Goods held for resale in the ordinary course of business. (333)

Merger Occurs when one company purchases all of the net assets of another and the acquired company goes out of existence. (614)

N

Natural Resources Assets occurring in nature, such as mineral deposits, timber tracts, oil, and gas. (409)

Net Book Value (Book Value, Carrying Value) The acquisition cost of an asset less accumulated depreciation, depletion, or amortization. (173, 397)

Net Realizable Value The expected sales price less selling costs (e.g., repair and disposal costs). (346)

Noncash Investing and Financing Activities Transactions that do not have direct cash flow effects; reported as a supplement to the statement of cash flows in narrative or schedule form. (658)

No-Par Value Stock Capital stock that has no par value specified in the corporate charter. (557)

Notes (Footnotes) Provide supplemental information about the financial condition of a company, without which the financial statements cannot be fully understood. (16)

Notes Receivable Written promises that require another party to pay the business under specified conditions (amount, time, interest). (286)

O

Operating Cycle (Cash-to-Cash Cycle) The time it takes for a company to pay cash to suppliers, sell goods and services to customers, and collect cash from customers. (103)

Operating Lease Does not meet any of the four criteria established by GAAP and does not cause the recording of an asset and liability. (470)

Ordinary Repairs and Maintenance Expenditures for the normal operating upkeep of long-lived assets. (394)

Outstanding Shares The total number of shares of stock that are owned by stockholders on any particular date. (554)

P

Paid-In Capital (Additional Paid-in Capital, Contributed Capital in Excess of Par) The amount of contributed capital less the par value of the stock. (242)

Par Value (1) The nominal value per share of capital stock established by the board of directors; serves as the basis for legal capital; it establishes the minimum amount a stockholder must contribute and has no relationship to the market price of the stock. (2) Also, another name for bond principal, or the maturity amount of a bond. (242, 507, 557)

Patent Granted by the federal government for an invention; gives the owner the exclusive right to use, manufacture, and sell the subject of the patent. (413)

Payment Date The date on which a cash dividend is paid to the stockholders of record. (561)

Percentage of Credit Sales Method Bases bad debt expense on the historical percentage of credit sales that result in bad debts. (290)

Periodic Inventory System An inventory system in which ending inventory and cost of goods sold are determined at the end of the accounting period based on a physical inventory count. (353)

Permanent (Real) Accounts The balance sheet accounts that carry their ending balances into the next accounting period. (183)

Perpetual Inventory System An inventory system in which a detailed inventory record is maintained, recording each purchase and sale during the accounting period. (353)

Post-Closing Trial Balance Prepared as the last step in the accounting cycle to check that debits equal credits and all temporary accounts have been closed. (186)

Preferred Stock Stock that has specified rights over common stock. (565)

Present Value The current value of an amount to be received in the future; a future amount discounted for compound interest. (471)

Press Release A written public news announcement normally distributed to major news services. (238)

Primary Objective of External Financial Reporting To provide useful economic information about a business to help external parties make sound financial decisions. (45)

Private Investors Individuals who purchase shares in companies. (236)

Public Company Accounting Oversight Board (PCAOB) The private sector body given the primary responsibility to work out detailed auditing standards. (20)

Purchase Discount Cash discount received for prompt payment of an account. (359)

Purchase Method Records assets and liabilities acquired in a merger or acquisition at their fair value on the transaction date. (614)

Purchase Returns and Allowances A reduction in the cost of purchases associated with unsatisfactory goods. (358)

R

Ratio (Percentage) Analysis An analytical tool that measures the proportional relationship between two financial statement amounts. (700)

Raw Materials Inventory Items acquired for the purpose of processing into finished goods. (334)

Record Date The date on which the corporation prepares the list of current stockholders as shown on its records; dividends can be paid only to the stockholders who own stock on that date. (561)

Relevant Information Information that can influence a decision; it is timely and has predictive and/or feedback value. (45, 236)

Reliable Information Information that is accurate, unbiased, and verifiable. (45, 236)

Replacement Cost The current purchase price for identical goods. (346)

Residual (or Salvage) Value The estimated amount to be recovered by the company, less disposal costs, at the end of an asset's estimated useful life. (398)

Retained Earnings Cumulative earnings of a company that are not distributed to the owners and are reinvested in the business. (49)

Revenue Expenditures Expenditures that maintain the productive capacity of an asset during the current accounting period only and are recorded as expenses. (394)

Revenue Principle Revenues are recognized when (1) goods or services are delivered, (2) there is evidence of an arrangement for customer payment, (3) the price is fixed or determinable, and (4) collection is reasonably assured. (108)

Revenues Increases in assets or settlements of liabilities from ongoing operations. (104)

S

Sales (or Cash) Discount Cash discount offered to encourage prompt payment of an account receivable. (282)

Sales Returns and Allowances A reduction of sales revenues for return of or allowances for unsatisfactory goods. (283)

Securities and Exchange Commission (SEC) The U.S. government agency that determines the financial statements that public companies must provide to stockholders and the measurement rules that they must use in producing those statements. (19)

Securities Available for Sale All passive investments other than trading securities and debt held to maturity (classified as either short term or long term). (602)

Separate-Entity Assumption States that business transactions are separate from the transactions of the owners. (45)

Specific Identification Method An inventory costing method that identifies the cost of the specific item that was sold. (339)

Stated Rate The rate of cash interest per period specified in the bond contract. (507)

Statement of Cash Flows (Cash Flow Statement) Reports inflows and outflows of cash during the accounting period in the categories of operating, investing, and financing. (14)

Statement of Retained Earnings Reports the way that net income and the distribution of dividends affected the financial position of the company during the accounting period. (12)

Stock Dividend A distribution of additional shares of a corporation's own stock. (563)

Stock Split An increase in the total number of authorized shares by a specified ratio; it does not decrease retained earnings. (564)

Stockholders' Equity (Owners' Equity or Shareholders' Equity) The financing provided by the owners and the operations of the business. (49)

Straight-Line Amortization A simplified method of amortizing a bond discount or premium that allocates an equal dollar amount to each interest period. (515)

Straight-Line Depreciation Method that allocates the cost of an asset in equal periodic amounts over its useful life. (399)

T

T-account A tool for summarizing transaction effects for each account, determining balances, and drawing inferences about a company's activities. (60)

Tangible Assets (or fixed assets) Assets that have physical substance. (389)

Technology Includes costs for computer software and Web development. (413)

Temporary (Nominal) Accounts Income statement (and sometimes dividends declared) accounts that are closed to Retained Earnings at the end of the accounting period. (183)

Temporary Differences Timing differences that cause deferred income taxes and will reverse, or turn around, in the future. (480)

Tests of Liquidity Ratios that measure a company's ability to meet its currently maturing obligations. (707)

Tests of Profitability Ratios that compare income with one or more primary activities. (702)

Tests of Solvency Ratios that measure a company's ability to meet its long-term obligations. (712)

Time Period Assumption The long life of a company can be reported in shorter time periods. (104)

Time Value of Money Interest that is associated with the use of money over time. (463)

Trademark An exclusive legal right to use a special name, image, or slogan. (412)

Trading Securities All investments in stocks or bonds that are held primarily for the purpose of active trading (buying and selling) in the near future (classified as short term). (602)

Transaction (1) An exchange between a business and one or more external parties to a business or (2) a measurable internal event such as the use of assets in operations. (50)

Transaction Analysis The process of studying a transaction to determine its economic effect on the business in terms of the accounting equation. (52)

Treasury Stock A corporation's own stock that has been issued but subsequently reacquired and is still being held by that corporation. (558)

Trial Balance A list of all accounts with their balances to provide a check on the equality of the debits and credits. (165)

Trustee An independent party appointed to represent the bondholders. (509)

U

Unearned (Deferred) Revenues Previously recorded liabilities that need to be adjusted at the end of the accounting period to reflect the amount of revenue earned. (169, 465)

Unit-of-Measure Assumption States that accounting information should be measured and reported in the national monetary unit. (46)

Units-of-Production Depreciation Method that allocates the cost of an asset over its useful life based on the relation of its periodic output to its total estimated output. (400)

Unqualified (Clean) Audit Opinion Auditor's statement that the financial statements are fair presentations in all material respects in conformity with GAAP. (233)

Unrealized Holding Gains or Losses Amounts associated with price changes of securities that are currently held. (602)

W

Work in Process Inventory Goods in the process of being manufactured. (334)

Working Capital The dollar difference between total current assets and total current liabilities. (467)

Y

Yield (Effective-Interest Rate) The current rate of interest on a debt when incurred; also called the *market interest rate*. (510)

CREDITS

Chapter 1

Opener: © Mark Richards/PhotoEdit.
Page 9: AP Photo/Matthias Rietschel.
Page 12: © Reed Kaestner/Corbis.
P&G logo courtesy of Proctor & Gamble Corporation.
Tootsie Roll logo courtesy of Tootsie Roll Industries.
Walgreens logo courtesy of Walgreens.
Urban Outfitters logo courtesy of Urban Outfitters, Inc.

Chapter 2

Opener: © Ezio Peterson/UPI Photo/NewsCom.
Papa John's logo courtesy of Papa John's Pizza.
Wendy's logo registered trademark of Wendy's International, Inc. and are used with permission.
Lance ® and the LANCE ® logo are registered trademarks of Lance Inc. and are used with permission.
Yum! logo courtesy of Yum! Brands, Inc.
Nike logo registered trademark of Nike, Inc. and are used with permission.
BMW logo registered trademark of Bayerische Motoren Werke AG and are used with permission.
Sheraton, Four Points, W, Aloft, The Luxury Collection, LeMéridien, Element Westin, St. Regis and their respective logos are the trademarks of Starwood Hotels & Resorts World wide, Inc or its affiliates and are used with permission.
Exxon logo is registered trademark of ExxonMobil Corporation and are used with permission.
Dell logo is a trademark of Dell Inc. and are used with permission.
Mattel is a trademark of Matell, Inc. and are used with permission.
Ethan Allen logo courtesy of Ethan Allen Interiors Inc.

Chapter 3

Opener: © Michael Newman/PhotoEdit.
Papa John's logo courtesy of Papa John's Pizza.
Mattel is a trademark of Mattel, Inc. and are used with permission.
Wendy's logo registered trademark of Wendy's International, Inc. and are used with permission.
Exxon logo is registered trademark of ExxonMobil Corporation and are used with permission.
Cedar Fair logo is a trademark of Cedar Fair, L.P. and are used with permission.

Chapter 4

Opener: © Kurt Brady/Alamy.
Papa John's logo courtesy of Papa John's Pizza.
Dell logo is a trademark of Dell Inc. and are used with permission.

Chapter 5

Opener: © Hunter Martin/Getty.
Page 241: © Kim Kulish/Corbis.
Callaway Golf logo is a registered trademark of Callaway Golf Company and are used with permission.
Yahoo! Finance screenshot is reproduced with permission of Yahoo! Inc. ©2010 Yahoo! Inc. YAHOO! and the YAHOO! logo are registered trademarks of Yahoo! Inc.
CFO Magazine, "How Green is my Company?" Russ Banham, October 2004 pp. 97-100. Copyright © 2004. Reprinted by permission.
Analyst's Accounting Observer Excerpt Used with permission.
Campbell Soup is a registered trademark of Campbell Soup Company and are used with permission.
Kroger logo is a registered trademark of The Kroger Co. of Michigan and is used with permission.
Lance ® and the LANCE ® logo are registered trademarks of Lance Inc. and are used with permission.
Tiffany and Co. logo is a registered trademark of Tiffany LLC and are used with permission.
Aeropostale logo is a trademark of Aeropostale and are used with permission.
Rubbermaid logo is a registered trademark of Newell Rubbermaid and are used with permission.
Ahold logo is a trademark of Royal Ahold and are used with permission.

Chapter 6

Opener: © Zuma Sports/NewsCom.
Page 281: © TRBfoto/Getty Images.
Page 299: © Jeff Greenberg/The Image Works.
Page 303: © Spencer Grant/PhotoEdit.
Deckers logo is a trademark of Decker's Outdoor Corporation and are used with permission.
Siemens logo is a trademark of Siemens AG and are used with permission.
Wendy's logo registered trademark of Wendy's International, Inc. and are used with permission.
Dell logo is a trademark of Dell Inc. and are used with permission.
Wall Street Journal excerpt "Ex-official at Symbol pleads guilty" Kara Scannel, The Wall Street Journal, March 26, 2003. Copyright © 2003 Dow Jones & Co. Inc. Used with permission.

Chapter 7

Opener AP Photo/Patrick Lux.
Page 335: © Steven Rubin/The Image Works.
Page 353: © Creatas/Digital Vision.
Caterpillar logo is a registered trademark of Caterpillar Inc and are used with permission.
Dell logo is a trademark of Dell Inc. and are used with permission.
JC Penney logo is a trademark of JC Penney Company Inc. and are used with permission.
Ford logo is a trademark of Ford Motor Company and are used with permission.
Gibson logo Trademark is owned by AGC, Inc. Reproduced by permission. American Greetings Corporation. ©AGC, Inc.
GM logo is a trademark of General Motors Company and are used with permission.
GE logo is a trademark of General Electric Company and are used with permission.
Dana logo is courtesy of Dana Holding Corporation.

Chapter 8

Opener © CNS Photo courtesy of PRNewsFoto/NewsCom.
Page 394: © AP Photo/Ted S. Warren.
Page 408: © Juan Silva/Iconica/Getty Images.
Page 412: © Martin Sasse/Laif/Aurora.
Southwest logo is a trademark of Southwest Airlines Co. and are used with permission.
Exxon logo is registered trademark of ExxonMobil Corporation and are used with permission.
Macy's logo is a trademark of Macy's Inc. and are used with permission.
Ford logo is a trademark of Ford Motor Company and are used with permission.
GM logo is a trademark of General Motors Company and are used with permission.

FM (Freeport) logo is a trademark of Freeport-McMoRan Copper & Gold Inc. and are used with permission.
Singapore Airlines logo is a trademark of Singapore Airlines Limited and are used with permission.

Chapter 9

Opener: © Jonathan Fickies.
Page 462: AP Photos/Kevin P. Casey.
Page 465: © Mark Richards/PhotoEdit.
General Mills Logo is a registered trademark of General Mills, Inc. and is used with permission.
Pepsi logo—this material contains valuable trademarks owned and used by PepsiCo, Inc. and its subsidiaries and affiliates to distinguish products and services of outstanding quality. Used with permission.
Dell logo is a trademark of Dell Inc. and are used with permission.
Ford logo is a trademark of Ford Motor Company and are used with permission.
Exxon logo is registered trademark of ExxonMobil Corporation and are used with permission.

Chapter 10

Opener: © Jonathan Alcorn/Bloomberg/Getty.
Page 509: © Artville/Getty.
Page 518: © John Gress/Reuters/Corbis.
General Mills Logo is a registered trademark of General Mills, Inc. and is used with permission.
JC Penney logo is a trademark of JC Penney Company Inc. and are used with permission.
Kroger logo is a registered trademark of The Kroger Co. of Michigan and is used with permission.
P&G logo courtesy of Proctor & Gamble Corporation.
Phelps Dodge logo is a trademark of Freeport-McMoRan Copper & Gold Inc. and are used with permission.
Ford logo is a trademark of Ford Motor Company and are used with permission.

Chapter 11

Opener: AP Photo/Al Behrman, file.
Page 557: © David Young-Wolff/PhotoEdit.
Page 562: © Monika Graff/The Image Works.
Page 563: © Joel Gordon.
Radio Shack logo is a registered trademark of Radio Shack Corporation and are used with permission.
Dillard's logo courtesy of Dillard's.
Duke Energy logo is a registered trademark of Duke Energy Corporation and are used with permission.
Haynes International is a trademark of Haynes International Corp. and are used with permission.

Chapter 12

Opener: AP Photo/Gerald Herbert.
Page 602: © Tim Sloan/AFP/Getty.
Page 614: © Studio 101/Alamy.
Macy's logo is a trademark of Macy's Inc. and are used with permission.

Chapter 13

Opener: Courtesy of National Beverage Corp.
Page 650: © mauritius images GmbH/Alamy.
National Beverage logo is a registered trademark of National Beverage Corporation and are used with permission.
Snapple logo is a registered trademark of Dr. Pepper Snapple Group and are used with permission.
Lion Nathan logo is a trademark of Lion Nathan National Foods and are used with permission.
Redhook Ale Brewery logo is a registered trademark of Craft Brewers Alliance, Inc. (CBAI) and are used with permission.
MillerCoors logo courtesy of MillerCoors.
Samuel Adams is a registered trademark of Boston Beer Co and are used with permission.
Stanley Furniture logo courtesy of Stanley Furniture Company.
Time Warner logo is a registered trademark of Time Warner Inc. and are used with permission.
Pepsi logo—this material contains valuable trademarks owned and used by PepsiCo, Inc. and its subsidiaries and affiliates to distinguish products and services of outstanding quality. Used with permission.
Gibraltar Industries logo courtesy of Gibraltar Industries, Inc.
Rocky Mountain Chocolate Factory logo is a registered trademark of Rocky Mountain Chocolate Factory and are used with permission.

Chapter 14

Opener: © EPA/Joshua Gates Weisberg/Corbis.
Page 702: © Jim McIsaac/Getty.
Page 709: © Michael Newman/PhotoEdit.
P&G logo courtesy of Proctor & Gamble Corporation.
Cintas logo is a registered trademark of Cintas Corporation and are used with permission.
JC Penney logo is a trademark of JC Penney Company Inc. and are used with permission.
Pepsi logo—this material contains valuable trademarks owned and used by PepsiCo, Inc. and its subsidiaries and affiliates to distinguish products and services of outstanding quality. Used with permission.
Dell logo is a trademark of Dell Inc. and are used with permission.

COMPANY INDEX

Page numbers followed by n indicate notes.

Page numbers followed by n indicate notes.

A